Tricks of the 3D Game Programming Gurus

Advanced 3D Graphics and Rasterization

André LaMothe

201 West 103rd Street, Indianapolis, Indiana 46290

Tricks of the 3D Game Programming Gurus: Advanced 3D Graphics and Rasterization

International Standard Book Number: 0-672-31835-0

Library of Congress Catalog Card Number: 99-067392

Printed in the United States of America

First Printing: June 2003

06 05 04 03 4 3 2 1

Sams Publishing offers excellent discounts on this book when ordered in quantity for bulk purchases or special sales. For more information, please contact

U.S. Corporate and Government Sales

1-800-382-3419

corpsales@pearsontechgroup.com

For sales outside of the U.S., please contact

International Sales

1-317-581-3793

international@pearsontechgroup.com

Trademarks

Warning and Disclaimer

Associate Publisher
Michael Stephens

Acquisitions Editor
Kim Spilker

Development Editor
Mark Renfrow

Managing Editor
Charlotte Clapp

Project Editor
George E. Nedeff

Copy Editors
Seth Kerney
Mike Henry

Indexer
Erika Millen

Proofreaders
Kevin Ober
Suzanne Thomas

Technical Editor
David Franson

Team Coordinator
Cindy Teeters

Multimedia Developer
Dan Scherf

Graphic Designer
Gary Adair

Cover Illustrator
Alex Varanese

Contents at a Glance

Table of Contents

Foreword

I am honored to be asked to write the foreword to this important work, teaching technical programmers the skills necessary for the creation of next-generation 3D video games from the ground up. There aren't many books that show you how to create a real-time 3D engine, starting with the plotting of a pixel. I reflect on how far the technology has come, and how primitive our games at Atari were. We were really pushing the state of the art then, but they really seem lame now.

To reminisce a bit, the early games were not even computer games in a technical sense. They were really just very fancy signal generators and state machines using counters and shift registers based on simple Boolean logic, built with nothing more than some slapped-together MSI (medium-scale integration) gates. You may remember that my first game (*Computer Space*) was created in 1970, four years *before* the Intel 4004, and six years before the 8080. I wish I had had a microprocessor to do them! Even then, the typical clock speed was much too slow for any significant real-time computing. The first game in which we used a microprocessor was *Asteroids*, and even then there was a great deal of hardware around it to augment the program, because the microprocessor couldn't do everything we needed in software.

Today, we march toward the capability to create images that are indistinguishable from a photograph (if we aren't already there). To create these images on the fly is truly a joy to behold. The realism and ability to create any world, environment, or character that these software and hardware tools give the game creator is a remarkable power. This palette of capability can shrink time, expand richness, and in general make new projects possible.

André LaMothe not only understands this technology intimately, but he also has an extraordinary game "sense." I have found over the years that many technologists are great practitioners of the art, but lack the sense of timing or tension that is necessary for a fun game. Others have a sense of gameplay, but are mediocre programmers. In André's case, you have both a true gamer and a software guru, and it comes through in every book he has written.

In a recent project that we did together, I was impressed not only with his knowledge of the state of the art, but also his extensive knowledge of the history of and intimacy with even some obscure games from the early days (ones that I thought only I remembered). Not to mention he wrote an entire game in 19 days for me! It is easy to remember the hits, but another thing to be knowledgeable about the stinkers (yes, Atari did a few that were really bad). But we did a lot that were great, and classics, as you know.

I hope you enjoy this book and use it as a launching pad for some great games that will keep me happily playing into the future.

Nolan Bushnell

Founder of Atari, Inc.

About the Author

André LaMothe has been involved in the computing industry and technology for more than a quarter century. He holds degrees in mathematics, computer science, and electrical engineering, and is one of the rare individuals that actually *did* work at NASA at the age of 20 doing research. His early teens and twenties were filled with consulting for numerous Silicon Valley companies, where he learned the realities of running a business and worked on his multidisciplinary background in fields such as telecommunications, virtual reality, robotics, compiler design, 3D engines, artificial intelligence, and other areas of computing and engineering.

His company Xtreme Games LLC was one of the first and last true "indie" publishers with a soul. Later he founded the Xtreme Games Developer Conference (XGDC) to give game developers a low-cost alternative to the GDC.

Lately he has been working on a number of projects, including eGamezone Networks, an online distribution system for games that's fair, fun, and has zero ads. Last but not least, he founded a new company, Nurve Networks LLC, to create handheld video game systems for value-minded consumers and hobbyists alike. Finally, he is the series editor for the world's largest game development series.

On a personal level, he likes everything extreme, from weightlifting, motorcycles, jet skis, and hotrods to "railing" on his blades. He has even trained extensively with the Shamrock Submission Fighting Team under the tutelage of Crazy Bob Cook, Frank Shamrock, and Javier Mendez. You probably don't want to get in an argument with him over DirectX or OpenGL—right or wrong, he will probably make you say uncle!

About the Technical Editor

David Franson has been a professional in the field of networking, programming, and 2D and 3D computer graphics since 1990. In 2000, he resigned his position as Information Systems Director of one of the largest entertainment law firms in New York City to pursue a full-time career in game development. He is also the author of *2D Artwork and 3D Modeling for Game Artists* (Premier Press), and is currently authoring *Xbox Hackz and Modz* (to be released June 2003).

Dedication

I dedicate this book to anyone with integrity—it's a lonely road, but someone has to walk it. Your actions do not go unnoticed...

Acknowledgments

First, I want to thank all the people at Sams Publishing. Let me make it clear that they have a very formulaic system for book publishing, and the *Tricks* series has always bent it way out of shape. We have to really applaud their ability to unplug from "Corporate America" once in a while and give everyone the latitude to create something that's a little special, so keep that in mind when reading their names below.

I would like to thank the publisher Michael Stephens, my acquisitions editor Kim Spilker, my trusty development editor Mark Renfrow, and of course, the project editor that keeps everything running smoothly, George Nedeff. There's also the nuts and bolts that go into a book, starting with the primary copy editor Seth Kerney, and of course, the technical editor David Franson (David also contributed some of the 3D models, including the Jet Ski, as well as many textures used in the demos).

Finally, no book would be complete without a CD, thanks to media developer Dan Scherf, and last but not least, the unsung hero that creates the index for the book—which is VERY important when you want to find something—anyway, thank you Erika Millen, for making a detailed and complete index for the book.

There's a special person that was part of this book when it first started the process that I don't want to go unmentioned; her name is Angela Kozlowski. She worked with me on the first 25% of the book, and really helped me define the overall "envelope" we were going to push; that is, "it's my way or the highway." She made everyone else understand how important and different this book would be. She never got to see the book finished because she moved on to another job, but now I am sure she will.

Next up are some of the companies and individuals that gave, loaned, or otherwise helped guide into my hands software and/or hardware. First is David Hackson of Intel Corporation for giving me copies of their latest advanced C++ and Fortran compiler products, as well as VTune. Then there was Kristine Gardner of Caligari Corporation, who gave me every version of trueSpace ever created. Long-time cohort Stacey Tsurusaki of Microsoft gave me that little inside edge at Microsoft. And of course, there are the companies that gave me evaluation copies of their products, or allowed me in one way or another to place their software on the CD, such as JASC Inc. for the use of Paint Shop Pro, and Sonic Foundry for the use of Sound Forge, and Right Hemisphere's Mary Alice Krayecki for sending me copies of Deep Exploration and Deep Paint UV.

The next set of individuals are friends that dealt with me while I wrote this book; I know I am an "intense" person, but that's what makes me so much fun at parties!

Anyway, I would like to thank Mike Perone for helping get "software," and dealing with networking issues.

Mark Bell for listening to me complain—only another entrepreneur can understand the "hell" we go through—thanks Mark.

Sellam Ismail of the Vintage Computer Festival for getting me lots of cool "retro" stuff, and really cheap "junk."

John Romero for his frequent communications and giving me hope that at least someone in this business is having a little fun!

Also, to Nolan Bushnell for having me down to uWink Inc. and taking the time to talk to me about video games. It's not every day you get to spend time with the guy that invented Atari! And thanks for writing the foreword!

Also, Alex Varanese, my new apprentice, for putting up with my constant lecturing about perfection, deadlines, pushing the limits, visualizing success—okay, okay, I'll stop!

Last but not least, the people that really got the sharp point of my aggressive and demanding personality—mom, dad, and my patient girlfriend Anita and my puppy Ariel.

We Want to Hear from You!

As the reader of this book, *you* are our most important critic and commentator. We value your opinion and want to know what we're doing right, what we could do better, what areas you'd like to see us publish in, and any other words of wisdom you're willing to pass our way.

As an associate publisher for Sams Publishing, I welcome your comments. You can email or write me directly to let me know what you did or didn't like about this book—as well as what we can do to make our books better.

Please note that I cannot help you with technical problems related to the *topic* of this book. We do have a User Services group, however, where I will forward specific technical questions related to the book.

When you write, please be sure to include this book's title and author as well as your name, email address, and phone number. I will carefully review your comments and share them with the author and editors who worked on the book.

Email: feedback@samspublishing.com

Mail: Michael Stephens
Associate Publisher
Sams Publishing
201 West 103rd Street
Indianapolis, IN 46290 USA

For more information about this book or another Sams Publishing title, visit our Web site at `www.samspublishing.com`. Type the ISBN (excluding hyphens) or the title of a book in the Search field to find the page you're looking for.

Introduction

"Come get some..."

—Duke Nukem

Game Programming Principles and Practice

A long time ago, in a galaxy far, far, away, I wrote a book about game programming called *Tricks of the Windows Game Programming Gurus*. For me, it was an opportunity to create something that I had always wanted—a book that teaches readers how to make games. Anyway, it's been a few years, and I'm a little older, a little wiser, and I've definitely learned a lot of TRICKS <VBG>. You can get along fine without ever reading the first *Tricks*, but I warn you—this volume is definitely more advanced, focuses on 3D, and assumes a lot.

With that in mind, this book is going to continue where the first *Tricks* left off, and further continue 3D concepts. I'm going to cover every major topic in 3D game programming that I can fit within the bounds of time and space.

Now, I'm not going to assume that you are a master programmer, or that you even know how to make games. However, this book is for not for beginners, and is really targeted toward intermediate to advanced game programmers, or intermediate to advanced programmers in general. If you don't know how to program in C/C++, you're going to be lost! So, newbies beware! There are many great books on C/C++, and I suggest anything by Stephen Prata or Robert Lafore—they are the best C/C++ authors in the world as far as I am concerned.

Today is probably the coolest time in history to be in the game business. We now have the technology to create games that do look real! Imagine what will come next—and you think the PlayStation 2, Xbox, and GameCube are cool! But all this technology isn't easy or trivial to understand—it takes really hard work and lots of Red Bull.

The difficulty level of game programming has definitely been cranked up these days in relation to the skill set needed to make games. But if you're reading this, you are probably one of those people that likes a challenge, right? Well, you came to the right place, because when you're done with this book, you will be able to create a full 3D, texture-mapped, fully-lit video game for the PC with a software rasterizer you write yourself. Moreover, you will understand the underlying principles of 3D graphics and be able to better understand and utilize 3D hardware today and in the future.

What You're Going to Learn

In this book, you're going to learn about 100^{10} teraquads of information! I'm going to fill your neural net so full of info, you'll have synaptic leakage! Seriously though, this book covers all the elements necessary to create a Windows 9x/2000-based game for the PC, including such topics as:

- A basic understanding of the engine from the first *Tricks*
- Win32 programming and DirectX Foundation 7.0+
- Advanced mathematics, including quaternions
- 2D/3D graphics and algorithms
- 3D projections and camera manipulation
- Wireframe and solid rendering
- Lighting and texture mapping
- Advanced visibility algorithms
- 3D animation techniques

And a lot more...

The first thing that you might be wondering about is, does this book focus on using 3D hardware, or does it show how to actually implement 3D software rasterizers with code? Well, the answer is software, primarily (with a "but" that I will get to in a minute)! Only wimps rely on 3D hardware. A real game programmer can write a 3D engine from scratch with blood pouring out of his eyes, on fire, and with needles in his eardrums, as well as use 3D hardware, if available. So, we're going to focus on real 3D programming in this book. With that knowledge, you can learn any 3D API in a couple of weeks.

My philosophy is: If you can understand how to write a texture mapper or a viewing system, you will have that much more of an advantage in using hardware. Furthermore, it will be some time before every computer has *good* 3D hardware, so you can't assume it exists, and it would be a bad thing to cut out all those computers from your target market just because they don't have 3D hardware (the Midwest and Europe are perfect examples of geographic areas that don't have the latest and greatest). Especially if you want to get into the game market without millions of dollars—you will start in the value software market, which is primarily non-3D accelerated. Finally, it's just more fun!

Finally, I'm sure you are a little worried about this whole "Windows-DirectX" deal. Well, with the right approach, Windows programming is actually very simple, fun, and takes care of a lot of problems that we had with DOS32. Don't think of Windows programming as a problem—think of it as an opportunity to spend more time on game code, rather than trivial details like GUI stuff, I/O, and graphics drivers. Believe me, you would spend 24 hours a day if you had to write graphics drivers for every 2D/3D accelerator that came on the market. Then there are sound cards, joysticks, blah, blah, blah...

What You Absolutely Need to Know

This book assumes that you can program, and program pretty well. You're going to be fairly lost if you can't write C code and don't know how to use a compiler in your sleep. However, the book uses some C++—enough to make a C coder just a little uneasy. I'll warn you if I'm doing anything weird. Also, there's a decent C++ primer in Appendix D, so check it out if you need a crash course. Basically, C++ is only needed here and there for examples using DirectX.

Nevertheless, I've decided that I'm going to use C++ a little more on this book because there are so many things in game programming that are object-oriented, and it's sacrilege to force them to be C-like structures. Bottom line: If you can program in C, you should be fine. If you program in C/C++, you shouldn't trip out at all.

Everyone knows that a computer program is nothing more than logic and math. Well, 3D video games have the emphasis on the math part! 3D graphics is all math. However, luckily for us, it's cool math! Yes, math can be cool. About the only thing you need to know is basic algebra and geometry. The vector, matrix, and calculus stuff I'll teach you along the way. Heck, if you can add, subtract, multiply, and divide, you will still be able to understand 90% of what's going on, even though you might not be able to re-derive it. But as long as you can use the code, that's all the matters in the end. And that Carmen Electra is single again <GRIN>.

That's really all you need to know. Of course, you'd better call all your friends and tell them that they won't see you for about two years because you're going to be a little busy. But just think of all the movies you'll get to rent when you're done with your training!

How This Book Is Organized

This book is separated into six major parts:

- Part I: Introduction to 3D Game Programming—This section introduces you to game programming, Windows, and DirectX, and we build up the virtual computer interface used to create all the demos.
- Part II: 3D Math and Transformation—This section introduces all the mathematical concepts and builds up a complete mathematics library for use in the book. The latter parts of the section cover 3D graphics, data structures, cameras, and wireframe rendering.
- Part III: Basic 3D Rendering—This section covers lighting, basic shading, and hidden surface removal. Full 3D clipping is also covered.
- Part IV: Advanced 3D Rendering—This section covers texture mapping, advanced lighting, shadows, and spatial partitioning algorithms, such as BSP trees, portals, and more.

- Part V: Advanced Animation, Physics Modeling, and Optimization—This section covers animation, motion, collision detection, and simple physics modeling. Hierarchical modeling is also covered, along with loading large worlds. We'll also cover numerous optimization techniques.

Installing the CD-ROM

The CD-ROM contains all the source, executables, sample programs, stock art, 3D modelers, sound effects, and bonus technical articles that make up the book. Here's the directory structure:

```
T3DIIGAME\

SOURCE\
        T3DIICHAP01\
        T3DIICHAP02\
                .
                .
        T3DIICHAP16\

TOOLS\
GAMES\
MEDIA\
         BITMAPS\
         3DMODELS\
         SOUND\


DIRECTX\


ARTICLES\
```

Each main directory contains specific data that you'll need. Here's a more detailed breakdown:

- `T3DGAMEII`—The root directory that contains all other directories. Be sure to read the `README.TXT` within it for any last-minute changes.
- `SOURCE`—Contains all the source directories for the book in chapter order. Simply drag the entire `SOURCE\` directory to your hard drive and work from there.
- `MEDIA`—Contains stock 2D artwork,3D models, and sounds that you may use royalty-free in your games.
- `DIRECTX`—Contains the latest version of the DirectX SDK.

- GAMES—Contains a number of 2D and 3D shareware games that I think are cool!
- ARTICLES—Contains articles written by various experts in the field of game programming for your edification.
- TOOLS—Contains various applications and tools you might find useful. Most can be downloaded from internet, but they are rather large, so these versions will save you the download time.

There isn't any general installation program for the CD because there are so many different types of programs and data. I leave the installation to you. However, in most cases, you'll simply copy the SOURCE\ directory to your hard drive and work within it. As for the other programs and data, you'll probably install them as you need them.

Installing DirectX

About the only important part of the CD that you must install is the DirectX SDK and runtime files. The installation program is located within the DIRECTX\ directory, along with a README.TXT file explaining any last-minute changes.

NOTE

You must install the DirectX 8.1 SDK or better to work with demos and source from this book (DirectX 9.0 is on the CD though), so if you're not sure that you have the latest files on your system, run the installation and it will tell you.

Compiling the Programs

I wrote the programs in this book with Microsoft Visual C++ 6.0. However, the programs will work with any Win32-compliant compiler in most cases. Nevertheless, I suggest Microsoft Visual C++ or .NET, because they work the best for this type of work.

If you are unfamiliar with your compiler's IDE, you are going to be wildly lost when compiling Windows programs. Please take the time to learn your way around the compiler, and at least how to compile a "Hello World" console program or something before you dive into compiling the programs.

To compile Windows Win32 .EXE programs, all you need to do is set the target of your program project to Win32 .EXE and compile. However, to create DirectX programs, you must include the DirectX import libraries in your project. You might think that you can simply add the DirectX libraries to your include path, but this won't work! Save yourself a headache and include the DirectX .LIB files in your project or workspace manually. You can find the .LIB files in the LIB\ directory, right under the main DirectX SDK directory that you installed under. This way, there won't be any linker confusion. In most cases, you'll need the following:

- `DDRAW.LIB`—DirectDraw import library
- `DINPUT.LIB`—DirectInput import library
- `DINPUT8.LIB`—DirectInput import library
- `DSOUND.LIB`—DirectSound import library
- `WINMM.LIB`—Windows Multimedia Extensions

I'll go into more detail on these files when you actually start working with them, but at least keep them in mind when you start getting "unresolved symbol" errors from your linker. I don't want any emails on this subject from rookies!

In addition to the DirectX .LIB files, you must include the DirectX .H header files in your header search path, so keep that in mind. Also, make sure to make the DirectX SDK directories first in the search path list, because many C++ compilers have old versions of DirectX within them, and the old headers might be found in the compiler's own `INCLUDE\`, which is wrong. The proper place is the DirectX SDK include directory, which is located in the main installation directory of the DirectX SDK in `INCLUDE\`.

Finally, for those of you that use Borland products, make sure that you use the Borland versions of the DirectX .LIB files. They can be found in the `BORLAND\` directory of the DirectX SDK installation.

PART I

Introduction to 3D Game Programming

IN THIS PART

CHAPTER 1

Getting Started with 3D Game Programming

IN THIS CHAPTER

- A Brief Introduction
- The Elements of a 2D/3D Game
- General Game Programming Guidelines
- Using Tools
- A Sample 3D Game: *Raiders 3D*

"1.21 Gigawatts!!!"

—Dr. Emmett Brown, *Back to the Future*

In this chapter we're going to cover some general game programming topics, like game loops and the differences between 2D and 3D games, to get you warmed up. Then we'll finish off with a little 3D game to get you set up on the compiler and DirectX correctly. If you have already read the first book of my grand series, *Tricks of the Windows Game Programming Gurus*, you can probably skim this chapter and only focus on the content at the end. But if you haven't, you should definitely read it—even if you're an intermediate or advanced game programmer. Here's what's in store:

- A brief introduction
- The elements of a 2D/3D game
- General game programming guidelines
- Using tools
- A sample 16-bit/windowed game: *Raiders 3D*

A Brief Introduction

This book is really the second volume of a two- (possibly three) volume series about 2D and 3D game programming. The first volume, *Tricks of the Windows Game Programming Gurus*, primarily covered the following:

- Windows programming
- The Win32 API

- DirectX foundation
- Artificial intelligence
- Basic physics modeling
- Sound and music
- Algorithms
- Game programming
- 2D raster and vector graphics

This book is really just a continuation of the previous book. However, I've attempted to write it so that if you haven't read the first book, you can still get a lot out of it in relation to real-time 3D graphics as it pertains to writing 3D games. Hence, the ideal reader of the book is either someone that has read the first *Tricks* book and is interested in 3D, or someone that is already a 2D game programmer and wants to learn 3D techniques from a software and algorithmic point of view.

With that in mind, I'm going to focus on 3D math and graphics in this book, and move very fast over anything related to game programming. I assume that you know it—if you don't, I suggest picking up *Tricks of the Windows Game Programming Gurus* (or any other good game programming book) and sitting at the computer until you feel comfortable with Windows, DirectX, and game programming in general.

On the other hand, even if you haven't read the previous *Tricks* and know nothing of game programming, you will still get something out of this book, because this is a graphics book. We are going to build the 3D engine(s) for the book chapter by chapter, but to save time (and about 1,500 pages), we're going to start off with the basic DirectX engine developed in the first book. (This will help with 2D, sound, music, input, and so forth.) Of course, this engine is a DirectX 7–8 engine, and now DirectX has changed a bit in Version 8.0+ to make 2D harder, because DirectDraw has been merged with Direct3D. We are going to stick with the DirectX 7 and 8 interfaces, but compile under the DirectX 9.0 SDK.

NOTE

This book is about software and algorithms, not DirectX, so I could write it in DOS and the material would be applicable. We just need reasonably advanced graphics, I/O, and a sound layer, so DirectX 8.0+ is fine. In other words, if you're a fan of Linux, porting the engine to SDL will be a snap!

Therefore, if you've already read the previous *Tricks*, the engine and functions will be very familiar. If you haven't, you'll just have to think of it as a black box API (source included, of course), because in this book we'll be adding the 3D aspect to it as we go.

Don't worry—in the next chapter, we'll cover the entire 2D engine API and structure, and you'll know what every function does; I'll also throw you a number of demos to get you warmed up using the basic DirectX engine created in the first book.

In this book, I want to try and take as much of a generic, or better yet, "virtual" point of view of the graphics system. Although the code will be based on my previous engine from the first *Tricks*, the point is that my previous engine does nothing more than set up a double-buffered graphics system in a standard, linearly addressable manner.

Thus, if you want to port any of the code to a Mac or Linux box, it should literally take anywhere from a few hours to a weekend. My goal here is to teach 3D graphics and math in general. It just so happens that the Windows platform under DirectX is the most prevalent computing system in the world at this time, so that's what I based the low-level stuff on. It's the high-level concepts that we are interested in here.

I have written about 20 or so 3D engines in my life, and I have them all here on my hard drives. But when I write a book, I like to write a new engine as I (we) go, so that I write the engine for the book, and not a book about that engine. The point of this book is not to regurgitate a 3D engine, but to make one. Thus, I'm not sure what we will end up with! In fact, I'm kind of excited to see what will happen. I'm shooting for a *Quake*-like 6DOF (degree of freedom) engine, but who knows? You will learn everything necessary to make a *Quake* engine, but I might get really focused on outdoor engines or something else—who knows. The point is that it will be a learning experience, and not the typical code dump with author annotations. I'm sure you know what I'm talking about!

Lastly, readers from the first book might notice that some of the material is the same here and there. Truthfully, I can't just jump into 3D graphics without some overlap with the last book. I can't assume someone has my other book, or force them to buy it (it's not like it makes me rich or anything, but maybe they don't have access). Whatever the case, the first few chapters will have a bit of overlap here and there in relation to DirectX, the engine, and Windows.

The Elements of a 2D/3D Game

As a review, let's take a look at what makes a video game program different from any other kind of program. Video games are extremely complex pieces of software. In fact, they are without a doubt the hardest programs to write. Sure, writing something like MS Word is harder than writing an asteroids game, but writing something like *Unreal*, *Quake Arena*, or *Halo* is harder than any program I can think of—including military weapons control software!

This means that you have to learn a new way of programming that's more conducive to real-time applications and simulation, rather than single-line, event-driven, or sequential logic programs that you might be used to. A video game is basically a continuous loop that performs logic and draws an image on the screen—usually at a rate of 30–60 fps (frames per second) or more. This is similar to how a movie is displayed, except that you are making the movie as you go.

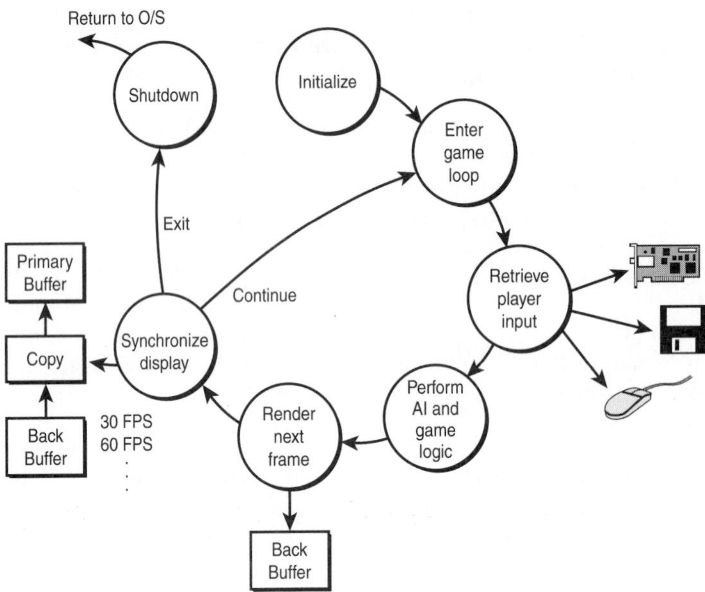

FIGURE 1.1 General game loop architecture.

Let's begin by taking a look at a simplified game loop, as shown in Figure 1.1. The following sections describe each section.

Section 1: Initialization

In this section, you perform the standard operations you would for any program, such as memory allocation, resource acquisition, loading data from the disk, and so forth.

Section 2: Enter Game Loop

In this section, the code execution enters into the main game loop. This is where the action begins and continues until the user exits out of the main loop.

Section 3: Retrieve Player Input

In this section, the player's input is processed and/or buffered for later use in the AI and logic section.

Section 4: Perform AI and Game Logic

This section contains the majority of the game code. The artificial intelligence, physics systems, and general game logic are executed, and the results are used to draw the next frame on the screen.

Section 5: Render Next Frame

In this section, the results of the player's input and the execution of the game AI and logic are used to generate the next frame of animation for the game. This image is usually drawn on an offscreen buffer area, so you can't see it being rendered. Next the image is very quickly copied to the visible display, creating the illusion of animation. In the case of a 3D software-based engine, thousands (or millions in some cases) of polygons are rendered that compose the world by a very complex 3D graphics pipeline. In the case of a 3D hardware-accelerated engine based on OpenGL or Direct3D, much of the work is offloaded to the hardware.

Section 6: Synchronize Display

Many computers will speed up or slow down due to the level of complexity that the game is currently exhibiting. For example, if there are 1,000 objects running around on the screen, the CPU is going to have a higher load than if there are only 10 objects. Therefore, the frame rate of the game will vary, which isn't acceptable. Hence, you must synchronize the game to some maximum frame rate and try and hold it there using timing and/or wait functions. Usually, 30 fps is considered to be minimum frame rate these days, with 60 fps being ideal. Frame rates over 60 fps are hardly an improvement, because your brain has problems processing information any faster that 60 fps—this is a waste, unless you are a Borg.

NOTE

Even though some games ideally update each frame 30–60 times a second, this frame rate might drop as the complexity level of the 3D rendering increases. However, using time-based calculations in the game logic, physics, and AI sections of the code will at least attempt to keep the display somewhat steady, as far as how much objects move in real time. That is, if time (*t*) is used in each of the calculations for motion and animation control, the result is much more temporally consistent animation.

Section 7: Loop

This section is fairly simple—just loop back to the beginning of the game loop and do it all again.

Section 8: Shutdown

This is the end of the game, meaning that the user has exited the main body or game loop and wants to return to the operating system. However, before doing this, you must release all resources and clean up the system, as you would for any other piece of software.

Now you might be wondering about all the details of a real game loop. Granted, the preceding explanation is a little oversimplified, but it captures the essence of what's going on. In reality, the game loop will in most cases be a *FSM (finite state machine)* that contains a number of states. For example, the following listing is a more detailed version of what a C/C++ game loop might look like in real code.

LISTING 1.1 A Simple Game Event Loop

```
// defines for game loop states
#define GAME_INIT     // the game is initializing
#define GAME_MENU     // the game is in the menu mode
#define GAME_START    // the game is about to run
#define GAME_RUN     // the game is now running
#define GAME_RESTART  // the game is going to restart
#define GAME_EXIT     // the game is exiting

// game globals
int game_state = GAME_INIT; // start off in this state
int error   = 0;    // used to send errors back to OS


// main begins here

void main()
{
// implementation of main game-loop

while (game_state!=GAME_EXIT)
  {
  // what state is game loop in
    switch(game_state)
  {
    case GAME_INIT: // the game is initializing
       {
       // allocate all memory and resources
      Init();

      // move to menu state
      game_state = GAME_MENU;
      } break;

     case GAME_MENU: // the game is in the menu mode
       {
       // call the main menu function and let it switch states
       game_state = Menu();
```

LISTING 1.1 Continued

```
        // note: we could force a RUN state here
        } break;

      case GAME_START:  // the game is about to run
        {
        // this state is optional, but usually used to
        // set things up right before the game is run
        // you might do a little more housekeeping here
        Setup_For_Run();

        // switch to run state
        game_state = GAME_RUN;
        } break;

      case GAME_RUN:  // the game is now running
        {
        // this section contains the entire game logic loop

        // clear the display
        Clear();

        // get the input
        Get_Input();

        // perform logic and ai
        Do_Logic();

        // display the next frame of animation
        // render 2D or 3D world
        Render_Frame();

        // synchronize the display to 30 fps+
        Wait();

        // the only way that state can be changed is
        // thru user interaction in the
        // input section or by maybe losing the game..
        } break;

      case GAME_RESTART: // the game is restarting
        {
        // this section is a cleanup state used to
```

LISTING 1.1 Continued

```
          // fix up any loose ends before
          // running again
          Fixup();
          // switch states back to the menu
          game_state = GAME_MENU;
          } break;

       case GAME_EXIT:  // the game is exiting
          {
          // if the game is in this state then
          // it's time to bail, kill everything
          // and cross your fingers
          Release_And_Cleanup();

          // set the error word to whatever
          error = 0;

          // note: we don't have to switch states
          // since we are already in this state
          // on the next loop iteration the code
          // will fall out of the main while and
          // exit back to the OS
          } break;

    default: break;
    } // end switch

  } // end while

// return error code to operating system
return(error);

} // end main
```

Although the code is nonfunctional, I think that you can get a good idea of the structure of a real game loop by studying it. All game loops—2D, 3D, whatever—pretty much follow this structure in one way or another. Take a look at Figure 1.2 to see the state transition diagram for the game loop logic. As you can see, the state transitions are fairly sequential.

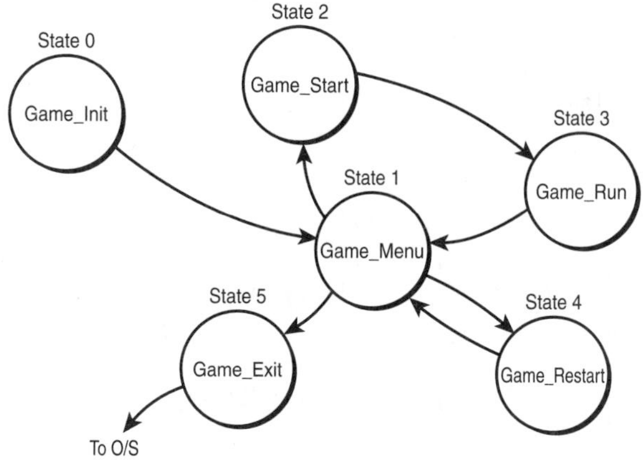

FIGURE 1.2 State transition diagram for the game loop logic.

General Game Programming Guidelines

The next thing I want to talk about is general game programming techniques and philosophies that you should think about and try to adopt (if you can) that will make game programming much easier for you.

To begin with, video games are ultra-high performance computer programs. This means that no longer can you use high-level APIs for time-critical or memory-critical code sections. You must, for the most part, write everything that is related to the inner loop of your game code yourself, or your game will suffer terrible speed and performance problems. Obviously, this doesn't mean that you can't trust APIs like DirectX, because DirectX was written to be as high performance and "thin" as possible. But in general, avoid high-level function calls based on the Win32 API. For example, you might think that `memset()` is very fast, but it only fills using single `BYTE`s. A much better fill would use `QUAD`s, so that four `BYTE`s can be written at once. For example, here's an inline assembly language function that I use to do `QUAD-BYTE` fills:

```
inline void Mem_Set_QUAD(void *dest, UINT data, int count)
{
// this function fills or sets unsigned 32-bit aligned memory
// count is number of quads

_asm
  {
```

```
  mov edi, dest  ; edi points to destination memory
  mov ecx, count ; number of 32-bit words to move
  mov eax, data  ; 32-bit data
  rep stosd     ; move data
  } // end asm

} // end Mem_Set_QUAD
```

And here's a WORD, or 2-BYTE version:

```
inline void Mem_Set_WORD(void *dest, USHORT data, int count)
{
// this function fills or sets unsigned 16-bit aligned memory
// count is number of words

_asm
  {
  mov edi, dest  ; edi points to destination memory
  mov ecx, count ; number of 16-bit words to move
  mov ax, data  ; 16-bit data
  rep stosw    ; move data
  } // end asm

} // end Mem_Set_WORD
```

These few lines of code can speed the frame rate of your game by two to four times in some cases! So, you definitely need to know what's inside of an API call if you are going to use API calls.

NOTE

Additionally, the Pentium III, 4, and greater support SIMD (Single Instruction Multiple Data) instructions that allow parallel processing of simple mathematical operations, so there's a lot of room to optimize basic math operations, like vector mathematics and matrix multiplications, but we'll get to that later.

Let's take a look at a list of tricks to keep in mind as you're programming.

TRICK

Back up your work all the time. When writing game code, you are going to lock the system up fairly frequently. Redoing a sorting algorithm is one thing, but redoing the AI for a character and the collision detection is another.

TRICK

When you start on your game projects, be organized. Use reasonable filenames and directory names, come up with a consistent variable naming convention, and try to use separate directories for graphics and sound data rather than dumping everything in one directory.

TRICK

Use inline functions. You can get rid of the function call completely by using the inline directive. The inline directive instructs the compiler to make its best attempt to put the code for the function right where it's called, rather than making the actual function call. Of course, this makes bigger programs, but speed is more important. Here's an example:

```
inline void Plot_I(int x, int y, int color)
{
// plots a pixel on the screen
video_buffer[x + y*MEMORY_PITCH] = color;
} // end Plot_I
```

Notice in this case I didn't use globals, because the compiler will in effect perform the same type of data aliasing. However, globals would come in handy if only one or two of the parameters were changing between calls, because the old values can be used without reloading.

TRICK

Always use 32-bit variables rather than 8- or 16-bit when possible. The Pentium and later processors are totally 32-bit, and the Itanium is 64-bit. This means that they don't like 8- or 16-bit data words. In fact, smaller data can slow them down because of caching and other related memory addressing anomalies. For example, you might create a structure that looks something like this:

```
struct CPOINT
{
short x,y;
unsigned char c;
} // end CPOINT
```

Although this might seem like a good idea, it's not! First, the structure itself is now 5 bytes long `(2*sizeof(short) + sizeof(char))` = 5. This is really bad, and will wreak havoc on the memory addressing. A better approach is the following structure:

```
struct CPOINT
{
int x,y;
int c;
} // end CPOINT
```

NOTE

STRUCTs in C++ are just like CLASSes, except that they have default PUBLIC visibility.

This new structure is much better. For one thing, all the elements are the same size—that is, `sizeof(int)` = 4 bytes. Therefore, a single pointer can be incremented on a DWORD boundary to access any member. Of course, the new structure is now `(3*sizeof(int))` = 12 bytes, but at least it's a multiple of 4 or on a DWORD boundary; this is definitely going to improve performance.

In fact, if you really want to make things rock, you can pad all structures to make them a multiple of 32 bytes. This is the optimal length because of standard on-chip cache line sizes in the Pentium class processors. Padding can be accomplished manually by adding dummy variables, or with a compiler directive (the easy way). Of course, this might waste a lot of memory, but it might be worth the speed.

TRICK

Don't be afraid to use global variables. Many video games don't use parameters for a lot of time-critical functions, and simply use a global parameter-passing area instead. For example, if a function looks like this:

```
void Plot(int x, int y, int color)
{
// plots a pixel on the screen
video_buffer[x + y*MEMORY_PITCH] = color;
} // end Plot
```

The body of the function takes less time than the function call! This is because of the parameter pushing and popping on the stack. In this case, a better method might be to first create a global parameter-passing area, and then make assignments before a call:

```
int gx,gy,gz,gcolor; // define some globals

void Plot_G(void)
{
// plot a pixel using globals
video_buffer[gx + gy*MEMORY_PITCH] = gcolor;

} // end Plot_G
```

TRICK

Program in a RISC (Reduced Instruction Set Computer)-like manner. Make your code simple rather than complex. Pentium processors especially like simple instructions rather than complex ones. Also, making your code longer with simpler instructions makes it easier for the compiler. For example, don't do this:

```
if (x+=(2*buffer[index++])>10)
{
// do work
} // end if
```

Do this:

```
x+=(2*buffer[index]);
index++;

if (x > 10)
{
// do work
} // end if
```

There are two reasons for coding like this. First, it allows a debugger to put break points in between code sections, and second, it makes it easier for the compiler to send simplified code to the PentiumX, which allows it to process more code in parallel using multiple execution units. Complex code is bad!

TRICK

Use binary shifts for the simple multiplication of integers by powers of two. Because all data in a computer is stored in binary form, shifting the bit pattern to the left or right is equivalent to multiplication and division, respectively. For example:

```
int y_pos = 10;

// multiply y_pos by 64
y_pos = (y_pos << 6); // 2^6 = 64
```

Similarly,

```
// to divide y_pos by 8
y_pos = (y_pos >> 3); // 1/2^3 = 1/8
```

Of course, these days (especially on the Pentium 4), there are single-cycle multiplications, but shifting is always a safe bet to multiply and divide by two really fast.

TRICK

Write efficient algorithms. All the assembly language in the world isn't going to make an $O(n^2)$ algorithm go faster. It's better to use clean, efficient algorithms rather than brute force.

TRICK

Don't optimize your code as you program. When writing game code, it's tempting to optimize as you go. This is usually a waste of time. Wait until you are done with a major code block or until you're done with the game before you start heavy optimization (Intel's VTUNE is a great tool for profiling). This will save you time in the end, because you won't have to deal with cryptic code or optimizations that aren't necessary. When the game is done, that's when you start profiling and finding problem areas to optimize. On the other hand, don't program sloppily.

TRICK

Use C++ sparingly. If you're a seasoned professional, go ahead and do as you please, but don't go class crazy or overload everything to death. In the end, simple, straightforward code is the best and easiest to debug. And I never want to see multiple inheritance! If C is good enough for *Doom* and *Quake*, there's no Earth-shattering reason to use C++. If it helps you, great; if not, stay away from it for game programming until you are comfortable with game programming and C++.

TRICK

If you see that you're going down a rocky road, stop, back up, and take a detour. I have seen many game programmers start down a bad programming line and bury themselves. It's better to realize you've made a mistake and redo 500 lines of code than to have a generally undesirable code structure. So, if you see a problem with what you're doing, re-evaluate and make sure that the time you're saving is worth it.

TRICK

Don't write a lot of complex data structures for simple objects. Just because linked lists are cool doesn't mean you should use them for a fixed array that you know will always be around 256 items. Just allocate it statically and be done with it. Video game programming is 90% data manipulation. Keep your data as simple and visible as possible, so you can access it quickly, do what you need to, and move on. Make sure the data structure fits the problem.

Using Tools

Writing video games used to be nothing more than a text editor and maybe homemade paint and sound programs. However, today things are a little more complicated. To write a 3D game, at a minimum you need a C/C++ compiler, 2D paint program, sound processing program, and some kind of minimal 3D modeler (unless you're going to enter all the 3D model data as ASCII data). Additionally, you'll need a music sequencing program if you're going to use any MIDI, or at least make changes to presequenced MIDI.

Let's take a look at some of the more popular products and what they do.

- C/C++ compilers—For Windows 9*x*/Me/XP/2000/NT development, there simply is no better compiler than MS VC++, shown in Figure 1.3. It does everything you need it to do and more. The .EXEs generated are the fastest code available. The Borland compiler will also work fine (and is a bit cheaper), but has a much smaller feature set. In either case, you don't need the full-blown version of either—a student version that makes Win32 .EXEs is more than enough.

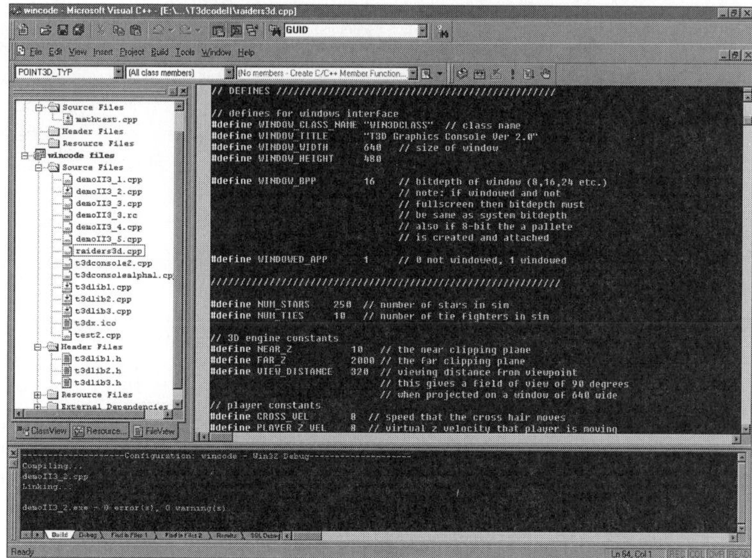

FIGURE 1.3 The Microsoft VC++ environment.

- 2D bitmap art software—Here you have paint programs, drawing programs, and image processing. Paint programs primarily allow you to draw images pixel by pixel with primitives and to manipulate them. As far as I'm concerned, Paint Shop Pro by JASC, shown in Figure 1.4, is the leader of the pack for price versus performance. But the ultimate favorite of most artists is Adobe Photoshop—it has more firepower than you'll ever need.

- 2D vector art software—Drawing programs, on the other hand, allow you to create images that are mostly constructed from curves, lines, and 2D geometrical primitives. The types of programs aren't as useful, but if you need one, Adobe Illustrator is the way to go.

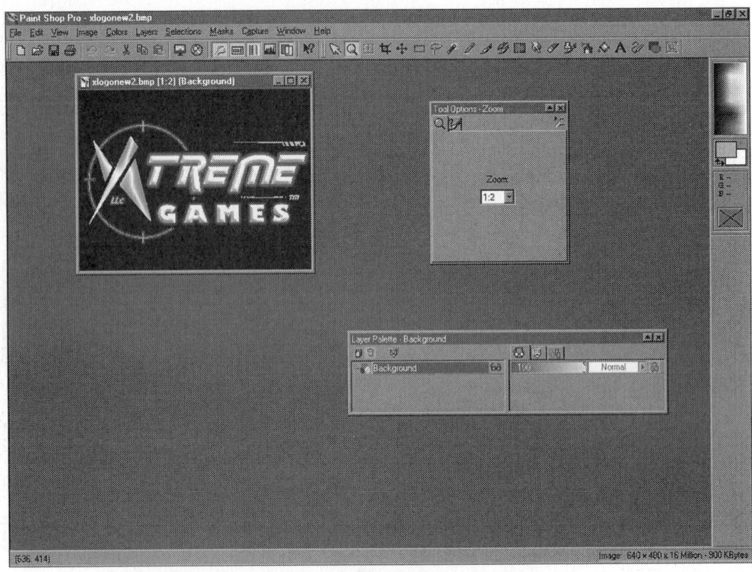

FIGURE 1.4 Paint Shop Pro by JASC Software.

- Post-production image processing—Image processors are the final class of 2D art programs. These programs are more for post-production rather than art creation. In this area, Adobe Photoshop is the favorite in most circles, but I think Corel Photo-Paint is better—you decide.
- Sound processing software—Ninety percent of all sound FX used in games today are digitized samples. To work with sound data of this type, you're going to need a digital sound processing program. One of the best programs in this genre is Sound Forge, shown in Figure 1.5. It is by far one of the most complex sound processing programs I have ever seen, and ironically the simplest to use as well. I'm still trying to figure out all the cool features! Cool Edit Pro is also very powerful, but I have less experience with it.
- 3D modelers—This is where things get financially challenging. 3D modelers can cost in the tens of thousands of dollars, but recently a number of low-cost modelers have shown up that have enough power to literally make a movie. The modeler that I primarily use for simple to medium-scale 3D models and animation is Caligari trueSpace, shown in Figure 1.6. This is the best 3D modeler for the price—it only costs a few hundred dollars, and has the best interface there is, in my opinion.

If you want a little more firepower and absolute photo-realism, 3D Studio Max, shown in Figure 1.7, is the way to go, but it costs around $2,500 or more, so that might be something to think about. However, because we are going to use these modelers just to create 3D meshes for the most part, and not for rendering, all the bells and whistles aren't really needed—trueSpace is the way to go, or perhaps a freeware or shareware modeler.

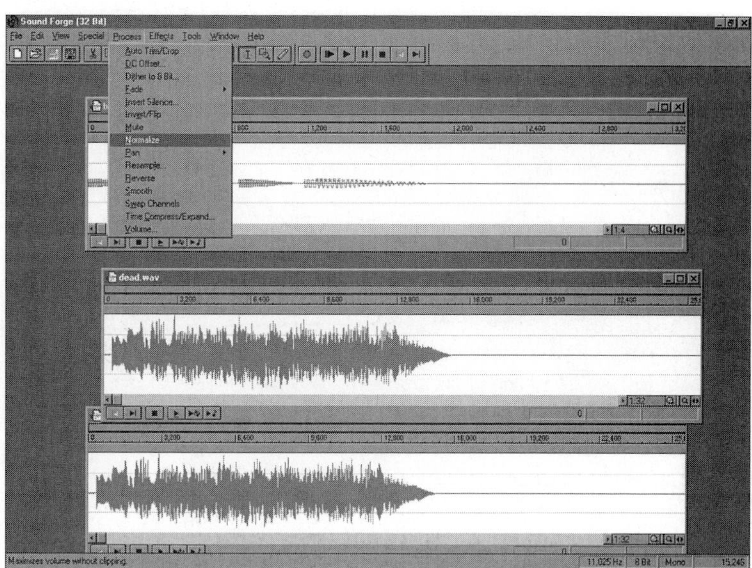

FIGURE 1.5 Sound Forge in action.

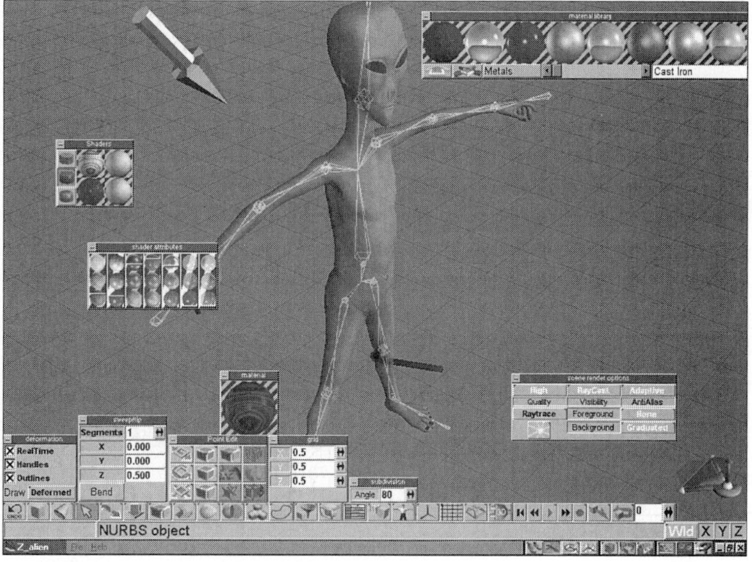

FIGURE 1.6 Caligari's trueSpace 3D modeler.

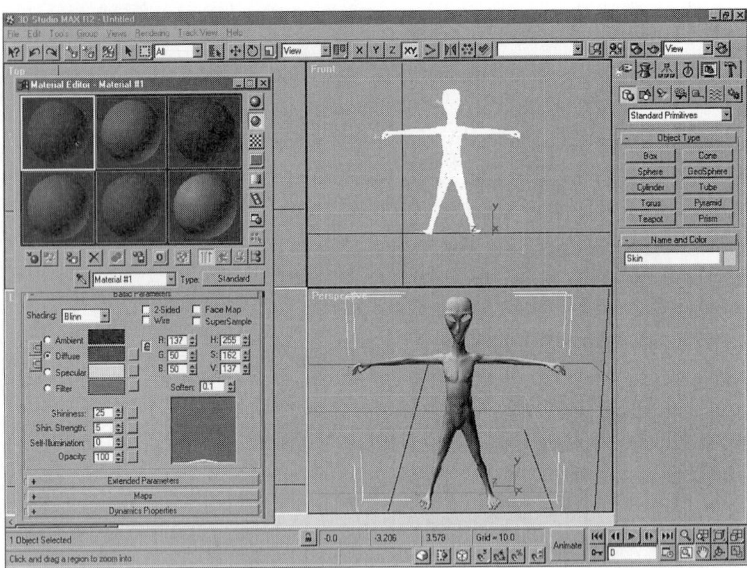

FIGURE 1.7 3D Studio Max (Heavy Metal).

NOTE

The Internet is full of free or shareware 3D modelers that are in some cases as powerful as the real thing. So, if cash is a problem, hunt around and see what you can find.

3D Level Editors

In this book, we are going to write a software-based 3D engine. However, we aren't going to write a complex tool to create 3D interior models. It's possible to create a 3D world with a 3D modeler, but there are much better programs to do this, such as WorldCraft, shown in Figure 1.8. Hence, the best approach to use when writing a 3D game and engine is to use a file format and data structure that is compatible with the types output by a commonly available editor such as WorldCraft (or a similar editor), so you can use someone else's tool to create your worlds. Of course, the file format of most of these editors is ultimately based on the work of id Software and the *Quake* engine, but whether it's based on the *Quake* file format or whatever, it's a proven file format, and obviously works well.

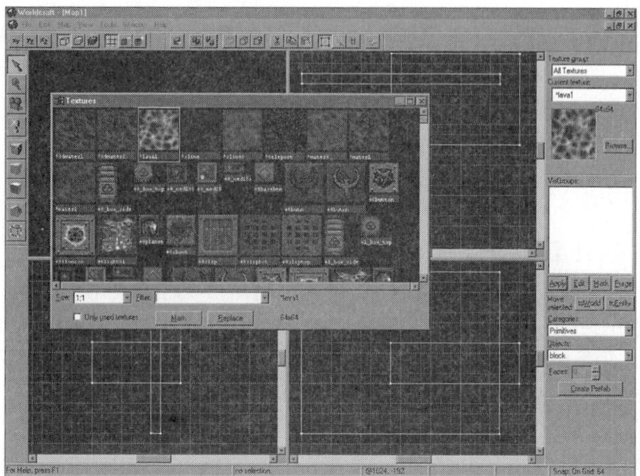

FIGURE 1.8 The WorldCraft level editor.

- Music and MIDI sequencing programs—There are two kinds of music in today's games: pure digital (like a CD), and MIDI (Musical Instruments Digital Interface), which is a synthesized performance based on note data. If you want to manipulate MIDI information and songs, you'll need a sequencing package. One of the best is called CakeWalk, shown in Figure 1.9. CakeWalk is also reasonably priced, so I suggest that you look into this program if you plan on recording and manipulating any MIDI music. We'll talk about MIDI data when covering DirectMusic.

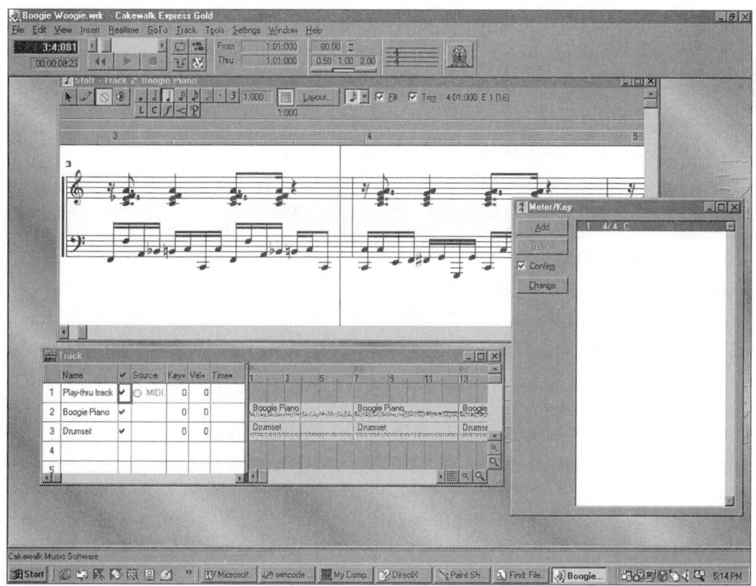

FIGURE 1.9 CakeWalk MIDI track sequencer.

NOTE

And now for the cool part ... A number of the manufacturers of the software listed previously have allowed me to put shareware or evaluation versions on the CD, so make sure to check them out!

Setting Up to Get Down—Using The Compiler

One of the most frustrating parts of learning 3D windows game programming is learning how to use the compiler. In most cases, you're so excited to get started that you dive into the IDE and try to compile, and a million compiler and linker errors pop up! To help with this problem, let's cover a few basic compiler concepts here.

NOTE

The details listed here are Visual C++-specific, but the ideas are the same for any compiler.

1. Read the entire compiler manual—please, please, I beg you!
2. You must install the DirectX 9.0 SDK on your system. To do this, navigate into the DirectX SDK directory on the CD, read the `README.TXT`, and do what it says, which should be nothing more than click on the DirectX SDK installation programs. And remember, we are using DirectX 9.0 for this book (but only using the interfaces from 7 and 8), so you need to use the DirectX SDK on the CD. However, you can compile everything with DirectX 8.0, if you really want to.
3. We are going to make Win32 .EXE application programs, ***not*** .DLLs, ActiveX components, CONSOLE applications, or anything else (unless I tell you to). So the first thing you need to do with your compiler if you want to compile is create a new project or workspace and set the target output file to Win32 .EXE. This step is shown for the Visual C++ 6.0 compiler in Figure 1.10.

NOTE

There are two types of .EXEs that you can build when compiling: Release and Debug. Release is faster code and optimized, whereas Debug is slower and has debugger hooks in it. I suggest that while you are developing, you build the Debug version until it works, then go ahead and set the compiler to Release mode.

4. Add the source files to the project using the Add Files command from the main menu, or from the project node itself. This is shown for the Visual C++ 6.0 compiler in Figure 1.11.

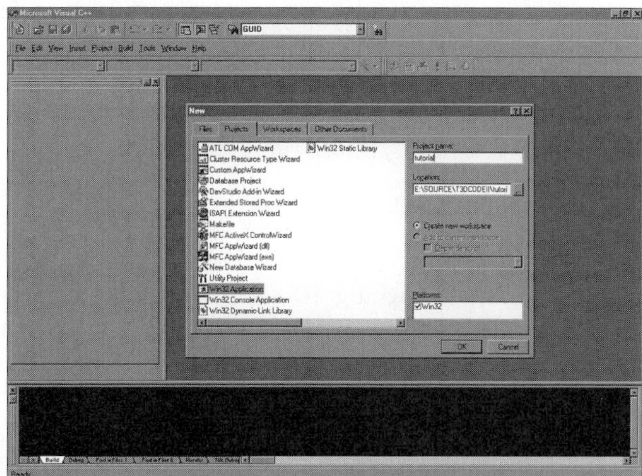

FIGURE 1.10 Creating a Win32 .EXE with Visual C++ 6.0.

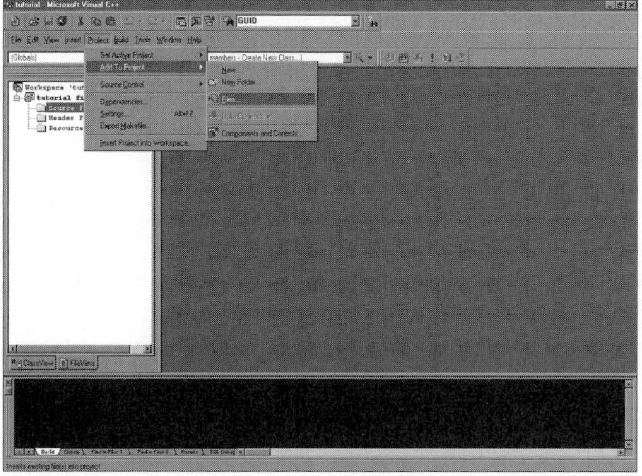

FIGURE 1.11 Adding files to a project with Visual C++ 6.0.

5. When you compile anything that needs DirectX, you're going to have to include in the search path of the compiler the location of the DirectX header files, as well as the location of the DirectX .LIB files. You can make these additions under the Options, Directories menu item in the main menu of the IDE. Then make the appropriate additions to the Include Files and Library Files variables. This is shown in Figure 1.12. (Of course, make sure you point them to your particular installation of DirectX and the newest libraries and header files.)

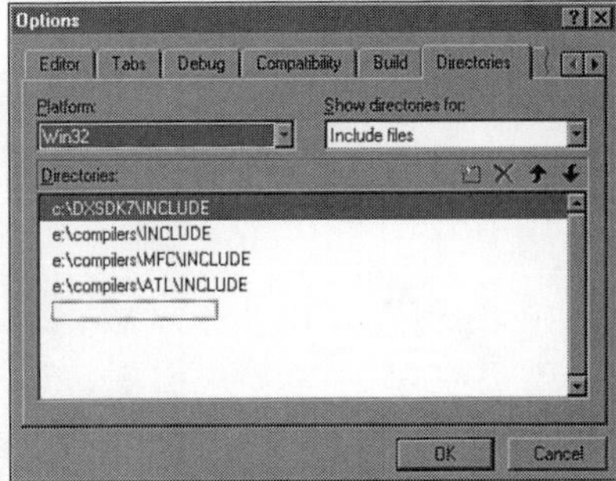

FIGURE 1.12 Setting up the search paths in Visual C++ 6.0.

> **NOTE**
>
> Make sure that the DirectX search nodes are **FIRST** in the list(s). You don't want the compiler finding old versions of DirectX that might have come with the compiler.

6. Additionally, you have to actually include the DirectX COM interface import libraries, listed here and shown in Figure 1.13, to the link list of your project or to the project resource list.

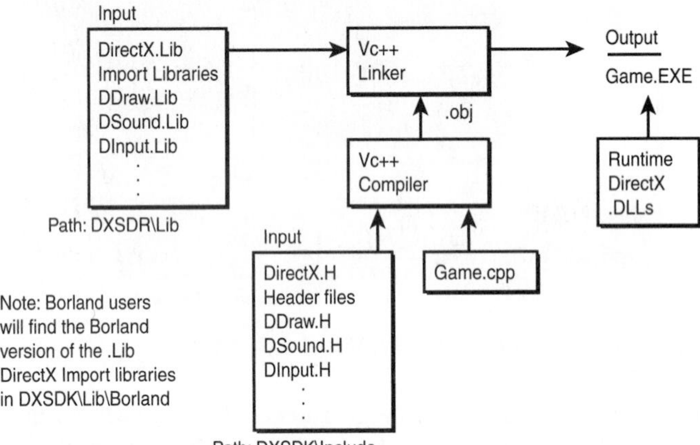

FIGURE 1.13 The resources needed to create a Win32 DirectX application.

- `DDRAW.LIB`
- `DSOUND.LIB`
- `DINPUT.LIB`

- `DINPUT8.LIB`
- Any others that I mention for a particular example

These DirectX .LIB files are located in the `LIB\` directory wherever you installed the DirectX SDK. **You MUST add these .LIB files to your project or workspace**. You can't just add the `LIB\` directory to the search path alone—that simply indicates where to search, but doesn't tell the compiler/linker to actually link the DirectX .LIB files. I have received thousands (that's right, thousands) of emails from people that don't do this and have problems. Once again: **You must manually include the DirectX .LIB files in the compiler's link list with the other libraries OR in the project along with your .CPP files**. You can do this in the Project, Settings submenu in the Link, General dialog in the Object/Library-Modules list. This is shown in Figure 1.14.

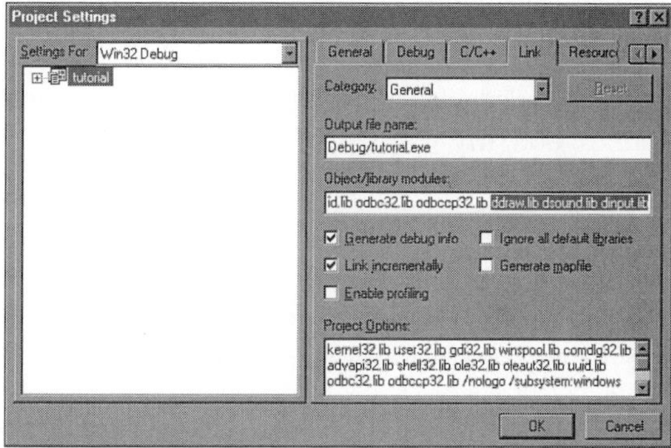

FIGURE 1.14 Adding the DirectX .LIB files to the link list in Visual C++ 6.0.

> **NOTE**
>
> While you're at it, you might have to add the Windows Multimedia Extensions library `WINMM.LIB` to your project if you're using Visual C++. This file is located in the `LIB\` directory of your Visual C++ compiler installation. If it's not there, just use the FIND command from the Start menu to find it. Once found, add it to the link list.

7. You're ready to compile your programs.

> **NOTE**
>
> If you're a Borland user, there is a separate `BORLAND\` library directory within the DirectX SDK, so make sure to add the .LIB files found in there for DirectX and NOT the higher Visual C++ DirectX .LIB files up higher in the directory tree, which are MS-Visual C++ compatible.

If you still have questions about this, don't worry—I will revisit the steps a number of times throughout the book when compiling the programs. But if I get one email about compiling and it's something that is right here in the preceding paragraphs—I'm going to explode!

NOTE

I'm sure you have heard of the new Visual .NET System. Technically, it's the newest of Microsoft's compiler and development technologies, but it's brand new. It only runs on Windows XP/2000 decently, and is overkill for our purposes, so we will stick with Visual C++ 6.0. However, everything works with .NET just as well: Win32 is Win32!

A Sample 3D Game: *Raiders 3D*

Before we both lose our minds talking about math, 3D game programming, and graphics, I would like to take a pause and show you a complete 3D space game—a simple one, but a game nonetheless. This way you can see a real game loop, some graphics calls, and give a shot at compilation. Sound good, my young Jedi?

The problem is we are only on Chapter 1, so it's not like I can use stuff from later chapters—that would be cheating, right? And I haven't showed you the API engine from the previous *Tricks*. So, I've decided to get you accustomed to using "black box" APIs for game programming. Hence, this sample game will get you accustomed to the idea of using an API such as DirectX and the engine from the first book.

NOTE

Although in the 70s, 80s, and early 90s you could get away with doing everything yourself, in the 21st century, there are simply too many hardware and software subsystems in a computer—it's nearly impossible to write everything yourself. Alas, we finally have to give in as game programmers and use a few APIs such as Win32, DirectX, and so forth.

Therefore, based on the "black box" requirement, I wondered what, at the absolute minimum, would be needed to create a 16-bit 3D wireframe space game?

All we really need is the following functionality from an API:

- Change into any graphics mode using DirectX
- Draw colored lines and pixels on the screen
- Get the keyboard input
- Play a sound from a .WAV file on disk
- Play a MIDI file from a .MID file on disk

- Synchronize the game loop using some timing functions
- Draw strings of colored text on the screen
- Copy the double buffer, or offscreen rendering page to the display

All this functionality is of course in the game library modules `T3DLIB*`, created in the previous *Tricks*, which is composed of six files: `T3DLIB1.CPP¦H`, `T3DLIB2.CPP¦H`, and `T3DLIB3.CPP¦H`. Module 1 contains most of the DirectX stuff, Module 2 contains most of the DirectInput and DirectSound, and Module 3 contains DirectMusic for the most part.

Based on using the absolute minimum set of functions from the `T3DLIB*` game library, I wrote a game called *Raiders 3D* that demonstrates a number of the concepts that we have discussed in the chapter. Additionally, since the game is wireframe 3D, there's a lot of code that might not make any sense to you—that's good! Although I will briefly explain the 3D math and algorithms, don't take too much time trying to understand what's going on; this is just to give you some perspective.

Raiders 3D illustrates all the major components of a real 3D game, including a game loop, scoring, AI (the intelligence of slugs), collision, sound, and music. Figure 1.15 is a screenshot of the game in action. Granted, it's not *Star Wars*, but it's not bad for a few hours of work!

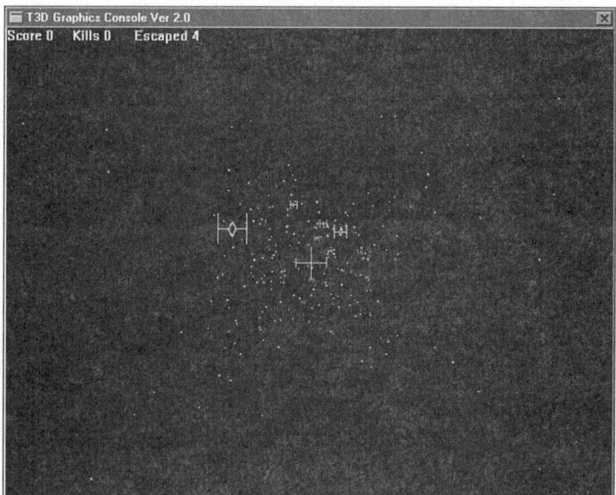

FIGURE 1.15 A screenshot of *Raiders 3D*.

NOTE

You might notice a bit of a similarity to the ancient game *Tail Gunner*. Mike, if you're reading this, did you ever get that *Tail Gunner* in your living room working?

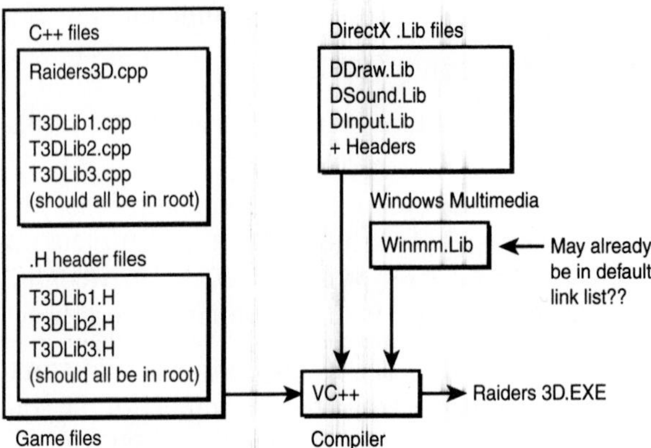

FIGURE 1.16 The code structure of *Raiders 3D*.

Before I show you the source code for the game, I want you to take a look at how the project and its various components fit together—refer to Figure 1.16. As you see from the figure, the game is composed of the following files that must be part of the project:

- `RAIDERS3D.CPP`—The main game logic that uses the functionality of `T3DLIB` and creates a minimum Win32 application.
- `T3DLIB1.CPP`—The `T3DLIB` game library source files.
- `T3DLIB2.CPP`
- `T3DLIB3.CPP`
- `T3DLIB1.H`—The header files for the game library.
- `T3DLIB2.H`
- `T3DLIB3.H`
- `DDRAW.LIB`—DirectDraw is the 2D graphics component of DirectX. The `DDRAW.LIB` import library is needed to build the application. This doesn't contain the real DirectX code; it's more of an intermediary library that you make calls to, which in turn loads the `DDRAW.DLL` dynamic link library that does the real work. You can find this in the DirectX SDK installation under `LIB\`.
- `DINPUT.LIB/DINPUT8.LIB`—DirectInput is the device input component of DirectX. The `DINPUT.LIB` and `DINPUT8.LIB` import libraries are needed to build the application. This doesn't contain the real DirectX code; it's more of an intermediary library that you make calls to, which in turn loads the `DINPUT.DLL/DINPUT8.DLL` dynamic link libraries that do the real work. You can find this in the DirectX SDK installation under `LIB\`.

- DSOUND.LIB—DirectSound is the digital sound component of DirectX. The DSOUND.LIB import library is needed to build the application. This doesn't contain the real DirectX code; it's more of an intermediary library that you make calls to, which in turn loads the DSOUND.DLL dynamic link library that does the real work. You can find this in the DirectX SDK installation under LIB\.

NOTE

Note that there isn't a DMUSIC.LIB file, even though DirectMusic is used by T3DLIB. That's because DirectMusic is a pure COM (Component Object Model) object. In other words, there isn't an import library full of nice wrapper functions to make calls to DirectMusic—you have to do all the work yourself. Luckily I did it for you!

These files aren't needed by the compiler or linker, but are the actual DirectX runtime DLLs that will be loaded when the game application starts up:

- DINPUT.DLL/DINPUT8.DLL—These are the runtime DirectDraw libraries that actually contain the COM implementation of the DirectInput interface functions that are called through the DINPUT.LIB import library. You don't need to worry about this per se, you just need to make sure that the DirectX runtime files are installed.
- DDRAW.DLL—This is the runtime DirectDraw library that actually contains the COM implementation of the DirectDraw interface functions that are called through the DDRAW.LIB import library. You don't need to worry about this per se, you just need to make sure that the DirectX runtime files are installed.
- DSOUND.DLL—This is the runtime DirectSound library that actually contains the COM implementation of the DirectSound interface functions that are called through the DSOUND.LIB import library. You don't need to worry about this per se, you just need to make sure that the DirectX runtime files are installed.
- DMUSIC.DLL—This is the runtime DirectMusic library that actually contains the COM implementation of the DirectMusic interface functions that are called directly through COM calls. You don't need to worry about this per se, you just need to make sure that the DirectX runtime files are installed.

Based on making a few calls to the library, I have created the game RAIDERS3D.CPP, which is shown in the listing below. The game runs in windowed mode with 16-bit graphics, so make sure that your desktop is in 16-bit color mode.

Anyway, take a good look at the code: especially the main game loop, 3D math, and the calls to the game processing functions:

```
// Raiders3D - RAIDERS3D.CPP -- our first 3D game
// READ THIS!
// To compile make sure to include DDRAW.LIB, DSOUND.LIB,
```

```
// DINPUT.LIB, WINMM.LIB in the project link list, and of course
// the C++ source modules T3DLIB1.CPP,T3DLIB2.CPP, and T3DLIB3.CPP
// in the project!!! And the T3DLIB1.H,T3DLIB2.H, and T3DLIB3.H
// header files in the working directory, so the compiler
// can find them

// to run the game make sure that your desktop is in 16bit
// color mode with a resolution of 640x480 or higher

// INCLUDES ///////////////////////////////////////////////

#define INITGUID    // make sure al the COM interfaces are available
            // instead of this you can include the .LIB file
            // DXGUID.LIB

#define WIN32_LEAN_AND_MEAN

#include <windows.h>  // include important windows stuff
#include <windowsx.h>
#include <mmsystem.h>
#include <iostream.h> // include important C/C++ stuff
#include <conio.h>
#include <stdlib.h>
#include <malloc.h>
#include <memory.h>
#include <string.h>
#include <stdarg.h>
#include <stdio.h>
#include <math.h>
#include <io.h>
#include <fcntl.h>

#include <ddraw.h> // directX includes
#include <dsound.h>
#include <dmksctrl.h>
#include <dmusici.h>
#include <dmusicc.h>
#include <dmusicf.h>
#include <dinput.h>
#include "T3DLIB1.h" // game library includes
#include "T3DLIB2.h"
#include "T3DLIB3.h"

// DEFINES ////////////////////////////////////////////////
```

```
// defines for windows interface
#define WINDOW_CLASS_NAME "WIN3DCLASS" // class name
#define WINDOW_TITLE   "T3D Graphics Console Ver 2.0"
#define WINDOW_WIDTH   640  // size of window
#define WINDOW_HEIGHT   480

#define WINDOW_BPP    16  // bitdepth of window (8,16,24 etc.)
                // note: if windowed and not
                // fullscreen then bitdepth must
                // be same as system bitdepth
                // also if 8-bit the a pallete
                // is created and attached

#define WINDOWED_APP   1    // 0 not windowed, 1 windowed

///////////////////////////////////////////////////////////

#define NUM_STARS  250 // number of stars in sim
#define NUM_TIES   10  // number of tie fighters in sim

// 3D engine constants
#define NEAR_Z     10  // the near clipping plane
#define FAR_Z      2000 // the far clipping plane
#define VIEW_DISTANCE  320 // viewing distance from viewpoint
               // this gives a field of view of 90 degrees
               // when projected on a window of 640 wide
// player constants
#define CROSS_VEL    8 // speed that the cross hair moves
#define PLAYER_Z_VEL  8 // virtual z velocity that player is moving
              // to simulate motion without moving

// tie fighter model constants
#define NUM_TIE_VERTS   10
#define NUM_TIE_EDGES   8

// explosiond
#define NUM_EXPLOSIONS  (NUM_TIES) // total number of explosions

// game states
#define GAME_RUNNING   1
#define GAME_OVER     0

// TYPES ///////////////////////////////////////////////////
```

```
// this a 3D point
typedef struct POINT3D_TYP
    {
    USHORT color;    // color of point 16-bit
    float x,y,z;   // coordinates of point in 3D
    } POINT3D, *POINT3D_PTR;

// this is a 3D line, nothing more than two indices into a vertex list
typedef struct LINE3D_TYP
    {
    USHORT color; // color of line 16-bit
    int v1,v2;    // indices to endpoints of line in vertex list

    } LINE3D, *LINE3D_PTR;

// a tie fighter
typedef struct TIE_TYP
    {
    int state;    // state of the tie, 0=dead, 1=alive
    float x, y, z; // position of the tie
    float xv,yv,zv; // velocity of the tie
    } TIE, *TIE_PTR;

// a basic 3D vector used for velocity
typedef struct VEC3D_TYP
    {
    float x,y,z; // coords of vector
    } VEC3D, *VEC3D_PTR;

// a wireframe explosion
typedef struct EXPL_TYP
    {
    int state;     // state of explosion
    int counter;    // counter for explosion
    USHORT color;   // color of explosion

    // an explosion is a collection of edges/lines
    // based on the 3D model of the tie that is exploding
    POINT3D p1[NUM_TIE_EDGES]; // start point of edge n
    POINT3D p2[NUM_TIE_EDGES]; // end point of edge n

    VEC3D  vel[NUM_TIE_EDGES]; // velocity of shrapnel
```

```
    } EXPL, *EXPL_PTR;

// PROTOTYPES ////////////////////////////////////////////////

// game console
int Game_Init(void *parms=NULL);
int Game_Shutdown(void *parms=NULL);
int Game_Main(void *parms=NULL);

// game functions
void Init_Tie(int index);

// GLOBALS //////////////////////////////////////////////////

HWND main_window_handle      = NULL; // save the window handle
HINSTANCE main_instance      = NULL; // save the instance
char buffer[256];             // used to print text

// the tie fighter is a collection of vertices connected by
// lines that make up the shape. only one tie fighter see if
// you can replicate it?

POINT3D tie_vlist[NUM_TIE_VERTS]; // vertex list for the tie fighter model
LINE3D tie_shape[NUM_TIE_EDGES]; // edge list for the tie fighter model
TIE   ties[NUM_TIES];      // tie fighters

POINT3D stars[NUM_STARS]; // the starfield

// some colors, note we can't build them until we know the bit
// depth format 5.5.5 or 5.6.5, so we wait a minute and do it in the
// Game_Init() function
USHORT rgb_green,
    rgb_white,
    rgb_red,
    rgb_blue;

// player vars
float cross_x = 0, // cross hairs
   cross_y = 0;

int cross_x_screen = WINDOW_WIDTH/2,  // used for cross hair
  cross_y_screen = WINDOW_HEIGHT/2,
```

```
  target_x_screen = WINDOW_WIDTH/2,  // used for targeter
  target_y_screen = WINDOW_HEIGHT/2;

int player_z_vel = 4; // virtual speed of viewpoint/ship
int cannon_state = 0; // state of laser cannon
int cannon_count = 0; // laster cannon counter

EXPL explosions[NUM_EXPLOSIONS]; // the explosiions

int misses = 0; // tracks number of missed ships
int hits   = 0; // tracks number of hits
int score = 0; // take a guess :)

// music and sound stuff
int main_track_id = -1, // main music track id
  laser_id    = -1, // sound of laser pulse
  explosion_id = -1, // sound of explosion
  flyby_id    = -1; // sound of tie fighter flying by

int game_state = GAME_RUNNING; // state of game

// FUNCTIONS //////////////////////////////////////////////////

LRESULT CALLBACK WindowProc(HWND hwnd,
                  UINT msg,
               WPARAM wparam,
               LPARAM lparam)
{
// this is the main message handler of the system
PAINTSTRUCT  ps;        // used in WM_PAINT
HDC       hdc;    // handle to a device context

// what is the message
switch(msg)
  {
  case WM_CREATE:
    {
    // do initialization stuff here
    return(0);
    } break;

  case WM_PAINT:
     {
```

```
     // start painting
     hdc = BeginPaint(hwnd,&ps);

     // end painting
     EndPaint(hwnd,&ps);
     return(0);
    } break;

  case WM_DESTROY:
    {
    // kill the application
    PostQuitMessage(0);
    return(0);
    } break;

  default:break;

  } // end switch

// process any messages that we didn't take care of
return (DefWindowProc(hwnd, msg, wparam, lparam));

} // end WinProc

// WINMAIN ////////////////////////////////////////////////

int WINAPI WinMain(  HINSTANCE hinstance,
          HINSTANCE hprevinstance,
          LPSTR lpcmdline,
          int ncmdshow)
{
// this is the winmain function

WNDCLASS winclass;  // this will hold the class we create
HWND    hwnd;    // generic window handle
MSG    msg;    // generic message
HDC    hdc;    // generic dc
PAINTSTRUCT ps;   // generic paintstruct

// first fill in the window class stucture
winclass.style    = CS_DBLCLKS | CS_OWNDC |
             CS_HREDRAW | CS_VREDRAW;
winclass.lpfnWndProc  = WindowProc;
```

```
winclass.cbClsExtra   = 0;
winclass.cbWndExtra   = 0;
winclass.hInstance  = hinstance;
winclass.hIcon     = LoadIcon(NULL, IDI_APPLICATION);
winclass.hCursor  = LoadCursor(NULL, IDC_ARROW);
winclass.hbrBackground  = (HBRUSH)GetStockObject(BLACK_BRUSH);
winclass.lpszMenuName  = NULL;
winclass.lpszClassName  = WINDOW_CLASS_NAME;

// register the window class
if (!RegisterClass(&winclass))
  return(0);

// create the window, note the test to see if WINDOWED_APP is
// true to select the appropriate window flags
if (!(hwnd = CreateWindow(WINDOW_CLASS_NAME, // class
       WINDOW_TITLE,   // title
 (WINDOWED_APP ? (WS_OVERLAPPED ¦ WS_SYSMENU) : (WS_POPUP ¦ WS_VISIBLE)),
       0,0,     // x,y
       WINDOW_WIDTH, // width
            WINDOW_HEIGHT, // height
       NULL,     // handle to parent
       NULL,     // handle to menu
       hinstance,// instance
       NULL)))  // creation parms
return(0);

// save the window handle and instance in a global
main_window_handle = hwnd;
main_instance    = hinstance;

// resize the window so that client is really width x height
if (WINDOWED_APP)
{
// now resize the window, so the client area is the actual size requested
// since there may be borders and controls if this is going to be a windowed app
// if the app is not windowed then it won't matter
RECT window_rect = {0,0,WINDOW_WIDTH,WINDOW_HEIGHT};

// make the call to adjust window_rect
AdjustWindowRectEx(&window_rect,
   GetWindowStyle(main_window_handle),
```

```
   GetMenu(main_window_handle) != NULL,
   GetWindowExStyle(main_window_handle));

// save the global client offsets, they are needed in DDraw_Flip()
window_client_x0 = -window_rect.left;
window_client_y0 = -window_rect.top;

// now resize the window with a call to MoveWindow()
MoveWindow(main_window_handle,
      CW_USEDEFAULT, // x position
      CW_USEDEFAULT, // y position
      window_rect.right - window_rect.left, // width
      window_rect.bottom - window_rect.top, // height
      FALSE);

// show the window, so there's no garbage on first render
ShowWindow(main_window_handle, SW_SHOW);
} // end if windowed

// perform all game console specific initialization
Game_Init();

// disable CTRL-ALT_DEL, ALT_TAB, comment this line out
// if it causes your system to crash
SystemParametersInfo(SPI_SCREENSAVERRUNNING, TRUE, NULL, 0);

// enter main event loop
while(1)
  {
  if (PeekMessage(&msg,NULL,0,0,PM_REMOVE))
    {
    // test if this is a quit
    if (msg.message == WM_QUIT)
      break;

    // translate any accelerator keys
    TranslateMessage(&msg);

    // send the message to the window proc
    DispatchMessage(&msg);
    } // end if
```

```
  // main game processing goes here
  Game_Main();

  } // end while

// shutdown game and release all resources
Game_Shutdown();

// enable CTRL-ALT_DEL, ALT_TAB, comment this line out
// if it causes your system to crash
SystemParametersInfo(SPI_SCREENSAVERRUNNING, FALSE, NULL, 0);

// return to Windows like this
return(msg.wParam);

} // end WinMain

// T3D II GAME PROGRAMMING CONSOLE FUNCTIONS ////////////////

int Game_Init(void *parms)
{
// this function is where you do all the initialization
// for your game

int index; // used for looping

Open_Error_File("error.txt");

// start up DirectDraw (replace the parms as you desire)
DDraw_Init(WINDOW_WIDTH, WINDOW_HEIGHT, WINDOW_BPP, WINDOWED_APP);

// initialize directinput
DInput_Init();

// acquire the keyboard
DInput_Init_Keyboard();

// initialize directsound
DSound_Init();

// load in sound fx
explosion_id = DSound_Load_WAV("exp1.wav");
laser_id    = DSound_Load_WAV("shocker.wav");
```

```
// initialize directmusic
DMusic_Init();

// load and start main music track
main_track_id = DMusic_Load_MIDI("midifile2.mid");
DMusic_Play(main_track_id);

// add calls to acquire other directinput devices here...

// hide the mouse
ShowCursor(FALSE);

// seed random number generator
srand(Start_Clock());

// all your initialization code goes here...

// create system colors
rgb_green = RGB16Bit(0,31,0);
rgb_white = RGB16Bit(31,31,31);
rgb_blue = RGB16Bit(0,0,31);
rgb_red  = RGB16Bit(31,0,0);

// create the starfield
for (index=0; index < NUM_STARS; index++)
  {
  // randomly position stars in an elongated cylinder stretching from
  // the viewpoint 0,0,-d to the yon clipping plane 0,0,far_z
  stars[index].x = -WINDOW_WIDTH/2 + rand()%WINDOW_WIDTH;
  stars[index].y = -WINDOW_HEIGHT/2 + rand()%WINDOW_HEIGHT;
  stars[index].z = NEAR_Z + rand()%(FAR_Z - NEAR_Z);

  // set color of stars
  stars[index].color = rgb_white;
  } // end for index

// create the tie fighter model

// the vertex list for the tie fighter
POINT3D temp_tie_vlist[NUM_TIE_VERTS] =
// color, x,y,z
{ {rgb_white,-40,40,0},  // p0
 {rgb_white,-40,0,0},  // p1
```

```
 {rgb_white,-40,-40,0},  // p2
 {rgb_white,-10,0,0},  // p3
 {rgb_white,0,20,0},   // p4
 {rgb_white,10,0,0},   // p5
 {rgb_white,0,-20,0},  // p6
 {rgb_white,40,40,0},   // p7
 {rgb_white,40,0,0},   // p8
 {rgb_white,40,-40,0}};  // p9

// copy the model into the real global arrays
for (index=0; index<NUM_TIE_VERTS; index++)
   tie_vlist[index] = temp_tie_vlist[index];

// the edge list for the tie fighter
LINE3D temp_tie_shape[NUM_TIE_EDGES] =
// color, vertex 1, vertex 2
{ {rgb_green,0,2   },  // l0
 {rgb_green,1,3   },  // l1
 {rgb_green,3,4   },  // l2
 {rgb_green,4,5   },  // l3
 {rgb_green,5,6   },  // l4
 {rgb_green,6,3   },  // l5
 {rgb_green,5,8   },  // l6
 {rgb_green,7,9   } }; // l7

// copy the model into the real global arrays
for (index=0; index<NUM_TIE_EDGES; index++)
   tie_shape[index] = temp_tie_shape[index];

// initialize the position of each tie fighter and its velocity
for (index=0; index<NUM_TIES; index++)
  {
  // initialize this tie fighter
  Init_Tie(index);

  } // end for index

// return success
return(1);

} // end Game_Init

///////////////////////////////////////////////////////////
```

```
int Game_Shutdown(void *parms)
{
// this function is where you shutdown your game and
// release all resources that you allocated

// shut everything down

// release all your resources created for the game here....

// now directsound
DSound_Stop_All_Sounds();
DSound_Shutdown();

// directmusic
DMusic_Delete_All_MIDI();
DMusic_Shutdown();

// shut down directinput
DInput_Shutdown();

// shutdown directdraw last
DDraw_Shutdown();

// return success
return(1);
} // end Game_Shutdown

//////////////////////////////////////////////////////////

void Start_Explosion(int tie)
{
// this starts an explosion based on the sent tie fighter

// first hunt and see if an explosion is free
for (int index=0; index < NUM_EXPLOSIONS; index++)
  {
  if (explosions[index].state==0)
    {
    // start this explosion up using the properties
    // if the tie figther index sent

    explosions[index].state   = 1; // enable state of explosion
    explosions[index].counter = 0; // reset counter for explosion
```

```
    // set color of explosion
    explosions[index].color = rgb_green;

    // make copy of of edge list, so we can blow it up
    for (int edge=0; edge < NUM_TIE_EDGES; edge++)
      {
      // start point of edge
      explosions[index].p1[edge].x = ties[tie].x+tie_vlist
➥[tie_shape[edge].v1].x;
      explosions[index].p1[edge].y = ties[tie].y+tie_vlist
➥[tie_shape[edge].v1].y;
      explosions[index].p1[edge].z = ties[tie].z+tie_vlist
➥[tie_shape[edge].v1].z;

      // end point of edge
      explosions[index].p2[edge].x = ties[tie].x+tie_vlist
➥[tie_shape[edge].v2].x;
      explosions[index].p2[edge].y = ties[tie].y+tie_vlist
➥[tie_shape[edge].v2].y;
      explosions[index].p2[edge].z = ties[tie].z+tie_vlist
➥[tie_shape[edge].v2].z;

      // compute trajectory vector for edges
      explosions[index].vel[edge].x = ties[tie].xv - 8+rand()%16;
      explosions[index].vel[edge].y = ties[tie].yv - 8+rand()%16;
      explosions[index].vel[edge].z = -3+rand()%4;

      } // end for edge

    // done, so return
    return;
    } // end if found

  } // end for index

} // end Start_Explosion

////////////////////////////////////////////////////////////

void Process_Explosions(void)
{
// this processes all the explosions
```

```
// loop thru all the explosions and render them
for (int index=0; index<NUM_EXPLOSIONS; index++)
  {
  // test if this explosion is active?
  if (explosions[index].state==0)
    continue;

  for (int edge=0; edge<NUM_TIE_EDGES; edge++)
    {
    // must be exploding, update edges (shrapel)
    explosions[index].p1[edge].x+=explosions[index].vel[edge].x;
    explosions[index].p1[edge].y+=explosions[index].vel[edge].y;
    explosions[index].p1[edge].z+=explosions[index].vel[edge].z;

    explosions[index].p2[edge].x+=explosions[index].vel[edge].x;
    explosions[index].p2[edge].y+=explosions[index].vel[edge].y;
    explosions[index].p2[edge].z+=explosions[index].vel[edge].z;
    } // end for edge

  // test for termination of explosion?
  if (++explosions[index].counter > 100)
    explosions[index].state = explosions[index].counter = 0;

  } // end for index

} // end Process_Explosions

///////////////////////////////////////////////////////////

void Draw_Explosions(void)
{
// this draws all the explosions

// loop thru all the explosions and render them
for (int index=0; index<NUM_EXPLOSIONS; index++)
  {
  // test if this explosion is active?
  if (explosions[index].state==0)
    continue;

  // render this explosion
  // each explosion is made of a number of edges
  for (int edge=0; edge < NUM_TIE_EDGES; edge++)
```

```
  {
  POINT3D p1_per, p2_per; // used to hold perspective endpoints

  // test if edge if beyond near clipping plane
  if (explosions[index].p1[edge].z < NEAR_Z &&
    explosions[index].p2[edge].z < NEAR_Z)
    continue;

  // step 1: perspective transform each end point
  p1_per.x = VIEW_DISTANCE*explosions[index].p1[edge].x/explosions
➥[index].p1[edge].z;
  p1_per.y = VIEW_DISTANCE*explosions[index].p1[edge].y/explosions
➥[index].p1[edge].z;
  p2_per.x = VIEW_DISTANCE*explosions[index].p2[edge].x/explosions
➥ [index].p2[edge].z;
  p2_per.y = VIEW_DISTANCE*explosions[index].p2[edge].y/explosions
➥ [index].p2[edge].z;

  // step 2: compute screen coords
  int p1_screen_x = WINDOW_WIDTH/2 + p1_per.x;
  int p1_screen_y = WINDOW_HEIGHT/2 - p1_per.y;
  int p2_screen_x = WINDOW_WIDTH/2 + p2_per.x;
  int p2_screen_y = WINDOW_HEIGHT/2 - p2_per.y;

  // step 3: draw the edge
  Draw_Clip_Line16(p1_screen_x, p1_screen_y, p2_screen_x, p2_screen_y,
           explosions[index].color,back_buffer, back_lpitch);

  } // end for edge

  } // end for index

} // end Draw_Explosions

//////////////////////////////////////////////////////////

void Move_Starfield(void)
{
// move the stars

int index; // looping var
```

```
// the stars are technically stationary,but we are going
// to move them to simulate motion of the viewpoint
for (index=0; index<NUM_STARS; index++)
  {
  // move the next star
  stars[index].z-=player_z_vel;

  // test for past near clipping plane
  if (stars[index].z <= NEAR_Z)
    stars[index].z = FAR_Z;

  } // end for index

} // end Move_Starfield

/////////////////////////////////////////////////////////

void Draw_Starfield(void)
{
// draw the stars in 3D using perspective transform

int index; // looping var

for (index=0; index<NUM_STARS; index++)
  {
  // draw the next star
  // step 1: perspective transform
  float x_per = VIEW_DISTANCE*stars[index].x/stars[index].z;
  float y_per = VIEW_DISTANCE*stars[index].y/stars[index].z;

  // step 2: compute screen coords
  int x_screen = WINDOW_WIDTH/2 + x_per;
  int y_screen = WINDOW_HEIGHT/2 - y_per;

  // clip to screen coords
  if (x_screen>=WINDOW_WIDTH || x_screen < 0 ||
    y_screen >= WINDOW_HEIGHT || y_screen < 0)
    {
    // continue to next star
    continue;
    } // end if
  else
    {
```

```
    // else render to buffer
    ((USHORT *)back_buffer)[x_screen + y_screen*(back_lpitch >> 1)]
              = stars[index].color;
    } // end else

  } // end for index

} // Draw_Starfield

////////////////////////////////////////////////////////

void Init_Tie(int index)
{
// this function starts a tie fighter up at the far end
// of the universe and sends it our way!

// position each tie in the viewing volume
ties[index].x = -WINDOW_WIDTH + rand()%(2*WINDOW_WIDTH);
ties[index].y = -WINDOW_HEIGHT + rand()%(2*WINDOW_HEIGHT);
ties[index].z = 4*FAR_Z;

// initialize velocity of tie fighter
ties[index].xv = -4+rand()%8;
ties[index].yv = -4+rand()%8;
ties[index].zv = -4-rand()%64;

// turn the tie fighter on
ties[index].state = 1;
} // end Init_Tie

////////////////////////////////////////////////////////

void Process_Ties(void)
{
// process the tie fighters and do AI (what there is of it!)
int index; // looping var

// move each tie fighter toward the viewpoint
for (index=0; index<NUM_TIES; index++)
  {
  // is this one dead?
  if (ties[index].state==0)
    continue;
```

```
  // move the next star
  ties[index].z+=ties[index].zv;
  ties[index].x+=ties[index].xv;
  ties[index].y+=ties[index].yv;

  // test for past near clipping plane
  if (ties[index].z <= NEAR_Z)
    {
    // reset this tie
    Init_Tie(index);

    // another got away
    misses++;

    } // reset tie

  } // end for index

} // Process_Ties

//////////////////////////////////////////////////////////

void Draw_Ties(void)
{
// draw the tie fighters in 3D wireframe with perspective

int index; // looping var

// used to compute the bounding box of tie fighter
// for collision detection
int bmin_x, bmin_y, bmax_x, bmax_y;

// draw each tie fighter
for (index=0; index < NUM_TIES; index++)
  {
  // draw the next tie fighter

  // is this one dead?
  if (ties[index].state==0)
    continue;

  // reset the bounding box to impossible values
  bmin_x = 100000;
```

```
bmax_x = -100000;
bmin_y = 100000;
bmax_y = -100000;

// based on z-distance shade tie fighter
// normalize the distance from 0 to max_z then
// scale it to 31, so the closer the brighter
USHORT rgb_tie_color = RGB16Bit(0,(31-31*(ties[index].z/(4*FAR_Z))),0);

// each tie fighter is made of a number of edges
for (int edge=0; edge < NUM_TIE_EDGES; edge++)
{
POINT3D p1_per, p2_per; // used to hold perspective endpoints

// step 1: perspective transform each end point
// note the translation of each point to the position of the tie fighter
// that is the model is relative to the position of each tie
➥fighter -- IMPORTANT
p1_per.x =
    VIEW_DISTANCE*(ties[index].x+tie_vlist[tie_shape[edge].v1].x)/
    (tie_vlist[tie_shape[edge].v1].z+ties[index].z);

p1_per.y = VIEW_DISTANCE*(ties[index].y+tie_vlist[tie_shape[edge].v1].y)/
      (tie_vlist[tie_shape[edge].v1].z+ties[index].z);

p2_per.x = VIEW_DISTANCE*(ties[index].x+tie_vlist[tie_shape[edge].v2].x)/
      (tie_vlist[tie_shape[edge].v2].z+ties[index].z);

p2_per.y = VIEW_DISTANCE*(ties[index].y+tie_vlist[tie_shape[edge].v2].y)/
      (tie_vlist[tie_shape[edge].v2].z+ties[index].z);

// step 2: compute screen coords
int p1_screen_x = WINDOW_WIDTH/2 + p1_per.x;
int p1_screen_y = WINDOW_HEIGHT/2 - p1_per.y;
int p2_screen_x = WINDOW_WIDTH/2 + p2_per.x;
int p2_screen_y = WINDOW_HEIGHT/2 - p2_per.y;

// step 3: draw the edge
Draw_Clip_Line16(p1_screen_x, p1_screen_y, p2_screen_x, p2_screen_y,
         rgb_tie_color,back_buffer, back_lpitch);
```

```
// update bounding box with next edge
int min_x = min(p1_screen_x, p2_screen_x);
int max_x = max(p1_screen_x, p2_screen_x);

int min_y = min(p1_screen_y, p2_screen_y);
int max_y = max(p1_screen_y, p2_screen_y);

bmin_x = min(bmin_x, min_x);
bmin_y = min(bmin_y, min_y);

bmax_x = max(bmax_x, max_x);
bmax_y = max(bmax_y, max_y);

} // end for edge

// test if this guy has been hit by lasers???
if (cannon_state==1)
  {
  // simple test of screen coords of bounding box contain laser target
  if (target_x_screen > bmin_x && target_x_screen < bmax_x &&
    target_y_screen > bmin_y && target_y_screen < bmax_y)
   {
   // this tie is dead meat!
   Start_Explosion(index);

   // start sound
   DSound_Play(explosion_id );

   // increase score
   score+=ties[index].z;

   // add one more hit
   hits++;

   // finally reset this tie figher
   Init_Tie(index);

   } // end if

  } // end if

} // end for index
```

```
} // end Draw_Ties

///////////////////////////////////////////////////////////

int Game_Main(void *parms)
{
// this is the workhorse of your game it will be called
// continuously in real-time this is like main() in C
// all the calls for your game go here!

int     index;     // looping var

// start the timing clock
Start_Clock();

// clear the drawing surface
DDraw_Fill_Surface(lpddsback, 0);

// read keyboard and other devices here
DInput_Read_Keyboard();

// game logic here...

if (game_state==GAME_RUNNING)
{
// move players crosshair
if (keyboard_state[DIK_RIGHT])
  {
  // move cross hair to right
  cross_x+=CROSS_VEL;

  // test for wraparound
  if (cross_x > WINDOW_WIDTH/2)
   cross_x = -WINDOW_WIDTH/2;

  } // end if
if (keyboard_state[DIK_LEFT])
  {
  // move cross hair to left
  cross_x-=CROSS_VEL;

  // test for wraparound
  if (cross_x < -WINDOW_WIDTH/2)
```

```
     cross_x = WINDOW_WIDTH/2;
    } // end if
if (keyboard_state[DIK_DOWN])
    {
    // move cross hair up
    cross_y-=CROSS_VEL;

    // test for wraparound
    if (cross_y < -WINDOW_HEIGHT/2)
     cross_y = WINDOW_HEIGHT/2;
    } // end if
if (keyboard_state[DIK_UP])
    {
    // move cross hair up
    cross_y+=CROSS_VEL;

    // test for wraparound
    if (cross_y > WINDOW_HEIGHT/2)
     cross_y = -WINDOW_HEIGHT/2;
    } // end if

// speed of ship controls
if (keyboard_state[DIK_A])
    player_z_vel++;
else
if (keyboard_state[DIK_S])
    player_z_vel--;

// test if player is firing laser cannon
if (keyboard_state[DIK_SPACE] && cannon_state==0)
    {
    // fire the cannon
    cannon_state = 1;
    cannon_count = 0;

    // save last position of targeter
    target_x_screen = cross_x_screen;
    target_y_screen = cross_y_screen;

    // make sound
    DSound_Play(laser_id);

    } // end if
```

```
} // end if game running

// process cannon, simple FSM ready->firing->cool

// firing phase
if (cannon_state == 1)
  if (++cannon_count > 15)
   cannon_state = 2;

// cool down phase
if (cannon_state == 2)
  if (++cannon_count > 20)
   cannon_state = 0;

// move the starfield
Move_Starfield();

// move and perform ai for ties
Process_Ties();

// Process the explosions
Process_Explosions();

// lock the back buffer and obtain pointer and width
DDraw_Lock_Back_Surface();

// draw the starfield
Draw_Starfield();

// draw the tie fighters
Draw_Ties();

// draw the explosions
Draw_Explosions();

// draw the crosshairs

// first compute screen coords of crosshair
// note inversion of y-axis
cross_x_screen = WINDOW_WIDTH/2 + cross_x;
cross_y_screen = WINDOW_HEIGHT/2 - cross_y;
```

```
// draw the crosshair in screen coords
Draw_Clip_Line16(cross_x_screen-16,cross_y_screen,
         cross_x_screen+16,cross_y_screen,
         rgb_red,back_buffer,back_lpitch);

Draw_Clip_Line16(cross_x_screen,cross_y_screen-16,
         cross_x_screen,cross_y_screen+16,
         rgb_red,back_buffer,back_lpitch);

Draw_Clip_Line16(cross_x_screen-16,cross_y_screen-4,
         cross_x_screen-16,cross_y_screen+4,
         rgb_red,back_buffer,back_lpitch);

Draw_Clip_Line16(cross_x_screen+16,cross_y_screen-4,
         cross_x_screen+16,cross_y_screen+4,
         rgb_red,back_buffer,back_lpitch);

// draw the laser beams
if (cannon_state == 1)
  {
  if ((rand()%2 == 1))
   {
   // right beam
   Draw_Clip_Line16(WINDOW_WIDTH-1, WINDOW_HEIGHT-1,
       -4+rand()%8+target_x_screen,-4+rand()%8+target_y_screen,
       RGB16Bit(0,0,rand()),back_buffer,back_lpitch);
   } // end if
  else
   {
   // left beam
   Draw_Clip_Line16(0, WINDOW_HEIGHT-1,
       -4+rand()%8+target_x_screen,-4+rand()%8+target_y_screen,
       RGB16Bit(0,0,rand()),back_buffer,back_lpitch);
   } // end if

  } // end if

// done rendering, unlock back buffer surface
DDraw_Unlock_Back_Surface();

// draw the informtion
sprintf(buffer, "Score %d   Kills %d   Escaped %d", score, hits, misses);
Draw_Text_GDI(buffer, 0,0,RGB(0,255,0), lpddsback);
```

```
if (game_state==GAME_OVER)
  Draw_Text_GDI("G A M E O V E R", 320-8*10,240,RGB(255,255,255), lpddsback);

// check if the music has finished, if so restart
if (DMusic_Status_MIDI(main_track_id)==MIDI_STOPPED)
  DMusic_Play(main_track_id);

// flip the surfaces
DDraw_Flip();

// sync to 30ish fps
Wait_Clock(30);

// check for game state switch
if (misses > 100)
  game_state = GAME_OVER;

// check of user is trying to exit
if (KEY_DOWN(VK_ESCAPE) || keyboard_state[DIK_ESCAPE])
  {
  PostMessage(main_window_handle, WM_DESTROY,0,0);

  } // end if
// return success
return(1);
} // end Game_Main

//////////////////////////////////////////////////////////
```

Pretty short for a 3D game, huh! That's an entire 3D Win32/DirectX game. Well, almost—there's a few thousand lines of code in the T3DLIB modules, but we'll just pretend that it's like DirectX and someone else wrote it.

Before we move on to analyzing the code, I want you to compile this bad boy yourself. You are not allowed to move on until you get a successful compile! Fair enough? So, follow the steps that we outlined as far as setting up the compiler to create a Win32 .EXE application with all the search paths and link lists ready for DirectX. Then, once you have your project ready, you must include the source files:

```
T3DLIB1.CPP, T3DLIB2.CPP, T3DLIB3.CPP, RAIDERS3D.CPP
```

Of course, the header files

```
T3DLIB1.H, T3DLIB2.H, T3DLIB3.H
```

must be in the working directory of the compiler. And finally, you need to make absolutely sure you have included the DirectX .LIB files in the project along with the .CPP files OR in the link list. You will only need the following DirectX .LIB files:

```
DDRAW.LIB, DSOUND.LIB, DINPUT.LIB, DINPUT8.LIB
```

You can call the .EXE anything you like—maybe `TEST.EXE` or `RAIDERS3D_TEST.EXE`—but don't move on until you can compile.

The Event Loop

`WinMain()` is the main entry point for all Windows programs, just like `main()` is the entry point for all DOS/Unix programs (please wash your mouth out if you said Unix out loud). In any case, the `WinMain()` for *Raiders3D* creates a window and then enters right into the event loop. If Windows needs to do something, it does it. In any case, `WinMain()` begins by creating a Windows class and registering it. Next the game window is created, then a call is made to our function `Game_Init()` that handles all the initialization of the game. When all the initialization is complete, a standard Windows event loop is entered that "peeks" for a message. If a message is found, the Windows procedure, or *WinProc* is called, which handles it. Otherwise, a call to our main game programming function `Game_Main()` is called. This is where the real action occurs for our game.

NOTE

Readers from the previous *Tricks* will notice that there is some extra code in `WinMain()`'s initialization to handle windowed graphics and the resizing of the window. This new feature, along with 16-bit support, is part of the revised `T3DLIB` game engine. However, the majority of the 3D for this book will still support 8-bit graphics, because getting speed out of 16-bit software 3D is still too slow in general.

If you want to, you could loop in `Game_Main()` forever, never releasing back to the main event loop in `WinMain()`. This would be bad because Windows would never receive any messages, and you would starve the system. What we need to do is perform one frame of animation and logic and then return back to `WinMain()`. This way, Windows will continue to function and process messages. This process is shown in Figure 1.17.

The Core 3D Game Logic

Once in `Game_Main()`, the logic for *Raiders3D* executes, and the 3D game image is rendered into an offscreen workspace (the double buffer, or in DirectX lingo, "back buffer"). It is finally displayed on the physical display at the end of the loop via the call to `DDraw_Flip()`, which creates the illusion of animation. The game loop consists of the standard sections as defined previously in the elements of a 2D/3D game. The area that I want to focus on is the 3D graphics.

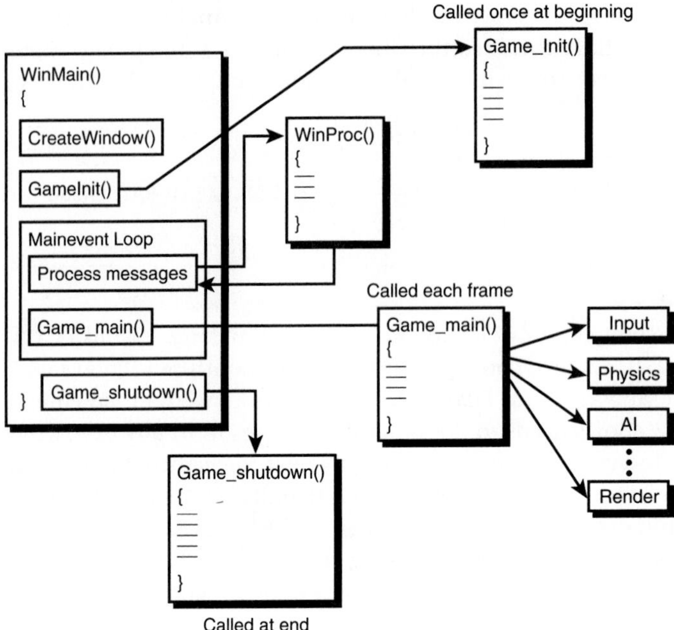

FIGURE 1.17 The entire message-processing system.

The game logic for the enemy AI is fairly simple. An alien ship is generated at a random position in 3D space at a distance just beyond view. Figure 1.18 shows the 3D space of the *Raiders3D* universe. As you can see, the camera or viewpoint is fixed along the negative z-axis at a position (0,0,-zd), where –zd is the viewing distance from the virtual window that the image is projected on. The 3D space is called a left-handed system because the positive z-axis goes into the screen.

After an enemy ship is generated, it follows a trajectory vector along a fixed path that intersects the player's viewing position—thus it's on a collision course, more or less. The vector and initial position are generated in the function `Init_Tie()`. Your goal as the player is to target the enemy and fire—that's it.

So, the question is, how is the 3D display generated? The enemy ships are nothing more than polygon objects (collections of lines) that outline the shape of the 3D object. That is, they are 2D outlines, rather than full 3D objects. The key to all 3D is perspective. Figure 1.19 shows the difference between an orthographic-projected house and a perspective-projected house. These are the two basic types of projections used in 3D graphics systems.

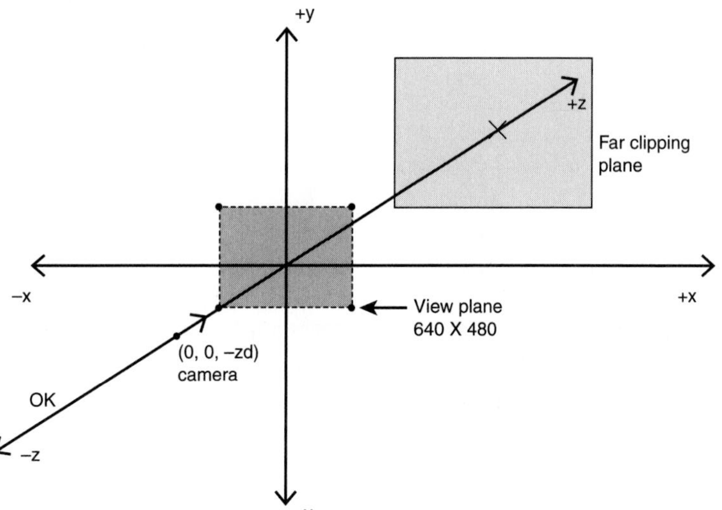

FIGURE 1.18 The universe of *Raiders3D*.

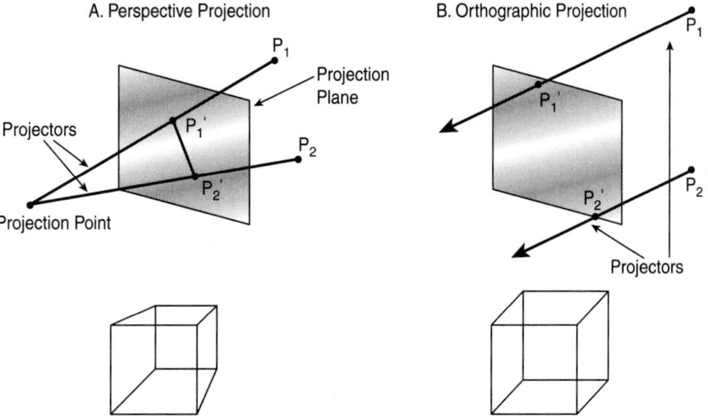

FIGURE 1.19 Orthographic versus perspective projections.

3D Projections

The orthographic projection is good for technical drawings and images where perspective warping is not desired. The math for an orthographic projection is very simple—basically, the z coordinates of each point are simply thrown away, as shown below:

EQUATION 1.1 The Orthographic Projection

Given (x,y,z) in 3D space:

$x_{ortho} = x$

$y_{ortho} = y$

The perspective projection is a little complex, and at this point I don't want to get too much into its derivation. In general, we want to take the z coordinate into consideration along with the viewing distance to arrive at a projected (x_{per}, y_{per}) in 2D that can be plotted on the 2D screen. The mathematics are based on the image shown in Figure 1.20, which is based on a similar triangles argument. It can be shown that the point (x_{per}, y_{per}) can be calculated with the following equations.

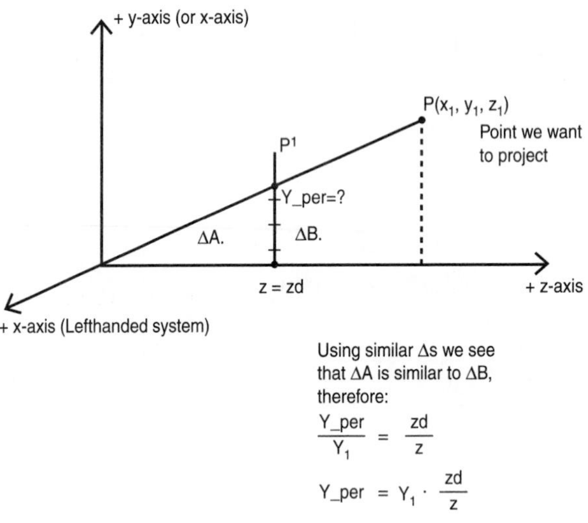

FIGURE 1.20 The derivation of the perspective transformation.

EQUATION 1.2 The Perspective Projection

Given (x,y,z) and the viewing distance zd in 3D space:

$x_{per} = zd*x/z$

$y_{per} = zd*y/z$

With that simple equation, we can move the polygon objects in 3D just like 2D objects, use the perspective projection equations to warp the points before rendering, and then the objects will look and move correctly in 3D. Of course, there are some details about converting the final coordinates (x_{per}, y_{per}) to actual screen coordinates, but that's not important right now. All you need to know is that 3D is nothing more than objects represented in 3D that move in 3D, and that they are projected from 3D onto a 2D viewing surface (the screen) with mathematics that take perspective into consideration.

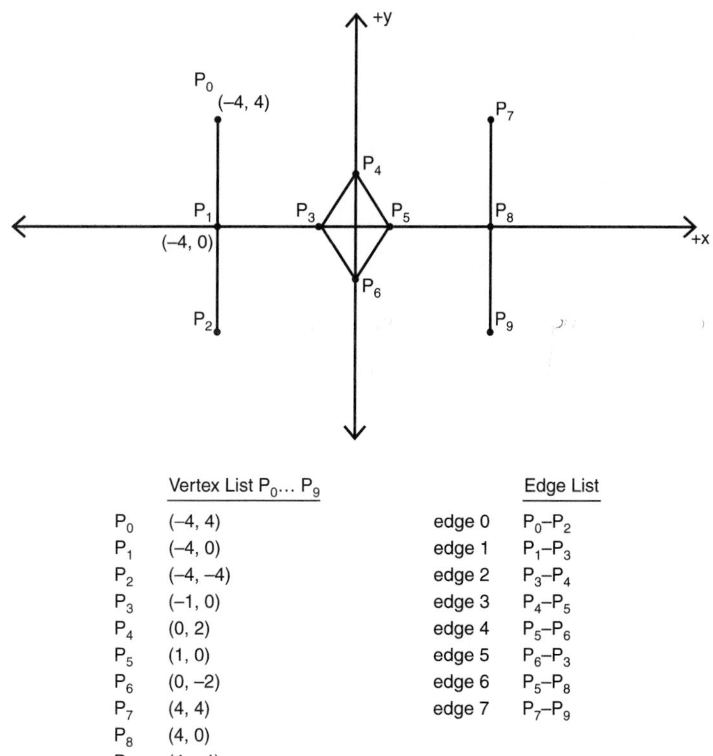

FIGURE 1.21 The wireframe model of the TIE fighter.

Based on this knowledge, each enemy ship is transformed with the perspective projection and rendered onto the screen. Figure 1.21 shows a wireframe model on graph paper of the TIE fighter enemy. Basically, this model is used as the basis for the rendering. A table of the actual positions of each TIE fighter is kept in an array of the following structures:

```
// a tie fighter
typedef struct TIE_TYP
    {
    int state;    // state of the tie, 0=dead, 1=alive
    float x, y, z; // position of the tie
    float xv,yv,zv; // velocity of the tie
    } TIE, *TIE_PTR;
```

When it's time to draw the enemy fighters, the data in the form of a TIE structure and the TIE 3D model are used along with the perspective projection. Presto—a moving 3D image!

You'll also notice that the TIE fighters get brighter as they get closer. This is an easy effect to implement. Basically, the z-axis distance is used as a scaling factor to control the brightness of the TIE fighter as it's drawn.

The Star Field

The star field is nothing more than a collection of single points generated from an emitter out in space. Furthermore, they are recycled as they pass the viewpoint of the player and go behind him. The points are rendered as full 3D objects with the perspective transform, but have a size of 1×1×1 pixel, so they are true "points" and always look like single pixels.

The Laser Cannons and Collision Detection

The laser cannons that the player fires are nothing more than 2D lines projected from the corners of the screen that converge on the crosshairs. The collision detection is accomplished by looking at the 2D projection of all the 3D ships on the viewing screen and testing if the lasers are contained within the bounding box of each projection. This is shown graphically in Figure 1.22.

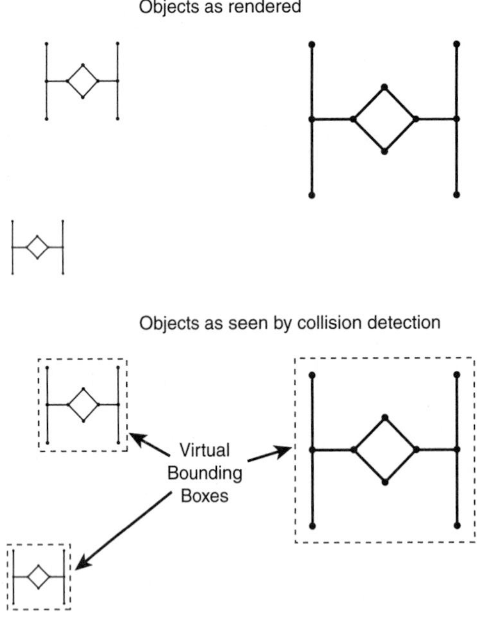

FIGURE 1.22 Using the 2D projected bounding box for collision detection.

This algorithm works because lasers travel at the speed of light. It doesn't matter if the target is 10 meters or 10,000 km away—if you target it with a laser beam and the laser beam intersects even the projection of the 3D image, there is a collision.

The Explosions

The explosions for this game are fairly impressive for the amount of code. When a TIE is hit by a laser pulse, I copied the lines that make up the 3D model of the TIE into a secondary data structure. The lines are then moved apart randomly in 3D, as if they were pieces of the TIE. The pieces move for a couple of seconds, and then the explosion terminates. The effect is very realistic, and is implemented in less than 100 lines of code.

Playing *Raiders3D*

To play the game, simply click on `RAIDERS3D.EXE` on the CD and the program will launch immediately. The controls are as follows:

Arrow keys	Move crosshair
Space bar	Fire lasers
Esc	Exits game

Note: If 100 enemies get by you, the game is over!

The game uses DirectDraw, DirectInput, DirectSound, and DirectMusic, so make sure that your runtime DirectX system is operational.

NOTE

At the end of the book, just for fun we will rewrite *Raiders3D* with the fully lit, full 3D-modeled, textured polygon engine, just to see the difference!

Summary

This chapter has been nothing more than a get-your-feet-wet introduction to 3D game programming. The most important thing to get out of it is compiling DirectX programs, if nothing else! However, we did cover game programming, game loops, general 3D perspective transforms, and using the compiler. You were also introduced to the `T3DLIB` game engine from the previous *Tricks* that we will use to help get a DirectX system up and running, so we can focus on 3D game programming and not on creating surfaces, querying for interfaces, and loading sound FX! Now that you can compile, try messing with the game—add more aliens, some asteroids, and whatever else—and meet me in the next chapter …

CHAPTER 2

A Crash Course in Windows and DirectX

IN THIS CHAPTER

- The Win32 Programming Model
- The Bare Minimum for a Windows Program
- A Basic Windows Application
- DirectX and COM Crash Course
- Flash Introduction to COM

"No, Lieutenant, your men are already dead."

—Agent Smith, *The Matrix*

In this chapter, we are basically going to take a crash course in Windows and DirectX programming. This book mostly assumes that you know Win32 and DirectX programming. However, I tried to write the book so that if you don't know Win32/DirectX programming, you can simply use the APIs that I create and focus on the 3D part. However, for those that don't have the pleasure of knowing Win32/DirectX programming, let me indulge you just a bit. Here's what we'll cover:

- Windows programming
- Event loops
- Writing a simple Windows shell
- DirectX fundamentals
- Component object model

The Win32 Programming Model

Windows is a multitasking/multithreaded O/S, but it's also an *event-driven* O/S. Unlike most DOS programs (all, actually), most Windows programs sit and wait for the user to do something (which fires an event) and then Windows responds to the event and takes action. Take a look at Figure 2.1 to see this graphically. Figure 2.1 depicts a number of application windows, each sending their events or messages to Windows to be processed. Windows does some of the processing, but the majority of the messages or events are passed through to your application program for processing.

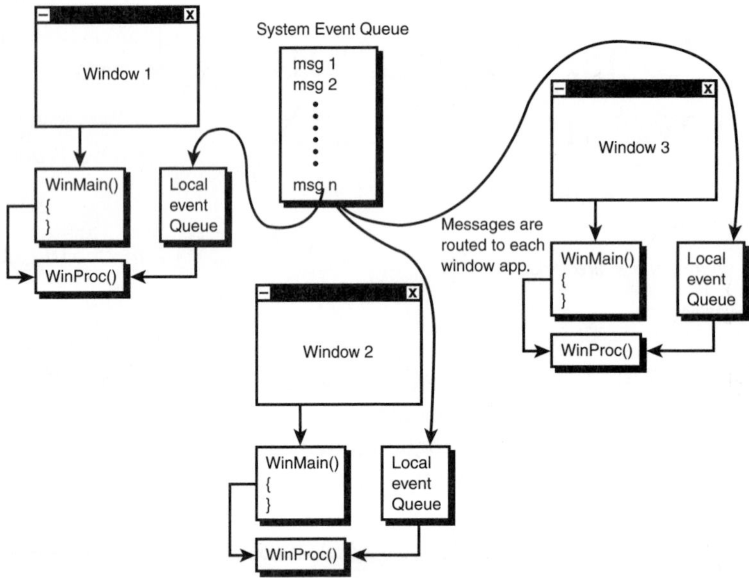

FIGURE 2.1 Windows event handling.

The good news is that for the most part you don't need to concern yourself with other applications that are running—Windows will handle them for you. All you have to worry about is your own application and the processing of messages for your application's window(s). This wasn't the entire truth in Windows 3.0/3.1. These versions of Windows weren't true multitasking O/Ss, and each application had to yield to the next. This made for a rather rough or sluggish feel for applications running under these versions. If other applications were hogging the system, there wasn't anything that compliant applications could do. However, with Windows *9x*/Me/2000/XP/NT, this isn't the case. The O/S will pull the rug from under your application whenever it feels like it—of course, it pulls it so quickly that you'll never notice!

NOTE

At this point, you know all you need to about O/S concepts. Luckily, Windows is such a nice O/S to write games for these days that you won't have to worry about scheduling and so on. All you need to worry about is the game code and pushing the machine to its limits.

The Bare Minimum for a Windows Program

Now that you have a general overview of the Windows O/S and some of its properties and underlying design, let's begin our crash course into Windows programming with our first Windows program.

It's customary to write a "Hello World" program in any new language or O/S that you're learning, so we'll do the same. The following listing is the standard DOS-based "Hello World."


```
// DEMOII2_1.CPP - hello world standard version
#include <stdio.h>

// main entry point for all standard DOS/console programs
void main(void)
{
printf("\nTHERE CAN BE ONLY ONE!!!\n");
} // end main
```

Now let's see how it's done with Windows.

NOTE

By the way, if you want to compile `DEMOII2_1.CPP`, you can actually create what's called a *console application* with the Visual C++ or Borland compilers. These are like DOS applications, but 32-bit. They only run in text mode, but are great for testing out ideas and algorithms.

It All Begins with `WinMain()`

All Windows programs begin execution at the function named `WinMain()`. This is equivalent to `main()` in a straight DOS/Unix program. What you do in `WinMain()` is up to you. If you want, you can create a window, start processing events, draw images on the screen and so on. On the other hand, you can just make a call to one of the hundreds (or thousands) of Win32 API functions. This is what we're going to do next.

As an example, I just want to print something on the screen in a little message box. There just so happens to be a Win32 API function that does just that—`MessageBox()`. The following listing is a complete, compilable Windows program that creates and displays a message box that you can move around and close if you want.

```
// DEMOII2_2.CPP - a simple message box
#define WIN32_LEAN_AND_MEAN // no MFC

#include <windows.h>    // the main windows headers
#include <windowsx.h>    // a lot of cool macros
```

```
// main entry point for all windows programs
int WINAPI WinMain(HINSTANCE hinstance,
          HINSTANCE hprevinstance,
        LPSTR lpcmdline,
        int ncmdshow)
{
// call message box api with NULL for parent window handle
MessageBox(NULL, "THERE CAN BE ONLY ONE!!!",
          "MY FIRST WINDOWS PROGRAM",
          MB_OK | MB_ICONEXCLAMATION);

// exit program
return(0);

} // end WinMain
```

To compile the program, follow these steps:

1. Create a new Win32 .EXE Application Project and include `DEMOII2_2.CPP` from `T3DIICHAP02\` on the CD-ROM.
2. Compile and link the program.
3. Run it! (Or, run the precompiled version `DEMOII2_2.EXE` on the CD.)

And you thought that a basic Windows program had hundreds of lines of code! Anyway, when you compile and run the program, you should see something like what's depicted in Figure 2.2.

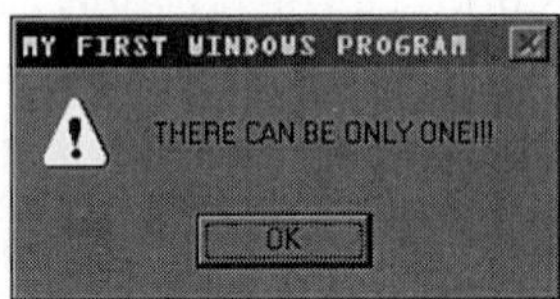

FIGURE 2.2 Screenshot of `DEMOII2_2.EXE` running.

Now that you have a complete Windows program, let's take it apart line by line and see what's going on.

The very first line of code is

```
#define WIN32_LEAN_AND_MEAN
```

This deserves a bit of explanation. There are two ways to write Windows programs: with *MFC (The Microsoft Foundation Classes)*, or with the *SDK (Software Development Kit)*. MFC is much more complex, based totally on C++ and classes, and it is 10 times more overkill than you will ever need for games. The SDK, on the other hand, is manageable, can be learned in a week or two (at least the rudiments of it), and uses straight C. Hence, the SDK is what I'm going to use in this book.

Back to the explanation: `WIN32_LEAN_AND_MEAN` instructs the compiler (header file logic, actually) to not include extraneous MFC overhead.

Next the following header files are included:

```
#include <windows.h>
#include <windowsx.h>
```

The first include of `windows.h` really includes all the Windows header files—and there are a lot of them, so this is like an inclusion macro with nested includes to save you from manually including dozens of explicit header files.

The second include `windowsx.h` is the macro and constant header that contains a number of important macros and constants that make Windows programming easier.

And now for the important part—the main entry point of all Windows applications, `WinMain()`:

```
int WINAPI WinMain(HINSTANCE hinstance,
          HINSTANCE hprevinstance,
       LPSTR lpcmdline,
       int ncmdshow);
```

First off, you should notice that weird `WINAPI` declarator. This is equivalent to the PASCAL function declarator, which forces the parameters to be passed from left to right, rather than the normal right-to-left order with the default `CDECL`. However, the PASCAL calling convention declarator is now obsolete, and `WINAPI` has taken its place. You ***must*** use `WINAPI` for the `WinMain()` function; otherwise, the startup code will end up passing the parameters incorrectly to the function!

Next let's look at each of the parameters in detail.

- `hinstance`—This parameter is the instance handle that Windows generates for your application. *Instances* are pointers or numbers used to track resources. In this case, `hinstance` is used to track your application, like a name or address. When your application is executed, Windows will supply this parameter to your application.
- `hprevinstance`—This parameter is no longer used, but in previous versions of Windows, it tracked the previous instance of the application. In other words, the instance of the application that launched the current one. No wonder Microsoft got rid of it! It's like time travel—it gives me a headache thinking about it.

- `lpcmdline`—A `NULL`-terminated string similar to the command-line parameters of the standard C/C++ `main(int argc, char **argv)` function, except that there isn't a separate parameter analogous to `argc` indicating the number of command-line parameters. For example, if you create a Windows application called `TEST.EXE` and launch it with the following parameters:

  ```
  TEST.EXE one two three
  ```

  then `lpcmdline` will contain the following data:

  ```
  lpcmdline = "one two three"
  ```

  Notice that the name of the .EXE itself is *not* part of the command line.

- `ncmdshow`—This final parameter is simply an integer that is passed to the application during launching, indicating how the main application window is to be opened. Thus, the user has a little control over how the application starts up. Of course, you as the programmer can disregard this if you want, but it's there if you want to use it (you pass it to `ShowWindow()`, but we're getting ahead of ourselves). Table 2.1 contains a list of the most common values `ncmdshow` can take on.

TABLE 2.1 Windows Codes for `ncmdshow`

Value	Meaning
`SW_SHOWNORMAL`	Activates and displays a window. If the window is minimized or maximized, Windows restores it to its original size and position. An application should specify this flag when displaying the window for the first time.
`SW_SHOW`	Activates the window and displays it in its current size and position.
`SW_HIDE`	Hides the window and activates another window.
`SW_MAXIMIZE`	Maximizes the specified window.
`SW_MINIMIZE`	Minimizes the specified window and activates the next top-level window in the Z order.
`SW_RESTORE`	Activates and displays the window. If the window is minimized or maximized, Windows restores it to its original size and position. An application should specify this flag when restoring a minimized window.
`SW_SHOWMAXIMIZED`	Activates the window and displays it as a maximized window.
`SW_SHOWMINIMIZED`	Activates the window and displays it as a minimized window.
`SW_SHOWMINNOACTIVE`	Displays the window as a minimized window. The active window remains active.
`SW_SHOWNA`	Displays the window in its current state. The active window remains active.
`SW_SHOWNOACTIVATE`	Displays a window in its most recent size and position. The active window remains active.

As you can see from Table 2.1, there are a lot of settings for `ncmdshow` (many of which make no sense at this point). In reality, the majority of them will never be sent in ncmdshow; you will use them with another function ShowWindow(), which actually displays a window after it's created. However, we will get to this a little later in the chapter.

The point I want to make is that Windows has a lot of options, flags, and so on that you will never use, but they are still there. It's like VCR programming options—more is always better, as long as you don't need to use them if you don't want to. Windows is designed this way. It has to make everybody happy, so that means a lot of options. In fact, we will use SW_SHOW, SW_SHOWNORMAL, and SW_HIDE 99% of the time.

Finally, let's talk about the actual function call to MessageBox() within WinMain(). This does all the work for us. MessageBox() is a Win32 API function that does something useful for us, so we don't have to do it. In the case of MessageBox(), it is used to display messages with various icons along with a button or two. You see, displaying simple messages is so common in Windows applications that a function was written just to save application programmers the half-hour or so needed to write one every time.

MessageBox() doesn't do much, but it does enough to get a window up on the screen, ask a question, and wait for the user's input. The following is the prototype for MessageBox():

```
int MessageBox( HWND  hwnd,    // handle of owner window
        LPCTSTR lptext,  // address of text in message box
        LPCTSTR lpcaption,// address of title of message box
        UINT  utype);  // style of message box
```

- hwnd—This is the handle of the window you want the message box attached to. At this point, we haven't covered window handles, so just think of it as the parent of the message box. In the case of DEMOII2_2.CPP, we are setting it to NULL, which means use the Windows Desktop as the parent window.
- lptext—This is a NULL-terminated string containing the text you want displayed.
- lpcaption—This is a NULL-terminated string containing the caption for the window of the message box dialog.
- utype—This is about the only exciting parameter of the bunch. It controls what kind of message box is displayed. Take a look at Table 2.2 to see a list (somewhat abridged) of the various options.

TABLE 2.2 MessageBox() Options

Flag	Meaning
The following settings group control the general style of message box.	
MB_OK	The message box contains one push button: OK. This is the default.
MB_OKCANCEL	The message box contains two push buttons: OK and Cancel.
MB_RETRYCANCEL	The message box contains two push buttons: Retry and Cancel.
MB_YESNO	The message box contains two push buttons: Yes and No.

TABLE 2.2 Continued

Flag	Meaning
The following settings group control the general style of message box.	
`MB_YESNOCANCEL`	The message box contains three push buttons: Yes, No, and Cancel.
`MB_ABORTRETRYIGNORE`	The message box contains three push buttons: Abort, Retry, and Ignore.
This group controls the addition of a graphic icon to add a little poor man's multimedia.	
`MB_ICONEXCLAMATION`	An exclamation point icon appears in the message box.
`MB_ICONINFORMATION`	An icon consisting of a lowercase letter *i* in a circle appears in the message box.
`MB_ICONQUESTION`	A question mark icon appears in the message box.
`MB_ICONSTOP`	A stop sign icon appears in the message box.
And finally, this flag group controls which button is highlighted by default.	
`MB_DEFBUTTON`*n*	Where *n* is a number (1...4) indicating which button is the default, numbered from left to right.

(Note: There are additional advanced O/S level flags, but we aren't concerned with them. You can always look them up in the online compiler Win32 SDK Help if you want to know more.)

You can logically `OR` the values together in Table 2.2 to create the desired message box. Usually, you will only `OR` one flag from each group.

And of course, like all good Win32 API functions, `MessageBox()` returns a value to let you know what happened. In our case, who cares, but in general, you might want to know the return value if the message box was a yes/no question, and so forth. The possible return values are listed in Table 2.3.

TABLE 2.3 Return Values for `MessageBox()`

Value	Meaning
`IDABORT`	Abort button was selected.
`IDCANCEL`	Cancel button was selected.
`IDIGNORE`	Ignore button was selected.
`IDNO`	No button was selected.
`IDOK`	OK button was selected.
`IDRETRY`	Retry button was selected.
`IDYES`	Yes button was selected.

Finally, a table where I can list all the values without defoliating an entire forest! Anyway, this completes the line-by-line analysis of our first Windows program—click!

Now I want you to get comfortable making changes to the program and compiling it in different ways. Try altering the various compiler options, like optimization, code generation, and so on. Then try running the program through the debugger and see whether you can figure that out. When you're done, come back. I'm going to get something to eat—I'm ready to pass out ....

If you want to hear some sound, a cheap trick is to use the `MessageBeep()` function. You can look it up in the Win32 SDK. It's similar to the `MessageBox()` function as far as simplicity of use. Here it is:


```
BOOL MessageBeep(UINT utype); // the sound to play
```

where the different sounds can be one of the constants shown in Table 2.4.

TABLE 2.4 Sound Identifiers for `MessageBeep()`

Value	Meaning
MB_ICONASTERISK	System asterisk sound.
MB_ICONEXCLAMATION	System exclamation sound.
MB_ICONHAND	System hand sound.
MB_ICONQUESTION	System question sound.
MB_OK	System default sound.
0xFFFFFFFF	Standard beep using the computer speaker—yuck!

(Note: if you have an MS-Plus theme installed, you're sure to get some interesting results.)

See how cool the Win32 API is? There are literally hundreds of functions to play with. Granted, they aren't the fastest things in the world, but for general housekeeping, I/O, and GUI stuff, the Win32 API is very convenient.

Let's take a moment to summarize what we know at this point about Windows programming. The first thing is that Windows is multitasking/multithreaded, so multiple applications can run at once. However, we don't have to do anything to make this happen. What does concern us is that Windows is event-driven. This means that we have to process events (which we have no idea how to do at this point) and respond to them. Okay, sounds good. Finally, all Windows programs start with the function `WinMain()`, which has a few more parameters than the normal DOS `main()`, but is within the realm of logic and reason.

With all that in mind, it's time to write a very basic Windows application that will in fact be the basis for the game engine template we will write later in the chapter.

A Basic Windows Application

Because the goal of this book is to write 3D games that run on Windows, we don't need to know much about Windows programming. Actually, all you need is a basic skeleton Windows program that opens a window, processes messages, and calls the main game loop—that's it. My goal in this section is to first teach you how to create simple Windows programs, but at the same time to lay the groundwork for a game programming "shell" application that looks like a 32-bit DOS/Unix machine. So let's get started.

The main point of any Windows program is to open a window. A Window is nothing more that a workspace that displays information such as text and graphics with which the user can interact. To create a fully functional Windows program, you only have to follow these steps:

- Create a Windows class.
- Create an event handler, or `WinProc`, as it's called.
- Register the Windows class with Windows.
- Create a window with the previously created Windows Class.
- Create a main event loop that retrieves and dispatches Windows messages to the event handler.

Let's take a look at each step in detail.

The Windows Class

Windows is really an object-oriented O/S, and therefore there are a lot of concepts and procedures in Windows that have their roots in C and C++—one of which is *Window Classes*. Each window, control, list box, dialog box, gadget, and so forth in Windows is actually a window. What makes them all different is the "Class" that defines them. A Windows Class is a description of a window type that Windows can handle.

There are a number of predefined Window Classes, such as buttons, list boxes, file selectors, and so on. However, you are free to create your own Window Classes. In fact, you will create at least one Window Class for each application you write. Otherwise, your program would be rather boring. So you can think of the Window Class as a template for Windows to follow when drawing your window, as well as processing messages for it.

There are two data structures available to hold Windows Class information: `WNDCLASS` and `WNDCLASSEX`. `WNDCLASS` is the older of the two, and will probably be obsolete soon, so we will use the new extended version `WNDCLASSEX`. The structures are very similar, and if you are interested, you can look up the old `WNDCLASS` in the Win32 Help. Anyway, let's take a look at `WNDCLASSEX` as defined in the Windows header files:

```
typedef struct _WNDCLASSEX
    {
    UINT  cbSize;      // size of this structure
    UINT  style;       // style flags
    WNDPROC lpfnWndProc;  // function pointer to handler
    int   cbClsExtra;  // extra class info
    int   cbWndExtra;  // extra window info
    HANDLE hInstance;   // the instance of the application
```

```
HICON   hIcon;       // the main icon
HCURSOR hCursor;     // the cursor for the window
HBRUSH hbrBackground; // the background brush to paint the window
LPCTSTR lpszMenuName; // the name of the menu to attach
LPCTSTR lpszClassName; // the name of the class itself
HICON   hIconSm;     // the handle of the small icon
} WNDCLASSEX;
```


So what you do is create one of these structures and then fill in all the fields.

```
WNDCLASSEX winclass; // a blank windows class
```

Let's see how to fill in each field now.

The first field `cbSize` is very important. It is the size of the `WNDCLASSEX` structure itself. You might be wondering why the structure needs to know how big it is. That's a good question. The reason is that if this structure is passed as a pointer, the receiver can always check the first field (4 bytes) to decide how long the data chunk is at the very least, and jump over it to get to the end. It's like a precaution and a little helper info, so other functions don't have to compute the class size during runtime. Therefore, all you have to do is set it up:

```
winclass.cbSize = sizeof(WNDCLASSEX);
```

The next field deals with the style information flags that describe the general properties of the window. There are a lot of these flags, so I'm not going to show them all, but suffice it to say that you can create any type of window with them. A good working subset of the possible flags is shown in Table 2.5. You can logically `OR` these values together to derive the type of window you want.

TABLE 2.5 Style Flags for Window Classes

Flag	Meaning
`CS_HREDRAW`	Redraws the entire window if a movement or size adjustment changes the width of the window.
`CS_VREDRAW`	Redraws the entire window if a movement or size adjustment changes the height of the window.
`CS_OWNDC`	Allocates a unique device context for each window in the class (more on this later).
`CS_DBLCLKS`	Sends double-click messages to the window procedure when the user double-clicks the mouse while the cursor is within a window belonging to the class.
`CS_PARENTDC`	Sets the clipping region of the child window to that of the parent window so that the child can draw on the parent.
`CS_SAVEBITS`	Saves the client image in a window, so you don't have to redraw it every time the window is obscured, moved, and so on. However, this takes up more memory and is slower than doing it yourself.
`CS_NOCLOSE`	Disables the Close command on the System menu.

(Note: the most commonly used flags are highlighted.)

There are a lot of flags in Table 2.5, and I can't blame you if you're confused. For now though, we'll just set the style flags to indicate that we want the window redrawn if it is moved or resized, and we want a static device context along with the capability to handle double-click events.

Device contexts are used for GDI graphics rendering into a window. Hence, if you want to do graphics, you need to request a device context for the particular window you are interested in. If we set the Windows Class such that it has its own device context via CS_OWNDC, we can save some time instead of requesting one all the time. Did that help at all, or did I make it worse? Windows is like that—the more you know, the more you don't. Anyway, here's how to set the style field to make a window that suits our needs:

```
winclass.style = CS_VREDRAW ¦ CS_HREDRAW ¦ CS_OWNDC ¦ CS_DBLCLICKS;
```

The next field of the WNDCLASSEX structure lpfnWndProc is a function pointer to the event handler. Basically, what we are setting here is a *callback* function for the class. Callback functions are fairly common in Windows programming. A callback function works like this: When something happens, instead of you randomly polling for it, Windows notifies you by calling a callback function you supply. Then within the callback function, you take whatever action needs to be taken.

This metaphor is how the basic Window event loop and event handler works. You supply a callback function to the Windows Class (of course, with a specific prototype), and when an event occurs, Windows calls it for you. This is shown graphically in Figure 2.3. Again, we will cover this more in later sections. For now, let's just set it to the event function that we'll write in a moment.

```
winclass.lpfnWndProc = WinProc; // this is our function
```

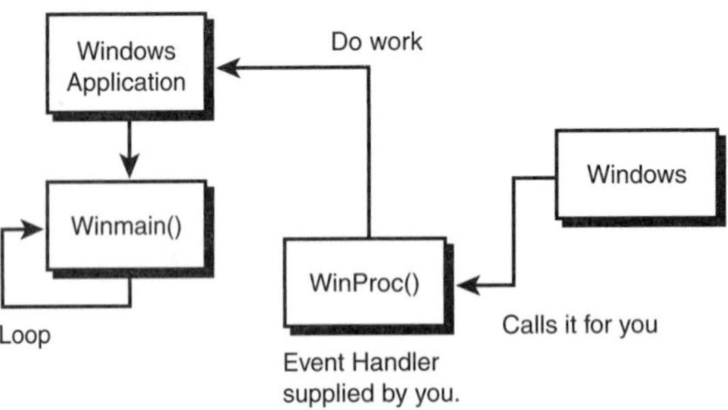

FIGURE 2.3 The Windows event handler callback in action.

NOTE

If you're not familiar with function pointers, they are like virtual function in C++. If you're not familiar with virtual functions, I guess I have to explain it <BG>. Suppose you have two functions that operate on two numbers:

```
int Add(int op1, int op2) {return(op1+op2);}
int Sub(int op1, int op2) {return(op1-op2);}
```

You want to be able to call either function with the same call—this can be done with a function pointer:

```
// define a function pointer that takes two int and returns an int
int (Math*)(int, int);

Then you can assign the function pointer like this:

Math = Add;
int result = Math(1,2); // this really calls Add(1,2)
// result will be 3

Math = Sub;
int result = Math(1,2); // this really call Sub(1,2)
// result will be -1
```

Cool, huh?

The next two fields `cbClsExtra` and `cbWndExtra` were originally designed to instruct Windows to save some extra space in the Windows Class to hold extra runtime information. However, most people don't use these fields, and simply set them to 0:

```
winclass.cbClsExtra = 0; // extra class info space
winclass.cbWndExtra = 0; // extra window info space
```

The next field is `hInstance`. This is simply the `hinstance` that is passed to the `WinMain()` function on start-up, so just copy it in from `WinMain()`:

```
winclass.hInstance = hinstance; // assign the application instance
```

The remaining fields relate to graphical aspects of the Window Class, but before I discuss them, I want to take a quick moment to review handles.

You're going to see handles again and again in Windows programs and types. Handles to bitmaps, handles to cursors, handles to everything. Remember, *handles* are just identifiers based on an internal Windows type. In fact, they are really integers, but Microsoft might change this, so it's a good idea to be safe and use the MS types. In any case, you are going to see more and more "handles to blank," so don't trip out on me! And remember: Any `type` prefixed by `h` is usually a handle. Okay, back to the white board.

The next field sets the type of icon that will represent your application. You have the power to load your own custom icon, but for now we are going to use a system icon—which, as you guessed it—you need a handle for. To retrieve a handle to a common system icon, you can use the `LoadIcon()` function:

```
winclass.hIcon = LoadIcon(NULL, IDI_APPLICATION);
```

This code loads the standard application icon; boring, but simple. If you're interested in the `LoadIcon()` function, take a look at the Win32 API—there are a number of premade icon values that you can use.

Alright, we're about half way through all the fields. Take another breath and let's forge on to the next field, `hCursor`. This is similar to `hIcon` in that it's a handle to a graphics object. However, it differs in that `hCursor` is the handle to the cursor that will be displayed that represents the mouse pointer when the pointer enters the client region of the window. `LoadCursor()` is used to obtain a handle to a cursor that's a resource or a predefined system cursor. Like I said, we will cover resources a bit later, but they are simply data-like bitmaps, cursors, icons, sounds, and so on that are compiled into your application and can be accessed at runtime. Anyway, here's how we set the cursor to the standard arrow for the Windows Class:

```
winclass.hCursor = LoadCursor(NULL, IDC_ARROW);
```

Again, if you're interested in more cursor styles, check out the Win32 API.

Now we're cooking! We're almost done. The remaining fields are a little more interesting. Let's move on to `hbrBackground`.

Whenever a window is drawn or refreshed, at the very least Windows will repaint the background of the window's client area for you with a predefined color, or *brush* in Window-speak. Hence, `hbrbackground` is a handle to the brush that you want to refresh the window. Brushes, pens, colors, and graphics are all part of the *Graphics Device Interface (GDI)*, which we don't need to worry about because we are primarily going to use DirectX. For now, I'm going to show you how to request a basic system brush with which to paint the window. This is accomplished with the `GetStockObject()` function, as shown in the following line of code:

```
winclass.hbrBackground = (HBRUSH)GetStockObject(WHITE_BRUSH);
```

CAUTION

Note the cast to `(HBRUSH)`. This is necessary for Visual C++ 6.0+ compilers! However, it won't hurt to add it with other compilers.

`GetStockObject()` is a general function that retrieves a handle to one of Windows' "stock" brushes, pens, palettes, or fonts. `GetStockObject()` takes a single parameter indicating which one of these resources to load. Table 2.6 contains a list of possible stock objects for brushes and pens only.

TABLE 2.6 Stock Object Identifiers for `GetStockObject()`

Value	Meaning
BLACK_BRUSH	Black brush
WHITE_BRUSH	White brush
GRAY_BRUSH	Gray brush
LTGRAY_BRUSH	Light gray brush
DKGRAY_BRUSH	Dark gray brush
HOLLOW_BRUSH	Hollow brush
NULL_BRUSH	Null brush
BLACK_PEN	Black pen
WHITE_PEN	White pen
NULL_PEN	Null pen

In most cases, the background brush of the window will be irrelevant, because after DirectX takes over, it won't matter. It's still good to know.

The next field in the `WNDCLASS` structure is the menu field `lpszMenuName`. This is a `NULL`-terminated ASCII string of the name of the menu resource to load and attach to the window. Because we aren't going to do much with menus, we'll just set it to `NULL`:

```
winclass.lpszMenuName = NULL; // the name of the menu to attach
```

As I mentioned a while ago, each Window Class represents a different type of window that your application can create. Classes are like templates in a manner of speaking; therefore, Windows needs to track and identify them. Hence, the next field `lpszClassName` is for just that. This field is filled with a `NULL`-terminated ASCII string that contains a text identifier for your class. I personally like using identifiers like `WINCLASS1`, `WINCLASS2`, and so forth. It's up to you, but it's better to keep it simple:

```
winclass.lpszClassName = "WINCLASS1"; // the name of the class itself
```

After this assignment, you can refer to the new Window Class by its class name, such as `WINCLASS1`—kinda cool, huh?

Last but not least is the "small" application icon. This is a new addition to the Window Class `WNDCLASSEX` structure and wasn't available in the older `WNDCLASS`. Basically, this handle points to the icon you want displayed on your window's title bar and on the Windows Desktop taskbar. Usually you would load a custom resource, but for now, let's just use one of the standard Windows icons via `LoadIcon()`:

That's it—now let's take a look at the whole class definition at once:

```
WNDCLASSEX winclass; // this will hold the class we create

// first fill in the window class structure
winclass.cbSize = sizeof(WNDCLASSEX);
winclass.style   = CS_DBLCLKS ¦ CS_OWNDC ¦ CS_HREDRAW ¦ CS_VREDRAW;
winclass.lpfnWndProc = WindowProc;
winclass.cbClsExtra = 0;
winclass.cbWndExtra = 0;
winclass.hInstance  = hinstance;
winclass.hIcon     = LoadIcon(NULL, IDI_APPLICATION);
winclass.hCursor    = LoadCursor(NULL, IDC_ARROW);
winclass.hbrBackground  = (HBRUSH)GetStockObject(BLACK_BRUSH);
winclass.lpszMenuName  = NULL;
winclass.lpszClassName  = "WINCLASS1";
winclass.hIconSm    = LoadIcon(NULL, IDI_APPLICATION);
```

And of course, if you want to save some typing, you could initialize the structure inline like this:

```
WNDCLASSEX winclass = {
        winclass.cbSize = sizeof(WNDCLASSEX),
        CS_DBLCLKS ¦ CS_OWNDC ¦ CS_HREDRAW ¦ CS_VREDRAW,
        WindowProc,
        0,
        0,
        hinstance,
        LoadIcon(NULL, IDI_APPLICATION),
        LoadCursor(NULL, IDC_ARROW),
        (HBRUSH)GetStockObject(BLACK_BRUSH),
        NULL,
        "WINCLASS1",
        LoadIcon(NULL, IDI_APPLICATION)};
```

It saves typing!

Registering the Windows Class

Now that the Windows Class is defined and stored in `winclass`, you must let Windows know about the new class by *registering* it. This is accomplished via the function `RegisterClassEx()`, which simply takes a pointer to the new class definition:

```
RegisterClassEx(&winclass);
```

CAUTION

Notice that I'm not yet using the class name (WINCLASS1 in the case of our example). For RegisterClassEx(), you must use the actual structure holding the class, because at the point before the call to the function, Windows does not yet know of the existence of the new class. So, the name WINCLASS1 is not yet available for reference.

Also, to be complete, there is the old RegisterClass() function, which is used to register a class based on the older structure WNDCLASS.

After the class is registered, we are free to create a window with it. Let's see how to do that, and then revisit the details of the event handler and main event loop to see what kind of processing needs to be done for a Windows application to work.

Creating the Window

To create a window (or any window-like object, such as a control), you use the CreateWindow() or CreateWindowEx() functions. The latter is a bit more recent and supports an additional style parameter, so we'll use it. This is where the Windows Class that we took so long to dissect piece by piece comes in. When you create a window, you must supply the text name of the window class—which in our case is WINCLASS1. This is what identifies your window class and differentiates it from other classes, along with the built-in types like buttons, text boxes, and so on.

Here's the function prototype for CreateWindowEx():

```
HWND CreateWindowEx(
   DWORD dwExStyle,    // extended window style
   LPCTSTR lpClassName, // pointer to registered class name
   LPCTSTR lpWindowName, // pointer to window name
   DWORD dwStyle,     // window style
   int x,         // horizontal position of window
   int y,         // vertical position of window
   int nWidth,      // window width
   int nHeight,      // window height
   HWND hWndParent,    // handle to parent or owner window
   HMENU hMenu,      // handle to menu, or child-window identifier
   HINSTANCE hInstance, // handle to application instance
   LPVOID lpParam);    // pointer to window-creation data
```

If the function is successful, it will return a handle to the newly created window, or NULL otherwise.

Most of the parameters are self-explanatory, but let's cover them anyway:

- dwExStyle—The extended styles flag is an advanced feature, and for most cases you'll set it to NULL. However, if you're interested in all the possible values, take a look at the Win32 SDK Help—there are a lot of them. About the only one I ever use is WS_EX_TOPMOST, which makes the window stay on top.
- lpClassName—This is the name of the class you want to create a window based on, such as WINCLASS1.
- lpWindowName—This is a NULL-terminated text string containing the title of the window, for example, My First Window.
- dwStyle—These are the general window flags that describe what the window looks and behaves like—very important! See Table 2.7 for a list of some of the more popular values used for DirectX applications. Of course, you can logically OR these values together to get the various features you want.
- x,y—Position of the upper left-hand corner of the window in pixel coordinates. If you don't care, use CW_USEDEFAULT and Windows will decide.
- nWidth, nHeight—Width and height of the window in pixels. If you don't care, use CW_USEDEFAULT and Windows will decide.
- hWndParent—Handle to the parent window if there is one. Use NULL if there isn't a parent; then the Desktop will be the parent.
- hMenu—Handle to the menu to attach to the window. More on this in the next chapter. Use NULL for now.
- hInstance—The instance of the application. Use hinstance from WinMain() here.
- lpParam—Advanced. Set to NULL.

TABLE 2.7 General Style Values for dwStyle

Style	Meaning
WS_POPUP	Creates a pop-up window.
WS_OVERLAPPED	Creates an overlapped window. An overlapped window has a title bar and a border. Same as the WS_TILED style.
WS_OVERLAPPEDWINDOW	Creates an overlapped window with the WS_OVERLAPPED, WS_CAPTION, WS_SYSMENU, WS_THICKFRAME, WS_MINIMIZEBOX, and WS_MAXIMIZEBOX styles.
WS_VISIBLE	Creates a window that is initially visible.

And here's how you would create a basic overlapped window with the standard controls at position (0,0) with a size of (400,400) pixels:

```
HWND hwnd; // window handle

// create the window, bail if problem
if (!(hwnd = CreateWindowEx(NULL, // extended style
             "WINCLASS1",     // class
          "Your Basic Window", // title
         WS_OVERLAPPEDWINDOW | WS_VISIBLE,
          0,0,    // initial x,y
         400,400, // initial width, height
         NULL,    // handle to parent
         NULL,    // handle to menu
         hinstance,// instance of this application
         NULL)))  // extra creation parms
return(0);
```

After the window has been created, it may or may not be visible. However, in this case, we added the style flag `WS_VISIBLE` that does this automatically. If this flag isn't added, use the following function call to manually display the window:

```
// this shows the window
ShowWindow(hwnd, ncmdshow);
```

Remember the `ncmdshow` parameter of `WinMain()`? This is where it comes in handy. Although we have overridden it by adding `WS_VISIBLE`, you would normally send it as the parameter to `ShowWindow()`. The next thing that you might want to do is force Windows to update your window's contents and generate a `WM_PAINT` message. This is accomplished with a call to `UpdateWindow()`:

```
// this sends a WM_PAINT message to window and makes
// sure the contents are refreshed
UpdateWindow();
```

The Event Handler

I don't know about you, but I'm starting to get the hang of this Windows stuff! It's not that bad—it's like a mystery novel, except the mystery is figuring out what language the novel is written in! Let's tackle the main event handler, or at least take a first look at it. Remember that the event handler is a callback function called by Windows from the main event loop whenever an event occurs that your window must handle. Take a look at Figure 2.3 again to refresh your memory of the general data flow.

This event handler is written by *you*, and it handles as many (or as few) events that you want to take care of. The rest you can pass on to Windows and let it deal with them. Of course, the more events and messages your application handles, the more functionality it will have, so keep that in mind.

Before we get into some code, let's talk about some of the details of the event handler and exactly what it does and how it works. First, for each Windows Class that you create, you can have a separate event handler that I will refer to as Windows Procedure, or simply `WinProc` from now on. The `WinProc` is sent messages from the main event loop as messages are received from the user and/or Windows and placed in the main event queue. That's a mental tongue twister, so I'll say it in another way ....

As the user and Windows do stuff, events and messages are generated that are for your window and/or other applications' windows. All of these messages go into a queue, but the ones for your window are sent to your window's own private queue. Then the main event loop retrieves these messages and sends them to your window's `WinProc` to be processed. This is shown in Figure 2.1.

There are literally hundreds of possible messages and variations, so we aren't going to cover them all, but luckily you only have to handle a very few to get a Windows application up and running.

So, in a nutshell the main event loop feeds the `WinProc` with messages and events, and the `WinProc` does something with them. Hence, not only do we have to worry about the `WinProc`, but also the main event loop. However, we will get to this shortly. For now, let's assume that the `WinProc` is simply going to be fed messages. Now that you know what the `WinProc` does, let's take a look at its prototype:

```
LRESULT CALLBACK WindowProc(
         HWND hwnd, // window handle of sender
         UINT msg, // the message id
         WPARAM wparam, // further defines message
         LPARAM lparam); // further defines message
```

Of course, this is just a prototype for the callback. You can call the function anything you want, because you are only going to assign the function's address as a function pointer to `winclass.lpfnWndProc`:

```
winclass.lpfnWndProc = WindowProc;
```

Remember? Anyway, the parameters are fairly self-explanatory.

- `hwnd`—This is the window handle. This is only important if you have multiple windows open with the same Windows Class. `hwnd` is then the only way you can tell which messages are coming from which window. Figure 2.4 shows this possibility graphically.
- `msg`—This is the actual message ID that the `WinProc` should handle. This ID might be one of dozens of main messages.
- `wparam` and `lparam`—These further qualify or subclass the message sent in the `msg` parameter.
- And finally, the return type and declaration specifier are of interest — `LRESULT CALLBACK`. These keywords are a must, so don't forget them!

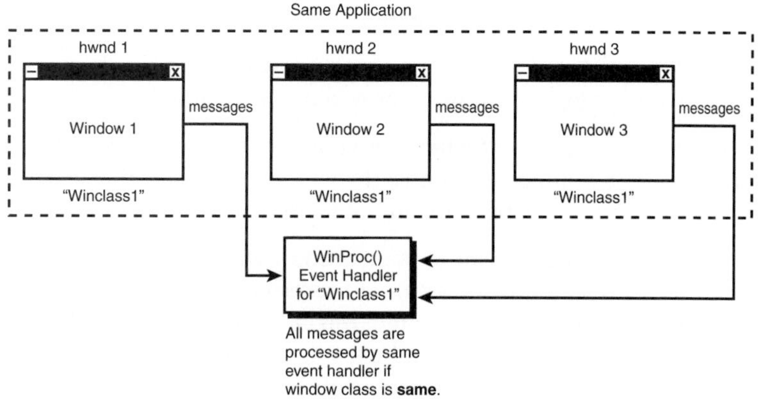

FIGURE 2.4 Multiple windows based on the same class.

What most people do is `switch()` on the `msg` and then write code for each case. Based on `msg` you will know whether you need to further evaluate `wparam` and/or `lparam`. Cool? Let's take a look at some of the possible messages that might come through the `WinProc` and then we'll see a bare bones `WinProc`. Take a look at Table 2.8 to see a short list of some basic message IDs.

TABLE 2.8 A Short List of Message IDs

Value	Meaning
WM_ACTIVATE	Sent when a window is activated or becomes the focus.
WM_CLOSE	Sent when a window is closed.
WM_CREATE	Sent when a window is first created.
WM_DESTROY	Sent when a window is about to be destroyed.
WM_MOVE	Sent when a window has been moved.
WM_MOUSEMOVE	Sent when the mouse has been moved.
WM_KEYUP	Sent when a key is released.
WM_KEYDOWN	Sent when a key is pressed.
WM_TIMER	Sent when a timer event occurs.
WM_USER	Enables you to send messages.
WM_PAINT	Sent when a window needs repainting.
WM_QUIT	Sent when a Windows application is finally terminating.
WM_SIZE	Sent when a window has changed size.

(Note: I have highlighted the messages that we are going to make the most use of.)

Take a good look at Table 2.8. Basically, the `WinProc` is sent one or more of these messages as the application runs. The message ID itself will be in `msg`, and any remaining info is stored in `wparam` and `lparam`. Thus, it's always a good idea to reference the online Win32 SDK Help and see what all the parameters of a particular message do.

Fortunately, we are only interested in three messages right now:

- WM_CREATE—This message is sent when the window is first created, and gives you a chance to do any setup, initialization, or resource allocation.
- WM_PAINT—This message is sent whenever your window's contents need repainting. This can occur for a number of reasons: the window was moved or resized by the user, another application popped up and obscured yours, and so on.
- WM_DESTROY—This message is sent to your window when the window is about to be destroyed. Usually, this is a direct result of the user clicking on the window's close icon or closing from the window's system menu. Either way, this is where you should de-allocate all the resources and tell Windows to terminate the application completely by sending a WM_QUIT message yourself—more on this later.

So without further ado, let's see a complete WinProc that handles all these messages. Take a look at the following listing:

```
LRESULT CALLBACK WindowProc(HWND hwnd,
              UINT msg,
              WPARAM wparam,
              LPARAM lparam)
{
// this is the main message handler of the system
PAINTSTRUCT  ps;  // used in WM_PAINT
HDC    hdc;  // handle to a device context

// what is the message
switch(msg)
  {
  case WM_CREATE:
    {
  // do initialization stuff here

    // return success
  return(0);
  } break;

  case WM_PAINT:
  {
  // simply validate the window
  hdc = BeginPaint(hwnd,&ps);
  // you would do all your painting here
    EndPaint(hwnd,&ps);
```

```
      // return success
    return(0);
    } break;

    case WM_DESTROY:
    {
    // kill the application, this sends a WM_QUIT message
    PostQuitMessage(0);

      // return success
    return(0);
    } break;

    default:break;

    } // end switch

// process any messages that we didn't take care of
return (DefWindowProc(hwnd, msg, wparam, lparam));

} // end WinProc
```

As you can see, the function is composed of empty space for the most part, which is a good thing! While I'm on the subject of empty space, did you know that most solid matter is composed mostly of empty space? And there's a finite probability that you can walk through a solid wall given enough attempts?

Let's begin with the processing of `WM_CREATE`. Here all the function does is `return(0)`. This simply tells Windows that we handled it, so don't take any more action. Of course, you could do all kinds of initialization in the `WM_CREATE` message, but that's up to you.

The next message `WM_PAINT` is very important. This message is sent whenever your window needs repainting. This means that you have to do the repainting, for the most part. This isn't going to matter for DirectX games because we are going to redraw the screen 30—60 fps (frames per second), but for a normal Windows application, it does. Nevertheless, for our DirectX applications, we don't want Windows to think that we aren't repainting the screen, so we have to let it know we are processing the `WM_PAINT` messages.

To accomplish this feat, you must "validate the client rectangle of the window." There are a number of ways to do this, but the simplest is with a call to `BeginPaint()` and `EndPaint()`. This calling pair validates the window and fills the background with the background brush previously stored in the Windows Class variable `hbrBackground`. Here's the code once again for the validation:

```
   // begin painting
 hdc = BeginPaint(hwnd,&ps);
 // you would do all your painting here
   EndPaint(hwnd,&ps);
```

There are a couple of things going on here that I want to address. First, notice that the first parameter to each call is the window handle `hwnd`. This is necessary because the `BeginPaint()/EndPaint()` function can potentially paint in any window of your application; so the window handle indicates which window you're interested in painting in. The second parameter is the address of a `PAINTSTRUCT` structure that contains the rectangle that you must redraw. That is, it's possible that only a small region needs repainting, so this structure defines that region. Here's what a `PAINTSTRUCT` looks like:

```
typedef struct tagPAINTSTRUCT
    {
    HDC hdc;
    BOOL fErase;
    RECT rcPaint;
    BOOL fRestore;
    BOOL fIncUpdate;
    BYTE rgbReserved[32];
    } PAINTSTRUCT;
```

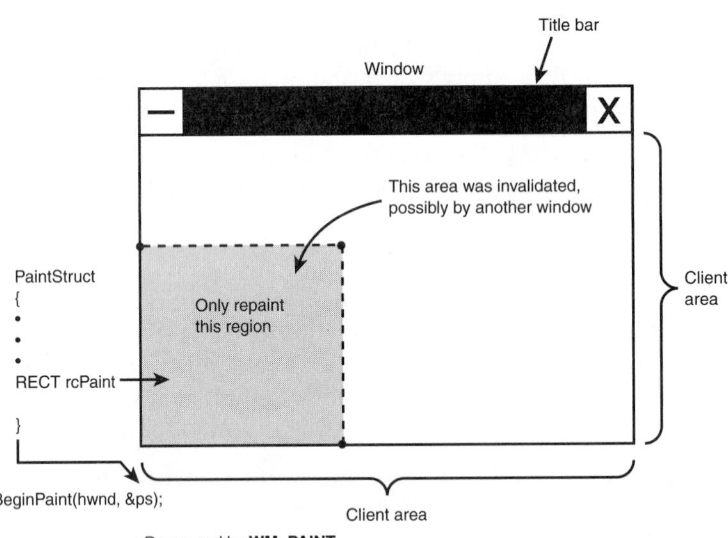

FIGURE 2.5 Repainting the invalid region only.

You mostly don't need to worry about this until later, when we talk about the GDI, but the most important field is `rcPaint`, which is a `RECT` structure that contains the minimum rectangle that needs to be repainted. Take a look at Figure 2.5 to see this graphically. You see, Windows tries to do the least amount of work possible, so when the contents of a window are mangled, Windows at least tries to tell you the smallest rectangle that you can repaint to restore the contents. If you're interested in the RECT structure, it's nothing more than the four corners of a rectangle, as shown in the following:


```
typedef struct tagRECT
    {
    LONG left;  // left x-edge of rect
    LONG top;  // top y-edge of rect
    LONG right; // right x-edge of rect
    LONG bottom; // bottom y-edge of rect
    } RECT;
```

The last thing you'll notice about the call to BeginPaint() is that it returns a handle to a graphics context, or hdc:

```
HDC hdc; // handle to graphics context
hdc = BeginPaint(hwnd,&ps);
```

A *graphics context* is a data structure that describes the video system and drawing surface. It's magic as far as we are concerned (but it wouldn't hurt you to take a look at its data structure in the header files); you just have to retrieve one if you want to do any graphics. That's about it for the WM_PAINT message—for now.

The WM_DESTROY message is actually quite interesting. WM_DESTROY is sent when the user closes the window. However, this only closes the window, not the application. The application will continue to run, but without a window. Therefore, you need to do something about this. In most cases, when the user kills the main window, he intends for the application to terminate. Thus, you must facilitate this by sending a quit message yourself! The message is called WM_QUIT. Because it's so common a message, there is a function to send it for you called PostQuitMessage().

All you need to do in the WM_DESTROY handler is clean up everything and then tell Windows to terminate your application with a call to PostQuitMessage(0). This in turn puts a WM_QUIT into the message queue, which at some point causes the main event loop to bail.

There are a couple of details you should be aware of in the WinProc handler we have been analyzing. First, I'm sure you have noticed the return(0) after each handler's body. This serves two purposes: to exit the WinProc, and to tell Windows that we have handled the message. The second important detail is the *default message handler* DefaultWindowProc(). This function is a *pass through*, which passes messages that you don't process on to Windows for default processing. Therefore, if you don't handle the message, make sure to always end all your event handler functions with a call like this:

```
// process any messages that we didn't take care of
return (DefWindowProc(hwnd, msg, wparam, lparam));
```

I know this might all seem like overkill and more trouble than it's worth. Nevertheless, after you have a basic Windows application skeleton, then you just copy it and add your own code. In fact, after we have our virtual computer set up, we can use it and almost forget that any Windows stuff is going on. Anyway, stay with me and let's move on to the last part: the main event loop.

The Main Event Loop

The hard part is over! The main event loop is so simple that I'm just going to blurt it out and then talk about it, so here it is:

```
// enter main event loop
while(GetMessage(&msg,NULL,0,0))
   {
   // translate any accelerator keys
   TranslateMessage(&msg);

   // send the message to the window proc
   DispatchMessage(&msg);
   } // end while
```

That's it? Yup! Let's see what's going on here, shall we? The main `while()` executes as long as `GetMessage()` returns a nonzero value. `GetMessage()` is the workhorse of the main event loop, and its sole purpose is to get the next message from the event queue and process it. You'll notice that there are four parameters to `GetMessage()`. The first one is important to us, but the remaining are set to `NULL` and zeros. Here's the prototype for reference:

```
BOOL GetMessage(
   LPMSG lpMsg,      // address of structure with message
   HWND hWnd,       // handle of window
   UINT wMsgFilterMin, // first message
   UINT wMsgFilterMax); // last message
```

The `msg` parameter is (you guessed it) the storage where Windows will place the next message. However, unlike the `msg` parameter for `WinProc()`, this `msg` is a complex data structure, rather than just an integer ID. Remember, by the time a message gets to the `WinProc`, it has been "cooked" and split into its constituent parts. Anyway, here is the `MSG` structure:

```
typedef struct tagMSG
    {
    HWND hwnd;    // window where message occurred
```

```
UINT message; // message id itself
WPARAM wParam; // sub qualifies message
LPARAM lParam; // sub qualifies message
DWORD time;  // time of message event
POINT pt;    // position of mouse
} MSG;
```


Starting to make sense? Notice that the parameters to `WinProc()` are all contained within this structure, along with some others, like the time and position of the mouse when then event occurred.

We know `GetMessage()` retrieves the next message from the event queue, but then what? `TranslateMessage()` is called next. `TranslateMessage()` is a virtual accelerator key translator, or in other words, an input cooker. Just call it and don't worry about what it does. The final function `DispatchMessage()` is where all the action occurs. After the message is retrieved with `GetMessage()` and potentially processed and translated a bit with `TranslateMessage()`, the actual `WinProc()` is called by the call to `DispatchMessage()`.

`DispatchMessage()` makes the call to the `WinProc`, sending the appropriate parameters from the original `MSG` structure. Figure 2.6 shows the whole process in its final glory.

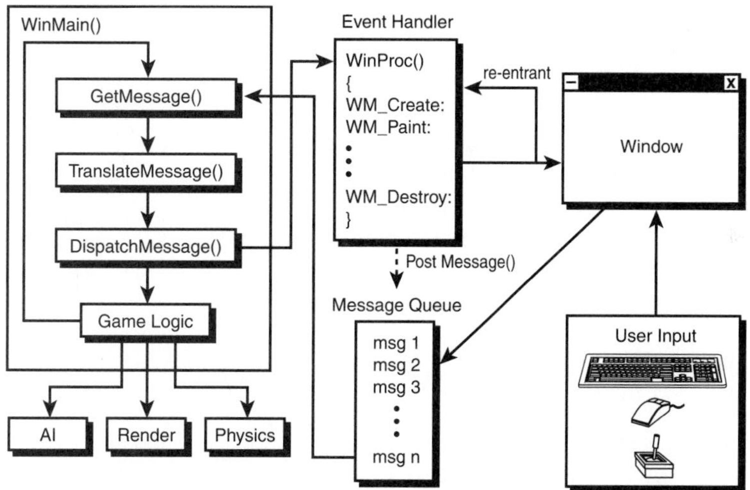

FIGURE 2.6 The mechanics of event loop message processing.

That's it—you're a Windows expert! The rest is just details, but if you grasp the concepts we just covered and the importance of the event loop, event handler, and so on, that's 90% of the battle. With that in mind, take a look at the following listing—it's a complete Windows program that creates a single window and waits for you to close it.

```
// DEMOII2_3.CPP - A complete windows program

// INCLUDES ///////////////////////////////////////////////
#define WIN32_LEAN_AND_MEAN // just say no to MFC

#include <windows.h>  // include all the windows headers
#include <windowsx.h> // include useful macros
#include <stdio.h>
#include <math.h>

// DEFINES ////////////////////////////////////////////////

// defines for windows
#define WINDOW_CLASS_NAME "WINCLASS1"

// GLOBALS ////////////////////////////////////////////////


// FUNCTIONS //////////////////////////////////////////////
LRESULT CALLBACK WindowProc(HWND hwnd,
         UINT msg,
              WPARAM wparam,
              LPARAM lparam)
{
// this is the main message handler of the system
PAINTSTRUCT  ps;  // used in WM_PAINT
HDC    hdc;  // handle to a device context

// what is the message
switch(msg)
  {
  case WM_CREATE:
    {
  // do initialization stuff here

    // return success
  return(0);
  } break;

  case WM_PAINT:
  {
  // simply validate the window
  hdc = BeginPaint(hwnd,&ps);
```

```
  // you would do all your painting here
    EndPaint(hwnd,&ps);

    // return success
  return(0);
  } break;

  case WM_DESTROY:
  {
  // kill the application, this sends a WM_QUIT message
  PostQuitMessage(0);

    // return success
  return(0);
  } break;

  default:break;

  } // end switch

// process any messages that we didn't take care of
return (DefWindowProc(hwnd, msg, wparam, lparam));

} // end WinProc

// WINMAIN ////////////////////////////////////////////////
int WINAPI WinMain(HINSTANCE hinstance,
      HINSTANCE hprevinstance,
      LPSTR lpcmdline,
      int ncmdshow)
{

WNDCLASSEX winclass; // this will hold the class we create
HWND    hwnd;   // generic window handle
MSG    msg;     // generic message

// first fill in the window class stucture
winclass.cbSize = sizeof(WNDCLASSEX);
winclass.style    = CS_DBLCLKS ¦ CS_OWNDC ¦
         CS_HREDRAW ¦ CS_VREDRAW;
winclass.lpfnWndProc   = WindowProc;
winclass.cbClsExtra   = 0;
winclass.cbWndExtra   = 0;
```

```
winclass.hInstance  = hinstance;
winclass.hIcon    = LoadIcon(NULL, IDI_APPLICATION);
winclass.hCursor  = LoadCursor(NULL, IDC_ARROW);
winclass.hbrBackground  = (HBRUSH)GetStockObject(BLACK_BRUSH);
winclass.lpszMenuName  = NULL;
winclass.lpszClassName  = WINDOW_CLASS_NAME;
winclass.hIconSm   = LoadIcon(NULL, IDI_APPLICATION);

// register the window class
if (!RegisterClassEx(&winclass))
  return(0);

// create the window
if (!(hwnd = CreateWindowEx(NULL, // extended style
              WINDOW_CLASS_NAME,  // class
        "Your Basic Window", // title
        WS_OVERLAPPEDWINDOW ¦ WS_VISIBLE,
         0,0,    // initial x,y
        400,400,    // initial width, height
        NULL,    // handle to parent
        NULL,    // handle to menu
        hinstance,   // instance of this application
        NULL)))    // extra creation parms
return(0);

// enter main event loop
while(GetMessage(&msg,NULL,0,0))
   {
   // translate any accelerator keys
   TranslateMessage(&msg);

   // send the message to the window proc
   DispatchMessage(&msg);
   } // end while

// return to Windows like this
return(msg.wParam);

} // end WinMain

///////////////////////////////////////////////////////////
```

To compile DEMOII2_3.CPP, simply create a Win32 .EXE application and add DEMOII2_3.CPP to the project. Or if you like, you can run the precompiled program DEMOII2_3.EXE from the CD-ROM. Figure 2.7 shows the program in action. It's not much to look at, but what do you want—this is a paperback book!

FIGURE 2.7 Screenshot of DEMOII2_3.EXE in action.

There are a couple of issues that I want to hit you with before moving on. First, if you take a closer look at the event loop, it doesn't look like it works in real time—while the program waits for a message via GetMessage(), the main event loop is basically blocked. This is very true, and we must get around it somehow, because we need to perform our game processing continuously and handle Windows events if and when they come.

Making a Real-Time Event Loop

A real-time non-waiting/blocking event loop is easy to make. All we need is a way to test whether there is a message in the message queue. If there is, we can process it; otherwise, we can continue processing other game logic and repeat. The function that performs just this test is called PeekMessage(). Its prototype is almost identical to GetMessage()'s, as shown here:

```
BOOL PeekMessage(
   LPMSG lpMsg,     // pointer to structure for message
   HWND hWnd,      // handle to window
   UINT wMsgFilterMin, // first message
   UINT wMsgFilterMax, // last message
   UINT wRemoveMsg);  // removal flags
```

Returns nonzero if a message is available.

The difference is in the last parameter. This controls how the messages should be retrieved from the message queue. The valid flags for `wRemoveMsg` are the following:

- `PM_NOREMOVE`—Messages are not removed from the queue after processing by `PeekMessage()`.
- `PM_REMOVE`—Messages are removed from the queue after processing by `PeekMessage()`.

Taking these two possibilities into consideration, we can do one of two things: use `PeekMessage()` with `PM_NOREMOVE`, and if there is a message, call `GetMessage()`; or use `PM_REMOVE` and use `PeekMessage()` itself to retrieve messages. We'll use the latter. Here's the core logic, changed to reflect this new technique in the main event loop:

```
while(TRUE)
  {
  // test if there is a message in queue, if so get it
  if (PeekMessage(&msg,NULL,0,0,PM_REMOVE))
    {
    // test if this is a quit
     if (msg.message == WM_QUIT)
       break;

    // translate any accelerator keys
    TranslateMessage(&msg);

    // send the message to the window proc
    DispatchMessage(&msg);
    } // end if

    // main game processing goes here
  Game_Main();
  } // end while
```

I've highlighted important points in the code. The first section highlighted is shown here:

```
if (msg.message == WM_QUIT)
  break;
```

This is how we must detect to bail out of the infinite `while(TRUE)` loop. Remember, when a `WM_DESTROY` message is processed in the `WinProc`, it's our job to send a `WM_QUIT` message via the call to `PostQuitMessage()`. The `WM_QUIT` then trickles through the event queue, and we can detect it to bail out of the loop.

The last section of highlighted code simply indicates where you would put the call to your main game code loop. But remember, the call to `Game_Main()` (or whatever you call it) must return after one frame of animation or game logic; otherwise, messages won't be processed by the main windows event loop.

As an example of this new real-time structure that is more appropriate for game logic processing, take a look at the source DEMOII2_4.CPP and the associated DEMOII2_4.EXE on the CD-ROM. This structure will in fact be our model for the virtual computer used for the remainder of the book. We will build on it in the next chapter.

Now that you have a handle on basic Windows programming, let's talk about the graphics, sound, and input interface that we'll be using for our games: DirectX.

DirectX and COM Crash Course

DirectX might take one more bit of control from you as a programmer, but in truth it's worth its weight in Monolithic DIMMS (Dual Inline Memory Modules). DirectX is basically a system of software that abstracts graphics, audio, input, networking, installation, and more, so no matter what the hardware configuration of a particular PC, you can use the same code. In addition, DirectX technology is many times faster and more robust than GDI and/or MCI (the Media Control Interface), which is native to Windows. Figure 2.8 illustrates how you would make a Windows game with and without DirectX. Notice how clean and elegant the DirectX solution is.

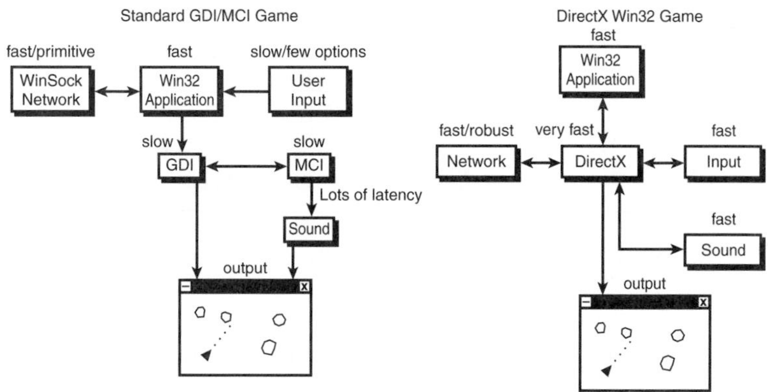

FIGURE 2.8 DirectX versus GDI/MCI.

So how does DirectX work? DirectX gives you almost hardware-level control of all devices. This is possible through a technology called *COM (Component Object Model)* and sets of drivers and libraries written by both Microsoft and the hardware vendors themselves. Microsoft came up with a set of conventions, functions, variables, data structures, and so on that must be used by the hardware vendors when implementing drivers to talk to the hardware.

As long as these conventions are followed, you don't need to worry about the details of the hardware—you just make calls to DirectX and DirectX handles the details for you. No matter what kind of video card, sound card, input device, network card, or whatever, as long as there is DirectX support, your program will be able to use it without you knowing anything about it!

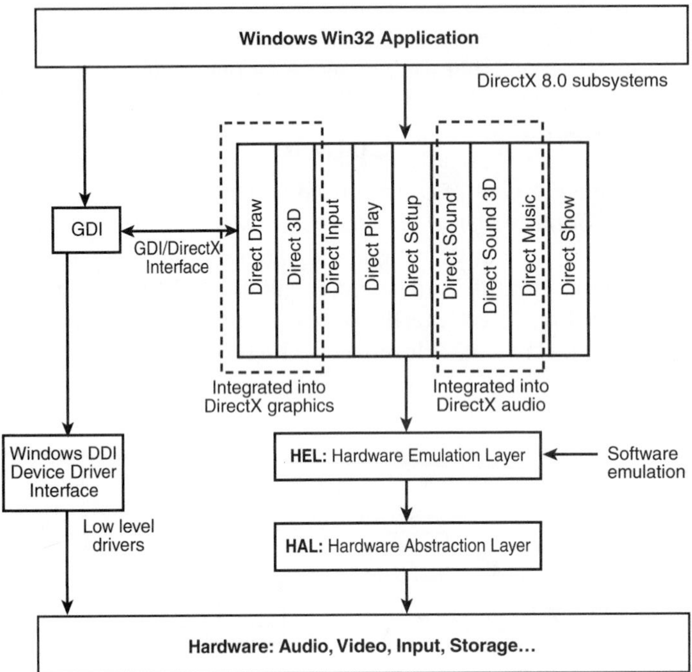

FIGURE 2.9 The architecture of DirectX 8.0+ and its relationship to Win32.

Currently there are a number of DirectX components that make up the DirectX 8.0+ foundation system. They are listed here and shown graphically in Figure 2.9.

- DirectDraw
- DirectSound
- DirectSound3D
- DirectMusic
- DirectInput
- DirectPlay
- DirectSetup

- Direct3DRM
- Direct3DIM

In DirectX 8.0, DirectDraw was merged with Direct3D and renamed DirectGraphics, and DirectSound and DirectMusic were merged and renamed DirectAudio. Thus, under DirectX 8.0+, there is no more DirectDraw. However, one of the rules of DirectX and COM is that you can always request a previous interface. Thus, in this book we will use DirectDraw under DirectX 7.0a for graphics, and the newer 8.0+ interfaces for sound and input. In any case, we are going to abstract graphics, sound, and input into our virtual computer, so truthfully even DirectX 3.0 would work! We will use the latest versions of DirectX (except for DirectDraw) to be as up-to-date as possible.

The HEL and HAL

You might notice on Figure 2.9 that there are two layers under DirectX called the *HEL (Hardware Emulation Layer)* and the *HAL (Hardware Abstraction Layer)*. Here's the deal—DirectX is a very forward-looking design, so it assumes advanced features are implemented by hardware. However, if the hardware doesn't support some feature, what happens? This is the basis of the dual-mode HAL and HEL design.

- HAL—The Hardware Abstraction Layer is the "to-the-metal layer." It talks directly to the hardware. This layer is usually the device driver from the vendor, and you communicate to it directly through generic DirectX calls. HAL is used when the feature you're requesting is supported directly by the hardware, and is thus accelerated.
- HEL—The Hardware Emulation Layer is used when the hardware doesn't support the feature that you are requesting. Let's suppose that you ask the video card to rotate a bitmap. If the hardware doesn't support rotation, the HEL kicks in and software algorithms take over. Obviously, this is slower, but the point is that it does NOT break your program. It will still work—just slower. In addition, the switching between the HAL and HEL is transparent to you. If you request DirectX to do something and the HAL does it directly, hardware will do it; otherwise, a software emulation will be called to get the job done with HEL.

You might be thinking that there are a lot of layers of software here. That's a concern, but the truth is that DirectX is so clean that the only penalty you take for using it is maybe an extra function call or two. A small price to pay for 2D/3D graphics, network, and audio acceleration. Can you imagine writing drivers to control all the video accelerators on the market? Trust me, it would take literally thousands of man-years—it just can't be done. DirectX is really a massively distributed engineering effort by Microsoft and all the hardware vendors to bring you an ultra-high performance standard.

The DirectX Foundation Classes in Depth

Now let's take a quick look at each of the DirectX components and what they do:

- DirectDraw (DirectX 7.0a only, not available in DirectX 8.0+)—This is the primary rendering and 2D bitmap engine that controls the video display. It is the conduit that all graphics must go through. This is probably the most important of all the DirectX components. The DirectDraw object more or less represents the video card(s) in your system.
- DirectSound—This is the sound component of DirectX. However, it only supports digital sound—no MIDI. However, this component makes your life a hundred times easier, because no longer do you have to license a third-party sound system to do your sound. Sound programming is a black art, and in the past no one wanted to keep up with writing all the drivers for all the sound cards. Hence, a couple of vendors cornered the market on sound libraries: Miles Sound System and DiamondWare Sound Toolkit. Both were very capable systems that enabled you to simply load and play digital and MIDI sounds from your DOS or Win32 programs. However, with the introduction of DirectSound, DirectSound3D, and the latest DirectMusic components, third-party libraries are much less useful now.
- DirectSound3D—This is the 3D sound component of DirectSound. It enables you to position 3D sounds in space and simulate 3D sound as if objects are floating around the room! This technology is relatively new, but maturing quickly. Today most sound cards support hardware-accelerated 3D effects, including Doppler shift, refraction, reflection, and more. However, if software emulation is used, all of this stuff comes to a halt!
- DirectMusic—DirectMusic is the missing MIDI technology that DirectSound didn't support. But more than that, DirectMusic has a new *DLS* system *(Downloadable Sounds)* that enables you to create digital representations of instruments and then play them back with MIDI control. This is much like a Wave Table synthesizer, but in software. Also, DirectMusic has a new Performance Engine that is an artificial intelligence system of sorts, and can make changes to your music in real time based on templates you give it. In essence, the system can create new music on the fly. Wild, huh?
- DirectAudio—In version 8.0+ of DirectX, DirectSound and DirectMusic were merged into a unified interface. You can still use them separately if you like, but if you prefer you can now use the new DirectAudio interface as well.
- DirectInput—This system handles all input devices, including the mouse, keyboard, joystick, paddles, track balls, and so forth. Moreover, DirectInput now supports force feedback devices. These are devices that have electro-mechanical actuators and force sensors, enabling you to physically manifest forces that the user can feel. It's going to really put the cybersex industry into overdrive!

- DirectPlay—This is the networking aspect of DirectX. It enables you to make abstract "connections" using the Internet, modems, direct connection, or any other kind of medium that might come up. The cool thing about DirectPlay is that it enables you to make these connections without knowing anything about networking. You don't have to write drivers, use sockets, or anything like that. In addition, DirectPlay supports the concepts of *sessions*, which are games in progress, and *lobbies*, which are places for gamers to congregate to play. Also, DirectPlay doesn't force you into any kind of multiplayer network architecture—it's up to you how you want to do things. All DirectPlay does is send and receive packets for you. What they contain and if they are reliable is up to you.

- Direct3DRM (DirectX 7.0a only, not available in DirectX 8.0+)—This is Direct3D Retained Mode, which is a high-level object and frame-based 3D system that you can use to create basic 3D programs. It takes advantage of 3D acceleration, but isn't the fastest thing in the world. It's great for making walkthru programs, 3D model manipulators, or extremely slow demos.

- Direct3DIM—This is Direct3D Immediate Mode, which is the low-level 3D support for DirectX. Originally, this was incredibly hard to work with, and was the cause for many flame wars with OpenGL. The old Immediate Mode used what are called *execute buffers*—basically, arrays of data and instructions that you would create that describe the scene to be drawn—very ugly. However, since DirectX 5.0, Immediate Mode now supports a much more OpenGL-like interface through the `DrawPrimitive()` and `DrawIndexedPrimitive()` functions. This enables you to send triangle strips, fans, and so on to the rendering engine, and make state changes with function calls rather than execute buffers. Although this book is a software-based 3D game book, Direct3D Immediate Mode will be covered at the end of the book for completion's sake.

- DirectGraphics—In DirectX 8.0+, DirectDraw is no longer supported, but that's not entirely true—from a philosophical point of view, at least. What Microsoft did was merge all the graphics software into a single interface called DirectGraphics that handles everything. It doesn't have any DirectDraw interfaces, but you can perform 2D with Direct3D interfaces if you want, or just use IDirectDraw7 and standard DirectDraw—I know, it's a mess, huh?

- DirectSetup/AutoPlay—These are quasi-DirectX components that enable you to install DirectX from your application on the user's machine and start the game up directly when the CD is placed in the system. DirectSetup is a small set of functions that basically loads the runtime DirectX files on a user's machine and registers them in the registry. AutoPlay is the standard CD subsystem that looks for the `AUTOPLAY.INF` file on the CD root, and if found, executes the batch command functions in the file.

Finally, you might be wondering what the deal is with all the versions of DirectX—it seems to be revised on a six-month basis. This is for the most part true. It's a manifestation of the business we are in—graphics and game technology move very fast. However, because DirectX is based on COM technology, programs that you write for, say, DirectX version 3.0, are guaranteed to work on DirectX version 8.0, 9.0, and so on because of their COM implementation. Let's see how that works ....

Flash Introduction to COM

COM was originally invented many years back as a simple white paper on a new software paradigm that was similar to how computer chips or LEGO blocks work—you simply plug them together and they work. Both computer chips and LEGO blocks know how to be computer chips and LEGO blocks, so everything works out automatically. To implement this kind of technology with software, you need some kind of very generic interface that can take on the form of any type of function set you can imagine. This is what COM does.

One of the cool things about computer chips is that when you add more computer chips to a design, you don't have to tell all the other chips that you changed something. However, as you know, this is a little harder with software programs. You at least have to recompile to make an executable. Fixing this problem is another goal of COM. You should be able to add new features to a COM object without breaking software that uses the old COM object. In addition, COM objects can be changed without recompiling the original program, which is very cool.

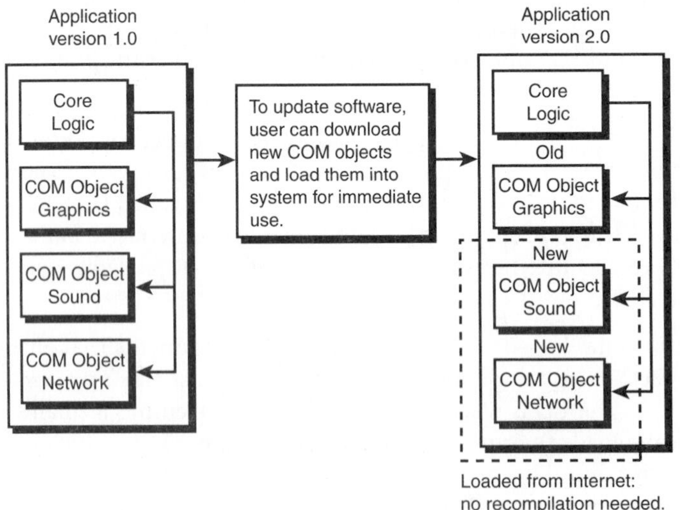

FIGURE 2.10 An overview of COM.

Because you can upgrade COM objects without recompiling your program, you can also upgrade your software without patches and new versions. For example, suppose that you have a program that uses three COM objects: one that implements graphics, one for sound, and one for networking, as shown in Figure 2.10. Now imagine that you sell 100,000 copies of your program that uses these COM objects, but you don't want to send out 100,000 upgrades! To update the graphics COM object, all you do is give users the new COM object for graphics, and the program will automatically use it. No recompiling, linking, or anything like that—easy. Of course, all this technology is very complex at the low level, and writing your own COM objects is a bit challenging, but using them is easy.

The next question is how are COM objects distributed or contained, given their plug-n-play nature? The answer is that there are no rules on this. However, in most cases COM objects are *.DLLs (Dynamic Link Libraries),* which can be downloaded or supplied with the program that uses them. This way they can be easily upgraded and changed. The only problem with this is that the program that uses the COM object must know how to load the COM object from a .DLL—but we'll get to that later.

What Exactly Is a COM Object?

A COM object is really a C++ class or a set of C++ classes that implement a number of *interfaces*. These interfaces are used to communicate to the COM object. Basically, an interface is a set of functions that perform a service. Take a look at Figure 2.11. Here we see a single COM object that has three interfaces named `IGRAPHICS`, `ISOUND`, and `IINPUT`.

Each one of these interfaces has a number of functions that you can call (when you know how) to do work. So, a single COM object can have one or more interfaces, and you may have one or more COM objects. Moreover, the COM specification states that all interfaces you create must be derived from a special base class interface called `IUnknown`. For you C programmers, all this means is that `IUnknown` is like the starting point to build the interface from.

Let's take a look at the `IUnknown` class definition:

```
struct Iunknown
{

// this function is used to retrieve other interfaces
virtual HRESULT __stdcall QueryInterface(const IID &iid, (void **)ip) = 0;

// this is used to increment interfaces reference count
virtual ULONG __stdcall AddRef() = 0;

// this is used to decrement interfaces reference count
virtual ULONG __stdcall Release() = 0;

};
```

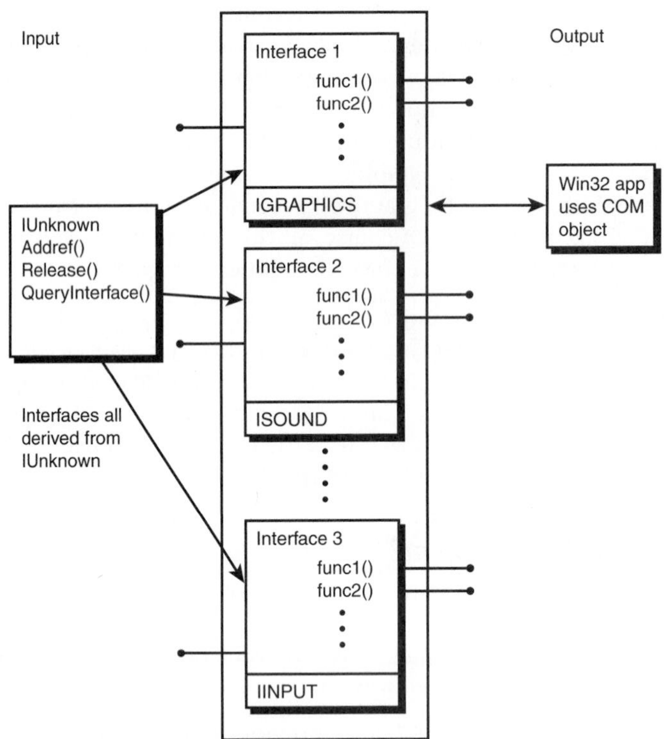

FIGURE 2.11 The interfaces of a COM object.

NOTE

Notice that all methods are pure and virtual. In addition, the methods use `__stdcall` in deference to the standard C/C++ calling convention. Remember that `__stdcall` pushes the parameters on the stack from right to left.

Even if you're a C++ programmer, the preceding class definition might look a bit bizarre if you're rusty on virtual functions. Anyway, let's dissect `IUnknown` and see what's up. All interfaces derived from `IUnknown` must implement at very minimum each of the methods `QueryInterface()`, `AddRef()`, and `Release()`.

`QueryInterface()` is the key to COM—it is used to request a pointer to the interface functions that you desire. To make the request happen, you must have an interface ID. This interface ID is a unique number 128 bits long that you assign to your interface. There are 2^{128} different possible interface IDs, and I guarantee that in a billion years, even if everybody on this planet does nothing but make COM objects, we won't run out! More on the ID when we get to a real example a little later in the chapter. Furthermore, one of the rules of COM is that if you have an interface, you can always request any other interface from it as long as it's from the same COM object. This means that you can get anywhere from anywhere else. Take a look at Figure 2.12 to see this graphically.

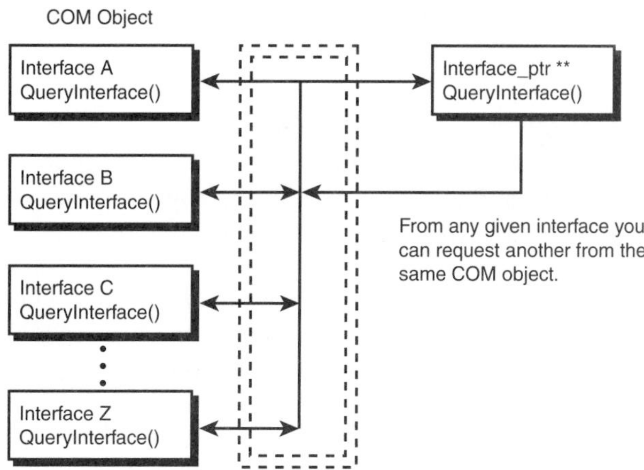

FIGURE 2.12 Navigating the interfaces of a COM object.

`AddRef()` is a curious function. COM objects use a technique called *reference counting* to track their life. This is because one of the specifications of COM is that it's not language-specific. Hence, `AddRef()` is called when a COM object is created and when interfaces are created to track how many references there are to the objects. If COM objects were to use `malloc()` or `new[]`, that would be C/C++-specific. When the reference count drops to `0`, the object(s) are destroyed internally.

TIP

Usually you don't have to call `AddRef()` yourself on interfaces or COM objects; it's done internally by the `QueryInterface()` function. However, sometimes you might have to if you want to up the reference count to trick the COM object into thinking that there are more references to it than there really is.

This brings us to a problem—if COM objects are C++ classes, how can they be created or used in Visual Basic, Java, Active X, and so on? It just so happens that the designers of COM used virtual C++ classes to implement COM, but you don't need to use C++ to access them, or even to create them. As long as you create the same binary image that a Microsoft C++ compiler would when creating a virtual C++ class, the COM object will be COM-compliant. Of course, most compiler products have extras or tools to help make COM objects, so that's not too much of a problem. The cool thing about this is that you can write a COM object in C++, Visual Basic, or Delphi, and then that COM object can be used by any of those languages! A binary image in memory is a binary image in memory.

`Release()` is used to decrement the reference count of a COM object or interface. In most cases, you must call this function yourself when you're done with an interface. However, sometimes if you create an object and then from that object create another object, killing the calling `Release()` on the parent will trickle down and `Release()` the child or derived object, but either way, it's a good idea to `Release()` in the opposite order that you queried.

Creating and Using DirectX COM Interfaces

At this point, I think we all understand that COM objects are collections of interfaces that are simply function pointers, and are more specifically, `VTABLE`s. Hence, all you need to do to work with a DirectX COM object is create it, retrieve an interface pointer, and then make calls to the interface using the proper syntax. Of course, this is all for your edification, because we are going to use an API that builds on all this stuff. I doubt you will ever make a COM call (maybe for DirectMusic and DirectInput), but it's good to know. As an example, I'll use the main DirectDraw interface to show how this is done.

First off, to experiment with DirectDraw you need three things:

- The DirectDraw runtime COM object(s) and .DLLs must be loaded and registered. This is what the DirectX installer does.
- You must include the `DDRAW.LIB` import library in your Win32 programs, so that the wrapper functions you call are linked in.
- You need to include `DDRAW.H` in your program, so the compiler can "see" the header information, prototypes, and data types for DirectDraw.

With that in mind, here's the data type for a DirectDraw 1.0 interface pointer:

```
LPDIRECTDRAW lpdd = NULL;
```

To create a DirectDraw 1.0 COM object and retrieve an interface pointer to the DirectDraw object (which represents the video card), all you need to do is use the wrapper function `DirectDrawCreate()`:

```
DirectDrawCreate(NULL, &lpdd, NULL);
```

Don't worry about the parameters. If you're interested, take a look at the DirectX SDK, but 99 out of a 100 times, the function will look as it does in the preceding. That is, only one parameter is used, and that's the address of the interface pointer to fill in with the DirectDraw COM interface. So for now, just believe that this call creates a DirectDraw object and assigns the interface pointer to `lpdd`.

NOTE

Of course, there is a lot going on in the function. It opens a .DLL, loads it, makes calls and does about a million other things, but you don't have to worry about it.

Now we're in business and can make calls to DirectDraw. But wait a minute! We don't know the methods or functions that are available—that's why you're reading this book <BG>. However, as an example, here's how you would set the video mode to 640×480 with 8-bit (256) color:

```
lpdd->SetVideoMode(640, 480, 8);
```

Is that simple or what? About the only extra work done is the pointer de-reference from the DirectDraw interface pointer `lpdd`—that's it. Of course, what's really happening is a lookup in the virtual table of the interface, but we aren't concerned about that.

In essence, any call to DirectX takes the form

```
interface_pointer->method_name(parameter list);
```

Also, for any other interfaces that you might want to work with (for example, Direct3D), you will get from the original DirectDraw interface by using `QueryInterface()`. Because there are multiple versions of DirectX floating around, Microsoft stopped writing wrapper functions a while ago to retrieve the latest interface. What this means is that you must manually retrieve the latest DirectX interface yourself with `QueryInterface()`. Let's take a look at that.

Querying for Interfaces

The weird thing about DirectX is that all the version numbers are out of sync. This is a bit of a problem, and definitely a cause for confusion. When the first version of DirectX came out, DirectDraw interface was named like this:

```
IDIRECTDRAW
```

Then when DirectX 2.0 came out, DirectDraw was upgraded to version 2.0, so we had

```
IDIRECTDRAW

IDIRECTDRAW2
```

Now at version 7.0a, we have this:

```
IDIRECTDRAW

IDIRECTDRAW2

IDIRECTDRAW4

IDIRECTDRAW7
```

And with version 8.0 and 9.0, there is no more `IDIRECTDRAW` upgrade because it was merged with Direct3D, but the other interfaces are still there:

```
IDIRECTDRAW

IDIRECTDRAW2

IDIRECTDRAW4

IDIRECTDRAW7
```

I mention 8.0 and 9.0 in the same breath because they are almost identical—there were no major changes, as there were from 7.0 to 8.0. The only differences in 9.0 are more advanced 3D support for shader programming, some more DirectPlay software, and a number of other enhancements. But more or less the major changes happened in the transition from 7.0 to 8.0—things will never be the same. Now you might be thinking "Wait a minute—what happened to interfaces 3 and 5?" I have no idea, and this is the problem. The idea is, even though you are using DirectX 8.0+, it doesn't mean that the interfaces are up to that version. Moreover, they can all be out of sync. DirectX 6.0 might have DirectDraw interfaces up to `IDIRECTDRAW4`, but DirectSound is only up to 1.0, which is simply called `IDIRECTSOUND`. You can see the mess we are in! The moral of the story is that whenever you use a DirectX interface, make sure that you are using the latest version. If you're not sure, use the revision 1 interface pointer from the generic "create" function to get the latest version. Here's an example of what I'm talking about.

`DirectDrawCreate()` returns a revision 1.0 interface pointer, but DirectDraw is really up to `IDIRECTDRAW7`, so how do we take advantage of this new functionality?

TIP

If you're having a panic attack over this stuff, don't feel alone. I was using the version 1.0 interfaces up until version 5.0 of DirectX because the DirectX docs are nebulous in this area—typical!

There are two ways to do this from the DirectDraw 1.0 interface: With low-level COM functions, or with `QueryInterface()`; let's use the latter. The process goes like this:

1. You create the DirectDraw COM interface with a call to `DirectDrawCreate()`. This returns a boring `IDIRECTDRAW` interface pointer.
2. Using the pointer retrieved from step 1, you make a call to `QueryInterface()` using the interface ID (GUID) for `IDIRECTDRAW7`, and you retrieve the new interface.

Here's an example of querying for the DirectDraw7 interface:

```
LPDIRECTDRAW lpdd;  // version 1.0
LPDIRECTDRAW7 lpdd7; // version 7.0

// create version 1.0 DirectDraw object interface
DirectDrawCreate(NULL, &lpdd, NULL);

// now look in DDRAW.H header, find IDIRECTDRAW7 interface
// ID and use it to query for the interface
lpdd->QueryInterface(IID_IDirectDraw7, &lpdd7);
```

At this point, you have two interface pointers, but you don't need the pointer to IDIRECT-DRAW, so you should release it:

```
// release, decrement reference count
lpdd->Release();

// set to NULL to be safe
lpdd = NULL;
```

Remember that you should release any interface when you are done with it—so when your program terminates, you would also release the IDIRECTDRAW7 interface:

```
// release, decrement reference count
lpdd7->Release();

// set to NULL to be safe
lpdd7 = NULL;
```

You might wonder whether there's a helper function to get a DirectDraw 7.0 interface. Well, actually there is, but I needed a good example to show off QueryInterface(), so don't be mad at me for not telling until now! Anyway, here's the easy way to get a DirectDraw 7.0 interface:

```
LPDIRECTDRAW7 lpdd7; // version 7.0 interface

// request the interface
DirectDrawCreateEx(NULL, (void **)&lpdd, IID_IDirectDraw7, NULL);
```

The function almost looks identical to the DirectDraw 1.0 version, but it has slightly different parameters, as shown in the following:

```
HRESULT WINAPI DirectDrawCreateEx(
 GUID FAR *lpGUID, // the GUID of the driver, NULL for active display
 LPVOID *lplpDD,  // receiver of the interface
```

```
 REFIID iid,    // the interface ID of the interface you are requesting
 IUnknown FAR *pUnkOuter // advanced COM, NULL
);
```

That's all there is to using DirectX and COM. Of course, you haven't seen all the hundreds of functions that DirectX components have and all the interfaces, but you will one way or another <BG>.

Summary

At this point, you should have a handle on very basic Windows programming, and at least what DirectX is and its relationship to Windows. The cool thing is that you really don't need to know too much about Windows or DirectX (or all the versions of it) to get a lot out of this book, because in the next chapter we are going to build a virtual computer of sorts to run our 3D experiments and write code on. This way, you are insulated from the underlying mechanics of Win32/DirectX, and can focus on the 3D part. Win32/DirectX is nice to know, so if you want more info, try *Tricks of the Windows Game Programming Gurus*, along with any good Windows programming book.

CHAPTER 3

3D Game Programming with a Virtual Computer

IN THIS CHAPTER

- Introduction to the Virtual Computer Interface
- Building the Virtual Computer Interface
- The T3DLIB Game Console
- The T3DLIB1 Library
- The T3DLIB2 DirectX Input System
- The T3DLIB3 Sound and Music Library
- The DirectMusic API Rapper
- Building the Final T3D Game Console
- Sample T3LIB Applications

"N O P E A C E…"

—Captured alien, *Independence Day*

In this chapter, we're basically going to build up a virtual computer system based on a software interface. It will support a linear 8- or 16-bit frame buffer (double buffered) and input devices, along with sound and music capabilities. With this interface, we can focus the remainder of the book on 3D math, graphics, and game programming. Here's what's in store:

- The design of a virtual computer graphics interface
- Building a Windows game console
- The API listing of the enhanced T3DLIB library from *Tricks of the Windows Game Programming Gurus*
- Implementing the virtual computer with T3DLIB
- The final game console
- Using the T3DLIB game library

Introduction to the Virtual Computer Interface

The goal of this book is to teach 3D graphics and game programming. However, my dilemma as an author is how to focus the book on just that, without talking about all the low-level details of Win32 programming, DirectX, and so on. Even though you should have some idea of Win32 programming and DirectX after reading the last chapter, it's still a bummer. Alas, my solution is to create a "virtual computer" based on the engine I developed in *Tricks of the Windows Game Programming Gurus* that you will simply use as a black box, so we can focus on the 3D graphics and game programming part. However, because of the sheer size of the engine, we still have a lot to discuss.

NOTE

This is basically the approach that OpenGL takes. You use GL libraries and/or add-ons that handle the low-level device-specific interfacing and housekeeping of whatever system you're on, including opening windows and getting input.

Ultimately, this really makes a lot of sense for a number of reasons. As long as you can communicate with a double-buffered, linearly-addressable graphics system that has support for input, sound, and music, who cares how it works? We are interested in the 3D graphics programming, not the low-level setup. Because 99% of our work is going to be related to rasterization, texture mapping, lighting, hidden surface removal, and so forth, this approach is feasible. So, all we really need is a black screen, the capability to talk to the joystick, keyboard, and mouse, and to maybe play some sound effects and music—right?

Therefore, instead of trying to explain every single detail of Win32, the DirectX foundation, and all that stuff (which I did in the first *Tricks*), we are simply going to use the API I wrote for that book as a tool to create a generic virtual computer on which we can run our 3D graphics experiments and write our games. Sound like a planetoid?

Using this layer of indirection, most of the 3D code will be generic enough that you could port it to Mac or Linux with very little work. All you would have to do is emulate the low-level interfaces, such as the double-buffered graphics system, sound, music, and input devices. The algorithms will stay the same for all the 3D code.

The only drawback to using the engine from the first *Tricks* is that a few of the data structures, and the design itself, were predicated on DirectX itself. I wanted the thinnest layer to DirectX for performance reasons. Hence, we could write another layer of software on top of my layer (which has some DirectX-centric parts to it) and totally be machine-independent, but I don't think it's worth the time. Bottom line is, if you want to port the 3D stuff, and as long as you can create a double-buffered display, everything will work. Sound, music, and input can be completely thrown away, because my functions make nothing more than a call to the DirectX functions anyway.

However, the thing to remember is that as long as you understand the API that I give you, you really do *not* need to know anything about Win32 or DirectX, because everything we do with 3D graphics simply consists of us, a frame buffer, and C/C++ code.

The fun part about this book is that we are only going to focus on 3D graphics and game programming. We are going to literally forget about all the details of setting up DirectX, getting input, and making sounds, and simply call API functions. We are going to accomplish this feat by creating a *virtual*, or *abstract*, graphics computer specification, and then implement it with the function API from the first *Tricks*. However, the main point of the virtual computer is to help us focus on 3D and not the details of the setup. With that in mind, here's the feature list you need to write a 3D game on any computer in the world:

1. Be able to create a window or screen on the display with a desired bit depth that is linearly addressable as a 2D matrix of pixels. Additionally, have support for an offscreen page or double buffer, so that images can be rendered offscreen and then copied or "flipped" to the primary display to create smooth animation.
2. Be able to get input from the system input devices such as the keyboard, mouse, and joystick. The input should be fairly raw and in a simple format.
3. **(Optional)** Be able to load and play sounds and music in common formats such as .WAV and .MID.

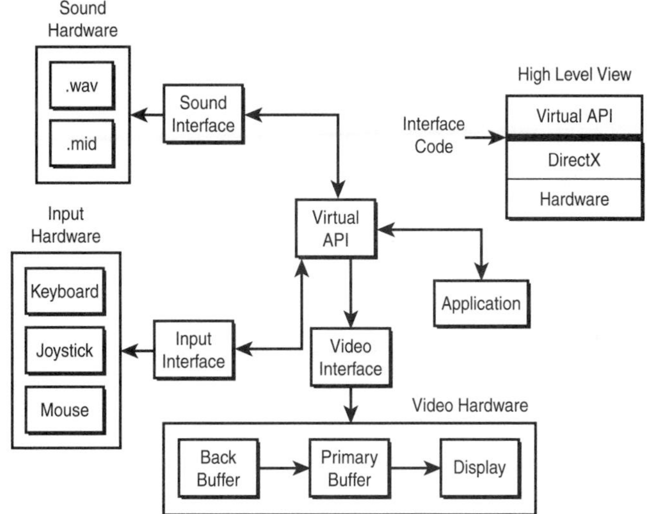

FIGURE 3.1 Systems-level diagram of the virtual computer.

Figure 3.1 illustrates a systems-level diagram of the virtual computer we want to design with software. I used to say, "If I can plot a pixel and read the keyboard, I can write *Doom*." It's true, all you need is the capability to access the frame buffer, and then everything else is simple. Moreover, because this book is about software 3D programming and rasterization, none of our algorithms will use any form of 3D acceleration. We are going to draw the polygons, compute the lighting, and everything else ourselves pixel-by-pixel in the frame buffer(s).

NOTE

You might be saying, why use software when hardware is available? The answer is threefold: First, to be a great graphics programmer, you need to know how to do it yourself; second, knowing how things work helps you better understand acceleration; and last but not least, who will write the hardware code?

Building the Virtual Computer Interface

Building the virtual computer interface is rather easy if you have a functional library that can implement features (1) through (3) from the preceding section—which of course we do. That is, the library from the first *Tricks*. But before we get into really specific details, let's design a "model" of the functions and data structures that we would like to have in the virtual computer interface. Of course, this is just an example, and is going to be very high-level. Moreover, I'm just going to make the function names up as we go, so we have something to refer to. Alas, the final version of the virtual computer will be different, because when implementing it, we must take details into consideration. However, the following exercise will give you an idea of the big picture.

The Frame Buffer and Video System

Before we get started, let's assume that there is a way to initialize the video system and open a window with a specific resolution and bit depth. Let's call it `Create_Window()`, and here's what it might look like:

```
Create_Window(int width, int height, int bit_depth);
```

To create a 640×480 display with 8-bits per pixel, you would make the following call:

```
Create_Window(640, 480, 8);
```

And to create a 800×600 display with 16-bits per pixel, you would make the following call:

```
Create_Window(800, 600, 16);
```

Remember, this is all academic, and the real code to create a window and initialize the system might be a set of functions, but you get the idea. In reality, the "window" might actually be a Windows window, or it might be full screen. So we know that we aren't going to get away this easy. But let's move on now assuming that we have a window.

As I said, we are interested in designing a system that is based on a primary display buffer that is visible, and a secondary offscreen buffer that is not visible. Both buffers should be linearly addressable, where one *word*, be it a `BYTE`, `WORD`, or `QUAD` represents a single pixel, depending on the bit depth. Figure 3.2 represents our frame buffer system.

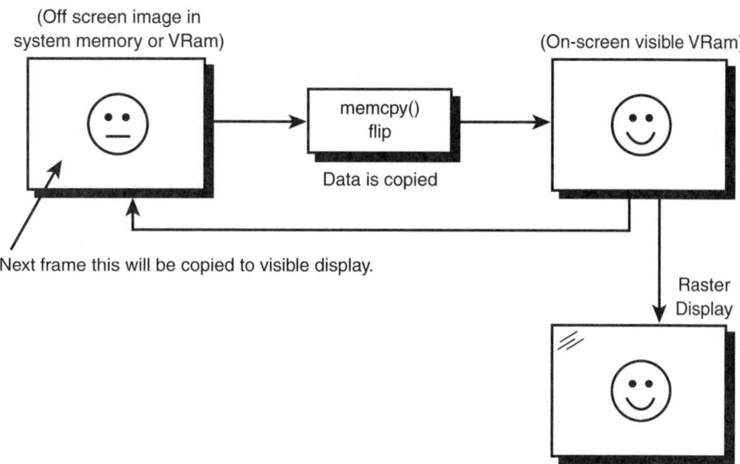

FIGURE 3.2 The frame buffer system.

You will notice that there is a *memory padding* region in the frame buffer memory in each of the primary and secondary display buffers. This models the fact that some video systems might be linear per row, but jump addresses row to row. For example, in Figure 3.3, we see this up close. In the example, the video system is set to 640×480×8, therefore, there is 1 byte per pixel, and there should be a total of 640 bytes per video line. But there's not! In this example, there are 1024 bytes per video line. This is a manifestation of the video card memory addressing, and is very common for many video cards. Hence, we need to model this discrepancy with what is commonly referred to as *memory pitch*.

Memory pitch models the fact that a video card might have extra memory per line because of caches or hardware addressing. This isn't a problem as long as we don't assume that memory pitch equals the *video pitch* (in the case of our example, 640 bytes = 640×1 byte per pixel). To locate a pixel on an 8-bit per pixel video system, we use the following code:

```
UCHAR *video_buffer; // ptr to the video buffer
int x,y;         // coordinates to the pixel
int memory_pitch;   // number of bytes per line

video_buffer[x + y*memory_pitch] = pixel;
```

On a 16-bit system, we would use slightly different code:

```
USHORT *video_buffer; // ptr to the video buffer
int x,y;         // coordinates to the pixel
int memory_pitch;    // number of bytes per line

video_buffer[x + y*(memory_pitch >> 1)] = pixel;
```

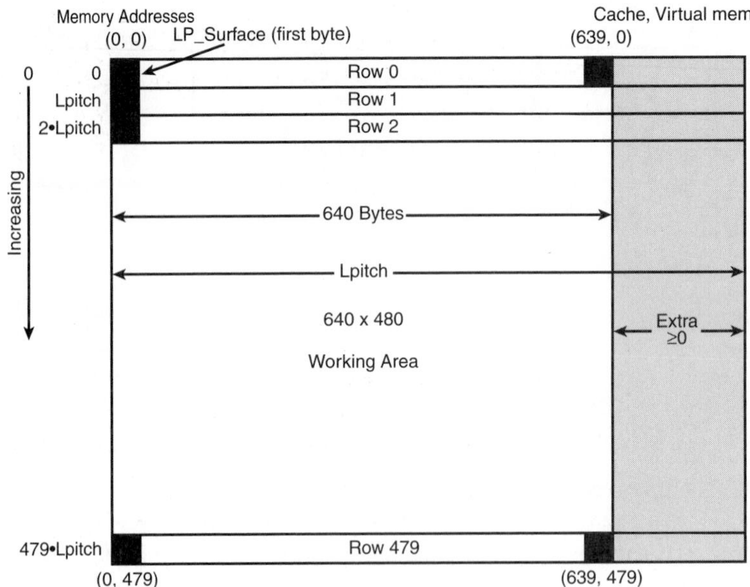

FIGURE 3.3 Close-up view of the hardware frame buffer.

Of course, if `memory_pitch` were the number of `USHORT`s per line, the bit shift operator >> used to divide by 2 wouldn't be needed.

With that in mind, let's create a model of the primary and secondary buffers. Remember, this is just a model, and the details will change when we actually implement the model with the `T3DLIB` game engine. Anyway, it looks like we need a pointer to both the primary and secondary buffers, along with variables to hold the memory pitch. For example, here's some globals that do the job:

```
UCHAR *primary_buffer; // the primary buffer
int  primary_pitch; // the memory pitch in bytes

UCHAR *secondary_buffer; // the secondary buffer
int  seconday_pitch;  // the memory pitch in bytes
```

Notice that both pointers are `UCHAR*`, and that the memory pitch is in terms of bytes? That's great if we are working with an 8-bit mode, but what about 16-bit modes, where there are 2 bytes per pixel, and each word is a `USHORT`? The answer is that I want to keep the data types simple and homogeneous. If you are working in a 16-bit mode, you can simply cast the pointers to `USHORT*`, or whatever. The point is that keeping the pointers `UCHAR*` is cleaner, along with always knowing memory pitch is in terms of bytes. This way, all the functions we write will have the same pointer/pitch parameter footprint.

Locking Memory

Alright, we are getting there, but there is one other feature that we should work in—*locking the memory*. Many video cards have special memory that might be multi-ported, cached, or whatever. What this means is that when you access the memory, and you're reading and writing to and from the frame buffer(s), you must let the system know that you are accessing the memory, so that the system does not alter it during this time. When you're done, you unlock and release the memory and the system can go about its business.

> **TIP**
>
> If you're an old Windows programming guru from the 80s and early 90s, you should feel right at home, because in the earlier versions of Windows (1.0, 2.0, and 3.0), you had to lock memory—yuck!

All this means to us as programmers is that the pointers `primary_buffer` and `secondary_buffer` are only valid during a locked period. Furthermore, you can't assume that the addresses will be the same in the next lock. That is, maybe during one lock-unlock period the primary buffer was at

0x0FFF**E**FF**C**00000000

and during the next lock it's at

0x0FFF**F**FF**D**00000000

This is a manifestation of the hardware. It might move the frame buffer(s), so watch out! In any case, the locking procedure is as follows:

1. Lock the buffer of interest (either primary or secondary) and retrieve the starting memory address, along with the memory pitch.
2. Manipulate the video memory.
3. Unlock the buffer.

And of course, in 99% of the cases you will only lock-Read/Write-unlock the secondary buffer rather than the primary buffer, because you wouldn't want the user to "see" you altering the primary display buffer.

Based on this new feature, let's create a few functions that perform the locking and unlocking operations:

```
Lock_Primary(UCHAR **primary_buffer, int *primary_pitch);
Unlock_Primary(UCHAR *primary_buffer);

Lock_Secondary(UCHAR **secondary_buffer, int *secondary_pitch);
Unlock_Secondary(UCHAR *secondary buffer);
```

Basically, to lock a buffer you call the function with the addresses of the storage for the frame buffer and memory pitch. The function then locks the surface and alters the sent variables (writes to them). Then you are free to use them. When you're done, you unlock the surface with a call to `Unlock_*()` with a pointer to the locked surface. Simple, huh?

As an example, let's see how we would write a single pixel in 800×600 mode to the screen of the secondary buffer in both 8-bit mode and 16-bit mode. First, here's the 8-bit example:

```
UCHAR *primary_buffer; // the primary buffer
int  primary_pitch; // the memory pitch in bytes

UCHAR *secondary_buffer; // the secondary buffer
int  seconday_pitch;  // the memory pitch in bytes

UCHAR pixel; // the pixel to write
int x,y;   // coordinates of pixel

// step 0:create the window
Create_Window(800, 600, 8);

// step 1: lock the secondary surface
Lock_Secondary(&secondary_buffer, &secondary_pitch);

// write the pixel to the center of the screen
secondary_buffer[x + y*secondary_pitch] = pixel;

// we are done, so unlock the secondary buffer
Unlock_Secondary(secondary_buffer);
```

That was easy! Now here's the same code, assuming that the system is in 16-bit mode or 2 bytes per pixel.

```
UCHAR *primary_buffer; // the primary buffer
int  primary_pitch; // the memory pitch in bytes

UCHAR *secondary_buffer; // the secondary buffer
int  seconday_pitch;  // the memory pitch in bytes

USHORT pixel; // the pixel to write, 16-bits
int x,y;   // coordinates of pixel

// step 0:create the window
Create_Window(800, 600, 16);
```

```
// step 1: lock the secondary surface
Lock_Secondary(&secondary_buffer, &secondary_pitch);

// at this point, we have to be careful since the
// locked pointer is a UCHAR * and not a USHORT *
// hence we need to cast it

USHORT *video_buffer = (USHORT *)secondary_buffer;

// write the pixel to the center of the screen
video_buffer[x + y*(secondary_pitch >> 1)] = pixel;

// we are done, so unlock the secondary buffer
Unlock_Secondary(secondary_buffer);
```


Note that we also had to divide the memory pitch by 2 (using the >> operator) because it's in terms of bytes, and if we want to use the built-in pointer arithmetic properly, we need to convert the memory pitch to the number of `USHORT`s per line. Of course, there are a hundred ways you can write this code, but you get the point. Get it—point? You could say I have a one-dimensional sense of humor <GRIN>.

Finally, there is one detail that we have left out—the 8- or 16-bit pixel data format. Oops!

Working with Color

We are primarily going to work with 8-bit palettized video modes and 16-bit RGB modes in our 3D game programming for speed reasons. In 8-bit mode, there is 1 byte per pixel, and in 16-bit mode, there are 2 bytes per pixel. However, the encoding is completely different.

8-Bit Color Mode

8-bit mode uses a standard 256-entry *color lookup table (CLUT)*, as shown in Figure 3.4. 16-bit mode uses a standard RGB encoding. When working with the 8-bit mode, we must fill the color lookup table with RGB values for each color entry in the table for 0...255. We assume that there is a function(s) to access this table and read/alter each entry, so let's not worry about it for now.

I just want you to know that there aren't any surprises about 8-bit mode—it's the standard 1 byte per pixel system, where each pixel value is an index into the color lookup table, and each table entry is composed of a color triad with 8-bits for each channel, (red, green, blue), for a total of 24-bits per entry.

TIP

Some cards only use 6 bits of each 8-bit channel entry, or in other words, there are only $2^6 = 64$ shades of each primary—red, green, blue—rather than the standard $2^8 = 256$ shades, with a full 8 bits per channel color lookup.

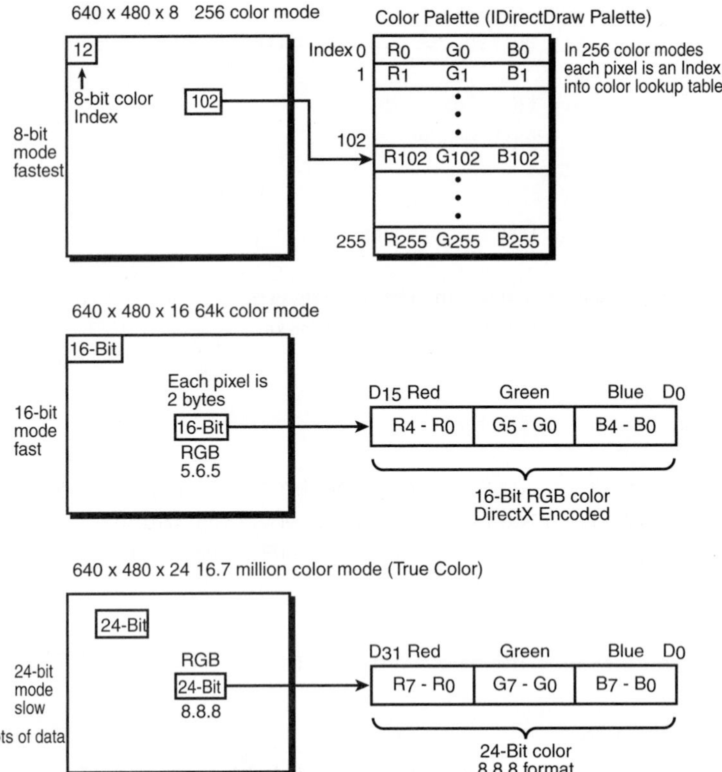

FIGURE 3.4 Comparisons of various color depths and their implementations.

16-Bit Color Mode

Working with 16-bit color is a little simpler than 8-bit—sorta. In the case of 16-bit color, there isn't a lookup table anymore. In fact, each pixel is in the form of a concatenated bit string word of RGB. In this form, the pixel format is either 5.5.5 (RGB) or 5.6.5 (RGB) format; that is, 5 bits of red, 5 bits of green, 5 bits of blue, or 5 bits of red, 6 bits of green, and 5 bits of blue, respectively. This is shown in Figure 3.5. This RGB pixel format concept sometimes gives people a lot of trouble (I have thousands of emails asking about it). The common question is how to build a pixel up? I think that the problem is that everyone thinks it's more complex than it really is. There is nothing to it really, just some bit manipulations.

In 5.5.5 RGB mode, there are 5 bits for every pixel, or $2^5 = 32$ intensities for each color channel. Therefore, a single pixel's RGB values each range from 0–31 (5 bits each), and there are a total of 32*32*32 = 32,768 different colors possible. Hence, all you need to do is write some code that takes a triad of three values. Suppose you have `r,g,` and `b`, each ranging from 0–31 (31 being the highest intensity) and you use bit manipulation operators to build the pixel up. Here's one such macro for 5.5.5 mode:

```
// this builds a 16 bit color value in 5.5.5 format (1-bit alpha mode)
#define _RGB16BIT555(r,g,b) ((b & 31) + ((g & 31) << 5) + ((r & 31) << 10))
```

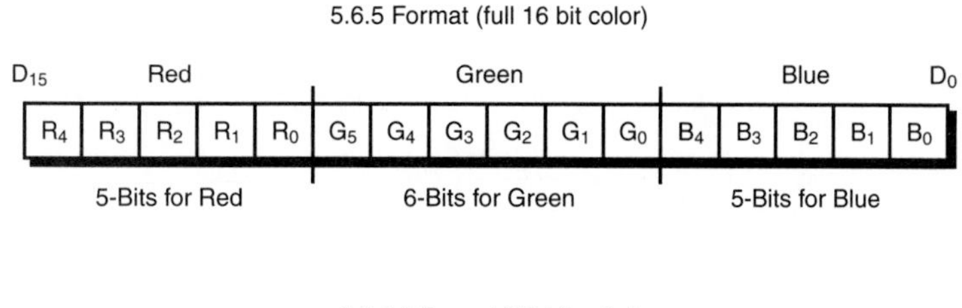

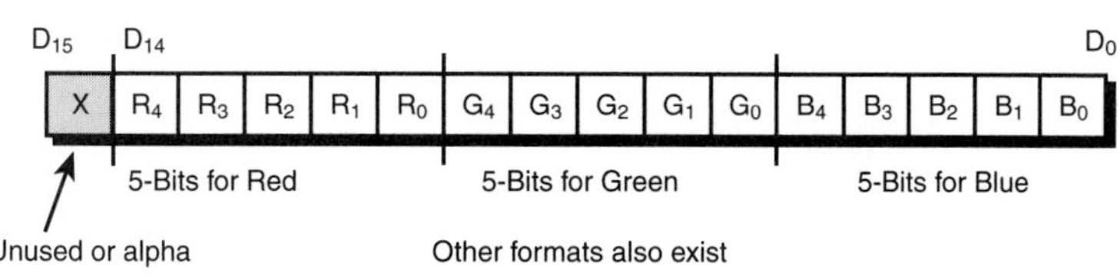

FIGURE 3.5 16-bit color encodings for both the 5.5.5 and 5.6.5 formats.

Similarly, in 5.6.5 mode, there is an extra bit for green, so the range of RGB pixel values is 0–31 for red, 0–63 for green, and 0–31 for blue. This gives us a total of 32*64*32 = 65,536 possible colors. Once again, here's a macro to build a pixel from a triad of values `r,g,` and `b`:

```
// this builds a 16 bit color value in 5.6.5 format (green dominate mode)
#define _RGB16BIT565(r,g,b) ((b & 31) + ((g & 63) << 5) + ((r & 31) << 11))
```

This problem has given people so much trouble in the past that we are going to work some logic into the system to take this into account. The graphics system, when selected into 16-bit mode, will determine the pixel format (either 5.5.5 or 5.6.5) and set flags and function pointers, so you can always use the same macro to build up a 16-bit color pixel. However, this feature will be in the "real" library we make later. For now, just make note of this detail, because I don't want to hear about how everything "looks green" when someone assumes a pixel format. Now, let's talk about animating the display.

Animating the Display

The final bit of functionality we need to implement is a way to flip the display, or copy the secondary buffer to the primary buffer, as shown in Figure 3.6. Of course, we could simply lock both surfaces and do a line-by-line copy of memory. However, many cards have special hardware to flip the display and copy them faster than we can with the processor. Hence, we will allow for this option and use a black box approach to flipping the display via an API call. Let's call the function `Flip_Display()`. It takes no parameters, and simply copies the secondary buffer to the primary buffer (with software or hardware, but we don't know which).

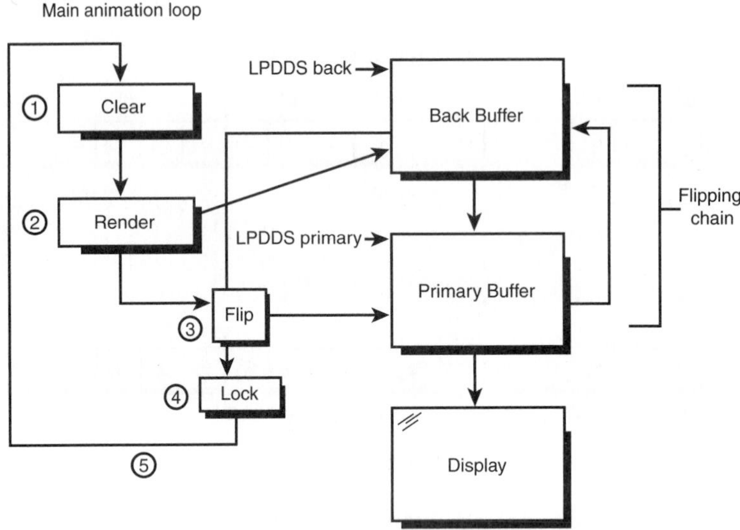

FIGURE 3.6 A page-flipped animation system.

CAUTION

You might wonder why I said to copy the secondary buffer line by line, rather than use a `memcpy()` function. This is because the secondary buffer may or may not be contiguous from line to line, and `memcpy()` has no way of knowing this. Alas, you must copy the buffers line by line, and then address each row by the appropriate memory pitch if you want to do it yourself.

However, there is a rule we are going to follow—when you make a call to `Flip_Display()`, you must make sure that both the primary and secondary buffers are *unlocked*. If they aren't, the flip won't occur, and an error will be thrown—or you will get some exercise with your index finger pressing the reset button on your computer. Therefore, before your call to `Flip_Display()`, you should always make sure that both buffers are unlocked and that the system has access to them.

Additionally, there are two more helper functions that come in handy when performing animation: functions to *clear* the buffers. You could once again just lock the buffers and use `memset()` or something to clear the buffer(s) line by line, but many cards have hardware-fill capabilities to clear memory buffers. Let's assume that where hardware filling is available it will be used; otherwise, software will be used to fill the memory. In either case, we don't care, because we will make up API functions to do this for both the secondary and primary buffers:

```
Fill_Primary(int color);
Fill_Secondary(int color);
```

The functions assume that the buffers are unlocked and the `color` parameter would be either 8- or 16-bit, depending on the mode. In most cases, you want to clear the buffer with black, so you would use `0`. This is because most palettes use index `0` as black, and the `USHORT` value of `0` is equivalent to RGB (0,0,0), which is black, also.

Using the clear function is simple. At the top of your animation loop, you would make a call to clear the screen out. However, because you are going to later copy the secondary buffer to the primary buffer at the end of the animation cycle, there is no need to clear the primary buffer, so all you need to do is clear the secondary buffer.

As an example, here's how you would draw an animated display of randomly positioned pixels in 800×600×8 mode, at 30 fps:

```
UCHAR *primary_buffer; // the primary buffer
int  primary_pitch; // the memory pitch in bytes

UCHAR *secondary_buffer; // the secondary buffer
int  seconday_pitch;  // the memory pitch in bytes

UCHAR pixel; // the pixel to write, 8-bits
int x,y;   // coordinates of pixel

// step 0:create the window
Create_Window(800, 600, 8);

// enter infinite loop
while(1)
{
// clear the secondary buffer
Fill_Secondary(0);

// step 1: lock the secondary surface
Lock_Secondary(&secondary_buffer, &secondary_pitch);

for (int num_dots=0; num_dots < 1000; num_dots++)
  {
  // get a random x,y,pixel
  x = rand()%800;
```

```
    y = rand()%600;
    pixel = rand()%256;

    // write the pixel to the center of the screen
    video_buffer[x + y*secondary_pitch)] = pixel;
    } // end for num_dots

// we are done, so unlock the secondary buffer
Unlock_Secondary(secondary_buffer);

// flip the display
Flip_Display();

// wait a sec
Sleep(33);

} // end while
```

Of course, the loop is infinite, and in a real Windows application, we can't be this greedy and not release each frame back to the main event loop—but you get the idea.

The Complete Virtual Graphics System

At this point, we have enough functionality to implement the virtual graphics system, so let's briefly summarize what we have thus far to make sure we all have the same quantum numbers:

- We assume that we can call functions that will set the graphics system up and open a window (it could be full-screen) with any size and bit depth that we desire. However, most of the time, we are only going to work with 8- and 16-bit modes for speed.
- The system is composed of both a primary and secondary offscreen display buffer. The buffers are linearly addressable, but have a memory pitch associated with them. Moreover, to access the actual memory of either buffer, the buffer must be locked. When the operation is complete, the buffer must be unlocked.
- To animate the display and "flip" one page to another, we assume there is a function that takes advantage of hardware blitting (blocking image transfers) acceleration to accomplish this. However, before making the call, we must make sure that both the primary and secondary buffers are unlocked. Also, there are buffer-clearing functions available that use hardware acceleration (if it's available).

Hopefully, you can see that if we can implement this virtual software system, the 3D graphics aspect of our programming is the only problem left. All we have to interface with to get our image on the screen is the frame buffers and a few API calls here and there.

I/O, Sound, and Music

Because the idea of this book is to make 3D games that are playable, we need to be able to obtain input from the player, as well as play sounds and music. Otherwise, people are going to think you are weird when you use mind control to play the game along with your own sound effects <GRIN>.

Of course, all of this functionality is part of DirectX, and I have written wrappers around all of it to make it as painless as possible. But the point I want to make here is that even if you port the code from the book to another system that doesn't support DirectX, you have very little work. The engine from the first *Tricks* really only has the following fundamental capabilities (in order):

1. Initialize and detect all input devices: keyboard, mouse, and joystick.
2. Read the data or *state* of all input devices, and put the data in simple data structures.
3. Initialize the sound and music system.
4. Load a sound off disk in .WAV format and play it once or loop it. Load a MIDI song off disk and play it once or loop it. Also be capable of testing the status of sounds and music when playing.
5. Shut everything down.

The preceding list is the exact functionality that we will implement. However, if you need to, you can simply "rip" all the I/O and sound code from any of the demos and port them with just the graphics interface. Of course, you need some kind of input, even if it is `getch()`!

As a sample API that looks something like what we will end up with, you might create something like this:

```
// this initializes all the input devices
Init_Input_Devs();

// this shuts down the input system
Shutdown_Input_Devs();

// this reads the keyboard, where data is some structure that
// holds the keyboard state, maybe an array
Read_Keyboard(&data);

// this reads the mouse, where data is some structure that
// holds the mouse state, maybe the position and buttons
Read_Mouse(&data);
```

```
// this reads the joystick, where data is some structure that
// holds the joystick state, maybe the position and buttons
Read_Joystick(&data);

// this initializes the sound and music system
Init_Sound_Music();

// this shuts down the sound and music system
Shutdown_Sound_Music();

// this loads a .WAV file and returns an id
int id = Load_WAV(char *filename);

// this plays a .WAV file based on an id
Play_WAV(int id);

// this loads a .MID file and returns an id
int id = Load_MID(char *filename);

// plays a .MID file based on an id
Play_MID(int id);
```

If we (you) can implement these functions, that's all you need for the I/O and sound interfaces.

Well, that's about it for the abstract design of the virtual computer interface. Remember, this was just an exercise in software design. Now we need to bang out the details—that is, the actual implementation of all the functions—I can't wait!

TIP

What we just did is actually a very useful exercise in design. We basically designed a portable graphics system. This is exactly how you would go about designing a game engine that you can port to other platforms just by implementing the "insides" of a very small set of functions.

The T3DLIB Game Console

At this point, I have another dilemma brewing. I want to show you the generic Windows Game Console prototype we are going to use to shell our games. However, within it are calls to the API. Should I show you the library function API now, or should I wait? Well, I'm in a top-down mood right now, and because you are an intermediate or advanced game programmer, I think you can handle waiting. If there is anything that you can't follow, simply take a peek at the Library API listings and descriptions.

T3DLIB System Overview

Based on our discussion of the virtual computer design, our goal is to abstract the Win32/DirectX model into a very simple double-buffered graphics system that we can access along with support for input and sound. Along the lines of this goal, I have created what's called the *T3D Game Console*. The Game Console is really the first step in creating the virtual computer interface. Before we can get into DirectX, input, and sound, first we have to remove Windows from the equation. How I'm going to do this is by creating a template, or Game Console as I call it, around Windows, so that from our point of view, a Windows application looks like a standard DOS/Unix application with a `main()` and that's it.

What we're going to do is build up the Game Console layer by layer until we have our virtual computer. Let's first start with removing Windows from the equation as best we can.

The Basic Game Console

The first iteration of the Game Console should perform the following tasks:

1. Open a window.
2. Call a user-defined initialization function: `Game_Init()`.
3. Enter into the main Windows event loop, process any messages for you, and return.
4. Call a user-defined "main" work function `Game_Main()` that performs one cycle of game logic and then returns.
5. Loop to step 3 until the user kills the application.
6. Call a user-defined shutdown function `Game_Shutdown()` that cleans up.

Figure 3.7 depicts the flow diagram of the Game Console. You will notice that I have decided to call the initialization, runtime, and shutdown functions `Game_Init()`, `Game_Main()`, and `Game_Shutdown()`, respectively.

If we can implement a shell program that performs the functionality of steps 1 through 6, we can completely forget about Windows and focus on the functions `Game_Init()`, `Game_Main()`, and `Game_Shutdown()` only. First, let's prototype out the three functions with some generic interfaces:

```
// game console
int Game_Init(void *parms=NULL);
int Game_Shutdown(void *parms=NULL);
int Game_Main(void *parms=NULL);
```

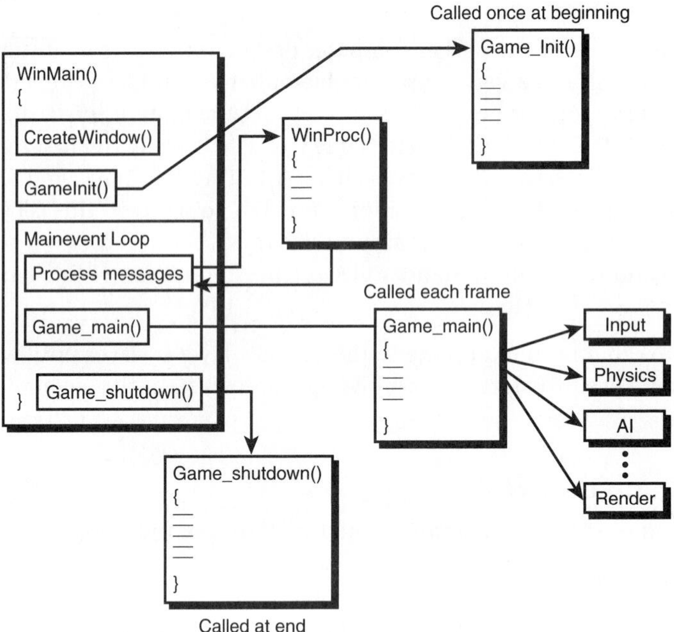

FIGURE 3.7 The control flow of the Game Console.

Not much to them, huh? Basically, I have written them so you can (if you want) send a structure to the functions, but I find I never use the feature. In any case, with that in mind, we need to write a Windows program shell program that does the following:

1. Creates a Windows class and registers the class.
2. Creates a window.
3. Has an event loop and a `WinProc()` that handles the basic messages `WM_CREATE`, `WM_PAINT`, and `WM_DESTROY`.
4. Before the event loop is called, a call to `Game_Init()` is called, so you can do your initialization here.
5. During the event loop, `Game_Main()` is called each cycle, so your game can process and run.
6. When the Window is terminated, a call to `Game_Shutdown()` is made, so you can clean up.

The following is a `T3DCONSOLEALPHA1.CPP` from the CD, a complete Windows program that does all of these steps. I have highlighted the function calls to our worker functions:

```
// T3DCONSOLEALPHA1.CPP - First alpha iteration of game console

// INCLUDES ///////////////////////////////////////////////

#define WIN32_LEAN_AND_MEAN

#include <windows.h>  // include important windows stuff
#include <windowsx.h>
#include <mmsystem.h>
#include <iostream.h> // include important C/C++ stuff
#include <conio.h>
#include <stdlib.h>
#include <malloc.h>
#include <memory.h>
#include <string.h>
#include <stdarg.h>
#include <stdio.h>
#include <math.h>
#include <io.h>
#include <fcntl.h>


// DEFINES ////////////////////////////////////////////////

// defines for windows interface
#define WINDOW_CLASS_NAME "WIN3DCLASS" // class name
#define WINDOW_TITLE   "T3D Graphics Console Alpha 1.0"
#define WINDOW_WIDTH   320 // size of window
#define WINDOW_HEIGHT   240

// these read the keyboard asynchronously
#define KEY_DOWN(vk_code) ((GetAsyncKeyState(vk_code) & 0x8000) ? 1 : 0)
#define KEY_UP(vk_code)  ((GetAsyncKeyState(vk_code) & 0x8000) ? 0 : 1)

// PROTOTYPES /////////////////////////////////////////////

// game console
int Game_Init(void *parms=NULL);
int Game_Shutdown(void *parms=NULL);
int Game_Main(void *parms=NULL);

// GLOBALS ////////////////////////////////////////////////
```

```
HWND main_window_handle  = NULL; // save the window handle
HINSTANCE main_instance  = NULL; // save the instance
char buffer[256];          // used to print text


// FUNCTIONS ////////////////////////////////////////////////

LRESULT CALLBACK WindowProc(HWND hwnd,
         UINT msg,
              WPARAM wparam,
              LPARAM lparam)
{
// this is the main message handler of the system
PAINTSTRUCT  ps;    // used in WM_PAINT
HDC     hdc;    // handle to a device context

// what is the message
switch(msg)
  {
  case WM_CREATE:
    {
  // do initialization stuff here
  return(0);
  } break;

    case WM_PAINT:
    {
    // start painting
    hdc = BeginPaint(hwnd,&ps);

    // end painting
    EndPaint(hwnd,&ps);
    return(0);
    } break;

  case WM_DESTROY:
    {
  // kill the application
  PostQuitMessage(0);
  return(0);
  } break;

  default:break;
```

```
  } // end switch

// process any messages that we didn't take care of
return (DefWindowProc(hwnd, msg, wparam, lparam));

} // end WinProc

// WINMAIN ////////////////////////////////////////////////

int WINAPI WinMain(  HINSTANCE hinstance,
      HINSTANCE hprevinstance,
      LPSTR lpcmdline,
      int ncmdshow)
{
// this is the winmain function

WNDCLASS winclass;  // this will hold the class we create
HWND   hwnd;     // generic window handle
MSG   msg;   // generic message
HDC   hdc;  // generic dc
PAINTSTRUCT ps; // generic paintstruct

// first fill in the window class stucture
winclass.style     = CS_DBLCLKS | CS_OWNDC |
             CS_HREDRAW | CS_VREDRAW;
winclass.lpfnWndProc  = WindowProc;
winclass.cbClsExtra   = 0;
winclass.cbWndExtra   = 0;
winclass.hInstance   = hinstance;
winclass.hIcon     = LoadIcon(NULL, IDI_APPLICATION);
winclass.hCursor    = LoadCursor(NULL, IDC_ARROW);
winclass.hbrBackground  = (HBRUSH)GetStockObject(BLACK_BRUSH);
winclass.lpszMenuName  = NULL;
winclass.lpszClassName  = WINDOW_CLASS_NAME;

// register the window class
if (!RegisterClass(&winclass))
  return(0);

// create the window, note the test to see if WINDOWED_APP is
// true to select the appropriate window flags
if (!(hwnd = CreateWindow(WINDOW_CLASS_NAME, // class
       WINDOW_TITLE,   // title
```

```
            WS_OVERLAPPED ¦ WS_SYSMENU ¦ WS_CAPTION,
        0,0,     // x,y
       WINDOW_WIDTH, // width
            WINDOW_HEIGHT, // height
       NULL,     // handle to parent
       NULL,     // handle to menu
       hinstance,// instance
       NULL)))  // creation parms
return(0);

// save the window handle and instance in a global
main_window_handle = hwnd;
main_instance    = hinstance;

// make sure window is visible
ShowWindow(main_window_handle, SW_SHOW);

// perform all game console specific initialization
Game_Init();

// enter main event loop
while(1)
  {
  if (PeekMessage(&msg,NULL,0,0,PM_REMOVE))
    {
    // test if this is a quit
     if (msg.message == WM_QUIT)
       break;

    // translate any accelerator keys
    TranslateMessage(&msg);

    // send the message to the window proc
    DispatchMessage(&msg);
     } // end if

  // main game processing goes here
  Game_Main();
  } // end while

// shutdown game and release all resources
Game_Shutdown();
```

```
// return to Windows like this
return(msg.wParam);

} // end WinMain

// T3D II GAME PROGRAMMING CONSOLE FUNCTIONS ////////////////

int Game_Init(void *parms)
{
// this function is where you do all the initialization
// for your game

// return success
return(1);

} // end Game_Init

////////////////////////////////////////////////////////////

int Game_Shutdown(void *parms)
{
// this function is where you shutdown your game and
// release all resources that you allocated

// return success
return(1);
} // end Game_Shutdown

///////////////////////////////////////////////////////////

int Game_Main(void *parms)
{
// this is the workhorse of your game it will be called
// continuously in real-time this is like main() in C
// all the calls for your game go here!

// game logic here...

// check if user is trying to exit
if (KEY_DOWN(VK_ESCAPE))
  {
  PostMessage(main_window_handle, WM_DESTROY,0,0);
  } // end if
```

```
// return success
return(1);

} // end Game_Main
```

The name of the source code on the CD is T3DCONSOLEALPHA1.CPP, and the executable is, of course, T3DCONSOLEALPHA1.EXE. If you run the .EXE, all you will see is the image in Figure 3.8—basically a little window with nothing happening. However, behind the scenes a lot is really going on: a window was created, Game_Init() was called, and Game_Main() is being called over and over each event cycle. Finally, when you close the window, Game_Shutdown() is called.

FIGURE 3.8 Alpha game console T3DCONSOLEALPHA1.EXE in action.

So all you need to do is put your entire game functionality within those three functions. That's all there is to it—we have abstracted a Windows application to three function calls, and everything else is done for us.

NOTE

It's really too bad that most of the books on Windows programming make it so hard. It really isn't—and it's kind of fun!

Based on this first version of the Game Console, we have all the Windows functionality that we need. Now we need the DirectX interface that emulates our virtual computer for us and gives us the basic double-buffered graphics system with sound and input capabilities. At this point, we could dive right in and take a look at the final Game Console that does all this, but I think it's a better idea to take a look at the API that I am going to use to build it up. Now remember, you don't need to completely understand the API and all the functions. Simply take a look at all of them and their associated explanations and examples.

After you have reviewed the tools that we will use to build the final Game Console, we will take the T3DGAMECONSOLEALPHA1.CPP file and add to it in various areas, so that the results are the final virtual computer interface that we need. Then we will use this "template" as a starting point for all the demos and games in the book. Additionally, before ending the chapter, I will give a number of examples that show how to use the T3DLIB's graphics, sound, and input abilities. Alrighty then, let's move on to the three subsystems that make up the T3DLIB game engine from the first *Tricks*.

The T3DLIB1 Library

At this point, we're ready to take a look at all the #defines, macros, data structures, and functions that compose the graphics module API of the T3DLIB game library—T3DLIB1.CPP.

NOTE

If you have already read the first *Tricks*, you will notice that the engine is almost identical except for the additional 16-bit support sprinkled throughout, along with windowed support. However, the code is still compatible, so you can take the demos from the first *Tricks* and compile them with this new version of T3DLIB1.CPP and they will still work! And of course, everything will compile with DirectX 8.0 or 9.0+.

The module consists of two files: T3DLIB1.CPP|H. Hence, you simply link these into your programs and then use the API.

The DirectX Graphics Engine Architecture

T3DLIB1 is a fairly simple 2D engine, as shown in Figure 3.9. Basically, it's a 2D, 8–16-bit color, doubled-buffered DirectX engine that has support for any resolution along with clipping. The engine also supports both windowed and full-screen displays, and takes care of all the setup. So, whether you're in a windowed display or full-screen mode, you always write to the offscreen or secondary buffer, and logic takes care of the detailed process of copying or flipping the secondary buffer to the primary display. This is done regardless of whether the primary display window is a window or full-screen.

To build an application using the library, you'll need to include T3DLIB1.CPP|H, along with DDRAW.LIB (DirectDraw Library) and WINMM.LIB (Win32 Multimedia Library).

NOTE

You only need WINMM.LIB if you are using Visual C++.

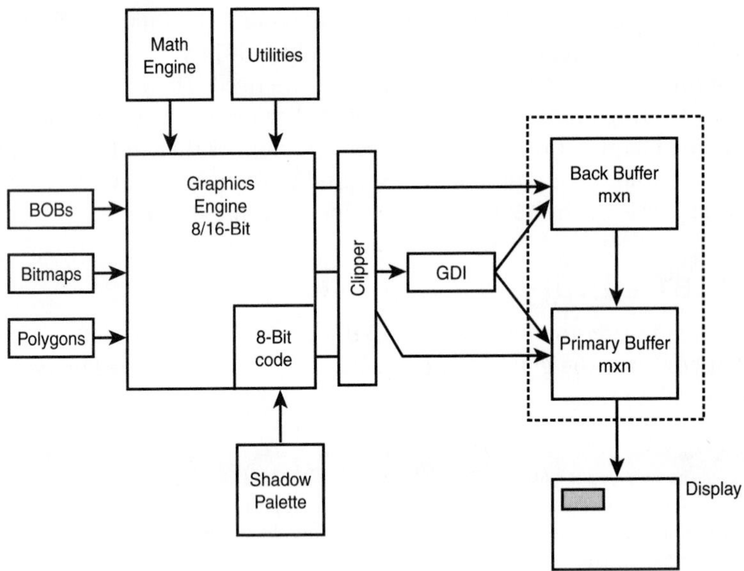

FIGURE 3.9 The architecture of the graphics engine.

Basic Definitions

The engine has one header file, `T3DLIB1.H`, and within are a number of `#defines` that the engine uses. Here they are for your reference:

```
// watch for multiple inclusions
#ifndef T3DLIB1
#define T3DLIB1

// DEFINES ////////////////////////////////////////////////

// default screen values, these are all overriden by the
// call to DDraw_Init() and are just here to have something
// to set the globals to instead of constant values
#define SCREEN_WIDTH    640 // size of screen
#define SCREEN_HEIGHT    480
#define SCREEN_BPP      8  // bits per pixel
#define MAX_COLORS_PALETTE 256


#define DEFAULT_PALETTE_FILE "PALDATA2.PAL"
```

```
// used for selecting full screen/windowed mode
#define SCREEN_FULLSCREEN  0
#define SCREEN_WINDOWED    1

// bitmap defines
#define BITMAP_ID       0x4D42 // universal id for a bitmap
#define BITMAP_STATE_DEAD  0
#define BITMAP_STATE_ALIVE  1
#define BITMAP_STATE_DYING  2
#define BITMAP_ATTR_LOADED  128

#define BITMAP_EXTRACT_MODE_CELL 0
#define BITMAP_EXTRACT_MODE_ABS  1

// directdraw pixel format defines, used to help
// bitmap loader put data in proper format
#define DD_PIXEL_FORMAT8    8
#define DD_PIXEL_FORMAT555   15
#define DD_PIXEL_FORMAT565   16
#define DD_PIXEL_FORMAT888   24
#define DD_PIXEL_FORMATALPHA888 32

// defines for BOBs
#define BOB_STATE_DEAD      0  // this is a dead bob
#define BOB_STATE_ALIVE     1  // this is a live bob
#define BOB_STATE_DYING     2  // this bob is dying
#define BOB_STATE_ANIM_DONE   1  // done animation state
#define MAX_BOB_FRAMES      64  // maximum number of bob frames
#define MAX_BOB_ANIMATIONS   16  // maximum number of animation sequences

#define BOB_ATTR_SINGLE_FRAME  1  // bob has single frame
#define BOB_ATTR_MULTI_FRAME  2  // bob has multiple frames
#define BOB_ATTR_MULTI_ANIM   4  // bob has multiple animations
#define BOB_ATTR_ANIM_ONE_SHOT 8  // bob will perform the animation once
#define BOB_ATTR_VISIBLE     16 // bob is visible
#define BOB_ATTR_BOUNCE      32 // bob bounces off edges
#define BOB_ATTR_WRAPAROUND   64 // bob wraps around edges
#define BOB_ATTR_LOADED      128 // the bob has been loaded
#define BOB_ATTR_CLONE      256 // the bob is a clone

// screen transition commands (256 color modes only)
#define SCREEN_DARKNESS 0      // fade to black
#define SCREEN_WHITENESS 1      // fade to white
```

```
#define SCREEN_SWIPE_X  2      // do a horizontal swipe
#define SCREEN_SWIPE_Y  3      // do a vertical swipe
#define SCREEN_DISOLVE  4      // a pixel disolve
#define SCREEN_SCRUNCH  5      // a square compression
#define SCREEN_BLUENESS 6      // fade to blue
#define SCREEN_REDNESS  7      // fade to red
#define SCREEN_GREENNESS 8      // fade to green

// defines for Blink_Colors
#define BLINKER_ADD      0  // add a light to database
#define BLINKER_DELETE    1  // delete a light from database
#define BLINKER_UPDATE    2  // update a light
#define BLINKER_RUN      3  // run normal

// pi defines
#define PI      ((float)3.141592654f)
#define PI2     ((float)6.283185307f)
#define PI_DIV_2  ((float)1.570796327f)
#define PI_DIV_4  ((float)0.785398163f)
#define PI_INV   ((float)0.318309886f)

// fixed point mathematics constants
#define FIXP16_SHIFT   16
#define FIXP16_MAG    65536
#define FIXP16_DP_MASK  0x0000ffff
#define FIXP16_WP_MASK  0xffff0000
#define FIXP16_ROUND_UP 0x00008000
```

Working Macros

Next are all the macros we've written thus far. Again, you've seen them all in one place or another, but here they all are at once:

```
// these read the keyboard asynchronously
#define KEY_DOWN(vk_code) ((GetAsyncKeyState(vk_code) & 0x8000) ? 1 : 0)
#define KEY_UP(vk_code)  ((GetAsyncKeyState(vk_code) & 0x8000) ? 0 : 1)

// this builds a 16 bit color value in 5.5.5 format (1-bit alpha mode)
#define _RGB16BIT555(r,g,b) ((b & 31) + ((g & 31) << 5) + ((r & 31) << 10))

// this builds a 16 bit color value in 5.6.5 format (green dominate mode)
#define _RGB16BIT565(r,g,b) ((b & 31) + ((g & 63) << 5) + ((r & 31) << 11))
```

```
// this builds a 24 bit color value in 8.8.8 format
#define _RGB24BIT(a,r,g,b) ((b) + ((g) << 8) + ((r) << 16) )

// this builds a 32 bit color value in A.8.8.8 format (8-bit alpha mode)
#define _RGB32BIT(a,r,g,b) ((b) + ((g) << 8) + ((r) << 16) + ((a) << 24))

// bit manipulation macros
#define SET_BIT(word,bit_flag)  ((word)=((word) ¦ (bit_flag)))
#define RESET_BIT(word,bit_flag) ((word)=((word) & (~bit_flag)))

// initializes a direct draw struct,
// basically zeros it and sets the dwSize field
#define DDRAW_INIT_STRUCT(ddstruct) {
memset(&ddstruct,0,sizeof(ddstruct));ddstruct.dwSize=sizeof(ddstruct); }

// used to compute the min and max of two expresions
#define MIN(a, b) (((a) < (b)) ? (a) : (b))
#define MAX(a, b) (((a) > (b)) ? (b) : (a))

// used for swapping algorithm
#define SWAP(a,b,t) {t=a; a=b; b=t;}

// some math macros
#define DEG_TO_RAD(ang) ((ang)*PI/180)
#define RAD_TO_DEG(rads) ((rads)*180/PI)

#define RAND_RANGE(x,y) ( (x) + (rand()%((y)-(x)+1)))
```

Data Types and Structures

The next set of code elements are the types and data structures that the engine uses. Many of them aren't really of concern, because a lot of them are for the 2D aspect from the first *Tricks*, but it doesn't hurt to see all of it.

```
// basic unsigned types
typedef unsigned short USHORT;
typedef unsigned short WORD;
typedef unsigned char UCHAR;
typedef unsigned char BYTE;
typedef unsigned int  QUAD;
typedef unsigned int  UINT;
```

```
// container structure for bitmaps .BMP file
typedef struct BITMAP_FILE_TAG
{
BITMAPFILEHEADER bitmapfileheader; // contains the bitmapfile
➥header
BITMAPINFOHEADER bitmapinfoheader; //info including
➥the palette
PALETTEENTRY   palette[256];    // palette
➥stored here
UCHAR       *buffer;        // pointer to the data

    } BITMAP_FILE, *BITMAP_FILE_PTR;

// the blitter object structure BOB
typedef struct BOB_TYP
    {
    int state;      // the state of the object (general)
    int anim_state;    // an animation state variable, up to you
    int attr;       // attributes pertaining to the object (general)
    float x,y;      // position bitmap will be displayed at
    float xv,yv;     // velocity of object
    int width, height; // the width and height of the bob
    int width_fill;    // internal, used to force 8*x wide surfaces
    int bpp;       // bits per pixel
    int counter_1;    // general counters
    int counter_2;
    int max_count_1;   // general threshold values;
    int max_count_2;
    int varsI[16];    // stack of 16 integers
    float varsF[16];   // stack of 16 floats
    int curr_frame;    // current animation frame
    int num_frames;    // total number of animation frames
    int curr_animation; // index of current animation
    int anim_counter;   // used to time animation transitions
    int anim_index;    // animation element index
    int anim_count_max; // number of cycles before animation
    int *animations[MAX_BOB_ANIMATIONS]; // animation sequences

    // the bitmap images DD surfaces
    LPDIRECTDRAWSURFACE7 images[MAX_BOB_FRAMES];
    } BOB, *BOB_PTR;

// the simple bitmap image
typedef struct BITMAP_IMAGE_TYP
```

```
    {
    int state;       // state of bitmap
    int attr;        // attributes of bitmap
    int x,y;        // position of bitmap
    int width, height; // size of bitmap
    int num_bytes;    // total bytes of bitmap
    int bpp;        // bits per pixel
    UCHAR *buffer;    // pixels of bitmap

    } BITMAP_IMAGE, *BITMAP_IMAGE_PTR;

// blinking light structure
typedef struct BLINKER_TYP
    {
    // user sets these
    int color_index;      // index of color to blink
    PALETTEENTRY on_color;  // RGB value of "on" color
    PALETTEENTRY off_color; // RGB value of "off" color
    int on_time;         // number of frames to keep "on"
    int off_time;        // number of frames to keep "off"

    // internal member
    int counter;         // counter for state transitions
    int state;          // state of light, -1 off, 1 on, 0 dead
    } BLINKER, *BLINKER_PTR;

// a 2D vertex
typedef struct VERTEX2DI_TYP
    {
    int x,y; // the vertex
    } VERTEX2DI, *VERTEX2DI_PTR;

// a 2D vertex
typedef struct VERTEX2DF_TYP
    {
    float x,y; // the vertex
    } VERTEX2DF, *VERTEX2DF_PTR;

// a 2D polygon
typedef struct POLYGON2D_TYP
    {
    int state;     // state of polygon
    int num_verts;  // number of vertices
```

```
    int x0,y0;    // position of center of polygon
    int xv,yv;    // initial velocity
    DWORD color;   // could be index or PALETTENTRY
    VERTEX2DF *vlist; // pointer to vertex list

    } POLYGON2D, *POLYGON2D_PTR;



// matrix defines
typedef struct MATRIX3X3_TYP
    {
    union
    {
    float M[3][3]; // array indexed data storage

    // storage in row major form with explicit names
    struct
       {
       float M00, M01, M02;
       float M10, M11, M12;
       float M20, M21, M22;
       }; // end explicit names

    }; // end union
    } MATRIX3X3, *MATRIX3X3_PTR;

typedef struct MATRIX1X3_TYP
    {
    union
    {
    float M[3]; // array indexed data storage

    // storage in row major form with explicit names
    struct
       {
       float M00, M01, M02;

       }; // end explicit names
    }; // end union
    } MATRIX1X3, *MATRIX1X3_PTR;

typedef struct MATRIX3X2_TYP
    {
```

```
    union
    {
    float M[3][2]; // array indexed data storage

    // storage in row major form with explicit names
    struct
       {
       float M00, M01;
       float M10, M11;
       float M20, M21;
       }; // end explicit names

    }; // end union
    } MATRIX3X2, *MATRIX3X2_PTR;

typedef struct MATRIX1X2_TYP
    {
    union
    {
    float M[2]; // array indexed data storage

    // storage in row major form with explicit names
    struct
       {
       float M00, M01;

       }; // end explicit names
    }; // end union
    } MATRIX1X2, *MATRIX1X2_PTR;
```

You'll notice some math support at the end. This is from the 2D polygon transformation support from the first *Tricks*. We are going to rewrite much of it when we create the new 3D math library.

Function Prototypes

Next I want you to take a look at the complete function prototype list, so you can see everything at once. I'm not going to cover every single function in the function API in the following sections because many functions are different versions of each other.

```
// DirectDraw functions
int DDraw_Init(int width, int height, int bpp, int windowed=0);
int DDraw_Shutdown(void);
```

```
LPDIRECTDRAWCLIPPER DDraw_Attach_Clipper(LPDIRECTDRAWSURFACE7 lpdds,
                        int num_rects, LPRECT clip_list);

LPDIRECTDRAWSURFACE7 DDraw_Create_Surface(int width, int height,
                    int mem_flags=0, USHORT color_key_value=0);

int DDraw_Flip(void);
int DDraw_Wait_For_Vsync(void);

int DDraw_Fill_Surface(LPDIRECTDRAWSURFACE7 lpdds, USHORT color,
            RECT *client=NULL);

UCHAR *DDraw_Lock_Surface(LPDIRECTDRAWSURFACE7 lpdds,int *lpitch);
int DDraw_Unlock_Surface(LPDIRECTDRAWSURFACE7 lpdds);
UCHAR *DDraw_Lock_Primary_Surface(void);
int DDraw_Unlock_Primary_Surface(void);
UCHAR *DDraw_Lock_Back_Surface(void);
int DDraw_Unlock_Back_Surface(void);

// BOB functions
int Create_BOB(BOB_PTR bob,int x, int y,int width, int height,
        int num_frames,int attr,
        int mem_flags=0, USHORT color_key_value=0, int bpp=8);

int Clone_BOB(BOB_PTR source, BOB_PTR dest);
int Destroy_BOB(BOB_PTR bob);
int Draw_BOB(BOB_PTR bob, LPDIRECTDRAWSURFACE7 dest);

int Draw_Scaled_BOB(BOB_PTR bob, int swidth, int sheight,
          LPDIRECTDRAWSURFACE7 dest);

int Draw_BOB16(BOB_PTR bob, LPDIRECTDRAWSURFACE7 dest);

int Draw_Scaled_BOB16(BOB_PTR bob, int swidth, int sheight,
           LPDIRECTDRAWSURFACE7 dest);

int Load_Frame_BOB(BOB_PTR bob, BITMAP_FILE_PTR bitmap,
          int frame, int cx,int cy,int mode);

int Load_Frame_BOB16(BOB_PTR bob, BITMAP_FILE_PTR bitmap,
           int frame, int cx,int cy,int mode);
```

```
int Animate_BOB(BOB_PTR bob);
int Move_BOB(BOB_PTR bob);

int Load_Animation_BOB(BOB_PTR bob, int anim_index,
            int num_frames, int *sequence);

int Set_Pos_BOB(BOB_PTR bob, int x, int y);
int Set_Vel_BOB(BOB_PTR bob,int xv, int yv);
int Set_Anim_Speed_BOB(BOB_PTR bob,int speed);
int Set_Animation_BOB(BOB_PTR bob, int anim_index);
int Hide_BOB(BOB_PTR bob);
int Show_BOB(BOB_PTR bob);
int Collision_BOBS(BOB_PTR bob1, BOB_PTR bob2);

// general utility functions
DWORD Get_Clock(void);
DWORD Start_Clock(void);
DWORD Wait_Clock(DWORD count);

int Collision_Test(int x1, int y1, int w1, int h1,
          int x2, int y2, int w2, int h2);

int Color_Scan(int x1, int y1, int x2, int y2,
        UCHAR scan_start, UCHAR scan_end,
        UCHAR *scan_buffer, int scan_lpitch);

int Color_Scan16(int x1, int y1, int x2, int y2,
         USHORT scan_start, USHORT scan_end,
         UCHAR *scan_buffer, int scan_lpitch);

// graphics functions
int Draw_Clip_Line(int x0,int y0, int x1, int y1, int color,
          UCHAR *dest_buffer, int lpitch);

int Draw_Clip_Line16(int x0,int y0, int x1, int y1, int color,
           UCHAR *dest_buffer, int lpitch);

int Clip_Line(int &x1,int &y1,int &x2, int &y2);

int Draw_Line(int xo, int yo, int x1,int y1, int color,
       UCHAR *vb_start,int lpitch);
```

```
int Draw_Line16(int xo, int yo, int x1,int y1, int color,
        UCHAR *vb_start,int lpitch);

int Draw_Pixel(int x, int y,int color,
        UCHAR *video_buffer, int lpitch);

int Draw_Rectangle(int x1, int y1, int x2, int y2,
          int color,LPDIRECTDRAWSURFACE7 lpdds);

void HLine(int x1,int x2,int y,int color, UCHAR *vbuffer, int lpitch);
void VLine(int y1,int y2,int x,int color, UCHAR *vbuffer, int lpitch);
void HLine16(int x1,int x2,int y,int color, UCHAR *vbuffer, int lpitch);
void VLine16(int y1,int y2,int x,int color, UCHAR *vbuffer, int lpitch);
void Screen_Transitions(int effect, UCHAR *vbuffer, int lpitch);
int Draw_Pixel(int x, int y,int color,UCHAR *video_buffer, int lpitch);
int Draw_Pixel16(int x, int y,int color,UCHAR *video_buffer, int lpitch);

// palette functions
int Set_Palette_Entry(int color_index, LPPALETTEENTRY color);
int Get_Palette_Entry(int color_index, LPPALETTEENTRY color);
int Load_Palette_From_File(char *filename, LPPALETTEENTRY palette);
int Save_Palette_To_File(char *filename, LPPALETTEENTRY palette);
int Save_Palette(LPPALETTEENTRY sav_palette);
int Set_Palette(LPPALETTEENTRY set_palette);
int Rotate_Colors(int start_index, int end_index);
int Blink_Colors(int command, BLINKER_PTR new_light, int id);

// simple bitmap image functions
int Create_Bitmap(BITMAP_IMAGE_PTR image, int x, int y,
         int width, int height, int bpp=8);

int Destroy_Bitmap(BITMAP_IMAGE_PTR image);

int Draw_Bitmap(BITMAP_IMAGE_PTR source_bitmap,UCHAR *dest_buffer,
        int lpitch, int transparent);

int Draw_Bitmap16(BITMAP_IMAGE_PTR source_bitmap,UCHAR *dest_buffer,
         int lpitch, int transparent);

int Load_Image_Bitmap(BITMAP_IMAGE_PTR image,BITMAP_FILE_PTR bitmap,
           int cx,int cy,int mode);
```

```
int Load_Image_Bitmap16(BITMAP_IMAGE_PTR image,BITMAP_FILE_PTR bitmap,
            int cx,int cy,int mode);

int Scroll_Bitmap(BITMAP_IMAGE_PTR image, int dx, int dy=0);

int Copy_Bitmap(BITMAP_IMAGE_PTR dest_bitmap, int dest_x, int dest_y,
        BITMAP_IMAGE_PTR source_bitmap, int source_x, int source_y,
        int width, int height);

int Flip_Bitmap(UCHAR *image, int bytes_per_line, int height);

// bitmap file functions
int Load_Bitmap_File(BITMAP_FILE_PTR bitmap, char *filename);
int Unload_Bitmap_File(BITMAP_FILE_PTR bitmap);

// gdi functions
int Draw_Text_GDI(char *text, int x,int y,
         COLORREF color, LPDIRECTDRAWSURFACE7 lpdds);

int Draw_Text_GDI(char *text, int x,int y,
         int color, LPDIRECTDRAWSURFACE7 lpdds);

// error functions
int Open_Error_File(char *filename, FILE *fp_override=NULL);
int Close_Error_File(void);
int Write_Error(char *string, ...);

// 2d 8-bit, 16-bit triangle rendering
void Draw_Top_Tri(int x1,int y1,int x2,int y2, int x3,int y3,
         int color,UCHAR *dest_buffer, int mempitch);

void Draw_Bottom_Tri(int x1,int y1, int x2,int y2, int x3,int y3,
           int color,UCHAR *dest_buffer, int mempitch);

void Draw_Top_Tri16(int x1,int y1,int x2,int y2, int x3,int y3,
          int color,UCHAR *dest_buffer, int mempitch);

void Draw_Bottom_Tri16(int x1,int y1, int x2,int y2, int x3,int y3,
            int color,UCHAR *dest_buffer, int mempitch);

void Draw_Top_TriFP(int x1,int y1,int x2,int y2, int x3,int y3,
          int color,UCHAR *dest_buffer, int mempitch);
```

3

```
void Draw_Bottom_TriFP(int x1,int y1, int x2,int y2, int x3,int y3,
            int color,UCHAR *dest_buffer, int mempitch);

void Draw_Triangle_2D(int x1,int y1,int x2,int y2,int x3,int y3,
           int color,UCHAR *dest_buffer, int mempitch);

void Draw_Triangle_2D16(int x1,int y1,int x2,int y2,int x3,int y3,
            int color,UCHAR *dest_buffer, int mempitch);

void Draw_TriangleFP_2D(int x1,int y1,int x2,int y2,int x3,int y3,
            int color,UCHAR *dest_buffer, int mempitch);

inline void Draw_QuadFP_2D(int x0,int y0,int x1,int y1,
              int x2,int y2,int x3, int y3,
              int color,UCHAR *dest_buffer, int mempitch);


// general 2D 8-bit, 16-bit polygon rendering and transforming functions
void Draw_Filled_Polygon2D(POLYGON2D_PTR poly, UCHAR *vbuffer, int mempitch);
void Draw_Filled_Polygon2D16(POLYGON2D_PTR poly, UCHAR *vbuffer, int mempitch);
int Translate_Polygon2D(POLYGON2D_PTR poly, int dx, int dy);
int Rotate_Polygon2D(POLYGON2D_PTR poly, int theta);
int Scale_Polygon2D(POLYGON2D_PTR poly, float sx, float sy);
void Build_Sin_Cos_Tables(void);
int Translate_Polygon2D_Mat(POLYGON2D_PTR poly, int dx, int dy);
int Rotate_Polygon2D_Mat(POLYGON2D_PTR poly, int theta);
int Scale_Polygon2D_Mat(POLYGON2D_PTR poly, float sx, float sy);
int Draw_Polygon2D(POLYGON2D_PTR poly, UCHAR *vbuffer, int lpitch);
int Draw_Polygon2D16(POLYGON2D_PTR poly, UCHAR *vbuffer, int lpitch);

// math functions
int Fast_Distance_2D(int x, int y);
float Fast_Distance_3D(float x, float y, float z);

// collision detection functions
int Find_Bounding_Box_Poly2D(POLYGON2D_PTR poly,
               float &min_x, float &max_x,
               float &min_y, float &max_y);

int Mat_Mul_1X2_3X2(MATRIX1X2_PTR ma,
          MATRIX3X2_PTR mb,
          MATRIX1X2_PTR mprod);
```

```
int Mat_Mul_1X3_3X3(MATRIX1X3_PTR ma,
          MATRIX3X3_PTR mb,
          MATRIX1X3_PTR mprod);

int Mat_Mul_3X3(MATRIX3X3_PTR ma,
        MATRIX3X3_PTR mb,
        MATRIX3X3_PTR mprod);

inline int Mat_Init_3X2(MATRIX3X2_PTR ma,
            float m00, float m01,
            float m10, float m11,
            float m20, float m21);


// memory manipulation functions
inline void Mem_Set_WORD(void *dest, USHORT data, int count);
inline void Mem_Set_QUAD(void *dest, UINT  data, int count);
```

You'll notice that all the calls to any rasterization functions that take pointers to the frame buffer always take a `UCHAR*`. Additionally, all memory pitch parameters are always in terms of bytes. Remember, this was our convention. Also note that about 90% of the entire library supports 16-bit graphics, but some things only work for 8-bit color. Finally, there's a lot of 2D polygon functions in there. These are all from the first *Tricks*, and although we could just use them for this book, we are going to write all of them again from scratch. This is because they are part of the rasterization process in 3D graphics, and I'm going to have to think up new names for them!

Global Domination

You know that I like globals because they are so fast. Moreover, they are appropriate for a lot of system-level variables (which any game engine has a lot of), so here are the globals for the engine—again, I know this is hard to follow, but just try and get a feel for them. I have commented them to help out.

```
FILE *fp_error;           // general error file
char error_filename[80];       // error file name

// notice that interface 7.0 is used on a number of interfaces
LPDIRECTDRAW7    lpdd;       // dd object
LPDIRECTDRAWSURFACE7 lpddsprimary;  // dd primary surface
LPDIRECTDRAWSURFACE7 lpddsback;    // dd back surface
LPDIRECTDRAWPALETTE lpddpal;     // a pointer to the created dd palette
LPDIRECTDRAWCLIPPER lpddclipper;   // dd clipper for back surface
LPDIRECTDRAWCLIPPER lpddclipperwin; // dd clipper for window
```

```
PALETTEENTRY     palette[256];  // color palette
PALETTEENTRY     save_palette[256]; // used to save palettes
DDSURFACEDESC2    ddsd;   // a direct draw surface description struct
DDBLTFX       ddbltfx; // used to fill
DDSCAPS2       ddscaps; // a direct draw surface capabilities struct
HRESULT       ddrval;  // result back from dd calls
UCHAR        *primary_buffer; // primary video buffer
UCHAR        *back_buffer;  // secondary back buffer
int         primary_lpitch; // memory line pitch
int         back_lpitch;   // memory line pitch
BITMAP_FILE     bitmap8bit;   // a 8 bit bitmap file
BITMAP_FILE     bitmap16bit;   // a 16 bit bitmap file
BITMAP_FILE     bitmap24bit;   // a 24 bit bitmap file

DWORD start_clock_count;  // used for timing
int  windowed_mode;    // tracks if dd is windowed or not

// these defined the general clipping rectangle for software clipping
int min_clip_x, // clipping rectangle
  max_clip_x,
  min_clip_y,
  max_clip_y;

// these are overwritten globally by DD_Init()
int screen_width,  // width of screen
  screen_height,  // height of screen
  screen_bpp,   // bits per pixel
  screen_windowed; // is this a windowed app?

int dd_pixel_format; // default pixel format

int window_client_x0; // used to track the starting (x,y) client area for
int window_client_y0; // for windowed mode directdraw operations

// storage for our lookup tables
float cos_look[360];
float sin_look[360];

// function ptr to RGB16 builder that builds 5.5.5 or 5.6.5 data
// depending on mode
USHORT (*RGB16Bit)(int r, int g, int b);
```

Make note of all the global names of the DirectX interface. Also, take a look at the various clipping and screen size globals.

The DirectDraw Interface

Now that you've seen all the data support, let's take a look at all the DirectDraw support functions. The DirectDraw system from the first *Tricks* (with a little upgrading) has the following features:

- Double-buffered, with both a primary and secondary (offscreen frame buffer)
- 8-bit color with palette
- 16-bit color with auto pixel format detection
- Windowed support for both 8- and 16-bit color modes
- 2D polygon and raster bitmap clipping
- Access to both the primary and secondary buffers
- Page flipping and buffer copying for windowed displays

NOTE

Note the last feature. DirectX does *not* allow Windowed applications to be double buffered, or in DirectX speak, to be *complex surfaces*. Therefore, when a windowed display is requested, instead of creating a standard full-screen complex surface with a primary buffer and a back buffer, only a primary buffer (which is the entire screen), and an offscreen plain buffer that's the size of the client area of the window are created. Then when a flip is requested, the logic manually copies the offscreen back buffer to the window's client area. Of course, this is all transparent to you.

Now let's take a look at each function, along with an example.

Function Prototype:

```
int DDraw_Init(int width, // width of display
        int height, // height of display
        int bpp,  // bits per pixel
        int windowed=0); // 0 for full screen, 1 for windowed
```

Purpose:

`DDraw_Init()` starts up and initializes DirectDraw. You can send any resolution and color depth. Also, if you want a windowed display, send a `1` for the last parameter; otherwise it defaults to full-screen. Returns `TRUE` if successful.

Examples:

```
// put the system into full screen 800x600 with 256 colors
DDraw_Init(800,600,8);
```

```
// put the system into windowed mode screen 400x400 with 16-bit color
// note that the desktop must be in 16-bit color
DDraw_Init(400,400,16,1);
```

Function Prototype:

```
int DDraw_Shutdown(void);
```

Purpose:

`DDraw_Shutdown()` shuts down DirectDraw and releases all interfaces.

Example:

```
// in your system shutdown code you might put
DDraw_Shutdown();
```

Function Prototype:

```
LPDIRECTDRAWCLIPPER
 DDraw_Attach_Clipper(
  LPDIRECTDRAWSURFACE7 lpdds, // surface to attach to
  int num_rects,    // number of rects
  LPRECT clip_list); // pointer to rects
```

Purpose:

`DDraw_Attach_Clipper()` attaches a clipper to the sent surface (the back buffer in most cases). In addition, you must send the number of rectangles in the clipping list and a pointer to the `RECT` list itself. Returns `TRUE` if successful.

Example:

```
// creates a clipping region the size of the screen
RECT clip_zone = {0,0,SCREEN_WIDTH-1, SCREEN_HEIGHT-1};
DDraw_Attach_Clipper(lpddsback, 1, &clip_zone);
```

Function Prototype:

```
LPDIRECTDRAWSURFACE7
  DDraw_Create_Surface(int width, // width of surface
       int height,      // height of surface
       int mem_flags=0,    // control flags
       USHORT color_key_value=0); // color key value
```

Purpose:

`DDraw_Create_Surface()` is used to create a generic offscreen DirectDraw surface in system memory, VRAM, or AGP memory. The default is `DDSCAPS_OFFSCREENPLAIN`. Any additional control flags are logically ORed with the default. They are the standard DirectDraw DDSCAP* flags, such as DDSCAPS_SYSTEMMEMORY and DDSCAPS_VIDEOMEMORY for system memory and VRAM, respectively. The function has internal logic to create either an 8- or 16-bit surface based on the previously set graphics mode. Additionally, the last parameter controls the value of the color key, which defaults to (int)0. In 8-bit color mode, this equates to index 0; in 16-bit color mode, this equates to RGB 0.0.0. If you want another value to be used as the transparent color key, send the value to override the default. If the function is successful, it returns a pointer to the new surface; otherwise it returns NULL.

Examples:

```
// let's create a 64x64 surface in VRAM
LPDIRECTDRAWSURFACE7 image = DDraw_Create_Surface(64,64, DDSCAPS_VIDEOMEMORY);

// let's create a 128x128 surface in off screen memory with a color key of 16
// assuming this is a 256 color mode
LPDIRECTDRAWSURFACE7 image =
      DDraw_Create_Surface(128,128, DDSCAPS_OFFSCREENPLAIN ,16);
```

Function Prototype:

```
int DDraw_Flip(void);
```

Purpose:

DDraw_Flip() simply flips the primary surface with the secondary surface in full-screen mode; in windowed mode, it copies the virtual secondary or back buffer to the client area of the windowed display. The call waits until the flip can take place, so it might not return immediately. Returns TRUE if successful.

Example:

```
// flip em baby
DDraw_Flip();
```

Function Prototype:

```
int DDraw_Wait_For_Vsync(void);
```

Purpose:

DDraw_Wait_For_Vsync() waits until the next vertical blank period begins (when the raster hits the bottom of the screen). Returns TRUE if successful, FALSE if something really bad happened.

Example:

```
// wait 1/70th of sec
DDraw_Wait_For_Vsync();
```

Function Prototype:

```
int DDraw_Fill_Surface(LPDIRECTDRAWSURFACE7 lpdds, // surface to fill
            int color, // color to fill
                 // either 8-bit index or 16-bit RGB
            RECT *client); // client area, null for whole surface
```

Purpose:

`DDraw_Fill_Surface()` is used to fill a surface with a color. The color must be in the color depth format of the surface. For example, a single byte in 256-color mode or an RGB descriptor in high-color modes. Also, if you want to fill a subregion of the entire surface, you can send a `RECT*` that defines it; otherwise, the entire surface is filled. Returns `TRUE` if successful.

Example:

```
// fill the primary surface with color 0
DDraw_Fill_Surface(lpddsprimary,0);
```

Function Prototype:

```
UCHAR *DDraw_Lock_Surface(LPDIRECTDRAWSURFACE7 lpdds,int *lpitch);
```

Purpose:

`DDraw_Lock_Surface()` locks the sent surface (if possible) and returns a `UCHAR` pointer to the surface, along with updating the sent `lpitch` variable with the linear memory pitch of the surface. While the surface is locked, you can manipulate it and write pixels to it, but the blitter will be blocked, so remember to unlock the surface ASAP. In addition, after unlocking the surface, the memory pointer and pitch are most likely invalid and should not be used. Returns the non-`NULL` address of the surface memory if successful, `NULL` otherwise.

Example:

```
// holds the memory pitch
int lpitch = 0;

// let's lock the little 64x64 image we made
UCHAR *memory = DDraw_Lock_Surface(image, &lpitch);
```

Function Prototype:

```
int DDraw_Unlock_Surface(LPDIRECTDRAWSURFACE7 lpdds);
```

Purpose:

DDraw_Unlock_Surface() unlocks a surface previously locked with DDraw_Lock_Surface(). You need only send the pointer to the surface. Returns TRUE if successful.

Example:

```
// unlock the image surface
DDraw_Unlock_Surface(image);
```

Function Prototype(s):

```
UCHAR *DDraw_Lock_Back_Surface(void);
UCHAR *DDraw_Lock_Primary_Surface(void);
```


Purpose:

These two functions are used to lock the primary and secondary rendering surfaces. However, in most cases you'll only be interested in locking the secondary surface, because this is a double-buffered system, but the capability to lock the primary surface is there if you need it. If you call DDraw_Lock_Primary_Surface(), the following globals will become valid:

```
extern UCHAR *primary_buffer;   // primary video buffer
extern int   primary_lpitch;    // memory line pitch
```

Then you are free to manipulate the surface memory as you want; however, the blitter will be blocked and all hardware acceleration is inhibited during a lock. Anyway, making the call to DDraw_Lock_Back_Surface() will lock the back buffer surface and validate the following globals:

```
extern UCHAR *back_buffer;      // secondary back buffer
extern int   back_lpitch;      // memory line pitch
```

NOTE

Do not change any of these globals yourself—they are used to track state changes in the locking functions. Changing them yourself might make the engine go crazy.

Example:

```
// let lock the primary surface and write a pixel to the
// upper left hand corner assuming an 8-bit mode
DDraw_Lock_Primary();

primary_buffer[0] = 100;
```

Function Prototype:

```
int DDraw_Unlock_Primary_Surface(void);
int DDraw_Unlock_Back_Surface(void);
```

Purpose:

These functions are used to unlock the primary or back buffer surfaces. If you try to unlock a surface that wasn't locked, there is no effect. Returns TRUE if successful.

Example:

```
// unlock the secondary back buffer
DDraw_Unlock_Back_Surface();
```

2D Polygon Functions

The next set of functions make up the 2D polygon system. This is by no means advanced, fast, or cutting edge, but it's great to build up demos. The functions work and do the job. However, there are better ways to do all of this stuff, but that's why you're glued to the book, right?

Function Prototype(s):

```
void Draw_Triangle_2D(int x1,int y1, // triangle vertices
         int x2,int y2,
         int x3,int y3,
         int color, // 8-bit color index
         UCHAR *dest_buffer, // destination buffer
         int mempitch); // memory pitch

// fixed point high speed version, slightly less accurate
void Draw_TriangleFP_2D(int x1,int y1,
            int x2,int y2,
            int x3,int y3,
            int color,
            UCHAR *dest_buffer,
            int mempitch);

// 16-bit version
void Draw_Triangle_2D16(int x1,int y1, // triangle vertices
         int x2,int y2,
         int x3,int y3,
         int color, // 16-bit RGB color
         UCHAR *dest_buffer, // destination buffer
         int mempitch); // memory pitch
```

Purpose:

Draw_Triangle_2D*() draws a filled triangle in the given memory buffer with the sent color. The triangle will be clipped to the current clipping region set in the globals, *not* by the DirectDraw clipper, because the function uses software and not the blitter to draw lines. Draw_TriangleFP_2D() does the exact same thing, but uses fixed-point math internally and is slightly faster, but with slightly less accuracy. All functions return nothing.

Examples:

```
// draw a triangle (100,10) (150,50) (50,60)
// with color index 50 in the back buffer surface
Draw_Triangle_2D(100,10,150,50,50,60,
         50, // color index 50
         back_buffer,
         back_lpitch);

// do the same with 16 bit version
// with RGB color pure red
Draw_Triangle_2D16(100,10,150,50,50,60,
         RGB16BIT565(31,0,0), // assume 5.6.5 format
         back_buffer,
         back_lpitch);
```

Function Prototype:

```
inline void Draw_QuadFP_2D(int x0,int y0, // vertices
      int x1,int y1,
      int x2,int y2,
      int x3,int y3,
      int color, // 8-bit color index
      UCHAR *dest_buffer, // destination video buffer
      int mempitch); // memory pitch of buffer
```

Purpose:

Draw_QuadFP_2D() draws the sent quadrilateral as a composition of two triangles in 8-bit mode only. Notice there isn't a 16-bit version. Returns nothing.

Example:

```
// draw a quadrilateral, note vertices must be ordered
// either in cw or ccw order
Draw_QuadFP_2D(0,0, 10,0, 15,20, 5,25,
        100,
        back_buffer, back_lpitch);
```

Function Prototype:

```
void Draw_Filled_Polygon2D(
     POLYGON2D_PTR poly, // poly to render
     UCHAR *vbuffer, // video buffer
     int mempitch); // memory pitch

// 16-bit version
void Draw_Filled_Polygon2D16(
     POLYGON2D_PTR poly, // poly to render
     UCHAR *vbuffer, // video buffer
     int mempitch); // memory pitch
```

Purpose:

`Draw_Filled_Polygon2D*()` draws a general filled polygon with *n* sides in either 8- or 16-bit color mode. The function simply takes the polygon to render, a pointer to the video buffer along with pitch, and that's it! Note that the function renders relative to the polys `(x0,y0)`, so make sure these are initialized. Returns nothing.

Examples:

```
// draw a polygon in the primary buffer
// in 8-bit mode
Draw_Filled_Polygon2D(&poly,
            primary_buffer,
            primary_lpitch);

// draw a polygon in the primary buffer
// in 16-bit mode
Draw_Filled_Polygon2D16(&poly,
            primary_buffer,
            primary_lpitch);
```

Function Prototype:

```
int Translate_Polygon2D(
      POLYGON2D_PTR poly, // poly to translate
      int dx, int dy); // translation factors
```

Purpose:

`Translate_Polygon2D()` translates the given polygon's origin `(x0,y0)`. Note that the function does not transform or modify the actual vertices making up the polygon. Returns `TRUE` if successful.

Example:

```
// translate polygon 10,-5
Translate_Polygon2D(&poly, 10, -5);
```

Function Prototype:

```
int Rotate_Polygon2D(
         POLYGON2D_PTR poly, // poly to rotate
         int theta); // angle 0-359
```


Purpose:

`Rotate_Polygon2D()` rotates the sent polygon in a counter-clockwise fashion about its origin. The angle must be an integer from 0–359. Returns `TRUE` if successful.

Example:

```
// rotate polygon 10 degrees
Rotate_Polygon2D(&poly, 10);
```

Function Prototype:

```
int Scale_Polygon2D(POLYGON2D_PTR poly, // poly to scale
          float sx, float sy); // scale factors
```

Purpose:

`Scale_Polygon2D()` scales the sent polygon by scale factors `sx` and `sy` in the x- and y-axes, respectively. Returns nothing.

Example:

```
// scale the poly equally 2x
Scale_Polygon2D(&poly, 2,2);
```

2D Graphic Primitives

This set of functions contains a few of everything—kind of a potpourri of graphics primitives. Nothing you haven't seen, at least I don't think so. Also, the 16-bit support is there, but not completely orthogonal to the 8-bit support.

Function Prototype:

```
int Draw_Clip_Line(int x0,int y0, // starting point
          int x1, int y1, // ending point
          int color,    // 8-bit color
          UCHAR *dest_buffer, // video buffer
          int lpitch); // memory pitch
```

```
// 16-bit version
int Draw_Clip_Line16(int x0,int y0, // starting point
          int x1, int y1, // ending point
          int color,   // 16-bit RGB color
          UCHAR *dest_buffer, // video buffer
          int lpitch); // memory pitch
```

Purpose:

`Draw_Clip_Line*()` clips the sent line to the current clipping rectangle and then draws a line in the sent buffer (8- or 16-bit). Returns `TRUE` if successful.

Examples:

```
// draw a line in the back buffer from (10,10) to (100,200)
//assume an 8-bit system
Draw_Clip_Line(10,10,100,200,
        5, // color index 5
        back_buffer,
        back_lpitch);

// draw a line in the back buffer from (10,10) to (100,200)
//assume an 16-bit system
Draw_Clip_Line16(10,10,100,200,
        RGB16BIT565(0,31,0), // RGB green
        back_buffer,
        back_lpitch);
```

Function Prototype:

```
int Clip_Line(int &x1,int &y1,  // starting point
       int &x2, int &y2); // ending point
```

Purpose:

`Clip_Line()` is for the most part internal, but you can call it to clip the sent line to the current clipping rectangle. Note that the function modifies the sent endpoints, so save them if you don't want this side effect. Also, the function does NOT draw anything, it only clips the endpoints mathematically, so bit depth is irrelevant. Returns `TRUE` if successful.

Example:

```
// clip the line defined by x1,y1 to x2,y2
Clip_Line(x1,y1,x2,y2);
```

Function Prototype:

```
int Draw_Line(int xo, int yo, // starting point
       int x1,int y1,  // ending point
       int color,    // 8-bit color index
       UCHAR *vb_start, // video buffer
       int lpitch);    // memory pitch


// 16-bit version
int Draw_Line16(int xo, int yo, // starting point
       int x1,int y1,  // ending point
       int color,    // 16-bit RGB color
       UCHAR *vb_start, // video buffer
       int lpitch);    // memory pitch
```


Purpose:

`Draw_Line*()` draws a line without any clipping, so make sure that the endpoints are within the display surface's valid coordinates. This function is slightly faster than the clipped version, because the clipping operation is not needed. Returns `TRUE` if successful.

Example:

```
// draw a line in the back buffer from (10,10) to (100,200)
// 8-bit mode
Draw_Line(10,10,100,200,
     5, // color 5
     back_buffer,
     back_lpitch);

// draw a line in the back buffer from (10,10) to (100,200)
// 16-bit mode
Draw_Line16(10,10,100,200,
      RGB16BIT(31,31,31), // RGB white
      back_buffer,
      back_lpitch);
```

Function Prototype:

```
inline int Draw_Pixel(int x, int y, // position of pixel
           int color, // 8-bit color
           UCHAR *video_buffer, // gee hmm?
           int lpitch); // memory pitch
```

```
// 16-bit version
inline int Draw_Pixel16(int x, int y, // position of pixel
          int color, // 16-bit RGB color
          UCHAR *video_buffer, // gee hmm?
          int lpitch); // memory pitch
```

Purpose:

Draw_Pixel*() draws a single pixel on the sent display surface memory buffer. In most cases, you won't create objects based on pixels, because the overhead of the call itself takes more time than plotting the pixel. If speed isn't your concern, the function does the job—at least it's inline! Returns TRUE if successful.

Example:

```
// draw pixel with color index 100 in the center of the 640x480x8 screen
Draw_Pixel(320,240, 100, back_buffer, back_lpitch);

// draw blue pixel in the center of the 640x480x16 screen
Draw_Pixel16(320,240, RGB16BIT(0,0,31), back_buffer, back_lpitch);
```

Function Prototype:

```
int Draw_Rectangle(int x1, int y1, // upper left corner
        int x2, int y2, // lower right corner
        int color, // 8-bit color index or
             // 16-bit RGB word
        LPDIRECTDRAWSURFACE7 lpdds); // dd surface
```

Purpose:

Draw_Rectangle() draws a rectangle on the sent DirectDraw surface. Note that the surface must be unlocked for the call to work. Moreover, the function uses the blitter, so it's very fast, and it works in either 8- or 16-bit color mode. Returns TRUE if successful.

Example:

```
// fill the screen using the blitter
Draw_Rectangle(0,0,639,479,0,lpddsback);
```

Function Prototype:

```
void HLine(int x1,int x2, // start and end x points
      int y,     // row to draw on
      int color,   // 8-bit color
      UCHAR *vbuffer, // video buffer
      int lpitch); // memory pitch
```

```
void HLine16(int x1,int x2, // start and end x points
      int y,      // row to draw on
      int color,    // 16-bit RGB color
      UCHAR *vbuffer, // video buffer
      int lpitch); // memory pitch
```

Purpose:

`HLine*()` draws a horizontal line very quickly compared to the general line drawing function. Returns nothing.

Example:

```
// draw a fast line in 8-bit mode from 10,100 to 100,100 with color index 20
HLine(10,100,100,
   20, back_buffer, back_lpitch);

// draw a fast line in 16-bit mode from 10,100 to 100,100 with blue
HLine(10,100,100,
   RGB16Bit(0,0,255), back_buffer, back_lpitch);
```

Function Prototype:

```
void VLine(int y1,int y2, // start and end row
      int x,      // column to draw in
      int color,    // 8-bit color
      UCHAR *vbuffer,// video buffer
      int lpitch);  // memory pitch

void VLine16(int y1,int y2, // start and end row
      int x,      // column to draw in
      int color,    // 16-bit RGB color
      UCHAR *vbuffer,// video buffer
      int lpitch);  // memory pitch
```

Purpose:

`VLine()` draws a fast vertical line. It's not as fast as `HLine()`, but it is faster than `Draw_Line()`, so use it if you know a line is going to be vertical in all cases. Returns nothing.

Example:

```
// draw a 8-bit line from 320,0 to 320,479 with color index 54
VLine(0,479,320,54,
   primary_buffer,
   primary_lpitch);
```

```
// draw a 16-bit line from 320,0 to 320,479 with green
VLine(0,479,320,RGB16Bit(0,255,0),
   primary_buffer,
   primary_lpitch);
```

Function Prototype:

```
void Screen_Transitions(int effect,  // screen transition
            UCHAR *vbuffer,// video buffer
            int lpitch);  // memory pitch

// screen transition commands
#define SCREEN_DARKNESS 0     // fade to black
#define SCREEN_WHITENESS 1     // fade to white
#define SCREEN_SWIPE_X  2     // do a horizontal swipe
#define SCREEN_SWIPE_Y  3     // do a vertical swipe
#define SCREEN_DISOLVE  4     // a pixel disolve
#define SCREEN_SCRUNCH  5     // a square compression
#define SCREEN_BLUENESS 6     // fade to blue
#define SCREEN_REDNESS  7     // fade to red
#define SCREEN_GREENNESS 8     // fade to green
```

Purpose:

`Screen_Transition()` performs various in-memory screen transitions as listed in the preceding header information. Note that the transformations are destructive, so please save the image and/or palette if you need them after the transition. Note that this only works for 8-bit color modes. Returns nothing.

Example:

```
// fade the primary display screen to black
Screen_Transition(SCREEN_DARKNESS, NULL, 0);
```

Function Prototype(s):

```
int Draw_Text_GDI(char *text, // null terminated string
      int x,int y, // position
      COLORREF color, // general RGB color
      LPDIRECTDRAWSURFACE7 lpdds); // dd surface

int Draw_Text_GDI(char *text, // null terminated string
        int x,int y, // position
        int color, // 8-bit color index
        LPDIRECTDRAWSURFACE7 lpdds); // dd surface
```

Purpose:

`Draw_Text_GDI()` draws GDI text on the sent surface with the desired color and position in either 8- or 16-bit color modes. The function is overloaded to take both a `COLORREF` in the form of the `RGB()` macro or a 256 (8-bit) color index. Note that the destination surface must be unlocked for the function to operate, because it locks it momentarily to perform the text blitting with GDI. Returns `TRUE` if successful.

Example:

```
// draw text with color RGB(100,100,0);
Draw_Text_GDI("This is a test",100,50,
       RGB16Bit(100,100,0),lpddsprimary);
```


Math and Error Functions

We will rewrite the math library quite a bit, but we might as well take a look at what there is to offer, because I might use it in some of the early demos. Additionally, there is some error support that you can use to write errors or diagnostic text as the engine runs. This is helpful, because debugging DirectX applications is so hard because of their resource sharing, or lack thereof <GRIN>.

Function Prototype:

```
int Fast_Distance_2D(int x, int y);
```

Purpose:

`Fast_Distance()` computes the distance from (0,0) to (x,y) using a fast approximation. Returns the distance within a 3.5% error truncated to an integer. It uses a Taylor series approximation, if you're interested.

Example:

```
int x1=100,y1=200; // object one
int x2=400,y2=150; // object two

// compute the distance between object one and two
int dist = Fast_Distance_2D(x1-x2, y1-y2);
```

Function Prototype:

```
float Fast_Distance_3D(float x, float y, float z);
```

Purpose:

`Fast_Distance_3D()` computes the distance from (0,0,0) to (x,y,z) using a fast approximation. The function returns the distance within an 11% margin of error.

Example:

```
// compute the distance from (0,0,0) to (100,200,300)
float dist = Fast_Distance_3D(100,200,300);
```

Function Prototype:

```
int Find_Bounding_Box_Poly2D(
        POLYGON2D_PTR poly, // the polygon
        float &min_x, float &max_x, // bounding box
        float &min_y, float &max_y);
```

Purpose:

`Find_Bounding_Box_Poly2D()` computes the smallest rectangle that contains the sent polygon in poly. Returns `TRUE` if successful. Also, notice the function takes parameters by reference.

Example:

```
POLYGON2D poly; // assume this is initialized
int min_x, max_x, min_y, max_y; // hold result

// find bounding box
Find_Bounding_Box_Poly2D(&poly,min_x,max_x,min_y,max_y);
```

Function Prototype:

```
int Open_Error_File(char *filename);
```

Purpose:

`Open_Error_File()` opens a disk file that receives error messages sent by you via the `Write_Error()` function. Returns `TRUE` if successful.

Example:

```
// open a general error log
Open_Error_File("errors.log");
```

Function Prototype:

```
int Close_Error_File(void);
```

Purpose:

`Close_Error_File()` closes a previously opened error file. Basically, it shuts down the stream. If you call this and an error file is not open, nothing will happen. Returns `TRUE` if successful.

Example:

```
// close the error system, note no parameter needed
Close_Error_File();
```

Function Prototype:

```
int Write_Error(char *string, ...); // error formatting string
```

Purpose:

`Write_Error()` writes an error out to the previously opened error file. If there is no file open, the function returns a `FALSE` and there is no harm. Note that the function uses the (...) variable parameter indicator, so you can use this function as you would `printf()`. Returns `TRUE` if successful.

Example:

```
// write out some stuff
Write_Error("\nSystem Starting...");
Write_Error("\nx-vel = %d", y-vel = %d", xvel, yvel);
```

Bitmap Functions

The following function set makes up the `BITMAP_IMAGE` and `BITMAP_FILE` manipulation routines. There are functions to load 8-, 16-, 24-, 32-bit bitmaps as well as to extract images from them and create simple `BITMAP_IMAGE` objects (which are not DirectDraw surfaces). In addition, functionality exists to draw these images in 8- and 16-bit modes only, but there is no clipping support. Hence, you can modify the source yourself if you need clipping support, or step up to the *BOB (Blitter Object)*, which is described at the end of the section. We will probably use these functions (or variants) to help load texture and light maps for our 3D rendering, so it's a good idea to take a close look at them.

Function Prototype:

```
int Load_Bitmap_File(BITMAP_FILE_PTR bitmap, // bitmap file
           char *filename); // disk .BMP file to load
```

Purpose:

`Load_Bitmap_File()` loads a .BMP format bitmap file off disk into the sent `BITMAP_FILE` structure, where you can manipulate it as you will. The function loads 8-, 16-, and 24-bit bitmaps, as well as the palette information on 8-bit .BMP files. Returns `TRUE` if successful.

Example:

```
// let's load "andre.bmp" off disk
BITMAP_FILE bitmap_file;

Load_Bitmap_File(&bitmap_file, "andre.bmp");
```

Function Prototype:

```
int Unload_Bitmap_File(BITMAP_FILE_PTR bitmap); // bitmap to close and unload
```

Purpose:

`Unload_Bitmap_File()` deallocates the memory associated with the image buffer of a loaded `BITMAP_FILE`. Call this function when you have copied the image bits and/or are done working with a particular bitmap. You can reuse the structure, but the memory must be freed first. Returns `TRUE` if successful.

Example:

```
// close the file we just opened
Unload_Bitmap_File(&bitmap_file);
```

Function Prototype:

```
int Create_Bitmap(BITMAP_IMAGE_PTR image, // bitmap image
         int x, int y, // starting position
         int width, int height, // size of bitmap
         int bpp=8); // the bit depth of bitmap
```

Purpose:

`Create_Bitmap()` creates an 8- or 16-bit system memory bitmap at the given position with the given size. The bitmap is initially blank and stored in the `BITMAP_IMAGE` image. The bitmap is not a DirectDraw surface, so there is no acceleration or clipping available. The function defaults to 8-bit bitmaps unless you override the `bpp` parameter with 16 for 16-bit. Returns `TRUE` if successful.

> **NOTE**
>
> There is a big difference between a `BITMAP_FILE` and a `BITMAP_IMAGE`. A `BITMAP_FILE` is a disk .BMP file, whereas a `BITMAP_IMAGE` is a system memory object like a sprite that can be moved and drawn.

Examples:

```
// let's create a 64x64 8-bit bitmap image at (0,0)
BITMAP_IMAGE ship;
Create_Bitmap(&ship, 0,0, 64,64);

// and now a 16-bit 32x32 image at (100,100)
BITMAP_IMAGE ship2;

// note the addition of 16 to override the default 8-bit depth
Create_Bitmap(&ship, 0,0, 32,32,16);
```

Function Prototype:

```
int Destroy_Bitmap(BITMAP_IMAGE_PTR image); // bitmap image to destroy
```

Purpose:

Destroy_Bitmap() is used to release the memory allocated during the creation of a BITMAP_IMAGE object (either 8- or 16-bit). You should call this function on your object when you're all done working with it—usually during the shutdown of the game, or if it's been destroyed in a bloody battle. Returns TRUE if successful.

Example:

```
// destroy the previously created BITMAP_IMAGE
Destroy_Bitmap(&ship);
```

Function Prototype:

```
int Load_Image_Bitmap(
 BITMAP_IMAGE_PTR image, // bitmap to store image in
 BITMAP_FILE_PTR bitmap, // bitmap file object to load from
 int cx,int cy, // coordinates where to scan (cell or abs)
 int mode); // image scan mode: cell based or absolute

// 16-bit version
int Load_Image_Bitmap16(
 BITMAP_IMAGE_PTR image, // bitmap to store image in
 BITMAP_FILE_PTR bitmap, // bitmap file object to load from
 int cx,int cy, // coordinates where to scan (cell or abs)
 int mode); // image scan mode: cell based or absolute


#define BITMAP_EXTRACT_MODE_CELL 0
#define BITMAP_EXTRACT_MODE_ABS  1
```

Purpose:

Load_Image_Bitmap*() is used to scan an image from a previously loaded BITMAP_FILE object into the sent BITMAP_IMAGE storage area—this is how you actually get objects and image bits into a BITMAP_IMAGE. Of course, the bitmap file and the bitmap object must be the same bit depth (8- or 16-bit), and you have to use the appropriate version of the function.

To use the function, you first must have a BITMAP_FILE loaded and have created the BITMAP_IMAGE. Then you make the call to scan an image of the same size out of the bitmap data stored in the BITMAP_FILE. There are two ways the function works: cell mode or absolute mode.

In cell mode (BITMAP_EXTRACT_MODE_CELL), the image is scanned, making the assumption that all the images are in the .BMP file in a template that is some given size *m*×*n*, with a 1 pixel-thick border between each cell, which usually range from 8×8, 16×16, 32×32, 64×64, and so on. Take a look at TEMPLATE*.BMP on the CD from this chapter—it contains a number of templates. Cell numbers range from left to right, top to bottom, and start with (0,0).

The second mode of operation is absolute coordinate mode (BITMAP_EXTRACT_MODE_ABS). In this mode, the image is scanned at the exact coordinates, sent in cx, cy. This method is good if you want to load your artwork with various sized images on the same .BMP. Hence, you can't template them.

Example:

```
8-bit example
// assume the source bitmap .BMP file is 640x480x8 and
// has a 8x8 matrix of cells that are each 32x32
// then to load the 3rd cell to the right on the 2nd
// row (cell 2,1), you would do this

// load in the .BMP file into memory
BITMAP_FILE bitmap_file;
Load_Bitmap_File(&bitmap_file,"images.bmp");


// initialize the bitmap
BITMAP_IMAGE ship;
Create_Bitmap(&ship, 0,0, 32,32);

// now scan out the data
Load_Image_Bitmap(&ship, &bitmap_file, 2,1,
        BITMAP_EXTRACT_MODE_CELL);

// the exact same example in 16-bit mode
// assume the source bitmap .BMP file is 640x480x16 and
// has a 8x8 matrix of cells that are each 32x32
// then to load the 3rd cell to the right on the 2nd
// row (cell 2,1), you would do this

// load in the .BMP file into memory
BITMAP_FILE bitmap_file;
Load_Bitmap_File(&bitmap_file,"images.bmp");
```

```
// initialize the bitmap
BITMAP_IMAGE ship2;
Create_Bitmap(&ship2, 0,0, 32,32,16);
************* 0,0,31,31,16? it's ok:al

// now scan out the data
Load_Image_Bitmap16(&ship2, &bitmap_file, 2,1,
         BITMAP_EXTRACT_MODE_CELL);
```

To load the exact same image assuming it's still in the template, but using the absolute mode, we have to figure out the coordinates—remember, there's a 1 pixel-thick partitioning wall on each side of the image.

```
// 8-bit example
Load_Image_Bitmap(&ship, &bitmap_file,
         2*(32+1)+1,1*(32+1)+1,
         BITMAP_EXTRACT_MODE_ABS);
```

Function Prototype:

```
int Draw_Bitmap(BITMAP_IMAGE_PTR source_bitmap, // bitmap to draw
        UCHAR *dest_buffer, // video buffer
        int lpitch, // memory pitch
        int transparent); // transparency?

// 16-bit version
int Draw_Bitmap16(BITMAP_IMAGE_PTR source_bitmap, // bitmap to draw
        UCHAR *dest_buffer, // video buffer
        int lpitch, // memory pitch
        int transparent); // transparency?
```

Purpose:

`Draw_Bitmap*()` draws the sent bitmap on the destination memory surface in either 8- or 16-bit mode with or without transparency. If transparent is 1, transparency is enabled and any pixel that is color index `0` or RGB word 0.0.0 in 16-bit mode will not be copied. Function returns `TRUE` if successful.

Example:

```
// draw our little ship on the back buffer
// in 8-bit mode
Draw_Bitmap( &ship, back_buffer, back_lpitch, 1);

// and now in 16-bit mode
Draw_Bitmap16( &ship2, back_buffer, back_lpitch, 1);
```

Function Prototype:

```
int Flip_Bitmap(UCHAR *image, // image bits to vertically flip
        int bytes_per_line, // bytes per line
        int height); // total rows or height
```

Purpose:

`Flip_Bitmap()` is usually called internally to flip upside down .BMP files during loading, but you might want to use it to flip an image yourself (8- or 16-bit). The function does an in-memory flip, and actually inverts the bitmap line by line, and your original sent data will be inverted, so watch out! Returns `TRUE` if successful.

Example:

```
// for fun flip the image bits of our little ship
// assuming 1 byte per pixel in 8 bit mode
Flip_Bitmap(ship->buffer, ship->width, ship->height);

// and here's the call for 16-bit mode, same call
// but we need to double the width since there are
// 2 bytes per pixel
Flip_Bitmap(ship2->buffer, 2*ship2->width, ship2->height);
```

Function Prototype:

```
int Copy_Bitmap(BITMAP_IMAGE_PTR dest_bitmap,
        int dest_x, int dest_y,
        BITMAP_IMAGE_PTR source_bitmap,
        int source_x, int source_y,
        int width, int height);
```

Purpose:

`Copy_Bitmap()` copies a rectangular region from one bitmap to another. The source and destination can be the same bitmap; however, the regions must *not* overlap—otherwise, undefined results might occur. Returns `TRUE` if successful.

Example:

```
// load in the .BMP file into memory
BITMAP_FILE bitmap_file;
Load_Bitmap_File(&bitmap_file,"playfield.bmp");


// initialize a bitmap to hold playfield
BITMAP_IMAGE playfield;
Create_Bitmap(&playfield, 0,0, 400,400,16);
```

```
// now scan out the data
Load_Image_Bitmap16(&playfield, &bitmap_file, 0,0,
         BITMAP_EXTRACT_MODE_ABSOLUTE);


// now copy the top portion of the same bitmap to the bottom
// really chunky scrolling!
Copy_Bitmap(&playfield, 0,200,
      &playfield, 0,0,
      200,200);
```


Function Prototype:

```
int Scroll_Bitmap(BITMAP_IMAGE_PTR image, int dx, int dy=0);
```

Purpose:

`Scroll_Bitmap()` scrolls the sent bitmap horizontally and/or vertically an amount *dx,dy* in the x- and y-axes, respectively. Positive numbers scroll right and down; negative numbers scroll left and up. Returns `TRUE` if successful.

Example:

```
// scroll the playfield 2 pixels to the right
Scroll_Bitmap(&playfield, 2,0);
```

8-Bit Palette Functions

The following functions make up the 8-bit 256 color palette interface. These functions are only relevant if you have the display set for a 256-color mode (8-bit color). However, in windowed display modes, the first and last 10 colors are used by Windows, and you can't alter them. (Of course, in full-screen mode you can.)

Additionally, the basic data structure used to hold a color is a native Win32 structure called `PALETTEENTRY`:

```
typedef struct tagPALETTEENTRY { // pe
  BYTE peRed;   // red channel 8-bits
  BYTE peGreen; // green channel 8-bits
  BYTE peBlue;  // blue channel 8-bits
  BYTE peFlags; // flags control, PC_EXPLICIT for windows colors
          // PC_NOCOLLAPSE for all others
} PALETTEENTRY;
```

With that in mind, let's look at the palette functions.

Function Prototype:

```
int Set_Palette_Entry(
        int color_index, // color index to change
        LPPALETTEENTRY color); // the color
```

Purpose:

`Set_Palette_Entry()` is used to change a single color in the color palette. You simply send the color index `0..255` along with a pointer to `PALETTEENTRY` holding the color, and the update will occur on the next frame. In addition, this function updates the shadow palette. Note that this function is slow, so if you need to update the entire palette, use `Set_Palette()`. Returns `TRUE` if successful, `FALSE` otherwise.

Example:

```
// set color 0 to black
PALETTEENTRY black = {0,0,0,PC_NOCOLLAPSE};
Set_Palette_Entry(0,&black);
```

Function Prototype:

```
int Get_Palette_Entry(
       int color_index, // color index to retrieve
       LPPALETTEENTRY color); // storage for color
```

Purpose:

`Get_Palette_Entry()` retrieves a palette entry from the current palette. However, the function is very fast because it retrieves the data from the RAM-based shadow palette. Hence, you can call this as much as you like, and it doesn't disturb the hardware at all. However, if you make changes to the system palette with the use of `Set_Palette_Entry()` or `Set_Palette()`, the shadow palette will not be updated and the data retrieved might not be valid. Returns `TRUE` if successful, `FALSE` otherwise.

Example:

```
// let's get palette entry 100
PALETTEENTRY color;
Get_Palette_Entry(100,&color);
```

Function Prototype:

```
int Save_Palette_To_File(
        char *filename, // filename to save at
        LPPALETTEENTRY palette); // palette to save
```

Purpose:

Save_Palette_To_File() saves the sent palette data to an ASCII file on disk for later retrieval or processing. This function is very handy if you generate a palette on the fly and want to store it on disk. However, the function assumes that the pointer in the palette points to a 256 entry palette—so watch out! Returns TRUE if successful, FALSE otherwise.

Example:

```
PALETTEENTRY my_palette[256]; // assume this is built

// save the palette we made
// note file name can be anything, but I like *.pal
Save_Palette_To_File("/palettes/custom1.pal",&my_palette);
```

Function Prototype:

```
int Load_Palette_From_File(
     char *filename, // file to load from
     LPPALETTEENTRY palette); // storage for palette
```

Purpose:

Load_Palette_From_File() is used to load a previously saved 256-color palette from disk via Save_Palette_To_File(). You simply send the file name along with storage for all 256 entries and the palette is loaded off disk into the data structure. However, the function does NOT load the entries into the hardware palette; you must do this yourself with Set_Palette(). Returns TRUE if successful, FALSE otherwise.

Example:

```
// load the previously saved palette
Load_Palette_From_File("/palettes/custom1.pal",&my_palette);
```

NOTE

When you create a 256-color display mode via a call to DDRAW_INIT(), the function will load a standard palette that has almost optimal color space coverage. The name of the palette file is PALDATA2.DAT. It's nothing more than an ASCII file with 256 line entries, each with a red, green, and blue value in the range of 0..255.

Function Prototype:

```
int Set_Palette(LPPALETTEENTRY set_palette); // palette to load into hardware
```

Purpose:

Set_Palette() loads the sent palette data into the hardware and updates the shadow palette, also. Returns TRUE if successful, FALSE otherwise.

Example:

```
// lets load the palette into the hardware
Set_Palette(&my_palette);
```

Function Prototype:

```
int Save_Palette(LPPALETTEENTRY sav_palette); // storage for palette
```

Purpose:

`Save_Palette()` scans the hardware palette out into `sav_palette` so that you can save it to disk or manipulate it. `sav_palette` must have enough storage for all 256 entries.

Example:

```
// retrieve the current DirectDraw hardware palette
PALETTEENTRY hardware_palette[256];
Save_Palette(&hardware_palette);
```

Function Prototype:

```
int Rotate_Colors(int start_index, // starting index 0..255
         int end_index); // ending index 0..255
```

Purpose:

`Rotate_Colors()` rotates a bank of colors in a cyclic manner. It manipulates the color palette hardware directly. Returns `TRUE` if successful, `FALSE` otherwise.

Example:

```
// rotate the entire palette
Rotate_Colors(0,255);
```

Function Prototype:

```
int Blink_Colors(int command, // blinker engine command
         BLINKER_PTR new_light, // blinker data
         int id); // id of blinker
```

Purpose:

`Blink_Colors()` is used to create asynchronous palette animation. The function is too long to explain here, but please refer to the previous chapter for a more in-depth description.

Example:

N/A

Utility Functions

Function Prototype:

```
DWORD Get_Clock(void);
```

Purpose:

`Get_Clock()` returns the current clock time in milliseconds since Windows was started.

Example:

```
// get the current tick count
DWORD start_time = Get_Clock();
```

Function Prototype:

```
DWORD Start_Clock(void);
```

Purpose:

`Start_Clock()` basically makes a call to `Get_Clock()` and stores the time in a global variable for you. Then you can call `Wait_Clock()`, which will wait for some number of milliseconds since your call to `Start_Clock()`. Returns the starting clock value at the time of the call.

Example:

```
// start the clock and set the global
Start_Clock();
```

Function Prototype:

```
DWORD Wait_Clock(DWORD count); // number of milliseconds to wait
```

Purpose:

`Wait_Clock()` simply waits the sent number of milliseconds since the call was made to `Start_Clock()`. Returns the current clock count at the time of call. However, the function will NOT return until the time difference has elapsed.

Example:

```
// wait 30 milliseconds
Start_Clock();

// code...

Wait_Clock(30);
```

NOTE

Later in the book, we will probably upgrade to using the high performance timers that Windows supports for better resolution.

Function Prototype:

```
int Collision_Test(int x1, int y1, // upper lhs of obj1
          int w1, int h1, // width, height of obj1
          int x2, int y2, // upper lhs of obj2
          int w2, int h2);// width, height of obj2
```

Purpose:

`Collision_Test()` basically performs an overlapping rectangle test on the two sent rectangles. The rectangles can represent whatever you like. You must send the upper-left hand corner coordinates of each rectangle, along with its width and height. Returns `TRUE` if there is an overlap, `FALSE` otherwise.

Example:

```
// do these two BITMAP_IMAGE's overlap?
if (Collision_Test(ship1->x,ship1->y,ship1->width,ship1->height,
          ship2->x,ship2->y,ship2->width,ship2->height))
  { // hit

  } // end if
```

Function Prototype:

```
int Color_Scan(int x1, int y1, // upper left of rect
        int x2, int y2, // lower right of rect
        UCHAR scan_start, // starting scan color
        UCHAR scan_end, // ending scan color
        UCHAR *scan_buffer, // memory to scan
        int scan_lpitch); // linear memory pitch
```

Purpose:

`Color_Scan()` is another collision detection algorithm that scans a rectangle for a single 8-bit value or sequence of values in some continuous range. You can use it to determine whether a color index is present within some area. Of course, it only works with 8-bit images, but the source is easily extensible to 16-bit or higher modes. Returns `TRUE` if the color(s) is found.

Example:

```
// scan for colors in range from 122-124 inclusive
Color_Scan(10,10, 50, 50, 122,124, back_buffer, back_lpitch);
```

The BOB (Blitter Object) Engine

Although with a bit of programming you can get the `BITMAP_IMAGE` type to do what you want, it is lacking in a serious way—it doesn't use DirectDraw surfaces, and hence there is no support for acceleration. Therefore, I have created a type called a *BOB*, or *blitter object,* that is very similar to a sprite. A *sprite* (for those of you that have been in a game programming cave) is nothing more than an object you can move around the screen that usually doesn't disturb the background. In our case, this isn't true; therefore, I called my animation object a BOB rather than a sprite, so there!

We will use the BOB engine very little in this book, but I still wanted you to see it, because it's a good example of using DirectDraw surfaces and full 2D acceleration. So let's talk briefly about what a BOB is. First here's the data structure for a BOB:

```
// the blitter object structure BOB
typedef struct BOB_TYP
    {
    int state;      // the state of the object (general)
    int anim_state;    // an animation state variable, up to you
    int attr;       // attributes pertaining to the object (general)
    float x,y;       // position bitmap will be displayed at
    float xv,yv;      // velocity of object
    int width, height; // the width and height of the bob
    int width_fill;    // internal, used to force 8*x wide surfaces
    int bpp;       // bits per pixel needed for 8/16 bit support
    int counter_1;    // general counters
    int counter_2;
    int max_count_1;   // general threshold values;
    int max_count_2;
    int varsI[16];    // stack of 16 integers
    float varsF[16];   // stack of 16 floats
    int curr_frame;    // current animation frame
    int num_frames;    // total number of animation frames
    int curr_animation; // index of current animation
    int anim_counter;   // used to time animation transitions
    int anim_index;    // animation element index
    int anim_count_max; // number of cycles before animation
    int *animations[MAX_BOB_ANIMATIONS]; // animation sequences
    // the bitmap images DD surfaces
    LPDIRECTDRAWSURFACE7 images[MAX_BOB_FRAMES];
    } BOB, *BOB_PTR;
```

A BOB is basically a graphical object represented by one or more DirectDraw surfaces (up to 64 as currently #defined). You can move a BOB, draw a BOB, animate a BOB, and set it in motion. BOBs consider the current DirectDraw clipper, so they are clipped as well as accelerated—which is a good thing! Figure 3.10 shows a BOB and it relationship to its animation frames.

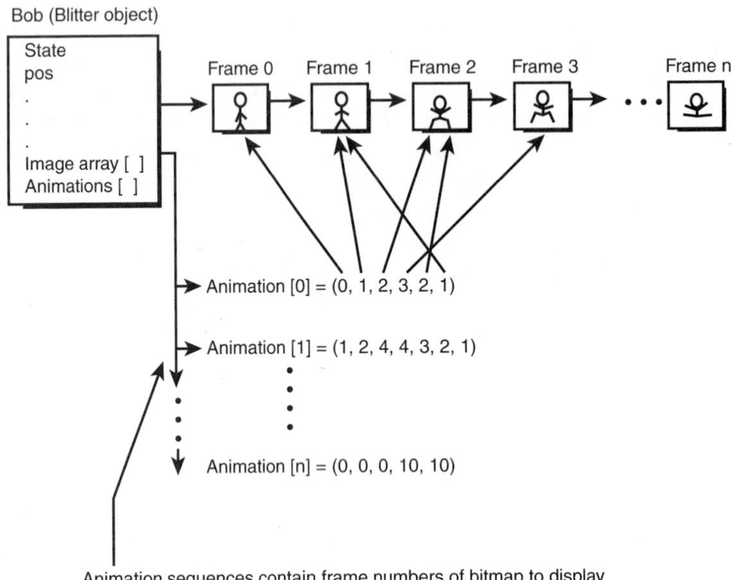

FIGURE 3.10 The BOB animation system.

Also, the BOB engine supports 8- or 16-bit images and animation sequences, so you can load in a set of frames and an animation sequence, and the sequence will play feeding from the frames. This is a very cool feature. Additionally, BOBs work with both 8- and 16-bit color, but most of the functions have internal logic that know what bit depth the system is in, so you don't have to worry it. The only functions that you need to explicitly call a different version for 16-bit mode are `Load_Frame_BOB*()` (when you load) and `Draw_BOB*()` (when you draw a BOB), but we will get to that, along with reviewing examples of both 8- and 16-bit demos, at the end of the chapter.

Finally, all the BOB functions return `TRUE` if successful and `FALSE` otherwise. So let's take a look at them all....

Function Prototype:

```
int Create_BOB(BOB_PTR bob, // ptr to bob to create
  int x, int y,       // initial position of bob
  int width, int height,  // size of bob
```

```
int num_frames, // total number of frames for bob
int attr,     // attributes of bob
int mem_flags=0, // surface memory flags, 0 is VRAM
USHORT color_key_value=0, // color key value is interpreted as
             // 8-bit index, or 16-bit RGB based
             // on the bpp setting below
int bpp=8); // bits per pixel, default is 8
```

Purpose:

`Create_BOB()` creates a single BOB object and sets it all up. The function assigns all the internal variables, in addition to creating a separate DirectDraw surface for each frame. Most of the parameters are self-explanatory—the only value that needs a little explanation is the attribute variable `attr`. Take a look at Table 3.1 to see a better description of each of the attributes you can logically `OR` together and send in this field.

TABLE 3.1 Valid BOB Attributes

Value	Meaning
`BOB_ATTR_SINGLE_FRAME`	Create a BOB with a single frame.
`BOB_ATTR_MULTI_FRAME`	Create a BOB with multiple frames, but the animation of the BOB will be a linear sequence through the frames `0..n`.
`BOB_ATTR_MULTI_ANIM`	Create a multiple frame BOB that supports animation sequences.
`BOB_ATTR_ANIM_ONE_SHOT`	If this is set then when an animation sequence plays, the animation sequence will only play once and then stop. At this point, the internal variable `anim_state` will be set. To play the animation again, reset this variable.
`BOB_ATTR_BOUNCE`	This flag tells the BOB to bounce off the screen boundaries like a ball. This only works if you use `Move_BOB()`.
`BOB_ATTR_WRAPAROUND`	This flag tells the BOB to wrap around to the other side of the screen as it moves. This only works if you use `Move_BOB()`.

Example:

Here are some examples creating BOBs. First, a single frame 8-bit BOB at (50,100) with a size of 96×64:

```
BOB car; // a car bob

// create the bob
if (!Create_BOB(&car, 50,100, // address of bob and initial position
        96,64,     // size of bob
        1,       // number of frames
        BOB_ATTR_SINGLE_FRAME, // attribute
        0, // memory flags
```

```
        0, // color key, for 8-bit this is the index
        8)) // bits per pixel, 8 for 256 color modes
  { /* error */ }
```

And here's a multiple frame 16-bit BOB with 8 frames and a size of 32×32:

```
BOB ship; // a space ship bob

// create the bob
if (!Create_BOB(&ship, 0,0, // address of bob and initial position
        32,32, // size of bob
        8,    // number of frames
        BOB_ATTR_MULTI_FRAME, // attribute
        0, // memory flags
        0, // color key, for 16-bit mode this is the RGB word
        16)) // bits per pixel, 16 for 16 bit modes
  { /* error */ }
```

Finally, a multiple frame 8-bit BOB that supports animation sequences:

```
BOB greeny; // a little green man bob

// create the bob
if (!Create_BOB(&greeny, 0,0,
  32,32,32,BOB_ATTR_MULTI_ANIM,0,0,8))
  { /* error */ }
```

TIP

Note that the last three parameters to `Create_BOB()` all have default values. Therefore, you don't need to override them if you don't want to. If 0,0,8 is okay with you, you don't have to type them.

Function Prototype:

```
int Destroy_BOB(BOB_PTR bob); // ptr to bob to destroy
```

Purpose:

`Destroy_BOB()` destroys a previously created BOB. It doesn't matter if it's 8- or 16-bit.

Example:

```
// destroy the BOB above, you would do this
Destroy_BOB(&greeny);
```

Function Prototype:

```
int Draw_BOB(BOB_PTR bob, // ptr of bob to draw
 LPDIRECTDRAWSURFACE7 dest); // dest surface to draw on

// and the 16-bit version
int Draw_BOB16(BOB_PTR bob, // ptr of bob to draw
 LPDIRECTDRAWSURFACE7 dest); // dest surface to draw on
```

Purpose:

`Draw_BOB*()` is a very powerful function. It draws the sent BOB on the DirectDraw surface you send it. The BOB is drawn in its current position and current frame (as defined by its animation parameters). Also, make sure to use the correct version of the function depending on whether your BOB is 8- or 16-bit; otherwise, you might get half a BOB!

> **CAUTION**
>
> For this function to work, the destination surface must NOT be locked.

Example:

```
// this is how you would position a multiframe BOB at
// (50,50) and draw the first frame of it on the back
// surface:
BOB ship; // a space ship bob

// create the bob, 8-bit default
if (!Create_BOB(&ship, 0,0,
        32,32,8,BOB_ATTR_MULTI_FRAME,0))

// load the bob images in..we'll get to this in a bit
// set the position and frame of bob
ship.x = 50;
ship.y = 50;
ship.curr_frame = 0; // this contains the frame to draw

// draw bob
Draw_BOB(&ship, lpddsback);
```

Function Prototype:

```
int Draw_Scaled_BOB(BOB_PTR bob, // ptr of bob to draw
 int swidth, int sheight, // new width and height of bob
 LPDIRECTDRAWSURFACE7 dest); // dest surface to draw on
```

```
// and the 16-bit version
int Draw_Scaled_BOB16(BOB_PTR bob, // ptr of bob to draw
 int swidth, int sheight, // new width and height of bob
 LPDIRECTDRAWSURFACE7 dest); // dest surface to draw on
```

Purpose:

`Draw_Scaled_BOB*()` works exactly like `Draw_BOB()`, except you can send any width and height to draw the BOB and the BOB will be scaled appropriately. This is very cool, and if you have acceleration, it's a great way to scale a BOB to make it look 3D! In fact, we will use a technique like this when we create billboards for our 3D applications.

> **NOTE**
>
> *Billboards* are simply 2D images that are drawn in 3D, but are always perpendicular to the view direction. For example, in *Doom*, all the creatures are billboard sprites, while the world is polygon-based.

Example:

```
// an example of drawing the ship 128x128 even though
// it was created as only 32x32 pixels
// 8-bit version
Draw_Scaled_BOB(&ship, 128,128,lpddsback);
```

Function Prototype:

```
int Load_Frame_BOB(
 BOB_PTR bob, // ptr of bob to load frame into
 BITMAP_FILE_PTR bitmap,// ptr of bitmap file to scan data
 int frame,   // frame number to place image into 0,1,2...
 int cx,int cy, // cell pos or abs pos to scan from
 int mode);    // scan mode, same as Load_Frame_Bitmap()

// and the 16-bit version
int Load_Frame_BOB16(
 BOB_PTR bob, // ptr of bob to load frame into
 BITMAP_FILE_PTR bitmap,// ptr of bitmap file to scan data
 int frame,   // frame number to place image into 0,1,2...
 int cx,int cy, // cell pos or abs pos to scan from
 int mode);    // scan mode, same as Load_Frame_Bitmap()
```

Purpose:

The `Load_Frame_BOB*()` function works identically to the `Load_Frame_Bitmap()` function, so refer to it for details. The only addition is the control of the frame to load via frame. If you create a BOB that has four frames, you will load the frames one by one. Additionally, you must call the correct version of the function (8- or 16-bit) based on the bit depth of the data and screen.

Example:

```
// here's an example of loading 4 frames into a 16-bit BOB from a
// bitmap file in cell mode

BOB ship; // the bob
// loads frames 0,1,2,3 from cell position (0,0), (1,0),
// (2,0), (3,0)
// from bitmap16bit bitmap file, assume it has been loaded

for (int index=0; index<4; index++)
   Load_Frame_BOB16(&ship,&bitmap16bit,
           index, index,0,
           BITMAP_EXTRACT_MODE_CELL );
```

> **NOTE**
>
> The next set of BOB manipulation functions work on the data structure elements of the BOB, so they work identically on both 8- and 16-bit BOBs.

Function Prototype:

```
int Load_Animation_BOB(
  BOB_PTR bob,  // bob to load animation into
  int anim_index, // which animation to load 0..15
  int num_frames, // number of frames of animation
  int *sequence); // ptr to array holding sequence
```

Purpose:

`Load_Animation()` takes a little explaining. The function is used to load one of 16 arrays internal to the BOB that contain animation sequences. Each sequence contains an array of indices or frame numbers to display in sequence. This is shown at the bottom of Figure 3.10.

Example:

You might have a BOB that has eight frames `0,1,…7`, but you might have four animations defined as follows:

```
int anim_walk[] = {0,1,2,1,0};
int anim_fire[] = {5,6,0};
int anim_die[]  = {3,4};
int anim_sleep[] = {0,0,7,0,0};
```

Then to load the animations into the BOB, you would do this:

```
// create a mutli animation bob
// create the bob
if (!Create_BOB(&alien, 0,0, 32,32,8,BOB_ATTR_MULTI_ANIM,0))
  { /* error */ }

// load the bob frames in...
// load walk into animation 0
Load_Animation_BOB(&alien, 0,5,anim_walk);

// load fire into animation 1
Load_Animation_BOB(&alien, 1,3,anim_fire);

// load die into animation 2
Load_Animation_BOB(&alien, 2,2,anim_die);

// load sleep into animation 3
Load_Animation_BOB(&alien, 3,5,anim_sleep);
```

After loading the animations, you can set the active animation and play them with functions you'll see in a minute.

Function Prototype:

```
int Set_Pos_BOB(BOB_PTR bob, // ptr to bob to set position
       int x, int y); // new position of bob
```

Purpose:

`Set_Pos_BOB()` is a simple way to set the position of the BOB. This does nothing more than assign the internal (x,y) variables, but it's nice to have a function.

Example:

```
// set the position of the alien BOB above
Set_Pos_BOB(&alien, player_x, player_y);
```

Function Prototype:

```
int Set_Vel_BOB(BOB_PTR bob, // ptr to bob to set velocity
     int xv, int yv); // new x,y velocity
```

Purpose:

Each BOB has an internal velocity contained in `(xv,yv)`. `Set_Vel_BOB()` simply assigns these values the new values sent in the function. The velocity values in the BOB won't do anything unless you use the function Move_BOB() to move your BOBs. However, even if you don't, you can use xv,yv to track the velocity of the BOB yourself.

Example:

```
// make the BOB move in a straight horizontal line
Set_Vel_BOB(&alien, 10,0);
```

Function Prototype:

```
int Set_Anim_Speed_BOB(BOB_PTR bob, // ptr to bob
         int speed); // speed of animation
```

Purpose:

Set_Anim_Speed() sets the internal animation rate for a BOB anim_count_max. The higher this number is, the slower the animation; the lower the number (0 is the lowest), the faster the animation. However, this function only matters if you use the internal BOB animation function Animate_BOB(). And of course, you must have created a BOB that has multiple frames.

Example:

```
// set the rate to change frames every 30 frames
Set_Anim_Speed_BOB(&alien, 30);
```

Function Prototype:

```
int Set_Animation_BOB(
     BOB_PTR bob, // ptr of bob to set animation
     int anim_index); // index of animation to set
```

Purpose:

Set_Animation_BOB() sets the current animation that will be played by the BOB. In the earlier example of Load_Animation_BOB(), we created four animations.

Example:

```
// make animation sequence number 2 active
Set_Animation_BOB(&alien, 2);
```

> **NOTE**
>
> This also resets the BOB animation to the first frame in the sequence.

Function Prototype:

```
int Animate_BOB(BOB_PTR bob); // ptr to bob to animate
```

Purpose:

`Animate_BOB()` animates a BOB for you. Normally, you would call this function once a frame to update the animation of the BOB.

Example:

```
// erase everything...
// move everything...
// animate everything
Animate_BOB(&alien);
```

Function Prototype:

```
int Move_BOB(BOB_PTR bob); // ptr of bob to move
```

Purpose:

`Move_BOB()` moves the BOB a delta of `xv,yv` (set with the `Set_Vel_BOB()` function), then, depending on the attributes, will either bounce the BOB off the walls, wrap it around, or do nothing. Similarly to the `Animate_BOB()` function, you would place this call once in the main loop right after (or before) `Animate_BOB()`.

Example:

```
// animate bob
Animate_BOB(&alien);

// move it
Move_BOB(&alien);
```

Function Prototype:

```
int Hide_BOB(BOB_PTR bob); // ptr to bob to hide
```

Purpose:

`Hide_BOB()` simply sets the BOB's internal visibility flag to `0`, after which `Draw_BOB()` won't display the BOB anymore.

Example:

```
// hide the bob
Hide_BOB(&alien);
```

Function Prototype:

```
int Show_BOB(BOB_PTR bob); // ptr to bob to show
```

Purpose:

Show_BOB() sets the visibility flag to 1 on a BOB, so it will be drawn (it undoes a Hide_BOB() call). Here's an example of hiding and showing a BOB because you are displaying a GDI object or something, and don't want the BOB to occlude it:

Example:

```
// Hide_BOB(&alien);
// make calls to Draw_BOB and GDI etc.
Show_BOB(&alien);
```


Function Prototype:

```
int Collision_BOBS(BOB_PTR bob1, // ptr to first bob
         BOB_PTR bob2); // ptr to second bob
```

Purpose:

Collision_BOBS() detects whether the bounding rectangles of two BOBs are overlapping. This can be used for collision detection in a game to see whether a player BOB hits a missile BOB or whatever.

Example:

```
// check if a missile BOB hit a player BOB:
if (Collision_BOBS(&missile, &player))
  { /* make explosion sound */ }
```

That's about it for the graphics module of the T3DLIB game library (T3DLIB1.CPP¦H). Now let's move on to the sound module.

The T3DLIB2 DirectX Input System

Writing a simple set of wrapper functions around DirectInput is almost a no-brainer. Well, it takes some brains, but for the most part it's fairly easy. All we need to do is create an API with a very simple interface and few parameters. The interface should support the following minimal functionality:

- Initialize the DirectInput system
- Set up and acquire the keyboard, mouse, and joystick—or any subset
- Read data from any of the input devices
- Shut down, unacquire, and release everything

I have created such an API, and it's available in T3DLIB2.CPP¦H on the CD. The API does everything you need to initialize DirectInput and read any device. Before reviewing the functions, take a look at Figure 3.11—it depicts the relationship between each device and the data flow.

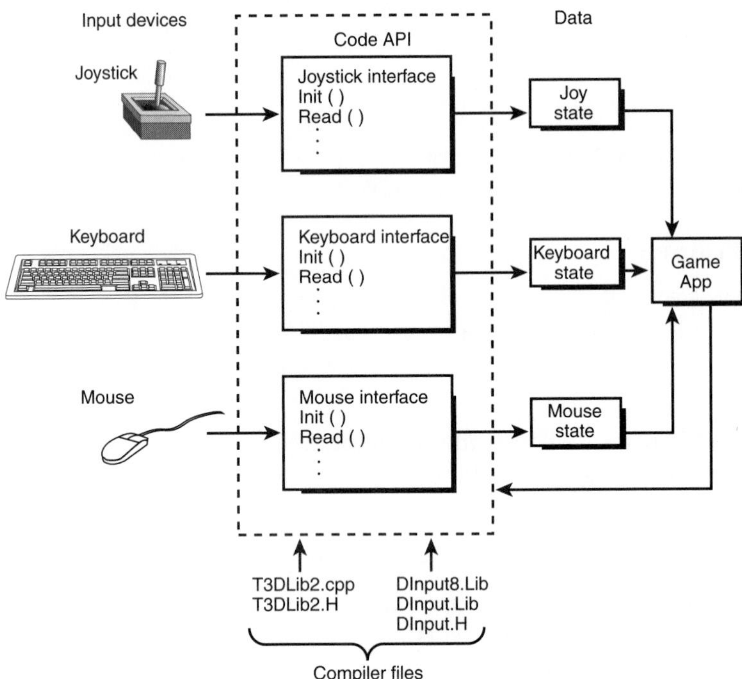

FIGURE 3.11 The DirectInput software system.

Here are the globals for the library:

```
LPDIRECTINPUT8    lpdi;     // dinput object
LPDIRECTINPUTDEVICE8 lpdikey;  // dinput keyboard
LPDIRECTINPUTDEVICE8 lpdimouse; // dinput mouse
LPDIRECTINPUTDEVICE8 lpdijoy;  // dinput joystick
GUID  joystickGUID; // guid for main joystick
char  joyname[80]; // name of joystick

// all input is stored in these records
UCHAR keyboard_state[256]; // contains keyboard state table
DIMOUSESTATE mouse_state; // contains state of mouse
DIJOYSTATE joy_state;   // contains state of joystick
int joystick_found;    // tracks if stick is plugged in
```

Input from the keyboard is placed in `keyboard_state[]`, the mouse data is stored in `mouse_state`, and the joystick data is stored in `joy_state` by the input system. The structure of each of these records is the standard DirectInput device state structures (except for the keyboard; it's just a Boolean array of BYTES) as shown in the following:

```
// for the mouse data
typedef struct DIMOUSESTATE {
  LONG lX; // x-axis
  LONG lY; // y-axis
  LONG lZ; // z-axis
  BYTE rgbButtons[4]; // state of the buttons
} DIMOUSESTATE, *LPDIMOUSESTATE;

// for the joystick data
typedef struct DIJOYSTATE {
  LONG  lX; // x-axis
  LONG  lY; // y-axis
  LONG  lZ; // z-axis
  LONG  lRx; // rotation about x-axis
  LONG  lRy; // rotation about y-axis
  LONG  lRz; // rotation about z-axis
  LONG  rglSlider[2]; // u,v slider positions
  DWORD  rgdwPOV[4];  // point of view hat state
  BYTE  rgbButtons[32]; // state of buttons 0..31
} DIJOYSTATE, *LPDIJOYSTATE;
```

In general, the mouse and joystick are roughly equivalent as far as the x,y position goes; that is, you access them via the fields lX, lY, and the buttons are BOOLEANs in rgbButtons[]. Let's get to the functions. The variable joystick_found is a BOOLEAN that is set when you request joystick access. If a joystick is found, it is TRUE, otherwise, it's FALSE. With it, you can conditional block out code that uses the joystick. So without further ado, here is the new API:

Function Prototype:

```
int DInput_Init(void);
```

Purpose:

DInput_Init() initializes the DirectInput input system. It creates the main COM object and returns TRUE if successful and FALSE otherwise. And of course, the global lpdi will be valid. The function does not create any devices, though. Here's an example of initializing the input system:

Example:

```
if (!DInput_Init())
  { /* error */ }
```

Function Prototype:

```
void DInput_Shutdown(void);
```

Purpose:

`DInput_Shutdown()` releases all the COM objects and any resources allocated during the call to `DInput_Init()`. Normally, you would call `DInput_Shutdown()` at the very end of your application after you have released all the input devices themselves—which we'll get to shortly. Anyway, here's an example of shutting down the input system:

Example:

```
DInput_Shutdown();
```

Function Prototype:

```
DInput_Init_Keyboard(void);
```

Purpose:

`DInput_Init_Keyboard()` initializes and acquires the keyboard. This should always work and return `TRUE`, unless another DirectX application has taken over in a really uncooperative way. Here's an example:

Example:

```
if (!DInput_Init_Keyboard())
  { /* error */ }
```

Function Prototype:

```
int DInput_Init_Mouse(void);
```

Purpose:

`DInput_Init_Mouse()` initializes and acquires the mouse. The function takes no parameters and returns `TRUE` if successful and `FALSE` otherwise. But it should always work, unless a mouse isn't plugged in or there's another DirectX application that has totally taken over! If everything goes well, `lpdimouse` becomes the valid interface pointer. Here's an example:

Example:

```
if (!DInput_Init_Mouse()) { /* error */ }
```

Function Prototype:

```
int DInput_Init_Joystick(int min_x=-256, // min x range
        int max_x=256, // max x range
        int min_y=-256, // min y range
        int max_y=256, // max y range
        int dead_zone=10); // dead zone in percent
```

Purpose:

`DInput_Init_Joystick()` initializes the joystick device for use. The function takes five parameters that define the x-y range of motion of the data sent back from the joystick and the dead zone with a percentage. If you want to use the defaults of -256 to 256 and 10% dead zone for each axis, you don't need to send parameters because they have default values (C++ thing). If the call returns back a `TRUE`, a joystick was found and it has been set up, initialized, and acquired. After the call, the interface pointer `lpdijoy` will be valid if you need it for anything. In addition, the string `joyname[]` will contain the "friendly" name of the joystick device, such as "Microsoft Sidewinder Pro," and so on.

Here's an example of initializing the joystick and setting its x-y ranges to -1024 to 1024 with a 5% dead zone:

Example:

```
if (!DInput_Init_Joystick(-1024, 1024, -1024, 1024, 5))
  { /* error */ }
```

Function Prototype(s):

```
void DInput_Release_Joystick(void);
void DInput_Release_Mouse(void);
void DInput_Release_Keyboard(void);
```

Purpose:

`DInput_Release_Joystick()`, `DInput_Release_Mouse()`, and `DInput_Release_Keyboard()` release each of the respective input devices when you are done with them. The functions can be called even if you haven't initialized the respective device, so you can just call them all at the end of your application if you want. Here's a complete example of starting up the DirectInput system, initializing all the devices and then releasing them and shutting down:

Example:

```
// initialize the DirectInput system
DInput_Init();

// initialize all input devices and acquire them
DInput_Init_Joystick();
DInput_Init_Mouse();
DInput_Init_Keyboard();

// input loop ....do work here
// now done...
```

```
// first release all devices, order is unimportant
DInput_Release_Joystick();
DInput_Release_Mouse();
DInput_Release_Keyboard();

// shutdown DirectInput
DInput_Shutdown();
```

Function Prototype:

```
int DInput_Read_Keyboard(void);
```

Purpose:

`DInput_Read_Keyboard()` scans the keyboard state and places the data in `keyboard_state[]`, which is an array of 256 `BYTE`s. This is the standard DirectInput keyboard state array, so you must use the DirectInput key constants `DIK_*` if you want to make sense of it. If a key is pressed, the array value will be `0x80`. Here's an example of testing whether the right and left keys are down using the manifest constants in DirectInput—which you can look up in the SDK or the abridged Table 3.2 following.

Example:

```
// read the keyboard
if (!DInput_Read_Keyboard())
  { /* error */ }

// now test the state data
if (keyboard_state[DIK_RIGHT])
  { /* move ship right */ }
else
if (keyboard_state[DIK_LEFT])
  { /* move ship left */ }
```

TABLE 3.2 The DirectInput Keyboard State Constants

Symbol	Meaning
`DIK_ESCAPE`	The Esc key
`DIK_0-9`	Main keyboard 0–9
`DIK_MINUS`	Minus key
`DIK_EQUALS`	Equals key
`DIK_BACK`	Backspace key
`DIK_TAB`	Tab key
`DIK_A-Z`	Letters A–Z
`DIK_LBRACKET`	Left bracket
`DIK_RBRACKET`	Right bracket

TABLE 3.2 Continued

Symbol	Meaning
DIK_RETURN	Return/Enter on main keyboard
DIK_LCONTROL	Left control
DIK_LSHIFT	Left shift
DIK_RSHIFT	Right shift
DIK_LMENU	Left Alt
DIK_SPACE	Spacebar
DIK_F1-15	Function keys 1–15
DIK_NUMPAD0-9	Numeric keypad keys 0–9
DIK_ADD	+ on numeric keypad
DIK_NUMPADENTER	Enter on numeric keypad
DIK_RCONTROL	Right control
DIK_RMENU	Right Alt
DIK_HOME	Home on arrow keypad
DIK_UP	UpArrow on arrow keypad
DIK_PRIOR	PgUp on arrow keypad
DIK_LEFT	LeftArrow on arrow keypad
DIK_RIGHT	RightArrow on arrow keypad
DIK_END	End on arrow keypad
DIK_DOWN	DownArrow on arrow keypad
DIK_NEXT	PgDn on arrow keypad
DIK_INSERT	Insert on arrow keypad
DIK_DELETE	Delete on arrow keypad

(Note: bolded entries simply mean to follow the sequence. For example, `DIK_0-9` means that there are constants `DIK_0`, `DIK_1`, `DIK_2`, and so forth.)

Function Prototype:

```
int DInput_Read_Mouse(void);
```

Purpose:

`DInput_Read_Mouse()` reads the relative mouse state and stores the result in `mouse_state`, which is a `DIMOUSESTATE` structure. The data is in relative delta mode. In most cases, you'll only need to look at `mouse_state.lX`, `mouse_state.lY`, and `rgbButtons[0..2]`, which are `BOOLEAN`s for the three mouse buttons. Here's an example of reading the mouse and using it to move a cursor around and draw:

Example:

```
// read the mouse
if (!DInput_Read_Mouse())
  { /* error */ }
```

```
// move cursor
cx+=mouse_state.lX;
cy+=mouse_state.lY;

// test if left button is down
if (mouse_state.rgbButtons[0])
  Draw_Pixel(cx,cy,col,buffer,pitch);
```

Function Prototype:

```
int DInput_Read_Joystick(void);
```

Purpose:

`DInput_Read_Joystick()` polls the joystick and then reads the data into `joy_state`, which is a `DIJOYSTATE` structure. Of course, if there isn't a joystick plugged in, the function returns `FALSE` and `joy_state` will be invalid, but you get the idea. If successful, `joy_state` contains the state information of the joystick. The data returned will be in the range you previously set for each axis, and the button values are `BOOLEAN`s in `rgbButtons[]`. As an example, here's how you would use the joystick to move a ship right and left and the first button to fire:

Example:

```
// read the joystick data
if (!DInput_Read_Joystick())
  { /* error */ }

// move the ship
ship_x+=joy_state.lX;
ship_y+=joy_state.lY;

// test for trigger
if (joy_state.rgbButtons[0])
  { // fire weapon // }
```

Of course, your joystick might have a lot of buttons and multiple axes. In this case, you can use the other fields of `joy_state` as defined in the `DIJOYSTATE` DirectInput structure.

> **NOTE**
>
> Even though we are using the `IDIRECTINPUTDEVICE8` interface, we don't need to use the `DIJOYSTATE2` structure. This is only for force feedback devices.

At this point, we are ready to take a look at one of the subsystems that most game programmers hate to deal with—sound and music! But under DirectX, along with my wrapper functions, making sound effects and playing music is so easy it's actually fun!

The T3DLIB3 Sound and Music Library

I have taken all the sound and music technology from the first *Tricks* and used it to create the last component to our game engine T3DLIB3. It is composed of two main source files:

- T3DLIB3.CPP—The main C/C++ source
- T3DLIB3.H—The header file

However, you'll also need to include the DirectSound import library DSOUND.LIB to make anything link. However, DirectMusic does *not* have an import library because it's a pure COM object, so there isn't a DMUSIC.LIB. On the other hand, you still need to point your compiler to the DirectSound and DirectMusic .H header files, so it can find them during compilation. Just to remind you, they are:

- DSOUND.H—The standard DirectSound header.
- DMKSCTRL.H—All of these are for DirectMusic.
- DMUSICI.H
- DMUSICC.H
- DMUSICF.H

With all that in mind, let's take a look at the main elements of the T3DLIB3.H header file.

NOTE

With DirectX 8.0+, Microsoft integrated DirectSound and DirectMusic much more tightly and called it DirectAudio. I see no point in changing to DirectAudio, so we will simply use each component separately in this book.

The Header

The header file T3DLIB3.H contains the types, macros, and externals for T3DLIB3.CPP. Here are the #defines you'll find in the header:

```
#define DM_NUM_SEGMENTS 64 // number of midi segments that can be cached in memory

// midi object state defines
#define MIDI_NULL    0  // this midi object is not loaded
#define MIDI_LOADED  1  // this midi object is loaded
```

```
#define MIDI_PLAYING 2  // this midi object is loaded and playing
#define MIDI_STOPPED 3  // this midi object is loaded, but stopped

#define MAX_SOUNDS   256 // max number of sounds in system at once

// digital sound object state defines
#define SOUND_NULL   0 // " "
#define SOUND_LOADED  1
#define SOUND_PLAYING 2
#define SOUND_STOPPED 3
```

Not much for macros—this is just a macro to help convert from 0–100 to the Microsoft decibels scale, and one to convert multibyte characters to wide characters:

```
#define DSVOLUME_TO_DB(volume) ((DWORD)(-30*(100 - volume)))

// Convert from multibyte format to Unicode using the following macro
#define MULTI_TO_WIDE( x,y )
     MultiByteToWideChar( CP_ACP,MB_PRECOMPOSED, y,-1,x,_MAX_PATH)
```

CAUTION

The column width of this book might be too small to fit the whole macro, so the definition might be on two lines. This is a no-no in real life. Macros must be on a single line!

Next up are the types for the sound engine. First, the DirectSound object.

The Types

There are only two types for the sound engine: one to hold a digital sample, and the other to hold a MIDI segment:

```
// this holds a single sound
typedef struct pcm_sound_typ
  {
  LPDIRECTSOUNDBUFFER dsbuffer; // the directsound buffer
                // containing the sound
  int state;  // state of the sound
  int rate;  // playback rate
  int size;  // size of sound
  int id;   // id number of the sound
  } pcm_sound, *pcm_sound_ptr;
```

And now the DirectMusic segment type:

```
// directmusic MIDI segment
typedef struct DMUSIC_MIDI_TYP
{
IDirectMusicSegment    *dm_segment; // the directmusic segment
IDirectMusicSegmentState  *dm_segstate; // the state of the segment
int             id;      // the id of this segment
int             state;    // state of midi song

} DMUSIC_MIDI, *DMUSIC_MIDI_PTR;
```


Both sounds and MIDI segments will be stored by the engine in the preceding two structures, respectively. Now let's take a look at the globals.

Global Domination

T3DLIB3 contains a number of globals. Let's take a look. First, here are the globals for the DirectSound system:

```
LPDIRECTSOUND  lpds;  // directsound interface pointer
DSBUFFERDESC  dsbd;  // directsound description
DSCAPS    dscaps; // directsound caps
HRESULT    dsresult // general directsound result
DSBCAPS    dsbcaps; // directsound buffer caps

pcm_sound  sound_fx[MAX_SOUNDS]; // array of sound buffers
WAVEFORMATEX  pcmwf; // generic waveformat structure
```

And here are the globals for DirectMusic:

```
// direct music globals
IDirectMusicPerformance  *dm_perf ;  // the directmusic performance manager
IDirectMusicLoader     *dm_loader; // the directmusic loader

// this hold all the directmusic midi objects
DMUSIC_MIDI     dm_midi[DM_NUM_SEGMENTS];
int dm_active_id;  // currently active midi segment
```

NOTE

I have highlighted lines in the arrays that hold sounds and MIDI segments.

You shouldn't have to mess with any of these globals, except to access the interfaces directly if you want. In general, the API will handle everything for you, but the globals are there if you want to tear them up.

There are two parts to the library: DirectSound and DirectMusic. Let's take a look at DirectSound first.

The DirectSound API Wrapper

DirectSound can be complicated or simple, depending on how you use it. If you want a "do it all" API, you're going to end up simply using most of the DirectSound functions themselves. But if you want a simpler API that enables you to initialize DirectSound and load and play sounds of a specific format, that is a lot easier to wrap up in a few functions.

So, what I've done is take much of our work in setting up DirectSound and formalize it into a set of functions for you. In addition, I've created an abstraction around the sound system, so you refer to a sound with an ID (same for the DirectMusic part) that is given to you during the loading process. Thus, you can use this ID to play the sound, check its status, or to terminate it. This way, there aren't any ugly interface pointers that you have to mess with. The new API supports the following functionality:

- Initializing and shutting down DirectSound with single calls
- Loading .WAV files with 11KHz 8-bit mono format
- Playing a loaded sound file
- Stopping a sound
- Testing the play status of a sound
- Changing the volume, playback rate, or stereo panning of a sound
- Deleting sounds from memory

Let's take a look at each function one by one.

> **NOTE**
>
> Unless otherwise stated, all functions return `TRUE` (`1`) if successful and `FALSE` (`0`) if not.

Function Prototype:

```
int DSound_Init(void);
```

Purpose:

`DSound_Init()` is used to initialize the entire DirectSound system. It creates the DirectSound COM object, sets the priority level, and so forth. Just call the function at the beginning of your application if you want to use sound. Here's an example:

Example:

```
if (!DSound_Init(void))
  { /* error */ }
```

Function Prototype:

```
int DSound_Shutdown(void);
```

Purpose:

`DSound_Shutdown()` is used to shut down and release all the COM interfaces created during `DSound_Init()`. However, `DSound_Shutdown()` will not release all the memory allocated to all the sound. You must do this yourself with another function. Anyway, here's how you would shut down DirectSound:

Example:

```
if (!DSound_Shutdown())
  { /* error */ }
```

Function Prototype(s):

```
int DSound_Load_WAV(char *filename);
```

Purpose:

`DSound_Load_WAV()` creates a DirectSound buffer, loads the sound data file into memory, and prepares the sound to be played. The function takes the complete path and filename of the sound file to be loaded (including the extension .WAV) and loads the file off disk. If successful, the function returns a non-negative ID number. You must save this number, because it is used as a handle to reference the sound. If the function can't find the file, or too many sounds are loaded, it will return `-1`. Here's an example of loading a .WAV file named `FIRE.WAV`:

Example:

```
int fire_id = DSound_Load_WAV("FIRE.WAV");

// test for error
if (fire_id==-1)
  { /* error */}
```

Of course, it's up to you on how you want to save the IDs. You might want to use an array or something else.

Finally, you might wonder where the sound data is, and how to mess with it. If you really must, then you can access the data within the `pcm_sound` array `sound_fx[]` using the ID you get back from either load function as the index. For example, here's how you would access the DirectSound buffer for the sound with ID sound_id:

Example:

```
sound_fx[sound_id].dsbuffer
```

Function Prototype:

```
int DSound_Replicate_Sound(int source_id); // id of sound to copy
```

Purpose:

DSound_Replicate_Sound() is used to copy a sound without copying the memory used to hold the sound. For example, suppose you have a gunshot sound, and you want to fire three gunshots, each right after the other? The only way to do this right now would be to load three copies of the gunshot sound into three different DirectSound memory buffers, which would be a waste of memory.

Alas, there is a solution—it's possible to create a duplicate or replicant (if you're a *Blade Runner* fan) of the sound buffer, except for the actual sound data. Instead of copying it, we just point a pointer to it, and DirectSound is smart enough to use it as a "source" for multiple sounds using the same data. The bottom line is, if you want to play a gunshot up to eight times, for example, you should load the gunshot once, make seven copies of it, and acquire a total of eight unique IDs. Replicated sounds work exactly the same as normal sounds, but instead of using DSound_Load_WAV() to load and create them, you copy them with DSound_Replicate_Sound(). Get it? Good! I'm starting to get dizzy! Here's an example of creating eight gunshots:

Example:

```
int gunshot_ids[8]; // this holds all the id's

// load in the master sound
gunshot_ids[0] = Load_WAV("GUNSHOT.WAV");

// now make copies
for (int index=1; index<8; index++)
  gunshot_ids[index] = DSound_Replicate_Sound(gunshot_ids[0]);

// use gunshot_ids[0..7] anyway you which they all go bang!
```

Function Prototype:

```
int DSound_Play_Sound(int id,     // id of sound to play
          int flags=0, // 0 or DSBPLAY_LOOPING
          int volume=0, // unused
          int rate=0,   // unused
          int pan=0);   // unused
```

Purpose:

DSound_Play_Sound() plays a previously loaded sound. You simply send the ID of the sound along with the play flags—0 for a single time, or DSBPLAY_LOOPING to loop it, and the sound will start playing. If the sound is already playing, it will restart at the beginning. Here's an example of loading and playing a sound:

Example:

```
int fire_id = DSound_Load_WAV("FIRE.WAV");
DSound_Play_Sound(fire_id,0);
```

I could have also left out the 0 for flags entirely, because its default parameter is 0:

```
int fire_id = DSound_Load_WAV("FIRE.WAV");
DSound_Play_Sound(fire_id);
```

Either way, the FIRE.WAV sound will play once and then stop. To make it loop, you would send DSBPLAY_LOOPING for the flags parameter.

Function Prototype(s):

```
int DSound_Stop_Sound(int id);
int DSound_Stop_All_Sounds(void);
```

Purpose:

DSound_Stop_Sound() is used to stop a single sound from playing (if it is playing). You simply send the ID of the sound, and that's it. DSound_Stop_All_Sounds() will stop all the sounds currently playing. Here's an example of stopping the fire_id sound:

Example:

```
DSound_Stop_Sound(fire_id);
```

At the end of your program, it's a good idea to stop all the sounds from playing before exiting. You could do this with separate calls to DSound_Stop_Sound() for each sound, or a single call to DSound_Stop_All_Sounds():

```
//...system shutdown code
DSound_Stop_All_Sounds();
```

Function Prototype:

```
int DSound_Delete_Sound(int id); // id of sound to delete
int DSound_Delete_All_Sounds(void);
```

Purpose:

DSound_Delete_Sound() deletes a sound from memory and releases the DirectSound buffer associated with it. If the sound is playing, the function will stop it first. DSound_Delete_All_Sounds() deletes all previously loaded sounds. Here's an example of deleting the fire_id sound:

Example:

```
DSound_Delete_Sound(fire_id);
```

Function Prototype:

```
int DSound_Status_Sound(int id);
```

Purpose:

DSound_Status_Sound() tests the status of a loaded sound based on its ID. All you do is pass the function the ID number of the sound, and the function will return one of these values:

- DSBSTATUS_LOOPING—The sound is currently playing and is in loop mode.
- DSBSTATUS_PLAYING—The sound is currently playing and is in single play mode.

If the value returned from DSound_Status_Sound() is neither of the preceding constants, the sound is not playing. Here's a complete example that waits until a sound has completed playing and then deletes it.

Example:

```
// initialize DirectSound
DSound_DSound_Init();

// load a sound
int fire_id = DSound_Load_WAV("FIRE.WAV");

// play the sound in single mode
DSound_Play_Sound(fire_id);

// wait until the sound is done
while(DSound_Sound_Status(fire_id) &
       (DSBSTATUS_LOOPING | DSBSTATUS_PLAYING));

// delete the sound
DSound_Delete_Sound(fire_id);
```

```
// shutdown DirectSound
DSound_DSound_Shutdown();
```

Pretty cool, huh? A lot better than the couple hundred or so lines of code to do it manually with DirectSound!

Function Prototype:

```
int DSound_Set_Sound_Volume(int id,  // id of sound
          int vol); // volume from 0-100
```

Purpose:

`DSound_Set_Sound_Volume()` changes the volume of a sound in real time. Send the ID of the sound along with a value from 0–100 and the sound will change instantly. Here's an example of changing the volume of a sound to 50% of what it was loaded as:

Example:

```
DSound_Set_Sound_Volume(fire_id, 50);
```

You can always change the volume back to 100% like this:

```
DSound_Set_Sound_Volume(fire_id, 100);
```

Function Prototype:

```
int DSound_Set_Sound_Freq(
        int id,  // sound id
        int freq); // new playback rate from 0-100000
```

Purpose:

`DSound_Set_Sound_Freq()` changes the playback frequency of the sound. Because all sounds must be loaded at 11KHz mono, here's how you would double the perceived playback rate:

Example:

```
DSound_Set_Sound_Freq(fire_id, 22050);
```

And to make you sound like Darth Vader, do this:

```
DSound_Set_Sound_Freq(fire_id, 6000);
```

Function Prototype:

```
int DSound_Set_Sound_Pan(
  int id,  // sound id
  int pan); // panning value from -10000 to 10000
```

Purpose:

`DSound_Set_Sound_Pan()` sets the relative intensity of the sound on the right and left speakers. A value of -10,000 is hard left and 10,000 is hard right. If you want equal power, set the pan to `0`. Here's how you would set the pan all the way to the right side:

Example:

```
DSound_Set_Sound_Pan(fire_id, 10000);
```

The DirectMusic API Rapper

Did you get my joke with the title? The DirectMusic API is even simpler than the DirectSound API. I have created functions to initialize DirectMusic, create all the COM objects for you, and enable you to focus on loading and playing MIDI files. Here's the basic functionality list:

- Initialize and shut down DirectMusic with single calls
- Load MIDI files off disk
- Play a MIDI file
- Stop a MIDI that is currently playing
- Test the play status of a MIDI segment
- Automatically connect to DirectSound if DirectSound has previously been initialized
- Delete MIDI segments from memory

Let's take a look at each function one by one.

> **NOTE**
>
> Unless otherwise stated, all functions return `TRUE` (1) if successful, and `FALSE` (`0`) if not.

Function Prototype:

```
int DMusic_Init(void);
```

Purpose:

`Dmusic_Init()` initializes DirectMusic and creates all necessary COM objects. You make this call before any other calls to the DirectMusic library. In addition, if you want to use DirectSound, make sure to initialize DirectSound before calling `DMusic_Init()`. Here's an example of using the function:

Example:

```
if (!DMusic_Init())
  { /* error */ }
```

Function Prototype:

```
int DMusic_Shutdown(void);
```

Purpose:

`DMusic_Shutdown()` shuts down the entire DirectMusic engine. It releases all COM objects, in addition to unloading all loaded MIDI segments. Call this function at the end of your application, but before the call to shutdown DirectSound—if you have DirectSound support. Here's an example:

Example:

```
if (!DMusic_Shutdown())
  { /* error */ }

// now shutdown DirectSound…
```

Function Prototype:

```
int DMusic_Load_MIDI(char *filename);
```

Purpose:

`DMusic_Load_MIDI()` loads a MIDI segment into memory and allocates a record in the `midi_ids[]` array. The function returns the ID of the loaded MIDI segment, or `-1` if not successful. The returned ID is used as a reference for all other calls. Here's an example of loading a couple of MIDI files:

Example:

```
// load files
int explode_id = DMusic_Load_MIDI("explosion.mid");
int weapon_id = DMusic_Load_MIDI("laser.mid");

// test files
if (explode_id == -1 || weapon_id == -1)
  { /* there was a problem */ }
```

Function Prototype:

```
int DMusic_Delete_MIDI(int id);
```

Purpose:

`DMusic_Delete_MIDI()` deletes a previously loaded MIDI segment from the system. Simply supply the ID to delete. Here's an example of deleting the previously loaded MIDI files in the preceding example:

Example:

```
if (!DMusic_Delete_MIDI(explode_id) ||
  !DMusic_Delete_MIDI(weapon_id) )
{ /* error */ }
```

Function Prototype:

```
int DMusic_Delete_All_MIDI(void);
```

Purpose:

`DMusic_Delete_All_MIDI()` simply deletes all MIDI segments from the system in one call. Here's an example:

Example:

```
// delete both of our segments
if (!DMusic_Delete_All_MIDI())
  { /* error */ }
```

Function Prototype:

```
int DMusic_Play(int id);
```

Purpose:

`DMusic_Play()` plays a MIDI segment from the beginning. Simply supply the ID of the segment you want to play. Here's an example:

Example:

```
// load file
int explode_id = DMusic_Load_MIDI("explosion.mid");

// play it
if (!DMusic_Play(explode_id))
  { /* error */ }
```

Function Prototype:

```
int DMusic_Stop(int id);
```

Purpose:

DMusic_Stop() stops a currently playing segment. If the segment is already stopped, the function has no effect. Here's an example:

Example:

```
// stop the laser blast
if (!DMusic_Stop(weapon_id))
  { /* error */ }
```

Function Prototype:

```
int DMusic_Status_MIDI(int id);
```

Purpose:

DMusic_Status() tests the status of any MIDI segment based on its ID. The status codes are as follows:

```
#define MIDI_NULL    0  // this midi object is not loaded
#define MIDI_LOADED  1  // this midi object is loaded
#define MIDI_PLAYING 2  // this midi object is loaded and playing
#define MIDI_STOPPED 3  // this midi object is loaded, but stopped
```

Here's an example of changing state based on a MIDI segment completing:

Example:

```
// main game loop
while(1)
   {
   if (DMusic_Status(explode_id) == MIDI_STOPPED)
    game_state = GAME_MUSIC_OVER;

   } // end while
```

That's it for the DirectSound and DirectMusic APIs. As I said, later in the chapter you will see demo examples of both, but for now, let's continue with putting together the final T3D Game Console and bring our virtual computer interface all together in one glorious ...Whoooaaa! I'm getting a little carried away here. I'm mean, let's finish up.

The T3DLIB Library at a Glance

At this point, we have three main .CPP|H modules that make up the T3D library:

- T3DLIB1.CPP¦H—DirectDraw plus graphics algorithms
- T3DLIB2.CPP¦H—DirectInput
- T3DLIB3.CPP¦H—DirectSound & DirectMusic

Keep this in mind when compiling programs. If you want to compile a demo program, call it `DEMOX_Y.CPP`, and then look at its .H includes. If you see it include any of the preceding related .H library modules, you'll obviously need to include the .CPP files, too.

To compile any of the programs, make sure to include both the library source files, as well as all the DirectX .LIB files—and please, for the sake of God, set your compiler to Win32 .EXE as the target!

Building the Final T3D Game Console

At this point, we have more than enough to implement our virtual graphics interface, including support for sound and input. Moreover, the virtual interface model can almost be implemented one-to-one with the data structures, globals, and functions you just reviewed that make up the three `T3DLIB` library modules from the first *Tricks*. Remember, our goal was to implement a double-buffered graphics system that supports 8- and 16-bit windowed and full-screen graphics, and that models our virtual computer interfaces functionality. We have exactly what we need to do that now.

The next step is to create a really solid Game Console "template" based on the alpha version we made a few sections back. However, before we go there, let's take a moment to look at the functionality of the virtual graphics interface, and the exact mapping to the real graphics interface in `T3DLIB1.CPP`. The sound and music stuff is much easier to grasp, so I'm not going to show the mapping. Moreover, the demos that follow in the final sections of this chapter have numerous examples of sound, music, and input, so you can see the functions in real programs. Even so, taking a look at the graphics part is worth the work, so let's do it.

Mapping the Real Graphics to the Unreal Graphics of the Virtual Interface

Earlier in this chapter, we went through a mental experiment and came up with the most generic graphics interface that we could think of as the minimum necessary to perform software-based 3D graphics on any computer. Now, with the tools of the libraries at hand, let's take a look at what the final mappings are from virtual to real.

Starting the System

In the virtual computer's graphics interface, we assumed that there was a function called `Create_Window()` with the prototype

```
Create_Window(int width, int height, int bit_depth);
```

that would take care of all the details of getting the graphics system ready, along with opening a window of the desired size and bit depth. In our real implementation, this functionality has to be split into two function calls, because we want to try and keep windows and DirectX separate. The first function calls are standard Windows calls to create a standard Windows window.

Now, listen up: If you are creating a full-screen application, you should use the window flags of WM_POPUP, but if you want a windowed application, you should use something like WM_OVERLAPPEDWINDOW. Hence, getting the graphics system ready is a two-step process:

1. Make a call to the Win32 API function Create_Window() with the appropriate parameters for either a full-screen window or a windowed application. With a full-screen window, you don't usually want any controls.

2. Call the DirectX wrapper function, along with the handle to the window (which is global) and the appropriate parameters to finish the job.

All the action really happens during step 2. This is where DirectDraw is initialized, the frame buffers are created, the palette for 8-bit modes is generated, and the clippers are attached to the graphics window and back buffer.

Because we are going to use the Game Console template, the plan of attack is to let the WinMain() function open the window up, and then in the call to Game_Init(), make a call to the function DDraw_Init(), which does all the dirty work. If you recall, here's its prototype:

```
int DDraw_Init(int width, int height, int bpp, int windowed=0);
```

Simple, huh? Well, just look inside the code to really appreciate all it does. Anyway, to recap, the single call in our virtual computer interface to create a window (in fantasy land) was Create_Window(). In real life, we need two calls to implement this functionality: one to create a Windows window, and the second to initialize DirectDraw and connect it to the window.

Global Mappings

The first things that we designed into our virtual graphics interface were two frame buffers: one visible, and one offscreen. We called these the primary and secondary (back) buffers, as shown in Figure 3.12.

Additionally, we agreed that for any given resolution and bit depth, these buffers would be linearly addressable, with the one constraint that the memory pitch to jump from line to line might not be the same as the pixel pitch, and that there would be variables to track this. The names of the virtual frame buffer pointers and the pitch variables were as follows:

```
UCHAR *primary_buffer; // the primary buffer
int  primary_pitch; // the memory pitch in bytes

UCHAR *secondary_buffer; // the secondary buffer
int  seconday_pitch;  // the memory pitch in bytes
```

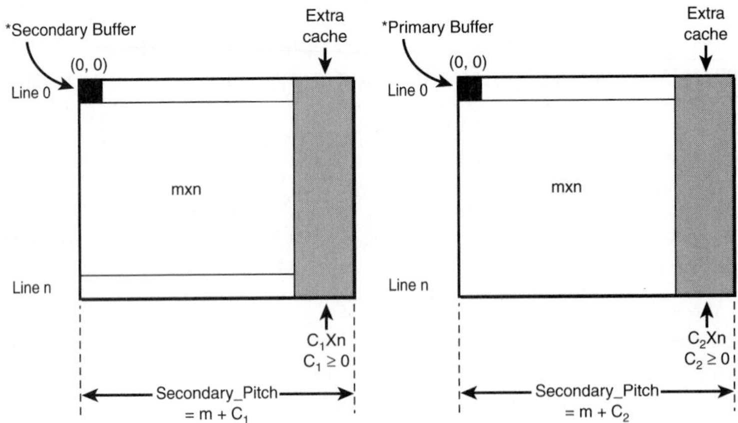

FIGURE 3.12 The frame buffers.

In the real graphics library under `T3DLIB1.CPP`, there is almost an identical mapping. The variables that serve the same purpose are as follows:

```
LPDIRECTDRAWSURFACE7 lpddsprimary;    // dd primary surface
LPDIRECTDRAWSURFACE7 lpddsback;     // dd back surface

UCHAR        *primary_buffer; // primary video buffer
UCHAR        *back_buffer;   // secondary back buffer
int         primary_lpitch;  // memory line pitch
int         back_lpitch;   // memory line pitch
```

You'll notice two extra DirectX-centric variables: `lpddsprimary` and `lpddsback`. These are DirectDraw surface pointers to both the primary and secondary (back) surfaces. They are needed for some calls, and hence you should know them. Additionally, the width and height of the primary and secondary buffers are always the same. Although the primary buffer's client area might only be a window and not the entire desktop, the secondary buffer will *always* be the same size as the client area. Bottom line—the visible primary frame buffer and the invisible secondary frame buffer are always the same size and bit depth.

256-Color Modes

Although you saw the 256-color palette manipulation functions in the graphics API listing of `T3DLIB1.CPP|H`, I just wanted to reinforce them. The functions that enable you to manipulate the palette are as follows:

```
int Set_Palette_Entry(int color_index, LPPALETTEENTRY color);
int Get_Palette_Entry(int color_index, LPPALETTEENTRY color);
int Load_Palette_From_File(char *filename, LPPALETTEENTRY palette);
```

```
int Save_Palette_To_File(char *filename, LPPALETTEENTRY palette);
int Save_Palette(LPPALETTEENTRY sav_palette);
int Set_Palette(LPPALETTEENTRY set_palette);
```

I have highlighted the functions of most interest. They are used to alter a single palette entry, or the entire palette at once. In most cases, it's inefficient to change one palette entry at a time. It's better to make all the changes at once. The data structure you pass is either a pointer to a single PALETTENTRY or to an array of them. Here's the PALETTENTRY data structure to refresh your memory:

```
typedef struct tagPALETTEENTRY { // pe
  BYTE peRed;   // red channel 8-bits
  BYTE peGreen; // green channel 8-bits
  BYTE peBlue;  // blue channel 8-bits
  BYTE peFlags; // flags control, PC_EXPLICIT for the first and last 10
          // colors if windowed mode, else use PC_NOCOLLAPSE
} PALETTEENTRY;
```

Finally, if you do select a 256-color mode, the palette data in PALDATA2.PAL will be loaded. This is a palette that I like to use, and it has good color space coverage. You can take a look at it by opening PALDATA2.BMP. Of course, you can always load your own 256-color palette off disk or from a bitmap's attached palette.

Locking/Unlocking Function Mappings

Alright, everything is looking good. Now let's take a look at the four functions we made up to lock/unlock the primary and secondary surfaces. In the virtual computer interface, they looked like this:

```
Lock_Primary(UCHAR **primary_buffer, int *primary_pitch);
Unlock_Primary(UCHAR *primary_buffer);

Lock_Secondary(UCHAR **secondary _buffer, int *secondary _pitch);
Unlock_Secondary(UCHAR *secondary _buffer);
```

In the real graphics library, we have these functions that implement that functionality:

```
UCHAR *DDraw_Lock_Primary_Surface(void);
int DDraw_Unlock_Primary_Surface(void);

UCHAR *DDraw_Lock_Back_Surface(void);
int DDraw_Unlock_Back_Surface(void);
```

The only difference is that the real functions alter the globals

```
UCHAR *primary_buffer;    // primary video buffer
UCHAR *back_buffer;       // secondary back buffer
int  primary_lpitch;      // memory line pitch
int  back_lpitch;        // memory line pitch
```

directly, and hence don't need any parameters.

Animation Function Mapping

The last function that I want to mention the mapping for is the animation function that flips the secondary surface buffer to the primary (or copies it in some cases). If you remember, we called it `Flip_Display()` in the virtual computer software interface model. This function is what makes smooth animation possible. In the real library, the function that does the job is

```
int DDraw_Flip(void);
```

Nothing more than a different name, really. The functionality of the desired virtual model is exactly implemented in this function. `DDraw_Flip()` will work perfectly for both full-screen and windowed applications.

Well, that's it for the function mapping of the virtual computer model with our real functions. I just wanted you to really understand what we are trying to do—create a generic graphics system with an API that we have handy that abstracts the graphics rendering enough that we only think in terms of two frame buffers and a few functions. I really hate dumping an API on you, but my hands are tied (all eight of them), and I had to use something to implement the virtual computer interface for which we had the source.

The Final `T3DLIB` Game Console

Now we're finally ready to see the complete Game Console that we are going to use to create all of the demos and game programs from here on out. Of course, we might add to it, but for the most part what you are about to see captures all the functionality we need. The upgraded Game Console is named `T3DCONSOLE2.CPP`. Its source is shown in the following.

> **NOTE**
>
> You might be wondering what happened to `T3DCONSOLE.CPP¦EXE`. In the first *Tricks*, I created `T3DCONSOLE.CPP¦EXE`, so it only seems appropriate to append a "2" onto the new version, because this book is really a continuation of the previous *Tricks* and we want to keep our naming conventions consistent.

```
// T3DCONSOLE2.CPP - First template for Tricks 3D Vol II
// Use this as a template for your applications if you wish
// you may want to change things like the resolution of the
```

```
// application, if it's windowed, the directinput devices
// that are acquired and so forth...
// currently the app creates a 640x480x16 windowed display
// hence, you must be in 16 bit color before running the application
// if you want fullscreen mode then simple change the WINDOWED_APP
// value in the #defines below value to FALSE (0). Similarly, if
// you want another bitdepth, maybe 8-bit for 256 colors then
// change that in the call to DDraw_Init() in the function
// Game_Init() within this file.


// READ THIS!
// To compile make sure to include DDRAW.LIB, DSOUND.LIB, DINPUT.LIB,
// DINPUT8.LIB, WINMM.LIB in the project link list, and of course
// the C++ source modules T3DLIB1.CPP,T3DLIB2.CPP, and T3DLIB3.CPP
// and the headers T3DLIB1.H,T3DLIB2.H, and T3DLIB3.H must
// be in the working directory of the compiler

// INCLUDES ///////////////////////////////////////////////

#define INITGUID    // make sure al the COM interfaces are available
            // instead of this you can include the .LIB file
            // DXGUID.LIB

#define WIN32_LEAN_AND_MEAN

#include <windows.h>  // include important windows stuff
#include <windowsx.h>
#include <mmsystem.h>
#include <iostream.h> // include important C/C++ stuff
#include <conio.h>
#include <stdlib.h>
#include <malloc.h>
#include <memory.h>
#include <string.h>
#include <stdarg.h>
#include <stdio.h>
#include <math.h>
#include <io.h>
#include <fcntl.h>

#include <ddraw.h> // directX includes
#include <dsound.h>
```

3

```
#include <dmksctrl.h>
#include <dmusici.h>
#include <dmusicc.h>
#include <dmusicf.h>
#include <dinput.h>
#include "T3DLIB1.h" // game library includes
#include "T3DLIB2.h"
#include "T3DLIB3.h"

// DEFINES ////////////////////////////////////////////////

// defines for windows interface
#define WINDOW_CLASS_NAME "WIN3DCLASS" // class name
#define WINDOW_TITLE   "T3D Graphics Console Ver 2.0"
#define WINDOW_WIDTH   640  // size of window
#define WINDOW_HEIGHT   480

#define WINDOW_BPP    16  // bitdepth of window (8,16,24 etc.)
                // note: if windowed and not
                // fullscreen then bitdepth must
                // be same as system bitdepth
                // also if 8-bit the a pallete
                // is created and attached

#define WINDOWED_APP   1   // 0 not windowed, 1 windowed

// PROTOTYPES /////////////////////////////////////////////

// game console
int Game_Init(void *parms=NULL);
int Game_Shutdown(void *parms=NULL);
int Game_Main(void *parms=NULL);

// GLOBALS ////////////////////////////////////////////////

HWND main_window_handle      = NULL; // save the window handle
HINSTANCE main_instance      = NULL; // save the instance
char buffer[256];             // used to print text



// FUNCTIONS //////////////////////////////////////////////
```

```
LRESULT CALLBACK WindowProc(HWND hwnd,
              UINT msg,
              WPARAM wparam,
              LPARAM lparam)
{
// this is the main message handler of the system
PAINTSTRUCT  ps;    // used in WM_PAINT
HDC    hdc;    // handle to a device context

// what is the message
switch(msg)
  {
  case WM_CREATE:
    {
  // do initialization stuff here
  return(0);
  } break;

  case WM_PAINT:
     {
     // start painting
     hdc = BeginPaint(hwnd,&ps);

     // end painting
     EndPaint(hwnd,&ps);
     return(0);
    } break;

  case WM_DESTROY:
    {
    // kill the application
    PostQuitMessage(0);
    return(0);
    } break;

  default:break;

  } // end switch

// process any messages that we didn't take care of
return (DefWindowProc(hwnd, msg, wparam, lparam));

} // end WinProc
```

```
// WINMAIN ////////////////////////////////////////////////

int WINAPI WinMain(  HINSTANCE hinstance,
      HINSTANCE hprevinstance,
      LPSTR lpcmdline,
      int ncmdshow)
{
// this is the winmain function

WNDCLASS winclass; // this will hold the class we create
HWND   hwnd;      // generic window handle
MSG    msg;      // generic message
HDC    hdc;     // generic dc
PAINTSTRUCT ps;   // generic paintstruct

// first fill in the window class stucture
winclass.style  = CS_DBLCLKS | CS_OWNDC | CS_HREDRAW | CS_VREDRAW;
winclass.lpfnWndProc  = WindowProc;
winclass.cbClsExtra  = 0;
winclass.cbWndExtra  = 0;
winclass.hInstance  = hinstance;
winclass.hIcon    = LoadIcon(NULL, IDI_APPLICATION);
winclass.hCursor  = LoadCursor(NULL, IDC_ARROW);
winclass.hbrBackground  = (HBRUSH)GetStockObject(BLACK_BRUSH);
winclass.lpszMenuName  = NULL;
winclass.lpszClassName  = WINDOW_CLASS_NAME;

// register the window class
if (!RegisterClass(&winclass))
  return(0);

// create the window, note the test to see if WINDOWED_APP is
// true to select the appropriate window flags
if (!(hwnd = CreateWindow(WINDOW_CLASS_NAME, // class
       WINDOW_TITLE,   // title
       (WINDOWED_APP ? (WS_OVERLAPPED | WS_SYSMENU | WS_CAPTION) :
             (WS_POPUP | WS_VISIBLE)),
        0,0,    // x,y
        WINDOW_WIDTH, // width
             WINDOW_HEIGHT, // height
        NULL,    // handle to parent
       NULL,    // handle to menu
       hinstance,// instance
```

```
       NULL))) // creation parms
return(0);

// save the window handle and instance in a global
main_window_handle = hwnd;
main_instance   = hinstance;

// resize the window so that client is really width x height
if (WINDOWED_APP)
{
// now resize the window, so the client area is the actual size requested
// since there may be borders
// alsocontrols if this is going to be a windowed app
// if the app is not windowed then it won't matter
RECT window_rect = {0,0,WINDOW_WIDTH-1,WINDOW_HEIGHT-1};

// make the call to adjust window_rect
AdjustWindowRectEx(&window_rect,
   GetWindowStyle(main_window_handle),
   GetMenu(main_window_handle) != NULL,
   GetWindowExStyle(main_window_handle));

// save the global client offsets, they are needed in DDraw_Flip()
window_client_x0 = -window_rect.left;
window_client_y0 = -window_rect.top;

// now resize the window with a call to MoveWindow()
MoveWindow(main_window_handle,
      0, // x position
      0, // y position
      window_rect.right - window_rect.left, // width
      window_rect.bottom - window_rect.top, // height
      FALSE);

// show the window, so there's no garbage on first render
ShowWindow(main_window_handle, SW_SHOW);
} // end if windowed

// perform all game console specific initialization
Game_Init();

// disable CTRL-ALT_DEL, ALT_TAB, comment this line out
// if it causes your system to crash
SystemParametersInfo(SPI_SCREENSAVERRUNNING, TRUE, NULL, 0);
```

```
// enter main event loop
while(1)
   {
   if (PeekMessage(&msg,NULL,0,0,PM_REMOVE))
    {
  // test if this is a quit
    if (msg.message == WM_QUIT)
      break;

  // translate any accelerator keys
  TranslateMessage(&msg);

  // send the message to the window proc
  DispatchMessage(&msg);
  } // end if

    // main game processing goes here
    Game_Main();

   } // end while

// shutdown game and release all resources
Game_Shutdown();

// enable CTRL-ALT_DEL, ALT_TAB, comment this line out
// if it causes your system to crash
SystemParametersInfo(SPI_SCREENSAVERRUNNING, FALSE, NULL, 0);

// return to Windows like this
return(msg.wParam);

} // end WinMain

// T3D II GAME PROGRAMMING CONSOLE FUNCTIONS ////////////////

int Game_Init(void *parms)
{
// this function is where you do all the initialization
// for your game

// start up DirectDraw (replace the parms as you desire)
DDraw_Init(WINDOW_WIDTH, WINDOW_HEIGHT, WINDOW_BPP, WINDOWED_APP);
```

```
// initialize directinput
DInput_Init();

// acquire the keyboard
DInput_Init_Keyboard();

// add calls to acquire other directinput devices here...


// initialize directsound and directmusic
DSound_Init();
DMusic_Init();

// hide the mouse
ShowCursor(FALSE);

// seed random number generator
srand(Start_Clock());

// all your initialization code goes here...


// return success
return(1);

} // end Game_Init

///////////////////////////////////////////////////////////

int Game_Shutdown(void *parms)
{
// this function is where you shutdown your game and
// release all resources that you allocated

// shut everything down

// release all your resources created for the game here....


// now directsound
DSound_Stop_All_Sounds();
DSound_Delete_All_Sounds();
DSound_Shutdown();
```

```
// directmusic
DMusic_Delete_All_MIDI();
DMusic_Shutdown();

// release all input devices
DInput_Release_Keyboard();

// shut down directinput
DInput_Shutdown();

// shutdown directdraw last
DDraw_Shutdown();

// return success
return(1);
} // end Game_Shutdown

//////////////////////////////////////////////////////////

int Game_Main(void *parms)
{
// this is the workhorse of your game it will be called
// continuously in real-time this is like main() in C
// all the calls for you game go here!

int index; // looping var

// start the timing clock
Start_Clock();

// clear the drawing surface
DDraw_Fill_Surface(lpddsback, 0);

// read keyboard and other devices here
DInput_Read_Keyboard();

// game logic here...



// flip the surfaces
DDraw_Flip();
```

```
// sync to 30ish fps
Wait_Clock(30);

// check of user is trying to exit
if (KEY_DOWN(VK_ESCAPE) || keyboard_state[DIK_ESCAPE])
  {
  PostMessage(main_window_handle, WM_DESTROY,0,0);

  } // end if

// return success
return(1);

} // end Game_Main
```


Let's take a look at some of the key points of the Game Console, and then we'll move on to using it. First, you'll notice that some of the code is highlighted in bold to indicate important code sections. Let's take a look at what does what.

Opening the Game Console Window

The first lines of code that are highlighted are in the `#defines` section:

```
#define WINDOW_WIDTH   640  // size of window
#define WINDOW_HEIGHT   480

#define WINDOW_BPP     16  // bitdepth of window (8,16,24 etc.)
                // note: if windowed and not
                // fullscreen then bitdepth must
                // be same as system bitdepth
                // also if 8-bit the a palette
                // is created and attached

#define WINDOWED_APP   1    // 0 not windowed, 1 windowed
```

These are very important because they control the size of the window (or full-screen size), the bit depth, and whether you want a windowed display rather than full screen. Currently, I have them set to 640×480 for the window size, 16-bits per pixel, and a windowed display. These parameters are used in a number of places in the code. However, the two most important are when the window is created in `WinMain()` along with the call to `DDraw_Init()` in `Game_Main()`. Let's talk about the call in `WinMain()` first.

If you take a look at the `Create_Window()` call in `WinMain()` (copied in the following fragment for your convenience), you will notice that there is a ternary conditional operator that tests whether the application is windowed.

```
// create the window, note the test to see if WINDOWED_APP is
// true to select the appropriate window flags
if (!(hwnd = CreateWindow(WINDOW_CLASS_NAME, // class
       WINDOW_TITLE,    // title
       (WINDOWED_APP ? (WS_OVERLAPPED ¦ WS_SYSMENU ¦ WS_CAPTION) :
            (WS_POPUP ¦ WS_VISIBLE)),
        0,0,     // x,y
        WINDOW_WIDTH, // width
            WINDOW_HEIGHT, // height
        NULL,     // handle to parent
       NULL,     // handle to menu
       hinstance,// instance
       NULL)))  // creation parms
return(0);
```

This is so the window is created with the proper Windows flag. If we want a windowed display, we want to see the window borders and have a couple of controls such as a close box, so the Window flags (WM_OVERLAPPED ¦ WM_SYSMENU ¦WS_CAPTION) are used.

On the other hand, if the code selects a full-screen mode, the window is made the same size as the DirectDraw surface, but with no controls; hence the window style WM_POPUP is used. Additionally, once the window is created (either in preparation for a windowed application or full-screen) the next section of code is rather tricky. It basically resizes the window so that the client area is the size that we are requesting, rather than the size we are requesting minus the size of the border and controls.

If you recall from Windows programming, when you create a window with size WINDOW_WIDTH x WINDOW_HEIGHT, it doesn't mean the client area will be WINDOW_WIDTH x WINDOW_HEIGHT. It means the window's entire area will be WINDOW_WIDTH x WINDOW_HEIGHT. Therefore, if there are no controls or borders, the client area *will be* WINDOW_WIDTH x WINDOW_HEIGHT, but if there are controls, we lose a little, as shown in Figure 3.13.

To solve this problem, we need to resize the window on the fly so that the size of the client area is the exact size that we are requesting for the window. Here's the code that does this:

```
// resize the window so that client is really width x height
if (WINDOWED_APP)
{
// now resize the window, so the client area is the actual size requested
// since there may be borders and controls if this is going to be a windowed app
// if the app is not windowed then it won't matter
RECT window_rect = {0,0,WINDOW_WIDTH-1,WINDOW_HEIGHT-1};

// make the call to adjust window_rect
AdjustWindowRectEx(&window_rect,
```

```
   GetWindowStyle(main_window_handle),
   GetMenu(main_window_handle) != NULL,
   GetWindowExStyle(main_window_handle));

// save the global client offsets, they are needed in DDraw_Flip()
window_client_x0 = -window_rect.left;
window_client_y0 = -window_rect.top;

// now resize the window with a call to MoveWindow()
MoveWindow(main_window_handle,
      0, // x position
      0, // y position
      window_rect.right - window_rect.left, // width
      window_rect.bottom - window_rect.top, // height
      FALSE);

// show the window, so there's no garbage on first render
ShowWindow(main_window_handle, SW_SHOW);
} // end if windowed
```

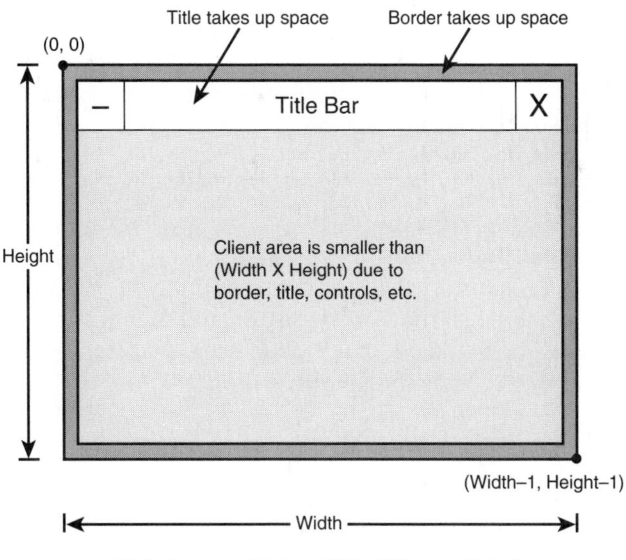

FIGURE 3.13 Total window area compared to client area.

There are a couple of other ways to do this, but this is the one I usually use. Another way is to know what controls you have, query Windows for the size of the controls, and then compute the size the window should be with the controls. Whatever way you do it, just make sure that if a windowed app is selected, the client area is exactly WINDOW_WIDTH x WINDOW_HEIGHT.

> **NOTE**
>
> If you set WINDOWED_APP to 0, this logic isn't executed, because a WM_POPUP window has no controls and we don't need to resize.

After the window is created and resized (if needed), at some point a call to Game_Init() is made. Within it you will add all your logic and initialization in the future. However, at this point, it has the bare minimum to get things going. In line with our discussion, a call to DDraw_Init() is made:

```
// start up DirectDraw (replace the parms as you desire)
DDraw_Init(WINDOW_WIDTH, WINDOW_HEIGHT, WINDOW_BPP, WINDOWED_APP);
```

You will notice that you don't have to do anything. Just make sure to set the #defines up at the top of the file to what you want and whammo—you're Kid Rock!

> **NOTE**
>
> You might notice those calls to SystemParametersInfo() around the main event loop. These calls make Windows think that the screensaver is on, and to ignore ALT+TAB. DirectX applications can get really mangled if you don't handle ALT+TAB-ing correctly (which we don't), so this way you hopefully don't have to worry about it. If you're interested, take a look at the DirectX SDK, but in general when your application loses focus, you have to restore all lost surfaces and reacquire all input devices and so on. It's a real pain!

Using and Compiling the Game Console

Basically T3DCONSOLE2.CPP is just a "shell" or template that you will use to create applications. You can use it to handle all the Windows stuff, and then just drop your code into the game functions Game_Init(), Game_Main(), and Game_Shutdown(). However, to compile it, you still need to include the following files:

- T3DLIB1.CPP¦H—The DirectDraw module
- T3DLIB2.CPP¦H—The DirectInput module
- T3DLIB3.CPP¦H—The DirectSound and DirectMusic module

These files must be in your root:

- PALDATA1¦2.PAL—The default palettes for 256-color mode

And you must, of course, link with

- DDRAW.LIB, DSOUND.LIB, DINPUT.LIB, and DINPUT8.LIB

Please set the compiler target to `Win32 .EXE application`. Don't forget to add the DirectX .LIB files to the link list, and to set the search paths for the compiler to find all the headers.

Just for fun, I have compiled the Game Console without anything in it, creating the `T3DCONSOLE2.EXE`. The application doesn't do much, but creates a 640×480×16-bit windowed display. However, to run it you must have your desktop in 16-bit mode.

CAUTION

Windowed applications based on the Game Console will *not* change the bit depth of the desktop. You can alter it to do this if you want, but it can be catastrophic. Here's why: If you have other applications running and you then start up a DirectDraw application that changes the bit depth of the screen, but creates a windowed display rather than a full-screen display, the other application might function improperly and/or crash the system if you switch focus to it. As a rule of thumb for full-screen applications, do what you will with resolution and bit depth. But for windowed applications, you might want to test for the bit depth and see whether it meets your target before starting your application and letting the user switch the desktop.

I could have just as easily made the application a full-screen 640×480×16 application with a single change to the `#defines`:

```
#define WINDOWED_APP   0    // 0 not windowed, 1 windowed
```

However, windowed applications are more fun and a little easier to debug, so I am supporting them heavily in this book. Nevertheless, when your game is finally ready to run, I suggest dumping the system into full-screen mode.

Sample T3LIB Applications

We are almost done with this chapter—whoooweee! I'm getting sick of this stuff—I'm dying to get to the 3D part! Anyway, just to be complete, what I want to do now is show you a number of sample applications that use the Game Console `T3DCONSOLE2.CPP` as the starting point for real demos that show off graphics, sound, music, and input. The demos are going to actually *do something*, because I am hijacking them from the first *Tricks*. However, they are all updated now. This way, you can see some real examples of using the console template. However, note that the sound and music demos are less glamorous, and don't really need much.

Lastly, as we proceed through the book and build the `T3DLIB` game engine, we will add modules `T3DLIB4`, `5`, `6`, and so forth each chapter or so.

Windowed Applications

As it stands, the `T3DCONSOLE2.CPP` is really a demonstration of windowed 16-bit applications, but I always like to see something with a little more girth to it—don't you?

Therefore, I converted one of the artificial intelligence demos from the first *Tricks* (pattern systems demo) to 16-bit and put it in a window. The name of the program on the CD is DEMOII3_1.CPP¦EXE and a screenshot is shown in Figure 3.14. To run the program, make sure the desktop is in 16-bit color mode. Also, if you want to compile it, make sure you include all the library modules!

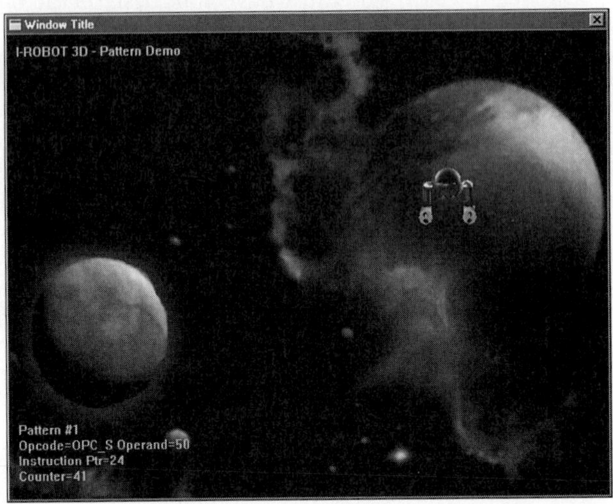

FIGURE 3.14 A screenshot of a windowed application AI demo.

In any case, the demo not only shows off 16-bit windowed mode, but it shows how to load bitmaps, use the BOB library, make sounds, and a lot more all in 16-bit graphics mode. Lots to learn by studying the code.

Full-Screen Applications

Writing a full-screen application is no different with our library; in fact, it's better because there is less chance of resource sharing problems. Moreover, in 256-color modes, you have full control over the entire palette, rather than losing access to the first and last ten entries, as with windowed 256-color modes. Additionally, you can switch into any bit depth and resolution with full-screen modes and not worry about the desktop.

As a demo of a full-screen application, I have taken one of the 256-color physics demos from the first *Tricks* and worked it into our new Game Console template. The name of the program is DEMOII3_2.CPP¦EXE. Figure 3.15 shows a screenshot of the program in action. This program again illustrates the use of bitmaps, BOBs, and palettized 256-color modes.

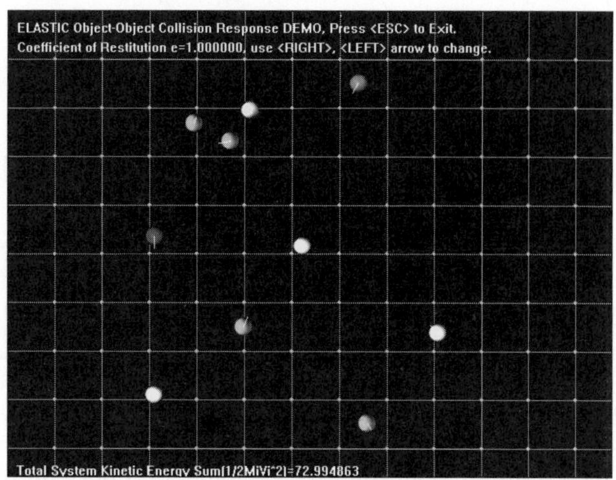

FIGURE 3.15 A screenshot of a 256-color, full-screen physics demo.

Sound and Music

Working with sound and music under DirectSound and DirectMusic isn't hard, but it's not easy, either. The systems are very complex, and have a lot of functionality. However, all we want to be able to do is load sound and music off disk and play the darn things! The T3DLIB2.CPP|H module handles all this in a very clean and simple way.

With that in mind, the sound and music demo is going to be rather plain graphically, so you can focus on just the calls to make sound and music work. Therefore, I have taken a demo from the first *Tricks* that basically works with both DirectSound and DirectMusic at the same time. The demo is a simple Windows application that has a menu and enables you to select a MIDI song to play, while at the same time you can "fire" off sound effects. Also, the demo structure is based on a stripped down version of the Game Console to minimize anything extraneous.

The name of the demo is DEMOII3_3.CPP|EXE, and Figure 3.16 features a screenshot of the application in action (what there is of it). Additionally, this demo uses a couple of resources such as a menu and cursor; thus, there are a few extra files that you need to add to your project:

- DEMOII3_3.RC—The Windows resource file with the menu
- DEMOII3_3RES.H—The header with identifiers for the resources
- T3DX.ICO—The cursor icon used by the program

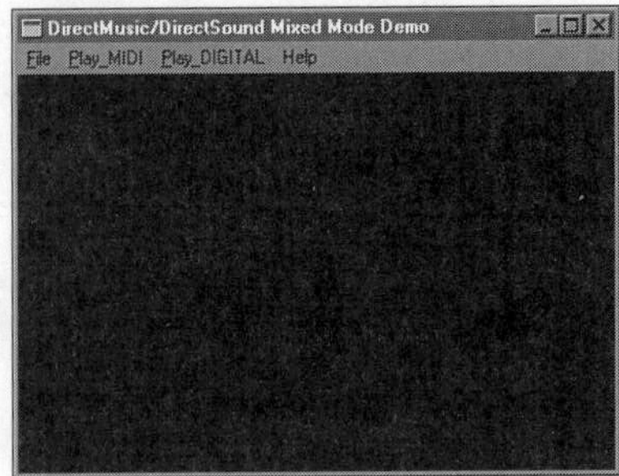

FIGURE 3.16 A screenshot of the sound and music demo.

As usual, this is still a DirectX application, and you need to include the DirectX .LIB files. Technically, you don't need `DDRAW.LIB`, but you should always keep all of them in your link list to be safe. Also, because there aren't any graphics or input calls to `T3DLIB1.CPP` or `T3DLIB2.CPP`, do *not* include the .CPP files in the build—you will get link errors if you do!

Working with Input

The last examples of using the library are input demos. As you know, there are three primary input devices used in a game:

- Keyboard
- Mouse
- Joystick

Of course, these days a joystick means a lot of things, but usually we can classify all devices that aren't a mouse or keyboard as a joystick.

Using the input library is very simple. It's contained in `T3DLIB2.CPP¦H` and supports the keyboard, mouse, and joystick devices. With just a few function calls, you can initialize DirectInput, acquire an input device, and read from it in your main loop. What we are going to do is review demos of each device: keyboard, mouse, and joystick. Of course, you are more than free to use all input devices together, but the demos will keep them separate, so you can better see what's going on.

Keyboard Demo

As usual, the demo are based on code from the first *Tricks*. Let's begin with the keyboard demo `DEMOII3_4.CPP¦EXE`. A screenshot is shown in Figure 3.17. Basically, this demo enables you to move a BOB skeleton around the screen. If you look at the code that reads the keyboard, you will notice that the data structure returned is nothing more than a 256 `BYTE` array of `BOOLEAN`s, each representing one key. The table is shown here:

```
UCHAR keyboard_state[256]; // contains keyboard state table
```

FIGURE 3.17 A screenshot of the keyboard demo.

To access the table, you use the DirectInput keyboard constants, which are all of the form `DK_*`. Table 3.2 from a previous section lists some of the more common constants. All you need to do to test whether a key is pressed. After you have retrieved the keyboard data with a call to `DInput_Read_Keyboard()`, you can use the following simple test:

```
if (keyboard_state[DIK_UP])
  {
  // if the up arrow is pressed this will execute
  } // end if
```

To compile the demo program, you will need all the DirectX .LIB files, along with `T3DLIB1.CPP¦H`, `T3DLIB2.CPP¦H`, and `T3DLIB3.CPP¦H`.

Mouse Demo

The mouse demo is again based on code from the first *Tricks*. It's a little paint program, as shown in Figure 3.18. The code is in the file `DEMOII3_5.CPP¦EXE`. The program shows off a number of interesting things about GUI programming, such as object picking, mouse tracking, and so forth. So, make sure to check out the painting code in addition to the mouse tracking code.

The mouse input device can operate in two modes: absolute or relative. I prefer relative because I can always figure out where I am, so the API wrapper puts the system in that mode. Hence, each time you read the mouse, you get deltas from the last call. The mouse is read each time you call `DInput_Read_Mouse()` and is stored in the following global mouse record:

```
DIMOUSESTATE mouse_state; // contains state of mouse
```

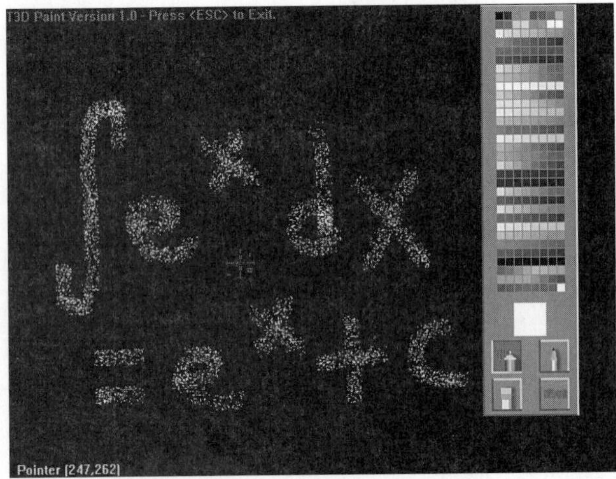

FIGURE 3.18 A screenshot of the mouse-based painting program.

Once again, the structure of a `DIMOUSESTATE` object is as follows:

```
typedef struct DIMOUSESTATE {
  LONG lX; // x-axis
  LONG lY; // y-axis
  LONG lZ; // z-axis
  BYTE rgbButtons[4]; // state of the buttons
} DIMOUSESTATE, *LPDIMOUSESTATE;
```

To compile this program, you will need all the DirectX .LIB files, along with `T3DLIB1.CPP¦H`, `T3DLIB2.CPP¦H`, and `T3DLIB3.CPP¦H`.

Joystick Demo

The "joystick" device on computers these days can be almost anything from gamepads to paddles. However, any joystick-like device is nothing more than a collection of two types of input devices:

- Analog axes
- Buttons

For example, if you take a look at Figure 3.19, we see four different joystick-like devices: a typical joystick, an advanced joystick, a game pad, and a steering wheel/paddle. You might hesitate to call these all joysticks, but they really are. The joystick has two axes: the x and y, along with two buttons. The gamepad is all buttons. And finally, the paddle consists of a rotational axis along with a couple of buttons.

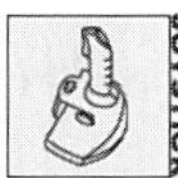

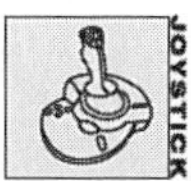

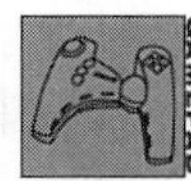

FIGURE 3.19 Four basic joystick devices.

Of course, in DirectInput speak, there are constants to define some of the most prevalent subtypes of joysticks, like plain joysticks, flight sticks, paddles, and gamepads, but in general they are all used in the same way. That is, you retrieve either smoothly varying data back from an analog slider or yoke, and a number of digital on/off signals representing the buttons. The data record returned the call to `DInput_Read_Joystick()` from the DirectInput module of our library is stored in the global

```
DIJOYSTATE joy_state;    // contains state of joystick
```

which is of the form

```
typedef struct DIJOYSTATE {
  LONG  lX; // x-axis
  LONG  lY; // y-axis
  LONG  lZ; // z-axis
  LONG  lRx; // rotation about x-axis
  LONG  lRy; // rotation about y-axis
  LONG  lRz; // rotation about z-axis
  LONG  rglSlider[2]; // u,v slider positions
  DWORD  rgdwPOV[4];  // point of view hat state
  BYTE  rgbButtons[32]; // state of buttons 0..31
} DIJOYSTATE, *LPDIJOYSTATE;
```

As a demo of using the joystick device, I have hijacked yet another program from the first *Tricks* that is a little *Centipede*-like game (not much of a game, though). The program is named `DEMOII3_6.CPP¦EXE` on the CD. A screenshot is shown in Figure 3.20. As usual, you will need all the DirectX .LIB files, along with `T3DLIB1.CPP¦H`, `T3DLIB2.CPP¦H`, and `T3DLIB3.CPP¦H` to compile.

NOTE

Make sure you check out some of the aspects of the demo relevant to game programming, such as the primitive game logic, collision detection, and weapon systems.

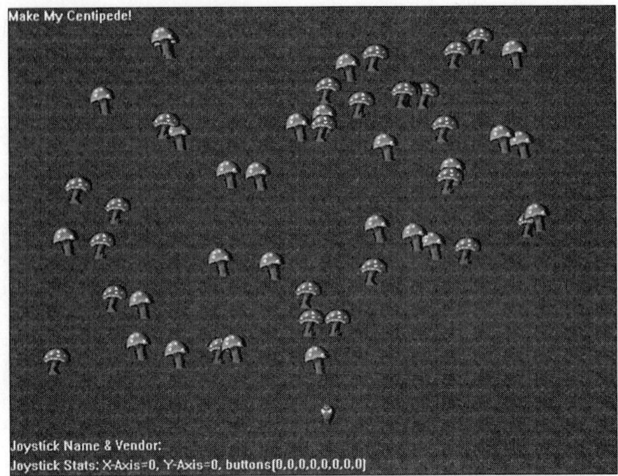

FIGURE 3.20 A screenshot of the joystick demo.

Summary

This chapter has really been a "transition" from the first *Tricks* to this book. You should understand that 3D graphics isn't about DirectX or Windows; it's about math, math, and more math. And all we need to experiment with 3D graphics is a platform that has a few functions and a couple of frame buffers. Also, even if you haven't read the first *Tricks*, you should have a decent handle on the API that we are going to use throughout the book. Either way, you should feel confident because we're only going to use a few functions to implement our virtual graphics computer needed for the rest of the text. For those of you that have read the first *Tricks*, I bet that you are happy that the `T3DLIB` now has 16-bit windowed support! Me too. It's cool <GRIN>.

PART II

3D Math and Transformation

IN THIS PART

CHAPTER **4**

It's a Math, Math, Math World—Trigonometry, Vectors, Matrices, and Quaternions

IN THIS CHAPTER

- Mathematical Notation
- 2D Coordinate Systems
- 3D Coordinate Systems
- 3D Cylindrical Coordinates
- 3D Spherical Coordinates
- Trigonometry
- Vectors
- Matrices and Linear Algebra
- Basic Geometric Entities
- Using Parametric Equations
- Introduction to Quaternions
- Basic Calculus

"For the last time—It's Bigboo-TAY'! Tay, Tay!!!" John Bigboote'!!!"

—John Bigboote', *Buckaroo Banzai*

It used to be that you could write computer games with a fleeting knowledge of trig and a bit of algebra. Things have definitely changed these days. I remember trying to get the editor of *Game Developer Magazine* to let me write an article about vectors just a few years ago, and his reply was that the math was too advanced. Now I routinely pick the magazine up, and it's full of advanced vector calculus! With that in mind, this chapter is going to be a refresher course (for most) on some of the basic mathematics you need for 3D computer graphics. I can't teach four years of college math in a single chapter, but I can at least jar your memory, and you can always pick up a real math book if you want more. Of course, if you are a math whiz, just skip to the next chapter where we start building the math library. Anyway, here's what we'll cover:

- Mathematical notation
- Coordinate systems
- Trigonometry
- Vectors
- Matrices and linear algebra
- Basic geometric entities

- Using parametric equations
- Introduction to quaternions
- Basic calculus

Mathematical Notation

Mathematics is like any language. It consists of a set of symbols that are used to represent mathematical concepts, formulas, equations, and operations. The problem with higher mathematics is that much of the symbology is literally Greek! So before we start, I want to show you some tables of commonly used symbols and conventions that I am going to try and stick to throughout the book when I am working with pure math. Although some of the concepts might be meaningless at this point, at least you have a "map" of definitions early on, rather than later in the chapter. Let's begin with Table 4.1, which contains the basic types of math objects we will work with.

TABLE 4.1 Mathematical Object Types

Type	Notation	Example
Scalar	Lower-case	a, b, x, y_1
Infinity	∞	$+\infty$, $-\infty$
Angle	Lower-case Greek	θ, ϕ, α, β
Vector	Lower-case bold	$\mathbf{u}$, $\mathbf{v}$, $\mathbf{a}_x$, $\mathbf{a}_y$
Quaternion	Lower-case bold	$\mathbf{p}$, $\mathbf{q}$, $\mathbf{r}_x$, $\mathbf{s}_y$
Elements of Vector	<components>	<ux, uy, uz>
Row Vector	[components]	[ux, uy, uz]
Point	Lower-case bold	$\mathbf{a}$, $\mathbf{p}_1$, $\mathbf{p}_2$
Matrix	Upper-case bold	$\mathbf{A}$, $\mathbf{B}$, $\mathbf{M}_2$
Triangle	Δ followed by points	$\Delta\mathbf{p}_0\mathbf{p}_1\mathbf{p}_2$, $\Delta\mathbf{abc}$

Note: All types can be subscripted or superscripted.

Now that we have a "general" guideline for types (although I might get sloppy from time to time based on context), let's take a look at some standard mathematical operators, as shown in Table 4.2.

TABLE 4.2 Mathematical Operators

Operation	Notation	Example
Scalar Multiplication	x,* Lower-case	3x5, a*b
Matrix Multiplication	x, Lower-case	**A**x**B**
Dot Product	.	**u . v**
Summation	Σ expr	

TABLE 4.2 Continued

Operation	Notation	Example
Absolute Value	|expr|	|-35|
Length	|expr|	|**u**|
Determinate	det(expr)	det(**M**)
Transpose	Superscript T	$\mathbf{v}^T$
Integration	∫ expr	
Differentiation	Prime Symbol '	x', x''

Note: "expr" stands for general expression.

Of course, we might make up some more notation as we go along, but Tables 4.1 and 4.2 are relatively decent conventions that most math books follow.

CAUTION

Generally, most mathematics books denote the determinate of matrix **M** by |**M**|, and length or norm of vector **v** by ||**v**||. The double vertical bars are too hard to lay out for general trade books like this, so we are going to use the symbology det(**M**) for determinate and |**v**| for the length and norm of a vector to simplify things, so keep that in mind. I think I am stressing the editors out enough with the Greek symbols!

2D Coordinate Systems

Just as we created some conventions for mathematical notation, we must make sure we are on the same page geometrically. Let's begin with describing and understanding the general 2D coordinate systems and then move on to the more complex 3D coordinate systems.

2D Cartesian Coordinates

The most common 2D coordinates that everyone has worked with are called *Cartesian coordinates*. Cartesian coordinates are based on a pair of perpendicular axes labeled x and y, as shown in Figure 4.1. The positive x-axis is to the right, and the negative x-axis is to the left. Conversely, the positive y-axis is in the upward direction, and the negative y-axis is in the downward direction. The point where both x = 0 and y = 0 is called the *origin*. Also, if you want to get technical, the y-axis is also called the *ordinate*, and the x-axis is the *abscissa*.

Additionally, there are four quadrants in the 2D x-y coordinate system labeled QI, QII, QIII, and QIV. The quadrants separate the four spaces by the sign on the x-y axis in that particular space. For example, Table 4.3 shows the signs of x-y in each quadrant.

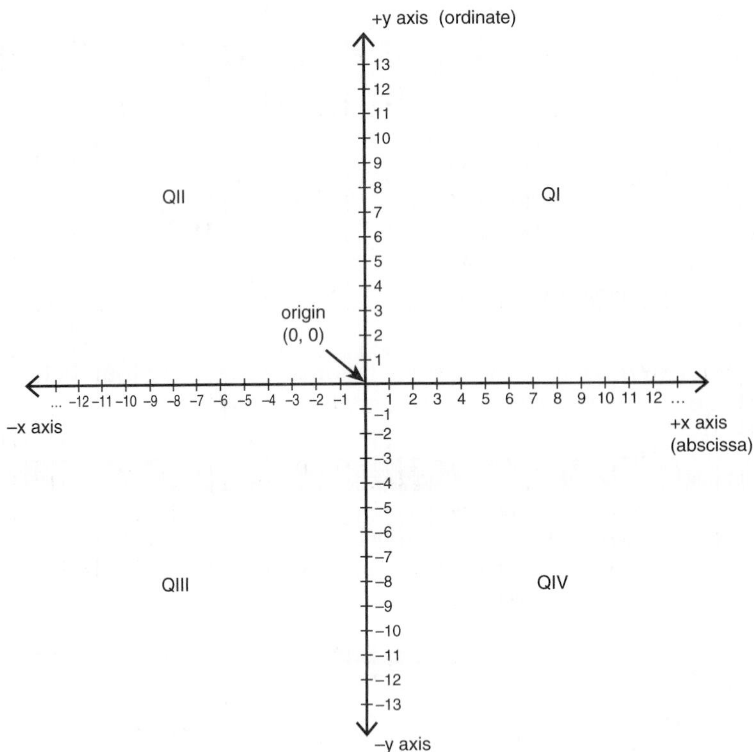

FIGURE 4.1 The Cartesian coordinate system.

TABLE 4.3 Signs in Each Quadrant

Quadrant	Sign (x)	Sign (y)
I	+	+
II	-	+
III	-	-
IV	+	-

TIP

Many graphics algorithms are optimized by solving the problem only for QI and then reflecting the solution based on symmetry to the other quadrants (or octants in a 3D system).

Finally, to locate any point in a 2D Cartesian coordinate system, you need both the x and y components. For example, the point **p**(5,3) means that x = 5 and y = 3, as shown in Figure 4.2. Easy enough? Okay, tough guy, let's move on then.

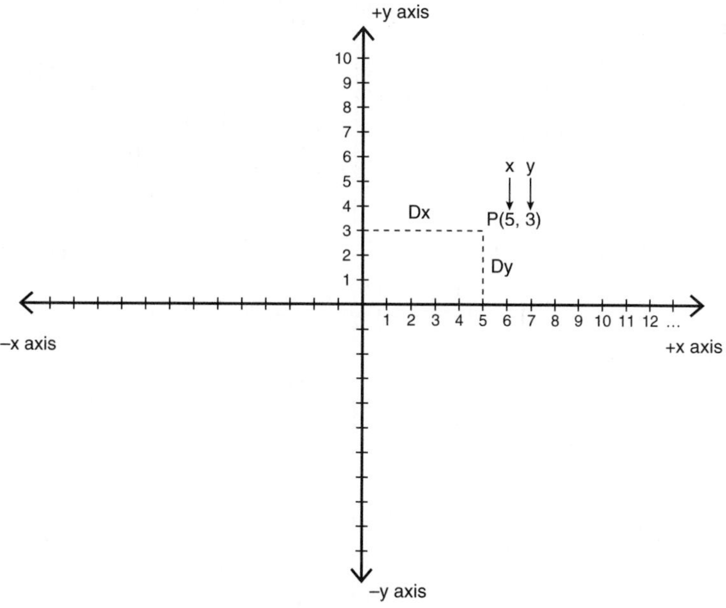

FIGURE 4.2 Locating points in the Cartesian coordinate system.

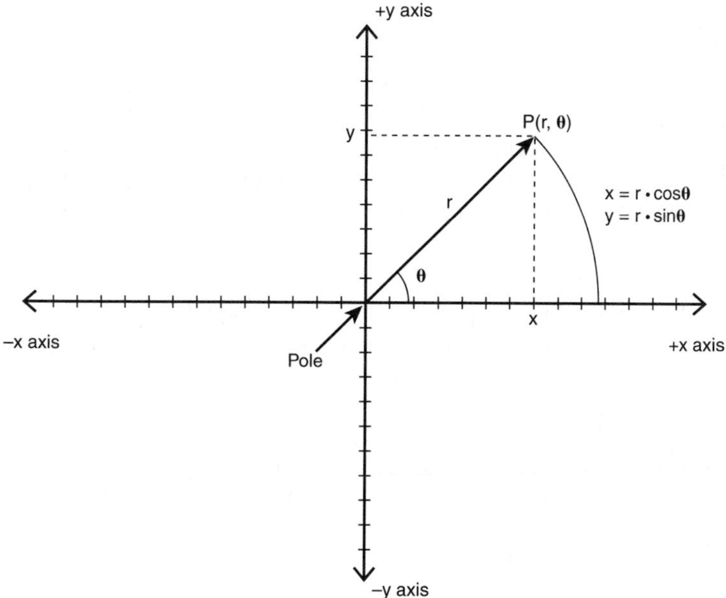

FIGURE 4.3 The 2D polar coordinate system.

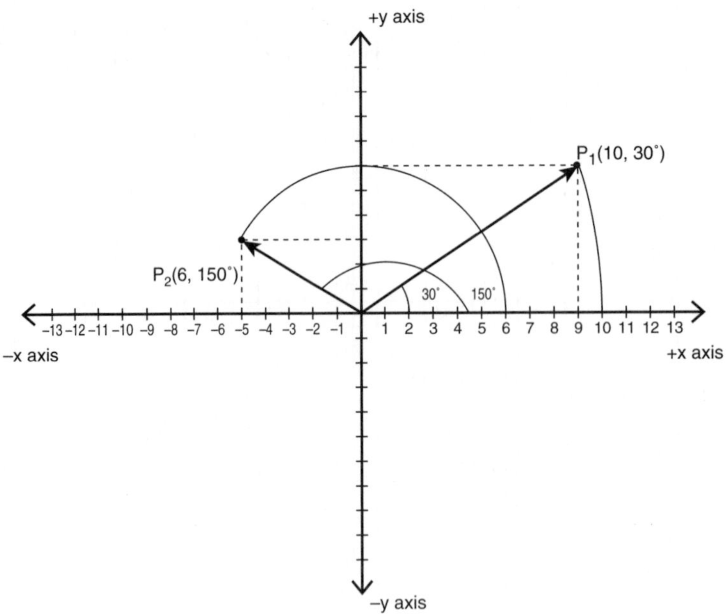

FIGURE 4.4 Locating points in a 2D polar system.

2D Polar Coordinates

The next type of coordinate system that two degrees of freedom supports is called *polar coordinates*. Polar coordinates are the entire basis of the game *Wolfenstein* and the technique of *ray-casting*. Polar coordinates are based on the desire to locate points in a 2D plane based on a heading and a distance, rather than an explicit (x,y) pair. Figure 4.3 depicts the standard 2D polar coordinate system. As you see, there are two variables used to locate a point: a distance r from the origin or *pole*, and a heading or angle θ (theta). Thus, the notation **p**(r, θ) would mean that the point **p** is located an angle θ degrees (or radians) relative to a reference ray (usually the x-axis) measured counter-clockwise and a distance r on that directional heading. Figure 4.4 shows examples of the points $\mathbf{p}_1(10,30°)$, and $\mathbf{p}_2(6,150°)$ using the x-y system as the reference.

Converting Between 2D Polar and Cartesian Coordinates

That's all fine and dandy, but polar coordinates are usually converted at some point into Cartesian coordinates to be useful. So how do we convert? Converting from Cartesian to polar and vice versa is easy if we just use a little geometry and the right triangle. Take a look at Figure 4.5—it shows a standard right triangle in quadrant I of a 2D Cartesian system. If we think of the tip of the hypotenuse as the "locator," or P, we can use the following formulas to convert from polar to Cartesian.

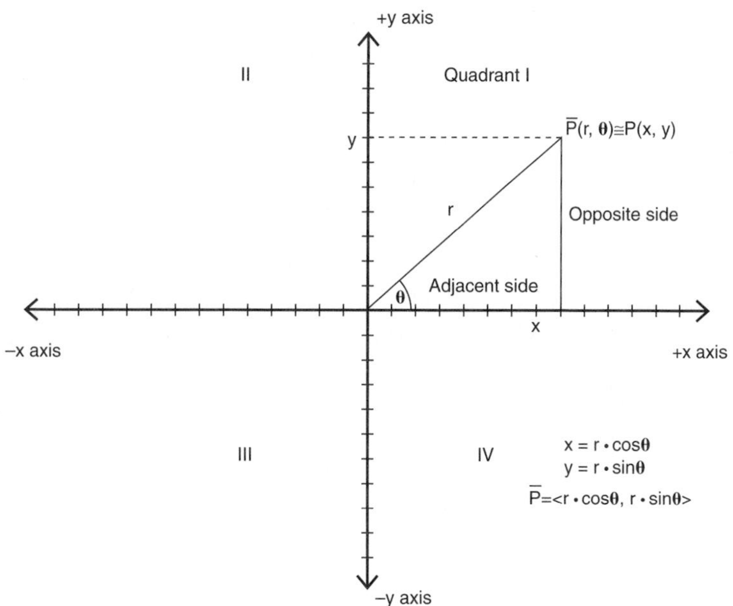

FIGURE 4.5 Geometrical interpretation of conversion between polar and Cartesian coordinates.

4

EQUATION 4.1 Converting 2D Polar Coordinates **p**(r,θ) to Cartesian Coordinates **p**(x,y)

```
x = r*cos(θ)
y = r*sin(θ)
```

> **TIP**
>
> If you are rusty on trigonometry, we will cover it a little later in the chapter, so for now just use the equations.

Converting from Cartesian to polar coordinates is a little more tricky. The problem is that we need the angle that the hypotenuse of the triangle formed by the point **p**(x,y) makes with the x-axis, along with its length. Again, trigonometry to the rescue. We can use the tangent to solve for the angle θ and the Pythagorean theorem to solve for *r*.

EQUATION 4.2 Converting 2D Cartesian Coordinates **p**(x,y) to Polar Coordinates **p**(r,θ)

Given: $x^2 + y^2 = r^2$

```
r = sqrt(x² + y²)
θ = tan⁻¹(y/x)
```

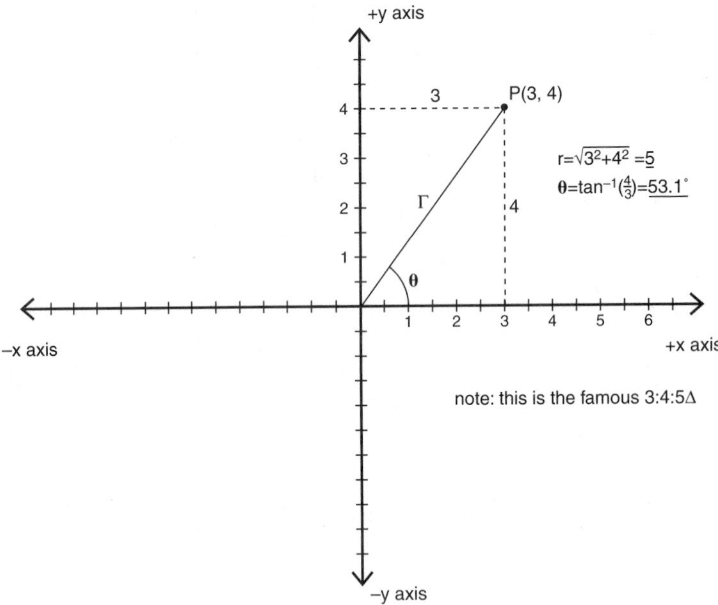

FIGURE 4.6 An example of converting from Cartesian to polar coordinates.

Let's give that a try for the point (3,4), which is located in QI and shown in Figure 4.6.

x = 3, y = 4, plugging into Equation 4.2:

```
r = sqrt(3² + 4²) = 5
θ = tan⁻¹(4/3) = 53.1°
```

Which, referring to Figure 4.6, looks about right.

TIP

If you are awake, you will notice that there is a problem with Equation 4.2—there is a *pole* (y goes to infinity) at x = 0! Or in other words, at the angles θ = 90° and θ = 270°, tangent is undefined (actually it's infinity [∞]). So to use Equation 4.2, you must test for x = 0 beforehand. In that case, you know the angle is 90°.

In conclusion, polar coordinates are very useful, and understanding them and how to convert back and forth is very important in many problems with trajectory, targeting, and navigation. If I had a dollar for every time I received an email about converting polar to Cartesian or vice versa, I would be a billionaire, so remember the equations—please! Otherwise, I'm going to start charging!

3D Coordinate Systems

Now that you have a good grasp of 2D coordinates, let's move on to 3D coordinates. If you have been game programming for a while, you are probably already familiar with 3D systems. But I want to cover the cylindrical and spherical systems as well, because they will help us later on with texture mapping and other special effects. We will start off with the standard Cartesian 3D systems and work our way into cylindrical and spherical systems.

3D Cartesian Coordinates

The 3D Cartesian coordinate system is identical to the 2D system with the addition of the z-axis, for a total of three degrees of freedom based on three mutually *orthogonal* (perpendicular) axes. Therefore, to locate a point **p** in 3D-space, you need three coordinates: x, y, z, or in compact form, **p**(x,y,z). Additionally, the three axes form three planes: the x-y plane, the x-z plane, and the y-z plane, as shown in Figure 4.7. These planes are very important, and each divides space into two regions, or half spaces. This concept is important, and we will revisit it in a number of algorithms. Now for a little work—there are three planes; each plane divides space into two half spaces. How many unique sub-spaces are there in a 3-axis system? The answer is eight! Therefore, in a 3-space system, there are eight *octants*. This is shown in Figure 4.8.

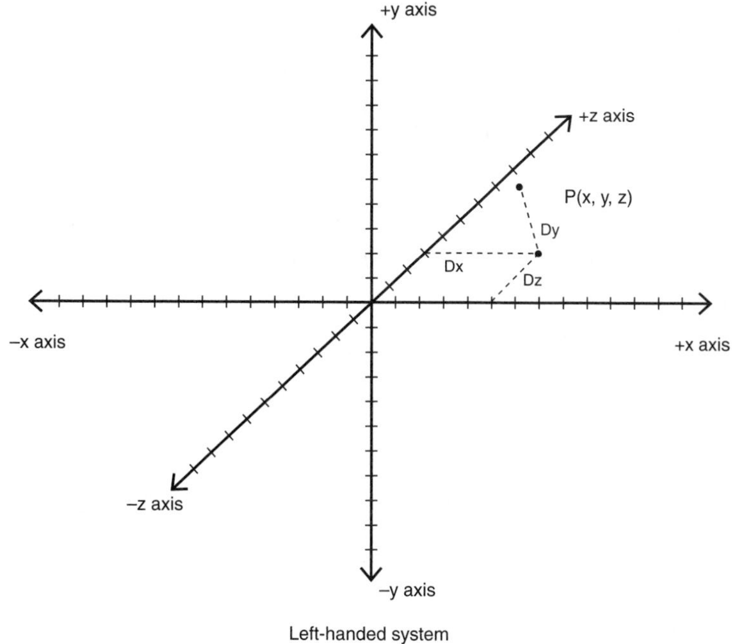

FIGURE 4.7 The 3D Cartesian coordinate system.

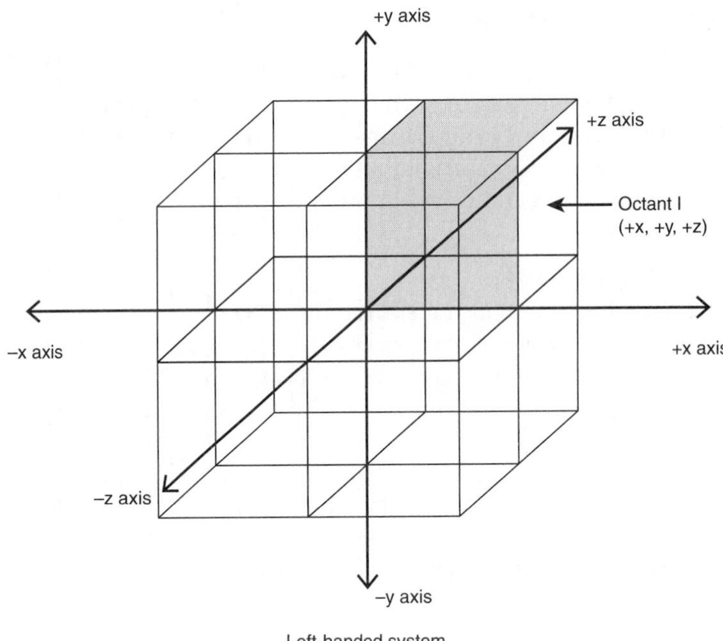

FIGURE 4.8 The octants of the 3D system.

This is all fantastic; however, this new z-axis creates a slight problem, as we must decide on two different orientations for the positive and negative half spaces for z, thus there are two distinct 3D Cartesian coordinate systems: the *left-handed system* and the *right-handed system*.

> **TIP**
>
> The names left-handed and right-handed come from the fact that if you wrap your right or left hand around the z-axis from x to y then your thumb will point in the direction of positive z.

The Left-Handed System

The left-handed system (LHS) is shown in Figure 4.9. In the LHS, the positive z-axis runs into the paper if we look straight down on it, or into the screen if we map x-y to the horizontal and vertical axes of the screen.

The Right-Handed System

The right-handed system (RHS) is shown in Figure 4.10. In the RHS, the positive z-axis runs out of the paper if we look straight down on it, and the negative z-axis runs into the paper. Thus, if we map the x-y to the screen as before, the negative z-axis runs into the screen and the positive z-axis out of the screen.

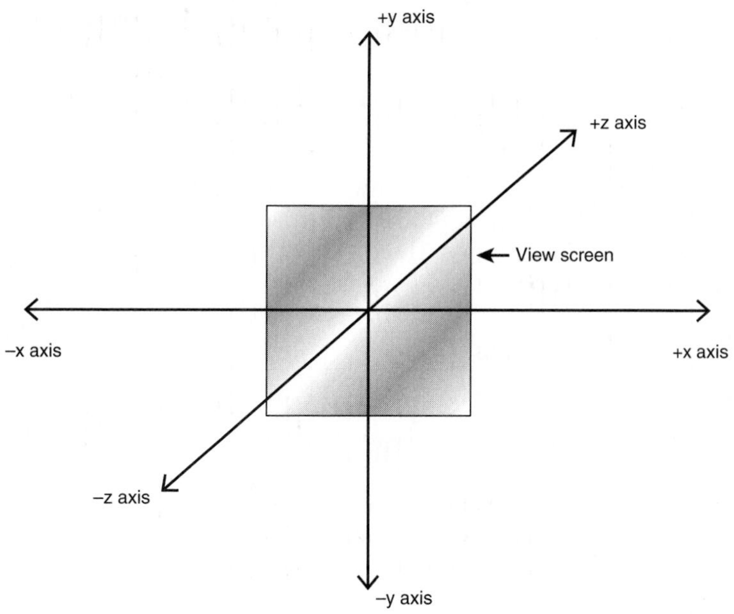

FIGURE 4.9 The left-handed 3D system.

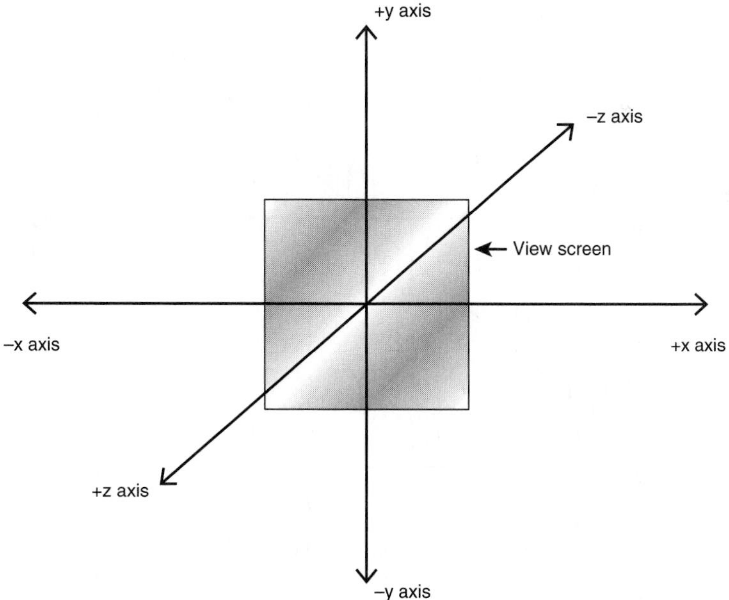

FIGURE 4.10 The right-handed 3D system.

NOTE

There isn't any real difference between either system, but in this book we will primarily use the LHS for the 3D engine. However, I might use the RHS to make 3D figures easier to understand.

We will generally use 3D Cartesian coordinates for everything in this book, but sometimes it's easier to think in terms of angles or directions when solving a particular problem—working with 3D cameras, for example. Therefore, understanding the two other common 3D coordinate systems is a good idea, so let's take a look.

3D Cylindrical Coordinates

Interestingly enough, there are polar coordinates in 2D, but in 3D there are both cylindrical and spherical coordinates because we have one more degree of freedom. We are free to interpret the other two as we wish, giving us two more distinct coordinate systems. Of course, they are all mappable to each other, but each has its uses. The 3D *cylindrical coordinate system* is the closest to the 2D polar system, because it is basically nothing more than a 2D x-y polar system with z tacked onto it.

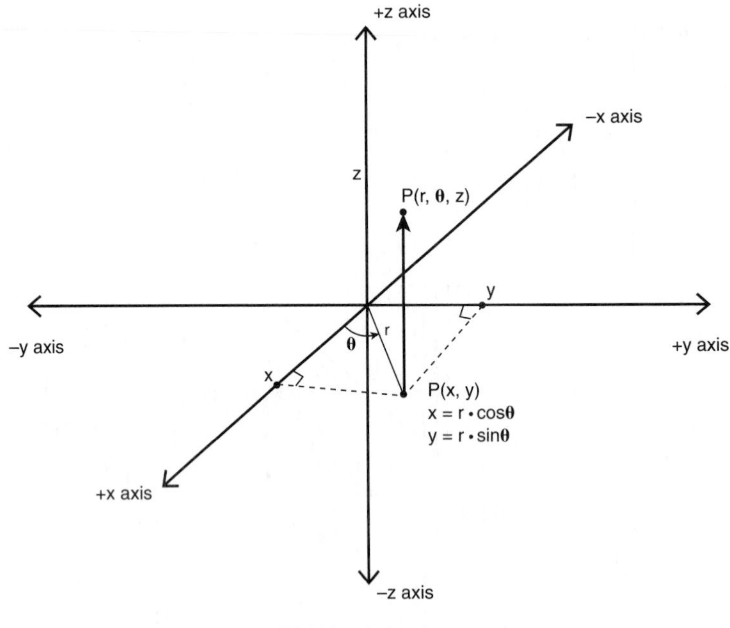

FIGURE 4.11 The cylindrical coordinate system.

Take a look at Figure 4.11 to see the standard cylindrical coordinate system. You will notice that the x-y plane at z = 0 is the standard 2D polar system, and the cylindrical coordinate locates a point by first locating the 2D point **p**(r, θ) in the x-y axis at z = 0 and then "climbing" up the z-axis an amount z. Also, note that a right-handed system is used, and it's rotated on its side to make the illustration easier to see.

Converting Between 3D Cartesian and Polar Coordinates

Converting between 3D Cartesian coordinates and cylindrical coordinates is trivial. We just use the 2D transform and then let z = z.

EQUATION 4.3 Converting 3D Polar Coordinates **p**(r,θ,z) to Cartesian Coordinates **p**(x,y,z)

```
x = r*cos(θ)
y = r*sin(θ)
z = z
```

4

In converting Cartesian coordinates to cylindrical, we again first use the 2D Cartesian-to-polar transform and then once again let z = z.

EQUATION 4.4 Converting 3D Cartesian Coordinates **p**(x,y,z) to Polar Coordinates **p**(r,θ,z)

Given: $x^2 + y^2 = r^2$

```
r = sqrt(x² + y²)
θ = tan⁻¹(y/x)
z = z
```

CAUTION

Again, the problem for the tangent still exists at the angles θ = 90° and θ = 270°.

Cylindrical coordinates are handy for a number of problems, such as controlling the camera in a first-person shooter to environment mapping.

3D Spherical Coordinates

3D spherical coordinates are a little more complex than all the other coordinate systems. In general, a point is located via two angles and a distance from the origin of the system (usually x-y-z). Figure 4.12 shows a spherical coordinate system. To locate a point with spherical coordinates, you need two angles and the distance from the origin. Conventionally, this is written **p**(ρ,ϕ,θ); that is, "rho," "phi," and "theta," where:

- ρ is the distance from the origin to the point **p**.
- ϕ is the angle that the directed line segment from the origin (**o**) to **p** makes with the positive z-axis (thus we will use a RHS system in this analysis).
- θ is the angle that the projection of the line from **o** to **p** makes on the x-y plane, which is just the standard 2D polar θ. Also, $0 <= \theta <= 2\pi$; that is, θ must be in the interval from 0 to 2π inclusive.

Hence, once again we see that we can derive spherical coordinates by using what we know about 2D polar coordinates. Let's see how to convert back and forth from 3D Cartesian and spherical coordinates, shall we?

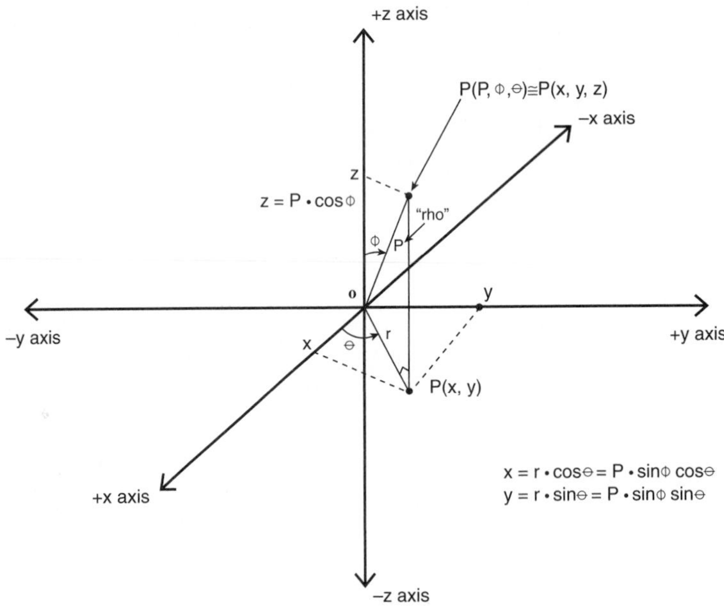

FIGURE 4.12 Spherical coordinates and conversion.

First, pay close attention to Figure 4.12, because the text description of the conversion is going to be confusing. To convert the spherical coordinates to 3D Cartesian coordinates (x,y,z), we can use a two-step process. First, we can project the line segment **o->p** onto the x-y plane and kill the z-axis. After we have done this, the problem becomes 2D and we already have a solution to it. Then we can back up and find z in terms of (ρ,ϕ,θ). This is the plan...

EQUATION 4.5 Converting 3D Spherical Coordinates **p**(ρ,φ,θ) to Cartesian Coordinates **p**(x,y,z)

From the projection of the line segment **o->p** onto the x-y plane, we see that:

$$r = \rho*\sin(\phi)$$
$$z = \rho*\cos(\phi)$$

and in the x-y plane, we know that:

$$x = r*\cos(\theta)$$
$$y = r*\sin(\theta)$$

Therefore, substituting r into x,y and collecting equations gives:

$$x = \rho*\sin(\phi)*\cos(\theta)$$
$$y = \rho*\sin(\phi)*\sin(\theta)$$
$$z = \rho*\cos(\phi)$$

EQUATION 4.6 Converting 3D Cartesian Coordinates **p**(x,y,z) to Spherical Coordinates **p**(ρ,φ,θ)

Given: $x^2 + y^2 + z^2 = \rho^2$

Similarly: $x^2 + y^2 = r^2$

Therefore:

$$r = \mathrm{sqrt}(x^2 + y^2)$$
$$\rho = \mathrm{sqrt}(x^2 + y^2 + z^2)$$
$$\theta = \tan^{-1}(y/x)$$

And we can solve for φ after we have r and ρ from the relationship:

$$r = \rho*\sin(\phi)$$

Solving for φ gives:

$$\phi = \sin^{-1}(r/\rho)$$

Also, we can use:

$$z = \rho*\cos(\phi)$$

Therefore:

$$\phi = \cos^{-1}(z/\rho)$$

Trigonometry

Trigonometry is the study of angles, shapes, and their relationships. Most trigonometry is based on the analysis of a *right triangle,* as shown in Figure 4.13. The right triangle has three interior angles and three sides. The angle opposite the 90 degree angle is usually used as the reference point, and is sometimes referred to as the *base angle*. From it, we can label the triangle. The side adjacent to the base angle is called the *adjacent side*. The side opposite the base angle is called the *opposite side*, and the side connecting them is called the *hypotenuse*. Don't underestimate the power of the triangle and similar triangles. I have seen few graphics algorithms that don't use triangles or similar triangles in some manner, so although it might seem trivial, expertise working with triangles is very important in graphics programming.

The Right Triangle

With all that in mind, let's just review some commonly known facts about triangles.

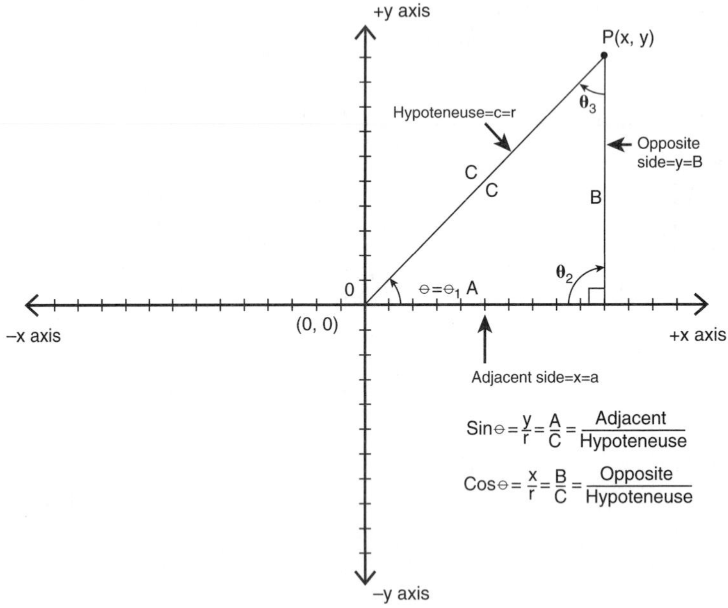

FIGURE 4.13 The right triangle.

> **NOTE**
>
> I will use *PI* and the symbol π interchangeably throughout the book. However, PI will usually mean the computer constant in the MATH.H header, whereas π means 3.14159....

TABLE 4.4 Radians Versus Degrees

Angle in Degrees	Angle in Radians
360 degrees	2*PI radians (approx. 6.28 radians)
180 degrees	PI radians (approx. 3.14159 radians)
57.296 degrees	360 degrees/2*PI radians = 1 radian
1.0 degrees	2*PI radians/360 degrees = 0.0175 radians

Fact 1: There are 360 degrees in a complete circle, or *2*PI* radians. Hence, there are *PI* radians in 180 degrees. The computer functions *sin()* and *cos()* work in radians, ***NOT*** degrees—remember that! Table 4.4 lists the values.

Fact 2: The sum of the interior angles $\theta_1 + \theta_2 + \theta_3 = 180$ degrees, or *PI* radians.

Fact 3: Once again referring to the right triangle in Figure 4.13, the side opposite θ_1 is called the opposite side, the side below it is called the adjacent side, and the long side is called the hypotenuse.

Fact 4: The sum of the squares of the sides of a right triangle equals the square of the hypotenuse. This is called the *Pythagorean Theorem*. Mathematically, we write it like this:

$$\text{hypotenuse}^2 = \text{adjacent}^2 + \text{opposite}^2$$

or sometimes using a, b, and c for dummy variables:

$$c^2 = a^2 + b^2$$

Therefore, if you have two sides of a right triangle, you can always find the third.

Fact 5: There are three main trigonometric ratios that mathematicians like to use. They are called the *sine*, *cosine*, and *tangent*. They are defined as:

```
          adjacent side       x
cos(θ)  = --------------- = -------
           hypotenuse         r
```

DOMAIN: 0 <= θ <= 2*PI

RANGE: -1 to 1

```
          opposite side       y
sin(θ)  = -------------- = -------
            hypotenuse        r
```

DOMAIN: 0 <= θ <= 2*PI

RANGE: -1 to 1

```
            sin(θ)         opposite/hypotenuse
tan(θ)  = ------------- = -------------------
            cos(θ)         adjacent/hypotenuse

      opposite         y
  = ------------ = ----- = slope = M
      adjacent         x
```

DOMAIN: -PI/2 <= θ <= PI/2

RANGE: -infinity to +infinity

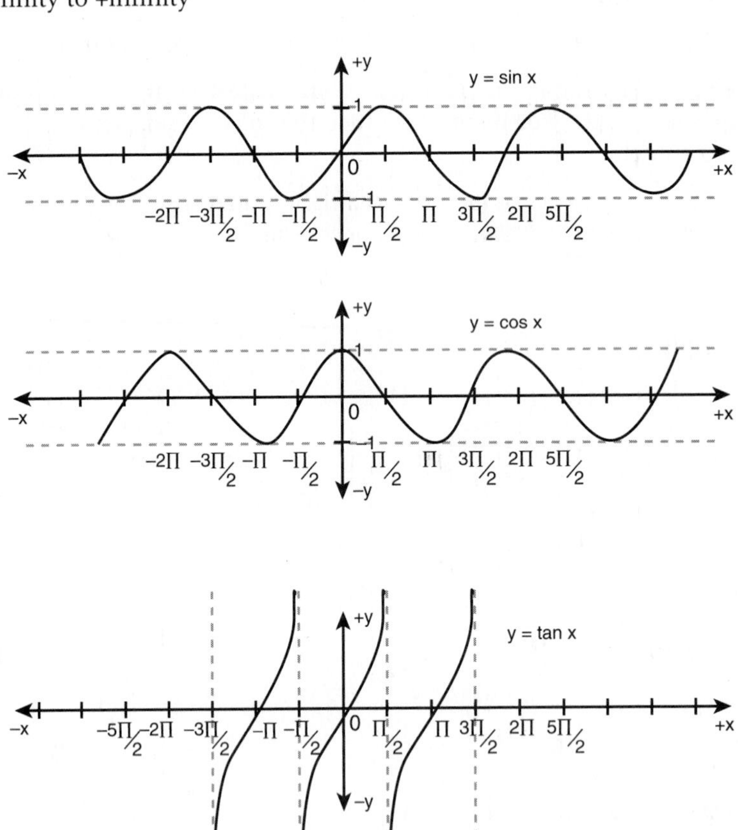

FIGURE 4.14 Graphs of basic trigonometric functions.

Figure 4.14 shows graphs of all the functions. Notice that all the functions are periodic (repeating) and that *sin(θ)* and *cos(θ)* have periodicity of *2*PI* while tangent has periodicity of *PI*. Also, notice that *tan(θ)* goes to + or -infinity whenever θ modulus *PI* is *PI/2*.

MATH

You might note the use of the terms *DOMAIN* and *RANGE*. These simply mean the input and the output, respectively.

Inverse Trigonometric Functions

Many times when using trig functions like sine, cosine, and tangent, you create a formula based on some geometry and need the initial angle back. That is, you want to use the function in reverse to find the angle that some given ratio represents in terms of sine, cosine, or tangent. This is called the inverse, and is written using a superscript -1:

$\theta = \cos^{-1}(x)$, where $0 <= \theta <= 2*PI$ and $-1 <= x <= 1$

$\theta = \sin^{-1}(x)$, where $0 <= \theta <= 2*PI$ and $-1 <= x <= 1$

$\theta = \tan^{-1}(x)$, where $-PI/2 <= \theta <= PI/2$ and $-\infty < x < +\infty$

NOTE

Of course, on a computer there usually isn't a representation for infinity, but in this context we mean numbers sufficiently large that for all intents and purposes they are many times larger than any other number in the number space we are considering. For example, if your game is working with a grid of 1000x1000, then 100,000,000 is close enough to infinity.

Using the preceding inverse functions is easy: Just plug in a number for x and solve for θ (actually, let the computer do it). However, there is a catch. Although standard sine, cosine, and tangent are slow (even on a computer), the inverse functions are 10 times slower! So, make sure you really need to know the actual angle. Many times you can just use the x itself in your algorithms. Of course, you can always use tricks like look-up tables and interpolation if you really need angles back.

Trigonometric Identities

Now, there are about a gazillion trigonometric identities and tricks, and it would take a math book to prove them all, so I'm just going to give you a table of the ones that a game programmer should know. Table 4.5 lists some other trigonometric ratios, as well as some neat identities.

TABLE 4.5 Useful Trigonometric Identities

Reciprocal Functions

Cosecant: $csc(\theta) = 1/sin(\theta)$
Secant: $sec(\theta) = 1/cos(\theta)$
Cotangent: $cot(\theta) = 1/tan(\theta)$

Pythagorean Theorem in terms of trig functions:

$sin(\theta)^2 + cos(\theta)^2 = 1$

Conversion identity:

$sin(\theta) = cos(\theta - PI/2)$

Reflection identities:

$sin(-\theta) = -sin(\theta)$
$cos(-\theta) = cos(\theta)$

Angle Addition identities:

$sin(\theta_1 + \theta_2) = sin(\theta_1)*cos(\theta_2) + cos(\theta_1)*sin(\theta_2)$
$cos(\theta_1 + \theta_2) = cos(\theta_1)*cos(\theta_2) - sin(\theta_1)*sin(\theta_2)$
$sin(\theta_1 - \theta_2) = sin(\theta_1)*cos(\theta_2) - cos(\theta_1)*sin(\theta_2)$
$cos(\theta_1 - \theta_2) = cos(\theta_1)*cos(\theta_2) + sin(\theta_1)*sin(\theta_2)$

Of course, you could derive identities until you turn many shades of green. In general, identities help you reduce complex trigonometric formulas into simpler ones, so you don't have to do the math. Hence, when you come up with an algorithm based on sine, cosine, tangent, and so on, always take a look in a trigonometry book and see whether you can simplify your math, so that fewer computations are needed to get to the result. Remember: speed, speed, speed!!!

TRICK

When we get to matrix transformations, we might decide to concatenate a number of operations together, like translation, rotation, and scaling. The rotation operation itself might be a concatenation of two or more rotation transformations, all in terms of sine and cosine. Hence, if we look at the results of the matrix multiplications, we can simplify the matrix using trigonometric identities and write a specific function that performs the transformation, rather than using general matrix multiplications blindly.

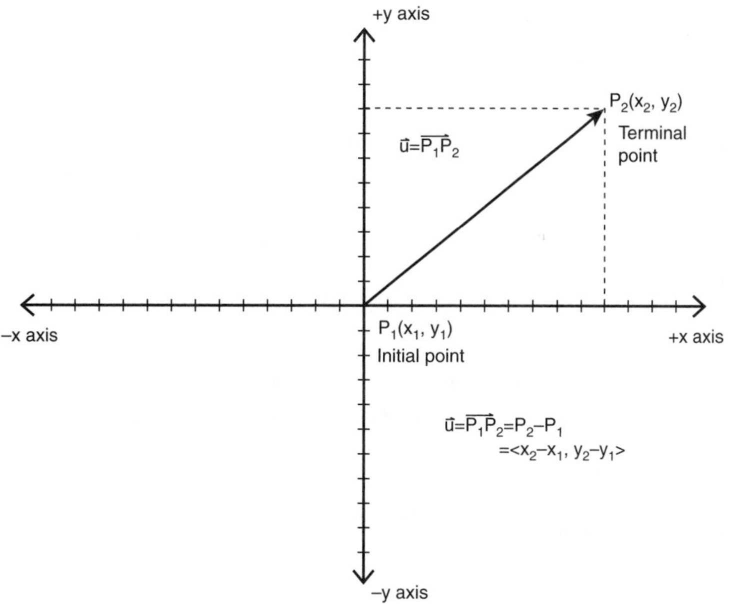

FIGURE 4.15 Definition of a vector.

Vectors

Vectors are the basis for all 3D algorithms, and thus are very important to a game programmer. Vectors are basically nothing more than a collection of two or more individual components that represent directed line segments in the 2- and 3-component case (which we are interested in). They are defined by an *initial point* and a *terminal point*, as shown in Figure 4.15. Referring to Figure 4.15, we see a vector **u** defined by the two points **p1** (the initial point) and **p2** (the terminal point). The vector **u** = $\langle u_x, u_y \rangle$ is from **p1**(x1,y1) to **p2**(x2,y2). To compute **u**, you simply subtract the initial point from the terminal point:

$$U = p2 - p1 = (x2-x1, y2-y1) = \langle u_x, u_y \rangle$$

Another way to represent the vector from **p1** to **p2** is to use bar notation by placing the two endpoints adjacent to each other and placing a bar over them, like this:

$$\overline{\mathbf{p1p2}}$$

which means the vector formed from point **p1** to **p2**. Also, we usually represent vectors by bolded lowercase (or uppercase) letters, like **u**, and the components are written within angled brackets, like $\langle u_x, u_y \rangle$.

Okay, so a vector represents a directed line segment from one point to another, but that segment can represent a lot of concepts, such as *velocity*, *acceleration*, or whatever. However, be warned: Once defined, vectors are always relative to the origin. This means that after you create a vector from point **p1** to **p2**, the initial point in vector space is always at (0,0), or (0,0,0) in 3D. This doesn't matter because the math takes care of everything, but if you think about it, it makes sense. A vector consists of two numbers in 2D and three numbers in 3D space, so it really only defines an endpoint in 2D or 3D space. Hence, the starting point is always thought of as the origin. This doesn't mean that you can't translate vectors around and perform various geometrical operations with the vectors themselves; it just means that you need to keep in mind what a vector really is.

The cool things about vectors are the operations that we can perform on them. Because vectors are really sets of ordered numbers, we can perform many of the standard mathematical operations on them by performing the mathematical operation on each component independently.

NOTE

Vectors can have any number of components. Usually, in computer graphics we deal with 2D and 3D vectors; that is, vectors of the form **a** = <x,y>, **b** = <x,y,z>. An *n*-dimensional vector has the form

c = <c1, c2, c3, …, cn>

n dimensional vectors are used to represent sets of variables rather than geometrical space, because after 3D we enter *Hyperspace*, as normal space only has three spatial dimensions. Right, Mr. Mallory?

Vector Length

The first thing that will pop up time and time again when working with vectors is how to compute the length of a vector or its magnitude. The length of a vector is called the *norm* and is represented by two vertical bars on either side of the vector (at least in this book), such as |**u**| and read as, "the length of **u**." The length is computed as the distance from the origin to the tip of the vector, or in general as the square root of the sum of the squares of the components. Hence, we can use the standard Pythagorean Theorem to find the length in the 2D and 3D case. Hence, |**u**| is equal to the following:

EQUATION 4.7 The Length of a 2D Vector $\mathbf{u} = <u_x, u_y>$

$$|\mathbf{u}| = \text{sqrt}(u_x^2 + u_y^2)$$

And if **u** happened to be a 3D vector, the length would be:

EQUATION 4.8 The Length of a 3D Vector $\mathbf{u} = <u_x, u_y, u_z>$

$$|\mathbf{u}| = \text{sqrt}(u_x^2 + u_y^2 + u_z^2)$$

Normalization

After you have the length of a vector, you can do something interesting—*normalize* it, or in other words, shrink the vector to make sure that its length is 1.0 while maintaining the direction. Unit vectors have a lot of nice properties, just like the scalar 1.0. For example, sometimes we might perform a number of operations and the resulting vector is of interest to us, but we don't care about its length; we just need a vector of length 1.0 in the direction of the computed vector. Normalization can give us this. Given a vector **n** = $<n_x,n_y>$, the normalized version of **n** is usually written as **n** with a "hat" over it, something like this:

```
^
n
```

But, again that's pressing my luck with the editors in layout, so we will use lowercase italic (along with a superscript prime symbol sometimes for unit vectors) like this:

n or *n*'

In any case, the normalized version of a vector **n** is computed like this:

EQUATION 4.9 Normalizing a Vector

n' = n/|n|

Very simple. The normalized version of a vector is simply the vector divided (multiplied by the inverse) by the length of the vector.

Scalar Multiplication

The first operation that you might want to perform on a vector is scaling. For example, suppose you have a vector representing speed and you want to go faster (or slower). Scaling is performed by multiplying each component by a single scalar number. For example:

Let **u** = $<u_x, u_y>$ and k be a real constant

$k*\mathbf{u} = k*<u_x, u_y> = <k*u_x, k*u_y>$

Figure 14.16 shows the scaling operation graphically. In addition, if you want to invert the direction of a vector, you can multiply any vector by –1 and invert the vector as shown in Figure 4.17, or mathematically:

Let

$\mathbf{u} = <u_x, u_y>$

then the vector in the opposite direction of **u** is

$-1*\mathbf{u} = -1*<u_x, u_y> = <-u_x, -u_y>$

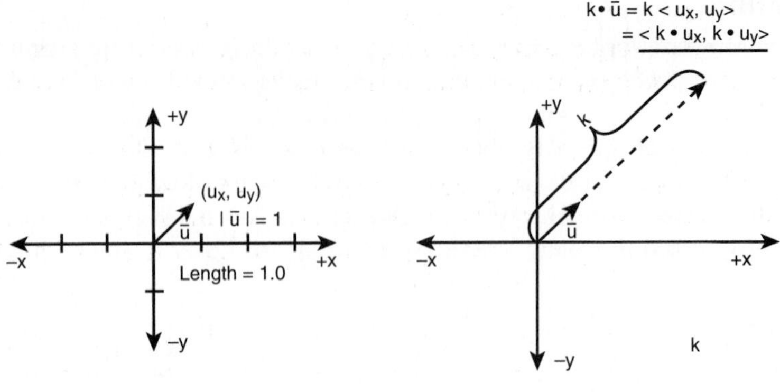

FIGURE 4.16 Vector scaling.

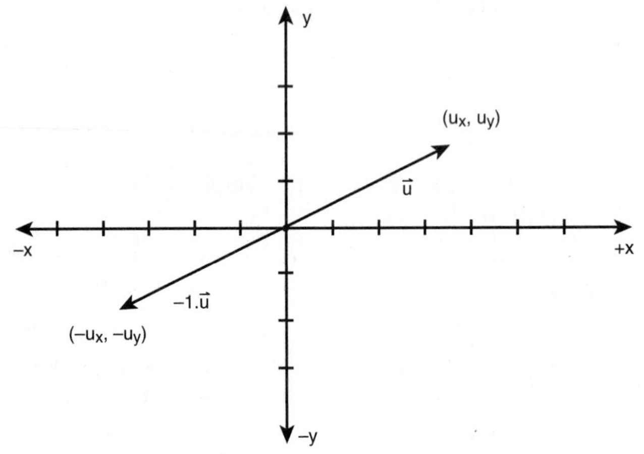

FIGURE 4.17 Vector inversion.

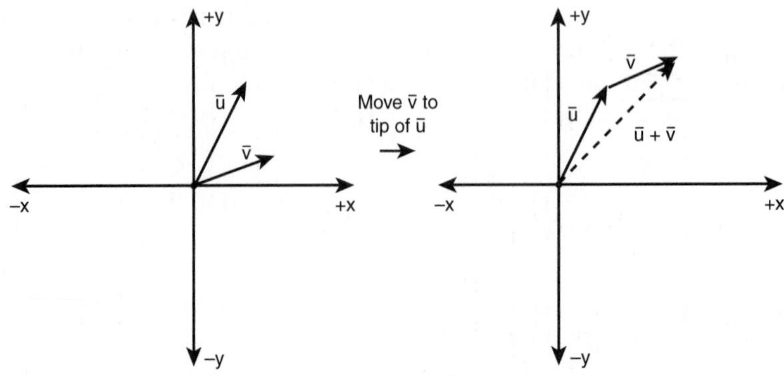

FIGURE 4.18 Vector addition.

Vector Addition

To add two (or more) vectors together, all you have to do is add the respective components together. Figure 4.18 illustrates this graphically for the 2D case (3D would tax my artistic abilities). Vector **u** is added to **v**, and the result is **r**. Notice how the addition was performed geometrically: I took **v** and moved it to the terminal point of **u** and then drew the other side of the triangle. Geometrically, this operation is equivalent to the following mathematical operation:

$$\mathbf{u} + \mathbf{v} = <u_x, u_y> + <v_x, v_y> = <u_x+v_x, u_y+v_y>$$

Thus, to add any number of vectors together on graph paper, you can simply add them "tip to tail," and when you add them all up, the vector from the origin to the last tip is the result.

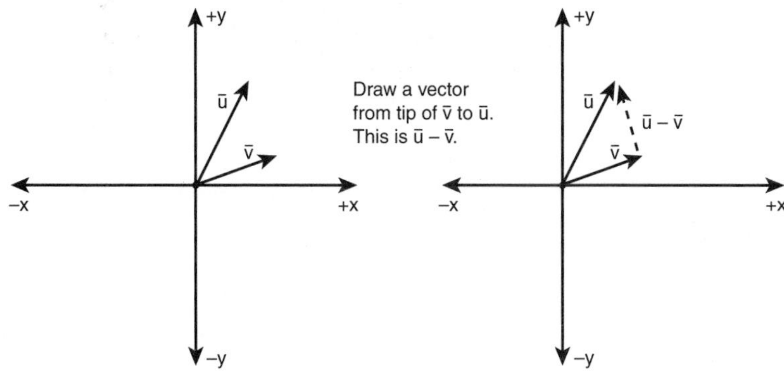

FIGURE 4.19 Vector subtraction.

Vector Subtraction

Vector subtraction is really vector addition with the opposite pointing vector; however, it is sometimes illustrative to see subtraction graphically. Take a look at Figure 4.19 to see **u** – **v** and **v** – **u**. Notice that **u** – **v** is computed by drawing a vector from **v** to **u**, and **v** – **u** is computed by drawing a vector from **u** (as the initial point) to **v** (the terminal point). Mathematically, we have:

$$\mathbf{u} - \mathbf{v} = <u_x, u_y> - <v_x, v_y> = <u_x-v_x, u_y-v_y>$$

which might be easier to remember, but a piece of graph paper can sometimes be a much better "computer" than doing the math manually because you can visualize the data quicker. Hence, it's a good idea to know how to add and subtract vectors on graph paper when you are working out rendering algorithms—trust me!

The Inner Product, or the "Dot" Product

At this point you might be asking, "Can you multiply two vectors together?" The answer is yes, but the straight component-wise multiplication represented by the symbol "⊗ " isn't very useful, it turns out:

$$\mathbf{u} \otimes \mathbf{v} = <u_x*v_x,\ u_y*v_y>$$

However, another kind of multiplication known as the dot product is very useful. It's defined like this:

EQUATION 4.10 The Dot Product

$$\mathbf{u}\ .\ \mathbf{v} = u_x*v_x + u_y*v_y$$

The dot product, usually represented by a dot (.), is computed by summing the products of the individual terms into a single scalar, rather than just multiplying the components and keeping the result in vector form. You might ask, what does the dot product do for us? We don't even have vectors anymore! True, but the dot product is also equal to this expression:

EQUATION 4.11 The Dot Product Related to the Angle Between the Vectors

$$\mathbf{u}\ .\ \mathbf{v} = |\mathbf{u}|*|\mathbf{v}|*\cos(\theta)$$

This states that **u** dot **v** is equal to the length of **u** multiplied by the length of **v** multiplied by the cosine of the angle between the vectors. If we combine the two different expressions, we get this:

$$\mathbf{u}\ .\ \mathbf{v} = u_x*v_x + u_y*v_y$$
$$\mathbf{u}\ .\ \mathbf{v} = |\mathbf{u}|*|\mathbf{v}|*\cos(\theta)$$
$$u_x*v_x + u_y*v_y = |\mathbf{u}|*|\mathbf{v}|*\cos\ \theta$$

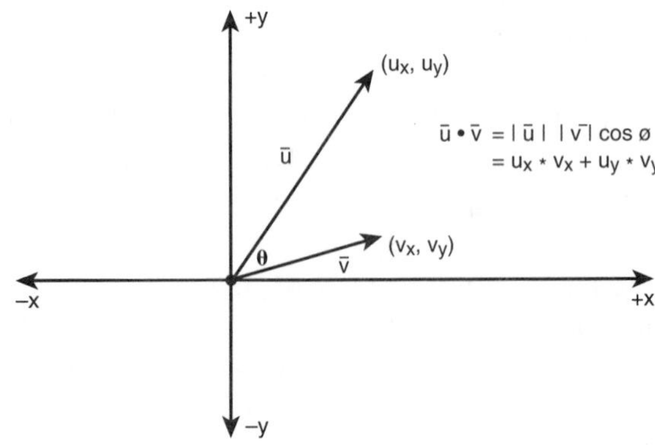

FIGURE 4.20 The dot product.

This is a very interesting formula—it basically gives us a way to compute the angle between two vectors, as shown in Figure 4.20, and that's a really useful operation. If you can't see that, then take a look at the equation after rearranging and taking the inverse cosine of both sides:

EQUATION 4.12 Computing the Angle Between Two Vectors

$$\theta = \cos^{-1} (u_x*v_x + u_y*v_y/|\mathbf{u}|*|\mathbf{v}|)$$

or more compactly, we assume that (**u.v**) means ($u_x*v_x + u_y*v_y$) and just write

$$\theta = \cos^{-1} (\mathbf{u.v}/|\mathbf{u}|*|\mathbf{v}|)$$

This is a very powerful tool and the basis of many 3D graphics algorithms. The cool thing is that if the **u** and **v** are already unit vectors—that is, the length of **u** and **v** are already 1.0—their product is 1.0 and the formula simplifies even more to

$$\theta = \cos^{-1} (\mathbf{u.v}), \text{ for } |\mathbf{u}|=|\mathbf{v}| = 1.0$$

And here are a couple interesting facts about the dot product:

Fact 1: If the angle between **u** and **v** is 90 (perpendicular), then **u.v** = 0.

Fact 2: If the angle between **u** and **v** is < 90 (acute), then **u.v** > 0.

Fact 3: If the angle between **u** and **v** is > 90 (obtuse), then **u.v** < 0.

Fact 4: If **u** and **v** are equal, then $\mathbf{u.v} = |\mathbf{u}|^2 = |\mathbf{v}|^2$.

These facts are all shown graphically in Figure 4.21.

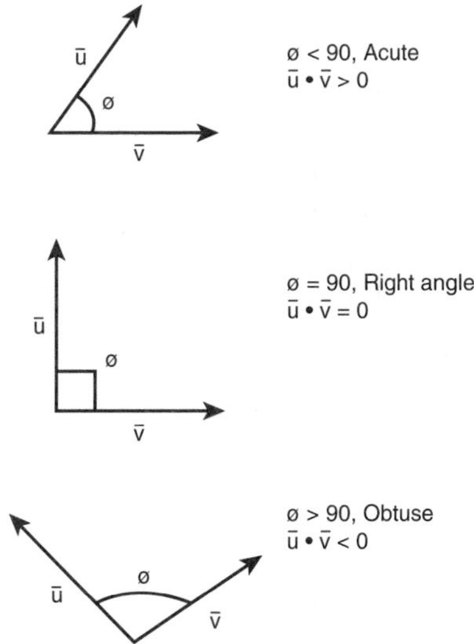

FIGURE 4.21 Angles and their relationship to the dot product.

Additionally, the dot product can be used for many other computations. One that is of great use in computer graphics and game programming is computing the components of one vector (or its projection) along a given test vector's direction. Figure 4.22 shows this graphically. For example, suppose you have a vector **v** that represents the trajectory of one character in your game, and you have a vector **u** that represents the trajectory of another character in your game. There are many cases when you want to know how much **u** is pointing in the direction of **v**. In other words, you want the vector projection of **u** onto **v**, which is called $\mathbf{Proj_v\ u}$. We can compute this vector using the dot product.

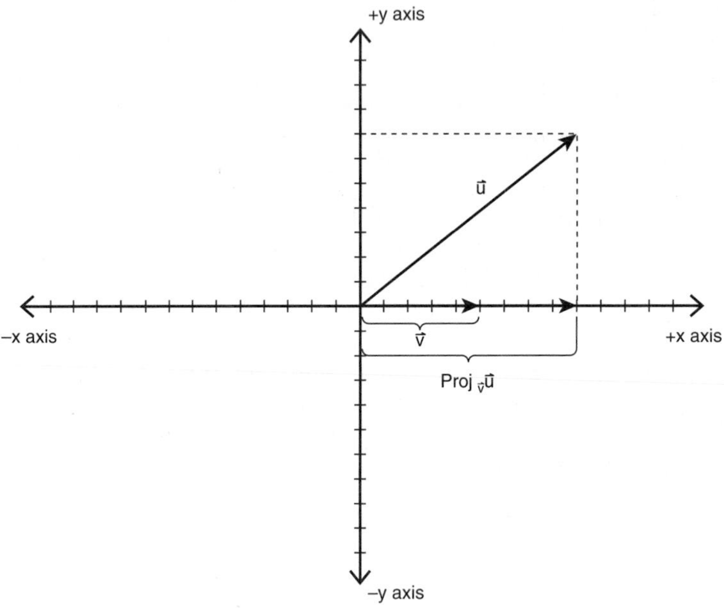

FIGURE 4.22 The projection of **u** on **v**.

Referring to Figure 4.22, we have both **u** and **v** and we want the length of the parallel projection of **u** onto **v** (we could just as well ask for the perpendicular length), then we can multiply this by the unit vector in the direction of **v** if we need a vector quantity. To compute this, we can use the dot product **u.v**. However, **v** must have length 1.0; that is, be normalized. Hence, the final equation for the vector of the projection **u** onto **v** is:

EQUATION 4.13 The Length of the Parallel Projection of **u** onto **v**

$$Proj_v\ \mathbf{u} = \frac{(\mathbf{u} \cdot \mathbf{v}) * \mathbf{v}}{|\mathbf{v}| * |\mathbf{v}|}$$

Let's see if we can understand what's happening here. In the numerator, we have **u**.**v**, which we know means

```
      u . v = |u|*|v|*cos(θ)
ux*vx + uy*vy = |u|*|v|*cos θ
```

Or in other words, **u**.**v** is equivalent to the length of **u** multiplied by the length of **v** times the cosine of the angle between them. In the context of this problem, we know that we are looking for the vector projection of **u** on **v**, but we need to convert **v** into a unit vector—that's what one of the |**v**| terms in the denominator does. You'll notice that I have deliberately aligned the **v**/|**v**| terms so you can see them. Thus, the |**v**| term is 1.0 and the dot product can be rewritten like this:

```
u . v = |u|*1*cos(θ) = |u|* cos(θ)
```

This is key. It states that as the angle θ becomes 0° (that is, as the vector **u** becomes co-linear with **v**), then |**u**|*cos(θ) becomes |**u**|, which is what we want. As the vectors align in the direction of **v**, then we should expect to get the total length of **u**, and we do. Now one last thing is up in the air—we need a vector, not just a magnitude! But this is easy. All we do is multiply the magnitude term

```
u . v
-----
 |v|
```

by the unit vector in the direction of **v**, and we are done. And the final result is exactly what we started with:

```
            (u . v) * v
Projv u = -------------
             |v| * |v|
```

The point of this exercise is to show how the dot product works to solve for projections. Basically, any time you want to find the amount that one vector is pointing in another vector's direction, you can use the dot product. However, remember that the test vector must be converted to a unit vector; **v** in this case.

Multiplicative Laws for Dot Products

Under normal multiplication of scalars, the associative, distributive, and commutative laws all work great. On the other hand, in vector space, sometimes these laws don't all work as you might think. Here's a list that encompasses all the laws relating to the dot product, so you don't do anything weird with them:

Given that **u**, **v**, and **w** are vectors and k is a scalar:

(a) **u . v** = **v . u**

(b) **u . (v + w) = (u . v + u . w)**

(c) k*(**u . v**) = (k*__u__) . **v** = (**u** . (k*__v__))

Note: the dot product always has higher precedence than addition.

The Cross Product

The next type of multiplication that can be applied to vectors is called the *cross product*. However, the cross product only makes sense on vectors with three or more components. Therefore, in our case we will use 3D space vectors as an example. Given **u** = $<u_x, u_y, u_z>$ and **v** = $<v_x, v_y, v_z>$, the cross product written (**u** × **v**) is defined as:

EQUATION 4.14 The Cross Product in Terms of the Normal Vector and the Angle Between **u** and **v**

```
u x v = |u|*|v|*sin(θ) * n
```

Alrighty then! Let's take this apart piece by piece. |**u**| denotes the length of **u**, |**v**| denotes the length of **v**, and sin(θ) is the sine of the angle between the vectors. Thus the product (|**u**|*|**v**|*sin(θ)) is a scalar; that is, a number. Then we multiply it by ***n***. But, what is ***n***? ***n*** is a unit normal vector, meaning that it's perpendicular to both **u** and **v** and has length 1.0. Figure 4.23 shows this graphically.

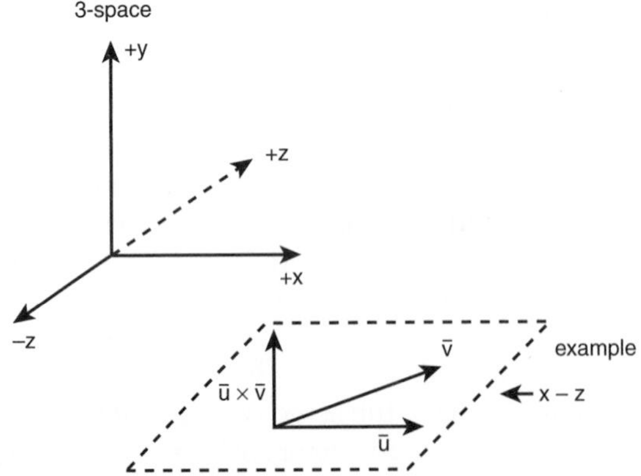

FIGURE 4.23 The cross product depicted graphically.

So the cross product tells us something about the angle between **u** and **v**, and the normal vector to both **u** and **v**. But without another equation, we aren't going to get anywhere. The question is, how to compute the normal vector from **u** and **v**? The answer is with another definition of the cross product.

The cross product is also defined as a very special vector product. However, it's hard to show without matrices, so bear with me. Assume that you want to compute the cross product of **u** and **v** (**u** × **v**): You would build a matrix like this:

$$\begin{vmatrix} \mathbf{i} & \mathbf{j} & \mathbf{k} \\ u_x & u_y & u_z \\ v_x & v_y & v_z \end{vmatrix}$$

where **i**, **j**, and **k** are unit vectors parallel to the x-, y-, and z-axes, respectively.

Then to compute the cross product of **u** and **v**, you perform this multiplication:

EQUATION 4.15 Computing the Normal Vector Between Two Vectors **u** and **v**

$$n = (u_y*v_z-v_y*u_z)*\mathbf{i} - (u_x*v_z-v_x*u_z)*\mathbf{j} + (u_x*v_y-v_x*u_y)*\mathbf{k}$$

n is just a linear combination of three scalars, each multiplied by mutually orthogonal (perpendicular) unit vectors that are each parallel to the x-, y-, and z-axes respectively. Thus we can forget **i**, **j**, and **k** and rewrite the equation as

$$n=\langle u_y*v_z-v_y*u_z,\ -u_x*v_z+v_x*u_z,\ u_x*v_y-v_x*u_y\rangle$$

n is the normal vector to both **u** and **v**; however, it is not necessarily a unit vector (if **u** and **v** were both unit vectors, **n** would be), so we must normalize it to find **n**. After this is done, we can plug everything into our cross product equation and do what we will.

In practice however, few people ever use the **u** x **v** = |**u**|*|**v**|*sin(θ)***n** formula; they simply use the matrix form to find the normal vector because θ is usually unknown. Once again, we see normalized vectors are very important in 3D graphics, and you will use them for lighting, back-face culling, defining planes, to comparing the orientation of polygons, and for collision detection, rendering, and so forth.

Multiplicative Laws for Cross Products

Here's a list that encompasses all the laws relating to the cross product, so you don't do anything weird with them:

Given that **u**, **v**, and **w** are vectors and k is a scalar:

(a) **u** × **v** = -(**v** × **u**) (very important!)

(b) **u** × (**v** + **w**) = (**u** × **v**) + (**u** × **w**)

(c) (**u** + **v**) × **w** = (**u** × **w**) + (**v** × **w**)

(d) k*(**u** × **v**) = (k***u**) × **v** = **u** × (k***v**)

The Zero Vector

Although you probably won't use the zero vector much, it does exist. The zero vector has zero length, no direction, and is simply a point, if you want to get technical. Thus in 2D, the zero vector is <0,0>, and in 3D it's <0,0,0>, and so on for higher dimensions.

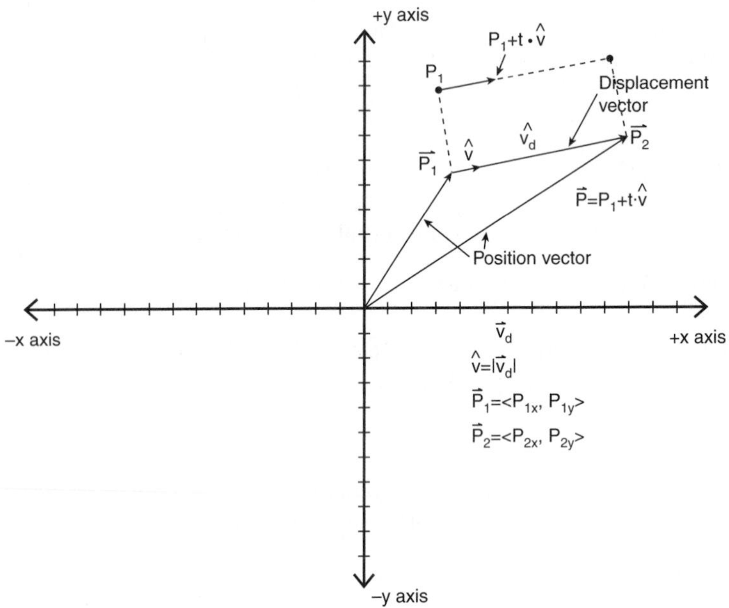

FIGURE 4.24 Position and displacement vectors.

Position and Displacement Vectors

The next topic I want to talk about is *position* and *displacement vectors*. These are really useful when tracing out geometrical entities like lines, segments, curves, and so on. Take a look at Figure 4.24—it depicts a position vector that can be used to represent a line segment. The line segment is from **p1** to **p2**, $\mathbf{v_d}$ is the displacement vector from **p1** to **p2**, and ***v*** is a unit vector in the direction of **p1** to **p2**. We then construct the vector **p** to trace out the segment. **p** looks like this mathematically:

```
p = p1 + t*v
```

where t is a parameter that varies from 0 to $|\mathbf{v_d}|$. If $t = 0$, then we have

```
p = p1 + 0*v = <p1> = <p1x, p1y>
```

Thus at $t = 0$, **p** is pointing to the beginning of the segment. On the other hand, when $t = |\mathbf{v_d}|$ we have

```
p = p1 + |vd|*v = p1 + vd = <p1+ vd>
        = <p1x+vx, p1y+vy>
        = p2 = <p2x, p2y>
```

Vectors as Linear Combinations

As you saw in the cross product, calculation vectors can also be written in the notation

```
U = ux*i + uy*j + uz*k
```

where **i**, **j**, and **k** are unit vectors parallel to the x-y-z axes. There is nothing magical about this; it's just another way to write vectors that you might need to know. All the operations still work exactly the same. For example:

let **u** = 3**i** + 2**j** + 3**k**

let **v** = -3**i** – 5**j** + 12**k**

```
u + v = 3i + 2j + 3k - 3i - 5j + 12k
      = 0i - 3j + 15k = <0, -3, 15>
```

Matrices and Linear Algebra

3D graphics involve nothing more than performing mathematical operations over and over on lists of numbers; hence the use of matrices simplifies the process of transforming and representing this type of data.

A *matrix* is a rectangular array of numbers with a given number of rows and columns. We usually say that a matrix is *m*×*n,* meaning it has *m* rows and *n* columns. The size *m*×*n* is also referred to as the *dimension* of the matrix. For example, here's a matrix **A** that has dimension 2×2:

```
A = |1  4|
    |9 -1|
```

Notice that I use uppercase bold to denote the matrix. In general, most texts use uppercase bold to denote matrices, but I have seen uppercase italics, too. However, in this book we will use uppercase bold. In the example preceding, the first row is <1 4>, and the second row is <9 –1>. Here's a 3×2 matrix:

```
    |5    6|
B = |2    3|
    |100 -7|
```

4

And here's a 2×3 matrix:

```
C = | 3  5  0 |
    |-8 12  4 |
```

To locate the <i,j>th element in the matrix, you simply look at the *i*th row and the *j*th column and look up the value. However, there is a gotcha—most math books start counting off matrix elements using 1 as the starting point, rather than 0 as we do in computer programs, so keep that in mind. We're going to start counting with 0 because this will make using C/C++ matrices work more naturally. For example, here's the labeling of a 3×3 matrix:

$$A = \begin{vmatrix} a_{00} & a_{01} & a_{02} \\ a_{10} & a_{11} & a_{12} \\ a_{20} & a_{21} & a_{22} \end{vmatrix}$$

Easy enough. So that's all there is to the actual matrix itself and the labeling conventions, but you might ask, "Where do matrices come from?" Matrices are simply mathematical tools to represent systems of equations. Basically, if you have a system of equations like

```
3*x + 2*y = 1
4*x - 9*y = 9
```

that's a lot of work writing all the variables down. You know that the equation is in terms of (x,y), so why keep writing them? Why not just create a compact format that contains only the stuff you want to work with? This is how matrices came to be. In the preceding example, there are three different sets of values that we can dump into matrices, and we can work with them together or independently.

1. The coefficients of the variables:

   ```
   3*x + 2*y = 1
   4*x - 9*y = 9
   A = |3  2|
       |4 -9|
   ```

   Note: Dimension of **A** is 2×2.

2. The variables themselves:

   ```
   3*x + 2*y = 1
   4*x - 9*y = 9
   X = |x|
       |y|
   ```

   Note: Dimension of **X** is 2×1.

3. And finally, the constants to the right:

```
3*x + 2*y = 1
4*x - 9*y = 9

B = |1|
    |9|
```

Note: Dimension of **B** is 2×1.

With all these nice matrices, we can focus on the coefficient matrix **A**, for example, without all the other stuff. Moreover, we can write matrix equations like

```
A*X = B
```

which, if you perform the math, (the multiplication), gives:

```
3*x + 2*y = 1
4*x - 9*y = 9
```

But how to perform the math? We learned that multiplication with vectors is non-intuitive, so what's the operation with matrices? Let's take a look by first understanding the concept of "1" in the context of matrices.

The Identity Matrix

The first thing we need to define in any mathematical system is 1 and 0. In matrix mathematics, there are analogs of both of these values. The analog of 1 is called the *identity matrix* **I**, and is created by placing all ones in the main diagonal of the matrix and zeros everywhere else. The identity matrix has the property:

```
A*I = I*A = A
```

Note: **I** and **A** must be the same size.

Furthermore, because matrices can be any size, there is obviously an infinite number of identity matrices, but there is one constraint—all identity matrices must be *square*, or in other words, *m*×*m*, where *m* >= 1. Here are a couple of examples:

```
I2 =  |1 0|
      |0 1|
```

Dimension 2×2

```
      |1 0 0|
I3 =  |0 1 0|
      |0 0 1|
```

Dimension 3×3

Technically, the identity matrix isn't exactly the analog of 1, but is under matrix multiplication (which we'll get to in a moment).

The second type of fundamental matrix is called the *zero matrix* **Z**, and is 0 under both addition and multiplication. It's nothing more than a matrix of dimension *m*×*n* with all entries 0. Other than that, there are no other special constraints.

```
       |0 0 0|
Z3x3 = |0 0 0|
       |0 0 0|

Z1x2 = |0 0|
```

The only interesting thing about the zero matrix is that it has the standard properties of scalar 0 for both matrix addition and multiplication. Other than that, it's pretty useless.

Matrix Addition

Addition and subtraction of matrices is performed by adding or subtracting each element in two matrices to arrive at the result for each entry. The only rule to addition and subtraction is that the matrices that the operation is being performed on must be the same dimension. Here are two examples:

Let

```
A = | 1 5|     B = |13 7  |
    |-2 0|         |5  -10|
```

then

```
A + B = | 1 5|  +  |13 7  | = |(1+13)     (5+7)| = |14 12|
        |-2 0|     |5  -10|   |(-2+5)   (0-10)|   |3 -10|
```

and

```
A - B = | 1 5|  +  |13 7  | = |(1-13) (5-7)      | = |-12 -2|
        |-2 0|     |5  -10|   |(-2-5) (0-(-10))|    |-7  10|
```

Transpose of a Matrix

Sometimes it's handy to be able to represent a matrix with its rows swapped with its columns. For example, for the 1×3 row matrix **M** = [x y z], the transpose $\mathbf{M}^t$ (or $[x\ y\ z]^t$) really means a 3×1 column matrix that looks like this:

```
       |x|
Mt  =  |y|
       |z|
```

For the general case of an *m*x*n* matrix, the transpose is computed simply by exchanging the rows with the columns. For example, for the 3×2 matrix **A** shown here:

```
      |5    6|
A =   |2    3|
      |100 -7|
```

The transpose is 2×3:

```
      |5  2  100|
At =  |6  3   -7|
```

That's all there is to it. When computing inverses and performing general matrix multiplications, the transpose of a matrix is sometimes employed.

Matrix Multiplication

There are two forms of matrix multiplication: *scalar-matrix* and *matrix-matrix*. Scalar matrix multiplication is simply the multiplication of a matrix by a scalar number. You simply multiply each element of the matrix by the number. The matrix can be any size *m*x*n*. Here's a general description for a 3×3 matrix:

Let k be any real constant.

```
        |a00 a01 a02|
Let A = |a10 a11 a12|
        |a20 a21 a22|

                |a00 a01 a02|   |k*a00 k*a01 k*a02|
Then k*A = k* |a10 a11 a12| = |k*a10 k*a11 k*a12|
                |a20 a21 a22|   |k*a20 k*a21 k*a22|
```

Here's an example:

```
3*| 1 4| = |(3*1)      (3*4)| = | 3 12|
  |-2 6|   |(3*(-2)) (3*6)|   |-6 18|
```

MATH

Scalar multiplication is also valid for matrix equations, as long as you perform the multiplication to both sides. This is true because you can always multiply the coefficients of any system of equations by a constant as long as you do so to both the right-hand side and the left-hand side of the system.

The second form is true matrix multiplication. Its mathematical basis is a bit complex, but more or less you can think of a matrix as an "operator" that operates on another matrix.

Anyway, any two matrices **A** and **B** that you want to multiply must have the same inner dimension, or in other words:

*If **A** is m×n, then **B** must be n×r.*

m and r may or may not be equal, but the inner dimension must. For example, you can multiply a 2×**2** by a **2**×2, a 3×**2** by a **2**×3, and a 4×**4** by a **4**×5, but you can't multiply a 3×**3** by a **2**×4 because the inner dimensions 3 and 2 are not equal. The resulting matrix of the multiplication will have a size that is equal to the outer dimension of the multiplier and multiplicand matrix. For example, a 2×3 multiplying a 3×4 would have dimension 2×4.

Matrix multiplication is one of those things that's very hard to describe with words, so take a look at Figure 4.25 while I give you the technical description of the multiplication algorithm.

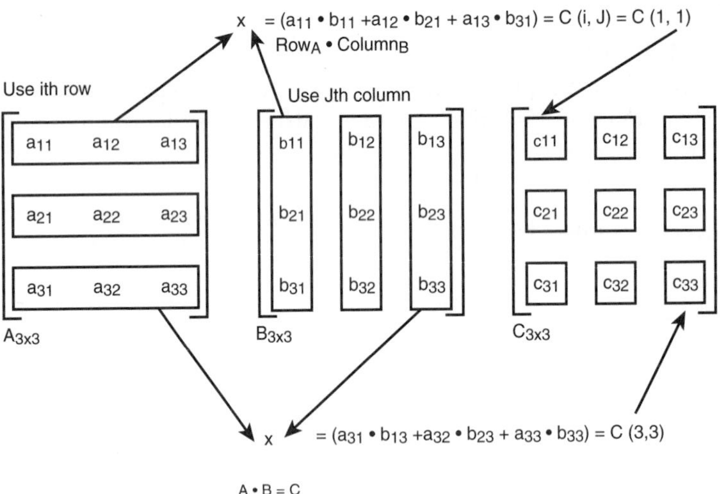

FIGURE 4.25 The mechanics of matrix multiplication.

Given a matrix **A** and **B**, to multiply them together (**A** × **B** = **C**) to compute each element of the resulting matrix **C**, you must take a row of **A** and multiply it by a column in **B**. To perform the multiplication, you will sum the products of each element or take the dot product. Here's an example for a 2×2 multiplying a 2×3—order counts!

```
Let A = |1 2|    B = |1 3 5|
        |3 4|        |6 0 4|


C = A x B = |(1*1 + 2*6) (1*3 + 2*0) (1*5 +2*4)|
            |(3*1 + 4*6) (3*3 + 4*0) (3*5 +4*4)|


 = |13 3 13|
   |27 9 31|
```

TIP

As an aside, I want to bring to your attention the bolded sum of products (1*1 + 2*6). This, and all the other elements of **C**, are really vector dot products of each row of **A** and each column of **B**. Hence, the $\mathbf{C}_{ij}$th element can also be computed as the ith row of **A** dotted with the jth column of **B**.

So that's how you multiply matrices. Another way to think of it is, if you want to compute the product of **A** × **B**, call it **C**. You can do this element by element. Hence, if you want the c_{ijth} element (where both i and j are zero-based), you can find it by taking the ith row of **A** and dotting (summing the products) with the jth column of **B**.

Laws for Matrix Operations

Just as the dot product and cross product have specific laws relating to addition and multiplication in the context of the associative, commutative, and distributive laws, so do matrices. Here they are:

(a) **A** + **B** = **B** + **A** (Commutative law for addition)

(b) **A** + (**B** + **C**) = (**A** + **B**) + **C** (Associative law for addition)

(c) **A***(**B***C**) = (**A***B**)***C** (Associative law for multiplication)

(d) **A***(**B**+**C**) = **A***B** + **A***C** (Distributive law)

(e) k*(**A** + **B**) = k***A** + k***B** (Distributive law)

(f) (**A**+**B**)***C** = **A***C** + **B***C** (Distributive law)

(g) **A***I** = **I***A** = **A** (Multiplicative property of identity)

Note: All the "+"s can be replaced with "-"s.

However, the following is not true in general:

(A*B) ≠ (B*A)

That is, the commutative law of multiplication does not hold for matrices. Thus, the order in which matrices are multiplied is very important.

NOTE

One case in which **(A*B)** does equal **(B*A)** is if **A** or **B** is equal to the identity matrix.

Computing the Inverse and Solving Systems

At this point, you know how to create and manipulate matrices, but there is one more mathematical object we need to learn to compute—the *multiplicative inverse*. In other words, if you have a scalar *x* and you want to find another number x^{-1} such that $x*x^{-1} = 1$, then x^{-1} is the multiplicative inverse, or simply the *inverse*. In the case of scalars, it's easy. Given x is a real number, x^{-1} can be computed as follows:

$$x^{-1} = 1/x, \text{ for all } x \neq 0.$$

That's pretty basic math. However, finding the multiplicative inverse for a matrix is rather complex. For example, in the matrix equation, we want to solve for **X**:

$$\mathbf{A}*\mathbf{X} = \mathbf{B}$$

If we had the inverse of **A** ($\mathbf{A}^{-1}$), we could multiply it by both sides:

$$(\mathbf{A}^{-1}*\mathbf{A})*\mathbf{X} = \mathbf{A}^{-1}*\mathbf{B}$$

And because we know that anything multiplied by its inverse is the identity matrix, we have

$$(\mathbf{I})*\mathbf{X} = \mathbf{A}^{-1}*\mathbf{B}$$

And any matrix multiplied by the identity matrix is that matrix, thus we have the solution for **X**:

$$\mathbf{X} = \mathbf{A}^{-1}*\mathbf{B}$$

Being able to solve systems of equations this way is very important in many areas of 3D game programming, such as graphics, physics, and animation. We don't really have time to cover how to find the inverse of a matrix **A** in general, but I will give you some starting places and show you how for the 2×2 case.

Given the matrix:

$$\mathbf{A} = \begin{vmatrix} a & b \\ c & d \end{vmatrix}$$

The inverse exists, and there is a unique solution to the system if the *determinate* of the matrix, that is, Det(**A**), is not zero. The determinate of an **A** (or any 2×2 matrix) can be computed as the following:

EQUATION 4.16 Determinate of a 2×2 Matrix

$$\text{Det}(\mathbf{A}) = (a*d - b*c)$$

If this result is not zero, the inverse of **A**, $\mathbf{A}^{-1}$ exists and can be computed as follows:

EQUATION 4.17 Inverse of a 2×2 Matrix

```
         1       ¦d -b¦
A-1 = ------ * ¦-c a¦
      det(A)
```

Multiplying this all out, we get:

```
        ¦ d/(a*d - b*c) -b/(a*d - b*c)¦
A-1 =  ¦-c/(a*d - b*c)  a/(a*d - b*c)¦
```

Let's put this to the test in a real system of equations. Assume you have the following two linear equations:

```
 3*x+5*y = 6
-2*x+2*y = 4
```

We want to solve for x,y using matrix techniques, so we first extract out the coefficient matrix **A**, the variable matrix X, and the constant matrix **B**:

```
A =    ¦ 3 5¦ =   ¦a  b¦
       ¦-2 2¦     ¦c  d¦

X =   ¦x¦
      ¦y¦

B =    ¦6¦
       ¦4¦
```

Therefore, we want to solve for X in

A*X = B, X = A-1*B

Computing the inverse of **A**, we get:

```
A =    ¦ 3 5¦ =   ¦a  b¦
       ¦-2 2¦     ¦c  d¦

(a*d - b*c) = (3*2 - (-2)*5) = (6+10) = 16

        ¦ d/(a*d - b*c) -b/(a*d - b*c)¦
A-1 =  ¦-c/(a*d - b*c)  a/(a*d - b*c)¦

        ¦2/16 -5/16¦
A-1 =  ¦2/16  3/16¦
```

Plugging into the matrix equation:

```
X = A-1*B

X =    |2/16 -5/16| * |6| = |(2/16)*6 +(4)*(-5)/16 |
       |2/16  3/16|   |4|   |(2/16)*6 +(4)*3/16    |

     = |12/16 - 20/16 |
       |12/16 + 12/16 |

     = |-8/16| = |-0.5|
       |24/16|   | 1.5|
```

Therefore, x = -0.5 and y = 1.5. Let's plug these values into the original system and see what's up:

```
   3*x   +    5*y     = 6
3*(-0.5)+    5*(1.5) = 6
 -1.5    +    7.5     = 6
```

That's correct. And just to make sure, let's check the second equation:

```
-2*x       +   2*y      = 4
-2*(-0.5) +   2*(1.5)  = 4
   1.0     +         3  = 4
```

Check-check! Cool, huh?

Cramer's Rule

The problem with solving a large system of equations that has three or more variables using Cramer's Rule is that the technique is bottlenecked by the computation needed to find the inverse of the coefficient matrix. This can be rather complex, and usually must be done iteratively for systems that have more than three variables by using techniques such as *Gaussian elimination*.

NOTE

Gaussian elimination is a process whereby a coefficient matrix is transformed into a form such that the solution to the system can literally be read off. The process is based on the fact that any row of a matrix can be multiplied by a number, or a multiple of another row can be added to any row as long as the same is done to the constant matrix. Using these basic rules, one can slowly convert a matrix into a form where only one non-zero coefficient in a row exists, which translates to a solved variable. Then the process can be continued, or you can employ back substitution to solve the rest of the system.

However, there is a closed form solution for a three-variable system based on *Cramer's Rule*, which you have probably heard of before. Cramer's Rule for a three-variable system is as follows:

Given a system:

$$a_{00}*x + a_{01}*y + a_{02}*z = b_0$$
$$a_{10}*x + a_{11}*y + a_{12}*z = b_1$$
$$a_{20}*x + a_{21}*y + a_{22}*z = b_2$$

We can convert it to matrix form as follows:

$$\mathbf{A} = \begin{vmatrix} a_{00} & a_{01} & a_{02} \\ a_{10} & a_{11} & a_{12} \\ a_{20} & a_{21} & a_{22} \end{vmatrix}$$

$$\mathbf{X} = \begin{vmatrix} x \\ y \\ z \end{vmatrix}$$

$$\mathbf{B} = \begin{vmatrix} b_0 \\ b_1 \\ b_2 \end{vmatrix}$$

At this point, we must compute the determinate of **A**, or Det(**A**), which for a 3×3 matrix is generally

$$\mathbf{A} = \begin{vmatrix} a_{00} & a_{01} & a_{02} \\ a_{10} & a_{11} & a_{12} \\ a_{20} & a_{21} & a_{22} \end{vmatrix}$$

EQUATION 4.18a Determinate of a 3×3 Matrix

$$Det(\mathbf{A}) = a_{00}*a_{11}*a_{22} + a_{01}*a_{12}*a_{20} + a_{02}*a_{10}*a_{21} - a_{02}*a_{11}*a_{20} - a_{01}*a_{10}*a_{22} - a_{00}*a_{12}*a_{21}$$

Note: 12 multiplications and 5 additions.

There is also another method of computing the determinate of a matrix based on *cofactor expansion*. This is rather advanced, so I will just give you the result:

EQUATION 4.18b Determinate of a 3×3 Matrix Using Cofactors

$$Det(\mathbf{A}) = a_{00}*(a_{11}*a_{22} - a_{21}*a_{12}) - a_{01}*(a_{10}*a_{22} - a_{20}*a_{12}) + a_{02}*(a_{10}*a_{21} - a_{20}*a_{11})$$

Note: 9 multiplications and 5 additions.

And just to be complete with the general notation, the determinate of a 2×2 matrix in general form is

$$A = \begin{vmatrix} a_{00} & a_{01} \\ a_{10} & a_{11} \end{vmatrix}$$

$$\text{Det}(\mathbf{A}) = a_{00}*a_{11} - a_{01}*a_{10}$$

Now that we have the Det(**A**) for the 3×3 system, Cramer's Rule can be written as a set of quotients that solve for x,y, and z. There's one quotient for each solution variable; x,y,z, where the numerator is the determinate of the coefficient matrix **A**, with the first, second, and third columns replaced with the column vector **B** to compute x,y, and z, respectively. Then the denominator of each quotient is simply Det(**A**). Or more specifically, we have

$$\mathbf{x} = \frac{\text{Det}\left(\begin{vmatrix} b_0 & a_{01} & a_{02} \\ b_1 & a_{11} & a_{12} \\ b_2 & a_{21} & a_{22} \end{vmatrix}\right)}{\text{Det}(\mathbf{A})}$$

Note: The first column of **A** was replaced with **B** to solve for x.

$$\mathbf{y} = \frac{\text{Det}\left(\begin{vmatrix} a_{00} & b_0 & a_{02} \\ a_{10} & b_1 & a_{12} \\ a_{20} & b_2 & a_{22} \end{vmatrix}\right)}{\text{Det}(\mathbf{A})}$$

Note: The second column of **A** was replaced with **B** to solve for y.

$$\mathbf{z} = \frac{\text{Det}\left(\begin{vmatrix} a_{00} & a_{01} & b_0 \\ a_{10} & a_{11} & b_1 \\ a_{20} & a_{21} & b_2 \end{vmatrix}\right)}{\text{Det}(\mathbf{A})}$$

Note: The third column of **A** was replaced with **B** to solve for z.

And of course, you must use one of the forms of Equation 4.18 to compute the determinate of each numerator, but you get the idea. Later we will write software to compute determinates and solve for systems of two and three variables.

Transformations Using Matrices

The whole point of learning all this stuff about matrices is to use them to perform 2D/3D transformations. Basically, what we're going to do is multiply the 2D/3D point **p** that we want transformed against the desired transformation matrix. Or mathematically:

$$p' = p*M$$

where **p'** is the transformed point, **p** is the original point, and **M** is the transformation matrix. Additionally, we can perform as many transformations as we want by multiplying transformation matrices together. That is, we can *concatenate* any number of matrices together by pre-multiplying them in a series, like this:

$$M = M_1*M_2*M_3*...M_n$$

The following transforms are equivalent:

$$p' = p*M = p*M_1*M_2*M_3*...M_n$$

Whether you multiply **p** by **M** or the product $\mathbf{M_1*M_2*M_3*...M_n}$, the results are the same. For example, say that we have three transformations $\mathbf{M_1}$, $\mathbf{M_2}$, and $\mathbf{M_3}$ that we want to apply to the point **p** in order to arrive at **p'**. These could represent a translation, rotation, and projection, for example. We could perform this series of transforms in the normal way, one at a time:

$$p1 = p*M_1$$

$$p2 = p1*M_2$$

$$p' = p2*M_3$$

Note: **p1** and **p2** are just temporary variables.

The preceding series of transforms is completely acceptable. But, what if we have thousands of **p**'s to transform, or even millions? It seems like those intermediate steps are a waste—and they are! We can concatenate the transforms together like this, via substitution:

$$p1 = p*M_1$$

$$p2 = p*M_1*M_2$$

$$p' = p*(M_1*M_2*M_3)$$

4

Hence, the transform to **p** can be represented by the transform **p** *(**M**), where $\mathbf{M}_{123} = (\mathbf{M}_1*\mathbf{M}_2*\mathbf{M}_3)$. Therefore, we can compute $\mathbf{M}_{123} = (\mathbf{M}_1*\mathbf{M}_2*\mathbf{M}_3)$ once and then use it instead of saving two matrix multiplies per point! Thus, the transform becomes

$$M_{123} = (M_1*M_2*M_3)$$

$$p' = p * M_{123}$$

Of course, we have to compute $\mathbf{M}_{123}$, but this has to be done only once, and then we can run as many points through the transform as we wish. The process of concatenating matrices together is very useful in the 3D pipeline, especially when transforming 3D vertices in object space into final points in screen space (but we'll get to that).

NOTE

Because of the noncommutative nature of matrix multiplication in the general case, order is very important, and $\mathbf{M}_1*\mathbf{M}_2*\mathbf{M}_3 \neq \mathbf{M}_3*\mathbf{M}_2*\mathbf{M}_1$.

Homogeneous Coordinates

The next topic I want to cover briefly is *homogeneous coordinates*. In most cases, we're going represent our 3D objects as lists of vertices, each having three components: **p**(x,y,z), or as a vector <x, y, z>, or as a row matrix [x y z]—note that all are equivalent and the difference is really notational. I will use the latter when I want to multiply with a matrix and/or I don't want to use commas. However, to be able to use the full power of matrix transformations, we are going to represent points in 2D and 3D using homogeneous coordinates, so we can perform all possible transformations using matrices. To convert a 2D or 3D point to homogeneous coordinates, we add a "w" term to each, as follows:

The homogeneous coordinate for a 3D point [x y z]:

```
[x y z w]
```

and for a 2D point [x y]:

```
[x y w]
```

w homogenizes the coordinate, but it's not artificial. To convert from homogenous coordinates to normal coordinates, we must divide by w. For example, in the 3D case:

Given

```
[x y z w]
```

the normal coordinate can be computed as

```
[x/w y/w z/w]
```

Therefore, if w = 1, the transform doesn't change x, y, or z. So what's the point of adding w? Well, w allows us to represent the concept of infinity. For example, as w approaches 0, then x/w approaches ∞. Or in other words, as the denominator of any fraction goes to 0, the quotient goes to infinity. Additionally, homogenous coordinates come from *homogenous equations*. For example, take a look at the following linear equation:

```
a*x + b*y + c = 0
```

This is a linear equation with degree 1, but two of the terms have degree 1 while the constant term has degree 0. What if we want all the degrees to be the same (homogenous)? We can convert the polynomial to a homogenous one by replacing x with x/w and y with y/w:

```
a*x/w + b*y/w + c = 0
```

And then we want to clear the w's in the denominator, so we multiply through by w, and the result is

```
a*x + b*y + c*w = 0
```

Now all the terms have degree 1, and thus the polynomial is homogenous. The point of all this is that if you represent geometric objects using homogenous coordinates, you can guarantee that all transformations are possible, including perspective transforms and translations. I don't want to belabor this anymore, but know that we are going to use a dummy variable w = 1 in many cases just so we can represent all transforms via matrices. In reality, we might not use any storage for w in our data structures because we are going to let w = 1 for most cases, and all homogenous coordinates [x y z w] with w = 1 are simply [x y z]. I just want you to know where this mathematical trick comes from.

Although we are going to cover the full gamut of 3D transformations in the next chapter in great detail, I just want to briefly show some of the most basic 3D transformations (*translation*, *scaling*, and *rotation*) and why we need homogeneous coordinates to support all three.

Applied Matrix Transformations

The following section illustrates some of the basic matrix transformations that we will perform to both 2D and 3D data. The examples are for 3D, but the 2D versions can easily be derived by dropping the z component in most cases. Note that w = 1 for all the examples.

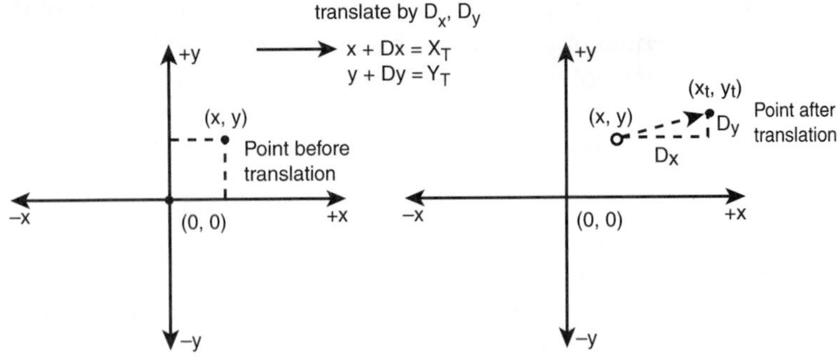

FIGURE 4.26 Translation depicted geometrically for the 2D case.

Translation

To perform translation in 3D, we want to translate the point **p**(x,y,z) to the new point **p**'(x+dx, y+dy, z+dz). This is shown in Figure 4.26 for the simplified case where the point is in the x-y plane. The following 4×4 matrix will do the job:

```
     |1  0  0  0|
Mt = |0  1  0  0|
     |0  0  1  0|
     |dx dy dz 1|
```

Given **p** = [x y z 1], we want to transform:

```
                        |1  0  0  0 |
p' = p*Mt = [x y z 1]*  |0  1  0  0 |
                        |0  0  1  0 |
                        |dx dy dz 1 |

= [(x+1*dx) (y+1*dy) (z+1*dz) (1*1)]

= [(x+dx) (y+dy) (z+dz) 1]
```

And dividing the first three components (which represent x, y, and z) by the w factor (1.0), we get:

```
= [(x+dx)/1 (y+dy)/1 (z+dz)/1]

= p'((x+dx), (y+dy), (z+dz))
```

NOTE

In reality, when we write the math library, we obviously aren't going to waste space and divide by 1.0 all the time. We are going to use a 4×3 matrix for most transforms and assume w = 1, but for now, let's just pretend.

And if we pull out the first three elements, we get

```
x' = x+dx
y' = y+dy
z' = z+dz
```

which is exactly what we wanted.

Translation Inverse

Also, it's interesting to note that the inverse of $\mathbf{M_t}$ is computed simply by changing the sign of dx, dy, and dz in the matrix $\mathbf{M_t}$:

```
          | 1   0   0  0|
Mt^-1 =   | 0   1   0  0|
          | 0   0   1  0|
          |-dx -dy -dz 1|
```

Let's check that by computing the product $\mathbf{M_t}*\mathbf{M_t}^{-1}$, which should be $\mathbf{I_{4x4}}$:

```
Mt*Mt^-1 =
      |1  0  0  0|   | 1   0   0  0|
  =   |0  1  0  0| * | 0   1   0  0|
      |0  0  1  0|   | 0   0   1  0|
      |dx dy dz 1|   |-dx -dy -dz 1|
          Mt              Mt^-1

      |1 0 0 0|
  =   |0 1 0 0| = I4x4.
      |0 0 1 0|
      |0 0 0 1|
```

> **NOTE**
>
> Computing the inverse efficiently for common transformation matrices is very important in 3D graphics, especially in the camera transform.

Scaling

To scale a point relative to the origin, we want to multiply the point $\mathbf{p}$(x,y,z) components by scaling factors sx, sy, and sz for the x- ,y-, and z-axes, respectively. This is shown in Figure 4.27 for the simplified case where all the points are in the x-y plane. In addition, we want no translation during the scaling operation. Here's the matrix we want:

```
     |sx 0  0  0|
Ms = |0  sy 0  0|
     |0  0  sz 0|
     |0  0  0  1|
```

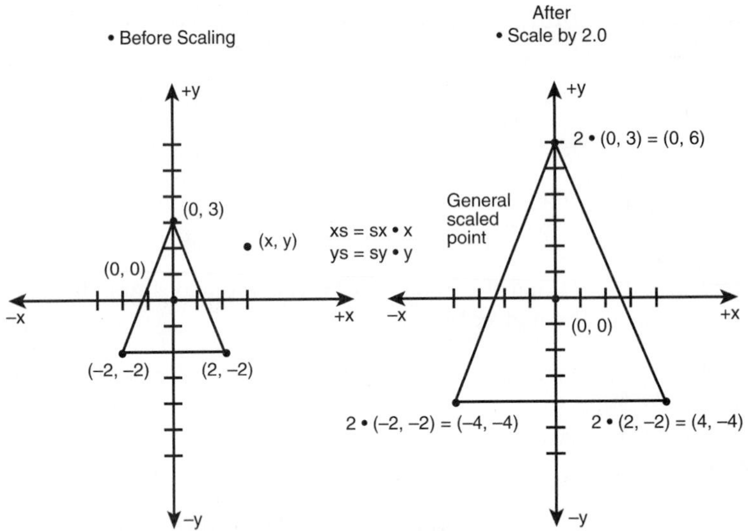

FIGURE 4.27 The scaling operation.

Given **p** = [x y z 1], we want to transform

```
                                |sx 0  0  0|
p' = p* M_s = [x y z 1] *       |0  sy 0  0|
                                |0  0  sz 0|
                                |0  0  0  1|

= [(x*sx) (y*sy) (z*sz) (1*1)]

= [(x*sx) (y*sy) (z*sz) 1]
```

And dividing the first three components (which represent x, y, z) by the w factor, we get

```
= [(x*sx)/1 (y*sy)/1 (z*sz)/1]

= p'((x*sx), (y*sy), (z*sz))
```

which again is the desired result for scaling; that is

```
x' = sx*x
y' = sy*y
z' = sz*z
```

MATH

Note the 1 in the lower-right bottom of the transformation matrix. Technically, it's not necessary because we aren't ever going to use the result from the fourth column for scaling. Hence, we are wasting math cycles. Again, as noted in the translation example, using the four-component representation to implement homogenous coordinates in our 3D points (or three-component for 2D points) forces us to use a 4×4 matrix to be mathematically correct. Later we will throw away all that we don't need.

Scaling Inverse

Although not as commonly used as the inverse of translation, computing the inverse of the scaling matrix can come in handy. Can you think of what the inverse is? Give up? The inverse of the scaling matrix $\mathbf{M_s}$ is computed simply by inverting each of the scaling factors sx, sy, and sz in the matrix $\mathbf{M_s}$:

4

```
        |1/sx 0    0    0|
Ms-1 =  |0    1/sy 0    0|
        |0    0    1/sz 0|
        |0    0    0    1|
```

Let's check that by computing the product $\mathbf{M_s}*\mathbf{M_s}^{-1}$, which should be $\mathbf{I_{4x4}}$:

```
Ms*Ms-1 =

   |sx 0  0  0|   |1/sx 0    0    0|
 = |0  sy 0  0| * |0    1/sy 0    0|
   |0  0  sz 0|   |0    0    1/sz 0|
   |0  0  0  1|   |0    0    0    1|
       Ms               Ms-1

   |1 0 0 0|
 = |0 1 0 0| = I4x4.
   |0 0 1 0|
   |0 0 0 1|
```

NOTE

Note that computing the inverse mathematically using Gaussian elimination or another method is very complex and tedious, whereas here we simply thought about the problem in terms of its geometrical properties to find the inverse. In general, when a transform represents a geometrical transformation in 2D or 3D, computing its inverse is trivial, and can usually be done with a little thought about simply inverting the geometrical transformation. Keep this in mind when we compute the inverses for the rotation matrices and see whether you can figure them out before getting to that section.

Rotation

The rotation matrix is the most complex of all the transformations because it's full of trig functions. Basically, we want to rotate the input point by using the rotation equations. To achieve this, we must look at the rotation equations and pick off the operators and then push them into a matrix. In addition, we don't want any translation, so the bottom row in positions 0, 1, and 2 will always be 0.

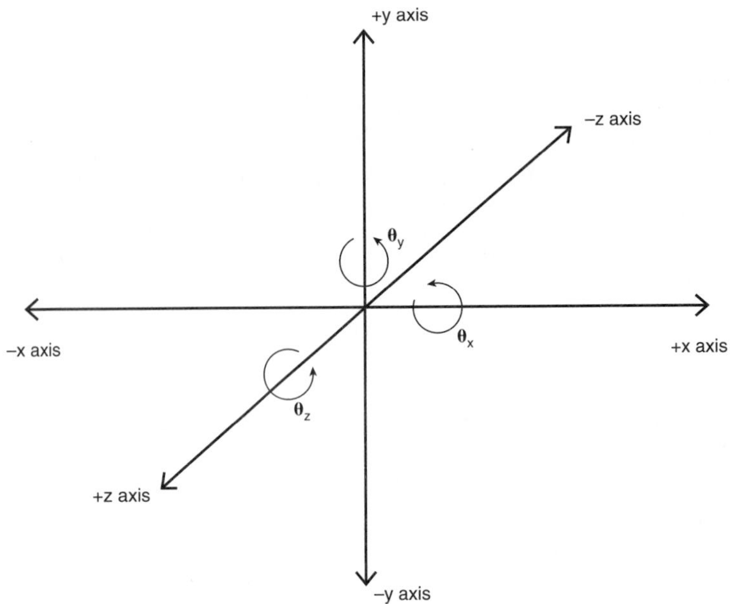

FIGURE 4.28 The axes of rotation.

There is also one more technical detail—in a 3D system, there are three axes that we can rotate in parallel to: the x, y, or z, as shown in Figure 4.28. With that in mind, we can start with the z-axis rotation and then use it as a model to create the x- and y-axis rotation matrices. The key is that during rotation around any axis, the axis component itself remains unchanged.

CAUTION

The direction of rotation for positive values of θ depends on the "handedness" of the system. If you are using a right-handed system, all rotations with positive θ will be counterclockwise. If you are using a left-handed system, positive θ will result in clockwise rotations.

Keeping all that in mind, here are the rotation equations for rotation parallel to the x-, y-, and z-axes:

Rotation parallel to the z-axis:

```
      | cosθ sinθ  0 0|
Mz =  |-sinθ cosθ  0 0|
      | 0    0     1 0|
      | 0    0     0 1|
```

NOTE

If you delete the last column and row, you'll have the matrix for 2D rotation in a plane.

Rotation parallel to the x-axis:

```
      |1   0     0     0|
Mx =  |0   cosθ  sinθ  0|
      |0  -sinθ  cosθ  0|
      |0   0     0     1|
```

Rotation parallel to the y-axis:

```
      | cosθ 0  -sinθ 0|
My =  | 0    1   0    0|
      | sinθ 0   cosθ 0|
      | 0    0   0    1|
```

Now, let's look at an example for rotation around the z-axis and see whether the transform works.

Given the point **p** = [x y z 1], we want to rotate an angle θ about the z-axis:

```
                             | cosθ sinθ 0 0|
p' = p*Mz = [x y z 1]  *     |-sinθ cosθ 0 0|
                             | 0    0    1 0|
                             | 0    0    0 1|
```

```
p' = [(x*cos θ - y*sin θ) (x*sin θ + y*cos θ) z (1*1)]
```

And dividing the first three components (which represent x, y, and z) by the w factor, we get:

```
p' = ((x*cos θ-y*sin θ), (x*sin θ + y*cos θ), z)
```

Note: z remained unchanged, as it should.

4

Rotation Inverse

The rotation inverses for $\mathbf{M}_x$, $\mathbf{M}_y$, and $\mathbf{M}_z$ are all computed in the same manner, so I'm only going to show you the derivation of $\mathbf{M}_z$—the others will follow from there. To compute the inverse of $\mathbf{M}_z$ for a given θ, you can take two approaches: one based on geometry, and the other based on linear algebra. Let's begin with the geometric computation of the inverse. It makes sense that if we rotate an object parallel to the z-axis by θ, then to rotate it back, we can simply rotate it by -θ. That's it! So all you need to do is take the rotation matrix and replace θ with -θ, and that's the inverse. Therefore, the inverse $\mathbf{M}_z^{-1}$ can be computed as follows:

$$\mathbf{M}_z^{-1} = \begin{vmatrix} \cos-\theta & \sin-\theta & 0 & 0 \\ -\sin-\theta & \cos-\theta & 0 & 0 \\ 0 & 0 & 1 & 0 \\ 0 & 0 & 0 & 1 \end{vmatrix}$$

Now, there's another simplification we can make here to get rid of the -θ terms. Using the *reflection identities* from Table 4.5, we have

$$\sin(-\theta) = -\sin(\theta)$$
$$\cos(-\theta) = \cos(\theta)$$

Using these formulas and rewriting $\mathbf{M}_z^{-1}$ in terms of positive θ, we have

$$\mathbf{M}_z^{-1} = \begin{vmatrix} \cos\theta & -\sin\theta & 0 & 0 \\ \sin\theta & \cos\theta & 0 & 0 \\ 0 & 0 & 1 & 0 \\ 0 & 0 & 0 & 1 \end{vmatrix}$$

Let's try the product $\mathbf{M}_z*\mathbf{M}_z^{-1}$ and see whether we get the identity matrix $\mathbf{I}_{4x4}$:

$$\mathbf{M}_z*\mathbf{M}_z^{-1} =$$

$$= \underbrace{\begin{vmatrix} \cos\theta & \sin\theta & 0 & 0 \\ -\sin\theta & \cos\theta & 0 & 0 \\ 0 & 0 & 1 & 0 \\ 0 & 0 & 0 & 1 \end{vmatrix}}_{\mathbf{M}_z} * \underbrace{\begin{vmatrix} \cos\theta & -\sin\theta & 0 & 0 \\ \sin\theta & \cos\theta & 0 & 0 \\ 0 & 0 & 1 & 0 \\ 0 & 0 & 0 & 1 \end{vmatrix}}_{\mathbf{M}_z^{-1}}$$

$$= \begin{vmatrix} (\cos^2\theta+\sin^2\theta) & (-\sin\theta*\cos\theta+\cos\theta*\sin\theta) & (0) & (0) \\ (-\sin\theta*\cos\theta+\cos\theta*\sin\theta) & (\sin^2\theta+\cos^2\theta) & (0) & (0) \\ (0) & (0) & (1) & (0) \\ (0) & (0) & (0) & (1) \end{vmatrix}$$

Which, using the identity $\cos^2\theta+\sin^2\theta = 1$, reduces to

$$= \begin{vmatrix} 1 & 0 & 0 & 0 \\ 0 & 1 & 0 & 0 \\ 0 & 0 & 1 & 0 \\ 0 & 0 & 0 & 1 \end{vmatrix} = \mathbf{I}_{4x4}.$$

See how powerful geometric interpretation is to compute inverses of geometry transforming matrices? Very cool! Anyway, now let's get a little mathematical. The rotation matrix itself is a special matrix in the wide world of matrices. In fact, it's part of a very unique class of matrices that are called orthonormal.

Orthonormal Matrices

Orthonormal matrices are matrices where each row or column is orthogonal to the previous for a given basis. A *basis* is a set of vectors that can represent all vectors in a space. In our case, the basis for standard 2D space is <i+j>, and the basis for 3D is <i+j+k>—remember this from a few sections ago? Remember, all vectors in a 3D space can be written as a linear combination:

$$\mathbf{u} = u_x*\mathbf{i} + u_y*\mathbf{j} + u_z*\mathbf{k}$$

Where **i** = <1,0,0>, **j** = <0,1,0>, and **k** = <0,0,1>. Therefore, i is orthogonal to j is orthogonal to k because for the set s1 = (**i**,**j**,**k**) with k = 0,1,2, and s2 = (**i**,**j**,**k**) with t = 0,1,2 and $k \neq t$, the dot product is 0; therefore, the vectors are perpendicular. For example, (**i**.**j**) equals:

```
<1,0,0> . <0,1,0> = 1*0 + 0*1 + 0*0 = 0.
```

This will hold true for all pairs of (**i**,**j**,**k**). Now, the point is that if a matrix contains a set of orthogonal vectors as its rows or columns, the matrix is said to be an orthogonal or orthonormal matrix. Let's take a look at $\mathbf{M}_z$ again:

$$\mathbf{M}_z = \begin{vmatrix} \cos\theta & \sin\theta & 0 & 0 \\ -\sin\theta & \cos\theta & 0 & 0 \\ 0 & 0 & 1 & 0 \\ 0 & 0 & 0 & 1 \end{vmatrix}$$

If we assume that the rows represent vectors in 3D, we have:

```
U1 = <cos θ, sin θ, 0, 0>
U2 = <-sin θ, cos θ, 0, 0>
U3 = <0, 0, 1, 0>
U4 = <0, 0, 0, 1>
```

Now, technically we are in 4D space because these transforms are based on homogeneous coordinates, but let's not worry about that for a moment and see whether all these vectors are orthogonal to one another.

- **u1** is orthogonal to **u4** because (**u1** . **u4**) = 0.
- It's easy to see that both **u1** and **u4** are orthogonal to both **u1** and **u2** because both **u1** and **u2** have zeros in the last two components, thus the products with either **u3** or **u4** will always be zero, and so will the dot product.

The only big question left is whether **u1** is orthogonal to **u2**. Let's see:

```
u1 = <cos θ, sin θ, 0, 0>
u2 = <-sin θ, cos θ, 0, 0>


u1 . u2 = (cos θ)*(-sin θ) + (sin θ)*(cos θ) + 0 + 0
      = 0.
```

Killer! The point is, we have shown what an orthogonal matrix is and how to check for it. Wonderful, but how does this help us find the inverse? Well, if a matrix is orthogonal, its transpose is its inverse. Therefore, if we compute $\mathbf{M}_z^t$, it should be equivalent to the inverse of $\mathbf{M}_z$ (that is, $\mathbf{M}_z^{-1}$).

Given

```
      | cosθ sinθ 0 0|
Mz =  |-sinθ cosθ 0 0|
      | 0    0    1 0|
      | 0    0    0 1|
```

its transpose is computed by exchanging each column with each row:

```
       |cosθ -sinθ 0 0|
Mz^t = |sinθ  cosθ 0 0|
       |0     0    1 0|
       |0     0    0 1|
```

which is indeed $\mathbf{M}_z^{-1}$! Amazing, huh? I scare myself sometimes <BG>.

Basic Geometric Entities

The next topic I want to discuss is basic geometric entities such as points, lines, planes, and surfaces, but with a focus on various mathematical representations and operations that are of interest in the world of 3D graphics. For example, all polygons are really planes with boundaries; therefore, being proficient at manipulating planes and plane equations is very useful.

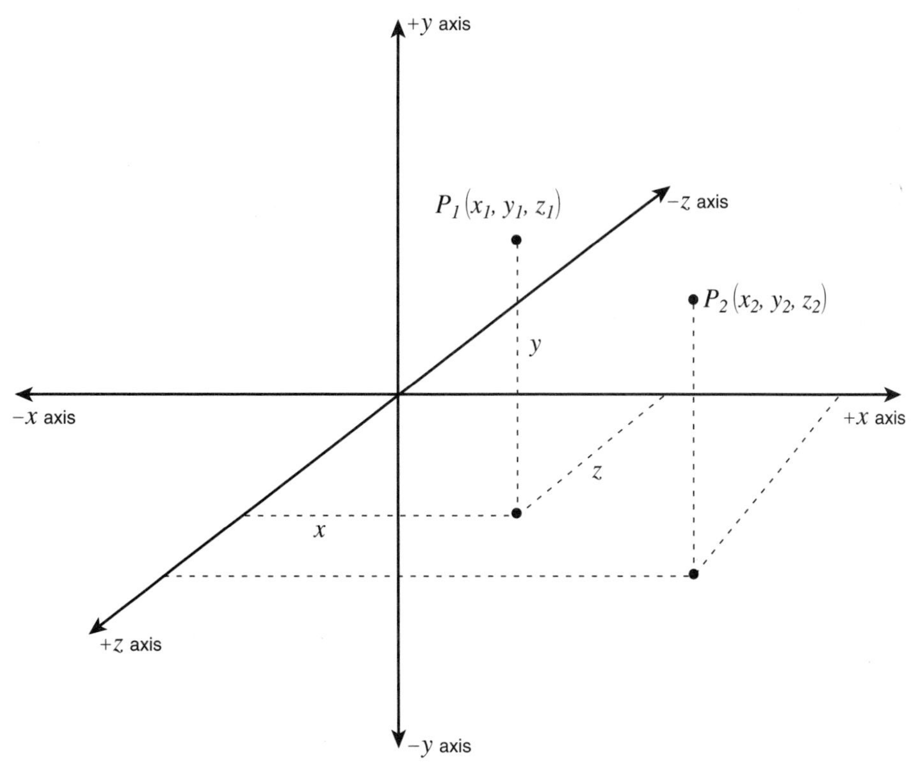

FIGURE 4.29 A plain old point in 3D.

Points

There's not much to say about a point. Figure 4.29 represents a point **p1**(x,y) in 2D and a point **p2**(x,y,z) in 3D. Of course, the homogeneous coordinates for **p1** and **p2** are [x y w] and [x y z w], respectively.

Lines

Lines are a bit more interesting, and a lot more complex to represent in 3D. Let's begin by looking at a line from **p1**(x1, y1) to **p2**(x2,y2) in 2D, as shown in Figure 4.30. Nothing special about this line. We can represent it in a number of ways, such as the *point-slope form*, the *slope-intercept form*, or the *general form*.

EQUATION 4.19 Slope-Intercept Form

```
y=m*x + b
```

where m is the slope of the line (dy/dx), and b is the y-axis intercept.

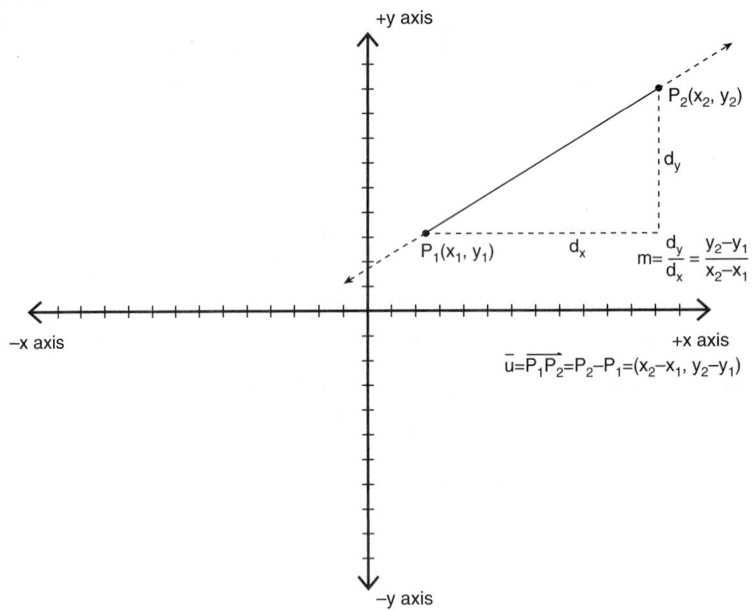

FIGURE 4.30 A line in 2D.

EQUATION 4.20 Point-Slope Form

```
(x-x0) = m*(y-y0)
```

where m is the slope and (x0,y0) is a point on the line.

EQUATION 4.21 General Form

```
a*x + b*y + c = 0
```

The general form, of course, is the most basic. Let's see whether we can convert it into the other forms. Converting to the slope-intercept form is trivial:

```
y = m*x + b
```

Rearranging, we get

```
m*x - 1*y + b = 0
```

We can now pick off a, b, and c in the general form:

```
a*x + b*y + c = 0
```

Therefore, a = m, b = -1, and c = b (the intercept). But what if you don't have the intercept? How can we find the values of (a,b,c) if we only have the coordinates (x0,y0) and (x1,y1)? Well, let's see whether the point-slope form can help out. Starting with the point-slope equation:

```
(y - y0) = m*(x - x0)
```

multiplying through by m,

```
y - y0 = m*x - m*x0
```

Collecting x and y on the LHS,

```
-m*x + y = y0 - m*x0
```

Moving the constant terms on the RHS to the LHS:

```
(-m)*x + (1)*y + (-1)*y0 + (m)*x0 = 0
```


MATH

The (-1) and the associated multiplications aren't necessary; they just make the extraction of (a,b,c) easier to see.

So it looks like a = -m, b = 1, and c = (m*x0 – y0). In general, any one of the forms may be appropriate for any particular application. However, if you have a problem where you want to compute the intersection of two lines, the general form is usually the most appropriate because you can push them into a matrix and then solve as follows:

```
a1*x + b1*y = c1
a2*x + b2*y = c2
A =   |a1  b1|
      |a2  b2|

X =  |x|
     |y|

B =   |c1|
      |c2|
```

We want to solve **A*X** = **B**. We can use the technique of multiplying each side by the inverse of **A**, $\mathbf{A}^{-1}$.

$$\mathbf{X} = \mathbf{A}^{-1}*\mathbf{B}$$

We have done this exercise, so I leave it to you to find a closed form solution.

MATH

If the determinate of **A**, Det(**A**), is zero, then no unique solution exists.

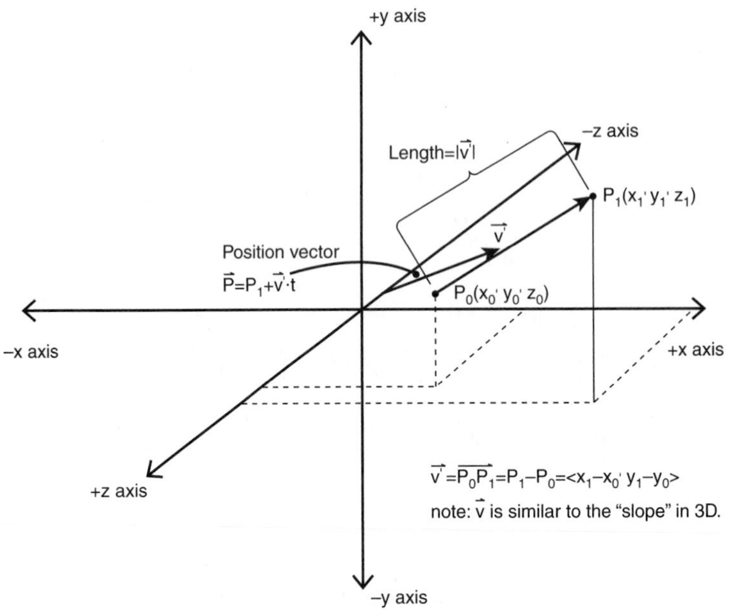

FIGURE 4.31 A line in 3D space.

Lines in 3D Space

Lines in 3D space are a little more complex to represent. In fact, they are downright ugly! In reality, we will use parametric representations of lines in many cases, but I want to talk about parametric representations as a whole; so for now, let's see whether we can figure out a way to represent a 3D line. Take a look at Figure 4.31, which depicts a line in 3D. Referring to the figure, we see a line that passes through points **p0**(x0,y0,z0) and **p1**(x1,y1,z1) and the unit vector **v**' = <x1-x0, y1-y0, z1-z0> = <a,b,c> in the direction of p0 to p1. So we know two points on the line, and we have **v**', which is analogous to the "slope" of the line.

Now, before showing you the equation of the line, let's take a quick look at the vector parametric form just for kicks:

EQUATION 4.22 Parametric Vector Form of a 3D Line

p(x,y,z) = **p0** + **v**'*t

As t varies from zero to |**v**|, **p** traces out **p0** -> **p1**. This should seem familiar, because we covered it when discussing position and 2D displacement vectors a few sections back. Anyway, we are looking for the explicit form of a line in 3D space, and here it is:

EQUATION 4.23 Explicit Symmetrical Form of a 3D Line

```
(x-x0)   (y-y0)   (z-z0)
------ = ------ = ------
  a        b        c
```

Interesting, huh? Basically, there are three equations here, but you only need two because they are coupled. Also, a,b,c are the (x,y,z) components of the unit vector **v**'. The problem with this form is that it's a bit clunky. For example, let's compute it for the line from **p0**(1,2,3) to **p1**(5,6,7).

Given

```
p0(1,2,3)
p1(5,6,7)
v = <p1-p0> = <5-1, 6-2, 7-3> = <4,4,4>
v' = v/¦v¦  = <4,4,4>/¦sqrt(4²+4²+4²)¦
            = <.57, .57, .57>
            = <a,   b,   c>
```

Plugging into Equation 4.23, we have

```
(x-1)     (y-2)    (z-3)
------ = ------ = ------
 .57       .57      .57
```

Multiplying by .57 to clear the denominator and separating the equations, we have

```
(x-1) = (y-2)
```

and

```
(y-2) = (z-3)
```

Simplifying, we get

```
x - y = -1
y - z = -1
```

As you can see in Figure 4.32, lines are fairly ugly in 3D in explicit form. The parametric form of lines is much cleaner.

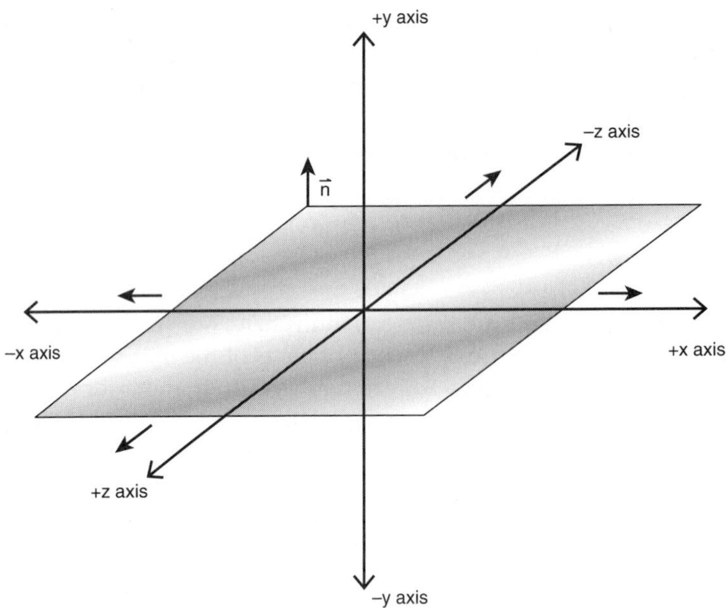

FIGURE 4.32 An infinite plane.

Planes

Planes are really the workhorse of 3D graphics. Technically, a plane is an infinite sheet that extends in all directions infinitely, as shown in Figure 4.32. However, when dealing with 3D graphics, we use the concept of a polygon many times, which is of course a closed (usually coplanar) object that lies in a plane, but is constructed of a set of edges or lines that make it up, as shown in Figure 4.33. However, because all polygons usually lie in a specific plane, we can tell a lot about a polygon from the plane information. Conversely, we can derive the information about a plane in which a polygon lies and use it for mathematical operations as well. Hence, understanding planes is very important. So let's first jot down a couple of the general conceptual attributes of planes:

- All planes are infinite sheets in 3D.
- All planes divide space into two half-spaces (very important for various space partitioning algorithms and collision detection).

A number of methods exist to generate an equation for a plane, but let's take a look at the problem geometrically and see whether we can come up with our own. This is a very important exercise—being able to derive something yourself. It will help you immensely in the future. Anyway, take a look at Figure 4.33, which depicts a plane that has the normal **n** = <a,b,c> with the points **p0**(x0, y0, z0) and **p**(x,y,z) that lie in the plane itself.

We can see the plane we want to define, but what's the equation? Let's begin by noticing that the vector **p0->p** lies within the plane, and should (must) be perpendicular (orthogonal) to **n** because both **p0** and **p** lie in the plane. Okay, now we have something to work with—a constraint that we can exploit. We know that for any **p**(x,y,z) in the plane, the vector <**p0->p**> dotted with **n** must be equal to zero, because the dot product of two orthogonal vectors is always zero. Therefore, we can write

```
n . (p0->p) = 0
```

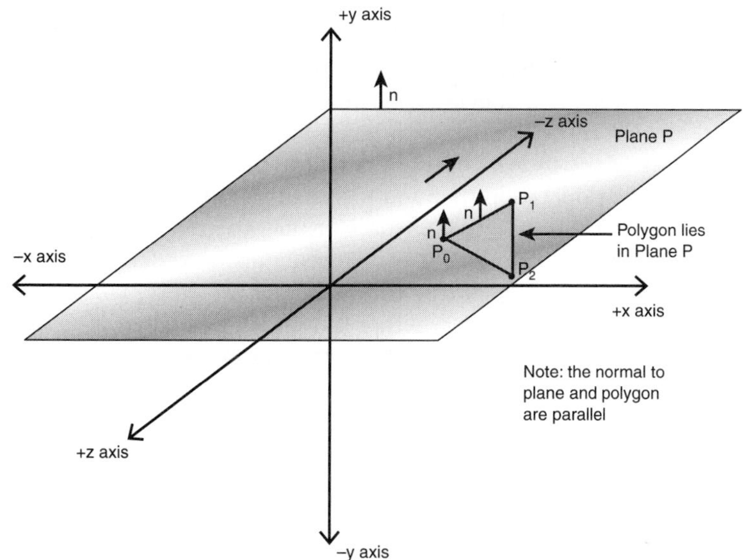

FIGURE 4.33 A plane constructed around a polygon.

That *is* the equation for the plane! Let's multiply it out now and see what it looks like:

EQUATION 4.24 Point-Normal Form of a Plane

```
<a,b,c> . <x-x0, y-y0, z-z0) = 0

a*(x-x0) + b*(y-y0) + c*(z-z0) = 0
```

This is called the *point normal form* of a plane. The reason is that (x0, y0, z0) is a point in the plane, and <a,b,c> is the normal to the plane. Now, if we multiply the terms out and collect the constants, we get the *general form* of a plane:

EQUATION 4.25 General Form of a Plane

Given

```
a*(x-x0) + b*(y-y0) + c*(z-z0) = 0
a*x + b*y + c*z + (-a*x0 - b*y0 - c*z0) = 0
```

and letting d = (-a*x0 - b*y0 - c*z0), we have

```
a*x + b*y + c*z + d = 0
```

The general form comes in handy when you want to compute the intersection of two or more planes. In that case, you have a system of two or more equations in terms of (x,y,z) and you want to solve them. Of course, this is most easily done with the general form.

Computing the Half-Space In Which a Point Is Contained

There is a very important operation that you will use over and over in relation to planes: computing whether a point is on one half-space or the other of a plane. For example, you might want to know whether a projectile has pierced a plane, or something similar. The plane equation can tell you this. Referring to Figure 4.34, we see a plane on its side, along with a point **p** that we want to decide whether it is on the positive half-space or the negative half-space of the plane. The positive half-space is the space into which the normal is pointing, and the negative is of course the other half-space.

To test for this, assuming that we have the equation of the plane in the form:

```
hs = a*(x-x0) + b*(y-y0) + c*(z-z0)
```

All you need to do is plug in the test point for (x,y,z) and test the result. Here are the outcomes:

- If hs = 0, then the point lies in the plane.
- If (hs > 0), then the point lies in the positive half-space.
- If (hs < 0), then the point lies in the negative half-space.

This is one way of writing a polygon point containment test. As an example, let's try a couple of test points, with the x-z plane as the test plane. The normal is <0,1,0> and a point on the plane is (0,0,0):

```
hs = 0*(x-0) + 1*(y-0) + 0*(z-0) = (y-0) = hs
```

First we see that the x-z coordinates are irrelevant, as they should be, because the plane in question is the x-z plane. Therefore, we really only have to look at the y-component of any point. For the point **p**(10,10,10), which is definitely in the positive half-space, we see that (y-y0) = (10-0) = 10 > 0, hence in the positive half-space. So in this case, the problem degenerated into a single component test. In general, it won't, but you get the point. That's what I call a singular sense of humor.

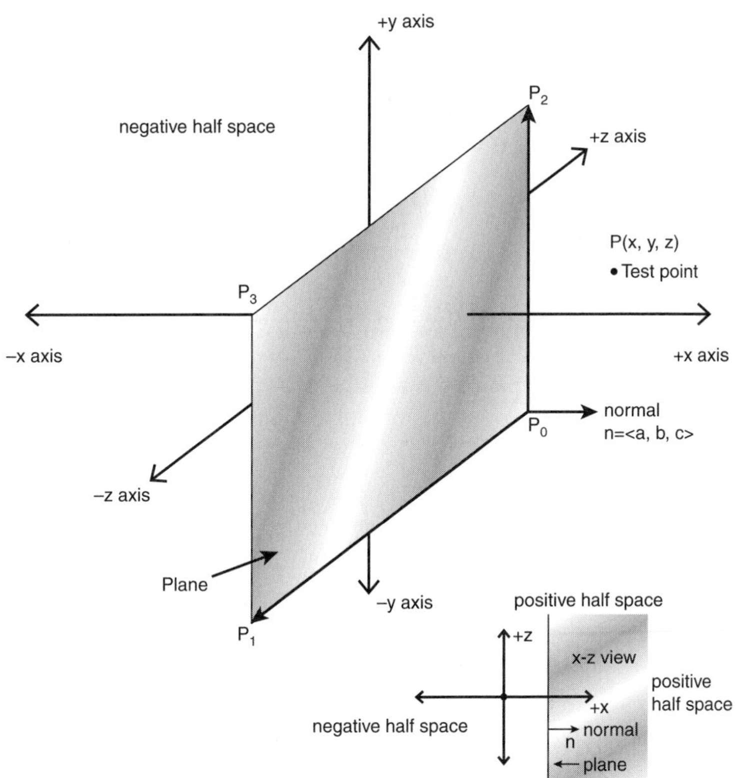

FIGURE 4.34 A plane and its half-spaces.

Intersection of a Plane and Line in 3D with Explicit Representations

As an example, let's see how we would compute the intersection of a line and plane in 3D. This is a very useful operation in a 3D game for a number of reasons: collision detection, clipping, and so forth. We'll use the plane and line shown in Figure 4.35. To make things easy, I have selected the x-z plane as the plane; therefore, the point **p0**(0,0,0) is contained within the plane, and the normal to the plane is **n** = <0,1,0>. The line we want to intersect with the plane goes through the points **p1**(4,4,4) and **p2**(5,-5,-4). Now, let's see whether we can solve for the intersection point $\mathbf{p_i}$(x,y,z) in the figure.

The general point normal equation for the plane is

```
a*(x-x0) + b*(y-y0) + c*(z-z0) = 0
```

Plugging in the normal for <a,b,c> and the point **p0** for (x0, y0, z0), we have

```
0*(x-0)+1*(y-0)+0*(z-0) = 0
                      y = 0
```

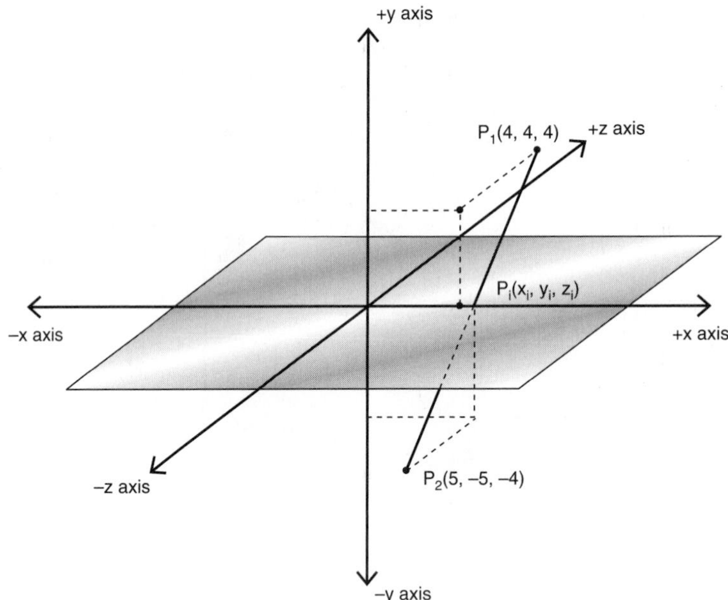

FIGURE 4.35 An illustration of a plane and line intersection.

The general equation for a line in 3D is

```
 (x-x0)  (y-y0)   (z-z0)
------ = ------ = ------
   a        b        c
```

> **NOTE**
>
> The variables are just dummy variables, and represent a point on the line (x0, y0, z0) and a vector parallel to the line <a,b,c>.

The variables <a,b,c> are the unit vector in the direction of the line **p1->p2**, which can be computed as follows:

```
v = p2-p1  = (5,-5,-4) - (4,4,4) = <1, -9, -8>
v' = v/|v| = <1, -9, -8>/<sqrt((1)²+(-9)²+(-8)²)
           = <0.08, -0.74, -0.66>
```

Plugging **p1** into (x0,y0,z0) and **v** into (a,b,c), we get

```
(x-4)      (y-4)     (z-4)
------ = ------ = ------
0.08      -0.74     -0.66
```

Collecting both the line equation and plane equation:

1. (x-4)/.08 = -(y-4)/.74 = -(z-4)/.66 (equation of line)
2. y = 0 (plane equation)

We can now solve the system. The plane equation is y = 0, and at this value, the line takes on values:

```
 (x-4)/.08 = -(y-4)/.74
-(y-4)/.74 = -(z-4)/.66
```

At y = 0, we get

```
 (x-4)/.08 = -(0-4)/.74
-(0-4)/.74 = -(z-4)/.66
x = 4+(.08)*4/.74 = 4.43
z = 4 -(0.66)*4/.74 = .43
```


Therefore, the line intersects at $\mathbf{p}_i$(4.43,0,.43), which looks right based on the figure. This example was a bit tedious, but it's important to see it at least once. Later we will derive quicker ways to compute intersections of lines and planes based on *a priori* knowledge of the geometry.

Using Parametric Equations

Parametric equations are infinitely more useful in computer graphics because they can be used to represent lines or curves as a function of a single variable, rather than 2- or 3-space variables. Moreover, they are a more natural method of representing motion and trajectories in computer games. Therefore, let's take a look at them in detail.

2D and 3D Parametric Lines

Referring to Figure 4.36, we see two points in the x-y plane: **p0**(x0, y0) and **p1**(x1, y1). We know that the vector is **v** = <vx, vy> = **p0->p1** = (x1-x0, y1-y0). Thus if we were to add **v** to **p0**, we would end up at **p1**. Now, the question is how can we write this parametrically, so that we can vary a value t (for example) in some closed interval [a,b], and so that as we vary the parameter t, a line is traced out from **p0** to **p1** along **v**? Of course, you have already seen this in the vector discussion on position vectors. Once again, the set of points (x,y) from **p0** to **p1** can be described by the following:

EQUATION 4.26 General Parametric Line

```
p = p0 + v*t, for t in the interval [a,b]
```

where **v** = <vx, vy> = **p0->p1** = (x1-x0, y1-y0).

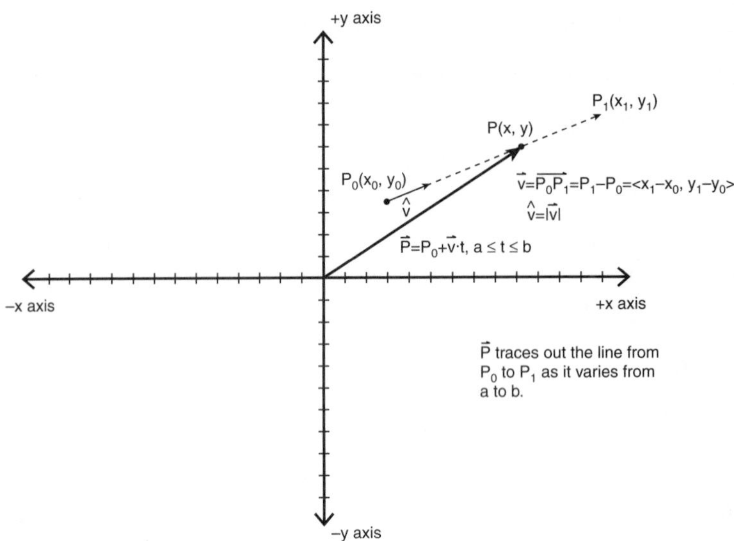

FIGURE 4.36 Parametric line development.

However, the only problem with the formulation is that the interval of *t* is not really known. We can compute it if we want, but there's a very subtle point here. Equation 4.26 is really a general parametric line equation, so lines go from -∞ to +∞; hence, we don't really care about the form of **v**, because we are allowed to set it equal to all real values. However, many times we want more control, with a parametric line segment rather than a parametric line. Now here's the cool part—parametric lines have the exact same form as parametric lines, but we define the interval more precisely, and there are two common ways to adjust the length of **v**. Let's take a look at both.

Parametric Line Segments with Standard Direction Vector v

In the previous discussion, we let **v** = <vx, vy> = **p0->p1** = (x1-x0, y1-y0). Therefore, the length of **v** or |**v**| is exactly the length or distance from **p0** to **p1**, as shown in Figure 4.36. So, if we do a little thinking on what values of t define just the line segment from **p0** to **p1**, it's fairly obvious that the interval is [0,1]. Let's plug in the interval and look at the results:

> **NOTE**
>
> The interval notation "[" and "]" means inclusive, and "(" and ")" mean non-inclusive. Thus, [0,1] defines the interval of all real numbers from 0 to 1 including 0 and 1, and the interval (0,1] means all real numbers from 0 to 1 including 1, but excluding 0.

We have the following formula for the parametric line:

```
p = p0 + v*t, for t in the interval [0,1]
```

where

```
v = <vx, vy> = p0->p1 = (x1-x0, y1-y0)
```

At t = 0, we get the following result:

```
p = p0 + v*t = p0
```

which is correct.

And at t = 1, we get the following result:

```
p = p0+v*1 = p0+v = p0+<vx, vy> = p1
```

which is also correct.

Hence, the interval [0,1] exactly traces the line from **p0** to **p1** as *t* varies from 0 to 1. Additionally, we see that it's perfectly legal to plug values into *t* that are beyond the interval, but these values are not on the desired segment. However, note that this is a very important property when trying to solve parametric systems. If you design a line segment interval from [0,1] and you get a parameter *t* outside of the interval for some calculation, then you know that the point is outside of the segment—this is a very important detail.

Also, using the standard v and interval from [0,1] is nice because 0 and 1 are both fantastic numbers! Now, let's see the other representation of a parametric line using a normalized v.

Parametric Line Segments with Unit Direction Vector |v| = 1

The next version of a parametric line is again the same as the previous, but with the one change that we normalize the direction vector **v**, call it **v**' so that |**v**'| = 1. Okay, let's see the equations with the normalized **v**' replacing v:

p = **p0** + **v'*t**, for *t* in the interval [a,b]

where **v** = <vx, vy> = **p0->p1** = (x1-x0, y1-y0) and **v**' = **v**/|**v**|.

Now, here's the problem: What is the interval that defines the line segment from **p0** to **p1**, as shown in Figure 4.37? If you're keeping awake, you should immediately see that the interval is [0, |**v**|]! Let's see why.

When t = 0, we have

```
p = p0 + v'*0 = p0
```

which is correct. When t = |v|, we have

```
p = p0 + v'*|v| = ?
```

which is equivalent to

```
          v
  = p0 + --- * |v|
         |v|
```

The |**v**|'s cancel out, giving us

```
= p0 + v
```

Plugging in for **v**, we get

```
p = p0+v = p0+<vx, vy> = p1
```

which is what we wanted. Ultimately, there is no difference between the two representations. They are both constructed the same, but in different intervals, so that in one case we vary *t* from [0,1], and in the other, we vary *t* from [0,|**v**|]. You could also construct a parametric so that as you varied *t* from [-1, 1], you would get the line from **p0** to **p1**. Try and see whether you can come up with the formula for this parametric line yourself.

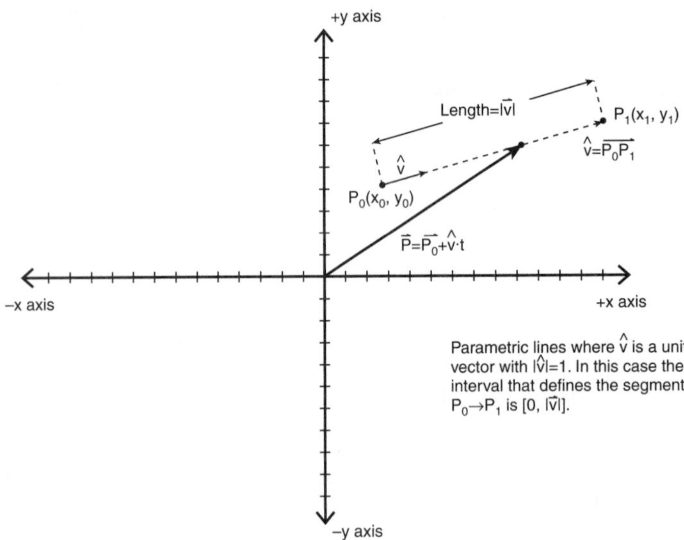

FIGURE 4.37 The interval that defines the line **p0** to **p1**.

Parametric Lines in 3D

3D parametric lines are absolutely identical to the 2D version: The points **p0**(x0, y0, z0) and **p1**(x1, y1, z1) have three components, and of course so does **v** = <vx, vy, vz> = <x1-x0, y1-y0, z1-z0>. The vector equation stays the same:

`p = p0 + v*t`, for *t* in the interval [a,b]

where

```
v = <vx, vy, vz> = p0->p1 = (x1-x0, y1-y0, z1-z0)
```

Other than the new parameter, everything stays the same. However, notice the simplicity from moving from 2D to 3D. Remember how complex a 3D explicit line was in terms of x, y, and z? It was ugly, but in parametrics, it's very simple. That's why working with lines in parametric form in a 3D engine is almost necessary, because the explicit form is nearly impossible to represent and do calculations on.

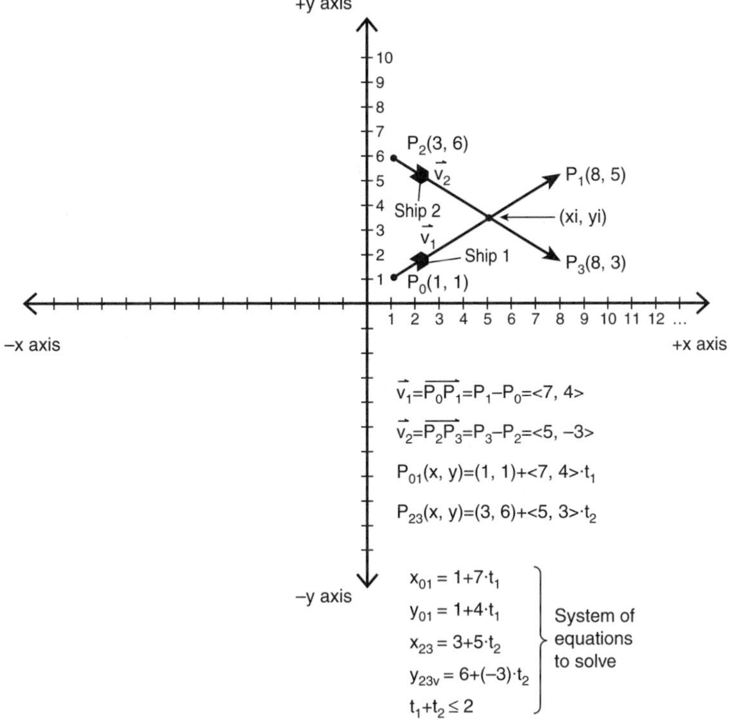

FIGURE 4.38 A pair of ships on 2D trajectories.

Computing the Intersection of Parametric Lines

Now, let's say that you have two ships traveling in 2D, as shown in Figure 4.38. From the figure, we see that:

- Ship 1 is traveling from **p0**(x0,y0) to **p1**(x1,y1).
- Ship 2 is traveling from **p2**(x2,y2) to **p3**(x3,y3).

We want to determine whether their trajectories will intersect. Now, we haven't said anything about whether the ships actually intersect because time hasn't been included into the problem. Remember, the objects not only have to collide in space, but at the same time! For now, let's just see whether their trajectories intersect. Your first attempt might be to construct two explicit lines for each trajectory and then see whether the lines intersect, but then you're hosed, because how can you tell whether the intersection is on the segments from **p0->p1** and **p2->p3**? That's why parametric lines are so useful. We can perform the calculations and find the solution value *t* at the intersection. However, if *t* is not in the interval that defines the lines, we know that their segments don't intersect. This case is shown in Figure 4.39.

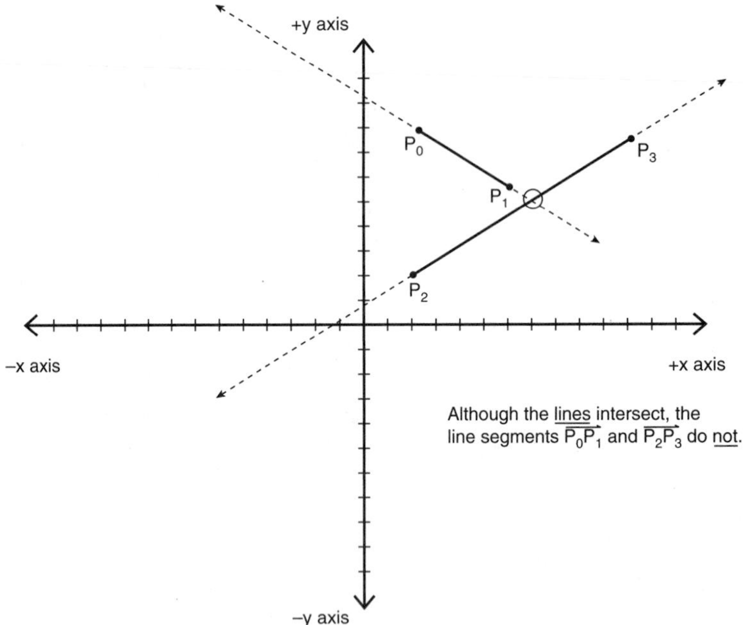

FIGURE 4.39 The point of intersection must lie on the lines' segments.

Let's begin by constructing the two parametric lines with intervals from [0,1] to make it easier. Note that if the lines each had different intervals, we would be comparing apples to oranges mathematically. Here are the definitions of the two lines parametrically:

Given

- Ship 1 is traveling from **p0**(1,1) to **p1**(8,5).
- Ship 2 is traveling from **p2**(3,6) to **p3**(8,3).

Computing the direction vectors for each line:

```
v1 = p0->p1 = <x1-x0, y1-y0> = <8-1, 5-1> = <7,4>
v2 = p2->p3 = <x3-x2, y3-y2> = <8-3, 3-6> = <5,-3>
```

For the parametric line equations, we have

```
p01 = p0 + v1*t1, t1 ∈ [0,1]
p23 = p2 + v2*t2, t2 ∈ [0,1]
```

And with the real values:

```
p01(x,y) = (1,1) + <7,4>*t1
p23(x,y) = (3,6) + <5,-3>*t2
```

Notice that the parameter variable is different in each line. We have *t1* and *t2* rather than *t*. This is because the parameters *are* different. It's true that each parameter varies in the interval from [0,1], but other than that, the *t* value on line one and the *t* value on line two where the intersection occurs (if any) need not be the same. Hence, we must track this by using two different parameters—this is very important, and forgetting to do it will cause lots of math problems.

Let's write all the equations in terms of their components:

```
x = 1 + 7*t1
y = 1 + 4*t1
```

and

```
x = 3 + 5*t2
y = 6 - 3*t2
```

We want to equate the x,y components together for each line and solve for *t1* and *t2*, then see whether *t1* and *t2* are both in the interval [0,1]. If so, we have an intersection, otherwise we don't. Equating terms, we have

```
x: 1 + 7*t1 = 3 + 5*t2
y: 1 + 4*t1 = 6 - 3*t2
```

Rearranging, we get

```
7*t1 - 5*t2 = 2
4*t1 + 3*t2 = 5
```

We have two equations and two unknowns, so we can solve using whatever technique we want: Gaussian elimination, Cramer's Rule, substitution, voodoo magic, whatever. The results are

```
t1 = .756
t2 = .658
```

We see that the lines intersect, because both *t1* and *t2* are in the interval of [0,1]. If we want the actual intersection point, we can plug *t1* or *t2* into either line equation. Let's plug both *t1* and *t2* into each and make sure that both result in the same (x,y), just to be safe:

For line 1:

```
x = 1 + 7*t1 = 1 + 7*(.756) = 6.29
y = 1 + 4*t1 = 1 + 4*(.756) = 4.02
```

And for line 2:

```
x = 3 + 5*t2 = 3 + 5*(.658) = 6.29
y = 6 - 3*t2 = 6 - 3*(.658) = 4.02
```

They check, thank Zeus! That should be enough to convince you that parametric representations are the best, and are simple to work with. Additionally, the same problem in 3D is absolutely identical. There are no weird formulas, just another variable. Hence, in 3D you would end up with something like this for each line:

```
p01(x,y,z) = (x0,y0,z0) + <vx1,vy1,vz1>*t1
p23(x,y,z) = (x2,y2,z2) + <vx2,vy2,vz2>*t2
```

And then you would break these into three equations and solve for *t1* and *t2*:

For line 1:

```
x = x0 + vx1*t1
y = y0 + vy1*t1
z = z0 + vz1*t1
```

For line 2:

```
x = x2 + vx2*t2
y = y2 + vy2*t2
z = z2 + vz2*t2
```

The only difference is that you have three equations and two unknowns, so you can pick any pair of the variables x,y,z and then solve for *t1* and *t2*. After you have solved the system, you must make sure that *t1* and *t2* result in the same point when plugged into the third equation variable that you didn't use. However, in most cases, you will never need to detect whether a 3D line intersects another 3D line segment because the probability of this happening in any context is remote. Most of the time, you will want to detect whether a 3D parametric line intersects with a plane. Let's take a look at this problem.

Computing the Intersection of a 3D Parametric Line and a 3D Plane

Computing the intersection of a 3D line and a plane can be extremely simple or fairly complex, depending on the plane. If the plane is x-y, x-z, y-z, or a plane parallel to them, it's trivial. However, for a general line plane intersection, we are going to have to work harder.

Let's start by writing down the formula for a parametric line and plane and solve the trivial case first. Here's the parametric line equation in 3D:

```
p = p0 + v*t, t ∈ [0,1]
```

Or more explicitly:

```
p(x,y,z) = p0(x0,y0,z0) + v<vx, vy, vz>*t
```

And here's the 3D plane equation:

```
n . (p - p0) = 0
nx*(x-x0) + ny*(y-y0) + nz*(z-z0) = 0
```

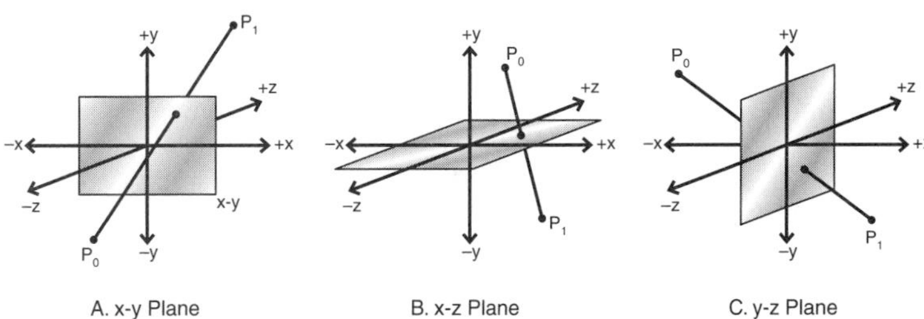

FIGURE 4.40 Intersections of lines and planes (trivial cases).

Referring to Figure 4.40, we see the three cases we are interested in:

- Case 1: Intersection of the line and the x-y plane when z = 0.
- Case 2: Intersection of the line and the x-z plane when y = 0.
- Case 3: Intersection of the line and the y-z plane when x = 0.

Solving all of these is trivial. Let's solve the x-y plane case as an example. In this case, we know that the z-coordinate must be 0, thus we can plug this into the parametric line equation for the z-component and see what *t* we get:

```
p(x,y,z) = p0(x0,y0,z0) + v<vx, vy, vz>*t
```

Component-wise:

```
x = x0 + vx*t
y = y0 + vy*t
z = z0 + vz*t
```

Plugging z = 0 into the z equation, we get

```
z = z0 + vz*t = 0
```

or

```
t = -z0/vz
```

If *t* is in the interval [0,1], then we have an intersection and we can plug the *t* into the x and y components of the parametric line and find those values, too:

```
x = x0 + vx*(-z0/vz)
y = y0 + vy*(-z0/vz)
```

Thus, intersecting lines with planes that are parallel to any of the standard planes in 3D is trivial—the problem is intersecting a 3D line and an arbitrary plane. Hmmm, let's take a look at the line again:

```
p(x,y,z) = p0(x0,y0,z0) + v<vx, vy, vz>*t
```

Component-wise:

```
x = x0 + vx*t
y = y0 + vy*t
z = z0 + vz*t
```

And here's an arbitrary plane:

```
                       n . (p - p0) = 0
      nx*(x-x0) + ny*(y-y0) + nz*(z-z0) = 0

nx*x + ny*y + nz*z + (-nx*x0-ny*y0-nz*z0) = 0
```

Written in general form:

```
a*x + b*y +c*z + d = 0
```

where a = nx, b = ny, c = nz, and d = (-nx*x0-ny*y0-nz*z0).

CAUTION

Don't confuse the x0, y0, z0 of the plane and the line—they are different! That's why I keep d in symbolic form, rather than long form.

Is the solution jumping out at you yet? If we plug in the values of the right-hand sides of x,y,z from the parametric line into the general form of the plane for x,y,z, we can solve for *t*! Here's the math:

EQUATION 4.27 Intersection of a Parametric Line and a Plane

```
a*(x0+vx*t) + b*(y0+vy*t) + c*(z0+vz*t) + d = 0
```

Solving for *t*:

```
t = -(a*x0 + b*y0 + c*z0 + d)/(a*vx + b*vy + c*vz)
```

where (x0,y0,z0, vx,vy,vz) are from the parametric line, and (a,b,c,d) are from the plane.

And of course, you just plug that back into the parametric equations to find the actual (x,y,z):

```
x = x0 + vx*t
y = y0 + vy*t
z = z0 + vz*t
```

The cool thing is that this *t* will be the solution no matter what interval the *t* of the segment is defined as. Thus, after you have *t*, just test whether it's in your interval [0,1] or whatever. The math will scale *t* to your interval no matter what, because the solution for *t* has the direction vector in it. Of course, watch out for a zero denominator before the division!

NOTE

Although I came up with the solution algebraically, it's more than obvious that a more beautiful geometric/vector solution is possible, because it's not hard to see that both the numerator and denominator are dot products—can you find one? If so, email it to me!

At this point, you are armed with enough math to handle 3D collision detection, wall following, clipping, weapon projectiles, and a lot more. We are going to use this stuff a lot later in the book, so make sure you understand it forward and backward.

Introduction to Quaternions

I remember talking to another game programmer in the early 80s about the mysterious speed of Atari's *Space Duel*. I couldn't believe how fast the 3D was working. My friend had some inside information that Atari was using "Matrix Multiplying." I was pretty impressed by that, because doing real math on 8-bit processors was quite a feat. These days, we have BSP trees, portals, and A-buffers, but you can't go anywhere without hearing the word *quaternion*.

Quaternions were invented in the 1800s by the mathematician William Rowan Hamilton (if you study graph theory, you should be familiar with Hamiltonian paths). Quaternions weren't specially designed for 3D graphics (obviously), but they have found their application in a couple of areas of 3D graphics for which they are well suited:

- 3D camera control
- Compact storage
- Smooth 3D interpolation

Quaternions are based on complex numbers, which are themselves a bit abstract to understand. And of course, they don't really mean anything in the real world—they only exist mathematically. However, complex numbers are a tool that can be used to represent mathematical ideas for which real numbers just don't work. With that in mind, first we are going to take a look at basic complex number theory, and then move on to quaternions and their mathematical properties. After that we'll see how they are applied in computer graphics and games.

Complex Number Theory

The set of real numbers ***R*** consists of all numbers in the interval $[-\infty, +\infty]$. Easy enough, but take a look at these equations:

```
x = sqrt(4) = 2
x = sqrt(1) = 1
x = sqrt(-1) = ???
```

The third equation is the problem—we don't have a number in the set of real numbers for the square root of –1 because there is no number that when multiplied by itself is equal to –1. You might say –1, but –1 * –1 = 1, so that's not correct. We need a new number, which we will call the *imaginary number i* (or *j* for electrical engineers). We are going to create the following rule:

```
let i = sqrt(-1)
```

And then

```
i*i = -1
```

Now we can compute things like sqrt(-4), which would be

```
sqrt(-4) = 2*i
```

because

```
(2*i)*(2*i) = 4*i² = 4*-1 = -4
```

Now, the cool thing about the imaginary number *i* is that you can think of it as a variable or coefficient; that is, all the rules of normal algebra still hold. You just pretend *i* is a variable like *x* and do what you would normally do. Then whenever you see i^2 terms, you can convert them into –1 if you like to simplify. For example, look at the following sum:

```
3 + 5*i + 3*i² - 10 + 6*i
```

Collecting terms, we get

```
= 3*i² + 5*i + 6*i + 3 - 10
 = 3*i² + 11*i - 7
 = 3*(-1) + 11*i - 7
 = -3 + 11*i - 7
 = -10 + 11*i
```


Nothing unordinary there. But, the imaginary number by itself is pretty boring, so mathematicians came up with the concept of a *complex number*, which is the sum of a real number and an imaginary one. Mathematically, a complex number looks like this:

```
z = (a + b*i)
```

a is called the *real part (RP)*, and *b* is called the *imaginary part (IM)*. Because *a* and *b* can never be added together because of the imaginary coefficient of *b*, you can also think of complex numbers as points in the complex plane, as shown in Figure 4.41.

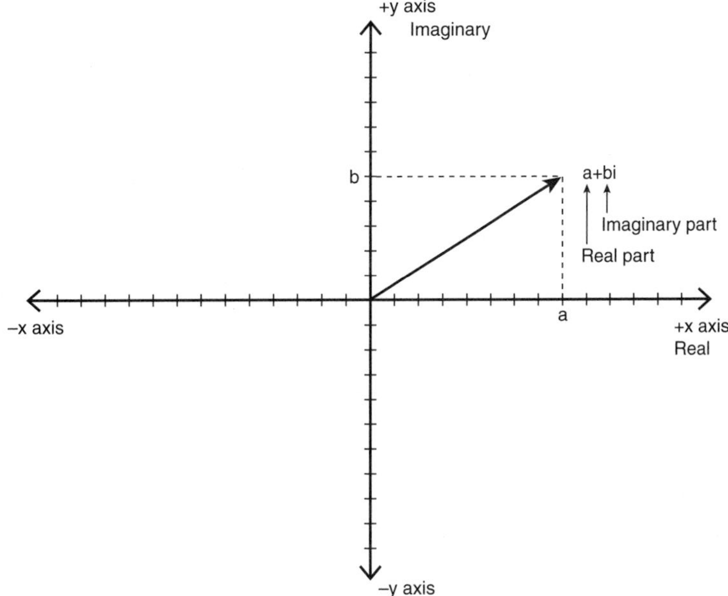

FIGURE 4.41 The complex plane.

As a convention, most people call the x-axis the real part, and the y-axis the imaginary axis. Thus, we have a geometrical interpretation of complex numbers based on the vector basis:

```
z = a*(1,0) + b*(0,i)
```

I want to come back to this concept a little later, so keep that in mind. However, let's look at the operations on complex numbers and figure out how to add, subtract, multiply, divide, and so on.

Complex Scalar Multiplication/Division

Multiplication of a scalar and a complex number is performed on a component-wise basis as follows:

Given:

```
z1   = (a+b*i)
k*z1 = k*(a+b*i) = (k*a + (k*b)*i)
```

Example:

```
3*(2+5*i) = (6 + 15*i)
```

That is, the scalar simply distributes over the complex number. Division of course is similar, because you can think of it as multiplication by the inverse.

Complex Addition and Subtraction

To add or subtract complex numbers, you simply add or subtract the real and the imaginary parts separately, as follows:

Given:

```
     z1 = (a+b*i)
     z2 = (c+d*i)
z1 + z2 = (a+b*i) + (c+d*i) = ( (a+c) + (b+d)*i)
```

Example:

```
(3 + 5*i) + (12 - 2*i) = (15 + 3*i)
```

Complex Additive Identity

Also, the *additive identity* (the complex number that, when added to any other complex number, is that number) is (0+0*i), because:

```
(0+0*i) + (a+b*i) = (0+a + (0+b)*i) = (a+b*i)
```

Complex Additive Inverse

The *complex additive inverse* (the number that, when added to any other complex number, is the additive identity (0 + 0*i)) is **z*** = (-a - b*i) for any complex number **z** = (a + b*i) because:

```
(a + b*i) + (-a - b*i) = (a-a) + (b-b)*i) = (0 + 0*i)
```

Complex Multiplication

Now for the fun part! Multiplying complex numbers is actually very easy. Let's do it, and pretend like *i* is a variable, as we have before.

z_1 = (a+b*i)
z_2 = (c+d*i)

z_1*z_2 = (a+b*i) * (c+d*i)
      = (a*c + a*d*i + b*c*i + b*d*i^2)

Noting that $i^2 = -1$ and collecting terms, we get

```
= (a*c + (a*d+b*c)*i + b*d*(-1))
```

Collecting terms once again, we have

```
= ((a*c-b*d) + (a*d+b*c)*i)
```

Therefore, we see that the real part equals (a*c - b*d), and the imaginary part equals (a*d + b*c). Let's do an example:

Example:

```
(1+2*i) * (-3 + 3*i) = ((-3-6) + (-6+3)*i) = (-9 - 3*i)
```

Complex Division

Division of complex numbers can be accomplished using brute force. For example, we can compute the quotient of two complex numbers z_1/z_2 in the following way:

z_1 = (a+b*i)
z_2 = (c+d*i)

```
          (a+b*i)
z1/z2 =  --------
          (c+d*i)
```

If c = 0 or d = 0, then the division is trivial, but if neither c nor d is equal to 0, then we are at a bit of an impasse. The question is how to perform the division so that the result is in the form (a + b*i) once again. The trick is to clear the denominator first and turn it into a pure scalar. This way, we can simply divide the scalar into the real part and imaginary part of the numerator. To turn the denominator into a pure scalar, we must multiply by the *complex conjugate*, usually denoted by a superscript asterisk (*).

The complex conjugate of **z** = (a + b*i) is **z***= (a - b*i). When we multiply a complex number and its conjugate, the result is always a pure real number. Take a look:

Given:

```
z = (a+b*i)
```

then

```
z * z* =
(a+b*i) * (a-b*i) = (a² + a*b*i - a*b*i - b²*i²)
                  = (a² + b²)
```

Cool, huh? With this trick we can convert the quotient problem into a more palatable form:

Given the quotient of two complex numbers

```
 (a+b*i)
-------
 (c+b*i)
```

We can always multiply by 1 and not change the results, so let's multiply by the complex conjugate of the denominator over itself:

```
 (a+b*i)  (c-d*i)
------- * --------
 (c+d*i)  (c-d*i)
```

Lots of steps go here...

```
  / (a*c+b*d)    ((b*c-a*d)*i) \
= | --------- + ------------- |
  \ (a² + b²)      (a² + b²)   /
```

Ugly as it might seem, rest assured it's of the form (a+b*i).

Multiplicative Inverse

The last mathematical property—complex numbers need to be a closed set—is a *multiplicative inverse*, which is a complex number that, when multiplied by another, results in "1"—where "1" in complex numbers is equal to (1+0*i). If you think about it long enough, you will definitely see that we can use the complex conjugate in some way. Let's just try the obvious and write an equation and see what happens. We want the following:

```
(a+b*i) * (c+d*i) = (1+0*i)
```

Amazingly, the multiplicative inverse of **z** = (a+b*i) is just

```
        1
1/z = ------
      (a+b*i)
```

But the problem is that we no longer have something in the form (real_part + imaginary_part*i); we have its inverse. We need to reform the preceding function so that it's of the form (a + b*i). We can multiply by the complex conjugate to find them, resulting in

```
   1     (a-b*i)        a           b
------   ------- = -------- + -------- * i
(a+b*i) (a-b*i)   (a² + b²)   (a² + b²)
```

Gnarly, huh? What this means is that if you are given the complex number (a+b*i), its inverse is 1/(a+b*i), but if you need the real part and imaginary part, you need to use the preceding equation.

Complex Numbers as Vectors

Last but not least, I want to revisit the representation of complex numbers and show you another way of thinking of them (if you haven't already figured it out). Complex numbers can also be thought of as vectors in a 2D plane. If you take a look at Figure 4.41, we've plotted an imaginary number on a 2D Cartesian plane with the real part as the x-coordinate and the imaginary part as the y-coordinate. So, there's no reason why we can't think of imaginary numbers as vectors with the basis:

```
z = a*(1,0) + b*(0,i)
```

Or, more compactly:

```
z = <a,b>
```

where a is the real part, and b is the imaginary part. Figure 4.42 shows our new representation in vector form.

The cool thing about representing complex numbers as vectors is that we can then transform them as vectors, and the results will all be perfectly valid. Moreover, representing complex numbers as vectors allows us to better visualize an abstract mathematical notion such as complex numbers, and to thus "see" relationships that might otherwise elude us in their pure mathematical form.

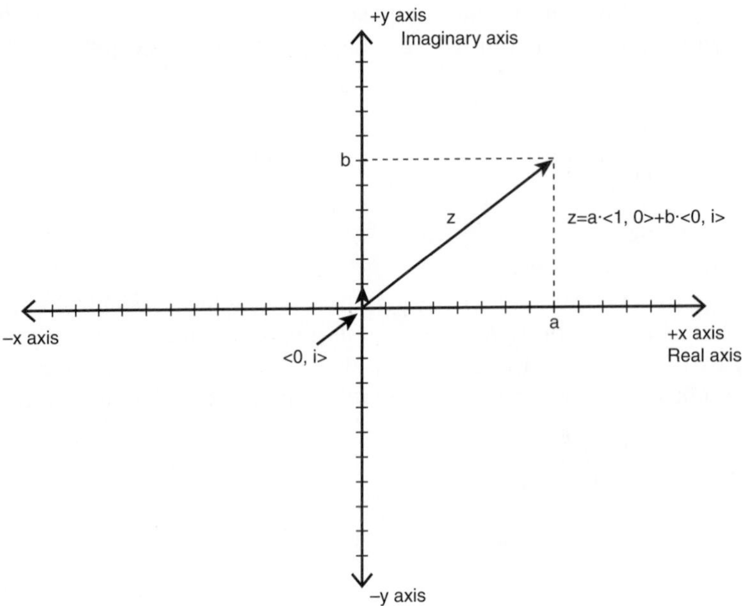

FIGURE 4.42 Complex numbers in a unit vector form.

Norm of a Complex Number

Many times we want to know the length of a complex number or the magnitude. Of course, this doesn't make much sense in a purely mathematical sense, but when we think of complex numbers as vectors in space, it's very natural and easy to understand. Anyway, the *norm* of a complex number can be computed in the following ways:

EQUATION 4.28 Norm of a Complex Number

Given

```
z = a+b*i
```

then

```
|z| = sqrt(a²+b²)
```

Also, take a look at the product of any complex number and its conjugate:

Given

```
z = a+b*i, z* = a-b*i
```

then

```
z * z* = a² + b*i - b*i + b² = a²+b²
```

Therefore, the norm is also equal to

$|z| = sqrt(z * z^*)$

Hyper-Complex Numbers

Quaternions are nothing more than *hyper-complex* numbers. The term *hyper-complex* can really mean anything mathematically, but usually it means a complex number that has more than one imaginary component. In our case, we are going to refer to hyper-complex numbers with one real part and three imaginary parts—otherwise known as quaternions.

A quaternion can be written many ways, but in general it's of the form seen in Equation 4.29:

EQUATION 4.29 The Form of a Quaternion

$$\mathbf{q} = q_0 + q_1*\mathbf{i} + q_2*\mathbf{j} + q_3*\mathbf{k}$$

or

$$\mathbf{q} = q_0 + \mathbf{q}_v, \text{ where } \mathbf{q}_v = q_1*\mathbf{i} + q_2*\mathbf{j} + q_3*\mathbf{k}$$

i = <1,0,0>, **j** = <0,1,0>, **k** = <0,0,1>, and $<q_0,q_1,q_2,q_3>$ are all real numbers, and **i**, **j**, and **k** are all imaginary numbers that form the vector basis of the quaternion **q**. Moreover, q_0 is real, and has no imaginary coefficient.

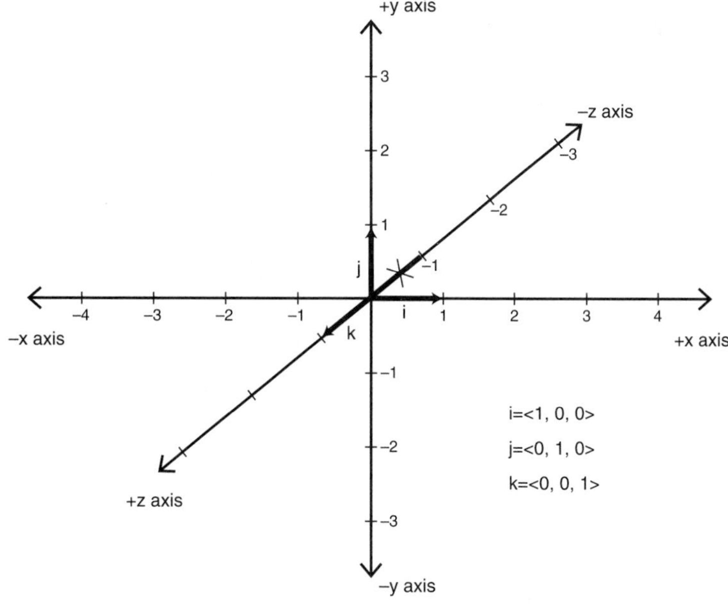

FIGURE 4.43 The hyper-complex basis interpreted as a 3D system.

4

Also, the imaginary basis <**i**,**j**,**k**> has some interesting properties. It can be thought of as a 3D mutually perpendicular set of unit vectors in an imaginary coordinate system that locates points in <**i**,**j**,**k**> space, as shown in Figure 4.43. But, the interesting thing about <**i**,**j**,**k**> is the following relationship:

EQUATION 4.30 The Quaternion Basis Products

$$i^2 = j^2 = k^2 = -1 = i*j*k$$

MATH

Note that I am bolding the imaginary basis **i**, **j**, **k**; thus, we would think they are vectors, and they are, but they can also be thought of as variables. They have a dualistic nature, and sometimes it's appropriate to think of them in their vector form, and sometimes it's not. I might switch back and forth, especially when I am using the i, j, or k alone or showing relationships among them.

The " = **i*j*k**" part takes a little getting used to, but it's correct. And of course, you can manipulate the relationship to arrive at the following:

Given

$$i^2 = j^2 = k^2 = -1 = i*j*k$$

therefore

$$i = j*k = -k*j$$
$$j = k*i = -i*k$$
$$k = i*j = -j*i$$

which intuitively seems right, because the cross-product of any two perpendicular vectors in an orthonormal basis should be perpendicular to the vectors themselves, or the third vector in a 3D orthonormal basis. And if we invert the order of multiplication, we should see an inversion or sign flip, and we do.

At this point, I want to establish some conventions about writing quaternions—otherwise, we are going to get caught up in notation. Many people like to write quaternions using lowercase letters to represent them, but they also break them up into a real and imaginary part, where they represent the imaginary part as a vector like this:

$$\mathbf{q} = q_0 + \mathbf{q}_v$$

where

$$\mathbf{q}_v = q_1*\mathbf{i} + q_2*\mathbf{j} + q_3*\mathbf{k}$$

So q_0 is the real part, and $\mathbf{q_v}$ is the imaginary part and is a vector <q_1, q_2, q_3>. That's cool, but I don't like the fact that **q**, the quaternion itself, is not bolded—it's confusing because it's a 4-tuple itself. We are going to use a notation in which quaternions are represented in lowercase bold, AND the vector part is also in lowercase bold. Here's an example:

```
a = -1 + 3*i + 4*j + 5*k
```

which in pure vector form is

```
a = <-1, 3, 4, 5>
```

or in real-vector form is

```
a = q0 + qv
```

where q_0 = -1, and $\mathbf{q_v}$ = <3,4,5> = 3*i + 4*j + 5*j.

The point is that we are going to use arrays obviously to represent quaternions in real life, and the first number will always be the real part, and the remaining three numbers will always be the imaginary coefficients of <i,j,k>. Moreover, from now on I want to start getting you into the habit of representing quaternions in this format:

```
q = q0 + x*i + y*j + z*k
```

Or in another way:

```
q = q0 + <x,y,z> . <i,j,k>
```

NOTE

Note that here we are taking advantage of the vector property of <**i**,**j**,**k**>.

That is, simply referring to the real part as q0 and the imaginary part as $\mathbf{q_v}$ = <x,y,z> gives us a little more to hold on to when relating quaternions to 3D space. However, depending on what we are doing, we might flip from one representation to another, but I think you get the point.

The cool thing about quaternions (or any hyper-complex number system) is that the mathematics of addition, multiplication, inverses, and so on are all the same as in standard complex number theory, but with more elements. Hence, we really already know how to do this stuff, but we just have to take into consideration that we now have three imaginary components rather than one, as we did with basic complex numbers or complex numbers of "rank 1."

Now let's take a look at the basic operations that we might need to perform on quaternions when doing calculations—I'm going to go fast because this should all be obvious at this point.

4

Quaternion Addition and Subtraction

Addition or subtraction of quaternions is accomplished by adding or subtracting the real part and the imaginary part, just as with normal complex numbers.

Example:

$$\mathbf{q} = q_0 + \mathbf{q}_v$$
$$\mathbf{p} = p_0 + \mathbf{p}_v$$

$$\mathbf{q} + \mathbf{p} = (q_0+p_0) + (\mathbf{q}_v+\mathbf{p}_v)$$

Example:

```
q = 3 + 4*i + 5*j + 6*k = <3,4,5,6> in vector form.
p = -5 + 2*i + 2*j - 3*k = <-5,2,2,-3> in vector form.

q + p = (3+ -5) + ( (4+2)*i + (5+2)*j + (6+ -3)*k)
      = -2 + 6*i + 7+j + 3*k
```

As you can see, the writing of the imaginary coefficients is getting rather tedious, and we could have just written

```
<3,4,5,6> + <-5,2,2,-3> = <-2,6,7, 3>.
```

However, we have to be careful, because although it works for addition and subtraction, for multiplication we need to recall that the last three components are complex. To avoid oversimplification, we need to keep the quaternions in a form that at least keeps the real and imaginary parts separate.

Additive Inverse and Identity

The additive inverse of any quaternion **q** is the number that, when added to **q**, results in zero. This is surprisingly just –q:

Given:

$$\mathbf{q} = q_0 + \mathbf{q}_v$$

The additive inverse is just

$$-\mathbf{q} = -q_0 - \mathbf{q}_v$$

because

$$\mathbf{q} - \mathbf{q} = (q_0-q_0)+ (\mathbf{q}_v - \mathbf{q}_v) = 0 + 0*i + 0*j + 0*j$$

The additive identity, or "0" in quaternion math, must be

```
q = 0 + 0*i + 0*j + 0*k = <0,0,0,0>.
```

Quaternion Multiplication

Addition and subtraction is always easy, huh? It's multiplication that ruins the party every time! And this is no exception. Because quaternions are nothing more than hyper-complex numbers based on real numbers with imaginary coefficients, we should be able to just multiply them out, taking into consideration the imaginary coefficients in the products and keeping track of them. Let's just try it and see what happens.

Given

$$\mathbf{p} = p_0 + p_1*\mathbf{i} + p_2*\mathbf{j} + p_3*\mathbf{k} = p_0 + \mathbf{p}_v$$
$$\mathbf{q} = q_0 + q_1*\mathbf{i} + q_2*\mathbf{j} + q_3*\mathbf{k} = q_0 + \mathbf{q}_v$$

then

$$\mathbf{p}*\mathbf{q} = (p_0 + p_1*\mathbf{i} + p_2*\mathbf{j} + p_3*\mathbf{k}) * (q_0 + q_1*\mathbf{i} + q_2*\mathbf{j} + q_3*\mathbf{k})$$
$$= p_0*q_0 +$$
$$p_0*q_1*\mathbf{i} + p_1*q_2*\mathbf{j} + p_2*q_3*\mathbf{k} +$$
$$p_1*\mathbf{i}*q_0 + p_1*\mathbf{i}*q_1*\mathbf{i} + p_1*\mathbf{i}*q_2*\mathbf{j} + p_1*\mathbf{i}*q_3*\mathbf{k} +$$
$$p_2*\mathbf{j}*q_0 + p_2*\mathbf{j}*q_1*\mathbf{i} + p_2*\mathbf{j}*q_2*\mathbf{j} + p_2*\mathbf{j}*q_3*\mathbf{k} +$$
$$p_3*\mathbf{k}*q_0 + p_3*\mathbf{k}*q_1*\mathbf{i} + p_3*\mathbf{k}*q_2*\mathbf{j} + p_3*\mathbf{k}*q_3*\mathbf{k}$$

If you have a good eye, you should see some structure to this product—maybe a cross-product here and there, and a dot product? Keep that in mind while we collect terms and use Equation 4.30 to simplify the imaginary product terms:

$$= p_0*q_0 +$$
$$p_0*q_1*\mathbf{i} + p_1*q_2*\mathbf{j} + p_2*q_3*\mathbf{k} +$$
$$p_1*q_0*\mathbf{i} + p_1*q_1*\mathbf{i}^2 + p_1*\mathbf{i}*q_2*\mathbf{j} + p_1*\mathbf{i}*q_3*\mathbf{k} +$$
$$p_2*\mathbf{j}*q_0 + p_2*q_1*\mathbf{j}*\mathbf{i} + p_2*q_2*\mathbf{j}^2 + p_2*q_3*\mathbf{j}*\mathbf{k} +$$
$$p_3*q_0*\mathbf{k} + p_3*q_1*\mathbf{k}*\mathbf{i} + p_3*q_2*\mathbf{k}*\mathbf{j} + p_3*q_3*\mathbf{k}^2$$

At this point, there are a lot of ways to format these products, but I will stop here and show you this equation.

EQUATION 4.31 Formula for Quaternion Products

Given

$$\mathbf{p} = p_0 + p_1*\mathbf{i} + p_2*\mathbf{j} + p_3*\mathbf{k} = p_0 + \mathbf{p}_v$$
$$\mathbf{q} = q_0 + q_1*\mathbf{i} + q_2*\mathbf{j} + q_3*\mathbf{k} = q_0 + \mathbf{q}_v$$

then

$$\mathbf{r} = \mathbf{p}*\mathbf{q} = (p_0*q_0 - (\mathbf{p}_v \cdot \mathbf{q}_v)) + (p_0*\mathbf{q}_v + q_0*\mathbf{p}_v + \mathbf{p}_v \times \mathbf{q}_v)$$
$$= r_0 + \mathbf{r}_v$$

NOTE

The *x* operator is the standard vector cross-product, and is calculated on the vector imaginary part of the quaternion as if the imaginary part was a standard 3-tuple vector.

And because dot products always result in scalars and cross products result in vectors, the first term (p_0*q_0 – ($\mathbf{p}_v$. $\mathbf{q}_v$)) is the real part r_0, and the term (p_0*$\mathbf{q}_v$ + q_0*$\mathbf{p}_v$ + $\mathbf{p}_v$ x $\mathbf{q}_v$) is the vector or imaginary part $\mathbf{r}_v$. I have to admit that quaternion multiplication is a very ugly thing in mathematics!

Also, note that the *multiplicative identity* (the analog of "1" in quaternion math) is

$\mathbf{q}_1$ = 1 + 0*i + 0*j + 0*k

This is true because any **q** * $\mathbf{q}_1$ = **q** = $\mathbf{q}_1$ * **q**.

Quaternion Conjugate

Computing the conjugate of a quaternion **q**, $\mathbf{q}^*$ is accomplished in the same manner as with complex numbers: You simply invert the sign of the imaginary component $\mathbf{q}_v$.

EQUATION 4.32 Computation of Complex Conjugate

Given

$\mathbf{q} = q_0 + q_1*\mathbf{i} + q_2*\mathbf{j} + q_3*\mathbf{k} = q_0 + \mathbf{q}_v$

The complex conjugate is computed by inverting the sign of the imaginary part:

$\mathbf{q}^* = q_0 - q_1*\mathbf{i} - q_2*\mathbf{j} - q_3*\mathbf{k} = q_0 - \mathbf{q}_v$

And take a look at the product of **q** and **q***—it's rather interesting (using Equation 4.31 to perform the multiplication):

EQUATION 4.33 The Quaternion-Conjugate Product

$$\begin{aligned}\mathbf{q} * \mathbf{q}^* &= (q_0 + \mathbf{q}_v) * (q_0 + (-\mathbf{q}_v)) \\ &= q_0*q_0 - (\mathbf{q}_v \cdot (-\mathbf{q}_v)) + q_0*\mathbf{q}_v + q_0*(-\mathbf{q}_v) + (\mathbf{q}_v \times (-\mathbf{q}_v)) \\ &= q_0^2 + q_1^2 + q_2^2 + q_3^2 + (q_0*\mathbf{q}_v - q_0*\mathbf{q}_v) + (\mathbf{0}) \\ &= q_0^2 + q_1^2 + q_2^2 + q_3^2\end{aligned}$$

Interestingly, the product is simply the square of each term. This property will come in handy when we deal with computing the norm and inverse of a quaternion.

Norm of a Quaternion

The norm of a quaternion is computed in the same manner as a complex number:

EQUATION 4.33 Norm of a Quaternion

Given

$$q = q_0 + q_1*i + q_2*j + q_3*k = q_0 + q_v$$

then

$$|q| = sqrt(q_0^2+q_1^2+q_2^2+q_3^2) = sqrt(q * q^*)$$

And of course,

$$|q|^2 = (q_0^2 + q_1^2 + q_2^2 + q_3^2) = (q * q^*)$$

MATH

Note that ($\mathbf{q} * \mathbf{q}^*$) = ($\mathbf{q}^* * \mathbf{q}$). The product of a quaternion and its conjugate is order-independent, but in general is $\mathbf{q}*\mathbf{p} \neq \mathbf{p}*\mathbf{q}$. Also, note that $\mathbf{q} + \mathbf{q}^* = 2*q0$.

4

Multiplicative Inverse

The multiplicative inverse of a quaternion is of special importance to us, because it can be used to simplify quaternion rotation. In fact, everything we have learned up until now is going to come to the single focus of rotating a vector using quaternions, and the inverse is needed for this operation. So put on your thinking cap and check it out...

Given a quaternion $\mathbf{q}$, we want to find another quaternion $\mathbf{q}^{-1}$ such that the following statement is true:

$$q*q^{-1} = 1 = q^{-1}*q$$

Don't blink and watch this...

Let's multiply each side by the complex conjugate $\mathbf{q}^*$:

$$(q * q^{-1}) * q^* = 1 = (q^{-1} * q) * q^* = q^*$$

Because the products in parentheses are 1, we know that 1 multiplied by the conjugate and the conjugate multiplied by 1 are both the conjugate, so we haven't changed anything or created a false statement. Alright, now's the cool part—let's stare at this a minute and see whether we can figure out what the inverse is. Do you see it? Let's look at the right side alone:

$$(q^{-1} * q) * q^* = q^*$$

or

$$q^{-1} * (q * q^*) = q^*$$

But

$$(\mathbf{q} * \mathbf{q}^*) = |\mathbf{q}|^2$$

The final result is as seen in Equation 4.34a.

Equation 4.34a Inverse of a Quaternion

$$\mathbf{q}^{-1} = \mathbf{q}^* / |\mathbf{q}|^2$$

Furthermore, if **q** is a unit quaternion, then $|\mathbf{q}|^2 = 1$ and we can further simplify the inverse to Equation 4.34b.

Equation 4.34b Inverse of a Unit Quaternion

$$\mathbf{q}^{-1} = \mathbf{q}^*$$

Pretty cool, huh? The preceding equation is the whole reason that makes using quaternions to perform rotations even possible. Thus, most of the time we will assume that all quaternions are unit quaternions, so we can use the preceding equation without a problem.

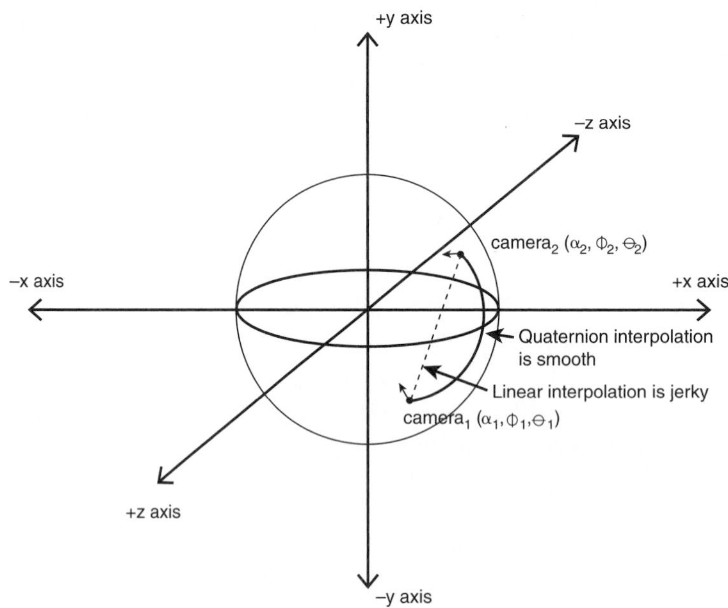

FIGURE 4.44 Interpolation from one orientation to another.

Applications of Quaternions

After all that work learning about quaternions, they probably seem just like interesting mathematical objects with little or no real use to us. However, the fact is that quaternions are very useful for a couple of functions in 3D graphics—rotation and the interpolation of rotations from one to another, as shown in Figure 4.44. In the figure you see two camera directions defined by two sets of angles relative to the x-y-z axis $camera_1 = (\alpha_1, \phi_1, \theta_1)$ and $camera_2 = (\alpha_2, \phi_2, \theta_2)$. How we point the camera in those directions is unimportant, but the point is, what if we want to smoothly interpolate from the orientation of $camera_1$ to $camera_2$? We could linearly interpolate based on the angles, but a number of problems can occur when you do this, such as jerky motion and the loss of a degree of freedom when the camera happens to align on an axis.

The point is that quaternions, by their 4D nature, can handle this problem much more elegantly than standard angles and rotation matrices; they are a bit slower, but worth it. We aren't going to use quaternions to perform standard 3D rotations and manipulations, but we will use them for advanced camera work, as manipulating a 3D camera with quaternions turns out to be more intuitive than using angles. I'm getting way ahead of myself here, so let's just learn how to perform a rotation of a vector with quaternions, and then when we get to camera work, we will revisit them and learn more about using quaternions to interpolate camera orientations and so forth. Right now, I just want you to see the math.

Quaternion Rotation

At some point you (as a mathematician) might wonder what operators can be represented by quaternion transformations—in other words, can they do anything interesting? The answer is yes. One of those interesting and useful operations is the capability to rotate a vector **v**. I would love to show you all the math to arrive at that result, but as usual, I am under both time and page constraints, and it's only interesting to a math maniac, so you're not missing anything. The end result is that given a vector $\mathbf{v} = <x,y,z>$, which in quaternion form we will call $\mathbf{v}_q = <0,x,y,z>$ in 3D (we use a dummy $0 = q_0$, so that we can use **v** as a quaternion), and a unit quaternion **q**, the following operations will rotate $\mathbf{v}_q$:

EQUATIONS 4.35 Quaternion Rotation

Right-handed system:

a. $\mathbf{v}_q' = \mathbf{q}^* * \mathbf{v}_q * \mathbf{q}$, clockwise rotation

b. $\mathbf{v}_q' = \mathbf{q} * \mathbf{v}_q * \mathbf{q}^*$, counter-clockwise rotation

Left-handed system:

c. $\mathbf{v}_q' = \mathbf{q} * \mathbf{v}_q * \mathbf{q}^*$, clockwise rotation

d. $\mathbf{v}_q' = \mathbf{q}^* * \mathbf{v}_q * \mathbf{q}$, counter-clockwise rotation

MATH

We can use $\mathbf{q}^*$ in this operator only for unit quaternions; otherwise, you must use the full inverse of $\mathbf{q}$.

So $\mathbf{v}_q$ is a vector encoded in a quaternion with $q_0 = 0$, and $\mathbf{q}$ is a quaternion, but what exactly does $\mathbf{q}$ represent? What's its relationship to the x-y-z axis and $\mathbf{v}_q$? You're going to love this—$\mathbf{q}$ defines both the axis of rotation and the angle θ to rotate about the axis! Of course, the result $\mathbf{v}_q'$ is technically a 4D vector or a quaternion. However, the first component, q_0, will always be zero, so we just throw it away and think of the last three elements as just a vector in 3D representing the original vector $\mathbf{v}$ after rotation.

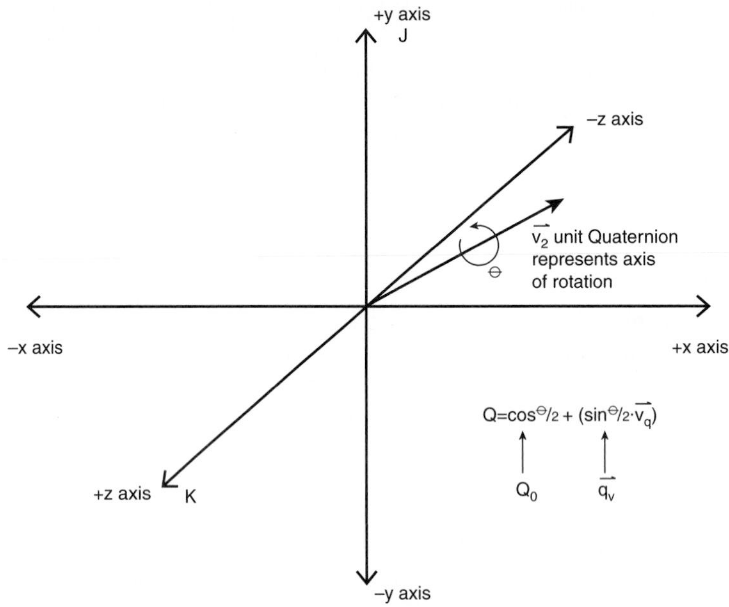

FIGURE 4.45 A geometrical interpretation of a rotation quaternion.

If you have ever tried to rotate a 3D object around an arbitrary axis, you know it's not that easy—but now it is. The axis that the quaternion $\mathbf{q}$ defines along with the angle isn't that obvious, but it's not that bad. Referring to Figure 4.45, we see that for a given unit quaternion $\mathbf{q} = q_0 + \mathbf{q}_v$, the axis of rotation is just the line defined by the vector part $\mathbf{q}_v$, and the angle of rotation θ is encoded in q_0 using the following transforms:

EQUATION 4.36 Conversion of Axis and Angle to Quaternion

$$\mathbf{q} = \cos(\theta/2) + \sin(\theta/2)*\mathbf{v}_q$$

Thus,

$$q_0 = \cos(\theta/2) \text{ and } \mathbf{q}_v = \sin(\theta/2)*\mathbf{v}_q$$

NOTE

Of course, $\mathbf{q}_v$ must be a unit vector itself, so that $\mathbf{q}$ remains a unit quaternion.

What if you don't have a vector that you want to rotate around, but have the standard Euler rotation angles? You can then create a quaternion from the angles by generating one of the products:

$$\begin{aligned}\mathbf{q}_{final} &= \mathbf{q}_{x\theta}*\mathbf{q}_{y\theta}*\mathbf{q}_{z\theta}\\ &= \mathbf{q}_{x\theta}*\mathbf{q}_{z\theta}*\mathbf{q}_{y\theta}\\ &= \mathbf{q}_{y\theta}*\mathbf{q}_{x\theta}*\mathbf{q}_{z\theta}\\ &= \mathbf{q}_{y\theta}*\mathbf{q}_{z\theta}*\mathbf{q}_{x\theta}\\ &= \mathbf{q}_{z\theta}*\mathbf{q}_{x\theta}*\mathbf{q}_{y\theta}\\ &= \mathbf{q}_{z\theta}*\mathbf{q}_{y\theta}*\mathbf{q}_{x\theta} \quad \text{<-most common transform}\end{aligned}$$

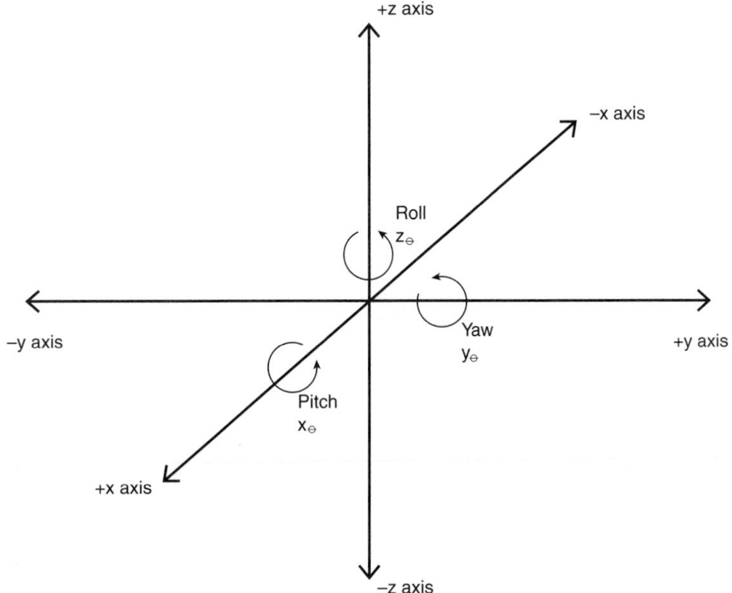

FIGURE 4.46 Yaw, pitch, and roll.

where x_θ refers to the *pitch* (angle parallel to the x-axis), y_θ refers to the *yaw* (angle parallel to the y-axis), and z_θ refers to the *roll* (angle parallel to the z-axis), as shown in Figure 4.46. Most people use the last transform most commonly in 3D engines, but all are just as valid. In any case, after you have the order of transforms, you can plug in the following formulas for the quaternions $\mathbf{q}_{x\theta}$, $\mathbf{q}_{y\theta}$, $\mathbf{q}_{z\theta}$ and perform the multiplication to arrive at $\mathbf{q}_{final}$.

EQUATION 4.37 Euler Angles to Quaternion

$$\mathbf{q}_{x\theta} = \cos(x_\theta/2) + \sin(x_\theta/2)*\mathbf{i} + 0*\mathbf{j} + 0*\mathbf{k}$$
$$q_0 = \cos(x_\theta/2),\ \mathbf{q}_v = \langle\sin(x_\theta/2),\ 0,\ 0\rangle$$

$$\mathbf{q}_{y\theta} = \cos(y_\theta/2) + 0*\mathbf{i} + \sin(y_\theta/2)*\mathbf{j} + 0*\mathbf{k}$$
$$q_0 = \cos(y_\theta/2),\ \mathbf{q}_v = \langle 0,\ \sin(y_\theta/2),\ 0\rangle$$

$$\mathbf{q}_{z\theta} = \cos(z_\theta/2) + 0*\mathbf{i} + 0*\mathbf{j} + \sin(z_\theta/2)*\mathbf{k}$$
$$q_0 = \cos(z_\theta/2),\ \mathbf{q}_v = \langle 0,0,\sin(z_\theta/2)\rangle$$

So to rotate a vector **v** using the Euler form, you are really doing the following for the example of roll, yaw, and pitch:

$$\mathbf{v}_q'(0,x',y',z') = (\mathbf{q}_{z\theta}*\mathbf{q}_{y\theta}*\mathbf{q}_{x\theta})*\ \mathbf{v}_q\ *\ (\mathbf{q}_{z\theta}*\mathbf{q}_{y\theta}*\mathbf{q}_{x\theta})^*$$

where $\mathbf{v}_q = \langle 0,x,y,z\rangle$, the initial vector or point we want to rotate cast into quaternion form.

Of course, you only need to compute the product in parentheses once. And because each of the factors $\mathbf{q}_{x\theta}$, $\mathbf{q}_{y\theta}$, $\mathbf{q}_{z\theta}$ is of the form below:

$$\mathbf{q}_{(i,j,k)} = \cos(\theta/2) + \sin(\theta/2)*(\mathbf{i},\mathbf{j},\mathbf{k})$$

The product of terms of this form have a lot of cancellations—thus the product $\mathbf{q}_{z\theta}*\mathbf{q}_{y\theta}*\mathbf{q}_{x\theta}$, for example, ends up looking like this:

$$q_0 = \cos(_{z\theta/2})*\cos(_{y\theta/2})*\cos(_{x\theta/2}) + \sin(_{z\theta/2})*\sin(_{y\theta/2})*\sin(_{x\theta/2})$$
$$q_1 = \cos(_{z\theta/2})*\cos(_{y\theta/2})*\sin(_{x\theta/2}) - \sin(_{z\theta/2})*\sin(_{y\theta/2})*\cos(_{x\theta/2})$$
$$q_2 = \cos(_{z\theta/2})*\sin(_{y\theta/2})*\cos(_{x\theta/2}) + \sin(_{z\theta/2})*\cos(_{y\theta/2})*\sin(_{x\theta/2})$$
$$q_3 = \sin(_{z\theta/2})*\cos(_{y\theta/2})*\cos(_{x\theta/2}) - \cos(_{z\theta/2})*\sin(_{y\theta/2})*\sin(_{x\theta/2})$$

NOTE

Note that each quaternion in the products can be thought of as an individual rotation operation, but it takes much less work to multiply quaternions than matrices. Therefore, if you find yourself doing a lot of matrix multiplications in a loop, you might be able to optimize it by converting to quaternions—doing all the matrix operations in quaternion form and then converting back.

The conversions from matrix to quaternion and quaternion to matrix are much more complex, and I don't have time to derive them here. However, I will hold off on them until we once again get to the camera stuff, so that it makes more sense to you within the context of something tangible. Also, we will cover interpolation of quaternions later in the camera animation coverage.

Basic Calculus

I never thought I would have to cover basic calculus in a game book, but these days you need to be a damn mathematician to write games! Calculus is nothing more than a form of mathematics invented independently by both Sir Isaac Newton and Baron Gottfried Wilhelm Leibniz in the 17th century—brainiacs deluxe! "The Calculus" (as it's referred to) was invented as a tool to help solve problems in motion, change, and dynamic systems that standard static algebra of the time couldn't handle. Thus, calculus is the mathematics of change, or systems in flux.

As far as we are concerned as game programmers, there is no way you can even think of creating a state-of-the-art 3D game these days without avoiding calculus and differential equations. 3D graphics used to be manageable with linear algebra and a good grasp of matrix mathematics and trig, but now the engines are getting more and more complex, and people want higher order surfaces, like spline and Bezier patches, and so forth. However, that's not the problem—we could all live without rendered curves in games, but lots of camera problems need splines and curves as well, and the mathematics of these objects sometimes take a little calculus to manipulate. However, the *real* problem that makes calculus an absolute necessity is *physics*.

Physics is why calculus was invented! These days friction and a little collision detection isn't going to cut it—people want to see real physics, and that means real math and real models. There is no way to avoid using calculus, so you might as well start learning it right now.

Of course, I can't hope to teach you four years of university math in 20 pages, but I am going to at least show you a couple of concepts. When I use them, you might not understand exactly what I am doing, but you won't be completely lost. I realize that many people reading this book will be in high school and many will be graduate students, but I don't want to leave anyone out in the cold (the biggest complaint I get about game programming books is that people want more math). I'm going to give you a very brief, very loose, and very abridged treatise on the most important things in calculus, and you can pick up a calculus book on your own if you are interested in further reading. I suggest *Calculus* by Howard Anton, or *Calculus* by Thomas & Finney—they rock.

The Concept of Infinity

The first topic I want to discuss might not change your whole life, but it's real, it works, and it's a mathematical reality—*infinity*, represented by the symbol ∞. Infinity is one of those things that we've all heard about, but can't really put our finger on. In calculus however, we love infinity and have no problem with it. In fact, there are all kinds of infinities; small, large, negative, and positive. These are all mathematical tools, and don't need to represent things that are physical, but many times they do.

In any case, I want you to be able to work with infinity because we might need it, and later we might get results that are infinite, which is perfectly fine in higher mathematics. We can start with infinity, or perform a mathematical operation that results in infinity. For example, take a look at the following quotient:

```
       1
q = ----
       y
```

That's a perfectly reasonable thing to do in a computer program, but what happens if y becomes very small? Let's see:

```
1/1 = 1, 1/.1 = 10, 1/.01 = 100, 1/.001 = 1000,…
```

As you can see, as we let y get smaller and smaller, the quotient of 1/y gets larger and larger. You might say, I can make the numerator 100,000,000,000. And I say, so what? I can make the denominator 10 times that and the result will be a small number. The point is that as the denominator gets very small, the quotient gets larger and larger without boundary. At some point, the denominator will become zero, but what will the quotient become? The answer is plus infinity.

```
x/0 = +∞, +infinity
```

It's irrelevant what x is. Also, interestingly enough, the following also holds true (sorta):

```
 x
--- = 0
 ∞
```

Which makes sense, because if you look at the following sequence, you can see it:

```
1/1 = 1, 1/10 = .1, 1/100 = .01, 1/1000 = .001, …
```

As the denominator gets larger and larger, the quotient gets smaller and smaller, and in the end the result will be zero.

The last question you might ask is what happens if both the numerator and the denominator go to infinity? Well, it depends on which one gets there faster. Let's think about it with common sense. Take a look at this:

```
      500*x
y = ---------
       x*x
```

The question is, what happens when x approaches infinity? Well, in the numerator we have 500*x, and in the denominator we have x*x. Here's a short run of the numerator and denominator for $x \in (0,1,2,3,4,5,6,7,8,9,10)$:

TABLE 4.6 A Run of Numbers in the Quotient $500*x/x^2$

x	Numerator (500*x)	Denominator(x*x)	Quotient
0	0	0	Indeterminate
1	500	1	500
2	1000	4	250
3	1500	9	166.66
4	2000	16	125
5	2500	25	100
6	3000	36	83.33
7	3500	49	71.42
8	4000	64	62.5
9	4500	81	55.55
10	5000	100	50

4

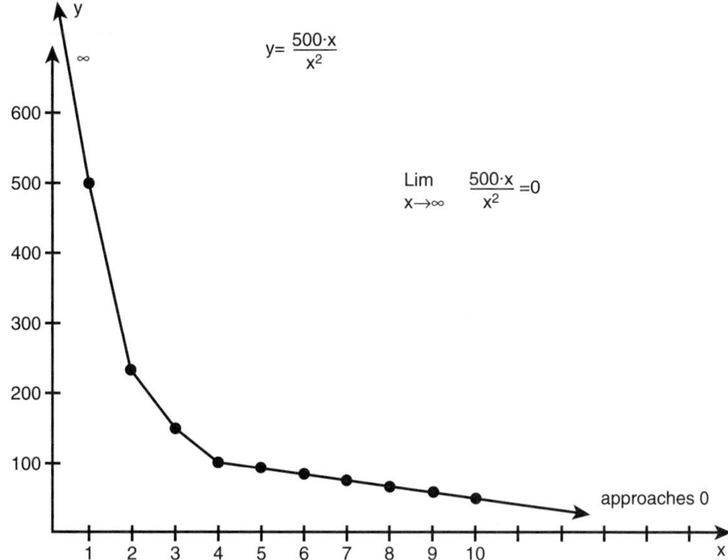

FIGURE 4.47 A graph of the quotient $500*x/x^2$.

Also, take a look at the graph in Figure 4.47. Although it seems that the numerator is moving very quickly, the denominator is quickly catching up, and thus the quotient is getting smaller and smaller. In fact, the end result will be zero. So does common sense seem right? Well, at first glance, if you didn't run the sequence, you might say that the numerator is much larger, and it is for small x. But as x gets large, the x*x is much larger than 500*x, so the end result is that the rate of increase of the denominator is greater than the numerator. Hence, the result will be zero in this case. We could have figured this out using a little algebra, actually.

If we look at the original quotient and simplify it, we can see the result of zero much easier.

```
     500*x
y = ------- = 500/x
      x*x
```

According to our first rule, we know that as x approaches infinity, anything divided by x approaches zero. This whole discussion leads into my next topic—limits.

Limits

The subject of limits is very large, but basically they are a formalization of what we have been doing in the previous section. In general, a *limit* is a mathematical statement that helps us write down a concept that has a changing variable that approaches a fixed constant. This is the very point of calculus—being able to write down in a consistent manner changing mathematical concepts. In any case, here's the general form of a limit statement:

```
Lim  f(x) = L
x->a
```

This is read "The limit of f(x) as x approaches a is equal to L." Computing limits are fairly simple for the more straightforward ones, but of course, they can get very complex. However, in our case, we will just stick to very simple ones. In essence, to compute a limit, you simply let x (or whatever the variable is) approach the limiting value (a in this case) and read off the result. This is best shown with examples:

Example 1: Simple limit

```
Lim 2*x = ?
x->3
```

As x approaches 3, nothing weird happens with f(x). Thus we can simply replace x with 3, and the limit is equal to

```
Lim 2*x = 2*(3) = 6
x->3
```

Example 2: Indeterminate limit

```
Lim x*x/3*x
x->0
```

Now this one is a bit tricky. If we let x approach 0, then we get

```
Lim 0*0/3*0 = ?
x->0
```

which is indeterminate (0/0 is not computable). We need to see whether we can simplify the limit first, so we can get a better grasp on what's happening:

```
Lim x*x/3*x
x->0
```

Canceling out the x terms in numerator and denominator gives us

```
Lim x/3 = 0
x->0
```

which clearly equals zero, because 0/3 = 0.

Example 3: Infinite limit

```
Lim 1/(5*x*x + 2*x) = ?
x->∞
```

We have seen this before, when we were talking about infinity. In this case, the bottom line is that as x gets larger and approaches infinity, (5*x*x + 2*x) gets larger and approaches infinity even faster. Thus the quotient goes to 1/∞, which is equal to zero.

> **NOTE**
>
> Limits can be useful, especially when you are trying to figure out what some expression will end up being as some variable approaches another.

Summation and Finite Series

The next topic I want to discuss isn't really hard-core calculus, but it's a nice way to ease into the subject of integrals, and has a real calculus feel to it. Many times when solving problems that are iterative or recursive in nature, we see sequences of numbers or terms that have patterns. For example, take a look at the following mathematical sequence or summation:

```
1+2+3+4+..n
```

Before we try to compute this, let's try and find a more compact way to write it using *sigma notation* (using the Σ symbol). The preceding sequence has a lower limit (1), an upper limit (n), and a rule. In this case, the rule is at each step simply add the next number in the sequence. It's really just a for loop:

```
for (int count = 1; sum =0; count <=100; count++)
  sum+=count; // <-the rule
```

This C/C++ code is written mathematically like this:

$$sum = \sum_{n=1}^{1000} n$$

which is read something like "sum equals the rule n as n varies from 1 to 1000." In general, the sigma or summation notation looks like this:

$$\sum_{n=a}^{b} f(n)$$

where a <= b (but not necessarily), a is called the "lower limit," and b is called the "upper limit."

Now, back to computing the answer. If n was equal to 1000, how long do you think it would take to add the numbers 1 to 1,000 up? Well, there's a formula for this (and many other sums) discovered by the great mathematician Karl Gauss:

EQUATION 4.38a The Sum of the First n Integers

$$\sum_{k=1}^{n} k = 1+2+3+\ldots+n = n*(n+1)/2$$

Plugging in `1000`, we get

```
1000*(1000+1)/2 = 500500
```

If you think that's impressive, Gauss was five years old when he figured that one out! Of course, throughout the years mathematicians have figured out many *closed forms* for various sequences. Here are two more that come in handy:

EQUATION 4.38b The Sum of the First n Squares

$$\sum_{k=1}^{n} k^2 = 1^2+2^2+3^2+\ldots+n^2 = n*(n+1)*(2*n+1)/6$$

EQUATION 4.38c The Sum of the First n Cubes

$$\sum_{k=1}^{n} k^3 = 1^3+2^3+3^3+\ldots+n^3 = (n*(n+1)/2)^2$$

MATH

Being able to work with series and sums helps with *asymptotic analysis* (see *Tricks of the Windows Game Programming Gurus*), which is the analysis of algorithms and deals with computing the runtime of inner loops and so on. So this is good stuff for 3D graphics.

Now that you have a couple of formulas under your belt, let's see whether we can figure out some sums that are a little bit different. For example:

```
n
Σ 3*k = ?
k = 1
```

The first thing we do is write out a few terms to see the pattern, and find out whether we can manipulate it into one of our formulas and solve it.

```
n
Σ 3*k = 3*1 + 3*2 + 3*3 +...+3*n
k = 1
```

Looks like 3 is always there, so let's factor it out of the sigma sign like this:

```
n
Σ 3*k = 3*1 + 3*2 + 3*3 +...+3*n
k = 1
  n
= 3*Σ k = 1 + 2 + 3 +...+n
  k = 1

= 3*n*(n+1)/2
```

Or in general, for any scalar *a*:

```
n
Σ a*k = a*n*(n+1)/2
k = 1
```

We can do this stuff all day long and come up with all kinds of cool summation formulas—it's good exercise for both your brain and your hands to tell you the truth! Now let's move on to infinite series that are more appropriate for some of the physics calculations you might make in your 3D programming career.

Infinite Series

Finite sums are things that are very tangible—they end somewhere. But there are mathematical sequences that go on forever, but aren't infinite! How can something go on forever, but not be infinite? Well, look at this, for example:

```
0 + 0 + 0 + ...
```

An infinite sum of zeros is definitely still zero. This is the theme of the next section.

There are many times when a complex system can run forever, but its height, energy, level, and so on are changing each time. These systems are real, and arise in nature and mathematics, so being able to come up with closed sums is very useful to us. Let's begin with some notation. A given series might look like this:

Domain:	0	1	2	3 ...	n
	↓	↓	↓	↓	↓
Range:	0	5	10	15	5*n

In this case, the domain is the positive integers 0, 1, 2 ... and the range is also the positive integers. The rule is multiply the integer by 5.

The question is, what is the sum of this infinite series? Common sense tells us that the series keeps getting larger and larger, and thus must grow unbounded, and hence the sum is infinity. However, there are other series that do converge to a finite value. For example, series of the following form *can* converge to a finite value, if the values of *a* and *r* satisfy certain constraints:

$$\sum_{n=1}^{\infty} a*r^{(n-1)} = a + a*r + a*r^2 + a*r^3 +...+ a*r^n + ...$$

where *a* and *r* are real numbers, and $a \neq 0$. Infinite series of this kind are called *geometric series*. Here's an example:

Example:

a = 5, r = 1/2

$$\sum_{n=1}^{\infty} a*r^{(n-1)} = a + a*r + a*r^2 + a*r^3 +...+ a*r^n + ...$$

$$= 5 + 5*1/2 + 5*(1/2)^2 + 5*(1/2)^3 + ...$$

$$= 5 + 5/2 + 5/4 + 5/8 + ...$$

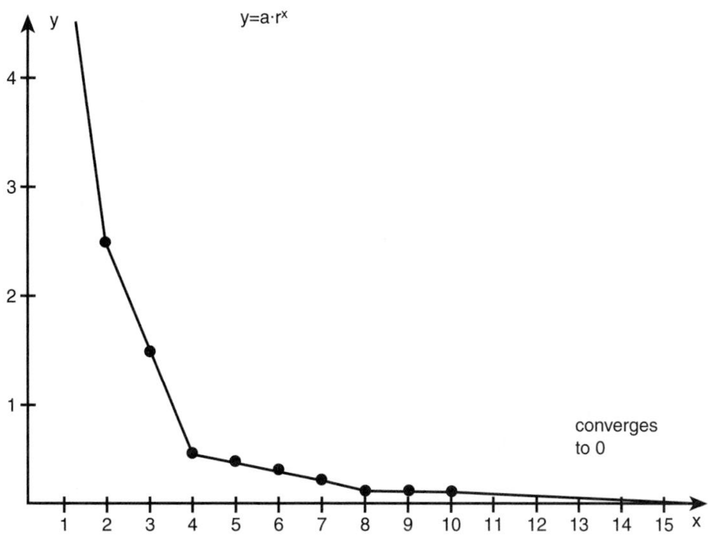

FIGURE 4.48 A plot of the geometric series a = 5, r = 1/2.

We can definitely see that the series is getting smaller and smaller, and this is confirmed by the plot of points in Figure 4.48. In fact, when n reaches infinity, the terms will approach zero. So, there does seem to be good reason to believe there is a finite sum—and of course there is!

EQUATION 4.39 Sum of a General Geometric Series

$$\sum_{n=1}^{\infty} a*r^{(n-1)} = a + a*r + a*r^2 + a*r^3 +...+ a*r^n+...$$

$$\text{the sum} = a/(1-r), \text{ for } |r|<1$$

That's got to be one of the coolest formulas in the world. It tells us how to compute the sum of an infinite collection of expressions in a closed form—math rocks! Using the formula on our series from the previous example with a = 5, and r = 1/2, |r| is less than 1, so it's cool to use, and the sum is

$$a/(1-r) = 5/(1/2) = 10.$$

Of course, there are many kinds of infinite series, but I leave it to you to explore more ...

Derivatives

Now we are finally ready to enter the twilight zone—real calculus. However, calculus is really baby math in the scheme of things, as it's the first course in college mathematics. On the other hand, I have not known many engineers that need to use it on a daily basis, but game programming is turning out to be a field where I see the need for it in the near future. This section and the next are going to be the briefest explanation of derivatives and integrals in the world, but you will at least have an idea of what's going on when I use them later in the book. Furthermore, I am going to be very loose with definitions and rigor.

For example, in high school they teach you that atoms are made of electrons, protons, and neutrons, and that's it. Of course, that's not really true. Furthermore, electrons do NOT orbit the nuclei of the atom. In general, they are a probability cloud. In the same vein, my math here is going to oversimplify reality, but be correct enough for our usage, or rather, detailed enough.

If you recall, the idea of calculus is to be able to discuss and manipulate mathematical objects that change as a function of time (or another variable); that is, functions that are not static. At the most basic level of this notion is the derivative function. The *derivative* of a function is the instantaneous rate of change of that function. For example, suppose you have an object in a game, and its position is described by the following formula, as shown in Figure 4.49:

```
x = x0 + vel*t
```

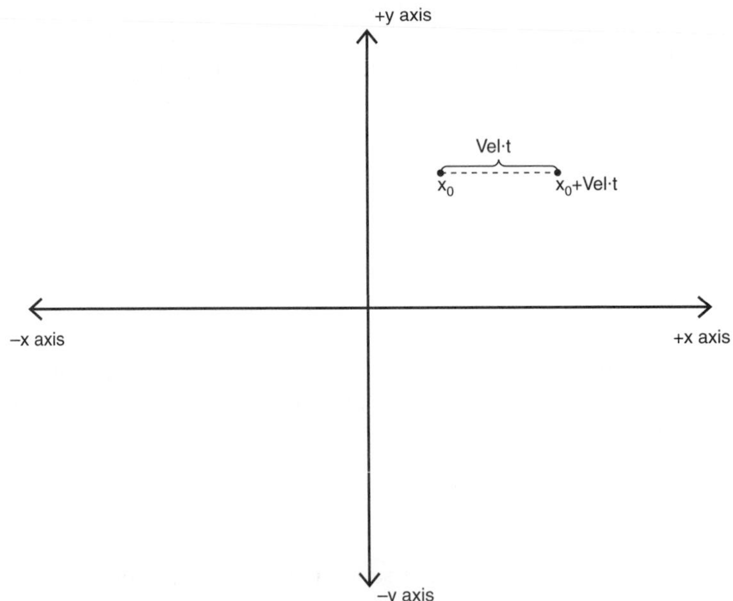

FIGURE 4.49 An object moving based on the motion model (x = x0 + vel*t).

This obviously means that the position x at any time is x0 plus the factor vel*t, where t could be time, or some artificial variable, like the current frame. In either case, we might ask the question, given the formula for *x*, what is the instantaneous rate of change of x? The answer to this is in the definition of x, because we know that with each increment of t, x will change by vel*dt, or velocity*1. Thus, the instantaneous rate of change is the rate factor vel itself. But what if we weren't so darn smart? How could we mathematically determine this without having seen this so many times that we just know? The answer is that the derivative tells us.

If we differentiate x with respect to t, the result is the rate of change of x with respect to t. Sounds pretty circular, huh? In other words, the derivative of the position *is* the velocity. Here's what taking the derivative looks like:

```
d/dt * x(t)
```

which means take the derivative of x with respect to t.

```
d/dt * x(t) = vel
```


Convenient, huh? Almost magical! At this point, if you are thinking "What the heck?" that's okay. Let's see how all this works.

Definition of Derivative

Later I will show you a couple of different notations for derivatives, but for now let's just forget about that and focus on what it is. If you take look at Figure 4.50, you see a curve that's a function of x, f(x). Also, you see two points on the curve: one labeled **a**, which has the value x0, and **b**, which has the value x0+h (h is just a number), and between the two points you see a tangent line with a slope. The slope of this tangent line is shown in Equation 4.40.

EQUATION 4.40 Definition of the Tangent Line

```
         dy  f(x0+h) - f(x0)
slope = --- ---------------
         dx         h
```

This slope is only an average or approximation, but what if we want the slope exactly at x0? We can just make h smaller and smaller to find this. We see this in Figure 4.51. We want to make it infinitely small (zero), so that we are dead on x0. Alas, there's a problem with this! Look at this limit:

```
lim     f(x0+h) - f(x0)
h->0    ---------------
               h
```

As *h* approaches zero, this limit looks like it might approach infinity, and we are fragged! However, this is the definition of the derivative:

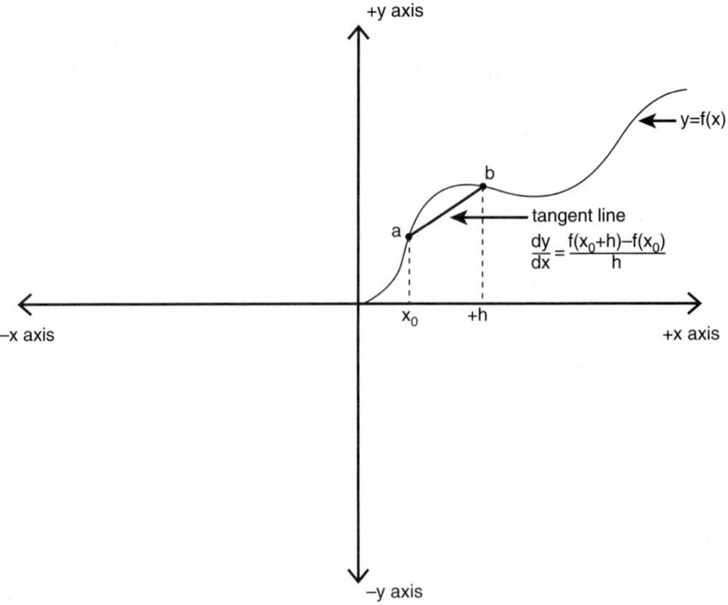

FIGURE 4.50 The definition of derivative.

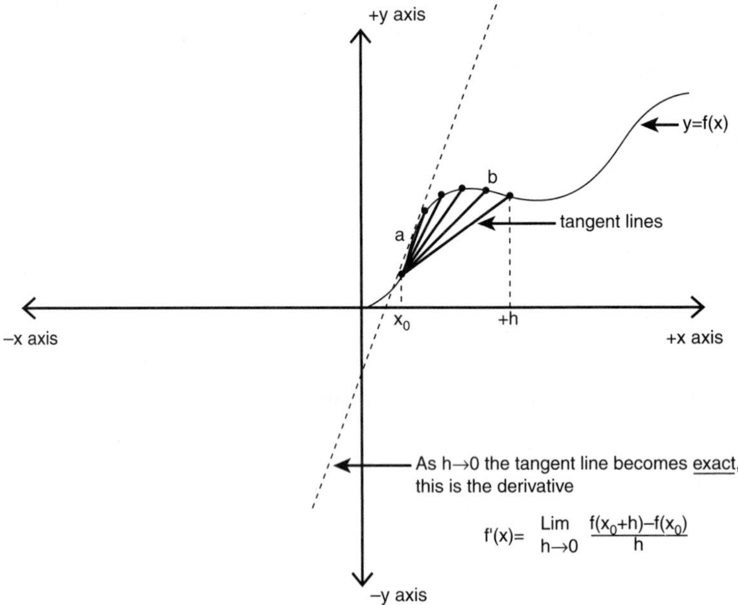

FIGURE 4.51 The tangent line becomes the derivative as h->0.

EQUATION 4.41 Definition of the Derivative

```
f'(x) =    lim     f(x0+h) - f(x0)
           h->0    ---------------
                          h
```

Just a sec, I know, I know. First, the new notation f'(x), or "f primed," means "the derivative of f with respect to x," so that's just notation. Similarly, f''(x) would mean "the second derivative of f with respect to x," or the derivative of the derivative. In general, these all mean the same thing:

1. f'(x)—The derivative of f with respect to x. Both the function and the variable are mentioned.
2. (d/dx)*f(x)—The derivative with respect to x of the function. Emphasizes that differentiation is an operator.
3. df/dx—Very similar to number 1, but in another format. Emphasizes both the function f and the variable to differentiate.

The important part about differentiation is the definition. If this limit exists, it is exactly the limit we need, and exactly the derivative. So how do we find the limit? Well, thankfully, a lot of really smart guys figured out hundreds (if not thousands) of general formulas to compute derivatives for us, so we don't have to (trust me, you don't want to use the definition!).

At this point, let's take a look at some of the more common mathematical expressions that we might have to differentiate in our domination of the universe and complete 3D simulation a la matrix techniques.

Derivatives of Simple Polynomials

Computing the derivatives of polynomials is the simplest, so let's start here. First, the derivative of the sum of terms in a polynomial is simply the sum of each of the derivatives:

$$f(x) = f_1(x) + f_2(x) + \ldots + f_n(x)$$
$$f'(x) = f_1'(x) + f_2'(x) + \ldots f_n'(x)$$

To compute the derivative of any polynomial term, here's what you do:

Let $f(x) = a*x^n$
$f'(x) = n*a*x^{(n-1)}$

Example 1:

$f(x) = 5*x^3$
$f'(x) = 3*5*x^{(3-1)} = 15*x^2$

Example 2:

```
f(x)    = 3*x² + 2*x + 5
```

or, writing out all the terms,

```
df/dx   = 3*x² + 2*x¹ + 5*x⁰
df/dx   = 2*3*x^(2-1) + 1*2*x^(1-1) + 0*5*x^(0-1)
        = 6*x¹ + 2*x⁰ + 0
        = 6*x + 2*1 = 6*x+2
```

NOTE

Note that the derivative of a constant is zero. Also, note that I switched notation for the fun of it, but it means the same thing. Many times, one notation is more convenient than another, as you will see.

Before moving on, let's look at a couple of general rules for computing derivatives.

Derivatives of Products: The Product Rule

Forget for a moment that you don't know how to differentiate everything, and just imagine that you have a product of two expressions. You can compute the derivative by thinking of each expression separately, rather than computing one big messy derivative. This is called the *product rule*. It looks like this:

Given u(x) and v(x) are functions of x,

```
(d/dx)*(u * v) = u*(dv/dx) + v*(du/dx)
```

which reads "The derivative of the product u multiplied by v is u multiplied by the derivative of v with respect to x added to v multiplied by the derivative of u with respect to x."

Example:

```
f(x) = (3*x² + 3) * (5*x)
```

Let

```
u(x) = (3*x² + 3), v(x) = (5*x)
```

then

```
f'(x)   = u(x)*v'(x) + v(x)*u'(x)
        = (3*x² + 3)*5 + (5*x)*(6*x)
```

Again, notice the change in notation, but it all means the same thing: d/dx, f'(x), df/dx.

Derivatives of Quotients: The Quotient Rule

Computing the derivative of a quotient can be accomplished using the product rule and inverses, but to make life easier, we usually just use what's called the *quotient rule* and leave the problem in its original form. Here it is again, in a slightly modified notation:

Given u(x) and v(x) are functions of x,

```
(d/dx) * (u/v) = [ v*(du/dx) - u*(dv/dx) ]
                 -------------------------------
                               v²
```

which reads "The derivative of the quotient u divided by v is equal to v multiplied by the derivative of u with respect to x minus u multiplied by the derivative of v with respect to x, quantity divided by v squared."

Example:

Given

```
        4*x³ - 3
f(x) = ---------
         -3*x²
```

Let

```
u(x) = (4*x³ - 3), v(x) = (-3*x²)
```

then

```
           [v(x)*u'(x) - u(x)*v'(x)]
f'(x)    = ------------------------
                    v(x)²

  = [(-3*x²)*(12*x²) - (4*x³ - 3)*(-6*x)]
  ---------------------------------------
                 (-3*x²)²
```

Again, note the change of notation. Also, we could simplify this if we wanted to.

The Chain Rule

I was hoping to leave this out, but after I wrote a few more pages, I decided I couldn't. It's just so hard to write math notation with MS Word—I'm dying here! In any event, sometimes when computing derivatives, you might come upon functions that are compositions of functions. For example, take a look at the following function:

```
f(x) = sqrt(x²+1) = (x²+1)^(1/2)
```

MATH

Taking the square root is the same as raising to the power of ½. I just can't make the square root symbol that easily!

We could attack this problem as it is and find the derivative of f(x) directly (if we can), or we could think of f(x) as a *composition* of two or more functions. *Composition* means nothing more than one function is the parameter to another. In this case, if we let g(x) = (x^2+1), and f(x) = sqrt(x), we can write this:

Given

$$f(x) = sqrt(x) = (x)^{1/2}$$

and

$$g(x) = (x^2+1)$$

If we replace the "x" in the definition of f(x) with the function for g(x), we have composed g with f, or mathematically:

$$f(g(x)) = (f \bullet g)(x) = (x^2+1)^{1/2}$$

NOTE

Note that the notation f(g(x)) and (f • g)(x) are equivalent.

As another example, let f(x) = sin x, and g(x) = (2*x+3), then f composed with g is

```
(f • g)(x) = sin (2*x+3)
```

The cool thing about thinking of functions as compositions is that it allows us to simplify them for a moment and work at a higher level. Now that you know what a composition is, let's get back to the chain rule for differentiation. The *chain rule* states that you can compute the derivative of a function by first computing the derivative of the composition, and then multiplying that by the derivative of the inside function. Then, if the inside function needs to be further simplified as more compositions, you continue the process. Mathematically, the chain rule can be stated as the following:

```
(d/dx)f(g(x)) = f'(g(x)) * g'(x)
```

Let's take another look at the first example with f(x) =$(x)^{1/2}$, g(x) = (x^2+1), and apply the rule.

$$f(g(x)) = (x^2+1)^{1/2}$$

Then applying the chain rule, we have

```
f'(g(x)) = f'(g(x)) * g'(x)
         = (d/dx)(g(x)^(1/2)) * (d/dx) g(x)
         = 1/2*((x^2+1)^(-1/2) * (2*x)
         = x/(x^2+1)^(1/2)
```

At this point, you can handle computing the derivative of just about anything you can think of. However, many times your functions might have trigonometric terms in them.

Derivatives of Trigonometric Functions

Showing the mathematical derivation for trigonometric functions is far beyond the scope of this book, so I am just going to give you a little table:

TABLE 4.7 Derivatives of Trigonometric Functions

Function	Derivative
sin x	cos x
cos x	-sin x
tan x	sec^2 x
cot x	$-csc^2$ x
sec x = 1/cos x	sec x * tan x
csc x = 1/sin x	-csc x * cot x

Simple enough. Unfortunately, most trig functions don't come in that pure of a flavor—they have functions of x as the parameter, and coefficients, and they might even be to the *n*th degree! However, these aren't that hard to handle. For example, suppose we have this:

```
f(x) = cos^2 x
```

Hmmmm. Let's try the product rule with

```
f(x) = cos(x) * cos(x)
```

Let

```
u = cos(x), let v = cos(x)
```

then

```
f'(x)   = u*(dv/dx) + v*(du/dx)
        = cos(x) * sin(x) + cos(x) * sin(x)
        = 2*cos(x) * sin(x)
```

Cool, huh? The point is, you can usually figure out something, and of course there are billions of little plastic cheat sheets that have all kinds of trig derivatives. Let's look at a couple more. What about this

```
f(x) = a*transcendental(x)
```

meaning any constant *a* multiplied by a trig function. To compute the derivative, we can again use the product rule like this:

```
f(x) = a*transcendental(x)
```

Let u = a, v = transcendental(x), where the trig function could be anything. Then we have:

```
f'(x)    = u*(dv/dx) + (du/dx)*v
         = a * transcendental'(x) + 0
         = a * transcendental'(x)
```

Note that the derivative of u is 0, so the product of the second term is also 0, thus leaving us with the original constant multiplied by the derivative of the transcendental function. Did you see that coming? Here's an example:

Given

```
f(x) = 3*cos(x)
f'(x) = -3*sin(x)
```

Finally, let's look at problems of this form:

```
f(x) = a*cos(b*x+c), a*sin(b*x+c), a*tan(b*x+c), etc.
```

That is, there's a multiplier in the parameter part, along with a constant that models the time multiplier and a shift. This is just a composition, so we can use the chain rule here, letting the inside function be g(x) and the outside function be f(x). Let's try figuring out a*sin(b*x), as all the others are absolutely identical. The first thing to realize is that we can forget about the leading multiplier *a* because we can pull it out of the derivative anyway based on our previous results:

Given

```
f(x) = a*sin(b*x+c)
f'(x) = a*[(d/dx)sin(b*x+c)]
```

Thus, our problem really boils down to computing this:

```
f(x) = sin(b*x+c)
```

Then we are done—we just multiply the answer by *a*. Let's use compositions and the chain rule for this baby. Here are the results:

Let

```
g(x) = (b*x+c)
f(x) = sin(x)
```

then

```
   f(g(x)) = sin (b*x+c)
f'(g(x))    = f'(g(x)) * g'(x)
            = (d/dx)sin(g(x)) * (d/dx)(b*x+c)
            = cos (b*x+c) * b
```

And now, multiply by the constant *a* to finish the problem (recall that we made the simplification f(x) = a*sin(b*x+c), f'(x) = a*[(d/dx)sin(b*x+c)]).

```
 f(x)    = a*sin(b*x)
f'(x)    = a*(cos(b*x+c)* b)
         = a*b*cos(b*x+c)
```

That's the quick tour of differentiation. At this point, you should be able to differentiate any polynomial or sum of polynomials that have transcendental terms that are themselves products of functions or compositions of functions. Hopefully, we won't need anything more complex than this!

Integrals

The next topic of discussion is integration. Integration is the opposite of differentiation—or *antiderivative*. If you were to differentiate f(x) to arrive at f'(x), what would you do to f'(x) to get back to the original f(x)? This process is called *integration*. Now, there are a lot of ways to mathematically define integration, along with ways to understand it geometrically or physically, so I'm going to give you several different points of view on the subject.

The first and purest way to look at the antiderivative is with its definition: Given a function f(x) and its derivative f'(x), the antiderivative F(x) is a function such that if you differentiate it, you get f(x):

```
F'(x) = f(x)
```

That seems fairly circular. It states that if you have a function f(x), and another function capital F(x) that you want to be the antiderivative of f(x), the derivative of F'(x) will equal the original function f(x). That's not that useful, so let's try an example like f(x) = 2*x. Now, the antiderivative of (2*x) is a function F(x), such that when I take the derivative of it, the result would be (2*x). Hmmmm. Let's write that down:

```
F'(x) = 2*x
```

What function, when we take the derivative, equals (2*x)? The answer is x^2 because

```
(d/dx)x² = 2*x^(2-1) = 2*x.
```

So it looks like we have found it. If you're astute, you should realize that we have found a way to find the antiderivative of any term of the form $a*x^n$. We just reverse the process of differentiation, which states to multiply by the exponent and then decrease the exponent. Reversing that, we get the process for integration, which must be to divide by the exponent and then add one to the exponent. Mathematically, the antiderivative of $a*x^n$ is

```
a*x^n = (a/(n+1))x*^(n+1) + c
```

Don't freak about the "c" term. I will get to it shortly.

Hold onto that thought for a moment, and let's talk about integration as an operator, now that we know what we want it to do.

Definition of Antiderivative

Integration is the process of computing the antiderivative of a function, and is written using the ∫ symbol, like this:

```
∫ f(x)dx = F(x) + c
```

f(x) is the function we want to find the antiderivative of, F(x) is the antiderivative, and c is the constant of integration. Let me show you what c represents. Let's say you have the function g(x) = 2*x+1 and you were to differentiate this:

```
 g(x)    = 2*x^1+1
g'(x)    = 1*2*x^(1-1) + 0
         = 2
```

The result is 2, which was just an example to show you that constants disappear when you differentiate. Now if we wanted to compute the antiderivative of that 2, knowing that we should end up back at (2*x+1), let's see what happens using our antiderivative rule relating functions of the form $a*x^n$ to the antiderivative $(a/(n+1))x^{*(n+1)}$:

```
F'(x) = 2*x^0
F(x) = (2/1)*x(0+1) = 2*x
```

Now you see there's a problem here. Basically, we took a function and found its derivative, and then used it as the new starting point and found its antiderivative thinking we would end up in the same place, but we didn't! We lost some information—the constant 1.0 in this case. This leads us back to the definition of an integral:

```
∫ f(x)dx = F(x) + c
```

The c takes this factor into consideration; that is, we know we could potentially lose information when we integrate to find the antiderivative. Only in cases where c = 0 can we forget about it; otherwise, we must keep this in mind. Thus in the example, we just computed that we need to add an arbitrary constant to the result, giving us (2*x+c). Hence, we really have a *family of functions*, or we have generated a function that is capable of generating all possible derivatives of the function 2. If this is confusing, don't worry about it too much. This is all theoretical, really; we just need to know how to integrate polynomials and transcendentals.

Let's recap now what we know. Integration is the opposite of differentiation, and the result is called the antiderivative. We know that the antiderivative of functions of the form $a*x^n$ is $[(a/(n+1))x^{*(n+1)} + c]$, where c is the constant of integration, and may be non-zero. In a moment we will talk about integrals of trig functions, but now I want to give you something more tangible to think about in relation to integration.

A Geometric Interpretation of Integration

As I said, differentiation is like computing the instantaneous rate of change or slope of a function. That is, when you differentiate a function f(x), you wind up with another function f'(x) that is the slope of f(x) for any x. Integration has a similar geometric interpretation in the opposite sense. Take a look at Figure 4.52. Here we see a common parabola function $f(x) = x^2$ in the interval of [0,5]. Additionally, I have shaded in the area under the curve. Interestingly enough, integration computes the area under the curve! Let's test that out. Given the initial function $f(x) = x^2$, let's integrate it using the formula:

$$\int f(x)dx = F(x) + c$$

and

$$f(x) = x^2$$
$$\int x^2dx = F(x) + c$$

Using our antiderivative formula $(a/(n+1))x^{*(n+1)}$, we get

$$\int x^2dx = x^3/3 + c$$

Now, that's great, but what's c? That's where the interval comes into play ([0,5]). We need this to lock into and compute c. The integrals we have been looking at thus far are called *indefinite integrals*—they compute a family of functions for the antiderivative because we don't know c, but definite integrals compute the *exact* value for c, and hence a single antiderivative. The only difference is that we write the definite integral a little differently.

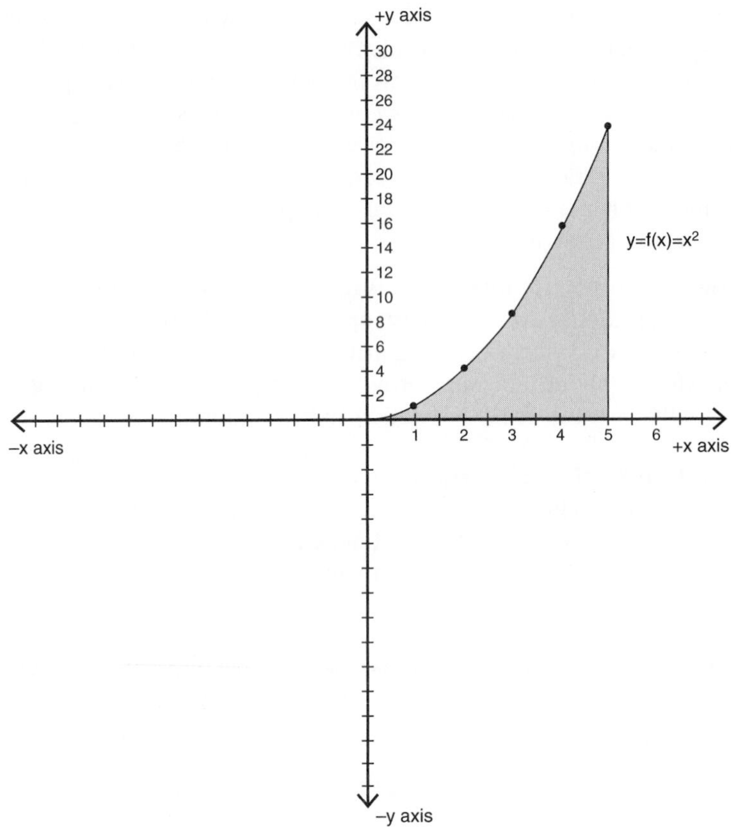

FIGURE 4.52 A geometric interpretation of integration.

EQUATION 4.42 The Definite Integral

$$\int_a^b f(x)dx$$

where [a,b] are the limits of integration. So, all you do is compute the integral as you normally would, but instead of just putting a generic "+c," we can compute it like this with the following notation and steps:

Step 1: Compute the integral.

$$\int_0^5 x^2 dx = [x^3/3 + c]$$

Step 2: Plug in the limits of integration and evaluate the integral at the upper limit and lower limit and subtract.

```
   5
= ∫[x³/3] = [(5)³/3 - (0)³/3]
   0
= [125/3 - 0]
= 41.66
```

A lot is going on here, but basically you compute the integral as usual, then after you have the general form of the integral, you plug the upper limit of integration into the result to arrive at a number, then do the same with the lower limit, and then subtract. This gives you an exact answer.

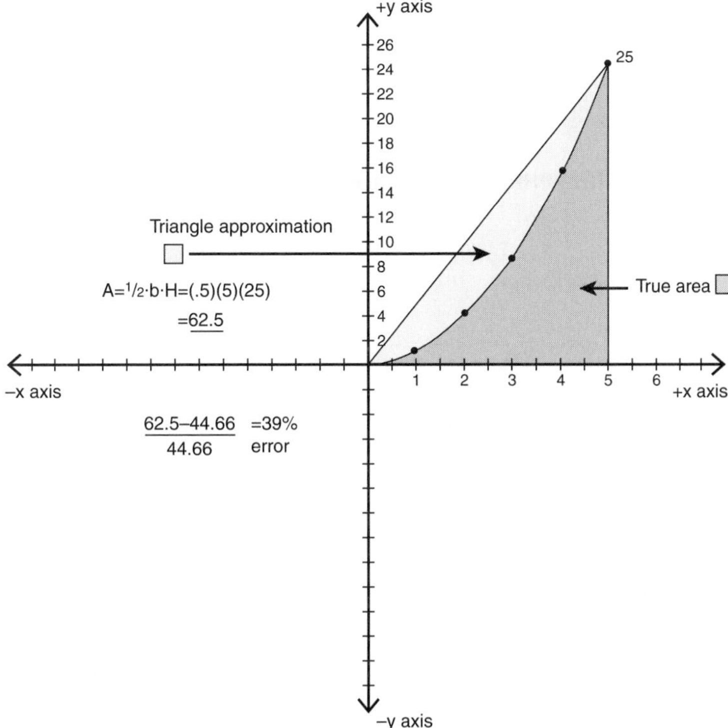

FIGURE 4.53 A triangular approximation of the area under the curve $f(x) = x^2$.

In this case, the answer should be the area under the curve $f(x) = x^2$ in the interval of [0,5]. We get 41.66 roughly; let's see whether that's in the ballpark. Because there are no formulas for computing areas under curves, we can use a triangular approximation, as shown in Figure 4.53. The height of the triangle is 25 and the width is 5, so the area is

```
A = 1/2*width*height = 1/2*5*25 = 62.5
```

which tells us that we are in the ballpark, because the area under the curve is of course less. In fact, take my word for it—the area is exactly 41.66.

Integration Formulas

Okay, so now we have mathematical definition for integral, a geometric interpretation, and we know how to integrate both indefinite and definite integrals. Now let's take a look at some formulas for integration, as shown in Table 4.8.

TABLE 4.8 Integration Formulas

Integral	Antiderivative
$\int a*u^n\,du$	$(a/n+1)*u^{(n+1)} + c$
$\int \sin u\,du$	$-\cos u + c$
$\int \cos u\,du$	$\sin u + c$
$\int \sec^2 u\,du$	$\tan u + c$
$\int \csc^2 u\,du$	$-\cot u + c$
$\int \sec u * \tan u\,du$	$\sec u + c$
$\int \csc u * \cot u\,du$	$-\csc u + c$

Summing Up Integration with a Physics Interpretation

Actually, summing is exactly what integration does! It sums a function from one point to another. That's a very useful operation, and absolutely necessary when calculating physics models. Why? Because most of the time, you will have a model like this:

```
Position: x(t) = x0 + v*t
Velocity: v(t) = v0 + a*t
```

where the acceleration a is constant. The point of my example is that we know that the time derivative of the position x(t) is equal the velocity v(t), or (dx/dt)x(t) = v(t), or put yet another way:

```
x'(t) = v(t)
```

That means if I have the formula for v(t), its antiderivative must be equal to x(t). Mathematically, we have

```
x'(t) = v(t)
```

So, integrating both sides:

```
∫ x'(t) dt = ∫ v(t) dt
```

The left-hand side is just x(t), because the antiderivative of the derivative of a function f'(x) must be f(x) again. Thus we have:

```
x(t) = ∫ v(t) dt
```

And we already know the form of $v(t) = v_0+a*t$; plugging it into the indefinite integral, we get

$$x(t) = \int v_0+a*t \, dt = [v_0*t + 1/2*a*t^2 + c]$$

And now all we need is c. But, if we use the initial conditions $t = 0$, $x = x_0$, and $v = v_0$, we get

$$[0 + 0 + c] = x_0$$

therefore $c = x_0$. Putting it all together, we get the final formula for motion as a function of time, and the initial position and velocity with constant acceleration:

$$x(t) = \int v_0+a*t \, dt = [v_0*t + 1/2*a*t^2 + x_0]$$

The point of this is that we needed to integrate the velocity function to find the position! This is exactly what physics modeling is all about. You run the model, compute collisions and forces, and then you need to integrate numerically to find the new position of all the objects in the game. So yes, we need to know this stuff. When we get to physics modeling, I will show you how to integrate numerically instead of symbolically.

Summary

At this point, I don't know what to say—I feel like I have barely scratched the surface mathematically of what is needed in a video game these days. I never thought I would be writing a math book—a Kama Sutra, yes, but math?—no. However, we just don't have any more time or pages, so we have to move on. On the other hand, I think that if your math skills were indeed rusty (or nonexistent), you should feel pretty good at this point. You covered a lot of complex material: vectors, matrices, parametrics, complex numbers, quaternions, calculus, and more.

However, I strongly suggest you get a couple of good books on linear algebra, calculus, and physics. They can only help. This game stuff is just going to get harder and harder these days, as we are now breaching the barrier of "toy" and entering into "simulation." There is no doubt in my mind that in 3–5 years we will have computer games that run physics models that are absolutely realistic in the Newtonian scale of things. And that means math, math, math! So be warned: I'm not going to explain all the math behind everything from now on. I'll assume you know this level of math at least…

CHAPTER 5

Building a Math Engine

IN THIS CHAPTER

- Brief Overview of the Math Engine
- Data Structures and Types
- Math Constants
- Macros and Inline Functions
- Prototypes
- Globals
- Math Engine API Listing
- Floating-Point Unit Math Primer
- Notes on Using the Math Engine
- Comments on Math Optimization

"I memorized them…"

—Lazlo Hollyfeld, *Real Genius*

Well, I was hoping that the math engine and the last chapter would fit together into one chapter, but as usual there seems to be an exponentially growing number of pages needed to explain everything as each day passes. Writing a book on 3D is like trying to hit an F-22 Raptor by throwing a rock at it! You have to throw the rock so far ahead of it to hit the darn thing! Thus, instead of cutting things out, I decided to make the math library a separate chapter. Basically, everything covered in Chapter 4," It's a Math, Math, Math World—Trigonometry, Vectors, Matrices, and Quaternions" is going to be implemented in one way or another in code: vectors, matrices, quaternions, and so forth. This chapter is a code dump for the most part, because we've already covered how the math works. Thus, I won't show the internals of all the functions, just some of the representative ones. In most cases, the math functions are verbatim implementations of the mathematics from Chapter 4 converted to C/C++. Here's the layout of this chapter:

- Brief overview of the math engine
- Math constants
- Data structures
- Macros and inline functions
- Prototypes
- Globals
- Coordinate system support
- Vector support

- Matrix support
- 2D and 3D parametric line support
- 3D plane support
- Quaternion support
- Fixed-point math support
- Floating-point math primer

Brief Overview of the Math Engine

As I mentioned in the introduction paragraph, I was hoping to fit the math primer and code in a single chapter, but this stuff is just too complicated and I don't want to cut corners. Alas, this chapter is going to continue where the last chapter ended and we're going to implement all of our mathematical findings in a math engine. This engine will be the starting point for our 3D engine and we'll continually add to it, modify it, and improve it as need be. It's not the most efficient math library because it's not optimized too aggressively at the low level. That's so I can remember what the heck I did!

However, where possible, I've optimized it at the high level algorithmically. That is, for example, when computing the determinate of a matrix, I use co-factor expansion rather than the brute force method of computing determinates—this saves multiplications. However, in a real production 3D engine, there are many shortcuts that can be taken once you know what the engine needs to do during runtime. The point is, now we'll have some tools to work with, and we can worry about optimizing them later. Finally, 1GHz+ processors are common now, so it's not like I'm that worried!

File Structure of the Math Engine

The math engine is relatively simple as far as the files are concerned. There are only two new files:

`T3DLIB4.CPP`—The C++ source file

`T3DLIB4.H`—The header file

Figure 5.1 depicts the relationship of the new math engine to the rest of the files in our system. Notice that the math library `T3DLIB4.CPP` relies on some structures in `T3DLIB1.CPP`; thus, we always need to link to `T3DLIB1.CPP¦H` (which you would always do anyway). Moreover, `T3DLIB1.CPP¦H` relies on `DDRAW.H`, hence, that's `#included` in `T3DLIB4.CPP` also. The point is that if you want to use this library module as a standalone in something else, you'll need to move a couple of functions from `T3DLIB1.CPP`, and the `defines` from `T3DLIB1.H` into `T3DLIB4.*`, respectively—just a heads up.

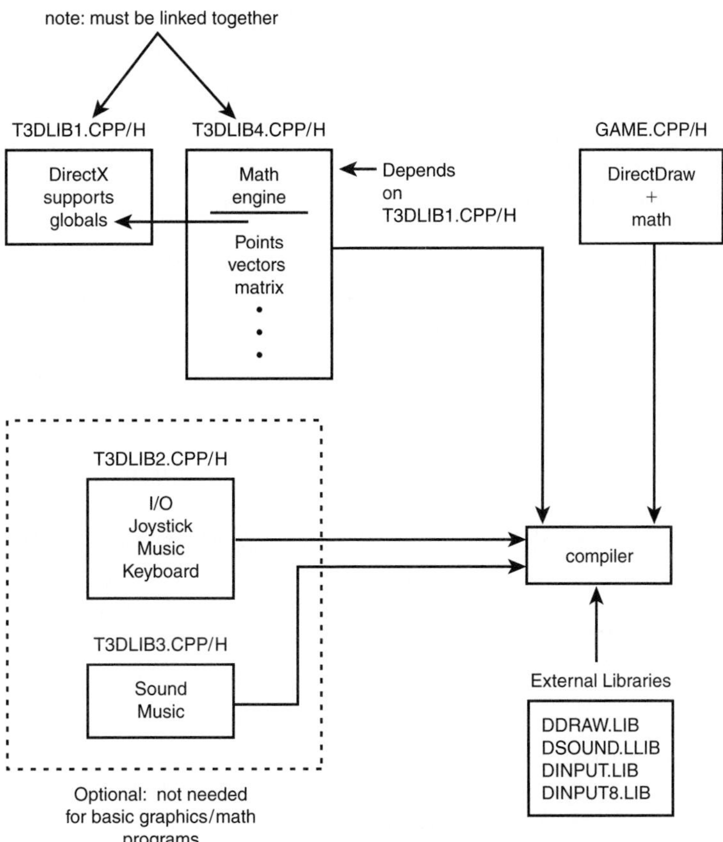

FIGURE 5.1 The relationship of the math engine to our game system.

The math engine itself is composed of numerous functions (and, believe me, it wasn't easy testing them all) that will help us work with points, vectors, lines, matrices, quaternions, and so on. Of course, I'm sure I've left stuff out, but we have a good foundation to work with.

Naming Conventions

As with the first *Tricks*, we'll use the convention that if we update a function, we'll append a number to the function name if the function performs the same operation, but only better or in a slightly different way. For example, a function named `Multiply()` might evolve into `Multiply2()` later in the book. Furthermore, naming functions is always one of those things everyone has a problem with because you want the function to have a reasonably intelligent name, but at the same time you don't want to type 80 billion characters! Therefore, I've decided on the convention that, in most cases, I'll use the class/structure name as part of the function name along with an almost-English description of what the function does and separate its data types by underscores (_). For example, the function that multiplies a vector and a matrix looks like this:

```
void Mat_Mul_VECTOR3D_3X3(VECTOR3D_PTR va,
          MATRIX3X3_PTR mb,
          VECTOR3D_PTR vprod);
```

The function declaration pretty much sums up what the function does. OpenGL has a nice naming convention something like this, so what the heck? This is much better than something like this:

```
MMV3D33(...)
```

Although you might want to use a more aggressive naming convention similar to the above in a production engine, for us, that little extra typing will make things more clear.

NOTE

Additionally, classes and structures are always defined in all uppercase, as well as `#defined` macros. However, some inline macros (short functions) are in mixed case like standard functions.

Error Handling

Error handling is simple—there is none! This book is for intermediate/advanced programmers; if you want error handling and exceptions thrown, add them yourself. In most cases, each function checks for really stupid errors like divide by 0, but there are barely any return codes for any of the functions. If there is a return code, usually `1` (`TRUE`) means success and `0` (`FALSE`) means there was a problem.

My Final Word on C++

Throughout the years of developing games and game programming books, along with writing the previous volume to this book, I think that I've finally arrived at this fact: C++ is a terrible teaching language! It's great in production, and I use it for my own games, but as for teaching, it's very, very bad. I'm not going to get into why I think that, but it is. For example, universities still teach many programming courses and data structure courses in Pascal, Modula II, and Ada—why? Because they're very structured languages, and you know what each line of code does. C++ is too hard to figure out without prior knowledge of the classes defined by the author. Meaning that when someone is trying to learn an algorithm, why complicate matters with classes and constructors and overloaded operators?

Alas, the one library that I was really excited about making completely in C++ has found its final state in what I call C+ (C with some function overloading and a bit of C++). My reasoning is that my C code version is as fast or faster than the C++ version, and it's easier to understand. On the other hand, please convert the math library or anything else you like to C++ if it helps you.

Personally, it's the coolest thing being able to do matrix and vector math with overloaded operators, but it's too hard to know what's going on from a teaching point of view. Moreover, every time I want to update a C++ class-based math library, I have to write a new class and derive and overload the previous class—this is just too much work. I'd much rather have a `Multiply()` function and call the new one `Multiply2()`—capice? And that's all I have to say about that.

Data Structures and Types

Let's start by taking a look at the data structures and types the math engine uses. For the most part, 90% of the types and structures are new, but there are some that we created back in `T3DLIB1.CPP|H` to do some simple matrix math. However, instead of breaking those up, I'm just going to make comments in the descriptions that they can be found in `T3DLIB1.H`.

The math engine supports numerous data types, including points, vectors, matrices, quaternions, parametric lines, 3D planes, polar coordinates, cylindrical coordinates, spherical coordinates, and fixed-point numbers. Let's take a look at each class of structures.

5

Vectors and Points

The math engine supports 2D, 3D, and 4D points and vectors, with 4D meaning homogenous coordinates of the form (x,y,z,w). However, in most cases, we'll never use w (because it will always be 1), but it's nice to have it. Anyway, because points and vectors are really the same thing—data-wise at least—the same data structure is used to hold them. Moreover, I've decided to use unions in the structures to allow multiple naming conventions. For example, sometimes it's nice to refer to a 3D point *p* as *p.x, p.y, p.z*, but other times, I want to use an algorithm that accesses x,y,z as an array *p.M[0], p.M[1], p.M[2]* or something like that. This is the theme throughout all the data structures. I want to give us a lot of room to refer to the data so that we can write clear algorithms. Hence, without further ado, here are the vector and point types:

```
// 2D vector, point without the w ////////////////////////
typedef struct VECTOR2D_TYP
{
union
  {
  float M[2]; // array indexed storage

  // explicit names
  struct
     {
```

```
      float x,y;
      }; // end struct

  }; // end union

} VECTOR2D, POINT2D, *VECTOR2D_PTR, *POINT2D_PTR;

// 3D vector, point without the w ////////////////////////
typedef struct VECTOR3D_TYP
{
union
  {
  float M[3]; // array indexed storage

  // explicit names
  struct
      {
      float x,y,z;
      }; // end struct

  }; // end union

} VECTOR3D, POINT3D, *VECTOR3D_PTR, *POINT3D_PTR;

// 4D homogenous vector, point with w ////////////////////
typedef struct VECTOR4D_TYP
{
union
  {
  float M[4]; // array indexed storage

  // explicit names
  struct
      {
      float x,y,z,w;
      }; // end struct
  }; // end union

} VECTOR4D, POINT4D, *VECTOR4D_PTR, *POINT4D_PTR;
```

And here are a couple of old vertex defines from T3DLIB1.H:

```
// a 2D vertex
typedef struct VERTEX2DI_TYP
    {
```

```
    int x,y; // the vertex
    } VERTEX2DI, *VERTEX2DI_PTR;

// a 2D vertex
typedef struct VERTEX2DF_TYP
    {
    float x,y; // the vertex
    } VERTEX2DF, *VERTEX2DF_PTR;
```

Later in the next chapter, when we start dealing with data structures to contain and represent 3D objects, we'll undoubtedly create 3D vertex representations.

Parametric Lines

In most cases, algorithms that use parametric representations of lines usually create them on the fly with points and variables that define the problem, but I thought that it might be nice to have an actual set of functions to work with explicit parametric lines. Hence, I created support for both 2D and 3D parametric lines. Here's the data structure for a 2D parametric line:


```
// 2D parametric line /////////////////////////////////////////
typedef struct PARMLINE2D_TYP
{
POINT2D p0; // start point of parametric line
POINT2D p1; // end point of parametric line
VECTOR2D v; // direction vector of line segment
       // |v|=|p0->p1|
} PARMLINE2D, *PARMLINE2D_PTR;
```

As shown in Figure 5.2, **p0** represents the starting or initial point, **p1** represent the ending or terminal point, and **v** is the vector from **p0->p1**. If we get a little more ambitious (and we will), 3D parametric lines are just as easy to represent:

```
// 3D parametric line /////////////////////////////////////////
typedef struct PARMLINE3D_TYP
{
POINT3D p0; // start point of parametric line
POINT3D p1; // end point of parametric line
VECTOR3D v; // direction vector of line segment
       // |v|=|p0->p1|
} PARMLINE3D, *PARMLINE3D_PTR;
```

Figure 5.3 represents a 3D parametric line. The values **p0**, **p1**, and **v** represent the same as with the 2D parametric line. However, you'll notice that I am using a left-handed system for the figure. Does this matter? No! A line is a line, no matter what the system. As long as you define the line and use the line in the same system, there won't be a problem.

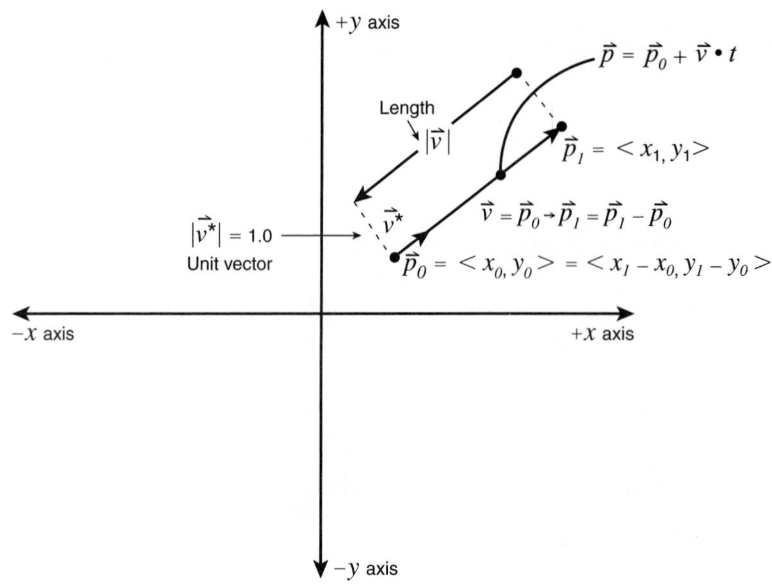

FIGURE 5.2 The 2D parametric line model.

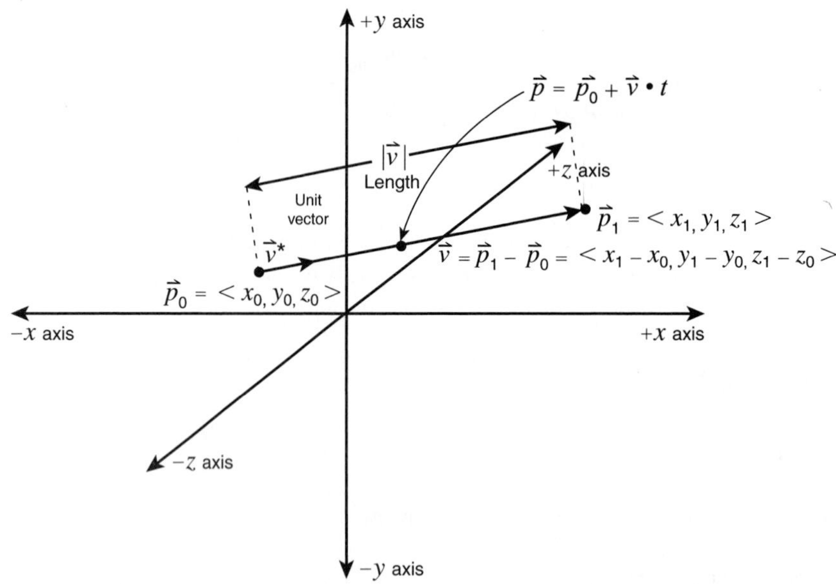

FIGURE 5.3 The 3D parametric line model.

3D Planes

Although most of the time we worry about 3D planes, it will be in the context of polygons. I thought that it might be nice to have a 3D plane type for a few reasons: to be able to perform partitioning algorithms, to ease writing clipping algorithms, and finally to help with collision detection algorithms between parametric 3D lines and 3D planes. Anyway, there are a number of ways to represent a plane in 3D, but ultimately they all represent the same object. Thus, I used the *point-normal* form rather than the explicit form to hold the representation. That doesn't mean that we can't store a plane in the form

```
a*x+b*y+c*z+d = 0
```

It just means that we need to write a function that converts it into the point normal form for storage. Furthermore, the point normal form is more suited for a number of computations and not having to perform the conversion from explicit form is helpful. In any case, here's the data structure we'll use for now:

```
// 3D plane ///////////////////////////////////////////////////
typedef struct PLANE3D_TYP
{
POINT3D p0; // point on the plane
VECTOR3D n; // normal to the plane (not necessarily a unit vector)
} PLANE3D, *PLANE3D_PTR;
```


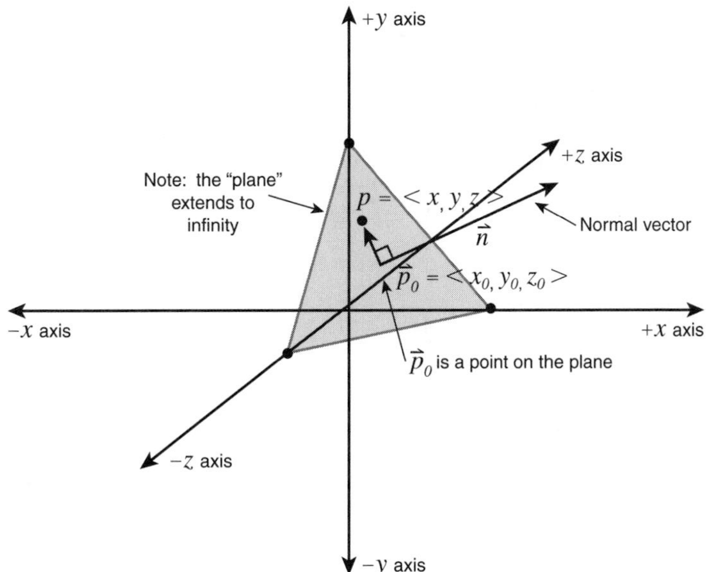

FIGURE 5.4 The 3D plane model.

Figure 5.4 depicts a 3D plane (in an LHS), **p0** is a point on the plane, and the vector **n** is normal to the plane. Note: we don't assume that **n** is a unit vector.

Matrices

The largest set of data structures in the math engine is the matrices. There is support for 1×2, 2×2, 1×3, 3×2, 3×3, 1×4, 4×4, and 4×3. The 1×*n* matrices are really data equivalent to *n*-element vectors. For example, a 1×3 matrix has the same data footprint as a VECTOR3D, which is good because we can cast data types and get functions written for one type to work transparently with another. Anyway, here's all the matrix types. Note that many of the 2×2 and 3×3 are defined in T3DLIB1.H and all matrices are in row major form and indexed [0..n][0..n] = [row_index][column_index].

```
// matrix defines

// 4x4 matrix /////////////////////////////////////////////
typedef struct MATRIX4X4_TYP
{
union
  {
  float M[4][4]; // array indexed data storage

  // storage in row major form with explicit names
  struct
     {
     float M00, M01, M02, M03;
     float M10, M11, M12, M13;
     float M20, M21, M22, M23;
     float M30, M31, M32, M33;
     }; // end explicit names

  }; // end union

} MATRIX4X4, *MATRIX4X4_PTR;

// 4x3 matrix /////////////////////////////////////////////
typedef struct MATRIX4X3_TYP
{
union
  {
  float M[4][3]; // array indexed data storage

  // storage in row major form with explicit names
  struct
     {
```

```
      float M00, M01, M02;
      float M10, M11, M12;
      float M20, M21, M22;
      float M30, M31, M32;
      }; // end explicit names

  }; // end union

} MATRIX4X3, *MATRIX4X3_PTR;

// 1x4 matrix ///////////////////////////////////////////////
typedef struct MATRIX1X4_TYP
{
union
  {
  float M[4]; // array indexed data storage

  // storage in row major form with explicit names
  struct
      {
      float M00, M01, M02, M03;
      }; // end explicit names

   }; // end union
} MATRIX1X4, *MATRIX1X4_PTR;


// 3x3 matrix ///////////////////////////////////////////////
// from T3DLIB1.H
typedef struct MATRIX3X3_TYP
    {
    union
    {
    float M[3][3]; // array indexed data storage

    // storage in row major form with explicit names
    struct
       {
       float M00, M01, M02;
       float M10, M11, M12;
       float M20, M21, M22;
       }; // end explicit names
```

```
    }; // end union
    } MATRIX3X3, *MATRIX3X3_PTR;

// 1x3 matrix ///////////////////////////////////////////////
// from T3DLIB1.H
typedef struct MATRIX1X3_TYP
    {
    union
    {
    float M[3]; // array indexed data storage

    // storage in row major form with explicit names
    struct
       {
       float M00, M01, M02;

       }; // end explicit names
    }; // end union
    } MATRIX1X3, *MATRIX1X3_PTR;

// 3x2 matrix ///////////////////////////////////////////////
// from T3DLIB1.H
typedef struct MATRIX3X2_TYP
    {
    union
    {
    float M[3][2]; // array indexed data storage

    // storage in row major form with explicit names
    struct
       {
       float M00, M01;
       float M10, M11;
       float M20, M21;
       }; // end explicit names

    }; // end union
    } MATRIX3X2, *MATRIX3X2_PTR;


// 2x2 matrix ///////////////////////////////////////////////
typedef struct MATRIX2X2_TYP
{
```

```
union
  {
  float M[2][2]; // array indexed data storage

  // storage in row major form with explicit names
  struct
     {
     float M00, M01;
     float M10, M11;
     }; // end explicit names

   }; // end union
} MATRIX2X2, *MATRIX2X2_PTR;

// 1x2 matrix ///////////////////////////////////////////////
// from T3DLIB1.H
typedef struct MATRIX1X2_TYP
    {
    union
    {
    float M[2]; // array indexed data storage

    // storage in row major form with explicit names
    struct
       {
       float M00, M01;

       }; // end explicit names
    }; // end union
    } MATRIX1X2, *MATRIX1X2_PTR;
```


Notice the naming conventions on all the matrices. For example, if we defined a 3×3 matrix like this:

```
MATRIX3X3 m = {0,1,2, 3,4,5, 6,7,8 };
```

Then the matrix would look like this in memory:

```
|0   1   2|
|3   4   5|
|6   7   8|
```

which is in row major form. To access the lower-right hand element and assign a 100.0 to it, both of the following statements are equivalent because of the union:

```
m.M22 = 100; // all elements are 0 indexed

m.M[2][2] = 100;
```

Quaternions

The next data type is the 4D hyper complex quaternion (I just love saying that). If you recall, quaternions have the form

```
q = q0 + q1*i + q2*j + q3*k
```

or

```
q = q0 + <q1, q2, q3>
```

or

```
q = q0 + qv
```

Any way you look at it, a quaternion is nothing more than a 4-tuple, where the real part is q0, and the vector part is imaginary. Moreover, because we're going to use quaternions in the context of rotation and camera work, it will be advantageous to be able to represent them in the form of a single real q0 or w along with a vector part <x,y,z>. That way we can use some of the other VECTOR3D functions to do work on quaternions—possibly because the data footprints are similar? With that in mind, take a look at the definition of a quaternion:

```
// 4d quaternion ///////////////////////////////////////////////
// note the union gives us a number of ways to work with
// the components of the quaternion
typedef struct QUAT_TYP
{
union
  {
  float M[4]; // array indexed storage w,x,y,z order

  // vector part, real part format
  struct
     {
     float  q0; // the real part
     VECTOR3D qv; // the imaginary part xi+yj+zk
     };
```

```
   struct
      {
      float w,x,y,z;
      };
   }; // end union

} QUAT, *QUAT_PTR;
```

Notice the union allows access to the quaternion in three different ways: as an array, as a float vector pair, and explicitly as w,x,y,z, which is great depending on the algorithm the quaternion is being processed with. For example, here's a quaternion defined and then the real part is altered:

```
QUAT q = {1, 1,2,3 };

q.w  = 5; // access with explicit name
q.q0  = 5; // access with real float/vector name
q.M[0] = 5; // access with array
```


NOTE

It was tempting to put quaternions into the form <x,y,z,w> so that their data footprint matched that of a VECTOR4D. However, tempting as it was, I wanted to keep the convention of the data type in the same format as used when writing them mathematically.

TIP

Later, we might create a new quaternion type if we find that a different data ordering speeds calculations or access.

Angular Coordinate System Support

Although I doubt we'll use coordinate systems other than Cartesian throughout the book, there might be a time when we need it just to make a representation more natural to model the problem. For example, if we were modeling a weapon turret (as shown in Figure 5.5), a polar coordinate system might be perfect because we need an angular direction about the axis. Hence, the math engine supports all angular 2D- and 3D-coordinate systems and transformation between systems. The systems supported are *polar 2D*, *cylindrical 3D*, and *spherical 3D*. All angles are in radians, and all conversions are relative to a right-handed system, so watch out if you're using a left-handed system—you might get a negative sign if you don't take the right-handedness into consideration.

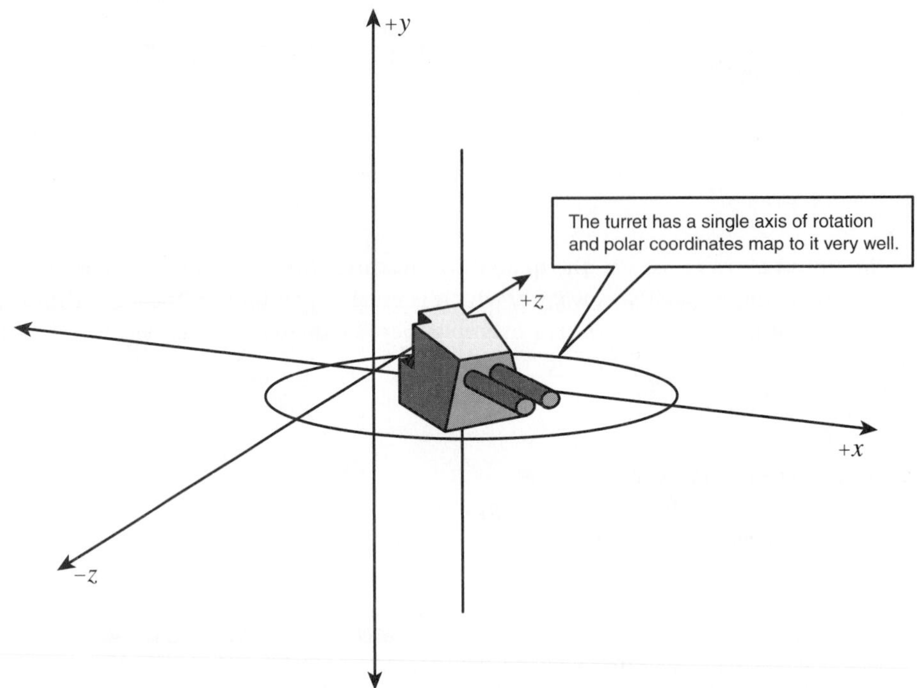
+y
The turret has a single axis of rotation and polar coordinates map to it very well.
+z
+x
−z

FIGURE 5.5 A weapon turret modeled with polar coordinates.

CAUTION

Watch out! All the angular functions assume that angles are in terms of radians NOT degrees!

Polar 2D

The polar 2D system is shown in Figure 5.6. A point is represented by a distance r from the origin or ***Pole***, and a heading or angle θ (theta). Thus, the notation **p**(r, θ) means that the point **p** is located an angle θ degrees (or radians) relative to a reference ray (usually the x-axis) measured counter-clockwise, and a distance r out on that directional heading. The data type is nothing more than this exact representation converted to C++:

```
// 2D polar coordinates ///////////////////////////////////////
typedef struct POLAR2D_TYP
{
float r;    // the radi of the point
float theta; // the angle in rads
} POLAR2D, *POLAR2D_PTR;
```

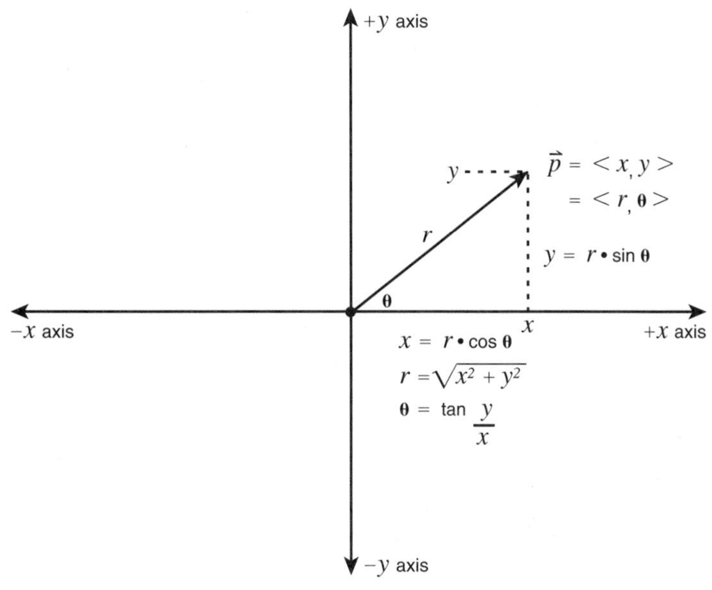

FIGURE 5.6 The polar 2D coordinate system.

Cylindrical 3D

The cylindrical 3D system is similar to the polar 2D system with the addition of a z-axis variable, as shown in Figure 5.7. Points are defined as a triple **p**(r,θ,z), meaning the point **p** is located an angle θ degrees (or radians) relative to a reference ray (usually the x-axis) measured counter-clockwise, and a distance r out on that directional heading. It's then raised or lowered an amount, z, on the z-axis. The data type contains exactly this information as shown in the following snippet:

```
// 3D cylindrical coordinates ////////////////////////////////
typedef struct CYLINDRICAL3D_TYP
{
float r;     // the radi of the point
float theta; // the angle in degrees about the z axis
float z;     // the z-height of the point
} CYLINDRICAL3D, *CYLINDRICAL3D_PTR;
```

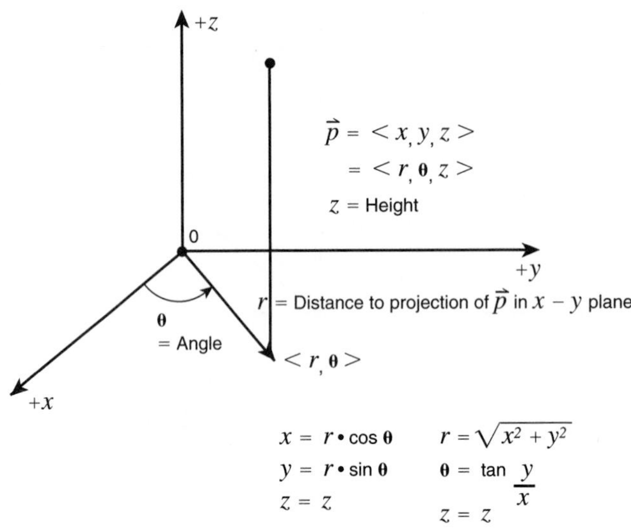

FIGURE 5.7 The cylindrical 3D coordinate system.

Spherical 3D

Spherical 3D coordinates are the most complex of all the angular systems. A point **p**(ρ,φ,θ) is defined by a distance and two angles as shown in Figure 5.8, where

ρ (rho) is the distance from the origin **o** to the point **p**.

φ (phi) is the angle that the directed line segment from the origin to **p** makes with the positive z-axis (thus, we'll use an RHS system in this analysis).

θ (theta) is the angle that projection of the line from **o** to **p** makes on the x-y plane, which is just the standard 2D polar θ. Also, $0 <= \theta <= \pi$; that is, θ must be in the interval from 0 to π, inclusive.

Of course, you've seen this before in the last chapter, but it can't hurt to show it again. Anyway, as you guessed the data structure is (drum roll please...):

```
// 3D spherical coordinates ////////////////////////////////////
typedef struct SPHERICAL3D_TYP
{
float p;     // rho, the distance to the point from the origin
float theta; // the angle from the z-axis and the line segment o->p
float phi;   // the angle from the projection if o->p onto the x-y
       // plane and the x-axis
} SPHERICAL3D, *SPHERICAL3D_PTR;
```

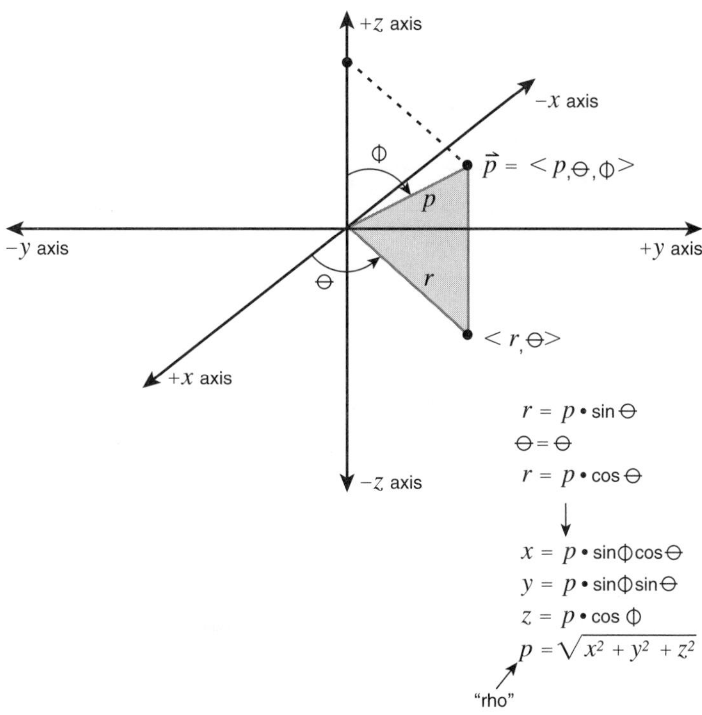

FIGURE 5.8 The 3D spherical coordinate system.

Fixed-Point Numbers

The last types are hardly types, but we need them nevertheless. Fixed-point numbers, as you know, are integers that are used to represent fractional or floating-point numbers with limited accuracy without the need of floating-point processing. Today the need for them is moot because Pentium+ and I64 processors can all perform floating-point math as quickly as fixed-point math. However, fixed-point sometimes still makes sense in tight inner loops where floating-point numbers can't be used, or when you want to use only integers, or on smaller handheld devices. In any case, for the majority of math in this book, we'll use the 16.16 format as shown in Figure 5.9; that is, 16 bits to represent the whole part and 16 bits to represent the decimal part. With that in mind, here are the data types:

```
// fixed point types ///////////////////////////////////////////
typedef int FIXP16;
typedef int *FIXP16_PTR;
```

Now, let's take a look the constants and defines used in the engine. Normally, they would come first, but I had some forward references to the data structures, so it was best to cover those first and the defines later.

A. A 16-Bit Fixed Point Format

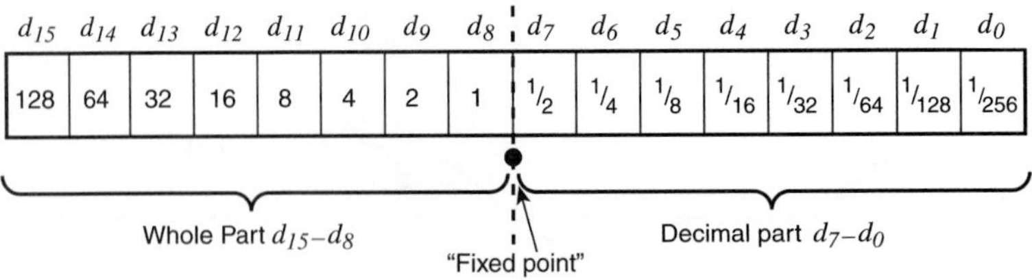

B. A 32-Bit Fixed Point Format

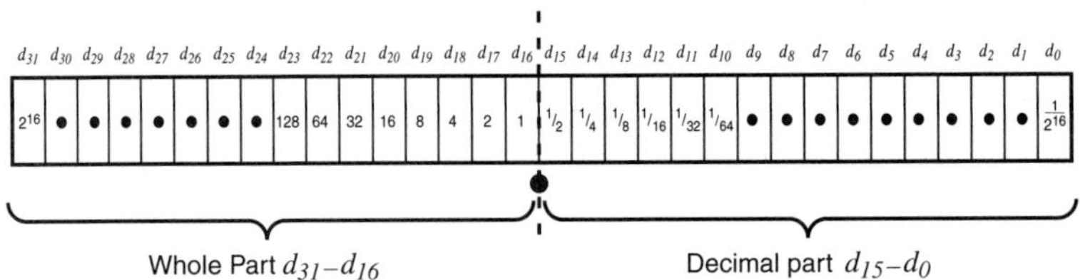

FIGURE 5.9 Fixed-point number representations.

Math Constants

The math engine is based on a number of defined constants. These constants are found in `T3DLIB4.H`, but there are a few legacy constants from `T3DLIB1.H` that are used. Here are the math constants that you'll find in `T3DLIB1.H` (just for review):

```
// math related constants from T3DLIB1.H

// pi defines
#define PI        ((float)3.141592654f)
#define PI2       ((float)6.283185307f)
#define PI_DIV_2  ((float)1.570796327f)
#define PI_DIV_4  ((float)0.785398163f)
#define PI_INV    ((float)0.318309886f)

// fixed point mathematics constants
#define FIXP16_SHIFT     16
#define FIXP16_MAG       65536
#define FIXP16_DP_MASK   0x0000ffff
#define FIXP16_WP_MASK   0xffff0000
#define FIXP16_ROUND_UP  0x00008000
```

Nothing more than pi and some fixed-point stuff. Note that we're using 16.16 fixed-point format, but more on that when we get to the fixed-point routines. Anyway, here are the constants from T3DLIB4.H broken down in sections with explanations where needed:

```
// defines for small numbers
#define EPSILON_E4 (float)(1E-4)
#define EPSILON_E5 (float)(1E-5)
#define EPSILON_E6 (float)(1E-6)
```

The *epsilon* constants help when performing math comparisons on small floating-point numbers. For example, it's common when doing floating-point math to test whether a number is equal to 0.0. However, 0.0 in floating-point is a rare thing once a few calculations have been performed and accuracy is lost, so a common strategy is to test for near 0.0 like this:

```
if (fabs(x) < 0.00001)
  {
  // that's close enough to 0
  } // end if
```

The next set of constants help with the parametric line functions and their return values (more on that when we get to the functions):

```
// defines for parametric line intersections
#define PARM_LINE_NO_INTERSECT      0
#define PARM_LINE_INTERSECT_IN_SEGMENT 1
#define PARM_LINE_INTERSECT_OUT_SEGMENT 2
#define PARM_LINE_INTERSECT_EVERYWHERE 3
```

And now for some identity matrices to make initializing matrices easier:

```
// identity matrices

// 4x4 identity matrix
const MATRIX4X4 IMAT_4X4 = {1,0,0,0,
              0,1,0,0,
              0,0,1,0,
              0,0,0,1};

// 4x3 identity matrix (note this is not correct mathematically)
// but later we may use 4x3 matrices with the assumption that
// the last column is always [0 0 0 1]t
const MATRIX4X3 IMAT_4X3 = {1,0,0,
              0,1,0,
```

```
                0,0,1,
                0,0,0,};


// 3x3 identity matrix
const MATRIX3X3 IMAT_3X3 = {1,0,0,
                0,1,0,
                0,0,1};

// 2x2 identity matrix
const MATRIX2X2 IMAT_2X2 = {1,0,
                0,1};
```

NOTE

Although only nxn matrices can have identity matrices (that is; 2x2, 3x3, 4x4, and so on), there's a 4x3 identity matrix in the preceding definitions. This technically isn't correct, but during many math operations, we use 4x3 matrices and assume the last column is $[0\ 0\ 0\ 1]^t$. Thus, we can create a 4x3 identity as long as we remember that there's an artificial extra column there when doing the math.

Amazingly enough, that's all there is to the math constants and defines!

Macros and Inline Functions

The problem with writing a math engine is that, in reality making function calls to perform operations on math objects can take as much time as the math operations themselves! Hence, using macros and inline functions is definitely the way to go. However, the problem with large inline functions is that inline functions **MUST** be available at compile time rather than at link time. That is, when you compile a program and call a function named `func()` in another module, the compiler doesn't need the code for `func()`, only the prototype:

```
int func(int x, int y);
```

With that, it can create a call in the compiled code and then later the linker can find `func()` and resolve the call to an address. The problem with inline functions is that during compile time the actual code **needs** to be available. Thus, the only way to cleanly implement large inline functions is with a header that defines the inline functions along with another pseudo C/C++ module named `*.inc` that you manually include in the module you're including. This way, the compiler has access to the actual code of the function you're requesting the inlining of. Figure 5.10 shows this setup.

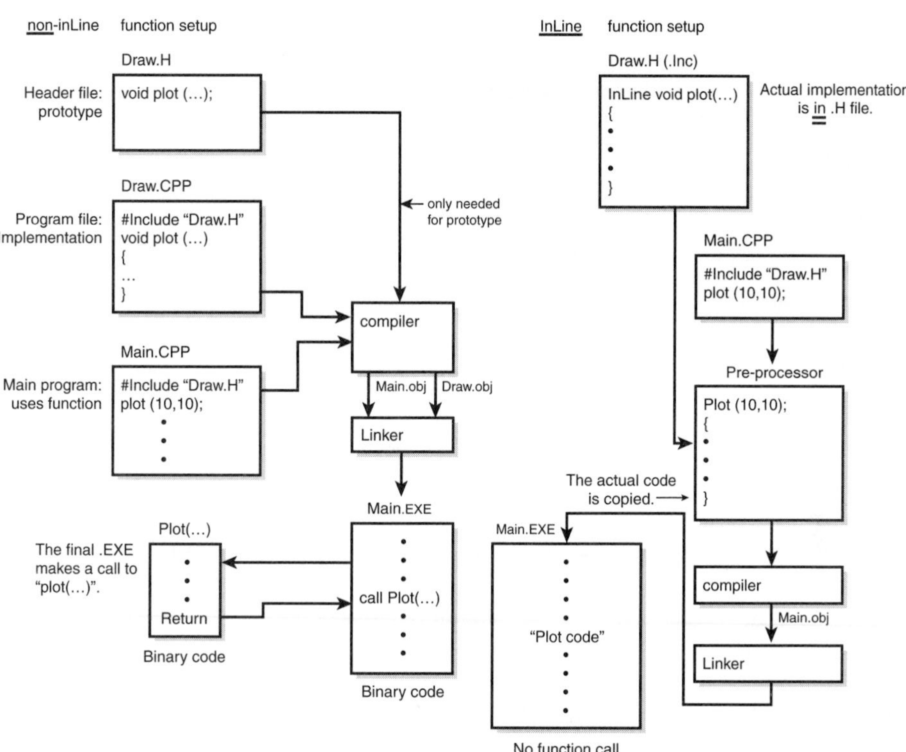

FIGURE 5.10 The inlining process in relation to the compiler and linker.

The point I am trying to make is this: When writing a math engine, all the functions should inline, for the most part, anything less than a few lines of code where the code itself takes on the same order of magnitude to run as does setting up the stack frame, making the call, and returning. For example, here's an example of a horrific function to call in an inner loop:

```
void Plot_Pixel(UCHAR *video_buffer, int mempitch, int x, int y, int color)
{
// plots a pixel
video_buffer[x+y*mempitch] = color;
} // end Plot_Pixel
```

If I make a call to this in my program, a function call will be generated. For example, take a look at the following code:

```
void main()
{
UCHAR *video_buffer = (UCHAR *)malloc(SCREEN_WIDTH*SCREEN_HEIGHT);
```

```
for (int y=0; y < SCREEN_HEIGHT; y++)
     for (int x=0; x < SCREEN_WIDTH; x++)
        Plot_Pixel(video_buffer, SCREEN_WIDTH, x,y,5); // slow call

} // end main
```

Although the function doesn't look bad, let's look at the disassembly of the code as generated by my Visual C++ 6.0 compiler:

```
_main PROC NEAR

; 52  : {

    push  ebp
    mov  ebp, esp
    sub  esp, 12                  ; 0000000cH

; 53  : UCHAR *video_buffer = (UCHAR *)malloc(SCREEN_WIDTH*SCREEN_HEIGHT);

    push  307200                  ; 0004b000H
    call  _malloc
    add  esp, 4
    mov  DWORD PTR _video_buffer$[ebp], eax

; 54  :
; 55  : for (int y=0; y < SCREEN_HEIGHT; y++)

    mov  DWORD PTR _y$[ebp], 0
    jmp  SHORT $L43914
$L43915:
    mov  eax, DWORD PTR _y$[ebp]
    add  eax, 1
    mov  DWORD PTR _y$[ebp], eax
$L43914:
    cmp  DWORD PTR _y$[ebp], 480       ; 000001e0H
    jge  SHORT $L43916

; 56  :    for (int x=0; x < SCREEN_WIDTH; x++)

    mov  DWORD PTR _x$43917[ebp], 0
    jmp  SHORT $L43918
$L43919:
    mov  ecx, DWORD PTR _x$43917[ebp]
    add  ecx, 1
```

```
    mov   DWORD PTR _x$43917[ebp], ecx
$L43918:
    cmp   DWORD PTR _x$43917[ebp], 640      ; 00000280H
    jge   SHORT $L43920

; 57  :          Plot_Pixel(video_buffer, SCREEN_WIDTH, x,y,5);

    push  5
    mov   edx, DWORD PTR _y$[ebp]
    push  edx
    mov   eax, DWORD PTR _x$43917[ebp]
    push  eax
    push  640                       ; 00000280H
    mov   ecx, DWORD PTR _video_buffer$[ebp]
    push  ecx
    call  ?Plot_Pixel@@YAXPAEHHHH@Z       ; Plot_Pixel
    add   esp, 20                   ; 00000014H
    jmp   SHORT $L43919
$L43920:
    jmp   SHORT $L43915
$L43916:

; 58  :
; 59  : } // end main

    mov   esp, ebp
    pop   ebp
    ret   0
_main  ENDP
```

I've highlighted all the code needed to make the call to `Plot_Pixel()` to set up the stack frame, the call, and the fix up during the return. Now, compare that to the actual code for the `Plot_Pixel()` function itself:

```
?Plot_Pixel@@YAXPAEHHHH@Z PROC NEAR          ; Plot_Pixel

; 45  : {

    push  ebp
    mov   ebp, esp

; 46  : // plots a pixel
; 47  : video_buffer[x+y*mempitch] = color;
```

5

```
    mov  eax, DWORD PTR _y$[ebp]
    imul  eax, DWORD PTR _mempitch$[ebp]
    mov  ecx, DWORD PTR _x$[ebp]
    add  ecx, eax
    mov  edx, DWORD PTR _video_buffer$[ebp]
    mov  al, BYTE PTR _color$[ebp]
    mov  BYTE PTR [edx+ecx], al

; 48  : } // end Plot_Pixel

    pop  ebp
    ret  0
?Plot_Pixel@@YAXPAEHHHH@Z ENDP             ; Plot_Pixel
```

As you can see, the call to `Plot_Pixel()` does almost as much work as the function does! However, if we inline the function, all this call overhead goes away. Here's the same example, but this time I tell the compiler to inline the function:

```
_main  PROC NEAR

; 52  : {

    push  ebp
    mov  ebp, esp
    sub  esp, 16                    ; 00000010H

; 53  : UCHAR *video_buffer = (UCHAR *)malloc(SCREEN_WIDTH*SCREEN_HEIGHT);

    push  307200                    ; 0004b000H
    call  _malloc
    add  esp, 4
    mov  DWORD PTR _video_buffer$[ebp], eax

; 54  :
; 55  : for (int y=0; y < SCREEN_HEIGHT; y++)

    mov  DWORD PTR _y$[ebp], 0
    jmp  SHORT $L43914
$L43915:
    mov  eax, DWORD PTR _y$[ebp]
    add  eax, 1
    mov  DWORD PTR _y$[ebp], eax
$L43914:
```

```
    cmp  DWORD PTR _y$[ebp], 480        ; 000001e0H
    jge  SHORT $L43916

; 56  :    for (int x=0; x < SCREEN_WIDTH; x++)

    mov  DWORD PTR _x$43917[ebp], 0
    jmp  SHORT $L43918
$L43919:
    mov  ecx, DWORD PTR _x$43917[ebp]
    add  ecx, 1
    mov  DWORD PTR _x$43917[ebp], ecx
$L43918:
    cmp  DWORD PTR _x$43917[ebp], 640     ; 00000280H
    jge  SHORT $L43920

; 57  :       Plot_Pixel(video_buffer, SCREEN_WIDTH, x,y,5);

    mov  DWORD PTR $T43941[ebp], 5
    mov  edx, DWORD PTR _y$[ebp]
    imul  edx, 640               ; 00000280H
    mov  eax, DWORD PTR _x$43917[ebp]
    add  eax, edx
    mov  ecx, DWORD PTR _video_buffer$[ebp]
    mov  dl, BYTE PTR $T43941[ebp]
    mov  BYTE PTR [ecx+eax], dl
    jmp  SHORT $L43919
$L43920:
    jmp  SHORT $L43915
$L43916:

; 58  :
; 59  : } // end main
```

This time, I've highlighted the inlined call to `Plot_Pixel()` and as you can see, it's much better! More code, but 200% faster on average.

I think I've shown that inlining is something that we want to do when the function being called has a small body, but it's a pain to implement because there's no good way to manage the files. I like .H and .CPP files, but I hate putting all my inline function listings along with code in the .H file, and I think adding a .INC file is asking for trouble. So, the moral to the story is this: Where possible, use `#define` macros as long as you don't foresee problems with the macro parameters being called multiple times.

Also, it's okay to use short inline functions (macros) in the header files as long as they aren't too big because most programmers hunting for source code clues won't go into the .H files, but into the .CPP files. Additionally, by having large code bases in .H files, headers take longer to compile (of course, using precompiled headers solves that). Bearing that in mind, when you're done with your engine, you might want to convert many functions to inline that are short in nature. The problem is that you end up migrating all your .CPP files into .H files, and that's a management problem for your source.

I tried to find a common ground for all this drama and convert only simple functions to inline macros and keep them in the .H file. All the real functions went into the .CPP file. However, sometimes I probably should have decided to convert some of my real functions to inline, and some of my inlines to non-inline and put them in the .CPP file, but I think you get the point I'm trying to make. A math engine needs to be wickedly fast; thus, as much as possible of it should be inlined.

Now that I've bored our optimization experts who are reading this, let's move on to all the macros. They're once again classed into working groups for general utility: vectors, matrices, lines, planes, quaternions, and so on. Hence, I'll present them in these groups. And finally, the macros and inline functions have comments describing what each group does (it isn't like you're not going to figure out five lines of code, anyway) <BG>.

General Utility and Conversion

In general, the only generic macros are in `T3DLIB1.H`, so let's get those out of the way:

```
// used to compute the min and max of two expressions
#define MIN(a, b) (((a) < (b)) ? (a) : (b))
#define MAX(a, b) (((a) > (b)) ? (b) : (a))

// used for swapping algorithm
#define SWAP(a,b,t) {t=a; a=b; b=t;}

// some math macros
#define DEG_TO_RAD(ang) ((ang)*PI/180.0)
#define RAD_TO_DEG(rads) ((rads)*180.0/PI)

#define RAND_RANGE(x,y) ( (x) + (rand()%((y)-(x)+1)))
```

All of these are straightforward. I find the *RAND_RANGE()* macro, along with `MIN()` and `MAX()`, very useful.

Points and Vectors

As I mentioned earlier in the chapter, the data format of a point and vector in 2D, 3D, and 4D is identical. Hence, I'm going to group the point and vector macros together here.

Also, some of the macros are written as inline functions to help with type checking. And many of them were too long to write as #defined macros.

```
// vector macros, note the 4D vector sets w=1
// vector zeroing macros
inline void VECTOR2D_ZERO(VECTOR2D_PTR v)
{(v)->x = (v)->y = 0.0;}

inline void VECTOR3D_ZERO(VECTOR3D_PTR v)
{(v)->x = (v)->y = (v)->z = 0.0;}

inline void VECTOR4D_ZERO(VECTOR4D_PTR v)
{(v)->x = (v)->y = (v)->z = 0.0; (v)->w = 1.0;}

// macros to initialize vectors with explicit components
inline void VECTOR2D_INITXY(VECTOR2D_PTR v, float x, float y)
{(v)->x = (x); (v)->y = (y);}

inline void VECTOR3D_INITXYZ(VECTOR3D_PTR v, float x, float y, float z)
{(v)->x = (x); (v)->y = (y); (v)->z = (z);}

inline void VECTOR4D_INITXYZ(VECTOR4D_PTR v, float x,float y,float z)
{(v)->x = (x); (v)->y = (y); (v)->z = (z); (v)->w = 1.0;}


// vector intialization macros to initialize with other vectors
inline void VECTOR2D_INIT(VECTOR2D_PTR vdst, VECTOR2D_PTR vsrc)
{(vdst)->x = (vsrc)->x; (vdst)->y = (vsrc)->y; }

inline void VECTOR3D_INIT(VECTOR3D_PTR vdst, VECTOR3D_PTR vsrc)
{(vdst)->x = (vsrc)->x; (vdst)->y = (vsrc)->y; (vdst)->z = (vsrc)->z; }

inline void VECTOR4D_INIT(VECTOR4D_PTR vdst, VECTOR4D_PTR vsrc)
{(vdst)->x = (vsrc)->x; (vdst)->y = (vsrc)->y;
(vdst)->z = (vsrc)->z; (vdst)->w = (vsrc)->w; }


// vector copying macros
inline void VECTOR2D_COPY(VECTOR2D_PTR vdst, VECTOR2D_PTR vsrc)
{(vdst)->x = (vsrc)->x; (vdst)->y = (vsrc)->y; }

inline void VECTOR3D_COPY(VECTOR3D_PTR vdst, VECTOR3D_PTR vsrc)
{(vdst)->x = (vsrc)->x; (vdst)->y = (vsrc)->y; (vdst)->z = (vsrc)->z; }
```

```
inline void VECTOR4D_COPY(VECTOR4D_PTR vdst, VECTOR4D_PTR vsrc)
{(vdst)->x = (vsrc)->x; (vdst)->y = (vsrc)->y;
(vdst)->z = (vsrc)->z; (vdst)->w = (vsrc)->w; }


// point initialization macros
inline void POINT2D_INIT(POINT2D_PTR vdst, POINT2D_PTR vsrc)
{(vdst)->x = (vsrc)->x; (vdst)->y = (vsrc)->y; }

inline void POINT3D_INIT(POINT3D_PTR vdst, POINT3D_PTR vsrc)
{(vdst)->x = (vsrc)->x; (vdst)->y = (vsrc)->y; (vdst)->z = (vsrc)->z; }

inline void POINT4D_INIT(POINT4D_PTR vdst, POINT4D_PTR vsrc)
{(vdst)->x = (vsrc)->x; (vdst)->y = (vsrc)->y;
(vdst)->z = (vsrc)->z; (vdst)->w = (vsrc)->w; }

// point copying macros
inline void POINT2D_COPY(POINT2D_PTR vdst, POINT2D_PTR vsrc)
{(vdst)->x = (vsrc)->x; (vdst)->y = (vsrc)->y; }

inline void POINT3D_COPY(POINT3D_PTR vdst, POINT3D_PTR vsrc)
{(vdst)->x = (vsrc)->x; (vdst)->y = (vsrc)->y; (vdst)->z = (vsrc)->z; }

inline void POINT4D_COPY(POINT4D_PTR vdst, POINT4D_PTR vsrc)
{(vdst)->x = (vsrc)->x; (vdst)->y = (vsrc)->y;
(vdst)->z = (vsrc)->z; (vdst)->w = (vsrc)->w; }
```

As you can see, there's a macro for everything! Zeroing, initialization with different data types, and copying. Lots of redundancy, but who cares?

Matrices

Next are the matrix macros. Note that some are `#defined` macros, whereas others are short inline functions.

```
// matrix macros

// macros to clear out matrices
#define MAT_ZERO_2X2(m) {memset((void *)(m), 0, sizeof(MATRIX2X2));}
#define MAT_ZERO_3X3(m) {memset((void *)(m), 0, sizeof(MATRIX3X3));}
#define MAT_ZERO_4X4(m) {memset((void *)(m), 0, sizeof(MATRIX4X4));}
#define MAT_ZERO_4X3(m) {memset((void *)(m), 0, sizeof(MATRIX4X3));}
```

NOTE

Many compilers use a byte-by-byte memory fill when calling the function `memset()`. We may be able to get more speed by using a quad-byte clear to zero out the matrices. Also note that, in general, integers do *NOT* equal their floating-point counterparts bit for bit for whole numbers; that is, the representation of (float)5.0 is completely different from (int)5. However, the 32-bit floating point representation of 0.0 is equal to the 32-bit integer representation of 0, thus we can use this trick and the memory functions to clear out floating-point arrays quickly.

```
// macros to set the identity matrix
#define MAT_IDENTITY_2X2(m) {memcpy((void *)(m), /
    (void *)&IMAT_2X2, sizeof(MATRIX2X2));}

#define MAT_IDENTITY_3X3(m) {memcpy((void *)(m), /
    (void *)&IMAT_3X3, sizeof(MATRIX3X3));}

#define MAT_IDENTITY_4X4(m) {memcpy((void *)(m), /
    (void *)&IMAT_4X4, sizeof(MATRIX4X4));}

#define MAT_IDENTITY_4X3(m) {memcpy((void *)(m), /
    (void *)&IMAT_4X3, sizeof(MATRIX4X3));}

// matrix copying macros
#define MAT_COPY_2X2(src_mat, dest_mat) {memcpy((void *)(dest_mat), /
          (void *)(src_mat), sizeof(MATRIX2X2) ); }
#define MAT_COPY_3X3(src_mat, dest_mat) {memcpy((void *)(dest_mat), /
          (void *)(src_mat), sizeof(MATRIX3X3) ); }
#define MAT_COPY_4X4(src_mat, dest_mat) {memcpy((void *)(dest_mat), /
          (void *)(src_mat), sizeof(MATRIX4X4) ); }
#define MAT_COPY_4X3(src_mat, dest_mat) {memcpy((void *)(dest_mat), /
           (void *)(src_mat), sizeof(MATRIX4X3) ); }

// matrix transposing macros
inline void MAT_TRANSPOSE_3X3(MATRIX3X3_PTR m)
{ MATRIX3X3 mt;
mt.M00 = m->M00; mt.M01 = m->M10; mt.M02 = m->M20;
mt.M10 = m->M01; mt.M11 = m->M11; mt.M12 = m->M21;
mt.M20 = m->M02; mt.M21 = m->M12; mt.M22 = m->M22;
memcpy((void *)m,(void *)&mt, sizeof(MATRIX3X3)); }

inline void MAT_TRANSPOSE_4X4(MATRIX4X4_PTR m)
{ MATRIX4X4 mt;
mt.M00 = m->M00; mt.M01 = m->M10; mt.M02 = m->M20; mt.M03 = m->M30;
```

5

```
mt.M10 = m->M01; mt.M11 = m->M11; mt.M12 = m->M21; mt.M13 = m->M31;
mt.M20 = m->M02; mt.M21 = m->M12; mt.M22 = m->M22; mt.M23 = m->M32;
mt.M30 = m->M03; mt.M31 = m->M13; mt.M32 = m->M22; mt.M33 = m->M33;
memcpy((void *)m,(void *)&mt, sizeof(MATRIX4X4)); }

inline void MAT_TRANSPOSE_3X3(MATRIX3X3_PTR m, MATRIX3X3_PTR mt)
{ mt->M00 = m->M00; mt->M01 = m->M10; mt->M02 = m->M20;
 mt->M10 = m->M01; mt->M11 = m->M11; mt->M12 = m->M21;
 mt->M20 = m->M02; mt->M21 = m->M12; mt->M22 = m->M22; }

inline void MAT_TRANSPOSE_4X4(MATRIX4X4_PTR m, MATRIX4X4_PTR mt)
{ mt->M00 = m->M00; mt->M01 = m->M10; mt->M02 = m->M20; mt->M03 = m->M30;
 mt->M10 = m->M01; mt->M11 = m->M11; mt->M12 = m->M21; mt->M13 = m->M31;
 mt->M20 = m->M02; mt->M21 = m->M12; mt->M22 = m->M22; mt->M23 = m->M32;
 mt->M30 = m->M03; mt->M31 = m->M13; mt->M32 = m->M22; mt->M33 = m->M33;}

// small inline functions that could be re-written as macros, but would
// be less robust

// matrix and vector column swaping macros
inline void MAT_COLUMN_SWAP_2X2(MATRIX2X2_PTR m, int c, MATRIX1X2_PTR v)
{ m->M[0][c]=v->M[0]; m->M[1][c]=v->M[1]; }

inline void MAT_COLUMN_SWAP_3X3(MATRIX3X3_PTR m, int c, MATRIX1X3_PTR v)
{ m->M[0][c]=v->M[0]; m->M[1][c]=v->M[1]; m->M[2][c]=v->M[2]; }

inline void MAT_COLUMN_SWAP_4X4(MATRIX4X4_PTR m, int c, MATRIX1X4_PTR v)
{m->M[0][c]=v->M[0]; m->M[1][c]=v->M[1];
 m->M[2][c]=v->M[2]; m->M[3][c]=v->M[3]; }

inline void MAT_COLUMN_SWAP_4X3(MATRIX4X3_PTR m, int c, MATRIX1X4_PTR v)
{m->M[0][c]=v->M[0]; m->M[1][c]=v->M[1];
 m->M[2][c]=v->M[2]; m->M[3][c]=v->M[3]; }
```

Notice that all the matrix functions use pointers. This theme is used throughout the majority of functions in the math library. Sometimes it's nice to use the real objects, but many times the stack pushing/popping and copying eat up too many cycles.

Quaternions

The next set of macros has to do with quaternions. Pretty much all the quaternion functions (including the ones in the T3DLIB4.CPP) should be inline macros; that would have made the code more complicated, but keep it in mind. Here they are:

```
// quaternion macros
inline void QUAT_ZERO(QUAT_PTR q)
{(q)->x = (q)->y = (q)->z = (q)->w = 0.0;}

inline void QUAT_INITWXYZ(QUAT_PTR q, float w, float x,float y,float z)
{ (q)->w = (w); (q)->x = (x); (q)->y = (y); (q)->z = (z); }

inline void QUAT_INIT_VECTOR3D(QUAT_PTR q, VECTOR3D_PTR v)
{ (q)->w = 0; (q)->x = (v->x); (q)->y = (v->y); (q)->z = (v->z); }

inline void QUAT_INIT(QUAT_PTR qdst, QUAT_PTR qsrc)
{(qdst)->w = (qsrc)->w; (qdst)->x = (qsrc)->x;
 (qdst)->y = (qsrc)->y; (qdst)->z = (qsrc)->z; }

inline void QUAT_COPY(QUAT_PTR qdst, QUAT_PTR qsrc)
{(qdst)->x = (qsrc)->x; (qdst)->y = (qsrc)->y;
(qdst)->z = (qsrc)->z; (qdst)->w = (qsrc)->w; }
```

Mostly they're macros to initialize a quaternion in whatever format you like.

Fixed-Point Math

Finally, here are the fixed-point math macros for conversion and extraction of fixed-point numbers. The rest of the fixed-point functions are written as real functions. They're definitely targets for inlining, but there's a lot of inline assembly language for the multiplication and division functions that I didn't want to hide in a header file.

```
// extract the whole part and decimal part from a fixed point 16.16
#define FIXP16_WP(fp) ((fp) >> FIXP16_SHIFT)
#define FIXP16_DP(fp) ((fp) && FIXP16_DP_MASK)

// convert integer and float to fixed point 16.16
#define INT_TO_FIXP16(i) ((i) << FIXP16_SHIFT)
#define FLOAT_TO_FIXP16(f) (((float)(f) * (float)FIXP16_MAG+0.5))

// convert fixed point to float
#define FIXP16_TO_FLOAT(fp) ( ((float)fp)/FIXP16_MAG)
```

Prototypes

At this point, let's take a look at all the function prototypes. Of course, you won't know what many of them do yet, but you should get an idea, and then when we do the function listing later, everything will become clear. Also, note that I will mark math functions from T3DLIB1.CPP¦H so that you can keep track of that. Again the functions are listed in groups for vectors, matrices, and so forth. Here they are:

```
// trig and general math functions
float Fast_Sin(float theta);
float Fast_Cos(float theta);

// distance functions (from T3DLIB1.CPP¦H)
int Fast_Distance_2D(int x, int y);
float Fast_Distance_3D(float x, float y, float z);

// polar, cylindrical, spherical functions
void POLAR2D_To_POINT2D(POLAR2D_PTR polar, POINT2D_PTR rect);
void POLAR2D_To_RectXY(POLAR2D_PTR polar, float *x, float *y);
void POINT2D_To_POLAR2D(POINT2D_PTR rect, POLAR2D_PTR polar);
void POINT2D_To_PolarRTh(POINT2D_PTR rect, float *r, float *theta);
void CYLINDRICAL3D_To_POINT3D(CYLINDRICAL3D_PTR cyl, POINT3D_PTR rect);
void CYLINDRICAL3D_To_RectXYZ(CYLINDRICAL3D_PTR cyl,
               float *x, float *y, float *z);
void POINT3D_To_CYLINDRICAL3D(POINT3D_PTR rect, CYLINDRICAL3D_PTR cyl);
void POINT3D_To_CylindricalRThZ(POINT3D_PTR rect,
                float *r, float *theta, float *z);
void SPHERICAL3D_To_POINT3D(SPHERICAL3D_PTR sph, POINT3D_PTR rect);
void SPHERICAL3D_To_RectXYZ(SPHERICAL3D_PTR sph, float *x, float *y, float *z);
void POINT3D_To_SPHERICAL3D(POINT3D_PTR rect, SPHERICAL3D_PTR sph);
void POINT3D_To_SphericalPThPh(POINT3D_PTR rect,
                float *p, float *theta, float *phi);

// 2d vector functions
void VECTOR2D_Add(VECTOR2D_PTR va, VECTOR2D_PTR vb, VECTOR2D_PTR vsum);
VECTOR2D VECTOR2D_Add(VECTOR2D_PTR va, VECTOR2D_PTR vb);
void VECTOR2D_Sub(VECTOR2D_PTR va, VECTOR2D_PTR vb, VECTOR2D_PTR vdiff);
VECTOR2D VECTOR2D_Sub(VECTOR2D_PTR va, VECTOR2D_PTR vb);
void VECTOR2D_Scale(float k, VECTOR2D_PTR va);
void VECTOR2D_Scale(float k, VECTOR2D_PTR va, VECTOR2D_PTR vscaled);
float VECTOR2D_Dot(VECTOR2D_PTR va, VECTOR2D_PTR vb);
float VECTOR2D_Length(VECTOR2D_PTR va);
float VECTOR2D_Length_Fast(VECTOR2D_PTR va);
void VECTOR2D_Normalize(VECTOR2D_PTR va);
void VECTOR2D_Normalize(VECTOR2D_PTR va, VECTOR2D_PTR vn);
void VECTOR2D_Build(VECTOR2D_PTR init, VECTOR2D_PTR term,
                    VECTOR2D_PTR result);
float VECTOR2D_CosTh(VECTOR2D_PTR va, VECTOR2D_PTR vb);
void VECTOR2D_Print(VECTOR2D_PTR va, char *name);
```

```
// 3d vector functions
void VECTOR3D_Add(VECTOR3D_PTR va, VECTOR3D_PTR vb, VECTOR3D_PTR vsum);
VECTOR3D VECTOR3D_Add(VECTOR3D_PTR va, VECTOR3D_PTR vb);
void VECTOR3D_Sub(VECTOR3D_PTR va, VECTOR3D_PTR vb, VECTOR3D_PTR vdiff);
VECTOR3D VECTOR3D_Sub(VECTOR3D_PTR va, VECTOR3D_PTR vb);
void VECTOR3D_Scale(float k, VECTOR3D_PTR va);
void VECTOR3D_Scale(float k, VECTOR3D_PTR va, VECTOR3D_PTR vscaled);
float VECTOR3D_Dot(VECTOR3D_PTR va, VECTOR3D_PTR vb);
void VECTOR3D_Cross(VECTOR3D_PTR va,VECTOR3D_PTR vb,VECTOR3D_PTR vn);
VECTOR3D VECTOR3D_Cross(VECTOR3D_PTR va, VECTOR3D_PTR vb);
float VECTOR3D_Length(VECTOR3D_PTR va);
float VECTOR3D_Length_Fast(VECTOR3D_PTR va);
void VECTOR3D_Normalize(VECTOR3D_PTR va);
void VECTOR3D_Normalize(VECTOR3D_PTR va, VECTOR3D_PTR vn);
void VECTOR3D_Build(VECTOR3D_PTR init, VECTOR3D_PTR term,
                    VECTOR3D_PTR result);
float VECTOR3D_CosTh(VECTOR3D_PTR va, VECTOR3D_PTR vb);
void VECTOR3D_Print(VECTOR3D_PTR va, char *name);

// 4d vector functions
void VECTOR4D_Add(VECTOR4D_PTR va, VECTOR4D_PTR vb, VECTOR4D_PTR vsum);
VECTOR4D VECTOR4D_Add(VECTOR4D_PTR va, VECTOR4D_PTR vb);
void VECTOR4D_Sub(VECTOR4D_PTR va, VECTOR4D_PTR vb, VECTOR4D_PTR vdiff);
VECTOR4D VECTOR4D_Sub(VECTOR4D_PTR va, VECTOR4D_PTR vb);
void VECTOR4D_Scale(float k, VECTOR4D_PTR va);
void VECTOR4D_Scale(float k, VECTOR4D_PTR va, VECTOR4D_PTR vscaled);
float VECTOR4D_Dot(VECTOR4D_PTR va, VECTOR4D_PTR vb);
void VECTOR4D_Cross(VECTOR4D_PTR va,VECTOR4D_PTR vb,VECTOR4D_PTR vn);
VECTOR4D VECTOR4D_Cross(VECTOR4D_PTR va, VECTOR4D_PTR vb);
float VECTOR4D_Length(VECTOR4D_PTR va);
float VECTOR4D_Length_Fast(VECTOR4D_PTR va);
void VECTOR4D_Normalize(VECTOR4D_PTR va);
void VECTOR4D_Normalize(VECTOR4D_PTR va, VECTOR4D_PTR vn);
void VECTOR4D_Build(VECTOR4D_PTR init, VECTOR4D_PTR term,
          VECTOR4D_PTR result);
float VECTOR4D_CosTh(VECTOR4D_PTR va, VECTOR4D_PTR vb);
void VECTOR4D_Print(VECTOR4D_PTR va, char *name);

// 2x2 matrix functions (note there others in T3DLIB1.CPP¦H)
void Mat_Init_2X2(MATRIX2X2_PTR ma,
         float m00, float m01, float m10, float m11);
void Print_Mat_2X2(MATRIX2X2_PTR ma, char *name);
float Mat_Det_2X2(MATRIX2X2_PTR m);
```

```
void Mat_Add_2X2(MATRIX2X2_PTR ma, MATRIX2X2_PTR mb, MATRIX2X2_PTR msum);
void Mat_Mul_2X2(MATRIX2X2_PTR ma, MATRIX2X2_PTR mb, MATRIX2X2_PTR mprod);
int Mat_Inverse_2X2(MATRIX2X2_PTR m, MATRIX2X2_PTR mi);
int Solve_2X2_System(MATRIX2X2_PTR A, MATRIX1X2_PTR X, MATRIX1X2_PTR B);

// 3x3 matrix functions

// from T3DLIB1.CPP|H
int Mat_Mul_1X2_3X2(MATRIX1X2_PTR ma,
          MATRIX3X2_PTR mb,
          MATRIX1X2_PTR mprod);

// from T3DLIB1.CPP|H
int Mat_Mul_1X3_3X3(MATRIX1X3_PTR ma,
          MATRIX3X3_PTR mb,
          MATRIX1X3_PTR mprod);

// from T3DLIB1.CPP|H
int Mat_Mul_3X3(MATRIX3X3_PTR ma,
        MATRIX3X3_PTR mb,
        MATRIX3X3_PTR mprod);

// from T3DLIB1.CPP|H
inline int Mat_Init_3X2(MATRIX3X2_PTR ma,
           float m00, float m01,
           float m10, float m11,
           float m20, float m21);

void Mat_Add_3X3(MATRIX3X3_PTR ma, MATRIX3X3_PTR mb, MATRIX3X3_PTR msum);
void Mat_Mul_VECTOR3D_3X3(VECTOR3D_PTR va, MATRIX3X3_PTR mb,
            VECTOR3D_PTR vprod);
int Mat_Inverse_3X3(MATRIX3X3_PTR m, MATRIX3X3_PTR mi);
void Mat_Init_3X3(MATRIX3X3_PTR ma,
           float m00, float m01, float m02,
           float m10, float m11, float m12,
           float m20, float m21, float m22);
void Print_Mat_3X3(MATRIX3X3_PTR ma, char *name);
float Mat_Det_3X3(MATRIX3X3_PTR m);
int Solve_3X3_System(MATRIX3X3_PTR A, MATRIX1X3_PTR X, MATRIX1X3_PTR B);

// 4x4 matrix functions
void Mat_Add_4X4(MATRIX4X4_PTR ma, MATRIX4X4_PTR mb, MATRIX4X4_PTR msum);
void Mat_Mul_4X4(MATRIX4X4_PTR ma, MATRIX4X4_PTR mb, MATRIX4X4_PTR mprod);
```

```
void Mat_Mul_1X4_4X4(MATRIX1X4_PTR ma, MATRIX4X4_PTR mb,
          MATRIX1X4_PTR mprod);
void Mat_Mul_VECTOR3D_4X4(VECTOR3D_PTR va, MATRIX4X4_PTR mb,
            VECTOR3D_PTR vprod);
void Mat_Mul_VECTOR3D_4X3(VECTOR3D_PTR va, MATRIX4X3_PTR mb,
            VECTOR3D_PTR vprod);
void Mat_Mul_VECTOR4D_4X4(VECTOR4D_PTR va, MATRIX4X4_PTR mb,
            VECTOR4D_PTR vprod);
void Mat_Mul_VECTOR4D_4X3(VECTOR4D_PTR va, MATRIX4X4_PTR mb,
            VECTOR4D_PTR vprod);
int Mat_Inverse_4X4(MATRIX4X4_PTR m, MATRIX4X4_PTR mi);
void Mat_Init_4X4(MATRIX4X4_PTR ma,
           float m00, float m01, float m02, float m03,
           float m10, float m11, float m12, float m13,
           float m20, float m21, float m22, float m23,
           float m30, float m31, float m32, float m33);
void Print_Mat_4X4(MATRIX4X4_PTR ma, char *name);

// quaternion functions
void QUAT_Add(QUAT_PTR q1, QUAT_PTR q2, QUAT_PTR qsum);
void QUAT_Sub(QUAT_PTR q1, QUAT_PTR q2, QUAT_PTR qdiff);
void QUAT_Conjugate(QUAT_PTR q, QUAT_PTR qconj);
void QUAT_Scale(QUAT_PTR q, float scale, QUAT_PTR qs);
void QUAT_Scale(QUAT_PTR q, float scale);
float QUAT_Norm(QUAT_PTR q);
float QUAT_Norm2(QUAT_PTR q);
void QUAT_Normalize(QUAT_PTR q, QUAT_PTR qn);
void QUAT_Normalize(QUAT_PTR q);
void QUAT_Unit_Inverse(QUAT_PTR q, QUAT_PTR qi);
void QUAT_Unit_Inverse(QUAT_PTR q);
void QUAT_Inverse(QUAT_PTR q, QUAT_PTR qi);
void QUAT_Inverse(QUAT_PTR q);
void QUAT_Mul(QUAT_PTR q1, QUAT_PTR q2, QUAT_PTR qprod);
void QUAT_Triple_Product(QUAT_PTR q1, QUAT_PTR q2, QUAT_PTR q3,
           QUAT_PTR qprod);
void VECTOR3D_Theta_To_QUAT(QUAT_PTR q, VECTOR3D_PTR v, float theta);
void VECTOR4D_Theta_To_QUAT(QUAT_PTR q, VECTOR4D_PTR v, float theta);
void EulerZYX_To_QUAT(QUAT_PTR q, float theta_z, float theta_y,
          float theta_x);
void QUAT_To_VECTOR3D_Theta(QUAT_PTR q, VECTOR3D_PTR v, float *theta);
void QUAT_Print(QUAT_PTR q, char *name);

// 2d parametric line functions
void Init_Parm_Line2D(POINT2D_PTR p_init, POINT2D_PTR p_term,
```

```
            PARMLINE2D_PTR p);
void Compute_Parm_Line2D(PARMLINE2D_PTR p, float t, POINT2D_PTR pt);
int Intersect_Parm_Lines2D(PARMLINE2D_PTR p1, PARMLINE2D_PTR p2,
              float *t1, float *t2);
int Intersect_Parm_Lines2D(PARMLINE2D_PTR p1, PARMLINE2D_PTR p2,
              POINT2D_PTR pt);

// 3d parametric line functions
void Init_Parm_Line3D(POINT3D_PTR p_init, POINT3D_PTR p_term,
            PARMLINE3D_PTR p);
void Compute_Parm_Line3D(PARMLINE3D_PTR p, float t, POINT3D_PTR pt);

// 3d plane functions
void PLANE3D_Init(PLANE3D_PTR plane, POINT3D_PTR p0,
          VECTOR3D_PTR normal, int normalize);
float Compute_Point_In_Plane3D(POINT3D_PTR pt, PLANE3D_PTR plane);
int Intersect_Parm_Line3D_Plane3D(PARMLINE3D_PTR pline, PLANE3D_PTR plane,
                float *t, POINT3D_PTR pt);

// fixed point functions
FIXP16 FIXP16_MUL(FIXP16 fp1, FIXP16 fp2);
FIXP16 FIXP16_DIV(FIXP16 fp1, FIXP16 fp2);
void FIXP16_Print(FIXP16 fp);
```

Lots of functions, huh? Like I said, this math engine has support for just about everything we'll need to write a 3D game, even with this early version. And if we need optimization, we'll optimize, but right now, we have a solid working set of math functions. I can't wait to show you how they work. Any volunteers?

Globals

There aren't that many globals in the math engine. In fact, the only globals that exist are from the original minimal math support in T3DLIB1.CPP¦H. The globals were the sine and cosine lookup tables, as shown here:

```
// storage for our lookup tables from T3DLIB1.CPP¦H
extern float cos_look[361]; // 1 extra so we can store 0-360 inclusive
extern float sin_look[361]; // 1 extra so we can store 0-360 inclusive
```

Notice that these tables are in degrees not radians, and there are 361 entries that represent [0..360] degrees, inclusive. Now, you might say that 360 degrees is exactly the same as 0 degrees. And yes, it is, but having that last entry makes some of the algorithms easier to write and saves a single compare. The only thing you have to do to initialize the tables is call Build_Sin_Cos_Tables() at the beginning of your application.

MATH

In a more robust math engine, you might have a number of global state variables that track states of the math engine, or more complex data structures such as matrix stacks (like those used in APIs such as D3D and OpenGL).

Math Engine API Listing

Now for the fun part! What we're going to do now is take a look at the entire math engine API from `T3DLIB4.CPP|H` and see what each function does along, with a simple example and demo program for some of the more complex math API functions. Additionally, I'll show you the inside of many of the functions that are representative of other similar functions so that you can see how everything is written. Finally, for functions that aren't part of `T3DLIB4.CPP|H` but are part of `T3DLIB1.CPP|H`'s math support, descriptions can be found in Chapter 3, "3D Game Programming with a Virtual Computer."

COOL

The Texas Instruments TI-89 calculator has got to be the coolest thing on earth (besides the TI-92 and the newer models, of course). But these next-generation calculators with 3D graphing, symbolic algebra, matrix mathematics, and calculus support are a must to check out your math. Unless you're a mathematical sadist and like doing page after page of multiplication and division—yuck!

Trigonometric Functions

Function Prototype(s):

```
float Fast_Sin(float theta);

float Fast_Cos(float theta);
```

Function Listing Reference:

```
float Fast_Sin(float theta)
{
// this function uses the sin_look[] lookup table, but
// has logic to handle negative angles as well as fractional
// angles via interpolation, use this for a more robust
// sin computation that the blind lookup, but with with
// a slight hit in speed

// convert angle to 0-359
theta = fmodf(theta,360);
```

```
// make angle positive
if (theta < 0) theta+=360.0;

// compute floor of theta and fractional part to interpolate
int theta_int  = (int)theta;
float theta_frac = theta - theta_int;

// now compute the value of sin(angle) using the lookup tables
// and interpolating the fractional part, note that if theta_int
// is equal to 359 then theta_int+1=360, but this is fine since the
// table was made with the entries 0-360 inclusive
return(sin_look[theta_int] +
    theta_frac*(sin_look[theta_int+1] - sin_look[theta_int]));

} // end Fast_Sin
```

Purpose:

`float Fast_Cos()` compute the sine and cosine of the sent parameter by using the `sin_look[]` and `cos_look[]` lookup table along with linear interpolation to arrive at a more accurate value than using the lookup table alone, while at the same time being faster than using the intrinsic C/C++ math library's `sin()` and `cos()` functions. The theta parameter must be in degrees. Figure 5.11 shows an illustration of the how the functions interpolate the value from the table.

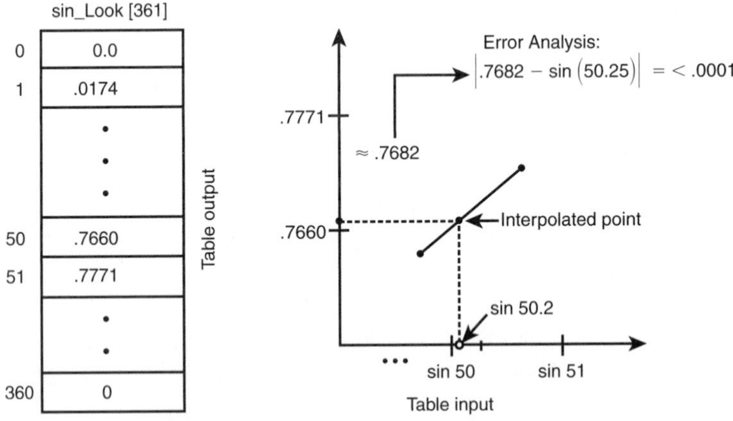

FIGURE 5.11 Interpolation to increase accuracy of trigonometric lookup tables.

Example:

As an example, here's how you would compute the sine and cosine values of 50.2 degrees.

```
// build look up tables first
Build_Sin_Cos_Tables();

float answer1 = Fast_Sin(50.2)
float answer2 = Fast_Cos(50.2)
```

Coordinate System Support Functions

The next section of the API deals with conversions to and from Cartesian coordinates—polar, cylindrical, and spherical. Each of the functions is implemented identically to the math from Chapter 4, so there's no need to look at the innards of any of them unless you want to see statements like

```
"x=r*sin(theta);"
```

be converted to C/C++:

```
"x=r*sin(theta);".
```

Also, all the functions have a return type void. So, without further ado, let's take a look at the functions.

Function Prototype:

```
void POLAR2D_To_POINT2D(POLAR2D_PTR polar, POINT2D_PTR rect);
```

Purpose:

`void POLAR2D_To_POINT2D()` converts a 2D polar point in terms of r and theta into an (x,y) point and stores it in a `POINT2D` structure.

Example:

```
POLAR2D pp = {5, PI2};
POINT2D pr = {0,0};

// convert polar to rectangular
POLAR2D_To_POINT2D(&pp, &pr);
```

Function Prototype:

```
void POLAR2D_To_RectXY(POLAR2D_PTR polar, float *x, float *y);
```

5

Purpose:

void POLAR2D_To_RectXY() converts a polar 2D point into explicit x,y coordinates.

Example:

```
POLAR2D pp = {5, PI2};
float x=0, y=0;

// convert polar point to x,y
POLAR2D_To_RectXY(&pp, &x, &y)
```

Function Prototype:

```
void POINT2D_To_POLAR2D(POINT2D_PTR rect, POLAR2D_PTR polar);
```

Purpose:

void POINT2D_To_POLAR2D() converts a point in rectangular format to 2D polar format.

Example:

```
POLAR2D pp = {0, 0};
POINT2D pr = {10,20};

// convert rectangular to polar
POINT2D_To_POLAR2D(&pr, &pp);
```

Function Prototype:

```
void POINT2D_To_PolarRTh(POINT2D_PTR rect, float *r, float *theta);
```

Purpose:

void POINT2D_To_PolarRTh() converts a polar 2D point into an explicit r and theta.

Example:

```
POLAR2D pp = {3, PI};
float r =0, theta = 0;

// convert polar to r, theta
POINT2D_To_PolarRTh(&pp, &r, &theta);
```

Function Prototype:

```
void CYLINDRICAL3D_To_POINT3D(CYLINDRICAL3D_PTR cyl, POINT3D_PTR rect);
```

Purpose:

void CYLINDRICAL3D_To_POINT3D() converts a cylindrical 3D point into a rectangular 3D point.

Example:

```
CYLINDRICAL3D pc = {10, PI/5, 20}; // r, theta, z
POINT3D pr = {0,0,0};

// convert cylindrical to rectangular
CYLINDRICAL3D_To_POINT3D(&pc, &pr);
```

Function Prototype:

```
void CYLINDRICAL3D_To_RectXYZ(CYLINDRICAL3D_PTR cyl, float *x, float *y, float *z);
```

Purpose:

void CYLINDRICAL3D_To_RectXYZ() converts a point from cylindrical 3D coordinates to explicit x,y,z coordinates.

Example:

```
CYLINDRICAL3D pc = {10, PI/5, 20}; // r, theta, z
float x=0, y=0, z=0;

// convert cylindrical to explicit x,y,z
CYLINDRICAL3D_To_RectXYZ(&pc, &x, &y, &z);
```

Function Prototype:

```
void POINT3D_To_CYLINDRICAL3D(POINT3D_PTR rect, CYLINDRICAL3D_PTR cyl);
```

Purpose:

void POINT3D_To_CYLINDRICAL3D() converts a rectangular 3D point into a cylindrical 3D point.

Example:

```
CYLINDRICAL3D pc = {0,0,0}; // r, theta, z
POINT3D pr = {1,2,3};

// convert rectangular to cylindrical
POINT3D_To_CYLINDRICAL3D(&pr, &pc);
```

Function Prototype:

```
void POINT3D_To_CylindricalRThZ(POINT3D_PTR rect, float *r,
                 float *theta, float *z);
```

Purpose:

void POINT3D_To_CylindricalRThZ() converts a 3D point into explicit cylindrical coordinates r, theta, z.

Example:

```
POINT3D pr = {1,2,3};
float r=0, theta=0, z=0;

// convert 3D point into explicit cylindrical coords
POINT3D_To_CylindricalRThZ(&pr, &r, &theta, &z);
```

Function Prototype:

```
void SPHERICAL3D_To_POINT3D(SPHERICAL3D_PTR sph, POINT3D_PTR rect);
```

Purpose:

void SPHERICAL3D_To_POINT3D() converts a spherical 3D point into a rectangular 3D point.

Example:

```
SPHERICAL3D ps = {1, PI/4, PI/2}; // p, theta, phi
POINT3D pr = {0,0,0};

// convert from spherical to rectangular
SPHERICAL3D_To_POINT3D(&ps, &pr);
```

Function Prototype:

```
void SPHERICAL3D_To_RectXYZ(SPHERICAL3D_PTR sph,
               float *x, float *y, float *z);
```

Purpose:

void SPHERICAL3D_To_RectXYZ() converts a spherical 3D point into explicit x,y,z coordinates.

Example:

```
SPHERICAL3D ps = {1, PI/4, PI/2}; // p, theta, phi
float x=0, y=0, z=0;

// convert from spherical to rectangular
SPHERICAL3D_To_RectXYZ(&ps, &x, &y, &z);
```

Function Prototype:

```
void POINT3D_To_SPHERICAL3D(POINT3D_PTR rect, SPHERICAL3D_PTR sph);
```

Purpose:

`void POINT3D_To_SPHERICAL3D()` converts a 3D point into spherical coordinates.

Example:

```
SPHERICAL3D ps = {1, PI/4, PI/2}; // p, theta, phi
POINT3D pr = {0,0,0};

// convert from rectangular to spherical
POINT3D_To_SPHERICAL3D(&pr, &ps);
```

Function Prototype:

```
void POINT3D_To_SphericalPThPh(POINT3D_PTR rect, float *p,
                float *theta, float *phi);
```

Purpose:

`void POINT3D_To_SphericalPThPh()` converts a 3D point into explicit spherical coordinates rho, theta, phi.

Example:

```
POINT3D pr = {10,20,30};
float p=0, theta=0, phi=0;

// convert the 3D point to spherical coords
POINT3D_To_SphericalPThPh(&pr, &p, &theta, &phi);
```

Vector Support Functions

The vector support for the math engine comes in three flavors: 2D, 3D, and 4D. The 2D and 3D support are easy enough to understand, but the 4D is worth a quickie. Remember homogenous coordinates? For example, **p** = <x,y,z,w>, and if we want to convert **p** into a real 3D coordinate **p**' then we perform the following transform:

```
p' = p/w = <x/w, y/w, z/w, w/w>
```

And then we typically throw away the last component, giving

```
p' = <x/w, y/w, z/w>
```

MATH

Note that many operations on 4D vectors treat w as a dummy, and work with only the first <x,y,z> components.

In any case, that's our refresher course on 4D homogenous coordinates. With that in mind, there are vector functions for all operations on 2D, 3D, and 4D vectors. Of course, some operations don't really make sense on each respective system. For example, taking the cross product of 2D vectors isn't defined. But, for the most part, there is a 2D, 3D, and 4D version of all vector functions, so I'm only going to show examples of one system. Moreover, vector functions that make sense only for a certain dimension will be illustrated separately, and vector functions that are similar will be grouped. Additionally, most of the functions return values that are either floats or the vector type of the function; for example, there are vector adding functions for 2D, 3D, and 4D vectors, and each returns a 2D, 3D, and 4D vector, respectively. Also, when referring to 2D, 3D, and 4D, I will use the notation "*D" to mean all of them. Get it? If not, you will!

NOTE

The data types for points and vectors are the same. Therefore, anywhere you use a `VECTOR3D` (for example), you can use a `POINT3D`. Of course, performing certain calculations on points doesn't really make sense. For example taking the cross product of two points. However, when building a vector, it makes sense to use a pair of points or a pair of vectors, or a point and a vector, and so forth.

Function Prototype(s):

```
void VECTOR2D_Add(VECTOR2D_PTR va, VECTOR2D_PTR vb, VECTOR2D_PTR vsum);

void VECTOR3D_Add(VECTOR3D_PTR va, VECTOR3D_PTR vb, VECTOR3D_PTR vsum);

void VECTOR4D_Add(VECTOR4D_PTR va, VECTOR4D_PTR vb, VECTOR4D_PTR vsum);
```

Purpose:

`void VECTOR*D_Add()` adds the sent vectors (`va+vb`) as shown in Figure 5.12, and stores the results in `vsum`.

Example:

```
VECTOR3D v1 = {1,2,3};
VECTOR3D v2 = {5,6,7};
VECTOR3D vsum; // holds result

// add em
VECTOR3D_Add(&v1, &v2, &vsum);
```

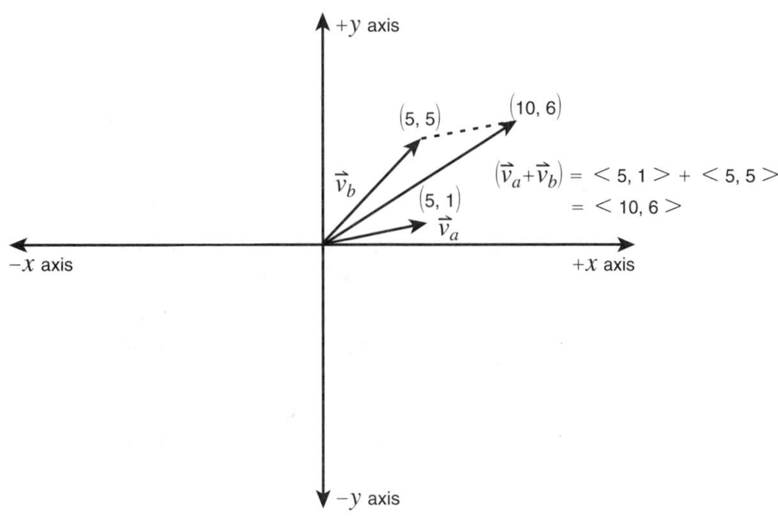

FIGURE 5.12 Vector addition setup.

Function Prototype(s):

```
VECTOR2D VECTOR2D_Add(VECTOR2D_PTR va, VECTOR2D_PTR vb);

VECTOR3D VECTOR3D_Add(VECTOR3D_PTR va, VECTOR3D_PTR vb);

VECTOR4D VECTOR3D_Add(VECTOR4D_PTR va, VECTOR4D_PTR vb);
```

Purpose:

`VECTOR*D VECTOR*D_Add()` is the stack version of the vector addition function that returns the result on the stack.

Example:

```
VECTOR2D v1 = {1,2};
VECTOR2D v2 = {5,6};

// add them and store result
VECTOR2D vsum = VECTOR2D_Add(&v1, &v2);
```

Function Prototype(s):

```
void VECTOR2D_Sub(VECTOR2D_PTR va, VECTOR2D_PTR vb, VECTOR2D_PTR vdiff);

void VECTOR3D_Sub(VECTOR3D_PTR va, VECTOR3D_PTR vb, VECTOR3D_PTR vdiff);

void VECTOR4D_Sub(VECTOR4D_PTR va, VECTOR4D_PTR vb, VECTOR4D_PTR vdiff);
```

Purpose:

void VECTOR*D_Sub() subtracts (vb-va) as shown in Figure 5.13, and stores the result in vdiff.

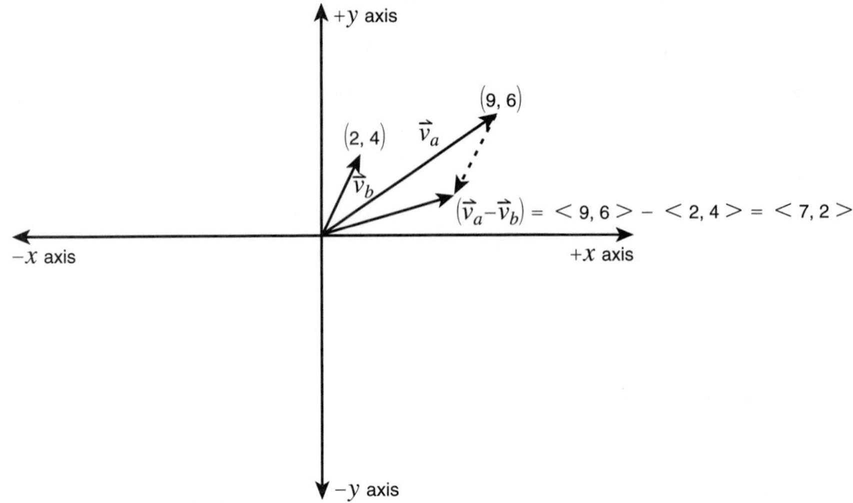

FIGURE 5.13 Vector subtraction setup.

Example:

```
VECTOR3D v1 = {1,2,3};
VECTOR3D v2 = {5,6,7};
VECTOR3D vdiff; // holds difference

// subtract em
VECTOR3D_Sub(&v1, &v2, &vdiff);
```

Function Prototype(s):

```
VECTOR2D VECTOR2D_Sub(VECTOR2D_PTR va, VECTOR2D_PTR vb);

VECTOR3D VECTOR3D_Sub(VECTOR3D_PTR va, VECTOR3D_PTR vb);

VECTOR4D VECTOR3D_Sub(VECTOR4D_PTR va, VECTOR4D_PTR vb);
```

Purpose:

VECTOR*D VECTOR*D_Sub() is the stack version of the vector subtraction function that returns the result on the stack.

Example:

```
VECTOR2D v1 = {1,2};
VECTOR2D v2 = {5,6};

// subtract them and store result
VECTOR2D vdiff = VECTOR2D_Sub(&v1, &v2);
```

Function Prototype(s):

```
void VECTOR2D_Scale(float k, VECTOR2D_PTR va, VECTOR2D_PTR vscaled);

void VECTOR3D_Scale(float k, VECTOR3D_PTR va, VECTOR3D_PTR vscaled);

void VECTOR4D_Scale(float k, VECTOR4D_PTR va, VECTOR4D_PTR vscaled);
```

Purpose:

`void VECTOR*D_Scale()` scales the sent vector `va` by `k` as shown in Figure 5.14, and stores the result (`k*va`) into `vscaled`.

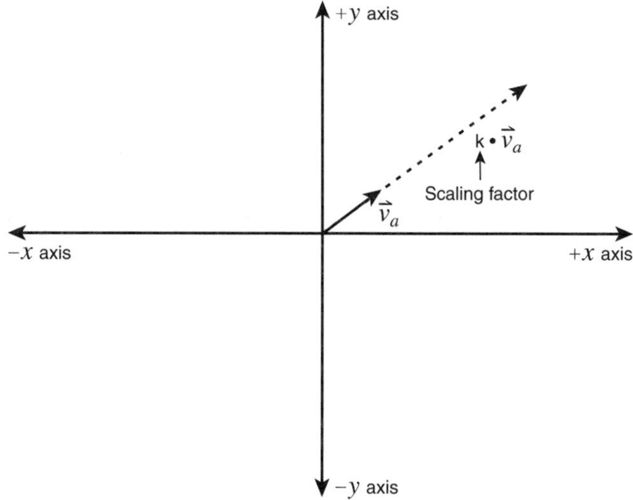

FIGURE 5.14 Vector scaling setup.

Example:

```
VECTOR3D v1 = {1,1,1};
VECTOR3D vs;
```

```
// scale v1 by 50
VECTOR3D_Scale(50, &v1, &vs);

// invert v1
VECTOR3D_Scale(-1, &v1, &vs);
```

Function Prototype(s):

```
float VECTOR2D_Dot(VECTOR2D_PTR va, VECTOR2D_PTR vb);

float VECTOR3D_Dot(VECTOR3D_PTR va, VECTOR3D_PTR vb);

float VECTOR4D_Dot(VECTOR4D_PTR va, VECTOR4D_PTR vb);
```

Purpose:

`float VECTOR*D_Dot()` computes the dot product (va.vb) and returns the scalar result. Note that for the `VECTOR4D` version, the w coordinate is disregarded.

Example:

```
VECTOR4D v1={1,0,0,1}; // the unit x-axis
VECTOR4D v2={0,1,0,1}; // the unit y-axis

// dot them together, the result better be 0!
float dp=VECTOR4D_Dot(&v1, &v2);
```

Function Prototype(s):

```
void VECTOR3D_Cross(VECTOR3D_PTR va,VECTOR3D_PTR vb,VECTOR3D_PTR vn);

void VECTOR4D_Cross(VECTOR4D_PTR va,VECTOR4D_PTR vb,VECTOR4D_PTR vn);
```

Purpose:

`void VECTOR*D_Cross()` computes the cross product (`va` x `vb`) as shown in Figure 5.15; that is, it computes the vector perpendicular to both `va` and `vb` and returns the result in `vn`. In the `VECTOR4D` case, w is disregarded as usual.

Example:

```
VECTOR3D vx = {1,0,0};
VECTOR3D vy = {0,1,0};
VECTOR3D vcross;

// cross the x-axis with the y-axis, the result should be
// the z-axis
VECTOR3D_Cross(&vx, &vy, &vcross);
```

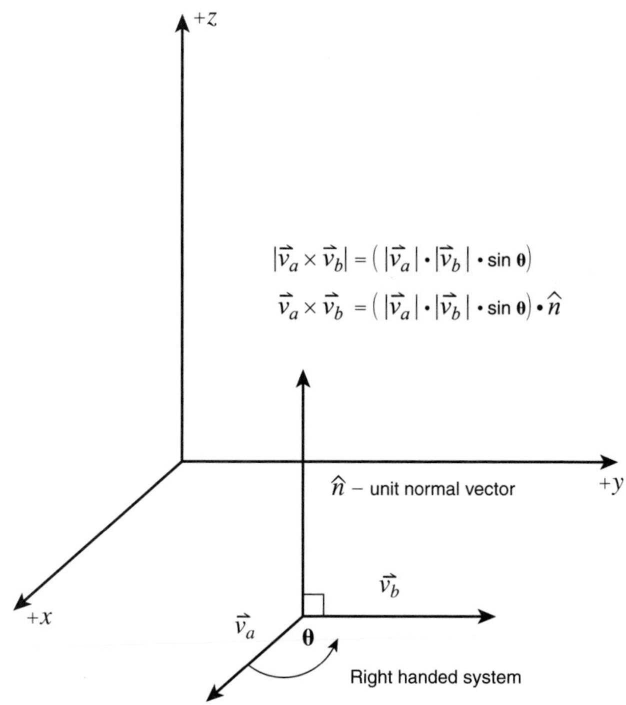

FIGURE 5.15 Vector cross product.

Function Prototype(s):

```
VECTOR3D VECTOR3D_Cross(VECTOR3D_PTR va, VECTOR3D_PTR vb);

VECTOR4D VECTOR4D_Cross(VECTOR4D_PTR va, VECTOR4D_PTR vb);
```

Purpose:

`VECTOR*D VECTOR*D_Cross()` computes the cross product (`va` x `vb`); that is, it computes the vector perpendicular to both `va` and `vb` and returns the result on the stack. In the `VECTOR4D` case, w is disregarded as usual.

Example:

```
VECTOR3D vx = {1,0,0};
VECTOR3D vy = {0,1,0};

// cross the x-axis with the y-axis, the result should be
// the z-axis
VECTOR3D vcross = VECTOR3D_Cross(&vx, &vy);
```

Function Prototype(s):

```
float VECTOR2D_Length(VECTOR2D_PTR va);
float VECTOR3D_Length(VECTOR3D_PTR va);
float VECTOR4D_Length(VECTOR4D_PTR va);
```

Purpose:

`float VECTOR*D_Length()` computes the length of the sent vector using the standard square root of the sum of squares algorithm.

Example:

```
VECTOR2D v1={3,4};

// compute length, should be 5
float length = VECTOR3D_Length(&v1);
```

Function Prototype(s):

```
float VECTOR2D_Length_Fast(VECTOR2D_PTR va);

float VECTOR3D_Length_Fast(VECTOR3D_PTR va);

float VECTOR4D_Length_Fast(VECTOR4D_PTR va);
```

Purpose:

`float VECTOR*D_Length_Fast()` computes the length of the sent vector by using a Taylor series approximation. Accurate to within a few percent, but 10 times faster than `VECTOR*D_Length()` function.

Example:

```
VECTOR2D v1={3,4};

// compute length, should be 5
float length = VECTOR3D_Length_Fast(&v1);
```

Function Prototype(s):

```
void VECTOR2D_Normalize(VECTOR2D_PTR va);

void VECTOR3D_Normalize(VECTOR3D_PTR va);

void VECTOR4D_Normalize(VECTOR4D_PTR va);
```

Purpose:

void VECTOR*D_Normalize() normalizes the vector va; that is, makes it a unit vector by dividing each component by the length of va. Note that va is modified.

Example:

```
VECTOR2D v={5,6};

// normalize v, v = v/¦v¦
VECTOR2D_Normalize(&v);
```

Function Prototype(s):

```
void VECTOR2D_Normalize(VECTOR2D_PTR va, VECTOR2D_PTR vn);

void VECTOR3D_Normalize(VECTOR3D_PTR va, VECTOR3D_PTR vn);

void VECTOR4D_Normalize(VECTOR4D_PTR va, VECTOR4D_PTR vn);
```

Purpose:

void VECTOR2D_Normalize() normalizes the vector va and stores it in vn.

Example:

```
VECTOR3D v={1,2,3};
VECTOR3D vn;

// vn = v/¦vn¦
VECTOR3D_Normalize(&v, &vn);
```

Function Prototype(s):

```
void VECTOR2D_Build(VECTOR2D_PTR init, VECTOR2D_PTR term, VECTOR2D_PTR result);

void VECTOR3D_Build(VECTOR3D_PTR init, VECTOR3D_PTR term, VECTOR3D_PTR result);

void VECTOR4D_Build(VECTOR4D_PTR init, VECTOR4D_PTR term, VECTOR4D_PTR result);
```

Purpose:

void VECTOR*D_Build() builds a vector from init->term and stores it in result. This is a good example of a function that works well using the data type alias POINT*D because in most cases you'll want to create a vector from two points.

Example:

```
POINT3D p1={1,2,3}, p2={4,5,6};
VECTOR3D v12; // use to store the result

// create a vector from point p1 to p2
VECTOR3D_Build(&p1, &p2, &v);
```

Note that we don't need to cast the types because points and vectors of the same dimension have the same types and data footprints. But, if you want to create a vector from two other vectors, you can do so, of course.

Function Prototype(s):

```
float VECTOR2D_CosTh(VECTOR2D_PTR va, VECTOR2D_PTR vb);

float VECTOR3D_CosTh(VECTOR3D_PTR va, VECTOR3D_PTR vb);

float VECTOR4D_CosTh(VECTOR4D_PTR va, VECTOR4D_PTR vb);
```

Purpose:

`float VECTOR*D_CosTh()` computes the cosine of the angle between the two vectors `va` and `vb`, respectively, as shown in Figure 5.16.

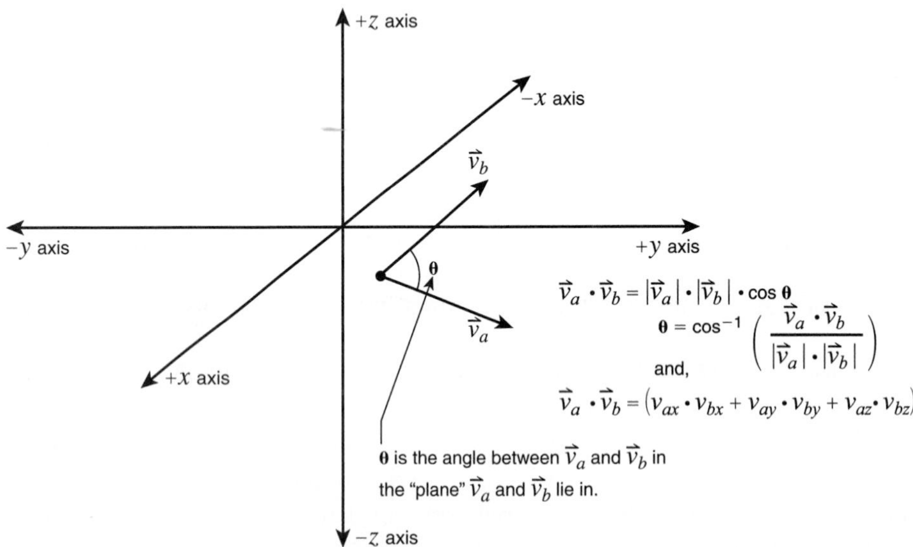

FIGURE 5.16 The dot product and interior vector angle.

In many 3D algorithms, the product formula

```
u.v = |u|*|v| * cos(θ)
```

is used to solve for θ; that is, the angle between the two vectors, **u** and **v**, using the following simplification:

```
θ = cos-1[(u . v)/(|u|*|v|)]
```

However, many times we don't need to go that far and the cos(θ) term will suffice:

```
cos(θ) = [(u . v)/(|u|*|v|)]
```

That's what this function is all about.

TRICK

There are many opportunities in game programming to exploit math and speed things up as in the preceding example. Another example is this: Say you have a number of objects, and when the objects get within 100 units of the black hole, you want them to get sucked in. You might blindly use the distance function and `sqrt()` function to compute the distance. If you're a little more clever though, you'll realize there's no need to use the exact distance—why not use the square of the distance? That is, use $d^2 = (x^2+y^2+z^2)$, and instead of 100 use (100*100) as the decision variable! This way, you lose the `sqrt()` function. The moral is that if $|x| < |y|$, $|x^2| < |y^2|$. But watch out for overflow!

5

Example:

```
VECTOR3D u = {0,1,0}; // the y-axis
VECTOR3D v = {1,1,0}; // a vector with a slope of 45 degrees

// find the angle between u and v
VECTOR3D_CosTh(&u, &v);
```

NOTE

This function is very useful in hidden surface removal where we need to detect if the angle between the view direction and the surface normal is acute or obtuse.

Function Prototype(s):

```
void VECTOR2D_Print(VECTOR2D_PTR va, char *name);

void VECTOR3D_Print(VECTOR3D_PTR va, char *name);

void VECTOR4D_Print(VECTOR4D_PTR va, char *name);
```

Purpose:

void VECTOR*D_Print() prints out a vector in "pretty form" along with a sent character name. This is used only as a debugging feature and writes the output to the error file previously opened with a call to Open_Error_File().

Example:

```
// open the error file
Open_Error_File("error.txt");

VECTOR3D v={1,2,3};

// print the vector
VECTOR3D_Print(&v,"Velocity");

// close the error file
Close_Error_File();
```

File dump of ERROR.TXT:

```
Opening Error Output File (error.txt) on Sat Jan 29 22:36:00.520, 2000

Velocity=[1.000000, 2.000000, 3.000000, ]

Closing Error Output File.
```

Matrix Support Functions

The next set of functions handles matrix mathematics and transformations. In general, a 3D engine uses 3×3 or 4×4 matrices depending on what you want to do, but sometimes we cheat and use a 4×3 and make assumptions about the last column and other tricks like that. Remember, we have both 3D and 4D homogenous points, so even though at some point we'll optimize the matrix math a lot, it doesn't hurt to generalize at this early stage. Moreover, although I've tried to think of all the cases of matrix multiplication and transformations we might need, I'm sure I've left some out—but we can always add them later. Finally, there is support for 2×2, 3×3, and 4×4 in general, but some of the older 2x2 support was in the T3DLIB1.CPP¦H modules.

NOTE

Although the matrix library is very similar to the vector library inasmuch as there is support for various dimensional data types, all with similar function names, there are enough differences that I've decided to separate each functional set in the reference, because some functions on higher dimensions sometimes work differently. Hence, we'll cover 2×2, 3×3, and 4×4, in that order.

Function Prototype:

```
void Mat_Init_2X2(MATRIX2X2_PTR ma, float m00, float m01, float m10, float m11);
```

Purpose:

`void Mat_Init_2X2()` initializes the matrix `ma` with the sent floating-point values in row major form.

Example:

```
MATRIX2X2 ma;

// initialize matrix to identity
Mat_Init_2X2(&ma, 1, 0, 0, 1);
```

Function Prototype:

```
void Mat_Add_2X2(MATRIX2X2_PTR ma, MATRIX2X2_PTR mb, MATRIX2X2_PTR msum);
```

Purpose:

`void Mat_Add_2X2()` adds the matrices (`ma+mb`) and stores the result in `msum`.

Example:

```
MATRIX2X2 m1 = {1,2, 3,4};
MATRIX2X2 m2 = {4,9, 5,6};
MATRIX2X2 msum;

// add em
Mat_Add_2X2(&m1, &m2, &msum);
```

Function Prototype:

```
void Mat_Mul_2X2(MATRIX2X2_PTR ma, MATRIX2X2_PTR mb, MATRIX2X2_PTR mprod);
```

Function Listing Reference:

```
void Mat_Mul_2X2(MATRIX2X2_PTR ma, MATRIX2X2_PTR mb, MATRIX2X2_PTR mprod)
{
// this function multiplies two 2x2 matrices together and
// and stores the result in mprod
mprod->M00 = ma->M00*mb->M00 + ma->M01*mb->M10;
mprod->M01 = ma->M00*mb->M01 + ma->M01*mb->M11;

mprod->M10 = ma->M10*mb->M00 + ma->M11*mb->M10;
mprod->M11 = ma->M10*mb->M01 + ma->M11*mb->M11;

} // end Mat_Mul_2X2
```

Purpose:

void Mat_Mul_2X2() matrix multiplies (ma*mb) and stores the result in mprod. Also refer to the earlier code listing and note that the matrices are explicitly multiplied out rather than using loop operations. This is optimal.

Example:

```
MATRIX2X2 m1 = {1,2, 3,4};
MATRIX2X2 m2 = {1,0, 0,1};
MATRIX2X2 mprod;


// multiply them, note that m1*m2 = m1 since m2=I
Mat_Mul_2X2(&m1, &m2, &mprod);
```

Function Prototype (from T3DLIB1.CPP¦H):

```
int Mat_Mul_1X2_3X2(MATRIX1X2_PTR ma,
           MATRIX3X2_PTR mb,
           MATRIX1X2_PTR mprod);
```

Function Listing Reference:

```
int Mat_Mul_1X2_3X2(MATRIX1X2_PTR ma,
           MATRIX3X2_PTR mb,
           MATRIX1X2_PTR mprod)
{
// this function multiplies a 1x2 matrix against a
// 3x2 matrix - ma*mb and stores the result
// using a dummy element for the 3rd element of the 1x2
// to make the matrix multiply valid i.e. 1x3 X 3x2

  for (int col=0; col<2; col++)
    {
    // compute dot product from row of ma
    // and column of mb

    float sum = 0; // used to hold result

    for (int index=0; index<2; index++)
       {
       // add in next product pair
       sum+=(ma->M[index]*mb->M[index][col]);
       } // end for index
```

```
    // add in last element * 1
    sum+= mb->M[index][col];

    // insert resulting col element
    mprod->M[col] = sum;

    } // end for col

return(1);

} // end Mat_Mul_1X2_3X2
```

Purpose:

`int Mat_Mul_1X2_3X2()` is a specialized function used to multiply a 1×2 matrix (basically a 2D point) against a 3×3 matrix that represents a rotation and a translation. The operation is mathematically undefined because the inner dimensions don't match. However, if we assume that the 1×2 is really 1×3 with the last element equal to 1, the multiplication can be carried out. Figure 5.17 illustrates what's being multiplied. Additionally, take a look at the code listing. This function is useful when transforming 2D points, but you want to save space on their representation and still want to support translation and homogenous coordinates.

Example:

```
MATRIX1X2 p1={5,5}, p2; // the point

// transformation rotation plus translation
MATRIX3X2 m = {cos(th), sin(th),
       -sin(th), cos(th),
        dx,    dy};

// perform matrix multiply
Mat_Mul_1X2_3X2(&p1, &m, &p2);
```

TIP

The function itself is rather slow. We could speed it up by unrolling the loops, but it's much clearer this way and you can see its iterative nature. Remember, never optimize until you need to, and start with your algorithms before you start looking at the actual code itself. Then, once you have optimal algorithms and code, if you really need the last step, inline assembly language is in order.

5

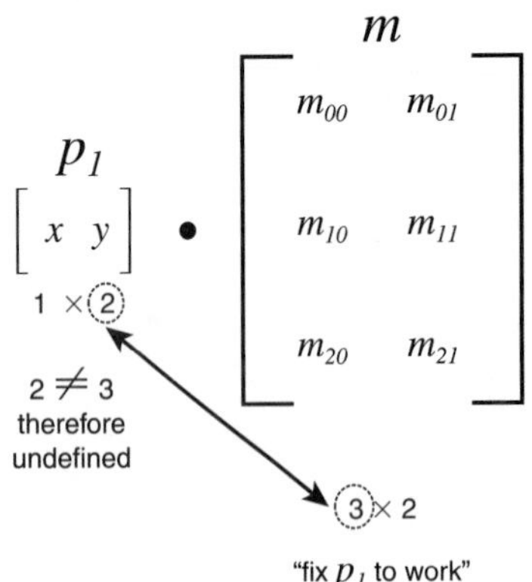

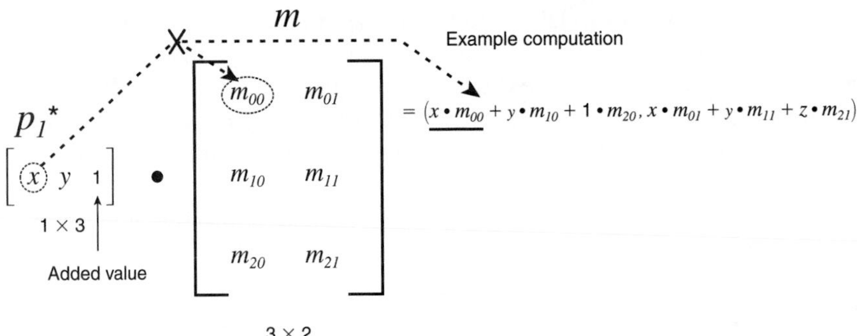

FIGURE 5.17 The methodology of undefined vector-matrix multiplication for the (1×2)*(3×2) case.

Function Prototype:

```
float Mat_Det_2X2(MATRIX2X2_PTR m);
```

Purpose:

`float Mat_Det_2X2()` computes the determinate of the matrix `m` and returns it on the stack.

Example:

```
MATRIX2x2 m = {1,2,4,8}; // this matrix is singular

// compute determinate
float det = Mat_Det_2X2(&m);
```

Function Prototype:

```
int Mat_Inverse_2X2(MATRIX2X2_PTR m, MATRIX2X2_PTR mi);
```

Purpose:

int Mat_Inverse_2X2() computes the inverse of m if it exists and returns it in mi. If the inverse exists, the function returns a 1; otherwise, it returns a 0 and mi is undefined.

Example:

```
MATRIX2X2 mA = {1,2, 4, -3};
MATRIX2X2 mI;

// compute the inverse of A
if (Mat_Inverse_2X2(&mA, &mI))
  {
  // inverse exists...
  } // end if
else
  {
  // inverse doesn't exist
  } // end else
```


Function Prototype:

```
void Print_Mat_2X2(MATRIX2X2_PTR ma, char *name);
```

Purpose:

void Print_Mat_2X2() prints out the matrix in "pretty" format along with the sent string in name as an identifier. All output, of course, goes to the error file previously opened with Open_Error_File().

Example:

```
MATRIX2X2 m = {1,2,3,4};

// open the error file and write to the screen
Open_Error_File("", stdout);

Print_Mat_2X2(&m,"Matrix m");

// close the error file
Close_Error_File();
```

Function Prototype:

```
void Mat_Init_3X3(MATRIX3X3_PTR ma,
         float m00, float m01, float m02,
         float m10, float m11, float m12,
         float m20, float m21, float m22);
```

Purpose:

void Mat_Init_3X3() initializes the matrix ma with the sent floating-point values in row major form.

Example:

```
MATRIX3X3 ma;

// initialize matrix to identity
Mat_Init_3X3(&ma, 1,0,0, 0,1,0, 0,0,1);
```

Function Prototype (from T3DLIB1.CPP|H):

```
inline int Mat_Init_3X2(MATRIX3X2_PTR ma,
            float m00, float m01,
            float m10, float m11,
            float m20, float m21);
```

Purpose:

void Mat_Init_3X2() initializes the matrix ma with the sent floating-point values in row major form.

Example:

```
MATRIX3X2 ma;

// initialize minor upper left hand 2x2
// matrix to identity matrix
Mat_Init_3X2(&ma, 1,0, 0,1, 0,0);
```

Function Prototype:

```
void Mat_Add_3X3(MATRIX3X3_PTR ma, MATRIX3X3_PTR mb, MATRIX3X3_PTR msum);
```

Purpose:

void Mat_Add_3X3() adds the matrices (ma+mb) and stores the result in msum.

Example:

```
MATRIX3X3 m1 = {1,2,3,4,5,6,7,8,9};
MATRIX3X3 m2 = {4,9,7, -1,5,6, 2,3,4};
MATRIX3X3 msum;

// add em
Mat_Add_3X3(&m1, &m2, &msum);
```

Function Prototype:

```
void Mat_Mul_VECTOR3D_3X3(VECTOR3D_PTR va, MATRIX3X3_PTR mb,VECTOR3D_PTR vprod);
```

Purpose:

`void Mat_Mul_VECTOR3D_3X3()` multiplies the 1×3 row vector `va` against the 3×3 matrix `mb`, and stores the result in the 1x3 row vector `vprod`. This is shown in Figure 5.18. Basically, this function performs a point or vector matrix multiplication.

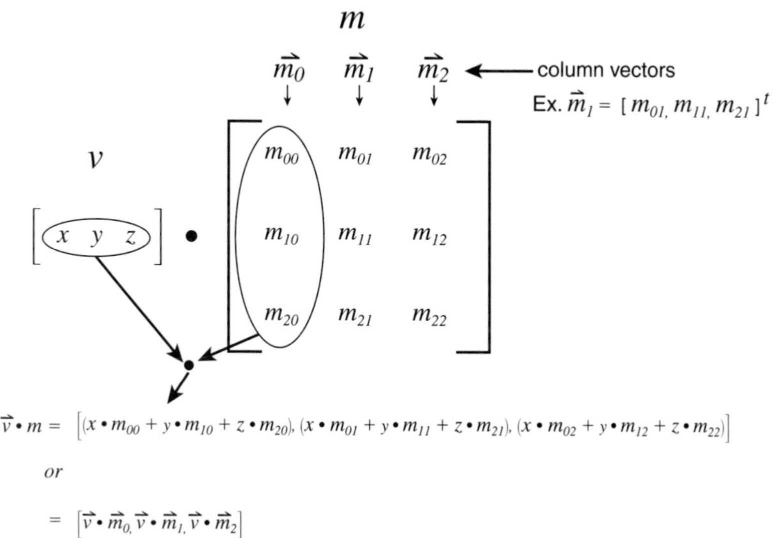

FIGURE 5.18 3D vector multiplied with 3×3 matrix.

Example:

```
VECTOR3D v={x,y,1}, vt;
MATRIX3X3 m = {1,0,0, 0,1,0,xt,yt,1};

// multiply v*m
Mat_Mul_VECTOR3D_3X3(&v, &m, &vt);
```

Can you figure out what this transform does? If we pretend that the `VECTOR3D` is really a 2D homogenous point, the transformation translates the point to

```
vt.x = v.x+xt;
vt.y = v.y+yt;
vt.z = 1;
```

Neat, huh? But a new Dodge Viper would be neater <VBG>.

Function Prototype (from T3DLIB1.CPP¦H):

```
int (MATRIX1X3_PTR ma,
          MATRIX3X3_PTR mb,
          MATRIX1X3_PTR mprod);
```

Purpose:

int Mat_Mul_1X3_3X3() multiplies a 1×3 matrix—basically a row vector—against a 3×3 matrix. This function is almost identical to Mat_Mul_VECTOR3D_3X3(). Only the types are different.

Example:

```
MATRIX1X3 v={x,y,1}, vt;
MATRIX3X3 m = {1,0,0, 0,1,0,xt,yt,1};

// multiply v*m
Mat_Mul_1X3_3X3(&v, &m, &vt);
```

Function Prototype (from T3DLIB1.CPP¦H):

```
int Mat_Mul_3X3(MATRIX3X3_PTR ma,
        MATRIX3X3_PTR mb,
        MATRIX3X3_PTR mprod);
```

Purpose:

void Mat_Mul_3X3() matrix multiplies (ma*mb) and stores the result in mprod.

Example:

```
MATRIX3X3 m1 = {1,2,3, 4,5,6, 7,8,9};
MATRIX3X3 m2 = {1,0,0, 0,1,0, 0,0,1};
MATRIX3X3 mprod;

// multiply them, note that m1*m2 = m1 since m2=I
Mat_Mul_3X3(&m1, &m2, &mprod);
```

Function Prototype:

```
float Mat_Det_3X3(MATRIX3X3_PTR m);
```

Purpose:

float Mat_Det_3X3() computes the determinate of the matrix m and returns it on the stack.

Example:

```
MATRIX3x3 m = {1,2,0, 4,8,9, 2,5,7};

// compute determinate
float det = Mat_Det_3X3(&m);
```

Function Prototype:

```
int Mat_Inverse_3X3(MATRIX3X3_PTR m, MATRIX3X3_PTR mi);
```

Purpose:

`int Mat_Inverse_3X3()` computes the inverse of `m` if it exists and returns it in `mi`. If the inverse exists, the function returns a `1`; otherwise, it returns a `0` and `mi` is undefined.

Example:

```
MATRIX3X3 mA = {1,2,9, 4,-3,6, 1,0,5};
MATRIX3X3 mI;

// compute the inverse of A
if (Mat_Inverse_3X3(&mA, &mI))
  {
  // inverse exists…
  } // end if
else
  {
  // inverse doesn't exist
  } // end else
```

Function Prototype:

```
void Print_Mat_3X3(MATRIX3X3_PTR ma, char *name);
```

Purpose:

`void Print_Mat_3X3()` prints out the matrix in "pretty" format along with the sent string in `name` as an identifier. All output, of course, goes to the error file previously opened with `Open_Error_File()`.

Example:

```
MATRIX3X3 m = {1,2,3, 4,5,6, 7,8,9};

// open the error file and write to a file
Open_Error_File("error.txt");
```

5

```
Print_Mat_3X3(&m,"Matrix m");

// close the error file
Close_Error_File();
```

Function Prototype:

```
void Mat_Init_4X4(MATRIX4X4_PTR ma,
      float m00, float m01, float m02, float m03,
      float m10, float m11, float m12, float m13,
      float m20, float m21, float m22, float m23,
      float m30, float m31, float m32, float m33);
```

Purpose:

`void Mat_Init_4X4()` initializes the matrix `ma` with the sent floating-point values in row major form.

Example:

```
MATRIX4X4 ma;

// initialize matrix to identity
Mat_Init_4X4(&ma, 1,0,0,0, 0,1,0,0, 0,0,1,0, 0,0,0,1);
```

Function Prototype:

```
void Mat_Add_4X4(MATRIX4X4_PTR ma, MATRIX4X4_PTR mb, MATRIX4X4_PTR msum);
```

Purpose:

`void Mat_Add_4X4()` adds the matrices (`ma+mb`) and stores the result in `msum`.

Example:

```
MATRIX4X4 m1 = {1,2,3,4, 5,6,7,8, 9,10,11,12, 13,14,15,16};
MATRIX4X4 m2 = {4,9,7,3, -1,5,6,7, 2,3,4,5, 2,0,5,3};
MATRIX4X4 msum;

// add em
Mat_Add_4X4(&m1, &m2, &msum);
```

Function Prototype:

```
void Mat_Mul_4X4(MATRIX4X4_PTR ma, MATRIX4X4_PTR mb, MATRIX4X4_PTR mprod);
```

Purpose:

`void Mat_Mul_4X4()` matrix multiplies (`ma*mb`) and stores the result in `mprod`.

Example:

```
MATRIX4X4 m1 = {1,2,3,4, 4,5,6,7, 7,8,9,10, 11,12,13,14};
MATRIX4X4 m2 = {1,0,0,0, 0,1,0,0, 0,0,1,0, 0,0,0,1};
MATRIX4X4 mprod;

// multiply them, note that m1*m2 = m1 since m2=I
Mat_Mul_4X4(&m1, &m2, &mprod);
```

Function Prototype:

```
void Mat_Mul_1X4_4X4(MATRIX1X4_PTR ma, MATRIX4X4_PTR mb, MATRIX1X4_PTR mprod);
```

Function Listing Reference:

```
void Mat_Mul_1X4_4X4(MATRIX1X4_PTR ma,
           MATRIX4X4_PTR mb,
           MATRIX1X4_PTR mprod)
{
// this function multiplies a 1x4 matrix against a
// 4x4 matrix - ma*mb and stores the result
// no tricks or assumptions here, just a straight multiply

  for (int col=0; col<4; col++)
    {
    // compute dot product from row of ma
    // and column of mb
    float sum = 0; // used to hold result

    for (int row=0; row<4; row++)
       {
       // add in next product pair
       sum+=(ma->M[row] * mb->M[row][col]);
       } // end for index

    // insert resulting col element
    mprod->M[col] = sum;

    } // end for col

} // end Mat_Mul_1X4_4X4
```

Purpose:

`void Mat_Mul_1X4_4X4()` multiplies a 1×4 row matrix against a 4×4 matrix and computes the product `mprod = (ma*mb)`. The function makes no assumptions about homogenous coordinates and so forth, so it's a straight matrix multiply as shown in the code listing. Also, note that we can speed this function up by explicitly performing all the math rather than using loops.

Example:

```
MATRIX1X4 v={x,y,z,1}, vt;
MATRIX4X4 m = {1,0,0,0 0,1,0,0, 0,0,1,0, xt,yt,zt,1};

// multiply v*m, this translates the 3D point x,y,z
Mat_Mul_1X4_4X4(&v, &m, &vt);
```

Function Prototype:

```
void Mat_Mul_VECTOR3D_4X4(VECTOR3D_PTR va, MATRIX4X4_PTR mb, VECTOR3D_PTR vprod);
```

Purpose:

`void Mat_Mul_VECTOR3D_4X4()` multiplies a 3D vector against a 4×4 matrix. However, to perform the multiplication, the function assumes that there's a phantom fourth element in `va` that's equal to 1.0. Moreover, when the multiplication completes, the result is a 3D vector, rather than a 4D vector. The bottom line is that this function is used to transform 3D points with 4×4 matrices that contain translation values and assume homogenous coordinates. Because a 3D point with only three elements [x y z] doesn't have enough space for the homogenous component w, we assume it's there and set it to 1.0. That was a mouthful! Figure 5.19 might clear this up for you a bit.

Example:

```
VECTOR3D v={10,10,10}, vrt;

// rotate around the x-axis and translate (tx,ty,tz)
MATRIX4X4 m = {1, 0, 0, 0,
         0, cos(th), sin(th),0,
         0,-sin(th), cos(th),0,
         tx, ty, tz, 1};

// do the transform
Mat_Mul_VECTOR3D_4X4(&v, &m, &vrt);
```

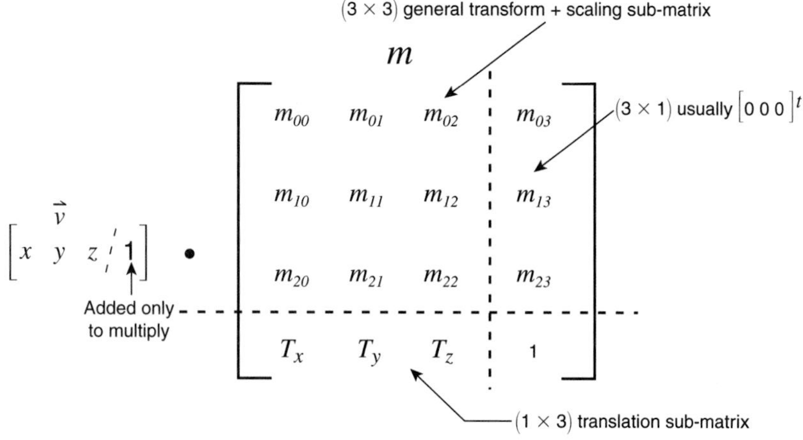

$$\vec{v} \cdot m = \left[(x \cdot m_{00} + y \cdot m_{10} + z \cdot m_{20} + T_x), (x \cdot m_{01} + y \cdot m_{11} + z \cdot m_{21} + T_y), (x \cdot m_{02} + y \cdot m_{12} + z \cdot m_{22} + T_z)\right]$$

Translation factors

FIGURE 5.19 3D vector multiplied against a 4×4 matrix.

Also, we could've defined the vectors as points made the same call because `VECTOR3D` and `POINT3D` are aliases:

```
POINT3D p1={10,10,10}, p2;

// rotate around the x-axis and translate (tx,ty,tz)
MATRIX4X4 m = {1, 0, 0, 0,
        0, cos(th), sin(th),0,
        0,-sin(th), cos(th),0,
        tx, ty, tz, 1};

// do the transform
Mat_Mul_VECTOR3D_4X4(&p1, &m, &p2);
```

Function Prototype:

```
void Mat_Mul_VECTOR3D_4X3(VECTOR3D_PTR va, MATRIX4X3_PTR mb, VECTOR3D_PTR vprod);
```

Purpose:

`void Mat_Mul_VECTOR3D_4X3()` is very similar to `Mat_Mul_VECTOR3D_4X4()`, but instead it multiplies a 3D vector against a 4×3 matrix rather than a 4×4 matrix. However, it also assumes that there's a phantom fourth element in `va` that's equal to 1.0 to carry out the multiplication. And because there are only three columns in the 4×3 matrix, the multiplication stops naturally rather than being cut off artificially as in `Mat_Mul_VECTOR3D_4X4()`.

Example:

```
POINT3D p1={10,10,10}, p2;

// rotate around the x-axis and translate (tx,ty,tz)
// note that we don't have to muck with the last column
// which is always [0 0 0 1]t anyway
MATRIX4X3 m = {1, 0, 0,
        0, cos(th), sin(th),
        0,-sin(th), cos(th),
        tx, ty, tz};

// do the transform
Mat_Mul_VECTOR3D_4X3(&p1, &m, &p2);
```

Function Prototype:

```
void Mat_Mul_VECTOR4D_4X4(VECTOR4D_PTR va, MATRIX4X4_PTR mb, VECTOR4D_PTR vprod);
```

Purpose:

`void Mat_Mul_VECTOR4D_4X4()` multiplies the 1×4 row vector `va` against the 4×4 matrix `mb`, and stores the result in the 1×4 row vector `vprod`. The function assumes nothing special and simply does a 1×4 * 4×4 matrix multiplication.

Example:

```
VECTOR4D v={10,10,10,1}, vrt;

// rotate around the x-axis and translate (tx,ty,tz)
MATRIX4X4 m = {1, 0, 0, 0,
        0, cos(th), sin(th),0,
        0,-sin(th), cos(th),0,
        tx, ty, tz, 1};

// do the transform
Mat_Mul_VECTOR4D_4X4(&v, &m, &vrt);
```

Note that the result is **vrt** = <x', y', z', 1>. That is, the w, or homogenous component, will be equal to 1.0.

Function Prototype:

```
void Mat_Mul_VECTOR4D_4X3(VECTOR4D_PTR va, MATRIX4X4_PTR mb, VECTOR4D_PTR vprod);
```

Purpose:

`void Mat_Mul_VECTOR4D_4X3()` is very similar to `Mat_Mul_VECTOR3D_4X3()`, but instead it multiplies a 4D vector against a 4×3 matrix rather than a 3D vector. And because there are only three columns in the 4×3 matrix, the multiplication stops naturally rather than being cut off artificially, as in `Mat_Mul_VECTOR3D_4X4()`. Finally, the w component from `va` is copied to `vprod`. Or, in other words, the last column of the 4×3 is assumed to be $[0\ 0\ 0\ 1]^t$.

Example:

```
POINT4D p1={10,10,10,1}, p2;

// rotate around the x-axis and translate (tx,ty,tz)
// note that we don't have to muck with the last column
// which is always [0 0 0 1]t anyway
MATRIX4X3 m = {1, 0, 0,
        0, cos(th), sin(th),
        0,-sin(th), cos(th),
        tx, ty, tz};

// do the transform
Mat_Mul_VECTOR4D_4X3(&p1, &m, &p2);
```

Function Prototype:

```
int Mat_Inverse_4X4(MATRIX4X4_PTR m, MATRIX4X4_PTR mi);
```

Purpose:

`int Mat_Inverse_4X4()` computes the inverse of `m` if it exists and returns it in `mi`. If the inverse exists, the function returns a `1`; otherwise, it returns a `0` and `mi` is undefined. Also, this function works only on matrices where the last column is $[0\ 0\ 0\ 1]^t$.

Example:

```
// note the last column is [0 0 0 1]t
MATRIX4X4 mA = {1, 2,9,0,
        4,-3,6,0,
        1, 0,5,0,
        2, 3,4,1};

MATRIX4X4 mI;

// compute the inverse of A
if (Mat_Inverse_4X4(&mA, &mI))
  {
  // inverse exists…
```

```
  } // end if
else
  {
  // inverse doesn't exist
  } // end else
```

Function Prototype:

```
void Print_Mat_4X4(MATRIX4X4_PTR ma, char *name);
```

Purpose:

`void Print_Mat_4X4()` prints the matrix out in "pretty" format along with the sent string in `name` as an identifier. All output, of course, goes to the error file previously opened with `Open_Error_File()`.

Example:

```
MATRIX4X4 m = {1,2,3,4,
        5,6,7,8,
        9,10,11,12,
        13,14,15,16};

// open the error file and write to a file
Open_Error_File("error.txt");

Print_Mat_4X4(&m,"Matrix m");

// close the error file
Close_Error_File();
```

2D and 3D Parametric Line Support Functions

When I started writing the math engine, I didn't think at all that I would add parametric line support into the engine. Why? Because most of the time, you would just manually code parametric lines in the algorithms where you need them with a vector and a parameter `t`. However, 9 times out of 10, you would use a vector and a parameter `t`, so why not encapsulate that in a structure (or class without methods) and then build on that for common functions such as intersection, and so forth? Hence, the math engine has support for both 2D and 3D parametric lines, along with a fairly complete set of functions to work with them.

To refresh your memory, here's the structure for a 2D parametric line:

```
typedef struct PARMLINE2D_TYP
{
POINT2D p0; // start point of parametric line
```

```
POINT2D p1; // end point of parametric line
VECTOR2D v; // direction vector of line segment
       // |v|=|p0->p1|
} PARMLINE2D, *PARMLINE2D_PTR;
```

The relationship of the values is shown in Figure 5.2. Note that the vector extends from **p0->p1**; that is, it's not normalized. And moving on, here's the structure for a 3D parametric line:

```
typedef struct PARMLINE3D_TYP
{
POINT3D p0; // start point of parametric line
POINT3D p1; // end point of parametric line
VECTOR3D v; // direction vector of line segment
       // |v|=|p0->p1|
} PARMLINE3D, *PARMLINE3D_PTR;
```

The only difference between the 2D version and the 3D version is the z-axis; other than that, each structure holds the same info in the same form. So, let's take a look at the functions now.

Function Prototype:

```
void Init_Parm_Line2D(POINT2D_PTR p_init, POINT2D_PTR p_term, PARMLINE2D_PTR p);
```

Purpose:

`void Init_Parm_Line2D()` initializes a 2D parametric line structure based on the sent points and computes the vector between them. Note that the vector is generated internally to the function.

Example:

```
POINT2D p1 = {1,2}, p2 = {10,20};
PARMLINE2D p;

// create a parametric line from p1 to p2
Init_Parm_Line2D(&p1, &p2, &p);
```

Function Prototype:

```
void Compute_Parm_Line2D(PARMLINE2D_PTR p, float t, POINT2D_PTR pt);
```

Purpose:

`void Compute_Parm_Line2D()` evaluates a 2D parametric line at the value `t` and returns the value in the sent point. Note that when parameter `t = 0`, the parametric line is equal to the initial point `p1`; when parameter `t = 1`, the parametric line equals the terminal point `p2`. That is, the line is traced from **p1** to **p2** as 0 <= t <= 1.

Example:

```
POINT2D p1 = {1,2}, p2 = {10,20}, pt;
PARMLINE2D p;

// create a parametric line from p1 to p2
Init_Parm_Line2D(&p1, &p2, &p);

// now evaluate the parametric line when t=.5
// and store the resulting point in pt
Compute_Parm_Line2D(&p, 0.5, &pt);
```

Function Prototype:

```
int Intersect_Parm_Lines2D(PARMLINE2D_PTR p1, PARMLINE2D_PTR p2,
              float *t1, float *t2);
```

Functional Listing:

```
int Intersect_Parm_Lines2D(PARMLINE2D_PTR p1, PARMLINE2D_PTR p2,
              float *t1, float *t2)
{
// this function computes the intersection of the two parametric
// line segments the function returns true if the segments
// intersect and sets the values of t1 and t2 to the t values that
// the intersection occurs on the lines p1 and p2 respectively,
// however, the function may send back t value not in the range [0,1]
// this means that the segments don't intersect, but the lines that
// they represent do, thus a return of 0 means no intersection, a
// 1 means intersection on the segments and a 2 means the lines
// intersect, but not necessarily the segments and 3 means that
// the lines are the same, thus they intersect everywhere

// basically we have a system of 2d linear equations, we need
// to solve for t1, t2 when x,y are both equal (if that's possible)

// step 1: test for parallel lines, if the direction vectors are
// scalar multiples then the lines are parallel and can't possible
// intersect unless the lines overlap
```

```
float det_p1p2 = (p1->v.x*p2->v.y - p1->v.y*p2->v.x);
if (fabs(det_p1p2) <= EPSILON_E5)
  {
  // at this point, the lines either don't intersect at all
  // or they are the same lines, in which case they may intersect
  // at one or many points along the segments, at this point we
  // will assume that the lines don't intersect at all, but later
  // we may need to rewrite this function and take into
  // consideration the overlap and singular point exceptions
  return(PARM_LINE_NO_INTERSECT);

  } // end if

// step 2: now compute the t1, t2 values for intersection
// we have two lines of the form
// p  = p0  + v*t, specifically
// p1  = p10  + v1*t1

// p1.x = p10.x + v1.x*t1
// p1.y = p10.y + v1.y*t1

// p2 = p20 + v2*t2

// p2.x = p20.x + v2.x*t2
// p2.y = p20.y + v2.y*t2
// solve the system when x1 = x2 and y1 = y2
// explained in chapter 4
*t1 = (p2->v.x*(p1->p0.y - p2->p0.y) - p2->v.y*(p1->p0.x - p2->p0.x))
   /det_p1p2;

*t2 = (p1->v.x*(p1->p0.y - p2->p0.y) - p1->v.y*(p1->p0.x - p2->p0.x))
   /det_p1p2;

// test if the lines intersect on the segments
if ((*t1>=0) && (*t1<=1) && (*t2>=0) && (*t2<=1))
  return(PARM_LINE_INTERSECT_IN_SEGMENT);
else
  return(PARM_LINE_INTERSECT_OUT_SEGMENT);

} // end Intersect_Parm_Lines2D
```

Purpose:

`int Intersect_Parm_Lines2D()` computes the intersection of two parametric lines, `p1` and `p2`, and sends back the parametric values `t1` and `t2` where the intersection takes place on each line segment, respectively. The function has the following return values based on whether there's an intersection on the parametric segment on the lines projected from the segments.

```
#define PARM_LINE_NO_INTERSECT      0
#define PARM_LINE_INTERSECT_IN_SEGMENT 1
#define PARM_LINE_INTERSECT_OUT_SEGMENT 2
```

Note that the function doesn't test whether the lines are co-linear because it would slow it down too much and there are too many cases (partial overlap, inclusion, point co-linearity). Therefore, it's up to you to check whether you need to know that. Or, you can add the functionality to the function. The thing to remember is that these parametric line segments are really finite segments, and all lines that aren't parallel intersect at some point, so the function determines the intersection regardless. However, if the `t` parameters coming back aren't in the range (0 <= `t` <= 1), you know that the intersection didn't occur on the original segment **p1->p2** of each line, respectively. Check out `DEMOII5_1.CPP|EXE` on the CD; it allows you to define parametric lines and test whether they intersect.

Example:

```
// these lines intersect
POINT2D p1 = {1,1}, p2 = {9,8};
POINT2D p3 = {2,8}, p4 = {7,1};

PARMLINE2D pl1, pl2;

// create a parametric line from p1 to p2
Init_Parm_Line2D(&p1, &p2, &pl1);

// create a parametric line from p3 to p4
Init_Parm_Line2D(&p3, &p4, &pl2);

float t1=0, t2=0; // storage for parameters

// compute intersection
int intersection_type = Intersect_Parm_Lines2D(&pl1, &pl2, &t1, &t2);
```

Function Prototype:

```
int Intersect_Parm_Lines2D(PARMLINE2D_PTR p1, PARMLINE2D_PTR p2, POINT2D_PTR pt);
```

Purpose:

`int Intersect_Parm_Lines2D()` computes the intersection of the parametric lines, but rather then sending back the parameters `t1` and `t2`, the function returns the actual point of intersection. Of course, care needs to be taken and the return value reviewed to see the type of intersection just as in the previous version.

Example:

```
// these lines intersect
POINT2D p1 = {1,1}, p2 = {9,8};
POINT2D p3 = {2,8}, p4 = {7,1};

POINT2D pt; // storage for intersection

PARMLINE2D pl1, pl2;

// create a parametric line from p1 to p2
Init_Parm_Line2D(&p1, &p2, &pl1);

// create a parametric line from p3 to p4
Init_Parm_Line2D(&p3, &p4, &pl2);

// compute intersection
int intersection_type = int Intersect_Parm_Lines2D(&pl1, &pl2, &pt);
```

C++

Pure C programmers might be a bit bewildered by two functions with the same name. This is a C++ feature. Basically, the parameter footprint of each function is different; thus, as far as the compiler is concerned, the functions are different. This is called *function overloading*, and is accomplished with name mangling based on the parameter list to come up with two unique names. This is covered in Appendix D, "C++ Primer."

And now here are the 3D parametric line functions. Note there are fewer because I classed some of them along with the 3D plane functions.

Function Prototype:

```
void Init_Parm_Line3D(POINT3D_PTR p_init, POINT3D_PTR p_term, PARMLINE3D_PTR p);
```

Purpose:

`void Init_Parm_Line3D()` initializes a 3D parametric line structure based on the sent points and the vector between them. Note that the vector is generated internally to the function.

Example:

```
POINT3D p1 = {1,2,3}, p2 = {10,20,30};
PARMLINE3D p;

// create a parametric line from p1 to p2
Init_Parm_Line3D(&p1, &p2, &p);
```

Function Prototype:

```
void Compute_Parm_Line3D(PARMLINE3D_PTR p, float t, POINT3D_PTR pt);
```

Purpose:

`void Compute_Parm_Line3D()` evaluates a 3D parametric line at the value `t` and returns the value in the sent point. Note that when parameter `t` = 0, the parametric line is equal to **p1**; when parameter `t` = 1, the parametric line equals **p2**. That is, the line is traced from **p1** to **p2** as 0 <= `t` <= 1.

Example:

```
POINT3D p1 = {1,2,3}, p2 = {10,20,30}, pt;
PARMLINE3D p;

// create a parametric line from p1 to p2
Init_Parm_Line3D(&p1, &p2, &p);

// now evaluate the parametric line when t=.5
// and store the resulting point in pt
Compute_Parm_Line3D(&p, 0.5, &pt);
```

3D Plane Support Functions

Although this might be a little premature, I decided to add some support for the abstract entity of 3D planes to the math engine. In reality, 99% of the time, we'll deal with closed polygons (that lie in planes), so these functions might need to be retrofitted later. Nevertheless, it's nice to be able to define planes and then work with them at least a little bit at this early stage.

I decided to go with the point-normal representation of a plane, which is shown in Figure 5.20.

```
nx*(x-x0) + ny*(y-y0) + nz*(z-z0) = 0
```

where **n** = <nx,ny,nz>, and **p0** = <x0,y0,z0>.

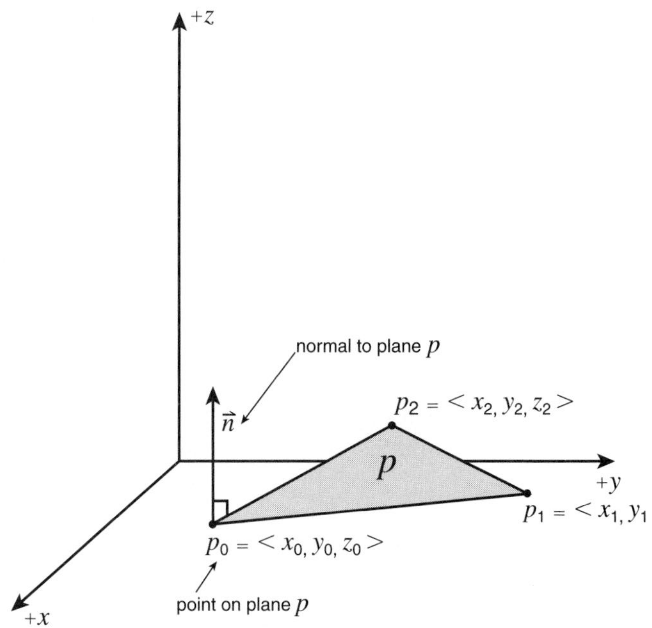

FIGURE 5.20 The point-normal-defined 3D plane.

Basically, in this format, we store a plane by means of its normal and a single point that lies on the plane. The normal need not be a unit normal. Once again, here's the structure for a 3D plane:

```
typedef struct PLANE3D_TYP
{
POINT3D p0; // point on the plane
VECTOR3D n; // normal to the plane (not necessarily a unit vector)
} PLANE3D, *PLANE3D_PTR;
```

Not much to it! Again, many of the functions in a math library just simplify repetitive calculations that you find yourself doing all the time, or ease the representation of mathematical or geometrical objects.

Function Prototype:

```
void PLANE3D_Init(PLANE3D_PTR plane, POINT3D_PTR p0,
             VECTOR3D_PTR normal, int normalize);
```

Purpose:

`void PLANE3D_Init()` initializes a 3D plane with the sent point and normal. Additionally, the function can normalize the sent normal vector and make its length 1.0 for you. To do this, set the parameter normalize to TRUE; otherwise, make it FALSE. This helps in many lighting and back face removal calculations to know that the normal to a polygon or plane has length 1.0.

Example:

```
VECTOR3D n={1,1,1};
POINT3D p={0,0,0};
PLANE3D plane;

// create the plane
PLANE3D_Init(&plane, &p, &n, TRUE);
```

Function Prototype:

```
float Compute_Point_In_Plane3D(POINT3D_PTR pt, PLANE3D_PTR plane);
```

Functional Listing:

```
float Compute_Point_In_Plane3D(POINT3D_PTR pt, PLANE3D_PTR plane)
{
// test if the point in on the plane, in the positive halfspace
// or negative halfspace
float hs = plane->n.x*(pt->x - plane->p0.x) +
      plane->n.y*(pt->y - plane->p0.y) +
      plane->n.z*(pt->z - plane->p0.z);

// return half space value
return(hs);

} // end Compute_Point_In_Plane3D
```

Purpose:

float Compute_Point_In_Plane3D() is a rather interesting function. It computes the half space that the test point lies in. In other words, many times we want to determine whether something is on one side of a plane or the other (or in the plane). That's what this function does. Figure 5.21 illustrates the logic. The function returns 0.0 if the point lies in the plane, a positive number if the point lies in the positive half space (that is, the half space the normal points to), and the function returns a negative number if the point lies in the negative half space. Check out DEMOII5_2.CPP¦EXE; it allows you to define a plane and then send test points to it to determine the half space.

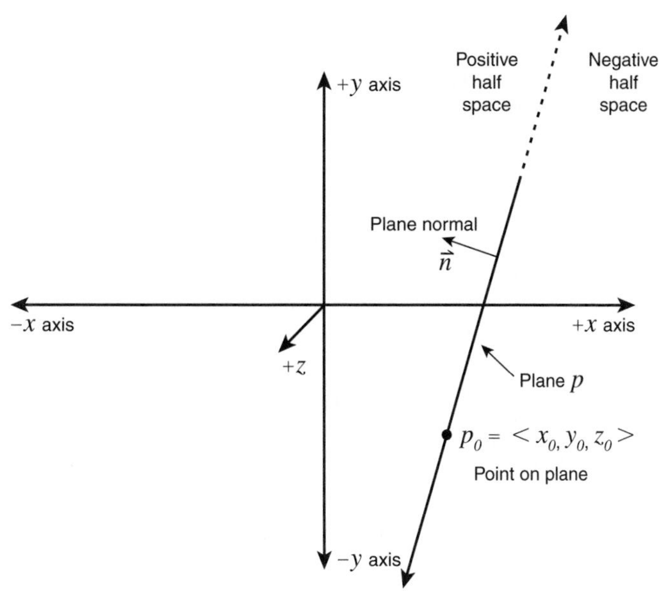

FIGURE 5.21 The half-space logic codes.

Example:

```
VECTOR3D n={1,1,1};
POINT3D p={0,0,0};
PLANE3D plane;

// create the plane
PLANE3D_Init(&plane, &p, &n, TRUE);

// this should be in the positive half space
POINT3D p_test = {50,50,50};

// test the point
float hs = Compute_Point_In_Plane3D(&p_test, &plane);
```

Function Prototype:

```
int Intersect_Parm_Line3D_Plane3D(PARMLINE3D_PTR pline, PLANE3D_PTR plane,
                     float *t, POINT3D_PTR pt);
```

Functional Listing:

```
int Intersect_Parm_Line3D_Plane3D(PARMLINE3D_PTR pline,
                     PLANE3D_PTR plane,
                     float *t, POINT3D_PTR pt)
{
// this function determines where the sent parametric line
// intersects the plane the function will project the line
// infinitely in both directions, to compute the intersection,
// but the line segment defined by p intersected the plane iff t e [0,1]
// also the function returns 0 for no intersection, 1 for
// intersection of the segment and the plane and 2 for intersection
// of the line along the segment and the plane 3, the line lies
// in the plane

// first test of the line and the plane are parallel, if so
// then they can't intersect unless the line lies in the plane!

float plane_dot_line = VECTOR3D_Dot(&pline->v, &plane->n);

if (fabs(plane_dot_line) <= EPSILON_E5)
  {
  // the line and plane are co-planer, does the line lie
  // in the plane?
  if (fabs(Compute_Point_In_Plane3D(&pline->p0, plane)) <= EPSILON_E5)
   return(PARM_LINE_INTERSECT_EVERYWHERE);
  else
   return(PARM_LINE_NO_INTERSECT);
  } // end if

// from chapter 4 we know that we can solve for the t where
// intersection occurs by
// a*(x0+vx*t) + b*(y0+vy*t) + c*(z0+vz*t) + d =0
// t = -(a*x0 + b*y0 + c*z0 + d)/(a*vx + b*vy + c*vz)
// x0,y0,z0, vx,vy,vz, define the line
// d = (-a*xp0 - b*yp0 - c*zp0), xp0, yp0, zp0, define the point on the plane

*t = -(plane->n.x*pline->p0.x +
    plane->n.y*pline->p0.y +
    plane->n.z*pline->p0.z -
    plane->n.x*plane->p0.x -
    plane->n.y*plane->p0.y -
    plane->n.z*plane->p0.z) / (plane_dot_line);
```

```
// now plug t into the parametric line and solve for x,y,z
pt->x = pline->p0.x + pline->v.x*(*t);
pt->y = pline->p0.y + pline->v.y*(*t);
pt->z = pline->p0.z + pline->v.z*(*t);

// test interval of t
if (*t>=0.0 && *t<=1.0)
  return(PARM_LINE_INTERSECT_IN_SEGMENT );
else
  return(PARM_LINE_INTERSECT_OUT_SEGMENT);

} // end Intersect_Parm_Line3D_Plane3D
```

Purpose:

`int Intersect_Parm_Line3D_Plane3D()` computes the intersection of a 3D parametric line and a 3D plane. The parametric value point of intersection is returned in `t` as well as the actual point of intersection in `pt`. However, before these data are used, the return value of `Intersect_Parm_Line3D_Plane3D()` can be tested to determine the details of the intersection. The values are the same as with the 2D intersection function, with the addition of a flag that indicates that the line lies in the plane itself. Here are the flags again for reference:

```
#define PARM_LINE_NO_INTERSECT      0
#define PARM_LINE_INTERSECT_IN_SEGMENT 1
#define PARM_LINE_INTERSECT_OUT_SEGMENT 2
#define PARM_LINE_INTERSECT_EVERYWHERE 3
```

Also take a look at `DEMOII5_3.CPP|EXE` on the CD; it allows you to define a 3D plane and parametric line and then computes their intersection.

Example:

```
POINT3D p1 = {5,5,-5}, p2 = {5,5,5},pt;
PARMLINE3D pl;
float t;

// create a parametric line from p1 to p2
// note this line is parallel to the z-axis
Init_Parm_Line3D(&p1, &p2, &pl);

VECTOR3D n={0,0,1};
POINT3D p={0,0,0};
PLANE3D plane;
```

```
// create the plane, note this plane
// is the x-y plane
PLANE3D_Init(&plane, &p, &n, TRUE);

// compute the point of intersection
// note it should be (5,5,0)
int intersection_type =
   Intersect_Parm_Line3D_Plane3D(&pl, &plane, &t, &pt);
```

Quaternion Support Functions

I have to tell you—writing the quaternion functions wasn't easy! The problem is making sure that they all work. To double-check everything, you have to do it on paper, and because quaternions don't really have a whole lot of physical meaning, you can't do those nice graph paper sanity checks. However, I think I finally have them all working. The only thing I left out is a couple matrix-quaternion conversion functions and spherical linear interpolation (SLERP). We'll add those when we need them, most probably in the camera work and or animation sections of the book. Nonetheless, I really like quaternions because they make many operations so simple. For example, rotation about an arbitrary line is trivial with quaternions, whereas it's a pain with Euler rotations. Anyway, to refresh your memory, a quaternion is a hyper complex number with four components where one of the components is the real part (usually referred to as q0 or w) and the other three components are the imaginary part (usually referred to as q1, q2, q3). Moreover, quaternions are usually written in one of the following ways:

$$\mathbf{q} = q_0 + q_1*\mathbf{i} + q_2*\mathbf{j} + q_3*\mathbf{k}$$

or

$$\mathbf{q} = q_0 + \mathbf{q}_v, \text{ where } \mathbf{q}_v = q_1*\mathbf{i} + q_2*\mathbf{j} + q_3*\mathbf{k}$$

So, we basically need to keep track of four floating-point numbers, and we should be able to access them in a number of ways. The data structure `QUAT` in the following code implements this functionality with a number of unions:

```
typedef struct QUAT_TYP
{
union
  {
  float M[4]; // array indexed storage w,x,y,z order

  // vector part, real part format
  struct
     {
     float  q0; // the real part
```

```
        VECTOR3D qv; // the imaginary part xi+yj+zk
        };
    struct
        {
        float w,x,y,z;
        };
    }; // end union

} QUAT, *QUAT_PTR;
```

With this structure, we can access the quaternion as an array, as a real and a vector, and as four unique identifiers. This makes writing various algorithms a snap! Anyway, here are the quaternion functions:

Function Prototypes:

```
void VECTOR3D_Theta_To_QUAT(QUAT_PTR q, VECTOR3D_PTR v, float theta);

void VECTOR4D_Theta_To_QUAT(QUAT_PTR q, VECTOR4D_PTR v, float theta);
```


Functional Listing:

```
void VECTOR3D_Theta_To_QUAT(QUAT_PTR q, VECTOR3D_PTR v, float theta)
{
// initializes a quaternion based on a 3d direction vector and angle
// note the direction vector must be a unit vector
// and the angle is in rads

float theta_div_2 = (0.5)*theta; // compute theta/2

// compute the quaternion, note this is from chapter 4
// pre-compute to save time
float sinf_theta = sinf(theta_div_2);

q->x = sinf_theta * v->x;
q->y = sinf_theta * v->y;
q->z = sinf_theta * v->z;
q->w = cosf( theta_div_2 );

} // end VECTOR3D_Theta_To_QUAT
```

Purpose:

`void VECTOR*D_Theta_To_QUAT()` creates a rotation quaternion based on a direction vector, `v`, and an angle, `theta`. Figure 5.22 illustrates the relationship. This function is primarily used to create quaternions for rotations of points. Note that the direction vector v must be a unit vector. Also, the 4D vector version disregards the w component of the vector.

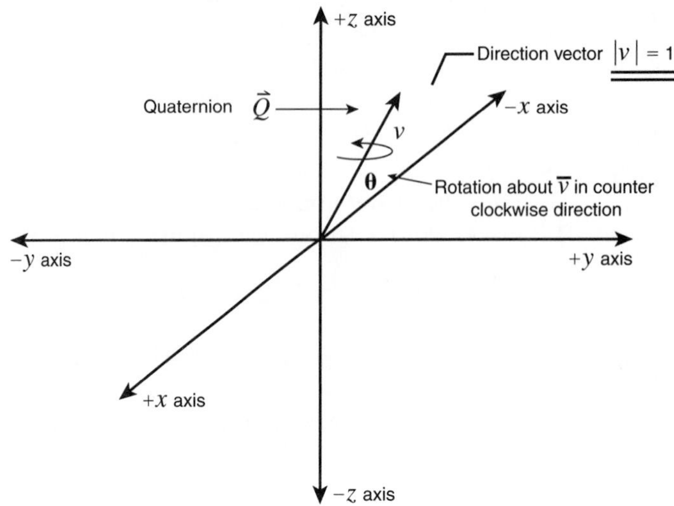

FIGURE 5.22 The rotation quaternion construction.

Example:

```
// create the vector to rotate about
// in this case the diagonal of the unit cube
// for octant 1
VECTOR3D v={1,1,1};
QUAT qr;

// normalize v
VECTOR3D_Normalize(&v);

float theta = DEG_TO_RAD(100); // 100 degrees

// create a rotation quaternion about v
// with angle theta
VECTOR3D_Theta_To_QUAT(&q, &v,theta);
```

Function Prototype:

```
void EulerZYX_To_QUAT(QUAT_PTR q, float theta_z, float
theta_y, float theta_x);
```

Functional Listing:

```
void EulerZYX_To_QUAT(QUAT_PTR q, float theta_z, float theta_y, float theta_x)
{
// this function initializes a quaternion based on the zyx
// multiplication order of the angles that are parallel to the
// zyx axis respectively, note there are 11 other possibilities
// this is just one, later we may make a general version of the
// the function

// precompute values
float cos_z_2 = 0.5*cosf(theta_z);
float cos_y_2 = 0.5*cosf(theta_y);
float cos_x_2 = 0.5*cosf(theta_x);

float sin_z_2 = 0.5*sinf(theta_z);
float sin_y_2 = 0.5*sinf(theta_y);
float sin_x_2 = 0.5*sinf(theta_x);

// and now compute quaternion
q->w = cos_z_2*cos_y_2*cos_x_2 + sin_z_2*sin_y_2*sin_x_2;
q->x = cos_z_2*cos_y_2*sin_x_2 - sin_z_2*sin_y_2*cos_x_2;
q->y = cos_z_2*sin_y_2*cos_x_2 + sin_z_2*cos_y_2*sin_x_2;
q->z = sin_z_2*cos_y_2*cos_x_2 - cos_z_2*sin_y_2*sin_x_2;

} // EulerZYX_To_QUAT
```

Purpose:

`void EulerZYX_To_QUAT()` creates a rotation quaternion based on the Euler angles parallel to the z, y, and x axes, respectively. This is your basic camera transform. Of course, there are a total of six ways (permutations = 3!) to multiply x*y*z together, but this is the most common. Use this function to convert your Euler rotation angles to a quaternion.

Example:

```
QUAT qzyx;

// create rotation angles
float theta_x = DEG_TO_RAD(20);
float theta_y = DEG_TO_RAd(30);
float theta_z = DEG_TO_RAD(45);

// create rotation quaternion
EulerZYX_To_QUAT(&qzyx,theta_z,theta_y,theta_x);
```

5

Function Prototype:

```
void QUAT_To_VECTOR3D_Theta(QUAT_PTR q, VECTOR3D_PTR v, float *theta);
```

Functional Listing:

```
void QUAT_To_VECTOR3D_Theta(QUAT_PTR q, VECTOR3D_PTR v, float *theta)
{
// this function converts a unit quaternion into a unit direction
// vector and rotation angle about that vector

// extract theta
*theta = acosf(q->w);

// pre-compute to save time
float sinf_theta_inv = 1.0/sinf(*theta);

// now the vector
v->x   = q->x*sinf_theta_inv;
v->y   = q->y*sinf_theta_inv;
v->z   = q->z*sinf_theta_inv;

// multiply by 2
*theta*=2;

} // end QUAT_To_VECTOR3D_Theta
```

Purpose:

`void QUAT_To_VECTOR3D_Theta()` converts a unit rotation quaternion into a unit 3D vector and a rotation angle theta about that vector. This function is basically the opposite of `VECTOR*D_Theta_To_QUAT()`.

Example:

```
QUAT q;
// assume q now has a unit rotation quaternion in it

// storage for the vector and angle
float theta;
VECTOR3D v;

// now convert the quat to a vector and an angle
QUAT_To_VECTOR3D_Theta(&q, &v, &theta);
```

Function Prototype:

```
void QUAT_Add(QUAT_PTR q1, QUAT_PTR q2, QUAT_PTR qsum);
```

Purpose:

void QUAT_Add() adds the quaternions q1 and q2 and stores the sum in qsum.

Example:

```
QUAT q1 = {1,2,3,4}, q2 = {5,6,7,8}, qsum;

// add em
QUAT_Add(&q1, &q2, &qsum);
```

Function Prototype:

```
void QUAT_Sub(QUAT_PTR q1, QUAT_PTR q2, QUAT_PTR qdiff);
```

Purpose:

void QUAT_Sub() subtracts the quaternion q2 from q1 and stores the difference in qdiff.

Example:

```
QUAT q1 = {1,2,3,4}, q2 = {5,6,7,8}, qdiff;

// subtract em
QUAT_Sub(&q1, &q2, &qdiff);
```

Function Prototype:

```
void QUAT_Conjugate(QUAT_PTR q, QUAT_PTR qconj);
```

Purpose:

void QUAT_Conjugate() computes the conjugate of the quaternion q and returns in qconj.

Example:

```
QUAT q = {1,2,3,4}, qconj;

// compute conjugate
QUAT_Conjugate(&q, &qconj);
```

Function Prototype:

```
void QUAT_Scale(QUAT_PTR q, float scale, QUAT_PTR qs);
```

Purpose:

`void QUAT_Scale()` scales the quaternion `q` by the factor `scale` and stores the result in `qs`.

Example:

```
QUAT q = {1,2,3,4}, qs;

// scale q by 2
QUAT_Scale(&q, 2, &qs);
```

Function Prototype:

```
void QUAT_Scale(QUAT_PTR q, float scale);
```

Purpose:

`void QUAT_Scale()` scales the quaternion `q` by the factor `scale` in place; that is, it modifies `q` directly.

Example:

```
QUAT q = {1,2,3,4};

// scale q by 2
QUAT_Scale(&q, 2);
```

Function Prototype:

```
float QUAT_Norm(QUAT_PTR q);
```

Purpose:

`float QUAT_Norm(QUAT_PTR q)` returns the norm of the quaternion `q`; that is, its length.

Example:

```
QUAT q = {1,2,3,4};

// whats the length of q?
float qnorm = QUAT_Norm(&q);
```

Function Prototype:

```
float QUAT_Norm2(QUAT_PTR q);
```

Purpose:

`float QUAT_Norm2(QUAT_PTR q)` returns the norm squared of the quaternion `q`; that is, its length squared. This function is useful because many times we need the norm of a quaternion squared. Thus, calling QUAT_Norm2() rather than calling QUAT_Norm() and then squaring the return value saves us both a sqrt() call and a multiplication.

Example:

```
QUAT q = {1,2,3,4};

// whats the length of q*q?
float qnorm2 = QUAT_Norm2(&q);
```

Function Prototype:

```
void QUAT_Normalize(QUAT_PTR q, QUAT_PTR qn);
```

Purpose:

void QUAT_Normalize() normalizes the quaternion q and sends the result back in qn.

> **TIP**
>
> Remember, all rotation quaternions must be unit quaternions.

Example:

```
QUAT q = {1,2,3,4}, qn;

// normalize q
QUAT_Normalize(&q, &qn);
```

Function Prototype:

```
void QUAT_Normalize(QUAT_PTR q);
```

Purpose:

void QUAT_Normalize() normalizes the quaternion q in place; that is, it modifies q itself.

Example:

```
QUAT q = {1,2,3,4};

// normalize q in place
QUAT_Normalize(&q);
```

Function Prototype:

```
void QUAT_Unit_Inverse(QUAT_PTR q, QUAT_PTR qi);
```

Purpose:

void QUAT_Unit_Inverse() computes the inverse of the quaternion q and returns the result in qi. However, q must be a unit quaternion for the function to work because the function is based on the fact that the inverse of a unit quaternion is its conjugate.

Example:

```
QUAT q = {1,2,3,4}, qi;

// normalize q first
QUAT_Normalize(&q);

// now compute inverse
QUAT_Unit_Inverse(&q, &qi);
```

Function Prototype:

```
void QUAT_Unit_Inverse(QUAT_PTR q);
```

Purpose:

void QUAT_Unit_Inverse() computes the inverse of the quaternion q in place, modifying q. However, q must be a unit quaternion for the function to work because the function is based on the fact that the inverse of a unit quaternion is its conjugate.

Example:

```
QUAT q = {1,2,3,4};

// normalize q first
QUAT_Normalize(&q);

// now compute inverse
QUAT_Unit_Inverse(&q);
```

Function Prototype:

```
void QUAT_Inverse(QUAT_PTR q, QUAT_PTR qi);
```

Purpose:

void QUAT_Inverse() computes the inverse of a general non-unit quaternion q and returns the result in qi.

Example:

```
QUAT q = {1,2,3,4}, qi;

// now compute inverse
QUAT_Inverse(&q, &qi);
```

Function Prototype:

```
void QUAT_Inverse(QUAT_PTR q);
```

Purpose:

void QUAT_Unit_Inverse() computes the inverse of a general non-unit quaternion q in place, modifying q.

Example:

```
QUAT q = {1,2,3,4};

// now compute inverse
QUAT_Inverse(&q);
```

Function Prototype:

```
void QUAT_Mul(QUAT_PTR q1, QUAT_PTR q2, QUAT_PTR qprod);
```

Functional Listing:

```
void QUAT_Mul(QUAT_PTR q1, QUAT_PTR q2, QUAT_PTR qprod)
{
// this function multiplies two quaternions

// this is the brute force method
//qprod->w = q1->w*q2->w - q1->x*q2->x - q1->y*q2->y - q1->z*q2->z;
//qprod->x = q1->w*q2->x + q1->x*q2->w + q1->y*q2->z - q1->z*q2->y;
//qprod->y = q1->w*q2->y - q1->x*q2->z + q1->y*q2->w - q1->z*q2->x;
//qprod->z = q1->w*q2->z + q1->x*q2->y - q1->y*q2->x + q1->z*q2->w;

// this method was arrived at basically by trying to factor the above
// expression to reduce the # of multiplies

float prd_0 = (q1->z - q1->y) * (q2->y - q2->z);
float prd_1 = (q1->w + q1->x) * (q2->w + q2->x);
float prd_2 = (q1->w - q1->x) * (q2->y + q2->z);
float prd_3 = (q1->y + q1->z) * (q2->w - q2->x);
float prd_4 = (q1->z - q1->x) * (q2->x - q2->y);
float prd_5 = (q1->z + q1->x) * (q2->x + q2->y);
float prd_6 = (q1->w + q1->y) * (q2->w - q2->z);
float prd_7 = (q1->w - q1->y) * (q2->w + q2->z);

float prd_8 = prd_5 + prd_6 + prd_7;
float prd_9 = 0.5 * (prd_4 + prd_8);

// and finally build up the result with the temporary products
```

```
qprod->w = prd_0 + prd_9 - prd_5;
qprod->x = prd_1 + prd_9 - prd_8;
qprod->y = prd_2 + prd_9 - prd_7;
qprod->z = prd_3 + prd_9 - prd_6;

} // end QUAT_Mul
```

Notice that at first I was using the brute-force method of multiplying the quaternions by the definition of multiplication (16 multiplications, 12 additions); and then with some algebra, I simplified the multiplication to 9 multiplications and 27 additions. Normally, you might think this is better, but that might not be the case on floating-point processors.

Purpose:

`void QUAT_Mul()` multiplies the quaternion q1*q2 and stores the result in `qprod`.

Example:

```
QUAT q1={1,2,3,4}, q2={5,6,7,8}, qprod;

// multiply q1*q2
QUAT_Mul(&q1, &q2, qprod);
```

> **CAUTION**
>
> The product `q1*q2` is not equal to `q2*q1` unless `q1` or `q2` is the multiplicative identity. Hence, multiplication is non-commutative for quaternions in general.

Function Prototype:

```
void QUAT_Triple_Product(QUAT_PTR q1, QUAT_PTR q2, QUAT_PTR q3, QUAT_PTR qprod);
```

Purpose:

`void QUAT_Triple_Product()` multiplies the three quaternions `q1*q2*q3` and stores the result in `qprod`. This function is useful for rotating points because the transform ($\mathbf{q}^*$)*($\mathbf{v}$)*($\mathbf{q}$) and ($\mathbf{q}$)*($\mathbf{v}$)*($\mathbf{q}^*$) are triple products that rotate vectors or points.

Example:

```
// let rotate the point (5,0,0)
// around the z-axis 45 degrees

// Step 1: create the rotation quaternion
VECTOR3D vz = {0,0,1};
```

```
QUAT qr, // this will hold the rotation quaternion
   qrc; // this will hold its conjugate

// create the rotation quaternion
VECTOR3D_Theta_To_QUAT(&qr, &vz, DEG_TO_RAD(45));

// now its conjugate
QUAT_Conjugate(&qr, &qrc);

// now create a the point to rotate with the q0
// element equal to 0 and the x,y,z as the point
QUAT qp={0,5,0,0};

// now we do the rotation which will rotate
// p about the z-axis 45 degrees, of course
// the rotation axis could have been anything
QUAT_Triple_Product(&qr, &qp, &qrc, &qprod);

// now the result will still have q0=0,
// so we can just extract the point from the
// x,y,z elements of the quaternion
```


Function Prototype:

```
void QUAT_Print(QUAT_PTR q, char *name);
```

Purpose:

`void QUAT_Print()` prints out a quaternion with the given name to the error file.

Example:

```
// set error file to screen
Open_Error_File("", stdout);

QUAT q={1,2,3,4};

QUAT_Print(&q);

// close the error file
Close_Error_File();
```

As a demo of some of the quaternion functions, check out `DEMOII5_4.CPP|EXE`. It enables you to enter a pair of quaternions and a point in 3D space, and then perform various operations on them and see the results.

Fixed-Point Math Support Functions

Although we didn't cover fixed-point math in the previous chapter, I felt the desire to add some functions to work with it just for the heck of it. If you're rusty on the topic, I refer you to the first *Tricks* for a more detailed discussion. Additionally, on Pentium+ processors, the floating-point unit(s) is as fast or faster than the integer unit(s), thus using fixed-point isn't needed to perform 3D math anymore. However, there are many times that you can write a really optimal algorithm that uses both the floating-point and integer units at the same time, so knowing how to represent and work with fixed-point is still a good thing.

In general, fixed-point is an old trick used on slower processors to perform multiplication and division using integers, but have decimal precision. The trick is using a "fixed point" that's artificially placed somewhere in the binary representation of a number, therefore breaking a number into both a whole part and a decimal part. For the representation for this iteration of the engine, I keep the format first created in the first *Tricks* of 16.16, meaning 16 bits of whole part and 16 bits of decimal part. That means that numbers can be represented that are signed in the magnitude range of +-32768, and a decimal accuracy of $1/2^{16}$.

Now the question is, how to represent a fixed-point number? The answer is just with a standard `int` or `long` data type (if you needed 64 bits, you would use `long`). So, the types in `T3DLIB4.H` define this for us:

```
typedef int FIXP16;
typedef int *FIXP16_PTR;
```

And in `T3DLIB1.H`, there are some legacy constants:

```
// fixed point mathematics constants
#define FIXP16_SHIFT    16
#define FIXP16_MAG      65536
#define FIXP16_DP_MASK  0x0000ffff
#define FIXP16_WP_MASK  0xffff0000
#define FIXP16_ROUND_UP 0x00008000
```

which just simplify working with fixed-point numbers.

Creating a Fixed-Point Number from an Integer

To create a fixed-point number from an integer, all you have do is shift the integer `FIXP16_SHIFT` times to the left, which places the integer in the whole part section of the fixed-point number. But remember not to overflow the fixed-point number. Here's an example:

```
FIXP16 fp1 = (100 << FIXP16);
```

And, of course, there's a macro called `INT_TO_FIXP16()` for this in the header file that does the same thing.

Creating a Fixed Point Number From a Float

Creating a fixed-point number from a float is a little trickier because the binary representation of an integer and a float are fairly alien to each other. So, what we need to do is scale the float by the equivalent magnitude that we shift the integers by. That is, we shift an `int` by 16 places to convert it to a fixed-point number. What we're really doing is multiplying the `int` by $2^{16} = 65536$. So, if we simply multiply the float we want to convert by 65536.0 and then convert it to an `int`, that will do the trick. Here's an example:

```
FIXP16 fp1 = (int)(100.5*65536.0);
```

Notice that we don't shift because the multiplication does that for us, in a manner of speaking. Of course, there's a macro for this called *`FLOAT_TO_FIXP16()`*, which is also in the header and performs the same function. However, you might want to round the number because part of it will be truncated during the conversion to an `int`. Hence, the addition of 0.5 before the conversion helps with loss of data and the final macro does this, which performs something like this:

```
FIXP16 fp1 = (int)(100.5*65536.0+0.5);
```


Converting Back to Floating-Point

If you do want to convert back to floating point, you simply need to extract the whole part of the fixed-point number, which isn't hard to do because it's in the upper 16 bits and it's in normal binary integer format. However, getting the decimal part out is a bit tricky. What you need to do is divide the decimal part by the magnitude it was scaled by originally, which is 65536. However, if you don't want to extract both the whole part and decimal part as separate entities, you can covert a fixed-point number to a float with the following transform:

```
float ((float)fp)/65536.0;
```

which is coded in the macro `FIXP16_TO_FLOAT()`.

Now, as a quick refresher, given two fixed-point numbers, here are the basic operations and how they have to be carried out.

Addition/Subtraction To add or subtract two numbers that are already in fixed-point format, you simply add or subtract them as you normally would. For example:

```
FIXP16 fp1 = FLOAT_TO_FIX(10.5);
FIXP16 fp2 = FLOAT_TO_FIX(20.7);

FIXP16 fpsum = fp1 + fp2;
FIXP16 fpdiff = fp1 - fp2;
```

As a more illustrative example, look at this:

```
int x=50, y=23;

// convert x,y to fixed point 16.16 format
FIXP16 fpx = x*65536;
FIXP16 fpy = y*65536;
FIXP16 fsum;

// now lets add them
fsum = fpx + fpy;
```

which simplifies to

```
fsum = x*65536 + y*65536 = (x+y)*65536;
```

Therefore, the result does indeed sum (x+y) and has the proper scale of 65536. The proof for subtraction is similar.

Multiplication Multiplication of fixed-point numbers is a little tricky. The reason why is that each number is scaled by a factor. In the case of 16.16 format, each fixed-point number is scaled by 65536. Thus, if we multiply two fixed-point numbers, we need to make sure that the result is scaled by only 65536 and not $(65536)^2$! The following example illustrates the problem by using a numeric example:

```
// numbers we are going to convert to fixed point
int x=50, y=23;

// convert x,y to fixed point 16.16 format
FIXP16 fpx = x*65536;
FIXP16 fpy = y*65536;
```

Now, the problem occurs when we try to multiply (`fpx*fpy`). If we look at the numeric results, we get this:

```
fpx*fpy = (x*65536) * (y*65536) = (x*y)*(65536*65536);
```

See the problem? The answer is scaled by 65536^2, rather than 65536. The solution is to simply scale the result back. However, the problem with that is that the act of multiplying the two fixed-point numbers (and then scaling after the fact) actually overflows a 32-bit number. Therefore, our only options are to use 64-bit math (which we'll see momentarily) or to pre-scale down both the multiplier and the multiplicand before the multiplication so that the resulting product is scaled by only 65536. Here's one way of doing it:

```
 = (fpx/256)*(fpy/256)
```

Substituting x,y:

```
= ((x*65536)/256) * ((y*65536)/256)
= (x*256)*(y*256) = (x*y)*65536
```

This is correct, but the problem with this approach is that during the scale down, we lose 8 bits of accuracy of both the multiplier and multiplicand, which isn't acceptable because that's the whole point of fixed-point math: to keep the decimal point accuracy. However, we can save the day with 64-bit math using assembly language.

Division Division has the same problem as multiplication does, but it's in reverse. The problem is when one fixed-point number is divided by another, the decimal portion is lost. That is, the scale of the result is 1.0, rather than 65536. Here's an example to illustrate this:

```
// numbers we are going to convert to fixed point
int x=50, y=23;

// convert x,y to fixed point 16.16 format
FIXP16 fpx = x*65536;
FIXP16 fpy = y*65536;
```

Now, let's divide and see what happens:

```
fpx/fpy = (x*65536) / (y*65536) = (x/y);
```

That's definitely not good. Again, we have a dilemma and there are two ways to solve it. We can use 64-bit division in assembly language, or we can pre-scale the numerator and denominator so that the results of the division are scaled by 65536. But again, we're trapped to the constraints of 32-bit math if we use the type `int`. Scaling the numerator up means losing accuracy on the whole part, and scaling the denominator down means losing accuracy on the decimal part, but that's our only choice. So, we can scale up the numerator by 256 (8-bits) and scale down the denominator by 256 (8-bits), and the result will be properly scaled by 65536. However, during the scaling transform, we turn the numerator from 16.16 into 8.16 and the denominator into 16.8, which means that if we want to handle signed numbers, the numerator can't be larger than 255 and the denominator can't be smaller than $1/2^8 \approx 0.0039$.

Here's our example fixed to work:

```
// numbers we are going to convert to fixed point
int x=50, y=23;

// convert x,y to fixed point 16.16 format
FIXP16 fpx = x*65536;
FIXP16 fpy = y*65536;
```

5

Now, let's divide with the scaling factors and see what happens:

```
= (x*256*65536) / (y*65536/256)
= (x*256*256/y)*65536/65536
= (x/y)*(256*256) = (x/y)*65536
```

TIP

These examples illustrate that there's no rule that states all fixed-point numbers have to be 16.16; some of your numbers may be 16.16, some 24.8, and still others 0.32. The point is that as long as you keep track of the decimal and overflow and underflow, the math will work out.

With all that in mind, let's take a look at the functions along with their assembly language internals.

Function Prototype:

```
FIXP16 FIXP16_MUL(FIXP16 fp1, FIXP16 fp2);
```

Function Listing:

```
FIXP16 FIXP16_MUL(FIXP16 fp1, FIXP16 fp2)
{
// this function computes the product fp_prod = fp1*fp2
// using 64 bit math, so as not to loose precision

FIXP16 fp_prod; // return the product

_asm {
   mov eax, fp1    // move into eax fp2
   imul fp2       // multiply fp1*fp2
   shrd eax, edx, 16 // result is in 32:32 format
            // residing at edx:eax
            // shift it into eax alone 16:16
   // result is sitting in eax
   } // end asm

} // end FIXP16_MUL
```

The assembly language is pretty straightforward; the only interesting thing is that the Intel 32-bit processors have support for 64-bit math!

Purpose:

`FIXP16 FIXP16_MUL()` multiplies the two fixed-point numbers `fp1*fp2` using 64-bit math and returns the result. Note that there's no loss of accuracy because 64-bit math is used.

Example:

```
FIXP16 fp1 = FLOAT_TO_FIX(10.5);
FIXP16 fp2 = FLOAT_TO_FIX(20.7);

// do the multiply
FIXP16 fpprod = FIXP16_Mul(fp1,fp2);
```

Function Prototype:

```
FIXP16 FIXP16_DIV(FIXP16 fp1, FIXP16 fp2);
```

Function Listing:

```
FIXP16 FIXP16_DIV(FIXP16 fp1, FIXP16 fp2)
{
// this function computes the quotient fp1/fp2 using
// 64 bit math, so as not to loose precision

_asm {
   mov eax, fp1    // move dividend into eax
   cdq         // sign extend it to edx:eax
   shld edx, eax, 16 // now shift 16:16 into position in edx
   sal eax, 16     // and shift eax into position since the
            // shld didn't move it -- DUMB! uPC
   idiv fp2      // do the divide
   // result is sitting in eax
   } // end asm

} // end FIXP16_DIV
```

The division algorithm is a little tricky. The main point is that first the dividend must be sign extended to 64 bits, and the 64-bit shifts to place the dividend properly are a little contrived since the 64-bit double-shift instructions don't shift the source register `eax`—it stays in place. Thus, we need an extra shift to place it after the initial 64-bit shift. Refer to any Intel assembly language manual for more details on these stupid 64-bit shifts that do half a job!

Purpose:

`FIXP16 FIXP16_DIV()` divides `fp1/fp2` and returns the result. Note that the function uses 64-bit math, so there's no loss of accuracy.

5

Example:

```
FIXP16 fp1 = FLOAT_TO_FIX(10.5);
FIXP16 fp2 = FLOAT_TO_FIX(20.7);

// do the divide
FIXP16 fpdiv = FIXP16_Mul(fp1,fp2);
```

> **NOTE**
>
> Although fixed-point math used to blow the doors off floating-point math, as you can see, there are quite a few instructions involved to perform both the multiplication and division. The rule of thumb is this. Fixed-point addition and subtraction are usually the same speed as floating-point; floating-point multiplication and division are, amazingly enough, as fast or faster than fixed-point.

Function Prototype:

```
void FIXP16_Print(FIXP16 fp);
```

Purpose:

`void FIXP16_Print()` prints out a fixed-point number as if it were a floating-point number.

Example:

```
FIXP16 fp1 = FLOAT_TO_FIX(10.5);
FIXP16_Print(fp1);
```

Finally, make sure to check out `DEMOII5_5.CPP|EXE` on the CD. It enables you to enter two floating-point values, converts them to fixed-point, performs all the operations on them, and prints the results so that you can see the accuracy.

Equation Solving Support

This next pair of functions is really cool. They enable you to solve systems of equations of the form **A*X** = **B**. All you need is the coefficient matrix **A** and the constant matrix **B**, and if a solution exists, the functions will find it. For example, given the 3x3 system:

```
3*x + 2*y - 5*z = 6
 x - 3*y + 7*z = -4
5*x + 9*y - 2*z = 5
```

We deduce that

```
     |3   2  -5|
A =  |1  -3   7|
     |5   9  -2|

X = [x y z]^t

B = [6 -4 6]^t
```

And we can use the transform **X** = **A**$^{-1}$***B**. This is exactly what the solvers do, more or less.

Function Prototype:

```
int Solve_2X2_System(MATRIX2X2_PTR A, MATRIX1X2_PTR X, MATRIX1X2_PTR B);
```

Function Listing Reference:

```
int Solve_2X2_System(MATRIX2X2_PTR A, MATRIX1X2_PTR X, MATRIX1X2_PTR B)
{
// solves the system AX=B and computes X=A(-1)*B
// by using cramers rule and determinates

// step 1: compute determinate of A
float det_A = Mat_Det_2X2(A);

// test if det(a) is zero, if so then there is no solution
if (fabs(det_A) < EPSILON_E5)
  return(0);

// step 2: create x,y numerator matrices by taking A and
// replacing each column of it with B(transpose) and solve
MATRIX2X2 work_mat; // working matrix

// solve for x /////////////////

// copy A into working matrix
MAT_COPY_2X2(A, &work_mat);

// swap out column 0 (x column)
MAT_COLUMN_SWAP_2X2(&work_mat, 0, B);

// compute determinate of A with B swapped into x column
float det_ABx = Mat_Det_2X2(&work_mat);
```

```
// now solve for X00
X->M00 = det_ABx/det_A;

// solve for y ////////////////

// copy A into working matrix
MAT_COPY_2X2(A, &work_mat);

// swap out column 1 (y column)
MAT_COLUMN_SWAP_2X2(&work_mat, 1, B);

// compute determinate of A with B swapped into y column
float det_ABy = Mat_Det_2X2(&work_mat);

// now solve for X01
X->M01 = det_ABy/det_A;

// return success
return(1);

} // end Solve_2X2_System
```

Purpose:

`int Solve_2X2_System()` solves the system of equations **A*X** = **B**, where **A** is 2×2, **X** is 1×2, and **B** is 1×2. If the solution exists, it is returned in **B** and the function returns a `1`; otherwise, the function returns a `0` and **B** is undefined. Also, take a look at the function listing to see what's going on inside. Basically, Cramer's rule is used to solve the system. `Solve_2X2_System()` is a good example of many matrix functions being used, so pay close attention. Also take a look at `DEMOII5_6.CPP|EXE` on the CD—it enables you to enter a system of equations and solves it for you!

Example:

`DEMOII5_6.CPP` allows you to input the coefficient matrix **A** along with constant matrix **B**, and then solves the system **A*X** = **B** with Cramer's rule. The following is a code dump of the main calls:

```
void main()
{
MATRIX2X2 mA;
MATRIX1X2 mB;
MATRIX1X2 mX;

// open the error system, so we can see output
```

```
// notice the last parameter "stdout" this tell the error
// system that we don't want to write errors to a text file
// but straight out to the screen!
Open_Error_File("", stdout);

// get matrix A
printf("\nEnter the values for the matrix A (2x2)");
printf("\nin row major form m00, m01, m10, m11?");
scanf("%f, %f, %f, %f", &mA.M00, &mA.M01, &mA.M10, &mA.M11);

printf("\nEnter the values for matrix B (2x1)");
printf("\nin column major form m00, m10?");
scanf("%f, %f", &mB.M00, &mB.M01);

// technically you can't multiply a 2x2 * 1x2,
// but you can multiply is a 2x2 * (1x2)t
// that is the transpose of a 1x2 is a 2x1,
// bottom line is the B matrix is just 2 numbers!

// now solve the system
if (Solve_2X2_System(&mA, &mX, &mB))
  {
  // now print results
  VECTOR2D_Print((VECTOR2D_PTR)&mX, "Solution matrix mX");
  } // end if
else
  printf("\nNo Solution!");

// close the error system
Close_Error_File();

} // end main
```

Function Prototype:

```
int Solve_3X3_System(MATRIX3X3_PTR A, MATRIX1X3_PTR X, MATRIX1X3_PTR B);
```

Purpose:

`int Solve_3X3_System()` solves the system if equations **A*X** = **B** where **A** is 3×3, **X** is 1×3, and **B** is 1×3. If the solution exists, it's returned in **B** and the function returns a `1`; otherwise, the function returns a `0` and **B** is undefined.

5

Example:

```
MATRIX3X3 mA = {1,2,9, 4,-3,6, 1,0,5};
MATRIX1X3 mB = {1,2,3};
MATRIX1X3 mX;

// solve the system
if(Solve_3X3_System(&mA, &mX, &mB))
  {
  // now print results
  VECTOR3D_Print((VECTOR3D_PTR)&mX, "Solution matrix mX");
  } // end if
else
  printf("\nNo Solution!");
```

Floating-Point Unit Math Primer

The old 80387 and internal math co-processor of PentiumX (FPU unit) are probably some of the most mysterious components of the PC's processing suite. To tell you the truth, it's next to impossible to find any good references on FPU programming other than a couple hard-to-find books and the Intel Instruction set docs. However, that's all going to change right now.

NOTE

These days, new generations of Pentium processors may have more than one FPU, so I'm going to generically refer to floating-point programming and floating-point co-processors as the FPU.

We're going to delve into the FPU at least to the point that we understand what's going on and how to actually program it using its own instruction set. Of course, the C/C++ compiler you're using generates FPU instructions when you compile code that uses floating-point operations. However, this code can be optimized in many cases with assembly language and full 64-bit instructions as our 64-bit multiply and divide illustrated using the integer unit to do fixed-point math.

Now, there's one other gotcha. On the Pentium models with MMX support, the FPU registers are aliased to the MMX registers, meaning that you can't mix MMX code and FPU code without doing a lot of context switching. Now, I'm not going to talk about MMX programming since it's its really added instructions to perform SIMD (single instruction multiple data) processing and really is a topic unto itself and better explained in a optimization book. If you're interested, Intel has a nice *MMX Programming Guide* that you can obtain from the developers section of Intel's site.

So, how does the FPU work? First, from a programming point of view, it doesn't matter whether there's one or more FPUs, whether they're internal or external (high-performance

FPUs), the instruction sets are roughly the same. At least the most common operations are, which is what we're interested in learning.

CAUTION

FPU programming must be done at the assembly language level. But we're going to at least use the inline assembler, so even if you aren't an assembly language guru, learning FPU programming is fairly easy because it's like a little computer with a stack—nothing more.

The FPU Architecture

The FPU is a stack-based machine that has only one mission in life: to compute mathematical floating-point calculations for the CPU core. Figure 5.23 shows the abstract model of the FPU in relationship to the CPU core. Basically, all instructions that the CPU comes across that are meant for the FPU are sent to the FPU where they are executed. Hence, FPU instructions don't directly affect the CPU or its internal registers. Many times the CPU's integer unit and FPU can't work at the same time, but in most cases, the CPU and FPU can work in parallel—especially with U-V pipe architectures like the Pentium. On more advanced models of the Pentium, things get a little weird, so you might want to read up on the Pentium I, II, III, Pro, and all the other flavors, since I gave up trying to keep up with all the rules!

Anyway, FPU can perform many common mathematical operations such as addition, subtraction, multiplication, and division. However, it's also equipped to handle logarithmic, transcendental, numerical conversions, and more. Furthermore, the FPU can actually perform many operations faster than the equivalent integer unit with much higher accuracy. Even in the cases in which the FPU is slower than pure integer operations using the integer unit, it might be worth the extra accuracy—especially in 3D graphics.

Programming the FPU is actually very simple. It has its own instruction set, which we'll cover shortly. Basically, whenever you want a FPU instruction to be executed, you simply place it in your code right with the other assembly language instructions. This brings us to a little problem, and that's that most FPU programming must be done using assembly language and, hence, either external assembly functions or inline (I prefer the inline). However, when I want to write a function that uses the FPU directly, I usually code the entire thing using inline assembly. But of course I do this for little functions that must run very quickly, not 500-line-long, high-level functions.

NOTE

When you set the compiler to high optimization and inline FPU instructions, it does a very good job at emitting FPU code that's nearly optimal.

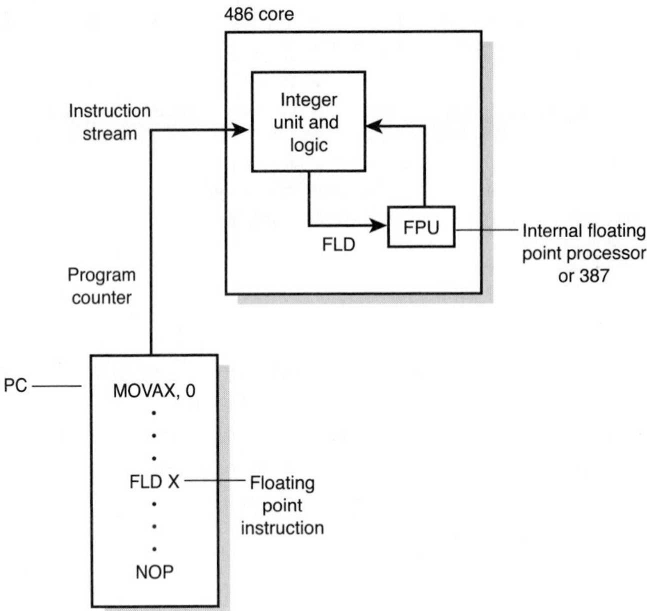

FIGURE 5.23 The floating-point processor performs all floating-point math.

The FPU Stack

Let's talk about the internal stack of the FPU since it's the basis of how everything works. Basically, there are eight stack elements in the FPU and a status word, as shown in Figure 5.24. Each stack element is 80 bits wide with 64 bits for the decimal part, 14 bits for the exponent, and 1 bit for the sign bit.

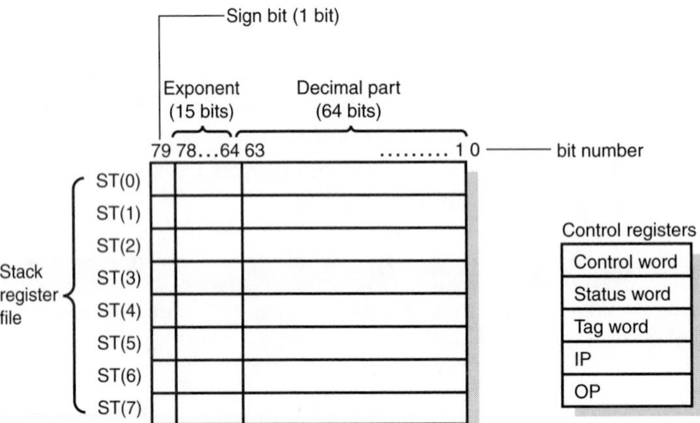

FIGURE 5.24 The FPU core architecture.

However, each stack element can hold different data types, as shown in Figure 5.25. We see that there are short, long, and 10-byte real numbers. The stack elements are used to hold inputs and return outputs; thus, they are the working registers for the FPU, in a sense. We can think of them as a register file, or we can think of them as a stack.

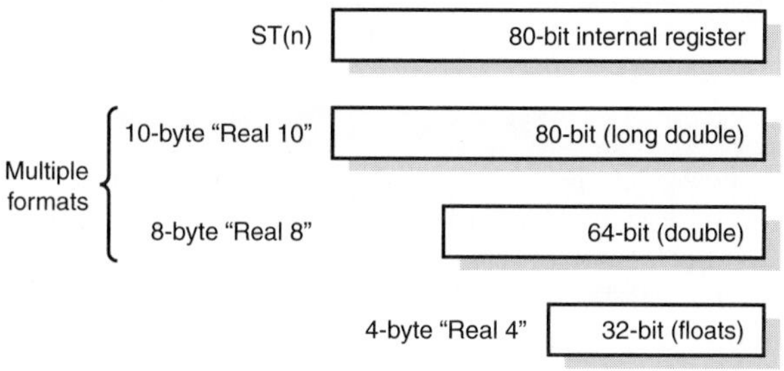

FIGURE 5.25 FPU data formats.

In any case, the stack is referred to using the syntax `ST(n)`, where *n* is the element. For example, take a look at Figure 5.26.

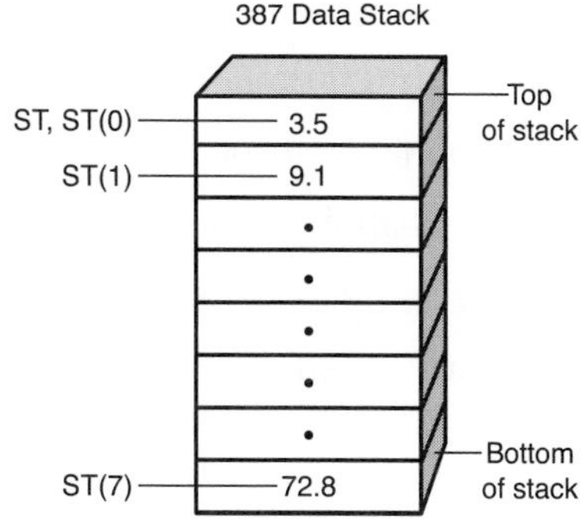

FIGURE 5.26 The FPU stack ordering and access.

Some examples:

`ST` is equivalent to the top of stack (TOS).

`ST(0)` is equivalent to the top of stack.

`ST(1)` is equivalent to the second element of the stack.

`ST(7)` is equivalent to the last element of the stack or element 8.

When programming the FPU, many of the instructions take zero, one, or two operands. This means that sometimes the operand(s) are implied. Also, the operands can either be constants, memory, or stack elements in most cases, so we have a bit of flexibility in defining what the data is for an operation. Furthermore, many of the instructions place the result on the top of the stack at `ST(0)`. This is a good thing to know if you're expecting some piece of data to remain valid after an operation and it gets obliterated.

Now that we have a bit of an idea of what the FPU does and how it does it, let's take a look at the instruction set and see how to use it.

NOTE

Because there are new Pentium processors popping up all the time, an exhaustive list of FPU instructions is pointless. Instead, Table 5.1 lists the majority of commonly used instructions that you'll probably never use more than 10% of anyway.

The FPU Instruction Set

The FPU is a complete processor with a rather large instruction set. The instructions fall into a few categories, they are

- Data Transfer—Used to move data between CPU and FPU
- Arithmetic—Used to perform standard arithmetic operations
- Transcendental—Used for non-linear operations, such as sin, cos, and so on
- Constants—Used to load commonly used constants such as 1, pi, and so on
- Comparison—Used to compare floating-point numbers
- Control—Used the control and set the state of the FPU

I don't know about you, but I like to see an instruction set first before I learn about it just to get a feel for what's what! Therefore, Table 5.1 lists all the FPU instructions available with a short description of what they do.

TABLE 5.1 The FPU Co-processor Instruction Set

Instruction Name	Description
Data Transfer Instructions	
FBLD	Loads a BCD number
FBSTP	Stores and pops a BCD number
FILD	Loads an integer
FIST	Stores an integer
FISTP	Stores an integer and pops the stack
FLD	Loads a real number
FSTP	Stores a real number and pops the stack
FXCH	Exchanges two stack elements

TABLE 5.1 Continued

Instruction Name	Description
Arithmetic Instructions	
FABS	Computes the absolute value
FADD	Adds real numbers
FIADD	Adds integers
FADDP	Adds real numbers and pops the stack
FCHS	Changes the sign of a number
FDIV	Divides real numbers
FIDIV	Divides integers
FDIVP	Divides real numbers and pops the stack
FDIVR	Divides real numbers, but reverses which operand is dividend and divisor
FIDIVR	Divides integers, but reverses which operand is dividend and divisor
FDIVRP	Divides real numbers and pops the stack, but reverses which operand is dividend and divisor
FMUL	Multiplies real numbers
FIMUL	Multiplies integers
FMULP	Multiples real numbers and pops the stack
FPREM	Computes partial remainder
FPREM1	Computes partial remainder using IEEE format
FRNDINT	Rounds the operand to an integer
FSCALE	Scales by a power of two
FSUB	Subtracts real numbers
FISUB	Subtracts integers
FSUBP	Subtracts real numbers and pops the stack
FSUBR	Subtracts real numbers, but reverses which operand is subtractor and subtrahend
FISUBR	Subtracts integers, but reverses which operand is subtractor and subtrahend
FSUBRP	Subtracts real numbers and pops the stack, but reverses which operand is subtractor and subtrahend
FSQRT	Computes the square root
FXTRACT	Extracts the exponents and signific and from real number
Transcendental Instructions (Note: all angles must be in radians)	
F2XM1	Computes the value (2*x-1)
FCOS	Computes the cosine
FPATAN	Computes the partial arctangent
FPTAN	Computes the partial tangent
FSIN	Computes the sine
FSINCOS	Computes both the sine and cosine
FYL2X	Computes the expression $y*\log_2 x$
FYL2XP1	Computes the expression $y*\log_2 (x+1)$

TABLE 5.1 Continued

Instruction Name	Description
Constants	
FLD1	Loads a 1.0
FLDL2E	Loads $\log_2 e$
FLDL2T	Loads $\log_2 10$
FLDLG2	Loads $\log_{10} 2$
FLDPI	Loads pi
FLDZ	Loads zero
Comparison Operators	
FCOM	Compares reals
FCOMP	Compares reals and pops the stack
FCOMPP	Compares reals and pops the stack twice
FICOM	Compares integers
FICOMP	Compares integers and pops the stack
FTST	Compares the top of stack to zero
FUCOM	Performs unordered compare
FUCOMP	Performs unordered compare along with a pop
FUCOMPP	Performs an unordered compare along with two pops
FXAM	Examine `st(0)` and place results in condition register
Control Instructions	
FCLEX	Clears all unmasked floating-point exceptions
FNCLEX	Clears all exceptions
FDECSTP	Decrements the stack pointer
FFREE	Clears a stack element making it seem like it was popped
FINCSTP	Increments stack pointer
FINIT	Initializes FPU and checks for exceptions
FNINIT	Initializes FPU without checking for exceptions
FLDCW	Loads the control word
FLDENV	Loads the FPU environment
FNOP	Equivalent to NOP
FRSTOR	Restores the state of the FPU with a given memory area
FSAVE	Saves the state of the FPU into a memory area, but checks for exceptions
FNSAVE	Saves the state of the FPU into a memory area without checking for exceptions
FSTCW	Stores the control word and checks exceptions
FNSTCW	Stores the control word without checking exceptions
FSTENV	Stores the environment and checks exceptions
FNSTENV	Stores the environment without checking exceptions
FSTSW	Stores the status word and checks exceptions
FNSTSW	Stores the status word without checking exceptions
FSTSW AX	Stores the status word into AX and checks exceptions
FNSTSW AX	Stores the status word into AX without checking exceptions
WAIT	Suspends CPU until FPU is complete with operation

Because there are so many instructions, listing an example of each of them would take up too much time; instead, Table 5.2 lists the general format of most instructions. Using this table, you should be able to deduce what the legal operands are for a particular instruction.

TABLE 5.2 The Operand Formats for the FPU

Instruction Format	Syntax Operands	Implied
Classical	`Finstruction`	ST,ST(1)
Memory	`Finstruction`	ST
	`memory_operand`	
Register	`Finstruction ST(n), ST`	None
	`Finstruction ST,ST(n)`	None
Register Pop	`FinstructionP ST(n),ST`	None

NOTE

Notice that all the FPU instructions start with a leading F and, in the case of register pop format, the instructions end with a P. Now let's discuss each of the instruction formats, so we know how to use them in programs.

Classical Instruction Format

The classical format treats the FPU's stack as if it were a classic stack. Meaning that all operations refer to the top of stack ST(0) and the second element ST(1). For example, if an addition is requested using the instruction:

```
FADD
```

then the operation that would be performed is ST(0) = ST(0) + ST(1). Therefore, the top of the stack would be replaced by the sum of the topmost two items, as shown in Figure 5.27. In general, classical instructions use ST(0) and ST(1) if two operands are needed, and ST(0) if only one is needed. If the instruction uses two operands, the source topmost operand is typically popped off the stack and the result is placed at the top also.

Memory Instruction Format

The memory instruction format is similar to the classical format in that the stack is still treated like a stack. However, memory format allows memory items to be pushed on the stack and popped off the stack into memory. For example, we might want to load the top of the stack with a memory operand like this:

```
FLD memory
```

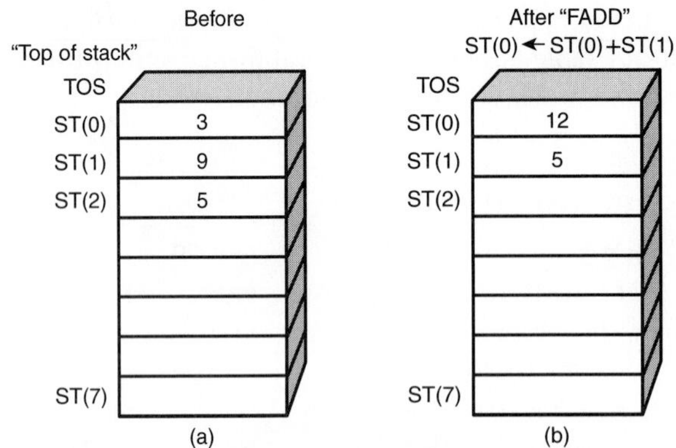

FIGURE 5.27 An example of a classical stack instruction.

And if we wanted to pop the top of stack into a memory location, we could write

```
FSTP memory
```

The results of both of these instructions are shown in Figure 5.28.

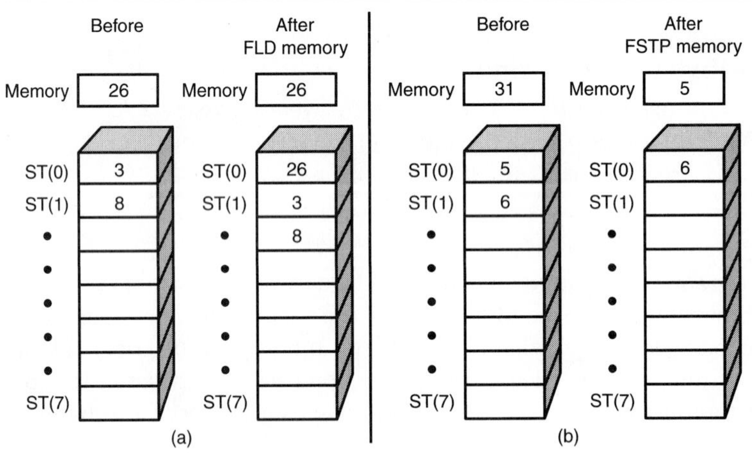

FIGURE 5.28 Examples of memory instruction format.

Register Instruction Format

The register instruction format simply allows the stack elements (registers) to be explicitly referred to. For example, say we want to add `ST(0)` and *`ST(4)`* together. We could write

```
FADD ST(0), ST(4)
```

and the top of stack would hold the sum of `ST(0) + ST(4)`, as is shown in Figure 5.29. Also, when using register instruction format with two operand forms, one of the operands must be the top of stack `ST(0)` or its abbreviation, `ST`.

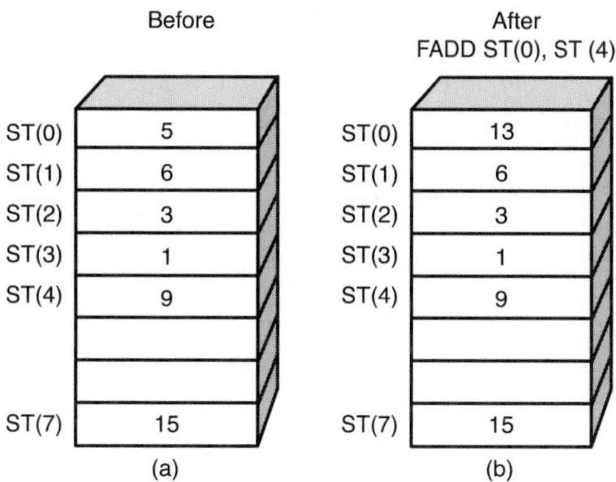

FIGURE 5.29 An example of register instruction format.

Register Pop Instruction Format

The register pop format is identical to the register instruction format except that after the result has been placed into the stack, the stack is popped once.

FPU Examples

Even though we aren't going to look at all the instructions the FPU has to offer, we'll take a look at some of the most representative instructions you'll need. They are

- `FLD`—In all its forms
- `FST`—In all its forms
- `FADD`—In all its forms
- `FSUB`—In all its forms
- `FMUL`—In all its forms
- `FDIV`—In all its forms

Also, the format of each instruction will be

1. Description
2. Instruction syntax and operands (if any)

FLD Examples

The FLD instruction and its various forms is used to load reals (FLD), integers (FILD), and constants such as pi (FLDPI). The FLD instruction has the following formats:

Load a real number:

FLD *op1*

32-bit short real

64-bit long real

80-bit temporary real

ST(n)

Load an integer:

FILD *op1*

16-bit word integer

32-bit short integer

64-bit long integer

Load a constant:

FLDcon

where *con* is the suffix that determines the constant to load. Refer to the section on constants in Table 5.1.

Let's see some examples now. To load a real 32-bit number from memory, we could write

```
FLD memory32
```

After the execution of the instruction, the top of stack ST(0) would contain the value in memory32. Figure 5.30a shows this.

To load a standard binary 16-bit integer in the FPU, we can write

```
FILD memory16
```

After the instruction executes the top of the stack would hold the 16-bit integer in IEEE format as shown in Figure 5.30b.

NOTE

All integers are converted to reals when processed by the floating-point processor.

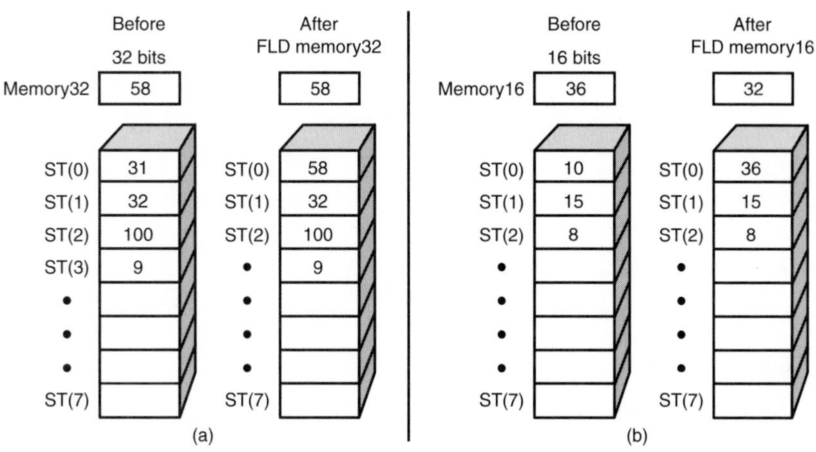

FIGURE 5.30 Examples of the load instruction.

FST Examples

The FST instruction is used to store reals (FST) and integers (FIST). Also, a P can be appended to both instructions, which instructs the FPU to pop the top of stack will after the store is executed. In essence, the top of stack ST(0) is stored into the destination and the stack pointer is adjusted when P is added to the instructions. The FST instruction has the following formats:

Store a real number:

FST *op1*

32-bit short real

64-bit long real

ST(n)

Store a real number and pop the stack:

FSTP *op1*

32-bit short real

64-bit long real

ST(n)

Round the top of stack and store it:

```
FIST    op1
```

16-bit word integer

32-bit short integer

64-bit long integer

Round the top of stack, pop, and store it:

```
FISTP   op1
```

16-bit word integer

32-bit short integer

64-bit long integer

Also, the top of the stack is always implied to be the source; hence *op1* is the destination. With that in mind, let's see some examples. To store the top of the stack in a standard floating-point location, we could write

```
FST memory32
```

The results of this are shown in Figure 5.31a; notice that the top of stack is not modified. On the other hand, if we were to execute this instruction:

```
FSTP memory32
```

the top of the stack would be popped into `memory32`. Now let's try some integer examples. If we wanted to store the top of the stack into a 32-bit integer, we could write

```
FIST memory32
```

and the value in the top of the stack would be converted to an integer by rounding and stored into `memory32` as shown in Figure 5.31b. `FISTP` works in the same way except the top of stack is popped as shown in Figure 5.31c.

FADD Examples

The `FADD` instruction adds two reals (`FADD`) or adds two integers (`FIADD`). Also, a `P` can be appended to the real version (`FADDP`) that pops the stack after the addition. However, this feature isn't supported for the integer version. The `FADD` instruction has the following forms:

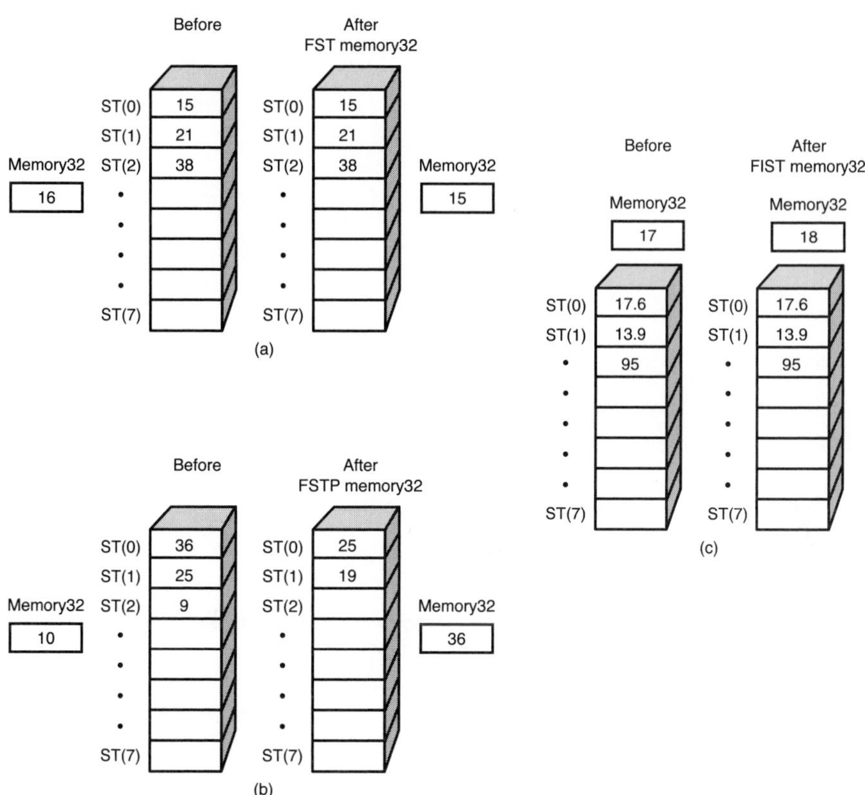

FIGURE 5.31 Examples of the store instructions.

Implied operands are `ST(0)` *and* `ST(1)`*. Also, the stack is popped after the addition.*

```
FADD
```

The top of stack is implied as the destination and one `memory32` *of the operands.*

```
FADD    op1
        memory64
        ST(n)
```

One of the operands must still be the top of stack `ST`*, but the destination need not be.*

```
FADD    op1, op2
        ST(n), ST
        ST, ST(n)
```

The operands are added and the result is popped off the top of stack.

```
FADDP   op1, op2
        ST(n), ST
        ST, ST(n)
```

The integer referred to by *op1* is converted to a real and added to the top of stack.

```
FIADD   op1
        memory16
        memory32
```

Alrighty then! Seems easy enough. Let's try some examples. First, let's add the two top most elements of the stack. The following instructions are equivalent:

```
FADD ST(1)

FADD ST,ST(1)
```

Figure 5.32a shows the results of executing either of the preceding instructions. As you can see, the top of the stack is obliterated with the sum.

However, if we were to use this instruction:

```
FADD ST(2), ST
```

the sum of ST(0) and ST(2) would be stored into ST(2) because it's the destination and ST(0) would be unscathed. This is shown in Figure 5.32b. Next, let's try one of the integer forms. Say we wanted to add a 32-bit integer number from memory with the top of the stack ST(0). We could use the following instruction:

```
FIADD memory32
```

The value within memory32 would be converted to a real and then added to ST(0). The result would be placed back into ST(0) as shown in Figure 5.32c. However, if we wanted to pop the top of stack after the addition, we would have to use a real addition because popping isn't supported after integer addition. But we could pop the stack manually with the instruction:

```
FINCSTP
```

Now let's put together a little program that adds two reals and stores the result in a 32-bit integer. Here's the code:

```
float fvalue_1 = 100.2;
float fvalue_2 = 50.5;
int ivalue_1 = 0;
```

```
_asm {
   FLD fvalue_1  // load the first 4 byte real
   FADD fvalue_2  // load and add second 4 byte real
   FISTP ivalue_1 // store the top of stack into the 4
          // byte integer
   } // end asm
```

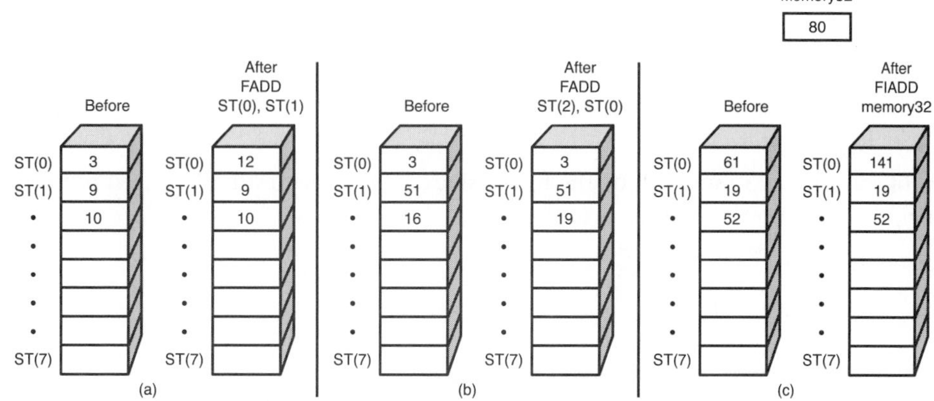

FIGURE 5.32 Examples of the add instructions.

Figure 5.33 shows the program executing step by step.

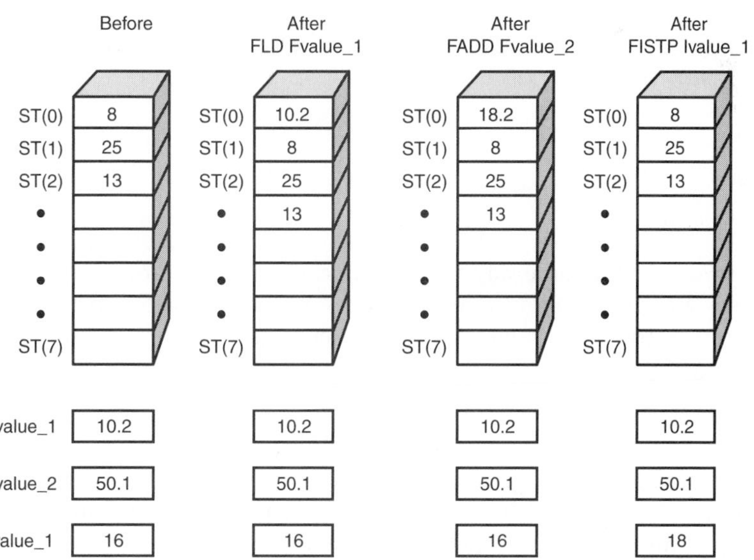

FIGURE 5.33 Execution of a floating-point program and the stack.

FSUB Examples

Implied operand and order are (ST(1) - ST(0)). Also, the stack is popped after the subtraction.

```
FSUB
```

The top of stack is implied as the destination and one of the operands; hence, the operation is (ST(0) – op1).

```
FSUB    op1
        memory32
        memory64
        ST(n)
```

One of the operands must still be the top of stack ST, but the destination need not be. Again, the operation performed is (*op1* - *op2*).

```
FSUB    op1, op2
        ST, ST(n)
        ST(n), ST
```

The expression (op1 - op2) is computed and the result is popped off the top of stack.

```
FSUBP   op1, op2
        ST, ST(n)
        ST(n), ST
```

The integer referred to by op1 is converted to a real and subtracted from the top of stack. The result is, of course, placed in ST(0).

```
FISUB   op1
        memory16
        memory32
```

Subtraction works in the same way as addition, except that the source and destination operands play a more important role because (a-b) is different from (b-a). That is, you need to keep an eye on the order in which the subtraction takes place! For example, the following instruction:

```
FSUB memory32
```

subtracts memory32 from the top of stack ST(0). That is, ST(0) = ST(0) - memory32, as is shown in Figure 5.34a. As another example, imagine that we wanted to subtract an integer from the top of the stack ST(0) (maybe to compute the decimal part). We could use this instruction:

```
FISUB memory16
```

and the top of stack would have the results `ST(0) - (real)(memory16)`, as shown in Figure 5.34b. Again, we see that all integers are converted into reals before they are used in calculations.

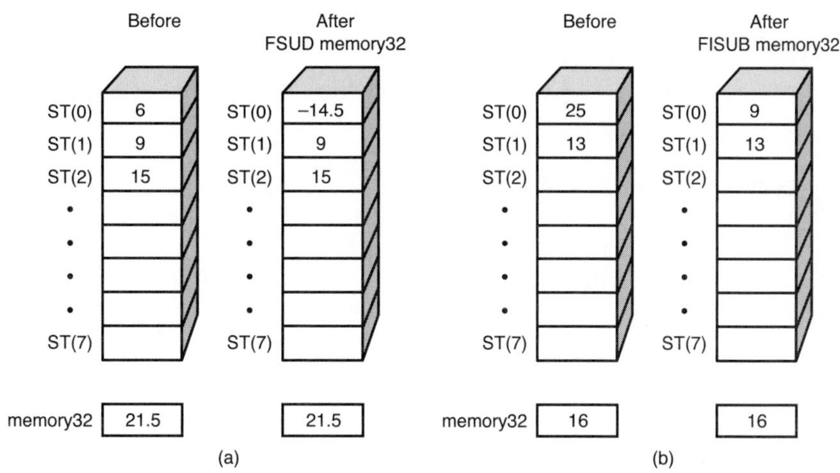

FIGURE 5.34 Examples of the subtract instructions.

`FMUL` Examples

The `FMUL` instruction is very similar to the `FADD` instruction. It can multiply two reals (`FMUL`), an integer and a real (`FIMUL`), and as usual, a `P` can be appended to the real version of the instruction (`FMULP`), which pops the stack after the multiplication. The *`FMUL`* instruction has the following forms:

Implied operand are `ST(0) * ST(1)`. Also, the stack is popped after the multiplication.

```
FMUL
```

The top of stack is implied as the destination and one of the operands.

```
FMUL    op1

        memory32

        memory64

        ST(n)
```

One of the operands must still be the top of stack `ST`, but the destination need not be.

```
FMUL    op1, op2

        ST, ST(n)

        ST(n), ST
```

The operands are multiplied and the result is popped off the top of stack.

```
FMULP   op1, op2
        ST, ST(n)
        ST(n), ST
```

The integer referred to by `op1` *is converted to a real and multiplied by the top of stack.*

```
FIMUL   op1
        memory16
        memory32
```

Hmmm … I'm running out of examples! Let's say that we wanted to do something useful, like compute 5!, which is read as "five factorial" and is equal to 5*4*3*2*1. This little program would do the trick:

```
_asm {
   FLD f_1 // load 1.0 into stack
   FLD f_2 // load 2.0 into stack
   FLD f_3 // load 3.0 into stack
   FLD f_4 // load 4.0 into stack
   FLD f_5 // load 5.0 into stack
   FMUL    // 5*4
   FMUL    // 5*4*3
   FMUL    // 5*4*3*2
   FMUL    // 5*4*3*2*1

    // top of stack ST(0) has 5*4*3*2*1 in it.
    } / /end asm
```

Figure 5.35 shows the factorial process and the stack, step-by-step, as the algorithm runs.

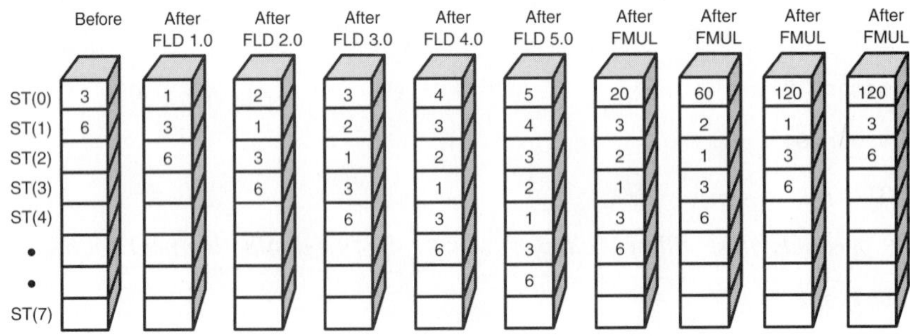

FIGURE 5.35 The stack step-by-step during a factorial calculation.

FDIV Examples

The final class of instruction we're going to look at is the division instruction: FDIV. It's similar to the subtraction instruction in that the order of operands makes a difference; that is, a/b, is different from b/a. As you would expect, the instruction has all the forms: real, integer, and stack popping. Here are the formats for review:

Implied operands are ST(1)/ST(0); also the stack is popped after the division.

```
FDIV
```

The top of stack is implied as the destination and one of the operands.

```
FDIV    op1
        memory32
        memory64
        ST(n)
```

One of the operands must still be the top of stack ST, but the destination need not be.

```
FDIV    op1, op2
        ST, ST(n)
        ST(n), ST
```

The operands op1/op2 are divided and the result is popped off the top of stack.

```
FDIVP   op1, op2
        ST, ST(n)
        ST(n), ST
```

The integer referred to by op1 is converted to a real and divided into the top of stack.

```
FIDIV   op1
        memory16
        memory32
```

As an example, let's use the formula:

```
velocity = distance/time
```

Let's see how long it takes to get to the moon with your average, run-of-the-mill rocket engine:

```
// Distance to moon: 250,000 miles
float f_dist = 250000.0;
```

5

```
// Velocity of Value Space Ship: 35,000 mph
float f_vel = 35000;

// the time?
float f_time;

_asm {
   FLD f_dist    // load the distance
   FDIV f_vel     // divide by velocity
   FSTP f_time    // store the result into f_time and pop
   // the stack
   } // end asm

printf("\ntime =%f",f_time);
```

TRICK

Notice how easy it is to mix C/C++ with inline asm and FPU code—pretty cool, huh?

When the code exits, `f_time` will have roughly 7.14 hours in it. Totally unacceptable. I much prefer space/time folding—that is, gravity drive—wherever you want to be, there you are. This was the idea behind the movie *Event Horizon*. Anyway, that's enough for floating-point! We'd better stop before we end up with a book within a book.

Notes on Using the Math Engine

Using the math engine in your programs is just like any other library module. However, there are a couple things to watch out for. First, the math engine is based on some legacy code from `T3DLIB1.CPP¦H`. Thus, you must make sure to include the header `T3DLIB1.H` in your programs that use the math library along with the C++ file `T3DLIB1.CPP`. However, you would do this anyway. Additionally, `T3DLIB1.CPP¦H` is based on DirectX 8.0+, so it needs `DDRAW.H` included for type info. The bottom line is that if you want to make a standalone `CONSOLE` math application, you need the following:

Source Files

`T3DLIB1.CPP`

`T3DLIB4.CPP`

Header Files

`T3DLIB1.H`

`T3DLIB4.H`

`DDRAW.H`

Library Files

N/A

Of course, you need to include the normal headers, too, if you want to make a standalone application. Don't forget to `#define INITGUID`; otherwise, the linker won't be able to find the DirectDraw stuff and bark at you even though you aren't doing any DirectDraw stuff with a standalone math application. Remember, `T3DLIB1.CPP¦H` needs DirectDraw types, and `T3DLIB4.CPP¦H` needs `T3DLIB1.CPP¦H`. For example, the test application I used to develop the math engine was a `CONSOLE` application with this header:

```
#define WIN32_LEAN_AND_MEAN

#ifndef INITGUID
#define INITGUID    // you need this or DXGUID.LIB
#endif

#include <windows.h>  // include important windows stuff
#include <windowsx.h>
#include <mmsystem.h>
#include <objbase.h>
#include <iostream.h> // include important C/C++ stuff
#include <conio.h>
#include <stdlib.h>
#include <malloc.h>
#include <memory.h>
#include <string.h>
#include <stdarg.h>
#include <stdio.h>
#include <math.h>
#include <io.h>
#include <fcntl.h>
#include <direct.h>
#include <wchar.h>

#include <ddraw.h>    // needed for defs in T3DLIB1.H
#include "T3DLIB1.H"  // T3DLIB4 is based on some defs in this
#include "T3DLIB4.H"
```

But of course, most of your applications will use the entire game library, so you would include the following:

5

Source Files

T3DLIB1.CPP	Graphics and utility support
T3DLIB2.CPP	Input support
T3DLIB3.CPP	Sound and music support
T3DLIB4.CPP	Math engine

Header Files

T3DLIB1.H

T3DLIB2.H

T3DLIB3.H

T3DLIB4.H

Library Files

DDRAW.LIB	DirectDraw
DSOUND.LIB	DirectSound
DINPUT.H	DirectInput
DINPUT8.H	DirectInput
DMKSCTRL.H	DirectMusic
DMUSICI.H	DirectMusic
DMUSICC.H	DirectMusic
DMUSICF.H	DirectMusic
WINMM.LIB	Windows multimedia extensions (Visual C++ users only)

I shouldn't have to tell you how to compile, but if you need yet another refresher course, take a look at Appendix B, "Installing DirectX Using the C/C++ Compiler," on compiling DirectX applications.

The Game Console

Because we have a new library module, we should update our game console template to reflect the addition of the new header files (that's about all there is to it). The new game console is named T3DCONSOLE3.CPP and the only thing I did to the file was add this line to the header section:

```
#include "T3DLIB4.h"
```

Other than that, the file is the same as version T3DCONSOLE2.CPP.

Comments on Math Optimization

The code from this chapter is reasonable solid algorithm-wise; that is, we used Taylor series for distance calculations, co-factor expansions to compute determinates, and so forth. The only speed-ups we can get are really in the low-level implementations of the functions by taking advantage of loop unrolling, using algebra to simplify calculations, collect terms, and so forth. Also, you'll notice in many algorithms I first compute the inverse of something and then multiply by it rather then dividing anywhere in the function.

TIP

Division will always suck on computers!

However, as I've mentioned, the best ways to optimize are at the algorithmic level or at the level where you can trade prior knowledge to make assumptions and, hence, gain speed. For example, we're going to be doing a ton of matrix multiplying. It doesn't take too much to realize that we're performing a lot of useless multiplies with most of the transformation matrices since they are so sparse; that is, they have lots of zeros in them. This is a common optimization. But, at some point, we can't make the algorithms any faster and inline assembly is the only way. Nevertheless, I'll be quite surprised if we need to go that far in the book to get the performance we need. I have high hopes for the C/C++ compiler's optimizer!

In closing, in terms of optimization, write clean code and strong algorithms, and then low-level optimize at the end.

Summary

Well, after this chapter, you should have nightmares about vector and matrices forever! That's such a nice thought—in an *Addams Family* kind of way <BG>. In any case, we covered a lot of ground, and you basically got a lot of code dumped on you. Normally, I would feel bad about this much code, but this is a programming book, and everything in this chapter is just the C/C++ version of what we talked about in the previous chapter. The header file macros are the only thing that I didn't cover line by line, but you shouldn't have any trouble figuring them out. Bottom line is, when you're coding using the math engine (if you want to use it), chances are I already wrote the function or macro you're looking for, so make sure to take a look before making it yourself.

The only problem I foresee in the near future is cornering ourselves with any particular system of representation; that is, should we use 3D points or homogenous 4D points? We'll just have to see, but at least we know how to handle them both. In reality, we're going to use 4x3 and 4x4 matrices, so technically we're going to work with homogenous points with an assumed w = 1 or a real w as a 4-tuple. But, I can't decide, so why try?

Finally, I can't overstate how helpful the TI-89/92 calculator was in writing this chapter, because it helped me check my work. If you're going to write any math functions, I highly recommend that you buy a calculator that can perform matrix, vector, and symbolic calculations so you can check your algorithms with test data. When writing the quaternion code, this was even more useful, because quaternions really have no visualization to speak of; that is, they're totally mathematical.

Boy, that was a long summary, huh? Weird…But then again, which way does a water vortex around down a sink if you're at the north pole, south pole, and equator? Think about it….

CHAPTER 6

Introduction to 3D Graphics

IN THIS CHAPTER

- 3D Engine Philosophy
- The Structure of a 3D Game Engine
- 3D Engine
- Game Engine
- 3D Coordinate Systems
- Basic 3D Data Structures
- 3D Tools
- Loading Data from the Outside World
- Basic Rigid Transformations and Animation
- Review of the Viewing Pipeline
- Types of 3D Engines
- Putting It All Together

"You aren't afraid of the dark, are you?"

—Riddick, *Pitch Black*

In this chapter, we're going to cover a lot of general ground on 3D graphics, so think of it as an executive summary with details. Then in the remaining chapters, we're going to focus on each of the main areas of expertise relative to 3D graphics. This chapter is an introduction, so I'm not going to get too freaky, but it's also a crash course in 3D, so you can get a feel for the whole process of 3D rather than having to read the whole book before you get the big picture. With that in mind, we're going to cover a number of topics, some with lots of detail, and some with very little detail. By the end of the chapter, you will have a good idea of what the remainder of the book is about. Here's the hit list:

- 3D engine philosophy
- The structure of a 3D game engine
- 3D coordinate systems
- Basic 3D data structures
- Transformations and basic animation
- Introduction to the viewing pipeline
- Types of 3D engines
- 3D tools
- Loading data from the outside world
- Putting it all together

3D Engine Philosophy

The primary goal of this book is to teach you 3D graphics—not how to use APIs and accelerators. Now, I want to be clear what that means. This book will give you the fundamental knowledge to create your own 3D graphics engine. This means that by the end of the book you will know every single step to creating a 3D engine from data representation, to final rasterization. In essence, if you got a job at NVIDIA, ATI, and so on, you would be able to create an entire engine API and underlying software algorithms that would then be implemented by hardware state machines. On the other hand, this book is *not* going to teach you how to use 3D APIs like Direct3D or OpenGL—they are cool, but if you really want to understand 3D, you need to understand how to write Direct3D or OpenGL yourself—and that's what I'm after. Bottom line is that I want you to be able to sit down on any machine on the planet with nothing more than the address of the video buffer and be able to write a software-based 3D engine. If you can do that, learning any 3D API will be trivial.

The Structure of a 3D Game Engine

There's a lot more to writing a 3D engine than writing a 3D engine! Because we are game programmers, the point of writing a 3D engine is to use it to render a 3D game. What this means is that the game engine, physics system, AI, and most of the game must all be integrated with the 3D engine itself. Otherwise, there's going to be lots of problems. Therefore, when you write a production 3D engine, you need to think about the relationship of the 3D engine and the game engine and how they are going to interact together, or else you will end up with a mess in the end. Figure 6.1 depicts a structural chart of some of the relationships a 3D game needs to have:

- 3D engine
- Game engine
- Input system and networking
- Animation system
- Collision detection and navigation system
- Physics engine
- Artificial intelligence system
- 3D model and imagery database

As you can see, there are a lot of things to think about! In a simple 2D game, collision detection, artificial intelligence (AI), and database issues are all fairly straightforward, but in a 3D game, you really have to think about these things. Of course, in this book we are focusing on the 3D engine part, but the others are obviously of concern. Let's talk about each of these and some issues you have to keep in mind with each.

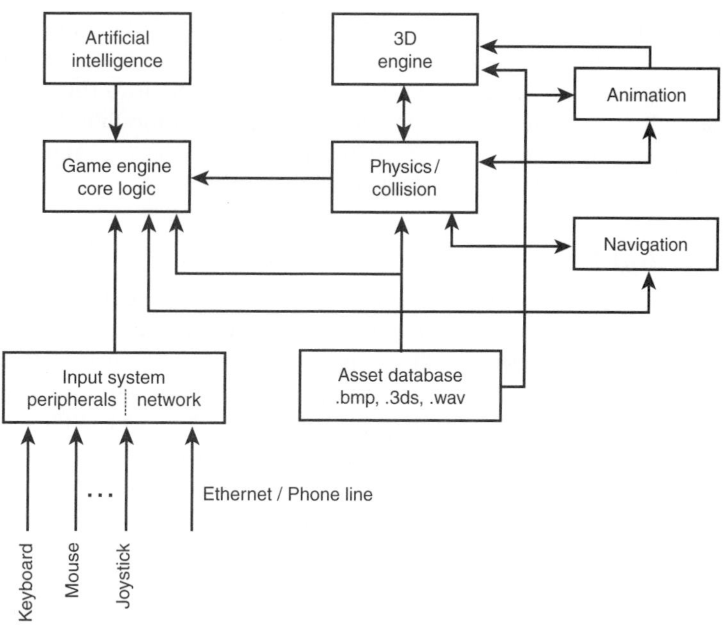

FIGURE 6.1 Structure of a general 3D game engine.

3D Engine

The 3D engine itself is the software that processes the 3D world's data structures, including all the lights, actions, and general state information, and renders the world from the viewpoint of the player or camera. This is relatively straightforward if the engine is designed in a modular way, such that there aren't lots of interrelationships with the 3D engine and the other game subsystems. One of the biggest mistakes you can make when writing a 3D engine is not making it solely responsible for 3D rendering. For example, it's tempting to do the physics modeling in the 3D engine code along with the 3D graphics—this is a big mistake! Another example might be to put some networking hooks in the 3D engine to help simplify your network—that's another no-no.

TIP

The 3D engine does one thing—3D rendering of the data, that's it.

Game Engine

The game engine in a 3D game can refer to a lot of things. Sometimes it doesn't really refer to anything. However, in most cases, the game engine is a system that processes everything, and is the controlling module that sends commands to all the subsystems.

Hence, the game engine needs to be designed so that it's connected to each of the game subsystems. A mistake that is sometimes made is to start on a 3D game with the 3D engine, and then at some point turn a portion of the 3D engine into the main control of the game—that's also a bad idea. From the beginning, design a module that will control everything—call it the "game engine," or whatever. Think of it as the container that holds all the other components and understands every part of the overall system.

Input System and Networking

The I/O and networking systems in a 3D game are notorious for being problems, and they are. The problem is that there is potentially so much data that must be sent over the network for a networked game that making any 3D networked game work is a miracle. Figure 6.2 shows two examples of network gaming models. However, the rule with the network portion of a 3D game is to think about the game first, and keep it separate from the network portion. The networking should not be part of the 3D engine, the AI, or the physics—it should be completely separate. Additionally, the network support for a 3D game needs to be thought out way ahead of any other part of the game. You need to think about what types of data and synchronization techniques you'll use to keep your 3D simulation in step, and then write the entire game with that in mind. Otherwise, you will definitely have a mess in the end.

TIP

If you are writing a 2D game, you can get away with adding networking at the end of development maybe five out of ten times with a lot of ugly code; but in a 3D game, it just won't happen. Decide on network support in the beginning and then create models, simulations, and test cases to test your system before implementing it.

Animation System

This is one of the first systems that may or may not be connected to another in a major way. For example, there are a number of animations that happen in a 3D game:

- Simple motion
- Complex animation
- Physically-based animation

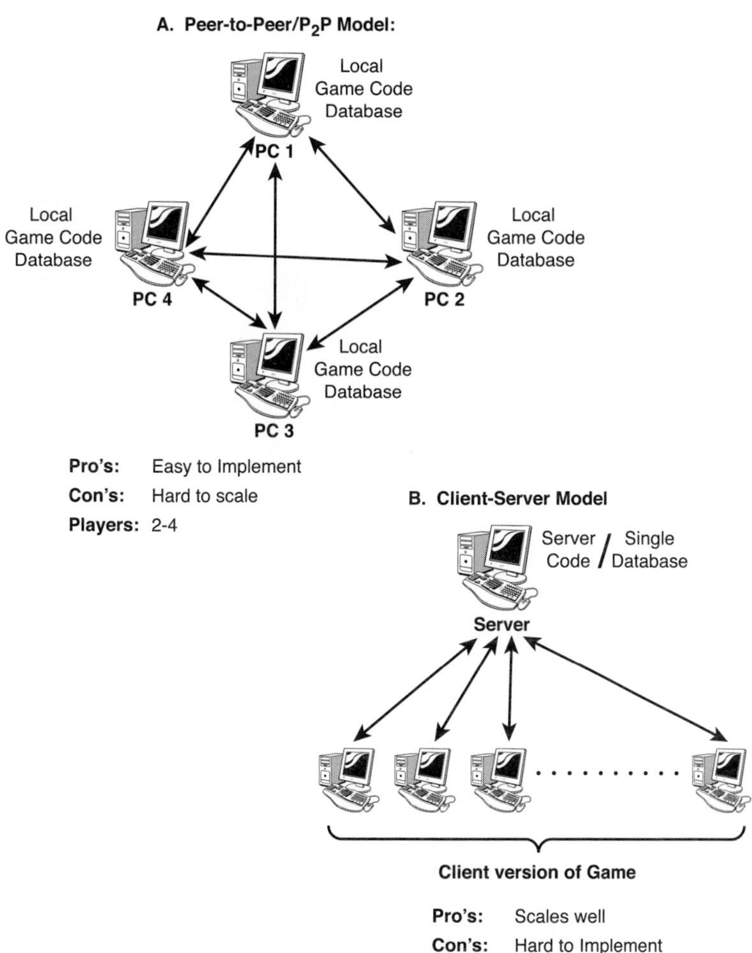

FIGURE 6.2 Network gaming models.

Simple Motion

Simple motion usually consists of the basic translation and rotation of your game objects, as shown in Figure 6.3. This motion can be controlled by data files, AI, patterns, simple logic, state machines, whatever. Nothing magical here. Nonetheless, whatever is driving the motion might be tied to others in a minor or major way. For example, say that you have a game where the artificial intelligence is moving around game units.

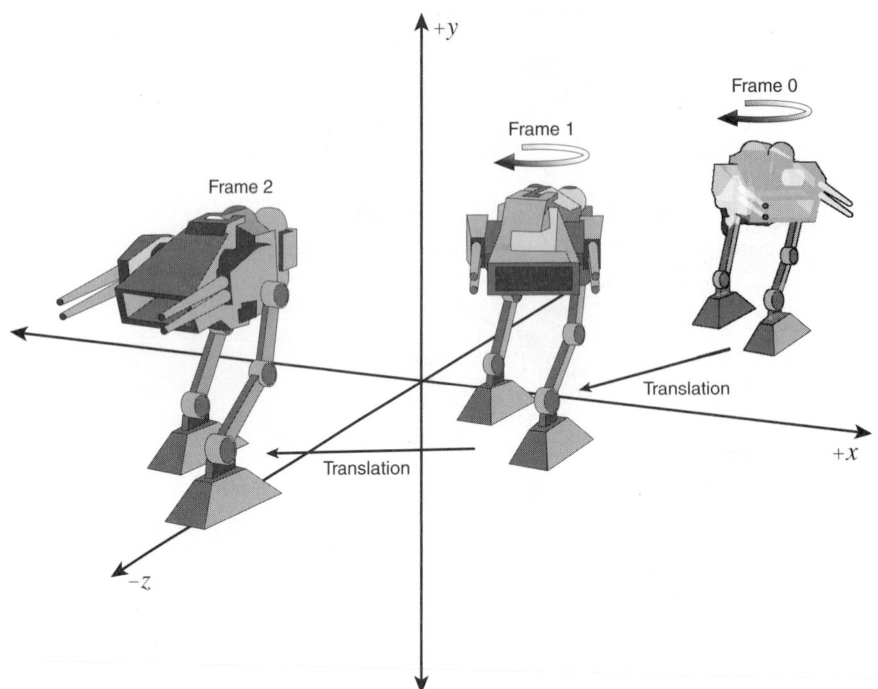

FIGURE 6.3 Simple translation and rotation.

These units move around in the map as shown in Figure 6.4. If the AI has a representation of this map, it can determine the collisions and make sure the units don't go through walls. On the other hand, perhaps the AI could send commands to the physics system, which also handles collision detection, and then it could determine whether the motion is possible. As you can see, in this example at least, you might have the AI, motion, and physics all within one tightly-knit system—and that's okay.

Complex Animation

Complex animation in 3D means a number of things. But, usually it means that you have *articulated-hierarchical* objects, with links that must move in relation to each other. An example seen in Figure 6.5 is a robotic tank with an upper body turret. For simplicity's sake, let's use the tank as the first example. It has a body and a single articulated link—the turret. The turret can rotate around the up axis of the tank body (usually parallel to the ground), but must stay connected to the top of the tank. Now, here's the problem: Is control of the turret going to be completely AI-based, or is it going to be data-based? In other words, suppose we want to make the tank turret do something interesting. It might be very difficult to do that with AI code, but very easy to do it with animation instructions or key framed data. Let's talk about that for a moment.

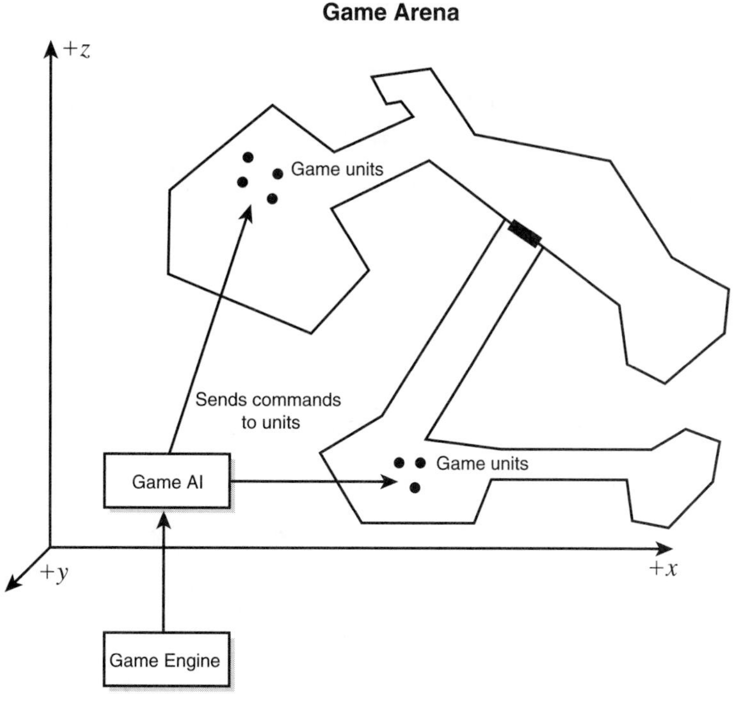

FIGURE 6.4 Artificial intelligence moving game units.

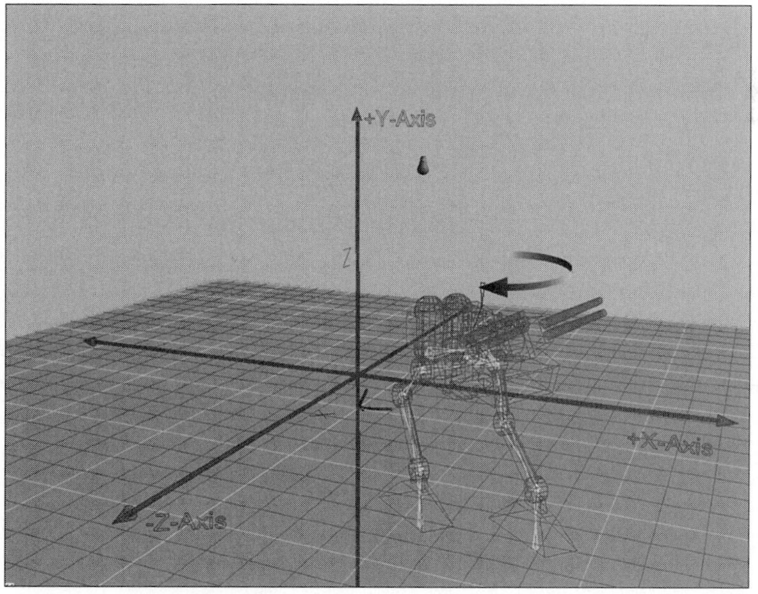

FIGURE 6.5 Animated articulated 3D model.

There are two ways to animate a 3D object that has components or linked objects. The first way is to animate them using a 3D modeling tool, import the meshes, and then animate as a function of time—simply load mesh 1, then mesh 2, then mesh 3, and so on. This technique is similar to standard 2D bitmap animation, except that the data is 3D data representing a 3D model. This method is memory-intensive, but fairly easy to implement. Figure 6.6 shows an example of this. Basically, we model the tank with its turret at one angle, then another, then another, and then save the mesh data output. Then to animate the tank, we load the meshes in and render them one at a time. This is the technique that *Quake* and *Quake II* use.

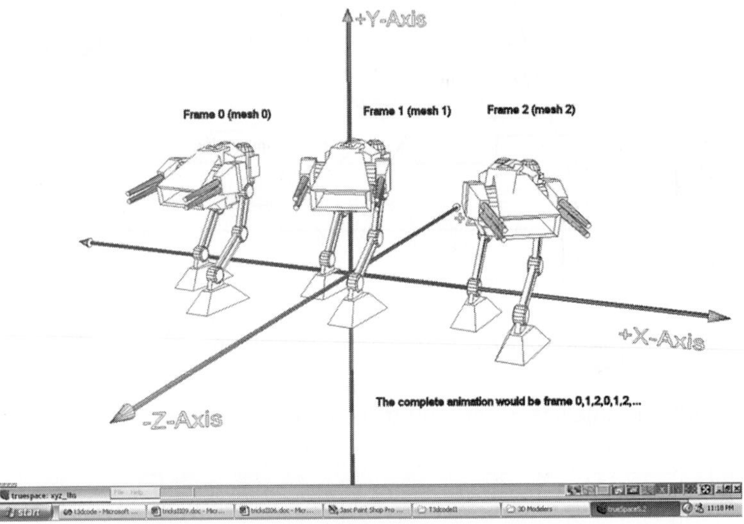

FIGURE 6.6 Using multiple frames to create an animation.

The second way to animate a 3D object is with *motion data*. One popular motion format is the BioVision .BVH format (a little sample is shown in the following code fragment). You can find the specification for this format within the directory for this chapter under `BIOVISION.DOC`. Basically, the data instructs the engine on what links to move relative to others, and the engine then moves each of the subcomponents of the 3D object. This technique is much more flexible, because once you create an animation engine that can read BioVision data, then the data can be anything from a walk to a dance, and your character will do it. This is the technique used in *Quake Arena, Doom III, Halo,* and most fighting games, like the *Tekken* series. If you're interested in purchasing motion data, then check BioVision out on the Web at `http://www.biovision.com`.

```
Example Biped-supported BVH File

HIERARCHY
ROOT Hips
{
    OFFSET    20    0.00    0.00
    CHANNELS 6 Xposition Yposition Zposition Zrotation Xrotation Yrotation
    JOINT LeftHip
    {
        OFFSET     3.430000     0.000000     0.000000
        CHANNELS 3 Zrotation Xrotation Yrotation
        JOINT LeftKnee
        {
            OFFSET     0.000000    -18.469999     0.000000
            CHANNELS 3 Zrotation Xrotation Yrotation
            JOINT LeftAnkle
            {
                OFFSET     0.000000    -17.950001     0.000000
                CHANNELS 3 Zrotation Xrotation Yrotation
                End Site
                {
                    OFFSET     0.000000    -3.119996     0.000000
                }
```


The problem with 3D animation is where to draw the line and put in a feedback loop, so that the animations make sense in the physical world? For example, suppose in the tank example that the tank is up against a wall, as shown in Figure 6.7, and a command is executed to rotate the turret around counter-clockwise 90 degrees. Now, the animation was probably initiated by the AI, because the tank wants to shoot an object behind it, but maybe the AI doesn't look ahead that far to see whether the turret will hit something as it rotates. This is a common omission in 3D games—we have all seen objects pass through others. The reason is that the designers didn't really care if once in a while the wheels went under the road, or the arms of the fighters went through the trees, or whatever. However, if we don't want these things to happen, somewhere we'll have to test for it.

The test might happen in the animation system itself—that is, when the turret is instructed to rotate, the animation system checks for possible collisions and then either performs the animation or doesn't. This brings us to yet another problem: Is it the job of the animation system, AI system, or physics system to do this? Again, it really depends on a lot of things. If your game has heavy physics modeling, then yes, the animation system needs to pass this off to the physics system. However, if you have very little physics, maybe it's okay for the animation system to do the testing.

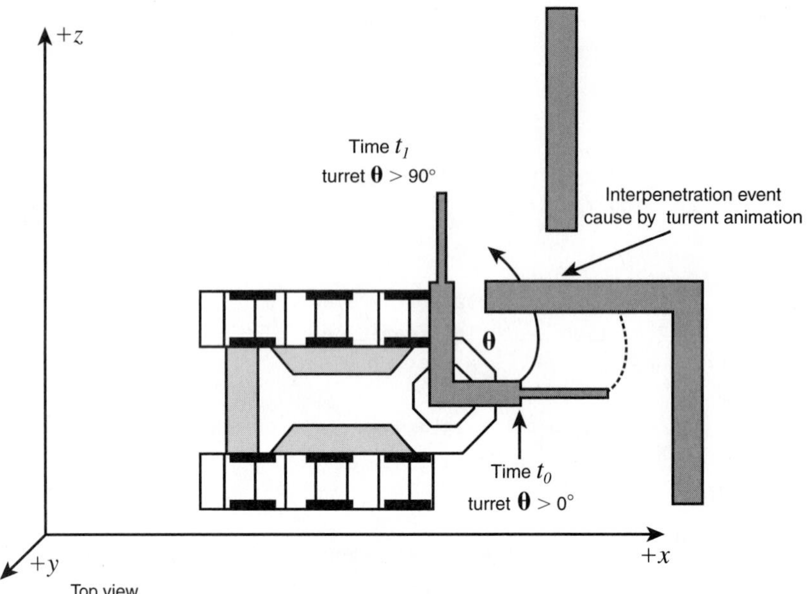

FIGURE 6.7 Physically impossible situations based on nonphysical animation.

I hope that you're seeing that there are a number of complex relationships that occur in a 3D engine!

Physically-Based Animation

This is the most complex of all animations. *Physically-based animation* means that the laws of physics for the most part are controlling how something animates or moves. For example, you might have a 3D fighting game where the fighting moves themselves are pre-canned motion capture data. However, this data is fed into the physically-based animation system, which basically controls physics-based models that perform the animation. They do this not blindly by rotating joints and translating objects, but by directing the model to do these things. Then the physics system determines whether it's possible. This is the best way to perform the most realistic simulation.

Continuing with the fighting game example, let's say that Fighter A throws a punch at Fighter B. The punch is really a set of motion capture data, but instead of just being "played" through the model, the data can be thought of as commands to the model's physics system. So, the physics system starts throwing the punch, then the hand of the punch hits a wall! The physics system then reacts to this by sending a force back through the motion controller and the hand stops dead in its tracks—this is what should happen. As another example, say that Fighter B throws Fighter A. The initial motions of the throw are motion captured, but after Fighter A hits the air, the physics system takes over completely, and he will hit the ground or whatever objects are in the way as the physics unfold based on the environment.

The point is, in a physically-based animation system, the animation and physics are intimately connected. However, once again they have nothing to do with the 3D rendering. By the time the 3D engine renders, all it should know about is a polygon list.

Collision Detection and Navigation System

We have already made reference to the physics system more than once, thereby showing that many systems in a 3D game can be connected. However, sometimes a full physics system is overkill, and all the game really needs is a simpler collision detection and navigation system to run right. We might call this a physics system, but unless it's based on forces, momentum, and other physical quantities, it's really just a glorified collision detection system. As an example, suppose you're creating a *Doom*-style first-person shooter (FPS), and you have almost no physics: The characters are animated by AI along with pre-canned mesh animations, and nothing slides (there's no momentum transfer, and so forth). The only thing you need to take into consideration is object-to-object and object-to-world penetration, as shown in Figure 6.8.

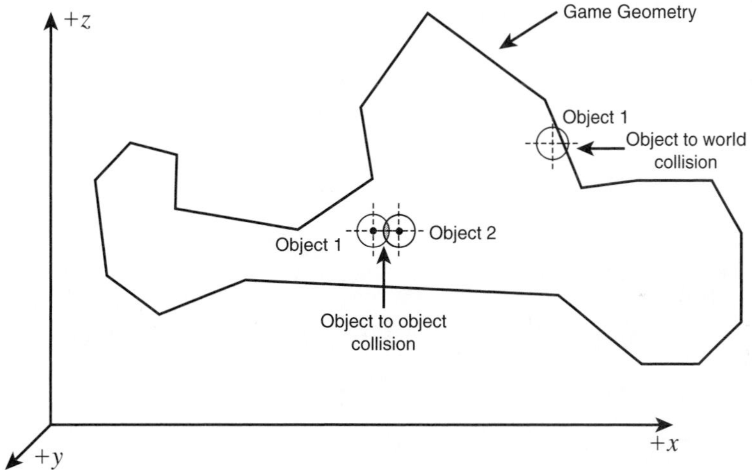

FIGURE 6.8 Object-to-object and object-to-world collision.

Thus, all you need is a simple collision detection system that feeds back the animation system (and/or the AI system) with information about what's happening as the animation system commands the game objects to walk, run, move, or whatever. However, with a system this simple, you might get objects penetrating each other, and creatures sliding on the ground unrealistically, and so forth.

Physics Engine

The physics system in a game can be very simple, as in the collision-only system mentioned previously, or very complex, based on real physics and closed-loop models.

The physics in a game engine really have nothing to do with the visual representation of 3D graphics at all. All the physics engine does is control and respond to actions that the objects in the game make or don't make, and then based on the physics models you've implemented, takes action. For example, a very simple physics model might have the following capabilities:

- Frictional forces and acceleration
- Elastic collision detection and response
- Linear momentum transfer

A good example of this kind of modeling is a simple 3D racing game consisting of a flat track and a number of cars, as shown in Figure 6.9. For each car, we might model the car as a point mass (or maybe a 4-point mass, one point for each wheel). Then as the cars drive around the track, either controlled by the player or the AI, the physics system keeps the cars on the road based on frictional forces only. That is, if a car is moving at 100 mph and then takes a turn at a certain angle, *centripetal force* (center seeking) is computed and compared to the *centrifugal force* (outward), and then the forces are modified appropriately and the acceleration of the car is altered. Furthermore, if a car hits another, they are modeled as spheres, perhaps, a simple elastic collision takes place, and momentum is transferred, but angular momentum is not computed—or it's faked.

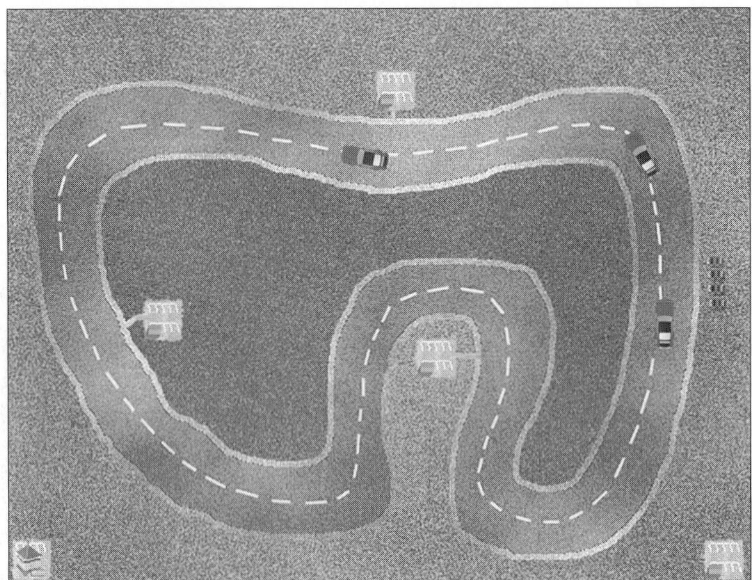

FIGURE 6.9 A simple racing game setup.

The preceding level of physics modeling is usually robust enough for a large class of 2D and 3D games, but if you want reality, you have to go farther. Farther means modeling objects based on their actual geometry, along with using full physics where the physics system is controlling the objects, rather than the AI system controlling the objects and taking feedback from a simplified system of collisions and friction. In a full physics model, each object is continually under simulation, and all the forces on the object are used in the standard physics equations that describe acceleration, velocity, and motion. Along with integration, these equations are used to arrive at the new position of any object, expressed as a function of time based on the forces that are being applied to the object—this is what *dynamics* does for us.

We will cover this in reasonable detail in the physics modeling part of the book. However, keep in mind that a 3D game with this level of simulation must have the animation and AI systems tied into the physics system, so that these other systems respond to the artificial reality imposed by the physics models, and don't continue to send commands to the game units that are impossible to execute because of the constraints of the game's physics.

Artificial Intelligence System

The AI in a 3D game can be an order of magnitude more complex than that of a 2D system or the same level, depending on the modeling of the game units. The problem with AI in a 3D environment is, of course, that it's 3D! Functions like navigation, path finding, and animation all become much more complex. In a 2D game, moving a collection of space ships around isn't that hard, but moving something in 3D is very hard. All the algorithms used in 3D are the same as 2D—deterministic, patterns, planning systems, finite state machines, fuzzy logic, neural nets, and so forth—it's just that a lot more thought has to be put into their implementation.

As an example, take a look at Figure 6.10a and Figure 6.10b. Here we see a 2D environment and a 3D environment from two different shooter games (*Valkyrie* and *Quake III*). The 2D scroller's AI is fairly straightforward because the environment is simple. The objects are nothing more than 2D bitmap animations, most of the object motion is controlled by patterns, tracking logic, and finite state machines. The 3D game works in a similar way, but it's about ten times harder to write! The problem is that everything is in 3D, and even moving the characters is now a large problem. When a 3D character approaches you, it has to look intelligent. This means its motion, animation, and logic have to take the 3D environment into consideration.

These constraints make programming AI for 3D game much harder. Operations like simply moving a unit from one point to another in a 3D world can be overwhelming because of the geometrical makeup of the world. It might be easy for us to "see" a simple path, but for the AI to invent one is not at all easy. Anyway, these are the kinds of issues that are going to come to light in 3D AI programming. Finally, the AI system in a 3D game is usually tied to the animation and the physics system, because the AI must have sensory input from the world, many times in response to its actions.

FIGURE 6.10 Examples of 2D and 3D environments.

3D Model and Imagery Database

The last large part of a 3D game is the data. And there's a lot of it! 3D games can have enormous data footprints. This is because of the nature of 3D. For example, a typical 3D game is going to have a number of the following data items:

- 3D meshes for objects
- 2D texture maps and light maps
- 3D worlds
- Motion and animation data
- Game map data

In most cases, the data that take up the most memory are the texture and light maps, because there might be hundreds, if not thousands, of texture maps. And with current texture maps possessing 24-bit color and up to 1024×1024 resolution, that's three megabytes per texture—wow! Of course, many games have user-selectable texture sizes and quality, but even at the 256×256 color level, that's still 65,536 bytes per texture—that's a lot of memory and memory management to go along with it. In this book, we will probably stick to textures in the range of 32×32 to 128×128 at most, just to keep things simple (and fast, because we are using software algorithms), but I think you get an idea of the massive amounts of memory needed for texture storage. Moreover, it's not just memory storage for the textures, but also for the meshes themselves.

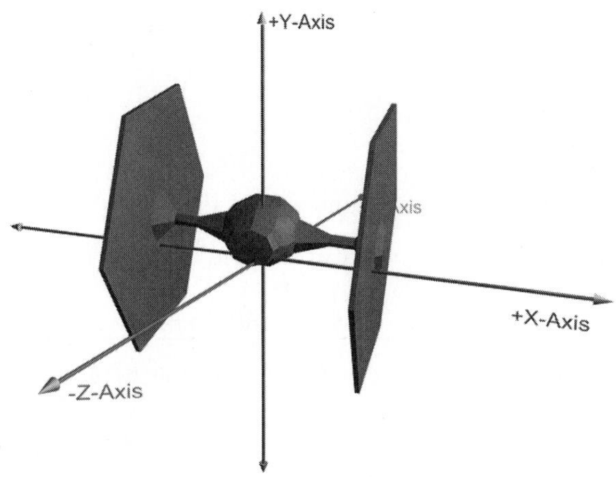

FIGURE 6.11 A low polygon model.

For example, if you decide to go with pre-canned animated meshes rather than motion data controlled animation, the amount of memory can quickly add up to hold an object's mesh animation. For example, suppose you have a character as shown in Figure 6.11 that has around 200–300 polygons and 200 vertices. Let's do the math to see what the storage is on this by making up a simple data structure to hold a 3D vertex that supports both the positional coordinates, along with texture and lighting information:

```
typedef VERTEX3Dptl_TYP
{
float x,y,z; // position
float u,v;   // texture coordinates
float l;     // light value

} VERTEX3Dptl, * VERTEX3Dptl_PTR;
```

That's roughly `6*sizeof(float) = 24` bytes per vertex (on a 32-bit system, at least). Our object has 200 vertices, so that's:

```
24 bytes per vertex * 200 vertices = 480 bytes per mesh.
```

However, we haven't factored in the higher-level stuff like the polygon mesh, color, and so on. Let's just forget about that for now, and continue with the example. Let's say that we want 32 frames of animation for each motion, and we need the following animation meshes:

- Walk
- Run
- Jump

- Duck
- Die
- Shoot

Okay, so that's 6 motions each with 32 frames, for a total of

```
6 motions * 32 frames each = 192 frames of motion.
```

And each frame takes 480 bytes, so we have a grand total of

```
192 frames of animation * 480 bytes per frame = 92,160 bytes.
```

That's a lot of freakin' memory! Multiply that by 32 different creatures in the game, and you have 32*92,160, or roughly three megs of vertices! So, you can see that this stuff adds up. The moral of the story is, in a 3D game, you're definitely going to need efficient data structure, databases, and on-demand loading and unloading of data. Of course, the virtual memory manager of Windows helps a lot with this, but you can't just load everything and then work with it—you will run out of memory.

> **TIP**
>
> You also have to think about bandwidth issues, too. When you are dealing with texture maps and large meshes, just the act of moving things around is going to eat up a lot of memory bandwidth on your system bus. That means that efficient data ordering is important, and that you use something and then you're done with it. You don't want to load object A, use it, discard it and use object B, then load A again. You want to try and order your data so that *cache coherence* is high—meaning you use something as much as possible before loading something else.

In conclusion, a 3D game (or any game, for that matter) is nothing more than a stream of bytes, but the representation of that stream of bytes is really important. Hence, good data structures and a well-thought out plan are always good ideas before you even think about coding. With that in mind, let's get to the 3D part!

3D Coordinate Systems

Now that you've had an introduction to 3D game programming from a high-level point of view, we're going to actually start talking about some 3D stuff, starting with 3D coordinate systems.

Although we've already covered Cartesian (2D/3D), cylindrical (3D), and spherical coordinates (3D), these are more like methods of representing 3D systems themselves. What we're interested in now is how a 3D graphics engine represents actual 3D objects in the various stages of processing.

In general, there can be many different coordinate systems that an object is transformed to as it makes its way to the video screen, through what's referred to as the *3D viewing pipeline*:

- Model coordinates
- World coordinates
- Camera coordinates
- Perspective coordinates
- Screen coordinates

These are the main classes of coordinates, but depending on the 3D engine, you can get pretty crazy with other types of transformations, such as normalizing or warping transformations. Nevertheless, the preceding list is what we'll talk about for now.

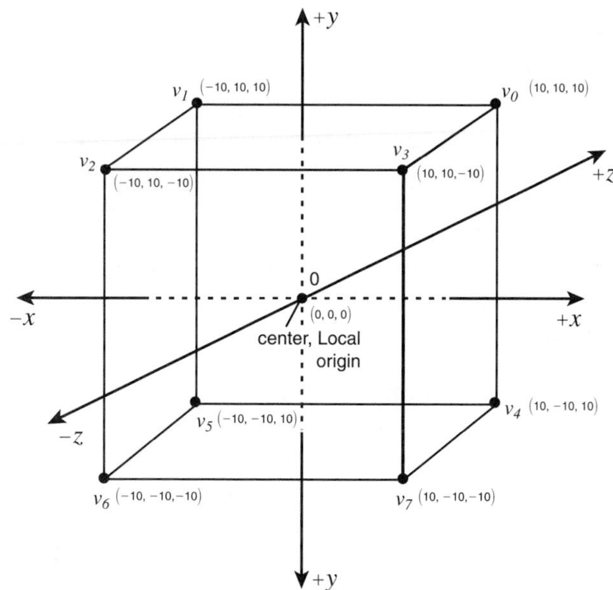

FIGURE 6.12 A basic cube in model/local coordinates for analysis.

Model Coordinates (Local Coordinates)

Model coordinates (also known as *local coordinates*, and I will use them interchangeably) are the coordinates of a 3D entity in its own local coordinate system. That is, every time you create a 3D object for a game, you usually create it with it's own set of local axes, where the center of the object is at (0,0,0) in 3D (or wherever you want the center to be). In

Figure 6.12, we see a cube defined in a left-handed coordinate system. The cube is 10 units on each side, and it has a center (0,0,0). The vertices (points) that make up the cube are

```
Vertex 0: (10,10,10)
Vertex 1: (-10,10,10)
Vertex 2: (-10,10,-10)
Vertex 3: (10,10,-10)
Vertex 4: (10,-10,10)
Vertex 5: (-10,-10,10)
Vertex 6: (-10,-10,-10)
Vertex 7: (10,-10,-10)
```

The idea behind model coordinates is that at some time during the 3D pipeline, you can translate your models to their real positions in the 3D world. This is how a 3D game works. On the other hand, sometimes you might actually want the local origin (0,0,0) of your 3D object not positioned at its geometric center. For example, suppose that you want to create a robot arm model as shown in Figure 6.13. You could define each link as a mesh of polygons, each with its local center at (0,0,0). Whenever the object is translated into world coordinates, it would be centered, so that its center moves to whatever that point is (if I'm losing you, just hold on). However, what if you want the links to rotate or move off center? That is, so that maybe the first link is the shoulder, and the second link is the forearm? There's no rule that states that an object's local coordinates must have (0,0,0) as the center of the object. Therefore, maybe you want the origin (0,0,0) to be at the end of the model's in Figure 6.13. This is actually a more intelligent position to call the origin for these types of objects, since a single point defines the rotation center and the rotating linkage is just a 3D line segment.

Orientation Issues

Lastly, I want to talk about orientation issues with model coordinates. By *orientation* I mean that you must have some kind of convention for defining or loading your 3D models; otherwise, you won't know what side is "up" or "forward." For example, suppose that you define two objects in a 3D game, as shown in Figure 6.14. The space ship has model coordinates such that the front of the ship is pointing in the negative z-axis, and the up direction, or top, is the positive y-axis. The mech, on the other hand, has its front pointing at the positive z-axis. Do you see the problem?

There are two ways to handle this. The first method is to come up with a convention during modeling that states that all models must have their "fronts" pointing in the positive z-axis, and their tops "pointing" in the positive y-axis (or whatever the convention is, as long as you stick to it). The second method is to model your objects anyway you like, but have software compute the major axis of each object (the axis that has the largest length), and align it to the positive z-axis (or whatever axis you choose), along with finding the second major axis and aligning that with the positive y-axis—or whatever, as long as you are consistent. This way, no matter what orientation the object is loaded in with, you always know that it will be reasonably oriented. My advice is to use the modeling convention rather than letting software do it, because software can only look at the geometry, and doesn't understand what an object really "looks" like.

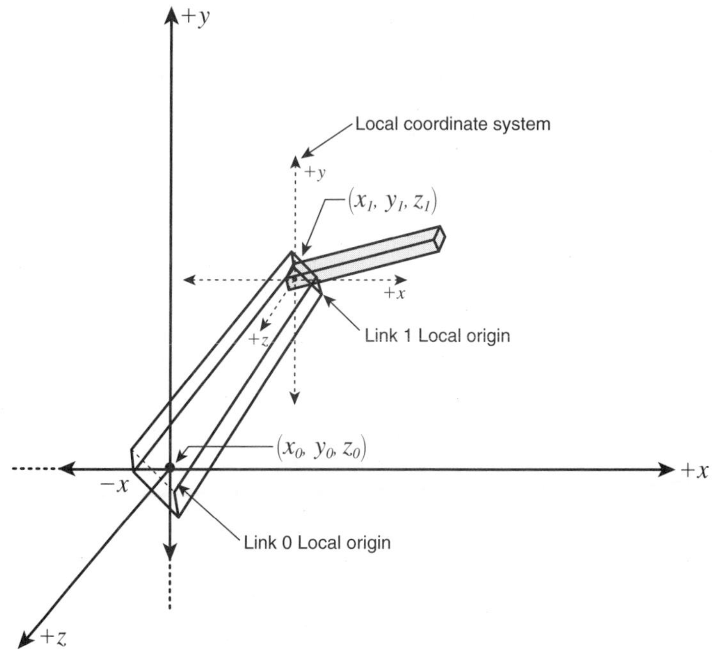

FIGURE 6.13 A robot arm hierarchical linkage.

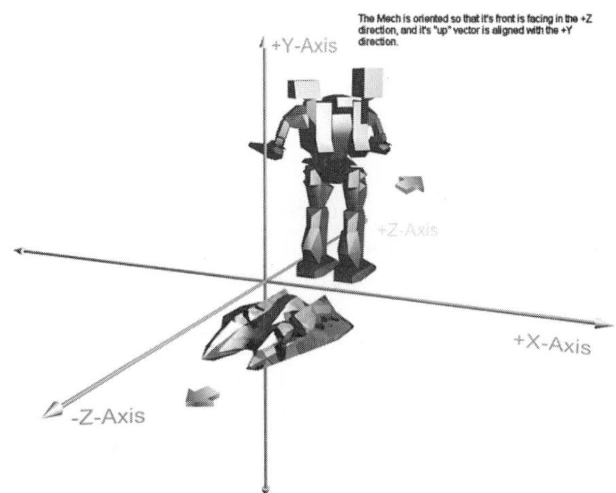

FIGURE 6.14 Arriving at an orientation convention for model loading.

For example, if you load a model of some of the newer 2000+ cars, the fronts look like the back, so you might be driving backwards! Especially that new Thunderbird—yuck!

TIP

Even with an orientation convention during modeling, you might want to rotate, scale, or translate each object during loading. This is a great added feature. For example, you might have a function `Load_3D_Mesh()` that loads an object, but also enables you to transform it during the load. That transformed version becomes the model coordinates that are then passed to the system.

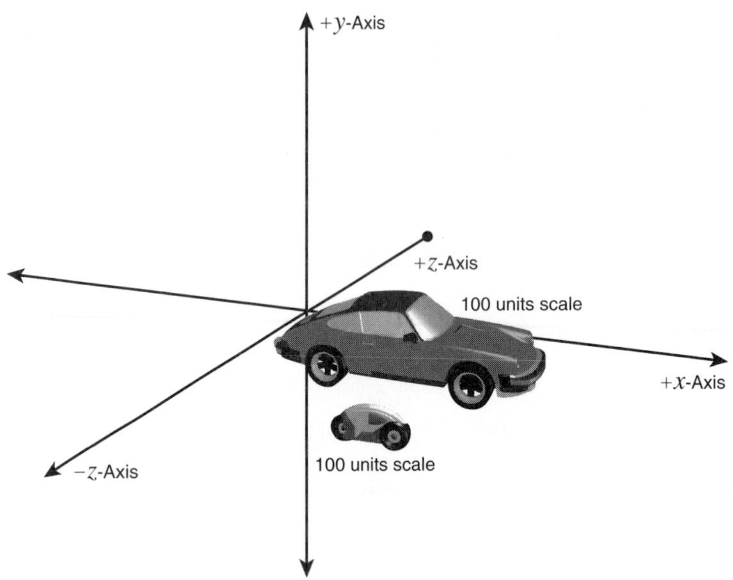

FIGURE 6.15 Differences in scale need to be normalized.

Scale Issues

There's also the issue of the scale of your models. What if one model that represents a car has a radius of 100, whereas another model that represents a light cycle also has the radius of 100, as shown in Figure 6.15? This doesn't make sense, because their 1:1 scales aren't correct. The solution to this problem is to again model all your objects at the same scale, meaning that maybe one unit in the modeling program is always 1 cm in the game engine. Or, you can model everything in a local world of 1×1×1 (normalized coordinates), and then scale the models as you load them. Personally, I just model all my objects using the same scale, so that one unit is something like 1 cm, 1 meter, or 1 km, but I use that same number for all my models as I create them. Again, your loader software function might allow you to specify x-y-z scaling factors, along with x-y-z rotation factors to load the same model, but change it. This is useful for simple objects, like asteroids. You load in the same model, but scale and rotate it on the fly, so that each loaded mesh seems completely different, which simplifies your 3D modeling work.

A Word on LHS/RHS Coordinate Systems

In a 3D game, you can use either a left-handed (LHS) system or right-handed (RHS) system to define each object with—it's up to you. Of course, you need to be consistent. I prefer to use left-handed coordinates, because all the other transformations are easier (along with projection), and I like the +z axis to go into the screen rather than out. However, sometimes drawing figures on paper is easier with a RHS, because the positive z-axis is pointing toward us. Even if you want to use a RHS for model coordinates and a LHS system for final 3D projection, you can do so with a simple reflection of the z-axis. But why make life hard? I already feel like I'm in the Matrix!

World Coordinates

After you have all your 3D models, you'll want to position them relative to the world. This is where *world coordinates* come into play. They are the actual real coordinates in the virtual universe in which objects move and are transformed. That is, if an object is at (50,100,200), it's *at* (50,100,200)—period! The first step in understanding world coordinates is understanding what their ranges mean in terms of some reference point. That is, how big should the world be? Should it be 1×1×1, 10×10×10, or 1,000,000×1,000,000×1,000,000?

Well, if you're using the convention that one unit in local coordinates is 1 meter, and you want to have a universe that's 100×100×100 km (a good size for a tank or racing sim), that means that your game grid has the following dimensions, given that there are 1,000 meters in a kilometer:

Example: World 100 km cubed with 1 meter/unit and origin (0,0,0):

x-axis: -50,000 <= x <= 50,000

y-axis: -50,000 <= y <= 50,000

z-axis: -50,000 <= z <= 50,000

That's also a nice number that is easily handled in a float. On the other hand, if you want each unit in model coordinates to represent 1 cm, and have a universe that's 1,000,000 km cubed, you might get into some range issues, because that world would have the following dimensions:

Example: World 1,000,000 km cubed with 1 cm/unit:

x-axis: -.5x10^{10} <= x <= .5x10^{10}

y-axis: -.5x10^{10} <= y <= .5x10^{10}

z-axis: -.5x10^{10} <= z <= .5x10^{10}

These numbers exceed an integer 32-bit representation, which is roughly +/- 2×10^9 and is getting into the range limits of a standard 32-bit floating number that has any accuracy at all. The bottom line is it's too big. The rule of thumb is that you need to constrain your universe so that you can represent the boundaries of the universe, along with having at least 3-4 decimal places of accuracy.

NOTE

The final scaling and camera transformations come into play along with your models sizes, too, so many times you end up resizing your universe to give it the right "feel" for the game objects, velocities, and scales. For example, I once made a 3D shooter and had a rather small universe (4096×4096×4096), but when the player ran from one end of the universe to the other at 30fps, it took about 15 seconds, which felt about right. A space game, on the other hand, would have to be ten times bigger because the relative velocities of the ships would be much faster. Of course, in reality, they would be thousands of times faster, but in a virtual world, ten times faster and larger would probably suffice.

Placing an Object in World Coordinates

Now that you have a handle on local and world coordinates, let's work through how you would actually transform an object from local coordinates to world coordinates. Remember, the whole point of local or model coordinates is to define the object, but then they must be placed in the world to arrive at the final world coordinates. As an example, take another look at Figure 6.12. Here we see our simple 3D cube object defined in model coordinates—it's a simple cube in this case, with each side having a length of 10 units. Thus, its local coordinates are as follows:

```
Vertex 0: (10,10,10)
Vertex 1: (-10,10,10)
Vertex 2: (-10,10,-10)
Vertex 3: (10,10,-10)
Vertex 4: (10,-10,10)
Vertex 5: (-10,-10,10)
Vertex 6: (-10,-10,-10)
Vertex 7: (10,-10,-10)
```

We could actually define this object using one of our data structures `POINT3D`, as follows:

```
POINT3D cube_model[8] = {
{10,10,10}, // vertex 0
{-10,10,10}, // vertex 1
{-10,10,-10}, // vertex 2
{10,10,-10}, // vertex 3
```

```
{10,-10,10}, // vertex 4
{-10,-10,10}, // vertex 5
{-10,-10,-10}, // vertex 6
{10,-10,-10}, // vertex 7
};
```

And of course, we could define each face that is a polygon that makes up the 3D solid representation as a set of four vertices as follows, if you want to get detailed:

```
Face 0: (0,1,2,3)
Face 1: (4,7,6,5)
Face 2: (0,3,7,4)
Face 3: (2,3,7,6)
Face 4: (1,5,6,2)
Face 5: (0,4,5,1)
```

However, the polygon definitions aren't needed for the transformation from local/model coordinates to world coordinates, so we don't really need the face list.

We have a vertex list of an object in local/model coordinates and we want to transform it into world coordinates. To do this, we simply need to know where in the game world we want the *center* of the object, and then translate the local/model coordinates to this position—simple. Assuming that our world is 1000×1000×1000 and we want to place the object at `(world_x, world_y, world_z)` as shown in Figure 6.16, the following translation algorithm will work nicely:

```
POINT3D cube_world[8]; // used to hold world coordinates

// translate each vertex by (x0, y0, z0)
for (int vertex = 0; vertex<8; vertex++)
    {
    cube_world[vertex].x=cube_model[vertex].x+world_x;
    cube_world[vertex].y=cube_model[vertex].y+world_y;
    cube_world[vertex].z=cube_model[vertex].z+world_z;
    } // end for
```

Notice that we did *not* modify the local/model coordinates of the cube. This is very important. If we did, we would lose our cube model. Rather we transformed them and stored the results in a new vertex list. This might seem like a waste of space, but it can't be avoided. In fact, there might be a number of different versions of coordinates as they are processed through the 3D pipeline. We will try to keep the number of copies to a minimum, but usually there are at least two to three copies of them.

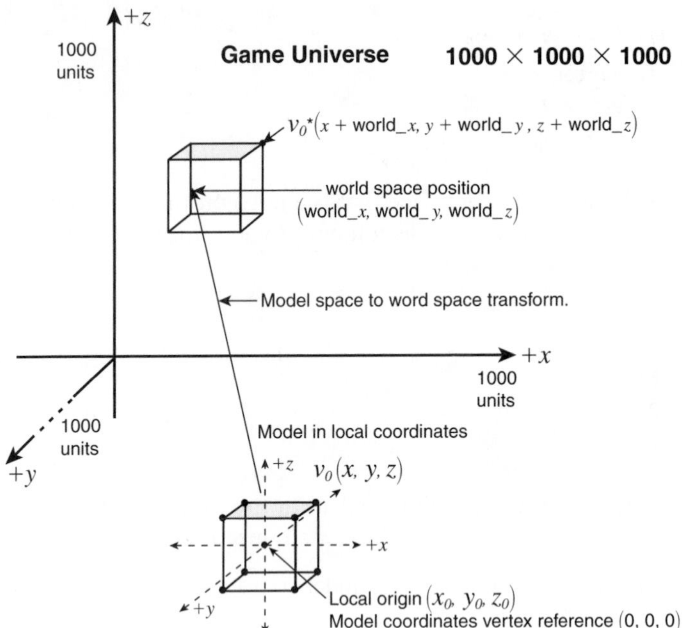

FIGURE 6.16 Placing an object in world space.

In any case, the preceding algorithm is nothing more than a translation. Thus, the local/model to world transformation can be represented with a standard matrix operation; call it T_{mw} for translation model to world. However, there's a gotcha—remember that to support translation in a matrix operation, we need 4D homogenous coordinates, so the matrix would like this:

```
         |1        0        0        0|
T mw =   |0        1        0        0|
         |0        0        1        0|
         |world_x  world_y  world_z  1|
```

NOTE

A word on matrix notation—many times I will name a matrix T with a subscript that further defines the transformation, such as T_{lw}, which might stand for the "local to world transformation matrix." Thus T stands for a general transform. However, other times, if the matrix is a translation or rotation matrix, T means translation and R means rotation. The point is, if you see a matrix named T with a subscript, it's either a general transformation or a translation matrix.

However, if you recall, we have a number of "smart" matrix multiply routines that know how to multiply a 3D vector by a 4×3 matrix, and/or a 4D vector by a 4×3 and 4×4 matrix, and so on. The point is—to implement a translation via matrix multiplication, you need that fourth row. With that in mind, here's the general matrix operation that must be performed to transform a point [x_m y_m z_m 1] in local/model coordinates to world coordinates.

FORMULA 6.1 Local/Model Coordinates to World Coordinates

$$= [x_m\ y_m\ z_m\ 1] * \mathbf{T}_{mw}$$

$$[x_m\ y_m\ z_m\ 1] * \begin{vmatrix} 1 & 0 & 0 & 0 \\ 0 & 1 & 0 & 0 \\ 0 & 0 & 1 & 0 \\ world\_x & world\_y & world\_z & 1 \end{vmatrix}$$

$$= [x_m + world\_x,\ y_m + world\_y,\ z_m + world\_z,\ 1]$$

$$= [x_w,\ y_w,\ z_w\ 1].$$

Of course, in this example we used 4D homogenous coordinates to make the math simple, but we could have used 3D coordinates as long as we assumed there's a phantom fourth element w equal to 1.0, so that the 4×3 or 4×4 matrix multiply makes some kind of sense. And finally, we would divide (x_w,y_w,z_w) by the last w factor to convert from homogeneous 4D to normal 3D coordinates, but because w = 1.0, there's no point to divide.

Summing up, the transformation from local/model coordinates to world coordinates is rather trivial; you simply translate each object's center to the desired position in the world: (world_x, world_y, world_z). This is in turn accomplished by translating all the vertices in the model and storing the results in a secondary data structure.

As far as the relationship of local/model and world coordinates to the 3D pipeline and the whole scheme of things, you basically transform the object's local coordinates only when you want to scale or rotate the object. Then you place the object in the world with the local/model-to-world coordinate transformation. Figure 6.17 depicts the current 3D pipeline we have up to world coordinates.

Camera Coordinates

Up until now, you've gotten off pretty easy. Now we're going crank up the positron flow... Both local and world coordinates are used to define 3D objects in space. Local/model coordinates define a single entity or collection of entities in their own 3D space and coordinate system relative to (0,0,0). World coordinates define the virtual 3D world in absolute terms—objects are virtually placed in this world. Okay, easy enough, but the point of a 3D game is playing it and moving around a 3D camera! Therefore, we need some way to view 3D objects. This is where *camera coordinates* and the *world-to-camera coordinate transformation* take place.

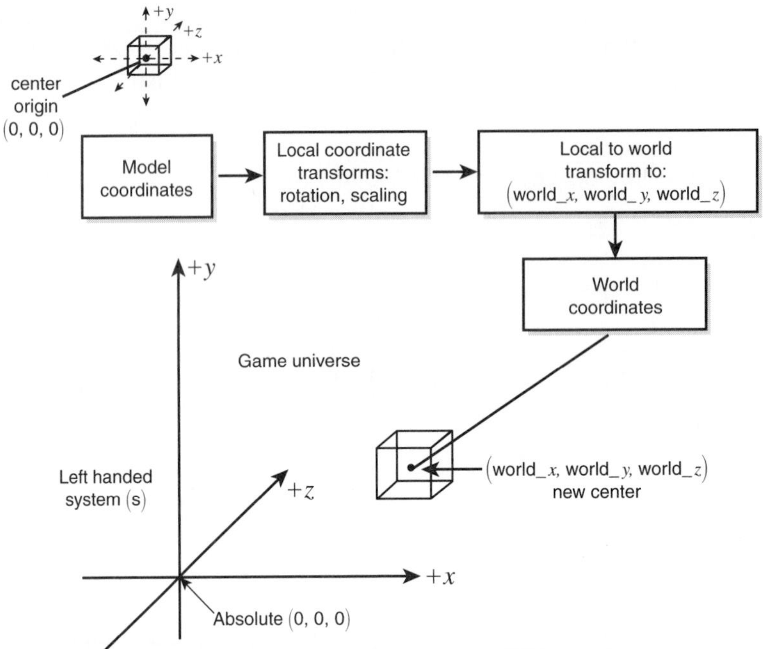

FIGURE 6.17 3D pipeline with local-to-world transform.

The Viewing Frustrum

To view a scene in a 3D world, the most common method is to place a virtual camera at a position in the world and then view the world with a specific field of view. This is shown in Figure 6.18. As you can see, we have a 3D world coordinate system with a virtual camera positioned at (cam_x, cam_y, cam_z) in a direction defined by (ang_x, ang_y, ang_z), or more commonly referred to as *(pitch, yaw, roll)*. Additionally, you see that there's a field of view, or *frustrum*, that the camera can "see in." This can be defined by the *field of view (FOV)* parameters in both the horizontal and vertical directions, which are usually in the range of 60–130 degrees. Additionally, there are near and far clipping planes, which represent the idea that objects beyond these regions are invisible. Only objects within the region are visible. Finally, there's a view plane, which is even more complicated, but ultimately it's the mathematical plane that we are going to project the 3D image on, so we can finally render it on a 2D computer screen. Now, let's talk a little more about the six walls that make up the viewing frustrum before moving on.

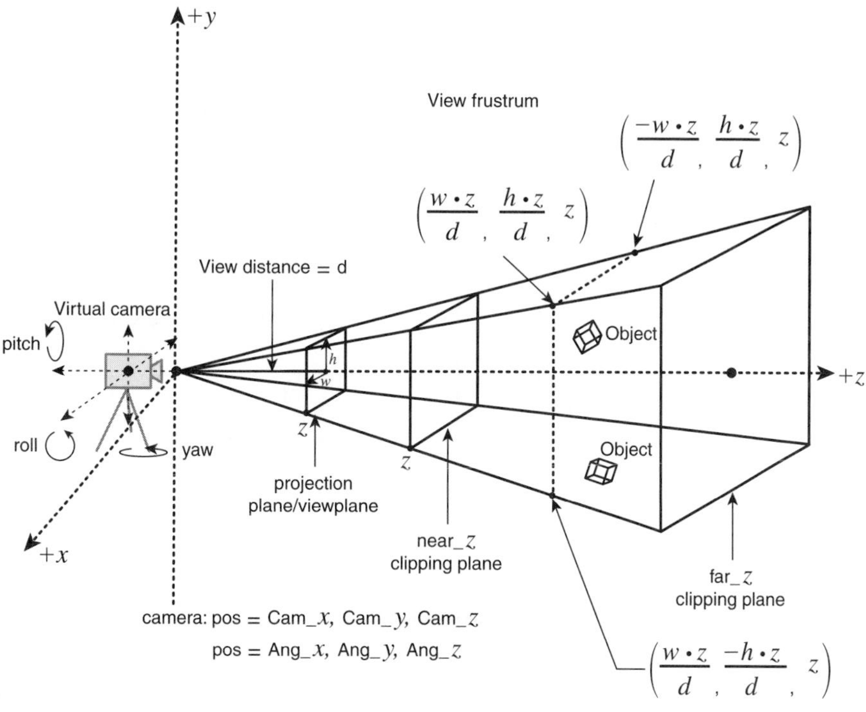

FIGURE 6.18 The 3D viewing frustrum.

Understanding the Near and Far Clipping Planes The near and far clipping planes are located at `near_z`, and `far_z`. Their plane equations are simply `z=near_z` and `z=far_z`, or more generally:

Near z-clip plane: `0*x + 0*y + 1*z  = near_z`

Far z-clip plane: `0*x + 0*y + 1*z  = far_z`

These planes are perpendicular to the viewing direction and represent the extents that valid 3D geometry can be rendered into. In other words, objects that are located farther than the far clipping plane will not be rendered, and objects that are nearer than the near clipping plane won't be rendered, either. Objects that are farther than the far clipping plane would be so small when rendered and projected that they are pointless to consider, because they would be little dots. Conversely, objects closer than the near clipping plane would be so close to the "eye" of the virtual camera that it would be like mashing your face up against a wall to look at it.

The Viewing Frustrum Walls The viewing frustrum is basically a truncated pyramid defined by the near, far, and side planes. These side planes or walls define the viewing volume of the frustrum. In our case, we are using a 90 degree viewing volume, so each of these planes is at a 45 degree angle to the view direction, as shown in Figure 6.19. Thus, the plane equations are simply ¦x¦=z, ¦y¦=z. Again, just as the near and far clipping planes, the side walls are used to clip objects, also. Objects that are not within these walls are not visible, and must be clipped and/or removed from the pipeline. (More on this later.)

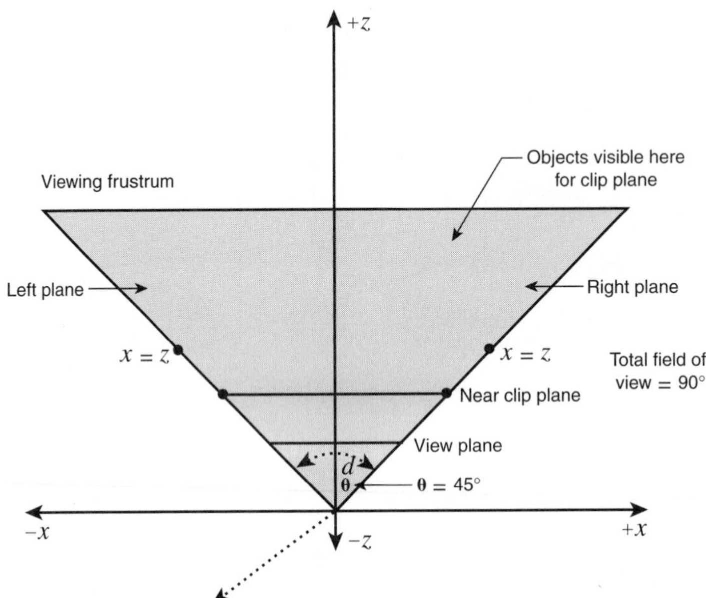

FIGURE 6.19 A simplified top-down view of the viewing frustrum.

The World-to-Camera Relationship The problem is this: We want to transform the objects in the 3D world so that they are relative to the camera. In other words, we want to be able to relate the world coordinates of the objects to the camera in as simple a manner as possible. This is the idea behind the world-to-camera coordinate transformation.

Take a look at Figure 6.19, where we see a camera placed at world coordinate position (0,0,0) looking straight down the positive z-axis with a horizontal and vertical field of view of 90 degrees (it's not necessary to have a FOV of 90, but makes the math easier because the plane equations are trivial). If there's an object in the viewing frustrum, it should be rendered, otherwise it shouldn't. Now, here's the tricky part—99.99999% of the time, the camera is *not* located at the origin looking straight down the positive z-axis (unless of course, you are looking at a DirectX 3D retained mode application of a rotating teapot), the camera is located at some position along with some orientation in the 3D world, usually connected to the front of the player's head.

The question then is this: If we were to artificially move the world so that the camera *was* at (0,0,0), with its orientation looking straight down the positive z-axis, along with the "up" direction pointing in the positive y-axis direction (that is, view angles equal to (0,0,0)), what transformation would we need to perform on all the world coordinates to make this consistent? This is the magic that the world-to-camera transformation performs and is actually really simple. Well, sorta!

TIP

If you decide to remove the rear end of your car, never under any circumstances take apart the spline gears—you will never get them aligned properly.

The World-to-Camera Transformation

The world-to-camera transformation is a transformation where we move the world around so that from the camera's point of view, the camera is at (0,0,0) looking straight down the positive z-axis, and the objects in the world move appropriately to make this happen. The transformation is accomplished in two steps: *translation*, followed by *rotation*. Let's start with the translation step.

The Translation Step

Take a look at Figure 6.20a. It's a simplified 3D world with a single object in it, along with a camera at some position (cam_x, cam_y, cam_z). We'll assume the camera angles are all (0,0,0) to simplify the example. Now, if we move the camera to (0,0,0) in the world, what would need to happen to the object located at (world_x, world_y, world_z) so that it has the same relationship to the camera? Referring to Figure 6.20b, we see that the camera is now at (0,0,0), but the object needs to be at (world_x, world_y, world_z)—(cam_x, cam_y, cam_z) to keep the relationship between the camera and the object the same. That is, the relative distance and angles have all been preserved. Or in other words, in the frame of the camera, nothing has changed. Only in the frame of the universe has something changed. Killer!

Now with the camera looking down the +z-axis, we can do some math to figure out whether the cube is either contained inside or outside the viewing frustrum, and then some more math to render the cube (with perspective) on the screen if it is. We'll get to that later—the point is, we have solved the translation half of the problem of the world-to-camera transformation.

In other words, the first step of the world-to-camera translation is to translate all world coordinates by an amount equal to the negative values of the camera's position in world space, or (-cam_x, -cam_y, -cam_z). The following code performs this step with our world coordinates from the previous section:

```
POINT3D cube_camera[8]; // used to hold camera coordinates

// translate each vertex by (-cam_x, -cam_y, -cam_z)
for (int vertex = 0; vertex<8; vertex++)
    {
```

```
cube_camera[vertex].x=cube_model[vertex].x-cam_x;
cube_camera[vertex].y=cube_model[vertex].y-cam_y;
cube_camera[vertex].z=cube_model[vertex].z-cam_z;
} // end for
```

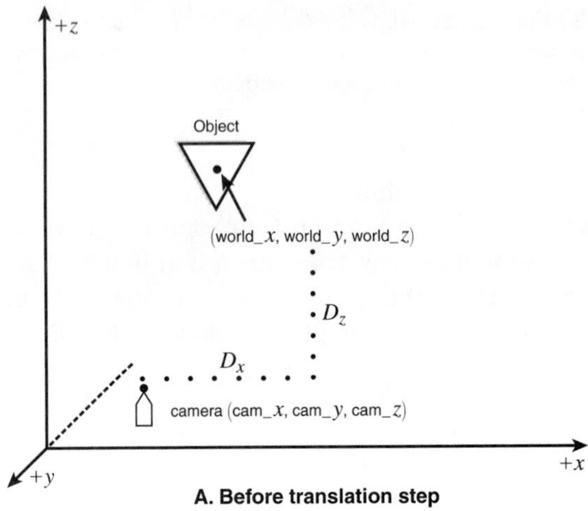

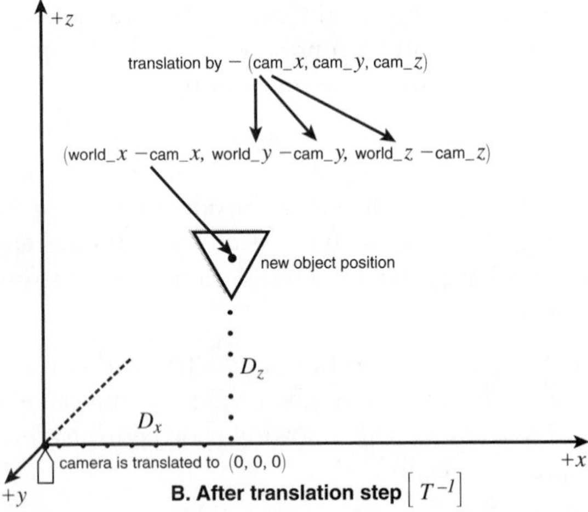

FIGURE 6.20 The translation step of the camera transformation.

Again, we see that yet another set of vertices is needed to hold the camera coordinates. Additionally, the first step of the camera transformation looks just like the local-to-world transform, so you might think of merging them into one transform. Although we are only half done with the world-to-camera transformation, I will say that it is possible to merge many of the 3D pipeline transformations together via matrix concatenation. However, many times it's better to do things in steps, because we might not transform all objects to camera coordinates. During the 3D pipeline, many objects and/or polygons defined by the vertices might get picked off because of clipping, hidden surface removal, or whatever. However, depending on how the final 3D engine works, it might indeed be true that a single matrix can transform a point from local coordinates all the way to screen coordinates! We'll get to that later, too.

Moving on, we can once again use a matrix transformation to perform the translation step. Assuming that the camera position translation matrix is T_{cam}, the inverse of the matrix T_{cam}^{-1} is formed by inverting each of the translation factors:

```
T_cam^-1 =   |1        0        0        0|
             |0        1        0        0|
             |0        0        1        0|
             |-cam_x   -cam_y   -cam_z   1|
```

MATH

Remember, the inverse of any translation matrix is formed by taking the negative of the translation factors in the bottom row of the matrix. Additionally, the inverse of any rotation matrix is formed by supplying the negative angles into each sine or cosine term of the matrix *or* by taking the transpose of the matrix.

So if we were to multiply each vertex in world coordinates against the matrix T_{cam}^{-1}, each vertex would be translated to the proper position to account for the camera being artificially repositioned at (0,0,0). Here's the actual matrix multiply to translate a vertex $[x_w\ y_w\ z_w\ 1]$ from world coordinates to camera coordinates (without taking into consideration the orientation of the camera, of course):

FORMULA 6.2 Translation Step of World-to-Camera Coordinates Transformation

```
= [x_w y_w z_w 1] * T_cam^-1

                     |1        0        0        0|
=[x_w y_w z_w 1] *   |0        1        0        0|
                     |0        0        1        0|
                     |-cam_x   -cam_y   -cam_z   1|

= [x_w-cam_x, y_w-cam_y, z_w-cam_z, 1]
```

Of course, if you want to code this portion of the world-to-camera transformation with matrices, you could do it with a simple matrix multiply, like this:

```
POINT3D cube_camera[8]; // used to hold camera coordinates

// define translation matrix
MATRIX4X4 Tcam_inv = { {1, 0, 0, 0},
                       {0, 1, 0, 0},
                       {0, 0, 1, 0},
                       {-cam_x, -cam_y, -cam_z, 1} };

// translate each vertex by (-cam_x, -cam_y, -cam_z)
// via a matrix multiply
for (int vertex = 0; vertex<8; vertex++)
    {
    // multiple the vector/point cube_world[]
    // against the translation matrix, note
    // that the matrix multiply assumes that there
    // is a phantom w=1 to make the matrix op
    // valid
    Mat_Mul_VECTOR3D_4X4(cube_world[vertex],
                         &Tcam_inv,
                         cube_camera[vertex]);

    } // end for
```

CAUTION

Now we have a partial transformation sitting in the `cube_camera[]` vertex array. When you perform matrix multiplies, be sure that the source and destination vertices are different; otherwise, partial values will be used, and the end results will be incorrect. Hence, always make sure that you transform one vertex into another by a matrix—don't transform a vertex by a matrix back into itself!

Now that we have the first part of the camera transformation done, let's work on the second part. Knowing that we need to move the world to the camera, and that the position part was nothing more than performing an inverse or negative translation operation to the world coordinates of each object or vertex an amount (-cam_x, -cam_y, -cam_z), it's fairly reasonable to think that we can do the same thing with the camera orientation.

The Rotation Step

In Figure 6.21a we see almost the same example that we worked with in Figure 6.20. However, in this case the camera is at location (cam_x, cam_y, cam_z), with view angles

(0, ang_y, 0). In other words, the camera has a nonzero heading or *yaw* angle. Thus, it's no longer pointing in the +z-axis direction. If we can figure out how rotating the camera to align it with the +z-axis affects the rest of the world (our little cube, in this case), we have the problem solved. So let's begin ...

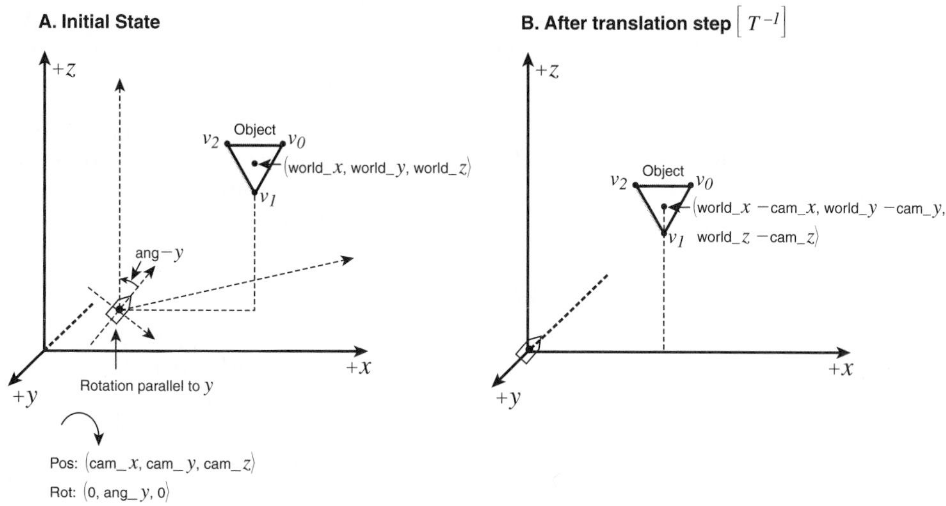

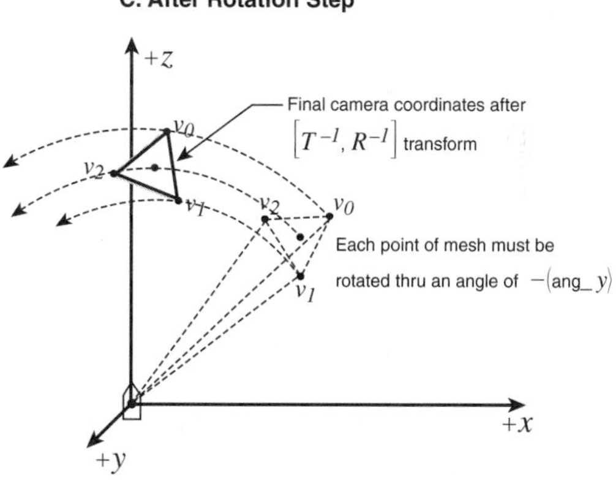

FIGURE 6.21 The rotation step of the camera transformation.

The first thing we do is translate the world coordinates of all objects so that the camera is at located at position (0,0,0) in world space. This is accomplished by translating all objects by the negative position of the camera, or (-cam_x, -cam_y, -cam_z), which is nothing more than multiplying each point in world coordinates against T_{cam}^{-1}.

At this point, we have the situation shown in Figure 6.21b. The camera is located at (0,0,0) and the relative position of the cube is the same, but the camera is still pointing at the location defined by the view angle (0, ang_y, 0). Now all we need to do to align the camera to the +z-axis is rotate the camera about the +y-axis at an angle (0,–ang_y,0), which is the inverse or negative angle that the camera is pointing (0, ang_y, 0). However, if we do this, we need to do the same thing to every vertex in the world, which in this case means the vertices that make up the cube. If we rotate the cube around the +y-axis at an angle (0, -ang_y, 0), the results are shown in Figure 6.21c.

In the figure, we have indeed positioned the camera at (0,0,0) with a view angle of (0,0,0). Nevertheless, the relative position and orientation of the object(s) in the world (the cube) are the same. What *has* changed are the actual absolute vertex positions in world space, but their relationship to the camera and each other has not. This is the complete world-to-camera transformation for a simple viewing system defined by a camera location (cam_x, cam_y, cam_z) and the Euler viewing angles (0, ang_y, 0).

But what about the general viewing angles (ang_x, ang_y, ang_z)? The transformation is the same: You must transform the world coordinates first by the negative or inverse translation matrix T_{cam}^{-1}, followed by a series of rotational transforms that rotate the world coordinates into place by the inverse of the camera orientation. Of course, as there are three angles that make up the camera orientation (ang_x, ang_y, ang_z), there are 3!=3*2*1 = 6 different ways to perform the rotation sequence:

Sequence 1: xyz

Sequence 2: xzy

Sequence 3: yxz

Sequence 4: yzx

Sequence 5: zxy

Sequence 6: zyx

However, most people use either Sequence 3 or 6, because it's more natural to first turn your head (yaw) and then tilt it up and down (pitch). The twist (roll) part isn't very natural (unless you're a dog). However, it's really up to you. The sequence doesn't really mean anything, other than if there were a virtual camera, this is how you would perform the rotation sequence. However, most of the time the camera is never seen in a game—only what it "sees" is viewed; hence, the sequence is arbitrary. In any case, we will assume Sequence 3 for the examples.

With that in mind, we need to perform three rotations: one parallel to the y-axis, which we will call R_{camy}^{-1}; followed by one around the x-axis, which we will call R_{camx}^{-1}; followed by a rotation around the z-axis, which we will call R_{camz}^{-1}. Additionally, the rotations must be the inverse of the camera angles, because we are trying to invert the whole system. Therefore, the entire rotation sequence that must be performed on every vertex to transform it to camera coordinates is as follows:

FORMULA 6.3 The Complete World-to-Camera Transformation for Arbitrary Camera Position (cam_x, cam_y, cam_z) and Orientation (ang_x, ang_y, ang_z)

$$\mathbf{T}_{wc} = \mathbf{T}_{cam}^{-1} * \mathbf{R}_{camy}^{-1} * \mathbf{R}_{camx}^{-1} * \mathbf{R}_{camz}^{-1}$$

Of course, you could concatenate all the matrices together into a single matrix and call it T_{wc} for the world-to-camera transformation, and then simply transform each point $[x_w\ y_w\ z_w\ 1]$ by the single matrix T_{wc}, as shown in the following to transform from world-to-camera coordinates:

$$[x_w\ y_w\ z_w\ 1] * \mathbf{T}_{wc}$$

Pretty cool, huh?

TIP

Note that we are using the inverse of the camera translation and rotation matrices. If we wanted to think of the camera as an object, to orient and place it we would transform it into world coordinates with the transformation sequence

$$\mathbf{R}_{camy} * \mathbf{R}_{camx} * \mathbf{R}_{camz} * \mathbf{T}_{cam}$$

Note that the rotation and translation steps have been reversed, and the matrices are not inverted. It's interesting to also note that the camera is really nothing more than a unit vector located at (cam_x, cam_y, cam_z), with orientation (ang_x, ang_y, ang_z).

In practice, you need to compute the matrix $\mathbf{T}_{wc}$, which equals $(\mathbf{T}_{cam}^{-1} * \mathbf{R}_{camy}^{-1} * \mathbf{R}_{camx}^{-1} * \mathbf{R}_{camz}^{-1})$. You can do this manually on paper and arrive at a single matrix that you can just initialize, or you can define the independent matrices and then multiply them together one by one and then use the result. Either way is fine, because you will only need to compute the world-to-camera transformation once per frame, and a couple matrix multiplies isn't going to kill you.

However, if you did want to manually compute $\mathbf{T}_{wc}$, it can be computed using algebra to simplify the matrix multiplies, and the resulting matrix will have the inverse translation along with the $(\mathbf{R}_{camy}^{-1} * \mathbf{R}_{camx}^{-1} * \mathbf{R}_{camz}^{-1})$ rotations all in one matrix. However, I want to hold off on this until later, because it's really nothing more than an exercise in algebra. For now, let's just use our formulas for translation and rotation and let the computer do the work:

```
// given the camera is at (cam_x, cam_y, cam_z) with
// view angle (ang_x, ang_y, ang_z) and a camera
// rotation sequence of y*x*z we have the following:

// here's the translation matrix
MATRIX4X4 Tcam_inv = { {1, 0, 0, 0},
                       {0, 1, 0, 0},
```

6

```
                    {0, 0, 1, 0},
                    {-cam_x, -cam_y, -cam_z, 1} };

// now we need the rotation matrices for x,y,z
// and remember the angles are ang_x, ang_y, ang_z

// here's the inverse rotation matrix for the x-axis
// remember all you need to do is plug in negative theta
// into the matrix and you will get the inverse rotation
// relative to positive theta
MATRIX4X4 Rcamx_inv = {
        {1,  0,           0,           0},
        {0,  cos(-ang_x), sin(-ang_x), 0},
        {0, -sin(-ang_x), cos(-ang_x), 0},
        {0,  0,           0,           1}};


// here's the inverse rotation matrix for the y-axis
// remember all you need to do is plug in negative theta
// into the matrix and you will get the inverse rotation
// relative to positive theta
MATRIX4X4 Rcamy_inv = {
          {cos(-ang_y), 0, -sin(-ang_y), 0},
          {0,           1,  0,           0},
          {sin(-ang_y), 0,  cos(-ang_y), 0},
          {0,           0,  0,           1}};

// finally, here's the inverse rotation matrix for the z-axis
// remember all you need to do is plug in negative theta
// into the matrix and you will get the inverse rotation
// relative to positive theta
MATRIX4X4 Rcamz_inv = {
          {cos(-ang_z), sin(-ang_z),  0, 0},
          {-sin(-ang_z), cos(-ang_z), 0, 0},
          {0,           0,            1, 0}
          {0,           0,            0, 1}};

// now were ready to go, let's multiply them all together
// Tcam_inv * Rcamy_inv * Rcamx_inv * Rcamz_inv

MATRIX4X4 Mtemp1, Mtemp2, Tcam;
```

```
Mat_Mul_4X4(&Tcam_inv, &Rcamy_inv, &Mtemp1);
Mat_Mul_4X4(&Rcamx_inv, &Rcamz_inv, &Mtemp2);

// watch your order!
Mat_Mul_4X4(&Mtemp1, &Mtemp2, &Tcam);

// and now we are finally ready to transform the world
// coords to camera coords

for (int vertex = 0; vertex<8; vertex++)
    {
    // multiple the vector/point cube_world[]
    // against the final camera matrix, note
    // that the matrix multiply assumes that there
    // is a phantom w=1 to make the matrix op
    // valid
    Mat_Mul_VECTOR3D_4X4(cube_world[vertex],
                         &Tcam,
                         cube_camera[vertex]);

    } // end for
```


MATH

If you want, you can simplify the `sin()` and `cos()` terms in the matrix definitions using the identities `sin(-x) = -sin(x)` and `cos(-x) = cos(x)`. However, I want you to see the negative signs and see how easy it is to compute the inverse of any rotation matrix.

At this point, we can further annotate our 3D viewing pipeline to add the world-to-camera transformation and arrive at the flow diagram shown in Figure 6.22. However, the diagram isn't really accurate. It's missing some intermediate steps, like object removal and clipping, but we will get to them shortly.

Final Word on Camera Coordinates

One last thing I want to bring to your attention is that the world-to-camera transformation depends on the representation of the virtual camera that you select. In this introductory chapter, we are using a fairly primitive camera system that has lots of problems, such as *gimbal lock*.

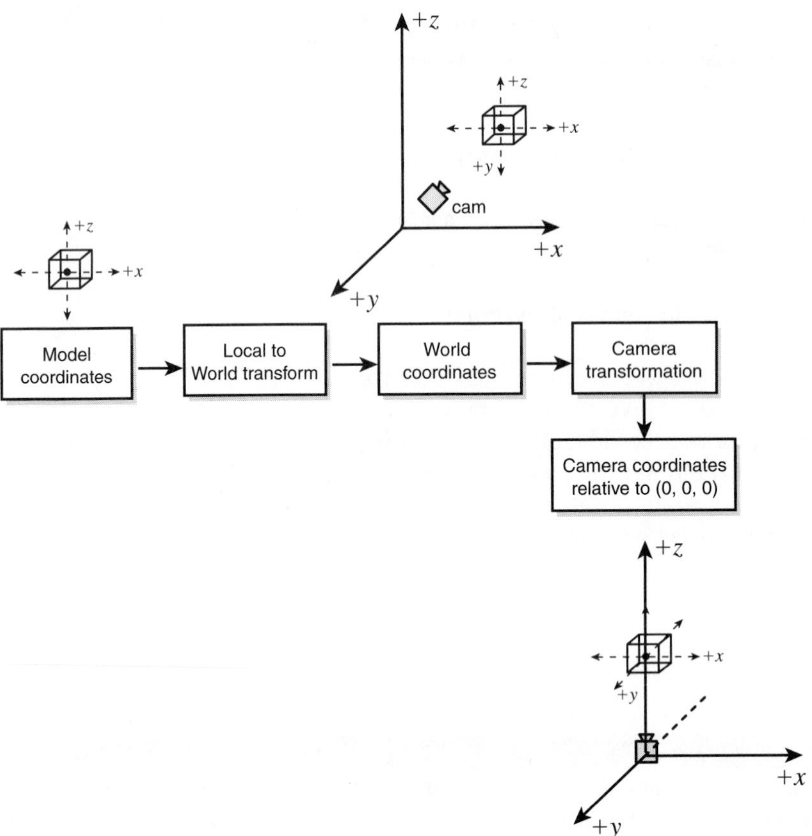

FIGURE 6.22 The 3D pipeline with the camera transformation added.

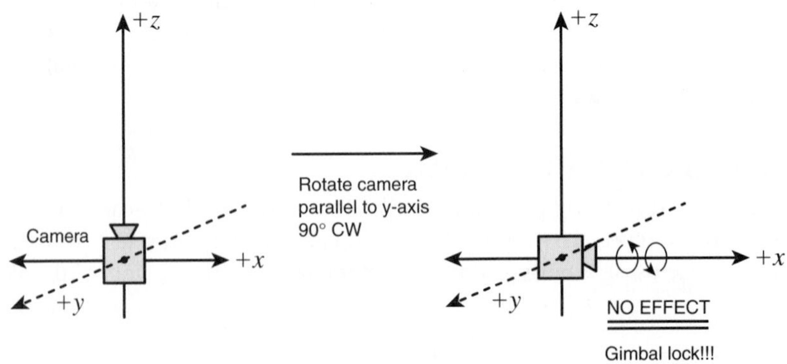

FIGURE 6.23 Gimbal lock.

Gimbal lock occurs when you rotate one axis to the point that it becomes aligned with another, and further rotation on that axis results in no motion at all. For example, take a look at Figure 6.23. In the figure, if we first rotate the camera around the y-axis 90 degrees so that it aligns with the x-axis, trying to rotate around the x-axis does nothing—this is gimbal lock.

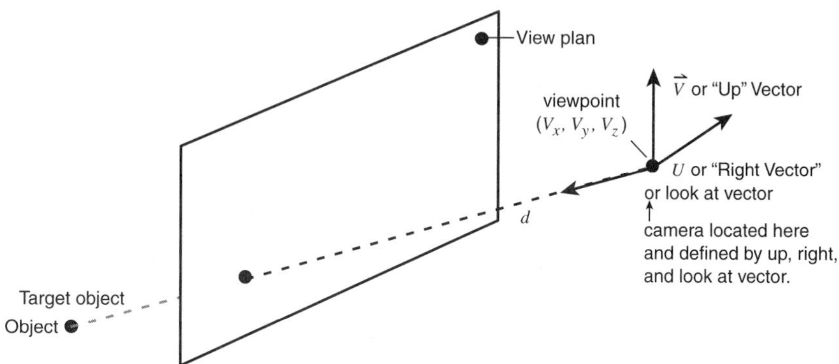

FIGURE 6.24 The UVN camera system.

Alas, there are better camera systems, based on a more natural representation of a camera, taking into account its position and orientation in terms of a focal point (or "look at" point, as shown in Figure 6.24), but we will get into that in more detail in the next chapter.

Hidden Object/Surface Removal and Clipping

Everything you have just learned is correct, but there are two topics I purposely left out because they really don't have anything to do with coordinates: *hidden surface/object removal* and *clipping*. Both of these topics are going to take some time to explain, so right now all I want to do is make you aware that we need to consider them in the 3D pipeline. Therefore, let's take a minute to talk about them, beginning with hidden object/surface removal.

When you perform the world-to-camera transformation (or before you perform it), there are a number of tests you can perform to determine what objects are visible to the camera. These tests are generally classed as hidden surface removal. That is, we need to determine what objects and/or geometry are visible to the camera, so that we don't mistakenly try to render them (or more importantly, not to push the objects through the camera transformation in the first place). With that in mind, two tests are generally performed: back-face removal and the bounding spheres test.

Back-Face Removal

In Figure 6.25, we see an object and we see the camera. However, right now the coordinate system is still in world coordinates. The back-face removal test is performed before the world-to-camera transformation in world-space. This test is used to limit the number of polygons that are transformed from world-to-camera coordinates that would be impossible to see because they are facing away from the viewpoint.

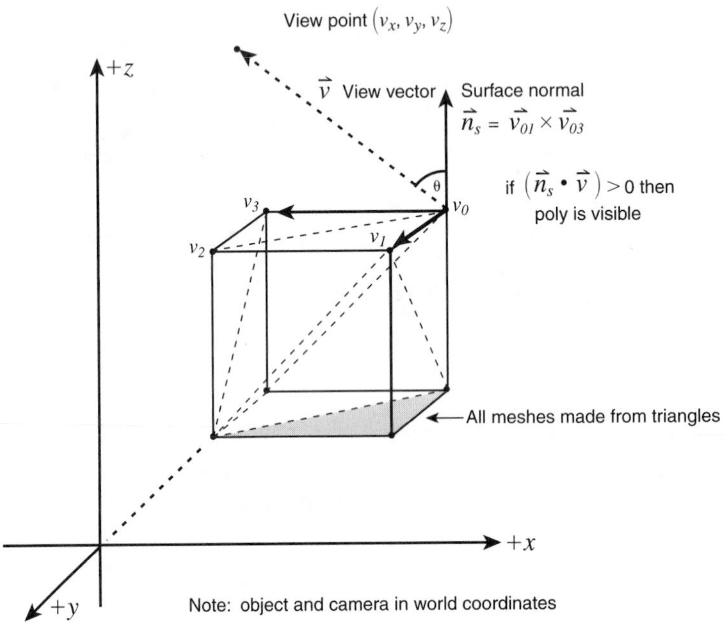

FIGURE 6.25 Back-face removal setup.

The logic of the back-face test works in the following way: All polygons that make up each object are labeled in a consistent way, either clockwise or counterclockwise (it doesn't matter). Then a surface normal $\mathbf{n}_s$ is computed with that knowledge for each polygon, and this normal is tested against the viewing vector **v**, as shown in Figure 6.25. If the angle between the normal and the viewing vector is less than or equal to 90 degrees, the polygon is visible to the viewer (of course, for two-sided polygons, this test doesn't work). Using this test, we can trivially reject half the geometry of each object.

The test itself is performed with the dot product, based on the fact that any pair of vectors that are dotted together have the following properties:

- u.v = 0, if and only if the angle between u and v is 90 degrees or pi/2 radians.
- u.v > 0, if and only if the angle between u and v is less than 90 degrees or pi/2 radians.
- u.v < 0, if and only if the angle between u and v is greater than 90 degrees or pi/2 radians.

Thus in our data structures that define objects as meshes of polygons (which we will get to shortly), we have a flag that indicates that a polygon is one-sided, so we can apply this test and filter out a great deal of the polygons from the expensive world-to-camera transformation with the following pseudo-code:

```
if (ns . v) > 0)
   {
   // poly is visible
   } // end if
```

NOTE

You might decide that polygons that are exactly 90 degrees relative to the view direction are visible, too—that is, polygons that are on edge, or *scathing*. However, this can cause problems with rendering, because these polygons will usually have a width of one pixel.

Bounding Spheres Test

After you perform the back-face removal step and filter out as many polygons in world coordinates from the camera position as you can, you then transform all the objects from world coordinates to camera coordinates. However, you can do one more test before you perform the back-face removal step at an even higher level. In fact, you should probably do this test before you perform the back-face removal, so you can throw entire objects away. However, this test only works if you have objects that are partitioned in convex areas. In other words, if you have a gameworld that takes place in space, for example, you can locate each asteroid and ship and put bounding boxes (or spheres) around them. On the other hand, with an indoor game composed of a single mesh, the world won't work with this type of test. However, you can surely partition rooms or areas and so forth. The point is simply this: Try to prevent large areas of the game geometry from being processed if they aren't visible whenever possible.

The idea of the test is to create a bounding sphere around all the objects in world space, as shown in Figure 6.26. Then you perform the world-to-camera transformation with only the center of the spheres (a single point). Then you test to see whether the spheres are contained within the viewing frustrum. If they aren't, you can throw the entire object away. If the spheres are partially contained in the frustrum, the test is inconclusive, and further testing is needed.

Therefore, if you have a world that is composed of objects composed of polygons, your first step might be to compute a bounding sphere around each object in world-space, performing the world-to-camera transformation only on the spheres (which are defined by a single point), and then testing whether the spheres are within the camera's viewing frustrum. Objects that aren't in the viewing frustrum at all would be thrown away. You must continue on with the back-face removal and finally perform the world-to-camera transform for the remaining polygon mesh geometry that is neither a back-face nor out of the viewing frustrum.

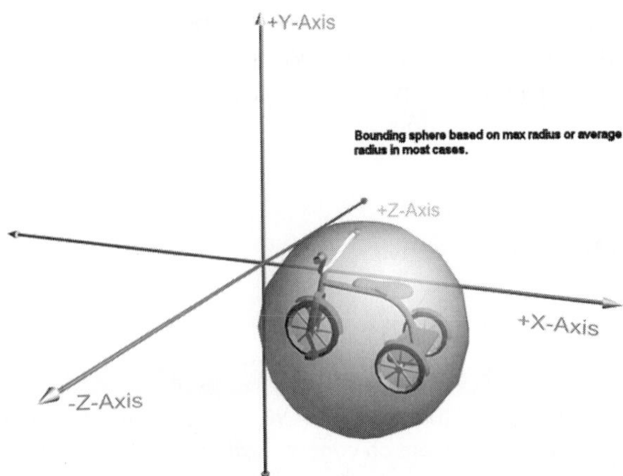

FIGURE 6.26 Placing a bounding sphere around objects to test for view frustrum culling.

Although I don't want to get into the details of the bounding sphere algorithm until we have a working wire-frame 3D engine, let's take a quick look at the math. The problem is very simple. Assume that we have an object **O**, which is a collection of vertices. We compute a bounding sphere around the object by determining the farthest vertex from the center of the object (this can be done ahead of time in a loading phase, rather than in real time), which is in essence its maximum radius. A possible algorithm is shown in the following, which you would run in local/model coordinates in most cases:

```
POINT3D cube_model[NUM_VERTICES]; // our 3D model

float max_radius = 0; // set to 0
float curr_radius;

// iterate thru the vertex list and keep updating
// the radius with the largest radius
for (int vertex=0; vertex < NUM_VERTICES; vertex++)
    {
    float x=cube_model[vertex].x;
    float y=cube_model[vertex].y;
    float z=cube_model[vertex].z;

    // have we found a larger bounding sphere?
    if (curr_radius = sqrt(x*x + y*y + z*z) > max_radius)
        max_radius = curr_radius;

    } // end for
```

Of course, I'm being pretty brutal by using `sqrt()`, and I could get along with an approximation, or even by using the 1-norm. That is, simply find the vertex that has the largest distance², and then take the `sqrt()` to find the real distance:

```
POINT3D cube_model[NUM_VERTICES]; // our 3D model

float max_radius = 0; // set to 0
float curr_radius;

// iterate thru the vertex list and keep updating
// the radius with the largest radius
for (int vertex=0; vertex < NUM_VERTICES; vertex++)
    {
    float x=cube_model[vertex].x;
    float y=cube_model[vertex].y;
    float z=cube_model[vertex].z;

    // have we found a larger bounding sphere?
    if (curr_radius = (x*x + y*y + z*z) > max_radius)
        max_radius = curr_radius;

    } // end for

// compute real distance now
max_distance = sqrt(max_distance);
```

9

TIP

The preceding trick works because if $|a| > |b|$, then $a^2 > b^2$, and the similar argument $|a| < |b|$, then $a^2 < b^2$.

Either way, it doesn't really matter, because you would run this algorithm in an initialization phase. After we compute `max_radius`, then we can do some work to create the bounding sphere: With the center of the object in world coordinates, calling it the point **p0**(x0, y0, z0) and its radius `max_radius`, we perform the world-to-camera transformation on the point **p0** as follows:

$$\mathbf{p1} = \mathbf{p0} * \mathbf{T}_{wc}$$

Now, **p1** is the center of our object's bounding sphere in camera coordinates, as shown in Figure 6.27. Here's the fun part: We define six other points relative to **p1** parallel to the +-x, +-y, and +-z axes that are a distance `max_radius` from **p1**, which define the boundaries of the bounding sphere S around **p1**. Then we are ready to determine whether the bounding sphere is within the viewing frustrum with some simple tests.

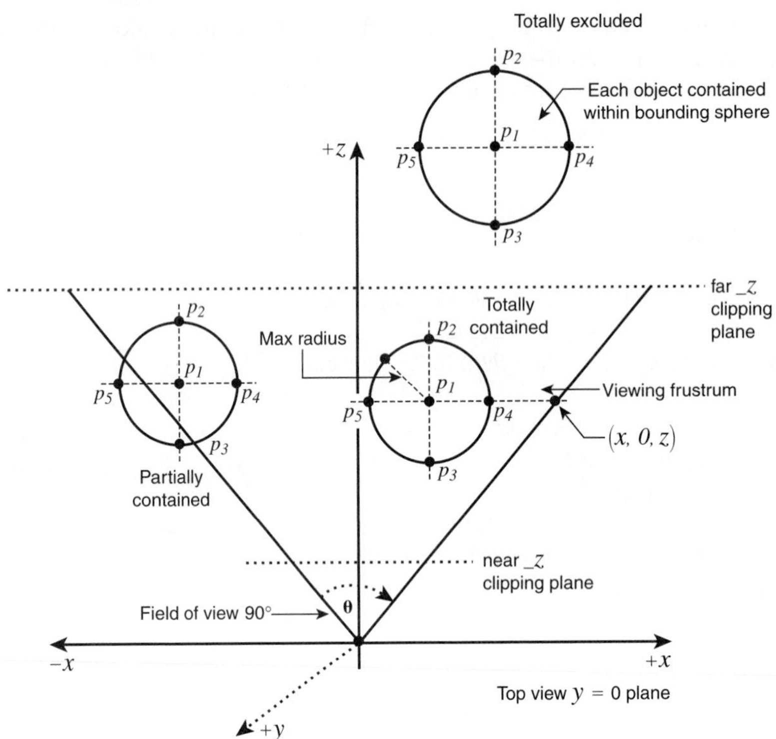

FIGURE 6.27 The details of the bounding sphere tests.

In Figure 6.27 we see a top view of the x-z plane. The tests for the y-z plane are identical, so we need not belabor them. There are a number of cases we need to consider—we need to compare the bounding sphere to the viewing frustrum and determine whether it's totally outside, totally inside, or partially inside. If the bounding sphere S is partially inside or totally inside, we simply include the entire sphere's mesh in the data stream and then perform further tests. At this point, you can either try and determine whether the bounding sphere is inside or partially inside the viewing frustrum or completely outside—it's up to you. However, sometimes using negative logic is cheaper, so that's the approach I will take in this example.

Okay, the problem can be stated as follows in 2D: We have a circle that is defined by a center $\mathbf{p_1}$ (x1,z1), along with four points that define its boundaries in the x and z directions, which are nothing more than

```
Center: p1(x1,z1)

Exterior points:
```

```
p2(x1, z1+max_radius)
p3(x1, z1-max_radius)
p4(x1+max_radius, z1)
p5(x1-max_radius, z1)
```

Theorem: If any of the points **p1–p5** are in the viewing frustrum, then the bounding circle/sphere must be in the viewing frustrum.

Corollary: If none of the points **p1–p5** are in the viewing frustrum, then no portion of the bounding circle/sphere can be in the viewing frustrum.

Take your pick, but I usually use the corollary and try to trivially reject the entire sphere. With that in mind, we need to really look at the viewing frustrum and come up with some equations so we can quickly plug in the vertex values **p1-p5** and make decisions. Referring to Figure 6.26, the near and far clipping planes are fairly easy to test against. If either of the following conditions are true, the object can't possibly be in the viewing frustrum:

Far clipping plane conditional:

```
If (p3.z > far_z)
   {
   // object is not in viewing frustrum
   } // end if
```

Near clipping plane conditional:

```
If (p2.z < near_z)
   {
   // object is not in viewing frustrum
   } // end if
```

We always hope for those! The problem is that the sides of the viewing frustrum (right, left, top, bottom) are defined by general planes. But again, we can use similar triangles or the plane equations along with a dot product to determine the relative position of the bounding sphere to the planes. For now, let's just stick to the 2D case and assume a 90 degree viewing volume. With those assumptions, the problem boils down to determining whether a point **p** (x,z) (for the x-z top-down case) is within the triangle defined by the left and right sides of the viewing frustrum. This can be solved with similar triangles.

However, if you're paying attention, there's an easier way. Remember that for a viewing volume of 90 degrees, the plane equations for the right and left sides of the frustrum are

$$|x| = z$$

Therefore, for a point **p** (x,z) that we want to test against the right clipping plane, if $x < z$, it means that the point **p** is on the left half space of the plane. If $x > z$, it means that the point is on the right half space of the plane, and $x = z$ means the point is right on the clipping boundary itself. A similar argument can be used for the left clipping plane, but the sign of x is simply inverted. With that in mind, we can complete our rules for the left and right clipping planes for 90 degree FOV:

Right clipping plane conditional:

```
if (p5.x > p5.z)
   {
   // object is not in viewing frustrum
   } // end if
```

Left clipping plane conditional (note the sign and comparison inversion because the left clipping plane has the equation $-x = z$):

```
if (-p4.x > p4.z)
   {
   // object is not in viewing frustrum
   } // end if
```

The same argument can be made for the top and bottom clipping planes; thus the general rules to test whether a point **p** (x,y,z) is outside the viewing frustrum are as follows:

```
if ((z > far_z)   || (z < near_z) || // z-axis
    (fabs(x) < z) || // x-z plane
    (fabs(y) < z))   // y-z plane
    {
    // point not in viewing frustrum
    } // end if
```

Now all you have to do is pick the right points to test—in this case, **p1–p5**—with the preceding rule.

> **NOTE**
>
> All this stuff sounds good, but remember one thing: So much depends on your data structures and representations of your objects. It might be that your whole game is composed of free polygons, and there's no real containable "objects." Perhaps it's pointless to remove back-faces, because meshes are based on vertex lists that must be transformed anyway, and there's no real "polygon" list that is a separate entity from the vertices that make up the object that the polygons skin. Or maybe all your objects are semitransparent, and thus all polygons have two sides. Alas, in many cases backface removal may not make sense.

Limitations of Object Removal

Before moving on, I want to bring up one point about object removal, which is this rule: If an object's bounding sphere is not in the viewing frustrum, the object itself cannot possibly be in the viewing frustrum. However, the opposite is not true: If a portion of the bounding sphere is inside the viewing frustrum, that does not necessarily mean the object is! Why? Because the bounding sphere might not be a good representation of the object. For example, take a look at Figure 6.28, where we see a very long object's bounding sphere and the viewing frustrum. Interestingly enough, the bounding sphere is in the viewing frustrum, although the object is not! This doesn't mean that the bounding sphere test doesn't work; it just means that it might not filter out all objects that are not in the viewing frustrum. Hence, sometimes bounding geometries that are geometrically more appropriate for the object are used, such as cubes or parallelepipeds.

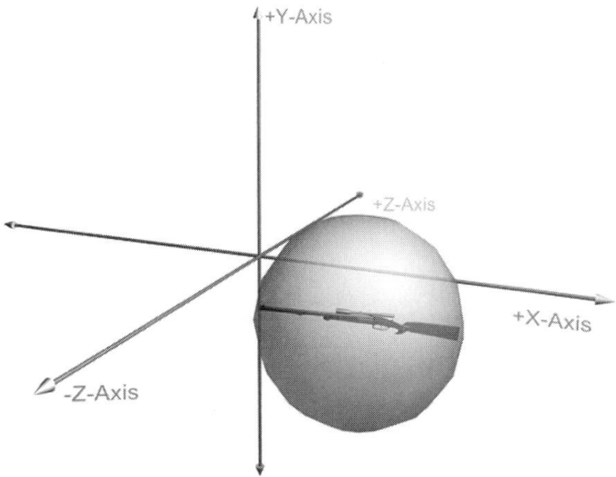

FIGURE 6.28 A bounding sphere might not be the best choice.

That's about it for the quick tour of object and back-face removal. Now take a look at Figure 6.29 to see our updated 3D pipeline—notice we're still a long way from the screen!

Perspective Coordinates

Now we're getting somewhere! Let's reiterate the major stages of the 3D pipeline:

Stage I: All 3D objects are usually defined in their own local space with their own local coordinate system. This representation is called the local or model coordinates representation.

Stage II: After you have all the 3D models that you want to place in the virtual 3D world, you place them by transforming the model coordinates to world coordinates. This is achieved with the local-to-world transformation. Furthermore, this transformation is nothing more than a translation of the vertices that make up each model to the desired center position at which you want the object placed in the world. Be careful not to frag your model coordinates in the process—you need another array to hold the results!

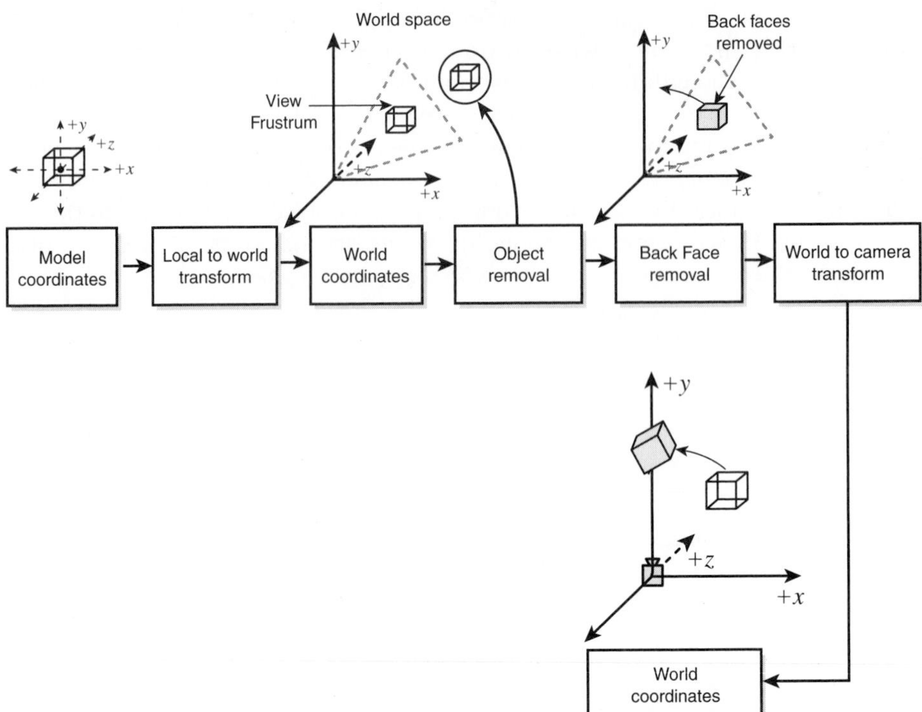

FIGURE 6.29 The 3D pipeline with back-face and object removal added.

Stage III: After you have all your objects placed in the world and they are defined with absolute world coordinates, you need to view the world through a virtual camera. There are a number of ways to represent the camera, but a position and orientation will suffice.

Stage IV: You might have a hidden object/surface back-face removal step at this point that minimizes the amount of geometry that is transformed to camera coordinates. You might first try to remove entire objects, and then for objects that remain visible, remove back-faces.

Stage V: There are a number of ways to compute how the objects would look through the lens of a virtual camera, but the process is greatly simplified when the camera is looking straight down the z-axis located at the origin. With this in mind, the world-to-camera transformation transforms all the geometry in the world as if the camera was at the origin looking down the z-axis. The transform is nothing more than a series of inverse transforms based on the translation and rotation transforms used to place the virtual camera.

Stage VI: Finally, with the camera at the origin (or similarly convenient position) with view angles all 0 (depending on convention), we have a viewing frustrum that represents what the camera's virtual lens can see. This frustrum usually has a near clipping plane and a far clipping plane, along with both a horizontal and vertical field of view. Objects within this frustrum are projected and rendered to the screen. This projection phase is the next part we are going to talk about.

Getting Ready for Projection

Before we talk about perspective coordinates, let's talk briefly about the entire projection process and the viewing frustrum once again. Assume that we have a 3D object made of a collection of vertices `v[]` that we want to render, and we have already performed all the transformations. The object is in the viewing frustrum as shown in Figure 6.18. The question is how to project this image onto the screen?

The answer is it depends on what you want to see. The first step is to look at the virtual camera system a little more so we can explain with the relationship between the camera, the world, and screen a little better.

Referring again to Figure 6.18, and assuming a 90 degree field of view system aligned to the z-axis and looking in the +z direction (a nice left handed system), this is the system we will use for the following discussion.

The Projection/Viewing Plane

The projection plane is where the action happens. Of course, the viewing frustrum itself determines what we process, but ultimately the viewing plane is used to form the virtual image of the 3D world, which is then used to display on the raster 2D screen. With our first camera system, we have decided that the camera will finally be positioned at location (0,0,0) looking straight down the +z-axis. With this setup, we can select the near, far, and view plane anywhere we like. However, the selection of the view plane will make some things easier or harder down the line in the viewing pipeline.

For example, because we are already assuming a 90 degree field of view, we can look at the 3D system from a top view without loss of generality, as shown in Figure 6.30, to arrive at some facts. These facts can then be generalized to full 3D. First, the distance that we place the view plane from the viewpoint (0,0,0) is sometimes called the viewing distance d. Now, the selection of d has a lot to do with the perspective transform and its relationship to the screen coordinates.

Now here's the clincher—after we define all these values and then place a 3D object in the frustrum, to render it onto the view plane we simply project mathematical *projectors* from each point that make up the object through the view plane that terminate at the viewpoint. This is all there is to projection! The image formed on the virtual view plane is then rendered on the screen of your computer.

Of course, there are some details we are missing here that have to do with scale, but we will get to that in a minute. At this point, let's take a closer look at the perspective transformation.

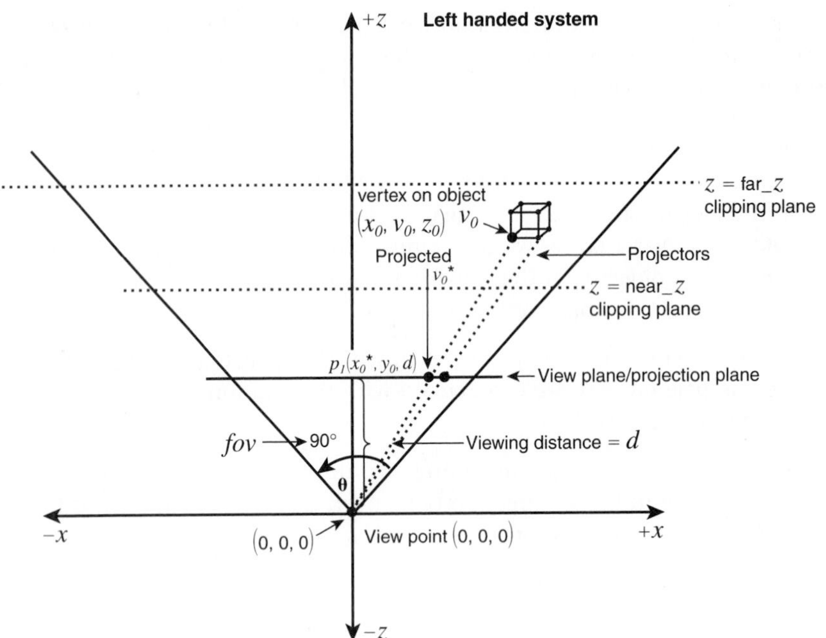

FIGURE 6.30 A simplified 2D top-down projection of the viewing frustrum in the x-z plane.

The Perspective Transformation

The perspective projection is nothing more than projecting an object's vertices through an arbitrary view plane, as shown in Figure 6.31. The formulation is as follows: Given that the view plane is a distance d from the point of projection (the camera viewpoint), then the math can easily be worked out to compute the intersection point in the view plane of a ray from the viewpoint through the view plane to a point on the object, or vice versa.

This geometry problem can be worked out using the 2D case and then generalized to the 3D case, so let's do that. In Figure 6.31, we see our 3D system on its side viewing the y-z plane. We also see a point **p**(y0,z0) that we want projected on our view plane, which is located a distance d from the origin at position z = d. The math is trivial, and nothing more than similar triangles that can be stated as follows: The side d is as to z as the y_p is to y. Thus, we can write the relationship as

$$d/z0 = y_p/y0$$

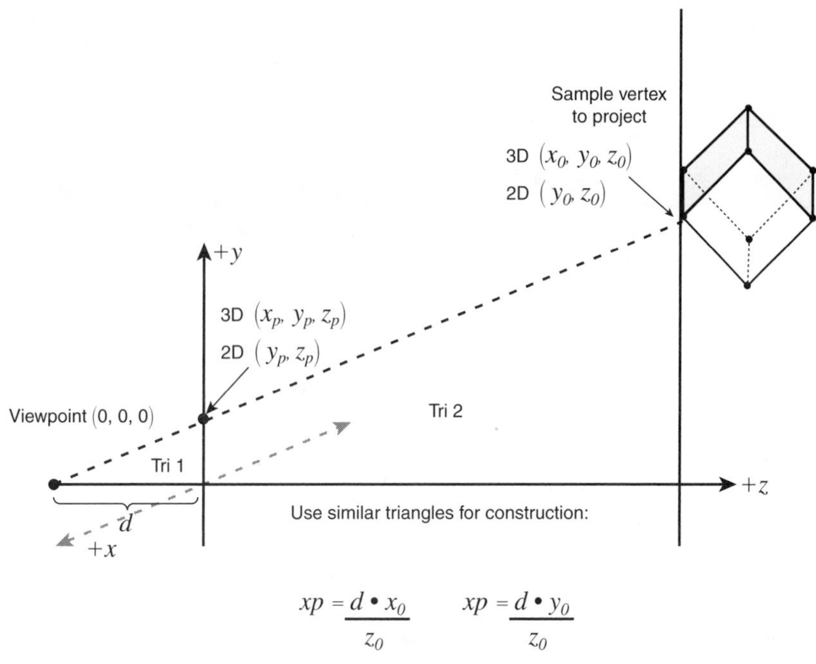

FIGURE 6.31 The construction of the perspective transform.

Rearranging this, we get

```
yp = d*y0/z0
```

which means that the projected point y_p on the projection plane z = d from the projection point (0,0,0) (which is the camera, of course) is equal to the product of the distance from the camera d multiplied by y0, then divided by z0. Additionally, if we were to do the same analysis from the x-z plane, we would get the following relationship:

```
d/z0 = xp/x0
```

Rearranging here, we get

```
xp = d*x0/z0
```

Putting them together, we get the final perspective transformation for a view plane located at z = d from the viewpoint located at (0,0,0):

FORMULA 6.4 The Perspective Transformation

```
xper = d*x/z
yper = d*y/z
```

First let's talk a little about problems with this formula. There's a *pole* at z = 0. That is, the equations go to infinity when z = 0, which is a bad thing. Alas, you can't project vertices with z = 0. Furthermore, objects with negative z values will get inverted, but still projected. That's why we need a near clipping plane, so this stuff can't happen.

NOTE

There's also a parallel or orthographic projection that is sometimes used in 3D for mechanical and CAD programs. In this projection, the z coordinates are simply thrown away. Of course, there's no perspective, but many times when designing parts and homes, you don't want to see any perspective. Thus, during the projection phase of a vertex (x0,y0,z0), the point is simply projected at (x0,y0), and sometimes z0 is used as an intensity value to shade the near imagery relative to z distance.

As always, let's take a look at the perspective transformation in terms of a code and a matrix formulation. The perspective transformation is very simple in terms of code. But we have to use homogenous coordinates—*period*! The reason is that there's no easy way to get a division by z with a matrix that doesn't contain z for each vertex, so hold that thought and look at how we would do the transform with brute force:

```
POINT3D cube_camera[8]; // used to hold camera coordinates
POINT3D cube_per[8]; // used to hold perspective coordinates

// perform the perspective transform on the camera
// coordinates, assume viewing distance is d
for (int vertex = 0; vertex<8; vertex++)
    {
    float z = cube_model[vertex].z;

    cube_per[vertex].x=d*cube_camera[vertex].x/z;
    cube_per[vertex].y=d*cube_camera[vertex].y/z;

    // we don't need this, so just copy it
    cube_per[vertex].z=cube_camera[vertex].z;
    } // end for
```

Brute force is good sometimes, isn't it? Hence, we can perform the perspective transform as shown and be done, but if we want to create a completely matrix-based system, we have to be able to represent everything with matrices. Therefore, here's the matrix T_{per} that performs the perspective transformation on 4D homogenous coordinates.

$$\mathbf{T}_{per} = \begin{vmatrix} 1 & 0 & 0 & 0 \\ 0 & 1 & 0 & 0 \\ 0 & 0 & 1 & 1/d \\ 0 & 0 & 0 & 0 \end{vmatrix}$$

Let's see whether it works with an example point in camera coordinates $p = [x_c\ y_c\ z_c\ 1]$:

$$\mathbf{p} * \mathbf{T}_{per} =$$

$$[x_c\ y_c\ z_c\ 1] * \begin{vmatrix} 1 & 0 & 0 & 0 \\ 0 & 1 & 0 & 0 \\ 0 & 0 & 1 & 1/d \\ 0 & 0 & 0 & 0 \end{vmatrix}$$

$$= [x_c,\ y_c,\ z_c,\ (z_c/d)]$$

Then if we divide the components (x,y,z) by $w = (z_c/d)$ to convert from homogenous coordinates back to normal coordinates, we get the final point:

$$= [x_c*d/z_c,\ y_c*d/z_c,\ z_c*d/z_c]$$

And of course, we don't need to even look at the z coordinate, because after projection, we are only interested in the (x,y) coordinates, which are

$$x = x_c*d/z_c$$
$$y = y_c*d/z_c$$

This performs the perspective transformation via a matrix. However, this is the first time we've had to convert from 4D homogenous coordinates back to 3D. We might want to rethink whether we really need to perform the perspective transform using a matrix. The answer is that it depends on how we build the engine. That is, do we want a totally matrix-based system, or are we going to use matrices for the majority of the transformations, but in the quest for speed use simple code for operations like the perspective transformation and screen transformation? We won't worry about that right now, but it is an issue.

We're just about to slay the projection dragon, but there's still another detail we need to consider—the viewing distance d. What value should we pick for d? This is a good question, but you might not like the answer: anything! Yes, you can pick anything you like for d. Changing d will artificially change the scale of imagery that is the amount of perspective. So then, what's the best d? I usually pick d in one of two ways. First, if I want to really simplify my math, I select d = 1, which turns the perspective projection into the following:

FORMULA 6.5 Perspective Projection with d = 1 (Normalized Coordinates)

$$x_{per} = 1*x/z$$
$$y_{per} = 1*y/z$$

The matrix for this operation is obtained by setting d = 1:

```
           |1    0    0    0 |
T      =   |0    1    0    0 |
 per1      |0    0    1    1 |
           |0    0    0    0 |
```

If you perform the preceding operation, you are going to end up with *normalized view plane coordinates*. In other words, all the vertices that are projected will fall in the range of –1 to +1 on both the x and y axes. Additionally, you need to map the view plane coordinates to screen coordinates for viewing. That is, map –1 to 1 on both the x and y axes to the screen resolution of width×height. There's a problem with this, though, because we are mapping a square view plane to the view port, and the view port must be square. Otherwise, one of the axes will end up being distorted, so in cases where the final view port or screen is nonsquare, we must take this into consideration and give the view plane the same ratio of width to height as the view port, or perform a secondary scaling on one of the axes at some point from the perspective-to-screen coordinates transformation. More on this later, but keep it in mind.

The other way to find d is to compute it based on the final screen coordinates that you want to generate. If you are going to project onto a screen that's 640×480, you can pick d such that the field of view is 90 on the x-axis, and all projections will lie in the range 640×480. However, there's a little problem here, because the x and y sizes are different. That means that you would think you would need a d for both the x-axis perspective transform and the y-axis transform. But if you use a different d for each, you will end up distorting the image on the screen. So in the case where you are projecting onto a screen of width×height and computing the d that gives a specific FOV for the x-axis, you MUST use that same d for both the x and y perspective transforms, and the end result will be that the y-axis field of view will be slightly different.

When you have a nonsquare projection view plane or view port, you need to be aware that the nice square projection won't work anymore, and that there's a factor that relates the x and y-axes together. This is called the *aspect ratio*. The aspect ratio is usually defined as width/height, so in the case of a 640×480 screen, the aspect is 4:3, or 1.33333. This number comes in handy during the perspective-to-screen projection for nonsquare view planes. In this case, you must multiple the aspect ratio times the focal distance during the perspective calculations.

Take a look at Figure 6.32 to see the construction and solution to find d. Then we simply use the same d for the vertical axis because we must use the same focal length.

NOTE

As a side effect, the vertical field of view will not in general be the same as the horizontal field of view, because the ratio of width/height is not 1.0.

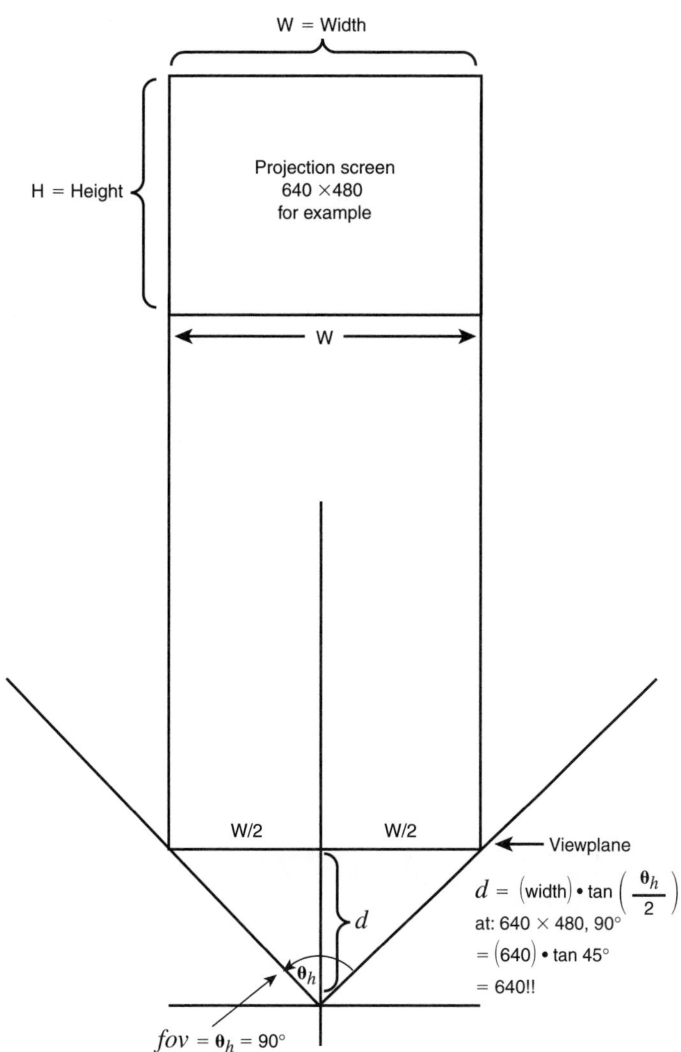

FIGURE 6.32 Computing d as a function of screen size and field of view.

FORMULA 6.6 Computation of Distance Values for Perspective Projection onto View Plane with Dimensions (Width×Height)

```
d = (0.5)*width*tan(θh/2)
```

Stated in plain English: The distance is equal to one half the width (or height, if you want that to be the major axis) of the projection plane times the tangent of the viewing angle divided by two. If you don't follow this, just look closely at the figure and remember that tan(θ) = opposite/adjacent = y/x, and in this case, y is the distance and x is related to the width.

Now that we have our distance factors for the projection onto a virtual view plane of size width×height, let's plug them back into the equations:

FORMULA 6.7a The Perspective Transformation onto a Square View Plane

x_{per} = d*x/z
y_{per} = d*y/z

To generalize this, we need to add in the aspect ratio factor ar. We can do this by multiplying it against the y component in the calculation—this generalizes the perspective transform:

FORMULA 6.7b The Perspective Transformation Generalized to Nonsquare View Planes

x_{per} = d*x/z
y_{per} = d*y*ar/z

And if you want to put it into matrix form the following matrix would perform desired transform:

```
            |d   0     0   0|
Tperd   =   |0   d*ar  0   0|
            |0   0     1   1|
            |0   0     0   0|
```

NOTE

Notice the repositioning of the d terms.

Given a point p [x_c y_c z_c 1], let's multiply it against the matrix and check the results:

```
p * Tperd    =

                      |d   0     0   0|
[xc yc zc 1]  *       |0   d*ar  0   0|
                      |0   0     1   1|
                      |0   0     0   0|
```

= [($d*x_c$) ($d*ar*y_c$) z_c z_c]

Dividing the x,y components by the w component $w = z_c$, we get

$$= [(d*x_c)/z_c \quad (d*ar*y_c)/z_c \quad 1]$$

or

$$x = (d*x_c)/z_c$$
$$y = (d*ar*y_c)/z_c$$

which is identical to Formula 6.7b, and is indeed the transformation we were looking for!

The point is that you can do this stuff with either matrix or manual methods. You might ask, why use a matrix at all? The answer lies in the fact that matrices are much more convenient, and you can concatenate many matrix operations together: that is, $\mathbf{M} = \mathbf{M}_1*\mathbf{M}_2*\ldots\mathbf{M}_i*\ldots\mathbf{M}_n$. Thus, it's possible to concatenate local object transforms with the local-to-world, then world-to-camera, then camera-to-perspective, all in one matrix! The point being if you have to multiply any point by a matrix, the matrix multiplier doesn't know that you have 100 operations in the single matrix. That's the power of matrix multiplication, if you set it up right. But let's move on, keeping that in the back of your mind.

Perspective Projection and 3D Clipping

Simply stated, the perspective projection operates on the camera coordinates of the vertices of geometry that you want to display (which is determined in a previous step). The perspective projection T_{per} (or various derivatives that we have explored) basically transforms the points in camera coordinates within the viewing volume onto the view plane, readying them for display in the final step to screen coordinates, which we will get to in a moment. However, there is another use for the perspective transformation in the context of clipping: turning the pyramid shaped viewing volume into a *cuboid* shape.

In Figure 6.33, we have a simple 2D projection of what I'm talking about. Suppose that we have two points **p1**(x1,y1,z1) and **p2**(x2,y2,z2) that define a line. We haven't yet talked about 2D or 3D clipping, but let's talk about it now. Imagine that we have a single line defined by **p1** and **p2**, and that the line as it's shown in Figure 6.33 is partially in the viewing frustrum. Further assume that we have a wireframe 3D engine, so we need to draw this line. The line can't be removed with object removal because it really doesn't define an object, and the line doesn't have a back-face because it's not a polygon.

Basically we have to clip the line to the viewing frustrum to actually draw it. This step is very important, because all objects that are totally contained within the viewing frustrum can trivially be projected and rendered. Similarly, all objects that are entirely out of the viewing frustrum can be trivially rejected. However, geometry that is partially within the viewing frustrum must be clipped somehow, just as you would clip lines or bitmaps in a 2D window. Of course, I'm simplifying all this, and in real life, we are going to have to clip polygons to the viewing frustrum, but bear with me.

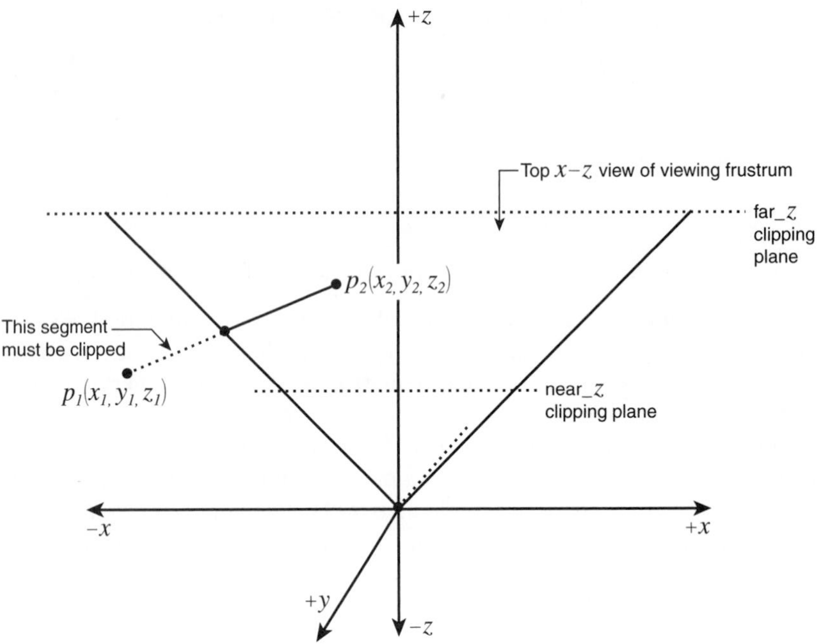

FIGURE 6.33 Simple clipping example.

There are two ways we can handle the line clipping—with the first method, we can blindly perform the perspective projection of the line (assuming that z > 0 on both end points), wait until we get to the rasterization phase of the 3D pipeline, and then clip the line in 2D against the window. This is called *image space clipping*. In other words, image space clipping involves waiting until all the objects to be rendered are already transformed into screen coordinates (although they might be out of range of the screen) and then clipping them in screen space or to the view port, as shown in Figure 6.34.

Image space clipping works great and is easy to implement, but it means that every single object gets clipped in 2D—even the objects that are entirely in the viewing window. This can be a great load on the processor, especially if you are rasterizing polygons and testing on a per pixel basis. But in the case of drawing lines, image space clipping in 2D is probably cheaper than clipping in 3D (which I'll explain in a minute).

The second way to clip is in *object space*; that is, in the mathematical space that the object(s) or geometry exist in. If you recall, we tried to remove entire objects from the pipeline and/or back-faces, so we didn't have to transform them to camera coordinates. This was an object space operation. However, some of the objects and geometry will of course be visible in a game (or you wouldn't have a game). Some of those objects will not be totally in the viewing volume, and hence must be clipped against it. Therefore, the problem boils down to this: Before you perform the perspective transformation on your geometry, if you want to perform object space clipping, all geometry (lines or polygons) that are only partially in the viewing frustrum must be clipped in 3D space to the viewing frustrum. This is called *3D clipping*, and it is not trivial unless you're Chris Knight.

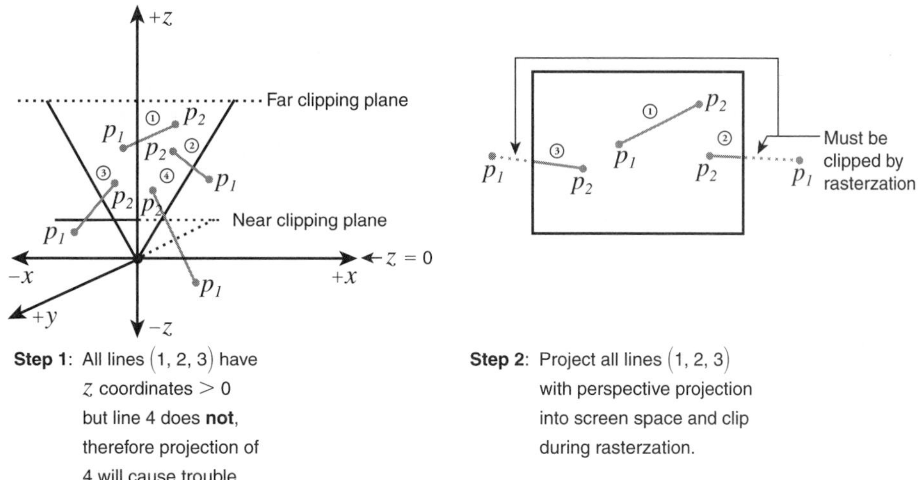
+z
Far clipping plane
Near clipping plane
−x
+x
+y
−z
z = 0
Step 1: All lines (1, 2, 3) have z coordinates > 0 but line 4 does **not**, therefore projection of 4 will cause trouble.
Must be clipped by rasterzation
Step 2: Project all lines (1, 2, 3) with perspective projection into screen space and clip during rasterzation.

FIGURE 6.34 The image space clipping pipeline.

In general, we have been dealing with a viewing frustrum that is fairly simple: There's a near and far clipping plane, the sides of the frustrum on the x and y axes are at 90 degrees FOV, and assuming a square projection plane, the plane equations are |x| = z and |y| = z, but still, clipping a 3D line to these six faces can be tedious. If the view plane isn't square, |x| = z, but |y| = z/ar.

Additionally, if the four side walls are not based on a 90 degree viewing angle, it's much harder, because the plane equations will be in general form.

The point is if you first clip all the geometry that is partially within the viewing frustrum to the viewing frustrum in 3D space (object space clipping) as shown in Figure 6.33, you are guaranteed that all the projected geometry will lie within the view plane. As I've mentioned, performing 3D clipping is a bit tricky, and when we get to it, you will see that not only do the polygon vertices have to be clipped, but the texture and lighting coordinates do, too—but more on that later in the book.

However, clipping to a cube or cuboid is much easier in 3D, because it's basically like clipping to a rectangle in each plane. Okay, now I can finally get to my point about the relationship between the *perspective transformation* and *clipping*. If you're willing to perform a perspective transformation on everything that is potentially visible, the perspective transform itself will warp the viewing volume into a cuboid, and the four sides that were at angles (90 degrees in our examples) will become parallel to each other on the x and y axes, and you will end up with a cube to which you can then clip your perspective coordinates. Amazing, huh? Let's see an example of this and see whether it's true.

Because anything we do to one plane works the same for the others, let's look at the top view of the x-z plane of the viewing frustrum, labeled as shown in Figure 6.35a, with a far clipping plane at z = far_z, a near clipping plane at z = near_z, and a projection, or view plane, at d = 1. The view angle is of course 90 degrees, and let's assume a square projection plan. What we want to do is perform the perspective projection on the corner points of the viewing pyramid (in the 2D case) and see what they look like after the transform. That is, what is the shape of the viewing frustrum itself if we were to perspective transform it?

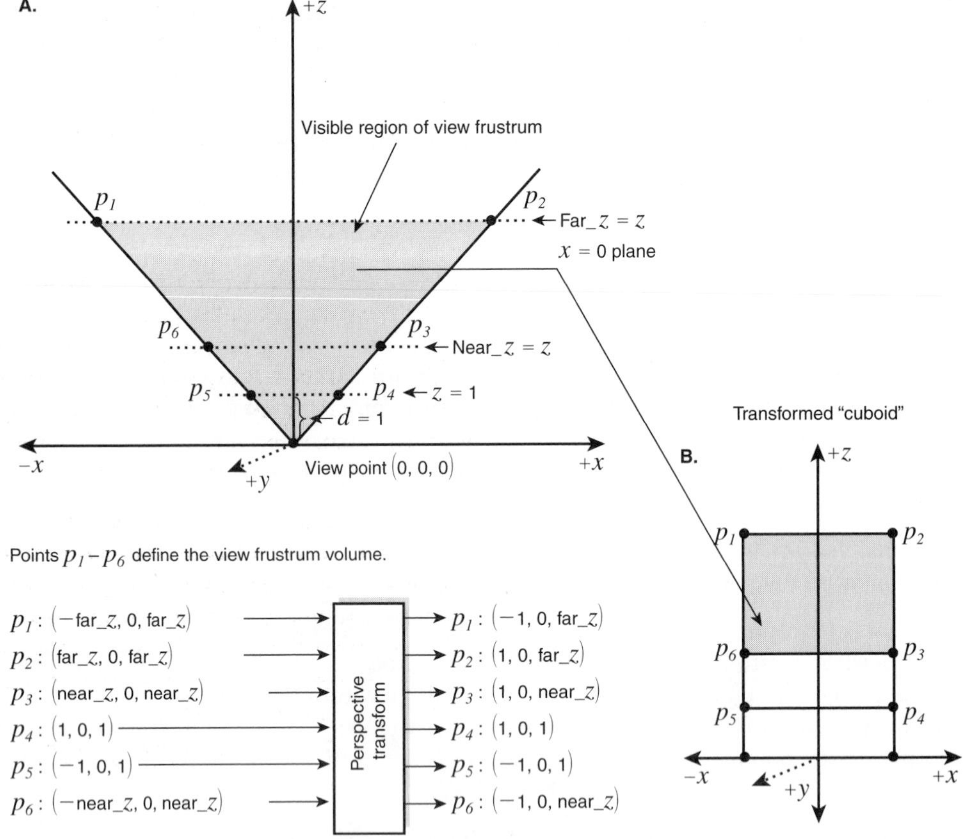

FIGURE 6.35 The perspective projection magically converts the viewing frustrum to a cuboid shape.

With that in mind, the points that make up the 2D projection on the x-z plane of the viewing volume are **p1–p6**, and they have the following actual coordinates in the form **p**(x,0,z):

```
p1(-far_z, 0, far_z)
p2(far_z, 0, far_z)
p3(near_z, 0, near_z)
p4(1,0,1) ← note the x components are 1 since d=1
p5(-1,0,1)
p6(-near_z, 0, near_z)
```

TIP

You might be concerned that the x components of some of the points are in terms of z. This is because we are using a 90 degree field of view with a square projection plane; thus |x| = z, and |y| = z, so at any z value from the origin, {x,y} = z.

Now watch this baby! If we perform the perspective projection on these points with d = 1 (that is, multiply each component by d), and then divide by z, we get this:

```
p1'(-far_z/far_z, 0/far_z, far_z)       = (-1, 0, far_z)
p2'(far_z/far_z, 0/far_z, far_z)        = (1, 0, far_z)
p3'(near_z/near_z, 0/near_z, near_z)    = (1, 0, near_z)
p4'(1/1, 0/1, 1)                        = (1, 0, 1)
p5'(-1/1, 0/1, 1)                       = (-1, 0, 1)
p6'(-near_z/near_z, 0/near_z, near_z)   = (-1, 0, near_z)
```

Of course, we can ignore the y components, because we know we are in the x-z plane.

Now, let's re-plot **p1'–p6'** and take a look at Figure 6.35b. Look, it's a rectangle. Aha! We have transformed the ugly pyramid into a nice clean rectangle, which is trivial to clip against, even in 3D. Of course, we can perform the same analysis on the y-z plane and come up with the same results. Merging them together, we get the new cuboid viewing volume shown in Figure 6.35b. The point of this exercise is to show you that the perspective transform can also be used to *normalize* all the geometry, so you can clip it trivially. Of course, you will see this in action in the upcoming chapters.

In conclusion, our 3D pipeline has more than just a perspective transform added onto it. The pipeline has a possible 3D clipping phase (if you don't want to clip in image space), so our new pipeline with 3D clipping up to the perspective transform is shown in Figure 6.36. Additionally, if we decide to transform all geometry from camera coordinates through the perspective transform, we can clip in 3D after the perspective transform, also shown in Figure 6.36—it's up to you how you want to do this.

Finally, let's get to the last step in the viewing pipeline—screen coordinates.

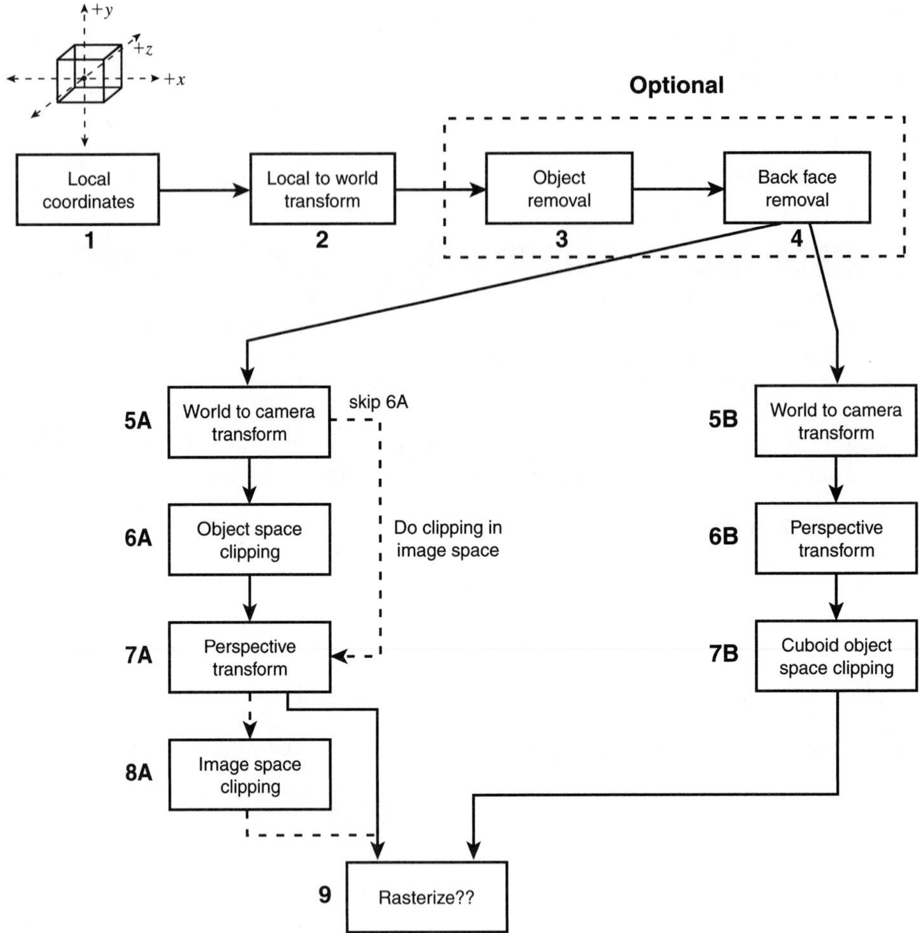

FIGURE 6.36 The next iteration of the 3D pipeline with the perspective transform and clipping.

The End of the Pipeline: Screen Coordinates

Before I describe the screen coordinate transform component of the pipeline, let it be known that we are still leaving out the entire lighting and texturing phases of the 3D pipeline. These are advanced topics and not appropriate for this chapter, but at least make note that somewhere between the world and screen coordinates we must light and texture our polygons. But for now, let's keep it simple, because I'm trying to stick to coordinate transforms.

At this point in the pipeline, we have a set of points that represent what we want to see on the screen. These points have already passed through the perspective transform, but may or may not be clipped to the final screen dimensions. For now, let's just assume that we don't care and come back to it. However, computing the final screen coordinates does rely on the type of perspective transform that took place; that is, what was the size of the view plane in virtual space? This matters because we need to map it to the screen. So let's look at some of the cases.

Field of View 90 Degrees with View Plane at d = 1

With a field of view of 90 degrees and the view plane at a distance d = 1 with a square projection plane, the perspective transform transforms all geometry and projects it onto a virtual view plane of width and height 2×2 (x:{-1 to 1} X y:{-1 to 1}). In the case of a nonsquare projection plane (the more common), the perspective projection projects everything onto a virtual view plane of width and height 2×(2/ar) (x:{-1 to 1} X y:{-1/ar to 1/ar}), where ar is of course the aspect ratio. The cool thing is when we get to the screen transform, we don't care about this anymore, because we assume that the perspective transform handled the aspect ratio. However, it's VERY important that somewhere the aspect ratio is taken into consideration—otherwise, your imagery will be squished!

In any case, the projections can be verified for your sanity by viewing Figure 6.37. So, we want to map coordinates from the view plane, which is 2×2 for square projections and 2×(2/ar) for nonsquare projections, to our view port or screen coordinates. Read that sentence once more—we want to map the view plane coordinates onto the view port. Remember that the view plane is in virtual camera space, and may or may not have the same dimensions as the view port, which is the final raster window.

This transformation step can be interpreted in different ways, but the way we are going to assume that things work for now is that we render into a view port buffer with origin (0,0) at the upper left-hand corner with dimensions (`SCREEN_WIDTH` × `SCREEN_HEIGHT`), as shown in Figure 6.38. In this case, the width and height are equal. This is the exact setup of the virtual computer system we designed back in Chapters 2 and 3.

With this in mind, we merely have to come up with the following transform from view plane coordinates to screen coordinates (which is our *view port*):

x_{per}: (-1 to 1) -> x_{screen}: (0 to SCREEN_WIDTH-1)
y_{per}: (-1/ar to 1/ar) -> y_{screen}: (SCREEN_HEIGHT-1 to 0)

NOTE

The y-axis is inverted, and details count here, boys and girls—we can't afford to be "off by one;" we need to be perfect!

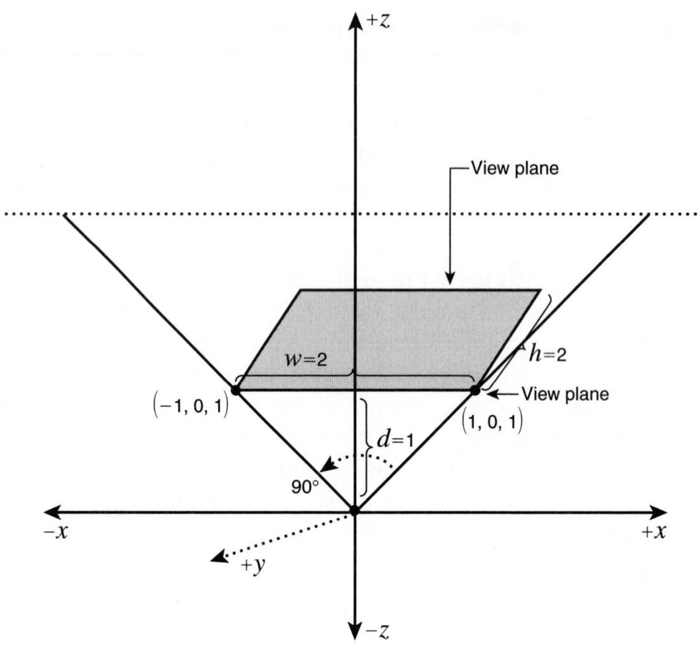

When the fov = 90 and aspect ratio = 1.0
then view plane = (2×2) at d = 1

When the fov = 90 and aspect ratio ≠ 1.0
then view plane = (2×2/ar) at d = 1

FIGURE 6.37 Projection details for FOV = 90 and d = 1 onto 2×2 projection plane.

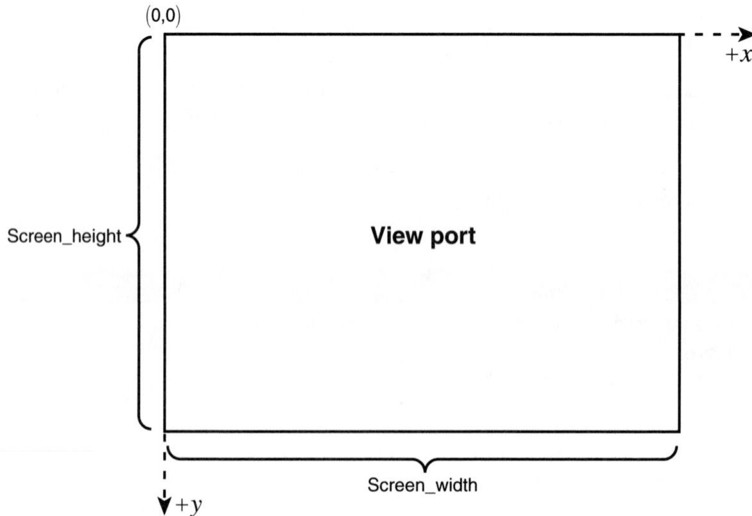

FIGURE 6.38 The viewport definition.

There are a number of ways to derive the math here, but the easiest is to find the center of the screen and transform from there. However, there is one thing to remember: The y-axis is inverted, so we need to take that into consideration. With that in mind, to transform the point **p**(x,y) to screen coordinates, we use the following transform:

FORMULA 6.7 Conversion to Screen Coordinates for d = 1 Case

```
x_screen = (x_per+1)*(0.5*SCREEN_WIDTH-0.5)
y_screen = (SCREEN_HEIGHT-1) - (y_per+1)*(0.5*SCREEN_HEIGHT-0.5)
```

Let's test this with some boundary conditions, like the four points that make up the bounding box of the view plane and transform them to screen coordinates. Performing this operation with Formula 6.7 we get

```
p1(-1,1)     = p1'(0, 0)
p2(1,1)      = p2'(SCREEN_WIDTH-1, 0)
p3(1,-1)     = p3'(SCREEN_WIDTH-1, SCREEN_HEIGHT-1)
p4(-1,-1)    = p4'(0, SCREEN_HEIGHT-1)
```

which is exactly the bounding box of the addressable screen with extents (`SCREEN_WIDTH` × `SCREEN_HEIGHT`). Of course, there are a number of ways that you can formulate the screen transformation by multiplying out the terms and collecting them in different ways. For example:

```
x_screen     = (x_per+1)*(0.5*SCREEN_WIDTH-0.5)
           = (x_per)*(0.5*SCREEN_WIDTH-0.5) +
             (0.5*SCREEN_WIDTH-0.5)
```

And if we let α = (`0.5*SCREEN_WIDTH-0.5`), we get

```
x_screen = α + xper*α

y_screen = (SCREEN_HEIGHT-1)-(yper+1)*(0.5*SCREEN_HEIGHT-0.5)

         = -(y_per)*(0.5*SCREEN_HEIGHT-0.5) -
           (0.5*SCREEN_HEIGHT-0.5) + (SCREEN_HEIGHT-1)

       = -(y_per)* (0.5*SCREEN_HEIGHT-0.5) + (0.5*
         SCREEN_HEIGHT-0.5)
```

If we let β = (`0.5*SCREEN_HEIGHT-0.5`), we get

```
y_screen = β - yper*β
```

Thus, we have the following final results:

$$x_{screen} = \alpha + x_{per}*\alpha$$
$$y_{screen} = \beta - y_{per}*\beta$$

where α = (0.5*SCREEN_WIDTH-0.5), and β = (0.5*SCREEN_HEIGHT-0.5).

What's interesting is that (α,β) is the exact center of our view screen (SCREEN_WIDTH × SCREEN_HEIGHT), which makes sense because we are mapping (0,0) there. The cool thing about the preceding formulation is that it's much easier to put in matrix format. However, we are at the point were we are really dealing with 2D screen coordinates, and using 4D homogenous coordinates isn't necessary. That is, if our perspective points are in the form (x,y), there's no point in using a 4×4 matrix. You could use a 3×3 matrix if you want. Sometimes it's nice to just keep everything in 3×3 or 4×4 matrices and disregard the z component at some point—whatever you decide is up to you, but I will show you both just to be complete.

With that in mind, let's look at a 4×4 version of the transformation, assuming that the view plane coordinates in perspective are in the form $[x_{per}, y_{per}, z, 1]$, where z is irrelevant and could be zero because it's already served its usefulness. Because this is the perspective-to-screen transform for viewing distance d = 1, we will call the matrix T_{scr1}:

$$\mathbf{T}_{scr1} = \begin{vmatrix} \alpha & 0 & 0 & 0 \\ 0 & -\beta & 0 & 0 \\ 0 & 0 & 1 & 0 \\ \alpha & \beta & 0 & 1 \end{vmatrix}$$

And if we multiply a test point $p = [x_{per}\ y_{per}\ 0\ 1]$, we get

$$\mathbf{p}^*\ \mathbf{T}_{scr1} =$$

$$[x_{per}\ y_{per}\ 0\ 1] * \begin{vmatrix} \alpha & 0 & 0 & 0 \\ 0 & -\beta & 0 & 0 \\ 0 & 0 & 1 & 0 \\ \alpha & \beta & 0 & 1 \end{vmatrix}$$

$$[x_{per}*\alpha + \alpha,\ -y_{per}*\beta + \beta,\ 0,\ 1]$$

And picking off the (x,y) components we get:

$$x = x_{per}*\alpha + \alpha$$
$$y = -y_{per}*\beta + \beta$$

which is correct! Of course, that was a lot of excess drama, because we could just use the preceding formula and forget the matrix transform! Remember: the idea is that at some point, we might be able to do 50 different things in a single matrix by concatenation, so that's why we're learning how to do everything in a matrix. Let's move on to a second example, assuming that we have a single 2D point (x_{per}, y_{per}) that represents the point that we want to transform into screen coordinates with a matrix, as we did previously. The problem is that we need to get a translation by (α,β), so we need homogenous coordinates. What we're going to do is use homogenous 2D coordinates—which will look like 3D coordinates, but with an (x, y, w)—then we can use a 3×3 matrix to perform the screen transform. With that in mind, let's say we want to transform the point p (x_{per}, y_{per}, 1) to screen coordinates, with d = 1 as usual. This matrix would do the trick:

```
          |α    0    0 |
Tscr1  =  |0   -β    0 |
          |α    β    1 |
```

And if we multiply a test point p = [x_{per} y_{per} 1], we get

```
p * Tscr1
                          |α   0   0 |
[xper yper  1]   *        |0   β   0 |
                          |α   β   1 |

[xper*α + α, -yper*β + β, 1]
```

Picking off the (x,y) components, we get

```
x = xper*α + α
y = -yper*β + β
```

which is again correct! My point is that you can do this stuff in a number of ways. Finally, let's look at some code to perform this operation, assuming that the perspective coordinates are already in the array `cube_per[8]`:

```
POINT3D cube_per[8]; // used to hold perspective coordinates

POINT2D cube_screen[8]; used to hold screen coordinates
// perform the perspective to screen transform
// on the perspective coordinates, assume screen has
// dimensions SCREEN_WIDTH x SCREEN_HEIGHT and
// view plane is at d=1 so perspective coords are
// normalized to -1 to 1 on each axis

// pre-compute alpha and beta
alpha = (0.5*SCREEN_WIDTH-0.5);
beta  = (0.5*SCREEN_HEIGHT-0.5);
```

6

```
// loop and transform
for (int vertex = 0; vertex<8; vertex++)
    {
    cube_screen[vertex].x=alpha+alpha*cube_per[vertex].x;
    cube_screen[vertex].y=beta-beta*cube_per[vertex].y;
    } // end for
```

As you can see, doing the transformation manually without matrices is a lot less complex.

NOTE

Although I am being cavalier with the definitions of view plane, viewport, and screen coordinates, remember that the view plane is what we initially project on in virtual space, and the viewport is the window that we map the view plane coordinates on (which in many cases is the exact same as the screen window).

View Plane with Arbitrary Field of View and General Viewing Distance d

Now that you've seen the construction of the perspective-to-screen transformation where d = 1, and the field of view is 90 degrees where the view plane coordinates in perspective space are normalized to –1 to 1 (on each axis for square projections), let's talk about the more general case, where we compute the d's like this:

```
d = (0.5)*viewplane_width*tan(θh/2)
```

Remember, in this case we solve for d based on the major axis (usually the x) field of view angle: θ_h (which would normally be 90 degrees for a square projection plane, but could be anything in this case). Additionally, we need the view plane dimensions we want to project the final image on, which would be (`SCREEN_WIDTH` × `SCREEN_HEIGHT`) in case we want the view plane to be the same size as the screen or view port. However, we need to be careful, because screen coordinates have the following ranges:

```
x: (0..SCREEN_WIDTH-1)
y: (0..SCREEN_HEIGHT-1)
```

So, in the previous formulas, we must replace `viewplane_width` and `viewplane_height` with the slightly different ranges `(SCREEN_WIDTH-1)` and `(SCREEN_HEIGHT-1)`, like this:

```
d = (0.5)*(SCREEN_WIDTH-1)*tan(θh/2)
```

This calculation will give us the correct d value if we want to merge the perspective transform *and* screen transform into one. However, the `SCREEN_HEIGHT` seems to have been left out—NO! Normally, we first project the image onto the view plane with a focal distance d for both the x and y axes, with the view plane size {x:-1 to 1, y:-1/ar to +1/ar}. Then we would map that onto the screen by multiplying by the SCREEN_WIDTH and SCREEN_HEIGHT on the x and y axes. But, because the ratio of SCREEN_WIDTH/SCREEN_HEIGHT is exactly the aspect ratio ar, the multiplication and division cancel out. Thus, when you map directly to the screen without the intermediate step of first going to view plane coordinates and then to viewport screen coordinates, the aspect ratio terms cancel out, and you are left with

$$x_{per} = (d*x_c)/z_c$$
$$y_{per} = (d*y_c)/z_c$$

The results will already be scaled to (SCREEN_WIDTH × SCREEN_HEIGHT), so you get the screen transformation free during the perspective transformation! Well, almost. There are a couple problems with this ... Give up? First, the y-axis is inverted for raster display, because 0 is at the top of a raster display and at the bottom of quadrant I (which is where the projection is working). That's no problem: We can simply invert the y coordinates:

$$y_{per} = (SCREEN\_HEIGHT - 1) - y_{per}$$
$$x_{per} = x_{per}$$

The second problem is a bit more subtle, and much worse. Although the projection will have a total range of (SCREEN_WIDTH-1) on the x-axis and (SCREEN_HEIGHT-1) on the y-axis, the actual coordinates pumped out will be in the range of

X-axis: -(SCREEN_WIDTH-1)/2 to (SCREEN_WIDTH-1)/2

Y-axis: -(SCREEN_HEIGHT-1)/2 to (SCREEN_HEIGHT-1)/2

Centered about (0,0), the range is split into a positive and negative half about zero on each axis! Just as the normalized projection gave us coordinates –1 to 1 on each axis, we now have similar, although scaled, coordinates. Alas, although we've gotten rid of our post-perspective normalized-to-screen transform scaling operation, it looks like we are still stuck with some translation of the origin. This is true, but we can fix it, along with the y-axis inversion, with this simple transform after the initial perspective transform:

$$x_{screen} = x_{per} + (0.5*SCREEN\_WIDTH-0.5)$$
$$y_{screen} = -y_{per} + (0.5*SCREEN\_HEIGHT-0.5)$$

If you analyze the preceding operations, you will come to the conclusion that they are almost identical to the normalized screen projection *without* the scaling operation. So, as you can see, this projection stuff all ends up being the same thing in the end—it's just how you want to think about it. In fact, if we let a = (0.5*SCREEN_WIDTH-0.5) and b = (0.5*SCREEN_HEIGHT-0.5) as before, we have Formula 6.8:

FORMULA 6.8 Screen Projection from View Plane Scaled Coordinates to Viewport Coordinates

$$x_{screen} = x_{per} + \alpha$$
$$y_{screen} = -y_{per} + \beta$$

And in matrix form, we have only to perform the translation to (x_{per}, y_{per}). Thus the transform, called $\mathbf{T}_{scr}$, would be

$$\mathbf{T}_{scr} = \begin{vmatrix} 1 & 0 & 0 & 0 \\ 0 & -1 & 0 & 0 \\ 0 & 0 & 1 & 0 \\ \alpha & \beta & 0 & 1 \end{vmatrix}$$

The preceding transform only differs from our more complex normalized-to-screen coordinate transform shown in the following by only the scaling factors (α,β) multiplied by x_{per} and y_{per}, respectively, which does nothing more than scale the view plane to a size ($|2*\alpha| \times |2*\beta/ar|$), because the actual coordinate range is from x: ($-\alpha$ to α) and y: ($-\beta$ to β):

$$x_{screen} = \alpha + x_{per}*\alpha$$
$$y_{screen} = \beta - y_{per}*\beta$$

The point is that we can scale the view plane coordinates before the screen transform as part of the perspective transform (but this gives us non-normalized coordinates), or we can scale the normalized coordinates to screen (view port) coordinates during the perspective-to-screen transformation.

Finally, we come to my last point—we have seen how to perform the perspective transform in its two flavors: normalized and view plane scaled to viewport, along with the two screen transforms that handle these previous types of perspective projections. But there's one little detail that I want to bring up—the conversion from homogenous 4D coordinates to 3D in the middle of the process. We have assumed that we are breaking the perspective transform and the screen transform up into two matrix multiplies with a quick homogenous-to-3D conversion of each vertex between the two transforms, but what if we want to perform the entire camera-to-screen transform all at once, both manually and with a single matrix? Let's look at it manually first.

Basically, we would perform the perspective transform along with scaling and translation all at once, and the math would look like this:

$$x_{screen} = d*x_{cam}/z_{cam} + (0.5*SCREEN\_WIDTH-0.5)$$
$$y_{screen} = -d*ycam/z_{cam} + (0.5*SCREEN\_HEIGHT-0.5)$$

Amazingly trivial, huh? Anyway, the simplicity of the preceding math is why many engines (mostly software) don't use matrix-based perspective and screen transforms. After vertices are in camera coordinates, the preceding two lines of code are used to transform all the way from camera coordinates to screen coordinates. But if we want to use a single matrix operation, it's a bit tricky because we have to assume 4D homogeneous coordinates, and that there will be a final conversion from homogenous to 3D (actually 2D) at the end via the division by w. With that in mind, take a look at the following matrix, which is a first attempt:

$$\mathbf{T}_{camscr} = \begin{vmatrix} d & 0 & 0 & 0 \\ 0 & -d & 0 & 0 \\ 0 & 0 & 1 & 1 \\ \alpha & \beta & 0 & 0 \end{vmatrix}$$

That looks about right. Let's try it out with a vertex in camera coordinates $p = [x_c\ y_c\ z_c\ 1]$:

$$\mathbf{p*T}_{camscr} = [d*x_c + \alpha,\ -d*y_c + \beta,\ z_c,\ z_c]$$

Although this looks right, when we convert from 4D homogenous coordinates to 3D, we divide x,y by $w = z_c$ and get

$$x_{screen} = d*x_c/z_c + [\ \alpha/z_c\ ] \quad \text{<- last terms are wrong}$$
$$y_{screen} = -d*y_c/z_c + [\ \beta/z_c\ ]$$

which is almost correct, but during the 4D to 3D conversion, we had to divide everything by $w = z_c$, resulting in the α and β terms being wrong (see the factor of z_c in the denominator of each). So what we need to do is scale them by z_c in the initial matrix, so that during the final conversion from homogenous coordinates to 3D, we get what we want. We can accomplish this by moving the α and β factors in the matrix up a row:

$$\mathbf{T}_{camscr} = \begin{vmatrix} d & 0 & 0 & 0 \\ 0 & -d & 0 & 0 \\ \alpha & \beta & 1 & 1 \\ 0 & 0 & 0 & 0 \end{vmatrix}$$

If we perform the same multiplication of the camera vertex $p = [x_c\ y_c\ z_c\ 1]$, we get

$$\mathbf{p*T}_{camscr} = [d*x_c + zc*\alpha,\ -d*y_c + zc*\beta,\ z_c,\ z_c]$$

which, after dividing by $w = z_c$, gives us our desired transformation:

$$x_{screen} = d*x_c/z_c + \alpha$$
$$y_{screen} = -d*y_c/z_c + \beta$$

CAUTION

The two things to remember about using the matrix-based perspective and screen transforms are that the resulting coordinates are homogenous out of the perspective transform and must be converted to 3D, and there are a lot of matrix multiplications and additions that are a complete waste of time.

Finally, you might ask, "Where did the aspect ratio factor go?" The answer is that is has been canceled out by combining the perspective-to-view plane and view plane-to-viewport (screen coordinate) transforms.

So, the question is, what methods should we use for both projection and the math itself? Well, they all have their place: normalized or scaled to the view port perspective transform, manual math, or matrix transformations, and so forth. In the exercises and demos in the next chapter, we will experiment with all of them, but in the end I think we will end up with the d = 1 with the FOV equal to 90 degrees on the x-axis formulation, because I like the normalized coordinates. However, later on we might find that merging the screen transform with the perspective transform is faster in real code.

Furthermore, as you can see we have 3–4 degrees of freedom with the view angle, focal distance, and the width and height. However, in most cases we *really* want to stick to FOV values that equal 90 degrees for the x-axis and let the math compute the FOV of the vertical axis, but in any case, use the same focal distance for the projection on both axes. However, for nonsquare projections, there must be a multiplication of the aspect ratio somewhere in there.

In conclusion, you might think that I have really beat down the whole projection process, but my goal is for you to really understand the relationship between camera coordinates, perspective coordinates, the view plane, the view port, and screen coordinates, as well as all the ways of arriving at them with various transformation sequences, both manual and matrix-based. The bottom line is that in this book, in most cases we will use a horizontal field of view of 90 degrees, and a focal distance of 1.0. That same focal distance will be used on the y-axis as well, so for nonsquare projections we will get distortion, but if we multiply the y component during the perspective calculation by the aspect ratio, it will cancel out when we scale by the `SCREEN_HEIGHT` in the screen mapping.

Another Look at the Viewing Pipeline

Now we have a complete picture of the viewing pipeline as far as geometry is concerned. Granted, we aren't doing lighting, shading, or texturing, but that really is a different part of 3D, under the topic of rendering, and we are only interested in the geometry transformations of the pipeline at this point. With that in mind, take a look at Figure 6.39, which depicts our system thus far.

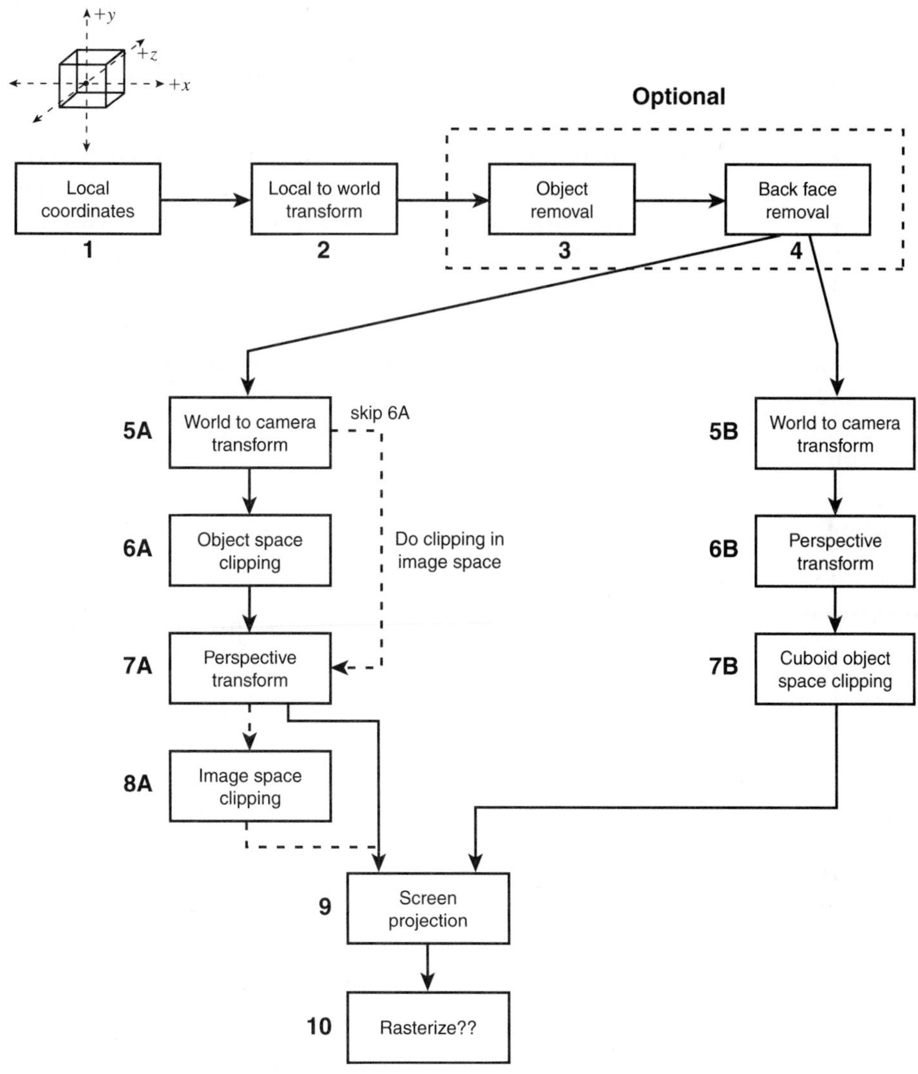

FIGURE 6.39 The next iteration of the 3D pipeline with the screen projection step added.

Basic 3D Data Structures

At this point, we are ready to start talking about general methods to represent 3D data. I think that you see there are a number of transformations that 3D data must go through, and there are a number of different representations as the data flows. Hence, there is no single correct way to do something—just the way that works in some specific context. For example, the way you store your data for a space game will probably be much different than that of an indoor game. Moreover, depending on how you clip your imagery, vertices might have to be inserted or deleted from your final rendered polygons, which takes some forethought. My buddy John Amato found this out writing his first 3D engine "SOL."

The bottom line is you need to really think out your engine, and many times you will end up redoing all of it because you might find that there's a better way to implement something. The approach I'm going to take in this book is a generic one. We will use some rough data structures to begin, and then tweak them as necessary. Again, the proper selection of data structures only comes after you know everything about 3D, but that won't happen until the end of the book, so at this point, we are just going to start off with something that works, along with some simplifications and assumptions.

My goal by the next chapter is to create a working wireframe 3D engine that enables you to move a camera around a space or terrain-like environment. The engine will do minimal clipping, and will probably be a hybrid of object space and image space algorithms. What I want to do now is discuss a couple of basic data structures that will help us represent 3D objects with a very simple generic 3D system in mind.

Considerations of Representing Polygonal Data in 3D

The first decision you have to make when designing a 3D engine is if you are going to support triangles, quadrilaterals, or general *n*-sided polygons, as shown in Figure 6.40. The majority of 3D engines (both software and hardware) only deal with triangles. The reasons are many, but most importantly, triangles are easy to render—three points define a plane, and many 3D algorithms work best with triangular meshes.

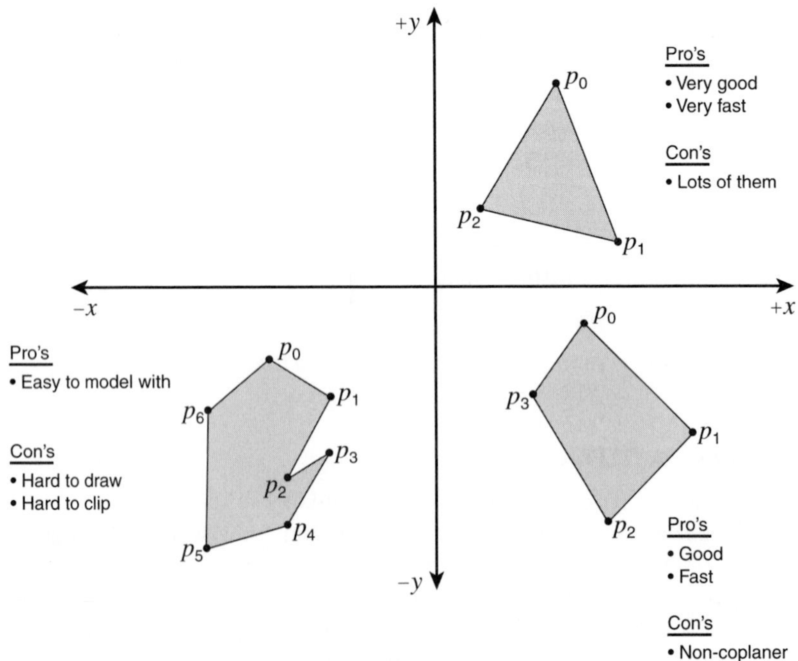

FIGURE 6.40 Potential polygonal primitives for a 3D engine to use.

Of course, your models in the modeling tool might have general *n*-sided polygons, but at some point everything is triangulated. Because using triangles is the norm, we are going to go along with this convention and have the rule that all models must be built of three-sided polygons or converted to triangles before we render them. At this point, we're not sure where we are going to get the data for the objects. Is it algorithmically generated, entered by hand, loaded from files, and so on? And we don't care—we just know that we are going to deal with triangular-based geometry.

Even with this constraint there's a problem. Take a look at Figure 6.41, which shows a number of triangles being clipped to a rectangular region. In essence, during the clipping phase we can introduce more vertices into each polygon. For example, in the worst case, we might insert (add) three new vertices to any triangle after it's clipped. Hence, we have to have data structures that can deal with this.

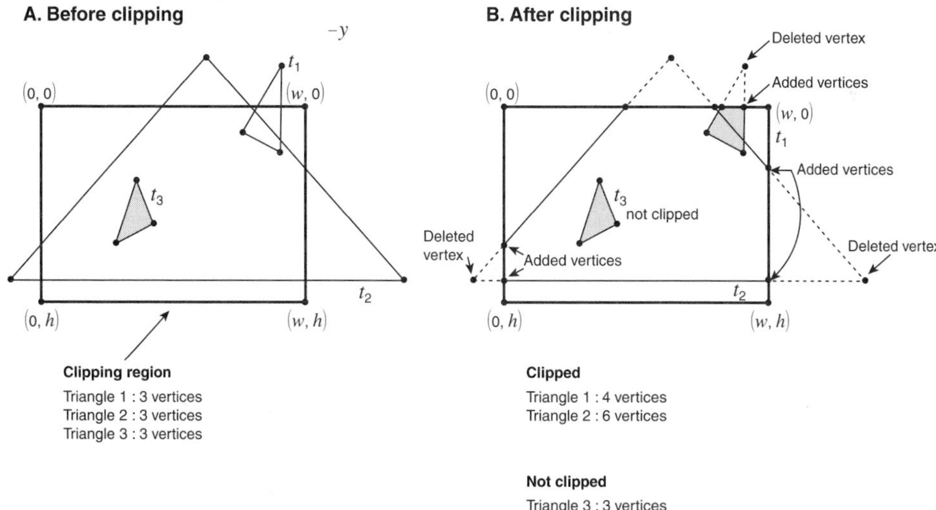

FIGURE 6.41 Triangle clipping in object space introducing extra vertices.

Now, you could say that we aren't going to clip at all in object space, but wait until the rasterization phase. This is fine, but then you run into the problem of polygons that pierce the near clipping plane, as shown in Figure 6.42, and worse yet, extend beyond the z = 0 plane! The operation of projecting these polygons will cause problems, so that's something else to think about. Of course, if all the polygons are small and their longest edge is smaller than the distance from the near clipping plane and the z = 0 plane, you can simply trivially reject whole polygons that fall into that range and not clip them, and then do pixel image space clipping during rasterization.

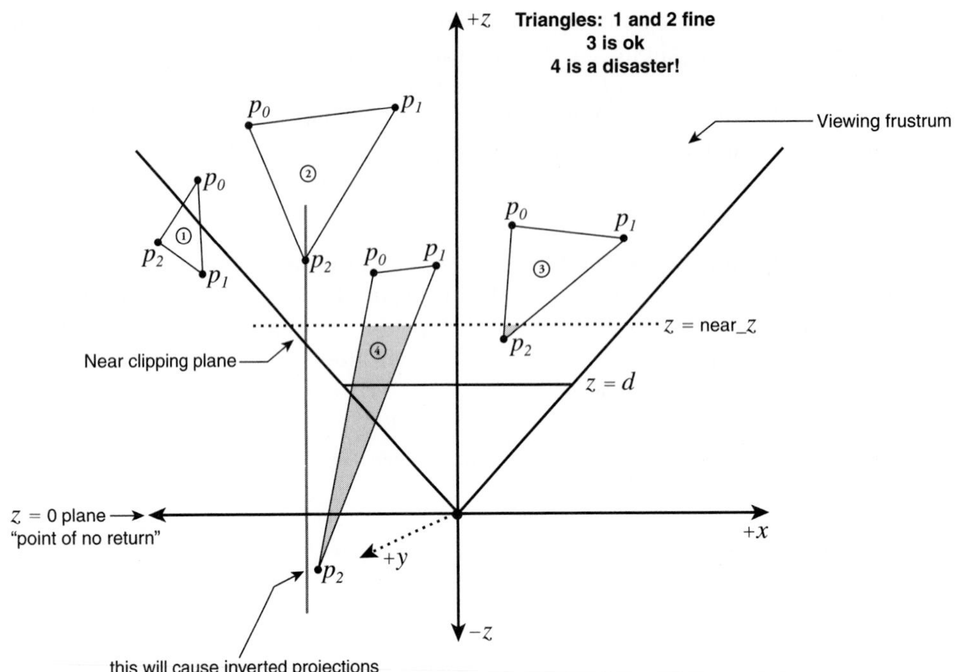

FIGURE 6.42 Triangles piercing the near clipping plane and z = 0 plane.

The moral of the story is that we are going to have to think long and hard about data structures, depending on the types of geometry we will envision and the clipping process we want to use. These factors will play into the representation of polygons, and will be the deciding factor if polygons can have more than three vertices.

You might say, "Let's just have the rule that all models must be built triangles, and then if a polygon ends up with more than three vertices during the 3D pipeline and clipping phase, we can handle those as a special case, either via triangulation, or we can have a special rasterizer for *n*-sided polygons." Again, this is a reasonable approach, and I have used it, too. So in conclusion, you need to think about all these factors at some point, but for now let's just keep things simple.

Defining Polygons

For our first shot at defining polygons, we are going to use the triangle rule and assume that no clipping ever occurs in world space that would necessitate the addition of vertices. That is, if we do any clipping in world space or camera space, we will throw the entire polygon away or keep it and let the rasterizer clip the polygon to the screen during rasterization (this will be fairly easy in our first engine, because it will be wireframe). This simplification enables us to get through this chapter without knowing about 3D clipping algorithms, which we want to hold off on. Anyway, when we define a polygon, we first have to decide a few things about our 3D worlds, such as what are we going to try and model?

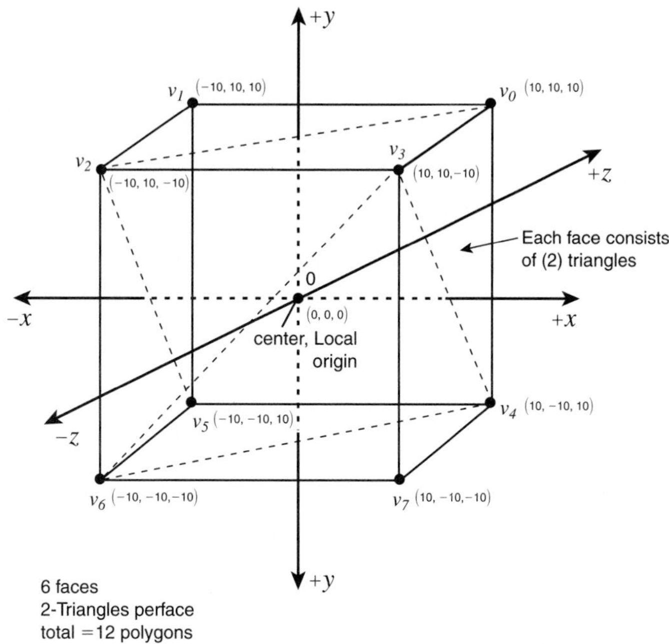

FIGURE 6.43 Modeling a cube.

For example, suppose that you want to model the 3D cube in Figure 6.43. The cube has six faces, which can each be modeled by two triangles (remember, no quadrilaterals allowed). That's a total of 12 polygons and 36 vertices. Or is it? Yes, there are 12 polygons, but are there 36 vertices, or 8 vertices? The answer depends on how you want to store the model. If we decide that every polygon is a unique entity, we would define it as a list of three vertices:

```
struct typedef POLY_EX_TYP_1
{
POINT3D v[3]; // the vertex list
} POLY_EX_1, *POLY_EX_1_PTR;
```

And to define any polygon, we would use something like this:

```
POLY_EX_1 face_1 = { {x0, y0, z0},
                     {x1, y1, z1},
                     {x2, y2, z2}, };
```

That's fine, and works okay. But it's a waste of space, because the cube only has eight total vertices, and if we define a cube with this structure, we will end up with 12 polygons, each containing three vertices. We should be able to reuse the vertex data better. Hence, we can come up with a more indirect method to define a polygon based on a vertex list.

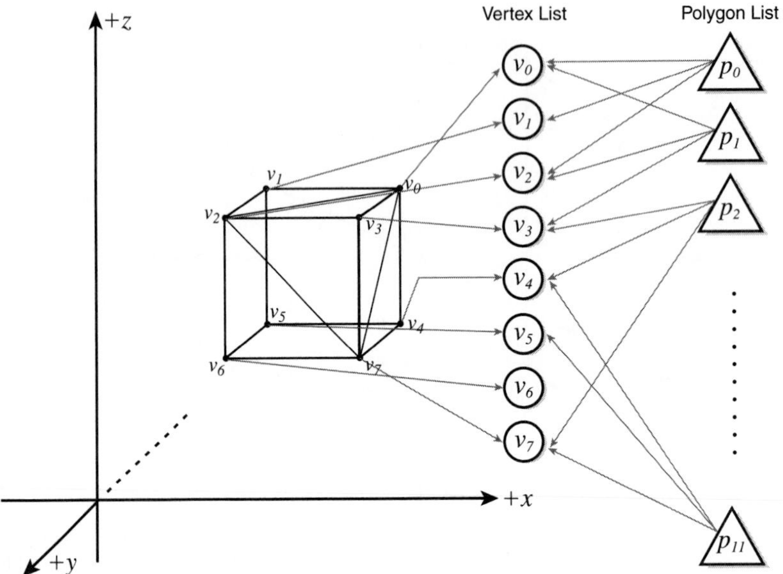

FIGURE 6.44 Geometry can be defined by a vertex list.

A *vertex list* is nothing more than a list of vertices that we reference to construct geometry, as shown in Figure 6.44. Therefore, we first define the vertices of the cube as a list or array, and then define the polygons based on pointers or references to that array. For example, here's how we might define a vertex list:

```
POINT3D vertex_list[NUM_VERTICES]; // the vertex list
```

Then we would initialize each vertex with the proper data from the eight points of the cube:

```
vertex_list[0] = {x0, y0, z0};
vertex_list[1] = {x1, y1, z1};
vertex_list[2] = {x2, y2, z2};
vertex_list[3] = {x3, y3, z3};
vertex_list[4] = {x4, y4, z4};
```

```
vertex_list[5] = {x5, y5, z5};
vertex_list[6] = {x6, y6, z6};
vertex_list[7] = {x7, y7, z7};
```

Now we can define a new polygon type that uses a vertex list to generate the polygon:

```
struct typedef POLY_EX_TYP_2
{
POINT3D_PTR vlist; // the vertex list itself
int vertices[3];   // the indices into the vertex list

} POLY_EX_2, *POLY_EX_2_PTR;
```

Now you can see the indirection. Instead of wasting space in each polygon storing the same vertices over and over, there is a single vertex list referenced by each polygon, so now we can define a single polygon

```
POLY_EX_2 face_1 = {vertex_list, 0, 1, 2};
```

which states that `face_1` is based on the vertex list `vertex_list`, and consists of the vertices (0,1,2), which equal {x0, y0, z0}, {x1, y1, z1}, {x2, y2, z2}, respectively.

There's a another little detail here that's important when we get to solid modeling, and that's *vertex ordering*. That is, when we define polygons or triangles, we need to order them in a specific way, so that we can determine what side is *outward*.

6

Referring to Figure 6.45, we see a triangle with its vertices ordered in *clockwise* order. Remember when we talked about back-face removal? The only way to perform back-face removal is to first decide what side is the front and back of a polygon, and then project a normal from it (of course, if the polygon is visible from both sides, this is irrelevant). To do this, we need to use a vertex ordering scheme, so we can compute the outward normal in a uniform manner.

If we are using a left-handed system and a clockwise vertex ordering, we can use the *left hand rule* by following the incremental vertex numbers, and our thumbs will point in the outward direction. Or in other words, if we create a vector u = $\mathbf{p_0}$->$\mathbf{p_1}$ and v = $\mathbf{p_0}$->$\mathbf{p_2}$, and then compute the cross product of u × v, this will be the normal n = $<v_x, v_y, v_z>$, as shown in the figure. This is, of course, the direction of the outward face. This vector n is exactly what we will use during back-face removal (if there is any). Therefore, for this book, we will always use a clockwise vertex ordering that will define the outward direction of any polygon. However, this of course only works for a left-handed system. In a right-handed system, we would have to invert the sign of the normal or use a right-handed rule. It's all in how you want to look at it.

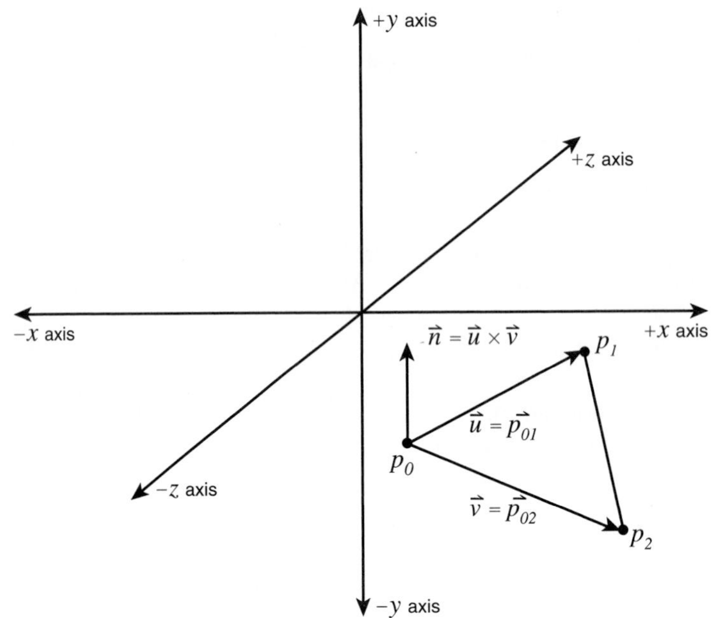

FIGURE 6.45 Vertex ordering.

> **TIP**
>
> Note that for any *n*-sided polygon, there are *n* different orderings that will keep the clockwise ordering (or counterclockwise, for that matter) satisfied—meaning the orderings are not unique. Many times though, if you can order the vertices so that lower numbers are accessed first, you can get better data coherence. For example, suppose that the order (0,5,12) is a clockwise ordering of a polygon. That's a good order to leave it in, even though (12,0,5) and (5,12,0) are also valid because the sequence is the same. But in both cases, data is accessed out of order in the vertex arrays, so the (0,5,12) order will end up having better access characteristics in most cases. However, many times accessing the last element, forcing the cache to be updated, *then* accessing the first elements, is faster.

Anyway, getting back to vertex lists—the vertex list representation is a nice representation, and we get a lot of cool freebies from using it. For example, if we want to transform the object, we don't have to transform the polygons it's made of; we only transform the vertex list. Moreover, when you have vertex copies that represent the same vertex, then many times you get *numerical drift*. That is, you have two polygons that share a common vertex, but each has its own copy of the vertex. Then you transform each polygon and its own copy of the vertex, but during the transform something happens and a slight error occurs in one of the copies, so now the two vertices that are supposed to represent the same vertex don't! This can cause cracking in your geometry. Just take a look at *Tomb Raider* to see what I'm talking about.

Now let's look at the dark side of the coin relating to using vertex lists. Many times as you get farther down the pipeline, you want to separate polygons and vertex lists. The reasons are many, but for example, imagine you have a mesh that has 1,000 vertices, and only one polygon is visible. Because all transformations are done at the vertex list level, you still end up transforming all that data for nothing—just for that single polygon! Of course, there are tricks to get around this, but it's an issue, so keep it in mind. Also, many times it's easier to write a rasterizer that just blasts polygons based on three vertices in a list, and not a list of pointers to a vertex list. Again, this all depends on the final architecture.

Finally, during the clipping stage, it might be very hard to clip the geometry if it's a vertex list and you don't really look at it as polygons. Then again, if you clip one vertex, all polygons that share that vertex will be clipped, but I think you are starting to see that there are a lot of things you have to think about.

With all that in mind, we are going to use a hybridized approach and define and transform all our objects based on vertex lists. However, at some point we will convert them to single polygons, even if they have common vertices. We will change this later, but for now it will simplify things.

Alright—there's yet another detail that I have glossed over that I want to take a look at before we make our final first draft of the polygon structure: the decision to use 3D or 4D homogenous coordinates. This is a tough question, but the right way to do it is to use both. In the end, we will use 3D coordinates and make assumptions that there's a phantom w = 1 with all of them and use the special 4×3 matrix multiplier code that we have written. For now I think we should use 4D points along with 4×4 matrices, so the next couple of chapters will further illustrate the use of matrices to perform clipping, perspective, and projection in a uniform manner. Although we all know that we don't need the extra w = 1 that the 4D homogenous coordinates give us and that we can assume it with special code, I don't want to make that assumption for now. Hence, we will assume that all points and vertices are in 4D homogenous coordinates with w = 1 in most cases, just to make the math and matrix operations uniform. With that in mind, let's create a more solid vertex list and polygon data structure based on these conventions.

Our First Polygon

We have left out a lot of details about the polygons, because at this point, we don't know enough about rendering to add them. However, for the next chapter, where we design a working wireframe engine, we will need at least the following for each polygon:

- Color—General color of the polygon. This could be a color index for 8-bit color, or an actual 16-bit or 24-bit RGB value for high-color modes. It could also be something else that you make up.
- State—State of the polygon. This will hold state information that changes dynamically as the polygon is processed. For example, is the polygon active, is it clipped, is it damaged?—things like that.

- Attributes—Physical attributes of the polygon. This might hold a number of flags that describe the polygon. For example, is it two-sided, does it reflect light, is it made of steel, is it transparent, and so forth.

As stated in our conventions, we are always going to assume that all polygons never have more than three vertices—just for now. With that in mind, here's the first version of the polygon structure:

```
typedef struct POLY4DV1_TYP
{
int state;    // state information
int attr;     // physical attributes of polygon
int color;    // color of polygon

POINT4D_PTR vlist; // the vertex list itself
int vert[3];       // the indices into the vertex list

} POLY4DV1, *POLY4DV1_PTR;
```

NOTE

The naming convention is [*root*][*coordinate type*][*version*]. POLY is the type of this object, 4D is the coordinate type, and V1 is the version.

Of course, the vertex list that vlist points to is of the type POINT4D[]. We're not going to further define state, attr, or color, because we want to keep them abstract and don't want to lock ourselves down. Let's continue on with another data structure that we might need, which I'm going to call a *face*.

Remember that we might need a simple list of polygons not associated with objects or general vertex lists during the rasterization phase. That is, we want a simple array or linked list of polygon faces that are each self-contained that we can send to the rasterizer. We might want to have this capability, so let's just create a data structure right now called POLYF4DV1 to hold this object. It should be identical to a POLY4DV1 structure, except that it's self-contained and doesn't reference an external vertex list.

```
typedef struct POLYF4DV1_TYP
{
int state;    // state information
int attr;     // physical attributes of polygon
int color;    // color of polygon

POINT4D vlist[3];  // the vertices of this triangle
POINT4D tvlist[3]; // the vertices after transformations
```

```
POLYF4DV1_TYP *next; // pointer to next polygon in list
POLYF4DV1_TYP *prev; // pointer to previous polygon in list

} POLYF4DV1, *POLYF4DV1_PTR;
```

Notice that there's a next and prev pointer. These are to help form a linked list of polygons like the one shown in Figure 6.46 that we can pass the rasterizer—we may or may not need them, but just some forward thinking. Also, notice that there are two copies of vertices vlist[] and tvlist[]. The second list tvlist[] is used to hold transformed versions of the first list. That is storage, so we don't have to overwrite the polygon as we manipulate it—again, we may or may not need this. Later, we might have extra space for world coordinates, camera coordinates, perspective coordinates, and screen coordinates!

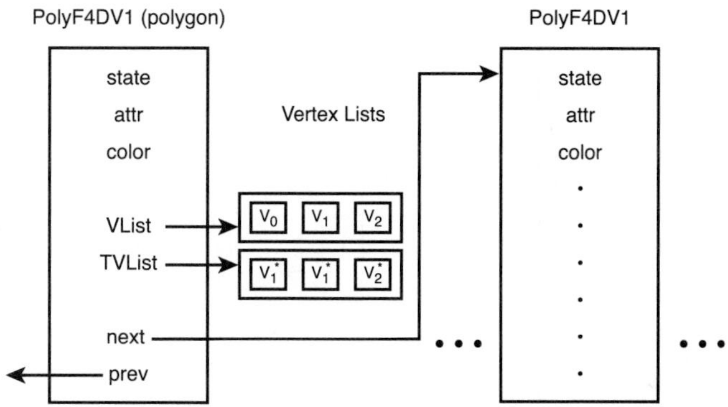

FIGURE 6.46 The POLYF4DV1 structure.

> **NOTE**
>
> Make a note that we cannot destroy the original 3D models' local coordinates. We must either copy them or transform them into another data structure at some point, because they are always the source of everything. On the other hand, if you perform local transformations like rotation and scaling, you usually want the model to stay that way, so it's okay to overwrite the original vertex data.

Alright, we have a vertex list, a polygon structure, and a face structure that we can use for rendering, so we have just barely enough to work with. Now let's increase the level of hierarchy a bit and talk about objects.

Defining Objects

An object in a 3D game is usually a collection of polygons that defines a single object, as shown in Figure 6.47. However, in a more advanced 3D system, an object might be a collection of objects interconnected with links, as shown in Figure 6.48. We will deal with the second type later, but for now, let's deal with the simple object that is composed of a rigid mesh of polygons with no moving parts, as shown in Figure 6.47. In this case, we have an object that is composed of a set of polygons that is itself based on a vertex list. With this abstract model, we can very easily come up with a data structure to hold a general object. However, it's at this point that we have to make some decisions about data storage in relation to the 3D pipeline.

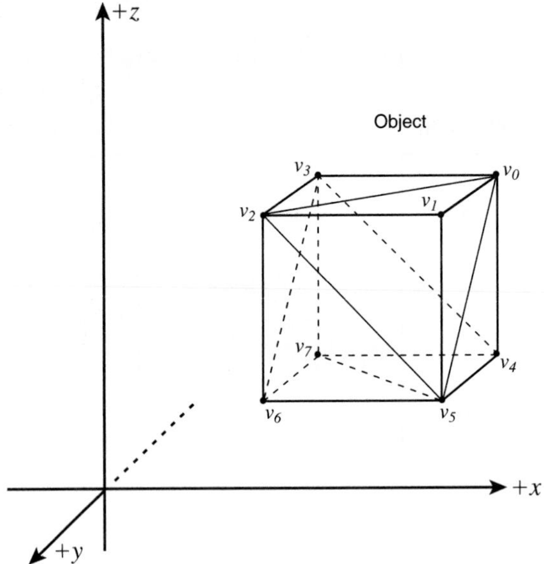

FIGURE 6.47 A single object made of polygons.

Remember that there are local coordinates, world coordinates, camera coordinates, perspective coordinates, and screen coordinates. The question is, do we need storage for each set of vertices as they propagate down the pipeline? The answer depends on a lot of things, but at the very least, we need the local coordinates of every object. Then the determination of necessary secondary storage really depends on how the 3D pipeline works internally. This means that if we pass a single object to the pipeline, do we put the responsibility on the pipeline or on the object for secondary storage.

This is a hard question, and there's no good answer. I have done it both ways—that is, create objects that internally have storage for local, world, and camera coordinates. On the other hand, I have also completely implemented it in the viewing pipeline.

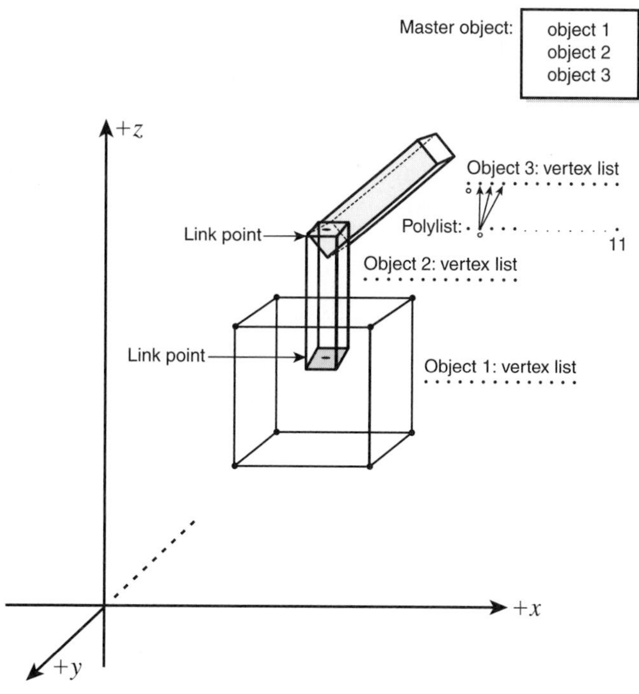

FIGURE 6.48 An interlinked object composed of many sub-objects.

For now, I think that I want to keep things relatively simple, so we are going to think of an object as a container of everything—even the transformations of the pipeline. However, we are only going to have storage for the local coordinates, along with the transformed coordinates. The transformed coordinates could be world, camera, perspective, or screen; we only know which by finding at which stage the data is in the pipeline. This minimizes storage. Okay, so that takes care of that. Now, what else do we need to define an object? Well, we need the number of vertices, maybe some attributes, state, and a name or `id`, along with a bounding radius that we will use later. So, our first shot at an object will look like this:

```
// an object based on a vertex list and list of polygons
typedef struct OBJECT4DV1_TYP
{
int  id;            // numeric id of this object
char name[64];      // ASCII name of object just for kicks
int  state;         // state of object
int  attr;          // attributes of object
```

```
float avg_radius;  // average radius of object used for collision detection
float max_radius;  // maximum radius of object

POINT4D world_pos;  // position of object in world

VECTOR4D dir;       // rotation angles of object in local
                    // cords or unit direction vector user defined???

VECTOR4D ux,uy,uz;  // local axes to track full orientation
                    // this is updated automatically during
                    // rotation calls

int num_vertices;   // number of vertices of this object

POINT4D vlist_local[64]; // array of local vertices
POINT4D vlist_trans[64]; // array of transformed vertices

int num_polys;         // number of polygons in object mesh
POLY4DV1 plist[128];   // array of polygons

} OBJECT4DV1, *OBJECT4DV1_PTR;
```

The first thing that you will notice is the incredible waste of space that `OBJECT4DV1` exhibits because of the static arrays. This is not an oversight, but on purpose, because I want to avoid memory allocation/deallocation issues at the juncture. Obviously, later versions will dynamically allocate the vertex and polygon lists. But for now, 64 vertices and 128 polygons should be more than enough to model cubes, rocks, and sex toys? Also notice that there are fields for the average and maximum radius of the object—these are to help with object culling.

And of course, there's a general position of the object `world_pos`, along with a general orientation of the object in its local space, named `dir`. You see, when we transform the object's orientation in local coordinates, we will modify the local coordinates and lose them, so we need some method to track these changes. Of course, we could use the convention that each time an object is processed through the pipeline, we perform all the local rotations to it on the fly and leave the original unscathed, but this might be a waste of time if we have 1,000 rocks in a desert that never rotate. In many cases, 3D engines will rotate objects in their local spaces and overwrite the local coordinates, but this rotation needs to be tracked, and that's what `dir` is for.

Moreover, we can store the angles there, or even a unit vector that's aligned with the z-axis initially (dir = <0,0,1>) and rotate each time along with the object, so we can keep track of the object's orientation relative to load time. Additionally, the basis vectors u_x, u_y, u_z are also to keep track of the object's orientation. That is, every time the object is transformed, so are u_x, u_y, u_z, which tracks the orientation of the object. For example, suppose we want to define a basic cube (as you have seen about ten times now), based on the following vertex list:

```
p0(10,10,10)
p3(-10,10,10)
p2(-10,10,-10)
p1(10,10,-10)
p4(10,-10,10)
p5(-10,-10,10)
p6(-10,-10,-10)
p7(10,-10,-10)
```

Here's the code that does it:

```
// define the cube object manually (very tedious)
OBJECT3DV1 cube_1;

cube_1.id    = 0;          // unused for now
cube_1.state = 0;          // unused for now
cube_1.attr  = 0;          // unused for now

cube_1.avg_radius  = 17.3;  // average radius of object
cube_1.max_radius  = 17.3;  // maximum radius of object
                            // sqrt(10*10+10*10+10*10)


cube_1.world_pos.x = 0; // position of object in world
cube_1.world_pos.y = 0; // who cares right now
cube_1.world_pos.z = 0;

cube_1.local_ang.x = 0; // the current orientation of
cube_1.local_ang.y = 0; // the object since loading
cube_1.local_ang.z = 1; // this will be default for
                        // all objects

cube_1.num_vertices =  8; // number of vertices

// create a vertex list to simplify initialization
POINT3D temp_verts[8] = { {10,10,10},      // p0
                          {10,10,-10},     // p1
                          {-10,10,-10},    // p2
                          {-10,10,10},     // p3
                          {10,-10,10},     // p4
                          {-10,-10,10},    // p5
                          {-10,-10,-10},   // p6
                          {10,-10,-10}};   // p7
```

9

```
// define the local vertices

for (int vertex=0; vertex < 8; vertex++)
    {
    cube_1.vlist_local[vertex].x = temp_verts[vertex].x;
    cube_1.vlist_local[vertex].y = temp_verts[vertex].y;
    cube_1.vlist_local[vertex].z = temp_verts[vertex].z;
    cube_1.vlist_local[vertex].w = 1;
    } // end for index

cube_1.num_polys = 12; // number of polygons

// define the polygons now, note that I am setting
// the state, attr, and color all to 0 for this exercise
// and the vertex pointer is pointing to the local coords
// but it doesn't really matter what list we point it to
// since we know that all polygon defined in this object
// are based on ITS vertex list and not something external

// create a list of triads that define each polygon to
// simplify initialization, note all in clockwise
// order, so we have an outward direction
int temp_poly_indices[12*3] = {
0,1,2, 0,2,3,    // polygons 0 and 1
0,7,1, 0,4,7,    // polygons 2 and 3
1,7,6, 1,6,2,    // polygons 4 and 5
2,6,5, 2,3,5,    // polygons 6 and 7
0,5,4, 0,3,5,    // polygons 8 and 9
5,6,7, 4,5,7 }; // polygons 10 and 11

// now initialize each triangle
// triangle 0

for (int tri=0; tri < 12; tri++)
    {
    // all of these are unused as of yet
    cube_1.plist[tri].state = 0;
    cube_1.plist[tri].attr  = 0;
    cube_1.plist[tri].color = 0;

    // point the vertex list to local coords
    cube_1.plist[tri].vlist = cube_1.vlist_local;

    // now assign the vertex indices
    cube_1.plist[tri].vert[0] = temp_poly_indices[tri*3+0];
```

```
cube_1.plist[tri].vert[1] = temp_poly_indices[tri*3+1];
cube_1.plist[tri].vert[2] = temp_poly_indices[tri*3+2];
} // end for
```

Wow, that seems like a ton of code for something so simple as a cube—and it is! This is one of the first problems with 3D graphics: the huge amounts of data. You would never represent a bitmap as individual bytes of data in a game, and likewise you would never represent an object or mesh as data in a real 3D game. Meshes and worlds are always loaded in from files because they can be made of hundreds, thousands, or millions of vertices. For now, we are going to use manual input along with some primitive ASCII-based file formats to represent our 3D objects, until we get more sophisticated.

At this point we have the cube, and we would proceed to push it through the 3D pipeline with a camera, viewing frustrum, and all the stuff we have been talking about. Then at the end, we would render the object, maybe with shaded polygons or wireframe, but that's for the next chapter.

Representing Worlds

Right now, our view of a 3D world is a composition of 3D objects, in which each object is a collection of polygons that are based on a vertex list (or maybe not). This is fine, but what about if we want to make a game like *Quake*, or a tank simulation with a huge amount of terrain? Sure, the objects in the game map nicely to our objects, but the indoor environment of *Quake* or the huge terrain maps of an outdoor tank simulation might not fit into our little object definition.

Indoor and outdoor worlds (or more generally, environments) are usually special cases of objects, and more advanced data structures must be employed to represent them properly because of their sheer size. For example, a typical game object of a tank or character might have about 20–500 polygons. This is manageable with the object data structure that we have designed. On the other hand, imagine a world that has tens of thousands, or even tens of millions of polygons. We can't just have a huge list of these polygons and throw them at the pipeline. We need to be smarter about how we load the data in, because at any time only a small fraction of the polygons in a world will be visible. Along those lines, we've already talked about how we might represent a terrain world in some of the previous sections of this chapter, and one of our solutions was to arrange the world as a matrix of sectors. Perhaps the sectors could be objects? On the other hand, some of our algorithms fall apart (object-removal) because there's no sense of objects when dealing with terrain or an indoor environment. On the other hand, these concepts are replaced with the concepts of rooms, areas, and portals, and we use analogous methods to cull them.

Additionally, most of the time terrain and indoor environments don't change much, so we can do lots of precalculations and optimizations on them and employ *binary space partitions*, *octrees*, or *portals* to simplify and minimize the amount of data that we have to process each frame. For instance, an environment can be defined completely in world coordinates because it won't move, thus saving us the local-to-world transformation.

Therefore, in most cases after we decide on the parts of the environment that are visible, we need only push them through the camera and projection matrices.

We will talk about all these concepts as the book progresses, but I want you to fully understand that we can get away with simple wireframe and flat-shaded 3D games with what we have so far. For more advanced games, we are going to have to think of much more robust data structures and algorithms to cut down all the data processed with each frame.

With all that in mind, there's no reason to even try to come up with a 3D data structure right now for general worlds, because we don't know enough about 3D, and truthfully, we need to tailor the design to the world itself. However, we can imagine that for a game similar to *Quake*, we might design the engine so that each room is a separate node in a tree. For every room, there are links to all the other rooms that are visible from that room. Thus, at any time we could refer to this data structure, and based on our position, cull out all but a few rooms. This is shown in Figure 6.49.

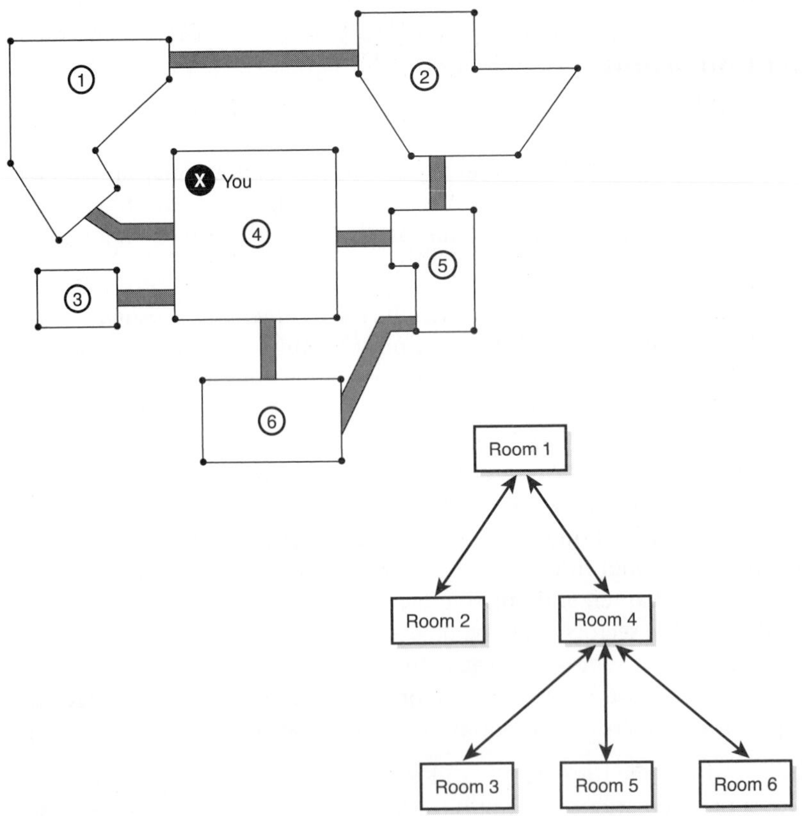

FIGURE 6.49 A possible level data structure.

Of course, this falls apart if we can see outside, or there are lots of windows, and so on. But if you write a game with rooms all connected with long hallways, you can have a billion rooms and the engine would be able to instantly cull them. These are some of the ideas behind BSP trees, octrees, and portals—more on this later, though. I'm getting ahead of myself, or at least the entity that is currently inhabiting my body is ...

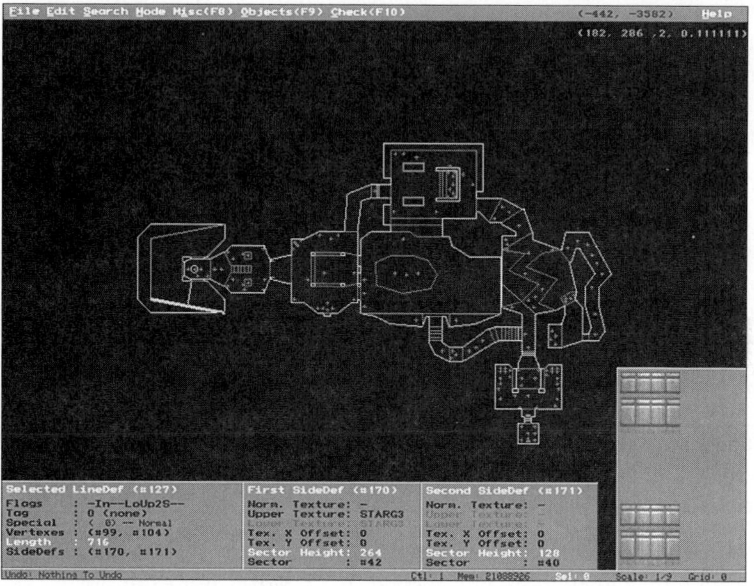

FIGURE 6.50 A screenshot of DoomEdit in action.

3D Tools

Alrighty, then. Where to even begin? Well, making a 3D game these days is a lot of work, mostly because of the 3D aspect of game and the amount of data needed. Alas, one of the most vexing problems facing a game programmer/designer is how on Earth all the data for the game will be generated and worked with. There are many solutions to this problem. For simple 3D games, you might create tools yourself for 3D modeling and world generation. For example, Figure 6.50 shows an old screenshot of the *Doom* editor. As you can see, the tool is bitmapped/line-drawn-based and features a top-down view. The tool reads in various data files and then enables the level designer to place objects, geometry, switches, creatures, lights, and so forth to create the world. DoomEdit and other "build engines" were used to generate the entire 3D world for the games, and were all-in-one solutions. Of course, other game assets like scripts, bitmaps, and sounds were created in other tools.

These days things have become much more complex, because the worlds are totally 3D, with arbitrary geometry. With this in mind, there are two routes to take: You can still write your own 3D tool, but realize that you're going to end up writing a 3D modeling package in essence; or you can use an existing 3D modeler like Caligari trueSpace, Maya, LightWave, 3D Studio Max, Blender, or Moray (coupled with the Persistence of Vision POV ray-tracer), completely design your objects and worlds with these modelers, and then interface the tools to your game engine via extra software and or plug-ins. This is probably the best approach, because you leverage someone else's work. On the other hand, 3D modelers aren't good at placing monsters, adding switches to doors, and so on, but they are getting better, and many of the aforementioned modelers have lots of hooks and API additions that enable you to modify the base functionality of the modeler to your needs.

Originally for this book I was going to use the *Quake* format for 3D worlds, and use something like WorldCraft to create the worlds. However, the developers of WorldCraft have kind of gone out of business (transferred the program to Valve, Inc. now under the name of the Hammer Editor), *Quake* is a proprietary format, and on second thought, I don't want to lock myself into it. Thus, we are going to use one or more of the standard file formats, like Caligari .COB, 3D Studio Max .3DS or .MAX files, .DXF, .NFF (neutral file format) and so on in this book, so you can use commonly available tools and well-documented formats. Moreover, this book is about 3D graphics and game programming, not really writing level design tools, so I want to stick to the point. With that in mind, you can use whatever 3D modeling tool you like, as long as it supports the file format(s) that I am going to read in this book.

Along those lines, I have placed a number of 3D modeler demos on the CD, along with some shareware modelers that are pretty good, too—Moray, for example, rocks. Even if the shareware modelers don't support the file format you like, I have also included a number of 3D file format converters on the CD.

Animation and Motion Data

Additionally, at some point you're going to want to create animated articulated creatures. This gets really complex. If you recall, we learned that you can animate creatures by mesh animations or by animated skeletal animation. In the first case, you'll need to get the 3D modeler to spit out the character mesh key frames and then you will need to read that out. In the second case, you'll need to be able to read in a mesh with articulation points and then pump motion data (like BioVision motion files) through the mesh links to animate the creature or object (if we go that far). This is again a very complex task, and the tools will get you the object and even give you the motion data (or you can make it or buy it), but you have to write the code that feeds the data into your engine. We will talk more about this later. Tools like 3D Studio Max, Maya, and trueSpace all have good character animation packages that will let you do both. However, in the end we may use a more basic keyframe system like *Quake*'s .MD2 format — we will see.

Loading Data from the Outside World

As I said, we are going to write code as we need it, but just to get you in the spirit of things, I want to show you a couple of file formats that we can use and just let you see what they look like. The whole point of a file format is to be able to represent 3D objects with enough information for our engine. At this point, we don't need to know anything about textures, lighting, and so on—we just basically want a description of an object as a vertex list and a polygon mesh.

However, as the book progresses, we are going to want to know a lot! For example, if we use the 3D modeler to create a tank, for example, we are going to want to know the vertex list, polygon mesh, texture coordinates, polygon attributes, and so on, so a more sophisticated file format will be needed. Additionally, if we want to model entire worlds with a 3D modeler, the modeler will have to support exported light sources or tagged information that our engine can use, and so on.

Describing all the file formats in complete detail is beyond the scope of this book, and beyond the scope of this chapter for that matter, but I just want to give you a taste for some of the more popular formats.

PLG Files

The PLG file format was invented by the people who made REND386, one of whom is Bernie Roehl (actually, I think he wrote the entire thing). The format is simple and to the point, so it's a good place to start. Unfortunately it lacks a bit in the texturing and two-sided polygon area, but it will suffice with a bit of finesse as a quick way for us to hand-edit models if we have to. The main reason to use it is that there are 3D modelers that generate PLG files, and utilities that convert .DXF files to PLG files. But most of all, writing a parser to read the files only takes an hour or two instead of a week, like it would for one of the more advanced formats.

PLG Header Line

A PLG file starts off with the name of the object and the number of vertices and polygon faces in the format:

```
object_name num_vertices num_polygons
```

For example,

```
pyramid 5 5
```

which says that the data to follow is for the object `pyramid`, which has five vertices and five faces.

PLG Vertex List

The next part of the data are the vertices in order of 0 to *n*. Each vertex should be separated by whitespace and be in x-y-z order. For the pyramid shown in Figure 6.51, the vertex data is

```
0   20  0
 30 -10  30
 30 -10 -30
-30 -10 -30
-30 -10  30
```

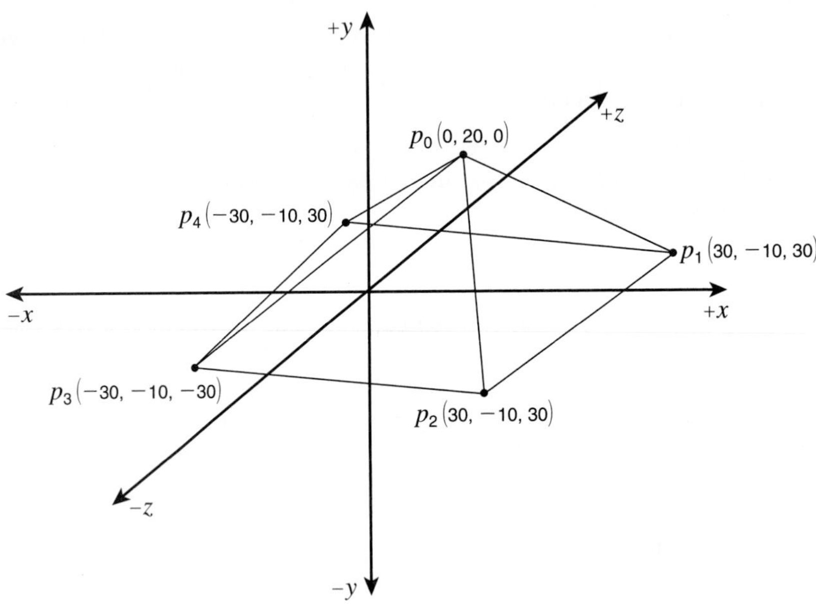

FIGURE 6.51 Five-faced pyramid.

PLG Polygon List

The next part of the file is the polygon description which is a series of lines that describe the color of the polygon, the number of vertices in the polygon, and the index number of the vertices. The format is

```
surface_description n v1 v2 v3 … vn
```

where `surface_description` is a surface descriptor we will get to in a moment, *n* is the number of vertices, and *v1, v2, ... vn* is the vertex list in counter-clockwise order. Note that in the actual file, there are no commas. In our pyramid example, the polygon list would look like this:

```
10  3 0 2 1
10  3 0 3 2
10  3 0 4 3
10  3 0 1 4
10  4 1 2 3 4
```

which means that there are five polygon faces. The first number on each row is called the surface descriptor and the next number is the number of vertices in that particular polygon. For example, the polygon in the second row has three vertices (0,3,2) and the polygon in the fifth row has four vertices (1,2,3,4). Remember, we are going to force all our models to be triangulated, but this is for illustrative purposes, to show that the format supports *n*-sided polys.

The only mystery at this point is the first number in each row, which is called the *surface descriptor* (in the case of the pyramid, this is 10 for all faces). Let's take a look at the meaning of the surface color descriptor.

PLG Surface Descriptor

The first number in each of the polygon definitions is called the *surface descriptor*. The surface descriptor can either be a decimal integer or in hex, with a 0x (or 0X) followed by a hexadecimal integer value. The surface descriptor is a 16-bit value, which is interpreted as bit fields in the following manner:

$H_{15}\ R_{14}\ S_{13}S_{12}\ C_{11}C_{10}C_9C_8\ B_7B_6B_5B_4B_3B_2B_1B_0$

- The R bit is reserved, and should be set to zero.
- If the H bit is set, it indicates that this is a "mapped" surface descriptor, and the lower 14 bits are taken to be an index into a surface map.
- If the H bit is zero, the SS bits are interpreted as shown in Table 6.1 following:

TABLE 6.1 Bit Definition for SS Bits of PLG Surface Descriptor

$S_{13}S_{12}$	Definition
00	This polygon is *solid shaded*; that is, it should be drawn in a fixed color with no special effects. If the CCCC bits are zero, the BBBBBBBB bits directly specify one of the 256 available colors in 256 color modes. If the CCCC bits are nonzero, they specify one of sixteen hues, and the top four bits of BBBBBBBB specify which shade of that hue to use.
01	This polygon is *flat shaded*; that is, it should be drawn with a constant shading that is determined by the angle at which light is striking it. Thus, as the polygon moves around, its apparent brightness will change. The CCCC bits specify one of sixteen hues, and the bottom 8 bits BBBBBBBB represent the "brightness" of the color. This brightness value is multiplied by the cosine of the angle between the polygon's normal vector and the vector from the polygon to the light source. The result is used to specify an offset into the given color's array of shades. Note that if the CCCC value is 0, the color will always be black.

TABLE 6.1 Continued

$S_{13}S_{12}$	Definition
10	This polygon should be treated as being "metallic." The CCCC bits (which should be nonzero) specify one of the 16 hues, and the top five bits of the BBBBBBBB value are used as an offset into a range of shades to cycle through to give the metallic effect; that is, a starting offset into the color cycle.
11	This polygon should be treated as being "transparent." It is just like surface type 10, except that alternating rows of dots are used instead of solid colors, allowing you to "see through" the polygon.

Note that Table 6.1 reflects the original definition of the PLG file format, and is a bit antiquated because it's obviously designed for 4- and 8-bit color modes. Although the 8-bit support will work for us here and there, we really need 16-bit colors. So what we will do is slightly modify the format when we get to using it in the next chapter to support 16-bit RGB colors. Of course, programs that export the files won't know this, but at least we will get hand-made support for our experiments.

Loading Objects with PLG Files

Loading in a PLG file isn't too much trouble. Basically, PLGs are standard ASCII files with one or more lines of text that describe the object. The only thing that makes reading PLG files a bit complicated is that color descriptors can be in either hex or decimal format, depending on a leading `0x`, and the files can have comments within them that can be started with the character #. Anyway, at this point we aren't going to write a parser, but it doesn't look that hard to do: not much more than reading lines one at a time and parsing out some numbers. Relatively speaking, this is a great format to hand-generate models for experimental uses, and we will probably use this in the next chapter just to get going. Here's the final object though, so you can see it in its entirety:

```
pyramid 5 5

# vertex list

 0   20  0
 30 -10  30
 30 -10 -30
-30 -10 -30
-30 -10  30

# polygon list

10  3 0 2 1
10  3 0 3 2
```

```
10  3 0 4 3
10  3 0 1 4
10  4 1 2 3 4
```

That's basically the entire PLG format description, so you can see why I like it. It's simple, down and dirty, gives you something to start with, and it's easy to write a reader for it. Of course, most modelers don't support it directly because it's so basic, but there are converters. The only issue is that PLG files refer to a right-handed system with vertices in counterclockwise order, so we must take that into consideration when loading objects exported from a tool, because we are using a left-handed system.

NFF Files

The next file format that is fairly easy to work with is called *neutral file format (NFF)*. I first used this format many years ago on VR games and it seemed to work well, so I think we might support it. It was originally developed by Eric Haines of Sense-8. Those were the days ... Anyway, the NFF file format is about up to version 3.1, so we will cover that.

The NFF format was designed to define simple worlds in addition to objects, in contrast to the PLG format, which just defines objects. Entities like the camera, background color, positions of lights, and so forth are supported in the NFF format. These features have very minimal impact on the parsing complexity of NFF, so it's a great format for what we want to do, as well as testing algorithms and try things.

3D Entities Supported by NFF

NFF supports the following entities:

- A simple perspective frustum
- A background color description
- A positional (versus directional) light source description
- A surface properties description
- Polygon, polygonal patch, cylinder/cone, and sphere descriptions

NFF files are output as lines of text. For each entity, the first field defines its type. The remainder of the line and possibly other lines contain further information about the entity itself. Entities types include the following:

`v`—Viewing vectors and angles

`b`—Background color

`l`—Positional light location

`f`—Object material properties

`c`—Cone or cylinder primitive

s—Sphere primitive

p—Polygon primitive

pp—Polygonal patch primitive

Let's take a brief look at the more important entities that we will deal with. I'll bold all the keywords and leave the parameters alone, which are usually floating point values.

Viewpoint Location Format The viewpoint location defines the viewpoint, along with some of the viewing frustrum parameters we have covered, but not all. Here it is:

```
v
from Fx Fy Fz
at Ax Ay Az
up Ux Uy Uz
angle angle
hither hither
resolution xres yres
```

Parameters:

`from`—The viewpoint location in world coordinates

`at`—A "look at" position to be at the center of the image, in world coordinates

`up`—A vector defining which direction is up relative to the `at` vector

`Angle`—Viewing angle in degrees, defined from the center of the top pixel row to the bottom pixel row, and left column to right column.

`hither`—The distance to hither/near clipping plane (if any) from the viewpoint/eye.

`resolution`—The resolution of the view plane in pixels.

NOTE

Note that no assumptions are made about normalizing the data (for example, the from-at distance does not have to be 1). Also, vectors are not required to be perpendicular to each other. Also, the far clipping plane is at infinity by default, and the aspect ratio is 1.0.

By convention, a view entity must be defined before any objects are defined, so if the NFF file is used to define the view point, the engine knows where to view from!

Background Color Format The background color is simply an RGB with values, with each channel from 0 to 1:

```
b R G B
```

If no background color is set, assume RGB = {0,0,0}.

Positional Light Format Lights are defined by their position and color as follows:

```
l X Y Z [R G B]
```

where `X Y Z` is the position of the light, and `R G B` is its color (which is optional). Also, all light entities must be defined before any objects are defined. However, lights that aren't colored will be assigned a nonzero intensity, which is undefined.

Fill Color and Shading Parameters Format The fill color and shading specifies the lighting properties of all entities that follow until a new fill color and shading are specified.

```
f red green blue Kd Ks Shine T index_of_refraction
```

Parameters:

> `red`, `green`, `blue`—RGB values from 0.0 to 1.0
>
> `Kd`—The diffuse reflection component
>
> `Ks`—The specular reflection component
>
> `Shine`—The Phong cosine exponentiation power for highlights
>
> `T`—The transmittance

Most of these parameters don't mean much to you yet because we haven't covered lighting, but in general there's a simple formula that defines the reflection of light off a surface in terms of its diffuse and specular (highlights) values, and that's what most of the preceding parameters are referring to.

Polygon Format A polygon is defined by a set of vertices that must be coplanar. In NFF files, all polygons are one-sided by definition, with the order of the vertices counter-clockwise as you face the polygon in a right-handed system. Also, the first two edges must form a nonzero convex angle, so that the normal and side visibility can be determined by using just the first three vertices.

> **CAUTION**
>
> The NFF file format is based on a right-handed coordinate system. Watch out!

```
p num_vertices
v1.x v1.y v1.z
v2.x v2.y v2.z
.
.
vn.x vn.y vn.z
```

where *num_vertices* is simply the number of vertices in the polygon, and v1 represents each vertex.

Polygonal Patch Format A polygonal patch is defined by a set of vertices and their normals. It's almost identical to a polygon p, but with the added feature that each vertex has a normal along with it.

```
pp num_vertices
v1.x v1.y v1.z n1.x n1.y n1.z
v2.x v2.y v2.z n2.x n2.y n2.z
.
.
vn.x vn.y vn.z nn.x nn.y nn.z
```

where *num_vertices* defines the number of vertices in the polygon patch, and v1 and n1 represent each vertex and its normal, respectively.

> **NOTE**
>
> The NFF format has a number of other features, such as allowing primitives like spheres and cones to be defined, but for the most part, the preceding entities cover everything we will need, except maybe the comment character #.

A Sample NFF File

To finish up our introductory discussion of NFF files, here's an actual 2×2×2 cube in NFF format:

```
v
from 0 2.0 2.0
at 0 0 0
up 0 1 0
angle 40
hither 1
resolution 512 512
l 0 5 0
l 0 2.0 2.0
f 0.000000 0.000000 0.000000 1 0 0 0 0
p 3
1.000000 -1.000000 -1.000000
-1.000000 -1.000000 -1.000000
-1.000000 -1.000000 1.000000
p 3
1.000000 -1.000000 -1.000000
-1.000000 -1.000000 1.000000
```

```
1.000000 -1.000000 1.000000
p 3
-1.000000 1.000000 -1.000000
-1.000000 -1.000000 -1.000000
1.000000 -1.000000 -1.000000
p 3
-1.000000 1.000000 -1.000000
1.000000 -1.000000 -1.000000
1.000000 1.000000 -1.000000
p 3
1.000000 1.000000 -1.000000
1.000000 -1.000000 -1.000000
1.000000 -1.000000 1.000000
p 3
1.000000 1.000000 -1.000000
1.000000 -1.000000 1.000000
1.000000 1.000000 1.000000
p 3
1.000000 1.000000 1.000000
1.000000 -1.000000 1.000000
-1.000000 -1.000000 1.000000
p 3
1.000000 1.000000 1.000000
-1.000000 -1.000000 1.000000
-1.000000 1.000000 1.000000
p 3
-1.000000 1.000000 -1.000000
1.000000 1.000000 -1.000000
1.000000 1.000000 1.000000
p 3
-1.000000 1.000000 -1.000000
1.000000 1.000000 1.000000
-1.000000 1.000000 1.000000
p 3
-1.000000 -1.000000 -1.000000
-1.000000 1.000000 -1.000000
-1.000000 1.000000 1.000000
p 3
-1.000000 -1.000000 -1.000000
-1.000000 1.000000 1.000000
-1.000000 -1.000000 1.000000
```

3D Studio Files

3D Studio and its newer offspring, 3D Studio Max (or just plain Max) are some of the most widely used 3D modelers in the world for both games and the movie industry. The original 3D Studio has been around for a long time, but it was actually an offspring of an even older program called AutoCad, written by AutoDesk. It was AutoCad that originally supported the DXF file format, and then later, when 3D Studio was developed, the 3DS file format, and finally the new MAX file formats came to be that includes the entire scene data as well as each mesh. The unfortunate thing about these formats is that they are way complicated, and can come in either ASCII or binary flavors. So, I'm not going to get into the details of either as I did with PLG or NFF, because we don't have the room right here. What I will do is give a brief description of each and a tiny sample. However, later we will probably end up supporting DXF and/or 3DS.

DXF Files

DXF (Data eXchange Format) files were originally supported by Autodesk's AutoCAD program. There is both a binary and ASCII version of the format, but both share the same name. The format isn't really that bad, but it was never really designed for high-end 3D modeling of solid, lit, textured geometry like we are interested in; this is because the original designers were more interested in modeling 3D mechanical and architectural objects, not aesthetically pleasing imagery. Hence, there is 3D support, but the support isn't complete. Moreover, there's a lot of overhead in DXF files for all the entities it supports, and the sheer amount of technical details that have to be part of a technical drawing that have nothing to do with the object itself. Therefore, we usually have to parse past all the garbage to get to our models. After we get to our 3D model data, reading the file is rather easy.

Format of a DXF File A standard ASCII DXF file has the following main sections:

- `HEADER` section—This contains general information about the model.
- `TABLES` section—This contains definitions of named items.
- `BLOCKS` section—This section contains *block definition* entities describing the entities comprising each block in the drawing.
- `ENTITIES` section—This contains the actual entities that describe the model itself, along with any block references.
- `END OF FILE` marker—Every DXF file ends with the string `EOF`.

And of course, there is going to be all kinds of data in each one of these possible sections. This data is indicated and grouped into classes with what are called group codes. These group codes help you write parsers, because if you just look at the group code, you can quickly determine the context of the data. Table 6.3 lists the basic group codes.

TABLE 6.3 DXF File Group Code Classes

Group Code Range	Meaning
0–9	String value
10–59, 210–239	Floating point value
60–79	Integer value
999	A comment

Whenever there is anything in a DXF file, first there will be a group code to class the data. Thus, for every single number or string in a DXF file, first you will see a group code—if this seems like a lot of overhead and waste, it is—but it makes parsing easier. Going further with group codes, they are subclassed in each range to further detail the data, but keep in mind that 99% of the group codes are irrelevant to us. Table 6.4 lists the group codes in greater detail.

TABLE 6.4 DXF File Group Codes in Detail

Group Code	Meaning
0	Identifies the start of a file, entity or table
1	The primary text value for an entity
2	A name of some kind
3–4	Other textual or information
6	Line type
7	Line style
8	Layer name
9	Variable name identifier, used in the HEADER section
10	Primary x coordinate
11–18	Additional x coordinates
20	Primary y coordinate
21–28	Additional y coordinates
30	Primary z coordinate
31–37	Additional z coordinates
38	Elevation
39	Thickness
40–48	General floating point values
49	Repeat value
50–58	Angles
62	Color number
66	"Entities follow" flag
70–78	Integer values
210, 220, 230	X, Y, Z of an extrusion follow
999	Comments

> **TIP**
>
> I am only going this far with DXF files because when I first learned them about 10 years ago, all the numbers confused me, so I don't want you to have that same feeling. Alas, you at least have an idea of what all the numbers represent now, and why they are all over the place. There seems to more overhead that 3D data!

The group code values always come first, then the "thing." For example, at the start of every DXF file, you will find a string value that indicates the beginning of a file. Referring to Table 6.3 and Table 6.4, string values are `0–10`, and the start of file is `0`, so we would see something like this at the beginning of every DXF file:

```
0
SECTION
```

Suppose you want to add a comment—you would use group code `999` and then put the comment like this:

```
999
This is a comment, stupid huh!
```

Now let's take a look at a generic, empty DXF file. Note that I have added comments using the C++ `//`, but they are for illustrative purposes only, and do not exist in the DXF file format:

```
0 // Begin HEADER section group code
SECTION

2 // group code
HEADER
 // Header variable items go here

0 // group code
ENDSEC  // End HEADER section

0       // Begin TABLES section group code
SECTION

2       // TABLES group code
TABLES

0       // TABLE group code
TABLE
```

```
2       // view port ENTITY group code
VPORT
70

// viewport table maximum item count)
// viewport table items go here>>>>

0       // end the TABLE group code
ENDTAB

0       // TABLE group code
TABLE

2      // group code allows any of these
LTYPE, LAYER, STYLE, VIEW, UCS, or DWGMGR
70
// Table maximum item count
// Table items go here

0       // end TABLE group code
ENDTAB

0
ENDSEC  // End TABLES section

0    // Begin BLOCKS section
SECTION

2    // BLOCKS group code
BLOCKS

// Block definition entities go here

0
ENDSEC //  End BLOCKS section

0       // Begin ENTITIES section
SECTION

2       // and here's where the ENTITIES start
ENTITIES
// Drawing entities go here
```

```
0      // end SECTION group code
ENDSEC // End ENTITIES section

0
EOF // End of file
```

As you can see, there's a lot of stuff in an empty file, but luckily the only thing we are interested in is the ENTITIES section, because this is where the 3D data will be. There are many entities as shown in Table 6.5.

TABLE 6.5 Useful DXF File Entities

ENTITY **Tag**	**Description**
LINE	A line
POINT	A point
CIRCLE	A circle
ARC	An arc
TRACE	A trace in space
SOLID	A solid object
TEXT	A text string
SHAPE	A shape
POLYLINE	A connected collection of lines
VERTEX	A single vertex
3DFACE	A 3D face or polygon

We are only interested in the 3DFACE entity, which is what all the 3D geometry exported using DXF files is stored in. Note however that there's no lighting, texturing, or camera information at all. DXF is very simple mesh data, and that's it. Anyway, the 3DFACE entity looks like this for a four-sided polygon (I'll use // for comments again, but remember that they are illegal; 999 is the real comment group code):

```
0 // this is the start of something,
  // so 0 for the group code
3DFACE
10 // x component of vertex 0 of face
x0 // and here's the value

20 // y component of vertex 0 of face
y0 // and here's the value

30 // z component of vertex 0 of face
z0 // and here's the value
```

```
// now for the next vertex we increment the
// XYZ group codes by 1

11 // x component of vertex 1 of face
x1 // and here's the value

21 // y component of vertex 1 of face
y1 // and here's the value

31 // z component of vertex 1 of face
z1 // and here's the value

// and for the next vertex we again increment
// the XYZ group codes by 1

12 // x component of vertex 2 of face
x2 // and here's the value

22 // y component of vertex 2 of face
y2 // and here's the value

33 // z component of vertex 2 of face
z2 // and here's the value

// and for the next vertex we again increment
// the XYZ group codes by 1

13 // x component of vertex 3 of face
x3 // and here's the value

23 // y component of vertex 3 of face
y3 // and here's the value

33 // z component of vertex 3 of face
z3 // and here's the value
```

NOTE

If you wanted to define a triangle, the last vertex v3 would have the same values as v2 (v0, v1, v2, v2).

And here is our cube in DXF format (I am using columns and a really small font so you can see the majority of the file at once, because DXF files are written out line by line):

```
0
SECTION
2
HEADER
0
ENDSEC
0
SECTION
2
TABLES
0
TABLE
2
LAYER
70
153
0
LAYER
2
Cube
70
0
62
15
6
CONTINUOUS
0
ENDTAB
0
ENDSEC
0
SECTION
2
ENTITIES
0
3DFACE
8
CUBE
10
1.000000
20
-1.000000
30
```

```
0
SECTION
2
HEADER
0
ENDSEC
0
SECTION
2
TABLES
0
TABLE
2
LAYER
70
153
0
LAYER
2
Cube
70
0
62
15
6
CONTINUOUS
0
ENDTAB
0
ENDSEC
0
SECTION
2
ENTITIES
0
3DFACE
8
CUBE
10
1.000000
20
-1.000000
30
```

```
0
3DFACE
8
CUBE
10
-1.000000
20
1.000000
30
0.000000
11
-1.000000
21
-1.000000
31
0.000000
12
1.000000
22
-1.000000
32
0.000000
13
1.000000
23
1.000000
33
0.000000
62
0
0
3DFACE
8
CUBE
10
1.000000
20
1.000000
30
0.000000
11
1.000000
21
```

```
0
3DFACE
8
CUBE
10
1.000000
20
1.000000
30
2.000000
11
1.000000
21
-1.000000
31
2.000000
12
-1.000000
22
-1.000000
32
2.000000
13
-1.000000
23
1.000000
33
2.000000
62
0
0
3DFACE
8
CUBE
10
-1.000000
20
1.000000
30
0.000000
11
1.000000
21
```

```
0.000000
11
-1.000000
21
-1.000000
31
0.000000
12
-1.000000
22
-1.000000
32
2.000000
13
1.000000
23
-1.000000
33
2.000000
62
0
0.000000
11
-1.000000
21
-1.000000
31
0.000000
12
-1.000000
22
-1.000000
32
2.000000
13
1.000000
23
-1.000000
33
2.000000
62
0
-1.000000
31
0.000000
12
1.000000
22
-1.000000
32
2.000000
13
1.000000
23
1.000000
33
2.000000
62
0
1.000000
31
0.000000
12
1.000000
22
1.000000
32
2.000000
13
-1.000000
23
1.000000
33
2.000000
62
0
```


NOTE

Notice the `8` followed by `CUBE` before each `3DFACE` is defined. This is totally acceptable and the reason why there are group codes—you can just disregard it if you like. However, in this case the `8` is a *layer name* group code, and the `CUBE` string is the name of the layer. A layer in this case is the name of the 3D object I exported, which was called `CUBE`.

As you can see, parsing this file isn't as hard as you think. You simply find the `ENTITIES` section and then start reading each `3DFACE`. The only bummer is that DXF files do not use vertex lists—they use independent vertices for each face.

3DS/ASCII Files

3D Studio Max supports a number of file formats, but its most native formats are 3DS and ASCII. They are actually the same format, but 3DS is binary, and ASCII is human-readable. The formats are extremely robust and you can do just about anything with them, so I'm not going to try to explain them. Rather, I think that if you just look at a file dump of our little 2×2×2 cube located at (0,0,0), you will be able to see how the format works:

```
Ambient light color: Red=0.3 Green=0.3 Blue=0.3

Named object: "Cube"
Tri-mesh, Vertices: 8     Faces: 12
Vertex list:
Vertex 0:  X:-1.000000     Y:-1.000000     Z:-1.000000
Vertex 1:  X:-1.000000     Y:-1.000000     Z:1.000000
Vertex 2:  X:1.000000     Y:-1.000000     Z:-1.000000
Vertex 3:  X:1.000000     Y:-1.000000     Z:1.000000
Vertex 4:  X:-1.000000     Y:1.000000     Z:-1.000000
Vertex 5:  X:1.000000     Y:1.000000     Z:-1.000000
Vertex 6:  X:1.000000     Y:1.000000     Z:1.000000
Vertex 7:  X:-1.000000     Y:1.000000     Z:1.000000
Face list:
Face 0:    A:2 B:3 C:1 AB:1 BC:1 CA:1
Material:"r255g255b255a0"
Smoothing:  1
Face 1:    A:2 B:1 C:0 AB:1 BC:1 CA:1
Material:"r255g255b255a0"
Smoothing:  1
Face 2:    A:4 B:5 C:2 AB:1 BC:1 CA:1
Material:"r255g255b255a0"
Smoothing:  1
Face 3:    A:4 B:2 C:0 AB:1 BC:1 CA:1
Material:"r255g255b255a0"
Smoothing:  1
Face 4:    A:6 B:3 C:2 AB:1 BC:1 CA:1
Material:"r255g255b255a0"
Smoothing:  1
Face 5:    A:6 B:2 C:5 AB:1 BC:1 CA:1
Material:"r255g255b255a0"
Smoothing:  1
Face 6:    A:6 B:7 C:1 AB:1 BC:1 CA:1
Material:"r255g255b255a0"
Smoothing:  1
Face 7:    A:6 B:1 C:3 AB:1 BC:1 CA:1
Material:"r255g255b255a0"
Smoothing:  1
Face 8:    A:6 B:5 C:4 AB:1 BC:1 CA:1
Material:"r255g255b255a0"
Smoothing:  1
Face 9:    A:6 B:4 C:7 AB:1 BC:1 CA:1
Material:"r255g255b255a0"
```

```
Smoothing:  1
Face 10:     A:1 B:7 C:4 AB:1 BC:1 CA:1
Material:"r255g255b255a0"
Smoothing:  1
Face 11:     A:1 B:4 C:0 AB:1 BC:1 CA:1
Material:"r255g255b255a0"
Smoothing:  1
```

Caligari COB Files

Over the years, I have really come to be a strong proponent of Caligari trueSpace. It's a very powerful 3D modeler, and I challenge anyone to argue that its interface isn't the simplest to use in the world. Anyway, the COB format is similar to 3DS format, in as much as what's in the file, and there are both binary and ASCII versions of this format, too. Anyway, the format is much too complex to describe in detail, but once again a listing of our venerable cube shows much more than I can describe in a few pages about the format, so take a look at the following:

```
Caligari V00.01ALH
PolH V0.06 Id 16796788 Parent 0 Size 00000981
Name Cube
center 0 0 1
x axis 1 0 0
y axis 0 1 0
z axis 0 0 1
Transform
1 0 0 0
0 1 0 0
0 0 1 1
0 0 0 1
World Vertices 8
-1.000000 -1.000000 -1.000000
-1.000000 -1.000000 1.000000
1.000000 -1.000000 -1.000000
1.000000 -1.000000 1.000000
-1.000000 1.000000 -1.000000
1.000000 1.000000 -1.000000
1.000000 1.000000 1.000000
-1.000000 1.000000 1.000000
Texture Vertices 14
0.000000 0.333333
0.000000 0.666667
0.250000 0.333333
0.250000 0.666667
```

9

```
0.500000 0.000000
0.500000 0.333333
0.500000 0.666667
0.500000 1.000000
0.250000 0.000000
0.250000 1.000000
0.750000 0.333333
0.750000 0.666667
1.000000 0.333333
1.000000 0.666667
Faces 6
Face verts 4 flags 0 mat 0
<2,2> <0,0> <1,1> <3,3>
Face verts 4 flags 0 mat 0
<4,4> <0,8> <2,2> <5,5>
Face verts 4 flags 0 mat 0
<5,5> <2,2> <3,3> <6,6>
Face verts 4 flags 0 mat 0
<6,6> <3,3> <1,9> <7,7>
Face verts 4 flags 0 mat 0
<4,10> <5,5> <6,6> <7,11>
Face verts 4 flags 0 mat 0
<0,12> <4,10> <7,11> <1,13>
DrawFlags 0
Radiosity Quality: 0
Unit V0.01 Id 16796789 Parent 16796788 Size 00000009
Units 2
Mat1 V0.06 Id 16799524 Parent 16796788 Size 00000090
mat# 0
shader: phong  facet: auto32
rgb 1,1,1
alpha 1  ka 0.23  ks 0.81  exp 0.91  ior 1
ShBx V0.00 Id 16799525 Parent 16799524 Size 00000627
Shader class: color
Shader name: "chrome" (chrome)
Number of parameters: 3
base colour: color (255, 255, 255)
vector: vector (0, 1, 0.5)
mix: float 0.5
Shader class: transparency
Shader name: "none" (none)
Number of parameters: 0
Shader class: reflectance
```

```
Shader name: "caligari phong" (caligari phong)
Number of parameters: 8
ambient factor: float 0.23
diffuse factor: float 0.19
specular factor: float 0.81
exponent: float 43.8135
specular colour: color (61, 67, 255)
transmission factor: float 0
mirror factor: float 0.78084
refraction: float 1
Shader class: displacement
Shader name: "none" (none)
Number of parameters: 0
END  V1.00 Id 0 Parent 0 Size        0
```

As you can see, the beef is up at the top, but basically it's once again a vertex-based format with a nice face list. Also, it's darn near in plain English, so you almost don't even need to read a DOC on the format—you can try mucking with an object a bit and figure out the majority of the format in a couple hours, as far as orientation, lights, texture coordinates, and so forth, go.

Additionally, trueSpace has what is called the .SCN format, or "Scene," which supports entire scenes and worlds. 3D Studio Max supports this too, with the .MAX format. Thus, we can potentially use either modeler (or Maya or Lightwave for that matter) to not only define objects, but also entire worlds with lights, and so on. So as I said before, when you get ready to write a game, see whether you can leverage a 3D modeler along with some custom plug-in code, and use it as your game editor. Most of the time this approach works great, and 3D modeler developers are making it easier each day, with more and more support for game designers and editors with each iteration of their tools.

9

Icon Cool

3D Studio Max has a scripting language called MaxScript. With MaxScript, you can pretty much access anything you want in a 3D world. This way you can write scripts or macros that add functionality to 3D Studio Max, and you can basically turn it into a game editor!

Microsoft DirectX .X Files

The light dims … Last but not least is Microsoft's DirectX format. I am not an expert on this format, and I haven't used it for much, other than exporting it and letting Direct3D import it for me. That is, I have never written a parser. But I can tell you one thing—this format has everything but the kitchen sink. It's very complex, but also very powerful—definitely not something we are even going to think about writing a parser for. Therefore, we aren't going to touch .X files ourselves. But the 3D acceleration portion of the book (on the CD) loads and uses them at the API level, if you're interested.

3D File Format Summary

As you can see, various 3D file formats each have different pros and cons, but definitely anything that is human-readable (has an ASCII version) is a plus. For more information on 3D file formats, try *3D Graphics File Formats* by Keith Rule (Addison-Wesley), or searching on the Net is always a good thing. For example, here are two nice URLs for a list of file format descriptions:

```
http://www.informatik.uni-frankfurt.de/~amueller/FF02.HTM
```

or

```
http://astronomy.swin.edu.au/~pbourke/3dformats/
```

However, we will write a parser for each format we need for the book.

NOTE

The majority of file formats we've reviewed export the coordinates in a right-handed system. However, depending on the tool, this can be overridden. But I want to emphasize that it's an issue when we finally write parsers, and if for some reason down the road you load an object into your game that supports some specific file format and everything is inside out, you simply need to invert the order of vertices and flip the z-axis in most cases.

Basic Rigid Transformations and Animation

If you're reading this book, you should have a fairly good grasp on 2D animation techniques such as translation, bitmap scaling, and rotation. However, in 3D there's a lot more we can do with 3D objects, because we have a total of six degrees of freedom to move objects around, and we can deform the meshes themselves.

We've already talked a little about *key frame animation* and *motion data-based animation*, and we will actually implement these types of mesh animations later in the book when we talk about character animation. Right now, I want to cover some of the basic animation techniques to simply move your 3D objects around and change their orientation, so that you can at least create games that have rigid objects that move around and do things. So, let's take a brief look at how to approach the basic animation techniques of motion, rotation, and morphing.

3D Translation

Translation in 3D is trivial, and we have already covered both the manual and matrix derivations for it, so I won't belabor the mechanics of it. What I want to talk about is how to translate an entire mesh, or better yet, the best way to translate a mesh in a 3D game.

Because each object has a set of local or model coordinates that are all relative to a local origin of (0,0,0), we don't really want to translate the local coordinates of an object to translate it. The better approach is to have the position of the object and then use it as the reference point during the local-to-world transformation to translate the object—which we have already done. In fact, our object already has a field to track the position of the object that it represents, called `world_pos`. Thus, we leave the actual translation of every point in the mesh to the local-to-world transform and we only have to deal with translating a single point to move an entire object! Therefore, if you want to move an object by the vector t = <tx, ty, tz>, all you need to do is this:

```
object.world_pos.x+=t.x;
object.world_pos.y+=t.y;
object.world_pos.z+=t.z;
```

Relatively simple. Okay, now that we know we can do everything with a single translation to a single point, the next question is how to move objects in 3D? Well, this is really more of a question that applies to AI. Your AI will generate a proper stream of motion or translation values. But just for fun, let's try to make an object move around in a circle in 3D. All we need to do is compute either absolute position values or relative position values from the last position. To makes things simple, let's use absolute values rather than relative. Let's say that we want to move an object on a elliptical path in a plane that is parallel to the x-z plane. Here's the code that would do it:

```
float x_pos = a*cos(angle);
float y_pos = altitude;
float z_pos = b*sin(angle);
```


You would just plug in values for `a`, `b`, `angle`, and the altitude, and the math would outpost the positions of an elliptical path—too easy, huh? Okay, what about a spiral that spirals up each cycle—that's easy, too:

```
// initial conditions
float altitude = 0;
float rate     = .1;

// this code is iterated each cycle
float x_pos = a*cos(angle);
float y_pos = altitude+=rate;
float z_pos = b*sin(angle);
```

And that's it—the point `(x_pos, y_pos, z_pos)` will spiral up from the ground plane y = 0. As you can see, writing motion code for 3D is just as simple as it is for 2D, and we are even using curves here without any problem at all.

3D Rotation

Rotation is a bit trickier than translation. Math isn't the hard part (although it's much more complex), but the tracking of the orientation is more difficult. For example, when you move an object to (x,y,z), you know it's at (x,y,z), simple as that. On the other hand, when you rotate an object (ang_x, ang_y, ang_z), the orientation isn't necessarily (ang_x, ang_y, ang_z) relative to the axis—remember all that stuff about gimbal lock? Additionally, when you rotate an object, the order that you apply the rotation matters; that is, XYZ is completely different from YXZ, and so forth. Of course, if you are rotating an asteroid around and you create a rotation rate (rx, ry, rz) with which you rotate the asteroid each frame, who cares? But if you are rotating a tank or ship around, you need to be able to compute the orientation of the ship when you need it. Hold onto that thought for a moment.

To rotate an object in 3D, you always want to rotate the local coordinates of the object. You want to perform the rotation transformation in the local space with (0,0,0) being the object's local origin (and not in world space—otherwise your object will rotate off center). Now it's really up to you if you want to perform the rotation and then store the rotated coordinates back into the local coordinate storage, or if you want to make the current orientation of each object part of the viewing transform. That is, when an object is getting ready to be rendered, some code says to rotate the objects a certain angle and then pass it on in a temporary array. The pro of this technique is that your model never gets mangled, and it can be used as a master copy and other objects can just link to it. The downside to this technique is that for an object that isn't animating or that is fairly stable, it will have to go through a rotation transformation each cycle, even if it's not animating—wasting cycles.

Keeping that in mind, if you want to rotate an object, you would simply transform its local coordinates in place and then store the results back. For example, let's say that we have a tank simulation, and a tank object called `tank1` that we already have defined and loaded in is sitting there oriented straight down the +z axis. As the player turns right or left, we can rotate the model in local coordinates:

```
// initialization, assume tank drives around in
// x-z plane therefore rotation to turn is parallel
// to the y-axis, that is yaw
tank1.dir.x = 0;
tank1.dir.y = 0;
tank1.dir.z = 0;

// game code
if (turn_right)
   {
   for (int index=0; index<tank1.num_vertices; index++)
       {
       // rotate the point, assume the call does it
       Rotate_Point_On_Y(&tank1.vlist_local[index], -5);
```

```
        // update the current orientation, so we know
        // where the tank is pointing
        tank1.dir.y-=5;
        } // end for

    } // end if
else
if (turn_left)
    {
    for (int index=0; index<tank1.num_vertices; index++)
        {
        // rotate the point, assume the call does it
        Rotate_Point_On_Y(&tank1.vlist_local[index], 5);

        // update the current orientation, so we know
        // where the tank is pointing
        tank1.dir.y+=5;
        } // end for

    } // end if
```


Not much is going on in the code; if the player turns left, the entire vertex list is rotated parallel to the y-axis +5 degrees, and if the player turns right, the vertex list is rotated –5 degrees. However, here's the clincher—after you rotate a 3D object, you have no idea what its orientation is by just looking at the mesh.

Therefore, this information is exactly what is tracked in the direction field `object.dir` via the updates to `tank1.dir`. At any time, we can look at `tank1.dir` and know that the tank is pointing at that angle relative to the positive X-axis (which we assume is the 0-degree direction for y-axis rotation).

This method works great, but when you start rotating all three axes at the same time, it kind of falls apart. As I said, the actual orientation of an object might not be the sum of the rotations to the individual axes taken one at a time. However, there's a better way to track this—using an orientation vector. That is, for every object in your 3D world, when you load it and it's oriented toward the +z axis, you initialize a unit 3D vector that is also pointing down the 3D +z. Whenever you transform the 3D object, you transform the unit direction, too. This is shown in Figure 6.52. After 1,000,000 rotations, if you review the rotation vector, it will always reflect the current direction of the object. This is what the `dir` field is also used for. Alas, there's a catch. What if you rotate the object parallel to the z-axis and flip it upside down? The direction vector is still correct, but you have lost information because a vector has no "roll" tracking (but quaternions do!).

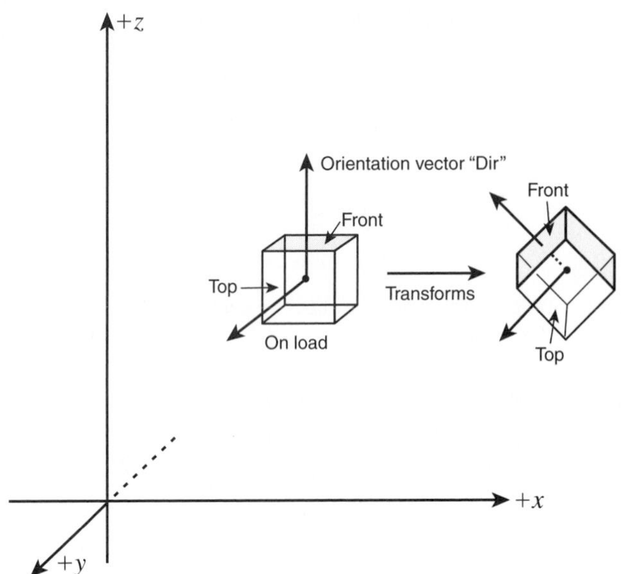

FIGURE 6.52 Tracking the orientation of an object after loading and transformations.

The point is that if you want absolute orientation tracking via a vector, you need three vectors inside your object structure/class, shown in Figure 6.53. You initialize these vectors to be the x-y-z local axis of the object, and then when you rotate the object, you rotate all three of the direction vectors. You will always be able to determine the absolute orientation of your object, because whenever you perform a rotation to the object, you perform the same rotation to the local axis, and thus they always reflect the transformations.

3D Morphing

The final simplistic type of animation that you can perform to a 3D mesh is morphing. I don't mean morphing from one mesh to another, but more scaling and shearing the mesh data in real time to make something look alive. For example, you could write the following code to make something look like it's breathing:

```
int up_down = 1; // -1 means get smaller
                 // 1 means get bigger

float scale = 1; // current scale

while(1)
{
// scale up or down?
if (up_down==1)
```

```
   {
   Scale_Object(&object, 1.05);
   scale*=1.05;
} // end scale
else
   {
   Scale_Object(&object, .95);
   scale*=.95;
   } // end else

// test if we are finishing cycle and changing
// directions
if (scale < .75 || scale > 1.25)
   up_down=-up_down;


} // end while
```

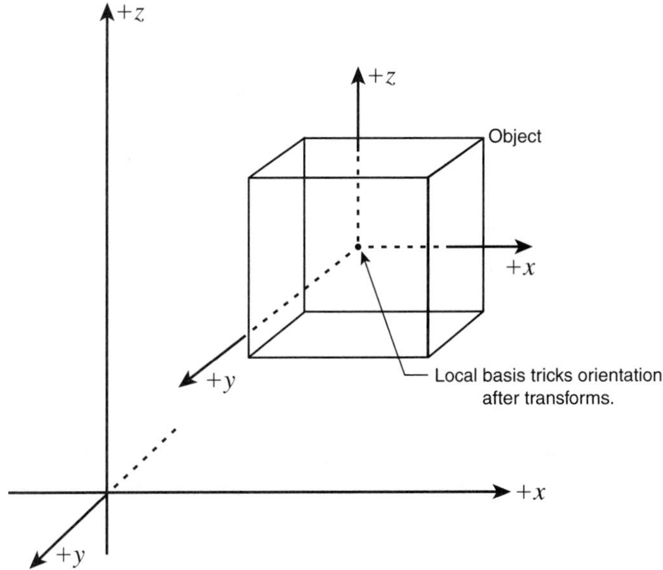

FIGURE 6.53 For total control of object orientation, an entire local axes basis must be stored.

The preceding code will scale an object by 5% up or down each cycle, making it look like it's breathing, or whatever. Of course, we have to write the function `Scale_Object()`, but that's nothing more than iterating through the sent objects vertex list and multiplying by the scale factor—easy. The point that I want to make is that we are assuming that we are modifying the local coordinates each cycle. This is fine, but slowly numerical errors will creep into the model, and it will deform hundreds, thousands, or tens of thousands of cycles, depending on the data. This is also true in the rotation animation.

CAUTION

Anytime you modify the local coordinates, there exists the possibility that after many modifications the original mesh data will be lost forever because of numeric errors, or *drift*.

The only real solution to this problem is to either keep a master copy of each mesh and refresh all objects every so often, or to make the rotation and morphing operations on the fly during the pipeline and apply them to the local coordinates of the object in question—but the results are stored in a temporary area, rather than overwriting the original mesh data.

Review of the Viewing Pipeline

We have covered so much ground once again. I'm cringing at this chapter's page count on MS Word, but hey—we aren't making grilled cheese sandwiches! Anyway, now that you know a little about all the parts of the 3D pipeline, let's recap the pipeline and try to fill in as much as possible, annotating the pipeline in places where we know we have lots of work to do.

In Figure 6.54, we see a fairly detailed view of the 3D pipeline, with all kinds of stuff hanging from it. The major parts are the following:

- Local transformations and animation—This stage is where the local coordinates of each object are transformed. There might be rotation, scaling, or other vertex operations that are performed in place.
- Local-to-world transformation—This stage is where the local coordinates are translated to world coordinates one at a time based on the position of the object, which is tracked relative to its local center at `world_pos` (in our object definition).
- Hidden surface removal and lighting—This stage is where we remove back-faces from the 3D models, as well as remove entire objects from the 3D pipeline. Additionally, lighting calculations are usually performed in world coordinates.
- Object removal—This stage is performed separately sometimes, and can be unlinked to the lighting phase. The only reason that lighting and hidden surface removal are performed at the same time is that surface normal calculations are made for the hidden surface removal that can be reused by the lighting models.
- World-to-camera transformation—This stage is where the final geometry that is potentially visible is transformed relative to the camera position and view angles.
- 3D clipping—This stage is where polygons are clipped to the 3D viewing volume.

- Perspective projection and clipping—This stage transforms the camera coordinates so that the objects have perspective. Additionally, the perspective transformation can normalize the viewing volume into a unit cube or cuboid shape, which makes 3D clipping easier to perform. Hence, sometimes 3D clipping is performed after the perspective transform.
- Screen projection—This is nearly the last stop in the pipeline. Here the view plane coordinates are mapped to the screen and passed to the rasterizer for final rendering.
- Rasterization and clipping—This is the last stage in the 3D pipeline. Here a list of polygons, vertex colors, texture maps, and so forth are passed to a rasterizer that just blasts the polygons down on the screen. Additionally, some polygons might extend past the edges of the screen (if they weren't clipped in a previous stage), and will be clipped at the pixel or scan line level.

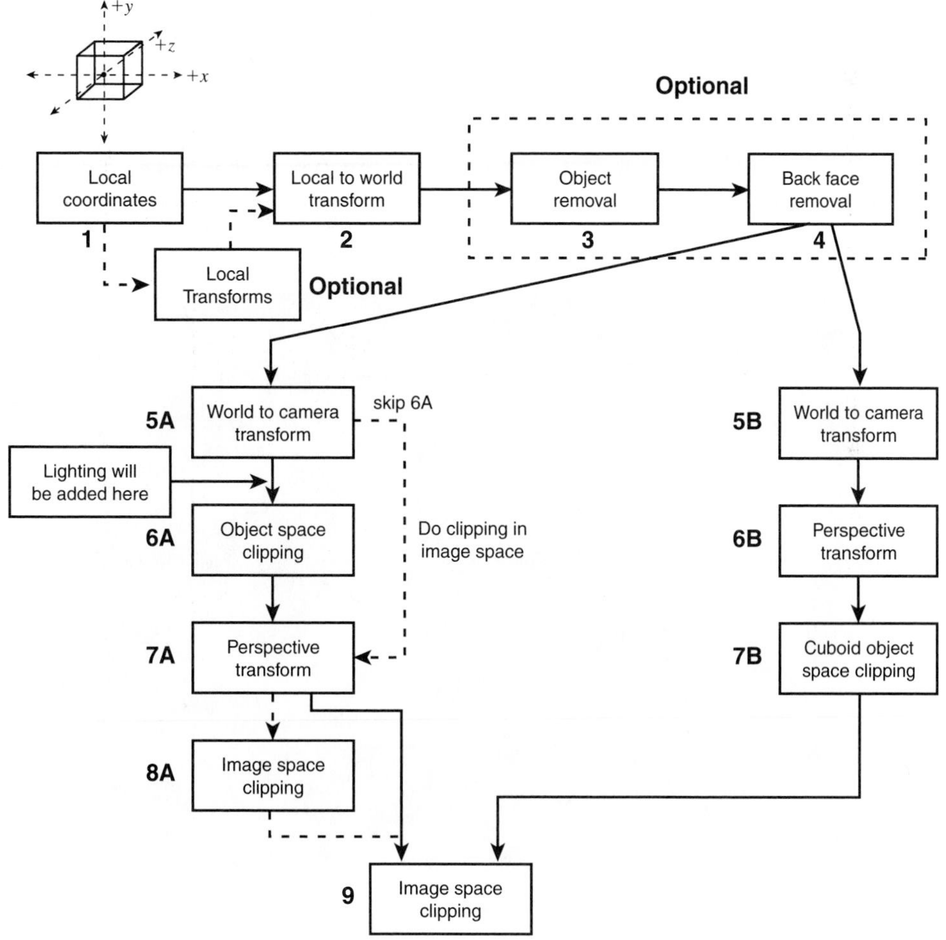

FIGURE 6.54 The final 3D pipeline review.

That's not a bad first shot at the 3D pipeline. Granted, there are a lot of details involved in making it work, but for the most part, that's it. Although we haven't talked much about lighting, you can imagine what's involved: lots of math, light sources, and the orientation of the polygons—but we will get to that in the upcoming chapters.

Types of 3D Engines

Now I want to take a moment to talk about the types of 3D engines out there. I don't want to get too much into the technology, but I just want you to get a feel for them—why they exist, and what they are each good at doing.

Space Engines

Figure 6.55 depicts a view of a good old space game: *Star Wars: X-Wing*. As you can see, the majority of the game is made out of objects floating in space. Games of this type are typically much simpler to write than first-person shooters for a number of reasons, including animation, collision detection, and database issues. However, in the most basic terms, space games are easier to write because the 3D engines aren't as complex. In most cases, 3D space games are object-based, meaning that all entities are objects, and during rendering, many of them are discarded from the pipeline. Then during the rendering phase, a simple painter's algorithm or Z-buffer is used to sort the polygons that make up each object. However, each object can be easily sorted against the other objects, because they represent ships in space.

FIGURE 6.55 A screenshot of *Star Wars: X-Wing*.

Additionally, most space games these days are written with polygon engines. However, some of the first 3D space games like *Wing Commander* were written using sprite engines, with lots of prerendered views, along with fast bitmap reflection and scaling algorithms. The positions of the ships and so forth were all represented by single points in 3D—so the engines were 3D in a sense, but the models were not. Anyway, space games these days are written with polygon engines for the most part, and lighting, animation, and so on are all handled in the normal manner.

The hard thing about space games is the motion. In a first-person shooter, it's very hard to animate bipeds walking around, but many times you have prerecorded animation files and you are usually walking on a 2D surface, like a floor. The problem with 3D space games is not so much the rendering, but the motion and AI for space ships. This is a bit more challenging, because the ships have to be able to make smooth turns, rolls, and operate in 3D. This means the use of 3D curves might have to be employed, along with other techniques. But as a rule of thumb, your first 3D games should be ground-based (in a desert, or in space) to simplify the rendering algorithms and database work.

Terrain Engines

Terrain engines are the next step up from space engines. A terrain engine can of course have more than terrain, but the terrain is a major component of the world, and a proper method of determining visible polygons is a must. Figure 6.56 is a screenshot from the game *Tread Marks* by Longbow Digital Arts, which is a 3D game with a lot of terrain. Aside from the terrain, the objects in a terrain (or any terrestrial) game are fairly easy to deal with. They can move around over the terrain (maybe some fly over), and in most cases are tanks or vehicles, so their animations aren't that bad. Of course, if you are making a mech warrior game, you have to deal with complex animation and biped terrain tracking. But the major problem with terrain engines is how to represent the world database, which can be quite large.

For example, suppose that you want to create a world that is a mesh of polygons 100,000×100,000 units in size, with each polygon no more than 200×200 units. That means you have a polygon mesh that is of the order

```
(100000/200)*(100000/200) = 250,000 polygons!
```

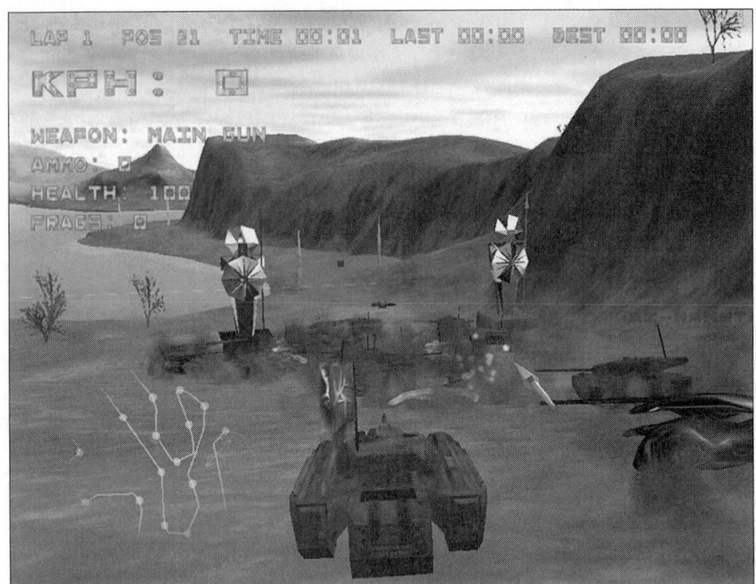

FIGURE 6.56 A screenshot of the most excellent game *Tread Marks*.

See what I mean?—that's a lot of polygons to track. Therefore, you have to use some kind of partitioning scheme to keep the number of active polygons that could potentially be visible at any time down to a reasonable minimum. One such technique is a *sectorizing* of the world. For example, take a look at Figure 6.57. Here I have sectorized our 100,000×100,000 game grid into an 8×8 matrix of sectors, each consisting of roughly 1,000 polygons per sector (250,000/256), which is manageable. And because I can only see maybe 1,000 units in front of me, I am guaranteed to only have to look in four sectors at once (worst case at a corner point), which means that at most I will have four sectors, or 4,000 polygons, to deal with at any one time. Not bad. Of course, that's minus objects.

Again, terrain or land-based games are a little more complex than space games because of the terrain and large database, but other than that, the rendering can be done using a modified painter's algorithm or binary space partition (if you want to get really big worlds), or a plain old Z-buffer. But you can get away with very little. Of course, another hard part about terrain engines is the motion of the objects and their tracking of the terrain contour. This is *terrain following,* nothing more than keeping your game objects oriented so their legs, feet, wheels, or whatever stay above ground, and that their center of masses up vectors are parallel to the terrain they are moving on.

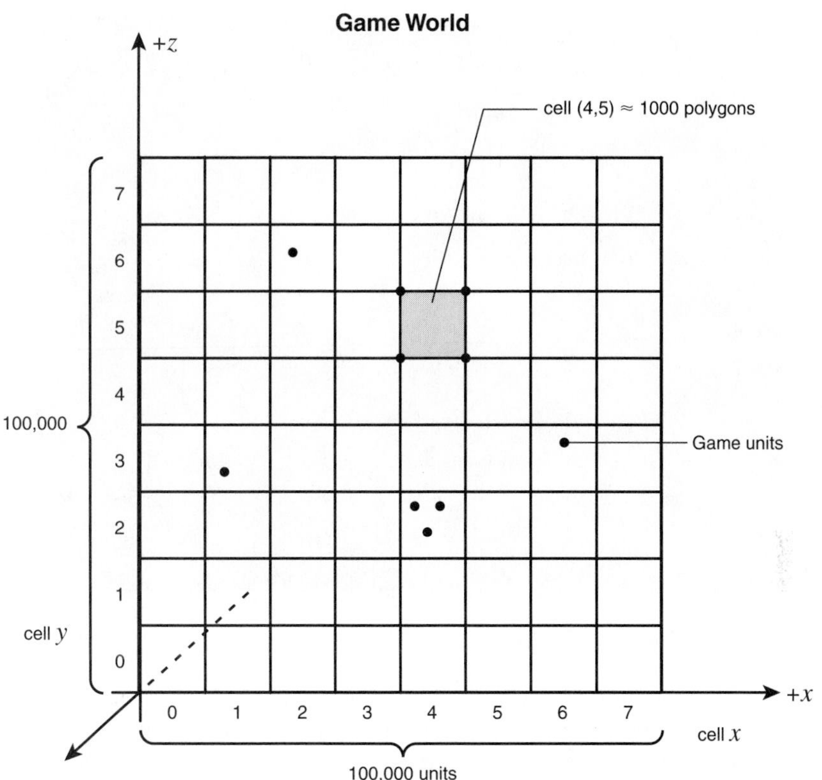

FIGURE 6.57 Sectorizing a large world into smaller blocks.

FPS Indoor Engines

These are the bad boys. Figure 6.58 is a screenshot of one of the quintessential 3D first-person shooter (FPS) games available: *Unreal Tournament*. First-person shooters are really the hardest games to write, for a number of reasons. First, you are indoors many times, and that means high detail and close quarters. Secondly, the worlds for FPS games are getting huge, and hence so are the polygon databases. This means that there is simply no way to just throw the whole world at the 3D pipeline—you have to sectorize your world using visibility schemes to minimize the number of polygons taken into consideration.

This means you'll need octrees, binary space partitions, portal engines, or whatever. In a space or terrain outdoor game, you can get by with the 3D models not looking right, polygons sorted incorrectly or missing, or whatever. But in a FPS game, you simply can't do that. Referring again to Figure 6.58, these games are solid as a rock, and really immerse the player in the worlds. Players simply won't accept an unstable, shaky, or ugly world. These things have to look real!

FIGURE 6.58 3D first-person shooter *Unreal Tournament.*

Finally, the physics modeling and AI for a FPS are very complex, again because of the intimate nature and close proximity of the games. The players "see" everything very well, and know what to expect. When a space ship blows up in a space shooter, that's not too hard to simulate, but when you fire a pulse at a player and he falls in the water, players want to see the water ripple and the box floating in it to bob up and down!

Ray Casters and Voxel Engines

So far we have talked about polygon-based engines, but there are other types of 3D engines based on ray casting and voxels. *Ray casting* is the technique used in many of the first 3D FPS games, like *Wolfenstein 3D*. These games are based on *forward ray tracing,* which is tracing a ray from the viewpoint of the player through the view plane until it hits a single object, as shown in Figure 6.59. Based on the geometry of the world and hints about the object, a 3D scene can be generated very quickly using this technique.

NOTE

Actually, a programmer named Paul Edelstein created the first 3D ray caster I ever saw on an Atari 800 game in the late 80s, but it was too ahead of its time for anyone to realize the power of the technique.

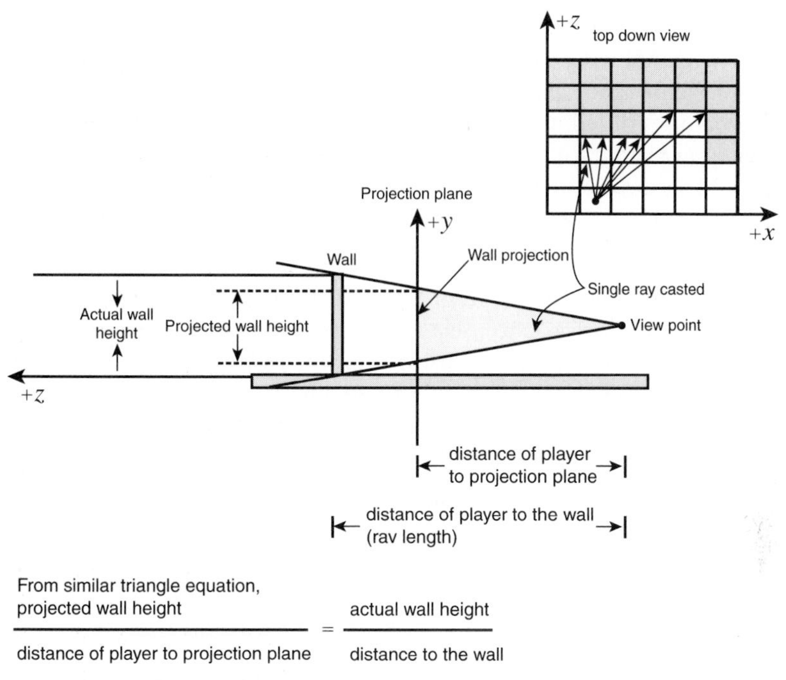

FIGURE 6.59 Ray casting mechanics.

The problem with ray casting is its limited capabilities. However, I believe that we will once again revisit advanced ray casters that perform a kind of ray casting/ray tracing hybrid in the next five years that will render in a more realistic way than with polygons—my two cents. Anyway, the other ray casting type technique is called *voxel graphics*, or *volumetric rendering*. One of the most notable games to use voxel graphics is Novalogic's *Comanche*. Technically, real voxel graphics are really not based on ray casting, but a technique called the *marching cubes algorithm*, which is used to render volumetric data. A 3D data set is used to render a 3D image—hence, the data is one-to-one with the image we desire to render. Medical imaging uses voxel systems. However, we have found that we can take voxel data and use other tricks based on ray casting to render the images very quickly. If you play with my voxel demo on the CD, you will see how fast it is.

The problem with ray casters and voxel engines is that you need a lot of data, and I mean a lot, to represent anything with detail. Alas, they aren't used that much in games these days, because polygons with texture maps are more efficient and look better. But as I said, I think we are going to see a comeback because ultimately all rendering will be based on light and ray tracing, and ray casting and voxel engines work well in these areas.

Hybrid Engines

The last type of engine I want to talk about is the hybrid. All this means is an engine that is designed to simulate space, land, and FPS all at the same time. This can also mean a single engine that uses different techniques in the same environment. For example, *Wolfenstein* uses ray casting for the world and sprites for the objects. *Doom* uses polygons for the world and sprites for the objects. *Quake* uses polygons for the world and some polygon models for the objects, and some sprites for others, and everything in *Quake III* is based on polygons.

The point is, many times you might want to create a game that has multiple environments, and it might behoove you to use a number of different engine types, so that each is better suited for the task, rather than using one and trying to make it work for everything. As another example, many 3D games these days have particle systems. Many times the particle systems are based on polygons that are *billboards*; that is, polygons that always face the viewer—hence, they are really like 3D sprites.

In conclusion, we are going to stick to full polygon 3D engines. If you're interested in some of the other techniques, maybe to make specific objects in your game easier to implement or whatever, there are a lot of other books on the subjects of sprite engines, ray casting, and other techniques.

Integrating Everything into a Final Engine

We have covered a lot of topics in this chapter, written a lot of pseudo-code, and reviewed lots of examples. At this point, we are ready to actually start writing working code that will enable us to create a crude 3D world, place objects in it, move the objects around, and view the world from a camera. We will do all this in the next chapter, and then each chapter thereafter will focus on specific topics (some that we have already discussed) and add lots of detail to each. However, there is a teenie-weenie bit of code we wrote in this chapter having to do with objects and data structures, and you can find it, along with all the stuff from the next chapter, in `T3DLIB5.CPP|H`.

So that's really it. No demos at all in this chapter, just a lot of high-level abstract ideas with some examples. Now I'm going to assume you know this stuff and pick up the pace a bit, so if you aren't completely comfortable with everything, please review this chapter again.

Summary

We have without a doubt covered a lot of ground in this chapter, and you probably have more questions than when you started. As we continue on, all will hopefully become clear. Our goal in this chapter was to learn coordinate systems in detail, because we are going to build on it directly in the next chapter, and additionally to get a general overview of everything 3D, just to give you something to think about as you learn each topic in detail. Like I said, 3D is so complex that to learn it, you need to start at the beginning, middle, and end all at the same time!

CHAPTER 7

Rendering Wireframe Worlds in 3D

IN THIS CHAPTER

- General Wireframe Engine Architecture
- Writing a 3D File Loader
- Building a 3D Pipeline
- Rendering a 3D World
- 3D Demos

"Would you say I have a plethora of piñatas?"

—El Guapo, *The Three Amigos*

Finally, we're ready to start writing 3D applications! You now have all the fundamental mathematical knowledge and at least a very general idea of all the parts of the 3D engine. In this chapter, we're going to write a simple wireframe 3D engine. As the book progresses, we'll upgrade to a flat-shaded engine, add lighting, texture mapping, and finally end up with something like a *Quake* software engine. Therefore, we're going to move in nice clean steps. Unlike the last chapter, this one is going to be code heavy, and we're going to explore a couple different ways to do everything. Moreover, we're going to be doing some more camera work in this chapter and discuss another camera model, called the UVN system, in addition to the Eulerian model. Here's the hit list:

- General wireframe engine architecture
- Writing a simple 3D file loader
- Building the 3D pipeline
- The local-to-world transform
- Camera models
- The world-to-camera transform
- The camera-to-perspective transform

- The perspective-to-screen view port transform
- Object removal
- Back-face removal
- Simple 2D/3D clipping
- Rendering the 3D imagery

General Wireframe Engine Architecture

Instead of just jumping into writing our first 3D engine, let's first lay the foundation of what we want to end up with. Remember, it's pointless for me to just give you a *Quake* engine and say, "here." The point of this book is to iterate version after version and for you to understand every single detail of building a 3D engine from the ground up. This also means making mistakes or simplifications for the sake of doing it.

TIP

In reference to the preceding statements about making mistakes or oversimplifications to make something understandable: One of the greatest simplifications in science is the model of an atom. During high school and even lower-level courses in college, the model of an atom is a nucleus composed of neutrons and protons along with a number of electrons orbiting in nice circular or elliptical orbits. Of course, this isn't true at all. Electrons hardly orbit; in fact, they're nothing more than a probability cloud and by their very nature, we can't locate them with certainty in both their momentum and position. But, for the purposes of many simple experiments, the orbital model works. In that same vein, many of the 3D techniques we'll learn can be improved on, but if you just see the end result, you're doomed to repeat history and make the same kind of mistakes if you don't learn why or when something is better than something else.

In the previous chapter, we covered a great deal of mathematical theory about 3D graphics. The fact is that whether you realize it or not, you know everything you need to about 3D graphics to make a fairly good engine (except maybe some rasterization techniques). So, what we're going to do is take all the mathematical and algorithmic concepts that we covered in relation to coordinate systems, projections, and data structures to build a simple wireframe 3D engine. This engine will allow polygons to be defined either independently or via higher-level objects loaded off disk and then rendered. Additionally, I've written all kinds of transformation functions (a plethora in fact), so we can create a number of different 3D pipelines to experiment with. For example, we might load an object and use hard-coded transforms all the way down the pipeline and render the object as a set of polygons. On the other hand, we might uses matrices to perform the various pipeline transformations and "rip" each object into its constituent polygons, and then render the polygons without caring about the original object(s) that they represented.

The point is that we're going to see more than one way to accomplish the same goal (and if you're an X Window System programmer, you'll feel right at home!). Very quickly, you'll learn that some basic 3D axioms, such as matrices, are beautiful but completely ridiculous when used to perform the local-to-world transform and so forth (with software engines, at least). Finally, we're going to explore two different camera models. The first is the simple Euler (or Eulerian) camera, which is nothing more than a position coupled with a set of rotation angles. The second camera (which we've covered descriptively, but didn't implement) is the UVN system, which is more like what a conventional movie director thinks in terms of; that is, a direction and focal point, along with an orientation relative to that direction.

By the way, if you don't own an advanced TI (or Casio) graphing calculator, buy one. I can't tell you how much it's been helping with the mathematics of the book and testing. Moreover, you can write games on them because many of them have 68000 32-bit processors in them!

The Data Structures and 3D Pipeline

There's not much to our first 3D engine. We're going to build it up as the chapter progresses, but right now, I want to at least lay out a rough diagram of the data sources and 3D pipeline. Figure 7.1 shows that the engine is based on three unique data structures:

- A structure for a general polygon based on a vertex list
- A structure for a general self-contained polygon
- A structure for objects that are composed of a number of polygons

These are implemented with the same data structures from the previous chapter. I've copied them here so you can refresh your memory (and mine—I'm going nuts naming things clearly):

```
// a polygon based on a vertex list
typedef struct POLY4DV1_TYP
{
int state;  // state information
int attr;   // physical attributes of polygon
int color;  // color of polygon

POINT4D_PTR vlist; // the vertex list itself
int vert[3];     // the indices into the vertex list

} POLY4DV1, *POLY4DV1_PTR;
```

```
// a self contained polygon used for the render list
typedef struct POLYF4DV1_TYP
{
int state;  // state information
int attr;   // physical attributes of polygon
int color;  // color of polygon

POINT4D vlist[3]; // the vertices of this triangle
POINT4D tvlist[3]; // the vertices after transformation if needed

POLYF4DV1_TYP *next; // pointer to next polygon in list??
POLYF4DV1_TYP *prev; // pointer to previous polygon in list??

} POLYF4DV1, *POLYF4DV1_PTR;
```

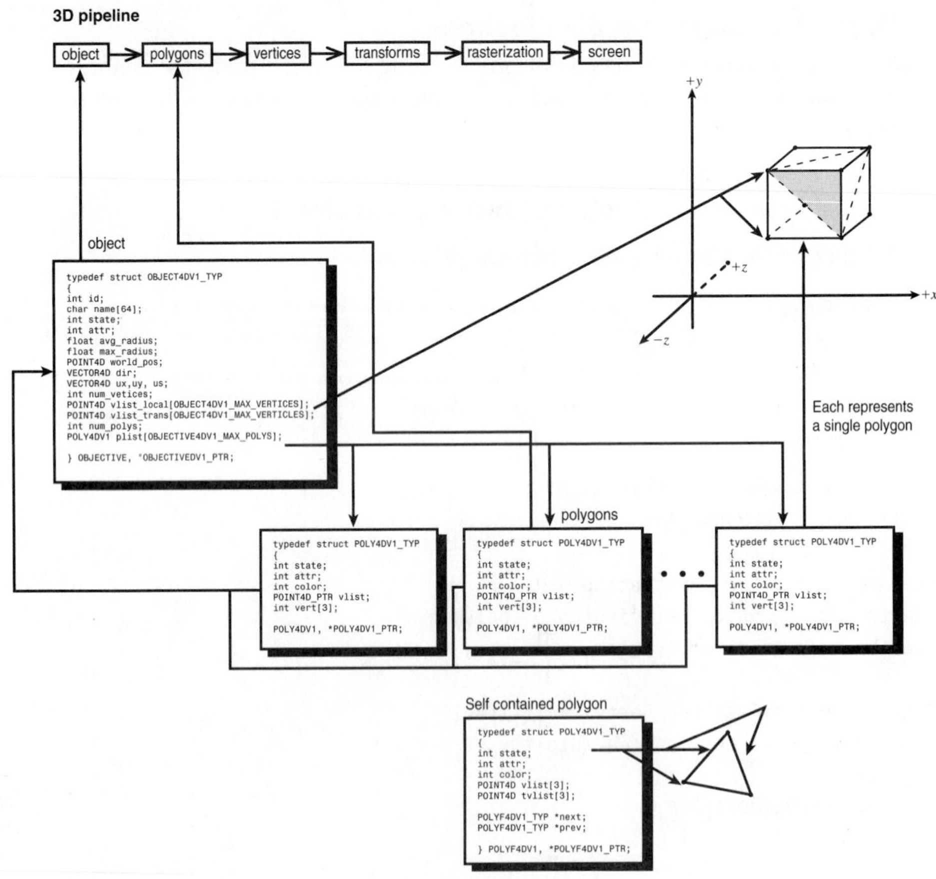

FIGURE 7.1 Data structures of our 3D engine.

Here are some of the #defines for the polygon structures to make life easier on us:

```
// defines for polygons and faces version 1

// attributes of polygons and polygon faces
#define POLY4DV1_ATTR_2SIDED        0x0001
#define POLY4DV1_ATTR_TRANSPARENT      0x0002
#define POLY4DV1_ATTR_8BITCOLOR      0x0004
#define POLY4DV1_ATTR_RGB16         0x0008
#define POLY4DV1_ATTR_RGB24         0x0010

#define POLY4DV1_ATTR_SHADE_MODE_PURE    0x0020
#define POLY4DV1_ATTR_SHADE_MODE_FLAT    0x0040
#define POLY4DV1_ATTR_SHADE_MODE_GOURAUD 0x0080
#define POLY4DV1_ATTR_SHADE_MODE_PHONG  0x0100

// states of polygons and faces
#define POLY4DV1_STATE_ACTIVE        0x0001
#define POLY4DV1_STATE_CLIPPED       0x0002
#define POLY4DV1_STATE_BACKFACE       0x0004
```

Some of the symbols may seem a bit alien, but they'll make sense as we build up the engine. Moving on, here's the object data structure:

```
// an object based on a vertex list and list of polygons
typedef struct OBJECT4DV1_TYP
{
int id;      // numeric id of this object
char name[64];   // ASCII name of object just for kicks
int state;     // state of object
int attr;      // attributes of object
float avg_radius; // average radius of object used for collision detection
float max_radius; // maximum radius of object

POINT4D world_pos; // position of object in world

VECTOR4D dir;     // rotation angles of object in local
          // cords or unit direction vector user defined???

VECTOR4D ux,uy,uz; // local axes to track full orientation
          // this is updated automatically during
          // rotation calls

int num_vertices;  // number of vertices of this object
```

7

```
POINT4D vlist_local[OBJECT4DV1_MAX_VERTICES]; // array of local vertices
POINT4D vlist_trans[OBJECT4DV1_MAX_VERTICES]; // array of transformed vertices

int num_polys;    // number of polygons in object mesh
POLY4DV1 plist[OBJECT4DV1_MAX_POLYS]; // array of polygons

} OBJECT4DV1, *OBJECT4DV1_PTR;
```

Nothing new, but a couple `#defines` are used to size the arrays. I've set them to reasonable values:

```
// change these if you need more
#define OBJECT4DV1_MAX_VERTICES      64
#define OBJECT4DV1_MAX_POLYS        128
```

NOTE

It would be more efficient to use arrays of pointers to polygons and vertices, but I'm not worried about memory at this point. Using dynamic arrays increases the complexity of the algorithms.

Continuing with our analysis of Figure 7.1, we see that there's a simplified 3D pipeline that takes either an object or a polygon and transforms it from local coordinates all the way to screen coordinates. Let's stop here for a moment and talk about what exactly we're going to process with the 3D engine.

In most cases, a 3D engine will have a number of objects and or individual polygons that represent the geometry. At some point, all these objects and polygons will be converted into polygons and placed into a render or rasterization list. However, with simpler 3D engines, it's quite possible to keep all objects separate (and intact) and to process and render them completely as individual entities. In most cases, you don't want high-level hierarchical objects to deal with at render time. Most 3D rasterizers like polygons, not "objects," but there's nothing wrong with it if you can make it work. In fact, at first, you may think that it might be impossible to deal with objects at raster time because you don't have a single list of polygons that represent all polygons that make up all geometry in the scene. Thus, how would you sort the polygons or Z-buffer them for correct rendering order (of course, I'm getting ahead of myself here).

Well, the key is that as long as you sort the objects themselves and then sort the polygons in the objects, you could theoretically render each object itself without problems because each object defines a *convex space* (roughly speaking, it can be thought of as a bounding sphere or box for sorting purposes). Of course, if you have a Z-buffer (which we'll discuss later), it's irrelevant if you have a polygon list or a list of objects made of polygons because at some point you're going to rasterize everything and use the Z-buffer for occlusion testing on a pixel-by-pixel basis.

The idea of the preceding paragraph is to reaffirm that we're going to do things in more than one way so that you can see the pros and cons of different techniques. Thus, I've written enough code to take a single polygon and rasterize it, or take a set of object(s) and keep them as objects all the way to rasterization, or to break objects into polygons and then add them to a master polygon list, which is what I want to talk about now.

The Master Polygon List

In most 3D engines (software or hardware), all the objects in the game are at some point converted into polygons from their high-level representations. These polygons are inserted into a master polygon list or stream, which is then pushed through the 3D pipeline (the high-level representation could be 3D meshes, parametric descriptions, or algorithmically generated on the fly). The list may be generated at the world-coordinate level or farther down the pipeline—maybe all objects are converted into polygons after the camera transformation? But, at some point, a single list of polygons will be thrown at the rasterizer. In our 3D engine toolkit, we have such a list, of course, and it's shown in Figure 7.2. If we like, we can use this list to hold the polygons. The data structure we're going to use for the first version of the polygon list is nothing more than an array of pointers to a static array, as shown in Figure 7.2 with the actual definitions following the figure.

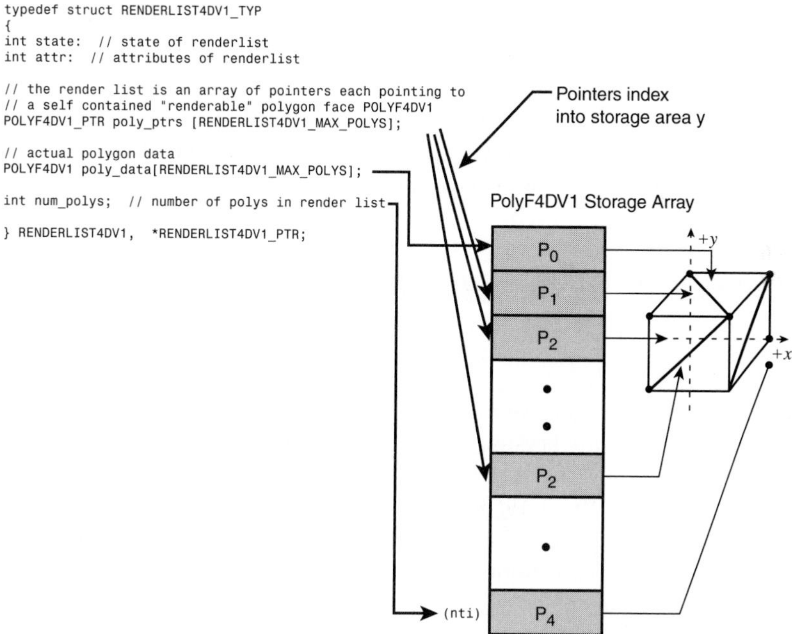
typedef struct RENDERLIST4DV1_TYP
{
int state: // state of renderlist
int attr: // attributes of renderlist
// the render list is an array of pointers each pointing to
// a self contained "renderable" polygon face POLYF4DV1
POLYF4DV1_PTR poly_ptrs [RENDERLIST4DV1_MAX_POLYS];
// actual polygon data
POLYF4DV1 poly_data[RENDERLIST4DV1_MAX_POLYS];
int num_polys; // number of polys in render list
} RENDERLIST4DV1, *RENDERLIST4DV1_PTR;
Pointers index
into storage area y
PolyF4DV1 Storage Array
P0
P1
P2
P2
P4
(nti)
+y
+x

FIGURE 7.2 The master polygon list.

```
// object to hold the render list, this way we can have more
// than one render list at a time
typedef struct RENDERLIST4DV1_TYP
{
int state; // state of renderlist ???
int attr; // attributes of renderlist ???

// the render list is an array of pointers each pointing to
// a self contained "renderable" polygon face POLYF4DV1
POLYF4DV1_PTR poly_ptrs[RENDERLIST4DV1_MAX_POLYS];

// additionally to cut down on allocatation, de-allocation
// of polygons each frame, here's where the actual polygon
// faces will be stored
POLYF4DV1 poly_data[RENDERLIST4DV1_MAX_POLYS];

int num_polys; // number of polys in render list

} RENDERLIST4DV1, *RENDERLIST4DV1_PTR;
```

As you can see, the `RENDERLIST4DV1` object has `state` and `attr` fields, which are used to track the state and attributes of the list (whatever we make that mean), but the important parts of the structure are the `poly_ptrs[]` and `poly_data[]` arrays. These arrays make up what's called an *indirection list* or an *indexed list*, meaning that the data is stored in the `poly_data[]` array, but instead of traversing the `poly_data[]` array directly, we traverse the `poly_ptrs[]` array, which has pointers (or it could as well have been indices into `poly_data[]`).

NOTE

The preceding technique is what Direct3D calls *indexed vertex buffers.*

Although you may think this is weird, we need it for a number of reasons. First, if I want to sort the polygons on some key—say, their z-values (for rendering order)—I can sort only the `poly_ptrs[]` list and not have to move around the `poly_data[]`! Second, if I want to disable a polygon node in the `poly_data[]` list, I would normally have to delete it and then move all the other nodes, if that was the only list I had. But with the indirection pointers in `poly_ptrs[]`, I can simply kill the link (and move the list up one if I want) to turn off a polygon node in the `poly_data[]` array. Finally, you might be thinking, "Why all this drama? Just use a linked list or something." I agree completely, but for now, a static array is easier to deal with, and only when we know that the number of polygons will vary from 2 to 2 million will using a linked list help us. For now, I know I'm going to be dealing with a few hundred polygons per frame maximum, so I can statically allocate the storage and not worry about it.

Finally, because you might have multiple render lists with many cameras, I decided not to use globals for the render list (or the camera, for that matter), so to define a render list you would do something like this:

```
RENDERLIST4DV1 rend_list;
```

Then you would make a call to the reset function, which resets the list for the next frame of animation:

```
void Reset_RENDERLIST4DV1(RENDERLIST4DV1_PTR rend_list)
{
// this function intializes and resets the sent render list and
// ready's it for polygons/faces to be inserted into it
// note that the render list in this version is composed
// of an array FACE4DV1 pointer objects, you call this
// function each frame

// since we are tracking the number of polys in the
// list via num_polys we can set it to 0
// but later we will want a more robust scheme if
// we generalize the linked list more and disconnect
// it from the polygon pointer list
rend_list->num_polys = 0; // that was hard!

} // Reset_RENDERLIST4DV1
```

Later, when we create more dynamic render lists (if we need them), this function would of course be more complex because it would probably deallocate memory and do cleanup of the last frame's polygon data.

NOTE

Data structures are so important in 3D graphics that I can't emphasize enough knowing your way around linked lists, double-linked lists, trees, graphs, and the various algorithms to search, insert, delete, and work with them. In *Tricks*, I covered a number of these data structures, but for a more complete treatise, try *Algorithms in C++*, by Sedgewick, or *Programs and Data Structures in C*, by Leendert Ammeraal.

Now that you're acquainted with the data structures, we're ready to start building a 3D wireframe engine. The funny thing is, there's not much to it, really (just a lot of details and connections, but nothing mind-boggling like filling out tax forms or anything). All we need to do is create a polygon or load an object (we'll need a function to do that) and then follow these steps:

1. Perform the local-to-world transform
2. Object removal (optional)

3. Perform back-face removal (optional)
4. Perform the world-to-camera transform
5. Perform 3D clipping (optional)
6. Perform the camera-to-perspective transform; that is, projection
7. Perform the perspective-to-view port or screen transform
8. Rasterize polygons

NOTE

Steps 6 and 7 are sometimes merged.

Of course, some of the steps may be rearranged, and it also matters whether we're dealing with objects or converting them to polygons (we'll have to perform the conversion at some time during the pipeline). Finally, we can opt to perform the transformations using matrices, manual methods, or a hybrid. For example, it's a waste of multiplications to perform a local-to-world transform with matrices because the same can be achieved with literally three additions per point rather than a matrix multiplications with 16 multiplies and 12 additions. On the other hand, the camera transform is almost always performed with a matrix transform because the camera matrix is non-sparse. The point is that there's no correct way to do anything—if it works, and it's fast, and it works for you, that's the correct way! But in this chapter, we'll do everything in a couple of different ways to get a good grip on the various methods to apply the pipeline and how ugly some can be—especially because we're using homogeneous coordinates, which can be a good and bad thing at the same time!

The New Software Modules

The new library modules for this chapter that contain all the functional code for the 3D wireframe engine are as follows:

- `T3DLIB5.H`—The header file
- `T3DLIB5.CPP`—The C/C++ source file

Of course, to compile any program in this chapter, you'll need to include all the previous `T3DLIB*.CPP¦H` files along with all the DirectX libraries, and set the compiler to Win32 .EXE target, but you knew that, right? Additionally, I always put a comment or two at the top of each demo program listing the requisite files to compile, so if you're unsure about the necessity of any particular library file, you can always refer to the comment.

CAUTION

Today I received about 13 emails about linker `error main() not found`. Unless I tell you we're making a DOS console application for some special reason, ALL Windows Win32/DirectX applications are Win32 .EXE and have `WinMain()` as the entry point. Thus, the only way you can get a linker error of `_main() not found` is if you're linking a Windows application as a DOS CONSOLE application and have the compiler set for CONSOLE application. I'm going to start a focus group called CAGA—Compilers Abuse Group of America—for abusers of various compiler products. If you're interested, email me at `compilerabuser@xgames3d.com` <GRIN>.

Writing a 3D File Loader

In the previous chapter, we covered a number of 3D file formats and hopefully you tried mucking with one of the 3D modelers on the CD or one you already own, can export a simple object such as a cube, and review the data in an ASCII editor. Now, writing a 3D file reader can be a simple task if you just finished a computer language course on compiler and parser design (Dragon book). Otherwise, writing a language parser might not be a nice experience for you because it's really not something you can hack together. You need to know what you're doing! So, one thing to consider is that if you're going to do a lot of 3D work, you might want to get yourself a set of 3D file import/export/conversion functions so that you don't have to write them. Nevertheless, I like doing everything myself, so I'm going to write every single format reader we use in this book rather than use third-party stuff. I'll try to make them short, clear, and to the point.

With that in mind, we're probably going to use the .PLG file format and the .NFF formats first in this book because they're simple to understand, and I can write a parser for either of them before Sci-Fi Channel's *First Wave* comes on tonight, and that's an important consideration. Moreover, they're both English-readable formats, and you can write the files by hand, which is what we're going to do for this chapter. Why? I want you to be able to work with 3D coordinates in your head before you delegate it to a 3D modeler.

7

We'll start with a .PLG parser, but I'm not going to go over the entire .PLG file format in detail because it's in the last chapter. I'm just going to give you a generic description of what a file we are trying to read looks like. Remember that the format is basically a vertex list–based format with a list of polygons referring to the vertex list as indices. Here's what a generic .PLG file looks like:

```
#this is a comment
#header line object name, number of vertices and polygons
object_name num_vertices num_polygons

# vertex list
# each vertex is in the form of x y z
x0 y0 z0
```

```
x1 y1 z1
x2 y2 z2
x3 y3 z3
.
.
xn yn zn

# polygon list
# each polygon is in the form
surface_descriptor num_vertices v0 v1 . vn
surface_descriptor num_vertices v0 v1 . vn
surface_descriptor num_vertices v0 v1 . vn
surface_descriptor num_vertices v0 v1 . vn
.
.
surface_descriptor num_vertices v0 v1 . vn
#where v0 v1 . vn are the vertex numbers that make up each polygon
```

And here's a simple cube object to give you something to look at for reference:

```
# begin plg/plx file

# simple cube, 8 vertices, 12 polygons
tri 8 12

# vertex list in x y z format
 5 5 5
-5 5 5
-5 5 -5
 5 5 -5
 5 -5 5
-5 -5 5
-5 -5 -5
 5 -5 -5

# polygon list
# each poly has 3 vertices
0xd0f0 3 0 1 2
0xd0f0 3 0 2 3
0xd0f0 3 0 7 4
0xd0f0 3 0 3 7
0xd0f0 3 4 7 6
0xd0f0 3 4 6 5
0xd0f0 3 1 6 2
```

```
0xd0f0 3 1 5 6
0xd0f0 3 3 6 7
0xd0f0 3 3 2 6
0xd0f0 3 0 4 5
0xd0f0 3 0 5 1
```

The only thing about PLG files is they are a bit "80s," so I've altered them a bit by adding some functionality; I call the new ones .PLX files. The point is that if you do actually find a 3D modeler that exports .PLG files, the reader we'll write will still read them, but the 16-bit surface descriptor will be invalid. The new surface descriptor I've made up for the modified .PLG files (which I sometimes refer to as .PLX files) is defined here:

```
Bit Number:    d15                    d0
Encoding:      CSSD ¦ RRRR¦ GGGG ¦ BBBB
```

where

- `C` is the RGB/indexed color flag.
- `SS` are two bits that define the shading mode.
- `D` is the double-sided flag.
- `RRRR`, `GGGG`, `BBBB` are the red, green, and blue bits for RGB mode.
- `GGGGBBBB` is the 8-bit color index for 8-bit mode and interpreted as the color index.

The following `#define`s help discriminate and extract these bit fields:

```
// bit masks to simplify testing????
#define PLX_RGB_MASK    0x8000// mask extracts RGB/indexed color
#define PLX_SHADE_MODE_MASK 0x6000// mask extracts shading mode
#define PLX_2SIDED_MASK   0x1000// mask for double sided
#define PLX_COLOR_MASK   0x0fff// xxxxrrrrggggbbbb, 4-bits per channel RGB
                    // xxxxxxxxiiiiiiii, indexed mode 8-bit index

// these are the comparison flags after masking
// color mode of polygon
#define PLX_COLOR_MODE_RGB_FLAG   0x8000 // poly uses RGB color
#define PLX_COLOR_MODE_INDEXED_FLAG 0x0000 // poly uses indexed 8-bit color

// double sided flag
#define PLX_2SIDED_FLAG      0x1000 // poly is double sided
#define PLX_1SIDED_FLAG      0x0000 // poly is single sided
```

```
// shading mode of polygon
#define PLX_SHADE_MODE_PURE_FLAG  0x0000 // poly is a constant color
#define PLX_SHADE_MODE_FLAT_FLAG  0x2000 // poly uses flat shading
#define PLX_SHADE_MODE_GOURAUD_FLAG 0x4000 // poly used gouraud shading
#define PLX_SHADE_MODE_PHONG_FLAG  0x6000 // poly uses phong shading
```

For example, if you want to define a polygon that's two-sided, 16-bit RGB color (0x3,0x8,0xF), with Gouraud shading, you would build the following surface descriptor.

Given that the 16-bit surface descriptor is in the format:

`CSSD ¦ RRRR¦ GGGG ¦ BBBB`

and

`C` = 1 for 16-bit color

`SS` = 10 for Gouraud shading

`D` = Double-sided bit; 1 for double sided

The `CCSD` nibble would look like this:

`1101`

The `RRRR ¦ GGGG ¦ BBBB` nibbles would simple be 0x3, 0x8, and 0xf. Thus, the result is

`1101 0011 1000 1111 = 0xD38F`

And that's all there is to it. The upper four bits of each descriptor describe the properties of the polygon and the color model, and the remaining 12 bits describe the color in the RGB model, or the index in the 8-bit model. All the file reader has to do is break these bits apart and set the appropriate bits in the polygon definition of whatever data structure(s) we load the object into. So, let's see the functions that read in a .PLG file.

The .PLG/X File Loader

The good thing about .PLG files is that their format is fixed, meaning that you can't put the polygons and then the vertices; you must put the vertices and then the polygons (.DXF files, for example, are a little more free form). Each data line in a .PLG must be in the correct format, which is usually one or more numbers separated by whitespace. So, the plan of attack is to write a simple parser that reads in each line along with a crude finite state machine that knows that the .PLG format is broken up into three sections:

Section 1: Header info

Section 2: Vertex data info

Section 3: Polygon data info

Each section has a particular format and is *line-based data*. Meaning we're guaranteed that each data line doesn't continue on to multiple lines. Thus, we can write a parser that reads single lines and then, depending on the state of the parser (what section we are in), we can parse the lines and extract the data elements (which are separated by whitespace). That's all there is to it. Of course, as the parser is parsing the data, the results are inserted into some data structure (which in this case will be an OBJECT4DV1 object).

To write the parser, I could use a single function, but it would be pretty ugly with all the various cases and the line reader/tokenizer. So, I decided to break it up into two functions which works pretty well.

TIP

If I did the parsing the right way, I would first write a suite of parsing functions and then leverage them to write this reader using a language specification. Of course, there are commercial tools to do this, including YACC and LEX, which are both Unix-based tools (but, of course, are available on PC) to write compilers and interpreters.

The first support function, Get_Line_PLG(), reads a single line of the .PLG file (it's based on fgets()) and is shown here:

```
char *Get_Line_PLG(char *buffer, int maxlength, FILE *fp)
{
// this little helper function simply reads past comments
// and blank lines in a PLG file and always returns full
// lines with something on them on NULL if the file is empty

int index = 0; // general index
int length = 0; // general length

// enter into parsing loop
while(1)
   {
   // read the next line
   if (!fgets(buffer, maxlength, fp))
   return(NULL);

  // kill the whitespace
  for (length = strlen(buffer), index = 0;
     isspace(buffer[index]); index++);

  // test if this was a blank line or a comment
  if (index >= length || buffer[index]=='#')
    continue;
```

```
  // at this point we have a good line
  return(&buffer[index]);
  } // end while

} // end Get_Line_PLG
```

There's not much to it. It basically understands whitespace and comments delineated by the # symbol. The function simply returns the next line in the file or NULL if the file is empty, which would occur only in an error condition because the .PLG file will have an exact deterministic number of data tokens based on the header information line. The function that reads the actual .PLG file is called Load_OBJECT4DV1_PLG() (note the naming convention) and is shown next:

```
int Load_OBJECT4DV1_PLG(OBJECT4DV1_PTR obj, // pointer to object
          char *filename,    // filename of plg file
          VECTOR4D_PTR scale,    // initial scaling factors
          VECTOR4D_PTR pos,    // initial position
          VECTOR4D_PTR rot)    // initial rotations
{
// this function loads a plg object in off disk, additionally
// it allows the caller to scale, position, and rotate the object
// to save extra calls later for non-dynamic objects

FILE *fp;      // file pointer
char buffer[256]; // working buffer

char *token_string; // pointer to actual token text, ready for parsing

// file format review, note types at end of each description
// # this is a comment

// # object descriptor
// object_name_string num_verts_int num_polys_int

// # vertex list
// x0_float y0_float z0_float
// x1_float y1_float z1_float
// x2_float y2_float z2_float
// .
// .
// xn_float yn_float zn_float
//
// # polygon list
// surface_description_ushort num_verts_int v0_index_int v1_index_int .
```

```
// vn_index_int
// .
// .
// surface_description_ushort num_verts_int v0_index_int v1_index_int .
// vn_index_int

// lets keep it simple and assume one element per line
// hence we have to find the object descriptor, read it in, then the
// vertex list and read it in, and finally the polygon list -- simple :)

// Step 1: clear out the object and initialize it a bit
memset(obj, 0, sizeof(OBJECT4DV1));

// set state of object to active and visible
obj->state = OBJECT4DV1_STATE_ACTIVE | OBJECT4DV1_STATE_VISIBLE;

// set position of object
obj->world_pos.x = pos->x;
obj->world_pos.y = pos->y;
obj->world_pos.z = pos->z;
obj->world_pos.w = pos->w;

// Step 2: open the file for reading
if (!(fp = fopen(filename, "r")))
  {
  printf("Couldn't open PLG file %s.", filename);
  return(0);
  } // end if

// Step 3: get first token string which should be the object descriptor
if (!(token_string = Get_Line_PLG(buffer, 255, fp)))
  {
  Write_Error("PLG file error with file %s (object descriptor invalid).",
        filename);
  return(0);
  } // end if

Write_Error("Object Descriptor: %s", token_string);

// parse out the info object
sscanf(token_string, "%s %d %d", obj->name,
                &obj->num_vertices,
                 &obj->num_polys);
```

7

```
// Step 4: load the vertex list
for (int vertex = 0; vertex < obj->num_vertices; vertex++)
  {
  // get the next vertex
  if (!(token_string = Get_Line_PLG(buffer, 255, fp)))
     {
     Write_Error("PLG file error with file %s (vertex list invalid).",
           filename);
     return(0);
     } // end if

  // parse out vertex
  sscanf(token_string, "%f %f %f", &obj->vlist_local[vertex].x,
                 &obj->vlist_local[vertex].y,
                 &obj->vlist_local[vertex].z);
  obj->vlist_local[vertex].w = 1;

  // scale vertices
  obj->vlist_local[vertex].x*=scale->x;
  obj->vlist_local[vertex].y*=scale->y;
  obj->vlist_local[vertex].z*=scale->z;

  Write_Error("\nVertex %d = %f, %f, %f, %f", vertex,
                    obj->vlist_local[vertex].x,
                    obj->vlist_local[vertex].y,
                    obj->vlist_local[vertex].z,
                    obj->vlist_local[vertex].w);

  } // end for vertex

// compute average and max radius
Compute_OBJECT4DV1_Radius(obj);

Write_Error("\nObject average radius = %f, max radius = %f",
      obj->avg_radius, obj->max_radius);

int poly_surface_desc = 0; // PLG/PLX surface descriptor
int poly_num_verts  = 0; // number of vertices for currpoly (always 3)
char tmp_string[8];    // string to hold surface descriptor in and
              // test if it need to be converted from hex

// Step 5: load the polygon list
for (int poly=0; poly < obj->num_polys; poly++)
  {
```

```
// get the next polygon descriptor
if (!(token_string = Get_Line_PLG(buffer, 255, fp)))
  {
  Write_Error("PLG file error with file %s (polygon descriptor invalid).",
         filename);
  return(0);
  } // end if

Write_Error("\nPolygon %d:", poly);

// each vertex list MUST have 3 vertices since we made this a rule
// that all models
// must be constructed of triangles
// read in surface descriptor, number of vertices, and vertex list
sscanf(token_string, "%s %d %d %d %d", tmp_string,
                &poly_num_verts, // should always be 3
                &obj->plist[poly].vert[0],
                &obj->plist[poly].vert[1],
                &obj->plist[poly].vert[2]);


// since we are allowing the surface descriptor to be in hex format
// with a leading "0x" we need to test for it
if (tmp_string[0] == '0' && toupper(tmp_string[1]) == 'X')
  sscanf(tmp_string,"%x", &poly_surface_desc);
else
  poly_surface_desc = atoi(tmp_string);

// point polygon vertex list to object's vertex list
// note this is redundant since the polylist is contained
// within the object and its up to the user to select
// whether the local or transformed vertex list is used when building
// polygon geometry, might be better to set to NULL in the context
// of polygons that are part of an object
obj->plist[poly].vlist = obj->vlist_local;

Write_Error("\nSurface Desc = 0x%.4x, num_verts = %d, /
       vert_indices [%d, %d, %d]",
                    poly_surface_desc,
                    poly_num_verts,
                    obj->plist[poly].vert[0],
                    obj->plist[poly].vert[1],
                    obj->plist[poly].vert[2]);
```

```
// now we that we have the vertex list and we have entered the polygon
// vertex index data into the polygon itself, now let's analyze the
// surface descriptor and set the fields for the polygon based on
// the description

// extract out each field of data from the surface descriptor
// first let's get the single/double sided stuff out of the way
if ((poly_surface_desc & PLX_2SIDED_FLAG))
  {
  SET_BIT(obj->plist[poly].attr, POLY4DV1_ATTR_2SIDED);
  Write_Error("\n2 sided.");
  } // end if
else
  {
  // one sided
  Write_Error("\n1 sided.");
  } // end else

// now let's set the color type and color
if ((poly_surface_desc & PLX_COLOR_MODE_RGB_FLAG))
  {
  // this is an RGB 4.4.4 surface, I know sucks!
  SET_BIT(obj->plist[poly].attr,POLY4DV1_ATTR_RGB16);

  // now extract color and copy into polygon color
  // field in proper 16-bit format
  // 0x0RGB is the format, 4 bits per pixel
  int red  = ((poly_surface_desc & 0x0f00) >> 8);
  int green = ((poly_surface_desc & 0x00f0) >> 4);
  int blue = (poly_surface_desc & 0x000f);

  // although the data is always in 4.4.4 format, the graphics card
  // is 5.5.5 or 5.6.5, but our virtual color system translates
  // 8.8.8 into 5.5.5 or 5.6.5 for us, but we have to first scale all
  // these 4.4.4 values into 8.8.8
  obj->plist[poly].color = RGB16Bit(red*16, green*16, blue*16);
  Write_Error("\nRGB color = [%d, %d, %d]", red, green, blue);
  } // end if
else
  {
  // this is an 8-bit color indexed surface
  SET_BIT(obj->plist[poly].attr,POLY4DV1_ATTR_8BITCOLOR);
```

```
      // and simply extract the last 8 bits and that's the color index
      obj->plist[poly].color = (poly_surface_desc & 0x00ff);

      Write_Error("\n8-bit color index = %d", obj->plist[poly].color);

      } // end else

    // handle shading mode
    int shade_mode = (poly_surface_desc & PLX_SHADE_MODE_MASK);

    // set polygon shading mode
    switch(shade_mode)
       {
       case PLX_SHADE_MODE_PURE_FLAG: {
       SET_BIT(obj->plist[poly].attr, POLY4DV1_ATTR_SHADE_MODE_PURE);
       Write_Error("\nShade mode = pure");
       } break;

       case PLX_SHADE_MODE_FLAT_FLAG: {
       SET_BIT(obj->plist[poly].attr, POLY4DV1_ATTR_SHADE_MODE_FLAT);
       Write_Error("\nShade mode = flat");

       } break;

       case PLX_SHADE_MODE_GOURAUD_FLAG: {
       SET_BIT(obj->plist[poly].attr, POLY4DV1_ATTR_SHADE_MODE_GOURAUD);
       Write_Error("\nShade mode = gouraud");
       } break;

       case PLX_SHADE_MODE_PHONG_FLAG: {
       SET_BIT(obj->plist[poly].attr, POLY4DV1_ATTR_SHADE_MODE_PHONG);
       Write_Error("\nShade mode = phong");
       } break;

       default: break;
       } // end switch

    // finally set the polygon to active
    obj->plist[poly].state = POLY4DV1_STATE_ACTIVE;

    } // end for poly

// close the file
fclose(fp);
```

```
// return success
return(1);

} // end Load_OBJECT4DV1_PLG
```

The function has a bit of error checking, which I probably went overboard with, but I wanted you to get in the habit of adding error handling to file loading functions because they can really go awry and write into memory. (Mr. Xenon, if you just initialized your variables, that wouldn't happen to you!) As a rule, I never do error handling in game code because if the code's not perfect, I'll make it perfect. But in a loader, you're counting on an external file to be correct, which might not be the case, depending the source of the file. Thus, some nice error states are dumped out to the error file as the loader is loading the data.

Moving on to how the function works, the function opens up the .PLG file requested by the string in ***filename***. Then the first line of the file is read in, which controls the number of vertices and polygons that need to be read in. The function then methodically reads in the vertex list, inserting the vertices into the sent `OBJECT4DV1` in `obj`. It then moves on to the polygons and inserts them along with determining their flags and color models via the surface descriptor for each polygon, which are translated into `POLY_ATTR_*` flags and logically `OR`ed. Additionally, you can send some parameters to the function to transform the objects as it's loaded: `scale`, `pos`, and `rot` are the initial scaling, position, and rotation factors for the object (note that they're vectors).

The only other interesting thing about the function is that it computes the average and maximum radius of the object for collision detection and object removal later down the line in the 3D pipeline. Anyway, to load an object off disk, all you do is this:

```
OBJECT4DV1 obj; // object storage

VECTOR4D scale = {1,1,1,1}, // no scaling basically
         pos   = {0,0,0,1}, // pos (0,0,0) in world
         rot   = {0,0,0,1}; // no rotation

// load the object
Load_OBJECT4DV1_PLG(&obj, "cube.plg", &scale, &pos, &rot);
```

That's it. If you use the debugger or something to read through the data structure `obj`, you'll see that the object data has been read into it and it's all correct (I hope!). The act of loading an external file into the `OBJECT4DV1` initializes the object and sets up the `state` and `attr` fields as well as setting the initial orientation basis defined by `ux`, `uy`, `uz` to `ux` = <1,0,0,1>, `uy` = <0,1,0,1>, and `uz` = <0,0,1,1>, which is in alignment with the world coordinate system axes for reference. Now, let's recap where we are as far as geometry.

At this point, we have three different data structures that we can work with:

- `POLY4DV1`—A single polygon, but needs an external vertex list.
- `POLYF4DV1`—A single polygon that has its own internal vertice storage. Also the basis of the master polygon list.
- `OBJECT4DV1`—A single object that's composed of a number of polygons. It has its own vertex and polygon storage; that is, it's self-contained.

We could write our engine to handle all of these types all the way down the pipeline, but I've opted to handle only the `POLYF4DV1` and the `OBJECT4DV1` because the `POLY4DV1` is just a `POLYF4DV1` without a vertex list. So, let's start building an engine to move these guys (yes...polygons are boys, but pixels are girls) through the pipeline!

Building the 3D Pipeline

We're ready to start implementing the 3D pipeline. We have our data structures, and we can load external objects in .PLG (enhanced .PLG, actually) format, so there's not much to do other than write the darn functions. Hold on one sec...let me write a couple thousand lines...okay, done!

CAUTION

The only regret I have is that we're going to have to write a lot of functions before we get to see any demos that put anything on the screen because the functions are all interrelated. But what I'll do at that point is create a number of demos that show some of the techniques leading up to the rendering stage of the pipeline.

Generic Transformation Functions

If you recall, anything that you can do in 3D, you can do via a 4x4 matrix transformation along with a post 4D homogeneous to 3D conversion (division by w, basically). However, this doesn't always mean it's the fastest way to do it! In general, any transformation that is a concatenation of rotations, translations, and projections is better to perform with a single 4x4 matrix because the matrix represents numerous transforms concantenated together and is usually non-sparse. However, if you're just trying to translate a single point, **p**, using a matrix multiple is overkill because it requires (4*4) = 16 multiplications, (4*3) = 12 additions to process the entire matrix multiple of **p*M** = **p**(1x4) * **M**(4x4). And if you do the translation manually, you only need three additions:

```
x=x+xt;
y=y+yt;
z=z+zt;
w=w;
```

The point is that in a production 3D engine, you might find a manual method faster and simpler. However, you might also find that although doing it manually is faster, it's not as clean or doesn't port well to hardware (which almost always uses 4x4 transforms for everything). Hence, as much as possible, we're going to allow both approaches in our engine design.

To facilitate the general transformation of a polygon or object by a 4x4 matrix, we need a function that takes as a parameter the polygon (`POLYF4DV1`) or the object (`OBJECT4DV1`) and performs a matrix multiplications on each vertex that makes up the geometry with a transformation matrix. Additionally, we have to take into consideration that both of these data structures have both local and transformed vertex storage.

If you recall, once you transform an object's vertex data, the transformation is lost. Thus, you better make sure that you want to do it. In many cases you do, but in some cases, the transformation is part of the pipeline, so you want to keep a copy of the original data unscathed, but transform and store the new data as it moves through the pipeline in secondary storage. Both the `POLYF4DV1` and `OBJECT4DV1` have such a secondary transformed storage space.

In the case of `POLYF4DV1`, the vertex data in the structure is stored in

```
POINT4D vlist[3]; // the vertices of this triangle

POINT4D tvlist[3]; // the vertices after transformation if needed
```

where `tvlist[]` is used to hold the transformed data. Similarly, in the `OJBECT4DV1` structure, vertex data is stored in these arrays:

```
POINT4D vlist_local[OBJECT4DV1_MAX_VERTICES]; // array of local vertices

POINT4D vlist_trans[OBJECT4DV1_MAX_VERTICES]; // array of transformed vertices
```

Hence, you can obliterate the secondary storage as much as you like because you always have a copy of the original data in the local storage array. However, sometimes you want to transform the local storage data (a scale or rotation operation, perhaps for animation) and want the new local model to remember the transform. In that case, you would modify the local data itself. Figure 7.3 shows a flowchart of the two operations we want to perform on vertex data.

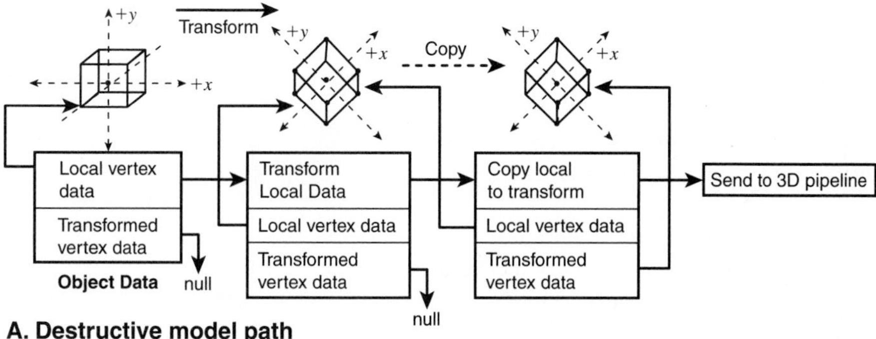

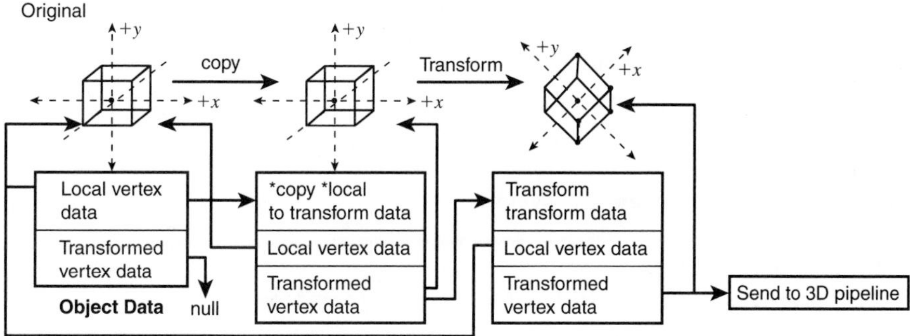

FIGURE 7.3 Flowchart of destructive and non-destructive transformations on vertex data.

So, we need a function to transform a `POLYF4DV1` by a transformation matrix. But, in most cases, you wouldn't want to transform a single polygon (it's a waste). You would wait until you had an entire list of them, so let's think in terms of transforming a list of polygons, such as the master polygon list object, which we called a `RENDERLIST4DV1` and is nothing more than an array of `POLYF4DV1`s. Here's a function that performs the transform defined by the matrix `mt` to a render list:

```
void Transform_RENDERLIST4DV1(RENDERLIST4DV1_PTR rend_list,
        MATRIX4X4_PTR mt,  // transformation matrix
        int coord_select)  // selects coords to transform
{
// this function simply transforms all of the
// polygons vertices in the local or trans
// array of the render list by the sent matrix

// what coordinates should be transformed?
switch(coord_select)
{
```

```
case TRANSFORM_LOCAL_ONLY:
{
for (int poly = 0; poly < rend_list->num_polys; poly++)
  {
  // acquire current polygon
  POLYF4DV1_PTR curr_poly = rend_list->poly_ptrs[poly];

  // is this polygon valid?
  // transform polygon if and only if it's not clipped, not culled,
  // active, and visible, note however the concept of "backface" is
  // irrelevant in a wire frame engine though
  if ((curr_poly==NULL) ||
       !(curr_poly->state & POLY4DV1_STATE_ACTIVE) ||
    (curr_poly->state & POLY4DV1_STATE_CLIPPED ) ||
    (curr_poly->state & POLY4DV1_STATE_BACKFACE) )
    continue; // move onto next poly

  // all good, let's transform
  for (int vertex = 0; vertex < 3; vertex++)
    {
    // transform the vertex by mt
    POINT4D presult; // hold result of each transformation

    // transform point
    Mat_Mul_VECTOR4D_4X4(&curr_poly->vlist[vertex], mt, &presult);

    // store result back
    VECTOR4D_COPY(&curr_poly->vlist[vertex], &presult);
    } // end for vertex
  } // end for poly

} break;

case TRANSFORM_TRANS_ONLY:
{
// transform each "transformed" vertex of the render list
// remember, the idea of the tvlist[] array is to accumulate
// transformations
for (int poly = 0; poly < rend_list->num_polys; poly++)
  {
  // acquire current polygon
  POLYF4DV1_PTR curr_poly = rend_list->poly_ptrs[poly];
  // is this polygon valid?
```

```
    // transform this polygon if and only if it's not clipped, not culled,
    // active, and visible, note however the concept of "backface" is
    // irrelevant in a wire frame engine though
    if ((curr_poly==NULL) || !(curr_poly->state & POLY4DV1_STATE_ACTIVE) ||
      (curr_poly->state & POLY4DV1_STATE_CLIPPED ) ||
      (curr_poly->state & POLY4DV1_STATE_BACKFACE) )
      continue; // move onto next poly

    // all good, let's transform
    for (int vertex = 0; vertex < 3; vertex++)
      {
      // transform the vertex by mt
      POINT4D presult; // hold result of each transformation

      // transform point
      Mat_Mul_VECTOR4D_4X4(&curr_poly->tvlist[vertex], mt, &presult);
      // store result back
      VECTOR4D_COPY(&curr_poly->tvlist[vertex], &presult);
      } // end for vertex
    } // end for poly

  } break;

  case TRANSFORM_LOCAL_TO_TRANS:
  {
  // transform each local/model vertex of the render list and store result
  // in "transformed" vertex list
  for (int poly = 0; poly < rend_list->num_polys; poly++)
    {
    // acquire current polygon
    POLYF4DV1_PTR curr_poly = rend_list->poly_ptrs[poly];

    // is this polygon valid?
    // transform polygon if and only if it's not clipped, not culled,
    // active, and visible, note however the concept of "backface" is
    // irrelevant in a wire frame engine though
    if ((curr_poly==NULL) ||
         !(curr_poly->state & POLY4DV1_STATE_ACTIVE) ||
      (curr_poly->state & POLY4DV1_STATE_CLIPPED ) ||
      (curr_poly->state & POLY4DV1_STATE_BACKFACE) )
      continue; // move onto next poly
```

7

```
    // all good, let's transform
    for (int vertex = 0; vertex < 3; vertex++)
      {
      // transform the vertex by mt
      Mat_Mul_VECTOR4D_4X4(&curr_poly->vlist[vertex], mt,
                    &curr_poly->tvlist[vertex]);
      } // end for vertex

    } // end for poly

  } break;

  default: break;

  } // end switch

  } // end Transform_RENDERLIST4DV1
```

The function is fairly straightforward. It simply applies the 4x4 transformation matrix `mt` to `rend_list` based on the coordinate transformation selection flag `coord_select`. Then, depending on the requested coordinates that should be transformed, the function starts looping and making calls to the matrix multiply function. The coordinate transformation selector is controlled by the parameter `coord_select` based on the following defines:

```
// transformation control flags
#define TRANSFORM_LOCAL_ONLY    0 // perform the transformation
                    // in place on the
                    // local/world vertex list
#define TRANSFORM_TRANS_ONLY    1 // perform the transformation
                    // in place on the
                    // "transformed" vertex list

#define TRANSFORM_LOCAL_TO_TRANS 2 // perform the transformation
                    // to the local
                    // vertex list, but store the
                    // results in the
                    // transformed vertex list
```

Thus, you can apply the transform to (1) the local storage, (2) the transformed storage, or (3) perform the transform to the local storage and store the results in the transformed storage. Did I leave anything out?

Using the function is trivial; assume that we have a render list named `rend_list` full of polygons and we want to transform the local coordinates of each polygon within it with the matrix m_trans and store the results in the transformed storage. The following call would do the job:

```
Transform_RENDERLIST4DV1(&rend_list, m_trans, TRANSFORM_LOCAL_TO_TRANS );
```

Wham, bam, the entire list is transformed with the 4x4 matrix. Cool, huh?

The second function we need is one to transform an object itself or the OBJECT4DV1. Basically, the function will be identical, but a little simpler because there's just a vertex list rather than a collection of polygons, each with its own vertex list. Of course, we still want the same coordinate transformation selection capability. With that in mind, here's the function:

```
void Transform_OBJECT4DV1(OBJECT4DV1_PTR obj, // object to transform
        MATRIX4X4_PTR mt,   // transformation matrix
        int coord_select,   // selects coords to transform
        int transform_basis) // flags if vector orientation
                   // should be transformed to
{
// this function simply transforms all of the vertices
// in the local or trans
// array by the sent matrix

// what coordinates should be transformed?
switch(coord_select)
   {
   case TRANSFORM_LOCAL_ONLY:
   {
   // transform each local/model vertex of the object mesh in place
   for (int vertex=0; vertex < obj->num_vertices; vertex++)
     {
     POINT4D presult; // hold result of each transformation

     // transform point
     Mat_Mul_VECTOR4D_4X4(&obj->vlist_local[vertex], mt, &presult);

     // store result back
     VECTOR4D_COPY(&obj->vlist_local[vertex], &presult);
     } // end for index
   } break;

   case TRANSFORM_TRANS_ONLY:
   {
   // transform each "transformed" vertex of the object mesh in place
   // remember, the idea of the vlist_trans[] array is to accumulate
```

```
    // transformations
    for (int vertex=0; vertex < obj->num_vertices; vertex++)
      {
      POINT4D presult; // hold result of each transformation

      // transform point
      Mat_Mul_VECTOR4D_4X4(&obj->vlist_trans[vertex], mt, &presult);

      // store result back
      VECTOR4D_COPY(&obj->vlist_trans[vertex], &presult);
      } // end for index

    } break;

    case TRANSFORM_LOCAL_TO_TRANS:
    {
    // transform each local/model vertex of the object mesh
    // and store result
    // in "transformed" vertex list
    for (int vertex=0; vertex < obj->num_vertices; vertex++)
      {
      POINT4D presult; // hold result of each transformation

      // transform point
      Mat_Mul_VECTOR4D_4X4(&obj->vlist_local[vertex], mt,
      &obj->vlist_trans[vertex]);

      } // end for index
    } break;

    default: break;

} // end switch

// finally, test if transform should be applied to orientation basis
// hopefully this is a rotation, otherwise the basis will get corrupted
if (transform_basis)
  {
  // now rotate orientation basis for object
  VECTOR4D vresult; // use to rotate each orientation vector axis

  // rotate ux of basis
  Mat_Mul_VECTOR4D_4X4(&obj->ux, mt, &vresult);
  VECTOR4D_COPY(&obj->ux, &vresult);
```

```
   // rotate uy of basis
   Mat_Mul_VECTOR4D_4X4(&obj->uy, mt, &vresult);
   VECTOR4D_COPY(&obj->uy, &vresult);

   // rotate uz of basis
   Mat_Mul_VECTOR4D_4X4(&obj->uz, mt, &vresult);
   VECTOR4D_COPY(&obj->uz, &vresult);
   } // end if

} // end Transform_OBJECT4DV1
```

Again, nothing more than the three different cases with the matrix multiplication math invoked, but there's something else here. Aha! There's a `transform_basis` flag. This is needed for the following reason: As shown in Figure 7.4, when you transform a 3D object, you lose its original load time orientation. That is, if you know you load an object with "up" pointing in the +Y direction and "forward" in the +Z direction, how will you track the result orientation after transforming an object?

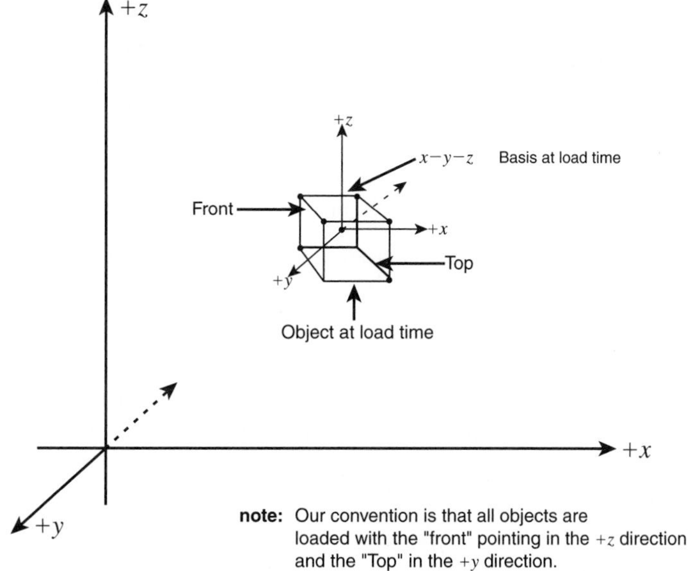

FIGURE 7.4 Load time orientation of an object.

The point is that you need to also transform the basis or local axes or the object, too. Then you can always use the basis of the object to figure the orientation of the object by comparing the basis to the world axes (a very common problem that I get billions of emails on…okay, maybe only hundreds of millions of emails). Figure 7.5 shows the same object after transformation with the object's local basis transformed in addition to the vertex data. Thus, the `transform_basis` flag determines whether you want the function also to transform the basis of the object itself. Remember that the basis of the object could be anything to start with, but usually it's [ux = <1,0,0,0>, uy = <0,1,0,0>, uz = <0,0,1,0>], which is the world unit coordinate axes basis.

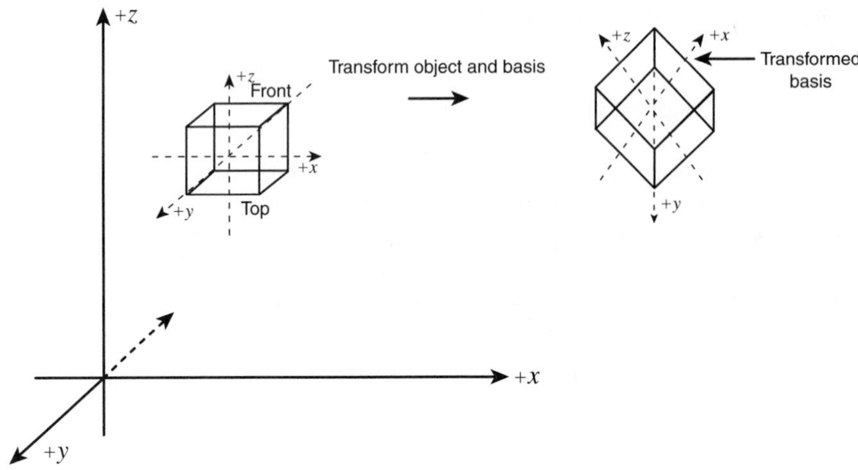

FIGURE 7.5 Local basis transformation to track an object's orientation.

As an example, say that we had previously loaded an object into the variable `obj` to transform its local coordinates by the matrix `m_trans` along with its basis. Here's the call:

```
Transform_OBJECTDV1(&obj, m_trans, TRANSFORM_LOCAL_TO_TRANS, 1 );
```

Easy as cheating on taxes! But of course, I would never do that.

Now that we have a general transformation function, we can implement any transformation as a 4x4 matrix and then call this function. But remember that many of the transforms are faster if performed manually. In the following sections, we'll see how to perform the various steps of the pipeline using manual and matrix methods on each geometry object: `OBJECT4DV1` and `RENDERLIST4DV1`.

The Local-to-World Transform

The local-to-world transformation transforms an object's (or polygon's) local or model coordinates into world coordinates (which are what defines the entire game universe), as shown in Figure 7.6. Therefore, given a point or vertex defined by **p** = <x,y,z,1> and a translation factor **dt** = <xt, yt, zt, 1>, the local-to-world transform is simply

```
p' = p + dt
```

leaving the w = 1 component the same.

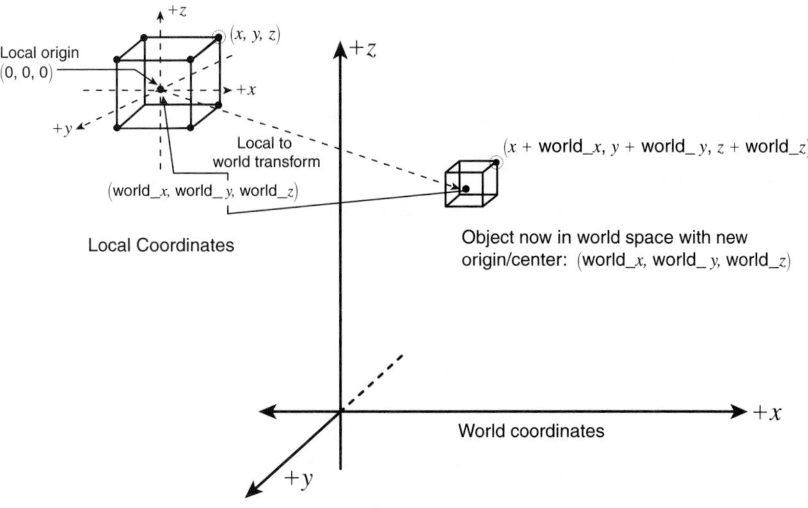

FIGURE 7.6 Local-to-world transformation.

Local-to-World Transformation for Objects

The function that performs the local (model)-to-world transformation on an `OBJECT4DV1` simply translates the vertices of the object stored in `local_vlist[]` by the amount `world_pos` and stores the results in `trans_vlist[]`. Here's the manual version:

```
void Model_To_World_OBJECT4DV1(OBJECT4DV1_PTR obj,
         int coord_select= TRANSFORM_LOCAL_TO_TRANS)
{
// NOTE: Not matrix based
// this function converts the local model coordinates of the
// sent object into world coordinates, the results are stored
// in the transformed vertex list (vlist_trans) within the object

// interate thru vertex list and transform all the model/local
// coords to world coords by translating the vertex list by
// the amount world_pos and storing the results in vlist_trans[]

if (coord_select == TRANSFORM_LOCAL_TO_TRANS)
{
for (int vertex=0; vertex < obj->num_vertices; vertex++)
  {
  // translate vertex
  VECTOR4D_Add(&obj->vlist_local[vertex], &obj->world_pos,
         &obj->vlist_trans[vertex]);
  } // end for vertex
```

```
} // end if local
else // TRANSFORM_TRANS_ONLY)
{
for (int vertex=0; vertex < obj->num_vertices; vertex++)
  {
  // translate vertex
  VECTOR4D_Add(&obj->vlist_trans[vertex], &obj->world_pos,
         &obj->vlist_trans[vertex]);
  } // end for vertex
} // end else trans

} // end Model_To_World_OBJECT4DV1
```

Given that you've already loaded a unit cube into the `OBJECT4DV1` cube and then set its `world_pos` to (100,200,400), you can translate the whole mesh with the call

```
Model_To_World_OBJECT4DV1(&cube);
```

Notice that there's a coordinate select function. This is useful in the cases where you perform another transformation to the model that's already in the transformed coordinates. In this case, the model to world transform should use the transformed coordinate rather than the original model coordinates. To control this, use the `coord_select` variable as usual.

Now, if you wanted to, you could perform this transformation with a matrix, but it would really be a waste of cycles. However, we need to look at it, because hardware loves matrices, and when you take advantage of it you will see this. The function that builds up translation matrix is called `void Build_Model_To_World_MATRIX4X4()` and is shown here:

```
void Build_Model_To_World_MATRIX4X4(VECTOR4D_PTR vpos, MATRIX4X4_PTR m)
{
// this function builds up a general local to world
// transformation matrix that is really nothing more than a translation
// of the origin by the amount specified in vpos

Mat_Init_4X4(m, 1,    0,    0,    0,
        0,    1,    0,    0,
        0,    0,    1,    0,
        vpos->x, vpos->y, vpos->z, 1 );

} // end Build_Model_To_World_MATRIX4X4
```

As you can see, the function takes the position to translate to and the matrix you want to store the computed transform matrix. Of course, you can use the matrix for general translation and not just the local-to-world transform. Anyway, to perform the local-to-world transformation with a matrix, we can make a call to Build_Model_To_Model_MATRIX4X4() to build up the matrix and then execute the transformation with Transform_OBJECT4DV1() like this:

```
MATRIX4X4 mt; // storage
VECTOR4D pos = {100,200,300, 1};

Build_Model_To_World_MATRIX4X4(&pos, &mt);

Transform_OBJECT4DV1(&obj, m_trans, TRANSFORM_LOCAL_TO_TRANS,1 );
```

So, that's all there is to performing the local-to-world transformation on OBJECT4DV1s.

NOTE

I know this is trivial stuff, but we're getting into good habits here—trust me....

Local-to-World Transformation for Render Lists

In most cases, you'll insert the polygons of an object into a render list after the object is already transformed from local to world coordinates. Thus, you'll probably never need to perform the local-to-world transform on an entire render list. But in the case when you don't want to use OBJECT4DV1 and you load polygons directly into a RENDERLIST4DV1 that happens to represent some large mesh (maybe a terrain, as Jonathan Blow, the world's expert on terrain rendering, would tell you), you'll need this step if the mesh isn't in world coordinates. Here's the function that manually performs the local to world transformation on a RENDERLIST4DV1 without a matrix:

```
void Model_To_World_RENDERLIST4DV1(RENDERLIST4DV1_PTR rend_list,
               POINT4D_PTR world_pos, int
               coord_select = TRANSFORM_LOCAL_TO_TRANS)
{
// NOTE: Not matrix based
// this function converts the local model coordinates of the
// sent render list into world coordinates, the results are stored
// in the transformed vertex list (tvlist) within the renderlist

// interate thru vertex list and transform all the model/local
// coords to world coords by translating the vertex list by
// the amount world_pos and storing the results in tvlist[]
// is this polygon valid?

if (coord_select == TRANSFORM_LOCAL_TO_TRANS)
  {
  for (int poly = 0; poly < rend_list->num_polys; poly++)
    {
```

```
    // acquire current polygon
    POLYF4DV1_PTR curr_poly = rend_list->poly_ptrs[poly];

    // transform this polygon if and only if it's not clipped,
    // not culled,
    // active, and visible,
    // note however the concept of "backface" is
    // irrelevant in a wire frame engine though
    if ((curr_poly==NULL) ||
      !(curr_poly->state & POLY4DV1_STATE_ACTIVE) ||
      (curr_poly->state & POLY4DV1_STATE_CLIPPED ) ||
      (curr_poly->state & POLY4DV1_STATE_BACKFACE) )
     continue; // move onto next poly

  // all good, let's transform
  for (int vertex = 0; vertex < 3; vertex++)
    {
    // translate vertex
    VECTOR4D_Add(&curr_poly->vlist[vertex], world_pos,
          &curr_poly->tvlist[vertex]);
    } // end for vertex

  } // end for poly
} // end if local
else // TRANSFORM_TRANS_ONLY
{
for (int poly = 0; poly < rend_list->num_polys; poly++)
  {
  // acquire current polygon
  POLYF4DV1_PTR curr_poly = rend_list->poly_ptrs[poly];

  // transform this polygon if and only if it's
  // not clipped, not culled,
  // active, and visible, note however the concept of "backface" is
  // irrelevant in a wire frame engine though
 if ((curr_poly==NULL) || !(curr_poly->state & POLY4DV1_STATE_ACTIVE) ||
   (curr_poly->state & POLY4DV1_STATE_CLIPPED ) ||
   (curr_poly->state & POLY4DV1_STATE_BACKFACE) )
    continue; // move onto next poly

  for (int vertex = 0; vertex < 3; vertex++)
    {
    // translate vertex
```

```
    VECTOR4D_Add(&curr_poly->tvlist[vertex], world_pos,
          &curr_poly->tvlist[vertex]);
    } // end for vertex

  } // end for poly

} // end else

} // end Model_To_World_RENDERLIST4DV1
```

Thus, if you have a render list named `rend_list` and you want to perform the local-to-world transform and move the geometry from its local position to the position `world_pos`, here's what you would do:

```
Model_To_World_RENDERLIST4DV1(&rend_list, &world_pos, TRANSFORM_LOCAL_TO_TRANS);
```

That would be very efficient. But, if you wanted to use a matrix, you could do so by creating the transform like this:

```
MATRIX4X4 mt; // storage
VECTOR4D pos = {100,200,300, 1};

Build_Model_To_World_MATRIX4X4(&pos, &mt);
```

And then use the generic `RENDERLIST4DV1` function to transform the geometry like this:

```
Transform_RENDERLIST4DV1(&rend_list, &mt, TRANSFORM_LOCAL_TO_TRANS);
```

7

NOTE

But this method would be waste of cycles due to the overhead of a matrix multiply per each vertex—ouch!

The Eulerian Camera Model

This isn't really a step of the 3D pipeline, but this is a good time to talk about the camera models we're going to use, because the next steps in the pipeline rely on them. If you recall, the camera that we've been using for our first system is called *Eulerian*, meaning that it's defined by a position and the rotation (or Euler angles) that make up its orientation. This is shown in Figure 7.7. Additionally, we're going to support the *UVN* camera, which needs only the addition of a look at target, and the **u**,**v**,**n** vectors themselves—more on that later, though.

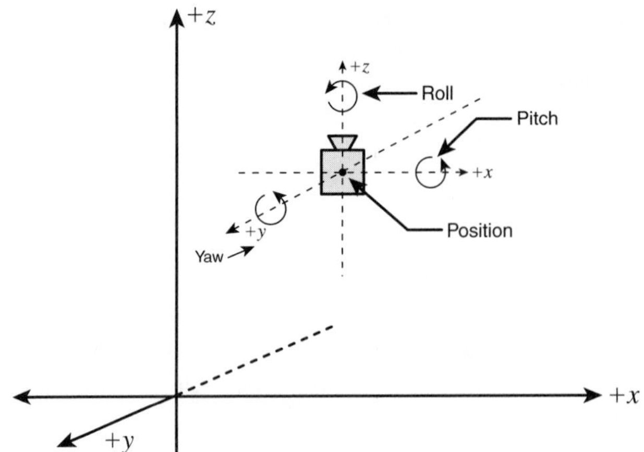

FIGURE 7.7 Euler camera model.

Whichever camera we use, we still need the viewing distance, a field of view, the near and far clipping planes, and a view plane of some width and height that represents the final image we want to display on the screen at some point, along with a viewport that has width and height and represents the actual raster window. All these aspects play into the camera model and create a viewing frustrum that encloses the camera's overall field of view and defines its properties. Objects within this field of view will be transformed and viewed.

Okay, so with all that in mind, I sat down and made up a structure to represent a simple camera. Really, I probably could have gotten away with the angles, position, near and far clipping planes, and a couple other things, but I wanted to start you off early thinking about all the information that a camera needs, even if we don't use it yet. Alas, there's some extra stuff that isn't really needed yet in this chapter—especially in relation to clipping. Anyway, here's the camera structure:

```
// camera version 1
typedef struct CAM4DV1_TYP
{
int state;    // state of camera
int attr;     // camera attributes

POINT4D pos;  // world position of camera used by both camera models

VECTOR4D dir;  // euler angles or look at direction of camera for UVN
        // models

VECTOR4D u;   // extra vectors to track the camera orientation
VECTOR4D v;   // for more complex UVN camera model
```

```
VECTOR4D n;
POINT4D target; // target or "look at" position for UVN model


float view_dist_h; // horizontal and vertical viewing distances
float view_dist_v;

float fov;      // field of view for both horizontal and vertical axes

// 3d clipping planes
// if view volume is NOT 90 degree then general 3d clipping
// must be employed
float near_clip_z;    // near z=constant clipping plane
float far_clip_z;    // far z=constant clipping plane

PLANE3D rt_clip_plane; // the right clipping plane
PLANE3D lt_clip_plane; // the left clipping plane
PLANE3D tp_clip_plane; // the top clipping plane
PLANE3D bt_clip_plane; // the bottom clipping plane

float viewplane_width; // width and height of view plane to project onto
float viewplane_height; // usually 2x2 for normalized projection or
            // the exact same size as the viewport or
            // screen window

// remember screen and viewport are synonomous
float viewport_width;    // size of screen/viewport
float viewport_height;
float viewport_center_x; // center of view port (final image destination)
float viewport_center_y;

// aspect ratio
float aspect_ratio;    // screen aspect width/height

// these matrices are not necessarily needed based on the method of
// transformation, for example, a manual perspective or screen transform
// and or a concatenated perspective/screen, however, having these
// matrices give us more flexibility

MATRIX4X4 mcam; // storage for the world to camera transform matrix
MATRIX4X4 mper; // storage for the camera to perspective transform matrix
MATRIX4X4 mscr; // storage for the perspective to screen transform matrix

} CAM4DV1, *CAM4DV1_PTR;
```

Although I commented the structure, let's review every single element so that there's no confision, I mean confusion!

`state`—Tracks the state of the camera. Nothing weird about that.

`attr`—Defines the particular attributes of the camera. Currently, there are only two type attributes: `CAM_MODEL_EULER` and `CAM_MODEL_UVN`.

`pos`—Defines the world position of the camera.

`dir`—Defines the axis angles for simple Eulerian camera model or, when using the UVN model, the x-component is the "elevation" for the spherical system and the y-component is the "heading."

`u,v,n`—Define vectors to track the camera orientation for the more complex UVN camera model we discuss later in the chapter.

`target`—Defines the target position that the UVN camera model looks at.

`view_dist_h`, `view_dist_v`—Define the horizontal and vertical viewing distances needed in the perspective transformation step.

`fov`—Defines the field of view for both horizontal and vertical axes.

`near_clip_z`, `far_clip_z`—Define the near and far constant z clipping planes.

`rt_clip_plane`, `lt_clip_plane`, `tp_clip_plane`, `bt_clip_plane`—Define the right, left, top, and bottom 3D clipping planes. For a field of view at 90 degrees, these planes are trivial at 45 degrees from the origin, but for arbitrary fields of view, these planes are no longer x = z, y = z, and so on, and must be generalized during 3D clipping.

`viewplane_width`, `viewplane_height`—Define the size of the viewing plane or viewplane that the perspective projection projects onto. This is 2x2 for normalized projection, or the exact same size as the view port or screen window if you want to merge the perspective transform and screen transform together (faster).

`viewport_width`, `viewport_height`—Define the size in pixel space of the final raster surface that you're rendering on.

`viewport_center_x`, `viewport_center_y`—Define the center of the viewport.

`aspect_ratio`—Simply the ratio of `viewport_width/viewport_height`.

`mcam`—Storage for the camera transformation only.

`mper`—Storage for the camera-to-perspective transformation.

`mscr`—Storage for the perspective-to-screen transformation.

Wow, a lot of stuff, huh? But remember, we aren't going to use or need all of it right away. The point of the structure is to hold all the camera information, but there's a lot of derived information in there that we don't want to have to define or compute ourselves.

Thus, we need a function that can take a set of simple inputs and build a camera. First, let's look at the prototype of such a function:

```
void Init_CAM4DV1(CAM4DV1_PTR cam,     // the camera object
         int cam_attr,      // camera attributes
         POINT4D_PTR cam_pos,  // initial camera position
         VECTOR4D_PTR cam_dir, // initial camera angles
         POINT4D_PTR cam_target, // initial target for UVN model
         float near_clip_z,    // near and far clipping planes
         float far_clip_z,
         float fov,        // field of view in degrees
         float viewport_width, // size of final screen viewport
         float viewport_height);
```

With this function, we can send the type of camera, position, orientation, distance of the clipping planes, the field of view, and viewport dimensions, and the function sets up the whole camera for us! Now, the only problem is that many of these parameters are related, and hence constrained by each other.

Therefore, I wrote the function so that, in all cases, it creates a viewplane such that the width is {-1 to 1}, and the height will be {-1/`aspect_ratio` to +1/`aspect_ratio`}. This has to be agreed upon, because during the perspective to screen projection or mapping, we need to know what we're mapping. Forcing this convention makes it easier.

In most cases, we're going to use a 90-degree field of view, which in turn results in a focal distance of 1.0, but I wanted to add the extra functionality to the camera setup function just so you could experiment with FOVs that are different from 90 degrees. Lastly, I decided that the camera function should NOT compute the camera matrix during initialization. The camera matrix should be created at a later time via calls to either the Euler or UVN camera helper function. So, let's take a look at the UVN camera now.

The UVN Camera Model

The Eulerian camera is okay for many setups, but it's fairly limited and doesn't work exactly the way you think it does when you supply the view angles. A more natural camera model is the UVN camera. It's much easier to work with, so what we're going to do now is come up with the derivation of the camera model and the camera transformation matrix. Figure 7.8 shows the standard UVN system.

Basically, the only difference between a Euler camera and a UVN camera is how we define the orientation of the camera; instead of using angles, we use vectors. These vectors describe the orientation or the basis of the camera's coordinate system:

UVN = { **X**:<ux, uy, uz>, **Y**:<vx, vy, vz>, **Z**:<nx, ny, nz>}

For example, a standard XYZ left-handed system would have the following basis, using the preceding notation:

XYZ = { **X**:<1, 0, 0>, **Y**:<0, 1, 0>, **Z**:<0, 0, 1>}

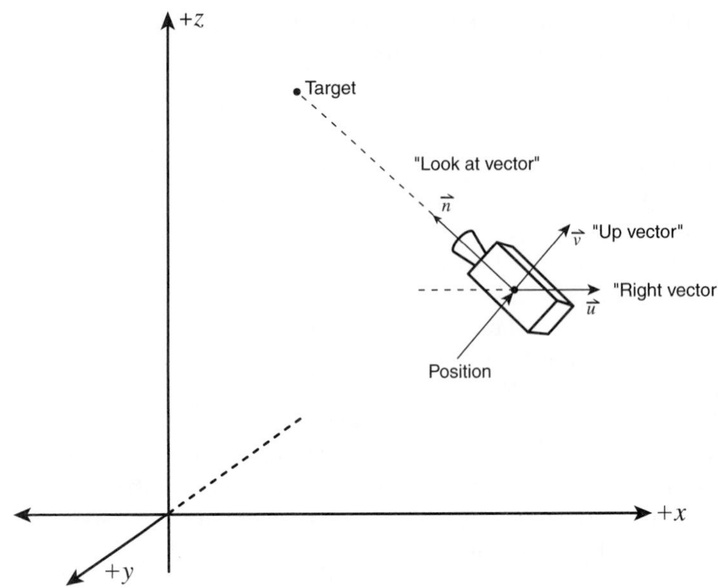

FIGURE 7.8 The UVN camera model.

The UVN system has the same properties as the XYZ system; it's mutually perpendicular, or *orthonormal*, and all the vectors are linearly independent and have unit length.

Additionally, the UVN system has what's called a *target* or *look at* point, which is nothing more than where the camera is looking. And, of course, the camera has a position in space that's called the *view reference point* (or VRP, in most cases).

Now let's talk about the UVN vectors and what they mean, but let's go a little out of order.

n—This vector is analogous to the z-axis of the UVN system and points toward the target position from the camera position. In other words, **n** = <target—VRP>. Of course, **n** must be a unit vector, so we would normalize this vector at some point.

v—This is called the "up" vector and begins life identical to the y-axis vector <0,1,0>. However, this value of **v** is only temporary and needed only to compute the "right" vector or **u**, and then a new **v** is computed.

u—This is called the "right" vector, and is computed from the cross product of **v** and **n** as **u** = (**v** x **n**). Here's where the temporary value of **v** comes in handy. Once **u** is computed, a recalculation of **v** is performed such that **v** = (**n** x **u**).

NOTE

Of course, all vectors must be normalized at some point.

Assuming that we've now computed the **u**, **v**, and **n** vectors of the UVN system, all that's left is to understand what they do!

Well, it's pretty simple, actually. UVN is basically the new orientation of the XYZ system that we want to transform everything into; or, in other words, it's the basis of the system. Thus, we need to somehow create a transformation matrix that will perform the mapping. That is, assuming that a UVN camera is out in space at some position looking at a target, what matrix will perform this transform? First, let's forget about the position of the camera. I think we both know that's a simple translation, so the hard part is the rotation part....

Computing the UVN Matrix

It turns out that all we need to transform any point **p**(x,y,z) in the standard XYZ system into a point in the UVN system is to take the dot product of **p**(x, y, z) with **u**, **v**, and **n**, respectively. In other words, we need to multiply x by the amount that the u-axis is colinear with the x, y by the amount the v-axis is colinear with the y-axis, and finally multiply z by the amount that the n-axis is colinear with the z-axis of the standard XYZ system. This will transform the point **p**(x,y,z) into the UVN space. Here's the matrix in 4x4 form:

```
        |ux  vx  nx 0|
M    =  |uy  vy  ny 0|
 uvn    |uz  vz  nz 0|
        |0   0   0  1|
```

Pretty slick, huh? So, the column vectors are just **u**,**v**, and **n**, respectively. Assuming that we take a point **p**(x,y,z,1) and transform it with this matrix to get **p'**, we get

```
p' = p * M
          uvn

                 |ux vx nx 0|
=[x y z 1]  *    |uy vy ny 0|
                 |uz vz nz 0|
                 |0  0  0  1|

= p'( (x*ux + y*uy + z*uz),
   (x*vx + y*vy + z*vz),
   (x*nx + y*ny + z*nz),1 )
```

which is indeed the dot product terms we were looking for:

```
p' = (p . u, p . v, p . n)
```

The last part of the puzzle is the positioning of the camera, but that's easy. We know that any camera transformation looks something like a translation step followed by a rotational transformation.

$$T_{cam}^{-1} * R_{cam}^{-1}$$

where $\mathbf{R}_{cam}^{-1}$ is a composition of one or more rotational transformations.

> **NOTE**
>
> The inverses are just to remind you that in the original derivation, we had the matrix that positioned the camera. To undo that, we needed the inverse of that matrix to bring the universe to the camera, and similarly for the rotation matrices.

We already have the rotational transform that we called $\mathbf{M}_{uvn}$, so all we need is the translation matrix. Assuming that the camera is located at position cam_pos=(cam_x, cam_y, cam_z) as usual, this is nothing more than

```
           | 1        0       0      0|
T_cam^-1 = | 0        1       0      0|
           | 0        0       1      0|
           |-cam_x  -cam_y  -cam_z   1|
```

Thus, we end up with the final transformation for the UVN camera of

```
T_uvn = T_cam^-1 * M_uvn

=

|1       0       0      0|   |ux vx nx 0|
|0       1       0      0|   |uy vy ny 0|
|0       0       1      0| * |uz vz nz 0|
|-cam_x  -cam_y  -cam_z 1|   |0  0  0  1|

=

| ux               vx               nx               0|
| uy               vy               ny               0|
| uz               vz               nz               0|
|-(cam_pos . u)   -(cam_pos . v)   -(cam_pos . n)    1|
```

The terms in the last row are the translation factors; `tx`, `ty`, and `tz`, which are nothing more than the negatives of the dot product of the camera position with each of the basis vectors **u**, **v**, and **n**, respectively.

That's all there is to the UVN camera system, so let's briefly review and then move on to how to actually compute and describe the UVN system.

The UVN system models the camera as usual via a camera position, but differs in that the camera has a target. Additionally, instead of representing the camera as a series of concatenated rotations parallel to each of the axes in some order, XYZ, YZX, and so on, the camera in a UVN system is made of a "look at" vector, **n**, an "up" vector, **v**, and finally a "right" vector, **u**. These correlate to the standard XYZ axes with the following mapping:

U -> X

V -> Y

N -> Z

Here are the exact steps to find **u**, **v**, and **n**:

Step 1: n = <target position—view reference point>

Step 2: Let **v** = <0,1,0>

Step 3: u = (**v** x **n**)

Step 4: v = (**n** x **u**)

Step 5 (Optional): Normalize **u**,**v**,**n** by dividing each vector by its length (if you haven't done so in previous steps)

Practical Implementations of the UVN System

As you can see, the UVN system is pretty cool and very natural to the way you might expect to use a camera in the real world. That is, you position the camera and then target a position (or subject) to view, as shown in Figure 7.8. The only problem is that many times you don't exactly know the coordinates of the position you're looking at, but know the general direction. Or, in other words, a more Eulerian model is appropriate, but as we've previously discovered, the Euler camera model doesn't always do what we want and suffers from gimbal lock and other issues. Therefore, if you know where you want to look, you can directly compute **u**, **v**, and **n** and be done with it. However, what about a more natural camera system based on a spherical system, where you give the position of the camera and then the "heading" and "elevation" (as shown in Figure 7.9), and the math computes **u**, **v**, and **n** for you? This isn't as hard as it seems. Take a look at Figure 7.9; it illustrates the setup we need.

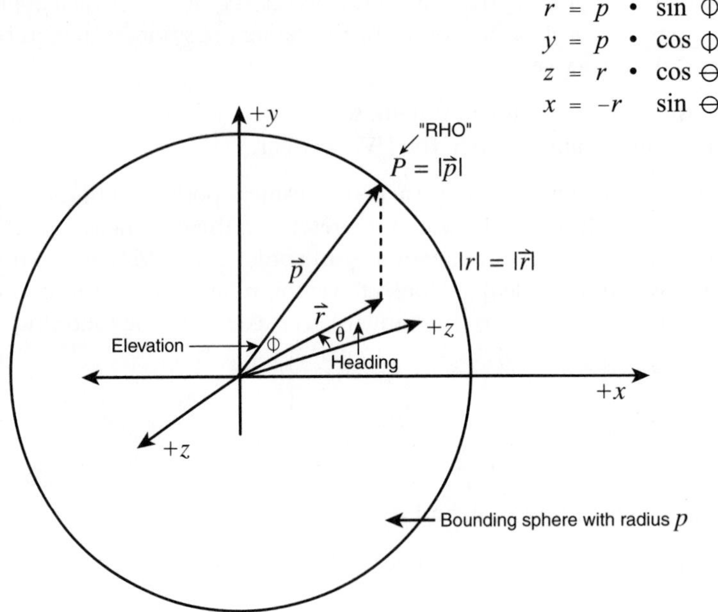

FIGURE 7.9 The spherical setup for the UVN system.

First, we assume that the camera is sitting at the origin (enclosed in a unit sphere) to make the derivation easier. Obviously, to move the camera anywhere, we just add in the translation step. Referring to the figure, the angular heading θ (theta) is the counter-clockwise angle around the positive y-axis with the convention that the 0 degree angle occurs when the heading is aligned with the positive z-axis. Next, the elevation φ (phi) is the angle measured from the ground plane (the x-z plane) to the direction vector, as shown in the figure. Now, based on our discussion of spherical coordinates, we usually refer to a point in spherical coordinates as **p**(ρ,φ,θ). However, in the derivation in Chapter 4, I assumed a right-handed system along with other conventions about the angles and so forth, so we want to be careful not to use the exact same formulas from Chapter 4. They need to be slightly modified as follows:

Given the spherical camera position **p**(ρ,φ,θ):

P = The target vector

ρ = The length of the target vector, which in this case is 1.0 because we're in a unit sphere

θ = The heading angle

φ = The elevation angle

r = The length of the projection of the target vector on the x-z plane

FORMULA 7.1 Computation of UVN Target Vector from Spherical Coordinates

then

$r = \rho*\sin(\phi)$

Therefore

$x = -r*\sin(\theta)$

$y = \rho*\cos(\phi)$

$z = r*\cos(\theta)$

If you look at the result from the function `SPHERICAL3D_To_POINT3D()`, the x,y,z it generates are based on a right-handed system. To map them to our system, we need the following transformation:

$x = -y$

$y = z$

$z = x$

Based on the computed value of **p**(x,y,z), this is exactly the look-at target, and thus we can completely define a UVN camera with just the heading, elevation, and position of the camera because we can compute the rest.

Well, that's it for the UVN system. With the Euler camera and the UVN system, you should be able to create any kind of camera you like. Shortly, we'll see the code that sets up cameras and the different calls to create the camera matrices for both systems.

7

Initializing the Camera

As I mentioned, the camera function isn't going to set up the actual camera transformation matrix (that will be handled by the helper functions), but is going to set up everything else having to do with the viewplane, clipping planes, and so forth. Here's the function:

```
void Init_CAM4DV1(CAM4DV1_PTR cam,    // the camera object
         int cam_attr,      // camera attributes
         POINT4D_PTR cam_pos,  // initial camera position
         VECTOR4D_PTR cam_dir, // initial camera angles
         POINT4D_PTR cam_target, // initial target for UVN model
         float near_clip_z,    // near and far clipping planes
         float far_clip_z,
         float fov,        // field of view in degrees
         float viewport_width, // size of final screen viewport
         float viewport_height)
{
```

```
// this function initializes the camera object cam, the function
// doesn't do a lot of error checking or sanity checking since
// I want to allow you to create projections as you wish, also
// I tried to minimize the number of parameters the functions needs

// first set up parms that are no brainers
cam->attr = cam_attr;        // camera attributes

VECTOR4D_COPY(&cam->pos, cam_pos); // positions
VECTOR4D_COPY(&cam->dir, cam_dir); // direction vector or angles for
                  // euler camera

// for UVN camera
VECTOR4D_INITXYZ(&cam->u, 1,0,0); // set to +x
VECTOR4D_INITXYZ(&cam->v, 0,1,0); // set to +y
VECTOR4D_INITXYZ(&cam->n, 0,0,1); // set to +z

if (cam_target!=NULL)
  VECTOR4D_COPY(&cam->target, cam_target); // UVN target
else
  VECTOR4D_ZERO(&cam->target);

cam->near_clip_z = near_clip_z;    // near z=constant clipping plane
cam->far_clip_z = far_clip_z;    // far z=constant clipping plane

cam->viewport_width = viewport_width;  // dimensions of viewport
cam->viewport_height = viewport_height;

cam->viewport_center_x = (viewport_width-1)/2; // center of viewport
cam->viewport_center_y = (viewport_height-1)/2;

cam->aspect_ratio = (float)viewport_width/(float)viewport_height;

// set all camera matrices to identity matrix
MAT_IDENTITY_4X4(&cam->mcam);
MAT_IDENTITY_4X4(&cam->mper);
MAT_IDENTITY_4X4(&cam->mscr);

// set independent vars
cam->fov       = fov;

// set the viewplane dimensions up, they will be 2 x (2/ar)
cam->viewplane_width = 2.0;
cam->viewplane_height = 2.0/cam->aspect_ratio;
```

```
// now we know fov and we know the viewplane dimensions plug into formula and
// solve for view distance parameters
float tan_fov_div2 = tan(DEG_TO_RAD(fov/2));

cam->view_dist = (0.5)*(cam->viewplane_width)*tan_fov_div2;

// test for 90 fov first since it's easy :)
if (fov == 90.0)
  {
   // set up the clipping planes -- easy for 90 degrees!
   POINT3D pt_origin; // point on the plane
   VECTOR3D_INITXYZ(&pt_origin,0,0,0);

   VECTOR3D vn; // normal to plane

   // right clipping plane
   VECTOR3D_INITXYZ(&vn,1,0,-1); // x=z plane
   PLANE3D_Init(&cam->rt_clip_plane, &pt_origin, &vn, 1);

   // left clipping plane
   VECTOR3D_INITXYZ(&vn,-1,0,-1); // -x=z plane
   PLANE3D_Init(&cam->lt_clip_plane, &pt_origin, &vn, 1);

   // top clipping plane
   VECTOR3D_INITXYZ(&vn,0,1,-1); // y=z plane
   PLANE3D_Init(&cam->tp_clip_plane, &pt_origin, &vn, 1);

   // bottom clipping plane
   VECTOR3D_INITXYZ(&vn,0,-1,-1); // -y=z plane
   PLANE3D_Init(&cam->bt_clip_plane, &pt_origin, &vn, 1);
  } // end if d=1
else
  {
   // now compute clipping planes yuck!
   POINT3D pt_origin; // point on the plane
   VECTOR3D_INITXYZ(&pt_origin,0,0,0);

   VECTOR3D vn; // normal to plane

   // since we don't have a 90 fov, computing the normals
   // are a bit tricky, there are a number of geometric constructions
   // that solve the problem, but I'm going to solve for the
   // vectors that represent the 2D projections of the frustrum planes
   // on the x-z and y-z planes and then find perpendiculars to them
```

7

```
    // right clipping plane, check the math on graph paper
    VECTOR3D_INITXYZ(&vn,cam->view_dist,0,-cam->viewplane_width/2.0);
    PLANE3D_Init(&cam->rt_clip_plane, &pt_origin, &vn, 1);

    // left clipping plane, we can simply reflect the right normal about
    // the z axis since the planes are symmetric about the z axis
    // thus invert x only
    VECTOR3D_INITXYZ(&vn,-cam->view_dist,0,-cam->viewplane_width/2.0);
    PLANE3D_Init(&cam->lt_clip_plane, &pt_origin, &vn, 1);

    // top clipping plane, same construction
    VECTOR3D_INITXYZ(&vn,0,cam->view_dist,-cam->viewplane_width/2.0);
    PLANE3D_Init(&cam->tp_clip_plane, &pt_origin, &vn, 1);

    // bottom clipping plane, same inversion
    VECTOR3D_INITXYZ(&vn,0,-cam->view_dist,-cam->viewplane_width/2.0);
    PLANE3D_Init(&cam->bt_clip_plane, &pt_origin, &vn, 1);
   } // end else

} // end Init_CAM4DV1
```

Please take some time to review the function. It's not that complicated at all, but it's a good example of the problems with cameras and projections and working around constraints.

Anyway, the function first determines what you're specifying and then, based on the field of view and the final viewport size, it computes everything based on that using the x-axis as the primary axis that must be equal to the selected field of view. Note that the function doesn't really care much about the camera model that's selected at this point. It just remembers it and sets up a couple fields, but for the most part, the camera helper functions build the actual camera matrix `mcam`. Now, let's take a look at some quick examples.

Example 1: Parameterization for Euler camera with normalized coordinates camera setup with FOV = 90, viewing distance 1.0, and screen dimension 400 × 400. The function computes the viewplane size, which in this case would be 2x2. Figure 7.10 shows what this camera model would look like.

```
// initialize the camera
Init_CAM4DV1(&cam,    // the camera object
       CAM_MODEL_EULER, // the camera model
       &cam_pos, // initial camera position
       &cam_dir, // initial camera angles
       NULL,    // not used in euler, send NULL
       50.0,    // near and far clipping planes
       500.0,
```

```
        90.0,    // field of view in degrees
        400,  // size of final screen viewport
        400);
```

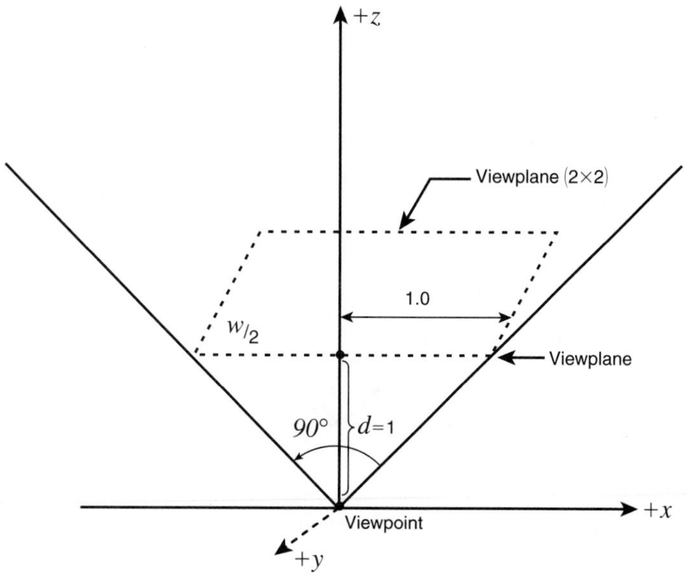

FIGURE 7.10 Camera setup with normalized coordinates, FOV of 90 with viewing distance 1.0.

Example 2: Parameterization for UVN camera with a FOV = 90 with the viewport 640x480, for a simplified screen projection. The function computes the viewing distance for us. Figure 7.11 shows what this camera model would look like.

```
// initialize the camera
Init_CAM4DV1(&cam,    // the camera object
       CAM_MODEL_UVN, // the camera type
       &cam_pos, // initial camera position
       &cam_dir, // initial camera angles
       &cam_target, // initial target
       50.0,    // near and far clipping planes
       500.0,
       90.0,    // field of view in degrees
       640,  // size of final screen viewport
       480);
```

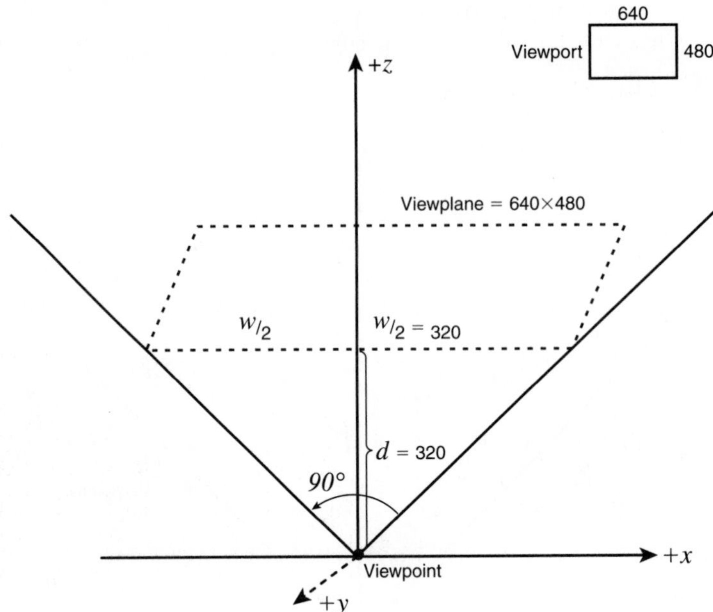

FIGURE 7.11 Camera setup for FOV of 90 with viewport dimensions equal to viewplane.

In both cases, the viewplane, focal distance, and aspect ratio are computed internally. In general, the setups from Examples 1 and 2 will suffice for all of our work. We always want FOV = 90 (or maybe 60), and we want either a nice normalized projection onto a viewplane of 2x2, or 2x2/`aspect_ratio` for non-square viewports.

Alright, we're almost done with the camera stuff. The last thing we need is a way to position the camera and compute the matrices in the camera object. So, here's a function that you can call with a position and the Euler angles that will take a camera object and compute all the matrices and other elements for you:

```
void Build_CAM4DV1_Matrix_Euler(CAM4DV1_PTR cam, int cam_rot_seq)
{
// this creates a camera matrix based on Euler angles
// and stores it in the sent camera object
// if you recall from chapter 6 to create the camera matrix
// we need to create a transformation matrix that looks like:

// Mcam = mt(-1) * my(-1) * mx(-1) * mz(-1)
// that is the inverse of the camera translation matrix mutilplied
// by the inverses of yxz, in that order, however, the order of
// the rotation matrices is really up to you, so we aren't going
// to force any order, thus its programmable based on the value
```

```
// of cam_rot_seq which can be any value CAM_ROT_SEQ_XYZ where
// XYZ can be in any order, YXZ, ZXY, etc.

MATRIX4X4 mt_inv, // inverse camera translation matrix
     mx_inv, // inverse camera x axis rotation matrix
     my_inv, // inverse camera y axis rotation matrix
     mz_inv, // inverse camera z axis rotation matrix
     mrot,  // concatenated inverse rotation matrices
     mtmp;  // temporary working matrix


// step 1: create the inverse translation matrix for the camera
// position
Mat_Init_4X4(&mt_inv, 1,  0,   0,   0,
           0,  1,   0,   0,
           0,  0,   1,   0,
           -cam->pos.x, -cam->pos.y, -cam->pos.z, 1);

// step 2: create the inverse rotation sequence for the camera
// rember either the transpose of the normal rotation matrix or
// plugging negative values into each of the rotations will result
// in an inverse matrix

// first compute all 3 rotation matrices

// extract out euler angles
float theta_x = cam->dir.x;
float theta_y = cam->dir.y;
float theta_z = cam->dir.z;

// compute the sine and cosine of the angle x
float cos_theta = Fast_Cos(theta_x); // no change since cos(-x) = cos(x)
float sin_theta = -Fast_Sin(theta_x); // sin(-x) = -sin(x)

// set the matrix up
Mat_Init_4X4(&mx_inv, 1,  0,       0,       0,
           0,  cos_theta, sin_theta, 0,
           0,  -sin_theta, cos_theta, 0,
           0,  0,       0,       1);

// compute the sine and cosine of the angle y
cos_theta = Fast_Cos(theta_y); // no change since cos(-x) = cos(x)
sin_theta = -Fast_Sin(theta_y); // sin(-x) = -sin(x)
```

7

```
// set the matrix up
Mat_Init_4X4(&my_inv,cos_theta, 0, -sin_theta, 0,
          0,     1, 0,     0,
          sin_theta, 0, cos_theta, 0,
          0,     0, 0,     1);

// compute the sine and cosine of the angle z
cos_theta = Fast_Cos(theta_z); // no change since cos(-x) = cos(x)
sin_theta = -Fast_Sin(theta_z); // sin(-x) = -sin(x)

// set the matrix up
Mat_Init_4X4(&mz_inv, cos_theta, sin_theta, 0, 0,
          -sin_theta, cos_theta, 0, 0,
          0,     0,     1, 0,
          0,     0,     0, 1);

// now compute inverse camera rotation sequence
switch(cam_rot_seq)
   {
   case CAM_ROT_SEQ_XYZ:
   {
   Mat_Mul_4X4(&mx_inv, &my_inv, &mtmp);
   Mat_Mul_4X4(&mtmp, &mz_inv, &mrot);
   } break;

   case CAM_ROT_SEQ_YXZ:
   {
   Mat_Mul_4X4(&my_inv, &mx_inv, &mtmp);
   Mat_Mul_4X4(&mtmp, &mz_inv, &mrot);
   } break;

   case CAM_ROT_SEQ_XZY:
   {
   Mat_Mul_4X4(&mx_inv, &mz_inv, &mtmp);
   Mat_Mul_4X4(&mtmp, &my_inv, &mrot);
   } break;

   case CAM_ROT_SEQ_YZX:
   {
   Mat_Mul_4X4(&my_inv, &mz_inv, &mtmp);
   Mat_Mul_4X4(&mtmp, &mx_inv, &mrot);
   } break;
```

```
    case CAM_ROT_SEQ_ZYX:
    {
    Mat_Mul_4X4(&mz_inv, &my_inv, &mtmp);
    Mat_Mul_4X4(&mtmp, &mx_inv, &mrot);
    } break;

    case CAM_ROT_SEQ_ZXY:
    {
    Mat_Mul_4X4(&mz_inv, &mx_inv, &mtmp);
    Mat_Mul_4X4(&mtmp, &my_inv, &mrot);

    } break;

    default: break;
    } // end switch

// now mrot holds the concatenated product of inverse rotation matrices
// multiply the inverse translation matrix against it and store in the
// camera objects' camera transform matrix we are done!
Mat_Mul_4X4(&mt_inv, &mrot, &cam->mcam);

} // end Build_CAM4DV1_Matrix_Euler
```

The function takes two parameters: the camera object itself and a flag that controls the rotation sequence for the Euler angles. The angles themselves and the position of the camera are internal to the camera, so you just set them in the camera object before making this call. Anyway, the various settings for the rotation control sequence are

```
// defines for camera rotation sequences
#define CAM_ROT_SEQ_XYZ 0
#define CAM_ROT_SEQ_YXZ 1
#define CAM_ROT_SEQ_XZY 2
#define CAM_ROT_SEQ_YZX 3
#define CAM_ROT_SEQ_ZYX 4
#define CAM_ROT_SEQ_ZXY 5
```

Assume that you've already created a camera called `cam` and initialized it with a call to `Init_CAM4DV1()`. To tell the camera to build up its matrices for a ZYX rotation sequence, here's the call:

```
// set position
cam.pos.x = 100;
cam.pos.y = 200;
cam.pos.z = 300;
```

7

```
// set viewing angles (degrees)
cam.dir.x = -45;
cam.dir.y = 0;
cam.dir.z = 0;

// generate camera matrix
Build_CAM4DV1_Matrix_Euler(&cam, CAM_ROT_SEQ_ZYX);
```

After the call, the matrix `cam.mcam` would be valid and you could use it as the world-to-camera transformation. Figure 7.12 shows the position and orientation of the virtual camera with these settings. However, the matrices `cam.mper` and `cam.mscr` are still undefined.

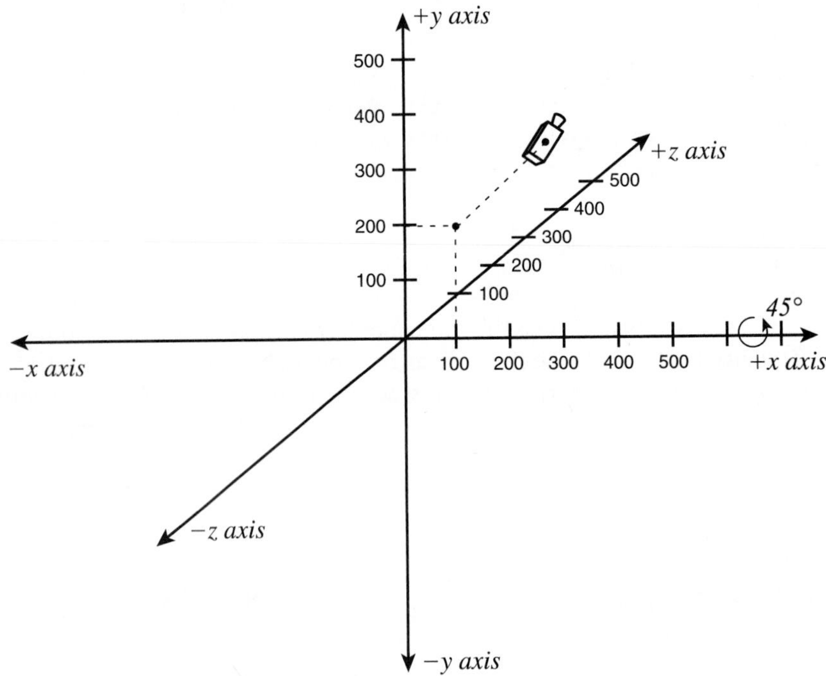

FIGURE 7.12 The results of the camera setup call.

Next, here's the camera function for the UVN model:

```
void Build_CAM4DV1_Matrix_UVN(CAM4DV1_PTR cam, int mode)
{
// this creates a camera matrix based on a look at vector n,
// look up vector v, and a look right (or left) u
// and stores it in the sent camera object, all values are
```

```
// extracted out of the camera object itself
// mode selects how uvn is computed
// UVN_MODE_SIMPLE - low level simple model,
// use the target and view reference point
// UVN_MODE_SPHERICAL - spherical mode, the x,y components will be used as the
//   heading and elevation of the view vector respectively
//   along with the view reference point as the position
//   as usual

MATRIX4X4 mt_inv, // inverse camera translation matrix
     mt_uvn, // the final uvn matrix
     mtmp;  // temporary working matrix

// step 1: create the inverse translation matrix for the camera
// position
Mat_Init_4X4(&mt_inv, 1,  0,   0,   0,
          0,  1,   0,   0,
          0,  0,   1,   0,
          -cam->pos.x, -cam->pos.y, -cam->pos.z, 1);


// step 2: determine how the target point will be computed
if (mode == UVN_MODE_SPHERICAL)
  {
  // use spherical construction
  // target needs to be recomputed

  // extract elevation and heading
  float phi   = cam->dir.x; // elevation
  float theta = cam->dir.y; // heading

  // compute trig functions once
  float sin_phi = Fast_Sin(phi);
  float cos_phi = Fast_Cos(phi);

  float sin_theta = Fast_Sin(theta);
  float cos_theta = Fast_Cos(theta);

  // now compute the target point on a unit sphere x,y,z
  cam->target.x = -1*sin_phi*sin_theta;
  cam->target.y = 1*cos_phi;
  cam->target.z = 1*sin_phi*cos_theta;
  } // end else
```

```
// at this point, we have the view reference point, the target and that's
// all we need to recompute u,v,n
// Step 1: n = <target position - view reference point>
VECTOR4D_Build(&cam->pos, &cam->target, &cam->n);

// Step 2: Let v = <0,1,0>
VECTOR4D_INITXYZ(&cam->v,0,1,0);

// Step 3: u = (v x n)
VECTOR4D_Cross(&cam->v,&cam->n,&cam->u);

// Step 4: v = (n x u)
VECTOR4D_Cross(&cam->n,&cam->u,&cam->v);

// Step 5: normalize all vectors
VECTOR4D_Normalize(&cam->u);
VECTOR4D_Normalize(&cam->v);
VECTOR4D_Normalize(&cam->n);


// build the UVN matrix by placing u,v,n as the columns of the matrix
Mat_Init_4X4(&mt_uvn, cam->u.x,  cam->v.x,   cam->n.x,   0,
           cam->u.y,  cam->v.y,   cam->n.y,   0,
           cam->u.z,  cam->v.z,   cam->n.z,   0,
           0,      0,      0,       1);

// now multiply the translation matrix and the uvn matrix and store in the
// final camera matrix mcam
Mat_Mul_4X4(&mt_inv, &mt_uvn, &cam->mcam);

} // end Build_CAM4DV1_Matrix_UVN
```

Alright, we can finally get back the 3D pipeline—that's what we call a *stall* <BG>.

The World-to-Camera Transform

Now that we have the camera modeled and set up, we can perform the world-to-camera transformation, but let's quickly review why the camera building functions work. Both the UVN and the Euler model do nothing more than take some representation of where the camera is and what it's orientation is and then build a matrix. This boils down to two steps: a translation step and a rotational step.

Figure 7.13 illustrates the steps in the world-to-camera transformation. The 3D world is viewed via a virtual camera positioned at some point with some orientation and with a given horizontal and vertical field of view. Through the lens of this virtual camera, we're interested in what the viewer would see if the camera and world were real. The trick is to create a transformation matrix that position transforms all the objects in the world so that we could artificially position the camera at the origin (0,0,0) looking straight down the +z axis. This way the math would be simplified for the final perspective projection later in the pipeline.

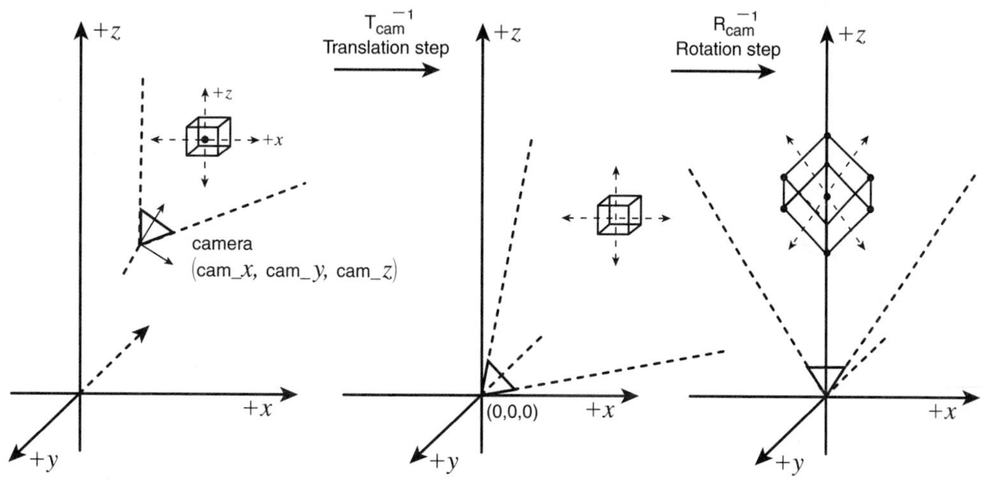

FIGURE 7.13 The world-to-camera transformation "reloaded."

We learned that this trick could be accomplished in the following way: If we assume that the camera is located in world space at `cam_pos` = *(*`cam_x, cam_y, cam_z`*)* defined by the transformation $\mathbf{T}_{cam}$, step one would be to translate all objects, vertices, polygons, or whatever in the world by the inverse of this matrix (value) or `-cam_pos` = *(*`-cam_x, -cam_y, -cam_z`*)*; that is, $\mathbf{T}_{cam}^{-1}$. The matrix for it looks like this:

```
         |1       0       0       0|
T    -1 =|0       1       0       0|
 cam     |0       0       1       0|
         |-cam_x -cam_y -cam_z   1|
```

Transforming each vertex by this matrix translates all the geometry relative to the camera being at the origin. Now, the next step in the camera transformation is the rotation step. Of course, this is a little trickier, and the model of the camera enters into the final 4x4 matrix that represents the camera orientation. With the Eulerian camera model we have been using, three angles to represent the orientation of the camera: `cam_ang` = *(*`ang_x, ang_y, ang_z`*)* as shown in Figure 7.14. Each angle represents the clockwise or counterclockwise (right-handed system) rotation around each positive axis. We call the separate transformations $\mathbf{R}_{camy}$, $\mathbf{R}_{camx}$, $\mathbf{R}_{camz}$. However, if you recall, the order in which you apply these rotations is important; XYZ, YZX, and so forth. But we decided to use YXZ and ZYX for most cases.

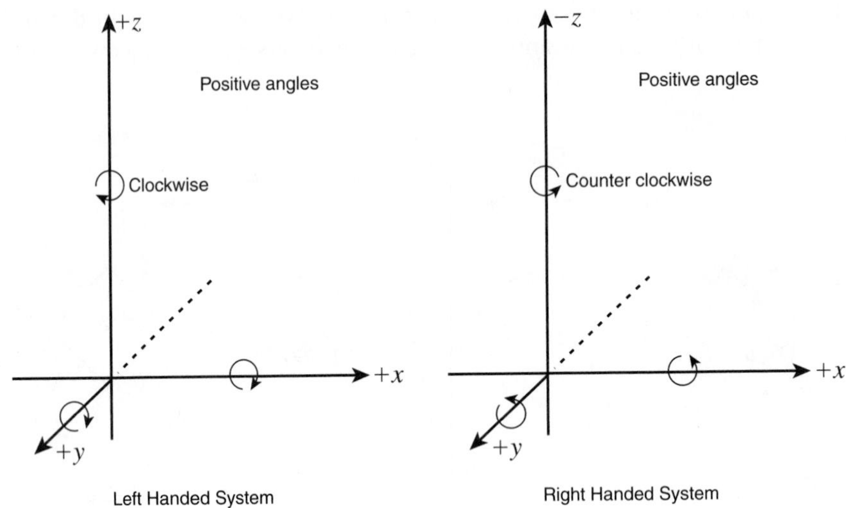

FIGURE 7.14 Relationship of camera rotation angles to coordinate systems.

So, to perform the rotation step of the camera transformation we need to apply the inverse rotations or the sequence:

$$\mathbf{R}_{camy}^{-1} * \mathbf{R}_{camx}^{-1} * \mathbf{R}_{camz}^{-1}$$

or maybe

$$\mathbf{R}_{camz}^{-1} * \mathbf{R}_{camy}^{-1} * \mathbf{R}_{camx}^{-1}$$

Putting this all together, the camera transform is $\mathbf{T}_{wc}$:

$$\mathbf{T}_{wc} = \mathbf{T}_{cam}^{-1} * \mathbf{R}_{camy}^{-1} * \mathbf{R}_{camx}^{-1} * \mathbf{R}_{camz}^{-1}$$

Or, if you want the ZYX rotation order:

$$\mathbf{T}_{wc} = \mathbf{T}_{cam}^{-1} * \mathbf{R}_{camz}^{-1} * \mathbf{R}_{camy}^{-1} * \mathbf{R}_{camz}^{-1}$$

Whichever you desire, the point is that you need a translation followed by three rotations. And, of course, these operations can be concatenated into a single matrix called $\mathbf{T}_{wc}$ as shown previously. All you do is multiply each vertex that you want to transform by the matrix, and that's it. That's what all the camera software does: It builds up this transform for you. All you do is transform each vertex by the matrix $\mathbf{T}_{wc}$ and you're done with the world-to-camera transformation! We already have a function to build the camera and initialize it, and one to compute the world-to-camera transformation matrix `Build_CAM4DV1_Matrix_Euler()`. And, of course, the `Build_CAM4DV1_Matrix_UVN()` function does the same thing, it just does it differently. That is, it uses the concept of the up, right, and target vectors rather than angles, but in the end, both functions arrive at a transformation that we need to apply to every vertex.

So, all we need is a function to apply the transform to an object and/or render list. Now, the interesting thing is that we already have a pair of generic transformation functions that take any matrix and can transform an object or render list: `void Transform_OBJECT4DV1()` and `void Transform_RENDERLIST4DV1()`. We can use either of those functions and walk away, but I like to write specific functions—sometimes for each step in the pipeline—instead of using the generalized ones so that I can take advantage of optimizations, so we'll see both.

World-to-Camera Transformation for Objects

As mentioned, we have the ability to apply any 4x4 transform matrix to an `OBJECT4DV1` with a call to `Transform_OBJECT4DV1()`, so let's look at that approach first. Assuming that we have an `object obj`, `camera cam`, and everything is initialized:

```
// generate camera matrix (use euler cam)
Build_CAM4DV1_Matrix_Euler(&cam, CAM_ROT_SEQ_ZYX);

// now apply the transform and make sure to use the
// world coordinates and transform them in place
Transform_OBJECT4DV1(&obj, &cam.mcam, TRANSFORM_TRANS_ONLY, 1 );
```

That would do the trick. The object would be in camera space all ready for a perspective projection and screen mapping. On the other hand, we can code the function a little more manually instead of using the `Transform_OBJECT4DV1()` function. Here's such a coding:

```
void World_To_Camera_OBJECT4DV1(CAM4DV1_PTR cam, OBJECT4DV1_PTR obj)
{
// NOTE: this is a matrix based function
// this function transforms the world coordinates of an object
// into camera coordinates, based on the sent camera matrix
// but it totally disregards the polygons themselves,
// it only works on the vertices in the vlist_trans[] list
// this is one way to do it, you might instead transform
// the global list of polygons in the render list since you
// are guaranteed that those polys represent geometry that
// has passed thru backfaces culling (if any)
```

7

```
// transform each vertex in the object to camera coordinates
// assumes the object has already been transformed to world
// coordinates and the result is in vlist_trans[]
for (int vertex = 0; vertex < obj->num_vertices; vertex++)
  {
  // transform the vertex by the mcam matrix within the camera
  // it better be valid!
  POINT4D presult; // hold result of each transformation

  // transform point
  Mat_Mul_VECTOR4D_4X4(&obj->vlist_trans[vertex], &cam->mcam, &presult);

  // store result back
  VECTOR4D_COPY(&obj->vlist_trans[vertex], &presult);
  } // end for vertex

} // end World_To_Camera_OBJECT4DV1
```

This function is a little faster and a little tighter. It takes the object and the camera as parameters and that's it. Here's the call you would make given that you have the object and camera already set up:

```
World_To_Camera_OBJECT4DV1(&cam, &obj);
```

NOTE

In a real 3D software engine, I might even hard-code the matrix and vector operations, but the rule of thumb is that doing so everywhere in your entire engine may give you 5–10%. If you need it, fine; otherwise, it's not worth the clutter. Better to design clean algorithms rather than to optimize code at that level during phase I design.

World-to-Camera Transformation for Render Lists

Performing the world-to-camera transform with the rendering is the same as with objects. We can use the generic transform function or write a manual function to transform the render list (call it `rend_list`). Again, let's do both. Here's the method using what we already have:

```
// generate camera matrix
Build_CAM4DV1_Matrix_Euler(&cam, CAM_ROT_SEQ_ZYX);

// now apply the transform and make sure to use the
// world coordinates and transform them in place
Transform_RENDERLIST4DV1(&rend_list, &cam.mcam, TRANSFORM_TRANS_ONLY);
```

Note that the transform_basis flag is not part of the parameter list to Transform_RENDERLIST4DV1(). This is because the polygon list represents many objects, and thus the orientation of these objects is irrelevant once the polygons have been extracted from each object and merged. Moving on, here's a manual function that performs the transformation. The only complexity is that each polygon of the list must be traversed, whereas in the OBJECT4DV1 version of the manual function, only a single vertex list had to be transformed. Here's the function:

```
void World_To_Camera_RENDERLIST4DV1(RENDERLIST4DV1_PTR rend_list,
                 CAM4DV1_PTR cam)
{
// NOTE: this is a matrix based function
// this function transforms each polygon in the global render list
// to camera coordinates based on the sent camera transform matrix
// you would use this function instead of the object based function
// if you decided earlier in the pipeline to turn each object into
// a list of polygons and then add them to the global render list
// the conversion of an object into polygons probably would have
// happened after object culling, local transforms, local to world
// and backface culling, so the minimum number of polygons from
// each object are in the list, note that the function assumes
// that at LEAST the local to world transform has been called
// and the polygon data is in the transformed list tvlist of
// the POLYF4DV1 object

// transform each polygon in the render list into camera coordinates
// assumes the render list has already been transformed to world
// coordinates and the result is in tvlist[] of each polygon object

for (int poly = 0; poly < rend_list->num_polys; poly++)
{
// acquire current polygon
POLYF4DV1_PTR curr_poly = rend_list->poly_ptrs[poly];

// is this polygon valid?
// transform this polygon if and only if it's not clipped, not culled,
// active, and visible, note however the concept of "backface" is
// irrelevant in a wire frame engine though
if ((curr_poly==NULL) || !(curr_poly->state & POLY4DV1_STATE_ACTIVE) ||
   (curr_poly->state & POLY4DV1_STATE_CLIPPED ) ||
   (curr_poly->state & POLY4DV1_STATE_BACKFACE) )
    continue; // move onto next poly
```

```
// all good, let's transform
for (int vertex = 0; vertex < 3; vertex++)
  {
  // transform the vertex by the mcam matrix within the camera
  // it better be valid!
  POINT4D presult; // hold result of each transformation

  // transform point
  Mat_Mul_VECTOR4D_4X4(&curr_poly->tvlist[vertex], &cam->mcam, &presult);

  // store result back
  VECTOR4D_COPY(&curr_poly->tvlist[vertex], &presult);
  } // end for vertex

} // end for poly

} // end World_To_Camera_RENDERLIST4DV1
```

And here's the call that would transform an entire render list `rend_list`, assuming that `cam` is defined and initialized as before:

```
World_To_Camera_RENDERLIST4DV1(&cam, &rend_list);
```

Simplataco! Yes, that's a word <BG>. At this point, we're about half way down the pipeline.

Now all we need is the perspective transformation projection and the screen projection, and that's it. However, there are a couple caveats.... First, we've said nothing about clipping, and that's a big issue. However, we did cover in the previous chapter that clipping can be performed in 3D object space, or in 2D raster image space; alas, we're going to have to do something about it.

However, we definitely can't wait all the way until rasterization because we surely can't project polygon vertices with negative or, worse yet, 0.0 z-values (divide by 0.0 error)! So, keep that in mind. We have to deal with that somewhat, but right now, let's talk about removing whole objects from the viewing pipeline.

Object Culling

Object culling is just that: removing objects so that they don't have to be processed through the entire 3D pipeline, as shown in Figure 7.15. However, object culling can be performed in world space *or* camera space. Nonetheless, I prefer to do it in camera space. "But," you might ask, "if you wait all the way until camera space to perform the culling of an object, didn't you already waste all those cycles transforming the object into camera space to see if it's invisible?" And the answer is, not necessarily.

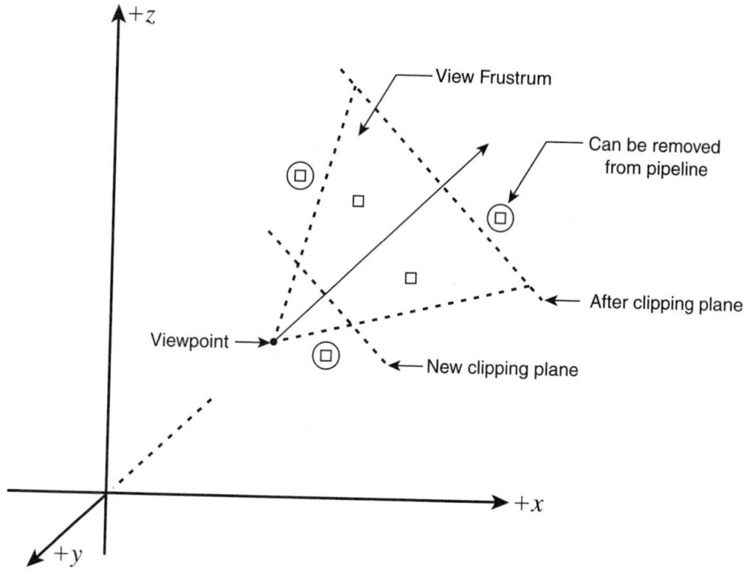

FIGURE 7.15 Removing objects from the 3D pipeline.

There's a trick. If you use the center of the object and its maximum radius to create a bounding sphere, you can perform the object culling test by transforming a single point from world-to-camera coordinates that represents the center of the object being tested. Then you basically test the bounding sphere for inclusion/exclusion in the viewing frustrum. This is detailed in the previous chapter, but if you recall, the math ended up being nothing more than testing a few points against the right, left, top, bottom, near, and far clipping planes. In any case, this is one of the *most important* steps in a 3D engine pipeline because in most cases, only a few objects will be in the scene at a time; the rest will be out of range or behind you, so there's no reason to process them. Therefore, we definitely want to add this functionality to our engine pipeline.

To accomplish the object culling step, we need a function that takes the object's current world position along with it's average/maximum radius (you might use either). The function then culls the object based on the current camera transformation. This only works for objects because the sense of "object" is lost once we convert an object into its constituent polygons and insert them into the master rendering list. Anyway, here's the object removal function:

```
int Cull_OBJECT4DV1(OBJECT4DV1_PTR obj, // object to cull
         CAM4DV1_PTR cam,    // camera to cull relative to
         int cull_flags)   // clipping planes to consider
{
```

```
// NOTE: is matrix based
// this function culls an entire object from the viewing
// frustrum by using the sent camera information and object
// the cull_flags determine what axes culling should take place
// x, y, z or all which is controlled by ORing the flags
// together
// if the object is culled its state is modified thats all
// this function assumes that both the camera and the object
// are valid!

// step 1: transform the center of the object's bounding
// sphere into camera space

POINT4D sphere_pos; //hold result of transforming cntr of bounding sphere

// transform point
Mat_Mul_VECTOR4D_4X4(&obj->world_pos, &cam->mcam, &sphere_pos);

// step 2: based on culling flags remove the object
if (cull_flags & CULL_OBJECT_Z_PLANE)
{
// cull only based on z clipping planes

// test far plane
if ( ((sphere_pos.z - obj->max_radius) > cam->far_clip_z) ||
   ((sphere_pos.z + obj->max_radius) < cam->near_clip_z) )
  {
  SET_BIT(obj->state, OBJECT4DV1_STATE_CULLED);
  return(1);
  } // end if

} // end if

if (cull_flags & CULL_OBJECT_X_PLANE)
{
// cull only based on x clipping planes
// we could use plane equations, but simple similar triangles
// is easier since this is really a 2D problem
// if the view volume is 90 degrees the the problem is trivial
// buts lets assume its not

// test the right and left clipping planes
// against the leftmost and rightmost
```

```
// points of the bounding sphere
float z_test = (0.5)*cam->viewplane_width*sphere_pos.z/cam->view_dist;

if ( ((sphere_pos.x-obj->max_radius) > z_test) || // right side
   ((sphere_pos.x+obj->max_radius) < -z_test) ) // left side
  {
  SET_BIT(obj->state, OBJECT4DV1_STATE_CULLED);
  return(1);
  } // end if
} // end if

if (cull_flags & CULL_OBJECT_Y_PLANE)
{
// cull only based on y clipping planes
// we could use plane equations, but simple similar triangles
// is easier since this is really a 2D problem
// if the view volume is 90 degrees the the problem is trivial
// buts lets assume its not

// test the the top and bottom clipping planes
// against the bottommost and topmost
// points of the bounding sphere
float z_test = (0.5)*cam->viewplane_height*sphere_pos.z/cam->view_dist;

if ( ((sphere_pos.y-obj->max_radius) > z_test) || // top side
   ((sphere_pos.y+obj->max_radius) < -z_test) ) // bottom side
  {
  SET_BIT(obj->state, OBJECT4DV1_STATE_CULLED);
  return(1);
  } // end if

} // end if

// return failure to cull
return(0);

} // end Cull_OBJECT4DV1
```

The function is a straightforward mathematical implementation of our findings on object culling in the last chapter, so there's no need to reiterate that. However, there are some interesting additions to the function. Basically, the function takes the object to test for culling, the current camera (you must make a call to initialize the `mcam` matrix before using the function), and a flags parameter `cull_flags` that defines the suite of tests to perform. Let's look at that....

7

The parameter cull_flags controls the axes that culling will be performed on. For example, if you want culling only on the z-axis (near and far clip planes), an object might still be invisible on the x and y axes, but at least you're guaranteed not to project polygons from an object that's behind you. In general, you should perform culling on all six faces of the 3D viewing frustrum because the tests are so cheap. Anyway, the flags that control the culling are as follows:

```
// general culling flags
#define CULL_OBJECT_X_PLANE   0x0001 // cull on the x clipping planes
#define CULL_OBJECT_Y_PLANE   0x0002 // cull on the y clipping planes
#define CULL_OBJECT_Z_PLANE   0x0004 // cull on the z clipping planes
#define CULL_OBJECT_XYZ_PLANES  (CULL_OBJECT_X_PLANE | CULL_OBJECT_Y_PLANE /
                      | CULL_OBJECT_Z_PLANE)
```

You just logically OR them together for what you want. For example, here's how you would cull an object to the entire frustrum:

```
if (Cull_OBJECT4DV1(&obj, &cam,
           CULL_OBJECT_X_PLANE |
           CULL_OBJECT_Y_PLANE |
           CULL_OBJECT_Z_PLANE))
{ /* object culled */ }
```

After culling, the function will alter the object's state flags and set a bit to indicate that the object was culled. To facilitate this, I've defined some constants for OBJECT4DV1 states:

```
// states for objects
#define OBJECT4DV1_STATE_ACTIVE        0x0001
#define OBJECT4DV1_STATE_VISIBLE       0x0002
#define OBJECT4DV1_STATE_CULLED        0x0004
```

We'll undoubtedly add to this, but for now, by setting and then testing the OBJECT4DV1_STATE_CULLED in rendering and transforming functions, we can disregard objects that have been culled. Additionally, an object may or may not be culled each frame. So, in each game frame, you need to reset your object's flags so that all the transient flags (such as the culling flag, for instance) are cleared. Here's a simple function that does that:

```
void Reset_OBJECT4DV1(OBJECT4DV1_PTR obj)
{
// this function resets the sent object and readies it for
// transformations, basically just resets the culled, clipped and
// backface flags, but here's where you would add stuff
// to ready any object for the pipeline
// the object is valid, let's rip it apart polygon by polygon
```

```
// reset object's culled flag
RESET_BIT(obj->state, OBJECT4DV1_STATE_CULLED);

// now the clipped and backface flags for the polygons
for (int poly = 0; poly < obj->num_polys; poly++)
  {
  // acquire polygon
  POLY4DV1_PTR curr_poly = &obj->plist[poly];

  // first is this polygon even visible?
  if (!(curr_poly->state & POLY4DV1_STATE_ACTIVE))
    continue; // move onto next poly

  // reset clipped and backface flags
  RESET_BIT(curr_poly->state, POLY4DV1_STATE_CLIPPED);
  RESET_BIT(curr_poly->state, POLY4DV1_STATE_BACKFACE);

  } // end for poly

} // end Reset_OBJECT4DV1
```

Making a call to the function resets the object's culling flag as well as resetting the back-face flag for each polygon that makes up the object's polygon mesh—let's talk about that next.

Back-face Removal

Back-face removal is shown in Figure 7.16. It's the process of removing polygons that are facing *away* from the viewpoint. We covered the mathematics of this in the last chapter, so I'm not going to go into detail. But in a nutshell, the test is performed on every single polygon of the object or render list. A direction vector is computed from the polygon to the viewpoint and the angle between this and the outward normal of the polygon is computed. If the angle is greater than 90 degrees or $\mathbf{n} \cdot \mathbf{l} <= 0$, the polygon is a back-face and can't possibly be visible.

Of course, the concept of back-face only makes sense for polygons that have one side. For polygons that are visible from both sides (two-sided), this test doesn't help us. Anyway, the test is usually performed in world space (because all we need is the viewpoint), not camera space, because we can usually kill a lot of polygons with back-face removal before pushing them through the world-to-camera transform, so it's a good way to remove another 50% of your geometry!

7

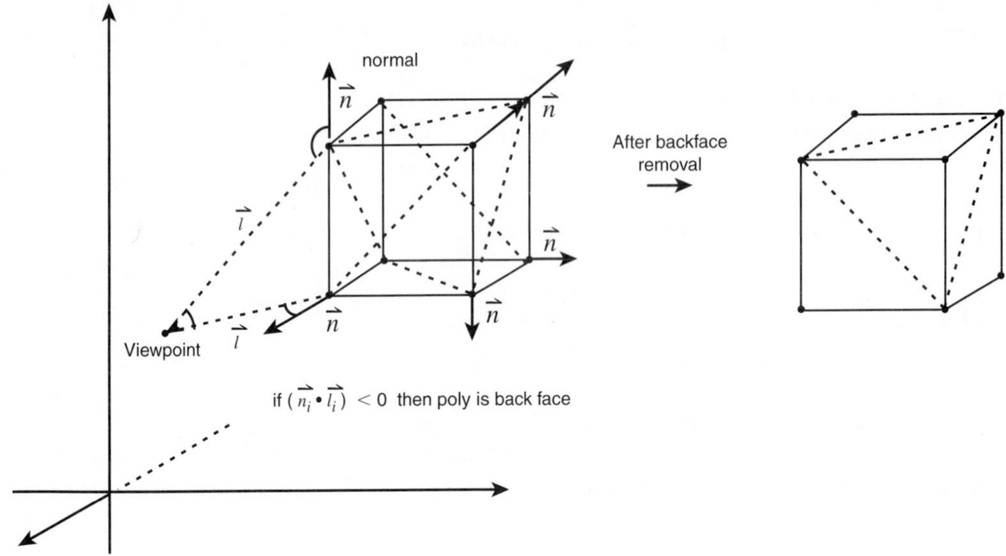

FIGURE 7.16 Backface removal in action.

Removing Back-faces in Objects

Here's the function that removes back-faces for objects contained in the OBJECT4DV1 structure:

```
void Remove_Backfaces_OBJECT4DV1(OBJECT4DV1_PTR obj, CAM4DV1_PTR cam)
{
// NOTE: this is not a matrix based function
// this function removes the backfaces from an object's
// polygon mesh, the function does this based on the vertex
// data in vlist_trans along with the camera position (only)
// note that only the backface state is set in each polygon

// test if the object is culled
if (obj->state & OBJECT4DV1_STATE_CULLED)
  return;

// process each poly in mesh
for (int poly=0; poly < obj->num_polys; poly++)
  {
  // acquire polygon
  POLY4DV1_PTR curr_poly = &obj->plist[poly];
```

```
// is this polygon valid?
// test this polygon if and only if it's not clipped, not culled,
// active, and visible and not 2 sided.
// Note we test for backface in the event that
// a previous call might have already determined this, so why work
// harder!
if (!(curr_poly->state & POLY4DV1_STATE_ACTIVE) ||
   (curr_poly->state & POLY4DV1_STATE_CLIPPED ) ||
   (curr_poly->attr & POLY4DV1_ATTR_2SIDED)  ||
   (curr_poly->state & POLY4DV1_STATE_BACKFACE) )
  continue; // move onto next poly

// extract vertex indices into master list, remember the polygons are
// NOT self contained, but based on the vertex list stored in the object
// itself
int vindex_0 = curr_poly->vert[0];
int vindex_1 = curr_poly->vert[1];
int vindex_2 = curr_poly->vert[2];

// we will use the transformed polygon vertex list since the backface removal
// only makes sense at the world coord stage further of the pipeline

// we need to compute the normal of this polygon face, and recall
// that the vertices are in cw order, u = p0->p1, v=p0->p2, n=uxv
VECTOR4D u, v, n;

// build u, v
VECTOR4D_Build(&obj->vlist_trans[ vindex_0 ],
        &obj->vlist_trans[ vindex_1 ], &u);
VECTOR4D_Build(&obj->vlist_trans[ vindex_0 ],
        &obj->vlist_trans[ vindex_2 ], &v);

// compute cross product
VECTOR4D_Cross(&u, &v, &n);

// now create eye vector to viewpoint
VECTOR4D view;
VECTOR4D_Build(&obj->vlist_trans[ vindex_0 ], &cam->pos, &view);

// and finally, compute the dot product
float dp = VECTOR4D_Dot(&n, &view);
```

7

```
    // if the sign is > 0 then visible, 0 = scathing, < 0 invisible
    if (dp <= 0.0 )
      SET_BIT(curr_poly->state, POLY4DV1_STATE_BACKFACE);

    } // end for poly

} // end Remove_Backfaces_OBJECT4DV1
```

Aren't you glad we wrote all those math and vector functions? I am! They made this function really easy to write. Anyway, take a few minutes to look at the function and see if it makes sense. Basically, it takes the object, traverses the polygon list, and tests whether all polygons that are active, visible, and one-sided are back-faces from the current viewpoint as defined in the camera object. Note that you don't need the `mcam` matrix defined for this function because all it needs is the camera's position. Here's how you would use the function:

```
Remove_Backfaces_OBJECT4DV1(&obj,&cam);
```

Hard, huh? And whamo! the polygon list in the object would have its flags altered for all back-faces. Specifically, each polygon that is a back-face gets its back-face bit set like this:

```
SET_BIT(curr_poly->state, POLY4DV1_STATE_BACKFACE);
```

TIP

Make sure that you perform back-face removal *after* object removal, but *before* the world-to-camera transformation.

Removing Back-faces in Render Lists

Now, if you decided to keep your objects in one piece before back-face removal and/or you just have a polygon list and no objects in your universe, you'll want to perform back-face removal on the render list. Of course, if you have objects and you performed this step previously and then inserted them into the rendering list, there's no point. Anyway, the function that tests for back-faces in a `RENDERLIST4DV1` object is almost identical to the `OBJECT4DV1` version, it's just a little different data structure access. Here it is:

```
void Remove_Backfaces_RENDERLIST4DV1(RENDERLIST4DV1_PTR rend_list, CAM4DV1_PTR cam)
{
// NOTE: this is not a matrix based function
// this function removes the backfaces from polygon list
// the function does this based on the polygon list data
// tvlist along with the camera position (only)
// note that only the backface state is set in each polygon
```

```
for (int poly = 0; poly < rend_list->num_polys; poly++)
  {
  // acquire current polygon
  POLYF4DV1_PTR curr_poly = rend_list->poly_ptrs[poly];

  // is this polygon valid?
  // test this polygon if and only if it's not clipped, not culled,
  // active, and visible and not 2 sided.
  // Note we test for backface in the event that
  // a previous call might have already determined this, so why work
  // harder!
  if ((curr_poly==NULL) || !(curr_poly->state & POLY4DV1_STATE_ACTIVE) ||
     (curr_poly->state & POLY4DV1_STATE_CLIPPED ) ||
     (curr_poly->attr & POLY4DV1_ATTR_2SIDED)  ||
     (curr_poly->state & POLY4DV1_STATE_BACKFACE) )
     continue; // move onto next poly

     // we need to compute the normal of this polygon face, and recall
     // that the vertices are in cw order, u = p0->p1, v=p0->p2, n=uxv
     VECTOR4D u, v, n;

     // build u, v
     VECTOR4D_Build(&curr_poly->tvlist[0], &curr_poly->tvlist[1], &u);
     VECTOR4D_Build(&curr_poly->tvlist[0], &curr_poly->tvlist[2], &v);

     // compute cross product
     VECTOR4D_Cross(&u, &v, &n);

     // now create eye vector to viewpoint
     VECTOR4D view;
     VECTOR4D_Build(&curr_poly->tvlist[0], &cam->pos, &view);

     // and finally, compute the dot product
     float dp = VECTOR4D_Dot(&n, &view);

     // if the sign is > 0 then visible, 0 = scathing, < 0 invisible
     if (dp <= 0.0 )
       SET_BIT(curr_poly->state, POLY4DV1_STATE_BACKFACE);

      } // end for poly

} // end Remove_Backfaces_RENDERLIST4DV1
```

7

Similar to the OBJECT4DV1 version, you want to remove back-faces before the world-to-camera transform because the transform is a waste if the polygons are back-faces and invisible! Finally, here's a sample call:

```
Remove_Backfaces_RENDERLIST4DV1(&rend_list, &cam);
```

After the call, the POLY4DV1_STATE_BACKFACE bit would be set in all polygons that were back-faces.

The Camera-to-Perspective Transform

The next stage in the 3D pipeline is the camera-to-perspective transformation. Figure 7.17 depicts the mathematics of the projection once again for your review. Basically, given a point **p** = (x_{world}, y_{world}, z_{world}, 1), the basic perspective transform is

```
x_per = viewing_distance*x_world/z_world
y_per  = viewing_distance*aspect_ratio*y_world/z_world
```

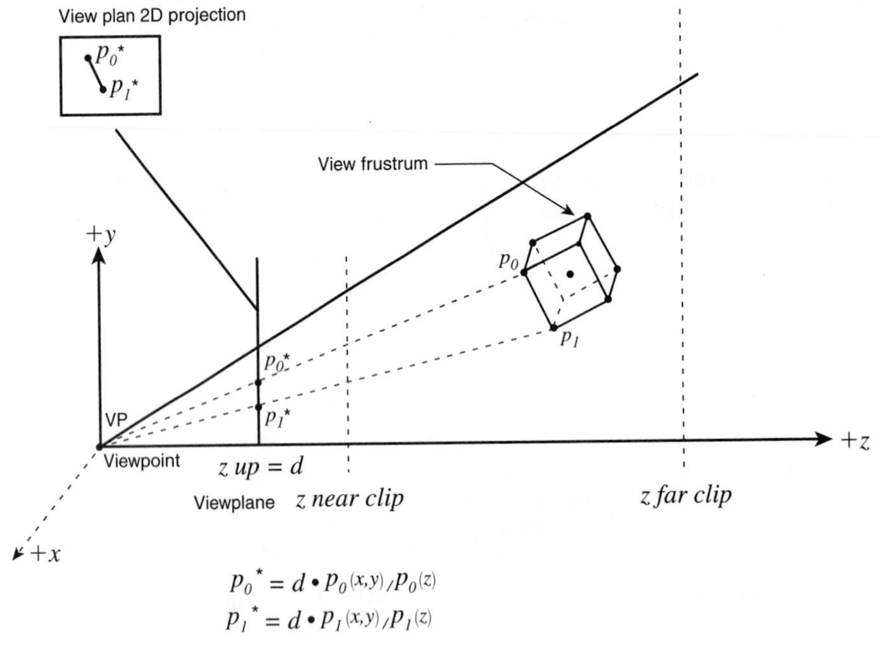

FIGURE 7.17 Review of perspective projection.

You recall that if we set the viewing distance (or d, for short) to 1.0, we ended up with normalized viewplane coordinates for the x and y axes in the range of x-axis—{x: –1 to 1}

y-axis—{y: -1/ar to 1/ar}

where ar is the aspect ratio width/height of the raster screen.

Additionally, a viewing distance of 1.0 forms a 90-degree field of view for both the x and y axes if the viewplane is square. Moving on, if we want to control the field of view or the viewing distance more, and project onto a viewplane of any size, we realized that viewing distance and field of view were dependent and we ended up with these formulas for the perspective transform:

```
d = (0.5)*viewplane_width*tan(θh/2)

xper = (d*xworld)/zworld
yper = (d*yworld*aspect_ratio)/zworld
```

Alright, enough review. The point of all this is to implement the transform with code and we have two different approaches: (1) perform the math manually (faster), or (2) perform the transform using matrices. But the problem with method 2 and using matrix transforms, as you recall, is that there's no way to perform a divide by z at the end via matrices. Thus, we must use 4D homogeneous coordinates and then convert the results from the matrix transform back to 3D non-homogeneous coordinates if we want to use a 4x4 matrix transform. The fact that the matrix multiplication is wasteful in addition to the post-homogeneous conversion makes using a matrix for the perspective transform a bad thing from a performance standpoint in software. But once again, many hardware implementations like only matrices. With all that in mind, let's take a look at both methods for the OBJECT4DV1 type along with the RENDERLIST4DV1 type.

7

The Perspective Transform for Objects

The camera object has all the information that we need to perform the perspective transform, including the viewing distance, the viewplane width and height, and the field of view (which is used to compute the viewing distance), so there's not much to the transform except performing the couple of lines of transformation math to each vertex. Here's the function that performs this on OBJECT4DV1:

```
void Camera_To_Perspective_OBJECT4DV1(OBJECT4DV1_PTR obj, CAM4DV1_PTR cam)
{
// NOTE: this is not a matrix based function
// this function transforms the camera coordinates of an object
// into perspective coordinates, based on the
// sent camera object, but it totally disregards the polygons themselves,
// it only works on the vertices in the vlist_trans[] list
// this is one way to do it, you might instead transform
// the global list of polygons in the render list since you
// are guaranteed that those polys represent geometry that
```

```
// has passed thru backfaces culling (if any)
// finally this function is really for experimental reasons only
// you would probably never let an object stay intact this far down
// the pipeline, since it's probably that there's only a single polygon
// that is visible! But this function has to transform the whole mesh!

// transform each vertex in the object to perspective coordinates
// assumes the object has already been transformed to camera
// coordinates and the result is in vlist_trans[]
for (int vertex = 0; vertex < obj->num_vertices; vertex++)
  {
  float z = obj->vlist_trans[vertex].z;

  // transform the vertex by the view parameters in the camera
  obj->vlist_trans[vertex].x = cam->view_dist_h *
                obj->vlist_trans[vertex].x/z;
  obj->vlist_trans[vertex].y = cam->view_dist_v *
                obj->vlist_trans[vertex].y *
                cam->aspect_ratio/z;
  // z = z, so no change

  // note that we are NOT dividing by the homogenous w coordinate since
  // we are not using a matrix op for this version of the function

  } // end for vertex

} // end Camera_To_Perspective_OBJECT4DV1
```

As you can see, the function is very short. Basically, it multiplies each vertex by the viewing distance (on both the x and y axes, which technically will be the same, but the aspect ratio takes the non-square viewplanes into consideration) and then divides by z. Here's a sample call:

```
Camera_To_Perspective_OBJECT4DV1(&obj, &cam);
```

NOTE

The function does not test for z values that are negative or 0.0. This is up to you to handle in a previous culling or clipping step. But for now, assume that the vertices are all projectable.

Now, what if you want to use a matrix to perform the projection? No problem. We can use our general `Transform_OBJECT4DV1()` function with a perspective matrix, which we can build with the following function:

```
void Build_Camera_To_Perspective_MATRIX4X4(CAM4DV1_PTR cam,
                     MATRIX4X4_PTR m)
{
// this function builds up a camera to perspective transformation
// matrix, in most cases the camera would have a 2x2 normalized
// view plane with a 90 degree FOV, since the point of the having
// this matrix must be to also have a perspective to screen (viewport)
// matrix that scales the normalized coordinates, also the matrix
// assumes that you are working in 4D homogenous coordinates and at
// some point there will be a 4D->3D conversion, it might be immediately
// after this transform is applied to vertices, or after the perspective
// to screen transform

Mat_Init_4X4(m,
cam->view_dist_h, 0,                 0, 0,
0,         cam->view_dist_v*cam->aspect_ratio, 0, 0,
0,         0,                1, 1,
0,         0,                0,0);

} // end Build_Camera_To_Perspective_MATRIX4X4
```

Then we just apply the transform to the OBJECT4DV1 like this (assuming that there's a camera object, of course):

```
MATRIX4X4 mper;
Build_Camera_To_Perspective_MATRIX4X4(&cam, &mper);
Transform_OBJECT4DV1(&obj, &mper, TRANSFORM_TRANS_ONLY,1);
```

Of course, there's one detail, right? After the transformation, the w factor in each vertex [x y z w] is no longer 1.0; thus, the coordinates are now completely homogeneous and we must convert them back to non-homogeneous before we use them. This is accomplished with a simple division by the w component of each vertex. Here's a function that performs the function on OBJECT4DV1:

```
void Convert_From_Homogeneous4D_OBJECT4DV1(OBJECT4DV1_PTR obj)
{
// this function converts all vertices in the transformed
// vertex list from 4D homogeneous coordinates to normal 3D coordinates
// by dividing each x,y,z component by w

for (int vertex = 0; vertex < obj->num_vertices; vertex++)
  {
```

```
  // convert to non-homogenous coords
  VECTOR4D_DIV_BY_W(&obj->vlist_trans[vertex]);
  } // end for vertex

} // end Convert_From_Homogeneous4D_OBJECT4DV1
```

So, as the last step to get real 3D coordinates, you just make the call:

```
Convert_From_Homogeneous4D_OBJECT4DV1(&obj);
```

The Perspective Transform for Render Lists

The perspective transform for the RENDERLIST4DV1 type works identically to the one for OBJECT4DV1. The functions more or less work the same, but must access the data structures a little differently—that's about it. Here's the primary non-matrix camera to perspective transform function:

```
void Camera_To_Perspective_RENDERLIST4DV1(RENDERLIST4DV1_PTR rend_list,
                                          CAM4DV1_PTR cam)
{
// NOTE: this is not a matrix based function
// this function transforms each polygon in the global render list
// into perspective coordinates, based on the
// sent camera object,
// you would use this function instead of the object based function
// if you decided earlier in the pipeline to turn each object into
// a list of polygons and then add them to the global render list

// transform each polygon in the render list into camera coordinates
// assumes the render list has already been transformed to world
// coordinates and the result is in tvlist[] of each polygon object

for (int poly = 0; poly < rend_list->num_polys; poly++)
{
// acquire current polygon
POLYF4DV1_PTR curr_poly = rend_list->poly_ptrs[poly];

// is this polygon valid?
// transform this polygon if and only if it's not clipped, not culled,
// active, and visible, note however the concept of "backface" is
// irrelevant in a wire frame engine though
if ((curr_poly==NULL) || !(curr_poly->state & POLY4DV1_STATE_ACTIVE) ||
   (curr_poly->state & POLY4DV1_STATE_CLIPPED ) ||
   (curr_poly->state & POLY4DV1_STATE_BACKFACE) )
    continue; // move onto next poly
```

```
// all good, let's transform
for (int vertex = 0; vertex < 3; vertex++)
  {
  float z = curr_poly->tvlist[vertex].z;

  // transform the vertex by the view parameters in the camera
  curr_poly->tvlist[vertex].x = cam->view_dist_h *
                curr_poly->tvlist[vertex].x/z;
  curr_poly->tvlist[vertex].y = cam->view_dist_v *
                curr_poly->tvlist[vertex].y *
                cam->aspect_ratio/z;
  // z = z, so no change

  // note that we are NOT dividing by the homogenous w coordinate since
  // we are not using a matrix op for this version of the function

  } // end for vertex

} // end for poly

} // end Camera_To_Perspective_RENDERLIST4DV1
```

It's used in the same as the OBJECT4DV1 version:

```
Camera_To_Perspective_RENDERLIST4DV1(&rend_list, &cam);
```

Next, to implement the matrix version, we once again build the matrix with a call to Build_Camera_To_Perspective_MATRIX4X4() and then make a call to Transform_RENDERLIST4DV1() like this:

```
MATRIX4X4 mper;
Build_Camera_To_Perspective_MATRIX4X4(&cam, &mper);

Transform_RENDERLIST4DV1(&rend_list, &mper, TRANSFORM_TRANS_ONLY);
```

You guessed it: We need to dehomogenize the coordinates because w is no longer 1.0 (actually w = z). Hence, here's the call to convert the homogeneous 4D back to 3D:

```
void Convert_From_Homogeneous4D_RENDERLIST4DV1(RENDERLIST4DV1_PTR rend_list)
{
// this function convertes all valid polygons vertices in the transformed
// vertex list from 4D homogeneous coordinates to normal 3D coordinates
// by dividing each x,y,z component by w
```

```
for (int poly = 0; poly < rend_list->num_polys; poly++)
{
// acquire current polygon
POLYF4DV1_PTR curr_poly = rend_list->poly_ptrs[poly];

// is this polygon valid?
// transform this polygon if and only if it's not clipped, not culled,
// active, and visible, note however the concept of "backface" is
// irrelevant in a wire frame engine though
if ((curr_poly==NULL) || !(curr_poly->state & POLY4DV1_STATE_ACTIVE) ||
   (curr_poly->state & POLY4DV1_STATE_CLIPPED ) ||
   (curr_poly->state & POLY4DV1_STATE_BACKFACE) )
    continue; // move onto next poly

// all good, let's transform
for (int vertex = 0; vertex < 3; vertex++)
  {
  // convert to non-homogenous coords
  VECTOR4D_DIV_BY_W(&curr_poly->tvlist[vertex]);
  } // end for vertex

} // end for poly

} // end Convert_From_Homogeneous4D_RENDERLIST4DV1
```

The final call sequence would of course look like this:

```
MATRIX4X4 mper;
Build_Camera_To_Perspective_MATRIX4X4(&cam, &mper);

Transform_RENDERLIST4DV1(&rend_list, &mper, TRANSFORM_TRANS_ONLY);

Convert_From_Homogeneous4D_RENDERLIST4DV1(&rend_list);
```

At this point, we have a virtual image sitting on the viewplane, so to speak. Now we need to project it onto the viewscreen or viewport, and that's the last step of the process (other than the actual rasterization, of course).

The Perspective-to-Screen Viewport Transform

The perspective-to-screen transform is more or less the last stage of the 3D pipeline. It basically takes the viewplane coordinates and scales them to screen coordinates, as shown in Figure 7.18. The transform must take into consideration that most raster screens have the origin (0,0) at the top-left corner, and the y-axis is inverted from the standard 2D Cartesian coordinate system. Of course, if during the perspective transform itself the viewplane was made the same size as the viewport, a scaling operation will not be needed. But a translation and inversion of the y-axis still will be needed in most cases, because during projection we assume that the center of the viewplane is the origin at (0,0) and positive x is to the right, whereas positive y is upward. Raster screens, of course, have their origin (0,0) at the upper-left corner and the y-axis is inverted. Therefore, no matter what you do, you're going to need a viewport transform of some kind.

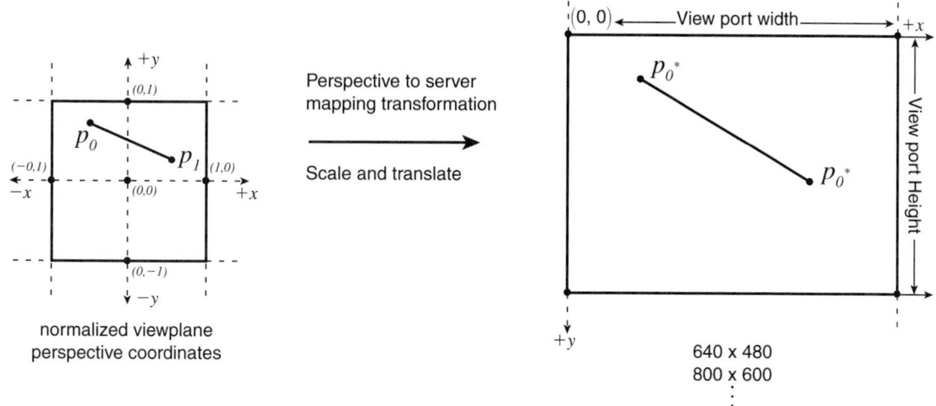

FIGURE 7.18 Transforming from perspective coordinates to screen coordinates.

With that in mind, let's take a look at a number of viewport transforms that I've written for both objects and render lists. But keep in mind that these transforms assume that the perspective transform was a normalizing one; that is, onto a viewplane of 2x2 for square projections, or 2/ar x 2/ar for non-square projections, so a scaling operation must be done. In the next section, we'll see the entire perspective/screen transform performed in a single step.

Viewport Transformation for Objects

First, we'll look at a manual function that performs the perspective to screen/viewport transformation. The function assumes that the perspective coordinates are in normalized form. So, the function must scale the coordinates to the size of the screen/viewport, and translate and invert the y-axis (of course, this is all in Chapter 6). Here's the function:

```
void Perspective_To_Screen_OBJECT4DV1(OBJECT4DV1_PTR obj, CAM4DV1_PTR cam)
{
// NOTE: this is not a matrix based function
// this function transforms the perspective coordinates of an object
// into screen coordinates, based on the sent viewport info
// but it totally disregards the polygons themselves,
// it only works on the vertices in the vlist_trans[] list
// this is one way to do it, you might instead transform
```

```
// the global list of polygons in the render list since you
// are guaranteed that those polys represent geometry that
// has passed thru backfaces culling (if any)
// finally this function is really for experimental reasons only
// you would probably never let an object stay intact this far down
// the pipeline, since it's probably that there's only a single polygon
// that is visible! But this function has to transform the whole mesh!
// this function would be called after a perspective
// projection was performed on the object

// transform each vertex in the object to screen coordinates
// assumes the object has already been transformed to perspective
// coordinates and the result is in vlist_trans[]

float alpha = (0.5*cam->viewport_width-0.5);
float beta = (0.5*cam->viewport_height-0.5);

for (int vertex = 0; vertex < obj->num_vertices; vertex++)
  {
  // assumes the vertex is in perspective normalized coords from -1 to 1
  // on each axis,scale them to viewport and invert y axis and project
  // to screen

  // transform the vertex by the view parameters in the camera
  obj->vlist_trans[vertex].x = alpha + alpha*obj->vlist_trans[vertex].x;
  obj->vlist_trans[vertex].y = beta - beta *obj->vlist_trans[vertex].y;

  } // end for vertex

} // end Perspective_To_Screen_OBJECT4DV1
```

The function really just maps the coordinates {x:–1 to 1} and {y:-1 to 1} (normalized viewplane coordinates) to the raster screen. However, there's one detail that we should mention: the 4D homogeneous conversion is unnecessary, because during the camera-to-perspective transform, there was a division by z. Thus, after this transform the (x,y) component of each vertex is ready to go and represents the real position on the raster screen to plot.

Now, it's possible that during the perspective transform we did not divide by z; that is, maybe we used a matrix formulation and left the coordinates in 4D homogeneous form (where w is not equal to 1.0). We can still use this function, but at some point we must divide each vertex by its w component to convert from homogeneous to non-homogeneous. However, in most cases, you don't leave the coordinate data in 4D form all the way down to the viewport transform, but there's no rule against doing it. Anyway, here's how you would use the function in the context of the perspective object transform:

```
// first camera to perspective transform
// after transform coordinates are already non-homogeneous
Camera_To_Perspective_OBJECT4DV1(&obj, &cam);

// now perform final viewport transform
Perspective_To_Screen_OBJECT4DV1(&obj, &cam);
```

Almost too easy!

Now let's talk about the perspective-to-screen transform using matrices. Here's the clincher: The matrix will be different depending on whether the perspective coordinates are still in 4D homogeneous form or if they've already been divided by w or z (depending on the transform was performed) and are the real 3D perspective coordinates (technically 2D; the x,y is all we need, though). So, let's take a look at both 4D and 3D versions.

Let's assume that we performed the perspective transform with this code:

```
MATRIX4X4 mper;
Build_Camera_To_Perspective_MATRIX4X4(&cam, &mper);

Transform_OBJECT4DV1(&obj, &mper, TRANSFORM_TRANS_ONLY,1);
```

The results would be in 4D form. Thus, to find the final coordinates, we need to divide each vertex by its w value. However, we can hold off on that and still perform the perspective-to-screen viewport transform in 4D coordinates with this matrix-building function:

```
void Build_Perspective_To_Screen_4D_MATRIX4X4(CAM4DV1_PTR cam, MATRIX4X4_PTR m)
{
// this function builds up a perspective to screen transformation
// matrix, the function assumes that you want to perform the
// transform in homogeneous coordinates and at raster time there will be
// a 4D->3D homogenous conversion and of course only the x,y points
// will be considered for the 2D rendering, thus you would use this
// function's matrix as if your perspective coordinates were still
// in homogeneous form when this matrix was applied, additionally
// the point of this matrix to scale and translate the perspective
// coordinates to screen coordinates, thus the matrix is built up
// assuming that the perspective coordinates are in normalized form for
// a 2x2 viewplane, that is, x: -1 to 1, y:-1/ar to 1/ar

float alpha = (0.5*cam->viewport_width-0.5);
float beta = (0.5*cam->viewport_height-0.5);
```

```
Mat_Init_4X4(m, alpha,  0,    0,  0,
        0,    -beta, 0,  0,
        alpha,  beta, 1,  0,
        0,     0,    0,  1);

} // end Build_Perspective_To_Screen_4D_MATRIX4X4()
```

So now we make a call to build the matrix and then transform the object like this:

```
MATRIX4X4 mscr;
Build_Perspective_To_Screen_4D_MATRIX4X4 (&cam, &mscr);
Transform_OBJECT4DV1(&obj, &mscr, TRANSFORM_TRANS_ONLY,1);
```

We almost have screen coordinates, but need to de-homogenize them with a call to

```
Convert_From_Homogeneous4D_OBJECT4DV1(&obj);
```

TIP

I know this stuff can be confusing, but the bottom line to remember is that we CANNOT perform division by z using a matrix, so we need to transfer z into the w component and then divide by it to obtain perspective transformations or non-affine transforms. That's the whole problem with 4D components. They're nice because you can use 4x4 matrices, but in most cases, I like to force w = 1 at all times and perform the perspective transform manually and divide by z myself, rather than having a separate de-homogenizing step where everything is divided by w.

Alright, that's the hard way. But let's assume that the vertices that make up the object have already been converted from 4D to 3D and are ready to go. So, all we need is a matrix version of the viewport transform that does the same math as the functional version we saw in `Perspective_To_Screen_OBJECT4DV1()`; that is, it assumes 3D coordinates and w = 1 already. Here's the matrix function that builds that matrix for us:

```
void Build_Perspective_To_Screen_MATRIX4X4(CAM4DV1_PTR cam, MATRIX4X4_PTR m)
{
// this function builds up a perspective to screen transformation
// matrix, the function assumes that you want to perform the
// transform in 2D/3D coordinates, that is, you have already converted
// the perspective coordinates from homogenous 4D to 3D before applying
// this matrix, additionally
// the point of this matrix is to scale and translate the perspective
// coordinates to screen coordinates, thus the matrix is built up
// assuming that the perspective coordinates are in normalized form for
// a 2x2 viewplane, that is, x: -1 to 1, y:-1/ar to 1/ar
// the only difference between this function and the version that
// assumes the coordinates are still in homogenous format is the
```

```
// last column doesn't force w=z, in fact the z, and w results
// are irrelevent since we assume that BEFORE this matrix is applied
// all points are already converted from 4D->3D

float alpha = (0.5*cam->viewport_width-0.5);
float beta = (0.5*cam->viewport_height-0.5);

Mat_Init_4X4(m, alpha,  0,   0,  0,
        0,   -beta, 0,  0,
        alpha,  beta, 1,  0,
        0,    0,   0,  1);

} // end Build_Perspective_To_Screen_MATRIX4X4()
```

With this function, we assume that the vertices are already in 3D form (technically 2D, and in perspective normalized coordinates, to boot). To use it, you would do this:

```
MATRIX4X4 mscr;
Build_Perspective_To_Screen_MATRIX4X4(&cam, &mscr);
Transform_OBJECT4DV1(&obj, &mscr, TRANSFORM_TRANS_ONLY,1);
```

The point of all these examples is to show you that once you convert from 4D to 3D (usually in the perspective transform), the pipeline math and matrices slightly change and you have to have two branches. Personally, I prefer to transform from 4D to 3D perspective coordinates during the perspective transformation.

Viewport Transformation for Render Lists

The viewport transformation for render lists is identical to that of the objects, other than the data structure access. First, let's look at the functional version that assumes there was a previous normalized perspective transform with a divide by z (or w, however it was done) and the perspective coordinates just need to be scaled and translated to screen coordinates. Here's that function:

```
void Perspective_To_Screen_RENDERLIST4DV1(RENDERLIST4DV1_PTR rend_list,
                        CAM4DV1_PTR cam)
{
// NOTE: this is not a matrix based function
// this function transforms the perspective coordinates of the render
// list into screen coordinates, based on the sent viewport in the camera
// assuming that the viewplane coordinates were normalized
// you would use this function instead of the object based function
// if you decided earlier in the pipeline to turn each object into
// a list of polygons and then add them to the global render list
// you would only call this function if you previously performed
// a normalized perspective transform
```

```
// transform each polygon in the render list from perspective to screen
// coordinates assumes the render list has already been transformed
// to normalized perspective coordinates and the result is in tvlist[]
for (int poly = 0; poly < rend_list->num_polys; poly++)
{
// acquire current polygon
POLYF4DV1_PTR curr_poly = rend_list->poly_ptrs[poly];

// is this polygon valid?
// transform this polygon if and only if it's not clipped, not culled,
// active, and visible, note however the concept of "backface" is
// irrelevant in a wire frame engine though
if ((curr_poly==NULL) || !(curr_poly->state & POLY4DV1_STATE_ACTIVE) ||
   (curr_poly->state & POLY4DV1_STATE_CLIPPED ) ||
   (curr_poly->state & POLY4DV1_STATE_BACKFACE) )
    continue; // move onto next poly

float alpha = (0.5*cam->viewport_width-0.5);
float beta = (0.5*cam->viewport_height-0.5);

// all good, let's transform
for (int vertex = 0; vertex < 3; vertex++)
  {
  // the vertex is in perspective normalized coords from -1 to 1
  // on each axis, simple scale them and invert y axis and project
  // to screen

  // transform the vertex by the view parameters in the camera
  curr_poly->tvlist[vertex].x = alpha + alpha*curr_poly->tvlist[vertex].x;
  curr_poly->tvlist[vertex].y = beta - beta *curr_poly->tvlist[vertex].y;
  } // end for vertex

} // end for poly

} // end Perspective_To_Screen_RENDERLIST4DV1
```

Nothing more than a scale and y-axis inversion, as we would expect. Here's an example of the function being used after a call to perform the camera-to-perspective conversion that results in non-homogeneous coordinates:

```
// do the camera to perspective and divide by z
Camera_To_Perspective_RENDERLIST4DV1(&rend_list, &cam);

// now map perspective cords to screen
Perspective_To_Screen_RENDERLIST4DV1(&rend_list, &cam);
```

At this point, I think you get the idea of the difference between 4D and 3D, so just as we did with objects, we can perform the transform with matrices. But we need to be careful to take into consideration of whether the perspective coordinates are in 4D or 3D. Here's the example of the coordinates staying in 4D form all way down:

```
MATRIX4X4 mscr;
Build_Perspective_To_Screen_4D(&cam, &mscr);

Transform_RENDERLIST4DV1(&rend_list, &mscr, TRANSFORM_TRANS_ONLY);
```

We almost have screen coordinates, but need to de-homogenize them with a call to

```
Convert_From_Homogeneous4D_RENDERLIST4DV1(&rend_list);
```

And finally, if the coordinates were already in 3D form, we can forget about the de-homogenizing phase and use the simpler perspective to screen transform that we've already seen. It builds a matrix, assuming 3D coordinates already, as shown here:

```
MATRIX4X4 mscr;

Build_Perspective_To_Screen_MATRIX4X4(&cam, &mscr);

Transform_RENDERLIST4DV1(&rend_list, &mscr, TRANSFORM_TRANS_ONLY);
```

As you can see, the cool thing about matrices is that we can use them for anything. In this case, the only difference between doing things with objects and render lists is the final call to `Transform_*()`, which performs the transformation.

7

TIP

In real life, I would write the `Transform_*()` functions as virtual (and all this stuff as classes) so that I could call a single function and it would transform whatever the underlying object was, but I have to leave something for you to do later!

Hybrid Perspective Screen Transforms

Now it's time to use some common sense and do a little optimizing. I want to show you all the ways to do things, so you have no doubt about how things work. But unless you're completely asleep, you should realize by now that matrices are pretty, but definitely not friendly to the perspective transform. Thus, performing the perspective transform is easier to do manually. Moreover, having separate functions to perform the perspective and then the screen mapping makes sense in a lot of cases. But if you just want to get the darn image into a buffer, there's no need for a second function call because all we're really doing is a second scale and translation after the perspective transform. Hence, it's trivial to put these two operations into a single function and create a single transform function that does both the perspective to viewplane, and then the viewplane to viewport/screen transform.

The Camera-to-Screen Transform for Objects

Basically, the fastest way to perform the camera-to-screen transform is with a function that manually does it and divides by z itself. Here it is for objects:

```
void Camera_To_Perspective_Screen_OBJECT4DV1(OBJECT4DV1_PTR obj, CAM4DV1_PTR cam)
{
// NOTE: this is not a matrix based function
// this function transforms the camera coordinates of an object
// into Screen scaled perspective coordinates, based on the
// sent camera object, that is, view_dist_h and view_dist_v
// should be set to cause the desired (width X height)
// projection of the vertices, but the function totally
// disregards the polygons themselves,
// it only works on the vertices in the vlist_trans[] list
// this is one way to do it, you might instead transform
// the global list of polygons in the render list since you
// are guaranteed that those polys represent geometry that
// has passed thru backfaces culling (if any)
// finally this function is really for experimental reasons only
// you would probably never let an object stay intact this far down
// the pipeline, since it's probably that there's only a single polygon
// that is visible! But this function has to transform the whole mesh!
// finally, the function also inverts the y axis, so the coordinates
// generated from this function ARE screen coordinates and ready for
// rendering

float alpha = (0.5*cam->viewport_width-0.5);
float beta = (0.5*cam->viewport_height-0.5);

// transform each vertex in the object to perspective screen coordinates
// assumes the object has already been transformed to camera
// coordinates and the result is in vlist_trans[]
for (int vertex = 0; vertex < obj->num_vertices; vertex++)
  {
  float z = obj->vlist_trans[vertex].z;

  // transform the vertex by the view parameters in the camera
  obj->vlist_trans[vertex].x = cam->view_dist_h *
                obj->vlist_trans[vertex].x/z;
  obj->vlist_trans[vertex].y = cam->view_dist_v *
```

```
                obj->vlist_trans[vertex].y *
                cam->aspect_ratio/z;
  // z = z, so no change

  // not that we are NOT dividing by the homogenous w coordinate since
  // we are not using a matrix operation for this version of the function

  // now the coordinates are in the range
  // x:(-viewport_width/2 to viewport_width/2)
  // and y:(-viewport_height/2 to viewport_height/2),
  // thus we need a translation and
  // since the Y-axis is inverted, we need to invert y
  // to complete the screen transform:
  obj->vlist_trans[vertex].x = obj->vlist_trans[vertex].x + alpha;
  obj->vlist_trans[vertex].y = -obj->vlist_trans[vertex].y + beta;

  } // end for vertex

} // end Camera_To_Perspective_Screen_OBJECT4DV1
```

Notice that we save even more math in the function. We don't have to scale the viewplane coordinates to the viewport because in the transform itself we project them onto a viewplane that's `viewport_width` × `viewport_height`, which saves a little more. Anyway, after this function, the coordinates in `vlist_trans[]` are totally ready to be drawn. Here's a sample call:

```
Camera_To_Perspective_Screen_OBJECT4DV1(&obj,&cam);
```

I have no idea why I keep giving examples of these incredibly trivial function calls, but it can't hurt! In any case, that's all there is to it! Of course, before the call, the coordinates better be in camera coordinates, but other than that, you're good to go.

The Camera-to-Screen Transform for Render Lists

There's nothing magic about performing the camera-to-screen transform at once for render lists either. It's just a slightly different data structure access. Here's the function:

```
void Camera_To_Perspective_Screen_RENDERLIST4DV1(RENDERLIST4DV1_PTR rend_list,
                             CAM4DV1_PTR cam)
{
// NOTE: this is not a matrix based function
// this function transforms the camera coordinates of an object
// into Screen scaled perspective coordinates, based on the
// sent camera object, that is, view_dist_h and view_dist_v
// should be set to cause the desired (viewport_width X viewport_height)
```

```
// it only works on the vertices in the tvlist[] list
// finally, the function also inverts the y axis, so the coordinates
// generated from this function ARE screen coordinates and ready for
// rendering

// transform each polygon in the render list to perspective screen
// coordinates assumes the render list has already been transformed
// to camera coordinates and the result is in tvlist[]
for (int poly = 0; poly < rend_list->num_polys; poly++)
{
// acquire current polygon
POLYF4DV1_PTR curr_poly = rend_list->poly_ptrs[poly];

// is this polygon valid?
// transform this polygon if and only if it's not clipped, not culled,
// active, and visible, note however the concept of "backface" is
// irrelevant in a wire frame engine though
if ((curr_poly==NULL) || !(curr_poly->state & POLY4DV1_STATE_ACTIVE) ||
   (curr_poly->state & POLY4DV1_STATE_CLIPPED ) ||
   (curr_poly->state & POLY4DV1_STATE_BACKFACE) )
    continue; // move onto next poly

float alpha = (0.5*cam->viewport_width-0.5);
float beta = (0.5*cam->viewport_height-0.5);

// all good, let's transform
for (int vertex = 0; vertex < 3; vertex++)
  {
  float z = curr_poly->tvlist[vertex].z;

  // transform the vertex by the view parameters in the camera
  curr_poly->tvlist[vertex].x = cam->view_dist_h *
                curr_poly->tvlist[vertex].x/z;
  curr_poly->tvlist[vertex].y = cam->view_dist_v *
                curr_poly->tvlist[vertex].y *
                cam->aspect_ratio/z;
  // z = z, so no change

  // not that we are NOT dividing by the homogenous w coordinate since
  // we are not using a matrix operation for this version of the function

  // now the coordinates are in the range
  // x:(-viewport_width/2 to viewport_width/2)
```

```
    // and y:(-viewport_height/2 to viewport_height/2),
    // thus we need a translation and
    // since the Y-axis is inverted, we need to invert y to complete the screen
    // transform:
    curr_poly->tvlist[vertex].x = curr_poly->tvlist[vertex].x + alpha;
    curr_poly->tvlist[vertex].y = -curr_poly->tvlist[vertex].y + beta;

    } // end for vertex

  } // end for poly

} // end Camera_To_Perspective_Screen_RENDERLIST4DV1
```

And here's a call to it:

```
Camera_To_Perspective_Screen_RENDERLIST4DV1(&rend_list,
&cam);
```

Wow! That's it. We're done with the major parts of the 3D pipeline! Probably the only confusing part is that when we get to the perspective transform, we have to decide whether to do it manually or with a matrix, and then whether we want to hold on to the 4D coordinates. On the other hand, we can perform the perspective and screen transform all at once and save a lot of time and drama. We'll end up using this method most of the time, or at least using manual functions for the perspective and screen transform that converts to 3D coordinates (that is, de-homogenizes) because we don't want to be converted 4D to 3D late in the pipeline. However, as I said when using hardware, we may not have this option, and matrices and 4D coordinates may be what the hardware likes.

Rendering a 3D World

I never thought we would get here—thank `char s[] = {71, 79, 68, 0}`! Of course, my dilemma was that for the previous zillion pages of this chapter, I couldn't show you a single demo because we have to first understand and code each step of the pipeline. But now we're done and we can write all the demos we want—and we will! But first, let's take yet another look at the 3D pipeline and then we'll write some simple graphics functions that draw wireframe meshes that feed from either `OBJECT4DV1`s or `RENDERLIST4DV1`s.

The 3D Pipeline As It Stands

Currently, we have all the code we need to load 3D objects off disk and store them in an `OBJECT4DV1` structure and then push one or more objects all the way through the 3D pipeline. Or we can push one or more `OBJECT4DV1`s down the 3D pipeline as far as we wish, rip it apart into its constituent polygons, and then insert them into a master polygon list via the data structure `RENDERLIST4DV1`. How you want to do it is really up to you; both methods have strengths and weaknesses. But in general, most 3D engines use a hybrid of both. They work with objects for the things that move around, but the environment might be a giant mesh that's sectorized and simply inserted into the render list along with the objects at some point. But for now, we're keeping things simple and assuming that our games are made from objects, and that there's no interior or exterior environments we need to deal with.

With that in mind, Figure 7.19 shows the different path ways geometry can take, but in general, the following steps must take place:

Stage 0: Load objects and position them

Stage 1: Local-to-world transform

Stage 2: Object and back-face removal

Stage 3: World-to-camera transform

Stage 4: Camera-to-perspective transform

Stage 5: Perspective-to-screen transform

Stage 6: Render the geometry

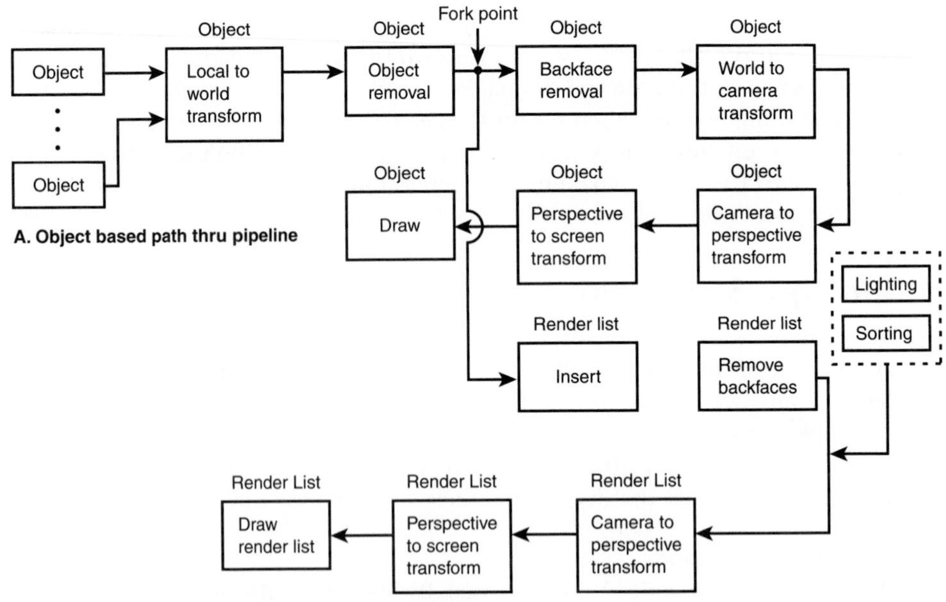

FIGURE 7.19 The viewing pipeline and multiple render paths.

Now, you might convert your objects into polygons anywhere after Stage 2 because you want to at least try to remove objects while they're intact. Once you convert them to polygons, you lose their structure and can't think of them as objects anymore. We've completely left out 3D clipping, but as long as we remove objects, we're somewhat safe at this point because we clip the objects to the near z-plane. For the most part, we won't get any geometry that has z = negative or z = 0 vertices, but we need to deal with this, and we will in the next chapter when we perform full 3D clipping. For now, we assume that all the projected vertices are reasonably safe, and if they *do* extend beyond the 2D viewport, they'll be clipped by the 2D drawing functions.

Okay, so no matter how you sequence our geometry down the 3D pipeline, at some point we're going to have one of two things: a list of OBJECT4DV1s that need to be rendered or a single RENDERLIST4DV1 that represents all the polygons and needs to be rendered. Of course, you could have more than one render list, but for now, let's assume one that basically would contain all the objects. So, what we need are two functions: one that can draw all the polygons in an OBJECT4DV1, and one that can draw all the polygons in a RENDERLIST4DV1.

Drawing an OBJECT4DV1 Before we begin, let's remember that we're going to use wireframe graphics without any hidden line removal or sorting. That means that you'll be able to see through the objects. Moreover, the objects may be drawn in the wrong order because we aren't taking into consideration their z-depth to sort them or use any other type of proper ordering, but who cares? They *are* hollow! Therefore, all we need to do is write a function that basically assumes that the vertex list in the transformed object's vertice list is valid and in screen coordinates, and just run through the geometry and draw each triangle. Here's the function that does the job. Note that the function tests to see if each polygon is visible, two-sided, can be clipped, or is a back-face.

```
void Draw_OBJECT4DV1_Wire16(OBJECT4DV1_PTR obj,
              UCHAR *video_buffer, int lpitch)

{
// this function renders an object to the screen in wireframe,
// 16 bit mode, it has no regard at all about hidden surface removal,
// etc. the function only exists as an easy way to render an object
// without converting it into polygons, the function assumes all
// coordinates are screen coordinates, but will perform 2D clipping

// iterate thru the poly list of the object and simply draw
// each polygon
for (int poly=0; poly < obj->num_polys; poly++)
  {
  // render this polygon if and only if it's not clipped, not culled,
  // active, and visible, note however the concecpt of "backface" is
  // irrelevant in a wire frame engine though
  if (!(obj->plist[poly].state & POLY4DV1_STATE_ACTIVE) ||
     (obj->plist[poly].state & POLY4DV1_STATE_CLIPPED ) ||
```

```
    (obj->plist[poly].state & POLY4DV1_STATE_BACKFACE) )
   continue; // move onto next poly

  // extract vertex indices into master list, rember the polygons are
  // NOT self contained, but based on the vertex list stored in the object
  // itself
  int vindex_0 = obj->plist[poly].vert[0];
  int vindex_1 = obj->plist[poly].vert[1];
  int vindex_2 = obj->plist[poly].vert[2];

  // draw the lines now
  Draw_Clip_Line16(obj->vlist_trans[ vindex_0 ].x,
           obj->vlist_trans[ vindex_0 ].y,
           obj->vlist_trans[ vindex_1 ].x,
           obj->vlist_trans[ vindex_1 ].y,
           obj->plist[poly].color,
           video_buffer, lpitch);

  Draw_Clip_Line16(obj->vlist_trans[ vindex_1 ].x,
           obj->vlist_trans[ vindex_1 ].y,
           obj->vlist_trans[ vindex_2 ].x,
           obj->vlist_trans[ vindex_2 ].y,
           obj->plist[poly].color,
           video_buffer, lpitch);

  Draw_Clip_Line16(obj->vlist_trans[ vindex_2 ].x,
           obj->vlist_trans[ vindex_2 ].y,
           obj->vlist_trans[ vindex_0 ].x,
           obj->vlist_trans[ vindex_0 ].y,
           obj->plist[poly].color,
           video_buffer, lpitch);

  } // end for poly

} // end Draw_OBJECT4DV1_Wire
```

The function is beautiful, huh? With our virtual computer system and graphics buffer, we can write 3D functions all day and not know a thing about the hardware—all we need is the address of the video buffer and the memory pitch. Anyway, the function makes use of a couple of the 2D functions for drawing clipped lines and does nothing more than traverse the polygon list and draw all the triangles that make up the 3D object. Here's a sample call where you would have already set up the graphics system, performed the 3D pipeline, and obj was ready to go:

```
Draw_OBJECT4DV1_Wire16(&obj, video_buffer,lpitch);
```

Drawing a `RENDERLIST4DV1` The drawing function for the render lists is identical to the objects, but with different data structure access. Here it is:

```
void Draw_RENDERLIST4DV1_Wire16(RENDERLIST4DV1_PTR rend_list,
              UCHAR *video_buffer, int lpitch)
{
// this function "executes" the render list or in other words
// draws all the faces in the list in wire frame 16bit mode
// note there is no need to sort wire frame polygons, but
// later we will need to, so hidden surfaces stay hidden
// also, we leave it to the function to determine the bitdepth
// and call the correct rasterizer

// at this point, all we have is a list of polygons and it's time
// to draw them
for (int poly=0; poly < rend_list->num_polys; poly++)
  {
  // render this polygon if and only if it's not clipped, not culled,
  // active, and visible, note however the concecpt of "backface" is
  // irrelevant in a wire frame engine though
  if (!(rend_list->poly_ptrs[poly]->state & POLY4DV1_STATE_ACTIVE) ||
     (rend_list->poly_ptrs[poly]->state & POLY4DV1_STATE_CLIPPED ) ||
     (rend_list->poly_ptrs[poly]->state & POLY4DV1_STATE_BACKFACE) )
    continue; // move onto next poly


  // draw the triangle edge one, note that clipping was already set up
  // by 2D initialization, so line clipper will clip all polys out
  // of the 2D screen/window boundary
  Draw_Clip_Line16(rend_list->poly_ptrs[poly]->tvlist[0].x,
        rend_list->poly_ptrs[poly]->tvlist[0].y,
        rend_list->poly_ptrs[poly]->tvlist[1].x,
        rend_list->poly_ptrs[poly]->tvlist[1].y,
        rend_list->poly_ptrs[poly]->color,
        video_buffer, lpitch);

  Draw_Clip_Line16(rend_list->poly_ptrs[poly]->tvlist[1].x,
        rend_list->poly_ptrs[poly]->tvlist[1].y,
        rend_list->poly_ptrs[poly]->tvlist[2].x,
        rend_list->poly_ptrs[poly]->tvlist[2].y,
        rend_list->poly_ptrs[poly]->color,
        video_buffer, lpitch);
```

7

```
  Draw_Clip_Line16(rend_list->poly_ptrs[poly]->tvlist[2].x,
        rend_list->poly_ptrs[poly]->tvlist[2].y,
        rend_list->poly_ptrs[poly]->tvlist[0].x,
        rend_list->poly_ptrs[poly]->tvlist[0].y,
        rend_list->poly_ptrs[poly]->color,
        video_buffer, lpitch);

  } // end for poly

} // end Draw_RENDERLIST4DV1_Wire
```

Calling it is no different, we just need a render list rather than an object:

```
Draw_RENDERLIST4DV1_Wire16(&rend_list, video_buffer,lpitch);
```

That's it, my large-brained friend! Now we're ready to see some demos. Now that we have the pipeline and rendering algorithms all done, I would like to write a number of demos to review all the different techniques we covered in the previous sections. So, the next section is going to run through a number of examples to give you a good idea how to do everything.

3D Demos

Finally, some full demos. It's been torture, hasn't it? Now, don't get too built up, we're not going to do anything other than basic wireframe examples based on all the functions we've built. But as I said, after this chapter, you could easily write *Battle Zone*, or something of that nature. Each demo will have a title and set of specifications that generally describe what's going on, so you can jump around this section of the chapter if you want and find something you're interested in. Additionally, I'm not going to show you the entire program for each demo because you've already seen all the functions themselves. Rather, just the important stuff in the main loop will be listed. To compile any of these demos, you'll need the following files in addition to the main .CPP file of the demo:

```
T3DLIB1.CPP¦H

T3DLIB2.CPP¦H

T3DLIB3.CPP¦H

T3DLIB4.CPP¦H

T3DLIB5.CPP¦H

DDRAW.LIB

DSOUND.LIB
```

DINPUT.LIB

DINPUT8.LIB

And all the .PLG files that are located in this chapter's directory, of course.

Single 3D Triangle—DEMOII7_1.CPP|EXE

Object(s) Loaded: None; manual creation of single polygon

Type of Camera: Euler, fixed position, 90 degree FOV normalized viewplane

Type of Projection: Perspective followed by viewport mapping

Math Used for 3D Pipeline: All manual function calls, no transforms based on individual matrices

Back-face Removal: None

Object Removal: None

Type of Rendering Geometry: Render list with single polygon

DEMOII7_1.CPP|EXE is as basic as it gets. The program creates a single polygon, rotates it around the +y-axis, and that's it! Here are the important globals for the demo:

```
// initialize camera position and direction
POINT4D cam_pos = {0,0,-100,1};
VECTOR4D cam_dir = {0,0,0,1};

// all your initialization code goes here...
VECTOR4D vscale={.5,.5,.5,1}, vpos = {0,0,0,1}, vrot = {0,0,0,1};

CAM4DV1    cam;           // the single camera
RENDERLIST4DV1 rend_list;         // the single renderlist
POLYF4DV1   poly1;          // our lonely polygon
POINT4D    poly1_pos = {0,0,100,1}; // world position of polygon
```

And here's the 3D code in the Game_Init() function:

```
// initialize math engine
Build_Sin_Cos_Tables();

// initialize a single polygon
poly1.state = POLY4DV1_STATE_ACTIVE;
poly1.attr  = 0;
poly1.color = RGB16Bit(0,255,0);

poly1.vlist[0].x = 0;
poly1.vlist[0].y = 50;
```

```
poly1.vlist[0].z = 0;
poly1.vlist[0].w = 1;

poly1.vlist[1].x = 50;
poly1.vlist[1].y = -50;
poly1.vlist[1].z = 0;
poly1.vlist[1].w = 1;

poly1.vlist[2].x = -50;
poly1.vlist[2].y = -50;
poly1.vlist[2].z = 0;
poly1.vlist[2].w = 1;

poly1.next = poly1.prev = NULL;

// initialize the camera with 90 FOV, normalized coordinates
Init_CAM4DV1(&cam,    // the camera object
       &cam_pos, // initial camera position
       &cam_dir, // initial camera angles
       50.0,    // near and far clipping planes
       500.0,
       90.0,    // field of view in degrees
       1.0,     // viewing distance
       0,      // size of viewplane-1
       0,
       WINDOW_WIDTH,  // size of final screen viewport
       WINDOW_HEIGHT);
```

Finally, here's the main core of the Game_Main() function that performs the entire 3D pipeline and rendering of the triangle:

```
int Game_Main(void *parms)
{
// this is the workhorse of your game it will be called
// continuously in real-time this is like main() in C
// all the calls for you game go here!

static MATRIX4X4 mrot; // general rotation matrix
static float ang_y = 0;    // rotation angle

int index; // looping var

// start the timing clock
Start_Clock();
```

```
// clear the drawing surface
DDraw_Fill_Surface(lpddsback, 0);

// read keyboard and other devices here
DInput_Read_Keyboard();

// game logic here...

// initialize the renderlist
Reset_RENDERLIST4DV1(&rend_list);

// insert polygon into the renderlist
Insert_POLYF4DV1_RENDERLIST4DV1(&rend_list, &poly1);

// generate rotation matrix around y axis
Build_XYZ_Rotation_MATRIX4X4(0, ang_y, 0, &mrot);

// rotate polygon slowly
if (++ang_y >= 360.0) ang_y = 0;

// rotate the local coords of single polygon in renderlist
Transform_RENDERLIST4DV1(&rend_list, &mrot, TRANSFORM_LOCAL_ONLY);

// perform local/model to world transform
Model_To_World_RENDERLIST4DV1(&rend_list, &poly1_pos);

// generate camera matrix
Build_CAM4DV1_Matrix_Euler(&cam, CAM_ROT_SEQ_ZYX);

// apply world to camera transform
World_To_Camera_RENDERLIST4DV1(&rend_list, &cam);

// apply camera to perspective transformation
Camera_To_Perspective_RENDERLIST4DV1(&rend_list, &cam);

// apply screen transform
Perspective_To_Screen_RENDERLIST4DV1(&rend_list, &cam);

// lock the back buffer
DDraw_Lock_Back_Surface();

// render the polygon list
Draw_RENDERLIST4DV1_Wire16(&rend_list, back_buffer, back_lpitch);
```

7

```
// unlock the back buffer
DDraw_Unlock_Back_Surface();

// flip the surfaces
DDraw_Flip();

// sync to 30ish fps
Wait_Clock(30);

// check of user is trying to exit
if (KEY_DOWN(VK_ESCAPE) || keyboard_state[DIK_ESCAPE])
  {
  PostMessage(main_window_handle, WM_DESTROY,0,0);
  } // end if

// return success
return(1);

} // end Game_Main
```

Figure 7.20 is a screenshot of DEMOII7_1.EXE in action. Very exciting, as you can see! The main point of this demo is to show that with a dozen or so calls, we can create a full 3D wireframe display—that's nothing to laugh at.

FIGURE 7.20 Screenshot of DEMOII7_1.EXE.

3D Wireframe Cube—DEMOII7_2.CPP|EXE

Object(s) Loaded: Simple Cube (CUBE1.PLG)

Type of Camera: Euler, fixed position, 90 degree FOV normalized viewplane of 2x2 with viewport of 400x400

Type of Projection: Perspective followed by viewport mapping

Math Used for 3D Pipeline: All manual function calls; no transforms based on individual matrices

Back-face Removal: None

Object Removal: None

Type of Rendering Geometry: Object rendering, no render list

Now that you've see a single polygon rotating, let's do something a little more exciting, shall we? `DEMOII7_2.CPP|EXE` is similar to the previous demo, but this time we're going to use our mesh-loading software to load in the cube mesh `CUBE1.PLG` shown here:

```
# begin plg/plx file

# simple cube
tri 8 12

# vertex list
 5 5 5
-5 5 5
-5 5 -5
 5 5 -5
 5 -5 5
-5 -5 5
-5 -5 -5
 5 -5 -5


# polygon list
0xd0f0 3 2 1 0
0xd0f0 3 3 2 0
0xd0f0 3 4 7 0
0xd0f0 3 7 3 0
0xd0f0 3 6 7 4
0xd0f0 3 5 6 4
0xd0f0 3 2 6 1
0xd0f0 3 6 5 1
0xd0f0 3 7 6 3
0xd0f0 3 6 2 3
0xd0f0 3 5 4 0
0xd0f0 3 1 5 0
```

Basically, it's a 10x10x10 cube. After the mesh is loaded as an `OBJECT4DV1`, it's slowly rotated in the main loop and transformed down the 3D pipeline. However, we will NOT convert the cube into polygons and insert them into a render list; we'll leave the cube as an object so that you can see that it's possible to keep an object intact all the way down the pipeline.

Here are the important globals for the demo:

```
// initialize camera position and direction
POINT4D cam_pos = {0,0,0,1};
VECTOR4D cam_dir = {0,0,0,1};

// all your initialization code goes here...
VECTOR4D vscale={5.0,5.0,5.0,1}, vpos = {0,0,0,1}, vrot = {0,0,0,1};

CAM4DV1  cam;    // the single camera
OBJECT4DV1 obj;    // used to hold our cube mesh
```

Notice the value of `vscale`. Remember that this vector scales the mesh during loading; hence, the 10x10x10 cube will be scaled during loading to 50x50x50. Of course, we could have just changed the model itself, but that's the point of the flexibility in the loading function: to use the same model and transform it during loading to allow slight morphing of the mesh.

Now, let's look at the 3D part of the initialization code in `Game_Init()`. It's the same as before, but you'll see the object loaded:

```
// initialize the camera with 90 FOV, normalized coordinates
Init_CAM4DV1(&cam,     // the camera object
       &cam_pos, // initial camera position
       &cam_dir, // initial camera angles
       50.0,    // near and far clipping planes
       500.0,
       90.0,    // field of view in degrees
       WINDOW_WIDTH,  // size of final screen viewport
       WINDOW_HEIGHT);

// load the cube
Load_OBJECT4DV1_PLG(&obj, "cube1.plg",&vscale, &vpos, &vrot);

// set the position of the cube in the world
obj.world_pos.x = 0;
obj.world_pos.y = 0;
obj.world_pos.z = 100;
```

Note that the object is positioned 100 units from the origin of the world. This is so it looks really big and we get a lot of perspective. Finally, here's the Game_Main() so that you can see the pipeline calls:

```
int Game_Main(void *parms)
{
// this is the workhorse of your game it will be called
// continuously in real-time this is like main() in C
// all the calls for you game go here!

static MATRIX4X4 mrot; // general rotation matrix

int index; // looping var

// start the timing clock
Start_Clock();

// clear the drawing surface
DDraw_Fill_Surface(lpddsback, 0);

// read keyboard and other devices here
DInput_Read_Keyboard();

// game logic here...

// reset the object (this only matters for backface and object removal)
Reset_OBJECT4DV1(&obj);

// generate rotation matrix around y axis
Build_XYZ_Rotation_MATRIX4X4(0, 5, 0, &mrot);

// rotate the local coords of single polygon in renderlist
Transform_OBJECT4DV1(&obj, &mrot, TRANSFORM_LOCAL_ONLY,1);

// perform local/model to world transform
Model_To_World_OBJECT4DV1(&obj);

// generate camera matrix
Build_CAM4DV1_Matrix_Euler(&cam, CAM_ROT_SEQ_ZYX);
```

```
// apply world to camera transform
World_To_Camera_OBJECT4DV1(&obj, &cam);

// apply camera to perspective transformation
Camera_To_Perspective_OBJECT4DV1(&obj, &cam);

// apply screen transform
Perspective_To_Screen_OBJECT4DV1(&obj, &cam);

// lock the back buffer
DDraw_Lock_Back_Surface();

// render the object
Draw_OBJECT4DV1_Wire16(&obj, back_buffer, back_lpitch);

// unlock the back buffer
DDraw_Unlock_Back_Surface();

// flip the surfaces
DDraw_Flip();

// sync to 30ish fps
Wait_Clock(30);

// check of user is trying to exit
if (KEY_DOWN(VK_ESCAPE) || keyboard_state[DIK_ESCAPE])
  {
  PostMessage(main_window_handle, WM_DESTROY,0,0);

  } // end if

// return success
return(1);

} // end Game_Main
```

Again, only a dozen or so important calls and we have an entire 3D demo up and running! Figure 7.21 is a screenshot of `DEMOII7_2.EXE` in action. Notice the amount of perspective. This is due to the field of view and the proximity of the object to the viewpoint.

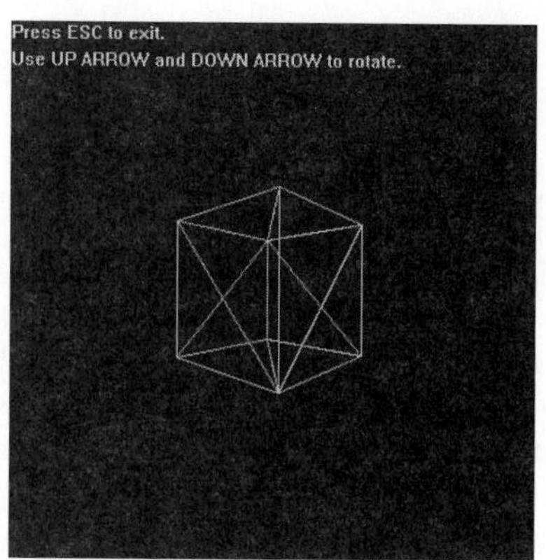

FIGURE 7.21 Screenshot of DEMOII7_2.EXE.

3D Wireframe Cube with Back-face Removal—DEMOII7_3.CPP¦EXE

Object(s) Loaded: Simple cube (CUBE2.PLG)

Type of Camera: Euler, fixed position, 90 degree FOV normalized viewplane of -1/ar to +1/ar with viewport of 640x480

Type of Projection: Perspective followed by viewport mapping

Math Used for 3D Pipeline: All manual function calls; no transforms based on individual matrices

Back-face Removal: Enabled

Object Removal: None

Type of Rendering Geometry: Object rendering; no render list

DEMOII7_3.CPP¦EXE is identical to DEMOII7_2.CPP¦EXE except that back-face removal has been enabled along with a larger viewport. Additionally, to make back-face removal work, we need to take a couple things into consideration. The first is in the model mesh itself. Remember that when loading a mesh, a polygon can be one- or two-sided. If it's one-sided, back-face removal makes sense. But if it's two-sided, it doesn't make sense because we can see the polygon from both sides. Now, in wireframe mode, it's obviously less important to have back-face removal, but we can still enable it in the mesh data if we like. The second thing we have to do is, of course, test for a back-face during the 3D pipeline somewhere after the world transform, but before the camera transform.

First, let's check to see whether back-faces were enabled in the CUBE1.PLG mesh data. Here's one of the polygon descriptor lines from the file:

```
# polygon list
0xd0f0 3 2 1 0 # polygon 0
```

The first number is the polygon descriptor, and if you recall from the code in the previous section on loading .PLG/.PLX files, the D bit in the 16-bit surface descriptor defines whether the polygon is two-sided or not:

```
CSSD ¦ RRRR¦ GGGG ¦ BBBB
```

In other words, the D bit is the lower bit of the leftmost hex digit. In the case of this surface descriptor, the digit is hex 0xD, which is 1101b in binary; therefore, the two-sided flag is on! We must disable it. To do so, we'll need another .PLG file, so I've created one and called it `CUBE2.PLG`. It's on the CD and has this bit reset, so the descriptor looks like 1100b, or 0xC in hex. The analogous polygon descriptor in the preceding example would now be

```
# polygon list
0xc0f0 3 2 1 0 # polygon 0
```

To remove the back-faces, a call is made to

```
// remove backfaces
Remove_Backfaces_OBJECT4DV1(&obj, &cam);
```

This call is made after the camera matrix is created for the viewing angles, but before the general world-to-camera transformation takes place. The call is placed at this particular point so that polygons that are not visible aren't transformed during the world-to-camera transformation.

Figure 7.22 is a screenshot of `DEMOII7_3.EXE` in action. Try pressing the up and down arrow keys and watch the cube rotate around the x-axis.

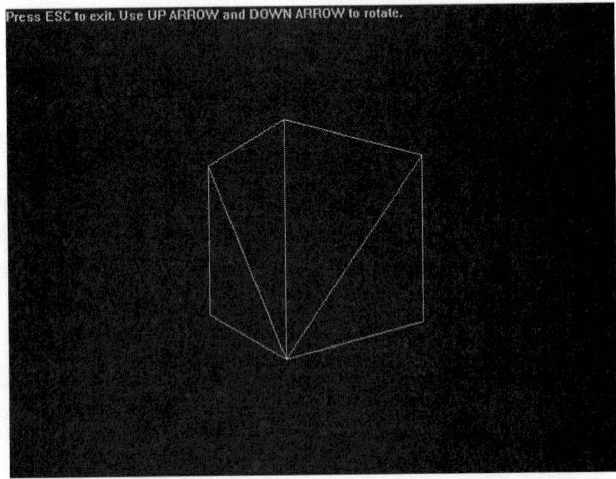

FIGURE 7.22 Screenshot of `DEMOII7_3.EXE`.

3D Tank Demo—DEMOII7_4.CPP¦EXE

Object(s) Loaded: Simple tank (TANK1.PLG)

Type of Camera: Euler, rotatable, 90 degree FOV normalized viewplane of -1/ar to +1/ar with viewport of 400x400

Type of Projection: Perspective followed by viewport mapping

Math Used for 3D Pipeline: All manual function calls; no transforms based on individual matrices

Back-face Removal: Disabled

Object Removal: Yes

Type of Rendering Geometry: Render list with multiple objects inserted

Figure 7.23 depicts the hard-hitting 3D gaming action of DEMOII7_4.CPP! Well, at least there's some tanks in there <BG>. Anyway, this is a fairly complex demo. The camera is set up as usual, the tank object is loaded, and the demo proceeds into the main loop.

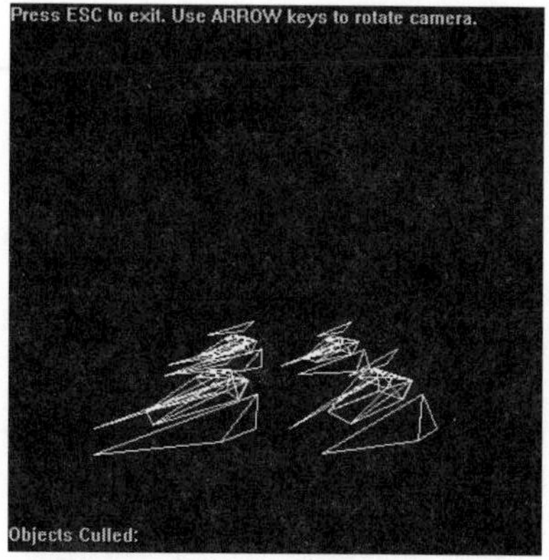

FIGURE 7.23 Screenshot of DEMOII7_4.EXE.

The interesting thing about this demo is how I created multiple copies of the tank: Instead of loading multiple tanks, I simply changed the position of the master tank and then inserted it into the master rendering list multiple times. Hence, the tank's polygons at a particular world position are transformed and then inserted into the rendering list, making it seem like there are multiple tanks. When the world-to-camera and perspective transformations are performed on the rendering list, we have multiple tanks! Here's an excerpt from the program that demonstrates the important parts of the main loop; I've bolded the copy/insertion code:

```
int Game_Main(void *parms)
{
// this is the workhorse of your game it will be called
```

```
// continuously in real-time this is like main() in C
// all the calls for you game go here!

static MATRIX4X4 mrot; // general rotation matrix
static float x_ang = 0, y_ang = 5, z_ang = 0;
char work_string[256];

int index; // looping var

// start the timing clock
Start_Clock();

// clear the drawing surface
DDraw_Fill_Surface(lpddsback, 0);

// read keyboard and other devices here
DInput_Read_Keyboard();

// game logic here...

// reset the render list
Reset_RENDERLIST4DV1(&rend_list);

// reset angles
x_ang = 0;
y_ang = 1;
z_ang = 0;

// is user trying to rotate camera
if (KEY_DOWN(VK_DOWN))
  cam.dir.x+=1;
else
if (KEY_DOWN(VK_UP))
  cam.dir.x-=1;

// is user trying to rotate camera
if (KEY_DOWN(VK_RIGHT))
  cam.dir.y-=1;
else
if (KEY_DOWN(VK_LEFT))
  cam.dir.y+=1;

// generate rotation matrix around y axis
Build_XYZ_Rotation_MATRIX4X4(x_ang, y_ang, z_ang, &mrot);
```

```
// rotate the local coords of the object
Transform_OBJECT4DV1(&obj, &mrot, TRANSFORM_LOCAL_ONLY,1);

// now cull the current object
strcpy(buffer,"Objects Culled: ");

for (int x=-NUM_OBJECTS/2; x < NUM_OBJECTS/2; x++)
  for (int z=-NUM_OBJECTS/2; z < NUM_OBJECTS/2; z++)
  {
  // reset the object (this only matters for backface and object removal)
  Reset_OBJECT4DV1(&obj);

  // set position of object
  obj.world_pos.x = x*OBJECT_SPACING+OBJECT_SPACING/2;
  obj.world_pos.y = 0;
  obj.world_pos.z = 500+z*OBJECT_SPACING+OBJECT_SPACING/2;

  // attempt to cull object
  if (!Cull_OBJECT4DV1(&obj, &cam, CULL_OBJECT_XYZ_PLANES))
    {
    // if we get here then the object is visible at this world position
    // so we can insert it into the rendering list
    // perform local/model to world transform
    Model_To_World_OBJECT4DV1(&obj);

    // insert the object into render list
    Insert_OBJECT4DV1_RENDERLIST4DV1(&rend_list, &obj);
    } // end if
  else
    {
    sprintf(work_string, "[%d, %d] ", x,z);
    strcat(buffer, work_string);
    }

  } // end for

Draw_Text_GDI(buffer, 0, WINDOW_HEIGHT-20, RGB(0,255,0), lpddsback);

// generate camera matrix
Build_CAM4DV1_Matrix_Euler(&cam, CAM_ROT_SEQ_ZYX);

// remove backfaces
Remove_Backfaces_RENDERLIST4DV1(&rend_list, &cam);
```

```
// apply world to camera transform
World_To_Camera_RENDERLIST4DV1(&rend_list, &cam);

// apply camera to perspective transformation
Camera_To_Perspective_RENDERLIST4DV1(&rend_list, &cam);

// apply screen transform
Perspective_To_Screen_RENDERLIST4DV1(&rend_list, &cam);

// draw instructions
Draw_Text_GDI("Press ESC to exit. Use ARROW keys to rotate camera.",
       0, 0, RGB(0,255,0), lpddsback);

// lock the back buffer
DDraw_Lock_Back_Surface();

// render the object
Draw_RENDERLIST4DV1_Wire16(&rend_list, back_buffer, back_lpitch);

// unlock the back buffer
DDraw_Unlock_Back_Surface();

// flip the surfaces
DDraw_Flip();

// sync to 30ish fps
Wait_Clock(30);

// check of user is trying to exit
if (KEY_DOWN(VK_ESCAPE) || keyboard_state[DIK_ESCAPE])
  {
  PostMessage(main_window_handle, WM_DESTROY,0,0);

  } // end if

// return success
return(1);

} // end Game_Main
```

Now you see why having a rendering list is so important, and is a better way to approach rendering than rendering separate objects themselves. Having objects is fine for transformations, animation, AI, logic, and so on, but once the rendering phase starts, it's better to simply decompose objects into polygons (after object culling) and then insert the polygons into a master list.

3D Tanks Demo with Flying Camera—DEMOII7_5.CPP¦EXE

Object(s) Loaded: Simple tank (TANK1.PLG)

Type of Camera: UVN, rotatable, 90 degree FOV normalized viewplane of -1/ar to +1/ar with viewport of 800x600, full-screen

Type of Projection: Perspective followed by viewport mapping

Math Used for 3D Pipeline: All manual function calls; no transforms based on individual matrices

Back-face Removal: Disabled

Object Removal: Yes

Type of Rendering Geometry: Render list with multiple objects inserted

FIGURE 7.24 Screenshot of DEMOII7_5.EXE.

Figure 7.24 is a screenshot of the most complex demo yet. I was shooting for a clone-wars-attack kind of thing! Anyway, this demo uses the UVN camera model, so the only thing that's really different from the other demos is the call to `Build_CAM4DV1_Matrix_UVN()` rather than the Euler function call. Moreover, the `UVN_MODE_SIMPLE` parameter is used, which tells the camera function that we're supplying only the target position manually.

Thus the function blindly computes the **u**,**v**,**n** vectors without further ado. The `Game_Main()` is very similar to the previous demo, but has a couple of interesting points: the computation of the camera position and, of course, the UVN camera model. Here's the code that positions the camera:

```
// compute new camera position, rides on a circular path
// with a sinuoid modulation
cam.pos.x = camera_distance*Fast_Cos(view_angle);
cam.pos.y = camera_distance*Fast_Sin(view_angle);
cam.pos.z = 2*camera_distance*Fast_Sin(view_angle);

// advance angle to circle around
if ((view_angle+=1)>=360)
  view_angle = 0;

// generate camera matrix
Build_CAM4DV1_Matrix_UVN(&cam, UVN_MODE_SIMPLE);
```

As you can see, there's not much to it! Figure 7.25 depicts the world setup and what's happening. This is a good example of very simple math creating a very interesting camera motion. In this case, I have a circular path for the camera (or elliptical, depending on the multiplication factors), along with bouncing the height of the camera above the x-z plane along a sine wave. The effect is a very nice camera motion. However, realize that this kind of camera control is possible only because we're using the UVN model. The UVN model gives the control we need in this case because it's well suited for the case in which you have a point of interest you want to "look at" and a camera position, which is the case in this demo. I position the camera on the circular ring surrounding the target, which is the center of the tank army, and that's it!

The interesting thing about this camera model is that it's great for viewing the action from a third-person perspective. That is, using the camera position and a target works when you want to look at some point of interest, and you want the math to figure out the UVN vectors, which in turn compute the rotation matrix. However, the second construction we developed for the UVN model (that is, where we give the camera position, but instead of a target we select the elevation and heading), works much better for a first-person game where you want to see through the character's eyes. Let's do a final demo using that technique and the spherical camera system plugged into the UVN model.

Battle Zone Walkthrough Demo—DEMOII7_6.CPP¦EXE

Object(s) Loaded: Tank (TANK1.PLG), Tower (TOWER1.PLG)

Type of Camera: Euler with heading, rotatable, 120 degree FOV normalized viewplane of -1/ar to +1/ar with viewport of 800x600, full-screen

Type of Projection: Perspective followed by viewport mapping

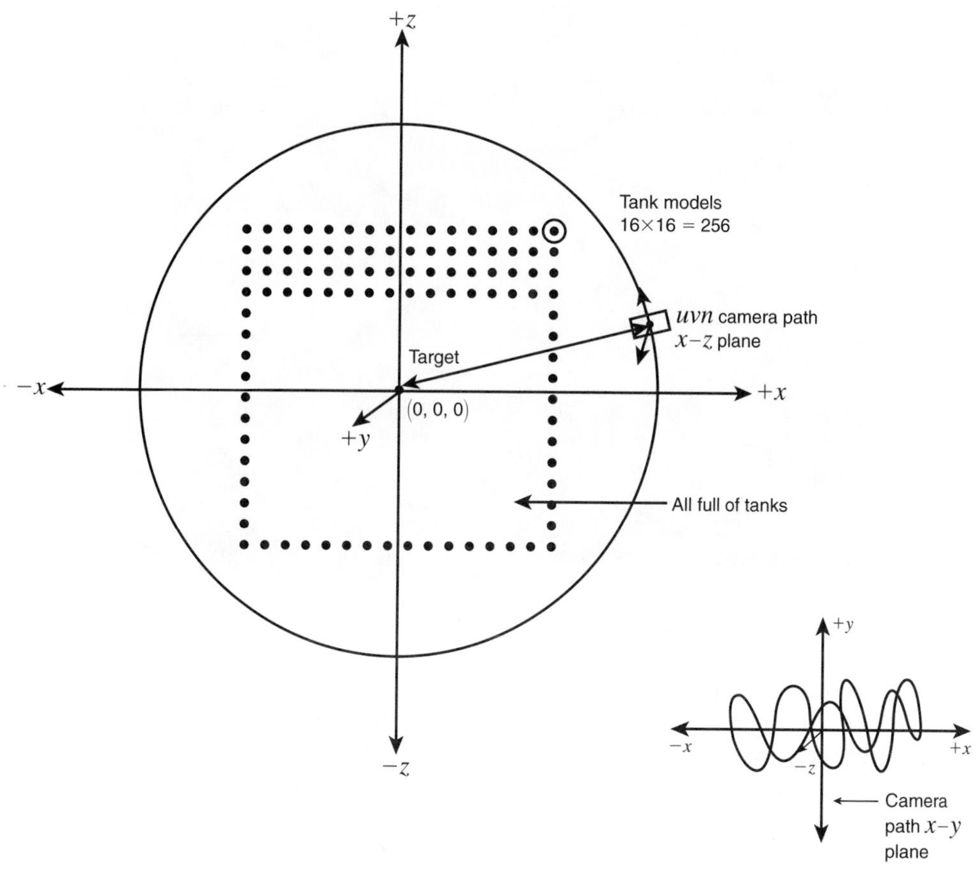

FIGURE 7.25 World setup for the demo.

Math Used for 3D Pipeline: All manual function calls; no transforms based on individual matrices

Back-face Removal: Disabled

Object Removal: Yes

Type of Rendering Geometry: Render list with multiple objects inserted

This is the coolest demo yet! Basically, the demo puts everything we have seen together and has a few game programming tricks thrown in. The demo consists of three object types: towers, tanks, and ground markers. Because we're still using wireframe rendering, it's difficult to create a feeling for depth, so I added a large number of regularly placed small pyramids all over the game arena to create a sense of a ground plane. Additionally, there's a sky and ground created with two blitter-filled rectangles. See Figure 7.26.

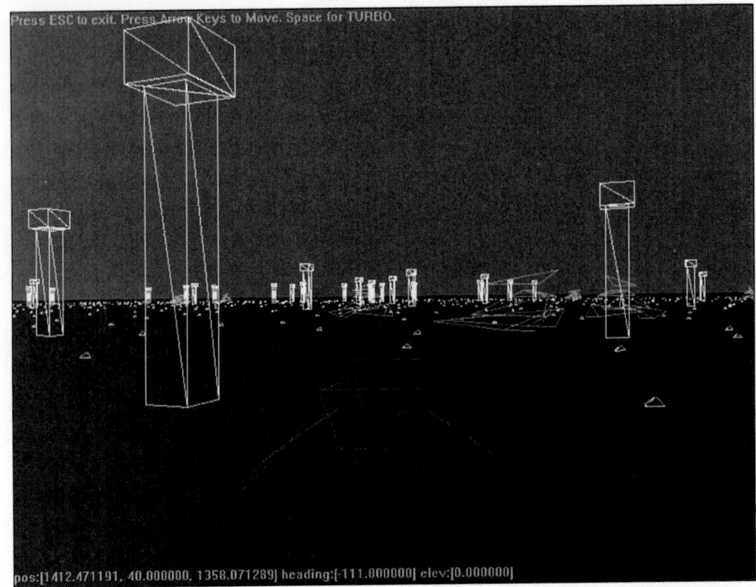

FIGURE 7.26 Screenshot of DEMOII7_6.EXE.

The important parts of the demo to review are how multiple objects are once again easily created by transforming a master object, and then inserting the transformed version into the rendering list without destroying the original. Of course, you need to keep track of the copies' positions and orientations, but that's nothing more than a couple of arrays of vectors. Now what I would like to do is describe the various elements of the demo and how they work. I'm going to excerpt code from the various parts of the demo because it's too long to list.

Loading and Initializing the Objects

As I said, there are three different types of objects: tanks, towers, and markers. All of them have what I call a *master object* that holds the original. I have secondary data structures to hold the unique information of the copies (which in this case is nothing more that position, because nothing is really moving). Here's the code that loads in and sets up the objects. Notice the scaling I performed to each mesh; sometimes it's necessary to tweak things like this.

```
// load the master tank object
VECTOR4D_INITXYZ(&vscale,0.75,0.75,0.75);
Load_OBJECT4DV1_PLG(&obj_tank, "tank2.plg",&vscale, &vpos, &vrot);

// load player object for 3rd person view
VECTOR4D_INITXYZ(&vscale,0.75,0.75,0.75);
Load_OBJECT4DV1_PLG(&obj_player, "tank3.plg",&vscale, &vpos, &vrot);
```

```
// load the master tower object
VECTOR4D_INITXYZ(&vscale,1.0, 2.0, 1.0);
Load_OBJECT4DV1_PLG(&obj_tower, "tower1.plg",&vscale, &vpos, &vrot);

// load the master ground marker
VECTOR4D_INITXYZ(&vscale,3.0,3.0,3.0);
Load_OBJECT4DV1_PLG(&obj_marker, "marker1.plg",&vscale, &vpos, &vrot);

// position the tanks
for (index = 0; index < NUM_TANKS; index++)
  {
  // randomly position the tanks
  tanks[index].x = RAND_RANGE(-UNIVERSE_RADIUS, UNIVERSE_RADIUS);
  tanks[index].y = 0; // obj_tank.max_radius;
  tanks[index].z = RAND_RANGE(-UNIVERSE_RADIUS, UNIVERSE_RADIUS);
  tanks[index].w = RAND_RANGE(0,360);
  } // end for


// position the towers
for (index = 0; index < NUM_TOWERS; index++)
  {
  // randomly position the tower
  towers[index].x = RAND_RANGE(-UNIVERSE_RADIUS, UNIVERSE_RADIUS);
  towers[index].y = 0; // obj_tower.max_radius;
  towers[index].z = RAND_RANGE(-UNIVERSE_RADIUS, UNIVERSE_RADIUS);
  } // end for
```


The Camera System

The camera is fairly simple. It's a Euler model that does nothing more than move around the game field, along with rotating parallel to the y axis. I also could have changed the angle relative to the x axis or the elevation, but the horizon is artificial and I would have had to compute where the artificial horizon rectangles would change when the elevation in 3D changed—too much of a pain! Anyway, here's the code that moves the camera around. Pay attention to the variable `turning`; it's used for an effect.

```
// allow user to move camera

// turbo
if (keyboard_state[DIK_SPACE])
  tank_speed = 5*TANK_SPEED;
```

```
else
  tank_speed = TANK_SPEED;

// forward/backward
if (keyboard_state[DIK_UP])
  {
  // move forward
  cam.pos.x += tank_speed*Fast_Sin(cam.dir.y);
  cam.pos.z += tank_speed*Fast_Cos(cam.dir.y);
  } // end if

if (keyboard_state[DIK_DOWN])
  {
  // move backward
  cam.pos.x -= tank_speed*Fast_Sin(cam.dir.y);
  cam.pos.z -= tank_speed*Fast_Cos(cam.dir.y);
  } // end if

// rotate
if (keyboard_state[DIK_RIGHT])
  {
  cam.dir.y+=3;

  // add a little turn to object
  if ((turning+=2) > 15)
   turning=15;

  } // end if

if (keyboard_state[DIK_LEFT])
  {
  cam.dir.y-=3;

  // add a little turn to object
  if ((turning-=2) < -15)
   turning=-15;

  } // end if
else // center heading again
  {
  if (turning > 0)
    turning-=1;
  else
```

```
  if (turning < 0)
    turning+=1;

  } // end else

// generate camera matrix
Build_CAM4DV1_Matrix_Euler(&cam, CAM_ROT_SEQ_ZYX);
```

That's basically the entire camera code. It's pretty straightforward. Depending on the keys being pressed, the camera position is moved along a vector based on its current heading or y-axis angle, and remember we are in the x-z, so that's why you see this code to move the camera:

```
cam.pos.x += tank_speed*Fast_Sin(cam.dir.y);
cam.pos.z += tank_speed*Fast_Cos(cam.dir.y);
```

Additionally, rotation of the camera is nothing more than updating the `cam.dir.y` variable because it's used by the camera construction call at the end of the code listing. Now the interesting thing is the variable `turning` and how it's used. If you play with the demo, you'll see a tank copy in front of the view screen. This of course represents you, but when you turn right or left, the tank model slowly turns and then turns back to straight when you let off the arrow keys. This is achieved by using the variable `turning` to track the state of the turn in a sense. When the player turns, I let the angle accumulate in the direction of the turn up to some value (15 degrees, in this case) and then it tops out. When the player stops turning, the tank centers itself again. This is a very cool effect used in many racing-type games with a third-person perspective and it takes only a few lines of code. Of course, in a real physics-based simulation, the physics model would do this, but for our purposes, it works fine at this point.

7

Generating the Game Arena

The game arena is composed of a number of static objects. These objects are copied from master objects and placed at static positions in the game arena. The code for each object basically performs a simple repositioning of the master object and then transforms the master and inserts it into the master polygon rendering list (a cull operation is attempted). The beauty of the system is that the originals are not destroyed. Because only the transformed vertices are used, the original models stay intact. I have two copies of vertices in the object for just such occasions. Here's the code that for example inserts all the tower models into the world:

```
// insert the towers in the world
for (index = 0; index < NUM_TOWERS; index++)
  {
  // reset the object (this only matters for backface and object removal)
  Reset_OBJECT4DV1(&obj_tower);
```

```
// set position of tower
obj_tower.world_pos.x = towers[index].x;
obj_tower.world_pos.y = towers[index].y;
obj_tower.world_pos.z = towers[index].z;

// attempt to cull object
if (!Cull_OBJECT4DV1(&obj_tower, &cam, CULL_OBJECT_XYZ_PLANES))
  {
  // if we get here then the object is visible at this world position
  // so we can insert it into the rendering list
  // perform local/model to world transform
  Model_To_World_OBJECT4DV1(&obj_tower);

  // insert the object into render list
  Insert_OBJECT4DV1_RENDERLIST4DV1(&rend_list, &obj_tower);
  } // end if

} // end for
```

Almost too easy, huh? Lastly, let's look at the player insertion model.

Rendering the Player's Tank Model

The engine we have so far isn't very advanced. Although we have a camera, it's not like we can attach the camera to an object and have it tag along. We must do this manually. Alas, in this demo, the position of the camera is known, so what I do is based on the heading of the camera. I draw a vector and then move the tank model out ahead a good distance (400 units approximately) and drop it down from the camera height a little. Then I rotate the tank model (which is a separate model from the one used by the object placer) based on the current viewing angle, transform the tank based on this information, place it in world coordinates and presto—we have a tank that looks like it's us!

The code that does all this magic is rather short:

```
// insert the player into the world
// reset the object (this only matters for backface and object removal)
Reset_OBJECT4DV1(&obj_player);

// set position of tank
obj_player.world_pos.x = cam.pos.x+400*Fast_Sin(cam.dir.y);
obj_player.world_pos.y = cam.pos.y-50;
obj_player.world_pos.z = cam.pos.z+400*Fast_Cos(cam.dir.y);

// generate rotation matrix around y axis
Build_XYZ_Rotation_MATRIX4X4(0, cam.dir.y+turning, 0, &mrot);
```

```
// rotate the local coords of the object
Transform_OBJECT4DV1(&obj_player, &mrot, TRANSFORM_LOCAL_TO_TRANS,1);

// perform world transform
Model_To_World_OBJECT4DV1(&obj_player, TRANSFORM_TRANS_ONLY);

// insert the object into render list
Insert_OBJECT4DV1_RENDERLIST4DV1(&rend_list, &obj_player);
```

Notice the bolded code. That's where I've added in the slight turning angle along with the current heading to create the effect of a turn.

NOTE

Although I've been using 16-bit graphics for most of the demos, the sad truth is that when we do more serious shaded and textured graphics, it's going to be very hard to keep a decent fill rate with software rasterization and 16-bit graphics. So, we'll do a lot of work with 8-bit modes to get more speed and to see the types of optimizations that can be used with paletted color modes.

Summary

Once again, I think I have worn the fingerprints off my fingers, but it's worth it, baby! There's so much to learn. Sure, you can learn just what you need to make a 3D engine, but I like knowing all the details and all the different ways to do things—I hope you agree. Anyway, we covered a lot of ground in this chapter, such as 3D data structures, loading objects off disk, the local-to-world transform, the world-to-camera transform, the camera-to-perspective transform, the screen transform, object culling, back-face removal, when to use 4D coordinates, why matrices aren't always the best way to perform transforms, rendering objects in wireframe, and finally the UVN camera model and a whole lot of demos! Now, it's time to make our 3D object a little more realistic with shading and lighting. Also, we need to handle 3D clipping because we can't avoid it too much longer. And we definitely need a better model loader!

PART III

Basic 3D Rendering

IN THIS PART

CHAPTER **8**

Basic Lighting and Solid Modeling

IN THIS CHAPTER

- Basic Lighting Models for Computer Graphics
- Lighting and Rasterizing Triangles
- Shading in the Real World
- Depth Sorting and the Painter's Algorithm
- Working with New Model Formats
- 3D Modeling Tools Review

"How's about now?"

—Tom Cruise, *Minority Report*

In this chapter, we are going to increase the amount of realism in a 3D scene by rendering objects as solids rather than wireframe. This means we have to cover shading and lighting. Additionally, the concept of back-face culling comes into play much more than in the wireframe case because we can no longer see through objects. In this chapter, we're going to discuss general lighting and shading and implement both 8-bit and 16-bit versions of everything. We're also going to revamp our little PLG/PLX file loader and support other formats so that we don't have to create models ourselves manually. Finally, this chapter will mix both the theoretical and the practical, but we won't leverage much of the theoretical until later chapters. Nevertheless, it's nice to start thinking about it now. Anyhow, here's the hit list:

- Basic lighting models
- Ambient light
- Diffuse light
- Specular lighting
- Directional lights
- Point lights
- Spotlights

- Rasterizing triangles
- Bit depth considerations for lighting
- Constant shading
- Flat shading
- Gouraud shading
- Phong shading
- Depth sorting
- Loading models

Basic Lighting Models for Computer Graphics

Lighting is a huge topic in computer graphics; it's the study of photons and the interaction with matter, more or less. Photons are, of course, pure energy that have both a wave and particle nature to them. Photons can have position and velocity (the particle aspect), as well as frequency (the wave aspect). Figure 8.1 depicts a chart of light and the various frequencies ranges of infrared, visible light, ultraviolet, X-rays, and so forth. Of course, all light travels at the speed of light (that's a bit redundant), which is referred to as *c* and is, more or less equal to

186,300 miles/sec or 3.0 x 10^8 meters/sec

And the relationship between frequency (measured in hertz) of light F, and the wave length λ (measured in meters) is

FORMULA 8.1 The Relationship Between Frequency and Wave Length

$$F = c / \lambda$$

For example, bright red, which is about 700 nm (nanometers 10^{-9} meters), has a frequency of

$$F = 3.0\times10^{8} \text{ m/s} / 700 \times 10^{-9} \text{ m} = 4.286 \times 10^{14} \text{ Hz}$$

You might think that light speed is fast, but it's terribly slow if you're trying to get somewhere in space. However, it *is* possible to go faster than the speed of light; one simply cannot accelerate to the speed of light because it would take infinite energy, but that's another story...

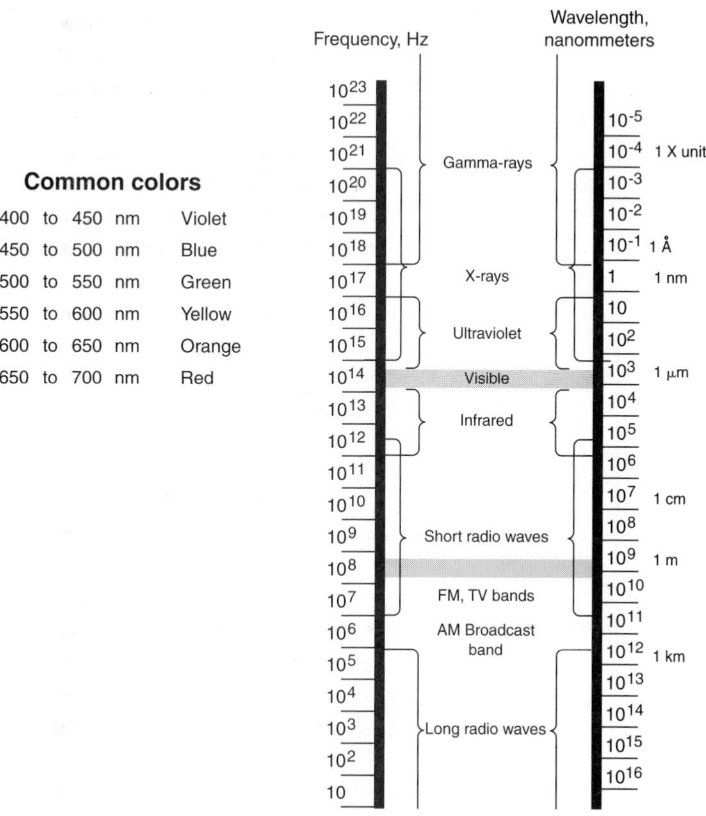

FIGURE 8.1 The electromagnetic light spectrum.

So, the color of light has to do with the frequency or wavelength. That's reasonable, but what about the intensity of light? Well, intensity has to do with the photons per second. Brightness is just the number of photons per second striking a surface, so the total energy per second a surface S absorbs is

$$\text{Energy/sec} = e_{photon}(\lambda) * \text{photons/sec}$$

Where the energy per photon is a function of the photon's frequency.

Of course, most 3D graphics engines don't rely on the use of real photons or real matter, but the models we use are getting there. Nearly all 3D rendering packages *ray trace*, which is the process of tracing single rays of light or photons from the view point through a scene, determining where they intersect the geometry of the scene, and then, based on this, coloring the pixel on the screen. Figure 8.2 illustrates this process with a couple of simple objects, and Figure 8.3 shows a ray-traced environment (notice the shadows, reflections, and shiny spots).

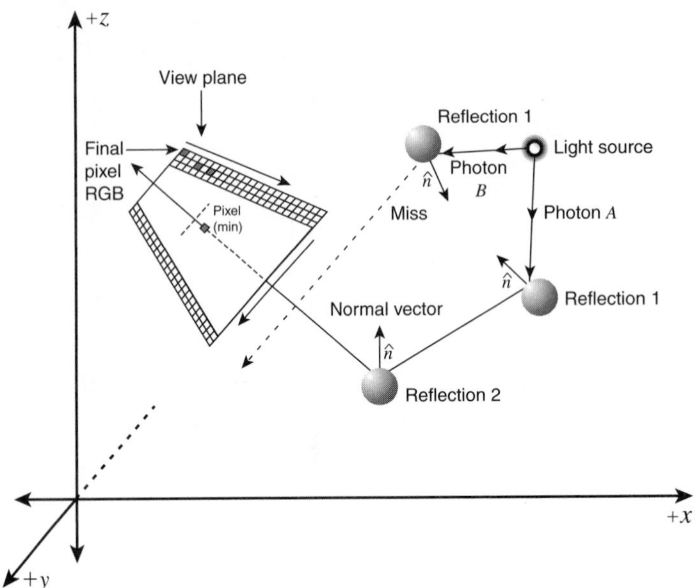

FIGURE 8.2 The physics of ray tracing.

FIGURE 8.3 A ray-traced scene.

Additionally, there are techniques that I'm sure you have heard of, such as *photon mapping*, *radiosity*, and others that simulate and model the interactions of energy or photons in a scene in a more complex manner. The point of these techniques is to create a scene where the lighting is as close to reality as possible.

Although we're interested in photo-realistic rendering as much as possible, there are limits depending on the hardware and software constraints you're working with. In our case, because we're creating a software-based engine, our lighting models can't be as complex as engines that are hardware based. However, that's the fun: to see how far we can push the software engine to perform real-time lighting. Based on this, our understanding of lighting becomes much deeper, which enables us to push hardware much more with techniques such as pixel and vertex shaders because we know what's what. So, let's get down to details, shall we?

Color Models and Materials

The material that an object is made of determines the way that light will interact with it when photons strike it. For example, say that white light (composed of all visible frequencies) strikes a surface. The surface will, in general, have a number of properties that determine the interactions that the light has. Some of the light is reflected from the surface; the color that's reflected defines the color of the object; the light that isn't reflected is absorbed by the surface. Also, it's possible that the object isn't completely opaque and that some of the light will be transmitted through the object or refracted. Finally, the act of the photons striking the material may cause it to emit light via fluorescence or phosphorescence. Moreover, all of these properties might be wavelength or intensity related. Thus, modeling the interaction a material has with light can be a big job. Usually, we model materials with a few parameters such as its reflectance, dispersion, specularity, and emissivity, and so forth.

Moving on to more practical concepts, you know that colors on the screen of a computer are usually represented in RGB or an indexed format for 8-bit colors. But, for this discussion, let's focus on RGB formats where each channel is represented by some value such as 0 to 1, or maybe 0 to 255, and so forth. For example, in a 24-bit RGB format, there would be 8 bits per channel, so pure red would be (255,0,0).

Conversely, in a floating-point format where each channel is represented by values from 0...1, pure red would be (1.0, 0.0, 0.0). Both are the same color. However, the floating-point format might be easier to work with than the byte-valued format for mathematical operations. But, on the other hand, the byte-valued format might be faster because the values can be directly written to the video buffer without conversion from floating point. In either case, let's look at a couple of operations we can perform to colors: addition and modulation.

8

Color Addition

Given RGB colors C1(r1, g1, b1) and C2(r2, g2, b2), we can add them together like this:

$C_{sum} = C1 + C2 = (r1 + r2, g1 + g2, b1 + b2)$

However, there's a problem with this, and that's *overflow*. No matter what representation we use for the colors, if we add two components, where their sum is larger than the maximum value per channel, we must clamp the results. Alas, if we're using a (0..255) 8-bit representation and we added colors C1 and C2, we would need to clamp the output of each channel as shown here:

C_{sum} = C1 + C2 = (MAX(r1 + r2, 255),

MAX(g1 + g2, 255),

MAX(b1 + b2, 255))

where MAX(x,y) simply returns the maximum of x,y.

This way we're guaranteed that the values never exceed 255, which could be disastrous because the values would overflow and wrap around in most cases, giving completely erroneous results.

Color Modulation

The next interesting process is color modulation, which is basically multiplication. Let's start with a simple example of scalar multiplication of our first color C1 by the value s:

$C_{modulated}$ = s*C1 = (s*r1, s*g1, s*b1)

In this case, s can be any number from 0 to infinity. A scale of 1.0 will leave the color unchanged, whereas a scale of 2.0 will brighten the color two times. A scale of .1 will make the color 1/10th as bright and so on. However, we must again be careful of overflow and clamp the results to 1.0, or 255, or whatever, depending on our final color representation. As an example of this color scaling by a uniform factor, try `DEMOII8_1.CPP|EXE`. By pressing the up and down arrow keys, you'll scale the brightness of the displayed texture by modulating the texture pixels. Also, you can change the texture with the right and left arrow keys. Notice how if you modulate the brightness too much, the texture will saturate various RGB channels and thus will distort. There's a way to fix this. During the modulation phase test, if any channel is already at maximum value (255, for example), leave the pixel alone. Increasing the other channels in this particular pixel will change the color because the channels will change and their ratios will not remain as they were.

This first form of modulation is really just brightness scaling; the second form of modulation I want to cover is straight RGB multiplication. In this case, we simply multiply two colors together; that is, color C1 modulates color C2 as shown here:

$C_{modulated}$ = C1*C2 = (r1*r2, g1*g2, b1*b2)

Now, color multiplication is a bit tricky. We have to agree on what we mean by *multiplication*. For example, if C1 is RGB format (0..1, 0..1, 0..1), of the format that C2 is in is irrelevant; the results will not overflow and C1 will basically intensity modulate C2. This is exactly how light mapping works. A given light texture named `LIGHT_TEXTURE[x][y]` is interpreted as light values from (0..1) for each pixel, which is then multiplied against a color texture `COLOR_TEXTURE[x][y]`. The results of this are shown in Figure 8.4. There we see a spotlight texture that represents the light texture we want to modulate the color texture with (notice that the light texture is monochrome). The results of the modulation are also shown. The only problem with modulation like this is that the results aren't always what you expect, so a more complex modulation pipeline might be needed. For example, we might want to do something like this:

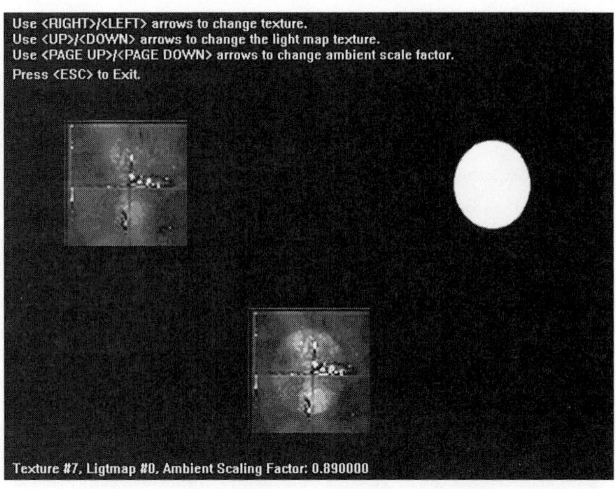

FIGURE 8.4 Light modulation in action.

FORMULA 8.2a Pixel Shading with Additive Component as Well as Modulation

$$\texttt{Pixel\_dest}[x,y]_{rgb} = \texttt{pixel\_source}[x,y]_{rgb} * \texttt{ambient} + \texttt{pixel\_source}[x,y]_{rgb} * \texttt{light\_map}[x,y]_{rgb}$$

FORMULA 8.2b Pixel Shading with Simpler Additive Modulation (looks better and is faster)

$$\texttt{Pixel\_dest}[x,y]_{rgb} = \texttt{pixel\_source}[x,y]_{rgb} + \texttt{ambient} * \texttt{light\_map}[x,y]_{rgb}$$

NOTE

The notation [x][y] simply means for all x,y of the image, and the subscript rgb means that the process must be done separately for each channel—red, green, and blue.

The earlier formula basically says that for each pixel in the texture map, we take a percentage of it and add that to the texture map modulated by the lighting texture. Figure 8.5 illustrates this process. As you can see, the results are a little brighter than straight modulation. Basically we're adding in the base texture as well as modulating it. The ambient term is simply a scalar that controls how much of the texture is added to the results, or in other words, how much of the texture we see in the output. Also, it turns out that Formula 8.2b looks a lot better in real life; that is, simply adding the light map (with a scaling factor) to the source map.

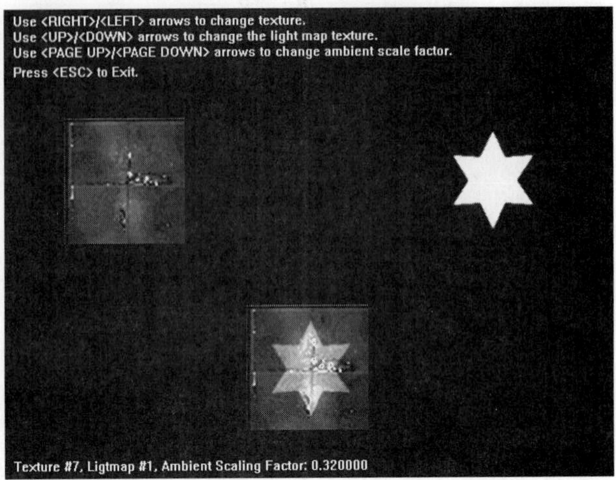

FIGURE 8.5 Additive and multiplicative modulation.

As an example of using light mapping and modulation, try `DEMOII8_2.CPP|EXE` (it uses the first) and `DEMOII8_2b.CPP|EXE` (it uses the second formula). The demos enable you to modulate a spotlight texture onto a wall texture using each formula. Notice the difference in the first and second demo. The second demo uses additive colors, so you can see the green lights, but the first uses modulation. Thus, only if there is green (in this case) in the base texture are you able to see the colored light. Both of these methods are useful; it just depends on if you want reality or what looks good. Anyway, use the arrow keys to control the demos.

Now, because this book is all about speed, we're already starting to see some of the problems associated with lighting. Even with simple lighting where we're taking one texture and applying a light map (which I'll explain in much better detail later), there are numerous multiplications, additions, and potential conditional logic to test for overflows, so we have our work cut out for us. Thus, we need to be aware that we have to use the best numerical model possible, along with the minimum number of conversions and steps in the model before we obtain the final pixel value. Moreover, if we're using an 8-bit mode that's palettized, the tricks become ever more complex, but 8-bit modes are faster for many processes because look up tables can be used.

Alpha Blending

The last thing I want to talk about is alpha blending because it leverages both the additive and modulation concepts. *Alpha blending* is the process of adding two or more pixel colors together to arrive at a destination pixel. The blending part comes into play because percentages of each source are used to arrive at the final pixel. Figure 8.6 show two source bitmaps and the alpha-blended results. Alpha blending is used to simulate transparency as well as other effects such as shadows. The math is rather simple, and works as follows: two (or more) sources are blended together by a blending factor (usually referred to as *alpha*), and the sum result is written as the destination color value. For example, here's how you would alpha blend two sources:

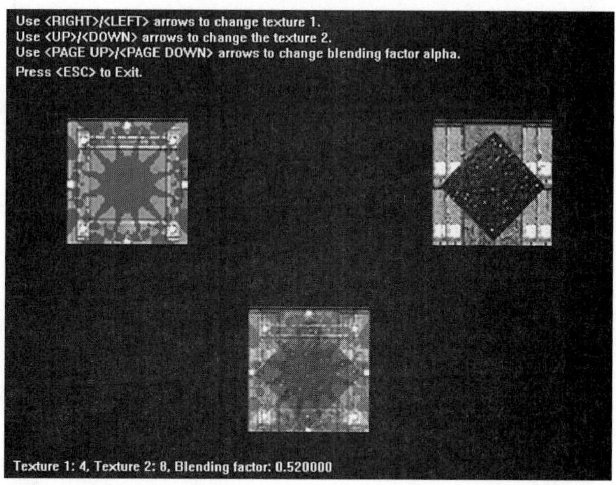

FIGURE 8.6 Alpha blending in action.

FORMULA 8.3 Basic Two-Source Alpha Blending

$$\texttt{Pixel\_dest[x][y]}_{rgb} = \texttt{alpha} \quad * \ \texttt{pixel\_source1[x][y]}_{rgb} + \\ \texttt{(1-alpha)* pixel\_source2[x][y]}_{rgb}$$

So, if we let alpha = 1, the destination pixels will be an exact copy of `pixel_source1[][]`. However, if we let alpha = .9, 90% of the destination pixel's color value will be from `pixel_source1[][]`, but 10% will be from `pixel_source2[][]`. It goes without saying that this process must be performed for each pixel and for each color channel, but the algorithm is quite simple. `DEMOII8_3.CPP|EXE` illustrates alpha blending; use the right and left arrow keys to change alpha from 0..1 and see the results of blending the two source textures together.

Now that you have a little idea about working with colors, let's talk about types of light.

Ambient Light

Ambient light is the light that's all around us. It has no source per se, but is the result of all the sources bouncing off all the objects, which results in an ambient light level. The ambient lighting term can be modeled simply by an additive ambient term, which is the product of an ambient reflectivity color of the surface $Cs_{ambient}$ and an ambient light intensity $I_{ambient}$. (Note that many texts like to use k for reflectivity, but when we get to modeling lights themselves, it's easier to think of both the surface material reflectivity and the light color as colors; thus, the use of C). This term can again be in RGB format or a general scalar that represents the general monochromatic brightness of the scene at a point, p. The point is that all polygons in the scene will have this light added to them, regardless of light sources. Thus, the total light hitting a surface S at a point p with ambient light is

$I_{total\mathbf{a}} = Cs_{ambient} * I_{ambient}$.

NOTE

To make the mathematics work out more easily, we'll assume that reflectivities are in floating-point RGB format (0..1, 0..1, 0..1) and intensity values are floating-point scalars. Also, notice the subscript under the intensity I has a bolded letter. It simply represents the type of light we're computing the final intensity for; "a" for ambient, in this case.

Diffuse Light

Diffuse light is the light that is scattered off an object due to a light source and the inherent roughness of the surface itself. Diffuse lighting is irrelevant of position of the viewer and scatters equally in all directions. Figure 8.7 shows a beam of light that hits a surface, S; the surface will scatter light in all directions, but the amount of light scattered depends on the angle of the surface relative to the light source. The final light intensity is proportional to the angle of the light vector with the normal to the surface.

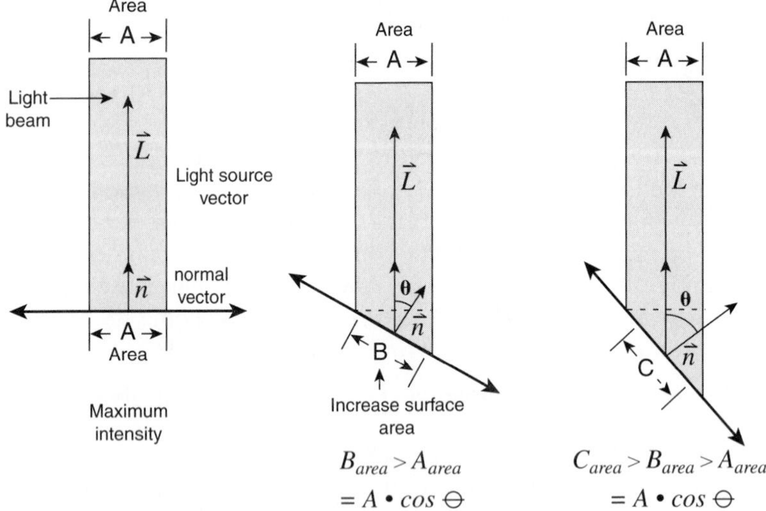

FIGURE 8.7 The geometry of diffuse reflection.

FORMULA 8.4 Intensity of Diffuse Lighting as a Function of the Angle θ Between the Surface Normal and the Incident Light Vector

$$I \approx (\mathbf{n} \cdot \mathbf{l}) = \cos \theta$$

Note: **n** and **l** must be unit vectors.

This is true because as the surface becomes parallel to the light source, the amount of surface area decreases (as θ approaches 90 degrees), so the amount of energy reflected per square unit is minimized. Conversely, as the surface becomes perpendicular to the direction of the light (as θ approaches 0 degrees), the amount of surface area gets larger, light scattering increases, and the amount of light per square unit increases. Finally, the maximum occurs when the normal vector **n** and the light source vector **l** are perpendicular.

Diffuse reflection is also called *Lambertian reflection,* and is based on the concept that surfaces are made of materials that interact with light in different ways. One of those ways is to scatter some component of the light in all directions due to randomly oriented microscopic surface detail. In reality, the physics is much more complex. Light may be scattered more or less depending on frequency, and the angle of scattering may change for different frequencies. However, for our model, we'll assume that each surface material has some diffuse reflectivity color $Rs_{diffuse}$ that determines the amount of light that diffusely scatters from the surface material. Note that $Rs_{diffuse}$ is an RGB color, not a scalar, meaning that it's quite possible that a surface may only scatter a specific frequency of light. For example, blue light if $Rs_{diffuse}$ = (0,0,1.0), or maybe the surface scatters all colors equally well and there is no other type of light scattering (specular, for example); thus $Rs_{diffuse}$ = (1.0, 1.0, 1.0). So, taking the diffuse reflectivity coefficient color $C_{diffuse}$ along with the light intensity $I_{diffuse}$, our final diffuse lighting equation for a single light source is Formula 8.5 Single-source diffuse lighting model

$$I_{total\mathbf{d}} = Rs_{diffuse} * I_{diffuse} * (\mathbf{n} \cdot \mathbf{l})$$

Now taking into consideration the new diffuse term, our lighting model for a single light source with intensity $I_{diffuse}$ looks like this:

FORMULA 8.6 Single-Source Ambient and Diffuse Lighting Model

$$I_{total\mathbf{ad}} = Rs_{ambient} * I_{ambient} + [Rs_{diffuse} * I_{diffuse} * (\mathbf{n} \cdot \mathbf{l})]$$

And for multiple light sources, we need only sum up the contributions of each diffuse term because the ambient term is the same:

FORMULA 8.7 Ambient and Diffuse Lighting Model for Multiple Sources

$$I_{total\mathbf{ad}} = Rs_{ambient} * I_{ambient} + Rs_{diffuse} * \sum_{i=1}^{n} [I(i)_{diffuse} * (\mathbf{n}_i \cdot \mathbf{l}_i)]]$$

NOTE

You might notice that some of this notation is redundant. For example, there's no need to have both intensities and reflectivities (especially in the ambient terms); we could just as well multiply them together and have single constants. However, the previous constructions are designed to show the independent components rather than optimal representations.

Specular Lighting

The next properties of light we see when looking at objects are the shiny reflections of the light sources themselves. This type of lighting is called *specular*. Specular reflections are caused, for the most part, by large numbers of microfacets on the surface having the same orientation in a regular way. Specular lighting models try to model this effect, which is related to the light source, the surface normal, and the position of the viewer in this case. (Remember that in diffuse lighting the position of the viewer didn't come into play.)

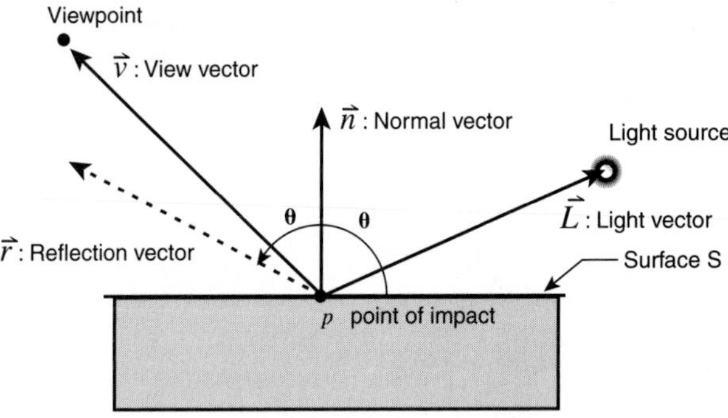

FIGURE 8.8 Specular lighting setup.

Figure 8.8 illustrates the setup for specular lighting. In this setup, we have the surface S, the normal **n**, the viewer vector **v**, and the reflection vector **r** (which is always symmetrical about the normal of the surface). As an experiment, try this: take a shiny object, maybe a plate or something plastic, and then hold it in front of you and slowly rotate the object around or move your head until you see the light sources in the room—that's specular reflection.

As the light source's reflection vector, **r**, and your viewing vector, **v**, align, you're basically seeing a reflection of the light source because the object surface acts like a mirror. The better the object's specular reflection coefficient, the sharper the highlights. And as the angle alpha between the reflection vector **r** and the viewing vector **v** tend toward zero, the reflection increases very rapidly. Similarly, as the angle alpha increases, the specular reflection decreases rapidly.

TIP

This model is usually referred to as the Phong illumination model (although most people refer to Phong shading as a technique that uses the interpolated normals during shading). Thus, the two different concepts are sometimes confused because they're related, but different. I think I'm confused now, too.

Thus, to model this, we need to take into consideration the viewing vector and the reflection vector, along with a constant that defines the shinyness—that is, the specularity—of the object's material we're trying to model. Common sense tells us that the specular reflection should increase as the angle between the viewing vector and light reflection vector decreases, while at the same time, if the normal and the light vector become negative, we know that the light source can't possibly light the surface anymore.

So, as usual, we'll need a reflectivity coefficient, which we'll call $Rs_{specular}$. Next, we need a light intensity, $I_{specular}$. Finally, one more variable, which is sometimes referred to as the *specular power* or *specular exponent*, which determines the concentration of the highlights. We'll call this variable sp. With all that in mind, here's a formula that models these properties for a single light source:

FORMULA 8.8 Specular Lighting Formula for a Single Source

$$I_{totals} = Rs_{specular} * I_{specular} * MAX(\mathbf{r} . \mathbf{v}, 0)^{sp}$$

Note: The use of the `MAX()` operator just prevents the value from being less than 0.

TIP

Although I've been using the dot product format to write these equations, we can also use the definition of dot product, which is $(\mathbf{u}.\mathbf{v}) = |\mathbf{u}|*|\mathbf{v}|*\cos\alpha$. Then the previous equation can be written as $Rs_{specular}*I_{specular}*\cos^{sp}\alpha$. Assuming, of course, that **r** and **v** are both unit vectors.

8

As I said, the angle between the light and the normal must be less than 90, so $(\mathbf{n}.\mathbf{l}) > 90$. So, if you like, you can add a Boolean operator $[(\mathbf{n}.\mathbf{l}) > 0 ? 1: 0]$ to the equation to disable the specular computation for points on the surface S that face away from the light source:

FORMULA 8.9 Specular Lighting Formula for a Single Source with Test for Light Source

$$I_{totals} = Rs_{specular}*I_{specular}*MAX(\mathbf{r}.\mathbf{v}, 0)^{sp} * [(\mathbf{n}.\mathbf{l}) > 0 ? 1: 0]$$

Next, let's see the multiple-source version. As usual, it's nothing more than iterating through the light sources:

FORMULA 8.10 Specular Lighting Formula for Multiple Sources with Test for Light Source

$$I_{totals} = Rs_{specular} * \sum_{i=1}^{n} [I(i)_{specular} * MAX(\mathbf{r}_i . \mathbf{v}_i, 0)^{sp} * [(\mathbf{n}_i . \mathbf{l}_i) > 0 ? 1 : 0]$$

Now let's put together the ambient, diffuse, and specular terms into one big lighting model:

$$I_{totalads} = I_{totala} + I_{totald} + I_{totals} =$$

$$Rs_{ambient} * I_{ambient} +$$

$$Rs_{diffuse} * \sum_{i=1}^{n} [I(i)_{diffuse} * (\mathbf{n}_i . \mathbf{l}_i)] +$$

$$Rs_{specular} * \sum_{i=1}^{n} [I(i)_{specular} * MAX(\mathbf{r}_i . \mathbf{v}_i, 0)^{sp} * [(\mathbf{n}_i . \mathbf{l}_i) > 0 ? 1 : 0]]$$

Emissive Lighting

Emissive lighting is the easiest to implement of all the lighting models, depending on how you implement it. When you set the emissivity of a surface, you're dictating how much light the surface gives off; that is, its self-illumination. Now, if this illumination were "real" light, you would consider it a light source and add it to the lighting calculations along with your other light sources through the diffuse and specular equations. But if you don't care that it doesn't emit light for the lighting calculations, you can just use the emissivity of a surface to self-illuminate a surface.

For example, say you have an object such as a beacon in a game world. The beacon might be made of a material that has only slight ambient and diffuse reflectivity coefficients. So, you can see the beacon's general shape as lights move around, but when you turn the beacon on, it lights up. However, because it's not really a light, it doesn't cast light—but it looks like a light. Figure 8.9 illustrates this: You see a beacon and an object by the beacon, but even though the beacon is on, notice that the object has no illumination from the beacon. Implementing emission is trivial:

FORMULA 8.11 Basic Emission

$$I_{totale} = Rs_{emission}$$

That is, the color of a pixel due to its own emission is simply $Rs_{emission}$—no need for a light source. Thus, our final lighting equation with all the bells and whistles is

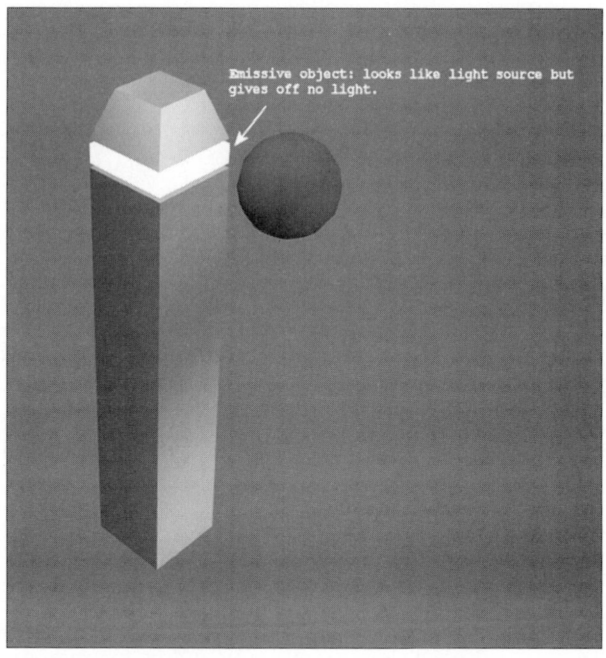

FIGURE 8.9 Emissive/constant lighting that doesn't cast light.

FORMULA 8.12 The Total Lighting Equation for a Single Pixel Due to Multiple Light Sources

$$I_{totalaeds} = R_{sambient} * I_{ambient} + Rs_{emission} +$$

$$R_{sdiffuse} * \sum_{i=1}^{n} [I(i)_{diffuse} * (\mathbf{n}_i \cdot \mathbf{l}_i)] +$$

$$R_{sspecular} * \sum_{i=1}^{n} [I(i)_{specular} * MAX(\mathbf{r}_i \cdot \mathbf{v}_i, 0)^{sp} * [(\mathbf{n}_i \cdot \mathbf{l}_i)>0?1:0]]$$

One last thing I want to mention is that the light intensities $I_{ambient}$, $I_{diffuse}$, and $I_{specular}$ may all be the same or different. That means you may have some lights that you want to affect only the diffuse component of the lighting model, some lights you want to affect the specular, and so forth. Hence, I've left the intensities the same. However, in many cases, the light intensity for the *i*th light I_i is the same and used in all the equations; thus, the equations would simplify to

8

$$I_{totalaeds} = Rs_{ambient} * I_{ambient} + Rs_{emission} + Rs_{diffuse} * \sum_{i=1}^{n} [I(i) * (\mathbf{n}_i \cdot \mathbf{l}_i)] + Rs_{specular} * \sum_{i=1}^{n} [I(i) * MAX(\mathbf{r}_i \cdot \mathbf{v}_i, 0)^{sp} * [(\mathbf{n}_i \cdot \mathbf{l}_i) > 0 \; ? \; 1:0]]$$

Ugly, huh? And we have to do that for every pixel and for every light in the scene. That's a lot of work, and what's sad is that we haven't even talked about lights yet! We've talked about *lighting*, but not lights. Now we need to talk about the lights themselves, and how we arrive at the intensity values for each light. Here's another nightmare.

Types of Lights

Even with the oversimplified lighting models we are using and the low count polygon meshes the final results are reasonable and can look quite striking. On the other hand, you have to remember that lighting is usually a per-pixel operation, and even with these crude lighting models, we still need to perform many, many, many operations per pixel to light the pixels correctly. And with software, this results in the use of a lot of tricks, so keep that in mind.

The next things we're going to talk about are lights themselves. Although you may think of lights as things in your office or living room shaped like little pears, the mathematical models are quite different. In most cases, computer models use only three types of lights:

- Directional
- Point
- Spot

Amazingly, the mathematics of each light that I'm about to describe are loosely based on real physics, so that's a comfort.

Directional Lights

Directional lights are lights that for all intents and purposes have no position because they're so far away (infinitely far away, in fact), and all the light that strikes any surface from them is parallel (see Figure 8.10). Hence, they're also referred to as *infinite lights*. Directional lights also have the property that the intensity of the light doesn't diminish as a function of distance from the light (because the light is already infinitely far away). However, directional lights can still have intensity and color. In any case, to define a directional light, all that's needed is its initial color and intensity. Now, we need to be careful with notation here. If you recall, we had a number of reflectivities for the ambient, diffuse, and specular properties of the surface materials and the lighting models. But, remember those were the reflectivities of the surface materials themselves—now we're talking about the color of the actual lights! So not to confuse anyone, let's use the notation that light colors are Cl_{xxx} where xxx is the type of light. And the initial intensity of light is $I0_{xxx}$ read as "I zero, sub xxx." Thus, for a directional light, the intensity is always

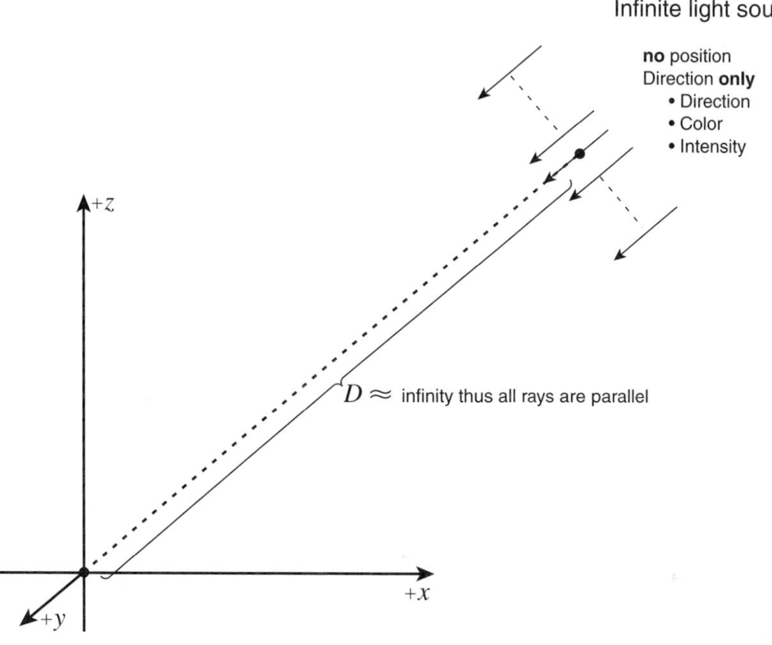

FIGURE 8.10 The properties of infinite lights.

FORMULA 8.13 Intensity of a Directional Light as a Function of Distance (it's the same!)

$$I(d)_{dir} = I0_{dir} * Cl_{dir}$$

Notice that as the distance changes, the light intensity doesn't—that's why it's not in the equation <BG>.

Point Lights

Point lights are modeled as single points in 3D space, as shown in Figure 8.11. Point lights actually are modeled after real point lights, and thus have falloff based on distance from the surface, S. The falloff, or *attenuation,* is usually modeled using three constants: a constant attenuation factor (k_c), a linear attenuation factor (k_l), and a quadratic attenuation factor (k_q). Taking these attenuation factors into consideration and assuming that the distance from the light source positioned at point **p** to a point **s** on the surface S called d, the intensity as a function of distance d is

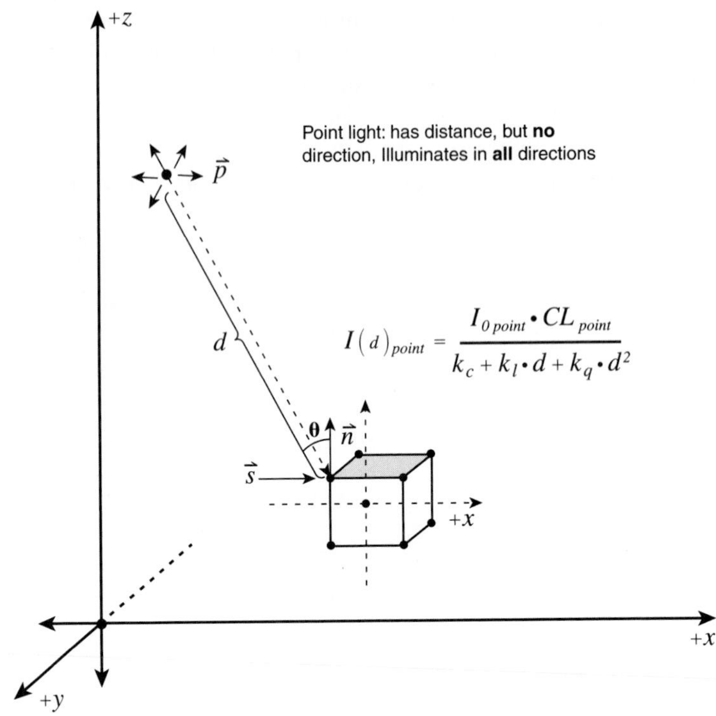

FIGURE 8.11 The properties of a point light.

FORMULA 8.14 Intensity of a Point Light as a Function of Distance with Constant, Linear, and Quadratic Attenuation Factors

$$I(d)_{point} = \frac{I0_{point} * Cl_{point}}{k_c + k_l*d + k_q*d^2}$$

Where d = |**p** - **s**|

Now, it might be interesting to see what this function looks like, so let's run some numbers through it. The first thing to remember is that all of our lighting equations are always in terms of RGB. That means each equation is really three equations: one for red, one for green, and one for blue. However, because the math is the same, we just write one equation and know what we are talking about. Therefore, without loss of generality (I love saying that), we can run the math for a single channel or, in other words, for a monochromatic system, and see what the curves look like to get an idea of the RGB response. Let's do that. First, let's set $I0_{point} = 1.0$ and $Cl_{point} = 1.0$ so that their product is 1.0, thereby normalizing our results. Now that we have that, let's run three different series:

Series 1: $k_c = 1$, $k_l = 0$, and $k_q = 0$

Series 2: $k_c = 0$, $k_l = 1$, and $k_q = 0$

Series 3: $k_c = 0$, $k_l = 0$, and $k_q = 1$

Figure 8.12 illustrates all the different curves for the various series. As you can see, the intensity of the light falls off fairly quickly for both the cases where the linear attenuation factor $k_l = 1$, and where the quadratic attenuation factor $k_q = 1$. In fact, for the quadratic case, by a distance of 10 and $k_q = 1$, the results are on the order of .01—basically nothing. Therefore, be careful when setting the attenuation factors. They have a strong effect on the attenuation. In fact, I suggest simply using the linear factor and setting it to (.001 - .0005).

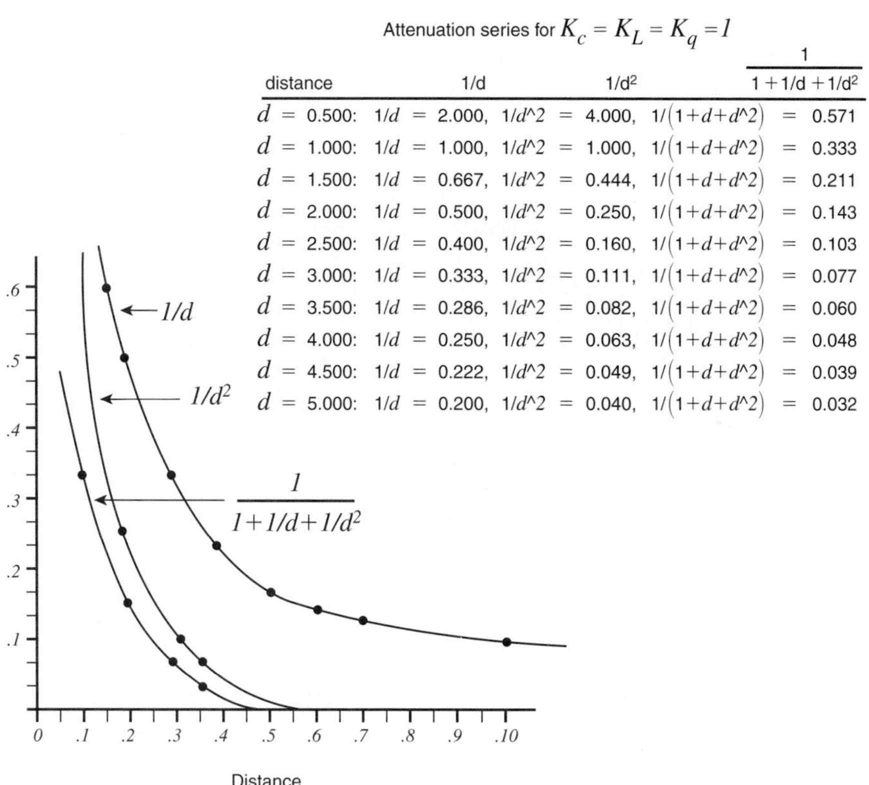

Attenuation series for $K_c = K_L = K_q = 1$

distance	1/d	1/d²	$\frac{1}{1+1/d+1/d^2}$
d = 0.500:	$1/d$ = 2.000,	$1/d$^2 = 4.000,	$1/(1+d+d^2)$ = 0.571
d = 1.000:	$1/d$ = 1.000,	$1/d$^2 = 1.000,	$1/(1+d+d^2)$ = 0.333
d = 1.500:	$1/d$ = 0.667,	$1/d$^2 = 0.444,	$1/(1+d+d^2)$ = 0.211
d = 2.000:	$1/d$ = 0.500,	$1/d$^2 = 0.250,	$1/(1+d+d^2)$ = 0.143
d = 2.500:	$1/d$ = 0.400,	$1/d$^2 = 0.160,	$1/(1+d+d^2)$ = 0.103
d = 3.000:	$1/d$ = 0.333,	$1/d$^2 = 0.111,	$1/(1+d+d^2)$ = 0.077
d = 3.500:	$1/d$ = 0.286,	$1/d$^2 = 0.082,	$1/(1+d+d^2)$ = 0.060
d = 4.000:	$1/d$ = 0.250,	$1/d$^2 = 0.063,	$1/(1+d+d^2)$ = 0.048
d = 4.500:	$1/d$ = 0.222,	$1/d$^2 = 0.049,	$1/(1+d+d^2)$ = 0.039
d = 5.000:	$1/d$ = 0.200,	$1/d$^2 = 0.040,	$1/(1+d+d^2)$ = 0.032

FIGURE 8.12 Attenuation curves.

Of course, when all the attenuation factors are nonzero, the intensity falls off even more rapidly. However, in practical usage, I find that the more simplified point light model works just as well without the quadratic term of

$$I(d)_{point} = \frac{I0_{point} * Cl_{point}}{k_c + k_l*d}$$

Where $d = |\mathbf{p} - \mathbf{s}|$

Spotlights

The last type of light source I want to discuss is the spotlight, as shown in Figure 8.13. Spotlights are extremely computationally expensive (even for hardware), and we'll definitely need tricks and simplifications to even begin simulating them in software, but that aside, let's take a look at the math. Figure 8.14 depicts the standard spotlight configuration. We see a spotlight at position **p**, with direction **l**, striking a surface S at a point **s**. Also, note we have a cone that the spotlight is to affect. This cone has two regions: the inner and the outer. The inner region, defined by α alpha, is usually referred to as the *umbra*, and the outer region (or soft shadow part) defined by ϕ (phi) is called the *penumbra*.

FIGURE 8.13 A spotlight illuminating objects.

The intensity of the spotlight is reasonably constant in the umbra, but falls off very quickly in the transition to the penumbra. Now, to model the falloff based on the umbra and penumbra, most engines simply use the following algorithm:

Case 1: If the angle between the light source and the surface point s is greater than the outer cone (that is, the penumbra), don't light the point.

Case 2: If the angle between the light source and the surface point s is within the inner cone (the umbra), use 100% intensity for the spotlight, only attenuating based on distance.

Case 3: If the angle between the light source and the surface point s is within the outer (penumbra) and inner (umbra) cones, use a falloff formula in addition to the attenuation based on distance.

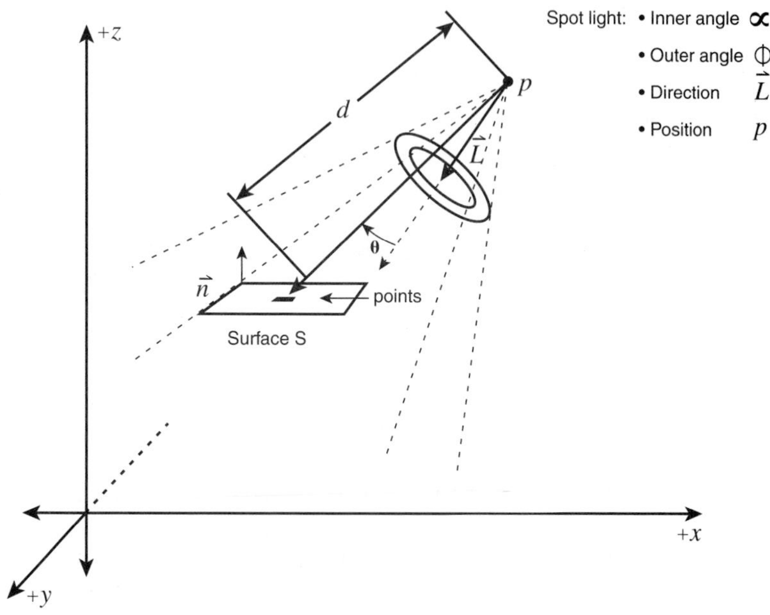

FIGURE 8.14 The setup for spotlight calculations.

Now, that sounds like a lot of work for a spotlight. The question is, do we really need it? Can we use a simpler model and get the same effect? The answer is probably, and I'll show you one in a moment. But for now, let's trek through this more complex model, which is the way Direct3D does it, so it's good practice.

So, to define our spotlight, we need a position (**p**), a direction vector (**l**), and two angles (α and ϕ) to define the inner and outer cones, respectively. Also, to make the math easier for angle comparisons, let's create two half-angles: α *= α /2 and ϕ *= ϕ /2. And ,of course, we need the color of the light $Cl_{spotlight}$ and its intensity $I0_{spotlight}$. What a disaster, huh?

Referring to Figure 8.15, we see the geometrical relationship of all the constituent players for the spotlight model. So, here's the deal: If the angle theta(θ) is ever greater than the spotlight angle alpha(α), there's no spotlight at all. However, if theta is within alpha, we need a spotlight—but the spotlight should be constant in the inner cone, and in the transition from the inner cone to the outer cone, the light should diminish.

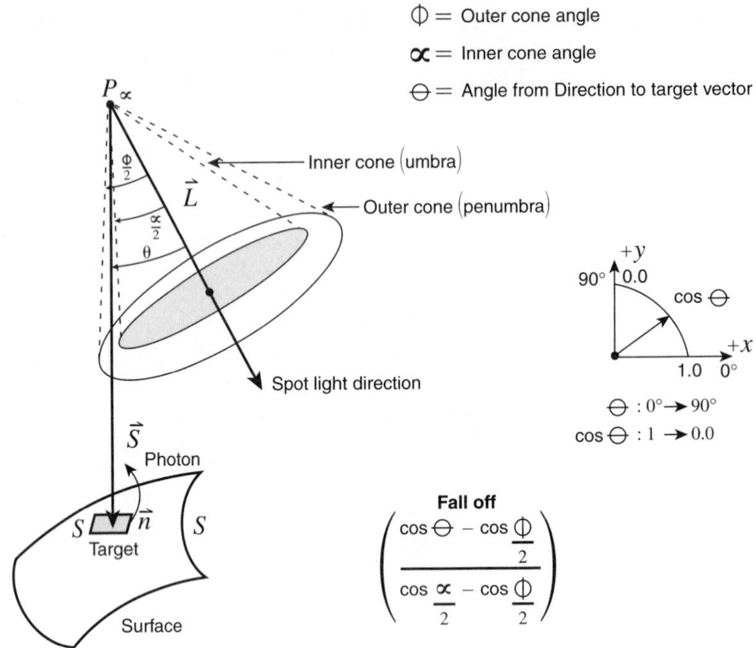

$$\left(\frac{\cos\theta - \cos\frac{\phi}{2}}{\cos\frac{\alpha}{2} - \cos\frac{\phi}{2}}\right)$$

FIGURE 8.15 A detailed analysis of the math behind the spotlight.

Finally, we need a power factor, concentration, or falloff factor that controls the overall intensity of the spotlight—let's call it pf. And last, but not least, because the spotlight is still a point type light source, we need to take attenuation into consideration over distance, so we need the attenuation factors Kc, Kl, and Kq once again. Considering that, here's the spotlight intensity formula:

Formula 8.15 Intensity of a Spotlight with Umbra Angle Alpha, Power Factor pf, as a Function of Distance with Constant, Linear, and Quadratic Attenuation Factors for all the Different Cases

Case 1: $\theta > \phi$ * (outside penumbra, don't light at all):

$$I(d)_{spotlight} = 0$$

Case 2: $\theta < \alpha$ * (inside umbra):

$$I(d)_{spotlight} = \frac{I0_{spotlight} * Cl_{spotlight}}{k_c + k_l*d + k_q*d^2}$$

Where $d = |\mathbf{p} - \mathbf{s}|$

Case 3: $\alpha^* < \theta < \phi^*$ (outside umbra, inside penumbra):

$$I(d)_{spotlight} = \frac{I0_{spotlight} * Cl_{spotlight}}{k_c + k_l*d + k_q*d^2} * \frac{(\cos\theta - \cos\phi^*)^{pf}}{(\cos\alpha^* - \cos\phi^*)}$$

Where $d = |p - s|$, and pf = power factor

If you're like me, you're probably saying, "That's a bit mysterious. The dot product thing I can understand, but the ratio of cosines (in bold) seems a bit shady," and I agree. Let's take a look at the math and see if it makes sense. As an example, let's assume that the umbra angle α is 40 degrees, the penumbra angle ϕ is 60 degrees, and that the angle θ is between the umbra and penumbra in the range of $40/2 < \theta < 60/2$ or $20 < \theta < 30$ (remember we need to use half-angles because θ is a half-angle itself). So, plugging all that into the right-most side of the lighting formula, we get

$$I = \frac{(\cos\theta - \cos 30)^{1.0}}{(\cos 20 - \cos 30)}$$

As you see, I've set the power factor to 1.0 to make things easy. Now, here's the thought process: The cosine of an angle approaches 1.0 as the angle approaches 0, and the cosine of an angle approaches 0 as the angle approaches 90 degrees. So, we want this ratio to approach 1.0 as the angle θ tends toward the inner cone (constant brightness area), and we want the ratio to approach 0.0 as the angle θ approaches the outer cone angle. Let's take a look at the ratio and see what it does. If we let θ = the inner cone angle of 20 degrees, we get

$$I = \frac{(\cos \mathbf{20} - \cos 30)^{1.0}}{(\cos 20 - \cos 30)} = 1.0$$

Amazingly, that's exactly what we want! Now, let's have θ equal the outer cone angle, which is where the ratio should immediately turn to 0.0:

$$I = \frac{(\cos \mathbf{30} - \cos 30)^{1.0}}{(\cos 20 - \cos 30)} = 0.0$$

Again, it's correct, so the question is, what does this falloff curve look like in-between? Take a look at Figure 8.16, which depicts the different response curves for pf = .2, 1.0, and 5.0, with and inner angle of 30 degrees, outer angle of 40 degrees, and theta varying from 30–40 (technically 15–20 because theta is the half angle from the direction vector). In most cases, a falloff based on a power factor of 1.0 works fine. Table 8.1 illustrates the data shown in Figure 8.16.

8

TABLE 8.1 Response Curve Data for Spotlight Falloff

Power Factor	Theta(θ)	Falloff
0.200000		
	15	1.000000
	16	0.961604
	17	0.912672
	18	0.845931
	19	0.740122
	20	0
1.000000		
	15	1.000000
	16	0.822205
	17	0.633248
	18	0.433187
	19	0.222083
	20	0.000000
5.000000		
	15	1.000000
	16	0.375752
	17	0.101829
	18	0.015254
	19	0.000540
	20	0.000000

Now, the question is, do we need all this? Well, it depends. If you're rendering offline 3D environments, yes, you need this. If you're rendering 3D games in real-time, probably not. Any model that even remotely models the spotlight will look good enough in a real-time game. In fact, we have all we need to model a poor man's spotlight right now. Let's do this: Instead of having a constant intensity region in the umbra, and then a falloff in the penumbra, let's just start from the middle and falloff. And let's make the falloff proportional to the angle θ without any kind of Boolean tests, but with the added feature that we exponentiate the falloff with our power factor, which in this case is more of a concentration. In any case, here's the simplified model:

$$I(d)_{spotlight} = \frac{I0_{spotlight} * Cl_{spotlight} * MAX((\mathbf{l} \cdot \mathbf{s}), 0)^{pf}}{k_c + k_l * d + k_q * d^2}$$

Where $d = |\mathbf{p} - \mathbf{s}|$, and pf = power factor

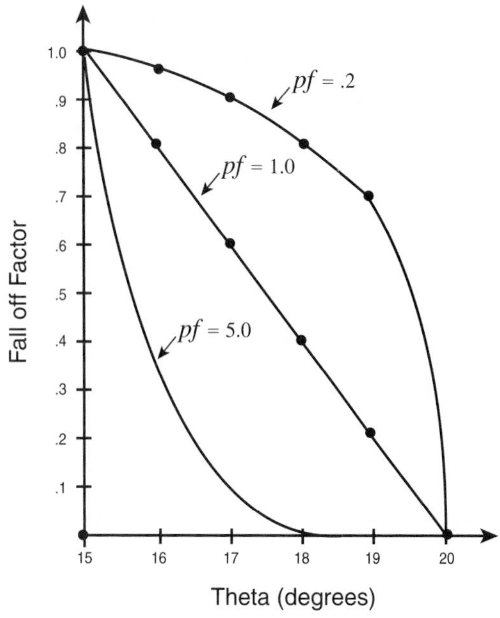

FIGURE 8.16 Response curves for intensity modulation term in spotlight calculations.

Lighting Summary

As you can see, there's a lot to lighting. The thing to remember is that lighting is about determining the pixel color of each pixel that makes up a polygon. To that end, we derive models that enable us to define virtual materials with properties such as reflection coefficients for ambient, diffuse, and specular light. Along with that, we then need virtual lights that generate the light for our virtual materials to interact with. These lights may be as simple as ambient lights that are everywhere, or as complex as spotlights.

At this point, our engine has absolutely no support for materials or lights, so that's something we need to add, and we will, but first things first. Now that you have an idea about materials and lighting, I want you to think about it, and while you're doing that, let's fill in our wireframe polygons with solid ones because we're going to need to do that anyway when we light them properly.

8

NOTE

All the software, structures, and so forth from this chapter can be found in `T3DLIB6.CPP|H`.

Lighting and Rasterizing Triangles

In Chapter 8, "Vector Rasterization and 2D Transformations" of *Tricks of the Windows Game Programming Gurus*, I covered how to rasterize triangles and polygons with a solid color. At this point, I'm not going to cover that material again because I'm going to re-derive it in a much deeper way in this book when we get to texture mapping in Chapter 9, "Interpolative Shading Techniques and Affine Texture Mapping." For now, I just want to give you a brief overview of the problem if you haven't read the first *Tricks*. First, we've already agreed that this 3D engine works with triangles. Thus, we don't need to worry about quadrilaterals or other more complex polygons. Taking that into consideration, Figure 8.17 shows a general triangle that we want to rasterize.

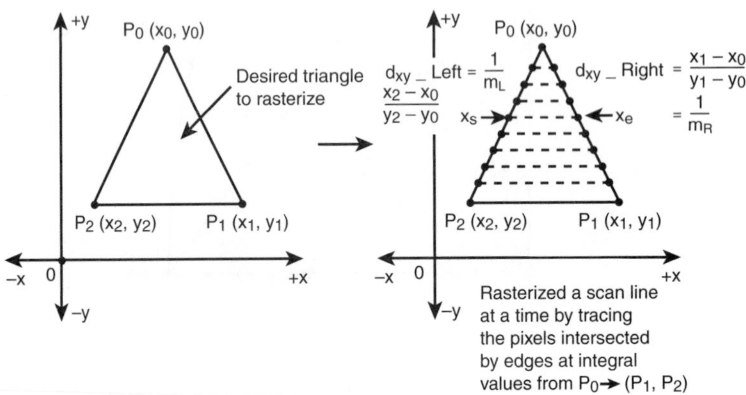

FIGURE 8.17 Triangle setup for rasterization.

Drawing a triangle is much like drawing a line: You must trace out the pixels of the left and right edges to be drawn and then fill the triangle line by line. This is shown in Figure 8.17. As you can see, after the slope of each edge is computed, you can simply move down each scan line, adjust the x-endpoints (`xs` and `xe`) based on the slope (or, more accurately, 1/slope), and then draw a connecting line.

You don't need to use Bresenham's algorithm because you aren't interested in drawing a line. You're only interested in seeing where the line intersects the pixel centers at each vertical integer interval. Here's the algorithm assuming that the bottom of the triangle is flat:

Step 1: First, compute the ratio dx/dy for the left side and the right side. Basically, this is 1/slope. You need it because you're going to use a vertically oriented approach. Thus, you want to know the change in x for each y, which is simply dx/dy or 1/M. Call these values `dxy_left` and `dxy_right` for the left and right side, respectively.

Step 2: Starting at the topmost vertex (`x0`,`y0`), set `xs = xe = x0` and `y = y0`.

Step 3: Add `dxy_left` to `xs` and `dxy_right` to `xe`. This will trace the endpoints to fill.

Step 4: Draw a line from (xs,y) to (xe,y).

Step 5: Go back to step 3 until the height of the triangle from the top to the bottom has been rasterized.

Of course, the initial conditions and boundary conditions for the algorithm take a little thought to get right, but that's all there is to it, more or less—fairly simple.

Let's implement the flat-bottom triangle rasterizer based on floating-point because at this point in the game (Pentium 4+), computers are fast enough for the most part. First, let's label the triangle as shown in Figure 8.17. Here's the algorithm:

```
// compute deltas
float dxy_left  = (x2-x0)/(y2-y0);
float dxy_right = (x1-x0)/(y1-y0);

// set starting and ending points for edge trace
float xs = x0;
float xe = x0;

// draw each scanline
for (int y=y0; y <= y1; y++)
    {
    // draw a line from xs to xe at y in color c
    Draw_Line((int)xs, (int)xe, y, c);
    // move down one scanline
    xs+=dxy_left;
    xe+=dxy_right;
    } // end for y
```

Now, let's talk about some of the details of the algorithm and what's missing. First off, the algorithm truncates the endpoints of each scanline. This is probably a bad thing because we're throwing away information. A better approach is to round the value of each endpoint by adding 0.5 before converting to integers. Another problem has to do with the initial conditions. On the first iteration, the algorithm draws a line that's a single pixel wide. This works, but it's definitely a place for optimization.

Now, let's see if you can write the algorithm for a flat-top triangle based on what you know. All you need to do is relabel the vertices so that **p0** and **p1** are the top-most vertices and **p2** is the bottom, and then change the algorithm's initial conditions slightly so that the left and right interpolants are correctly computed. Here are the changes:

```
// compute deltas
float dxy_left  = (x2-x0)/(y2-y0);
float dxy_right = (x2-x1)/(y2-y1);

// set starting and ending points for edge trace
float xs = x0;
float xe = x1;
```

```
// draw each scanline
for (int y=y0; y <= y2; y++)
    {
// draw a line from xs to xe at y in color c
Draw_Line((int)(xs+0.5), (int)(xe+0.5), y, c);
// move down one scanline
xs+=dxy_left;
xe+=dxy_right;

} // end for y
```

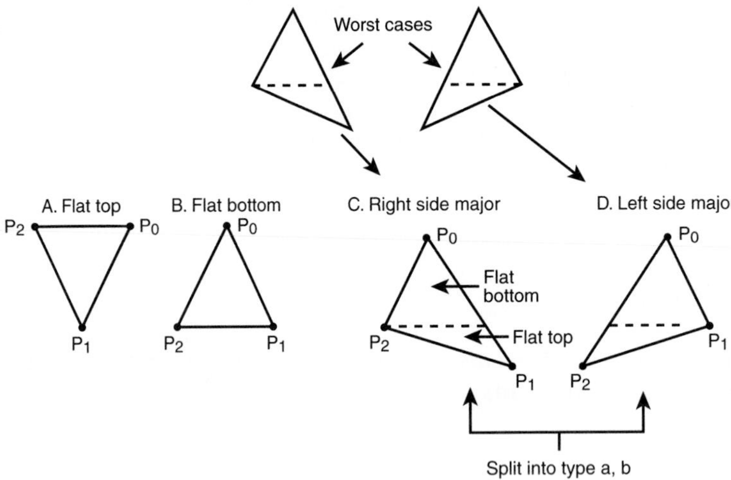

FIGURE 8.18 The various triangle rasterization cases.

At this point, you have a triangle rasterizer that can draw both flat-top and flat-bottom triangles. With this, you write a general rasterizer that decomposes triangles not in this format into two triangles and then makes calls to each individual triangle rasterization case, as shown in Figure 8.18. This simple triangle rasterizing function is already in our library in a number of forms, and the various prototypes are shown in the following code:

```
// 8-bit version of rasterizer
void Draw_Triangle_2D(int x1,int y1, // vertex 1
                      int x2,int y2, // vertex 2
                      int x3,int y3, // vertex 3
                      int color,     // color index of poly
                      UCHAR *dest_buffer, // dest buffer
                      int mempitch); // pitch of buffer
```

```
// 8-bit version of rasterizer based on fixed point math
void Draw_TriangleFP_2D(int x1,int y1, // vertex 1
                        int x2,int y2, // vertex 2
                        int x3,int y3, // vertex 3
                        int color,     // color index of poly
                        UCHAR *dest_buffer, // dest buffer
                        int mempitch); // pitch of buffer

// 16-bit version of rasterizer
void Draw_Triangle_2D16(int x1,int y1, // vertex 1
                        int x2,int y2, // vertex 2
                        int x3,int y3, // vertex 3
                        int color,   // RGB color of poly
                        UCHAR *dest_buffer, // dest buffer
                        int mempitch); // pitch of buffer
```

These can all be found in T3DLIB1.CPP¦H. Now, in this chapter, we're working on T3DLIB6.CPP¦H, so anything we add, we'll do there. For example, we could add a fixed-point 16-bit version of the rasterizer, but I doubt we will because we don't need to break any speed limits yet, not that fixed-point is any faster than floating-point these days (but you never know).

Anyway, now that we have a tool to draw triangles that are solid, let's add this functionality to our 3D engine. All we need to do is take the functions that draw wireframe objects and render lists, change the code to make the call to the triangle render functions, and we're done! Let's do exactly that. First, here's a complete list of all the new functions I've written to draw solid objects and render lists (you should be familiar with the parameters):

```
// draw a solid 8-bit object
void Draw_OBJECT4DV1_Solid(OBJECT4DV1_PTR obj,
                           UCHAR *video_buffer, int lpitch);

// draw a solid 16-bit object
void Draw_OBJECT4DV1_Solid16(OBJECT4DV1_PTR obj,
                             UCHAR *video_buffer, int lpitch);

// draw a solid 8-bit render list
void Draw_RENDERLIST4DV1_Solid(RENDERLIST4DV1_PTR rend_list,
                               UCHAR *video_buffer, int lpitch);

// draw a solid 16-bit render list
void Draw_RENDERLIST4DV1_Solid16(RENDERLIST4DV1_PTR rend_list,
                                 UCHAR *video_buffer, int lpitch);
```

8

Let's start with function that draws an OBJECT4DV1 in 8-bit color. Here's the code that does that:

```
void Draw_OBJECT4DV1_Solid(OBJECT4DV1_PTR obj,
                     UCHAR *video_buffer, int lpitch)
{
// this function renders an object to the screen in solid,
// 8 bit mode, it has no regard at all about hidden surface removal,
// etc. the function only exists as an easy way to render an object
// without converting it into polygons, the function assumes all
// coordinates are screen coordinates, but will perform 2D clipping
// iterate thru the poly list of the object and simply draw
// each polygon
for (int poly=0; poly < obj->num_polys; poly++)
    {
    // render this polygon if and only if it's not clipped, not culled,
    // active, and visible, note however the concecpt of "backface" is
    // irrelevant in a wire frame engine though
   if (!(obj->plist[poly].state & POLY4DV1_STATE_ACTIVE) ||
      (obj->plist[poly].state & POLY4DV1_STATE_CLIPPED ) ||
      (obj->plist[poly].state & POLY4DV1_STATE_BACKFACE) )
      continue; // move onto next poly

   // extract vertex indices into master list, remember the polygons are
   // NOT self contained, but based on the vertex list stored in the object
   // itself
   int vindex_0 = obj->plist[poly].vert[0];
   int vindex_1 = obj->plist[poly].vert[1];
   int vindex_2 = obj->plist[poly].vert[2];

   // draw the triangle
   Draw_Triangle_2D(obj->vlist_trans[ vindex_0 ].x, obj->vlist_trans[ vindex_0 ].y,
   obj->vlist_trans[ vindex_1 ].x, obj->vlist_trans[ vindex_1 ].y,
   obj->vlist_trans[ vindex_2 ].x, obj->vlist_trans[ vindex_2 ].y,
   obj->plist[poly].color, video_buffer, lpitch);
    } // end for poly
 } // end Draw_OBJECT4DV1_Solid
```

Rather short, huh? As you see, all we needed to do was extract the vertices and use them to send the actual x,y screen space coordinates for the three vertices that make up the triangle we want rendered.

TIP

You might be asking, "What about clipping?" Clipping is still performed in screen space at this point, other than 3D object culling. Hence, when we send polys down the rendering pipeline, the screen rasterization function is doing the clipping on a pixel-by-pixel basis, which is fine for now.

Next, let's take a look at version that draws a 16-bit solid render list:

```
void Draw_RENDERLIST4DV1_Solid16(RENDERLIST4DV1_PTR rend_list,
UCHAR *video_buffer, int lpitch)
{
// this function "executes" the render list or in other words
// draws all the faces in the list in wire frame 16bit mode
// note there is no need to sort wire frame polygons, but
// later we will need to, so hidden surfaces stay hidden
// also, we leave it to the function to determine the bitdepth
// and call the correct rasterizer

// at this point, all we have is a list of polygons and it's time
// to draw them
for (int poly=0; poly < rend_list->num_polys; poly++)
    {
    // render this polygon if and only if it's not clipped, not culled,
    // active, and visible, note however the concecpt of "backface" is
    // irrelevant in a wire frame engine though
   if (!(rend_list->poly_ptrs[poly]->state & POLY4DV1_STATE_ACTIVE) ||
      (rend_list->poly_ptrs[poly]->state & POLY4DV1_STATE_CLIPPED ) ||
      (rend_list->poly_ptrs[poly]->state & POLY4DV1_STATE_BACKFACE) )
   continue; // move onto next poly

   // draw the triangle
   Draw_Triangle_2D16(rend_list->poly_ptrs[poly]->tvlist[0].x,
                      rend_list->poly_ptrs[poly]->tvlist[0].y,
                      rend_list->poly_ptrs[poly]->tvlist[1].x,
                      rend_list->poly_ptrs[poly]->tvlist[1].y,
                      rend_list->poly_ptrs[poly]->tvlist[2].x,
                      rend_list->poly_ptrs[poly]->tvlist[2].y,
                      rend_list->poly_ptrs[poly]->color, video_buffer, lpitch);
   } // end for poly
} // end Draw_RENDERLIST4DV1_Solid16
```

As you can see, these functions are literally a few lines of code. Now, what we need to do next is make the connection between lighting and rendering, so that the polygons are drawn based on the lights and materials in the system.

8

Getting Ready for Lighting

Alright, now that we have materials, lights, and the mathematical models for them, let's take a look at the new 3D pipeline and see where everything fits (at least in an abstract way, because we're going to implement very little in this chapter). Referring to Figure 8.19, the new pipeline has an added lighting stage. The lighting stage is shown after the back-face and object removal steps, and thus is performed in world space. However, lighting can be performed in camera space just as well. The only place lighting can't be performed in is perspective or screen space because at this point we've lost 3D information and flattened the universe.

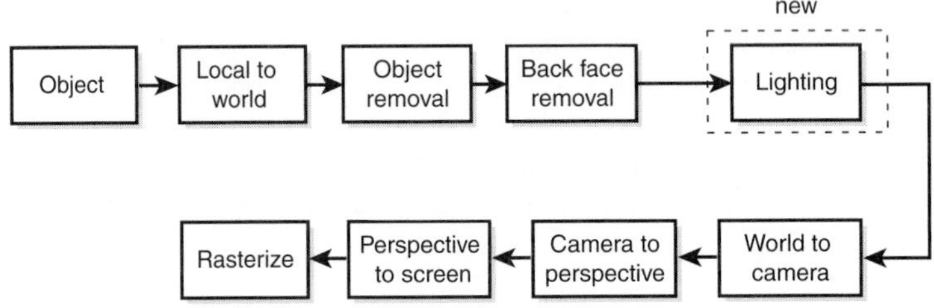

FIGURE 8.19 The new 3D pipeline with lighting.

The reason I want to direct your attention to the position of the lighting step in the 3D pipeline is that now it's really going to start to matter where and when we do things. For example, the lighting calculations are based on a lot of surface normals, right? Therefore, it behooves us to perform the lighting calculations on precomputed normals, *or* to at least perform lighting when we perform the back-face removal step, or to at least store the normals during the back-face removal step and then use them during the following lighting step.

As you can see, there's a lot to think about. The bottom line is that we want to write reasonably optimal code, but do so without losing too much generality or structure; otherwise, we might as well just program in assembly language!

Before we can actually light the polygons in the system, we need to talk about materials and lights themselves. There are a number of problems with this. First, the model format we're using right now. PLG/PLX format doesn't have a whole lot of material support (none in fact). It does have flags for constant, flat, Gouraud, and Phong shading, but there's nothing that even remotely describes all the reflectivity constants of materials and so forth. Additionally, we don't even have lights in the system, so we need some kind of support for those, too. Consistent with my philosophy of "keep it simple," I have no idea what I'll be thinking by next chapter, but I do know that the light models we use in reality and our materials will be very simplified; otherwise, we'll all be waiting for the Pentium 10 to come out! With that in mind, here's a rough first draft of a possible material definition that we can use to apply to surfaces of polygons. Although we may use very little of it, at least it's reasonably complete.

Defining Materials

As discussed earlier, materials have a number of properties, such as their reflectivities and colors. Additionally, we need to abstract materials to take into consideration things such as the type of shading we want applied, texture maps, and more. Currently, we have flags in the version 1.0 polygon attribute field that track a number of things:

```
// attributes of polygons and polygon faces
#define POLY4DV1_ATTR_2SIDED              0x0001
#define POLY4DV1_ATTR_TRANSPARENT         0x0002
#define POLY4DV1_ATTR_8BITCOLOR           0x0004
#define POLY4DV1_ATTR_RGB16               0x0008
#define POLY4DV1_ATTR_RGB24               0x0010

#define POLY4DV1_ATTR_SHADE_MODE_PURE       0x0020
#define POLY4DV1_ATTR_SHADE_MODE_CONSTANT   0x0020 // (alias)
#define POLY4DV1_ATTR_SHADE_MODE_FLAT       0x0040
#define POLY4DV1_ATTR_SHADE_MODE_GOURAUD    0x0080
#define POLY4DV1_ATTR_SHADE_MODE_PHONG      0x0100
#define POLY4DV1_ATTR_SHADE_MODE_FASTPHONG  0x0100 // (alias)
#define POLY4DV1_ATTR_SHADE_MODE_TEXTURE    0x0200

// states of polygons and faces
#define POLY4DV1_STATE_ACTIVE             0x0001
#define POLY4DV1_STATE_CLIPPED            0x0002
#define POLY4DV1_STATE_BACKFACE           0x0004
```


Remember those? Well, those are the kinds of things we now want to hand off a bit to materials. Rather than have this data stored in each separate polygon, we'll instead have a number of materials in a system that should be applied to various polygons during rendering. Figure 8.20 shows the relationship between materials and polygons with this new definition. With this model of solids, we can paint an object with a number of different materials. Then, during rendering, the engine looks up the material based on an ID or pointer, and uses that material rather than internal information of the polygon—cool, huh?

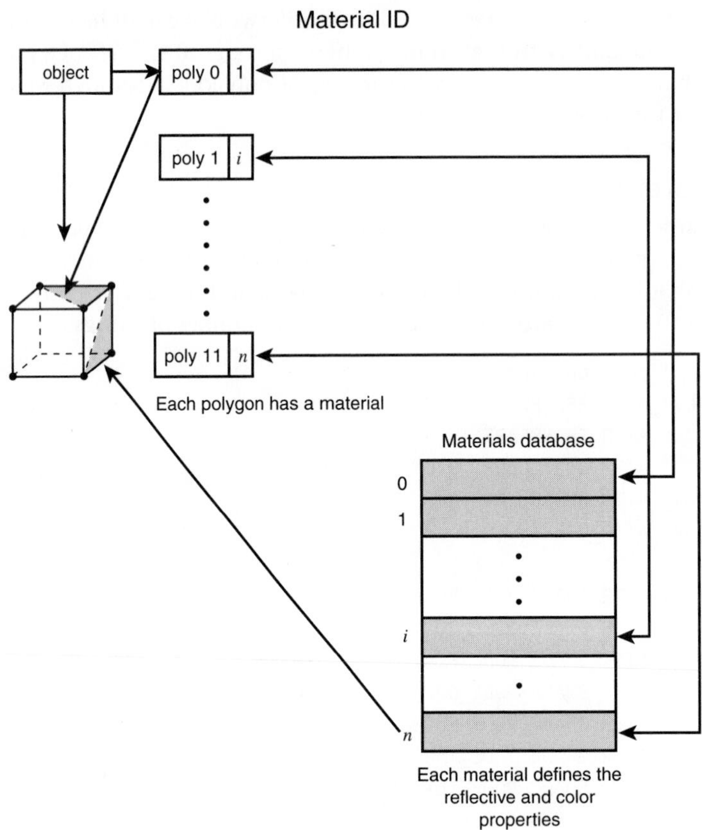

FIGURE 8.20 The relationship between materials and polygons.

So, here's what I came up with for a first-generation material structure. Of course, we may change this, and in this chapter we'll use it minimally, but let's start thinking along these lines. Anyway, here are the material definitions:

```
// defines for materials, follow our polygon attributes as much as possible
#define MATV1_ATTR_2SIDED                  0x0001
#define MATV1_ATTR_TRANSPARENT             0x0002
#define MATV1_ATTR_8BITCOLOR               0x0004
#define MATV1_ATTR_RGB16                   0x0008
#define MATV1_ATTR_RGB24                   0x0010

#define MATV1_ATTR_SHADE_MODE_CONSTANT     0x0020
#define MATV1_ATTR_SHADE_MODE_EMMISIVE     0x0020 // alias
#define MATV1_ATTR_SHADE_MODE_FLAT         0x0040
#define MATV1_ATTR_SHADE_MODE_GOURAUD      0x0080
```

```
#define MATV1_ATTR_SHADE_MODE_FASTPHONG   0x0100
#define MATV1_ATTR_SHADE_MODE_TEXTURE     0x0200


// states of materials
#define MATV1_STATE_ACTIVE                0x0001

// defines for material system
#define MAX_MATERIALS                     256
```

Now the material struct itself:

```
// a first version of a "material"
typedef struct MATV1_TYP
{
int state;          // state of material
int id;             // id of this material, index into material array
char name[64];      // name of material
int  attr;          // attributes, the modes for shading, constant, flat,
                    // gouraud, fast phong, environment, textured etc.
                    // and other special flags...

RGBAV1 color;            // color of material
float ka, kd, ks, power; // ambient, diffuse, specular,
// coefficients, note they are
// separate and scalars since many
// modelers use this format
// along with specular power

RGBAV1 ra, rd, rs;       // the reflectivities/colors pre-
                         // multiplied, to more match our
                         // definitions, each is basically
                         // computed by multiplying the
                         // color by the k's, eg:
                         // rd = color*kd etc.

char texture_file[80];   // file location of texture
BITMAP texture;          // actual texture map (if any)

} MATV1, *MATV1_PTR;
```

Nothing too strange there; I usually like to put `state`, `id`, `name`, and `attr` fields everywhere. But focus your attention on the rest of the fields—notice the `color` entry. Actually, it's a union that holds r, g, b, and alpha entries, along with a couple of convenient union access names/methods:

```
// RGB+alpha color
typedef struct RGBAV1_TYPE
{
union
    {
    int rgba;                    // compressed format
    UCHAR rgba_M[4];             // array format
    struct {  UCHAR a,b,g,r;  }; // explicit name format
    }; // end union

} RGBV1, *RGBV1_PTR;
```

Also, here's a helper macro to create an RGBA 32-bit word:

```
// this builds a 32 bit color value in 8.8.8.a format (8-bit alpha mode)
#define _RGBA32BIT(r,g,b,a) ((a) + ((b) << 8) + ((g) << 16) + (r << 24))
```

NOTE

We already had a macro `_RGB32BIT(a,r,g,b)` that creates DirectX-compatible 32-bit words, but I don't like alpha up top. I can see some places where having alpha in the lower byte might help, so we'll use the format RGBA.

Additionally, the structure contains the reflectivities `ka`, `kd`, `ks`, and power coefficients. This is due to the fact that many modelers like calling the reflectivities K's, so I used that convention. But, in my lighting model derivations, I used R's because those are easier to follow mathematically. Moreover, in our derivation, we basically merged the color and reflectivities together, but in the data structure, they're separate. But there are copies of them in `ra`, `rd`, and `rs`, which are pre-multiplied reflectivities more in line with our model. Bottom line: We may need one, the other, or both, so it's not going to kill us to store them in both formats. Here's an example using the scalars `ka`, `kd`, and `ks` and the ARGB color to compute our version of `ra`, `rd`, and `rs` (this is from the Caligari trueSpace object loader, which we'll see later in the chapter):

```
// compute material reflectivities in pre-multiplied format to help engine
for (int rgb_index=0; rgb_index < 3; rgb_index++)
    {
    // ambient reflectivity
    materials[material_index+num_materials].ra.rgba_M[rgb_index] =
    ( (UCHAR)(materials[material_index + num_materials].ka *
    (float)materials[material_index +
    num_materials].color.rgba_M[rgb_index] + 0.5) );
```

```
    // diffuse reflectivity
    materials[material_index+num_materials].rd.rgba_M[rgb_index] =
    ( (UCHAR)(materials[material_index + num_materials].kd *
    (float)materials[material_index +
     num_materials].color.rgba_M[rgb_index] + 0.5) );

    // specular reflectivity
    materials[material_index+num_materials].rs.rgba_M[rgb_index] =
    ( (UCHAR)(materials[material_index + num_materials].ks *
    (float)materials[material_index +
    num_materials].color.rgba_M[rgb_index] + 0.5) );

    } // end for rgb_index
```

Finally, there's support for a texture map and its name. That should about do it.

Okay, now that we have a material data structure, we need a global material library to store them in. So, here it is:

```
MATV1 materials[MAX_MATERIALS]; // materials in system
int num_materials;              // current number of materials
```

Very simple: just create a new material, insert it in the library, and then apply it to polygons! Of course, the problem is making the polygons and the engine do something with the material, but we'll get to that later. But let's at least write a function that initializes the material library to a known state:

```
int Reset_Materials_MATV1(void)
{
// this function resets all the materials
static int first_time = 1;

// if this is the first time then zero EVERYTHING out
if (first_time)
   {
   memset(materials, 0, MAX_MATERIALS*sizeof(MATV1));
   first_time = 0;
   } // end if

// scan thru materials and release all textures, if any?
for (int curr_matt = 0; curr_matt < MAX_MATERIALS; curr_matt++)
    {
    // regardless if the material is active check to see if there is a
    // dangling texture map
```

8

```
    Destroy_Bitmap(&materials[curr_matt].texture);
    // now it's safe to zero memory out
    memset(&materials[curr_matt], 0, sizeof(MATV1));
    } // end if

return(1);
} // end Reset_Materials_MATV1
```

To reset the material library array, simply call the function:

```
Reset_Materials_MATV1();
```

and you're all good. Next, let's look at an example of manually setting up a material because I'm still not sure if we're even going to think about a helper function until we really put materials to use and have a model format that supports them. In any case, say we want a material that reflects 100% of both ambient and diffuse light, has a color of pure blue, uses flat shading only, and no texture:

```
// load material into slot 0
MATV1_PTR m = &Materials[0];
// clear out structure
memset(m, sizeof(MATV1);

m->state = MATV1_ACTIVE;    // state of material

m->id = 0;                  // id of this material

strcpy(m->name, "blue mat 1"); // name
m->attr = MATV1_ATTR_2SIDED ¦ MATV1_ATTR_16BIT ¦
MATV1_ATTR_FLAT;    // attributes

m->color.rgba = _RGBA32BIT(0,0,255, 255); // set to blue
m->ka    = 1.0;  // set ambient reflectivity to 1.0
m->kd    = 1.0;  // set diffuse reflectivity to 1.0
m->ks    = 1.0;  // set specular reflectivity to 1.0
m->power = 0.0;  // not used, set to

// these are actual colors in RGBA format, so we need
// to scale the "blue" by the reflectivities and store
// we can do this without code, but let's do it the long
// way to see how, but only for the blue channel
m->ra.b = (UCHAR)(m->ka * (float)m->color.b +0.5);
m->rd.b = (UCHAR)(m->ka * (float)m->color.b +0.5);
m->rs.rgba = 0; // no specular reflectivity
```

Obviously, we're going to want a helper function(s) to do this, but because we aren't sure how we're going to define materials—that is, manually or by loading objects—let's hold off on that a bit. Now it's time to look at some lights.

Defining Lights

The practical implementation of lights is more or less like getting a root canal without Novocaine—it's nasty. Everything seems all rosy until you actually try to do it, and realize that you don't have billions of processor cycles to perform trillions of dot products, and quadrillions of trig functions....

I might be exaggerating a bit, but you get the point. In general, a good lighting engine would support infinite lights of any type, and the lighting calculations would be performed on a pixel-by-pixel basis for all the different material properties—that isn't going to happen. Even the most advanced 3D accelerators support only a handful of lights (8–16, in most cases). However, there are ways around this, such as light mapping, and we'll get to that. For now, keep in mind that we're NOT going to be able to do pixel-perfect lighting, and for the most part we're going to support only infinite and point lights. Moreover, all lighting calculations will be performed at triangle vertices only and then interpolation will be used to smooth lighting over surfaces (Gouraud/Phong shading).

Now that your dreams of writing a pixel shader in software have been crushed, let's define a basic light source structure that can handle the three types of lights we've discussed thus far (even though the spotlight has a photon's chance in hell of ever seeing the light of day) <BG>.

Here are the defines for the software lights (version 1.0). Notice that there are two subtypes for spotlights, so that later we might be able to use a standard and simplified model:

```
// defines for light types
#define LIGHTV1_ATTR_AMBIENT      0x0001  // basic ambient light
#define LIGHTV1_ATTR_INFINITE     0x0002  // infinite light source
#define LIGHTV1_ATTR_POINT        0x0004  // point light source
#define LIGHTV1_ATTR_SPOTLIGHT1   0x0008  // spotlight type 1 (simple)
#define LIGHTV1_ATTR_SPOTLIGHT2   0x0010  // spotlight type 2 (complex)

#define LIGHTV1_STATE_ON          1       // light on
#define LIGHTV1_STATE_OFF         0       // light off

#define MAX_LIGHTS                8       // good luck with 1!
```

Basically, we need to select the type of light and be able to set its state to on or off. Next, here's the data structure to store a light:

```
// version 1.0 light structure
typedef struct LIGHTV1_TYP
{
int state;          // state of light
int id;             // id of light
int attr;           // type of light, and extra qualifiers

RGBAV1 c_ambient;   // ambient light intensity
RGBAV1 c_diffuse;   // diffuse light intensity
RGBAV1 c_specular;  // specular light intensity
POINT4D  pos;       // position of light
VECTOR4D dir;       // direction of light
float kc, kl, kq;   // attenuation factors
float spot_inner;   // inner angle for spot light
float spot_outer;   // outer angle for spot light

float pf;           // power factor/falloff for spot lights

} LIGHTV1, *LIGHTV1_PTR;
```

Next is the global light array, which is much like the material array:

```
LIGHTV1 lights[MAX_LIGHTS];  // lights in system
int num_lights;              // current number of lights
```

And remember, we may use the materials, the lights, both, neither, or whatever, during the actual rendering, depending on what we're doing with the engine. At this early stage, we're just trying to create models of things that we're going to need in the future so that we don't do something stupid when we need them. Early planning in 3D engine design is important because as you're writing the engine, you can think about how something will work into it. If you wait until you're forced to add something, you pay. The best example of this I can think of is network support. Don't even *think* about thinking about adding network support after the engine is done!

Enough philosophy. Let's create some lights. Now, unlike materials, lights are something that I don't think there's much to think about. They're either there or they're not, and the engine can decide how much to use them and how far to go, but we can surely make a helper function to create lights that will work without many modifications. Basically, we just need to send the type of light, position, direction, and other values, based on what type of light we're creating. Also, because we're going to have so few lights (4–8), I'm going with the philosophy that we can turn on a particular light in the array, and then when the lighting stage runs, it simply runs through the (4–8) lights and lights that are on will be processed. Cool? Coool! First, let's start with a housekeeping function that initializes all the lights and turns them off:

```
int Reset_Lights_LIGHTV1(void)
{
// this function simply resets all lights in the system
static int first_time = 1;

memset(lights, 0, MAX_LIGHTS*sizeof(LIGHTV1));
// reset number of lights
num_lights = 0;

// reset first time
first_time = 0;

// return success
return(1);

} // end Reset_Lights_LIGHTV1
```

So, we would just make a call to `Reset_Lights_LIGHTV1()` in the initialization section of the engine/game. Moving on, here's the helper function to create a light:

```
int Init_Light_LIGHTV1(
    int           index,      // index of light to create (0..MAX_LIGHTS-1)
    int          _state,      // state of light
    int          _attr,       // type of light, and extra qualifiers
    RGBAV1       _c_ambient,  // ambient light intensity
    RGBAV1       _c_diffuse,  // diffuse light intensity
    RGBAV1       _c_specular, // specular light intensity
    POINT4D_PTR  _pos,        // position of light
    VECTOR4D_PTR _dir,        // direction of light
    float kc, kl, kq,         // attenuation factors
    float        _spot_inner, // inner angle for spot light
    float        _spot_outer, // outer angle for spot light
    float        _pf)         // power factor/falloff for spot lights
{
// this function initializes a light based on the flags sent in _attr, values that
// aren't needed are set to 0 by caller
// make sure light is in range
if (index < 0 || index >= MAX_LIGHTS)
   return(0);

// all good, initialize the light (many fields may be dead)
lights[index].state       = _state;      // state of light
lights[index].id          = index;       // id of light
lights[index].attr        = _attr;       // type of light, and extra qualifiers
```

8

```
lights[index].c_ambient   = _c_ambient;  // ambient light intensity
lights[index].c_diffuse   = _c_diffuse;  // diffuse light intensity
lights[index].c_specular  = _c_specular; // specular light intensity
lights[index].kc  = _kc;         // constant, linear, and quadratic attenuation fac-
tors
lights[index].kl  = _kl;
lights[index].kq  = _kq;

if (pos)
    VECTOR4D_COPY(&lights[index].pos, _pos;  // position of light
if (dir)
   {
   VECTOR4D_COPY(&lights[index].dir, _dir;  // direction of light
   // normalize it
   VECTOR4D_Normalize(&lights[index].dir);
   } // end if

lights[index].spot_inner  = _spot_inner; // inner angle for spot light
lights[index].spot_outer  = _spot_outer; // outer angle for spot light
lights[index].pf          = _pf;         // power factor/falloff for spot lights

// return light index as success
return(index);

} // end Create_Light_LIGHTV1
```

For the most part, the function simply copies the sent parameters into the light structure after performing a little error checking. After the function completes, it returns the index of the light it just created (of course, you sent this in, but what the heck). Referring to the function, let's create some lights....

Creating an Ambient Light

Every scene is (probably) going to have an ambient light; in fact, our first solid engine is going to have nothing but ambient light. In any case, here's how to set up an ambient light:

```
ambient_light = Init_Light_LIGHTV1(0,  // use index 0 for ambient lights
    LIGHTV1_STATE_ON,                  // turn the light on
    LIGHTV1_ATTR_AMBIENT,              // ambient light type
   _RGBA32BIT(255,255,255,0), 0, 0,    // pure white light for ambient term only
    NULL, NULL,                        // no need for pos or dir
    0,0,0,                             // no need for attenuation
    0,0,0);                            // spotlight info NA
```

Very cool, huh? Once a light is turned on, we can manually toggle it by accessing the state variable as follows:

```
Lights[ambient_light].state = LIGHTV1_STATE_OFF;
```

TIP

We could write helper functions all day long, but I just want to keep things simple; otherwise, I would program in Java <BG>.

Creating an Infinite Light (Directional Light)

Next, let's create an infinite diffuse light source similar to the sun. Hence, let's color it yellow and point it straight up (technically you might feel more comfortable with the direction being down, but it's just a vector and pointing toward the light source makes the math easier) from the positive y-axis as shown in Figure 8.21 (note that all directions must be unit vectors).

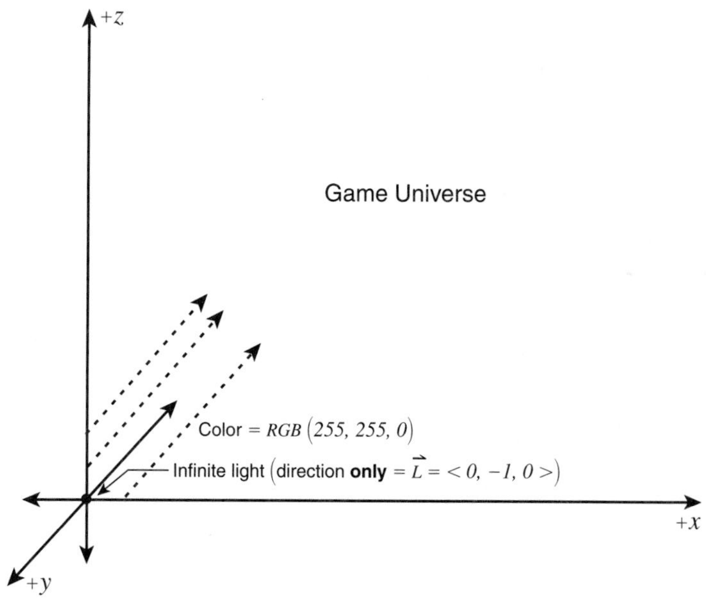

FIGURE 8.21 The infinite light setup for the example.

```
VECTOR4D sun_dir = {0, -1, 0, 0};

sun_light = Init_Light_LIGHTV1(1,         // use index 1 for sun light
            LIGHTV1_STATE_ON,             // turn the light on
            LIGHTV1_ATTR_INFINITE,        //  light type
            0, RGBA32BIT(255,255,0,0), 0, // pure yellow light for diffuse term only
            NULL, &sun_dir, // no need for pos, but dir is (0,-1,0)
            0,0,0,          // no need for attenuation
            0,0,0);         // spotlight info NA
```

Creating a Point Light

For a point light, let's use the sun model, but position it 10,000 units above on the positive y-axis (because point lights have position). Figure 8.22 illustrates this.

```
VECTOR4D sun_pos = {0, 10000, 0, 0};

sun_light = Init_Light_LIGHTV1(1,          // use index 1 for sun light
            LIGHTV1_STATE_ON,              // turn the light on
            LIGHTV1_ATTR_POINT,            //  light type
            0, RGBA32BIT(255,255,0,0), 0,// pure yellow light for diffuse term only
            &sun_pos, NULL,    // position above on y-axis, no need for direction
            0,1,0,             // linear attenuation = 1
            0,0,0);            // spotlight info NA
```

Creating a Spotlight

Finally, let's create a spotlight, if for nothing else than to help memorize the function call! Seriously though, as you can see from the math, real-time spotlights based on the full model are really out of the question. Moreover, we would be able to compute the spotlight only at vertices because doing it for each pixel would be insane. Thus, to even see the spotlight, we would need a lot of polygons on the object. That's not to say we can't make a demo of it, but in gameplay, it's not going to happen—it's just too slow. But, on the other hand, there are tricks such as light mapping to create spotlights, and we will cover them later in the book, so don't despair.

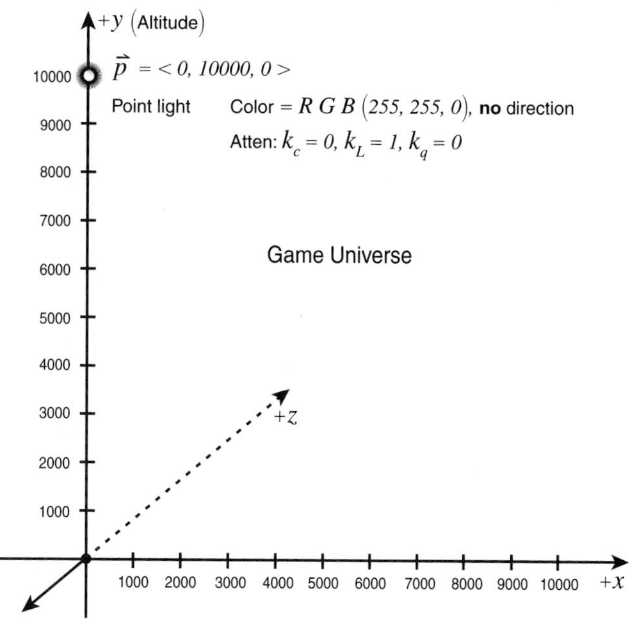

FIGURE 8.22 The point light setup for the example.

At any rate, let's define a spotlight at position **p** = (1000, 1000, -1000), directed toward the origin **o**(0,0,0), **v** = <-1, -1, 1>, with a 50% intensity of white light RGB = (128,128,128). It affects both diffuse and specular materials with an inner angle umbra of 30 degrees and an out angle penumbra of 60 degrees, with a falloff/power factor of 1.0. That's a mouthful! Referring to Figure 8.23, here's the code:

```
VECTOR4D spot_pos = {1000,1000,-1000, 0};
VECTOR4D spot_dir = {-1, -1, 1,0};
float umbra = 30, penumbra = 60, falloff = 1.0;

int spot_light = Init_Light_LIGHTV1(5, // use index 5 for this light
                  LIGHTV1_STATE_ON,     // turn the light on
                  LIGHTV1_SPOTLIGHT1,   //  light type (spotlight 1)
                 _0, RGBA32BIT(128,128,128,0), 0, // 50% white light for diffuse
term only
                  &spot_pos, &spot_dir,          // position of spot light
                  umbra,penumbra,falloff);       // spotlight info
```

8

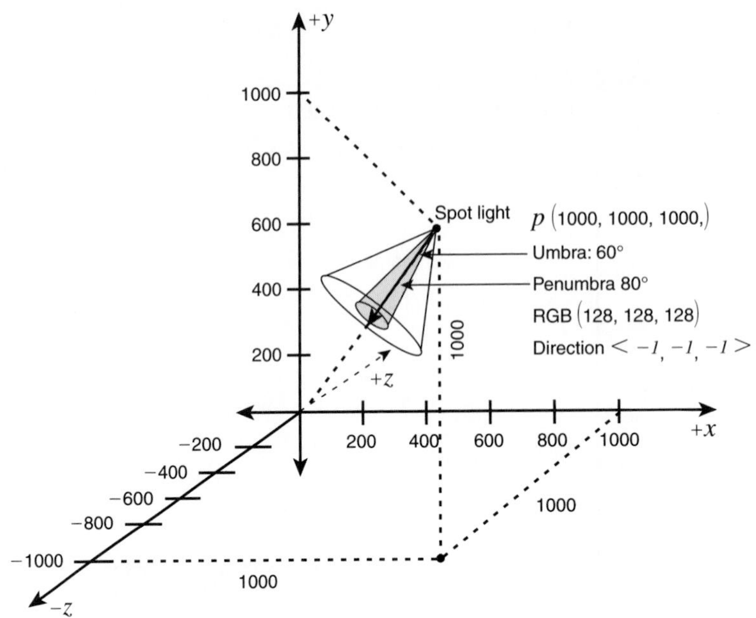

FIGURE 8.23 The spotlight setup for the example.

Shading in the Real World

We're almost ready to actually draw something! The funny part is that 50% of everything we learned in this chapter won't be utilized until later. But, as I said, materials and lighting are the kinds of things you need to know about before you learn them…if that makes any sense. In any event, I would like to take a moment to discuss practical implementations and optimizations as they relate to 8/16-bit graphics modes. I'm doing so because 8-bit modes are going to be three times faster than the 16-bit modes because we don't have to deal with the three RGB channels—we deal with only a single brightness or luminance value. So, let's talk a little about that.

16-Bit Shading

Shading begins with materials and lights. For the most part, the models that we've built are based upon RGB space. For example, our materials have RGB values for reflectivities, our lights have RGB colors, and so forth. Thus, in most cases, we can perform the lighting calculations just as we have outlined in the mathematical descriptions at the beginning of this chapter. Of course, the final implementation may cheat or use assumptions.

For example, we may decide that all lights are white to speed things up. We might also decide that all objects are only affected by ambient, diffuse, and emissive properties and leave it at that. However, whatever we do, at some point, we're going to have to compute the final color of a polygon, vertex, or pixel, and that means some math will have to be performed. But remember: we want to keep the math to a minimum. I can tell you that doing something on a per-polygon or per-vertex basis isn't going to kill you, but anything on a per-pixel basis will.

Next, the question may arise, what format should we use for the math? Why? Well, we're using 16-bit RGB mode. That means at some point we need to convert our calculations into 16-bit RGB mode. Alas, should we perform our lighting calculations knowing this or perform them in a more general way and simply "eat" the conversion? These are the kinds of things I want you thinking about. There are no good answers except this one: whichever method is fastest, use it.

8-Bit Shading

16-bit shading is mathematically easier to track than 8-bit shading. The reason, of course, is that there's a reasonable 1:1 mapping of intensities in RGB space to the actual pixels on the screen. For example, say we have a polygon that has diffuse reflection and ambient reflection and is pure blue RGB(0,0,255). Now assume that the light intensity turns out to be 50% or .5 for the active lights, and 20% or .2 for the ambient light level.

There are a couple of ways to think about this. First, let's talk about the ambient light. If a material has color blue and the ambient light has color red, you won't see anything if we're working totally in RGB space. The following is the reason why:

```
Final_pixelrgb = materialrgb*ambientrgb

= (0,0,255)*(1.0,0,0) = (0,0,0)
```

However, if we use the simplification that all lights are just intensities of pure white, it simplifies our math a bit. In that case, you would see something.

```
Final_pixelrgb = materialrgb*ambientrgb

= (0,0,255)*(1.0,1.0,1.0) = (0,0,255)
```

8

NOTE

Notice that the ambient light levels have been converted to floats in the range of (0..1) so that modulation calculations have the same range as the color space. We can easily use (0..255), but we'll have to scale after the calculations.

A Robust RGB Model for 8-Bit Modes

Keep that in your head, because our final engine is, for the most part, going to use white lights to ease calculations. Now, here's the problem: In either of the brief RGB examples you saw earlier, the resulting final pixels are in RGB 24-bit format or maybe even in (0..1, 0..1, 0..1) format, which can quickly be converted to RGB 24-bit format. The point is that we then take the RGB 24-bit value and convert it to 16-bit and write it to the screen.

However, in 8-bit mode, this means nothing! The screen is not in RGB format, but indexes into colors—therein lies the problem. So, what's the solution? How do we perform lighting in an indexed mode?

The answer is simple. We just need an intermediate step that converts RGB values into color indices and *then* writes those values to the screen. But the problem, of course, is that there can be only 256 colors at once, so when an RGB color is computed, we have to perform a closest-match scan in the color palette and use that color index as the final color; this process is shown in Figure 8.24. Basically, say you have a color RGB(10,45,34). The closest thing to that in the palette might be color index 45, which has the value (14,48,40)—that's the value that would be returned. But that would mean a "least-squares" computation and scan of the entire color palette each time a pixel had to be written—ouch! Therefore, we need to use lookup tables to perform the math ahead of time. What we need to do is the following: decide on an RGB space and then create a lookup table that maps the input RGB vector into an index. The RGB vector itself is used as an index into the table.

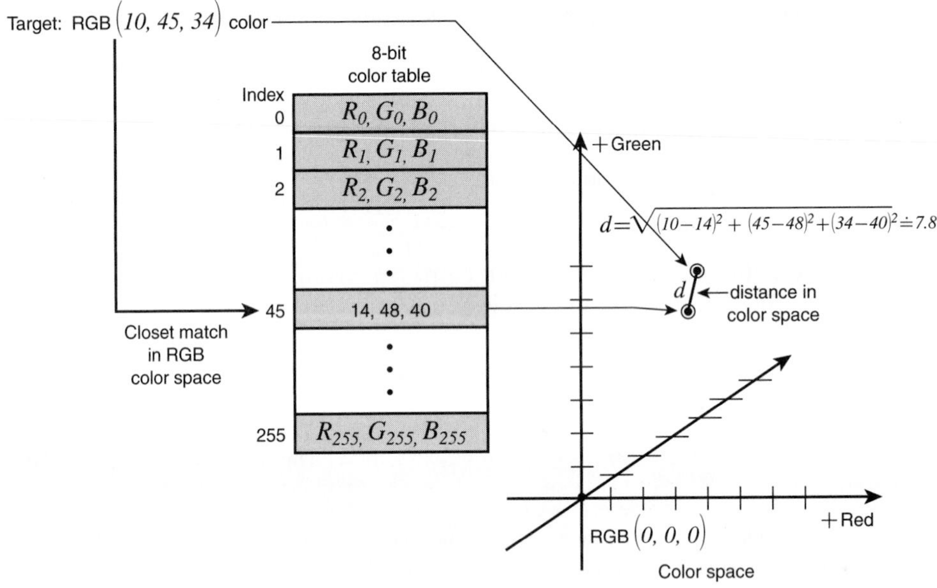

FIGURE 8.24 Searching for a closest match in the color table.

TIP

When using 8-bit color modes with real-time shading, you must use a color palette that covers a lot of RGB space and has lots of shades. If you use a palette that leans toward a portion of the color space, you're going to get woefully ugly lighting. The palettes I supply in the bitmap files `PALDATAxx.BMP|PAL` are good choices and have worked well for me. Of course, all your graphics *must* use these colors because there's only one palette in 8-bit modes.

Whether we perform our lighting calculations in RGB 8.8.8 mode or in a 16-bit mode itself (5.5.5 or 5.6.5 format), we surely can't create a lookup table that maps all 8.8.8 RGB values into indices—that would take 4 gigabytes, which is a bit excessive <BG>. However, what we can do is this: create a 16-bit RGB lookup table that maps any RGB value that's in 16-bit format into an 8-bit index. That will take only 64KB of memory—that I can deal with! Also, because we may have a 5.6.5 or 5.5.5 format, we need to be able to generate two possible tables, one for each input format. Now, make sure that you understand this: Given any 24-bit input RGB value, we're going to first convert it to 16-bit 5.5.5 or 5.6.5 format. That value is then going to be used as a single binary word as an index into a color table that's composed of single-byte entries that are each index values pointing in the 256-color palette that that has the closest RGB value. This is shown in Figure 8.25.

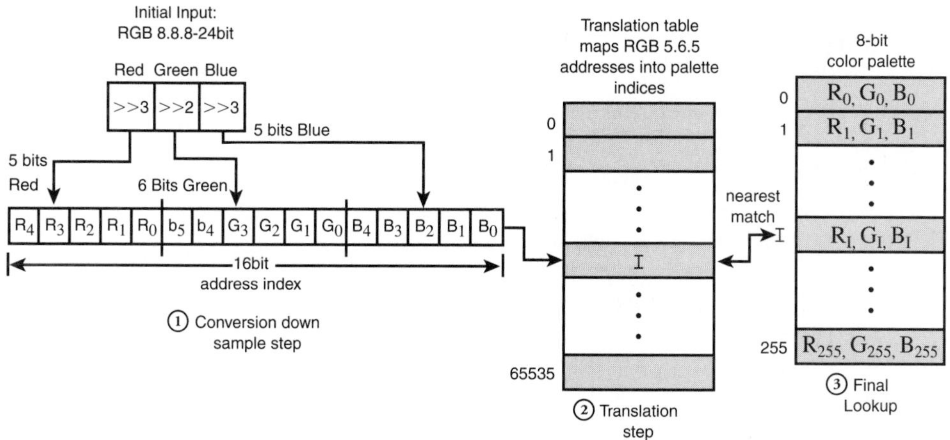

FIGURE 8.25 The structure of the indexed RGB color translation lookup table.

With that in mind, what we need is a function that works as follows: We supply it with the 16-bit format that we want it to generate a color translation table for, an 8-bit source palette for the translation, and a pointer to the data table it should fill. (We might want to have multiple palettes and lookups for different regions on the world; otherwise, I would use a global table in the function.) Here's the function that just does that:

```
int RGB_16_8_IndexedRGB_Table_Builder(
    int rgb_format,  // format we want to build table for
                     // 99/100 565
    LPPALETTEENTRY src_palette, // source palette
    UCHAR *rgblookup)           // lookup table
{
// this function takes as input the rgb format
// that it should generate the lookup table
// for;  dd_pixel_format = DD_PIXEL_FORMAT565, or DD_PIXEL_FORMAT555
```

```
// notice in 5.5.5 format the input has only 32K possible colors
// and the high most bit will be disregarded
//thus the look up table will only need to be 32K
// in either case, it's up to the caller
// to send in the rgblookup table pre-allocated
// the function doesn't allocate memory for the caller
// the function uses a simple least squares scan for all possible
// RGB colors in the 16-bit color space that map to the discrete RGB space

// in the 8-bit palette

// first check the pointers
if (!src_palette || !rgblookup)
   return(-1);

// what is the color depth we are building a table for?
if (rgb_format==DD_PIXEL_FORMAT565)
   {
   // there are a total of 64k entries,
   // perform a loop and look them up, do the least
   // amount of work, even with a pentium,
   // there are 65536*256 iterations here!
   for (int rgbindex = 0; rgbindex < 65536; rgbindex++)
   {
   int  curr_index  = -1;       // current color index of best match
   long curr_error  = INT_MAX;  // distance in color space to
                                // nearest match or "error"

       for (int color_index = 0; color_index < 256; color_index++)
       {
       // extract r,g,b from rgbindex
       // assuming an encoding of 5.6.5, then scale to 8.8.8 since
       // palette is in that format always
       int r = (rgbindex >> 11) << 3;;
       int g = ((rgbindex >> 5) & 0x3f) << 2;
       int b = (rgbindex & 0x1f) << 3;

       // compute distance to color from target
       long delta_red   = abs(src_palette[color_index].peRed   - r);
       long delta_green = abs(src_palette[color_index].peGreen - g);
       long delta_blue  = abs(src_palette[color_index].peBlue  - b);
       long error = (delta_red*delta_red) + (delta_green*delta_green) +
                    (delta_blue*delta_blue);
```

```
        // is this color a better match?
        if (error < curr_error)
           {
           curr_index = color_index;
           curr_error = error;
           } // end if

       } // end for color_index

   // best match has been found, enter it into table
   rgblookup[rgbindex] = curr_index;

  } // end for rgbindex

  } // end if
else
if (rgb_format==DD_PIXEL_FORMAT555)
   {
   // there are a total of 32k entries,
   // perform a loop and look them up, do the least
   // amount of work, even with a pentium,
   // there are 32768*256 iterations here!
   for (int rgbindex = 0; rgbindex < 32768; rgbindex++)
   {
   int  curr_index  = -1;      // current color index of best match
   long curr_error  = INT_MAX; // distance in color space to
                               // nearest match or

   for (int color_index = 0; color_index < 256; color_index++)
   {
   // extract r,g,b from rgbindex, assuming an encoding of 5.6.5
   // then scale to 8.8.8 since
   // palette is in that format always
   int r =  (rgbindex >> 10) << 3;;
   int g = ((rgbindex >> 5) & 0x1f) << 3;
   int b =  (rgbindex & 0x1f) << 3;

   // compute distance to color from target
   long delta_red   = abs(src_palette[color_index].peRed   - r);
   long delta_green = abs(src_palette[color_index].peGreen - g);
   long delta_blue  = abs(src_palette[color_index].peBlue  - b);
   long error = (delta_red*delta_red) + (delta_green*delta_green) +
                (delta_blue*delta_blue);
```

```
    // is this color a better match?
    if (error < curr_error)
       {
       curr_index = color_index;
       curr_error = error;
       } // end if
    } // end for color_index

   // best match has been found, enter it into table
   rgblookup[rgbindex] = curr_index;

} // end for rgbindex
} // end if
else
   return(-1); // serious problem! unsupported format,
               // what are you doing to me!!!!

// return success
return(1);

} // end RGB_16_8_IndexedRGB_Table_Builder
```

The function operates just as we outlined. That is, we know that with a 16-bit color, the possible input range varies from 0–65535. Thus, we simply create a lookup table that computes the nearest match for all these possibilities. To use the function, you call it after initializing DirectDraw and loading your 8-bit game palette as follows:

```
// create storage for look up table
UCHAR rgblookup = (UCHAR *)malloc(65536);

// use the global bit depth and palette in call
RGB_16_8_IndexedRGB Table_Builder(dd_pixel_format, palette, rgblookuptable);
```

On return from the function, `rgblookup[]` would contain the 16-bit to 8-bit translation table for either 5.6.5 or 5.5.5 mode. So, to use it, we simply perform our lighting calculations as usual. When they're complete, we convert the final pixel to 16-bit, and then write the pixel to the screen as follows:

```
final_pixel_index = rgblookup[final_pixelrgb16];
```

And that's it! Wheewww… Lots of details, huh? Now, let's take a look at what we gained here. By using a preprocessing step, we completely turned all the translations into a single lookup, which is great, but there's still a single lookup per pixel for 8-bit mode. The question is, do we need this? Well, the answer is as follows: You're never going to get rid of this step, no matter what. Whenever you perform lighting in 8-bit mode, the results are always going to have to be translated to 8-bit indices one way or another. Sure, you can use tricks. For example, you can create a color palette that has shades of each color and then the intensity can be used as an index from the base color into the table; but again, you're still using an index, in essence. The moral of the story is that if lighting is performed in RGB space, you're going to get hit no matter what because the calculations themselves must be carried out and then translated into an 8-bit index.

The question is; can we create a color model that is more 8-bit oriented in the first place, and minimize the 16-bit RGB intermediate steps? Of course, let's take a look at that.

A Simplified Intensity Model for 8-Bit Modes

The part of shading that will kill us in any mode is the calculation of the final RGB value. However, if we simplify the lighting model so that we aren't concerned with color in the lights or the materials, we can use an extremely simplified 8-bit shading model. Here's how it works: All polygons have a color in RGB space that's defined by the palette. Now, because we know we're dealing with 8-bit indices and 8.8.8 format in the palette, let's forget all the RGB stuff, think out of the box for a moment, and perform the lighting in the opposite direction. That is, based on the palette we have, compute all 256 possible intensity values for that color. Then create a table that has 256 rows, one row for each color in the real palette; each row contains 256 entries each that are the palette entries of that row's best matches to 256 intensity values. Figure 8.26 illustrates this.

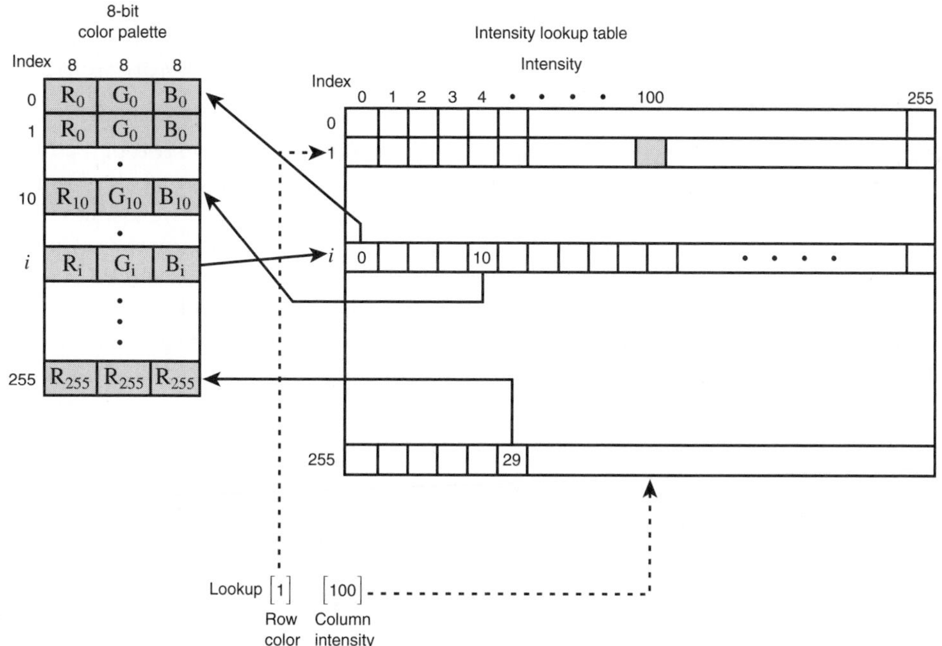

FIGURE 8.26 The structure of the intensity indexed color translation lookup table.

8

The point is, why compute general intensity values? Let's compute the intensity values around the colors that we know exist, and then when we perform the lighting step, we'll use the color as the index into the row and the intensity as an index in the column of the table. Again, we're using a lookup table, but we've completely cut out all the intermediate 16-bit RGB steps by forcing an 8-bit model and assuming that intensity values are in the range of (0..255), which is simple because even if they aren't, we can always scale them.

Now, if you're a little confused, listen to this. The first, more robust model uses RGB space throughout, meaning that the light calculations are performed in RGB space and then a 16-bit RGB desired color is sent to the lookup table for translation. However, we already know that we aren't in 16-bit mode, so why the drama? The reason, of course, is that it's more generalized. However, if we think of things from the point of view of "what colors are there in the palette to shade in the first place?" we can simply create a shader translation table that, for each color in the palette, contains 256 values that represent the intensity modulated versions of that particular color. The reason this works is that we know that the models in the 8-bit simulation will always be one of the colors in the palette! Of course, because we're synthetically searching for 256 shades of each color with a least-squares match, colors that don't have a lot of shades are going to look bad, but what the heck!

I'm going to show you a function shortly that performs the lookup, but the thing to remember is that we need to write two different shader front ends for 8-bit modes if we want to use both of these techniques, because one shader will perform all calculations in RGB space and then, at the last minute, translate to 8-bit indices via a call to `rgblookup[]` with the RGB color compressed into an index. However, the new model will use a 2D lookup table where the first index is the color and the second is the intensity, as follows `rgbintensitylookup[color][intensity]`.

To write the function that generates the table, we basically need to loop through all the colors in the palette and then compute all RGB-valued 256 shades of each color. And here's the gotcha: When we're computing the 256 shades of a color, do we assume that the color is at 100% intensity and then downscale from there? That is, say we're trying to compute all intensities of color index 5, which happens to have RGB values (100,40,30). The problem is that the RGB model isn't the greatest thing in the world to do this, and the reason why is that we really need the hue of a color and then create all 256 intensities of it.

As another example, and to put a finer point on it, say we have the color (100,0,0). That's a mid-intensity red, so do we create 256 shades of red assuming that (100,0,0) is the 100% version of red? Or do we do some math so that we compute a virtual color of (255,0,0) and then create all the shades of it because that's what's more intended by the user and gives better results for the lighting engine?

These questions are definitely issues, but at this point, I say we use the following convention: For any color index, we look at the RGB values of this color and then brighten the color so that we max out one or more of the channels without overflowing the channel.

We use that color as our "color," compute the 256 intensities for that color, and then look those up. This will have the effect of darkening models, but giving them a more uniform color space. Here's an example of taking a source color, c, and computing a maximized intensity color, c*.

Intensity Modulation Algorithm:
Given:

polygon color c = RGB(red,green,blue) = RGB(50,20,100)

c* = RGB(red*,green*,blue*)

Step 1 - Compute largest component:

Largest component = blue = 100

Step 2 - Set maximum component to 255, compute ratio:

blue = 100, blue* = 255, ratio = 255/100 = 2.55

Step 3 - Scale all other channels by ratio:

red* = red * ratio = 50 * 2.55 = 127.5

green* = green * ratio = 20 * 2.55 = 51.0

blue = 255

Rounding off, c* = RGB(128, 51, 255), which is the same "color," but a higher intensity; that is, the ratios of R:G:B are the same. Now, we can assume that this is the 100% intensity value for the color index we were working with and compute 256 intensity values, which is very similar to the previous function we wrote. But instead of searching for general RGB values, we're going to mathematically generate them and then search for them. The algorithm works as follows: For each color (after the intensity modulation phase), we assume that it's at 100% intensity, and then compute 256 intensity values from the color down to total 0 intensity for all channels. With each RGB value, we perform the standard least-squares search in the real color palette, find the nearest match, and write it to the row of the color index we're working with. For example, if we had the color 25 = RGB(255,0,0), we would scan for colors:

ROW25 = [RGB(0,0,0)i_1, RGB(1,0,0)i_2, RGB(2,0,0)i_3, ..., RGB(255,0,0)i_{256})]

where each RGB(x,x,x)i means the color index that closely matches RGB(x,x,x).

I hope I didn't belabor all this 8-bit stuff too much. But it's subtle and very useful in software engines and nonaccelerated handhelds, so I want you to really get a handle on all the sick and twisted tricks that are used to format the input domain and output range of the color translations that are performed in a game.

Okay, as promised, here's the function that creates an intensity table from a given palette. Note that the bit depth is irrelevant because all calculation are performed in RGB 8.8.8

space and the results are 8-bit palette indices. Therefore, we need only the input palette and the storage for the table (which is 64KB—256 rows of 256 intensities, 1 byte per entry):

```
int RGB_16_8_Indexed_Intensity_Table_Builder(LPPALETTEENTRY src_palette,
UCHAR rgbilookup[256][256],  // lookup table
int intensity_normalization=1)
{
// this function takes the source palette to compute
// the intensity shading table with
// the table will be formatted such that
// each row is a color index, and each column
// is the shade 0..255 desired, the output is a single byte index
// in either case, it's up to the caller to send in the
// rgbilookup table pre-allocated
// 64k buffer byte [256][256]the function doesn't
// allocate memory for the caller
// the function builds the table by looping thru each color
// in the color palette and then
// for each color, it scales the color to maximum intensity
// without overflow the RGB channels
// and then uses this as the 100% intensity value of the color,
// then the algorithm computes
// the 256 shades of the color, and then uses the
// standard least squares scan the find the
// colors in the palette and stores them in the row of the
// current color under intensity
// translation, sounds diabolical huh?
// Note: if you set intensity normalization to 0
// the maximization step isn't performed.
int ri,gi,bi;        // initial color
int rw,gw,bw;        // current working color
float ratio;         // scaling ratio
float dl,dr,db,dg;   // intensity gradients for 256 shades

// first check the pointers
if (!src_palette || !rgbilookup)
   return(-1);

// for each color in the palette, compute maximum intensity value then scan
// for 256 shades of it
for (int col_index = 0; col_index < 256; col_index++)
    {
```

```
// extract color from palette
ri = src_palette[col_index].peRed;
gi = src_palette[col_index].peGreen;
bi = src_palette[col_index].peBlue;

// find largest channel then max it out and scale other
// channels based on ratio
if (intensity_normalization==1)
    {
    // red largest?
   if (ri >= gi && ri >= bi)
      {
      // compute scaling ratio
      ratio = (float)255/(float)ri;

      // max colors out
      ri = 255;
      gi = (int)((float)gi * ratio + 0.5);
      bi = (int)((float)bi * ratio + 0.5);
      } // end if
  else // green largest?
  if (gi >= ri && gi >= bi)
     {
     // compute scaling ratio
     ratio = (float)255/(float)gi;

     // max colors out
     gi = 255;
     ri = (int)((float)ri * ratio + 0.5);
     bi = (int)((float)bi * ratio + 0.5);
     } // end if
  else // blue is largest
     {
     // compute scaling ratio
     ratio = (float)255/(float)bi;

     // max colors out
     bi = 255;
     ri = (int)((float)ri * ratio + 0.5);
     gi = (int)((float)gi * ratio + 0.5);
     } // end if

  } // end if
```

```
// at this point, we need to compute the intensity gradients for this color,
// so we can compute the RGB values for 256 shades of the current color
dl = sqrt(ri*ri + gi*gi + bi*bi)/(float)256;
dr = ri/dl,
db = gi/dl,
dg = bi/dl;

// initialize working color
rw = 0;
gw = 0;
bw = 0;

// at this point rw,gw,bw, is the color that we need to compute
// the 256 intensities for to
// enter into the col_index (th) row of the table
for (int intensity_index = 0; intensity_index < 256; intensity_index++)
    {
    int  curr_index  = -1;          // current color index of best match
    long curr_error  = INT_MAX;     // distance in color space to
                                    // nearest match or "error"

    for (int color_index = 0; color_index < 256; color_index++)
        {
        // compute distance to color from target
        long delta_red   = abs(src_palette[color_index].peRed   - rw);
        long delta_green = abs(src_palette[color_index].peGreen - gw);
        long delta_blue  = abs(src_palette[color_index].peBlue  - bw);
        long error = (delta_red*delta_red) +
                     (delta_green*delta_green) +
                     (delta_blue*delta_blue);
        // is this color a better match?
       if (error < curr_error)
           {
           curr_index = color_index;
           curr_error = error;
           } // end if

        } // end for color_index

// best match has been found, enter it into table
rgbilookup[col_index][intensity_index] = curr_index;

// compute next intensity level
// (test for overflow, shouldn't happen, but never know)
```

```
if (rw+=dr > 255) rw=255;
if (gw+=dg > 255) gw=255;
if (bw+=db > 255) bw=255;

} // end for intensity_index
} // end for c_index
// return success
return(1);

} // end RGB_16_8_Indexed_Intensity_Table_Builder
```

To create the table, you call it in much the same way as the RGB version:

```
UCHAR rgbilookup[256][256];
RGB_16_8_Indexed_Intensity_Table_Builder(palette, rgbilookup, 1);
```

To use the table, say that you have a polygon with color index 12. You could care less what the actual color is, but you want the final color to be color 12 with an intensity of 150 (255 max, of course):

```
Final_pixel = rgbilookup[12][15];
```

Simple as that!

NOTE

Setting the last parameter of the function `intensity_normalization` to `0` simply disables the maximization step. It takes a color RGB(100,0,0) and computes the 256 shades based on RGB(100,10,10), rather than our heuristic convention of maxing out the largest channel and then converting that value to 256 shades—which in this case would be the value RGB(255,25,25) into 256 shades.

Constant Shading

I don't know about you, but I'm really tired of talking about shading—I want to do it! Therefore, we're going to create both 8- and 16-bit versions of everything to give you the tools to use 8-bit on slower machines if you need to, and 16-bit on those Pentium 4+s. Anyway, the first kind of shading we're going to look at is constant shading. This is the absolute simplest model and doesn't take anything into consideration—no ambient light, no diffuse light, nothing. We just want the polygons to be solid and have a color. Hence, constant shading doesn't care about the lighting model whatsoever. We literally just take the index or RGB value for the color of the polygon and draw it. This is exactly how we're going to implement emissive polygons; that is, polygons that give off light. We're just going to draw them in whatever color they are defined. Of course, as I previously described, emissive polygons don't actually generate light, but they *look* like they do. If you really want them to generate light, you'll have to attach a real light to them.

In any event, we have everything we need for a constant-shaded demo right now. I'm going to take the tank demo from Chapter 7 and simply replace the call that draws the polygons from the wireframe version with the solid version we discussed earlier. Here's the old code (16-bit call):

```
// render the object
Draw_RENDERLIST4DV1_Wire16(&rend_list, back_buffer, back_lpitch);
```

And now here's the new call:

```
// render the object
Draw_RENDERLIST4DV1_Solid16(&rend_list, back_buffer, back_lpitch);
```

CAUTION

I had to generate new .PLG files for each of the objects in the demo (tank, marker, tower) to make certain that we have the winding order correct for each polygon and have the one-sided or two-sided flags correct. This is a must because we're drawing things solid now, and we want to make sure that the back-facing polygons are removed and not rendered.

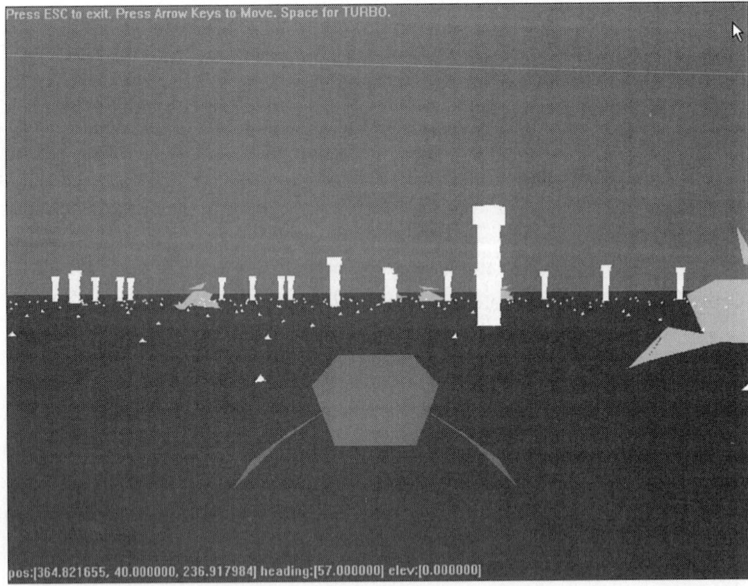

FIGURE 8.27 A screenshot of the first shaded demo.

The results of switching this single call are shown in Figure 8.27. The source and executable are DEMOII8_4.CPP¦EXE (DEMOII8_4_8b.CPP¦EXE). Now let's take a quick look at the shading support in the PLX/PLG format:

```
// double sided flag
#define PLX_2SIDED_FLAG              0x1000   // this poly is double sided
#define PLX_1SIDED_FLAG              0x0000   // this poly is single sided

// shading mode of polygon
#define PLX_SHADE_MODE_PURE_FLAG      0x0000  // this poly is a constant color
#define PLX_SHADE_MODE_CONSTANT_FLAG  0x0000  // alias
#define PLX_SHADE_MODE_FLAT_FLAG      0x2000  // this poly uses flat shading
#define PLX_SHADE_MODE_GOURAUD_FLAG   0x4000  // this poly used gouraud shading
#define PLX_SHADE_MODE_PHONG_FLAG     0x6000  // this poly uses phong shading
#define PLX_SHADE_MODE_FASTPHONG_FLAG 0x6000  // this poly uses phong shading
(alias)
```

The Draw_RENDERLIST4DV1*() functions at this point don't take the shading model into consideration. This makes sense because when we wrote them, there wasn't a model to model! However, at least the PLG/PLX format does have support to select the different kinds of shading you desire. In this case, that would be the PLX_SHADE_MODE_CONSTANT_FLAG flag, but the function doesn't even look at it, so it's moot. However, the code we write in the next chapter will look at it because we're going to fully support all these concepts in the lighting model and functions. However, at this point, I don't want to rewrite the entire engine because we don't have time in this chapter, and we've covered so many new ideas that I just want to implement them with what we have now, and clean it up next chapter.

With that in mind, play around with the demo for a minute and then come back here. I want to see if you notice something.... If you play with the demo or have been paying close attention to the book, there is a serious flaw in the renderer at this point: It's drawing polygons out of order! In other words, we need to implement some sort of depth sorting so that polygons are rendered back to front. One such method to fix this is called the *painter's algorithm*. It's a simple algorithm to implement, and for simple geometry, it can sort our polygons for us and render them in the correct way. I don't want to write an algorithm for it yet because this is an issue of visibility, but we'll write one by the end of this chapter just to hold you over before we get into more complex visibility and depth buffering algorithms. Briefly, the main idea is simple. Given a render list, we simply sort the polygons on their average z-values from back to front and then render, in that order. That takes care of most of the visual problems you're seeing in the demo. The process is shown in Figure 8.28, but we'll get to that later. Let's move on to more advanced lighting.

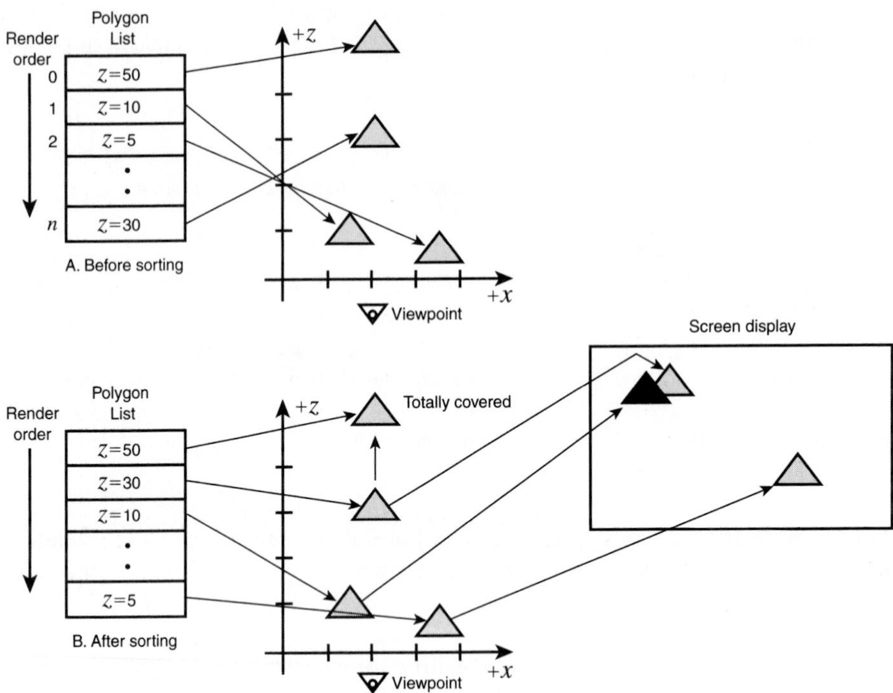

FIGURE 8.28 The painter's algorithm and z-sorting.

Flat Shading

Alright, here's where we finally get to some real lighting. *Flat shading* means shading an entire polygon based on the light that hits a single pixel of it. In other words, we assume that a polygon is composed of a single material, and because all polys in our engine are triangles, we know each polygon has the same surface normal. Therefore, we can perform lighting calculations on a single vertex of each polygon and then shade the polygon based on those results—this is flat shading or *faceted* shading. It looks okay for objects that are by nature made of flat surfaces, but for objects that are curved by nature and approximated by polygons, it makes them look like objects made of polygons <BG>. Figure 8.29 illustrates this. However, if we use smooth shading such as Gouraud or Phong, then the shading model makes the flat polygons look as if they are smooth, but more on that later. For now, let's figure out a way to implement flat shading.

Let's see what we have to work with. We have a PLG/PLX file loader, so we can import simple models in which we can define the type of shading and the color properties (RGB or color index) of a surface. That's good, but we really don't have any functions that perform lighting, so we need to think about that. Secondly, we need to determine where in the pipeline we're going to perform the lighting. As I've said, as long as lighting is performed in world or camera coordinates, you're good to go. Furthermore, the question arises: Should we have lighting support at the object level, the rendering list level, or both?

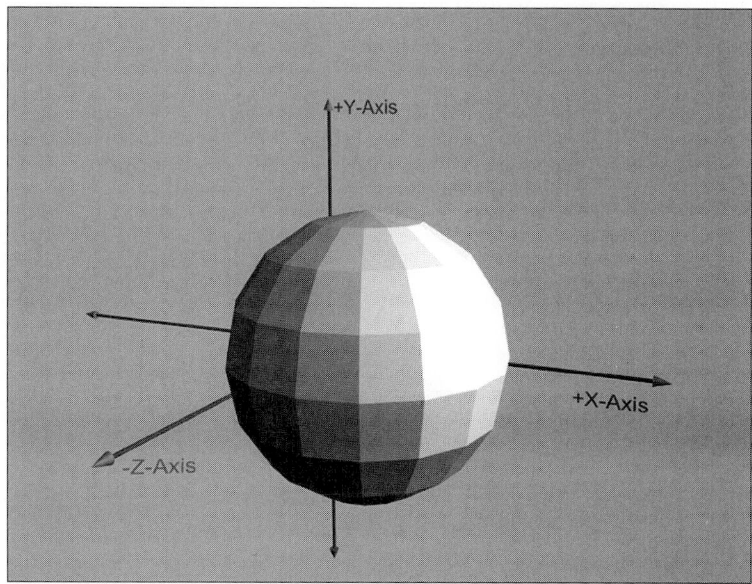

FIGURE 8.29 Approximating objects with polygons make objects look like they're made from polygons!

The first thing we need to look at is the general pipeline and see where we might perform lighting. As an example, here's the pipeline from the previous demo more or less with extraneous code deleted and generalized a bit to see the main flow:

```
// reset the render list
Reset_RENDERLIST4DV1(&rend_list);

// generate camera matrix
Build_CAM4DV1_Matrix_Euler(&cam, CAM_ROT_SEQ_ZYX);

// reset the object
Reset_OBJECT4DV1(&obj);

// perform world transform
Model_To_World_OBJECT4DV1(&obj, TRANSFORM_TRANS_ONLY);

// attempt to cull object
Cull_OBJECT4DV1(&obj, &cam, CULL_OBJECT_XYZ_PLANES))
```

```
// insert the object into render list
Insert_OBJECT4DV1_RENDERLIST4DV1(&rend_list, &obj);

// remove backfaces
Remove_Backfaces_RENDERLIST4DV1(&rend_list, &cam);

// apply world to camera transform
World_To_Camera_RENDERLIST4DV1(&rend_list, &cam);

// apply camera to perspective transformation
Camera_To_Perspective_RENDERLIST4DV1(&rend_list, &cam);

// apply screen transform
Perspective_To_Screen_RENDERLIST4DV1(&rend_list, &cam);

// render the object
Draw_RENDERLIST4DV1_Solid16(&rend_list, back_buffer, back_lpitch);
```

In this example, a single object, `obj`, is inserted in the rendering list and that's it. Along the way, there are a lot of stops though. First, the engine tries to cull the object completely; if it passes that test, the object is inserted in the rendering list. Once in the rendering list, the back-faces are removed, and the world-to-camera, and camera-to-perspective, and finally the perspective-to-screen transforms are performed. The final results are rendered with the call to `Draw_RENDERLIST4DV1_Solid16()`.

We can technically perform the lighting step anywhere after the `Model_To_World_OBJECT4DV1()` call, but before the `Camera_To_Perspective_RENDERLIST4DV1()` call. This is the dilemma. There are a couple good places to put the lighting code. We can add it as part of the object functions, meaning that we could create a separate function that lights an object itself and we could make the call after the object has been culled (so we don't waste time lighting objects that aren't visible). On the other hand, we could add lighting code right into the back-face removal function. The reason being that we're already dealing with polygon normals during back-face removal and those normals are key to performing lighting. However, merging back-face removal and lighting into one function might be a little ugly to you. However, we could let the back-face removal save the normal for the next step, which would be a lighting phase. That's a possibility. Lots to think about, huh?

There are no correct answers here, only answers that work for your particular situation. Because this is a teaching guide, let's write two lighting functions: one that performs lighting on objects themselves, and one that performs lighting after back-face removal (on rendering lists).

For now, we'll leave out merging back-face removal and lighting because, in the scheme of things, lighting has so many calculations that one extra normal calculation savings isn't worth the coding until we get into serious optimization. Later, when we cover optimization, we will probably do this. For now, though, let's light only objects and rendering lists and keep things nice and separate.

NOTE

You might notice that I always prefer to lean toward rendering list operations rather than on objects themselves. The reason, of course, is that a rendering list is a complete list of geometry to work on, which seems cleaner than performing lighting on objects one by one.

Now we need to think about details. For example, when we write a lighting module that lights objects, we need to change the color of each polygon, so do we have space for that? The same thing goes for rendering lists. Finally, if we were to perform lighting in the back-face removal function, do we have a place to store the normal to a polygon?

So, let's begin with the first problem. Assuming that we perform the lighting to an object that's already in world space (or we perform the transform ourselves to do this), where are we going to store the final polygon color? We can't overwrite the initial color of the polygon because during the next pass, we would lose the initial state of the polygon. With that in mind, let's take a look at the `OBJECT4DV1` structure:

```
// an object based on a vertex list and list of polygons
typedef struct OBJECT4DV1_TYP
{
int  id;            // numeric id of this object
char name[64];      // ASCII name of object just for kicks
int  state;         // state of object
int  attr;          // attributes of object
float avg_radius;  // average radius of object used for collision detection
float max_radius;  // maximum radius of object
POINT4D world_pos;  // position of object in world
VECTOR4D dir;       // rotation angles of object in local
                    // cords or unit direction vector user defined???

VECTOR4D ux,uy,uz;  // local axes to track full orientation
// this is updated automatically during
// rotation calls

int num_vertices;   // number of vertices of this object
POINT4D vlist_local[OBJECT4DV1_MAX_VERTICES]; // local vertices
POINT4D vlist_trans[OBJECT4DV1_MAX_VERTICES]; // transformed vertices
int num_polys;        // number of polygons in object mesh
POLY4DV1 plist[OBJECT4DV1_MAX_POLYS];  // array of polygons
} OBJECT4DV1, *OBJECT4DV1_PTR;
```

The actual polygons are stored in plist[], which is an array of the following structures:

```
// a polygon based on a vertex list
typedef struct POLY4DV1_TYP
{
int state;      // state information
int attr;       // physical attributes of polygon
int color;      // color of polygon

POINT4D_PTR vlist; // the vertex list itself
int vert[3];       // the indices into the vertex list
} POLY4DV1, *POLY4DV1_PTR;
```

Sad to say, we're out of luck! There is nowhere to store the shaded post-lighting version of the color. I don't want to rewrite our engine just yet. I want to go through the exercise of working the engine and data structures, so in the next chapter, we can create new versions, based on this information. So, let's get creative <VBG>.

The color is stored as a 32-bit integer, but only the lower 16-bits contain color information because the only color models we support are 16/8 bit. Thus, we can store the shaded color in the upper 16 bits. However, this is a problem because the rendering function itself uses the lower 16 bits to shade. So what we need to do is slightly change the object insertion code (or rewrite the rendering functions) so that the function assumes we've lit the polygon, stored the lit polygon color in the upper 16 bits, and then used the upper 16 bits as the color when it's ripping the polygons from the object and inserting them into the rendering list. Thus, we're going to have to (at the very least) write a new insertion function, which follows:

```
int Insert_OBJECT4DV1_RENDERLIST4DV2(RENDERLIST4DV1_PTR rend_list,
                                     OBJECT4DV1_PTR obj,
                                     int insert_local=0,
                                     int lighting_on=0)
{
// converts the entire object into a face list and then inserts
// the visible, active, non-clipped, non-culled polygons into
// the render list, also note the flag insert_local control
// whether or not the vlist_local or vlist_trans vertex list
// is used, thus you can insert an object "raw" totally untransformed
// if you set insert_local to 1, default is 0, that is you would
// only insert an object after at least the local to world transform
// the last parameter is used to control if their has been
// a lighting step that has generated a light value stored
// in the upper 16-bits of color, if lighting_on = 1 then
// this value is used to overwrite the base color of the
// polygon when its sent to the rendering list
```

```
// is this objective inactive or culled or invisible?
if (!(obj->state & OBJECT4DV1_STATE_ACTIVE) ||
    (obj->state & OBJECT4DV1_STATE_CULLED) ||
    !(obj->state & OBJECT4DV1_STATE_VISIBLE))
return(0);

// the object is valid, let's rip it apart polygon by polygon
for (int poly = 0; poly < obj->num_polys; poly++)
    {
    // acquire polygon
    POLY4DV1_PTR curr_poly = &obj->plist[poly];
    // first is this polygon even visible?
    if (!(curr_poly->state & POLY4DV1_STATE_ACTIVE) ||
       (curr_poly->state & POLY4DV1_STATE_CLIPPED ) ||
       (curr_poly->state & POLY4DV1_STATE_BACKFACE) )
    continue; // move onto next poly

// override vertex list polygon refers to
// the case that you want the local coords used
// first save old pointer
POINT4D_PTR vlist_old = curr_poly->vlist;
if (insert_local)
   curr_poly->vlist = obj->vlist_local;
else
   curr_poly->vlist = obj->vlist_trans;
// test if we should overwrite color with upper 16-bits
if (lighting_on)
   {
   // save color for a sec
   unsigned int base_color = (unsigned int)curr_poly->color;
   curr_poly->color = (int)(base_color >> 16);
   } // end if

// now insert this polygon
if (!Insert_POLY4DV1_RENDERLIST4DV1(rend_list, curr_poly))
   {
   // fix vertex list pointer
   curr_poly->vlist = vlist_old;

   // the whole object didn't fit!
   return(0);
   } // end if
```

```
// test if we should overwrite color with upper 16-bits
if (lighting_on)
   {
   // fix color upc
   curr_poly->color = (int)base_color;
   } // end if

// fix vertex list pointer
curr_poly->vlist = vlist_old;

} // end for
// return success
return(1);

} // end Insert_OBJECT4DV1_RENDERLIST4DV2
```

I've bolded the code that performs the save of the base color and shift of the upper 16 bits into the lower 16 bits. Remember, this will work for both 8/16 bit modes because we could care less what the value is in the lower 16 bits. We just need to restore it when we're inserting the object. If lighting has been performed, we must assume that the upper 16 bits have the lit RGB value or index. In either case, we just shift the upper 16 bits to the lower 16 bits and we're done.

Great, so now we've dealt with the ability to insert a lit object into the rendering list one object at a time (we still need the lighting function itself), but we need to address the other two cases where we potentially perform lighting during back-face removal and after back-face removal on the rendering list. Well, we have some luck here. First, because we're already dealing with a rendering list, we can obliterate the color of each polygon because the original is always in the objects themselves, so that's a nice side effect. Therefore, we can write lighting functions and not worry about the color-overwriting problem.

As an aside, we were thinking about trying to merge the back-face removal and lighting steps into one function with a new function that does both, but we decided not to do so at this point to keep the code clean. The question is, can we perform lighting as a separate step and take advantage of the normal calculated in the back-face removal step? That is, in the rendering list, is there any place that the normal can be stored for retrieval by a separate function? Figure 8.30 illustrates the two pipelines I'm talking about. So, let's take a quick look at the version 1.0 of rendering lists:

```
typedef struct RENDERLIST4DV1_TYP
{
int state; // state of renderlist ???
int attr;  // attributes of renderlist ???
```

```
// the render list is an array of pointers each pointing to
// a self contained "renderable" polygon face POLYF4DV1
POLYF4DV1_PTR poly_ptrs[RENDERLIST4DV1_MAX_POLYS];

// additionally to cut down on allocation, de-allocation
// of polygons each frame, here's where the actual polygon
// faces will be stored
POLYF4DV1 poly_data[RENDERLIST4DV1_MAX_POLYS];

int num_polys; // number of polys in render list
} RENDERLIST4DV1, *RENDERLIST4DV1_PTR;
```

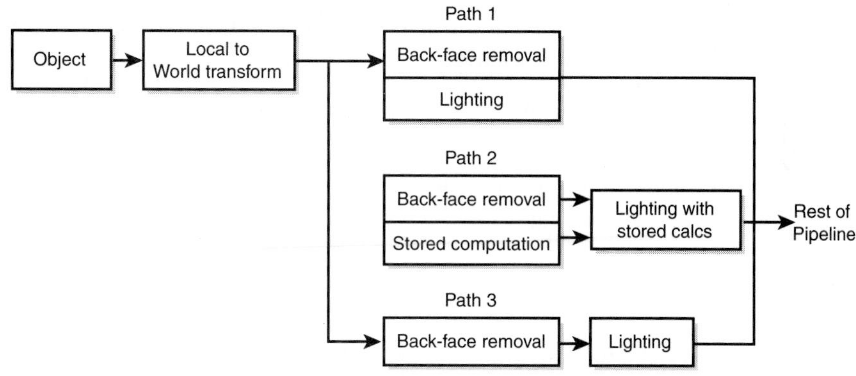

FIGURE 8.30 Various lighting integration pipelines.

You'll notice that the rendering list is composed of polygon faces `POLYF4DV1` rather than simple polygons, and they look like this:

```
typedef struct POLYF4DV1_TYP
{
int state;     // state information
int attr;      // physical attributes of polygon
int color;     // color of polygon

POINT4D vlist[3];  // the vertices of this triangle
POINT4D tvlist[3]; // the vertices after transformation if needed
POLYF4DV1_TYP *next; // pointer to next polygon in list??
POLYF4DV1_TYP *prev; // pointer to previous polygon in list??
} POLYF4DV1, *POLYF4DV1_PTR;
```

Unfortunately, this has no place to store a normal; each polygon has storage for the untransformed and transformed vertices, but that's about it. So, we're out of luck! Hence, we've determined that although it sounded like a good idea to save the normal information in the back-face removal function (at the very least, rather than merging back-face and lighting in the same function), we simply don't have room unless we get really tricky and store the normal in the pointers to `next` and `prev`, but that's too much work.

The point I want to make here is that we've found that our initial data structures are a little bit lacking. Of course they are, we didn't know where we were going!

Flat Shading in 16-bit Mode

Now that we know we're going to write only an object and rendering list lighting system, we can begin outlining what kind of lighting we're going to support. We've described a number of light types, from infinite light sources to spotlights. Additionally, we've defined how to create the lights and the materials. We need the code for both the 16-bit and 8-bit cases. Let's start with the 16-bit case. For our first functional lighting model, we're going to support only the following lighting model:

- Polygons with the constant/pure shading bit set will pass through the lighting model without any changes.
- Polygons with the flat shading bit set will be affected by ambient, infinite, point lights, and spotlights in the light list.

The lighting will work the same whether we're talking about the object or rendering list version, so without loss of generality, I'll talk in generic terms for a moment. (The rendering list version doesn't have to deal with saving the color; it can just overwrite the color because after the rendering list is rendered, it's discarded.)

Okay, for each polygon, we need to test the attributes of the polygon. If the polygon has the `POLY4DV1_ATTR_SHADE_MODE_CONSTANT` flag set, no lighting will be performed. However, if the polygon has the `POLY4DV1_ATTR_SHADE_MODE_FLAT` flag set, we'll perform lighting on the polygon. Referring to Figure 8.31, our pseudo code for the lighting engine version 1.0 will look something like this:

Step 1: Compute normal to surface.

Step 2: For each light source in the light list, compute light intensity.

Step 3: Sum results.

Step 4: Write results out to polygon color upper 16 bits.

Of course, the calculations must be performed based on the light models described in the first part of the chapter. Additionally, this first version of lighting has no concept of materials, so we're going to use a default material for all objects such that the color's themselves are the reflectivities. Finally, objects will only reflect ambient and diffuse light.

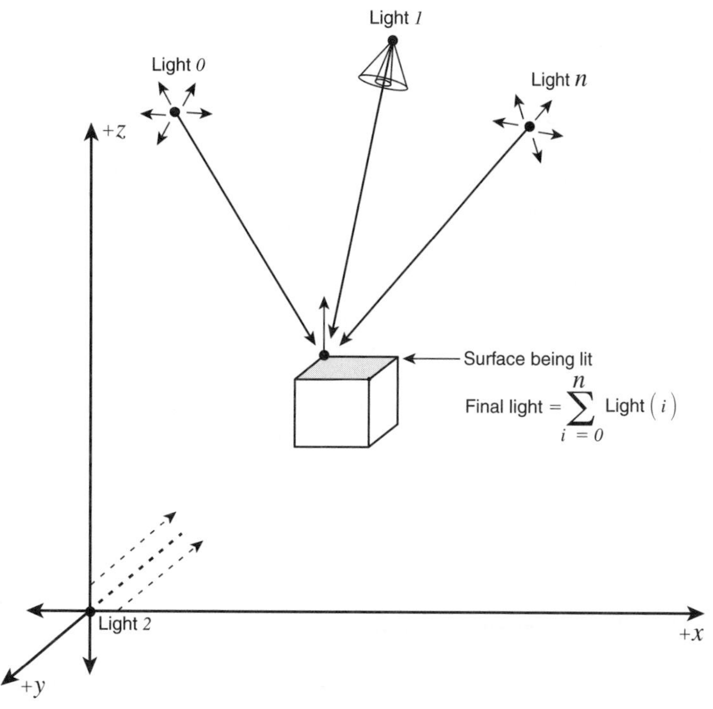

FIGURE 8.31 The lighting algorithm.

With all that in mind, here's a function that performs lighting on an object (it assumes the object is in world coordinates) based on the lights sent to the function:

```
int Light_OBJECT4DV1_World16(OBJECT4DV1_PTR obj,  // object to process
CAM4DV1_PTR cam,      // camera position
LIGHTV1_PTR lights,  // light list (might have more than one)
int max_lights)      // maximum lights in list
{
// 16-bit version of function
// function lights an object based on the sent lights and camera.
// the function supports
// constant/pure shading (emissive), flat shading with ambient,
// infinite, point lights, and spot lights
// note that this lighting function is rather brute force
// and simply follows the math, however
// there are some clever integer operations that are used in scale 256
// rather than going to floating
// point, but why? floating point and ints are the same speed.
// HOWEVER, the conversion to and from floating
// point can be cycle intensive, so if you can keep your calcs in ints
```

```
// then you can gain some speed
// also note, type 1 spot lights are simply point lights with direction,
// the "cone" is more of a function
// of the falloff due to attenuation, but they still look like spot lights
// type 2 spot lights are implemented with the intensity having
// a dot product relationship with the
// angle from the surface point to the light direction
// just like in the optimized model, but the pf term
// that is used for a concentration control must be 1,2,3,....
// integral and non-fractional

unsigned int r_base, g_base, b_base,  // base color being lit
             r_sum,  g_sum,  b_sum,   // sum of lighting process over all lights
             shaded_color;            // final color

float dp,     // dot product
      dist,   // distance from light to surface
      i,      // general intensities
      nl,     // length of normal
      atten;  // attenuation computations

// test if the object is culled
if (!(obj->state & OBJECT4DV1_STATE_ACTIVE) ||
   (obj->state & OBJECT4DV1_STATE_CULLED) ||
   !(obj->state & OBJECT4DV1_STATE_VISIBLE))
   return(0);

// process each poly in mesh
for (int poly=0; poly < obj->num_polys; poly++)
    {
    // acquire polygon
    POLY4DV1_PTR curr_poly = &obj->plist[poly];

    // is this polygon valid?
    // test this polygon if and only if it's not clipped, not culled,
    // active, and visible. Note we test for backface in the event that
    // a previous call might have already determined this, so why work
    // harder!
    if (!(curr_poly->state & POLY4DV1_STATE_ACTIVE) ||
        (curr_poly->state & POLY4DV1_STATE_CLIPPED ) ||
        (curr_poly->state & POLY4DV1_STATE_BACKFACE) )
        continue; // move onto next poly
```

```
// extract vertex indices into master list, remember the polygons are
// NOT self contained, but based on the vertex list stored in the object
// itself
int vindex_0 = curr_poly->vert[0];
int vindex_1 = curr_poly->vert[1];
int vindex_2 = curr_poly->vert[2];

// we will use the transformed polygon
// vertex list since the backface removal
// only makes sense at the world coord stage further of the pipeline
// test the lighting mode of the polygon (use flat for flat, gouraud))
if (curr_poly->attr & POLY4DV1_ATTR_SHADE_MODE_FLAT ||
   curr_poly->attr & POLY4DV1_ATTR_SHADE_MODE_GOURAUD)
   {
   // step 1: extract the base color out in RGB mode
   if (dd_pixel_format == DD_PIXEL_FORMAT565)
      {
     _RGB565FROM16BIT(curr_poly->color, &r_base, &g_base, &b_base);
      // scale to 8 bit
      r_base <<= 3;
      g_base <<= 2;
      b_base <<= 3;
      } // end if
  else
     {
     RGB555FROM16BIT(curr_poly->color, &r_base, &g_base, &b_base);
     // scale to 8 bit
     r_base <<= 3;
     g_base <<= 3;
     b_base <<= 3;
     } // end if

 // initialize color sum
 r_sum  = 0;
 g_sum  = 0;
 b_sum  = 0;

 // loop thru lights
for (int curr_light = 0; curr_light < max_lights; curr_light++)
    {
    // is this light active
    if (!lights[curr_light].state)
       continue;
    // what kind of light are we dealing with
```

```
if (lights[curr_light].attr & LIGHTV1_ATTR_AMBIENT)
   {
   // simply multiply each channel against the color of the
   // polygon then divide by 256 to scale back to 0..255
   // use a shift in real life!!! >> 8
   r_sum+= ((lights[curr_light].c_ambient.r * r_base) / 256);
   g_sum+= ((lights[curr_light].c_ambient.g * g_base) / 256);
   b_sum+= ((lights[curr_light].c_ambient.b * b_base) / 256);
   // there better only be one ambient light!
   } // end if
else if (lights[curr_light].attr & LIGHTV1_ATTR_INFINITE)
      {
      // infinite lighting, we need the surface normal,
      // and the direction of the light source

      // we need to compute the normal of this polygon face, and recall
      // that the vertices are in cw order, u=p0->p1, v=p0->p2, n=uxv
      VECTOR4D u, v, n;

      // build u, v
      VECTOR4D_Build(&obj->vlist_trans[ vindex_0 ],
                     &obj->vlist_trans[ vindex_1 ], &u);
      VECTOR4D_Build(&obj->vlist_trans[ vindex_0 ],
                     &obj->vlist_trans[ vindex_2 ], &v);

      // compute cross product
      VECTOR4D_Cross(&u, &v, &n);
      // at this point, we are almost ready,
      // but we have to normalize the normal vector!
      // this is a key optimization we can make later
      // we can pre-compute the length of all polygon
      // normals, so this step can be optimized

      // compute length of normal
      nl = VECTOR4D_Length_Fast(&n);

      // ok, recalling the lighting model for infinite lights
      // I(d)dir = I0dir * Cldir
      // and for the diffuse model
      // Itotald =   Rsdiffuse*Idiffuse * (n . l)
      // so we basically need to multiple it all together
      // notice the scaling by 128,
      // I want to avoid floating point calculations, not because they
```

```
            // are slower, but the conversion to and from cost cycles
            dp = VECTOR4D_Dot(&n, &lights[curr_light].dir);

            // only add light if dp > 0
            if (dp > 0)
               {
               i = 128*dp/nl;

               r_sum+= (lights[curr_light].c_diffuse.r * r_base * i) /
                       (256*128);
               g_sum+= (lights[curr_light].c_diffuse.g * g_base * i) /
                       (256*128);
               b_sum+= (lights[curr_light].c_diffuse.b * b_base * i) /
                       (256*128);
               } // end if
           } // end if infinite light
        else if (lights[curr_light].attr & LIGHTV1_ATTR_POINT)
           {
           // perform point light computations
           // light model for point light is once again:
           //              I0point * Clpoint
           //  I(d)point = ___________________
           //              kc +  kl*d + kq*d2
           //
           //  Where d = |p - s|
           // thus it's almost identical to the infinite light,
           // but attenuates as a function
           // of distance from the point source to the surface point being lit
           // we need to compute the normal of this polygon face, and recall
           // that the vertices are in cw order, u=p0->p1, v=p0->p2, n=uxv
           VECTOR4D u, v, n, l;

           // build u, v
           VECTOR4D_Build(&obj->vlist_trans[ vindex_0 ],
                          &obj->vlist_trans[ vindex_1 ], &u);
           VECTOR4D_Build(&obj->vlist_trans[ vindex_0 ],
                          &obj->vlist_trans[ vindex_2 ], &v);

           // compute cross product
           VECTOR4D_Cross(&u, &v, &n);
           // at this point, we are almost ready,
           // but we have to normalize the normal vector!
           // this is a key optimization we can make later,
           // we can pre-compute the length of all polygon
```

8

```
        // normals, so this step can be optimized
        // compute length of normal
        nl = VECTOR4D_Length_Fast(&n);

        // compute vector from surface to light
        VECTOR4D_Build(&obj->vlist_trans[ vindex_0 ],
                       &lights[curr_light].pos, &l);

        // compute distance and attenuation
        dist = VECTOR4D_Length_Fast(&l);

        // and for the diffuse model
        // Itotald =   Rsdiffuse*Idiffuse * (n . l)
        // so we basically need to multiple it all together
        // notice the scaling by 128
        // I want to avoid floating point calculations,
        // not because they are slower

        // but the conversion to and from cost cycles
        dp = VECTOR4D_Dot(&n, &l);

        // only add light if dp > 0
        if (dp > 0)
           {
           atten =  (lights[curr_light].kc + lights[curr_light].kl*dist +
                     lights[curr_light].kq*dist*dist);
           i = 128*dp / (nl * dist * atten );

           r_sum += (lights[curr_light].c_diffuse.r * r_base * i) /
                     (256*128);
           g_sum += (lights[curr_light].c_diffuse.g * g_base * i) /
                     (256*128);
           b_sum += (lights[curr_light].c_diffuse.b * b_base * i) /
                     (256*128);
           } // end if
        } // end if point
     else
     if (lights[curr_light].attr & LIGHTV1_ATTR_SPOTLIGHT1)
        {
        // perform spotlight/point computations simplified model that uses
        // point light WITH a direction to simulate a spotlight
        // light model for point light is once again:
        //                I0point * Clpoint
        //  I(d)point = ___________________
```

```
//              kc +  kl*d + kq*d2
//
//  Where d = |p - s|
// thus it's almost identical to the infinite light,
// but attenuates as a function
// of distance from the point source to the surface point being lit
// we need to compute the normal of this polygon face, and recall

// that the vertices are in cw order, u=p0->p1, v=p0->p2, n=uxv
VECTOR4D u, v, n, l;

// build u, v
VECTOR4D_Build(&obj->vlist_trans[ vindex_0 ],
               &obj->vlist_trans[ vindex_1 ], &u);
VECTOR4D_Build(&obj->vlist_trans[ vindex_0 ],
               &obj->vlist_trans[ vindex_2 ], &v);

// compute cross product (we need -n, so do vxu)
VECTOR4D_Cross(&v, &u, &n);
// at this point, we are almost ready,
// but we have to normalize the normal vector!
// this is a key optimization we can make later,
// we can pre-compute the length of all polygon
// normals, so this step can be optimized
// compute length of normal
nl = VECTOR4D_Length_Fast(&n);

// compute vector from surface to light
VECTOR4D_Build(&obj->vlist_trans[ vindex_0 ],
               &lights[curr_light].pos, &l);

// compute distance and attenuation
dist = VECTOR4D_Length_Fast(&l);

// and for the diffuse model
// Itotald =   Rsdiffuse*Idiffuse * (n . l)
// so we basically need to multiple it all together
// notice the scaling by 128,
// I want to avoid floating point calculations, not because they
// are slower, but the conversion to and from cost cycles
// note that I use the direction of the light here
// rather than a the vector to the light
// thus we are taking orientation into account
```

```
        // which is similar to the spotlight model
        dp = VECTOR4D_Dot(&n, &lights[curr_light].dir);

        // only add light if dp > 0
        if (dp > 0)
           {
           atten =  (lights[curr_light].kc +
                     lights[curr_light].kl*dist +
                     lights[curr_light].kq*dist*dist);

           i = 128*dp / (nl * atten );

           r_sum += (lights[curr_light].c_diffuse.r * r_base * i) /
                    (256*128);
           g_sum += (lights[curr_light].c_diffuse.g * g_base * i) /
                    (256*128);
           b_sum += (lights[curr_light].c_diffuse.b * b_base * i) /
                    (256*128);
           } // end if
        } // end if spotlight1
     else
     if (lights[curr_light].attr & LIGHTV1_ATTR_SPOTLIGHT2)
        // simple/complex version
        {
        // perform spot light computations
        // light model for spot light simple version is once again:
        //              I0spotlight * Clspotlight * MAX( (l . s), 0)^pf
        // I(d)spotlight = _______________________________________________
        //                            kc + kl*d + kq*d2
        // Where d = |p - s|, and pf = power factor
        // thus it's almost identical to the point,
        // but has the extra term in the numerator
        // relating the angle between the light source and the point on the
➥surface
        // we need to compute the normal of this polygon face, and recall
        // that the vertices are in cw order, u=p0->p1, v=p0->p2, n=uxv
        VECTOR4D u, v, n, d, s;

        // build u, v
        VECTOR4D_Build(&obj->vlist_trans[ vindex_0 ],
                       &obj->vlist_trans[ vindex_1 ], &u);
        VECTOR4D_Build(&obj->vlist_trans[ vindex_0 ],
                       &obj->vlist_trans[ vindex_2 ], &v);
```

```
// compute cross product (v x u, to invert n)
VECTOR4D_Cross(&v, &u, &n);
// at this point, we are almost ready,
// but we have to normalize the normal vector!
// this is a key optimization we can make later
// we can pre-compute the length of all polygon
// normals, so this step can be optimized
// compute length of normal
nl = VECTOR4D_Length_Fast(&n);

// and for the diffuse model
// Itotald =   Rsdiffuse*Idiffuse * (n . l)
// so we basically need to multiple it all together
// notice the scaling by 128, I want to avoid
// floating point calculations, not because they
// are slower, but the conversion to and from cost cycles
dp = VECTOR4D_Dot(&n, &lights[curr_light].dir);

// only add light if dp > 0
if (dp > 0)
    {
    // compute vector from light to surface
    // (different from l which IS the light dir)
    VECTOR4D_Build( &lights[curr_light].pos,
                    &obj->vlist_trans[ vindex_0 ], &s);

    // compute length of s (distance to light source)
    // to normalize s for lighting calc
    dist = VECTOR4D_Length_Fast(&s);

    // compute spot light term (s . l)
    float dpsl = VECTOR4D_Dot(&s, &lights[curr_light].dir)/dist;

    // proceed only if term is positive
    if (dpsl > 0)
       {
       // compute attenuation
       atten = (lights[curr_light].kc +
                lights[curr_light].kl*dist +
                lights[curr_light].kq*dist*dist);

       // for speed reasons, pf exponents that are
       // less that 1.0 are out of the question, and exponents
```

8

```
                    // must be integral
                    float dpsl_exp = dpsl;

                    // exponentiate for positive integral powers
                    for (int e_index = 1;
                         e_index < (int)lights[curr_light].pf; e_index++)
                         dpsl_exp*=dpsl;

                    // now dpsl_exp holds (dpsl)^pf power
                    // which is of course (s . l)^pf
                    i = 128*dp * dpsl_exp / (nl * atten );

                    r_sum += (lights[curr_light].c_diffuse.r * r_base * i) /
                                (256*128);
                    g_sum += (lights[curr_light].c_diffuse.g * g_base * i) /
                                (256*128);
                    b_sum += (lights[curr_light].c_diffuse.b * b_base * i) /
                                (256*128);
                    } // end if
                 } // end if
              } // end if spot light
        } // end for light

    // make sure colors aren't out of range
    if (r_sum  > 255) r_sum = 255;
    if (g_sum  > 255) g_sum = 255;
    if (b_sum  > 255) b_sum = 255;

    // write the color
    shaded_color = RGB16Bit(r_sum, g_sum, b_sum);
    curr_poly->color = (int)((shaded_color << 16) | curr_poly->color);

    } // end if
 else // assume POLY4DV1_ATTR_SHADE_MODE_CONSTANT
      {
      // emmisive shading only, copy base color into upper 16-bits
      // without any change
      curr_poly->color = (int)((curr_poly->color << 16) | curr_poly->color);
      } // end else

   } // end for poly
```

```
// return success
return(1);

} // end Light_OBJECT4DV1_World16
```

The lighting function is a straightforward implementation of what we discussed in the beginning of the chapter. Basically, it begins by determining the pixel format and then extracts the RGB components of the polygon's color and converts them to 8-bit each. Then the lighting loop is entered. If a polygon is constant shaded, the function continues to the next polygon; otherwise, the lights are used to light the polygon. The algorithm sums up the contributions of each light source that's currently active in the light list—ambient, point, infinite, and it even supports spotlights, but highly optimized/simplified versions. You'll notice that, in the constants for lights, we had a few different spotlight constants. This was to support different spotlight models that were simplified models. In any case, two spotlight models are supported in the lighting system:

- `LIGHTV1_ATTR_SPOTLIGHT1`—This spotlight is similar to the point light, except that it uses the direction vector. That's all. So, basically, set this up like you would a point light, but send in a direction vector for the direction of the spotlight. Interestingly, the attenuation effects seem to simulate the cone falloff well.
- `LIGHTV1_ATTR_SPOTLIGHT2`—This spotlight is basically the full spotlight model without an umbra and penumbra defined explicitly. If you recall, we covered two spotlight models, and one of them used a power factor or concentration factor that exponentiated the dot product term. This had the effect of controlling the radius of the spotlight. So, in this case, set the spotlight up as a real spotlight, except that the umbra and penumbra angles, alpha and phi, are not used—only the pf factor is used. Additionally, `pf` must be an integer greater than 1.0. I use an iterative multiplication for exponentiation because calling `exp()` is asking for an eternity.

Moving on, whatever light sources there may be in the light database are simply summed up, and then final RGB values are converted back to 5.6.5 or 5.5.5, depending on the pixel format. This value is copied into the upper 16 bits of the color field of the polygon where it's safe and won't destroy the real color of the polygon. That's it!

CAUTION

When performing lighting calculations, many times it's possible to overflow your RGB channels. Therefore, make sure that you test for overflows and don't allow any channel to exceed 255 or your maximum intensity. Use an inline function to test for this, of course.

Sadly, the function's so simple, there's not much to calling it. You just call it with the object you want lit, the camera (unused, but you might need later), the lights you want referenced, and the number of lights in the list. Here's a typical call. This assumes that the lights are in a global array called `lights`, and that three lights are active:

```
// perform lighting
Light_OBJECT4DV1_World(&obj_marker, &cam, lights, 3);
```

After this call, the object will be lit and the colors of the lit polygons will be in the upper 16 bits of each polygon color, which, when inserted via our new `Insert_OBJECT4DV1_RENDERLIST4DV2()` function, will work out perfectly.

The function that performs nearly the same logic, but on a rendering list, has the following prototype:

```
int Light_RENDERLIST4DV1_World16(
         RENDERLIST4DV1_PTR rend_list,  // rendering list to process
         CAM4DV1_PTR cam,      // camera position
         LIGHTV1_PTR lights,   // light list (might have more than one)
         int max_lights);      // maximum lights in list
```

Use it the same way as you would the object lighting function, but call it after back-face removal and while the rendering list is still in world or camera coordinates.

Now for a demonstration of lighting. Figure 8.32 is a screenshot of `DEMOII8_5.CPP|EXE` in action. Basically this demo creates an ambient light, point light, infinite light, and spotlight type 1, and places them in the world. When the demo starts, all the lights will be enabled and you'll see the results of all of them as you run the simulation. Additionally, I've set the vertical stabilizers on the tanks to emissive colors (in other words, constant shading), so they're like lights that don't emit light. Refer to Table 8.2 for the demo controls.

TABLE 8.2 Controls for `DEMOII8_5.CPP|EXE`

Key	Function
A	Toggles ambient light source
I	Toggles infinite light source
P	Toggles point light source
S	Toggles spotlight source
W	Toggles wireframe/solid mode
B	Toggles back-face removal
L	Toggles lighting engine
Right arrow	Rotates player right
Left arrow	Rotates player left
Up arrow	Moves player forward
Down arrow	Moves player backward
Space bar	Turbo
H	Toggles Help menu
Esc	Exits demo

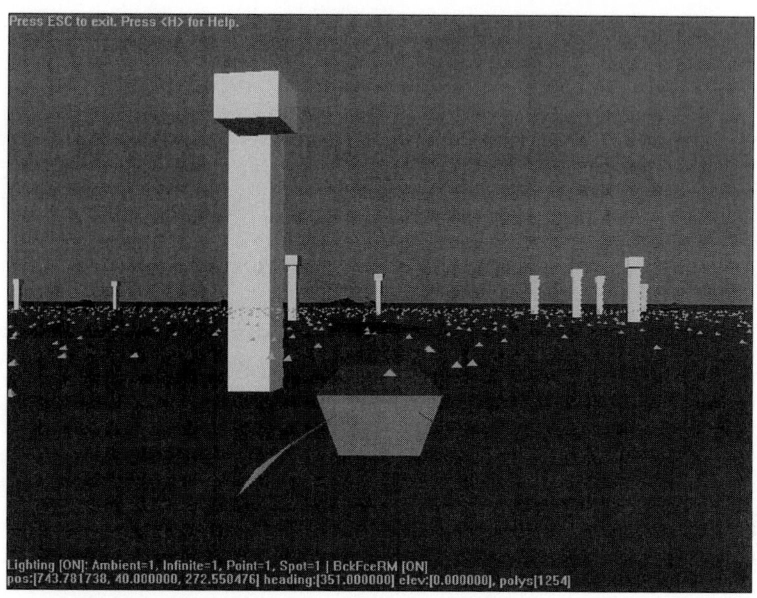

FIGURE 8.32 A screenshot of our fully lit engine in action.

TIP

As usual, to compile, just include all the `T3DLIB.CPP|H` files up to `T3DLIB6.CPP|H` and, of course, `DEMOII8_5.CPP` itself.

The demo is pretty cool. I like watching the lights move around in the world—especially the point and spotlight sources (they're colored)! Anyway, have fun, and experiment with the lights, change their colors, and so forth. Amazingly, this is a software demo of real-time colored lights in 16-bit mode—not bad!

8

Flat Shading in 8-bit Mode

Shading in 8-bit mode is challenging for a number of reasons. The first problem being that there are only 8 bits of color! But the main problem is that, no matter what, we have only a single palette. No matter what we do to light a surface, in the end, *everything* will be 8-bit and from the original palette. With that in mind, there are a couple ways to approach writing the 8-bit shader. We can approach it generically (as I've done) or with more constraints and simplifications, knowing we're in 8-bit mode. For example, forcing white lights and simplifying lights to have only intensities rather than color and so forth. Recall that we built two color lookup tables (refer back to Figures 8.24–8.26). We would definitely use the second table that was a collection of colors in rows where each row represented 256 shades of that color. Thus, for very fast color translation, an indexing scheme can be used of this form:

```
shaded_color = rgbilookup[color][shade];
```

Of course, the color and shade are both 0..255 and the resulting 8-bit index the table outputs is the nearest match in the REAL color palette, but at least it's sound.

However, I don't want to dumb down our lighting system at this point. I have high hopes that 16-bit lighting will continue to be fast enough, so we aren't going to optimize for 8-bit just yet; we're going to support it, but not natively. The good news is that writing an 8-bit lighting module takes little more than adding and deleting a few lines of code from our 16-bit version. The plan of attack is as follows: We don't need to worry about pixel formats anymore; we simply look at the color index of the polygon. Based on that index, we look up the real RGB values of the color from the system palette and then use those (which are already in 8-bit/channel form) for the lighting calculations. When the lighting is complete, we simply convert the final RGB values into a 5.6.5 encoded index and use that index to index into the table created with the call to `RGB_16_8_IndexedRGB_Table_Builder()`. If you recall, `RGB_16_8_IndexedRGB_Table_Builder()` takes any RGB value as an encoded 16-bit value, uses it as an actual index, and outputs the nearest 8-bit index match in the table, which then is used as an input into the real color palette. Very slick, huh? The entire process is shown in Figure 8.33.

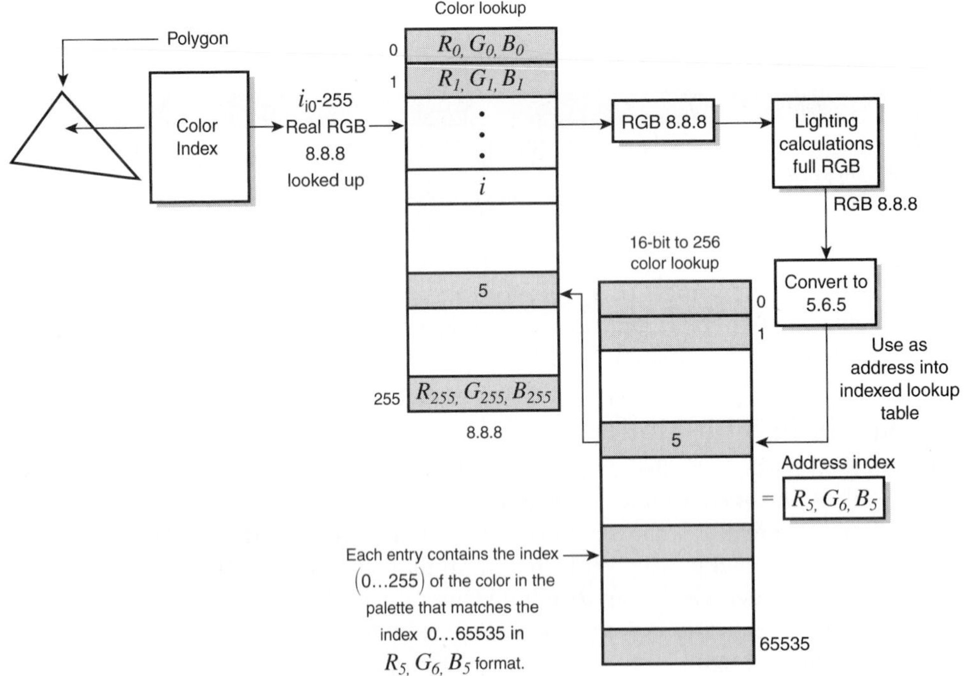

FIGURE 8.33 The complete 8-bit RGB lighting process.

I don't have room to show the function (plus it's nearly identical), but here's the prototype:

```
int Light_OBJECT4DV1_World(OBJECT4DV1_PTR obj,  // object to process
    CAM4DV1_PTR cam,      // camera position
    LIGHTV1_PTR lights,  // light list (might have more than one)
    int max_lights);      // maximum lights in list
```

NOTE

Remember that for 8/16-bit functions, we agreed on the convention that the 16-bit versions would have a 16 appended to the end of the function name. The function looks the same and works the same, but has a slightly different name. And, of course, I could have merged the two functions, but I wanted to keep them separate so that they would be a little faster and smaller.

Here's the rendering list version of the function. Once again, it works identically to the 16-bit version:

```
int Light_RENDERLIST4DV1_World(RENDERLIST4DV1_PTR rend_list,  // rendering list to
process
    CAM4DV1_PTR cam,      // camera position
    LIGHTV1_PTR lights,  // light list (might have more than one)
    int max_lights);      // maximum lights in list
```

For a demo of the 8-bit lighting system, check out `DEMOII8_5_8b.CPP|EXE`. It's identical to 16-bit demo (it uses the same controls) except that it's 8-bit! Notice that the lighting doesn't look too bad compared to the 16-bit version. Figure 8.34 is a screenshot of the demo running.

However, palettes count here, boys and girls. For this demo, the system uses the default 8-bit palette from the first *Tricks*, which is `PALDATA2.PAL`. `PALDATA2.BMP` is a blank bitmap with that bitmap, so you can load and look at the colors for the palette. Amazingly, you may say, "That looks like a good palette," but it's only good for colors that are in the palette. When you try to find a shade of fuchsia that's not in the palette, the nearest neighbor algorithm ends up with light brown or something else horrific, and the lighting looks bad.

To remedy this, you must use a palette that has a very small color space but a large intensity space. For example, if you're making a *Doom* clone, you would pick a palette with a lot of grays, browns, and such colors, and nothing more, and 8–16 shades of each. That way, all possible shades of each color are in the palette, so the lookup table doesn't have ridiculous entries in it.

Well, that's it for your first look at solid models and shading. Let's now see how to improve the flat shaded models with other shading models for the rasterization phase.

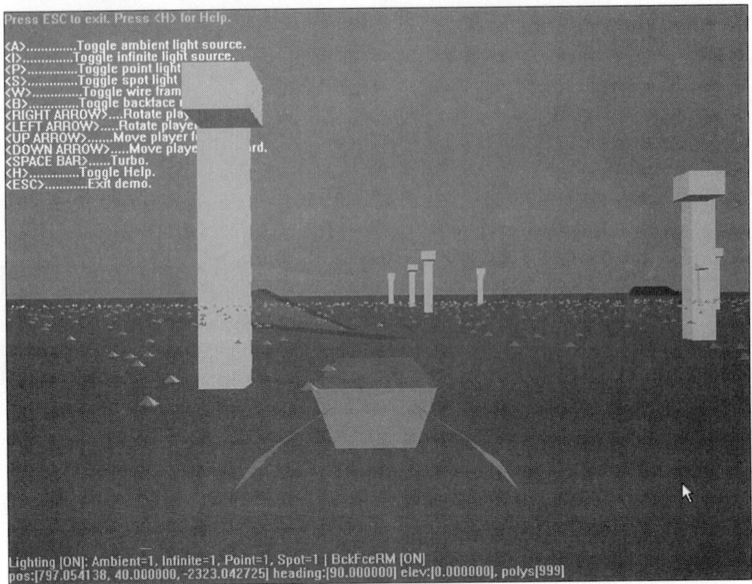

FIGURE 8.34 A screenshot of the 8-bit version of the lighting demo.

Gouraud Shading Preview

If you've been paying attention, we're thus far supporting only what is called flat shading. That means we select a single color for an entire polygon, and then shade the polygon with that same color. However, this makes objects look very faceted.

> **TIP**
>
> Gouraud is the name of a person, so technically, we should always capitalize it. Additionally, it's pronounced "gu-row."

Of course, for objects that *are* faceted, this is fine. For example, our lighting model works great on a cube, but bad on the sphere see Figure 8.35. What we need is a way to smooth the colors over the surface so that surfaces intended to be smooth look that way. Take a look at Figure 8.36. Here we see the same sphere, but this time it's Gouraud shaded. Notice the smoothness. However, a Gouraud-shaded cube is also shown in Figure 8.36. It looks bad due to the smooth. Therefore, objects that are supposed to be faceted should not be smoothed with Gouraud shading.

So, how does Gouraud shading work? Referring to Figure 8.37, we compute the color and intensity at each vertex of each polygon. For polygons that share more than one vertex, we average together the normals of the polygons that share that vertex. Then we perform the lighting calculations as usual and assign the final color to each vertex. Next comes the interesting part: Instead of using a single color to color the entire polygon in question, we use the colors at each vertex and interpolate the colors across and down the polygon. This process is shown in Figure 8.38. The polygon will look pixel-shaded, even though we did no such thing! Cool, huh?

A. Flat shaded cube

B. Flat shaded sphere

FIGURE 8.35 Flat-shaded objects.

A. Gouraud shaded cube

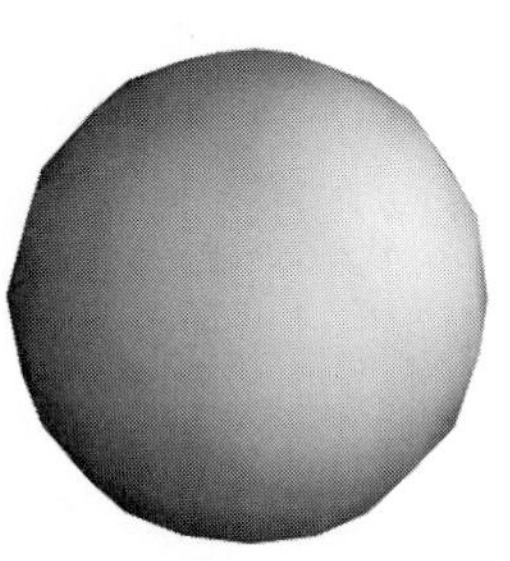

B. Gouraud shaded sphere

FIGURE 8.36 Smooth-shaded objects.

Of course, there's a downside to this. The shading phase occurs when we rasterize each polygon. Thus, it's performed in *screen space*, so there will be perspective distortion. Luckily, your eyes can't see it that well (not like textures at least), so it's not bad. The second problem is that we need to perform an interpolation algorithm and that can be costly during rasterization. However, the interpolation is exactly what we need to do when we texture map, so we can do all this at the same time.

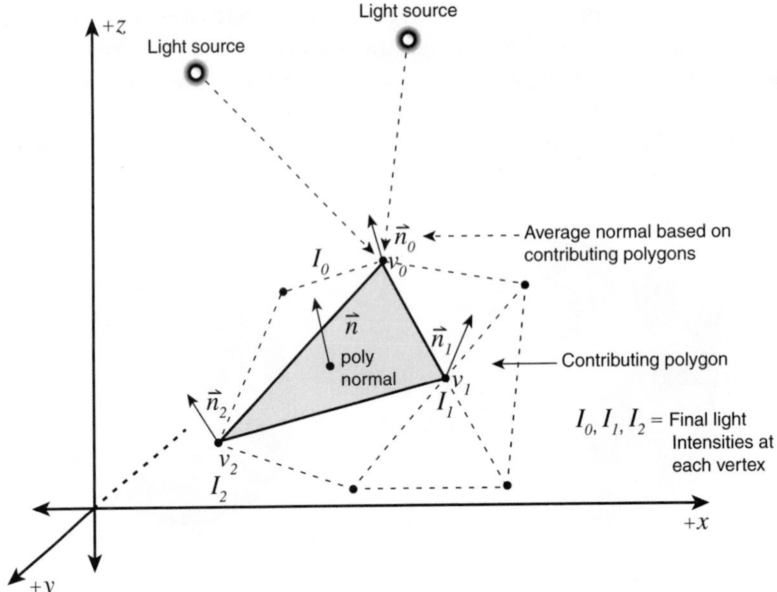

FIGURE 8.37 The setup for Gouraud shading.

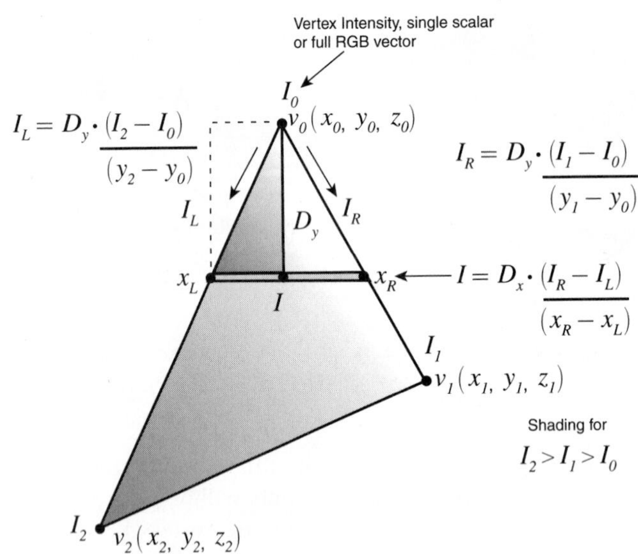

FIGURE 8.38 The Gouraud shading interpolation step.

Finally, no one ever said you have to compute the color intensities at each vertex. If you wish, you can manually assign them, too; that is, manual or preprocessed static lighting—just a thought. Anyway, before moving on, let's take a quick look at the math to interpolate the shades down a polygon and rasterize it. Referring to Figure 8.38, you see a flat-bottom triangle with various values marked off. Interpolating the colors is simple: We simply initialize two colors, one for the left side and one for the right side, and as the polygon rasterizer is drawing, we consult the current (x,y) position on each edge of the polygon. Based on that, we compute the intensity of the current scan line based on the gradient of the intensity as a function of y at both the left and right sides of the triangle. We then draw the scan line interpolating that value across the scan line and move on.

This should sound very familiar to you—it's the standard interpolation algorithm for everything from color to texture maps. Were going to use it extensively in this book. In the next chapter, we're going to study this in depth when we study affine texture mapping, so if you don't quite get it—you will....

Phong Shading Preview

Gouraud shading is the de facto standard for something like 99% of all graphics accelerators on the market, and it looks great, but it does have the shortcoming of not taking perspective into consideration. However, Phong shading addresses these issues (sort of) because it operates by computing the shading at every single pixel. Instead of interpolating the color values across a polygon in screen space, it interpolates the normal vectors across the polygon in screen space, and *then* lights the pixel based on the interpolated normal. This is shown in Figure 8.39. Phong shading looks slightly more realistic than Gouraud shading. It really picks up specular effects much better. It's impossible to have sharp specular regions with Gouraud shading because the line interpolator can simply increase or decrease a value from one value to another along a scan line, but a Phong shaded is pixel shading, so every pixel can change.

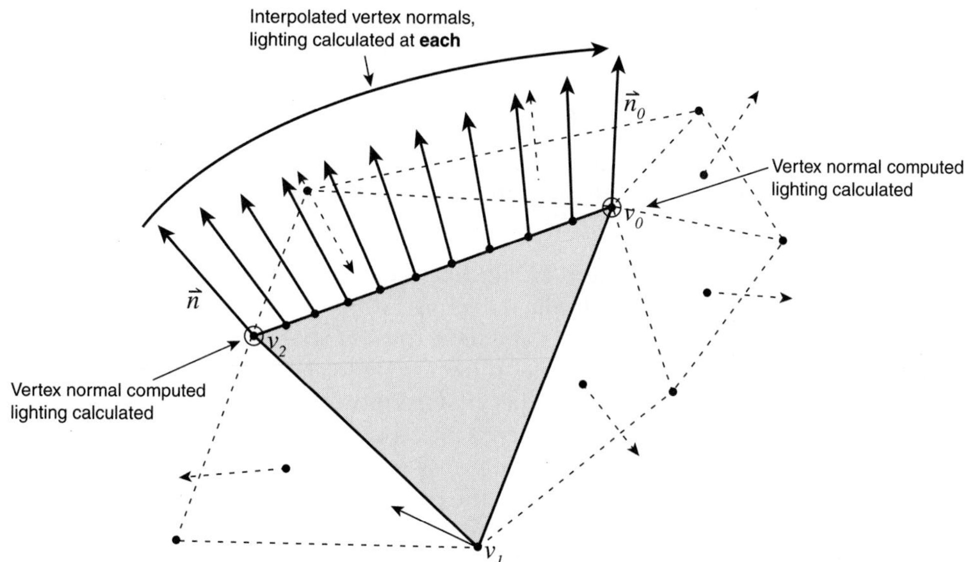

FIGURE 8.39 The Phong vertex normal interpolation algorithm.

The downside, of course, is that Phong shading can hardly be done in hardware, let alone in software, so we won't be implementing it at all in this book. But we will use some tricks to get Phong-like highlights (that's the main reason for Phong shading) when we get to advanced lighting.

Depth Sorting and the Painter's Algorithm

At this point in the game, your knowledge of 3D is fairly detailed, but one thing we haven't discussed very much is visibility and rendering order. The term *visibility* is thrown around quite a bit in 3D, but for the most part, it means "can you see the polygon?" But it also means "did you draw the polygons in the correct order?" The point is that even though we're culling objects and removing back-faces, we're generating a generic list of polygons and throwing them at the renderer in whatever order they come in. The renderer has no idea of what order to draw the polygons in! This is definitely an issue, and we're going to spend chapters discussing complex algorithms to determine the order, and figure out ways to cull even more geometry, and so forth. You can see why order is important if you play with the demos for more than a couple seconds; you'll notice objects that should be drawn behind things are being drawn in front and vice versa—it's a mess, to say the least <BG>. Things look fine in wireframe mode, but once you turn the shader on…yuck!

> **TIP**
>
> Remember, 3D graphics is about not drawing what you can't see!

What we're going to do is implement the simplest of rendering algorithms, called the painter's algorithm, and then we'll have something that works, at least for now. We can continue working with texturing and lighting and not be disturbed by the visual artifact caused by out-of-order rendering.

Alright, so let's talk about the painter's algorithm. It's basically modeled after how a painter paints: He paints the background, and then paints the foreground over it as shown in Figure 8.40. Thus, objects that are closer to the viewpoint automatically occlude the background.

Therefore, this algorithm is all we need to implement our polygon rendering. We know the z-values of every single polygon in the rendering list, so we can simply sort the polygons from back to front on their z-values and draw them as shown in Figure 8.28. This works for the most part until the anomalies shown in Figure 8.41 occur. Long polygons, overlapping polygons, and so forth won't be rendered properly sometimes. However, this isn't an issue because right now we're primarily interested in simply getting our displays to look more correct. Additionally, as long as polygons are kept small and there are no concave polyhedrons (shown in Figure 8.42), the painter's algorithm works fine. In fact, many 3D games that you've played use nothing more than a painter's algorithm or variant because it's simple.

FIGURE 8.40 A painter painting.

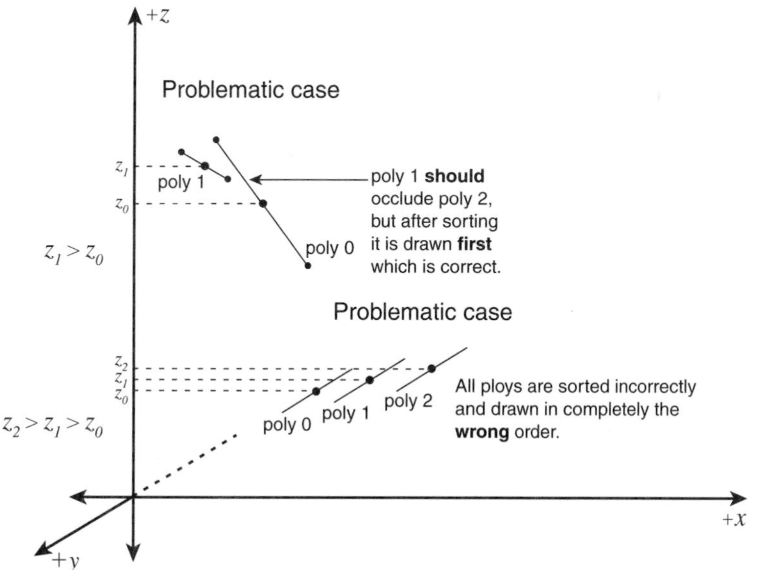

FIGURE 8.41 Special cases that z-sorting will fail on.

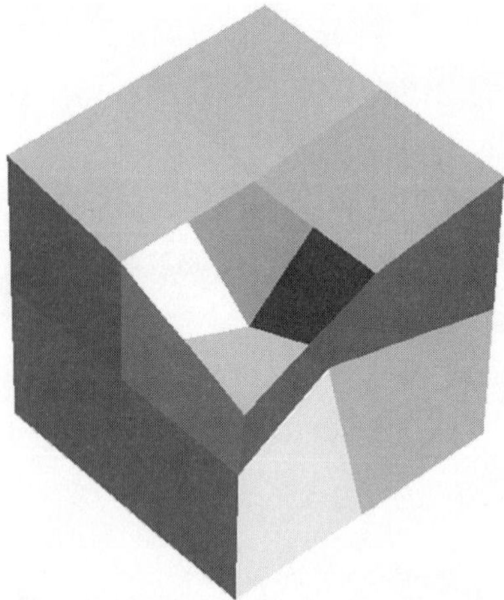

FIGURE 8.42 A concave polyhedron causes numerous rendering anomalies with the painter's algorithm.

NOTE

In fact, the z-buffer algorithm we'll discuss later in the book is in fact a painter's algorithm implemented on a pixel-by-pixel basis.

So, now comes the fun part: how to implement the algorithm with our current system and data structures. Well, there are two ways to do this. In method one, we sort the polygons in the rendering list and move them in place. In method two, we create a secondary index/pointer list into the rendering list, and then sort that! Method one might seem easier, but it's much too inefficient to move actual data around.

Additionally, there might be polygons in the rendering list that are disabled, and there's no need to sort them. Hence, we're going to create a secondary array of pointers, each of which points to a polygon in the rendering list. Then we'll sort the pointers, and render the pointer list rather than the rendering list itself. Figure 8.43 illustrates this.

Now, if you take a look at the original rendering list data structure, it's actually implemented in just this way!

```
// this is the indirection array used for
typedef struct RENDERLIST4DV1_TYP
{
int state; // state of renderlist ???
int attr;  // attributes of renderlist ???
```

```
// the render list is an array of pointers each pointing to
// a self contained "renderable" polygon face POLYF4DV1
POLYF4DV1_PTR poly_ptrs[RENDERLIST4DV1_MAX_POLYS];

// additionally to cut down on allocation, de-allocation
// of polygons each frame, here's where the actual polygon
// faces will be stored POLYF4DV1 poly_data[RENDERLIST4DV1_MAX_POLYS];
int num_polys; // number of polys in render list

} RENDERLIST4DV1, *RENDERLIST4DV1_PTR;
```

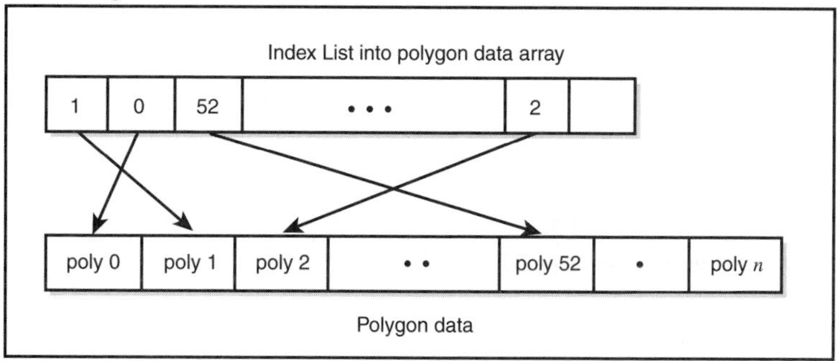

FIGURE 8.43 Rendering from an indexed array rather than the polygon data itself.

See the bolded code? That's the actual indirection array, so we're good to go. We just need the sorting algorithm. We'll use the built-in quicksort algorithm, the prototype for which is shown next:

```
void qsort(void *base, // Start of target array
     size_t num,    // array size in elements
     size_t width,  // element size in bytes
     int (cdecl *compare )(const void *elem1, // compare function and
     const void *elem2 ) );  // ptrs to the array elements to be compared with the
key
```

> **TIP**
>
> If you recall, quicksort sorts in **O**(n*log n), and is based on a recursive sort algorithm in which the list is split into pieces, the pieces are sorted, and then reassembled.

Although the function looks easy to use, it can be a bit harrowing when dealing with pointers. If you look closely at the prototype for the comparison function, it sends in a pointer to the key and the comparison item. But in our case, each key and comparison item are themselves pointers! Ouch! So, this means that in our comparison functions, we have to dereference the `const void *` pointers as if they were `**` pointers to polygon faces. This is just a bit tricky, and you have to get it right.

Also, the comparison function itself is worth discussing for a moment. We know that we're going to compare one polygon's z-value to another, but which z-value? We could use the largest, the smallest, or the average of the three vertices that make up each triangle. With this in mind, we'll support all three methods via a flag because some of your scenes may sort better depending on which sort key you use. Therefore, the sorting algorithm should case on a flag that determines this. With all this in mind, here's the sorting algorithm:

```
void Sort_RENDERLIST4DV1(RENDERLIST4DV1_PTR rend_list, int sort_method)
{
// this function sorts the rendering list based on the polygon z-values
// the specific sorting method is controlled by sending in control flags
switch(sort_method)
{
case SORT_POLYLIST_AVGZ:  //  - sorts on average of all vertices
     {
     qsort((void *)rend_list->poly_ptrs,
            rend_list->num_polys, sizeof(POLYF4DV1_PTR),
            Compare_AvgZ_POLYF4DV1);
     } break;
case SORT_POLYLIST_NEARZ: // - sorts on closest z vertex of each poly
     {
     qsort((void *)rend_list->poly_ptrs,
           rend_list->num_polys, sizeof(POLYF4DV1_PTR),
           Compare_NearZ_POLYF4DV1);
     } break;
case SORT_POLYLIST_FARZ:  //  - sorts on farthest z vertex of each poly
     {
     qsort((void *)rend_list->poly_ptrs,
     rend_list->num_polys, sizeof(POLYF4DV1_PTR), Compare_FarZ_POLYF4DV1);
     } break;

default: break;

} // end switch

} // end Sort_RENDERLIST4DV1
```

I bet you thought it would be big! And here are the sorting flags:

```
#define SORT_POLYLIST_AVGZ  0 - sorts on average of all vertices
#define SORT_POLYLIST_NEARZ 1 - sorts on closest z vertex of each poly
#define SORT_POLYLIST_FARZ  2 - sorts on farthest z vertex of each poly
```

And finally, here's a sample comparison function (average z compare, in this case):

```
int Compare_AvgZ_POLYF4DV1(const void *arg1, const void *arg2)
{
// this function compares the average z's of two polygons and is used by the
// depth sort surface ordering algorithm
float z1, z2;
POLYF4DV1_PTR poly_1, poly_2;
// dereference the poly pointers
poly_1 = *((POLYF4DV1_PTR *)(arg1));
poly_2 = *((POLYF4DV1_PTR *)(arg2));

// compute z average of each polygon
z1 = (float)0.33333*(poly_1->tvlist[0].z + poly_1->tvlist[1].z + poly_1-
>tvlist[2].z);

// now polygon 2
z2 = (float)0.33333*(poly_2->tvlist[0].z + poly_2->tvlist[1].z + poly_2-
>tvlist[2].z);
// compare z1 and z2, such that polys' will be sorted in descending Z order

if (z1 > z2)
   return(-1);
else
   if (z1 < z2)
return(1);
else
   return(0);
} // end Compare_AvgZ_POLYF4DV1
```

Now, the last question of the day is where to make the call to perform the sorting algorithm? This is very important—the sort must be performed in camera coordinates so that all the polygons are in the final positions before projection. Thus, we need to call it right after the world-to-camera transform, but before the camera-to-perspective transform, something like this:

```
// remove backfaces
Remove_Backfaces_RENDERLIST4DV1(&rend_list, &cam);

// light scene all at once
Light_RENDERLIST4DV1_World16(&rend_list, &cam, lights, 3);

// apply world to camera transform
World_To_Camera_RENDERLIST4DV1(&rend_list, &cam);
```

8

```
// sort the polygon list (hurry up!)
Sort_RENDERLIST4DV1(&rend_list,  SORT_POLYLIST_AVGZ);

// apply camera to perspective transformation
Camera_To_Perspective_RENDERLIST4DV1(&rend_list, &cam);

// apply screen transform
Perspective_To_Screen_RENDERLIST4DV1(&rend_list, &cam);
```

As an example of the code in action, take a look at Figure 8.44. It's a screenshot of `DEMOII8_6.CPP¦EXE` (`DEMOII8_6_8b.CPP¦EXE` is the 8-bit version) running. As you can see, the polygons are now properly sorted, and the world looks correct (for the most part). However, try running around in the world (it has the same controls as the previous demos), and see if you can mess up the painter's algorithm. Also, try experimenting by changing the sorting algorithm from average z, to near z, and far z.

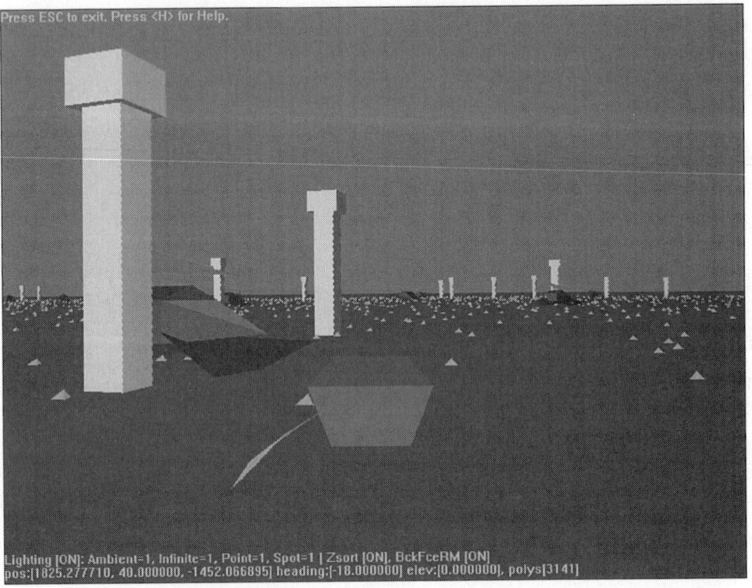

FIGURE 8.44 A screenshot of z-sorting in action.

> **TIP**
>
> We're sorting the polygons in the rendering list to make things easy, but this isn't necessarily the fastest way to create the proper rendering order, depending on the data set. It's also possible to sort all the objects themselves and then, based on their bounding spheres, sort the objects and insert them in order as complete polygon sets. In other words, sort the objects, and then as long as objects are convex for the most part and there are no inter-object intersections, you can then

do an insertion sort on the center of each object and get the proper rendering order, thus greatly decreasing your sort times. Of course, this works only for fast games that are outdoor, space games, and the like, where a few misplaced polys aren't going to kill you.

Working with New Model Formats

Although this hasn't been much of an issue until now, it's time to support more advanced model formats. I can tell that you creating cubes by hand is one thing, but creating mech warriors by hand is entirely another, and not going to happen! So, what we need to do is support some file formats in addition to the .PLG/PLX format we've used until now. That format is great because it's easy to read, easy to manipulate, and easy to parse, but there's nothing on the market that supports the format, and it's really limited anyway. Thus, let's write a couple more parsers for some current file formats.

To do this, though, I had to make a decision. Again, I'm torn between efficiency and education, and education usually wins. The point here is to learn, and writing a gnarly binary parser isn't that illustrative; I would rather work with ASCII file formats so that you can see the data and manually change it. Then, at a later time, you can always write a binary version loader yourself. With that in mind, I just wrote a couple new loaders: one that supports the 3D Studio Max .ASC ASCII format and one that supports the Caligari trueSpace .COB (version 4.0+) format. Articles on both of these formats can be found on the CD.

Both these formats have their pros and cons, but they give us the flexibility we need to create 3D models with real tools (or use premade models) and then export to these formats. Of course, even if you don't have Max or trueSpace, you can surely find a converter to switch from the format your particular tool saves in. Now, before I show you the file loaders themselves, we need to take a look at a C++ class (more of a C class) and helper functions that I wrote to facilitate parsing text files.

The Parser Class

8

Writing file loaders in any format, whether it be ASCII or binary, is an exercise in file I/O for the most part. So, it really pays to take the time to write a suite of functions that enable you to load a file, look for tokens, strip characters—whatever it is you need. Now because we're dealing with ASCII-formatted files, I wanted to write a parser that had the following capabilities:

- Open/close a file
- Read in a line of text
- Strip characters from the line
- Get tokens that are separated by whitespace
- Ignore anything after a comment character

- Count the lines and so forth
- Pattern matching

Figure 8.45 depicts a block diagram of the parser system. As you can see from the figure and outline, a parser with this functionality will seriously help us out. Let's talk about the pattern matching; it's the only interesting aspect of the parser.

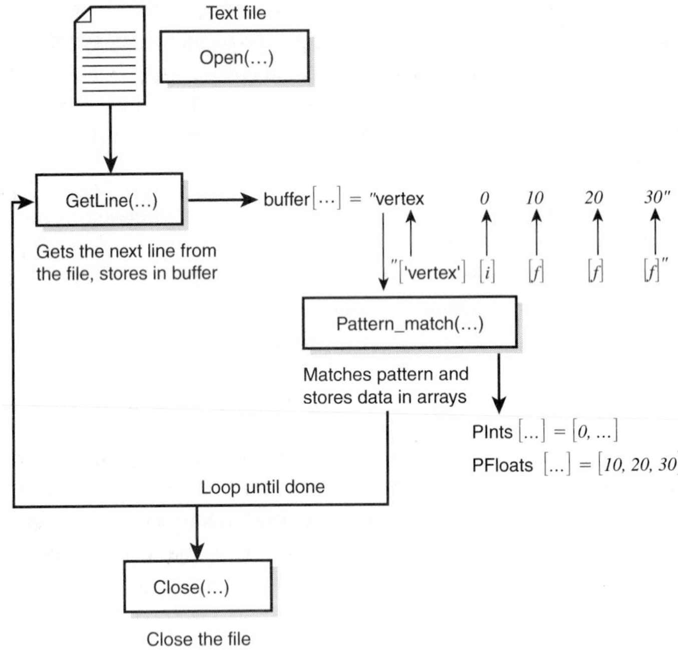

FIGURE 8.45 A block diagram of the parser system.

I wanted a pattern-matching system that allows me to scan for simple regular expressions when given a single line. For example, say we had the following line in a text buffer:

```
static char *buffer = "Polys: 10 Vertices: 20";
```

We can easily see that following `Polys:` is the number of polygons (integer). Following that is `Vertices:` and the number of vertices (integer). However, none of the `scanf()` class functions can really parse this line due to the commas and other extraneous characters. Thus, we need to write a pattern matcher to help parsing. That additional functionality has also been implemented in my parser class. Thus, I can write something like this:

```
Pattern_Match(buffer, "['Polys:'] [i] ['Vertices:'] [i]"));
```

So, the pattern matcher looks for the string "Polys:", consumes it, looks for an integer, consumes that, looks for the string "Vertices:", consumes that, and finally consumes the last integer. I'll shortly show you the entire pattern matching language after we see the class.

Okay, so far so good, but we also need functions that can do things like strip characters, replace characters, and so forth. Basically, we need a more robust set of string operations that C/C++ comes with. Of course, there are a million classes out there, but if you wanted to use engines and classes, you could just create MODs all day and be done—you're reading this because you want to know how yourself!

With that in mind, here's the parser class definition itself:

```
// parser class ///////////////////////////////////////////////
class CPARSERV1
{
public:
// constructor ///////////////////////////////////////////////
CPARSERV1();
// destructor ////////////////////////////////////////////////
~CPARSERV1() ;
// reset file system ////////////////////////////////////////
int Reset();
// open file /////////////////////////////////////////////////
int Open(char *filename);
// close file ////////////////////////////////////////////////
int Close();
// get line //////////////////////////////////////////////////
char *Getline(int mode);
// sets the comment string //////////////////////////////////
int SetComment(char *string);
// find pattern in line /////////////////////////////////////
int Pattern_Match(char *string, char *pattern, ...);

// VARIABLE DECLARATIONS /////////////////////////////////////
public:
FILE *fstream;                    // file pointer
char buffer[PARSER_BUFFER_SIZE];  // line buffer
int  length;                      // length of current line
int  num_lines;                   // number of lines processed
char comment[PARSER_MAX_COMMENT]; // single line comment string

// pattern matching parameter storage, easier that variable arguments
// anything matched will be stored here on exit from the call to pattern()
char  pstrings[PATTERN_MAX_ARGS][PATTERN_BUFFER_SIZE]; // any strings
    int   num_pstrings;
```

8

```
    float pfloats[PATTERN_MAX_ARGS];      // any floats
    int   num_pfloats;

    int   pints[PATTERN_MAX_ARGS];        // any ints
    int   num_pints;

}; // end CLASS CPARSERV1 ///////////////////////////////////////////////
typedef CPARSERV1 *CPARSERV1_PTR;
```

As I mentioned, it's a very basic C++ class. I hate C++ for teaching. You can look at code and have no idea what it means, so if I do use it, I use it sparingly. In any case, take a look at all the methods for a moment and then return here....

The system is incredibly simple, as you can see. The class has the following functions:

`int Open(char *filename)`—Opens the sent file path. Returns `1` if successful; `0` otherwise.

`int Reset()`—Resets the entire parser, closes all files, and resets all variables.

`int Close()`—Calls `Reset()`.

`char *Getline(int mode)`—Once a file has been opened for parsing, this gets the next line from the file. If there's another line, it returns the line; otherwise it returns `NULL`. The call has the following modes of operation:

```
#define PARSER_STRIP_EMPTY_LINES        1   // strips all blank lines
#define PARSER_LEAVE_EMPTY_LINES        2   // leaves empty lines
#define PARSER_STRIP_WS_ENDS            4   // strips ws space at ends of line
#define PARSER_LEAVE_WS_ENDS            8   // leaves it
#define PARSER_STRIP_COMMENTS           16  // strips comments out
#define PARSER_LEAVE_COMMENTS           32  // leaves comments in
```

When `Getline()` returns, the current line will be stored in the class variable buffer as well as returned as a pointer.

`int SetComment(char *string)`—This function enables you to set the comment string that will be used as a sentinel to begin a comment line. Use anything you wish, up to 16 characters, but it must not contain whitespace. In most cases, the strings `#`, `;`, and `//` make good comment sentinels; the default is `#`.

`int Pattern_Match(char *string, char *pattern, ...)` —This is the most complex function of them all. It enables you to pass a pattern that must be matched by the sent string. Notice that although `Pattern_Match()` is a method of the parser class, it allows you to send any string for pattern matching. The pattern-matching language is shown in Table 8.3.

TABLE 8.3 Pattern-Matching Language

Pattern	Meaning
`[i]`	Matches an integer
`[f]`	Matches a floating-point number
`[s=d]`	Matches any string that is exactly `d` characters long
`[s<d]`	Matches any string that is less than `d` characters long
`[s>d]`	Matches any string that is greater than `d` characters long
`['ssss...s']`	Matches the string between the single quotes exactly

For example, if you wanted to match the following schema:

```
"Vertex 3 34.56 23.67 10.90"
```

The pattern `"['Vertex'] [f] [f] [f]"` would be used. But where do the pattern-matched strings go? Inside the parser class object are some variables and arrays at the bottom of the class that are bolded—go take a look. For example, if you try to match floats, the floats themselves and the number of floats will be stored in

```
int   pfloats[PATTERN_MAX_ARGS];
int   num_pfloats;
```

So, in the preceding example match, `num_pfloats=3` and `pfloats[]={34.56, 23.67, 10.90}`.

> **NOTE**
>
> You may see the variable parameter list at the end of `Pattern_Match()`. I was going to export the found variables in these arrays, but didn't completely finish it because the output arrays seemed to work better, but later you may find this a cool feature and finish it.

Now, there are a couple limitations to the pattern matcher. It works only on tokens separated by whitespace, so if you had a string like this

```
"Vertex 3: 20.9, 90.8, 100.3"
```

it wouldn't work! But helper functions to the rescue. Let's take a look at all the cool string helper functions to make things like this easy.

Parsing Helper Functions

The following is a small library of string processing helper functions also in the `T3DLIB6.CPP|H` library. They're designed to be used standalone or with the parser—it's up to you. Here's a list of the functions:

```
char buffer[64]; // used for output
```

First let's start with the character-stripping function:

```
// strips characters from a string
int StripChars(char *string_in, char *string_out, char *strip_chars, int case_on=1);
```

You send `StripChars()` the string you want stripped, the string you want the stripped version saved in, and the characters you want stripped along with a case-sensitivity flag. Here's an example of stripping all : and , from a string:

```
StripChars("Vertex 3: 20.9, 90.8, 100.3", buffer, ":,", 1);
```

The result in the buffer will be `"Vertex 3 20.9 90.8 100.3"`.

Now, let's take a look at something that will replace characters rather than just stripping them:

```
// replaces characters from a string
int ReplaceChars(char *string_in, char *string_out,
                 char *replace_chars, char rep_char, int case_on=1);
```

Sometimes stripping a character isn't exactly what you want; sometimes you just need to replace it with a blank or whatever. `ReplaceChars()` serves this purpose. It's similar to `StripChars()`, but you send in an additional `char` parameter, which is the replacement character. So, as another example, imagine we had something like this:

```
"Vertex #3: 20.9,90.8,100.3"
```

If we ran `StripChars()` on this, stripping `"#,:"`, the result would be

```
"Vertex 320.990.8100.3"
```

Ouch! The problem is that we wanted to strip those, but then they weren't replaced and we lost the whitespace, mashing the string together. But with `ReplaceChars()`, we can make it do what we need:

```
ReplaceChars("Vertex #3: 20.9,90.8,100.3",
buffer, "#:,", ' ', 1);
```

The result in the buffer will be

```
"Vertex  3  20.9 90.8 100.3"
```

which is exactly what we want. Then we can make a call to `Pattern_Match(buffer,"[i] [f] [f] [f]")` and it will match the first integer and three floats.

Next, here are some whitespace-trimming functions:

```
// trims all whitespace from the left side of a string
char *StringLtrim(char *string);

// trims all white space from the right side of a string
char *StringRtrim(char *string);
```

These next two functions determine whether a string is a float or an int and, if so, return the value. They don't try to force the issue; thus, they do pattern-matching themselves. If the string sent in is not a float or an int, the functions return `FLT_MIN` and `INT_MIN`, respectively. These are defined in `limits.h` as an error.

```
// a robust function that converts a string to a float
float IsFloat(char *fstring);

// a robust function that converts an string to a float
int   IsInt(char *istring);
```

Take a look at the following code for `IsFloat()`. It's interesting, with lots of parsing techniques there:

```
float IsFloat(char *fstring)
{
// validates the sent string as a float and converts it, if it's not valid
// the function sends back FLT_MIN, the chances of this being the number
// validated is slim
// [whitespace] [sign] [digits] [.digits] [ {d | D | e | E }[sign]digits]
char *string = fstring;
// must be of the form
// [whitespace]
while(isspace(*string)) string++;

// [sign]
if (*string=='+' || *string=='-') string++;

// [digits]
while(isdigit(*string)) string++;

// [.digits]
if (*string =='.')
   {
string++;
while(isdigit(*string)) string++;
   }

// [ {d | D | e | E }[sign]digits]
if (*string =='e' || *string == 'E' || *string =='d' || *string == 'D')
   {
string++;
// [sign]
if (*string=='+' || *string=='-') string++;
```

8

```
// [digits]
while(isdigit(*string)) string++;
   }

// the string better be the same size as the other one
if (strlen(fstring) == (int)(string - fstring))
return(atof(fstring));
else
return(FLT_MIN);
} // end IsFloat

///////////////////////////////////////////////////////////////////////////
```

Alright, it wasn't my intent to get into parsing at all. I really hate it, and wanted to avoid it, but I didn't want to just dump a black box parser on you and then write magical functions that load the new model formats. So, you have now at least seen the functions and have an idea of what they do. Moreover, the helper functions are really useful! Anyway, as an example, `DEMOII8_7.CPP|EXE` (screen shown in Figure 8.46) enables you to load a text file, run it through the parser, and then search for patterns.

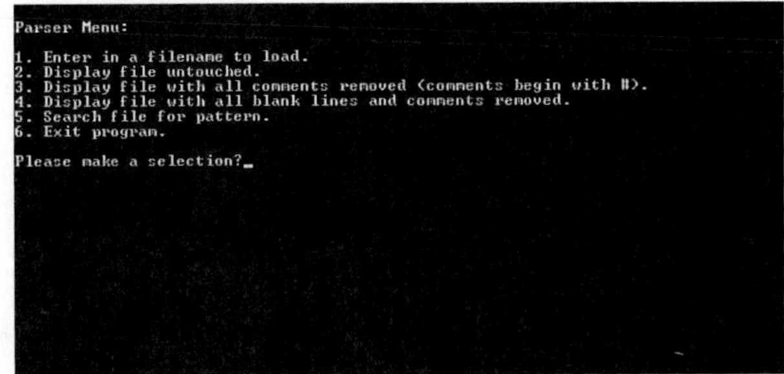

FIGURE 8.46 The parser testing bed running.

I've included a couple of text files in the directory for this chapter: `TEST1.TXT` and `TEST2.TXT`, as shown here:

```
# test 1
object name: tank
num vertices: 4

vertex list:
0 10 20
5 90 10
3 4 3
1 2 3

end object # this is a comment!
```

And the second file:

```
# test 2
This is a line...
# I am commented out!
And this a 3rd...
```

Basically, run the program, load the filename, and then try printing it out with the various parsing functions. Try looking for patterns such as `"[i] [i] [i]"` in `TEST1.TXT` and so on. Review the program; it shows you how to use the parser and helper functions a bit.

3D Studio MAX ASCII .ASC Format

The 3D Studio Max .ASC ASCII version format is a fairly simple format that contains vertex and polygon information in addition to the material for each polygon. Unfortunately, there's no texture information or reflectivity information, so the .ASC format isn't going to be robust enough for full-textured objects. However, it's ten times better than the .PLG format, and .ASC can actually be exported from 99% of all 3D modelers, so it's going to make my life and yours easier. On the other hand, there's no way to select shading models for the polygons in the .ASC format because it's so limited. Please refer back to Chapter 6 on file formats for more details, but for reference, I've listed a standard cube output in .ASC format:

```
Ambient light color: Red=0.3 Green=0.3 Blue=0.3
Named object: "Cube"
Tri-mesh, Vertices: 8     Faces: 12
Vertex list:
Vertex 0:  X:-1.000000     Y:-1.000000     Z:-1.000000
Vertex 1:  X:-1.000000     Y:-1.000000     Z:1.000000
Vertex 2:  X:1.000000     Y:-1.000000     Z:-1.000000
Vertex 3:  X:1.000000     Y:-1.000000     Z:1.000000
Vertex 4:  X:-1.000000     Y:1.000000     Z:-1.000000
Vertex 5:  X:1.000000     Y:1.000000     Z:-1.000000
Vertex 6:  X:1.000000     Y:1.000000     Z:1.000000
Vertex 7:  X:-1.000000     Y:1.000000     Z:1.000000
Face list:
Face 0:    A:2 B:3 C:1 AB:1 BC:1 CA:1
Material:"r255g255b255a0"
Smoothing:  1
Face 1:    A:2 B:1 C:0 AB:1 BC:1 CA:1
Material:"r255g255b255a0"
Smoothing:  1
Face 2:    A:4 B:5 C:2 AB:1 BC:1 CA:1
Material:"r255g255b255a0"
Smoothing:  1
Face 3:    A:4 B:2 C:0 AB:1 BC:1 CA:1
```

```
Material:"r255g255b255a0"
Smoothing:  1
Face 4:    A:6 B:3 C:2 AB:1 BC:1 CA:1
Material:"r255g255b255a0"
Smoothing:  1
Face 5:    A:6 B:2 C:5 AB:1 BC:1 CA:1
Material:"r255g255b255a0"
Smoothing:  1
Face 6:    A:6 B:7 C:1 AB:1 BC:1 CA:1
Material:"r255g255b255a0"
Smoothing:  1
Face 7:    A:6 B:1 C:3 AB:1 BC:1 CA:1
Material:"r255g255b255a0"
Smoothing:  1
Face 8:    A:6 B:5 C:4 AB:1 BC:1 CA:1
Material:"r255g255b255a0"
Smoothing:  1
Face 9:    A:6 B:4 C:7 AB:1 BC:1 CA:1
Material:"r255g255b255a0"
Smoothing:  1
Face 10:    A:1 B:7 C:4 AB:1 BC:1 CA:1
Material:"r255g255b255a0"
Smoothing:  1
Face 11:    A:1 B:4 C:0 AB:1 BC:1 CA:1
Material:"r255g255b255a0"
Smoothing:  1
```

To read in this file format, we need to write a parser that performs the following steps:

Step 1: Read the name of the object, number of vertices, and polygons.

Step 2: Read in the vertex list.

Step 3: Read in each polygon definition along with the RGB material color information.

If you review the file format, there's not much to it. Our parser routines will chew through this format easily. The only downside is that there's no way to set one or two sided polygons, texturing, light model, and so on. For the most part, we just get a color for each polygon and that's it. Alas, the reader we write must assume things, such as the lighting model. For now, I just wanted something that would load a .ASC file in either 8/16-bit graphics modes, and then fill in the proper data structures, set the lighting and so forth to default values. Before we see that, I want to review a single polygon definition to make sure that you get it:

Face 10: `A:1 B:7 C:4 AB:1 BC:1 CA:1`

Material:`"r255g255b255a0"`

Smoothing: `1`

This is face (10). It's composed of three polygons with vertices A, B, and C, which are actually vertex numbers 1,7, and 4, respectively. The AB, BC, and CA text describes the winding order of the polygon (unused by us), and the smoothing element has to do with whether polygon normals be averaged (unused also). For a more complete description of this format, please look on the CD in the directory `3D_DOCS\File Formats\`.

Alright, that's about all there is to the file format, so let's see the function prototype:

```
int Load_OBJECT4DV1_3DSASC(OBJECT4DV1_PTR obj,   // pointer to object
                       char *filename,       // filename of ASC file
                       VECTOR4D_PTR scale,   // initial scaling factors
                       VECTOR4D_PTR pos,     // initial position
                       VECTOR4D_PTR rot,     // initial rotations
                       int vertex_flags)     // flags to re-order vertices
```

The function has almost an identical prototype as the .PLG loader except for the added `vertex_flags` parameter. This is to give you a little control when loading objects. The reason being that when you create objects using modelers, many times coordinates will be inverted or swapped, winding orders will be backward, and so forth. This parameter gives you the ability to change these things during loading. For example, our engine uses a left-handed system, but your modeler might be right-handed, so you would have to invert the z-axis—these are the kinds of things I'm talking about. Here are the `vertex_flags` you can logically `OR` together:

```
#define VERTEX_FLAGS_INVERT_X           1 // inverts the Z-coordinates
#define VERTEX_FLAGS_INVERT_Y           2 // inverts the Z-coordinates
#define VERTEX_FLAGS_INVERT_Z           4 // inverts the Z-coordinates
#define VERTEX_FLAGS_SWAP_YZ            8 // transforms a RHS model to LHS
#define VERTEX_FLAGS_SWAP_XZ            16 // ???
#define VERTEX_FLAGS_SWAP_XY            32
#define VERTEX_FLAGS_INVERT_WINDING_ORDER 64 // invert winding order
                                         // from cw to ccw or ccw to cc
```

Here's how you would load the object `CUBE.ASC` with a reversed winding order:

```
int Load_OBJECT4DV1_3DSASC(&obj, "CUBE.ASC",
                           NULL, NULL, NULL,
                           VERTEX_FLAGS_INVERT_WINDING_ORDER);
```

CAUTION

The reader reads ASCII .ASC files only! Don't try to read a binary file; you'll crash the reader.

The code is way too long to list, so please review it in `T3DLIB6.CPP` on the CD. Its length is due to going overboard on error handling (purposely, so you can see it) even though errors will never occur if the files it loads are correct. The error handling is mostly illustrational, and also to help you if you decide to manually type in an object off the top of your head.

As an example of using the function, check out `DEMOII8_8.CPP|EXE`. A screenshot is shown in Figure 8.47. It allows you to load any .ASC object off disk via a menu. You must give the full path to the object. Here are a few objects I made that are in the directory `CHAPTER8\`:

`SPHERE01.ASC` (swap YZ and invert winding order)

`CAR01.ASC` (Swap YZ and invert winding order)

`HAMMER02.ASC`

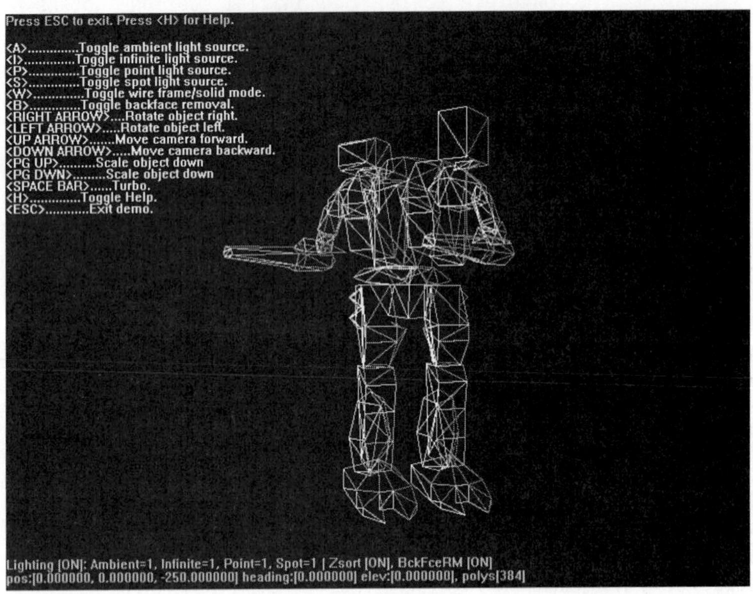

FIGURE 8.47 The 3D Studio .ASC loader up and running.

CAUTION

You can't load an object with more vertices or polygons than the engine can handle. Right now both vertices and polygons are set to a max of:

```
// defines for objects version 1
#define OBJECT4DV1_MAX_VERTICES    1024
#define OBJECT4DV1_MAX_POLYS       1024
```

These defines are, of course, in the previous library module `T3DLIB5.H`.

Additionally, the load file dialog has check boxes that enable you to swap the y- and z-coordinates and invert the winding order. You might have to play with these to get your object to load correctly.

trueSpace ASCII .COB Format

"Never underestimate the power of the Magic Ring." That's an inside joke if you like using trueSpace 5+. Otherwise, completely disregard it <BG>. Anyway, after much thought and compromise, I think that the best static file format on the market, other than Microsoft .X files, is the Caligari .COB format. It's very robust and supports everything we would ever need along with the concept of materials. Hence, we can select the type of shading model to apply to polygons by literally applying appropriate materials to the objects themselves. Moreover, .COB format has texture support and lots more. Of course, if you don't use trueSpace, you need to export to .COB to use the reader or use a converter such as Polytrans. I simply refuse to write a .3DS reader. The format is a disaster, and I hate cryptic aged formats. So, if you want .3DS format, you're more than welcome to write a reader. In truth, it's not that bad, but it's a binary format and harder to visualize.

In Chapter 6, we discussed the .COB format (full detailed analysis is on the CD in `3D_DOCS\File Formats\`, so check that out). But let's take a look at an ASCII file dump of a simple .COB object once again. The file is `CALIGARI_COB_FORMAT_EXAMPLE01.COB` and Figure 8.49 is a screenshot of it.

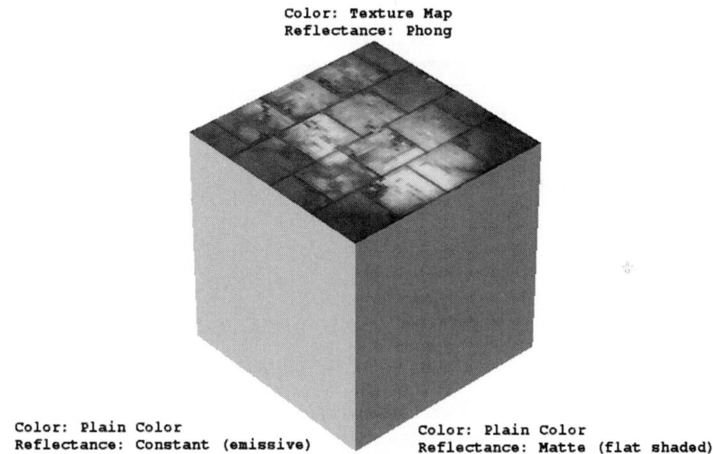

FIGURE 8.48 The cube model with multiple surface types.

Basically, it's a cube in trueSpace with a texture on a single face. The following is the ASCII file data itself. I've added some vertical whitespace, so imagine that it's not there, plus I've bolded areas of interest and removed a few advanced sections such as the thumbnail and radiosity stuff, so please refer to the original file for everything, but it's too long to list here. Anyway, go ahead and take a look at it for a moment to recall the format:

```
Caligari V00.01ALH
PolH V0.08 Id 18661892 Parent 0 Size 00001060
Name Cube,1
```

```
center 0 0 0
x axis 1 0 0
y axis 0 1 0
z axis 0 0 1

Transform
1 0 0 1.19209e-007
0 1 0 0
0 0 1 -1
0 0 0 1

World Vertices 8
1.000000 -1.000000 0.000000
1.000000 -1.000000 2.000000
1.000000 -1.000000 0.000000
1.000000 -1.000000 2.000000
1.000000 1.000000 0.000000
1.000000 1.000000 0.000000
1.000000 1.000000 2.000000
1.000000 1.000000 2.000000

Texture Vertices 6
0.000000 0.000000
0.000000 1.000000
0.000000 0.000000
0.000000 1.000000
1.000000 0.000000
1.000000 1.000000

Faces 12
Face verts 3 flags 0 mat 4
<0,0> <1,1> <3,5>
Face verts 3 flags 0 mat 4
<0,0> <3,5> <2,4>
Face verts 3 flags 0 mat 0
<0,1> <2,5> <5,4>
Face verts 3 flags 0 mat 0
<0,1> <5,4> <4,0>
Face verts 3 flags 0 mat 1
<2,2> <3,3> <6,5>
Face verts 3 flags 0 mat 1
<2,2> <6,5> <5,4>
Face verts 3 flags 0 mat 0
<1,0> <7,1> <6,5>
```

```
Face verts 3 flags 0 mat 0
<1,0> <6,5> <3,4>
Face verts 3 flags 0 mat 2
<4,4> <5,0> <6,1>
Face verts 3 flags 0 mat 2
<4,4> <6,1> <7,5>
Face verts 3 flags 0 mat 3
<0,4> <4,2> <7,3>
Face verts 3 flags 0 mat 3
<0,4> <7,3> <1,5>
Mat1 V0.06 Id 18659348 Parent 18661892 Size 00000102
mat# 1
shader: phong  facet: auto32
rgb 0.00784314,1,0.0352941
alpha 1  ka 0.1  ks 0.1  exp 0  ior 1
ShBx V0.03 Id 18659349 Parent 18659348 Size 00000383
Shader class: color
Shader name: "plain color" (plain) ß- this is an example of a non-textured material
Number of parameters: 1
colour: color (2, 255, 9)
Flags: 3
Shader class: transparency
Shader name: "none" (none)
Number of parameters: 0
Flags: 3
Shader class: reflectance
Shader name: "constant" (constant) ß this material is constant shaded, or emmisive
to us
Number of parameters: 0
Flags: 3
Shader class: displacement
Shader name: "none" (none)
Number of parameters: 0
Flags: 3

Mat1 V0.06 Id 18658628 Parent 18661892 Size 00000085
mat# 2
shader: phong  facet: auto32
rgb 1,0,0
alpha 1  ka 0.1  ks 0.1  exp 0  ior 1
ShBx V0.03 Id 18658629 Parent 18658628 Size 00000427
Shader class: color
Shader name: "plain color" (plain) ß again a plain colored material
Number of parameters: 1
```

```
colour: color (255, 0, 0)
Flags: 3
Shader class: transparency
Shader name: "none" (none)
Number of parameters: 0
Flags: 3
Shader class: reflectance
Shader name: "matte" (matte) ß this material is flat shaded in our engine
Number of parameters: 2
ambient factor: float 0.1
diffuse factor: float 1
Flags: 3
Shader class: displacement
Shader name: "none" (none)
Number of parameters: 0
Flags: 3

Mat1 V0.06 Id 18657844 Parent 18661892 Size 00000101
mat# 3
shader: phong  facet: auto32
rgb 0.0392157,0.0117647,1
alpha 1  ka 0.1  ks 0.5  exp 0  ior 1
ShBx V0.03 Id 18657845 Parent 18657844 Size 00000522
Shader class: color
Shader name: "plain color" (plain) ß again a colored material
Number of parameters: 1
colour: color (10, 3, 255)
Flags: 3
Shader class: transparency
Shader name: "none" (none)
Number of parameters: 0
Flags: 3
Shader class: reflectance
Shader name: "plastic" (plastic) ß this means use gouraud shading
Number of parameters: 5
ambient factor: float 0.1
diffuse factor: float 0.75
specular factor: float 0.5
roughness: float 0.1
specular colour: color (255, 255, 255)
Flags: 3
Shader class: displacement
Shader name: "none" (none)
```

```
Number of parameters: 0
Flags: 3

Mat1 V0.06 Id 18614788 Parent 18661892 Size 00000100
mat# 4
shader: phong  facet: auto32
rgb 1,0.952941,0.0235294
alpha 1  ka 0.1  ks 0.1  exp 0  ior 1
ShBx V0.03 Id 18614789 Parent 18614788 Size 00000515
Shader class: color
Shader name: "plain color" (plain) ß a plain colored material
Number of parameters: 1
colour: color (255, 243, 6)
Flags: 3
Shader class: transparency
Shader name: "none" (none)
Number of parameters: 0
Flags: 3
Shader class: reflectance
Shader name: "phong" (phong) ß actually use a phong shader in our engine
Number of parameters: 5
ambient factor: float 0.1
diffuse factor: float 0.9
specular factor: float 0.1
exponent: float 3
specular colour: color (255, 255, 255)
Flags: 3
Shader class: displacement
Shader name: "none" (none)
Number of parameters: 0
Flags: 3

Mat1 V0.06 Id 18613860 Parent 18661892 Size 00000182
mat# 0
shader: phong  facet: auto32
rgb 1,0.952941,0.0235294
alpha 1  ka 0.1  ks 0.1  exp 0  ior 1
texture: 36D:\Source\models\textures\wall01.bmp
offset 0,0  repeats 1,1  flags 2
ShBx V0.03 Id 18613861 Parent 18613860 Size 00000658
Shader class: color
Shader name: "texture map" (caligari texture) ß this means this material is a tex-
ture map
Number of parameters: 7
```

```
file name: string "D:\Source\models\textures\wall01.bmp" ß here the texture
S repeat: float 1
T repeat: float 1
S offset: float 0
T offset: float 0
animate: bool 0
filter: bool 0
Flags: 3
Shader class: transparency
Shader name: "none" (none)
Number of parameters: 0
Flags: 3
Shader class: reflectance
Shader name: "phong" (phong) ß the shader for this material should be phong
Number of parameters: 5
ambient factor: float 0.1
diffuse factor: float 0.9
specular factor: float 0.1
exponent: float 3
specular colour: color (255, 255, 255)
Flags: 3
Shader class: displacement
Shader name: "none" (none)
Number of parameters: 0
Flags: 3
END  V1.00 Id 0 Parent 0 Size        0
```

The format is fairly human-readable and makes sense for the most part. Let's gloss over the details so that you have some idea of how I coded the reader. Here are the general steps to read a .COB file:

Step 1: Read the header line at the top of the file.

Step 2: Read in the name line and then the center, x-axis, y-axis, and z-axis lines. These make up the local transform for the object. This transform must be applied to the object's vertices because all trueSpace objects are exported without transformations to the vertices for reasons of accuracy. In other words, when you rotate or move a cube in trueSpace, the modeler records the transform and renders it, but leaves the unit cube alone—this way you don't lose accuracy.

Step 3: Read in the transform line and following matrix. This matrix transforms the local space to world space; in most cases, it will be the identity matrix, but we'll support applying the transform as well as the previous to make sure that we get the model where the modeler intended it and in the proper orientation.

Step 4: Read in the World vertices line and then read the vertex list in (x, y, z) order.

Step 5: Read in the Texture vertices line and the <u,v> texture coordinates for each texture coordinate. There's a bit of compression here in the texture coordinates; that is, you would normally expect three texture coordinates per triangle. However, the .COB format seems to reuse common (u,v) values, so even though you have a mesh with 100 triangles and you would expect 300 texture coordinates, there will be fewer in most cases; also there can be duplicates even though they aren't needed. Whatever the logic is, I haven't figured it out. But it's irrelevant; you simply read them into an array and then store the values into the final texture coordinate array (which we don't have yet, so don't worry about it).

NOTE

If you aren't familiar with texture coordinates, they're the sample points in a texture that should be pinned to a polygon's surface. In most cases, textures have the coordinate system shown in Figure 8.49. u is the x-axis, v denotes the y-axis, and 99% of all textures are square. So, to map the texture shown in the figure to a pair of triangles, you would use the coordinates as shown in the figure. We'll cover this in heavy detail later.

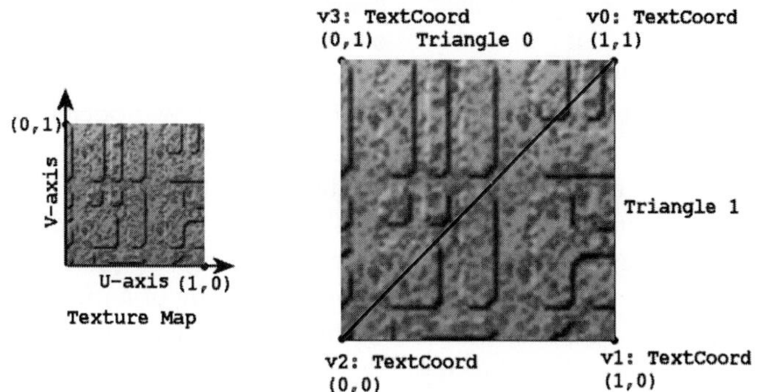

FIGURE 8.49 Standard texture coordinates.

Step 6: Read in the Face line and then read each polygon face. Faces can have many vertices, but we'll make sure that all exported meshes have three vertices, so our Face lines should look like this:

```
Face verts 3 flags ff mat mm
```

where `ff` and `mm` are the flags and material number, respectively. The flags are irrelevant, so disregard them, but the material number is important. This is a zero-based number that indicates the material that should be applied to the face. As we parse, we need to remember this material so that when we read in materials later in the file, we can fix this up.

Next is the polygon face itself, which is a set of vertex indices in the format <v1,t1> <v2, t2> .... The first element is the vertex index of the vertex that makes up the triangle and the second is the texture coordinate. So, <1,2> <9,5> <3,8> would mean that this triangle is composed of the three vertices: 1,9,3 and the texture coordinates for these vertices are 2, 5, 8 with a one to one and onto mapping.

Step 7: Here's where things get nasty. We have to read in the materials (and they can be out of order). Now, our engine isn't like a hardware HALO engine, so we don't support every single material option. We need to encode the following properties somehow:

```
#define MATV1_ATTR_2SIDED                  0x0001
#define MATV1_ATTR_TRANSPARENT             0x0002
#define MATV1_ATTR_8BITCOLOR               0x0004
#define MATV1_ATTR_RGB16                   0x0008
#define MATV1_ATTR_RGB24                   0x0010

#define MATV1_ATTR_SHADE_MODE_CONSTANT     0x0020
#define MATV1_ATTR_SHADE_MODE_EMMISIVE     0x0020 // alias
#define MATV1_ATTR_SHADE_MODE_FLAT         0x0040
#define MATV1_ATTR_SHADE_MODE_GOURAUD      0x0080
#define MATV1_ATTR_SHADE_MODE_FASTPHONG    0x0100
#define MATV1_ATTR_SHADE_MODE_TEXTURE      0x0200
```

We're going to have no luck with the two-sided thing. Very few modelers have the concept of two-sided encoded in the polygon list or materials, so that's moot. Additionally, all materials from all modelers are always in RGB space, so the color depth stuff is artificial and computed at load time based on the mode the models are loaded from. The only stuff we have any control over are the highlighted properties. We're lucky that the material support in the .COB format allows exporting of a number of different things that we can use to signal that we want to use a particular lighting model for the polygon.

For example, say we model a ship and want to make the engines constant-shaded, and the rest Gouraud-shaded. We need to apply material so we can extract this information. If the modeler doesn't support some way to export the information, we have to get really clever. For example, we might say that anything that's colored gray is an emissive polygon, and the color is 0–15 based on the shade of gray—crazy stuff like that.

Anyway, we don't have to do that because we can encode the material properties naturally using the modeler. However, there's not an exact 1:1 correspondence between the material's shading mode in the modeler and the one we want, for example, but I'll get to that in a minute. Now, let's talk about the actual encoding. What modeler we use is irrelevant as long as you export the object as a trueSpace 4.0+ .COB object, we should be fine. The encoding is performed as outlined here.

First, we find the material. They all start with something that looks like this (the second line is the material number):

```
Mat1 V0.06 Id 142522724 Parent 18646020 Size 00000182
mat# 0
```

Thus, this would be the definition for material 0, so any polygon that previously used material 0—this is the material for it. Moving on, the next lines of interest are of the form

```
rgb 0.0392157,0.0117647,1
alpha 1  ka 0.1  ks 0.5  exp 0  ior 1
```

The RGB is the color of the polygon (this is redundant and in more than one place). The next line, starting with `alpha`, determines the alpha, reflectivities, and a couple of other things, as outlined in Table 8.4.

TABLE 8.4 Alpha Line Encoding for .COB Materials

Variable	Meaning	Range
alpha	Transparency	0 - 1
ka	Ambient coefficient	0 - 1
ks	Specular coefficient	0 - 1
exp	Highlight power exponent	0 - 1
ior	Index of refraction	(Unused by us)

Cool, so now here's how I extract out the shading model. If you look at the each material definition in the listing, you'll see I've bolded a couple lines in each material as shown here:

```
Shader class: color
Shader name: "plain color" (plain)
.
.
.
.
Shader class: reflectance
Shader name: "phong" (phong)
.
.
```

We need to pay attention to these lines very carefully. The `Shader class: color` and the `Shader Class: reflectance` are going to be our key to encoding stuff. Here's the logic to figure out whether we have a plain color polygon (in which case the polygon is emissive, flat, Gouraud, or Phong) or a textured polygon.

First, we need to know the shading model. It's a bit tricky, but we need to look for the lines like this:

```
Shader class: color
```

After that, we need to look for this:

```
Shader name: "xxxxxx" (xxxxxx)
```

8

where the xxxxx part will be "plain color" and "plain" for colored polys. respectively or "texture map" and "caligari texture" for textures (I know this sucks). Then based on that, we hunt for

```
Shader class: reflectance
```

which is where the type of shading is encoded. We look for the line

```
Shader name: "xxxxxx" (xxxxxx)
```

Based on its value, we map it to our shading system, as shown in Table 8.5.

TABLE 8.5 Shader Mapping from .COB to our Engine

.COB Shader Model	Our Shader Model
"constant"	MATV1_ATTR_SHADE_MODE_CONSTANT
"matte"	MATV1_ATTR_SHADE_MODE_FLAT
"plastic"	MATV1_ATTR_SHADE_MODE_GOURAUD
"phong"	MATV1_ATTR_SHADE_MODE_FASTPHONG
And in the case that in the "color" class, we find "texture map", the "shading mode" is	
"texture map"	MATV1_ATTR_SHADE_MODE_TEXTURE

NOTE

Texture mapping must be logically ORed with the other previous modes so that the texture is shaded.

What a nightmare, huh? The problem is simple, though. Modelers don't have ways to export information about the models. For example, if you want to use Max to make a game world, great, but how are you going to indicate that a door is a door? See the problem? This is a similar situation—not as bad, granted—but still an issue. We have to find ways to encode information in the file format about our model.

Well, now that you're completely confused, let's briefly reiterate how you model something in trueSpace that our .COB reader can read. First, model your object as usual, and then you must apply materials to the object. If you want a polygon to be a plain color, leave the material's color as a "plain color" rather than texture. Then, in the reflectance part of the model, select the reflectance model of constant, matte, plastic, or Phong, depending on what you want our engine to do. Right now, of course, we support only constant (emissive) and flat shading. Now, if you want a texture on a surface, just texture it as you normally would; the modeler will set the color to "texture" and apply the texture. Then, once again, you need to set the reflectance model to how you want the texture lit. And, of course, our engine doesn't support textures yet, so don't try it!

Okay, now that all this drama about the .COB file format has been discussed, what are we doing with the materials? Well, in fact, they're actually being loaded into the material library when a .COB object is loaded, as shown in Figure 8.50. However, there are a couple of problems with this. First, our engine doesn't use materials yet, only lights. Second, the material that one object loads may be reusable by another object; hence, if you load 10 objects with their own materials and you use the same exact materials for the 5 objects, you're going to get 25 materials loaded into the material library! It's not going to kill you, but it's something to think about. Therefore, we might have to do something about this. But as I said, we aren't even supporting materials yet because we didn't have a 3D format that supported them until now.

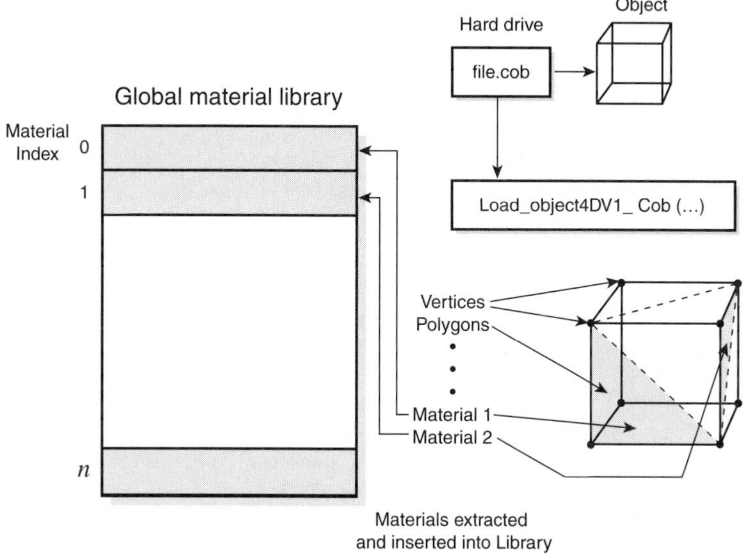

FIGURE 8.50 The .COB reader loading materials into the global material library.

CAUTION

It's imperative that you export all .COB objects as triangles only. Thus, triangulate all objects before exporting. I left the earlier example in quad format to save space, but our engine understands only triangles.

Okay, now that you have some idea of what's under the hood of the .COB format, take a look at the following prototype of the file loader. It's almost identical to the .ASC reader, except for a couple more features:

```
int Load_OBJECT4DV1_COB(OBJECT4DV1_PTR obj,   // pointer to object
          char *filename,        // filename of Caligari COB file
          VECTOR4D_PTR scale,    // initial scaling factors
          VECTOR4D_PTR pos,      // initial position
```

```
            VECTOR4D_PTR rot,       // initial rotations
            int vertex_flags)       // flags to re-order vertices
                                    // and perform transforms
```

The only differences are a couple of added `vertex_flags` that you can logical `OR` to enable the local or world transforms that we discussed for this format:

```
#define VERTEX_FLAGS_TRANSFORM_LOCAL         512   // if file format has
                                                   // local transform
                                                   // then do it!
#define VERTEX_FLAGS_TRANSFORM_LOCAL_WORLD  1024   // if file format has
                                                   // local to world
                                                   // then do it!
```

Here's an example of loading a typical .COB object with the flags set as most modelers export:

```
Load_OBJECT4DV1_COB(&obj_tank,"D:/Source/models/cobs/hammer03.cob",
                    &vscale, &vpos, &vrot,
                    VERTEX_FLAGS_SWAP_YZ ¦ VERTEX_FLAGS_TRANSFORM_LOCAL );
```

You can see here that scaling, position, and rotation vectors have been sent in; these are optional, of course.

Well, that's it for the .COB file format. As I said, take a look at the complete spec on the CD in `3D_DOCS\File Formats\` and, of course, review the code on the CD in the `T3DLIB6.CPP¦H` files. As an example of using the loader, give `DEMOII8_9.CPP¦EXE` a try; it's identical to the .ASC loader, but loads .COB files instead.

Additionally, the File, Load dialog has check boxes that enable you to swap the y-z coordinates, invert the winding order, and enable the local and world transforms. You might have to play with these to get your object to load correctly. Finally, remember we have room for only 1,024 vertices and 1,024 polys per object! Here are some .COB objects you can load:

`SPHERE01.COB` (Swap YZ and invert winding order)

`CAR01.COB` (Swap YZ, local, and world transforms)

`HAMMER03.COB` (Swap YZ, local, and world transforms)

CAUTION

When creating .COB files, remember that you MUST triangulate all meshes and that the reader reads only single objects. Also, make sure that you set the color of each polygon to `"plain color"` and the reflectance to `"matte"` for flat shading (which is all we support now).

Quake II Binary .MD2 Format Preview

The *Quake II* .MD2 format is one of the most popular formats for 3D animation. Of course, the format is designed for *Quake II* and thus for games, so the support in modelers like Max and trueSpace is nonexistent. There are tools to create and view these models, but I'll get to that. For now, I just want you to have a feel for what the format supports. Basically, an .MD2 file is a set of vertices, animation frames, skins, and a couple other things for a *Quake II* in-game model. Each file is a complete animation set for a *Quake II* character and contains all the animation sequences for each of the various animations a *Quake* character might have (384 frames total): walk, die, fire, turn, and so on.

The skins are basically square texture maps, usually 256×256 in .PCX file format, that are used as textures for the models. All the textures are in a single skin, and by using texture coordinates, you can cut out textures that you wish. Figures 8.51 and 8.52 show a skin to apply onto an .MD2 mesh.

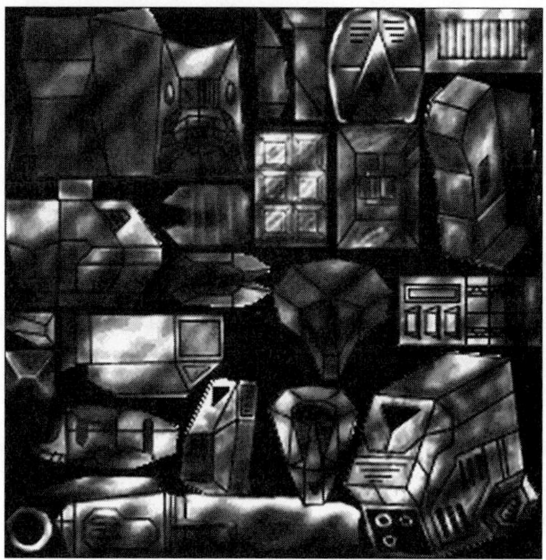

FIGURE 8.51 A *Quake II* .MD2 format skin.

And Figure 8.52 shows the actual mesh (as viewed in Milkshape 3D) from a .MD2 model that I downloaded from `http://www.planetquake.com/polycount`—a great place to get models. Of course, if you want to use this or any other model in a commercial game, you may need permission.

The format also supports simple compression schemes, such as offset bias, delta encoding of floats, and more. So all in all, it's a simple format to parse and a simple format to understand. Of course, it's completely binary, but oh well! We'll definitely use this format later when we get to animation. The only downside is that the format has no sense of materials, so when we load an object, we'll apply a default material so that our more advanced lighting engine knows what to do with the model.

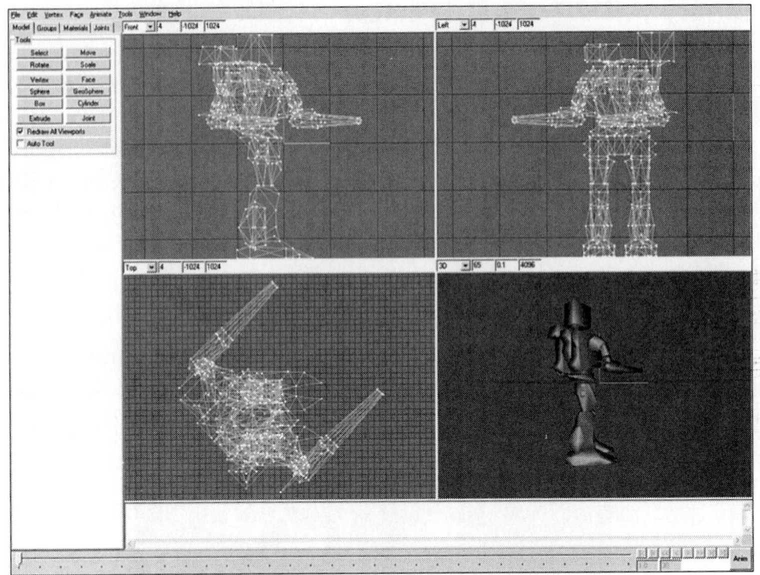

FIGURE 8.52 A single frame from a *Quake II* .MD2 mesh.

3D Modeling Tools Review

Well, this is it! We're almost done with this chapter, but before I go, I want to give you a rundown of some tools that I found useful for modeling and conversions for this chapter (some of them are on the CD in evaluation form):

- **Caligari trueSpace 4.0+** (Modeler primarily)—Shown in Figure 8.53. This is one of my favorite modelers. It's fast, easy, and reasonably priced. It also exports in a number of file formats. Find out more at `http://www.caligari.com`.
- **3D Studio Max 3.0+** (modeler primarily)—Shown in Figure 8.54. I don't need to say much here; Max is the #$@$%, period. It's used to make games, movies, you name it. Of course, the $2,500—$5,000 price tag might be a little prohibitive to you. Find out more at `http://www.discreet.com/products/3dsmax/`.
- **Gmax**—Similar to 3D Studio Max shown in Figure 8.54. This is an interesting product. Apparently it's a free, but slightly crippled version of 3D Studio Max. I have to read more, but it's definitely something to check out. Basically, you can license it as a game developer. Anyway, it's also on the Discreet site at `http://www.discreet.com/products/gmax/`.

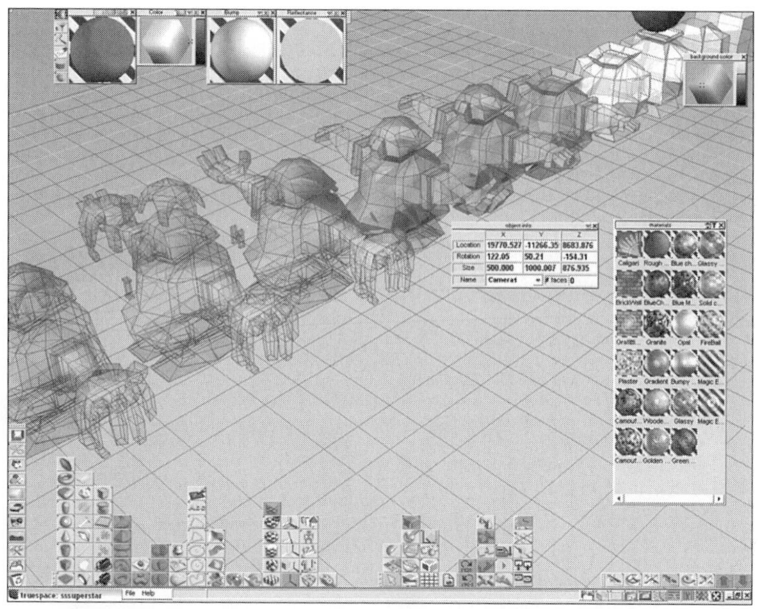

FIGURE 8.53 trueSpace in action.

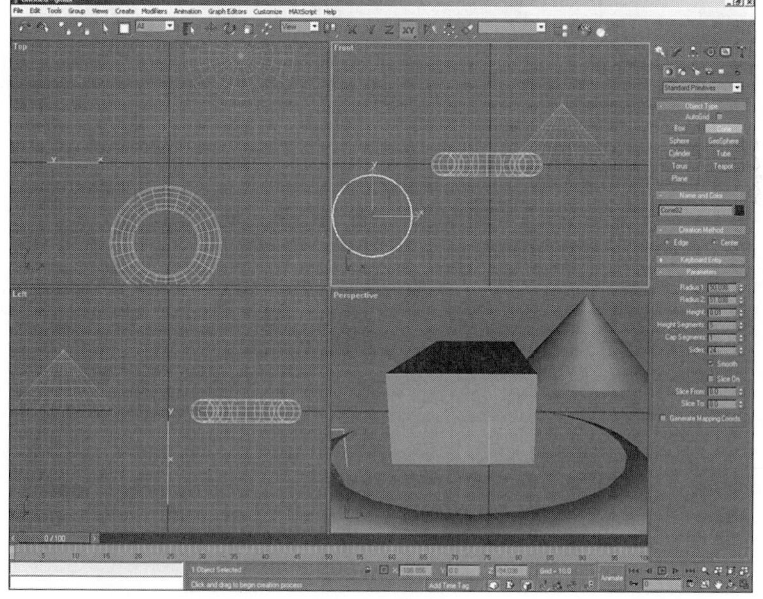

FIGURE 8.54 Gmax Game Studio in action.

- **Blender** (Modeler primarily)—Shown in Figure 8.55. This is a free modeler, but the company NaN has temporarily gone out of business, so I guess the "free-and-charge-for-tech-support idea" isn't really working in the real world. Anyway, the modeler is amazing. I really hope the designer can license it to someone or simply repackage it as a real product and sell it. Anyway, you can find out more at `http://www.blender.nl`.

FIGURE 8.55 Blender in action.

- **Milkshape 3D** (Modeler, viewer, and exporter)—Shown in Figure 8.52 previously. This is an awesome tool, completely designed for game file formats. However, it's one of those open source, floating-around tools, so different people play with it and upgrade it, which is good and bad. It's good because it's almost free, and bad because there isn't a single Web site for it. However, this one seems to be stable: `http://www.swissquake.ch/chumbalum-soft/index.html`.
- **Deep Exploration** (Viewer, exporter, and modeler)—Shown in Figure 8.56. This is one of the most advanced tools I have seen. It has a wicked interface, and allows you to view your data in all kinds of cool modes:

  `http://www.righthemisphere.com`.

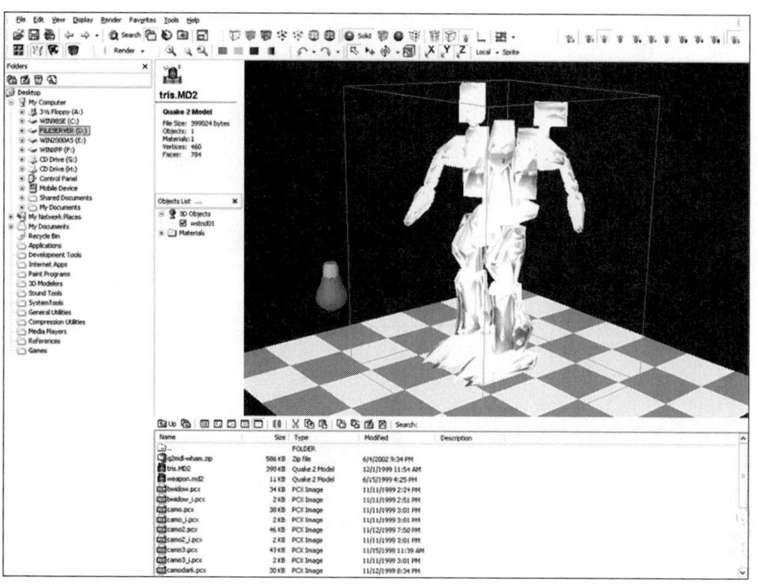

FIGURE 8.56 Deep Exploration in action.

- **Polytrans** (Viewer and exporter)—This product has one of the most complete import/export systems in existence. Pretty much every single 3D format is supported, but it has weak support for game file formats. Check it out at `http://www.okino.com/conv/conv.htm`.
- **WorldCraft Editor** (Level editor)—Shown in Figure 8.57. This is the tool behind about a trillion mods and many games such as *Half-Life*. This tool can be used to create gameworlds that can then be imported into your engine. At this point, we don't need something like this, but when we get to indoor stuff, this will be something to check out. There are lots of places working on WorldCraft, so you may have to look around, but this site is pretty stable: `http://www.valve-erc.com/`.

And here are some cool links to 3D Web sites and model resources:

- `http://www.planetquake.com/polycount/`
- `http://www.web3d.org/vrml/vft.htm`
- `http://www.gmi.edu/~jsinger/free3dmodels.htm`

In general, I use trueSpace and Max to model, and perform conversions and manipulations with Deep Exploration. However, I think that Milkshape 3D is a lot more powerful than it looks at first glance and I would like to play with it a little more.

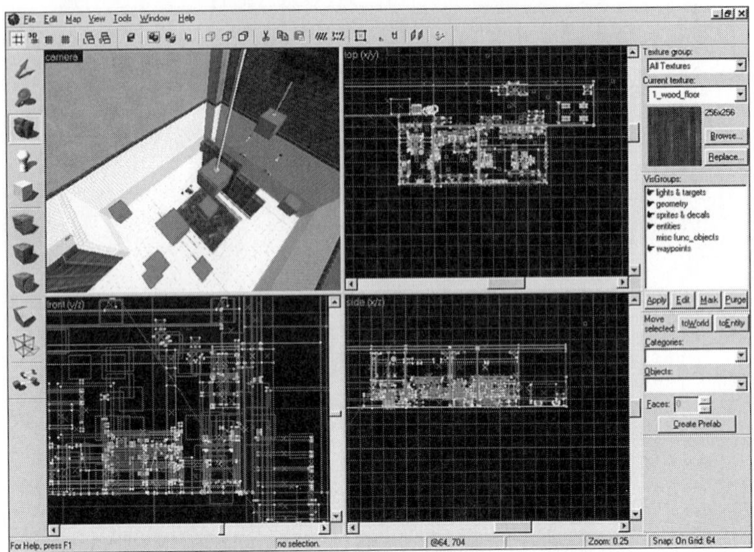

FIGURE 8.57 WorldCraft Editor in action.

Summary

This chapter has been nasty! It was both a theoretical download and a practical implementation. We covered a lot of material: basic light theory, materials, lights themselves, a lot of math, shading, depth sorting, new model formats, and a lot more. Your brain is probably swimming with ideas now—I know mine is. But there will be time for that later. Let's move right into Chapter 9, which will be much shorter (I am sure you are glad about that) and finish off with more advanced pixel-level shading, texturing, and talk in detail about triangle rasterization again. By the end of the next chapter, you'll have a complete texture-mapped, lit 3D engine (outdoor, of course).

CHAPTER 9

Interpolative Shading Techniques and Affine Texture Mapping

IN THIS CHAPTER

- The New T3D Engine Features
- Upgrading the T3D Data Structures and Design
- Rewriting the Object Loaders
- Polygon Rasterization Review
- Implementing Gouraud Shading
- Basic Sampling Theory
- Updating the Lighting/Rasterization Engine for Textures
- Final Thoughts on Optimization Strategies for 8- and 16-Bit Modes

"The things I'm going to do for my country."

—*Triple X*

I just finished writing all the software for this chapter! More than 15,000 lines of code had to be changed, written, and reworked just for the core engine, plus another 5,000 or so for the demos, but I think it's going to work for us. My goal has never been to give you a working 3D engine and say, "Here, have fun!" but rather to iteratively create multiple 3D engines step-by-step, purposely showing you the thinking process that one needs when undertaking such an endeavor. Or, in my case, the road to insanity <BG>.

In any event, I'm really excited about the performance I'm seeing from the 16-bit core of the engine. In fact, I'm so excited that this chapter may be the last of the 8-bit material because there's really no need for it anymore. However, I'll tell you why when we cross that bridge. For now, let's get started! Here's what we're going to be doing:

- Discussing the new engine
- Upgrading the 3D data structures
- Rewriting the object loaders
- Polygon rasterization review
- Implementing Gouraud shading
- Basic sampling theory
- Implementing affine texture mapping

- Adding lighting to textures
- Functional listing review
- Optimization strategies for 8- and 16-bit modes

The New T3D Engine Features

In the last chapter, we left our engine with the capability to render solid objects with a full-colored lighting system that supported ambient, infinite, point, and spotlights for a flat-shaded lighting model. In addition, we started on a material system and wrote a number of file loaders and support software to load 3D Studio .ASC and Caligari .COB files. The only remaining things to cover were Gouraud shading and basic texture mapping, which we put off until this chapter.

Although you may not think those are big subjects, you would be wrong. The reason is that writing a texture mapper or a Gouraud shader in itself is not that hard; the real problem is integrating it into the engine in a useable form. Anyone can write a program that spins a 3D cube in front of a camera with lights and a texture, but the hard thing is to write a generalized system that allows arbitrary cameras, lights, models, textures, resolutions, bit depths, file formats, and so forth. This is what we've been doing. Along those lines, I can tell you that integrating Gouraud shading and texture mapping have been quite a challenge. The entire engine needed rewriting to add the subtle details that we needed in the data structures, lighting modules, model loaders, and more. Also, I made optimization such as pre-computing the length of normals for polygon flat shading and other optimizations in the lighting modules to cache mathematical operations on a per-light basis to speed things up—lots of cool stuff, needless to say!

Although we took quite some time discussing the concept of materials and a material database, I'm still not ready to integrate a complete material system into the engine. Thus, to support textures, texture coordinates, and full Gouraud shading, I had to alter the data structures and come up with version 2.0 of many of them (which we'll discuss shortly). However, as a side effect, all the functions had to be rewritten—at least the ones that dealt with 3D.

Of course, in many cases, this simply meant changing prototypes and copying code. But in other cases, the new elements of the data structures had to be taken into consideration. Moreover, some design changes had to be made to the lighting system and the color information flow; that is, where post-lighting colors are stored for any polygon.

Then there are the speed issues that are really starting to crop up. I'm getting to the point where optimizing code is a necessity and I can no longer get away with writing understandable code. In other words, I've had to resort to using low-level tricks to get performance in some areas—the texture mapper, for example. Nonetheless, I haven't had to use assembly language, but I'm dying to use SIMD (single instruction multiple data) instructions to perform parallel processing, which could speed our code up at least four times. But I'll cover that in the optimization chapter.

Summing up, this new version of the engine supports both 8/16 modes with full Gouraud shading and lighting for single-colored polygons, and flat shading for texture mapped polygons—and did I mention it's all still in full RGB color? With that in mind, let's talk about the some of the new engine software. I promise to keep it reasonably short because I don't like code dumps without lots of theory behind them. But on the other hand, theory isn't very helpful without having an idea of where you're going—so let's see what we can learn about the new engine.

CAUTION

I did make one assumption in version 2.0 of the engine and that is that 16-bit mode is in 5.6.5 format. This had to be done because asking the question on the fly would kill performance. I could use conditional compilation and have the best of both worlds, but frankly I can't find any 5.5.5 cards anymore, so I think this is moot at this point.

Upgrading the T3D Data Structures and Design

First off, the name of the new library module is

`T3DLIB7.CPP`—The core C/C++ functions

`T3DLIB7.H`—The header

As usual, you must compile and link it with all the other library modules to create any of the programs from this chapter—that means `T3DLIB1.CPP` through `T3DLIB7.CPP`. Alright, as I mentioned in the introduction earlier, the entire point of this chapter is simply to add Gouraud shading and affine texture mapping (remember that affine texture mapping simply means linear and not perspective correct). However, my dilemma with this new material is that although it seems simple on the surface, a deeper analysis uncovers that many changes must be made to our data structures to support the new lighting and texturing features. Of course, this causes the side effect that all new functions must be created.

TIP

All the C++ people are probably gloating and saying with C++ this wouldn't be an issue! But, it's still an issue; true, we can just derive another class and then implement the changes, but the fact is that we must derive another class. However, in the end, I don't want a class hierarchy, I want a single data structure and single set of functions that work. So, the way we're developing this engine is the most efficient in that sense.

The bright side to all this is that, in most cases, the same functions can be used from the previous version of the engine with a few key code lines changed and, of course, a new prototype. Although we're going to cover everything new in this chapter, I always like to give you a preview of what you're looking at so that you don't have to skip to the end every time you see something new. So, let's take a look at the new `T3DLIB7.H` header file key elements and their significance to the engine.

CAUTION

Although this warning is out of context, if you try any of the 8-bit demos, there may be a delay of up to 1 minute while lookup tables are computed. You'll see a black screen during this period, so don't be alarmed.

New #defines

The following are the #defines for the new library module T3DLIB7.CPP. Of course, they're all contained in the T3DLIB7.H header file. Let's take a look at them one section at a time. Here are some constants to help the texture mapper function draw triangles:

```
// defines for texture mapper triangular analysis
#define TRI_TYPE_NONE       0
#define TRI_TYPE_FLAT_TOP     1
#define TRI_TYPE_FLAT_BOTTOM   2
#define TRI_TYPE_FLAT_MASK   3
#define TRI_TYPE_GENERAL     4
#define INTERP_LHS        0
#define INTERP_RHS        1
#define MAX_VERTICES_PER_POLY  6
```

Basically, the preceding constants are used internally by the state machine of the texture mapper to help it draw. You probably won't ever need to concern yourself with them, but one interesting thing is how I decided to make the texture mapping function render general triangles rather than breaking up triangles into two special case triangles with a flat top and bottom—these constants help that happen.

The next #defines are for the new POLY4DV2 polygon structure, which we'll get to shortly, but for now ,review these to see if they look at all familiar:

```
// defines for polygons and faces version 2

// attributes of polygons and polygon faces
#define POLY4DV2_ATTR_2SIDED         0x0001
#define POLY4DV2_ATTR_TRANSPARENT       0x0002
#define POLY4DV2_ATTR_8BITCOLOR        0x0004
#define POLY4DV2_ATTR_RGB16          0x0008
#define POLY4DV2_ATTR_RGB24          0x0010

#define POLY4DV2_ATTR_SHADE_MODE_PURE     0x0020
#define POLY4DV2_ATTR_SHADE_MODE_CONSTANT  0x0020 // (alias)
#define POLY4DV2_ATTR_SHADE_MODE_EMISSIVE  0x0020 // (alias)
```

```
#define POLY4DV2_ATTR_SHADE_MODE_FLAT     0x0040
#define POLY4DV2_ATTR_SHADE_MODE_GOURAUD  0x0080
#define POLY4DV2_ATTR_SHADE_MODE_PHONG    0x0100
#define POLY4DV2_ATTR_SHADE_MODE_FASTPHONG 0x0100 // (alias)
#define POLY4DV2_ATTR_SHADE_MODE_TEXTURE  0x0200

// new
#define POLY4DV2_ATTR_ENABLE_MATERIAL 0x0800 // use material for lighting
#define POLY4DV2_ATTR_DISABLE_MATERIAL 0x1000 // use basic color only
                    // for lighting (emulate ver 1.0)

// states of polygons and faces
#define POLY4DV2_STATE_NULL          0x0000
#define POLY4DV2_STATE_ACTIVE         0x0001
#define POLY4DV2_STATE_CLIPPED        0x0002
#define POLY4DV2_STATE_BACKFACE        0x0004
#define POLY4DV2_STATE_LIT          0x0008
```

If you've been experimenting with the engine at all, you should realize that nearly all the POLY4DV2_* #defines are identical to the previous POLY4DV1_*—only a few new #defines have been added, and I've highlighted them in bold. The new #defines again help us put some structure in place for the future addition of materials, and also to tag polygons that have been lit. This is needed because we have multiple pipeline paths now for lighting (or we will, by the end of the chapter), so once a polygon is lit, we don't want to light it again—ouch!

The next #defines are vertex control flags that are sent in when objects are loaded by the object loading functions. These flags help override certain properties such as shading models, and help straighten out things such as inverted texture coordinates and so forth.

```
// (new) used for simple model formats to override/control the lighting
#define VERTEX_FLAGS_OVERRIDE_MASK   0xf000 // this masks bits to
                      // extract them

#define VERTEX_FLAGS_OVERRIDE_CONSTANT 0x1000
#define VERTEX_FLAGS_OVERRIDE_EMISSIVE 0x1000 //(alias)
#define VERTEX_FLAGS_OVERRIDE_PURE   0x1000
#define VERTEX_FLAGS_OVERRIDE_FLAT   0x2000
#define VERTEX_FLAGS_OVERRIDE_GOURAUD 0x4000
#define VERTEX_FLAGS_OVERRIDE_TEXTURE 0x8000

#define VERTEX_FLAGS_INVERT_TEXTURE_U 0x0080  // invert u texture coord
#define VERTEX_FLAGS_INVERT_TEXTURE_V 0x0100  // invert v texture coord
#define VERTEX_FLAGS_INVERT_SWAP_UV  0x0800  // swap u,v texture coords
```

We'll clear up all the vertex overrides when we discuss the object loader functions. Moving on, the next #defines relate to the version 2.0 of the object container OBJECT4DV2 structure. Once again, most are duplicates with the same values simply renamed with the new OBJECT4DV2_* tag, but there are a couple interesting added defines that I've highlighted with bold:

```
// defines for objects version 2
// objects use dynamic allocation now, but keep as max values
#define OBJECT4DV2_MAX_VERTICES   1024
#define OBJECT4DV2_MAX_POLYS     2048

// states for objects
#define OBJECT4DV2_STATE_NULL     0x0000
#define OBJECT4DV2_STATE_ACTIVE   0x0001
#define OBJECT4DV2_STATE_VISIBLE   0x0002
#define OBJECT4DV2_STATE_CULLED   0x0004

// new
#define OBJECT4DV2_ATTR_SINGLE_FRAME 0x0001 // single frame object
                      // (emulates ver 1.0)
#define OBJECT4DV2_ATTR_MULTI_FRAME 0x0002 // multi frame object for
                      // .md2 support etc.
#define OBJECT4DV2_ATTR_TEXTURES   0x0004 // flags if object contains
                      // textured polys?
```

Only the last three #defines are of interest. The OBJECT4DV2_ATTR_SINGLE_FRAME and OBJECT4DV2_ATTR_MULTI_FRAME #defines help us with supporting objects that have multiple frames. Remember, we want to have "mesh animations" something like the *Quake II* .MD2 format. To support this, we need to somehow tag an object to indicate that it's holding multiple frames in its vertex lists. When the "current" frame is selected, only those specific vertices for that particular frame should be used, although the same polygons, colors, and so forth will be mapped to those vertices—more on this later. Finally, the OBJECT4DV2_ATTR_TEXTURES attribute simply flags an object as having textures on it somewhere; this helps us with certain optimizations.

Next we have the new rendering list maximum polygon setting. This is completely arbitrary, so feel free to change it. But I doubt we can render more than 10,000 polygons per frame at more than 15–30 fps, so 32,768 polygons should be more than enough:

```
// render list defines ver 2.0
#define RENDERLIST4DV2_MAX_POLYS      32768
```

The next set of #defines are rather interesting—read the inline comments to see why—but basically when we define a vertex from now on, we're going to use a much more robust vertex definition that supports not only the vertex, but also the normal, texture coordinates, and attribute flags:

```
// defines for vertices, these are "hints" to the transform and
// lighting systems to help determine if a particular vertex has
// a valid normal that must be rotated, or a texture coordinate
// that must be clipped etc., this helps us minimize load during lighting
// and rendering since we can determine exactly what kind of vertex we
// are dealing with, something like a (direct3d) flexible vertex format in
// as much as it can hold:
// point
// point + normal
// point + normal + texture coordinates
#define VERTEX4DTV1_ATTR_NULL       0x0000 // this vertex is empty
#define VERTEX4DTV1_ATTR_POINT      0x0001
#define VERTEX4DTV1_ATTR_NORMAL      0x0002
#define VERTEX4DTV1_ATTR_TEXTURE     0x0004
```

I'm very excited about the new vertex `VERTEX4DTV1` because it's going to make a lot of our work easier, but let's hold off on its definition until we get to the data structures in a few pages.

Amazingly, that's all there are to the added `#defines`. I told you there wasn't much. Keeping incremental is the key; that way you learn a lot and get a lot of experience at the same time. Remember, learning what not to do is just as important as learning what to do!

Added Math Structures

Have you looked at the math library we made lately? There's a lot of stuff in there! We went a little nuts I think, and I find myself needing very little additional math functionality each chapter. About the only thing that's ever required are some new data structures with cleaner names. In any event, almost the only thing I found myself needing in this chapter were some pure integer vector types, so here they are

```
// integer 2D vector, point without the w ////////////////////////
typedef struct VECTOR2DI_TYP
{
union
  {
  int M[2]; // array indexed storage

  // explicit names
  struct
     {
```

```
        int x,y;
        }; // end struct

    }; // end union

} VECTOR2DI, POINT2DI, *VECTOR2DI_PTR, *POINT2DI_PTR;

// integer 3D vector, point without the w ////////////////////////
typedef struct VECTOR3DI_TYP
{
union
  {
  int M[3]; // array indexed storage

  // explicit names
  struct
     {
     int x,y,z;
     }; // end struct

  }; // end union

} VECTOR3DI, POINT3DI, *VECTOR3DI_PTR, *POINT3DI_PTR;

// integer 4D homogenous vector, point with w ////////////////////
typedef struct VECTOR4DI_TYP
{
union
  {
  int M[4]; // array indexed storage

  // explicit names
  struct
     {
     int x,y,z,w;
     }; // end struct
  }; // end union

} VECTOR4DI, POINT4DI, *VECTOR4DI_PTR, *POINT4DI_PTR;
```

Basically these are 2D, 3D, and 4D integral vectors—nothing more. They simply help when doing texture mapping, or storing data in vector form (but integral) that I don't feel like converting to floats.

Utility Macros

Here's a nice floating-point comparison function:

```
// floating point comparison
#define FCMP(a,b) ( (fabs(a-b) < EPSILON_E3) ? 1 : 0)
```

As you may or may not know, when working with floating-point numbers, it's a bad idea to use the following code:

```
float f1, f2;

//..f1, f2 are set to some value

if (f1==f2)
  {
  // perform logic
  }
```

The problem lies within the `"if"` conditional. Even though `f1` and `f2` may be identical as far as you're concerned, `f1` and `f2` might have picked up some numeric "noise" along the way due to rounding and lack of accuracy. Alas, although they should be mathematically equal, they may not be as far as the comparison goes. Thus, it's a better idea to compute their absolute difference and compare it to some small value epsilon that's nearly 0 such as .001 or .0001. For all intents and purposes, both of those numbers are 0.0 because floating-point numbers are only accurate to 4–5 decimal places at best. In any case, that's why I needed that `FCMP()` macro.

The next inline macros are just copy functions used to copy the new `VERTEX4DTV1` objects into one another. Technically, we don't need copy operators for them, but until I optimize everything, I like to spell things out:

```
inline void VERTEX4DTV1_COPY(VERTEX4DTV1_PTR vdst, VERTEX4DTV1_PTR vsrc)
{ *vdst = *vsrc; }

inline void VERTEX4DTV1_INIT(VERTEX4DTV1_PTR vdst, VERTEX4DTV1_PTR vsrc)
{ *vdst = *vsrc; }
```

This last inline function is a slightly faster version of our previous length computation function. The only difference is that old `VECTOR4D_Length_Fast()` made a function call to the generic 3D distance calculation, and I didn't like that extra function call. So, here's a slightly better one:

```
inline float VECTOR4D_Length_Fast2(VECTOR4D_PTR va)
{
// this function computes the distance from the origin to x,y,z
```

```
int temp; // used for swaping
int x,y,z; // used for algorithm

// make sure values are all positive
x = fabs(va->x) * 1024;
y = fabs(va->y) * 1024;
z = fabs(va->z) * 1024;

// sort values
if (y < x) SWAP(x,y,temp)
if (z < y) SWAP(y,z,temp)
if (y < x) SWAP(x,y,temp)

int dist = (z + 11 * (y >> 5) + (x >> 2) );

// compute distance with 8% error
return((float)(dist >> 10));

} // end VECTOR4D_Length_Fast2
```

Adding Features to Represent 3D Mesh Data

Updating the 3D data structures was probably the most painful of all. The "thing of thing" is that it's pointless just to skip to the end and read the last page (if you get what I mean), so I want to smoothly iterate from version to version, adding just what we need to get the job done. But that's a lot of work!

Anyway, refreshing your memory from last chapter, we implemented a full-colored lighting system that supported both emissive and flat shaded illumination on a per-polygon basis. Both the PLG/PLX and .COB file formats enabled us to create models that could define which polygons had which properties (.ASC format just supports vertices, polygons, and colors). The PLG/PLX format allowed us to manually set the polygon shading type via these flags:

```
// defines for enhanced PLG file format -> PLX
// the surface descriptor is still 16-bit now in the following format
// d15            d0
//  CSSD ¦ RRRR¦ GGGG ¦ BBBB

// C is the RGB/indexed color flag
// SS are two bits that define the shading mode
// D is the double sided flag
// and RRRR, GGGG, BBBB are the red, green, blue bits for RGB mode
// or GGGGBBBB is the 8-bit color index for 8-bit mode
```

```
// bit masks to simplify testing????
#define PLX_RGB_MASK    0x8000 // mask to extract RGB or indexed color
#define PLX_SHADE_MODE_MASK 0x6000 // mask to extract shading mode
#define PLX_2SIDED_MASK   0x1000 // mask for double sided
#define PLX_COLOR_MASK 0x0fff // xxxxrrrrggggbbbb, 4-bits per channel RGB
               // xxxxxxxxiiiiiiii, indexed 8-bit index

// these are the comparision flags after masking
// color mode of polygon
#define PLX_COLOR_MODE_RGB_FLAG   0x8000  // poly uses RGB color
#define PLX_COLOR_MODE_INDEXED_FLAG 0x0000  // poly uses an indexed 8-bit color

// double sided flag
#define PLX_2SIDED_FLAG       0x1000  // poly is double sided
#define PLX_1SIDED_FLAG       0x0000  // poly is single sided

// shading mode of polygon
#define PLX_SHADE_MODE_PURE_FLAG   0x0000 // poly is a constant color
#define PLX_SHADE_MODE_CONSTANT_FLAG 0x0000 // alias
#define PLX_SHADE_MODE_FLAT_FLAG   0x2000 // poly uses flat shading
#define PLX_SHADE_MODE_GOURAUD_FLAG  0x4000 // poly used gouraud shading
#define PLX_SHADE_MODE_PHONG_FLAG   0x6000 // poly uses phong shading
#define PLX_SHADE_MODE_FASTPHONG_FLAG 0x6000 // poly uses phong shading
```

For the .COB models, we decided that we would use the `"color"` shader to define colored/textured polygons, and the `"reflectance"` shader to define the type of lighting based on the conventions outlined in the comments of the .COB loader:

```
// now we need to know the shading model, it's a bit tricky,
// we need to look for the lines
// "Shader class: color" first, then after this line is:
// "Shader name: "xxxxxx" (xxxxxx) "
// where the xxxxx part will be "plain color" and
// "plain" for colored polys
// or "texture map" and "caligari texture" for textures
// THEN based on that we hunt for "Shader class: reflectance"
// which is where the type
// of shading is encoded, we look for the
// "Shader name: "xxxxxx" (xxxxxx) " again,
// and based on it's value we map it to our shading system as follows:
// "constant" -> MATV1_ATTR_SHADE_MODE_CONSTANT
// "matte"  -> MATV1_ATTR_SHADE_MODE_FLAT
// "plastic" -> MATV1_ATTR_SHADE_MODE_GOURAUD
```

9

However, we had a little problem with the lighting calculations. If you recall, we didn't really think far enough ahead in the polygon structures to have any storage for a polygon's final color *after* lighting. In other words, a polygon's color was stored in 8/16 bit format in the `color` field of the polygon structures. That data was then used in the lighting calculations and a final color was computed based on the lights. Now, if lighting was performed at the rendering list stage, this wasn't too much of an issue because any polygon in the rendering list can be altered or destroyed because it's on its way to the screen. However, the problem is if we made a call to light an object while it was still intact as an object and not inserted into the rendering list, we walked into trouble.

The reason for the trouble is that we cannot destroy the color of any polygon with the lighting engine's final color. Thus, our strategy was to copy the lit color data into the upper 16 bits of the polygon's color as a hack. Figure 9.1 illustrates this.

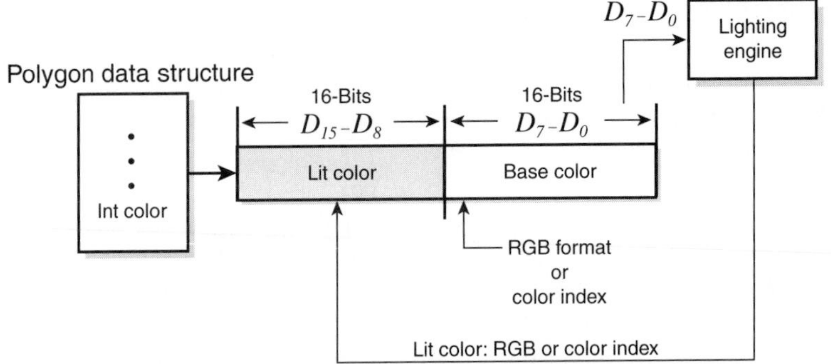

FIGURE 9.1 Using the upper 16 bits of the polygon color field to store the lit color.

This hack worked great, and in fact, we can pat ourselves on the back and say, "Wow, that's a great idea." But this technique won't work anymore when we're lighting polygons for full Gouraud shading. Hence, one of the major additions to the polygon data was added data field support for final color storage that doesn't disturb the base color.

The next thing we have to concern ourselves with is the Gouraud shading algorithm itself. Referring to Figure 9.2, we need a normal for each vertex (that's the point of Gouraud shading: to find the intensity at each vertex and interpolate). So, this is another thing we need to concern ourselves with in addition to the final color for each vertex, once again causing us to rethink our lit color storage for each polygon/vertex.

Finally, the last major things we need to add support for are animated meshes, such as those in *Quake II* .MD2 format. Figure 9.3 illustrates the concept, but in essence mesh animation is similar to standard bitmap animation—a series of frames is animated and rendered. Mesh animation works in just this way. Say you have a cube composed of 8 vertices and 12 polygons. Each polygon has a specific color and shading model, and is defined by three vertices in the master vertex list of the eight vertices. Now the trick is to add a frame. We create eight new vertices with the same ordering, but slightly changed positions, and then replace the original eight vertices with these new vertices. Therefore, the polygons are still defined, the colors are correct, and so are the textures, but the object is now animated!

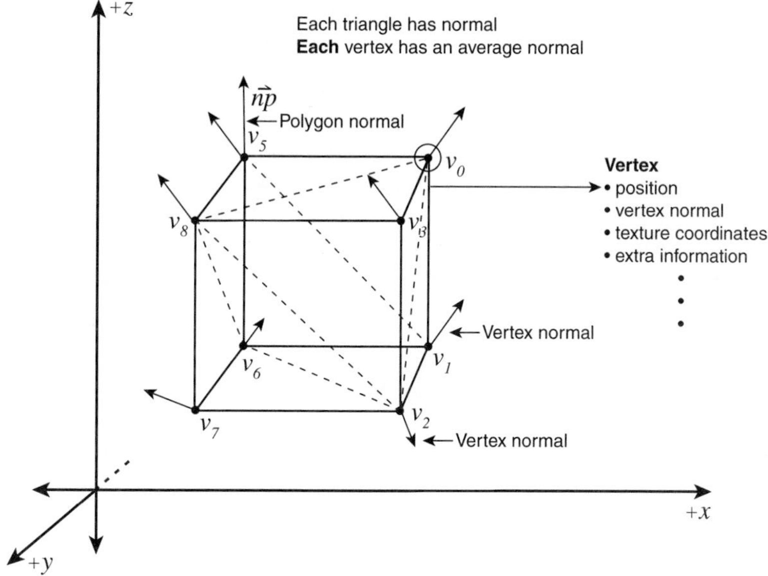

FIGURE 9.2 Gouraud shading requires vertex normals.

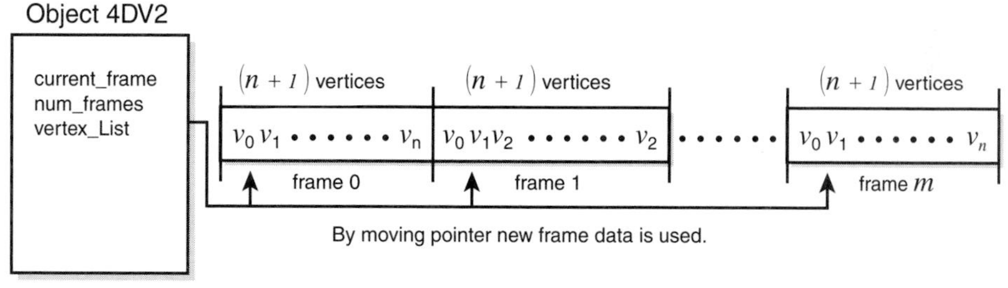

FIGURE 9.3 Supporting multiple mesh frames in our objects.

Quake II .MD2 uses this exact technique. The only rules are that each mesh animation must be composed of the same number of vertices and polygons. The positions of the vertices can change, but not their relationship to the polygons; that is, if polygon 22 is composed of vertices (12,90,200), it's always composed of those vertices.

In any case, we aren't going to add a .MD2 reader to this chapter because the chapter's material is way too large already. But we're going to add animation support for this file type soon, and having multiple frame support is important, thus I've added this functionality to the OBJECT4DV2 structure and taken it into consideration in most of the new rewritten functions.

With all that in mind, let's take a look at the new vertex and polygon data structures one by one.

Our First Real Vertex

Up to this point, we really haven't had a "vertex" type in the 3D graphics sense of the word; we've had vertex type data such as a point in 3D space and so on, but at this point, we need to start creating some more robust data structures that can handle our needs for a little while. Additionally, I tried to add a bit of control to allow a somewhat flexible vertex format by means of tag fields (defined earlier with the VERTEX4DTV1_ATTR_* #defines). This way, we can create various types of vertices that contain different types of information, but the structure and layout must always stay the same. Anyway, here's the new VERTEX4DTV1 structure.

NOTE

If you're a Direct3D programmer, you'll appreciate the flexible vertex formats and why they're so important. Before them, programmers had to use pre-defined vertex formats and that made programming more difficult.

```
// 4D homogeneous vertex with 2 texture coordinates
// and vertex normal, normal can be interpreted
// as vector or point
typedef struct VERTEX4DTV1_TYP
{
union
  {
  float M[12];       // array indexed storage

  // explicit names
  struct
     {
     float x,y,z,w;    // point
     float nx,ny,nz,nw; // normal (vector or point)
     float u0,v0;     // texture coordinates

     float i;        // final vertex intensity after lighting
     int  attr;      // attributes/ extra texture coordinates
     };          // end struct

   // high level types
   struct
```

```
    {
    POINT4D v;     // the vertex
    VECTOR4D n;     // the normal
    POINT2D t;     // texture coordinates
    };

  }; // end union

} VERTEX4DTV1, *VERTEX4DTV1_PTR;
```

Looks a little large, huh? Well, maybe, but I'm not trying to save space here. Referring to the structure, it's a union of a number of different types for ease of access, depending on the way you want to write your algorithms. For example, if you want to think of the vertex data as a stream of data (like Direct3D does), you might like accessing the data as an array—that's what the `M[]` part of the union is for. Similarly, you might like using slightly higher-level names; thus, there are explicit names for each part of the vertex:

x,y,z,w—The point locating the vertex

nx,ny,nz,nw—The vertex normal (more on this later)

u0,v0—The 2D texture coordinates

i—The intensity or color of the vertex (future expansion)

attr—The vertex tags that specify the type of vertex and what it contains

Additionally, there are structured names via another unnamed union: `v`, `n`, and `t`; they're the vertex, normal, and texture coordinates, respectively. However, there's nothing high level for the attribute and intensity because they aren't really components. Now, to use the union is automatic because it's unnamed. For example, to access the address of the 3D point, you would use the following code:

```
VERTEX4DTV1 p1;

&p1.v
```

And to access only the x component of the 3D point:

```
&p1.x
```

Or using the `v` union:

```
&p1.v.x
```

Cool, huh?

So, what's nice is that we can pass the entire vertex, normal, or texture coordinates as structures or we can drill down to the components themselves. Finally, when a vertex is created, we now have the ability to add a normal (important for lighting) and texture coordinates, but only if they're needed. This is accomplished via the `attr` field of the vertex type. For example, if we want to enable a vertex to support a 3D point and a normal, but no texture coordinates, we would use the following setup:

```
VERTEX4DTV1 p1;
p1.attr = VERTEX4DTV1_ATTR_POINT | VERTEX4DTV1_ATTR_NORMAL;
```

Of course, there's no magical force stopping you from accessing the point, normal, or texture coordinates at any time, but this attribute field is used as a message to let you and your functions know what is valid.

The New Internal POLY4DV2 Structures

The next big change to the engine data structures are the polygon structures. If you recall, we have two structures: one that refers to external vertex lists in another structure, such as an object, and another that's totally self-contained for entry into the rendering list. Refer to Figure 9.4, and let's take a look at the new `POLY4DV2`, structure which needs external vertex data:

```
// a polygon ver 2.0 based on an external vertex list
typedef struct POLY4DV2_TYP
{
int state;        // state information
int attr;        // physical attributes of polygon
int color;        // color of polygon
int lit_color[3];  // holds colors after lighting, 0 for flat shading
           // 0,1,2 for vertex colors after vertex lighting

BITMAP_IMAGE_PTR texture; // pointer to the texture
             // information for simple texture mapping

int mati;        // material index (-1) no material (new)

VERTEX4DTV1_PTR vlist; // the vertex list itself
POINT2D_PTR   tlist; // the texture list itself (new)
int vert[3];     // the indices into the vertex list
int text[3];     // the indices into the texture coordinate list (new)
float nlength;    // length of normal (new)

} POLY4DV2, *POLY4DV2_PTR;
```

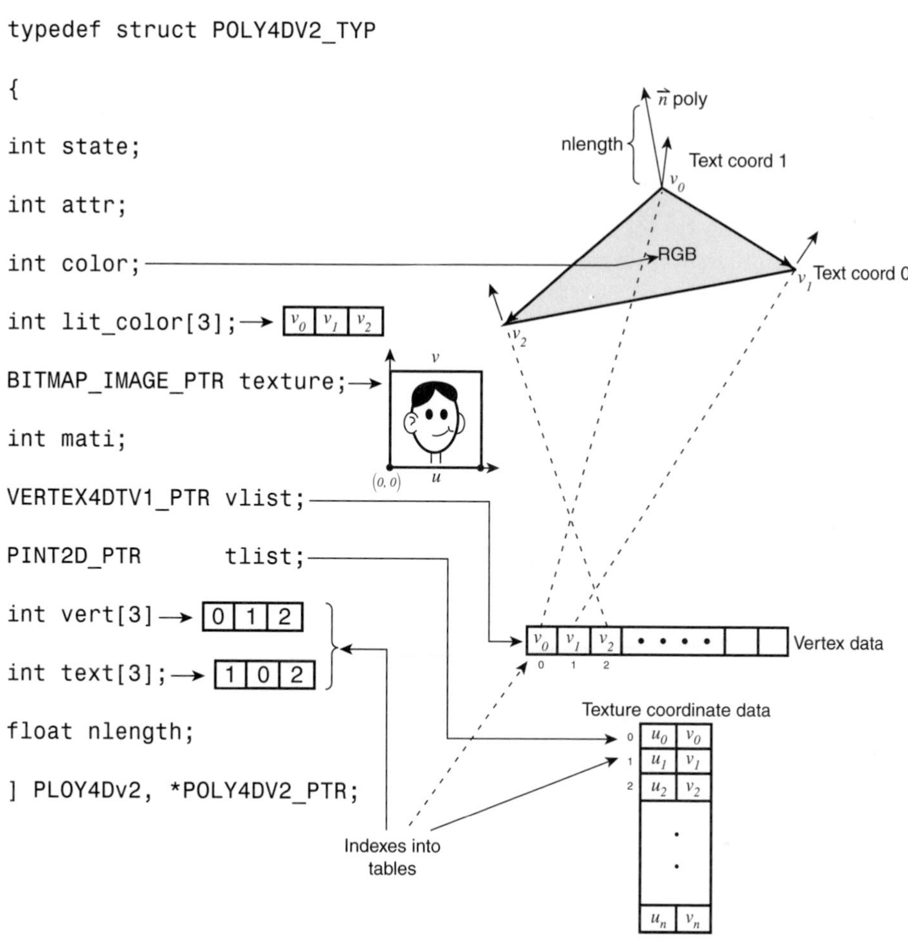
typedef struct POLY4DV2_TYP
{
int state;
int attr;
int color;
int lit_color[3];
BITMAP_IMAGE_PTR texture;
int mati;
VERTEX4DTV1_PTR vlist;
PINT2D_PTR tlist;
int vert[3]
0 1 2
int text[3];
1 0 2
float nlength;
] PLOY4Dv2, *POLY4DV2_PTR;
n poly
nlength
Text coord 1
RGB
Text coord 0
(0, 0)
Vertex data
Texture coordinate data
Indexes into tables

FIGURE 9.4 A graphical representation of the new `POLY4DV2` structure.

I've highlighted with bold all the new and changed fields—pretty much all of them! Let's discuss the motivation for each.

- **`lit_color[3]`**—The new lighting system needs support not only for a single color for the entire polygon, but also for three colors for each vertex when Gouraud shading is requested. Hence, `lit_colors[3]` supports this feature. When lighting calculations are performed for a flat-shaded polygon, the results do not overwrite the upper 16 bits of the color field, but are instead stored in `lit_colors[0]`. This is similar to when Gouraud shading calculations are performed; a final color for each vertex is computed and stored in `lit_colors[0,1,2]`, respectively.
- **`texture`**—To keep things as simple as possible, I'm still shying away from full material support, but we still need storage for each polygon's texture map for textured

polys. This field is a pointer to the texture map, if there is one for the polygon in question.

- **mati**—This is a material index into the material database for future planning of material support. I'm still not sure if we'll use it, but I decided to add it in this iteration of the data structure to save us some trouble.
- **tlist**—This is newly added support for texture mapping. As shown in Figure 9.4, when a texture map is textured onto a polygon, we need to specify "texture coordinates." Thus the new `OBJECT4DV2` structure has an array of texture coordinates that are indexed by `tlist`, just as the vertex array is indexed by `vlist`. These texture coordinates are then used during the texture mapping stage.
- **text[3]**—These are the actual texture indices into the texture coordinate list.
- **nlength**—This field contains the length of the polygon normal vector to speed up lighting calculations. This is a small optimization, but one that was bothering me. If you look at the math in the lighting engine, we're computing normals of polygons by taking the cross product of (**v0->v1** X **v0->v2**) and then normalizing the vector to length 1.0 or at least computing it's length.

The cross product doesn't worry me as much as the computation of length. Not only did we use an approximate value, but there's absolutely no need to perform the length calculation because it does *not* change when the polygon is rotated or translated. Thus we can precompute the normal length of all polygon normals as long as we always use the same two vectors (which we do) for the computation. Additionally, we get the second-order effect of having better accuracy because the normal length calculation is performed during offline load time, so we don't have to call the real-time (faster) length approximation function. In short, we save a lot of cycles with this optimization.

TIP

You might be asking, "Why not also pre-compute the normal vector to the polygon?" We could do this also, and then normalize it, but then we would have to rotate the vector when we transformed the mesh, so it's a wash. The rotation by a 4×4 matrix turns out to be an equal or greater amount of math than the cross product calculation, so although it seems like a good idea, precomputing the polygon normal doesn't help us, because we lose the gains due to the need to transform the normal by a 4×4 matrix.

The New External Self Contained `POLYF4DV2` Structures

The next newly updated polygon structure is the totally self-contained `POLYF4DV2` structure, which is used to store final polygon information in the rendering list. Take a look at the new structure definition:

```
// a self contained polygon used for the render list version 2
typedef struct POLYF4DV2_TYP
{
```

```
int state;       // state information
int attr;       // physical attributes of polygon
int color;       // color of polygon
int lit_color[3];  // holds colors after lighting, 0 for flat shading
             // 0,1,2 for vertex colors after vertex lighting
BITMAP_IMAGE_PTR texture; // pointer to the texture information for simple
             // texture mapping

int   mati;  // material index (-1) for no material (new)

float  nlength; // length of the polygon normal if not normalized (new)
VECTOR4D normal; // the general polygon normal (new)

float  avg_z;  // average z of vertices, used for simple sorting (new)

VERTEX4DTV1 vlist[3]; // the vertices of this triangle
VERTEX4DTV1 tvlist[3]; // the vertices after transformation if needed

POLYF4DV2_TYP *next;  // pointer to next polygon in list??
POLYF4DV2_TYP *prev;  // pointer to previous polygon in list??

} POLYF4DV2, *POLYF4DV2_PTR;
```

POLYF4DV2 is nearly identical to the POLY4DV2 structure. The only difference is that the storage for vertices are internal rather than external via a link. Additionally, the actual VERTEX4DTV1 representing each vertex now contains the texture coordinates as well, so the all the information we need for every vertex is contained within vlist[] and tvlist[]. Other than those differences, all the fields with the same names as contained in POLY4DV2 have the seem meaning.

Updating the Object Containers and Rendering List

Now for the big daddy! In our original design, we decided to contain "objects" in a general object structure that contained both vertex and polygon information for the object. This seems to work great for objects that move around in the game, but will it work for other higher-level data such as game levels and so forth? The answer is yes, for the most part. In fact, we may decide to compose a level by merging a list of objects, each representing a floor, or maybe even a room, so we are on the right track. Of course, when we get to spatial partitioning and so forth, we'll see what transformations and changes need to be made to objects to support the concept of level geometry. But for now these are working as good containers, so we'll stick with them.

The new version object container OBJECT4DV2 is roughly the same as the old one, but of course it has texture coordinate support, new attributes, and a global texture (which I'll get to in a moment). But the big change is that the new OBJECT4DV2 structure supports multi-mesh animation or frames. However, I haven't written anything to take advantage of it (an .MD2 reader would do the trick), but I'm placing the infrastructure for the support. Take a look back at Figure 9.3 to see a graphic illustration of the new OBJECT4DV2 structure and to see how each frame is stored. The structure follows; focus your attention on the bolded fields:

```
// an object ver 2.0 based on a vertex list and list of polygons
// new object has a lot more flexibility and supports "framed" animation
// that is this object can hold hundreds of meshes as lon as
// the mesh has the same polygons and geometry, but with changing
// vertex positions similar to the Quake II .md2 format
typedef struct OBJECT4DV2_TYP
{
int  id;      // numeric id of this object
char name[64];  // ASCII name of object just for kicks
int  state;    // state of object
int  attr;    // attributes of object
int  mati;    // material index overide (-1) - no material (new)
float *avg_radius; // [OBJECT4DV2_MAX_FRAMES]; // average radius of object
                        // used for collision detection
float *max_radius; // [OBJECT4DV2_MAX_FRAMES]; // maximum radius of object

POINT4D world_pos; // position of object in world

VECTOR4D dir;    // rotation angles of object in local
          // cords or unit direction vector user defined???

VECTOR4D ux,uy,uz; // local axes to track full orientation
          // this is updated automatically during
          // rotation calls

int num_vertices;  // number of vertices per frame of this object
int num_frames;   // number of frames (new)
int total_vertices; // total vertices
int curr_frame;   // current animation frame (0) if single frame (new)

VERTEX4DTV1_PTR vlist_local; // array of local vertices
VERTEX4DTV1_PTR vlist_trans; // array of transformed vertices

// these are needed to track the "head" of the vertex list for
// multi-frame objects
VERTEX4DTV1_PTR head_vlist_local;
VERTEX4DTV1_PTR head_vlist_trans;
```

```
// texture coordinates list (new)
POINT2D_PTR tlist;     // 3*num polys at max

BITMAP_IMAGE_PTR texture; // pointer to the texture information for
            // simple texture mapping (new)

int num_polys;       // number of polygons in object mesh
POLY4DV2_PTR plist;    // ptr to polygons (new)

// METHODS ///////////////////////////////////////////////////

// setting the frame is so important that it should be a member function
// calling functions without doing this can wreak havok!
int Set_Frame(int frame);

} OBJECT4DV2, *OBJECT4DV2_PTR;
```

Most of the new fields should make sense from their names and the previous polygon definitions. About the only interesting changes/additions are in relation to the vertex and texture coordinate lists and support for multi-frame objects, so let's look at those:

- **`*avg_radius, *max_radius`**—Because objects can now contain multiple frames, each mesh frame will have different vertex values. Hence the average and maximum radii will change from frame to frame. Therefore, these average and max radius values now need to be arrays to support this possibility.
- **`num_frames`**—Number of animation frames.
- **`curr_frame`**—Current active frame mesh.
- **`vlist_local`**—Pointer to the active frame's vertex mesh.
- **`vlist_trans`**—Pointer to the active frame's vertex mesh (transformed versions).
- **`head_vlist_local`**—Head of the entire vertex list.
- **`head_vlist_trans`**—Head of the entire vertex list (transformed versions).
- **`tlist`**—Pointer to the head of the texture coordinate list; we need only one list for all animation frames. Also, take a moment to make sure that you understand what this list contains. Even though, we haven't covered texture mapping yet, the point of this list is to hold the actual texture coordinates for the entire mesh. Geometrically, there are up to `3*num_vertices` texture coordinates; in other words, you might have a mesh such as a cube that only has texture coordinates (0,0), (0,1), (1,0), and (1,1). Therefore, there would be a total of four possible texture coordinates; thus, each polygon vertex has an index into this array indicating which texture coordinate to use. However, in the worst case scenario, each vertex may need a specific texture coordinate for each polygon; in this case, `3*num_vertices` texture coordinates would be needed.

9

So, let's talk a little more about mesh animations and the meanings of the fields discussed earlier. As I outlined, our first attempt at animation will be static multiple-frame animations whereby we load a number of meshes and then flip through the meshes just as we would bitmaps in a 2D animation. However, we're going to force a couple constraints on mesh animations: First, the number of vertices must be the same mesh to mesh; second, the polygon information of the vertices that make up each polygon must not change. The only things that we allow to change are the positions of the vertices for each mesh. These conventions are to support the *Quake II* .MD2 format for the most part. We aren't implementing any of the animation functionality in this chapter, but we're nonetheless getting ready for it later.

TIP

More advanced animation systems use forward or inverse kinematics that are based on physical models rather than static mesh information. A mathematical model runs on the mesh information that transforms the joints based on the external forces or animation data that's used to transform joints. Thus, an object is composed of a hierarchy of subobjects that animate individually to create a full-bodied animation.

Let's talk a moment about the multiple-frame support. When a frame is selected into "context," the head pointers are used along with the number of vertices and the current frame to find the address of the frame in question. Then the pointers `vlist_local` and `vlist_trans` are vectored to the frame and anything that's performed on `vlist_local` and `vlist_trans` is transparently performed on the correct frame. This is shown in Figure 9.5. Other than this, the only housekeeping is to be aware that when a frame changes, the average and maximum radius arrays must be accessed at the current frame element as well. Very few other changes need to be made because changing from static array to pointers to reference `vlist_local` and `vlist_trans` make all this multiple frame stuff trivial—just a pointer manipulation really.

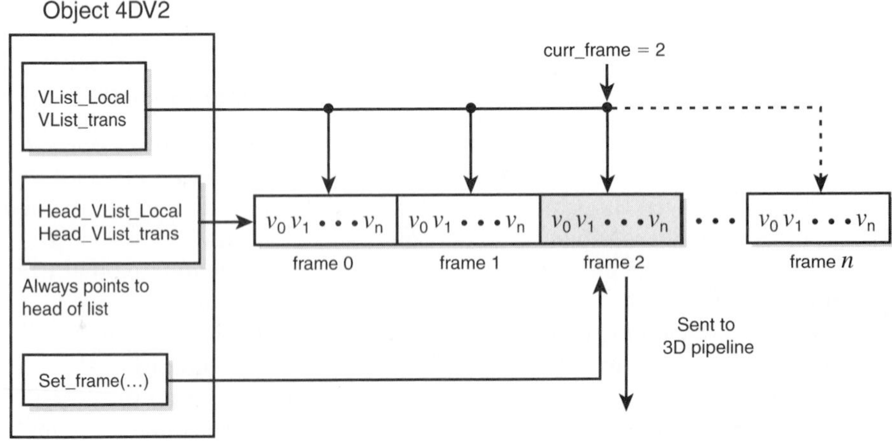

FIGURE 9.5 Data flow and transformations for multiple frames.

Next, we're using dynamically allocated arrays for more efficient memory consumption and to help implement the multiple frames support. The only problem with this is that not all file formats start with something like this:

```
"number of polygons, number of vertices, number of texture coordinates"
```

That would be nice! Therefore, a little legerdemain must be used when allocating the arrays (and re-allocating in a couple cases once the real values have been read out of the files). For example, I need to create the OBJECT4DV2 object first and then load the vertices and polygons into it, but when reading the .COB file format, for example, not until later do I know the real number of texture coordinates, so I have to approximate the worst case. Just as an aside, if you don't know how many of some object to allocate, just allocate the worst case, and later perform a new memory allocation, copy, and delete the old one.

Finally, I added a single method to the OBJECT4DV2 structure to help set a frame because calling functions if the frame isn't set up and copied correctly can cause a crash. The name of the method is Set_Frame(); to use it, you would simply do this:

```
object.Set_Frame(0);
```

That would set the frame to 0, which is how everything in this chapter works. Also, it might be good to take a look at the code for Set_Frame() just to drive home the simplicity of the pointer manipulation, so here it is

```
// setting the frame is so important that it should be a member function
int OBJECT4DV2::Set_Frame(int frame)
{
// this functions sets the current frame in a multi frame object
// if the object is not multiframed then the function has no effect

// test if object is valid?
if (!this)
  return(0);

// test if its multiframe?
if (!(this->attr & OBJECT4DV2_ATTR_MULTI_FRAME))
  return(0);

// we have a valid object and its multiframe, vector pointers to frame data

// check bounds on frame
if (frame < 0 )
  frame = 0;
else
```

```
if (frame >= this->num_frames)
  frame = this->num_frames - 1;

// set frame
this->curr_frame = frame;

// update ptrs to point to "block" of vertices that represent this frame
// the vertices from each frame are 1-1 and onto relative to the polys that
// make up the object, they are simply shifted, we need this to re-vector
// the pointers based on the head pointers

this->vlist_local = &(this->head_vlist_local[frame*this->num_vertices]);
this->vlist_trans = &(this->head_vlist_trans[frame*this->num_vertices]);

// return success
return(1);

} // end Set_Frame
```

NOTE

There's also an external version of the function `Set_OBJECT4DV2_Frame(OBJECT4DV2_PTR obj, int frame)`. It's identical, but can be called as a normal function rather than an object method call.

Lastly, each object has a root texture that's applied to the entire object, meaning that although the polygon structures support a different texture pointer for each polygon, objects support only one texture. We might change this later, but when texturing objects, it's easier to think of a texture as a "skin." Thus, when an object is loaded, the (single) texture map is loaded into the texture object of the `OBJECT4DV2`. Then as polygons are loaded, their internal texture pointer is pointed to the `OBJECT4DV2`'s internal texture. This is where it would be nice to have a material library because we could easily have multiple textures, but we'll see later.

Functional Listing Review and Prototypes

Because we've added so much new software for this chapter, I want to take a few moments to briefly review all the new functions. Remember, you have seen all the functions for the most part, but now we have version 2.0 of everything. So, I just want to cover each function, and give brief explanation of its use. I won't go into details about parameters or examples because as I said, these are not new, they're just new versions, so you know how to use them for the most part—I just want to show you what's available.

I know that most of the following prototypes might be a little confusing because you don't know what some of the new functions do, but I still want you to read each one of them so that when I'm discussing the theoretical material, you have at least an idea of what's available in the pipeline and the final functional support. Also, there are some added functions for testing and support that aren't really part of the final engine—they're for `OBJECT4DV1` and `RENDERLIST4DV1` support and for testing only. You don't need to use them at all for this chapter, but I wrote them as I was transitioning to the new version 2.0 data structures to help test things. You won't see them here, but they're in the .CPP and .H files, just to let you know. Anyway, here are the useful prototypes from this chapter and the `T3DLIB7.CPP|H` module of the engine. I've grouped similar functions together along with their purpose:

Function:

```
char *Extract_Filename_From_Path(char *filepath, char *filename);
```

Purpose: Extracts the filename from a complete filepath.

Function:

```
int Set_OBJECT4DV2_Frame(OBJECT4DV2_PTR obj, int frame);
```

Purpose: Sets the current frame in a multimesh animation.

Function:

```
int Destroy_OBJECT4DV2(OBJECT4DV2_PTR obj);
```

Purpose: Destroys the object and frees all memory.

Function:

```
int Init_OBJECT4DV2(OBJECT4DV2_PTR obj,  // object to allocate
          int _num_vertices,
          int _num_polys,
          int _num_frames,
          int destroy=0);
```

Purpose: Initializes and allocated memory for the object.

Function:

```
void Translate_OBJECT4DV2(OBJECT4DV2_PTR obj, VECTOR4D_PTR vt);
```

Purpose: Translates the object in 3D space.

Function:

```
void Scale_OBJECT4DV2(OBJECT4DV2_PTR obj, VECTOR4D_PTR vs, int all_frames=0);
```

Purpose: Scales one or all the frames of an object.

Function:

```
void Transform_OBJECT4DV2(OBJECT4DV2_PTR obj, MATRIX4X4_PTR mt,
             int coord_select,
             int transform_basis,
             int all_frames=0);
```

Purpose: Applies the sent transformation matrix to the current frame or all frames of the object.

Function:

```
void Rotate_XYZ_OBJECT4DV2(OBJECT4DV2_PTR obj,
             float theta_x,
             float theta_y,
             float theta_z,
             int all_frames);
```

Purpose: Rotates an object parallel to the x,y,z axes by the sent amounts.

Function:

```
void Model_To_World_OBJECT4DV2(OBJECT4DV2_PTR obj,
       int coord_select = TRANSFORM_LOCAL_TO_TRANS, int all_frames=0);
```

Purpose: Performs the model to world transform on the sent object.

Function:

```
int Cull_OBJECT4DV2(OBJECT4DV2_PTR obj, CAM4DV1_PTR cam, int cull_flags);
```

Purpose: Culls the object from the viewing pipeline, or more specifically, the viewing frustrum.

Function:

```
void Remove_Backfaces_OBJECT4DV2(OBJECT4DV2_PTR obj, CAM4DV1_PTR cam);
```

Purpose: Removes back-faces from the sent object relative to the sent camera.

Function:

```
void Remove_Backfaces_RENDERLIST4DV2(RENDERLIST4DV2_PTR rend_list, CAM4DV1_PTR cam);
```

Purpose: Removes back-faces from the sent rendering list relative to the sent camera.

Function:

```
void Camera_To_Perspective_OBJECT4DV2(OBJECT4DV2_PTR obj, CAM4DV1_PTR cam);
```

Purpose: Performs the camera-to-perspective transformation on the sent object using the sent camera.

Function:

```
void Perspective_To_Screen_RENDERLIST4DV2(RENDERLIST4DV2_PTR rend_list,
                     CAM4DV1_PTR cam);
```

Purpose: Performs the perspective-to-screen transformation on a rendering list using the sent camera.

Function:

```
void Camera_To_Perspective_Screen_RENDERLIST4DV2(RENDERLIST4DV2_PTR rend_list,
                         CAM4DV1_PTR cam);
```

Purpose: Performs the entire camera-to-screen transformation from the sent rendering list using the sent camera, in essence merging the -perspective and perspective-to-screen transforms.

Function:

```
void Camera_To_Perspective_RENDERLIST4DV2(RENDERLIST4DV2_PTR rend_list,
                     CAM4DV1_PTR cam);
```

Purpose: Performs the camera-to-perspective transform on the sent rendering list using the sent camera.

Function:

```
void World_To_Camera_OBJECT4DV2(OBJECT4DV2_PTR obj, CAM4DV1_PTR cam);
```

Purpose: Performs the world-to-camera space transformation on the sent object using the sent camera.

Function:

```
void World_To_Camera_RENDERLIST4DV2(RENDERLIST4DV2_PTR rend_list,
                  CAM4DV1_PTR cam);
```

Purpose: Performs the world-to-camera transformation on the sent rendering list using the sent camera.

Function:

```
void Camera_To_Perspective_Screen_OBJECT4DV2(OBJECT4DV2_PTR obj, CAM4DV1_PTR cam);
```

Purpose: Performs the camera-to-screen transform on the sent object using the sent camera, in essence merging the camera-to-perspective and perspective-to-screen transforms.

6

Function:

```
void Perspective_To_Screen_OBJECT4DV2(OBJECT4DV2_PTR obj, CAM4DV1_PTR cam);
```

Purpose: Performs the perspective-to-screen transform on the sent object using the sent camera.

Functions:

```
int Insert_POLY4DV2_RENDERLIST4DV2(RENDERLIST4DV2_PTR rend_list,
                 POLY4DV2_PTR poly);

int Insert_POLYF4DV2_RENDERLIST4DV2(RENDERLIST4DV2_PTR rend_list,
                  POLYF4DV2_PTR poly);
```

Purpose: Inserts the sent polygon into the rendering list.

Function:

```
int Insert_OBJECT4DV2_RENDERLIST4DV2(RENDERLIST4DV2_PTR rend_list,
                  OBJECT4DV2_PTR obj,
                  int insert_local);
```

Purpose: Inserts the sent object into the render list by breaking the object up into polygons.

Function:

```
void Reset_OBJECT4DV2(OBJECT4DV2_PTR obj);
```

Purpose: Resets the state values of an object.

Function:

```
int Compute_OBJECT4DV2_Poly_Normals(OBJECT4DV2_PTR obj);
```

Purpose: Computes the polygon normals for the sent object's mesh; primarily needed for lighting functions.

Functions:

```
void Draw_OBJECT4DV2_Wire(OBJECT4DV2_PTR obj,
             UCHAR *video_buffer, int lpitch);

void Draw_OBJECT4DV2_Wire16(OBJECT4DV2_PTR obj,
              UCHAR *video_buffer, int lpitch);
```

Purpose: Renders the sent object in wireframe mode on the screen.

Functions:

```
void Draw_RENDERLIST4DV2_Wire(RENDERLIST4DV2_PTR rend_list,
               UCHAR *video_buffer, int lpitch);

Function:
void Draw_RENDERLIST4DV2_Wire16(RENDERLIST4DV2_PTR rend_list,
               UCHAR *video_buffer, int lpitch);
```

Purpose: Renders the sent render list to the screen in wireframe mode.

Functions:

```
void Draw_RENDERLIST4DV2_Solid16(RENDERLIST4DV2_PTR rend_list,
               UCHAR *video_buffer, int lpitch);

void Draw_RENDERLIST4DV2_Solid(RENDERLIST4DV2_PTR rend_list,
               UCHAR *video_buffer, int lpitch);
```

Purpose: Renders the sent rendering list to the screen; supports emissive, flat-shaded, and textured polygons.

Function:

```
float Compute_OBJECT4DV2_Radius(OBJECT4DV2_PTR obj);
```

Purpose: Computes the average and maximum radius of an object and all its frames.

Function:

```
int Compute_OBJECT4DV2_Vertex_Normals(OBJECT4DV2_PTR obj);
```

Purpose: Computes the vertex normals of an object.

Function:

```
int Load_OBJECT4DV2_PLG(OBJECT4DV2_PTR obj, // pointer to object
         char *filename,     // filename of plg file
         VECTOR4D_PTR scale,   // initial scaling factors
         VECTOR4D_PTR pos,    // initial position
         VECTOR4D_PTR rot,    // initial rotations
         int vertex_flags=0);  // flags to re-order vertices
```

Purpose: Loads a .PLG/PLX format 3D mesh file from disk.

Function:

```
int Load_OBJECT4DV2_3DSASC(OBJECT4DV2_PTR obj, // pointer to object
             char *filename,   // filename of ASC file
             VECTOR4D_PTR scale, // initial scaling factors
```

9

```
            VECTOR4D_PTR pos,  // initial position
            VECTOR4D_PTR rot,  // initial rotations
            int vertex_flags=0); // flags to re-order vertices
```

Purpose: Loads a 3D Studio Max .ASC mesh file from disk; supports shading overrides via the `vertex_flags` parameter.

Function:

```
int Load_OBJECT4DV2_COB(OBJECT4DV2_PTR obj, // ptr to object
        char *filename,    // filename of Caligari COB file
        VECTOR4D_PTR scale, // initial scaling factors
        VECTOR4D_PTR pos,  // initial position
        VECTOR4D_PTR rot,  // initial rotations
        int vertex_flags=0);// flags to re-order vertices
                  // and perform transforms
```

Purpose: Loads a Caligari trueSpace 3D .COB mesh file from disk; supports objects with constant, flat-, Gouraud-, and texture-mapped polygons.

Function:

```
void Reset_RENDERLIST4DV2(RENDERLIST4DV2_PTR rend_list);
```

Purpose: Resets the sent rendering list for another pass through the pipeline.

Functions:

```
int Light_OBJECT4DV2_World16(OBJECT4DV2_PTR obj, // object to process
       CAM4DV1_PTR cam,   // camera position
       LIGHTV1_PTR lights, // light list (one or more lights)
       int max_lights);   // maximum lights in list


int Light_OBJECT4DV2_World(OBJECT4DV2_PTR obj, // object to process
        CAM4DV1_PTR cam,    // camera position
        LIGHTV1_PTR lights, // light list (one or more lights)
        int max_lights);    // maximum lights in list
```

Purpose: Lights the sent object using the sent camera and lights; both 8- and 16-bit versions.

Functions:

```
int Light_RENDERLIST4DV2_World16(RENDERLIST4DV2_PTR rend_list, // list
      CAM4DV1_PTR cam,    // camera position
      LIGHTV1_PTR lights, // light list (one or more)
      int max_lights);    // maximum lights in list
```

```
int Light_RENDERLIST4DV2_World(RENDERLIST4DV2_PTR rend_list, // list
        CAM4DV1_PTR cam,    // camera position
        LIGHTV1_PTR lights, // light list (might have more than one)
        int max_lights);    // maximum lights in list
```

Purpose: Lights the sent rendering list using the sent camera and light; both 8- and 16-bit versions.

Function:

```
void Sort_RENDERLIST4DV2(RENDERLIST4DV2_PTR rend_list, int sort_method);
```

Purpose: Performs a z-sort on the rendering list based on the sent sorting method key.

Functions:

```
int Compare_AvgZ_POLYF4DV2(const void *arg1, const void *arg2);

int Compare_NearZ_POLYF4DV2(const void *arg1, const void *arg2);

int Compare_FarZ_POLYF4DV2(const void *arg1, const void *arg2);
```

Purpose: Sorting methods for the sorting algorithm; called internally by `Sort_RENDERLIST4DV2()`.

Functions:

```
Drawvoid Draw_Textured_Triangle16(POLYF4DV2_PTR face,
              UCHAR *dest_buffer, int mem_pitch);

void Draw_Textured_Triangle(POLYF4DV2_PTR face,
              UCHAR *dest_buffer, int mem_pitch);
```

Purpose: Low-level affine texture rendering functions to draw triangles; both 8- and 16-bit versions.

Functions:

```
void Draw_Textured_TriangleFS16(POLYF4DV2_PTR face, // ptr to face
          UCHAR *_dest_buffer, // ptr to video buffer
          int mem_pitch);     // bytes per line, 320, 640 etc.


void Draw_Textured_TriangleFS(POLYF4DV2_PTR face, // ptr to face
          UCHAR *_dest_buffer, // pntr to video buffer
          int mem_pitch);    // bytes per line, 320, 640 etc.
```

Purpose: Low-level texture rendering functions with flat-shading lighting support to draw triangles; both 8- and 16-bit versions.

9

Functions:

```
void Draw_Gouraud_Triangle16(POLYF4DV2_PTR face, // ptr to face
         UCHAR *_dest_buffer, // pntr to video buffer
         int mem_pitch);   // bytes per line, 320, 640 etc.

void Draw_Gouraud_Triangle(POLYF4DV2_PTR face, // ptr to face
         UCHAR *dest_buffer, // pointer to video buffer
         int mem_pitch);   // bytes per line, 320, 640 etc.
```

Purpose: Low-level Gouraud shading rasterizer rendering functions to draw triangles; both 8- and 16-bit versions.

Functions:

```
void Draw_Top_Tri2_16(float x1, float y1,
          float x2, float y2,
          float x3, float y3,
          int color,
          UCHAR *_dest_buffer, int mempitch);

void Draw_Bottom_Tri2_16(float x1, float y1,
            float x2, float y2,
            float x3, float y3,
            int color,
            UCHAR *_dest_buffer, int mempitch);


void Draw_Top_Tri2(float x1, float y1,
          float x2, float y2,
          float x3, float y3,
          int color,
          UCHAR *_dest_buffer, int mempitch);

void Draw_Bottom_Tri2(float x1, float y1,
            float x2, float y2,
            float x3, float y3,
            int color,
            UCHAR *_dest_buffer, int mempitch);
```

Purpose: Low-level functions to draw flat-top and -bottom triangles; both 8- and 16-bit versions.

Functions:

```
void Draw_Triangle_2D2_16(float x1, float y1,
             float x2, float y2,
             float x3, float y3,
             int color,
             UCHAR *dest_buffer, int mempitch);


void Draw_Triangle_2D2(float x1, float y1,
             float x2, float y2,
             float x3, float y3,
             int color,
             UCHAR *dest_buffer, int mempitch);
```

Purpose: Low-level functions to draw general triangles; both 8- and 16-bit versions.

Function:

```
int Load_Bitmap_File2(BITMAP_FILE_PTR bitmap, char *filename);
```

Purpose: Bitmap loading function that supports both .BMP and .PCX file formats and loads it into a bitmap file object.

Function:

```
int Load_Bitmap_PCX_File(BITMAP_FILE_PTR bitmap, char *filename);
```

Purpose: Loads a .PCX file into a bitmap file object.

Rewriting the Object Loaders

I'm going insane constantly rewriting these loaders; it's getting to be a major pain! I'm glad though that we're getting them to a level of sophistication when we've topped out the file formats themselves. This is the case with the .PLG/PLX and .ASC formats; that is, they don't support all the new features that the engine does, so there's not much more work to do to them. I keep them around only because they're easy to work with by hand. The Caligari .COB format, on the other hand, has more than enough support for anything we can throw at it.

In any case, the .PLG/PLX format supports different shading modes (but not texture mapping), plus the format is very primitive and mostly for quick-and-dirty hand modeling of objects to test things out. Finally, the .PLG format's hard coded 8/16-bit support is a pain and making me nuts, but it's a good format to start any 3D engine off with, so I've been keeping it around.

Next, the .ASC format is nearly useless for anything other than mesh data and color. It doesn't support texture mapping, lighting models—nothing. Therefore, to support these features (lighting at least), I've added *overrides* to the object loader to force a lighting model. But there's still no texture support in .ASC or .PLG/PLX format because we have no way to define the texture coordinates. Finally, there's the .COB format, which has support for everything, so it's the only format that, with the modeler itself, can natively export 3D models with texture and lighting information that our engine can use. Therefore, my intuition tells me that as we proceed in the book, we'll be focusing more and more on the .COB format and less on the .PLG/PLX and .ASC formats, but we'll see. With that all in mind, let's take a look at the new loaders and what they support.

Updating the Good Old .PLG/PLX Reader

The .PLG/PLX reader has the fewest number of changes, but it's the only function that I can even think of listing in the text because it's not that large. In any event, the main changes to the function are in the support of the new `OBJECT4DV2` structure along with data element access and setting some of the new vertex flags. Remember, the new `VERTEX4DTV1` structure has attribute flags that control whether each vertex needs a point, normal, and texture coordinates. Hence, I think it will be illustrative to take a look at the .PLG/PLX file reader to see some of these modifications so that you can review the code for the other readers on the CD and not be lost. Here's the function for review with key elements highlighted:

```
int Load_OBJECT4DV2_PLG(OBJECT4DV2_PTR obj, // pointer to object
          char *filename,    // filename of plg file
          VECTOR4D_PTR scale, // initial scaling factors
          VECTOR4D_PTR pos,   // initial position
          VECTOR4D_PTR rot,   // initial rotations
          int vertex_flags)   // vertex flags, used to override
{
// this function loads a plg object in off disk, additionally
// it allows the caller to scale, position, and rotate the object
// to save extra calls later for non-dynamic objects
// there is only one frame, so load the object and set the fields
// appropriately for a single frame OBJECT4DV2

FILE *fp;      // file pointer
char buffer[256]; // working buffer

char *token_string; // pointer to actual token text, ready for parsing

// file format review, note types at end of each description
// # this is a comment
```

```
// # object descriptor
// object_name_string num_verts_int num_polys_int

// # vertex list
// x0_float y0_float z0_float
// x1_float y1_float z1_float
// x2_float y2_float z2_float
// .
// .
// xn_float yn_float zn_float
//
// # polygon list
// surface_description_ushort num_verts_int v0_index_int v1_index_int ..
// .
// .
// surface_description_ushort num_verts_int v0_index_int v1_index_int ..

// lets keep it simple and assume one element per line
// hence we have to find the object descriptor, read it in, then the
// vertex list and read it in, and finally the polygon list -- simple :)

// Step 1: clear out the object and initialize it a bit
memset(obj, 0, sizeof(OBJECT4DV2));

// set state of object to active and visible
obj->state = OBJECT4DV2_STATE_ACTIVE | OBJECT4DV2_STATE_VISIBLE;

// set position of object
obj->world_pos.x = pos->x;
obj->world_pos.y = pos->y;
obj->world_pos.z = pos->z;
obj->world_pos.w = pos->w;

// set number of frames
obj->num_frames = 1;
obj->curr_frame = 0;
obj->attr = OBJECT4DV2_ATTR_SINGLE_FRAME;

// Step 2: open the file for reading
if (!(fp = fopen(filename, "r")))
{
Write_Error("Couldn't open PLG file %s.", filename);
return(0);
} // end if
```

```
// Step 3: get the first token string which should be the object descriptor
if (!(token_string = Get_Line_PLG(buffer, 255, fp)))
{
Write_Error("PLG file error with file %s (object descriptor invalid).",
       filename);
return(0);
} // end if

Write_Error("Object Descriptor: %s", token_string);

// parse out the info object
sscanf(token_string, "%s %d %d",
    obj->name, &obj->num_vertices, &obj->num_polys);

// allocate the memory for the vertices and number of polys
// the call parameters are redundant in this case, but who cares
if (!Init_OBJECT4DV2(obj,  // object to allocate
        obj->num_vertices,
        obj->num_polys,
        obj->num_frames))
  {
  Write_Error("\nPLG file error with file %s (can't allocate memory).",
        filename);
  } // end if

// Step 4: load the vertex list
for (int vertex = 0; vertex < obj->num_vertices; vertex++)
  {
  // get the next vertex
  if (!(token_string = Get_Line_PLG(buffer, 255, fp)))
    {
    Write_Error("PLG file error with file %s (vertex list invalid).",
          filename);
    return(0);
    } // end if

  // parse out vertex
  sscanf(token_string, "%f %f %f", &obj->vlist_local[vertex].x,
                 &obj->vlist_local[vertex].y,
                 &obj->vlist_local[vertex].z);
  obj->vlist_local[vertex].w = 1;

  // scale vertices
  obj->vlist_local[vertex].x*=scale->x;
```

```
    obj->vlist_local[vertex].y*=scale->y;
    obj->vlist_local[vertex].z*=scale->z;

    Write_Error("\nVertex %d = %f, %f, %f, %f", vertex,
                obj->vlist_local[vertex].x,
                obj->vlist_local[vertex].y,
                obj->vlist_local[vertex].z,
                obj->vlist_local[vertex].w);

    // every vertex has a point at least, set that in the flags attribute
    SET_BIT(obj->vlist_local[vertex].attr, VERTEX4DTV1_ATTR_POINT);

    } // end for vertex

// compute average and max radius
Compute_OBJECT4DV2_Radius(obj);

Write_Error("\nObject average radius = %f, max radius = %f",
      obj->avg_radius, obj->max_radius);

int poly_surface_desc = 0; // PLG/PLX surface descriptor
int poly_num_verts  = 0; // num of vertices for current poly (always 3)
char tmp_string[8];   // tmp string to hold surface descriptor in and
           // test if it need to be converted from hex

// Step 5: load the polygon list
for (int poly=0; poly < obj->num_polys; poly++)
  {
  // get the next polygon descriptor
  if (!(token_string = Get_Line_PLG(buffer, 255, fp)))
  {
  Write_Error("PLG file error with file %s \
        (polygon descriptor invalid).",filename);
  return(0);
  } // end if

  Write_Error("\nPolygon %d:", poly);

  // each vertex list MUST have 3 vertices
  // since we made this a rule that all models
  // must be constructed of triangles
  // read in surface descriptor, number of vertices, and vertex list
  sscanf(token_string, "%s %d %d %d %d", tmp_string,
         &poly_num_verts, // should always be 3
```

9

```
        &obj->plist[poly].vert[0],
        &obj->plist[poly].vert[1],
        &obj->plist[poly].vert[2]);

// since we are allowing the surface descriptor to be in hex format
// with a leading "0x" we need to test for it
if (tmp_string[0] == '0' && toupper(tmp_string[1]) == 'X')
  sscanf(tmp_string,"%x", &poly_surface_desc);
else
  poly_surface_desc = atoi(tmp_string);

// point polygon vertex list to object's vertex list
// note that this is redundant since the polylist is contained
// within the object in this case and its up to the user to select
// whether the local or transformed vertex
// list is used when building up
// polygon geometry, might be a better to set to NULL in the context
// of polygons that are part of an object
obj->plist[poly].vlist = obj->vlist_local;

Write_Error("\nSurface Desc = 0x%.4x, num_verts = %d, \
       vert_indices [%d, %d, %d]",
               poly_surface_desc,
               poly_num_verts,
               obj->plist[poly].vert[0],
               obj->plist[poly].vert[1],
               obj->plist[poly].vert[2]);

// now we that we have the vertex list and we have entered the polygon
// vertex index data into the polygon itself,
// now let's analyze the surface
// descriptor and set fields for the polygon based on the description

// extract out each field of data from the surface descriptor
// first let's get the single/double sided stuff out of the way
if ((poly_surface_desc & PLX_2SIDED_FLAG))
  {
  SET_BIT(obj->plist[poly].attr, POLY4DV2_ATTR_2SIDED);
  Write_Error("\n2 sided.");
  } // end if
else
  {
  // one sided
```

```
  Write_Error("\n1 sided.");
  } // end else

// now let's set the color type and color
if ((poly_surface_desc & PLX_COLOR_MODE_RGB_FLAG))
  {
  // this is an RGB 4.4.4 surface
  SET_BIT(obj->plist[poly].attr,POLY4DV2_ATTR_RGB16);

  // now extract color and copy into polygon color
  // field in proper 16-bit format
  // 0x0RGB is the format, 4 bits per pixel
  int red  = ((poly_surface_desc & 0x0f00) >> 8);
  int green = ((poly_surface_desc & 0x00f0) >> 4);
  int blue = (poly_surface_desc & 0x000f);

  // although the data is always in 4.4.4 format, the graphics card
  // is either 5.5.5 or 5.6.5,
  // but our virtual color system translates
  // 8.8.8 into 5.5.5 or 5.6.5 for us,
  // however we have to first scale all
  // these 4.4.4 values into 8.8.8
  obj->plist[poly].color = RGB16Bit(red*16, green*16, blue*16);
  Write_Error("\nRGB color = [%d, %d, %d]", red, green, blue);
  } // end if
else
  {
  // this is an 8-bit color indexed surface
  SET_BIT(obj->plist[poly].attr,POLY4DV2_ATTR_8BITCOLOR);

  // and simple extract the last 8 bits and that's the color index
  obj->plist[poly].color = (poly_surface_desc & 0x00ff);

  Write_Error("\n8-bit color index = %d", obj->plist[poly].color);

  } // end else

// handle shading mode
int shade_mode = (poly_surface_desc & PLX_SHADE_MODE_MASK);

// set polygon shading mode
switch(shade_mode)
   {
```

9

```
case PLX_SHADE_MODE_PURE_FLAG: {
SET_BIT(obj->plist[poly].attr, POLY4DV2_ATTR_SHADE_MODE_PURE);
Write_Error("\nShade mode = pure");
} break;

case PLX_SHADE_MODE_FLAT_FLAG: {
SET_BIT(obj->plist[poly].attr, POLY4DV2_ATTR_SHADE_MODE_FLAT);
Write_Error("\nShade mode = flat");

} break;

case PLX_SHADE_MODE_GOURAUD_FLAG: {
SET_BIT(obj->plist[poly].attr, POLY4DV2_ATTR_SHADE_MODE_GOURAUD);

// the vertices from this polygon all need normals,
// set that in the flags attribute
SET_BIT(obj->vlist_local[ obj->plist[poly].vert[0] ].attr,
    VERTEX4DTV1_ATTR_NORMAL);
SET_BIT(obj->vlist_local[ obj->plist[poly].vert[1] ].attr,
    VERTEX4DTV1_ATTR_NORMAL);
SET_BIT(obj->vlist_local[ obj->plist[poly].vert[2] ].attr,
    VERTEX4DTV1_ATTR_NORMAL);

Write_Error("\nShade mode = gouraud");
} break;

case PLX_SHADE_MODE_PHONG_FLAG: {
SET_BIT(obj->plist[poly].attr, POLY4DV2_ATTR_SHADE_MODE_PHONG);

// the vertices from this polygon all need normals,
// set that in the flags attribute
SET_BIT(obj->vlist_local[ obj->plist[poly].vert[0] ].attr,
    VERTEX4DTV1_ATTR_NORMAL);
SET_BIT(obj->vlist_local[ obj->plist[poly].vert[1] ].attr,
    VERTEX4DTV1_ATTR_NORMAL);
SET_BIT(obj->vlist_local[ obj->plist[poly].vert[2] ].attr,
    VERTEX4DTV1_ATTR_NORMAL);

Write_Error("\nShade mode = phong");
} break;

default: break;
} // end switch
```

```
    // set the material mode to ver. 1.0 emulation
    SET_BIT(obj->plist[poly].attr, POLY4DV2_ATTR_DISABLE_MATERIAL);

    // finally set the polygon to active
    obj->plist[poly].state = POLY4DV2_STATE_ACTIVE;

    // point polygon vertex list to object's vertex list
    // note that this is redundant since the polylist is contained
    // within the object in this case and its up to the user to select
    // whether the local or transformed
    // vertex list is used when building up
    // polygon geometry, might be a better idea to set
    // to NULL in the context
    // of polygons that are part of an object
    obj->plist[poly].vlist = obj->vlist_local;

    // set texture coordinate list, this is needed
    obj->plist[poly].tlist = obj->tlist;

    } // end for poly

// compute the polygon normal lengths
Compute_OBJECT4DV2_Poly_Normals(obj);

// compute vertex normals for any gouraud shaded polys
Compute_OBJECT4DV2_Vertex_Normals(obj);

// close the file
fclose(fp);

// return success
return(1);

} // end Load_OBJECT4DV2_PLG
```

Okay, let's discuss each highlighted section of code because they each reflect the new changes. Starting from the top of the function, the first section you'll see highlighted is this:

```
// set number of frames
obj->num_frames = 1;
obj->curr_frame = 0;
obj->attr = OBJECT4DV2_ATTR_SINGLE_FRAME;
```

9

This is for the multiple frames support, and sets the frame to 0. These steps must be performed even for single-frame objects. Next we have the call that allocates the memory for the OBJECT4DV2:

```
if (!Init_OBJECT4DV2(obj,  // object to allocate
        obj->num_vertices,
        obj->num_polys,
        obj->num_frames))
  {
  Write_Error("\nPLG file error with file %s (can't allocate memory).",
         filename);
  } // end if
```

This function does nothing more than allocate memory and release any memory that's already there. Here's the functional listing of the actual Init_OBJECT4DV2():

```
int Init_OBJECT4DV2(OBJECT4DV2_PTR obj,  // object to allocate
           int _num_vertices,
           int _num_polys,
           int _num_frames,
           int destroy)
{
// function does nothing more than allocate the memory for an OBJECT4DV2
// based on the sent data, later we may want to create more robust version
// but the problem is that we don't want to tie the initializer to anything
// yet, in 99% of cases this all will be done by the call to load object
// we just might need this function if we manually want to build an object???


// first destroy the object if it exists
if (destroy)
  Destroy_OBJECT4DV2(obj);

// allocate memory for vertex lists
if (!(obj->vlist_local = (VERTEX4DTV1_PTR)malloc(sizeof(VERTEX4DTV1)*_
                   num_vertices*_num_frames)))
  return(0);

// clear data
memset((void *)obj->vlist_local,0,sizeof(VERTEX4DTV1)*_
              num_vertices*_num_frames);

if (!(obj->vlist_trans = (VERTEX4DTV1_PTR)malloc(sizeof(VERTEX4DTV1)*_
                  num_vertices*_num_frames)))
  return(0);
```

```
// clear data
memset((void *)obj->vlist_trans,0,sizeof(VERTEX4DTV1)*_
                 num_vertices*_num_frames);

// number of texture coordinates always 3*number of polys
if (!(obj->tlist = (POINT2D_PTR)malloc(sizeof(POINT2D)*_num_polys*3)))
  return(0);

// clear data
memset((void *)obj->tlist,0,sizeof(POINT2D)*_num_polys*3);


// allocate memory for radii arrays
if (!(obj->avg_radius = (float *)malloc(sizeof(float)*_num_frames)))
  return(0);

// clear data
memset((void *)obj->avg_radius,0,sizeof(float)*_num_frames);


if (!(obj->max_radius = (float *)malloc(sizeof(float)*_num_frames)))
  return(0);

// clear data
memset((void *)obj->max_radius,0,sizeof(float)*_num_frames);

// allocate memory for polygon list
if (!(obj->plist = (POLY4DV2_PTR)malloc(sizeof(POLY4DV2)*_num_polys)))
  return(0);

// clear data
memset((void *)obj->plist,0,sizeof(POLY4DV2)*_num_polys);

// alias head pointers
obj->head_vlist_local = obj->vlist_local;
obj->head_vlist_trans = obj->vlist_trans;

// set some internal variables
obj->num_frames    = _num_frames;
obj->num_polys    = _num_polys;
obj->num_vertices  = _num_vertices;
obj->total_vertices = _num_vertices*_num_frames;
```

```
// return success
return(1);

} // end Init_OBJECT4DV2
```

You might notice the function makes a call to `Destroy_OBJECT4DV2()`, which is listed here:

```
int Destroy_OBJECT4DV2(OBJECT4DV2_PTR obj)  // object to destroy
{
// this function destroys the sent object, basically frees the memory
// if any that has been allocated

// local vertex list
if (obj->head_vlist_local)
  free(obj->head_vlist_local);

// transformed vertex list
if (obj->head_vlist_trans)
  free(obj->head_vlist_trans);

// texture coordinate list
if (obj->tlist)
  free(obj->tlist);

// polygon list
if (obj->plist)
  free(obj->plist);

// object radii arrays
if (obj->avg_radius)
  free(obj->avg_radius);

if (obj->max_radius)
  free(obj->max_radius);

// now clear out object completely
memset((void *)obj, 0, sizeof(OBJECT4DV2));

// return success
return(1);

} // end Destroy_OBJECT4DV2
```

As usual, I'm probably being overzealous with error detection, but what the heck. Moving on with the .PLG loader, the next important section occurs for every vertex and sets the appropriate vertex point field:

```
// every vertex has a point at least, set that in the flags attribute
SET_BIT(obj->vlist_local[vertex].attr, VERTEX4DTV1_ATTR_POINT);
```

This must be done for every vertex that contains a point (which is pretty much all of them), but this is part of our new *flexible vertex format* system that allows points, normals, and texture coordinates. Along the same lines, if you move down the code some more, you'll see in the Gouraud and Phong shading sections the following code to enable the normal for each vertex making up the polygon:

```
// the vertices from this polygon all need normals,
// set that in the flags attribute
SET_BIT(obj->vlist_local[ obj->plist[poly].vert[0] ].attr,
                VERTEX4DTV1_ATTR_NORMAL);
SET_BIT(obj->vlist_local[ obj->plist[poly].vert[1] ].attr,
                VERTEX4DTV1_ATTR_NORMAL);
SET_BIT(obj->vlist_local[ obj->plist[poly].vert[2] ].attr,
                VERTEX4DTV1_ATTR_NORMAL);
```

The surface normal will be needed for each vertex for Gouraud shading and Phong shading (which we probably won't implement), so we set the attribute here to enable that part of the vertex. Finally, we have the two calls to calculate both the polygon normals and the vertex normals. You've seen the polygon normal calculation before:

```
// compute the polygon normal lengths
Compute_OBJECT4DV2_Poly_Normals(obj);
```

But the new function calculates the vertex normals for each polygon:

```
// compute vertex normals for any gouraud shaded polys
Compute_OBJECT4DV2_Vertex_Normals(obj);
```

Let's discuss this new function in detail.

9

Vertex Normal Calculation for Lighting

I'm going to cover the lighting and Gouraud shading algorithm in the next section, but at this point, let's forget about that and focus on the mechanics of computing vertex normals. The problem is as follows: Given a model mesh composed of p polygons and v vertices, for each vertex v_i, compute the normal to that vertex. Okay, sounds reasonable, but what normal are we talking about exactly? Well, for lighting purposes, we're going to need the average normal for each vertex. Referring to Figure 9.6, we see a simple mesh and the polygon normals for each polygon. To compute the vertex normals, we need to find each polygon that touches any given vertex and then average in the normal of that polygon. Moreover, we need to take into consideration the area of the polygon that's contributing to the vertex in question.

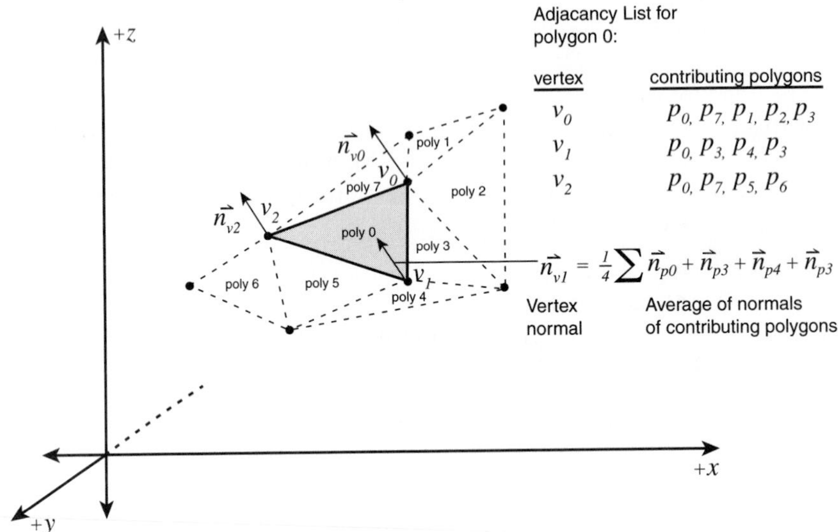

FIGURE 9.6 Calculating vertex normals using polygon contribution testing.

For example, say we have two polygons that share a single vertex, as shown in Figure 9.7. The normal from polygon 1 should have much more of a contribution to the vertex normal than polygon 2 because the area of polygon 1 is much greater than the area of polygon 2. In fact, this is trivial to code. We can use the trick that if we take the cross product of any two vectors of a triangle to compute the normal, the length of that cross product is actually proportional to the area of the triangle. In fact, based on the following equation, it's equal to the area of the parallelogram, as shown in Figure 9.8.

```
|u x v| = (base)(altitude) = Area of parallelogram
```

|u x v|/2 is the area of the triangle created by u,v. Thus, our algorithm to compute the vertex normals is as follows:

```
for each vertex vi in mesh begin
    let v_sum_normal = <0,0,0>

    for each polygon pi that touches vertex vi
      begin
```

```
        v_sum_normal+=p_i's normal
        end

    normalize v_n

next vertex
```

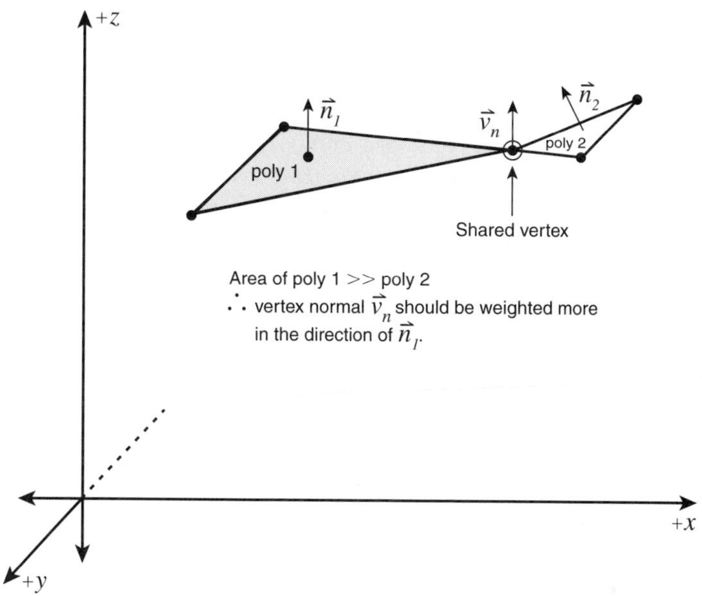

FIGURE 9.7 Calculating polygon normal contributions based on the area for each vertex.

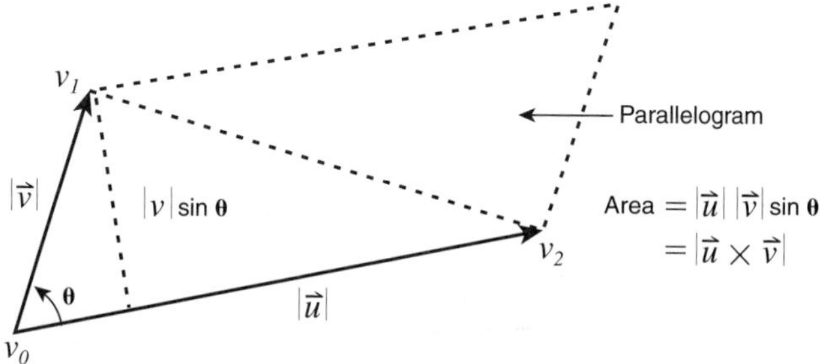

FIGURE 9.8 The absolute value of the signed cross product is equal to the area of the parallelogram defined by **u** and **v**.

Now, here's the tricky part. After the calculations are complete, we have a problem: We have a vertex normal vector, but as we transform the model mesh, we must also transform the vertex normal vector to keep it in sync with the model! This is key; otherwise, the normal will be useless. Alas, we've incurred an extra transformation operation per vertex; that is, we must also transform the normal vector, thereby doubling the number of vertices per polygon for Gouraud-shaded polygons. However, this is only for polygons that have Gouraud lighting and need them; hence, the overhead is minimized when the models have few or no Gouraud-shaded polygons.

Taking all that in, here's the function that computes vertex normals offline during loading:

```
int Compute_OBJECT4DV2_Vertex_Normals(OBJECT4DV2_PTR obj)
{
// the vertex normals of each polygon are commonly needed in a number
// functions, most importantly lighting calculations for gouraud shading
// however, we only need to compute vertex normals for polygons that are
// gouraud shader, so for every vertex we must determine the polygons that
// share the vertex then compute the average normal,
// to determine if a polygon contributes we look at the
// shading flags for the polygon

// is this object valid
if (!obj)
  return(0);

// algorithm: we are going to scan the polygon list and for
// every polygon that needs normals we are going to "accumulate"
// the surface normal into all vertices that the polygon touches,
// and increment a counter to track how many polys contribute
// to vertex, then when the scan is done the counts will be used
// to average the accumulated values, so instead of an O(n^2) algorithm,
// we get a O(c*n)

// this tracks the polygon indices that touch a particular vertex
// the array is used to count the number of contributors to the vertex
// so at the end of the process we can divide each "accumulated" normal
// and average
int polys_touch_vertex[OBJECT4DV2_MAX_VERTICES];
memset((void *)polys_touch_vertex,0,sizeof(int)*OBJECT4DV2_MAX_VERTICES);

// iterate thru the poly list of the object, compute its normal, then add
// each vertice that composes it to the "touching" vertex array
// while accumulating the normal in the vertex normal array
```

```
for (int poly=0; poly < obj->num_polys; poly++)
  {
  Write_Error("\nprocessing poly %d", poly);

  // test if this polygon needs vertex normals
  if (obj->plist[poly].attr & POLY4DV2_ATTR_SHADE_MODE_GOURAUD)
    {
    // extract vertex indices into master list, rember the polygons are
    // NOT self contained, but based on the vertex list
    // stored in the object itself
    int vindex_0 = obj->plist[poly].vert[0];
    int vindex_1 = obj->plist[poly].vert[1];
    int vindex_2 = obj->plist[poly].vert[2];

    Write_Error("\nTouches vertices: %d, %d, %d",
          vindex_0, vindex_1, vindex_2);

    // we need to compute the normal of this polygon face, and recall
    // that the vertices are in cw order, u=p0->p1, v=p0->p2, n=uxv
    VECTOR4D u, v, n;

    // build u, v
    VECTOR4D_Build(&obj->vlist_local[ vindex_0 ].v,
           &obj->vlist_local[ vindex_1 ].v, &u);
    VECTOR4D_Build(&obj->vlist_local[ vindex_0 ].v,
           &obj->vlist_local[ vindex_2 ].v, &v);

    // compute cross product
    VECTOR4D_Cross(&u, &v, &n);

    // update vertex array to flag this polygon as a contributor
    polys_touch_vertex[vindex_0]++;
    polys_touch_vertex[vindex_1]++;
    polys_touch_vertex[vindex_2]++;

Write_Error("\nPoly touch array v[%d] = %d, v[%d] = %d, v[%d] = %d",
       vindex_0,
       polys_touch_vertex[vindex_0],
       vindex_1, polys_touch_vertex[vindex_1],
       vindex_2, polys_touch_vertex[vindex_2]);

    // now accumulate the normal into the vertex normal itself
    // note, we do NOT normalize at this point since we want
```

9

```
    // the length of the normal
    // to weight on the average, and since the length is in fact
    // the area of the parallelogram constructed by uxv,
    // so we are taking the "influence" of the area into consideration
    VECTOR4D_Add(&obj->vlist_local[vindex_0].n, &n,
          &obj->vlist_local[vindex_0].n);
    VECTOR4D_Add(&obj->vlist_local[vindex_1].n, &n,
          &obj->vlist_local[vindex_1].n);
    VECTOR4D_Add(&obj->vlist_local[vindex_2].n, &n,
          &obj->vlist_local[vindex_2].n);
    } // end for poly

   } // end if needs vertex normals

// now we are almost done, we have accumulated all the vertex normals,
// but need to average them
for (int vertex = 0; vertex < obj->num_vertices; vertex++)
  {
  // if this vertex has any contributors then it must need averaging,
  // OR we could check the shading hints flags, they should be one to one
Write_Error("\nProcessing vertex:%d, attr:%d, contributors:%d", vertex,
                 obj->vlist_local[vertex].attr,
                 polys_touch_vertex[vertex]);

  // test if this vertex has a normal and needs averaging
  if (polys_touch_vertex[vertex] >= 1)
    {
    obj->vlist_local[vertex].nx/=polys_touch_vertex[vertex];
    obj->vlist_local[vertex].ny/=polys_touch_vertex[vertex];
    obj->vlist_local[vertex].nz/=polys_touch_vertex[vertex];

    // now normalize the normal
    VECTOR4D_Normalize(&obj->vlist_local[vertex].n);

    Write_Error("\nAvg Vertex normal: [%f, %f, %f]",
          obj->vlist_local[vertex].nx,
          obj->vlist_local[vertex].ny,
          obj->vlist_local[vertex].nz);

    } // end if

  } // end for
```

```
// return success
return(1);

} // end Compute_OBJECT4DV2_Vertex_Normals
```

When you run any of the demos, some of the analysis is always printed to the file ERROR.TXT. You might want to look at the file and review the vertex analysis phase—it's interesting to see the algorithm work.

Updating the 3D Studio .ASC Reader

The .ASC reader hasn't changed much since the previous version because it has no support for textures, lighting, and so forth. The only additions to the function are the support for the OBJECT4DV2 functionality as outlined in the .PLG/PLX loader. However, to give the format some oomph, I've decided to allow what I call *vertex overrides* to force or select the lighting model at least on an objectwide basis. Maybe next we'll add a global texturing with some generic texture coordinates that will work for rocks or simple geometrical primitives. The function is too large to list, but as I said, it performs the same additional logic as the .PLG/PLX loader function in relation to the object initialization and vertex type setting. Here's the prototype for the .ASC reader:

```
int Load_OBJECT4DV2_3DSASC(OBJECT4DV2_PTR obj, // pointer to object
           char *filename,    // filename of ASC file
           VECTOR4D_PTR scale, // initial scaling factors
           VECTOR4D_PTR pos,  // initial position
           VECTOR4D_PTR rot,  // initial rotations
           int vertex_flags)  // flags to re-order vertices
                    // and shading overrides
```

All the new functionality is basically in the vertex lighting overrides, which are shown here:

```
// (new) used for simple model formats to override/control the lighting
#define VERTEX_FLAGS_OVERRIDE_MASK    0xf000 // mask to extract overrides
#define VERTEX_FLAGS_OVERRIDE_CONSTANT 0x1000
#define VERTEX_FLAGS_OVERRIDE_EMISSIVE 0x1000 //(alias)
#define VERTEX_FLAGS_OVERRIDE_PURE    0x1000
#define VERTEX_FLAGS_OVERRIDE_FLAT    0x2000
#define VERTEX_FLAGS_OVERRIDE_GOURAUD 0x4000
#define VERTEX_FLAGS_OVERRIDE_TEXTURE 0x8000
```

As you can see, I've created an override for pretty much everything. At this point, only the pure, flat, and Gouraud overrides are working, as shown in the following code fragment from the function:

```
// first test to see if there is an override at all
int vertex_overrides = (vertex_flags & VERTEX_FLAGS_OVERRIDE_MASK);

if (vertex_overrides)
  {
  // which override?
  if (vertex_overrides & VERTEX_FLAGS_OVERRIDE_PURE)
    SET_BIT(obj->plist[poly].attr, POLY4DV2_ATTR_SHADE_MODE_PURE);

  if (vertex_overrides & VERTEX_FLAGS_OVERRIDE_FLAT)
    SET_BIT(obj->plist[poly].attr, POLY4DV2_ATTR_SHADE_MODE_FLAT);

  if (vertex_overrides & VERTEX_FLAGS_OVERRIDE_GOURAUD)
   {
   SET_BIT(obj->plist[poly].attr, POLY4DV2_ATTR_SHADE_MODE_GOURAUD);

   // going to need vertex normals!
   SET_BIT(obj->vlist_local[ obj->plist[poly].vert[0] ].attr,
       VERTEX4DTV1_ATTR_NORMAL);
   SET_BIT(obj->vlist_local[ obj->plist[poly].vert[1] ].attr,
       VERTEX4DTV1_ATTR_NORMAL);
   SET_BIT(obj->vlist_local[ obj->plist[poly].vert[2] ].attr,
       VERTEX4DTV1_ATTR_NORMAL);
   } // end if

   if (vertex_overrides & VERTEX_FLAGS_OVERRIDE_TEXTURE)
     SET_BIT(obj->plist[poly].attr,POLY4DV2_ATTR_SHADE_MODE_TEXTURE);

   } // end if
```

Notice that the Gouraud shading override causes the vertex attribute flag `VERTEX4DTV1_ATTR_NORMAL` to be set, which is correct because we need normals. As an example from one of the demos, here's how you would load an object and override the lighting to Gouraud mode:

```
Load_OBJECT4DV2_3DSASC(&obj_player,"tie01.asc",
            &vscale, &vpos, &vrot,
            VERTEX_FLAGS_OVERRIDE_GOURAUD);
```

Updating the Caligari .COB Reader

Last but not least is the new .COB object reader. This function is huge if you've looked at it, but for the most part, the basic changes are to support the new `OBJECT4DV2` structure. However, .COB files do have texture coordinate and texture support, so I've added full support for them.

Now, before getting into it, let's review how we process .COB files. We use the plain color shader to indicate pure color or texture mapped. Then we use the reflectance shader to select either emissive, flat, or Gouraud shading. The interesting thing is that when using textures, we still need a lighting model. In this version of the engine, I support both emissive and flat shading for textures; Gouraud interpolation would slow texturing down too much. But it means that when you create a model in .COB format, you must set the color of the polygon you want texture mapped to `"color: texture map"`, but also set the reflectance of the polygon to either emissive (`"constant"` model in trueSpace) or flat (`"matte"` in trueSpace) shading.

CAUTION

Objects for our engine can have only a single texture! They must be m×m, where m is a power of 2, and nothing larger than 256×256.

Pay attention to that warning, but the cool thing is that although each object must use the same texture, it doesn't mean that you can't texture map it in a cool way. You just need to use a large skin, say 128×128 or 256×256, to texture map the object and then map the texture coordinates onto the object. Figure 8.52 in the last chapter shows a nice skin from a *Quake II* model. As you saw, there are a lot of little pieces in the same texture map, so if we use that same texture map, all we need to do is use the correct texture coordinates.

Alright, so the new .COB loader does pretty much the same thing as the previous model, but it has the new capability to load and understand textures. It reads the texture information from the .COB file, which looks like this for a basic cube:

```
Texture Vertices 6
0.000000 0.000000
0.000000 1.000000
0.000000 0.000000
0.000000 1.000000
1.000000 0.000000
1.000000 1.000000
```

When the face list is read, the second component of each face vertex that defines a polygon is the texture coordinate (bolded):

```
Faces 12
Face verts 3 flags 0 mat 4
<0,0> <1,1> <3,5>
Face verts 3 flags 0 mat 4
<0,0> <3,5> <2,4>
Face verts 3 flags 0 mat 0
<0,1> <2,5> <5,4>
```

```
Face verts 3 flags 0 mat 0
<0,1> <5,4> <4,0>
Face verts 3 flags 0 mat 1
<2,2> <3,3> <6,5>
Face verts 3 flags 0 mat 1
<2,2> <6,5> <5,4>
Face verts 3 flags 0 mat 0
<1,0> <7,1> <6,5>
Face verts 3 flags 0 mat 0
<1,0> <6,5> <3,4>
Face verts 3 flags 0 mat 2
<4,4> <5,0> <6,1>
Face verts 3 flags 0 mat 2
<4,4> <6,1> <7,5>
Face verts 3 flags 0 mat 3
<0,4> <4,2> <7,3>

Face verts 3 flags 0 mat 3 ß face #11
<0,4> <7,3> <1,5>
```

For example, the very last polygon in the cube mesh, face 11, is a polygon with three vertices constructed from the vertices (0,7,1), but the texture vertices are (4,3,5). If we look up the texture coordinates for these vertices, they translate to the following:

(4,3,5) texture indices maps to:

((1.000000, 0.000000),

(0.000000, 1.000000),

(1.000000, 1.000000))

where each pair is in (u,v) format or the x,y axis of the texture map. We'll cover more of these mapping details when we cover texture mapping, but for now just understand the mechanics of it. Okay, cool, so we load in the texture coordinates, but then we need to load in the actual texture map. This is semi-tricky, but as long as we take care of details, we're all right. The first detail is that for every object, only one texture can be loaded. Hence, when a material is scanned in with a texture map, only the very first texture map is loaded—the rest are disregarded (if they exist). The code in the .COB reader that loads the textures is shown here:

```
// the OBJECT4DV2 is only allowed a single texture,
// although we are loading in all
// the materials, if this is the first texture map, load it,
// and set a flag disallowing
// any more texture loads for the object
if (!obj->texture)
```

```
{
// step 1: allocate memory for bitmap
obj->texture = (BITMAP_IMAGE_PTR)malloc(sizeof(BITMAP_IMAGE));

// load the texture, just use the final
// file name and the absolute global texture path
char filename[80];
char path_filename[80];
// get the filename
Extract_Filename_From_Path(materials[material_index +
            num_materials].texture_file, filename);

// build the filename with root path
strcpy(path_filename, texture_path);
strcat(path_filename, filename);

// buffer now holds final texture path and file name
// load the bitmap(8/16 bit)
Load_Bitmap_File(&bitmap16bit, path_filename);

// create a proper size and bitdepth bitmap
Create_Bitmap(obj->texture,0,0,
bitmap16bit.bitmapinfoheader.biWidth,
bitmap16bit.bitmapinfoheader.biHeight,
bitmap16bit.bitmapinfoheader.biBitCount);

// load the bitmap image (later make this 8/16 bit)
if (obj->texture->bpp == 16)
 Load_Image_Bitmap16(obj->texture,
          &bitmap16bit,0,0,BITMAP_EXTRACT_MODE_ABS);
else
 {
 Load_Image_Bitmap(obj->texture, &bitmap16bit,0,0,
         BITMAP_EXTRACT_MODE_ABS);
 } // end else 8 bit

// done, so unload the bitmap
Unload_Bitmap_File(&bitmap16bit);

// flag object as having textures
SET_BIT(obj->attr, OBJECT4DV2_ATTR_TEXTURES);

} // end if
```

The preceding section of code is important because it performs some housekeeping that I want you to be thinking about. First, this code is contained in the section after all the polygons have been loaded and the materials have been applied to each polygon. Remember that the .COB format uses a material index for each polygon, but the materials don't come until *after* the entire mesh is loaded. So, we have to wait until we're done loading the mesh, and then load the materials, and then fix up the material references. In our case, we aren't really using materials yet, but the information about textures are contained in them, so we do have to wait. In any case, once a material is loaded that's determined to have a texture applied to it, the preceding code executes.

The first step that the code takes is to determine whether a texture has already been loaded. If so, nothing happens. Otherwise, the code block is entered. Upon entry, the code first extracts only the filename portion of the texture map with a call to the new function `Extract_Filename_From_Path()` shown here:

```
char *Extract_Filename_From_Path(char *filepath, char *filename)
{
// this function extracts the filename from a complete path and file
// "../folder/.../filname.ext"
// the function operates by scanning backward and looking for the first
// occurance of "\" or "/" then copies the filename from there to the end
// test of filepath is valid
if (!filepath || strlen(filepath)==0)
  return(NULL);

int index_end = strlen(filepath)-1;

// find filename
while( (filepath[index_end]!='\\') &&
     (filepath[index_end]!='/') &&
     (filepath[index_end] > 0) )
   index_end--;

// copy file name out into filename var
memcpy(filename, &filepath[index_end+1],
     strlen(filepath) - index_end);

// return result
return(filename);

} // end Extract_Filename_From_Path
```

The necessity for this function is twofold: The ANSI string support in C/C++ sucks, and there simply isn't an easy way to get the darn filename from a complete path like this:

```
d:\path\...\filename.ext
```

so, I had to write one. Basically, the function works backward from the end and returns the string up to the last `\` or `/` character. Therefore, calling the function with a file path of `"d:\files\atari\object.cob"` like this:

```
char filename[80];

Extract_Filename_From_Path("d:\files\atari\object.cob", filename);
```

Results in *filename*=`"object.cob"`, which is exactly what we need. That's all fine and dandy, but has all the path information been completely lost? What if we want to place textures somewhere? Well, to provide that functionality, I decided to create a *texture root path*, meaning that all textures must be located in the root path. The root path is defined in `T3DLIB7.CPP` as

```
char texture_path[80] = "./"; // root path to ALL textures
```

In other words, the working directory of the .EXE that's executed is where textures will be searched for. Remember that `"./"` means current directory. So, for now, all demos must have all the media in the same working directory as the demo itself. When you create your own games later, you might want to create a directory `MEDIA\` with the following subdirectories:

```
TEXTURES\

MODELS\

SOUNDS\

..

etc.
```

and place all your textures there.

In any case, the second reason we're doing all this work with the filename is much more important. If you review Caligari .COB object with texturing, you'll see something quite disturbing. Take a look at the following sample texture material:

```
Mat1 V0.06 Id 18623892 Parent 18629556 Size 00000182
mat# 0
shader: phong facet: auto32
rgb 1,0.952941,0.0235294
alpha 1 ka 0.1 ks 0.1 exp 0 ior 1
texture: 36D:\Source\models\textures\wall01.bmp
offset 0,0 repeats 1,1 flags 2
ShBx V0.03 Id 18623893 Parent 18623892 Size 00000658
Shader class: color
Shader name: "texture map" (caligari texture)
Number of parameters: 7
```

```
file name: string "D:\Source\models\textures\wall01.bmp"
S repeat: float 1
T repeat: float 1
S offset: float 0
T offset: float 0
animate: bool 0
filter: bool 0
Flags: 3
Shader class: transparency
Shader name: "none" (none)
Number of parameters: 0
Flags: 3
Shader class: reflectance
Shader name: "phong" (phong)
Number of parameters: 5
ambient factor: float 0.1
diffuse factor: float 0.9
specular factor: float 0.1
exponent: float 3
specular colour: color (255, 255, 255)
Flags: 3
Shader class: displacement
Shader name: "none" (none)
Number of parameters: 0
Flags: 3
END V1.00 Id 0 Parent 0 Size    0
```

You'll notice that the texture paths are absolute—ouch! That means a demo from my computer won't work on yours unless we have the exact same paths. So, I think using the root filename plus a generic texture path is the best of both worlds.

NOTE

There's probably a setting in trueSpace to disable absolute paths, but after fighting with the "magic ring," I've given up <BG>.

To finalize our discussion of the new .COB reader: After the final texture path and name are derived, the actual texture is loaded. Nothing unusual here; a call to load the bitmap is made, and the texture bitmap is created and copied from the bitmap file into the bitmap image holding the texture. Of course, the bit depth is determined (8- or 16-bit) and the appropriate call is made based on that.

This leads me into a brief discussion about bit depth. At some point, we might want to hide the 8/16-bit functions with higher-level wrapper functions because it's kind of a pain to test and make the calls. Of course, the reason why I shy away from this is that if we're using 8- or 16-bit mode, we "know" we are, so why make the extra call? Of course, with function pointers or virtual functions, we can override this overhead and get it for free. Something to think about....

The next subject I want to talk about are vertex overrides for the .COB reader. It's pointless to override the lighting model (although you may want to), but something that we might need to muck with are the texture coordinates. The output of any modeler's .COB files might not have texture coordinates exactly how we like them. For example, u and v might be swapped, or inverted, and so forth. To add this functionality to the reader, I've introduced the following vertex flags:

```
// invert u texture coordinate
#define VERTEX_FLAGS_INVERT_TEXTURE_U     0x0080
// invert v texture coordinate
#define VERTEX_FLAGS_INVERT_TEXTURE_V     0x0100
// swap u and v texture coordinates
#define VERTEX_FLAGS_INVERT_SWAP_UV      0x0800
```

You simply logically `OR` them together with any other flags you might want for the .COB to take into consideration, such as the `VERTEX_FLAGS_TRANSFORM_LOCAL_WORLD` flag and so on.

Also, while we're talking about texture coordinates, I have an aside I want to discuss. Texture coordinates from most modelers use coordinates in the range: (0..1, 0..1). In other words, they're normalized to 1.0. Our rasterization functions do not (or will not) like this, so when texture coordinates are finally written to the texture array cache and the reader exits, we have to make sure that we scale the coordinates to the size of the texture. For example, if a texture that's loaded is 64 × 64 and a texture coordinate is (.2, .34), the final texture coordinate should be scaled by (64-1) = 63 on both axes:

(63*.2, 63*.34) = (12.6, 21.42)

NOTE

Texture coordinates are left in floating-point format, so we can have sub-pixel accuracy in the texture mapping, or at least plan for it.

Well, that about sums it up for the new .COB reader. The function works in the same way as before, as far as calling it. For example, here's an example from one of the later demos that loads a TIE fighter–looking model with textures, taking into consideration inverted-v texture coordinates as well as the right-handed modeling system of Caligari trueSpace:

```
Load_OBJECT4DV2_COB(&obj_player,"tie02.cob",
        &vscale, &vpos, &vrot,
        VERTEX_FLAGS_INVERT_TEXTURE_V |
        VERTEX_FLAGS_SWAP_YZ |
        VERTEX_FLAGS_TRANSFORM_LOCAL_WORLD );
```

Polygon Rasterization Review

Wow! It took a long time to discuss the basic changes to the engine, even if given only cursory coverage. The point is this stuff is getting complicated and big. However, anything I talk about, I want to try to implement and show you, but the setup for this material is getting rather large, so please bear with me. Before getting into Gouraud shading and texture mapping, I want to cover polygon rasterization one more time. I originally covered the subject in the first *Tricks*, and I briefly mentioned it in the last chapter, but it's something that keeps coming up everywhere in 3D graphics. 99% of everything has something to do with rasterization, interpolation, or sampling, so this is something it pays to know well.

Taking that into consideration, I've rewritten our basic polygon rasterizers to make them a little more accurate. The original rasterizers operated on integer coordinates only. I also define a "fill convention" and a number of other details; I want to discuss those things now so that you have an understanding of them.

Triangle Rasterization

There are a number of ways to draw triangles, including tracing the two edges of the triangle with a line drawing algorithm such as Bresenham's or with simple interpolation. I prefer interpolation because its more straightforward. Let's once again see how this works. Take a look at Figure 9.9. All we have to do is find the points that make up the rasterized version of the triangle. These points are shown in the figure as little dots. Once we find these pixel locations for each scan line that makes up the triangle, drawing the triangle is nothing more than performing a simple memory fill from point to point, as shown in Figure 9.10.

Finding these points is nothing more than interpolating the slope (well, almost) of each side of the triangle. The interpolation is performed as follows.

We know that the height of the triangle is

```
dy = (y2 - y0);
```

and the difference in X's between the lower-left vertex and the lower-right vertex is

```
dx_left_side = (x2 - x0);
dx_right_side = (x1 - x0);
```

Thus, the slope of the left-hand side is

```
slope_left_side = dy/dx_left_side = (y2 - y0)/(x2 - x0);
```

and the slope of the right-hand side is

```
slope_right_side = dy/dx_right_side = (y2 - y0)/(x1 - x0);
```

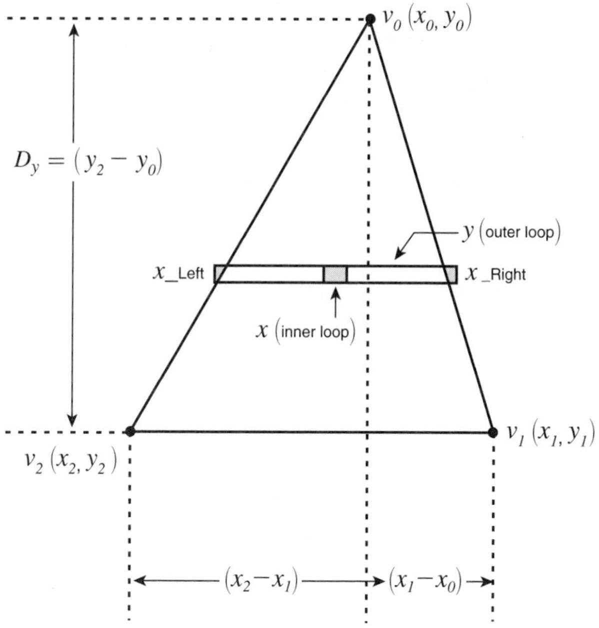

FIGURE 9.9 Setup for triangle rasterization.

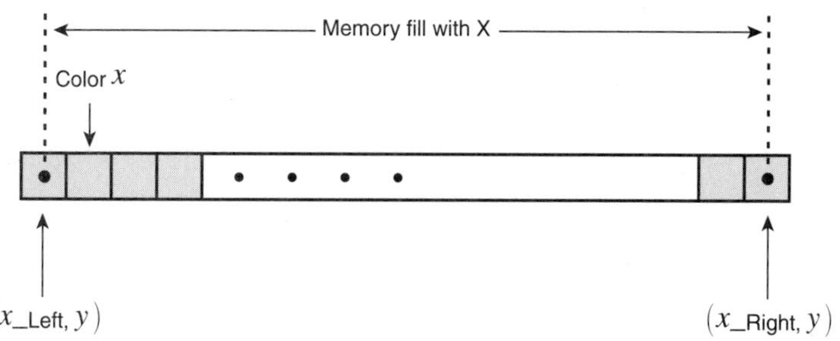

FIGURE 9.10 Rasterizing single scan line.

However, we don't exactly want the slope. The slope is the "change in y per change in x." This means that if we were to move over exactly one pixel in the x direction, the y would change by the slope. We don't want that; we want the opposite, or dx/dy. That's because we're drawing the triangle scan line by scan line, and incrementing y each time; hence, dy = 1, which is a constant, so:

```
dx_left_side = 1 * (x2 - x0)/(y2 - y0);
```

and

```
dx_right_side = 1 * (x1 - x0)/(y2 - y0);
```

That's it! That's the entire triangle-drawing algorithm for a flat-bottom triangle. A flat-top triangle is similar and I leave writing the interpolation algorithm up to you. Take a look at the following pseudo-code implementation of the triangle drawing algorithm:

```
void Draw_Triangle(float x0,float y0, // vertex 0
           float x1,float y1, // vertex 1
           float x2,float y2, // vertex 2
           int color)     // color
{
// this function rasterizes a triangle with a flat bottom

// compute left side interpolant
float dx_left = (x2 - x0)/(y2 - y0);

// compute right side interpolant
float dx_right = (x1 - x0)/(y2 - y0);

// seed left and right hand interpolators
float x_left = x0;
float x_right = x0;

// enter into rasterization loop
for (int y=y0; y<=y1; y++)
   {
   // draw the scanline
   Draw_Line(x_left, x_right, y, color);

   // advance interpolants
   x_left+=dx_left;
   x_right+=dx_right;

   } // end for y

} // end DRAW_Triangle
```

This function actually works fine and is the basis for our real triangle rasterizer. However, it has a few shortcomings. First, it's written in floating-point math. Ironically this isn't the problem, because floating point is as fast as integer math these days. Of course, you can get in trouble when converting back and forth from integers to floating point for the final rasterization phase, but let's hold off on that for a second.

The real problem is the `Draw_Line()` function. We're assuming that it takes floating-point values, and maybe it does, but at some point those floating-point values must be converted to integers and therein lies the dilemma. Should we truncate, round, use the mathematical ceiling function or the mathematical floor function? All these question relate to what is called a *fill convention*.

TIP

The mathematical `ceiling(x)` function shown in Figure 9.11 returns the smallest integer greater than or equal to `x`. Conversely, the `floor(x)` function shown in Figure 9.12 returns the largest integer less than or equal to `x`.

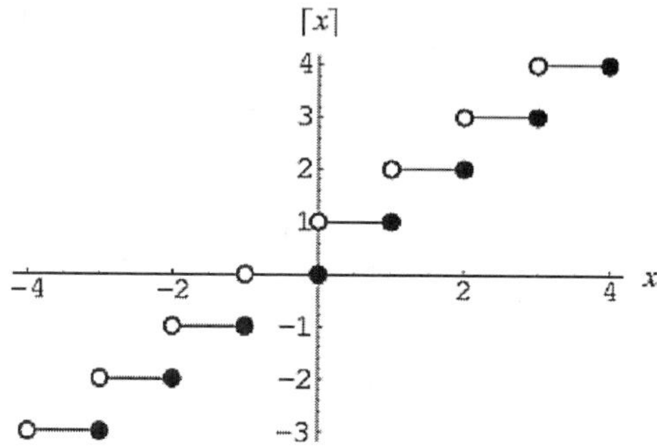

FIGURE 9.11 A graph of the `ceiling()` function.

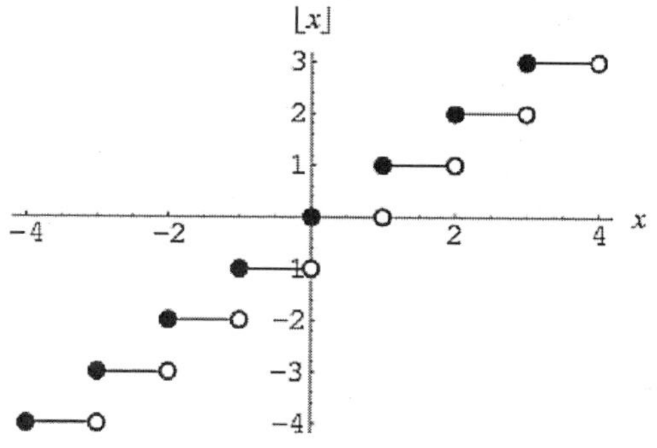

FIGURE 9.12 A graph of the `floor()` function.

Fill convention has to do with how polygons are rasterized in relation to the starting and stopping pixels from the top to bottom and from the left to right that are lit. We'll get to this in a moment because it's so important, but for now let's continue on with our rasterizer and talk about some more details.

So, aside from the fill convention issue, what else are we making assumptions about with the preceding rasterizer prototype?

1. There's no mention of general triangles, and we need to deal with that.
2. There's no mention of clipping, either image space or object space, and that needs to be addressed.

Let's discuss (1) first. In this book, I've been using the triangle rasterizers from the first *Tricks*. If you review those, you'll find that they all break up polygons into three different types:

Type 1: Triangles with a flat top

Type 2: Triangles with a flat bottom

Type 3: General triangles

These types are shown in Figure 9.13. I think you get the point by now that it might be faster to perform initial tests so that we don't have to write a more general triangle rasterizer that simply draws any triangle. Let me refresh your memory on my thinking process.

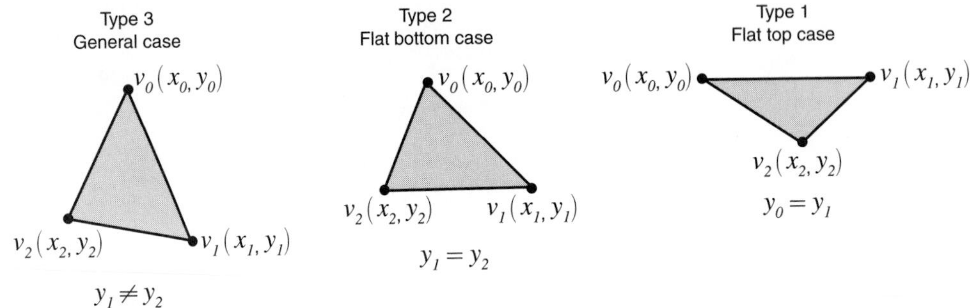

FIGURE 9.13 The special cases of triangles.

When drawing a triangle, you'll notice we have an inner loop from `y0` to `y1`. In this loop, we simply adjust the left- and right-pixel locations and draw the line. However, for a general triangle, the slope of either the right or left side of the triangle will change at some point. This means that we either have to place some test code within the `y0` to `y1` loop for this, or we need to break up the rasterization into two portions: a flat bottom and a flat top.

If we take the second approach, we're back to having special cases. If we take the first approach—that is, changing the slope midstream—we have an extra conditional something like what's shown next, assuming that we're rasterizing the triangle shown in Figure 9.14:

```
for (y=y0; y < y2; y++)
  {
  Draw_Line(x_left, x_right, y, color);

  x_left+=dx_left;
  x_right+=dx_right;
```

```
// test for change of slope
if (y==y1)
  dx_right = new_dx_right;

} // end for
```

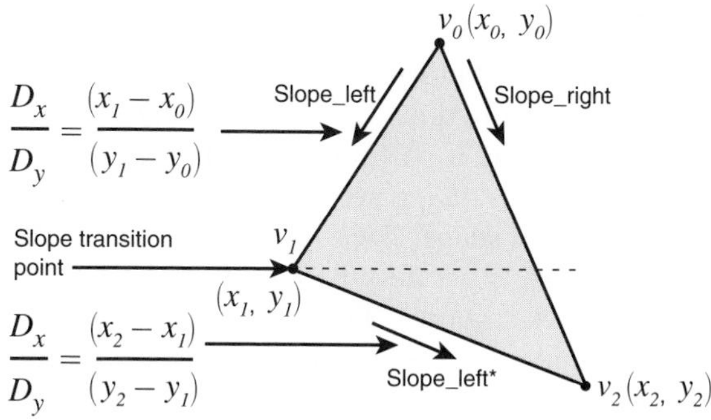

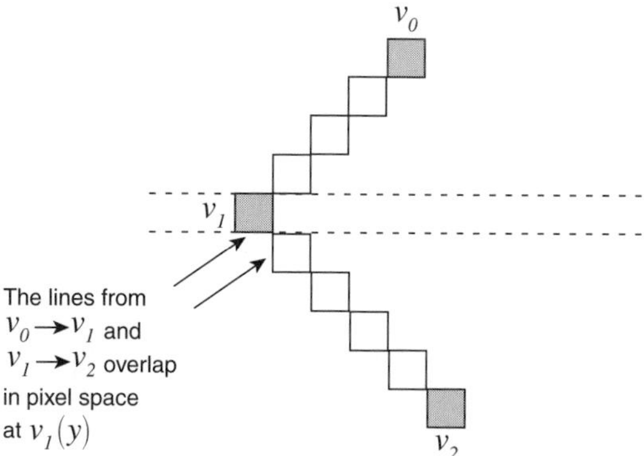

FIGURE 9.14 A closeup view of the slope transition during triangle rasterization.

Basically, during the inside loop, we have to test when the line interpolation hits the new triangle edge and update the slope appropriately. However, this uncovers a nasty subtlety: No matter how we break up the triangle—that is, two subtriangles, one flat bottom, one flat top, or have a conditional that flags a change in slope—there's potential for an error during this change of slopes. Take a look at Figure 9.14 to see this. The problem is that when we draw the last pixel on the left edge and then transition to the new slope of the new left edge, where do we start? Do we start on the current pixel? One below it? Basically, we have to be careful that we don't overdraw the pixel (which is harmless), but worse yet that we mess up the current y position. What has to be done is the following: We must pre-step down to the next line the exact amount from the exact (x1, y1) vertex location. Let me repeat that again. When the y position hits the transition vertex, depending on what kind of variable y is (integer or float), we must be careful not to advance the x component by the full slope `new_dx_right`, but by the differential difference based on the actual position of (*x1*, *y1*) at that point.

Fill Convention

When rasterizing polygons in a 3D engine, the point of rasterizing the polygons is usually to build up an image of some solid object. What this means is that when we're drawing polygons that define a mesh, many times the polygons share vertices. And if they do, we want to draw the polygons such that polygons that share vertices do not overdraw the same lines. Take a look at Figure 9.15a to see what I'm talking about. Here we see two triangles building up a diamond shape. The top triangle ends at row 20, but the bottom triangle starts at row 20! So, we either need to stop the top triangle at row 19 or start the bottom triangle at row 21. As a second example, take a look at Figure 9.15b. Here we see two triangles adjacent horizontally creating a diamond shape. Again, should the left triangle draw the last rightmost pixel at column 50, or should the rightmost triangle start at column 51, and so on? All of these questions define a fill convention.

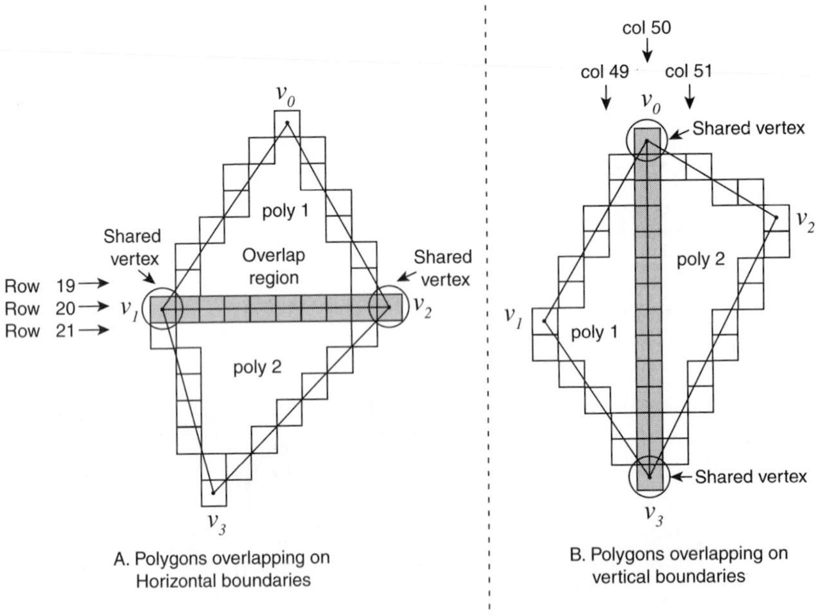

FIGURE 9.15 Polygons that share vertices and edges.

We're going to use what is termed as a *top-left fill convention*, which is what Direct3D uses for rasterization. That is, if you were to render a rectangle from (0,0) to (5,5), you would think that the pixels on the fifth row and fifth column would be filled, but they aren't; this is shown in Figure 9.16.

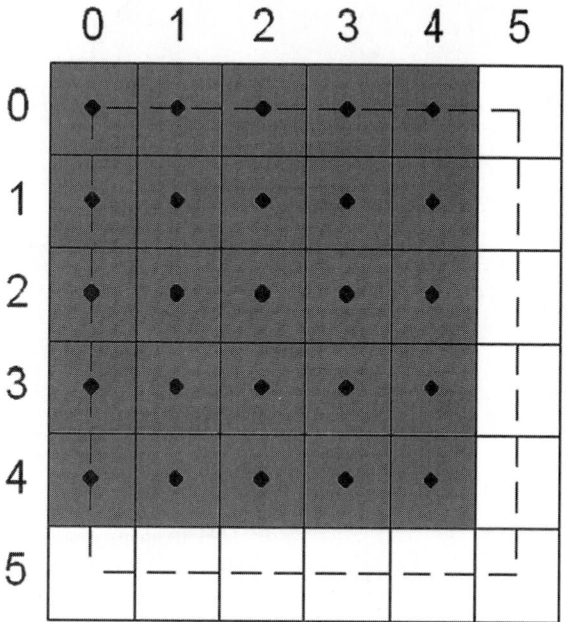

FIGURE 9.16 Top-left fill convention applied to a rectangle.

The rectangle depicted fills 25 pixels, just as you would expect. The width of the rectangle is defined as right minus left. The height is defined as bottom minus top, but the last row and last column are not yet filled.

The top-left filling convention determines the action taken when a triangle passes through the center of a pixel. In Figure 9.17, we see two triangles: one at (0, 0), (5, 0), and (5, 5), and the other at (0, 5), (0, 0), and (5, 5). The first triangle in this case gets 15 pixels (shown in black), whereas the second gets only 10 pixels (shown in gray) because the shared edge is the left edge of the first triangle.

This is the fill convention we want to employ because it's the standard as far as I can tell. In any event, to facilitate this fill convention, we simply need to snap the incoming pixel coordinates to integral positions with the ceiling function. So, for example, if we were rasterizing a flat-bottom triangle from `y0` to `y1`, these coordinates would change to

```
ystart = ceil(y0)
yend = ceil(y1)-1
```

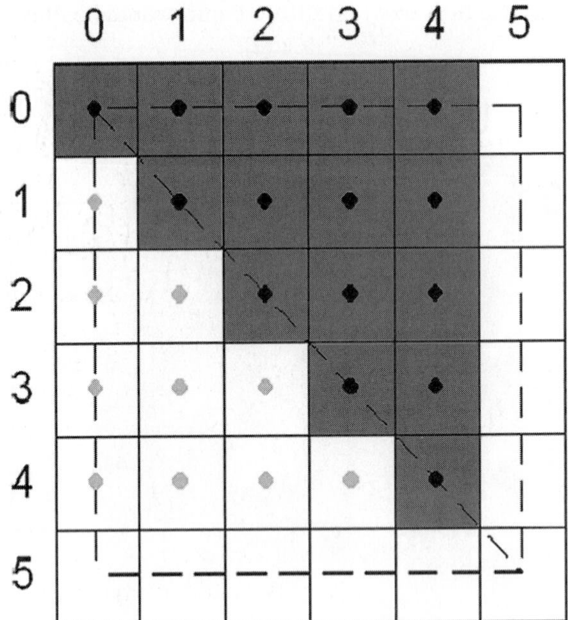

FIGURE 9.17 Top-left fill convention applied to triangles.

During the looping process, when we are generating x values for each scan line, we also need to compute the ceiling of those:

```
xs = ceil(x_left)
xe = ceil(x_right)-1
```

So, to sum up, we need to compute the ceiling function of both the initial y starting and ending loop values, and also compute the ceiling function of the x end points before we rasterize each scan line.

Alright, easy enough, but is there anything else we're missing? Actually, yes. Because we are throwing away information about the pixel locations before starting rasterization, we need to take this into consideration when prestepping the x positions. That means that the real vertical span was from `y0` to `y1`, but we decided on a top-left fill convention and thus took the `ceil(y0)` and `ceil(y1)-1` to compute our starting and ending positions. But we need to take this into consideration with the `x_left` and `x_right` (if we're drawing a flat-bottom triangle). Take a look at Figure 9.18.

We see the details of the top-left filling convention side effect in relation to the initial x-position for the left interpolant. The key here to make sure that we take the altered ystart position into consideration, this is easy though and nothing more than

```
x_left = x_left + (ystart - y0) * dx_left
```

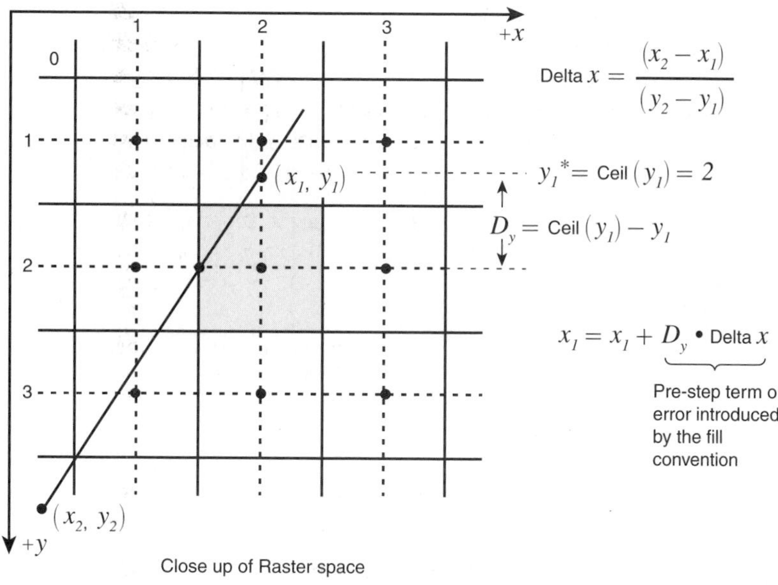

FIGURE 9.18 Taking coordinate truncation into consideration and pre-stepping properly.

In other words, we need to add the small differential change caused by snapping `y0` to the value `ceil(y0)` to x. Thus, we compute the difference from the original `y0` and the `ceil(y0)`, take the difference, and multiply by the gradient of the left edge to properly set the initial x position of the left side interpolant. A similar process must be performed for the right side interpolant.

Okay, I think that's about it. The only other housekeeping details to rasterize a triangle is that, on entry, we must sort the vertices from top to bottom and from left to right, so that we know the order they're in.

Clipping

The final topic I want to discuss before moving on to some real triangle code is clipping. We've discussed clipping a number of times, but let's review it once again in the context of triangle rasterization. We could clip all triangles to the screen rectangle as shown in Figure 9.19. However, I find that this is more of a pain than it's worth, and it's better to perform clipping during rasterization. To accomplish this is rather trivial. We need to determine what kind of clipping is needed—that is, y-clipping, x-clipping, or no clipping—and then select the code block that performs this, as shown in Figure 9.20. The case where no clipping is needed is the simplest, of course, and then comes the y-clipping case. In this case, part of the triangle extends beyond the top or bottom of the screen (or both for a large triangle).

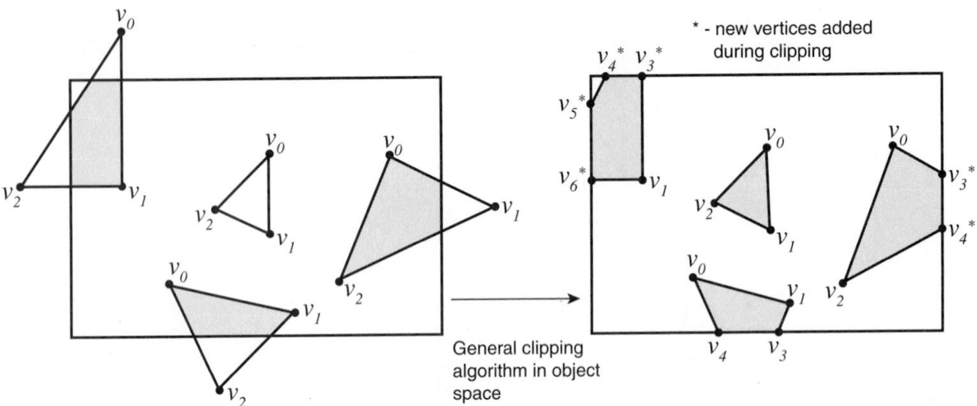

FIGURE 9.19 Screen rectangle clipping.

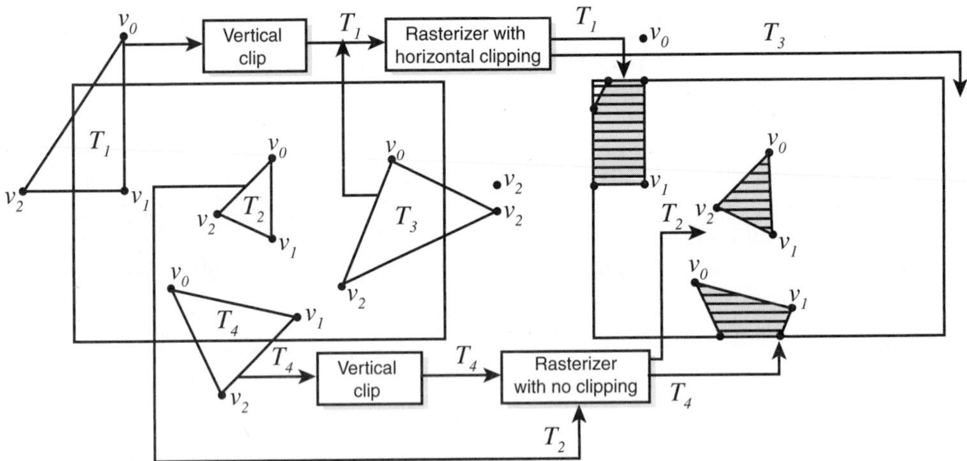

FIGURE 9.20 Special case clippers based on geometry.

For example, to clip to the top of the screen (y = 0 in most cases), we test if the topmost triangle vertex is less than 0. If so, we set the new y = 0, but we have to be careful here; we must step the left and right x coordinates down the edges of the triangle to account for the new y. Once again, this is a pre-stepping phase, and care must be taken not to lose accuracy. This is also shown in Figure 9.21.

Clipping the bottom of the triangle is much easier than the top: We simply stop rasterizing at the last screen row, but we don't need to recompute any left- or right-side x interpolants because we aren't scanning down the edges from the top; we're scanning down and stopping *before* the bottom.

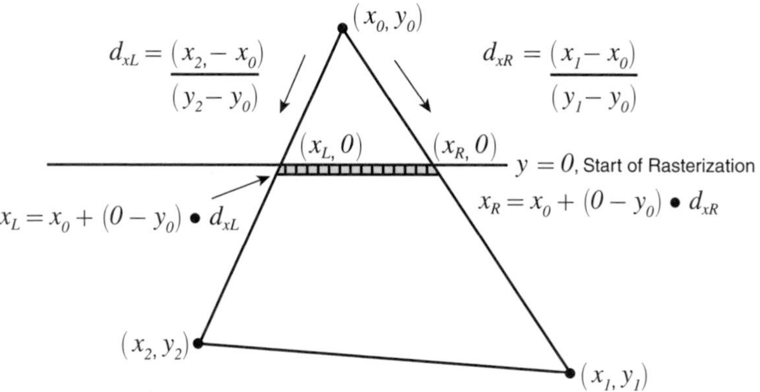

FIGURE 9.21 Properly recomputing or stepping x rasterization locations after clipping on the y-axis.

The final case is when, as the triangle is being rasterized, its starting and ending x positions extend beyond the right and left of the window. This is similar to the top y-clipping case. Starting with scan lines that are clipped to x = 0, we simply set the x position to 0, and then we perform the same test to the right side x position and clip it. The results are then stored and the scan line drawn—it's simple as that.

TIP

A little later, we're going to perform 3D clipping somewhat, but we'll find that it's not worth performing a full 3D clip against the view frustrum because a single triangle can end up having six sides after clipping. However, we'll absolutely have to perform near z-plane clipping, which can result in quadrilaterals that then need to be split into triangles once again. But that will be performed at the rendering list level, so it's not going to be a killer to split triangles that get clipped once in a while.

The New Triangle Functions

Now that we've reviewed some of the details to rasterize a triangle, let's take a look at the new triangle rendering functions that take some of these concepts into consideration. I basically rewrote all the triangle rendering functions for both 8- and 16-bit bit depths. My main concern was that the old versions didn't support floating-point coordinates, so the new ones do. Also, I have conditionally compilation flags to select how accurate you want the rasterizers because the more accurate they are, the slower they are. I felt that using conditional compilation was better than using assembly language optimization at this point. In any case, I don't want to list all the functions. I'm only going to show a couple that are indicative of the new functionality, so let's look at the triangle-splitting function that makes the call to the low-level top/bottom triangle drawing functions first (16-bit version):

```
void Draw_Triangle_2D2_16(float x1,float y1,
              float x2,float y2,
              float x3,float y3,
              int color,
              UCHAR *dest_buffer, int mempitch)
{
// this function draws a triangle on the destination buffer
// it decomposes all triangles into a pair of flat top, flat bottom

float temp_x, // used for sorting
   temp_y,
   new_x;

#ifdef DEBUG_ON
  // track rendering stats
  debug_polys_rendered_per_frame++;
#endif

// test for h lines and v lines
if ((FCMP(x1,x2) && FCMP(x2,x3)) || (FCMP(y1,y2) && FCMP(y2,y3)))
  return;

// sort p1,p2,p3 in ascending y order
if (y2 < y1)
  {
  SWAP(x1,x2,temp_x);
  SWAP(y1,y2,temp_y);
  } // end if

// now we know that p1 and p2 are in order
if (y3 < y1)
  {
  SWAP(x1,x3,temp_x);
  SWAP(y1,y3,temp_y);
  } // end if

// finally test y3 against y2
if (y3 < y2)
  {
  SWAP(x2,x3,temp_x);
  SWAP(y2,y3,temp_y);
  } // end if
```

```
// do trivial rejection tests for clipping
if ( y3 < min_clip_y || y1 > max_clip_y ||
  (x1 < min_clip_x && x2 < min_clip_x && x3 < min_clip_x) ||
  (x1 > max_clip_x && x2 > max_clip_x && x3 > max_clip_x) )
  return;

// test if top of triangle is flat
if (FCMP(y1,y2))
  {
  Draw_Top_Tri2_16(x1,y1,x2,y2,x3,y3,color, dest_buffer, mempitch);
  } // end if
else
if (FCMP(y2,y3))
  {
  Draw_Bottom_Tri2_16(x1,y1,x2,y2,x3,y3,color, dest_buffer, mempitch);
  } // end if bottom is flat
else
  {
  // general triangle that's needs to be broken up along long edge
  new_x = x1 + (y2-y1)*(x3-x1)/(y3-y1);

  // draw each sub-triangle
  Draw_Bottom_Tri2_16(x1,y1,new_x,y2,x2,y2,color, dest_buffer, mempitch);
  Draw_Top_Tri2_16(x2,y2,new_x,y2,x3,y3,color, dest_buffer, mempitch);
  } // end else

} // end Draw_Triangle_2D2_16
```

The function has the same prototype as the previous version, `Draw_Triangle_2D_16()`. The only differences are that all calculations are performed in floating-point math and the pixel coordinates are sent as floats. Next, let's take a look at the function that draws a flat-bottom 16-bit triangle:

```
void Draw_Bottom_Tri2_16(float x1, float y1,
             float x2, float y2,
             float x3, float y3,
             int color,
             UCHAR *_dest_buffer, int mempitch)
{
// this function draws a triangle that has a flat bottom

float dx_right,  // the dx/dy ratio of the right edge of line
   dx_left,   // the dx/dy ratio of the left edge of line
   xs,xe,    // the starting and ending points of the edges
```

```
    height,   // the height of the triangle
    temp_x,   // used during sorting as temps
    temp_y,
    right,    // used by clipping
    left;

int iy1,iy3,loop_y;

// cast dest buffer to ushort
USHORT *dest_buffer = (USHORT *)_dest_buffer;

// destination address of next scanline
USHORT *dest_addr = NULL;

// recompute mempitch in 16-bit words
mempitch = (mempitch >> 1);

// test order of x1 and x2
if (x3 < x2)
   {
   SWAP(x2,x3,temp_x);
   } // end if swap

// compute delta's
height = y3 - y1;

dx_left = (x2-x1)/height;
dx_right = (x3-x1)/height;

// set starting points
xs = x1;
xe = x1;

#if (RASTERIZER_MODE==RASTERIZER_ACCURATE)
// perform y clipping
if (y1 < min_clip_y)
   {
   // compute new xs and ys
   xs = xs+dx_left*(-y1+min_clip_y);
   xe = xe+dx_right*(-y1+min_clip_y);

   // reset y1
   y1 = min_clip_y;
```

```
        // make sure top left fill convention is observed
        iy1 = y1;
        } // end if top is off screen
    else
        {
        // make sure top left fill convention is observed
        iy1 = ceil(y1);

        // bump xs and xe appropriately
        xs = xs+dx_left*(iy1-y1);
        xe = xe+dx_right*(iy1-y1);
        } // end else

    if (y3 > max_clip_y)
        {
        // clip y
        y3 = max_clip_y;

        // make sure top left fill convention is observed
        iy3 = y3-1;
        } // end if
    else
        {
        // make sure top left fill convention is observed
        iy3 = ceil(y3)-1;
        } // end else
    #endif

    #if ((RASTERIZER_MODE==RASTERIZER_FAST) ||
       (RASTERIZER_MODE==RASTERIZER_FASTEST))
    // perform y clipping
    if (y1 < min_clip_y)
        {
        // compute new xs and ys
        xs = xs+dx_left*(-y1+min_clip_y);
        xe = xe+dx_right*(-y1+min_clip_y);

        // reset y1
        y1 = min_clip_y;
        } // end if top is off screen

    if (y3 > max_clip_y)
        y3 = max_clip_y;
```

```
// make sure top left fill convention is observed
iy1 = ceil(y1);
iy3 = ceil(y3)-1;
#endif

// compute starting address in video memory
dest_addr = dest_buffer + iy1*mempitch;

// test if x clipping is needed
if (x1 >= min_clip_x && x1 <= max_clip_x &&
  x2 >= min_clip_x && x2 <= max_clip_x &&
  x3 >= min_clip_x && x3 <= max_clip_x)
  {
  // draw the triangle
  for (loop_y = iy1; loop_y <= iy3; loop_y++, dest_addr+=mempitch)
    {
    // draw the line
    Mem_Set_WORD(dest_addr+(unsigned int)(xs),color,
           (unsigned int)((int)xe-(int)xs+1));

    // adjust starting point and ending point
    xs+=dx_left;
    xe+=dx_right;
    } // end for

  } // end if no x clipping needed
else
  {
  // clip x axis with slower version

  // draw the triangle
  for (loop_y = iy1; loop_y <= iy3; loop_y++,dest_addr+=mempitch)
    {
    // do x clip
    left = xs;
    right = xe;

    // adjust starting point and ending point
    xs+=dx_left;
    xe+=dx_right;

    // clip line
    if (left < min_clip_x)
```

```
      {
      left = min_clip_x;

      if (right < min_clip_x)
        continue;
      }

     if (right > max_clip_x)
      {
      right = max_clip_x;

      if (left > max_clip_x)
        continue;
      }
     // draw the line
     Mem_Set_WORD(dest_addr+(unsigned int)(left),color,
            (unsigned int)((int)right-(int)left+1));
     } // end for
   } // end else x clipping needed
} // end Draw_Bottom_Tri2_16
```

Again, the naming convention appends a 2 to the primary function name, but the interface stays the same. Reviewing the function, you can see the support for filling convention as well as the conditional compilation flags that I've highlighted in the code as bold and are defined here:

```
// these are defines for conditional compilation of the new rasterizers
// I don't want 80 million different functions, so I have decided to
// use some conditionals to change some of the logic in each
// these names aren't necessarily the most accurate, but 3 should be enough
#define RASTERIZER_ACCURATE 0 // sub-pixel accurate with fill convention
#define RASTERIZER_FAST    1 //
#define RASTERIZER_FASTEST  2

// set this to the mode you want the engine to use
#define RASTERIZER_MODE     RASTERIZER_ACCURATE
```

To change the conditional compilation, modify the bolded line in the preceding code in the `T3DLIB7.H` file to `RASTERIZER_FAST`; for example, to speed up the rasterizer a bit in exchange for accuracy. The function basically implements everything we've discussed; its sister function that renders flat-top triangles is similar. Additionally, there are versions for 8-bit modes as shown in the earlier functional listing.

Now that you've been completely bored out of your mind with rasterization, let's talk briefly about some optimizations that can be made to these rasterizers.

Optimizations

The beautiful thing about these rasterizers is that they're so short. The optimization domain is small, meaning that we can see the entire code at once. So, what are some areas to optimize? Well, the algorithms are sound, meaning that we aren't going to get much with changing the algorithm—rasterization is rasterization. Rasterization is not like sorting where huge gains can be realized with new algorithms. Additionally, the inner loops have very little in them—for the most part, a couple additions and a line draw, and that's it. The only thing we can get some speed out of is looking closely at data conversions and doing math we don't need to do. Take a look at the following fragment, which represents the inner loop of the rasterizer:

```
// draw the triangle
for (loop_y = iy1; loop_y <= iy3; loop_y++, dest_addr+=mempitch)
  {
  // draw the line
  Mem_Set_WORD(dest_addr+(unsigned int)(xs),
         color,(unsigned int)((int)xe-(int)xs+1));

  // adjust starting point and ending point
  xs+=dx_left;
  xe+=dx_right;
  } // end for
```

The only killer is the highlighted line, which makes the call to `Mem_Set_WORD()`. This is an inline function, but I still don't like the call, so that's something we might code directly with inline ASM to do the WORD move. Other things that disturb me are all the type conversions going on; this could potentially be a killer. Basically, I'm trying to implement the fill convention here for horizontal lines. And I'm only partially doing it because I'm not performing a ceiling operation on each scan line end point, so I'm overdrawing, but calling the `ceil()` function will take too long. Now, if we want to follow the fill convention explicitly, we need a faster `ceil()` function so that we can use it all the time and we have to really analyze how we're performing conversion to integer and so forth. The point is that this is an area for assembly language because the compiler is too coarse-grained to write tight code for this inner loop for us. Hence, we'll defer assembly optimization until the end of the book for the most part.

But let's briefly talk about the `ceil()` and `floor()` functions. They're implemented in standard C/C++ libraries and even though we're calling them only for the accurate version of the polygon rasterizer on a per-polygon basis, that's still 10–20,000 potential calls, so why not speed them up? One way to speed up the `ceil()` function is to write our own, based on the domain of numbers that we know are going to pass through it. In other words, we know that we're going to be rendering triangles that have coordinates somewhere in the range of `screen_width` × `screen_height` +- some negative and positive overlap, so it's possible to make a lookup table for `ceil()` and `floor()` based on this knowledge. For example, let's look at the functional mapping for the `ceil()` function for a second:

```
ceil(x) = { if x >= 0:
            if x=int(x) then ceil(x) = x
            else x=int(x)+1

     { if x < 0: ceil(x) = int(x)
```

Ultimately, the deciding factor for computing `ceil(x)` is if there's a decimal portion to x. If so, we bump x up to the next integer; otherwise, we leave x alone (for the *x* >= 0 case). For x < 0, we simply truncate the decimal portion. Here's an algorithm:

```
inline int Ceiling(float x)
{
if (x < 0) return (int)x;
else
if ((int)x < x) return((int)x+1);

} // end if
```

If you use inline floating point ASM, you can make this a few instructions. The analysis of `floor()` is similar. Hence, if you want to optimize these math functions, those are some ideas.

TIP

It's possible to convert ceiling to floor, and then use the modulus operator to compute the floor. However, all the work seems to cancel out in most cases, and I prefer the more straightforward approach. You might want to consult a math book on this transformation or try it yourself.

But the point of all this is to bring your attention to the simple fact that it doesn't matter how fast the floating-point processor or integer process is if you get penalized for conversions when you finally compute the integer pixel locations. That's why it makes sense sometimes to use fixed-point math: We can use a single data type `int` to perform all our math, and when it's time to rasterize, we simply use the upper 16 bits for the pixel locations. This makes a lot of sense, and is the approach I've taken for both the Gouraud shader and affine texture mapper.

Finally, although your main optimizations should always be focused on the innermost loops, as we saw, these polygon routines may be called 10–20,000 times each frame. Hence, anything you can shave off the "setup" phase per polygon is surely worth it. Thus, our philosophy of having a triangle function that breaks a triangle into a flat top, flat bottom, or general, and then makes either one or two calls to the specific polygon rasterizer might be a good place to optimize later and make rendering a polygon a single call.

Again, this is the strategy I took when writing the Gouraud shader and affine texture mapper; the rasterizers handle a general polygon all in one—no splitting.

Just food for thought. There are so many ways to rasterize triangles, and you can always make them faster. I would guess that you can get an approximate 2–10 times speed increase from what we have here if you muck with it, use assembly language, SIMD, and so forth.

Implementing Gouraud Shading

Alright, we're finally to the good part: the entire point of this chapter is to cover Gouraud shading and affine texture mapping, but we had to cover the preliminaries, you know! Anyway, take a look at Figure 9.22. It's a screenshot of the engine in action. Look at the colored lights on the textures and the smooth shading on the polygons— pretty cool, huh? Now let's see how this all works.

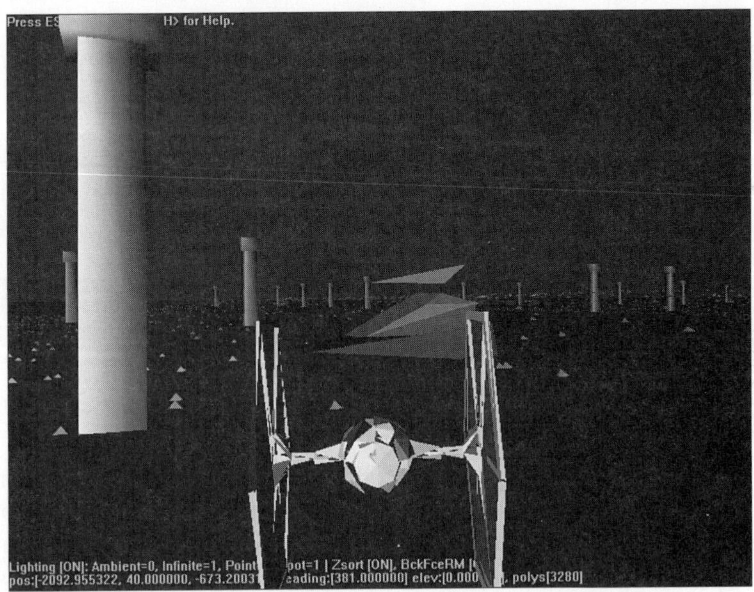

FIGURE 9.22 The Gouraud-shaded texture-mapped 3D engine in action.

As we discussed in the lighting material of the last chapter, Gouraud shading/lighting differs from flat shading in that instead of computing a single polygon normal per polygon and a light intensity for the entire surface, the Gouraud shading algorithm computes the light intensity at each vertex. When the rasterization phase occurs, the light intensities are interpolated across the triangle.

Figure 9.23 illustrates the interpolation process. Basically, we run the lighting engine for each polygon vertex normal rather than the single polygon normal, and then we compute the incident light intensity's RGB value, and store that value in the vertex as its color. We simply linearly interpolate the colors down the triangle and presto! We have a Gouraud-shaded polygon.

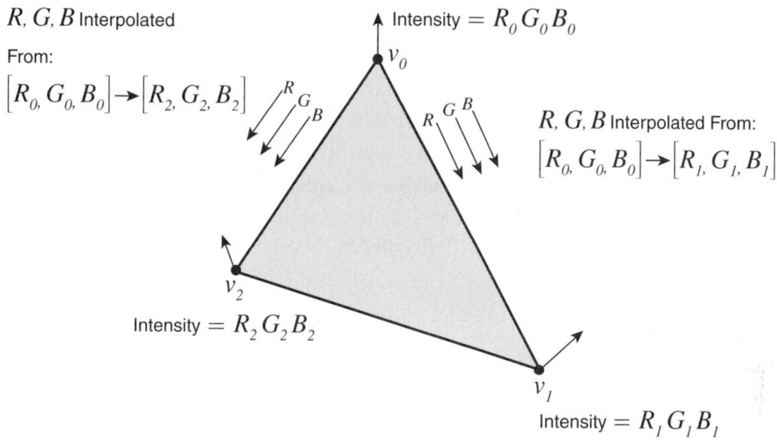

FIGURE 9.23 Gouraud interpolation across a polygon.

Now then, writing a Gouraud shading engine has two parts to it:

Part 1—We need a lighting engine that can compute light based on a surface normal, but we already have that. Therefore, all we need to do is light each vertex normal of any polygon that has Gouraud shading enabled and then compute the light intensities for each vertex.

Part 2—We need to write a Gouraud rasterizer that can handle different colors at each polygon vertex and interpolate between them.

Part 1 is already mostly done, so let's assume for a minute that we pass an `OBJECT4DV2` or a `RENDERLIST4DV2` through the lighting module and it outputs polygons lit as before: emissive, flat, and now Gouraud. If a polygon is Gouraud-shaded, the vertex colors for the lit vertices will be stored in `lit_color[0..2]`. Otherwise, for emissive and flat-shaded polys, `lit_color[0]` contains the color for the entire polygon. Therefore, if we assume that we have this lighting technology, the problem really become simple: We need a triangle rasterizer that rasterizes a single triangle, but such that it not only interpolates the pixels down the edges and draws lines from edge to edge, but also interpolates the colors from vertex to vertex and line to line. This is what we need to write.

Gouraud Shading Without Lighting

This section is so titled because I don't care how we get the vertex colors. They could be set manually, or computed with a light engine based on radiosity, or looked up as part of a static scene, whatever. The point is that I simply need to interpolate the values across the triangle as I'm rendering it. This problem is really simple and we've seen it many times now: interpolation.

Figure 9.24 illustrates the setup we need to implement. We have a general triangle with vertices **v0**, **v1**, **v2**, ordered as shown. Additionally, let's say that each vertex has a full RGB color in 8.8.8 format. Now, when we rasterized a triangle, what did we do? We computed the left and right edge gradients and called them `dx_left` and `dx_right`. Basically these gradients were nothing more than the change in x relative to the change in y; thus, as we moved from scan line to scan line we simply added `dx_left` and `dx_right` to the starting and ending x positions on the scan line and then drew a line. This is exactly what we need to do to Gouraud shade—we need to interpolate the colors down the edges of the triangle as a function of y. Let's try to do this for a simplified intensity-only version with some pseudo code. Writing an RGB version is the same; we simply need to do it three times, once for each color channel. Now, I'm not going to worry about fill convention, vertex sorting, and things like that right now, I just want to get the interpolation under control.

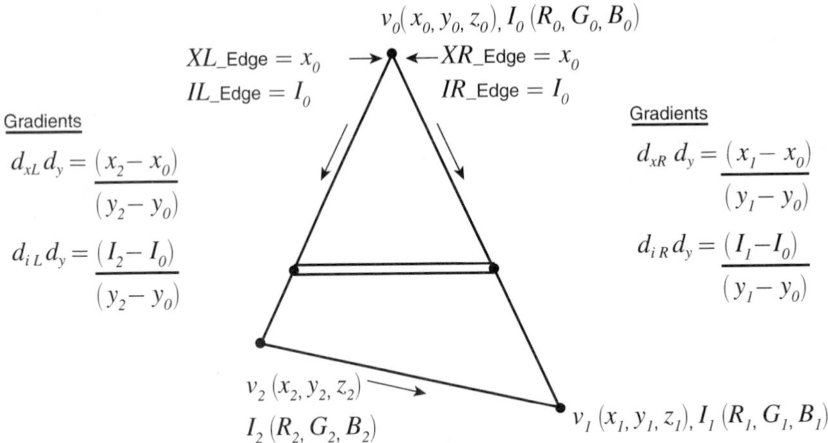

FIGURE 9.24 The setup for Gouraud interpolation.

Let's begin by working through the interpolation manually so that you can see what's going on. I'll use slightly different variable names in the final functions. These are just to make things easy for discussion. Anyway, referring to Figure 9.24, we see a general triangle labeled as before with vertices `v0`, `v1`, and `v2` in a clockwise fashion. Additionally, you see quite a few Vulcan-looking markings—these are all the gradients and coordinate location labels. Let's interpolate this triangle step by step:

Step 1: Initial setup and computation of left and right edge gradients.

These variables track the positions of the interpolation on the left and right edges of the triangle:

```
xl_edge = x0
xr_edge = x0
```

These variables track the intensity interpolation on the left and right edges of the triangle:

```
il_edge = i0
ir_edge = i0
```

Step 2: Compute all left and right gradients as a function of y.

This is the left edge gradient for the change in x with respect to y; the standard rasterization gradient:

```
dxldy = (x2 - x0)/(y2 - y0)
```

Similar for the right edge:

```
dxrdy = (x1 - x0)/(y1 - y0)
```

Now compute the intensity gradients. These are the changes in intensity as a function of y:

```
dildy = (i2 - i0)/(y2 - y0)
```

Similar for the right edge:

```
dirdy = (i1 - i0)/(y1 - y0)
```

Step 3: Enter into the y loop, for y = y0 to y2 (first half of the triangle).

Step 4: The horizontal rasterization step. At this point, we're going to draw a single scan line, but we have to draw it a pixel at a time because we're interpolating both vertically and horizontally.

Set up starting points for x and intensity:

```
i = il_edge
x = xl_edge
```

Compute horizontal intensity gradient i as a function of x:

```
dix = (ir_edge - il_edge) / (xr_edge - xl_edge)
```

Step 5: Rasterize line pixel by pixel with interpolation:

```
For (x = xl_edge to xr_edge)
   begin
   setpixel(x,y,i)
```

```
// update the intensity
i = i + dix
end
```

Step 6: Update vertical interpolants and loop.

First normal rasterization left and right edge positions:

```
xl_edge = xl_edge + dxldy
xr_edge = xr_edge + dyrdy
```

Now, update intensity interpolation values:

```
il_edge = il_edge + dildy
ir_edge = ir_edge + dirdy
```

Next y interation.

Step 7: Perform the same logic for the bottom half of the triangle, but update left edge gradients to reflect terminal vertex `v1`.

Take some time to review the pseudo-code algorithm to make sure that you understand it, but in a nutshell the rasterization works identically to the standard triangle rasterization except that we're tracking the intensities down the left and right edges of the triangle. For each scan line, instead of drawing a constant colored line, we must interpolate the scan line intensity from left to right where the value being interpolated is the current intensity on the left and right edge of the triangle. Now, just for fun, let's completely convert the pseudo-code to rough C/C++ code to see the entire algorithm at once:

```
void Draw_Gouraud_Triangle(float x0, float y0, float i0, // vertex 0
              float x0, float y0, float i0, // vertex 1
              float x0, float y0, float i0, // vertex 2
{
// assume that vertex positions are in the form as shown
// in the figure

// initialize positions
xl_edge = x0;
xr_edge = x0;


// initialize intensities
il_edge = i0;
ir_edge = i0;

// initialize vertical edge gradients
dxldy = (x2 - x0)/(y2 - y0);
```

```
dxrdy = (x1 - x0)/(y1 - y0);
dildy = (i2 - i0)/(y2 - y0);
dildy = (i1 - i0)/(y1 - y0);

// enter into y loop (first half of triangle only)
for (y=y0; y < y2; y++)
  {
  // setup starting points for x and intensity
  i = il_edge
  x = xl_edge

  // compute horizontal intensity gradient i
  // as a function of x:
  dix = (ir_edge - il_edge) / (xr_edge - xl_edge);

  // Rasterize line pixel by pixel with interpolation

  for (x = xl_edge; x < xr_edge; x++)
    {
     // draw the pixel at (x,y) with intensity i
     setpixel(x,y,i);

     // update the intensity
     i = i + dix
     } // end for


  // update vertical interpolants and loop
  xl_edge = xl_edge + dxldy;
  xr_edge = xr_edge + dyrdy;
  il_edge = il_edge + dildy;
  ir_edge = ir_edge + dirdy;

  } // end for y

// add code for second half of triangle here, need to
// update the left side gradients only and then perform
// same logic

} // end Draw_Gouraud_Triangle
```

In summary, rendering a Gouraud-shaded triangle or, more technically, rasterizing a triangle where the intensity or colors at each vertex are smoothly interpolated from vertex to vertex both vertically and horizontally, is nothing more than what's shown in the earlier pseudo-code and the minimal C/C++ function. So, what do we need to do this for real? Well, truthfully, we just need to interpolate red, green, and blue, instead of a single "intensity" values. For the final scan line horizontal interpolation, when we write the pixel, we just build the pixel back up. Or, in other words, we interpolate RGB down the left and right edge of the triangle, For every scan line, we interpolate RGB across the scan line, as shown in Figure 9.25.

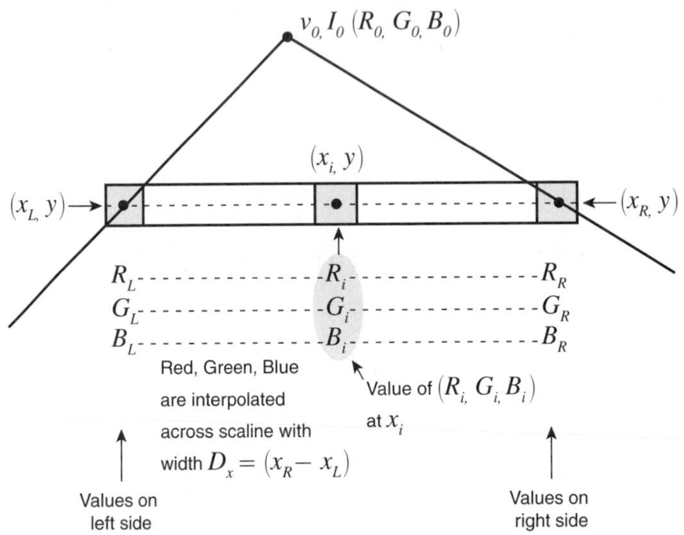

FIGURE 9.25 Rasterizing a single scan line with full-colored Gouraud shading.

The only program with all this interpolation is speed. We're interpolating six color channels and two rasterization channels, for a total of two values down the left and right edges in total. Furthermore, when we draw the scan line, we have to interpolate the RGB color from the left to right side of the scan line, which is three channels, as shown in Figure 9.25. This stuff has to go fast!

Keeping all that in mind, I wrote this a couple times, and I ended up using fixed-point 16.16 math. I did that not because fixed-point is faster than floating-point, but because I wanted to avoid the final floating-point-to-integral conversions when writing pixels and computing final RGB words because the compiler likes to use crappy code when doing this. I also wanted to avoid assembly at this point. In any case, I've decided to include the function listing even though it's rather large. This will be the only function listing I'm going to include in this chapter because the code is so long and complex. However, I think it's worth it because the code is written in a RISC-like manner to take advantage of the pipelining of the Pentium processors, so I've really coded things in a long drawn-out manner to get as much parallelism as possible. Of course, the function is approximately 30 pages, so I can't list it in its entirety. I'm going to only list the first triangle case handled in the code, but that contains everything you need to see:

```
void Draw_Gouraud_Triangle16(POLYF4DV2_PTR face,  // ptr to face
          UCHAR *_dest_buffer, // pointer to video buffer
          int mem_pitch)    // bytes per line, 320, 640 etc.
{
// this function draws a gouraud shaded polygon,
// based on the affine texture mapper, instead
// of interpolating the texture coordinates,
// we simply interpolate the (R,G,B) values across
// the polygons, I simply needed at another interpolant,
// I have mapped u->red, v->green, w->blue

int v0=0,
  v1=1,
  v2=2,
  temp=0,
  tri_type = TRI_TYPE_NONE,
  irestart = INTERP_LHS;

int dx,dy,dyl,dyr,    // general deltas
  u,v,w,
  du,dv,dw,
  xi,yi,       // the current interpolated x,y
  ui,vi,wi,      // the current interpolated u,v
  index_x,index_y,  // looping vars
  x,y,        // hold general x,y
  xstart, xend, ystart, yrestart, yend, xl,
  dxdyl, xr, dxdyr, dudyl, ul, dvdyl, vl, dwdyl,
  wl, dudyr, ur, dvdyr, vr, dwdyr, wr;

int x0,y0,tu0,tv0,tw0,  // cached vertices
  x1,y1,tu1,tv1,tw1,
  x2,y2,tu2,tv2,tw2;

int r_base0, g_base0, b_base0, // base colors
  r_base1, g_base1, b_base1,
  r_base2, g_base2, b_base2;

USHORT *screen_ptr = NULL,
    *screen_line = NULL,
    *textmap   = NULL,
    *dest_buffer = (USHORT *)_dest_buffer;

#ifdef DEBUG_ON
  // track rendering stats
```

```
  debug_polys_rendered_per_frame++;
#endif

// adjust memory pitch to words, divide by 2
mem_pitch >>=1;

// first trivial clipping rejection tests
if (((face->tvlist[0].y < min_clip_y) &&
   (face->tvlist[1].y < min_clip_y) &&
   (face->tvlist[2].y < min_clip_y)) ||

  ((face->tvlist[0].y > max_clip_y) &&
   (face->tvlist[1].y > max_clip_y) &&
   (face->tvlist[2].y > max_clip_y)) ||

  ((face->tvlist[0].x < min_clip_x) &&
   (face->tvlist[1].x < min_clip_x) &&
   (face->tvlist[2].x < min_clip_x)) ||

  ((face->tvlist[0].x > max_clip_x) &&
   (face->tvlist[1].x > max_clip_x) &&
   (face->tvlist[2].x > max_clip_x)))
  return;

// degenerate triangle
if ( ((face->tvlist[0].x==face->tvlist[1].x) &&
   (face->tvlist[1].x==face->tvlist[2].x)) ||
   ((face->tvlist[0].y==face->tvlist[1].y) &&
     (face->tvlist[1].y==face->tvlist[2].y)))
  return;

// sort vertices
if (face->tvlist[v1].y < face->tvlist[v0].y)
  {SWAP(v0,v1,temp);}

if (face->tvlist[v2].y < face->tvlist[v0].y)
  {SWAP(v0,v2,temp);}

if (face->tvlist[v2].y < face->tvlist[v1].y)
  {SWAP(v1,v2,temp);}

// now test for trivial flat sided cases
if (face->tvlist[v0].y==face->tvlist[v1].y)
  {
```

```
    // set triangle type
    tri_type = TRI_TYPE_FLAT_TOP;

    // sort vertices left to right
    if (face->tvlist[v1].x < face->tvlist[v0].x)
      {SWAP(v0,v1,temp);}

    } // end if
else
// now test for trivial flat sided cases
if (face->tvlist[v1].y==face->tvlist[v2].y)
    {
    // set triangle type
    tri_type = TRI_TYPE_FLAT_BOTTOM;
    // sort vertices left to right
    if (face->tvlist[v2].x < face->tvlist[v1].x)
      {SWAP(v1,v2,temp);}
    } // end if
else
    {
    // must be a general triangle
    tri_type = TRI_TYPE_GENERAL;
    } // end else

// assume 5.6.5 format -- sorry!
// we can't afford a function call in the inner loops, so we must write
// two hard coded versions, if we want support for both 5.6.5, and 5.5.5
_RGB565FROM16BIT(face->lit_color[v0], &r_base0, &g_base0, &b_base0);
_RGB565FROM16BIT(face->lit_color[v1], &r_base1, &g_base1, &b_base1);
_RGB565FROM16BIT(face->lit_color[v2], &r_base2, &g_base2, &b_base2);
// scale to 8 bit
r_base0 <<= 3; g_base0 <<= 2; b_base0 <<= 3;
// scale to 8 bit
r_base1 <<= 3; g_base1 <<= 2; b_base1 <<= 3;
// scale to 8 bit
r_base2 <<= 3; g_base2 <<= 2; b_base2 <<= 3;

// extract vertices for processing, now that we have order
x0 = (int)(face->tvlist[v0].x+0.5);
y0 = (int)(face->tvlist[v0].y+0.5);

tu0 = r_base0; tv0 = g_base0; tw0 = b_base0;
```

```
x1 = (int)(face->tvlist[v1].x+0.5);
y1 = (int)(face->tvlist[v1].y+0.5);

tu1 = r_base1; tv1 = g_base1; tw1 = b_base1;

x2 = (int)(face->tvlist[v2].x+0.5);
y2 = (int)(face->tvlist[v2].y+0.5);

tu2 = r_base2; tv2 = g_base2; tw2 = b_base2;

// set interpolation restart value
yrestart = y1;

// what kind of triangle
if (tri_type & TRI_TYPE_FLAT_MASK)
  {
  if (tri_type == TRI_TYPE_FLAT_TOP)
  {
  // compute all deltas
  dy = (y2 - y0);
  dxdyl = ((x2 - x0)  << FIXP16_SHIFT)/dy;
  dudyl = ((tu2 - tu0) << FIXP16_SHIFT)/dy;
  dvdyl = ((tv2 - tv0) << FIXP16_SHIFT)/dy;
  dwdyl = ((tw2 - tw0) << FIXP16_SHIFT)/dy;
  dxdyr = ((x2 - x1)  << FIXP16_SHIFT)/dy;
  dudyr = ((tu2 - tu1) << FIXP16_SHIFT)/dy;
  dvdyr = ((tv2 - tv1) << FIXP16_SHIFT)/dy;
  dwdyr = ((tw2 - tw1) << FIXP16_SHIFT)/dy;

  // test for y clipping
  if (y0 < min_clip_y)
    {
    // compute overclip
    dy = (min_clip_y - y0);
    // computer new LHS starting values
    xl = dxdyl*dy + (x0 << FIXP16_SHIFT);
    ul = dudyl*dy + (tu0 << FIXP16_SHIFT);
    vl = dvdyl*dy + (tv0 << FIXP16_SHIFT);
    wl = dwdyl*dy + (tw0 << FIXP16_SHIFT);
    // compute new RHS starting values
    xr = dxdyr*dy + (x1 << FIXP16_SHIFT);
    ur = dudyr*dy + (tu1 << FIXP16_SHIFT);
    vr = dvdyr*dy + (tv1 << FIXP16_SHIFT);
    wr = dwdyr*dy + (tw1 << FIXP16_SHIFT);
```

```
  // compute new starting y
  ystart = min_clip_y;
  } // end if
else
  {
  // no clipping
  // set starting values
  xl = (x0 << FIXP16_SHIFT);
  xr = (x1 << FIXP16_SHIFT);
  ul = (tu0 << FIXP16_SHIFT);
  vl = (tv0 << FIXP16_SHIFT);
  wl = (tw0 << FIXP16_SHIFT);
  ur = (tu1 << FIXP16_SHIFT);
  vr = (tv1 << FIXP16_SHIFT);
  wr = (tw1 << FIXP16_SHIFT);
  // set starting y
  ystart = y0;
  } // end else

} // end if flat top
else
{
// must be flat bottom
// compute all deltas
dy = (y1 - y0);
dxdyl = ((x1 - x0)  << FIXP16_SHIFT)/dy;
dudyl = ((tu1 - tu0) << FIXP16_SHIFT)/dy;
dvdyl = ((tv1 - tv0) << FIXP16_SHIFT)/dy;
dwdyl = ((tw1 - tw0) << FIXP16_SHIFT)/dy;
dxdyr = ((x2 - x0)  << FIXP16_SHIFT)/dy;
dudyr = ((tu2 - tu0) << FIXP16_SHIFT)/dy;
dvdyr = ((tv2 - tv0) << FIXP16_SHIFT)/dy;
dwdyr = ((tw2 - tw0) << FIXP16_SHIFT)/dy;

// test for y clipping
if (y0 < min_clip_y)
  {
  // compute overclip
  dy = (min_clip_y - y0);
  // computer new LHS starting values
  xl = dxdyl*dy + (x0 << FIXP16_SHIFT);
  ul = dudyl*dy + (tu0 << FIXP16_SHIFT);
  vl = dvdyl*dy + (tv0 << FIXP16_SHIFT);
```

```
    wl = dwdyl*dy + (tw0 << FIXP16_SHIFT);
    // compute new RHS starting values
    xr = dxdyr*dy + (x0 << FIXP16_SHIFT);
    ur = dudyr*dy + (tu0 << FIXP16_SHIFT);
    vr = dvdyr*dy + (tv0 << FIXP16_SHIFT);
    wr = dwdyr*dy + (tw0 << FIXP16_SHIFT);
    // compute new starting y
    ystart = min_clip_y;
    } // end if
  else
    {
    // no clipping
    // set starting values
    xl = (x0 << FIXP16_SHIFT);
    xr = (x0 << FIXP16_SHIFT);
    ul = (tu0 << FIXP16_SHIFT);
    vl = (tv0 << FIXP16_SHIFT);
    wl = (tw0 << FIXP16_SHIFT);
    ur = (tu0 << FIXP16_SHIFT);
    vr = (tv0 << FIXP16_SHIFT);
    wr = (tw0 << FIXP16_SHIFT);
    // set starting y
    ystart = y0;
    } // end else
  } // end else flat bottom
  // test for bottom clip, always
  if ((yend = y2) > max_clip_y)
    yend = max_clip_y;

    // test for horizontal clipping
  if ((x0 < min_clip_x) || (x0 > max_clip_x) ||
    (x1 < min_clip_x) || (x1 > max_clip_x) ||
    (x2 < min_clip_x) || (x2 > max_clip_x))
  {
    // clip version
  // point screen ptr to starting line
  screen_ptr = dest_buffer + (ystart * mem_pitch);
  for (yi = ystart; yi<=yend; yi++)
    {
    // compute span endpoints
    xstart = ((xl + FIXP16_ROUND_UP) >> FIXP16_SHIFT);
    xend  = ((xr + FIXP16_ROUND_UP) >> FIXP16_SHIFT);
    // compute starting points for u,v,w interpolants
```

```
ui = ul + FIXP16_ROUND_UP;
vi = vl + FIXP16_ROUND_UP;
wi = wl + FIXP16_ROUND_UP;
// compute u,v interpolants
if ((dx = (xend - xstart))>0)
  {
  du = (ur - ul)/dx;
  dv = (vr - vl)/dx;
  dw = (wr - wl)/dx;
  } // end if
else
  {
  du = (ur - ul);
  dv = (vr - vl);
  dw = (wr - wl);
  } // end else

///////////////////////////////////////////////////////////////////////

// test for x clipping, LHS
if (xstart < min_clip_x)
  {
  // compute x overlap
  dx = min_clip_x - xstart;

  // slide interpolants over
  ui+=dx*du;
  vi+=dx*dv;
  wi+=dx*dw;

  // reset vars
  xstart = min_clip_x;
  } // end if

// test for x clipping RHS
if (xend > max_clip_x)
  xend = max_clip_x;

///////////////////////////////////////////////////////////////////////

// draw span
for (xi=xstart; xi<=xend; xi++)
{
```

```
// write textel assume 5.6.5
  screen_ptr[xi] = ((ui >> (FIXP16_SHIFT+3)) << 11) +
             ((vi >> (FIXP16_SHIFT+2)) << 5) +
              (wi >> (FIXP16_SHIFT+3));

   // interpolate u,v
   ui+=du;
   vi+=dv;
   wi+=dw;
   } // end for xi

  // interpolate u,v,w,x along right and left edge
  xl+=dxdyl;
  ul+=dudyl;
  vl+=dvdyl;
  wl+=dwdyl;
  xr+=dxdyr;
  ur+=dudyr;
  vr+=dvdyr;
  wr+=dwdyr;
  // advance screen ptr
  screen_ptr+=mem_pitch;
  } // end for y

 } // end if clip

// . REMOVED NON-CLIPPED SUB-CASE to allow listing in book!!!!

 } // end if

// . REMOVED GENERAL CASE to allow listing in book!!!!

} // end Draw_Gouraud_Triangle16
```

What you're looking at is the 16-bit version of the Gouraud shader. This function `Draw_Gouraud_Triangle16()` has no concept of lighting or any of that; all it does is interpolate the vertex colors it finds in `lit_color[]` down the triangle. Now, there's some bad news: I've decided to use 5.6.5 format from now on where speed is important. In other words, I'm losing speed here and there by asking the question of what mode we're in or using the function pointers to access the correct bit-merging functions. Because 99.9% of cards are all 5.6.5, this shouldn't be a problem. However, if you happen to have a 5.5.5 card, you can rewrite the code that does the bit manipulations manually. For example, look at the inner horizontal loop rasterizer in the earlier function as shown in the following:

```
// draw span
for (xi=xstart; xi<=xend; xi++)
  {
  // write textel assume 5.6.5
  screen_ptr[xi] = ((ui >> (FIXP16_SHIFT+3)) << 11) +
           ((vi >> (FIXP16_SHIFT+2)) << 5) +
           (wi >> (FIXP16_SHIFT+3));
  // interpolate u,v,w
  ui+=du;
  vi+=dv;
  wi+=dw;
  } // end for xi
```

If you look closely at the final pixel assignment, I'm manually writing a 5.6.5 pixel. I would hate to make any calls here, so this is my motivation. If you need to change it, you will have to do so in anything that draws to the screen, but it's easy to find because you'll always see the shifting and masking operations, and I also comment it.

NOTE

You might be wondering why I have called the interpolants u, v, and w. Well, I actually wrote the texture mapper first, and instead of going nuts renaming everything to r, g, and b, I just used the texture mapper, which uses u and v, and added a w. Thus u, v, and w maps to red, green, and blue. They're just variable names, so if they bug you, YOU change them! There are too many of them and even with text replace, and changing them is asking for bugs.

Cool, so let's take a look at a demo of the Gouraud shader, which is nothing more than drawing triangles. Figure 9.26 is a screenshot of `DEMOII9_1.CPP¦EXE` in action. Try running the program for yourself. It randomly selects a vertex position for a triangle along with colors and then calls the Gouraud triangle function. Also, there's an 8-bit version called `DEMOII9_1_8b.CPP¦EXE`.

Adding Vertex Lighting for the Gouraud Shader

The next step is to use our lighting engine functions to actually compute the light intensity at each vertex, resulting in a final RGB color for each vertex. When we call the Gouraud shader function as a replacement for the standard flat shader function, presto! We have Gouraud-shaded triangles that change as a function of the lighting in the scene. So, let's reiterate what needs to be done to make this work. We already created new polygon structures that have color arrays to hold the final lit colors after the lighting stage. This array is named `lit_color[]` and it has three slots, one for each triangle vertex. Thus, all we really need to do is take our lighting function that lights either the rendering list or an object itself, and modify it so that it knows how to light emissive, flat-, and Gouraud-shaded polygons.

FIGURE 9.26 A screenshot of the Gouraud triangle rendering function in action.

We already have it working for emissive and flat-shaded polygons. In the case of emissive, the function does nothing but copy the polygon color field directly into `lit_color[0]` and it's done. But for flat-shaded polygons, the function processes each light that's active in the system and lights the polygon based on it's base color and it's normal. Hence, we simply need to copy this functionality in another loop so that polygons that are Gouraud-shaded will be lit on a vertex-by-vertex basis. This process is shown in Figure 9.27, where we see polygons coming down the pipeline, the lighting engine performing the lighting calculations on each polygon, and the steps that are involved.

As you can see in the figure, we basically need to replicate the lighting code to light Gouraud-shaded polygons to take into consideration that Gouraud-shaded polygons have their normals stored in the `VERTEX4DTV1` structure in the `n` (normal) field, and that's about it! The only downside, of course, is the triple calculations that must be performed for each polygon because we have to recompute the light for each vertex—ouch! However, there are some optimizations that we can apply here and I'll discuss them later in the section.

That's all good, so let's take a look at the new lighting functions that support vertex lighting and Gouraud shading for both 16- and 8-bit modes.

16-Bit Gouraud Lighting

As outlined earlier, adding vertex lighting support to the lighting functions is rather easy. It's nothing more than code copying and changing the polygon normals used for the flat shading to the vertex normals and performing the lighting three times, or once for each vertex. However, the only problem is that the lighting function becomes rather complicated because of this, and each polygon can take quite a long time to process. That's why you don't see too many software-based, colored-light systems with Gouraud shading. But this one isn't bad, and it's even fast enough for games.

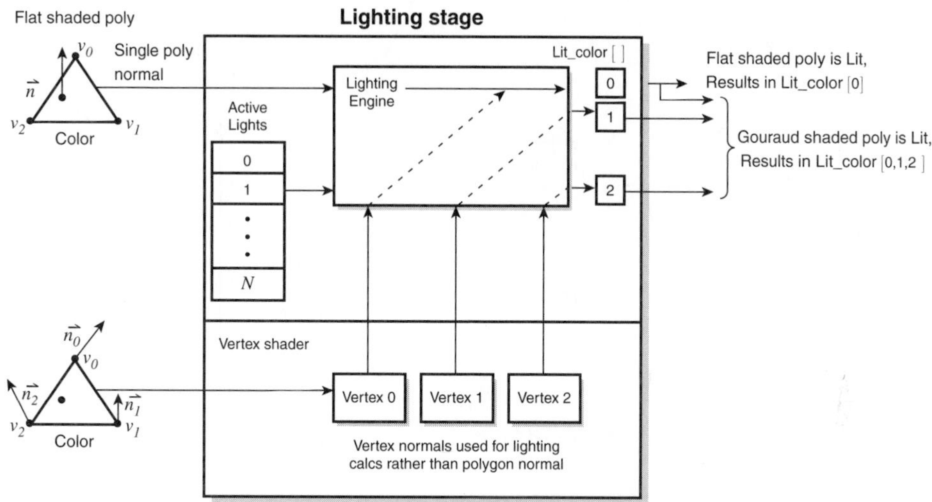

FIGURE 9.27 The new lighting pipeline supports both flat shading and Gouraud shading.

We need to rewrite two functions to enable Gouraud lighting; they're the object-based lighting function and the rendering list–based lighting function. I'm going to show you the rendering list version because we've been doing most of our work at the rendering list level, including lighting. Although even in the previous version of the engine, we had both object-level and rendering list–level lighting functions for both 8- and 16-bit, we tended to use the rendering list version. However, Gouraud lighting has a twist that necessitates a rethinking of this in relation to optimization.

Here's the deal. Take a look at Figure 9.28. We see a cube as a unified object and as separate polygons in a rendering list. The problem is that while in its `OBJECT4DV2` form, the cube only has eight vertex normal (because there are only eight vertices). But once the cube is "ripped" and inserted into the rendering list, the cube now has 12*3 = 36 vertex normals! This is of course due to the fact that we create a totally self-contained polygon for each polygon in the rendering list and we completely forego all indirection.

Alas, if we perform lighting at the `OBJECT4DV2` phase—that is, while an object is still intact as a single mesh—we can take advantage of the minimum number of vertex normals. However, if we wait until the object has been converted into polygons and then light the rendering list, we take a 300% or more over calculation hit recalculating copied vertex normals. This is obviously not acceptable and something we'll need to address later when we optimize.

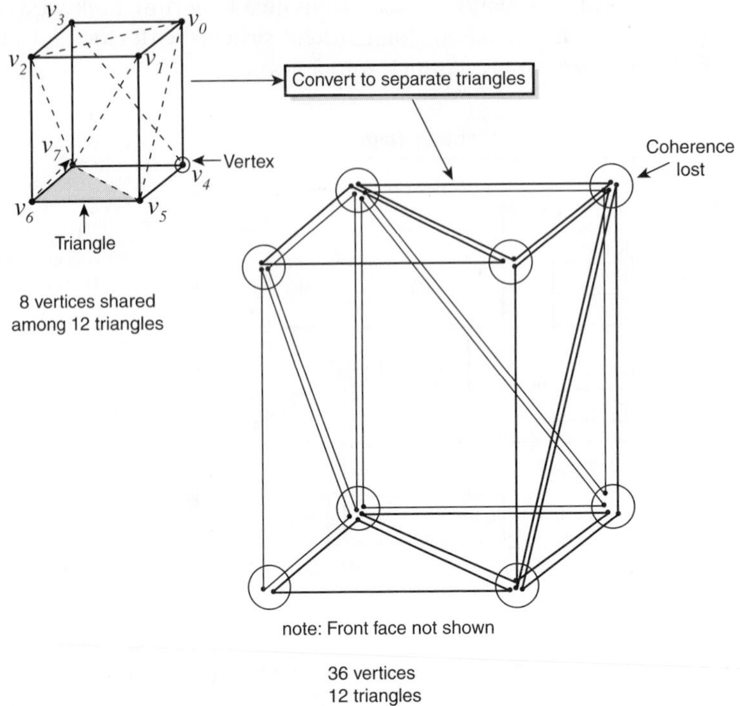

FIGURE 9.28 Objects have vertex coherence while intact, but once converted to polygons they lose coherence.

To that end, both the object-based lighting functions and the rendering list lighting functions light three vertex normals for each polygon. Even though the object lighting function could "tag" vertices it has already lit so that we can minimize calculations, this is complicated to get working for a first iteration, so I wanted to lay off it for now, but keep it in mind.

The reason it's complicated is that when a vertex is lit and the final vertex colors are computed and stored in `lit_colors[]`, the base color of the polygon that contains those vertices is used in the lighting calculations. Hence, to reuse vertices that have been lit, we have to break the lighting into two steps: the first step is an intensity-only lighting phase where we tag lit vertices and don't light them again for other polygons that share them. Then there's a post-processing step where we take the final vertex intensities and then modulate them by each polygon's actual color. The details of this make the code messy, and we're dealing with enough stuff right now. However, this is an optimization that I'll use in upcoming chapters, so keep your eyes peeled, or you may like to do it now yourself.

In any case, let's take a look at the 16-bit lighting functions in the source on the CD. They're way too large to list in the book (30+ pages), but basically we have two new functions:

```
int Light_RENDERLIST4DV2_World16(RENDERLIST4DV2_PTR rend_list,// list
            CAM4DV1_PTR cam,   // camera position
            LIGHTV1_PTR lights, // light list
            int max_lights)   // maximum lights in list
```

And the object-based version:

```
int Light_OBJECT4DV2_World16(OBJECT4DV2_PTR obj,// object to process
            CAM4DV1_PTR cam,  // camera position
            LIGHTV1_PTR lights,// light list
            int max_lights)  // maximum lights in list
```

The functions work in the same way as the previous versions did in the last chapter. What's changed are the versions of the rendering list and the objects themselves; other than that, there's nothing new to calling them. However, I do want to excerpt some code from the functions to show you some interesting additions in relation to the Gouraud shading. As I said, the functions are way too big to list, but let's at least take a look at some of the internal Gouraud shading code. Here's an example of the code that performs the ambient and infinite lighting calculations on a per-vertex basis in the Gouraud shading section of the code:

```
if (curr_poly->attr & POLY4DV2_ATTR_SHADE_MODE_GOURAUD) /////////////////
  {
  // gouraud shade, unfortunetly at this point in the pipeline,
  // we have lost the original mesh, and only have triangles,
  // thus, many triangles will share the same vertices and
  // they will get lit 2x since we don't have any way to tell this,
  // alas, performing lighting at the object level is a better idea
  // when gouraud shading is performed since the commonality of vertices
  // is still intact, in any case, lighting here is similar to polygon
  // flat shaded, but we do it 3 times, once for each vertex,
  // additionally there are lots of opportunities for optimization,
  // but I am going to lay off them for now, so the code
  // is intelligible, later we will optimize

  // step 1: extract the base color out in RGB mode
  // assume 565 format
  _RGB565FROM16BIT(curr_poly->color, &r_base, &g_base, &b_base);

  // scale to 8 bit
  r_base <<= 3;  g_base <<= 2;  b_base <<= 3;

  // initialize color sum(s) for vertices
  r_sum0 = 0;  g_sum0 = 0;  b_sum0 = 0;
```

```
r_sum1 = 0;  g_sum1 = 0;  b_sum1 = 0;
r_sum2 = 0;  g_sum2 = 0;  b_sum2 = 0;

  // new optimization:
  // when there are multiple lights in the system we will end up
  // performing numerous redundant calculations to minimize this
  // my strategy is to set key variables to to MAX values on each
  // loop then during the lighting calcs to test the vars for
  // the max value, if they are the max value then the first
  // light that needs the math will do it, and then save the
  // information into the variable (causing it to change state
  // from an invalid number) then any other lights that need
  // the math can use the previously computed value
  // loop thru lights
  for (int curr_light = 0; curr_light < max_lights; curr_light++)
    {
    // is this light active
    if (lights[curr_light].state==LIGHTV1_STATE_OFF)
     continue;

    // what kind of light are we dealing with
    if (lights[curr_light].attr & LIGHTV1_ATTR_AMBIENT) ///////////
     {
     // simply multiply each channel against the color of the
     // polygon then divide by 256 to scale back to 0..255
     // use a shift in real life!!! >> 8
     ri = ((lights[curr_light].c_ambient.r * r_base) / 256);
     gi = ((lights[curr_light].c_ambient.g * g_base) / 256);
     bi = ((lights[curr_light].c_ambient.b * b_base) / 256);

     // ambient light has the same affect on each vertex
     r_sum0+=ri; g_sum0+=gi; b_sum0+=bi;
     r_sum1+=ri; g_sum1+=gi; b_sum1+=bi;
     r_sum2+=ri; g_sum2+=gi; b_sum2+=bi;
     } // end if
    else
    if (lights[curr_light].attr & LIGHTV1_ATTR_INFINITE) //////////
     {
     // infinite lighting, we need the surface normal,
     // and the direction
     // of the light source
     // no longer need to compute normal or length,
     // we already have the vertex normal
     // and it's length is 1.0
```

```
// ....
// ok, recalling the lighting model for infinite lights
// I(d)dir = I0dir * Cldir
// and for the diffuse model
// Itotald =  Rsdiffuse*Idiffuse * (n . l)
// so we basically need to multiple it all together
// notice the scaling by 128, I want to avoid floating point
// calculations not because they are slower,
// but the conversion to and from cost cycles

// need to perform lighting for each vertex

// vertex 0
dp = VECTOR4D_Dot(&curr_poly->tvlist[0].n,
         &lights[curr_light].dir);

// only add light if dp > 0
if (dp > 0)
  {
  i = 128*dp;
  r_sum0+= (lights[curr_light].c_diffuse.r * r_base * i) /
      (256*128);
  g_sum0+= (lights[curr_light].c_diffuse.g * g_base * i) /
      (256*128);
  b_sum0+= (lights[curr_light].c_diffuse.b * b_base * i) /
      (256*128);
  } // end if

// vertex 1
dp = VECTOR4D_Dot(&curr_poly->tvlist[1].n,
         &lights[curr_light].dir);

// only add light if dp > 0
if (dp > 0)
  {
  i = 128*dp;
  r_sum1+= (lights[curr_light].c_diffuse.r * r_base * i) /
      (256*128);
  g_sum1+= (lights[curr_light].c_diffuse.g * g_base * i) /
      (256*128);
  b_sum1+= (lights[curr_light].c_diffuse.b * b_base * i) /
      (256*128);
  } // end if
```

```
        // vertex 2
        dp = VECTOR4D_Dot(&curr_poly->tvlist[2].n,
                &lights[curr_light].dir);

        // only add light if dp > 0
        if (dp > 0)
          {
          i = 128*dp;
          r_sum2+= (lights[curr_light].c_diffuse.r * r_base * i) /
              (256*128);
          g_sum2+= (lights[curr_light].c_diffuse.g * g_base * i) /
              (256*128);
          b_sum2+= (lights[curr_light].c_diffuse.b * b_base * i) /
              (256*128);
          } // end if

       } // end if infinite light
```

If you review this code, you'll notice that I'm using `r_sum0..2`, `g_sum0..2`, and `b_sum0..2` to store the red, green, and blue vertex results for vertices 0..2. And, of course, the base polygon color that's lit is `r_base`, `g_base`, and `b_base`. The calculations are the same as the flat-shaded calculations except they're tripled. I've highlighted the vertex calculations in the infinite light model so that you can see the redundancy.

However, there's a very interesting optimization that I've introduced into the new lighting functions—I call it *calculation caching*. Basically, I analyze the lighting loops and as each polygon is lit, we process multiple lights over the polygon surface: ambient, infinite, point, spotlights, and so forth. However, in each of these subcalculations, we recompute everything, meaning that if we need the distance from a light source to a polygon, we compute it; if we need the normal, we compute it; and so forth. The trick is to find common calculations that are light source invariant and cache them. For example, the distance to the light source is variant because it changes for each light. However, the polygon normal does not vary from light source to light source. Therefore, this is a candidate for caching. This is a great way to speed up the lighting, but it works only if you have multiple lights. I haven't gone nuts with it, and I've implemented only the surface normal calculation that's common in the point and spotlight calculations, but later I'll revisit the optimization and be more aggressive about it.

Unfortunately, the Gouraud shading excerpt can't take advantage of this. However, the flat shading section can. Therefore, here's an excerpt from the flat shading portion of the function that uses the optimization. It begins right before the light loop that processes each light:

```
// set surface normal.z to FLT_MAX to flag it as non-computed
n.z = FLT_MAX;

// loop thru lights
for (int curr_light = 0; curr_light < max_lights; curr_light++)
  {
```

I simply set one of the normal vector's components to infinity for all intents and purposes to "tag" it as invalid, and then during the lighting loop, light models that need the normal contained in this code:

```
// test if we already computed poly normal in previous calculation
if (n.z==FLT_MAX)
  {
  // we need to compute the normal of this polygon face, and recall
  // that the vertices are in cw order, u=p0->p1, v=p0->p2, n=uxv

  // build u, v
  VECTOR4D_Build(&curr_poly->tvlist[0].v, &curr_poly->tvlist[1].v, &u);
  VECTOR4D_Build(&curr_poly->tvlist[0].v, &curr_poly->tvlist[2].v, &v);

  // compute cross product
  VECTOR4D_Cross(&u, &v, &n);
  } // end if
```

A test is performed on `n.z`, and if it's still `FLT_MAX`, it's computed; otherwise, it's passed over. Therefore, if you have eight point lights, the normal will be computed only once! Pretty cool, huh?

TIP

This strategy can really speed things up, but, you can go too far and assume there will be lots of lights when in fact your game may only have one or two. In such a case, this optimization actually slows things down, so if you indulge in this optimization, make sure that the overhead of setup is outweighed by the many lights that need the calculations.

As a demo of Gouraud shading with light values generated from the lighting engine, check out `DEMOII9_2.CPP|EXE`. Figure 9.29 is a screenshot of the demo running. The program creates three water molecules and then spins them with multiple light sources in the scene. One is constant-shaded, one flat-shaded, and the last one is Gouraud-shaded—can you guess which is which? Notice how the edges of the Gouraud-shaded molecule look round even though the models are faceted—this is of course due to the vertex averaging at the corners.

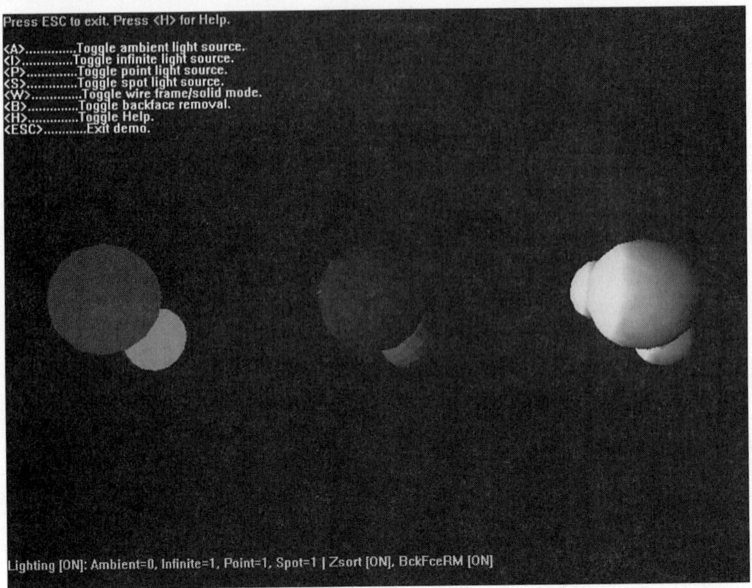

FIGURE 9.29 A full 3D demo of Gouraud lighting.

8-Bit Gouraud Lighting

This is where things get slightly ugly. Surprisingly, 8-bit lighting almost works the same as 16-bit lighting in the lighting stage now. In fact, almost the same code is used for the 8-bit versions of the functions. The only difference is that if a polygon is emissive or flat-shaded, the final color index is computed and stored into `lit_color[0]` with a call to the lookup table as follows:

```
curr_poly->lit_color[0] = rgblookup[RGB16Bit565(r_sum, g_sum, b_sum)];
```

If you recall, the lookup table works by taking an RGB 5.6.5 word (concatenating it) and using it as a 16-bit index into the table. The table then outputs the color index that is the closest match to the requested RGB color. We create the table with a call to

```
// create lookup for lighting engine
RGB_16_8_IndexedRGB_Table_Builder(DD_PIXEL_FORMAT565, // pixel format
                 palette,  // source palette
                 rgblookup); // storage for table
```

in the initialization phase of the program—remember from last chapter? Anyway, that's fine, but here's the problem: When we Gouraud shade a triangle, it's pointless to convert the final vertex colors to color indices because we can't interpolate them! We need actual RGB colors to interpolate; therefore, when a polygon is Gouraud lit in 8-bit mode, the actual RGB values are stored in each of the array elements `lit_colors[0..2]` just as we do with the 16-bit version. Then the real action takes place in the 8-bit Gouraud rasterizer.

The function that draws Gouraud triangles in 8-bit mode is

```
void Draw_Gouraud_Triangle(POLYF4DV2_PTR face,// ptr to face
        UCHAR *dest_buffer, // pointer to video buffer
        int mem_pitch)   // bytes per line, 320, 640 etc.
```

Just like the 16-bit version, but the difference is in the initial setup of the interpolants and the final pixel write to the screen. The function is too large to list, but let's take a look at these highlights. First, here's the initial RGB color extraction step:

```
// assume 5.6.5 format -- sorry!
// we can't afford a function call in the inner loops, so we must write
// two hard coded versions, if we want support for both 5.6.5, and 5.5.5
// notice that eventhough we will rasterize in 8-bit, the incoming data
// is still in RGB format
_RGB565FROM16BIT(face->lit_color[v0], &r_base0, &g_base0, &b_base0);
_RGB565FROM16BIT(face->lit_color[v1], &r_base1, &g_base1, &b_base1);
_RGB565FROM16BIT(face->lit_color[v2], &r_base2, &g_base2, &b_base2);

// scale to 8 bit
r_base0 <<= 3;
g_base0 <<= 2;
b_base0 <<= 3;

// scale to 8 bit
r_base1 <<= 3;
g_base1 <<= 2;
b_base1 <<= 3;

// scale to 8 bit
r_base2 <<= 3;
g_base2 <<= 2;
b_base2 <<= 3;
```

If you look closely, it's the same as the 16-bit version! And it should be because when a polygon is Gouraud lit in the 8-bit lighting functions, we store the final vertex colors as full 5.6.5 RGB words in `lit_colors[0..2]` instead of converting them to color indices. That would be a waste of time and cycles because we can't interpolate color indices. In any event, the real action happens in the final inner loop that rasterized a single line; take a look:

```
// draw span
for (xi=xstart; xi<=xend; xi++)
  {
  // write textel assume 5.6.5
```

9

```
screen_ptr[xi] = rgblookup[( ((ui >> (FIXP16_SHIFT+3)) << 11) +
                ((vi >> (FIXP16_SHIFT+2)) << 5) +
                (wi >> (FIXP16_SHIFT+3)) ) ];
// interpolate u,v
ui+=du;
vi+=dv;
wi+=dw;
} // end for xi
```

What's going on here? Well, what I did was this: I simply converted the RGB values into 5.6.5 format again, and then used our trusty RGB to the index lookup table to find the right color index that's closest to our desired color.

This brings me to a philosophical question? Is 8-bit slower than 16-bit? The answer is yes and no. Yes, if you're trying to do full lighting in a straightforward way; no, if you're using monochrome lighting designed specifically for 8-bit mode. It's pretty simple. If you have a computer that's really slow, writing 16-bit graphics would be out of the question, and so would colored light (sorta), so you would end up supporting white lights only and your Gouraud shader would interpolate only intensities. Then you would create a lookup table that has all 256 colors and 256 shades of each and then index the table with the color and intensity. Ironically we have one of these tables for just such an occasion. Hence, if we wanted to, we could cripple the lighting functions for 8-bit mode and have them output intensity only. Then, at each vertex, the 8-bit rasterizer would interpolate only one intensity channel, which would be three times faster than RGB interpolation. At rasterization time, we could use our color index/intensity lookup to look up the color index for each specific color/intensity combination and whammo! 8-bit fast monochrome Gouraud shading.

We could get creative and have multiple lookup tables for colored lights as shown in Figure 9.30. Then we could pump the intensity value through one of the color tables by first selecting the light color that's closest to the real light in the scene—get it? For example, assume that we know that for the most part we're going to have white, red, green, blue, and orange lights. Well then, we simply make five lookup tables that map color indices along with intensities to color indices that are "tinted" or colored as they would be if that particular colored light hit the surface. This is how you can do colored lights using lookup tables without a performance hit.

However, the moral of the story is that all this work for 8-bit mode isn't really necessary because 16-bit is fast enough these days. In fact, the 8-bit stuff is slowing us down because we're really targeting 16-bit and then converting to 8-bit mode! On the other hand, tricks like the lookup table stuff can come in handy—why? Well, no one ever said we can't do this in 16-bit mode. For example, if we know that we're never going to use lights other than red, green blue, white, orange, whatever, we can use single monochrome interpolation in the 16-bit Gouraud shader and for the light that's coloring the polygon, we can select the correct table on function entry and get rid of those other two interpolants—pretty neat, huh? We might do this later in the book when we optimize, but I don't want to start doing this stuff now; once I start on lookup tables, it's hard to say what will happen!

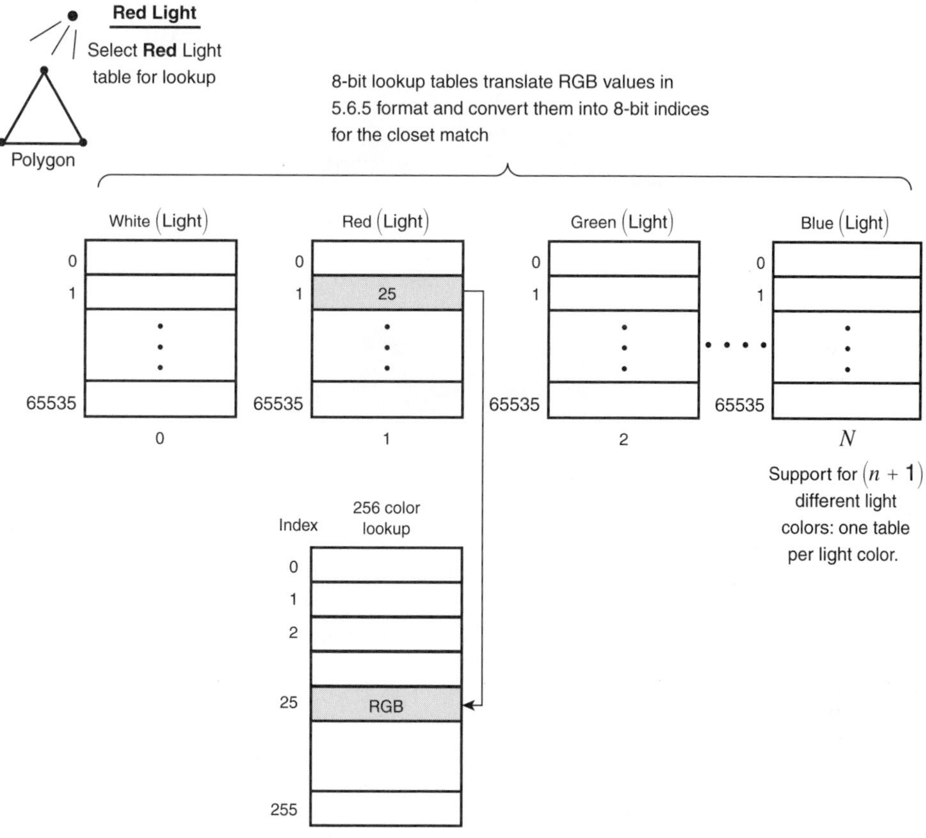

FIGURE 9.30 Using multiple lookup tables with precomputed lighting values for common light colors.

As a demo of an 8-bit Gouraud shading, check out `DEMOII9_2_8b.CPP|EXE` in action. Try running the program for yourself—it creates three water molecules and then spins them with multiple light sources in the scene. One is constant-shaded, one flat-shaded, and one is Gouraud-shaded. Notice how the edges of the Gouraud-shaded molecule look round, even though the models are the same. Amazingly, even with the limited color space it doesn't look too bad.

Alright, it's time for texture mapping!

Basic Sampling Theory

Guess what? You're already done with texture mapping! Seriously, there's nothing to it. Instead of interpolating color, you interpolate texture coordinates. Of course, there are some details, but for the most part, that's it. Now, I'm only talking about *affine* or *linear* texture mapping; perspective correction is an entirely different story. Figure 9.31 depicts the classic checkerboard example of linear and perspective correction texture mapping.

a. Affine texture mapping - notice no perspective cues.

b. Perspective texture mapping - notice 3D perspective both near and far.

FIGURE 9.31 Linear and perspective texture mapping.

However, if you're nervous about the subject of texture mapping, don't be. You already know how to do it. With that in mind, let's take yet another look at interpolation from a different point of view—a view in which we're sampling data with the interpolated coordinates.

Sampling in One Dimension

What we want to do is come up with an algorithm that samples the texture map, so that the sampled pixels can be used to color each pixel of each scan line of the target triangle polygon as it's being rendered. Figure 9.32 illustrates this for the three basic triangles that we usually break into cases: flat top, flat bottom, and general.

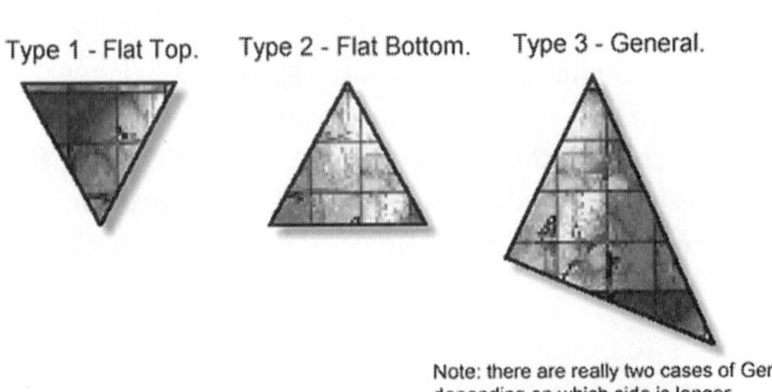
Type 1 - Flat Top.
Type 2 - Flat Bottom.
Type 3 - General.
Note: there are really two cases of General depending on which side is longer.

FIGURE 9.32 Texture mapping the three basic triangle cases.

Figure 9.33 shows the exact process that we want to implement. We want to texture-map a rectangular bitmap that is m×m pixels (8-/16-bit color) onto an arbitrary triangle with any coordinates. That means we need a way to take rotation and scaling of the triangle into consideration. To help design the algorithm, I've labeled a number of points of interest on Figure 9.33.

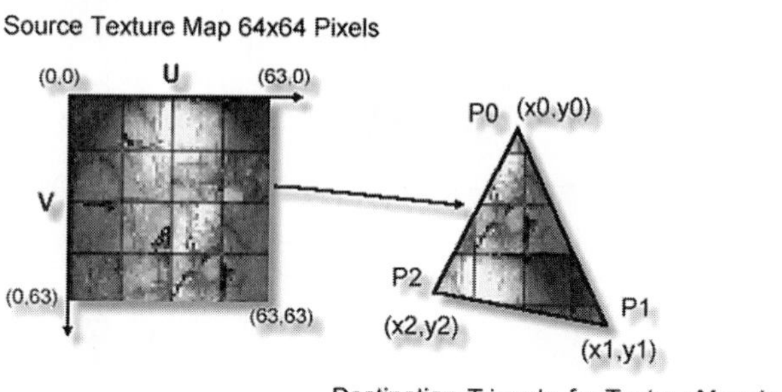

FIGURE 9.33 Details of mapping a texture in u, v space to a triangle.

First, you'll see that the destination triangle is made up of three vertices. These have been labeled **p0**, **p1**, and **p2**, with coordinates (x0, y0), (x1, y1), and (x2, y2), respectively. In addition, I've labeled the axes around the texture map as u and v, where u is the horizontal axis and v is the vertical axis. Note that both u and v range from (0,0) in the upper-left corner to (63,63) in the lower-right corner for this example. However, in many cases, u,v can range from 0..1 if they are normalized texture coordinates, or 0...(any power of 2).

Linearly texture mapping a triangle with a rectangular texture map is nothing more than a lot of interpolating, but there's so much interpolating that it's easy to make a mistake and or write a slow algorithm. Also, even though we've covered this for both triangle rasterization and Gouraud shading, we've *never* taken the point of view that we were sampling data. Thus, let's take our time and look at interpolation from another point of view; that is, with the goal of sampling data rather than interpolating rasterizer coordinates or color intensities. Let's start with the simplest case of sampling in one dimension.

Figure 9.34 illustrates the world's simplest texture mapper, the texture mapping of a single vertical line. In the figure, we have a texture map that's exactly one pixel thick and eight pixels high. We want to map this into a destination polygon that is exactly one-pixel thick, but any height. How do we do this? Sampling again comes to the rescue.

What we need to do is "sample" the texture map, which in this case is a single 1×8 pixel bitmap, and map it into the destination polygon which is 1xn pixels, where n can range from 1 to infinity. Refer to Figure 9.34 and let's take a look at some examples.

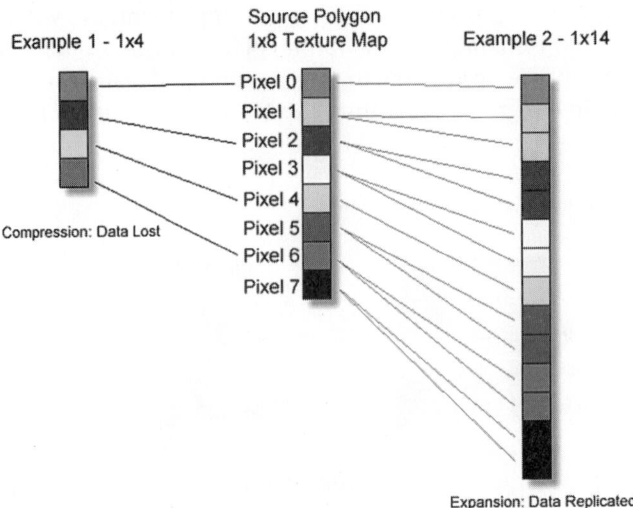

FIGURE 9.34 One-dimensional texture mapping.

As a first example, let's say that our destination polygon is 1×4 pixels. It makes sense that we want to sample every other pixel of the source texture, as shown in the figure. Thus, if we select pixels (0,2,4,6) of the source texture and map them into the destination polygon at positions (0,1,2,3), we're doing pretty good. But how did I arrive at (0,2,4,6)? The answer is by using a *sampling ratio*, which is nothing more than an interpolation factor. Here's the math:

In general:

```
sampling_ratio = source_height / destination_height
```

Thus the sampling ratio for this example is

```
sampling_ratio = 8/4 = 2.0
```

Hence, for every 1.0 pixels we move on the destination polygon in the vertical axis, we must move 2.0 pixels in the source to keep up. That's where the 2 comes from and, hence, the sampling sequence (0,2,4,6). If you're still with me, you should say, "Wait a minute, we lost color information!" Indeed we did—we had to throw away half the pixels. This is definitely a problem with sampling on an integer matrix without any averaging or filtering. If you were writing a high end 3D modeler like 3D Studio Max, you would probably average the pixels you're sampling (area sampling) so as to get a better approximation. But for games and real-time software, this first technique (which is referred to as *point sampling*) will do. Now let's see another example of the opposite extreme case.

In example 1, we saw that the source texture was compressed; that is, the destination was smaller than the source, so information was lost. The second case, of course, would be when the destination is bigger than the source and there isn't enough information to go around. In this case, the source data must be sampled more than once and replicated. This is where "chunkyness" comes from when texture-mapped polygons get too close to you in a 3D game. There isn't enough texture data, so some sample points are sampled—many times creating big blocks. Anyway, referring to the second example in Figure 9.34, we see that the source is again 1×8, but this time the destination is 1×14 pixels—yuck! Obviously, we're going to need a fractional sampling ratio, but let's let the math do it.

As usual,

```
sampling_ratio = source_height / destination_height
```

Thus the sampling ratio is

```
sampling_ratio = 8/14 = 0.57
```

Hence, for every pixel we draw on the destination polygon, we should sample it 0.57 units from the last sample point on the source. This gives us the following sample point sequence for destination pixels (0,1,2,3,...13):

Sample 0: 0.57

Sample 1: 1.14

Sample 2: 1.71

Sample 3: 2.28

Sample 4: 2.85

Sample 5: 3.42

Sample 6: 3.99

Sample 7: 4.56

Sample 8: 5.13

Sample 9: 5.7

Sample 10: 6.27

Sample 11: 6.84

Sample 12: 7.41

Sample 13: 7.98

To get the actual sample points, we simply truncate the sample points in integer space or take the floor of each value resulting in the sample points (0, 1, 1, 2, 2, 3, 3, 4, 5, 5, 6, 6, 7, 7) which sounds about right. Each point was sampled about two times, or 1/0.57 ~ 2.0.

Bilinear Interpolation

As an aside, let's briefly talk about basic filtering and why it's important. As shown in the previous example, when we compute the final sample pixels, we simply truncate the floating-point sample values to integral values. However, what if we were to take the fractional portion of the pixel values into consideration and sample more than one pixel based on a geometrical filter? Take a look at Figure 9.35. It depicts what I'm talking about by showing a point-sampled texture versus a filtered one. For example, if you look at sample 12 in the example, it uses the floating-point sample value of 7.41. However, when point sampling, we simply truncate this value and sample textel pixel 7.0, losing information.

A. Bilinear interpolation

B. Point sampling

FIGURE 9.35 Point sampling versus bilinear filtering.

This is faster, yes, but it doesn't look as nice. If we use a simple 1D box filter as shown in Figure 9.36, and assume that pixel 7.0 would be centered at the pixel center, we see that 7.41 slides the box filter over .41 pixels, thereby partially covering pixel 7.0 as well as partially covering pixel 8.0. The partial coverage, of course, is 59% pixel 7, and 41% pixel 8—do you see what's coming? Yes, a blending function. Here it is:

$$\text{final texture pixel} = (.59) * \text{pixel}(7)_{rgb} + (.41) * \text{pixel}(8)_{rgb}$$

Of course, we perform the blending in RGB space, and the final textel will be the blended pixel that we desire mixed from the color of pixel 7 *and* 8. The results will be much nicer and you won't see any jaggies. The only drawback to this is that we're performing yet another interpolation or, more simply, a blending operation per pixel rather than a simple sample operation. Although this isn't going to kill us, it'll hurt us.

Moreover, we have to do this in not just one dimension, but in two! Because of this we need to work in 2D for a real texture mapper—hence the term *bilinear interpolation*. However, once again, there are "tricks" to speed this up with lookup tables and other approximations. For example, if you perform the interpolation in fixed-point math, you can use say 2–3 bits of the decimal portion as a "mixing" factor, and create a table that contains from 0...100% of every color. Then you can access the table for each blending component and add the results—you get the idea.

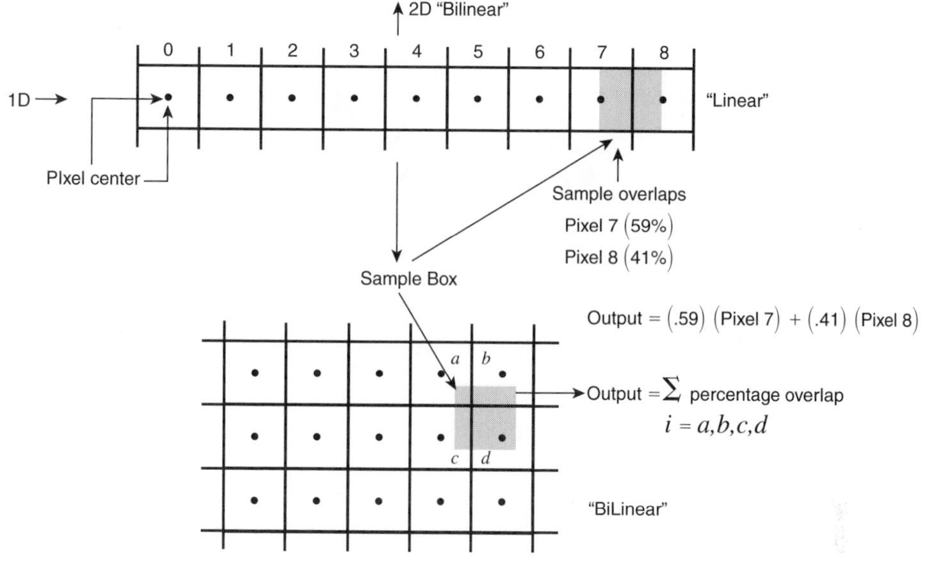

FIGURE 9.36 A simple box filter for bilinear interpolation.

TIP

We aren't going to implement bilinear filtering yet, but we might later if we can make it fast enough. Truthfully, it tends to blur textures and remove the high frequency aliasing that occurs during sampling. However, we can minimize the aliasing with point-sampled textures by pre-blurring or softening textures used in the engine in the art asset stage. You lose a bit of detail, but it's well worth it because it looks much better.

Interpolating u and v

The idea behind the algorithm is that we want to interpolate down the left and right edges of the triangle and draw each scan line strip as we go with the proper texture pixels. So, what we need to do first is assign full texture coordinates to the vertices of the destination triangle to give us a frame of reference for the interpolants. Thus we must assign each vertex a (u,v) texture coordinate, as shown in Figure 9.37. Therefore, each vertex has a total of four components (we throw away z). We'll need to perform the texture mapping (x, y, u, v). Of course, our new `VERTEX4DTV1` already has support for texture coordinates, and there are u,v texture coordinate arrays in the `OBJECT4DV2` structure, so we have everything we need to define a final texture mapping onto a triangle.

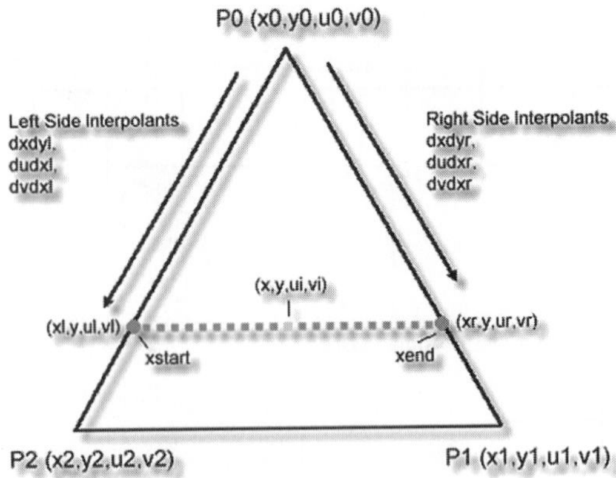

FIGURE 9.37 The setup for texture mapping.

Moving on, let's talk about the range of the texture coordinates. Because our source texture map must be m×m where m is a power of 2 and is usually 64×64, 128×128, or 256×256 pixels, it means that the texture coordinates must range from zero to these values minus 1. For sake of discussion, let's assume that all texture maps are 64×64. Therefore all texture coordinate must be (0…63, 0…63) for any vertex. This will map or stretch the texture map to each vertex.

For example, in Figure 9.38, we see a couple examples: one triangle with the texture coordinates (0,0), (63,0), and (63,63) mapped to vertices 0, 1, and 2, respectively. This basically copies half of the texture map to the destination triangle, which is what we would expect. In the second example in Figure 9.38, we see the same texture mapped onto two triangles that are adjacent to each other, forming a square. In this case, the texture coordinates are selected in such a way that half of the texture map is mapped to one triangle and the rest to the other; hence, a perfect texture wrapping around two triangles. Moreover, this is how you would make a quadrilateral with two triangles.

Now that you have a visual on the problem, refer to the labeling from Figure 9.37. Let's implement the algorithm mathematically. Note that the variable names used in the following analysis are based on Figure 9.37 and the final texture mapper, so that you can follow the program code more easily.

The left edge interpolants are as follows:

```
dxdyl = (x2 - x0)/(y2 - y0); // the x interpolant for the left hand side
dudyl = (u2 - u0)/(y2 - y0); // the u interpolant for the left hand side
dvdyl = (v2 - v0)/(y2 - y0); // the v interpolant for the left hand side
```

Similarly, the right edge interpolants are as follows:

```
dxdyr = (x1 - x0)/(y2 - y0); // the x interpolant for the right hand side
dudyr = (u1 - u0)/(y2 - y0); // the u interpolant for the right hand side
dvdyr = (v1 - v0)/(y2 - y0); // the v interpolant for the right hand side
```

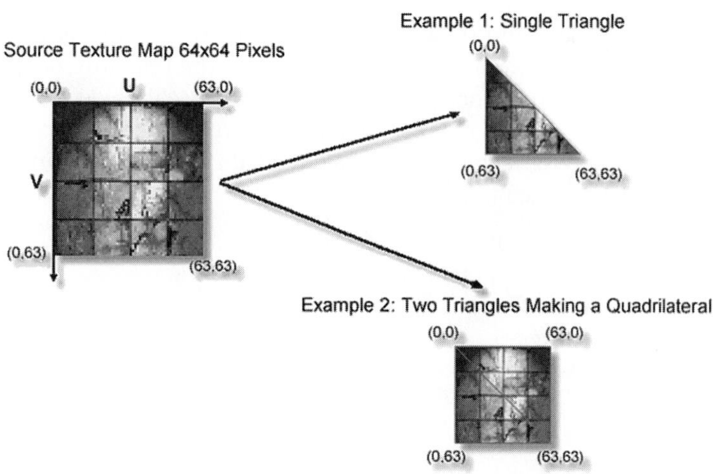

FIGURE 9.38 Example texture mappings on a triangle and quadrilateral.

Of course, there's a lot of room for optimization in the math. For example, the term (y2 - y0) is common and need only be computed once; furthermore, it's better to compute the reciprocal of (y2 - y0) and then multiply, but you get the idea. Anyway, now that we have the interpolants, we're almost ready to rock. The interpolants must be in reference to some starting point, right? This starts at the topmost vertex, vertex 0. Hence, we need to start the algorithm off like this:

```
xl = x0; // the starting point for the left hand side edge x interpolation
ul = u0; // the starting point for the left hand side edge u interpolation
vl = v0; // the starting point for the left hand side edge v interpolation
```

And for the right-hand side:

```
xr = x0; // the starting point for the right hand side edge x interpolation
ur = u0; // the starting point for the right hand side edge u interpolation
vr = v0; // the starting point for the right hand side edge v interpolation
```

Now we're almost ready to go. We can interpolate down the left-hand edge and the right edge with

```
xl+=dxdyl;
ul+=dudyl;
vl+=dvdyl;
```

and

```
xr+=dxdyr;
ur+=dudyr;
vr+=dvdyr;
```

But at each point on the left- and right-hand edge of the triangle, we still need to perform one more linear interpolation across the scan line! This is the final interpolation and the one that will give us our texture coordinates (ui,vi), which we'll use as [row, column] indices into the texture bitmap to obtain the textel. All we need to do is compute the u,v coordinate on the left and right sides and then use the *dx* to compute a linear interpolation factor for each. Here's the math:

```
dx = (xend - xstart); // the difference or delta dx
xstart = xl;      // left hand starting point
xend = xr;      // right hand starting point
```

Therefore, the interpolants across each scan line in u,v space are

```
du = (ul - ur)/dx;
dv = (vl - vr)/dx;
```

With du,dv, we have everything we need to interpolate across the scan line at vertical position y from xstart to xend. Here's a code fragment:

```
// initialize u,v interpolants to left and right hand side values
ui = ul;
vi = vl;

// now interpolate from left to right, i.e, in a positive x direction
for (x = xstart; x <= xend; x++)
   {
   // get texture pixel value
   pixel = texture_map[ui][vi];

   // plot pixel at x,y
   Plot_Pixel(x,y,pixel);

   // advance u,v interpolants
   ui+=du;
   vi+=dv;
   } // end for x
```

That's it. Of course, for the outer loop, you would still interpolate xl, ul, vl, xr, ur, vr down the triangle edges for each scan line of the triangle.

Again there are lots of details to writing the texture mapper that are left out in the preceding pseudo-functions, but as I mentioned, the Gouraud rasterizer *is* the texture mapper. That is, I wrote the texture mapper first and then converted it to the Gouraud shader, so you're already familiar with the function. Additionally, the texture mapper and the Gouraud shader use fixed point just, so I can save the conversions to and from floating point in the inner loops when the pixels are written because I don't trust the compiler.

Remember that floating math is as fast as integer, but sometimes the code emitted by the compiler for the conversion back and forth takes 10–100 times as long as the math!

Implementing Affine Texture Mapping

Alright, I think we have all the theory out of the way for texture mapping functions, so I want to discuss the details of the functions a little, and present the prototypes and a bit of code from each. Again, the functions are too large to list, so you'll have to refer to the CD. (Sorry, but until eBooks are available, we can't have 20–30 page listings all the time—it would make the book unbindable!) Nevertheless, I've implemented both 8- and 16-bit versions of the texture mapper. The only interesting facets of each are in the final inside loops that actually sample the textures and write to the screen. If you recall, the Gouraud rasterizers used the final interpolants as RGB values and then built up a pixel value from that. However, the texture mappers use the final u,v interpolants as the texture coordinates and then sample the texture map and render the pixel. Of course, there's no bilinear filtering—yet <BG>.

16-Bit Texture Mapping

The 16-bit texture mapping function is almost identical to the Gouraud shader. It has only a few differences as noted in the final inner loop that writes the pixel, but I'll get to that momentarily. Right now, let's take a look at the function prototype and talk about its use:

```
void Draw_Textured_Triangle16(POLYF4DV2_PTR face, // ptr to face
          UCHAR *_dest_buffer,// pointer to video buffer
          int mem_pitch) // bytes per line, 320, 640 etc.
```

Expecting more? Less is always more—Stephen Wolfram believes that the entire universe can be described in a few lines of code—therefore complexity can be derived from simplicity in many cases. Anyway, the function is called simply by setting up a `POLYF4DV2` structure with the vertices, texture map, destination buffer, and memory pitch. Bam! You'll see a textured, clipping triangle on the screen faster than a gnat can flap it's wings!

So, to solidify the use of the function, here's an example of how you might call the texture mapper. This is excerpted from one of the rendering functions:

```
if (rend_list->poly_ptrs[poly]->attr & POLY4DV2_ATTR_SHADE_MODE_TEXTURE)
  {
  // set the vertices
  face.tvlist[0].x = (int)rend_list->poly_ptrs[poly]->tvlist[0].x;
  face.tvlist[0].y = (int)rend_list->poly_ptrs[poly]->tvlist[0].y;
  face.tvlist[0].u0 = (int)rend_list->poly_ptrs[poly]->tvlist[0].u0;
  face.tvlist[0].v0 = (int)rend_list->poly_ptrs[poly]->tvlist[0].v0;

  face.tvlist[1].x = (int)rend_list->poly_ptrs[poly]->tvlist[1].x;
  face.tvlist[1].y = (int)rend_list->poly_ptrs[poly]->tvlist[1].y;
```

```
  face.tvlist[1].u0 = (int)rend_list->poly_ptrs[poly]->tvlist[1].u0;
  face.tvlist[1].v0 = (int)rend_list->poly_ptrs[poly]->tvlist[1].v0;

  face.tvlist[2].x = (int)rend_list->poly_ptrs[poly]->tvlist[2].x;
  face.tvlist[2].y = (int)rend_list->poly_ptrs[poly]->tvlist[2].y;
  face.tvlist[2].u0 = (int)rend_list->poly_ptrs[poly]->tvlist[2].u0;
  face.tvlist[2].v0 = (int)rend_list->poly_ptrs[poly]->tvlist[2].v0;

  // assign the texture
  face.texture = rend_list->poly_ptrs[poly]->texture;

 // is this a plain emissive texture?
 if (rend_list->poly_ptrs[poly]->attr & POLY4DV2_ATTR_SHADE_MODE_CONSTANT)
   {
   // draw the textured triangle as emissive
   Draw_Textured_Triangle16(&face, video_buffer, lpitch);
   } // end if
 else
   {
   // draw as flat shaded
   face.lit_color[0] = rend_list->poly_ptrs[poly]->lit_color[0];
   Draw_Textured_TriangleFS16(&face, video_buffer, lpitch);
   } // end else
```

Pay attention to the highlighted section; it's the setup for the triangle. As you can see, the (x,y,u,v) for each vertex is assigned to the face and then used in the call to `Draw_Textured_Triangle16()`. Also, you may notice that there is another `Draw_Textured_TriangleFS16()` function right below; this is the "shaded" version of the function that supports flat shading, but we'll get to that in a moment. Currently, the texture mapper inside the call to `Draw_Textured_Triangle16()` supports only constant or emissive shading. Meaning that, in your model, you must set the shading mode to `"constant"`, and then apply a texture. The lights in the scene will have no affect at all on the texture. We'll fix this shortly, but this is the first version of the texture mapper that supports only constant shading. Anyway, let's move on to some of the highlights of the `Draw_Textured_Triangle16()` function.

Here's the inner loop from the texture mapping function:

```
// draw span
for (xi=xstart; xi<=xend; xi++)
  {
  // write textel
  screen_ptr[xi] = textmap[(ui >> FIXP16_SHIFT) + (
              (vi >> FIXP16_SHIFT) << texture_shift2)];
```

```
// interpolate u,v
ui+=du;
vi+=dv;
} // end for xi
```

Let's discuss the highlighted code for a moment. First, the texture coordinates `ui`, `vi` are in 16.16 fixed-point format, thus the shifting operation, so the math looks like this functionally:

```
screen_ptr[xi] = textmap[ui + vi * word_pitch]
```

See that multiplication by `word_pitch`? That is of course implemented as a shift operation via `texture_shift2`, and because the texture maps are in row major form, we can access them as a 2D array using this expression. The only thing of interest is the derivation of the term `texture_shift2`. It's very simple; it's just the log base 2 of the texture width. So, a texture map that's 64×64 (remember they always have to be square) has a `texture_shift2` of 6 because $2^6 = 64$ or $\log_2 64 = 6$.

The thing that's kind of a bummer is that I use the `BITMAP_IMAGE` structure to hold texture maps, and even though it contains the width and height of a texture, it doesn't contain the nearest power of 2. So, I could have put that somewhere in the polygon, or hacked it into the `BITMAP_IMAGE` somewhere in the upper 4 bits of something, but that would be shady. Instead, for fun, I decided to make a $\log_2$ lookup table:

```
// logbase2ofx[x] = (int)log2 x, [x:0-256]
UCHAR logbase2ofx[257] =
{
0,0,1,1,2,2,2,2,3,3,3,3,3,3,3,3, 4,4,4,4,4,4,4,4,4,4,4,4,4,4,4,4,
5,5,5,5,5,5,5,5,5,5,5,5,5,5,5,5, 5,5,5,5,5,5,5,5,5,5,5,5,5,5,5,5,
6,6,6,6,6,6,6,6,6,6,6,6,6,6,6,6, 6,6,6,6,6,6,6,6,6,6,6,6,6,6,6,6,
6,6,6,6,6,6,6,6,6,6,6,6,6,6,6,6, 6,6,6,6,6,6,6,6,6,6,6,6,6,6,6,6,
7,7,7,7,7,7,7,7,7,7,7,7,7,7,7,7, 7,7,7,7,7,7,7,7,7,7,7,7,7,7,7,7,
7,7,7,7,7,7,7,7,7,7,7,7,7,7,7,7, 7,7,7,7,7,7,7,7,7,7,7,7,7,7,7,7,
7,7,7,7,7,7,7,7,7,7,7,7,7,7,7,7, 7,7,7,7,7,7,7,7,7,7,7,7,7,7,7,7,
7,7,7,7,7,7,7,7,7,7,7,7,7,7,7,7, 7,7,7,7,7,7,7,7,7,7,7,7,7,7,7,7, 8,
};
```

The table's operation is simple; send it any number from 0–256, inclusive, and it'll give you the nearest $\log_2$ of that number. For example, `logbase2ofx[128]` = 7, `logbase2ofx[129]` also is 7, and so forth. Therefore, on entry into the texture mapping function, we determine what power of 2 the texture is, store it in `texture_shift2`, and use that as the shift in the final textel computation, thereby supporting any size texture from 1×1 to 256×256. However, I wouldn't trust anything less than 16×16—the fixed point might freak out!

In any event, this is just another example of thinking out of the box and speeding things up with lookup tables. But what we really need in a new BITMAP storage structure that precomputes the power of 2 of the texture and stores it. A single table lookup per polygon isn't going to kill us, but remember: A single anything per polygon or pixel isn't going to kill us, but when you get lots of those, you find yourself dead! So, watch out! We're chipping away at performance.

8-Bit Texture Mapping

The 8-bit emissive texture mapper is nearly identical to the 16-bit because it's a sampling operation and not a color operation. Therefore, the code really has no changes. It just operates on BYTEs rather than SHORTs. Other than that it's exactly the same, and works the same, so there's no need to belabor it, the function prototype is

```
void Draw_Textured_Triangle(POLYF4DV2_PTR face, // ptr to face
        UCHAR *_dest_buffer, // pointer to video buffer
        int mem_pitch) // bytes per line, 320, 640 etc.
```

Updating the Lighting/Rasterization Engine for Textures

Now let's update the lighting engine itself to support textures. For the most part, this is already done! We literally don't have to add a single line of code to the lighting functions to support textures. But we do have to perform a slight hack—let me explain.

When a polygon is lit by the lighting system, we use the base color of the polygon as the material and then modulate that color with the lights. That is, a red polygon will reflect only red light and so forth. However, when texture mapping, we can't even begin to think of lighting each pixel of a texture map, so we need to use a trick. What we'll do is this: For any polygon that has a texture mapped to it, we'll set the underlying polygon to white (255,255,255), and then we'll perform lighting as usual on the polygon. However, I've written a rasterizer that deals only with flat-shaded textured polygons at this point, not Gouraud-shaded textured polygons, so the lighting model for any texture-mapped polygon must be constant or flat. In any case, back to the white base color trick. As I said, we'll color *every* polygon that is texture-mapped as white, and then run the lighting on the polygon as usual, ignoring the fact that the polygon is texture mapped.

This has the effect of the polygon picking up *all* the light that strikes the polygon. This is exactly what we want. Then, in the rasterization phase, when we draw the textured polygon, instead of just accessing the texture map, we modulate each textel with the after-lighting polygon coloring and presto: lit textured polys! With that in mind, let's look at the 16-and 8-bit implementations.

Adding Lighting to 16-Bit Texture Rendering

The final lighting and rasterization process for 16-bit flat-shaded textures is shown in Figure 9.39. The function that draws flat-shaded textured polys is shown here:

```
void Draw_Textured_TriangleFS16(POLYF4DV2_PTR face, // ptr to face
        UCHAR *_dest_buffer, // pointer to video buffer
        int mem_pitch)    // bytes per line, 320, 640 etc.
```

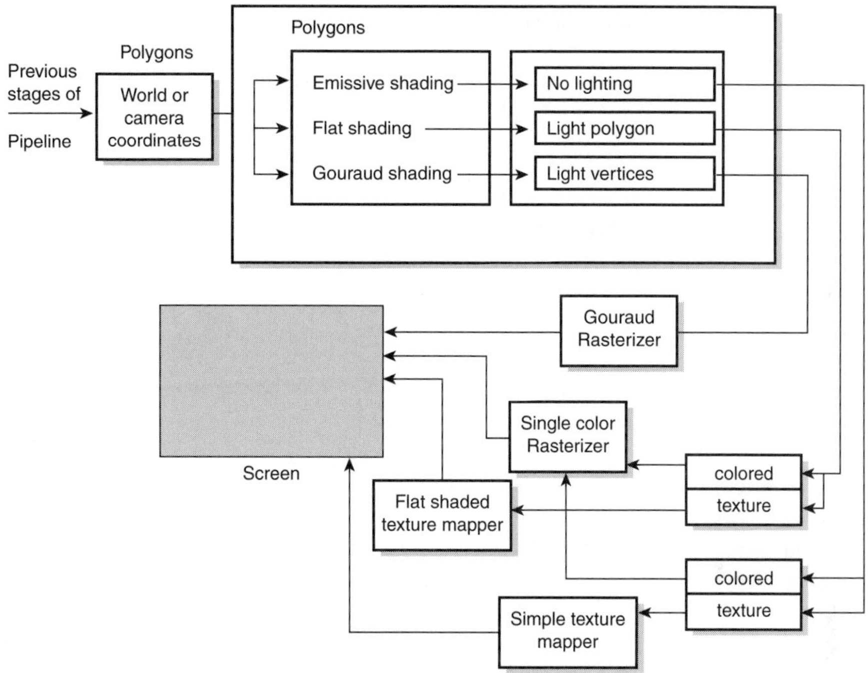

FIGURE 9.39 The final pipeline for lighting and rasterizing textures.

The prototype is identical to the non-flat-shaded version, except that this function has an added "FS" concatenated on the function name to remind you that it supports flat shading. Anyway, let's look at some excerpts from the function to see the lighting stuff in action. Now remember that the lighting function will light the polygon as if it were white and store the results in `lit_color[0]` for us. We simply need to modulate the texture color, or multiply it, in other words, and that will light the texture. First, let's look at the old inner loop from the constant-shaded texture rendering function `Draw_Textured_Triangle16()` for reference:

```
// draw span
for (xi=xstart; xi<=xend; xi++)
  {
```

```
  // write textel
  screen_ptr[xi] = textmap[(ui >> FIXP16_SHIFT) +
              ((vi >> FIXP16_SHIFT) << texture_shift2)];
  // interpolate u,v
  ui+=du;
  vi+=dv;
  } // end for xi
```

And now, here's the new inner loop with lighting modulation:

```
// draw span
for (xi=xstart; xi<=xend; xi++)
  {
  // write textel
  // get textel first
  textel = textmap[(ui >> FIXP16_SHIFT) +
          ((vi >> FIXP16_SHIFT) << texture_shift2)];

  // extract rgb components
  r_textel = ((textel >> 11)     );
  g_textel = ((textel >> 5) & 0x3f);
  b_textel =  (textel     & 0x1f);

  // modulate textel with lit background color
  r_textel*=r_base;
  g_textel*=g_base;
  b_textel*=b_base;

  // finally write pixel, note that we did the math such that the results
  // are r*32, g*64, b*32 hence we need to divide the results by 32,64,32
  // respetively, BUT since we need to shift the results to fit into the
  // destination 5.6.5 word, we can take advantage of the shifts
  // and they all cancel out for the most part, but we will need logical
  // anding, we will do it later when we optimize more...
  screen_ptr[xi] = ((b_textel >> 5) +
          ((g_textel >> 6) << 5) +
          ((r_textel >> 5) << 11));

  // interpolate u,v
  ui+=du;
  vi+=dv;
  } // end for xi
```

As you can see, we just totally annihilated our performance in the inner loop. We're doing like 10 times the work to add just flat shading, but still, amazingly enough, if you only have a few textured objects with flat shading in your game, this will work. The inner loop works as follows: We need to extract each textel from the texture map, and then it's modulated by the polygon color from the lighting engine, and written to the screen. The thing that kills us is all this bit manipulation and shifting. In assembly, we could do much better, and using single instruction multiple data instructions we could do four times better than that. Finally, by using lookup tables, we might be able to avoid some of the math.

Figure 9.40 is a screenshot of DEMOII9_3.CPP¦EXE in action. It's a demo of the fully lit, flat-shaded texture engine spinning a textured cube with lights.

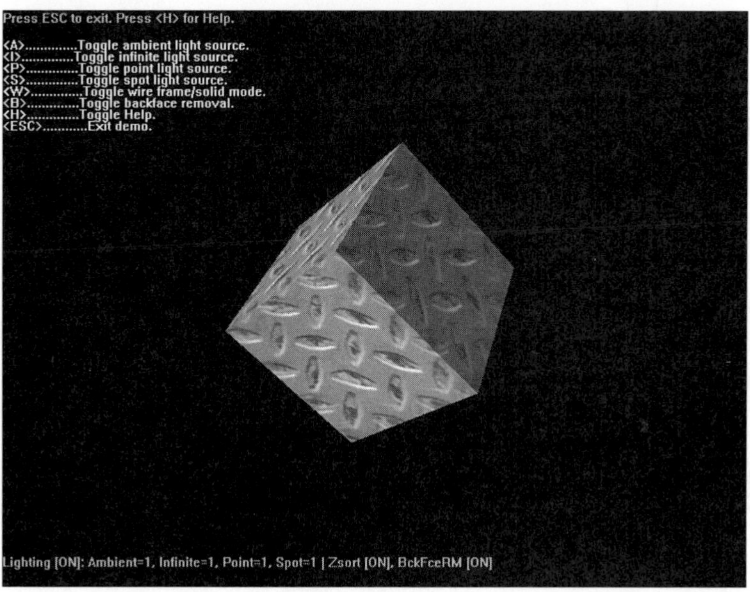

FIGURE 9.40 The fully lit 16-bit texture engine in action.

9

Adding Lighting to 8-Bit Texture Rendering

The 8-bit version of the flat-shaded textured rasterization function is identical to the 16-bit version all the way down to the inner loop, but that's where the magic happens. First, let's get the prototype out of the way:

```
void Draw_Textured_TriangleFS16(POLYF4DV2_PTR face,// ptr to face
          UCHAR *_dest_buffer, // pointer to video buffer
          int mem_pitch)    // bytes per line, 320, 640 etc.
```

Alright, take a look at Figure 9.41 to follow my algorithm. The problem with all the 8-bit lighting is that we've been using full RGB lighting rather than ramp or mono lighting; that's like putting brakes on a fast car. The whole reason we even wanted to support 8-bit was to make everything fast, but I decided to support full RGB for two reasons. You may want a full RGB 8-bit engine, for example, you're a GameBoy Advance programmer; secondly, the RGB calculations can always be reduced to monochrome calculations, but converting to RGB from monochrome is much harder, so I decided to stick to making things more robust rather than focusing on speed.

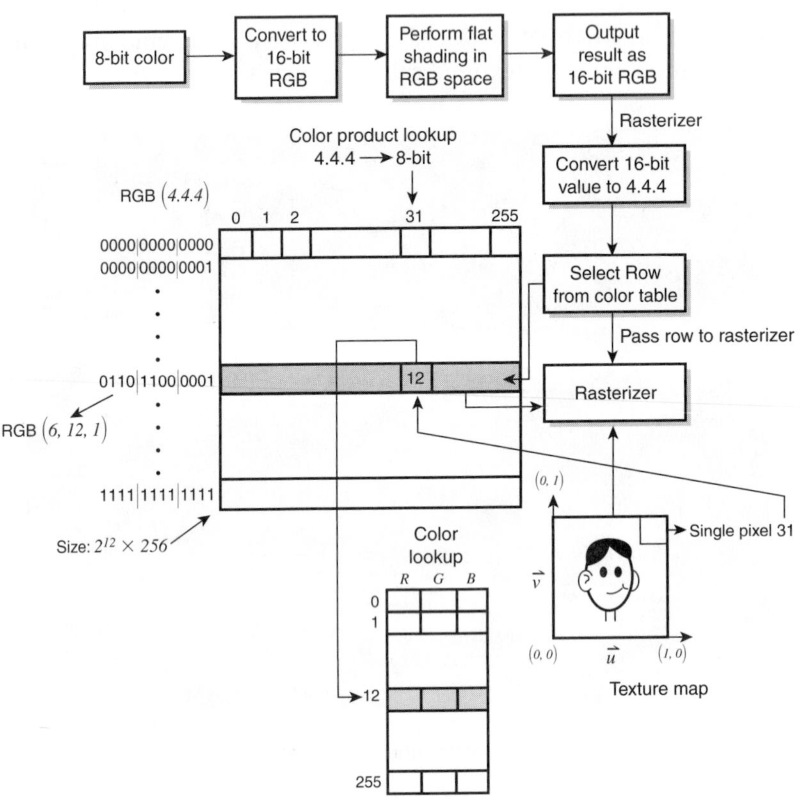

FIGURE 9.41 8-bit lighting data flow.

In any event, the problem when rasterizing 8-bit flat-shaded textured polygons is that we can't really modulate colors because we're in index space when accessing 8-bit texture maps. Sure, we could do something insane like read the textel out of the texture map in 8-bit mode, look up the RGB values in the color lookup table, modulate the RGB color in `lit_color[0]`, reconvert the final result to an index via the RGB to index lighting table, and then sit back and say 8-bit mode is two times slower than RGB mode! Or we can be clever <BG>.

Referring to Figure 9.41, my strategy is to create a lookup table that contains all possible products of any pair of colors. Now, this normally would take a lookup table that contains 2^{32} or 4 billion elements. However, in 256-color mode, we can get more devious about it.

In 8-bit mode, there are only 256 colors. Thus, we can create a lookup table that contains 65536 rows for full RGB coverage; that is, for any 5.6.5 RGB words, we compute all 256 possible products with that RGB word and color index 0..255, and then we scan the color table for the closest match. For example, say I wanted color index 26 modulated by RGB (5,10,12), which is in 5.6.5 format or ranges of (0..31, 0..63, 0..63). Thus, in 8.8.8 format, we need to multiply by (8,4,8)*(5,10,12) = (40, 40, 96).

We first extract out the RGB values from index 26; say they're (90,12,60). Remember they are in 8.8.8 mode. Then we multiply that by RGB color indexed by index 26, which is (40,40,96) in 8.8.8 format, so we have

```
final color = (90, 12, 60) * (40, 40, 96) = (3600, 480, 5760)
```

Now, we need to scale these back down to 0..255, so we must divide by 255, which results in the integral values of

```
(14, 1, 22)
```

So what does this all mean? The preceding RGB value is the resulting RGB color that would result in the modulation of color index 26 by the RGB 5.6.5 color of (5,10,12). Therefore, we've basically precomputed the light modulation step with one color index and one possible RGB value. So, to make this complete, we scan the color lookup table, find the closest index to (5,10,12), and store it. To look it up, you would use this lookup:

```
color_lookup[RGBcolor][color_index]
```

where `RGBcolor` varies from 0..65535, and `color_index` varies from 0..255. However, this is a huge table: 16.7MB. Do we really need all that? The answer is no! The trick is to prescale all RGB values from the lighting engine down to 4.4.4 format, or 16 shades of red, green, and blue, and then use that as the modulator with all 256 colors in the table. Therefore this table is only 2^{12} * 256 = 1MB, which is manageable. The only problem is making the table; it takes about 20 seconds on a Pentium 4! Anyway, a table like this is created by the following function:


```
int RGB_12_8_Lighting_Table_Builder(LPPALETTEENTRY src_palette,
                UCHAR rgblookup[4096][256])
{
// this function creates a lighting table used for 8-bit
// lighting inside the texture mapping function, what we
// need is a table that for every possible
// light color and textel color outputs the textel index
// that is the closest match for the given color modulation,
```

```
// however, that would be 256*65536! a little excessive, thus,
// we will scale the incoming light value down to 4.4.4
// format, or only 16 different intensities per channel,
// or a total of 12 bits, now we will only need 256*2^12 = 1meg
// which is reasonable for the speed gain
// additionally, the table is going to be 2d,
// where the row is the intensity and the column is the color,
// this format is more effective since tables are stored in
// row-major form, and since we are shading flat shaded polys with
// texture, we know the texture color will change during the calculations,
// but not the light color, thus, the cache coherence will be excellent
// if we access elements in the form:
// rgblookup[RGBcolor.12bit][textel index.8bit]
// finally, it's up to the caller to send in the rgblookup pre-allocated
// here it goes...

// first check the pointers
if (!src_palette || !rgblookup)
  return(-1);

// there are 4096 RGB values we need to compute, assuming that
// we are in RGB: 4.4.4 format
for (int rgbindex = 0; rgbindex < 4096; rgbindex++)
  {
  // for each RGB color 0..4095
  // we need to multiple by each palette entry 0..255
  // and then scan for the closest match, lots of loops!!!!
  for (int color_index = 0; color_index < 256; color_index++)
    {
    int curr_index = -1;    // current color index of best match
    long curr_error = INT_MAX; // dist to nearest match or "error"

    // extract r,g,b from rgbindex, assuming an encoding of 4.4.4
    int r = (rgbindex >> 8);
    int g = ((rgbindex >> 4) & 0x0f);
    int b = (rgbindex & 0x0f);

    // final target is this r,g,b value, simulating the light source
    // multiplied by the textel color, that IS our target...
    // modulate values together, make sure results 0..255, divide results
    // by 15 since the r,g,b values were normalized to 15 rather than 1.0
    r = (int)(((float)r *(float)src_palette[color_index].peRed) /15);
    g = (int)(((float)g *(float)src_palette[color_index].peGreen)/15);
    b = (int)(((float)b *(float)src_palette[color_index].peBlue)/15);
```

```
    // now scan palette to find this color
    for (int color_scan = 0; color_scan < 256; color_scan++)
      {
      // compute distance to color from target
      long delta_red   = abs(src_palette[color_scan].peRed   - r);
      long delta_green = abs(src_palette[color_scan].peGreen - g);
      long delta_blue = abs(src_palette[color_scan].peBlue - b);
      long error = (delta_red*delta_red) +
             (delta_green*delta_green) +
             (delta_blue*delta_blue);

      // is this color a better match?
      if (error < curr_error)
        {
        curr_index = color_scan;
        curr_error = error;
        } // end if
      } // end for color_scan

      // best match has been found, enter it into table
      rgblookup[rgbindex][color_index] = curr_index;
     } // end for color_index
  } // end for rgbindex
// return success
return(1);
} // end RGB_12_8_Lighting_Table_Builder
```

I've created a global variable to hold the table:

```
UCHAR rgblightlookup[4096][256]; // rgb 8.12 lighting table lookup
```

Thus, when working with 8-bit modes, you must create the table *after* loading your palette, but *before* you make any 3D lighting calls like this:

```
RGB_12_8_Lighting_Table_Builder(palette,      // source palette
                rgblightlookup); // lookup table
```

We simply call the function with the global table and the global palette, which happens to be in the variable palette from `T3DLIB1.CPP` <BG>.

Now, let's get back to the actual 8-bit flat-shaded rasterizer. Here's the deal: The table consists of 4,096 rows of 256 values; each row represents the 4.4.4 RGB value multiplied by all 256 colors, and the elements of that row are the nearest matches. Therefore, all we do on entry to the 8-bit rasterizer is alias a pointer to the row that we're trying to light the polygon as. In the inner loop of the rasterizer, we index into the one-dimensional table with the color index from the texture map, and the table basically performs the entire lighting modulation for us! Here's the code:

```
// draw span
for (xi=xstart; xi<=xend; xi++)
  {
  // write textel
  // get textel
  textel = textmap[(ui >> FIXP16_SHIFT) +
          ((vi >> FIXP16_SHIFT) << texture_shift2)];
  // modulate with base color via light table and write textel
  screen_ptr[xi] = lightrow444_8[textel];
  // interpolate u,v
  ui+=du;
  vi+=dv;
  } // end for xi
```

See that reference to `lightrow444_8[]`? That's the row that has all 256 colors "lit" or modulated by the incoming color of the white polygon under the texture. I hope you get this! If you're really paying attention, you'll see that we can use this same technique for 16-bit lighting! The tables will be huge, but if we're clever, we might be able to make the 16-bit inner loop look just like this one, or maybe two lookups at most!

As a demo of the 8-bit version of texture mapping with flat shading, check out `DEMOII9_3_8b.CPP|EXE`. It's a demo of the fully lit, flat-shaded texture engine spinning a textured cube in 8-bit mode.

Final Thoughts on Optimization Strategies for 8- and 16-Bit Modes

Throughout this chapter, I've mentioned many opportunities for optimization and lots of ideas. I avoided implementing 90% of them because the code would become nearly impossible to follow—for me especially <BG>. Nonetheless, I want to briefly recap some of the ideas to keep you thinking about them.

Lookup Tables

I can't say enough about this technique. You can use lookup tables for just about everything. I've barely touched the surface. I suggest that you look at every algorithm, and anything that has functional inputs that when concatenated together can be stored in a table that is a few KB with an upward bound of a couple of MB—do it! Computers have a ton of memory these days. The one I am writing on has 2.0GB of RAM, so even if your game has 32–64 megs of lookup tables, who cares?

The areas to concentrate your lookup table endeavors are obviously mathematical, but in 3D graphics there are many other places to use them in relation to color mapping, texture mapping, and other related operations. Also, try to use what I call *cascading lookup tables*. Let me explain.

Say that you have two inputs x,y that are both 16 bits, and you need a single-byte output for all possible x,y inputs. That's a total of 16+16 = 32 bits of input possibilities, or 4.2 billion bytes for a lookup table—ouch, a little big. However, the trick is to recast the problem in stages so that maybe you can work with only the upper 8 bits of each operand, perform a look up on them (which would take a total of (8+8) = 16, or 64K bytes), and based on that output, you would plug it into yet another lookup with the remaining 16 bits.

So maybe now the output from table 1 is 8 bits. You add that to the other 16-bit data and you have 24 bits you need to look up a single BYTE for each value—that's only 16 million bytes! Get it? 16 million is large, but it's a lot smaller than 4 billion! The point is that sometimes you can use a logarithmic breakdown of the search/computation space, so that if you break the problems input domain down into halves or chunks, you can use a 2-n step lookup table process and use much less space.

Also, don't be afraid to scale your input data down to make it manageable. For example, in the flat-shaded 8-bit texture mapper, I used a giant lookup table that worked in 4.4.4 RGB mode to find color indices that matched the desired 8.8.8 color indices. This table cost me nothing memorywise, but speeds up the process immensely. And in reality, we're working with 5.6.5 in screen space, so scaling down to 4.4.4 only loses half the color space for the most part, but in 8-bit mode no one notices anyway—these are the kinds of tricks you need to be thinking about.

Mesh Vertex Coherence

Although we didn't implement any mesh coherence in the vertex shading code for the Gouraud lighting model, this is screaming to be optimized. Why light 36 vertices for a cube when I need to light only 8? Remember, while objects are still intact, there is a one-to-one relationship between vertices and polygons because polygons share vertices—there are no duplicates. This goes for vertex normals, texture coordinates, and so forth; so, if there's optimization you can take advantage of while objects are still objects (such as lighting them), do it—we'll actually do this very soon. Of course, you don't want to light polygons that are backfaces and such, so you have to be careful that you aren't foolhardy and aren't paying attention to the minimum amount of work that needs to be performed.

Mathematical Caching

We saw a little of this in the new lighting functions when I cached the computation of the polygon normal that was re-used in the point and spotlight lighting functions. Of course, there are many more opportunities for this kind of caching. Simply look through code, and anything that's redundantly computed more than once is a candidate. The way to code it cleanly is to set the variable that contains the results or a field of it to infinity to "tag" the data in essence, and before the data is used, you test for infinity. If it's equal, compute the value and store it. Otherwise, jump the code; for example, here's a function before computational caching:

```
// code block
f1 = sin(x)*cos(y)+zeta
f2 = f1 * cos(y)
f3 = alpha + beta * sin(x)
```

Now, assuming that `x`, `zeta`, `alpha`, and `beta` change in this loop due to external forces, the one thing that stays constant is `y`. Thus, we can cache `cos(y)` as follows:

```
cosy = cos(y)

// code block
f1 = sin(x)*cosy+zeta
f2 = f1 * cosy
f3 = alpha + beta * sin(x)
```

Now, the problem with the preceding fragment is that we know that `cos(y)` needs to be used later down the line, so we compute it. But if we don't, we surely do *not* want to even waste the time computing it *until* it's needed—get it? For example, the earlier code block might never be called, and we would wastefully compute `cos(y)` for nothing. Thus, a more robust strategy to use when a value may or may not be needed is to set it to infinity (or some other impossible tag value) and *when* it's needed, compute it:

```
// initialization
float cosy = FLT_MAX;

//. code

// ..more code

// this code is executed only when we are certain
// that cosy is needed
if (cosy == FLT_MAX)
  cosy = cos(y);
```

SIMD

SIMD stands for *single instruction multiple data*. Its part of the Pentium III+ architecture that allows you to perform the same operation on multiple data streams. Meaning that you can multiply four numbers by four numbers, and so on. This is perfect for the types of operations we're doing in 3D. You may be saying, "'Isn't that MMX?" Yes and no. MMX, or multimedia extensions, was the first generation of this technology and didn't quite deliver. It basically gave the Pentium the ability to perform four integer operations simultaneously, but at the expense of the floating-point registers. On the other hand, I can tell you that SIMD does work!

With the Pentium 4 for example, we can speed up our math and 3D algorithms almost 400% by using inline SIMD instructions and/or the compiler-specific intrinsic functions. I'll cover this briefly at the end of the book, but it's definitely something to look at. Imagine how much faster we can light, Gouraud shade, texture map, and transform polygons—the list is limitless! Check out Intel's site at

```
http://www.intel.com
```

Search under "sse," "sse2," and "simd."

Also, you can download the Visual C++ processor pack for the Visual C++ compiler to give it support for SSE (streaming SIMD extensions)/SSE2 (streaming SIMD extensions 2) instructions at:

```
msdn.microsoft.com/vstudio/downloads/ppack/default.asp
```

Final Demos

Alrighty then! It's been while since I said that—I think I'll say it again: Alrighty then! Okay, now I feel better! It's time for a demo of the engine. I'm getting seriously sick of this tank thing, but I've been waiting until we had the technology to make something very cool before I spent the 20 hours or so needed to make a cool demo. However, because it's a no-brainer to upgrade the tank demo with all this stuff, `DEMOII9_4.CPP¦EXE` is the 16-bit version and `DEMOII9_4_8b.CPP¦EXE` is the 8-bit version. Check out the screenshot in Figure 9.42 to see the nice shading. Basically, it's the same demo we've been working with, but with Gouraud shading added to many of the objects in the scene along with a texture-mapped, flat-shaded craft that you control. As usual, you can control the demo with the keys shown in Table 9.1.

TABLE 9.1 Controls for `DEMOII9_4xx.CPP¦EXE`

Key	Function
A	Toggles ambient light source
I	Toggles infinite light source
P	Toggles point light source
S	Toggles spotlight source
W	Toggled wire frame/solid mode
B	Toggles backface removal
L	Toggles lighting engine
Right arrow	Rotates player right
Left arrow	Rotates player left
Up arrow	Moves player forward
Down arrow	Moves player backward
Space bar	Turbo
H	Toggles Help menu
Esc	Exits demo

FIGURE 9.42 The good old tank demo with Gouraud shading and texture mapping.

Raiders 3D II

Now for the fun stuff! I've decided to remake the initial Chapter 1 space demo in full solid 3D. Figure 9.43 is a screenshot from the demo. It supports everything we've created so far: colored lights, texture mapping, and a lot more. It's very basic and a technology demo, so feel free to add all kinds of stuff. The demo is `RAIDERS3D_2.CPP¦EXE` and `RAIDERS3D_2B.CPP¦EXE` (a slightly different color scheme), and you will need to link in all library modules `T3DLIB1.CPP¦H` through `T3DLIB7.CPP¦H`. And, of course, remember to copy all the assets into your executable directory. Also remember that all texture maps use a texture directory named

```
char texture_path[80] = "./";
```

You may want to set it to `"TEXTURE/"` or something, but then remember all the textures must be contained within this subdirectory contained within your working directory of your final .EXE.

The game is similar to the version in Chapter 1, but is quite a bit more advanced. Use the mouse to move the targeting reticule and the left mouse button to fire. To exit, press Esc. The gameplay logic is very simple: You must destroy the incoming enemies with your particle beam weapons. When 25 enemies escape your clutches, the game ends. To restart, simply press Return. Some of the other engine controls are still available, for example:

W—Toggles the wireframe mode

I—Toggles the primary sun point light

A—Toggles the ambient light

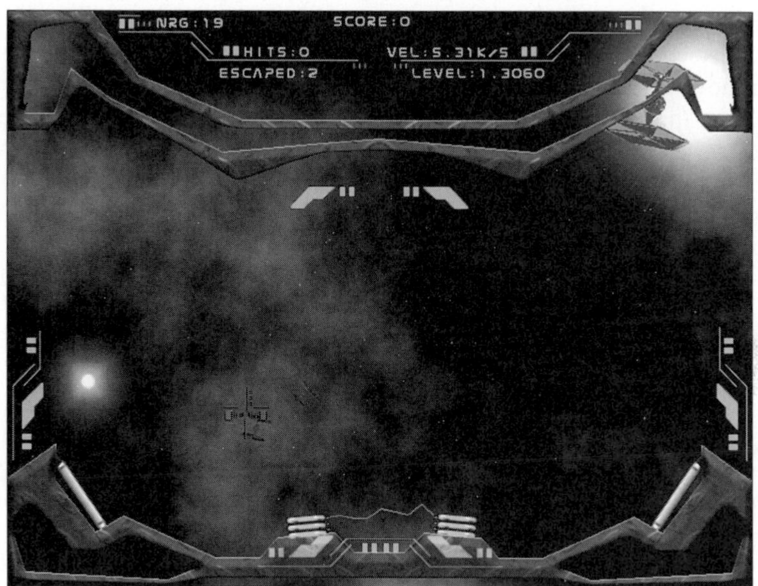

FIGURE 9.43 *Raiders 3D II.*

Even though the game is simple, there are a number of interesting features of the game that I would like to discuss one by one, so you can add to the game yourself.

The Stars

The 3D star field is implemented as a hack of sorts. Our engine has no support for stars, so to get them in there, I had to overlay them into the engine and render them in manually using the same view distance and window size for the perspective equations. However, for the most part, the star logic is straight out of Chapter 1's `RAIDERS3D.CPP|EXE` demo. Amazingly, we can get away with this because "particle"-like stars are so small, who cares if they're lit or z-sorted. However, we definitely need to add some support for particles in the engine soon so that we don't have to use hacks like this. On the other hand, I would hate to force something as simple as particles through the entire rendering process, so a happy medium is something we need to think about.

The Energy Weapons

This is a really cool effect. At first I had nothing more than straight lines to represent the weapons, but then I thought it would be cool to simulate a particle or plasma energy weapon that looked like lightning. To implement the weapons, I simply wrote code that took the two endpoints to draw the energy beam between, the number of segments to break the beam into, and finally the maximum amplitude. Amazingly, it worked on the first try and looks perfect!

The Collision Detection and Target Tracking

The collision detection is a bit of work to get right. Basically, you have a reticule that's in 2D that you move around on the screen. But the objects are in 3D space, so the trick is that you have to "project" the bounding box of each ship into 2D screen space and then test whether the center of the targeting reticule is within it. To accomplish this task, I simply found the bounding box of each ship, and then projected the four points defining the bounding box. Then I tested the reticule to see if it was in it. Nothing you haven't seen—it's just another application of it. However, this technique is important to be able to implement because it's the basis of 3D "picking" with a 2D position. But just remember: Project the 3D image's bounding box onto screen space and always work from there.

The Explosions

The explosions didn't quite turn out as dramatic as I had wished. The algorithm basically takes the polygon mesh of the alien ship and then copies it into an explosion mesh that's disposable. However, I purposely lose the vertex coherence, copy each polygon one by one, and replicate its vertices. This is done so that I can animate or transform each polygon individually in the object during the explosion phase. Then, during the explosion phase, I throw out the polygons (shrapnel) at different angles and velocities. It looks okay, but there's nothing like a bitmap explosion! Please add one on top of the polygon explosion—the game needs that, and I don't have time, but you do <BG>.

The Font Engine

As you know, GDI is very slow, and although displaying stats or other debugging information with it is okay, it's just too slow and clunky for game text. So, what I did was write a simple font engine for this game. The font engine uses two functions that you'll find in the `RAIDERS3D_2.CPP` itself, not the library:

```
int Load_Bitmap_Font(char *fontfile, BOB_PTR font);
```

The function loads a bitmap containing a templated font. The font must contain exactly 64 chanters in 4 rows of 16, and each character must be 16×14 pixels. The first character should be the SPACE char. Take a look at the file `tech_char_set_01.bmp` within the directory for this chapter. Also, you need to send the load font an empty BOB so that it will place the font in where each animation cell is a character.

The next function is used to display a string at any x,y position on the screen. You send it the BOB containing the bitmap font, the x,y string, and the horizontal and vertical spacing you would like, along with the surface to render on. Here's that function:

```
int Draw_Bitmap_Font_String(BOB_PTR font,
              int x, int y,
              char *string,
              int hpitch, int vpitch,
              LPDIRECTDRAWSURFACE7 dest);
```

Using them is trivial. I suggest reviewing the code to see them in action. I'll probably add them to our library next chapter with some cleanup.

Lighting in the Game

The whole point of this chapter is lighting! Well, this little demo has its share. There are four engine lights:

- An ambient light.
- A sun (white), which is a point light located in the upper-right sector of space.
- A sun (red), which is a point light located in the lower-left sector near the bitmap sun.
- An energy discharge, which is a point light, located a few hundred units in front of your ship. It's activated only when your weapons are engaged.

> **TIP**
>
> Try disabling the ambient light to see more dramatic lighting effects.

Final Comments

This game barely touches on the capabilities of our little engine. With some work, a complete 3D space game that you could probably sell could be constructed from this demo! It needs levels, goals, storyline, and so on, but the technology is there. And remember that this engine is 1/10 to 1/20 as fast as it could be after optimizations. Anyway, make sure to try both the red (`RAIDERS3D_2.EXE`) and green (`RAIDERS3D_2B.EXE`) versions of the game (they simply have different backgrounds).

Summary

This chapter was gigantic. I don't know what's happening, but I really want to try and cover as many details as possible. To cover both the theoretical ground as well as the practical and then write the code that does it is simply taking us places we never thought we would go! But I'm very happy with our progress. If you put this book down right now and forget the rest of it, you still have the capability to create a fully lit, colored, exterior 3D engine with texture mapping and 8/16-bit support—and that's pretty good.

I promise that the next chapter will be shorter, but please take some time and really mess with the code from this chapter and experiment with the demo. I don't have time to really ring out the engine and make really cool demos for you, but I have barely touched the surface of what our crude unoptimized engine can do. I'm sure you can make it do things that are amazing!

CHAPTER 10

Clipping in 3D++

IN THIS CHAPTER

"Don't worry, it's not a threat to you."

—Marla, *Fight Club*

We have avoided 3D clipping for quite some time, but it has finally caught up with us! There is simply no way we can avoid the issue any longer—not that I was trying to <BG>. In this chapter, I am going to cover both a theoretical as well as practical framework for clipping in 3D, the reasons behind the techniques, and what really works. Here are the general topic areas:

- Introduction to clipping
- Theoretical coverage of clipping algorithms
- Implementing view frustrum clipping
- A little fun with terrains

Introduction to Clipping

We have discussed clipping in general many times in both this book and in *Tricks of the Windows Game Programming Gurus, Second Edition*. Clipping is of the utmost importance in 3D graphics because geometry that is not clipped properly will not only be displayed incorrectly, but can cause divide-by-zero exceptions, memory crashes, and lots of other nasty problems. With that in mind, let's briefly recap the different kinds of clipping and the reasons for using each one.

Object Space Clipping

Object space clipping occurs when you clip the actual geometry of the primitives to some clipping region. The clipping region can be 2D or 3D, but the point is that object space clipping occurs in mathematical space using the mathematical representations of the objects, polygons, primitives, or whatever. The nice thing about object space clipping is that abstractly, it's very clean; you have an object or list of polygons, and you clip them to the view extents, either 2D or 3D, and you then send these clipping polygons (triangles in our case) to the next stage in the 3D pipeline.

The problem with the object space approach is, of course, in the details. We are always using triangles in our engine, so we must clip triangles to either 2D rectangles or 3D viewing pyramids. This can create polygons with more than three vertices (non-triangles). Put in another way, for each clipping plane, we have the potential to introduce extra vertices in each triangle during the clipping operation, making them quads or more; thus they have to be converted back into triangles. This might not be a clean process. If we had designed the engine so that polygons could have any number of vertices, this wouldn't be such an issue, but we have made numerous optimizations based on the knowledge that we are only using triangles. Secondly, performing clipping in any object space system means intersecting lines with lines, lines with planes, and so forth. This might seem easy, but again, it's a bit tricky, and there are lots of problems involved.

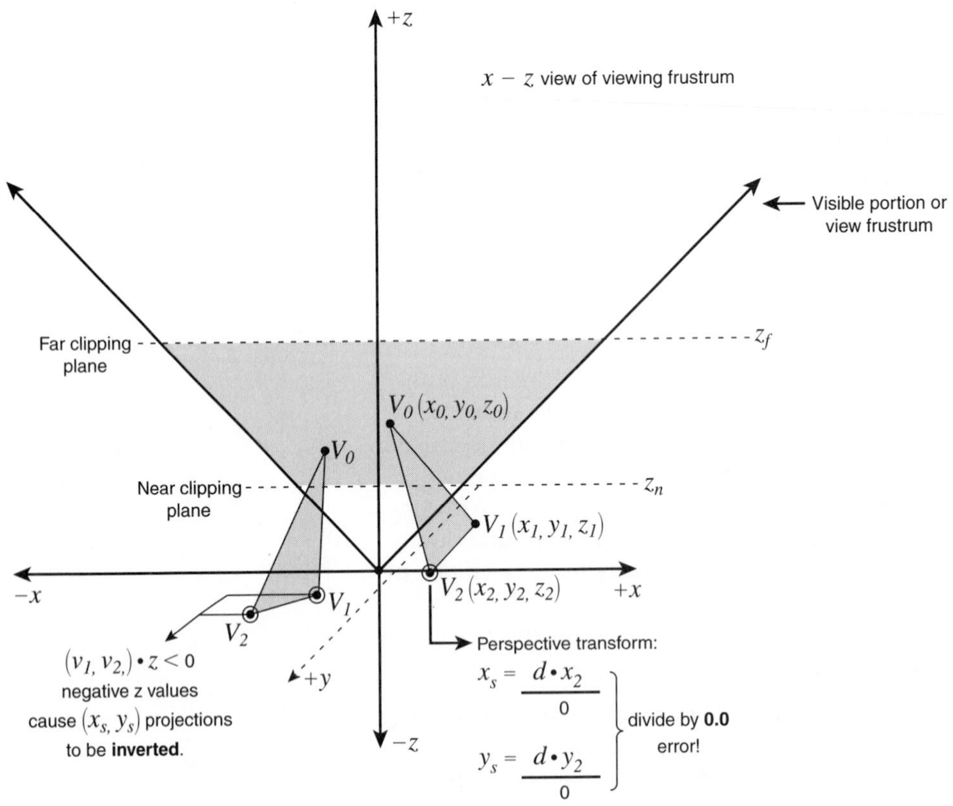

FIGURE 10.1 Projecting vertices with z less than or equal to 0 is bad.

2D Clipping in Object Space

2D clipping in object space is something that we have already performed, and have been doing for quite some time in 2D. The basic idea here is that we have lines or triangles that are *already* projected onto the viewplane and simply need to be clipped to the rectangular viewplane. The code to do this has been covered in both this book and more deeply in the first *Tricks*. Clipping in 2D isn't going to help us anymore because our major problem is that in 3D, we are projecting polygons that could potentially be so long that they not only pierce the near clipping plane in 3D, but also the z = 0 plane, and thus the projected vertices have negative z values. This is shown in Figure 10.1. Therefore, a more aggressive 3D clipping is needed in object space.

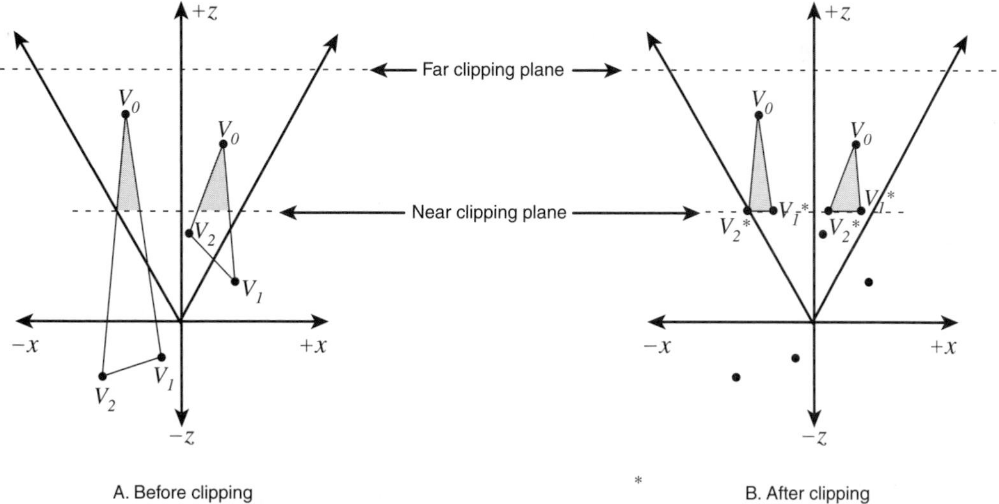

FIGURE 10.2 Long polygons must be clipped.

3D Clipping in Object Space

There is simply no way to avoid 3D clipping to the near clipping plane if you want to have geometry that has polygons with any size to it (the case shown in Figure 10.2). For example, you can get away with the trivial rejection and culling of polygons if they are small enough and move in their entirety beyond the near clipping plane, as shown in Figure 10.3, but if you are running around in an interior level, this isn't going to work.

At the very least, we must perform clipping of all polygons to the near clipping plane, and the resulting clipped polygons might no longer be triangles, but quads. Therefore we must split them once again into triangles, and re-insert them into the rendering list. So, at worst, we have to clip all polygons to the near clipping plane, which is a line/plane intersection. However, the details of this are more problematic. I have already mentioned the splitting triangle problem, but we *also* have to clip the texture coordinates, get any lighting information for Gouraud shading, and new vertex normals must be computed—lots of drama, but we will get to it.

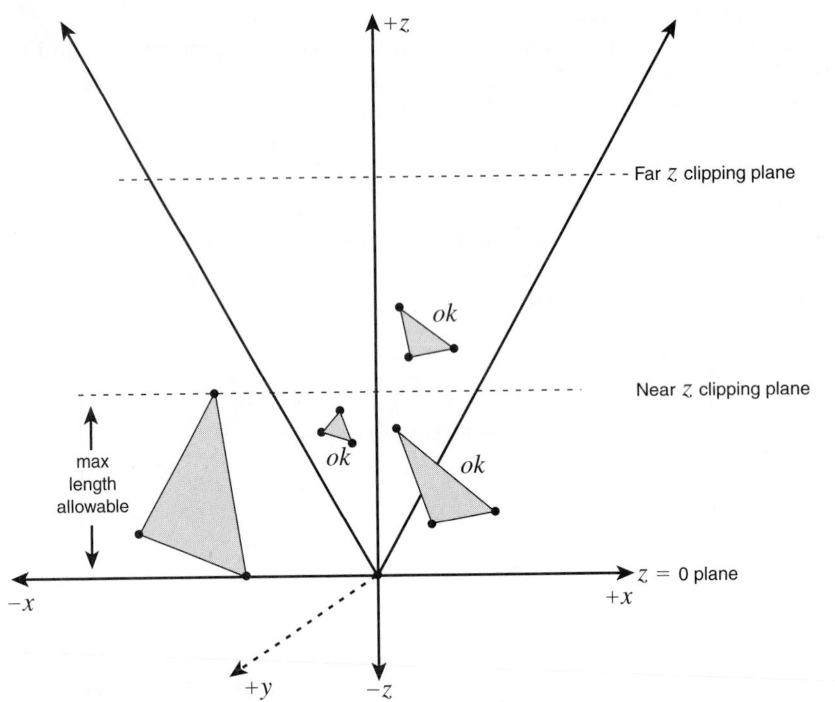

FIGURE 10.3 Little polygons can slip by.

On the other hand, we are going to learn that we do not need to clip our polygons to the other five view frustrum walls. Take a look at Figure 10.4. You see, clipping a polygon to the far z-clipping plane is a waste of time. What would we gain from that? Nothing, but it would waste time, so we will trivially reject polygons that are beyond the far clipping plane, no matter how long or short they are. If they are totally beyond the far z-clipping plane, we will cull them rather than try to clip them.

Similarly, the top/bottom and right/left clipping planes that make up the viewing frustrum also turn out to be a waste to clip to as well. The reason is that the clipping operations take a bit of time, and in the end, why are we clipping? We are clipping so that the final projected coordinates do not extend beyond the 2D view plane, but who cares? We can clip these polygons in image space during rasterization, which turns out to be as fast or faster. Plus, we don't mire the situation by adding even more polygons to the pipeline with top/bottom, right/left clipping to the viewing frustrum.

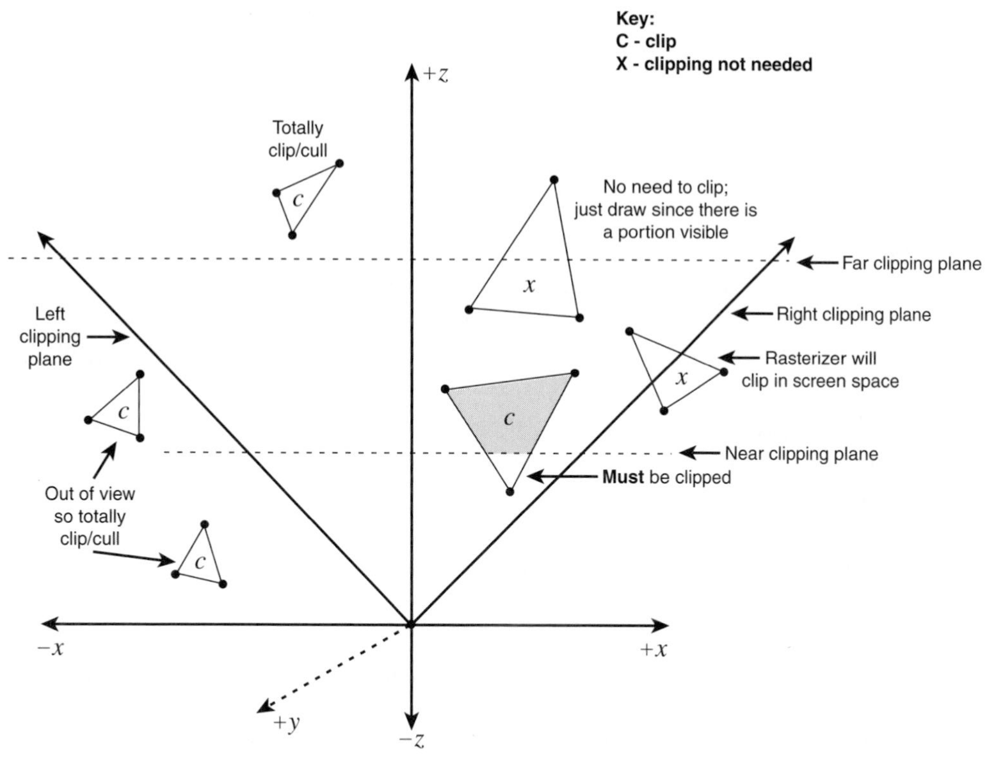

FIGURE 10.4 3D clipping need not be performed for all the view frustrum planes.

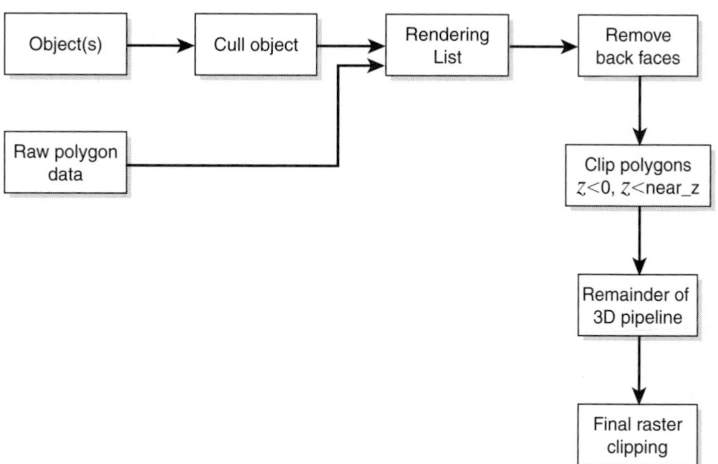

FIGURE 10.5 The steps in our 3D clipping pipeline.

Of course, if you want to do this for a clean design, you are more than welcome to do so, and I will show you how, but we are going to stick with the following steps for culling and clipping, as shown in Figure 10.5:

1. Cull all objects (if possible, you might not have objects in your system-only level data or large terrains).
2. Remove back-faces.
3. Clip all polygons to the viewing frustrum. Only the near z-clipping plane performs a full clip and split to polygons; the remaining five planes are a gross trivial accept-or-reject clip/cull. This means that if a triangle is entirely in the region or partially inside the viewing frustrum, pass it on; if it's completely outside the top/bottom, right/left clipping planes, cull it.
4. Pass all the polygons down the viewing pipeline, and any triangles that extend beyond the 2D boundaries of the viewing plane and screen space will be clipped in 2D during rasterization.

This is very easy system to implement, works perfectly, and is very fast.

Image Space Clipping

Finally, let's reiterate what we mean by image space clipping. Basically, we have the situation shown in Figure 10.6: A polygon is ready to be rasterized, but extends a bit over one of the 2D bounding lines that make up the viewplane/screen. This is no problem in the vertical cases. We just begin the rasterization loop lower from the top vertex by computing where the triangles begin on the screen. This takes one line of code to figure this out, and in the horizontal cases, we select a slightly different rasterizer that on each scanline as the primitive is being rendered we clip the line, but this is better than clipping every triangle to all four of the top/bottom, right/left clipping planes that make up the viewing frustrum and potentially adding many new polygons into the pipeline, clipping their texture coordinates, recomputing their normals, and so forth. It's bad enough clipping the polygons to the near clipping plane, and potentially splitting each one that intersects with it.

On the other hand, we don't want to image space clip polygons where we would lose any kind of 3D information; this is actually a very important point when we get to z-buffering and so forth. We must be careful about what we do in screen space when we start interpolating z values down polygon edges, and at least keeping the z components of vertices around will become important. What I am saying is that we might find that when we finally rasterize, we *cannot* clip in screen space anymore with only 2D coordinates. But let's see how things go, and worry about what happens later.

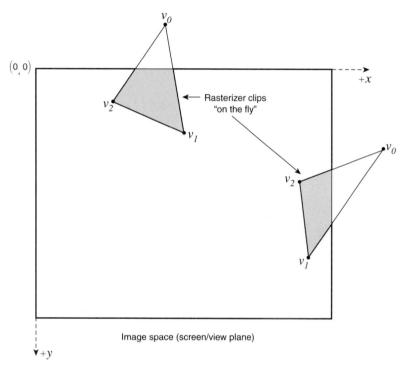

FIGURE 10.6 Image space clipping during rasterization.

Theoretical Coverage of Clipping Algorithms

Before I get started, I want to say one thing: I think it's almost ridiculous how there are all these "named" clipping algorithms. I have personally thought of every single one before I even knew they existed—which doesn't mean I am smart, it just means that they are simply common sense for anyone that writes graphics algorithms. Figuring out how not to pay taxes—that would make me smart <BG>. Algorithm naming is a problem prevalent in computer graphics: Someone "thinks" she's come up with a new "algorithm," publishes it, and from then on the algorithm has a name. Of course, this is many times not the author's intention; she just writes a paper, and then it's someone *else* that keeps referring to the algorithm by that name.

Clipping is far too simple to even think that it was "discovered." Every clipping algorithm is just a slight variation on intersecting lines and common sense. I personally just make all my algorithms to suit the job—sometimes I re-invent something, sometimes I don't. The point I am trying to make is that I am going to list the accepted clipping algorithms by

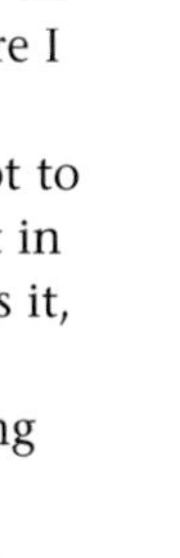

name, but do me a favor—please don't think that these are the only ways to do it. As I am sure you know, many times you spend hours trying to figure something out, only to find out later it's very similar to something else already solved. In the case of clipping, I wish the algorithms had more descriptive names—that's all. I don't know if they are algorithm names or law firms!

I think that for an algorithm to have a name, it should have a sufficient level of sophistication, and it has to be completely non-obvious to the average person in that field. I think something like Binary Space Partitioning should be named after the inventor because that's not something that's totally obvious; whereas the second you try to clip a polygon against another polygon, within 1–2 hours you go through every permutation of line clipping, vertex classification, bit encoding, parametric line representations there is. Guess what: You just thought of everything I am about to show you!

TIP

The point of the preceding paragraph is for you to try new things yourself. Ninety-nine percent of the time what you have thought of has been thought of before, but it might not be published, so just use it and be happy!

Now that I have complained about this, let's get to it! I'm going to cover some of the most popular clipping algorithms from a theoretical point of view, and then later we will actually implement one for our needs. Our algorithm will be a hybrid of many of the concepts, because I just made it up to solve the problem. Let's begin with a little background on clipping.

Clipping Fundamentals

Clipping polygons reduces to clipping lines, which reduces to determining whether points are within some region—either a 2D area or a 3D volume. Figure 10.7 illustrates the general problem. We have a collection of lines/geometry that make up the polygons of our scene that we are going to project at some point, and we must determine whether these entities are within some boundary. This simplifies to determining whether single points are within a boundary. In other words, all triangles are made of three points that define three edges. Although the edges make the geometry "solid" or "real," it's the points that really matter. Hence, at the lowest level, we need to determine whether a point (x,y) or (x,y,z) is inside or outside a bounding area/volume with *point testing*.

Point Testing 2D Case

Given a point in 2D **p0**(x,y) and a rectangular region bounded by xmin, xmax, ymin, ymax as seen in Figure 10.7, the point is inside if it satisfies the following inequalities:

```
{xmin <= x <=xmax} and {ymin <= y <=ymax}
```

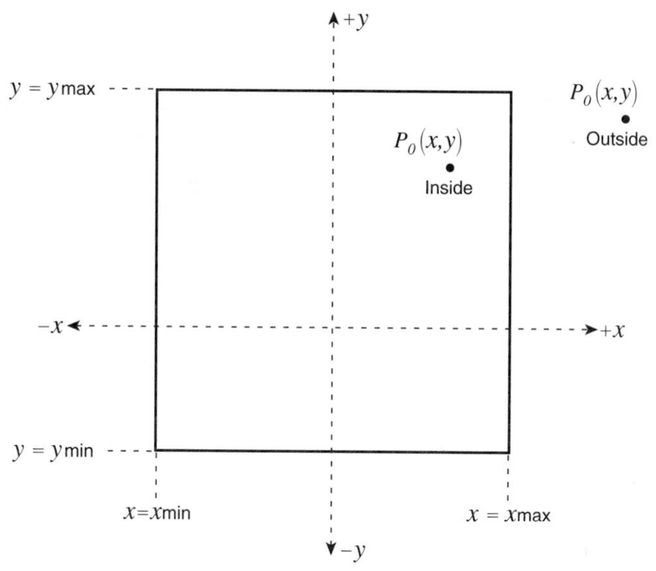

FIGURE 10.7 Point testing in 2D.

Point Testing 3D Cases
***Subcase 1**: Cuboid volume*

Given a point in 3D **p0**(x,y,z) and a rectangular cuboid region bounded by xmin, xmax, ymin, ymax, zmin, and zmax as seen in Figure 10.8, the point is inside if it satisfied the following inequalities:

```
{xmin <= x <=xmax} and {ymin <= y <=ymax} and {zmin <= z <=zmax}
```

You might wonder why we care about clipping to a cuboid when we know that the viewing frustrum is a pyramid shape made of six planes. This is true, but remember when we discussed projection, and the perspective projection had the effect of "straightening" out the viewing frustrum into a cuboid shape? In this case, the clipping volume is trivial and simple comparisons to the containment walls are all that is needed to perform the clipping operation. Additionally, no one ever said that clipping is only for the viewing frustrum—maybe you want to clip laser beams in a cube or rectangular solid somewhere out in the middle of a game universe.

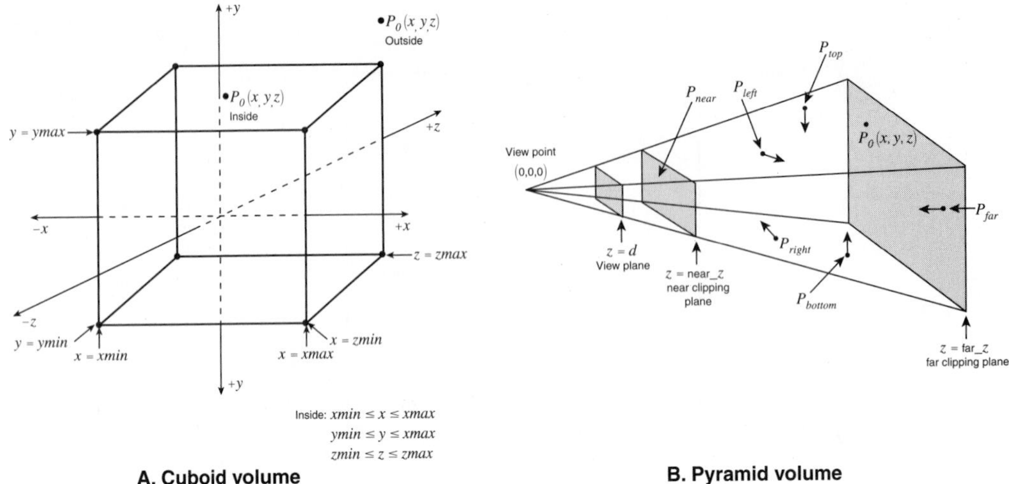

FIGURE 10.8 Point testing in 3D.

Subcase 2: *General pyramid shape viewing frustrum*

This case is the one that we are going to deal with. It's the standard case, in which we have six planes that make up the viewing frustrum that all geometry must be clipped to. In this case, we can define the viewing frustrum in a number of ways: the z position of the z-clipping planes, along with a field of view for the horizontal and vertical extents, for example, but the bottom line is that we are going to end up with six planes. Let's call them **P**top, **P**bottom, **P**right, **P**left, **P**far, and **P**near. Additionally, let's assume that we have defined the planes in such a way that they are consistently constructed with all normals pointing inward, toward the interior of the viewing frustrum. Then given a point **p0**(x,y,z) we compute the half space that the point is in. Positive half space means the point is on the interior side of the clipping plane, whereas a negative half space means that the point is on the negative side of the clipping plane, or outside the clipping plane and the viewing frustrum. If you recall, to determine whether a point is *on* a plane or in the positive or negative half space, we simply plug the point into the plane equation (this was covered in Chapter 4, " It's a Math, Math, Math World—Trigonometry, Vectors, Matrices, and Quaternions," and Chapter 5, "Building a Math Engine"). So, let's assume the operator HS(**p**, pln) outputs the half space value for the point **p**, and the plane pln, +1 for positive half space, -1 for negative, and 0 for on the plane itself.

So we need to determine whether the following inequalities are satisfied:

```
{HS(p0, Ptop)  > 0} and {HS(p0, Pbottom) > 0} and
{HS(p0, Pright) > 0} and {HS(p0, Pleft)  > 0} and
{HS(p0, Pnear) > 0} and {HS(p0, Pfar)  > 0}
```

That seems like a lot of work, but it's really not.

Line Clipping Basics

Now we can determine whether points are inside or outside a clipping region that is either 2D or 3D. The next step is to move up the hierarchy and clip the lines/edges that are defined by the points that make up the triangles of the mesh. Thus, we need tools to intersect line segments with infinite lines and/or finite segments. Once again, we covered all this in Chapters 4 and 5, so I am not going to cover it again in depth, but I will refresh your memory.

Polygon clipping is one baby step above line clipping, so I don't want to spoil everything, but basically we just need to think of how to clip a line segment against another infinite line (in 2D) or a plane (in 3D). A full clipping algorithm is nothing more than iteratively or recursively applying the clipping procedure over and over for every line segment that makes up the polygon against every clipping boundary. Of course, the point of the clipping algorithms is to minimize the work, but for the most part, that's clipping: 2D, 3D, whatever.

Line Clipping 2D Case Anyway, back to the line clipping problem. Let's do the 2D case first. Referring to Figure 10.9, we see a line from point **p0**(x0,y0) to **p1**(x1,y1) that we want to clip against the vertical line at x = xl.

NOTE

In most cases, we don't need to clip our triangles against arbitrary lines, so studying the horizontal or vertical clipping case is sufficient.

To clip the line, all we need to do is convert the line into parametric form and then plug in the vertical x value at which we want to find the intersection. Here's the derivation:

In vector form, the position of the point along the line segment is

```
p = p0 + (p1-p0)*t
```

In component form:

```
x = x0 + (x1 - x0)*t, {0 <= t <= 1}
y = y0 + (y1 - y0)*t, {0 <= t <= 1}
```

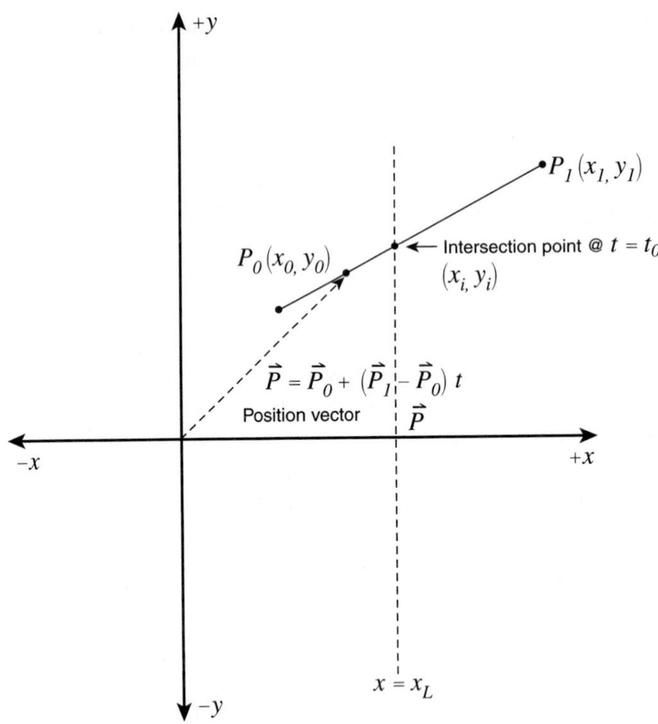

FIGURE 10.9 Simple line clipping.

If we want to test for an intersection of the line with a vertical line, we plug the x value that defines the vertical line (in this case, x = xL) into the left-hand side of the equation for x, and then solve for t. If {0 <= t <= 1}, there is an intersection; if there isn't:

```
x = x0 + (x1 - x0)*t
```

Plugging xL into the left-hand side, we get

```
xL = x0 + (x1 - x0)*t
```

Solving for t:

```
(xL - x0)/(x1 - x0) = t
```

If t is between 0 and 1, there was an intersection on the segment itself. Remember, a parametric line defined as we have defined it thus far exists from **p0** to **p1** when {0 <= t <= 1}; t values beyond this range are still on the line, but not on the *segment* from **p0** to **p1**. Anyway, assuming we have a good t, we just plug it into the equation for y:

```
y = y0 + (y1 - y0)*t
```

And then we have our (x,y) intersection with the vertical line defined by x = xL. Computing the horizontal case is just as trivial, but instead of solving for t in terms of the x equation, we use the y equation. Let's do it for a horizontal line y = yL:

Plugging yL into the left-hand side, we get

```
yL = y0 + (y1 - y0)*t
```

Solving for t:

```
(yL - y0)/(y1 - y0) = t
```

Again, a sanity check on t. If {0 <= t <= 1}, there is an intersection, and we plug t into the equation for x:

```
x = x0 + (x1 - x0)*t
```

And once again, we get the (x,y) of the intersection with the vertical line.

Of course, you need to use some common sense and trivial rejection tests here. If the endpoints **p0** and **p1** are the same, there's no need to perform intersection tests. Similarly, trying to intersect a horizontal line with another horizontal line doesn't make sense, and so on.

Line Clipping 3D Case The 3D case of line clipping is just as simple as the 2D case—it's all a matter of how you want to represent the planes. But at this point we're not using any tricks, so let's review the general case where we have a plane equation in 3D and a parametric line equation in 3D. Referring to Figure 10.10, let's construct the problem. First the plane equation—we define a plane using the point normal form:

Let **p0** = (x0, y0, z0) be a point on the plane, and n =< nx, ny, nz> be the normal to the plane:

```
nx*(x - x0) + ny*(y - y0) + nz*(z - z0) = 0
```

And now a parametric line from **p1** to **p2** in vector form:

```
p = p1 + (p2 - p1)*t, {0 <= t <= 1}
```

In component form:

```
x = x1 + (x2 - x1)*t
y = y1 + (y2 - y1)*t
z = z1 + (z2 - z1)*t
```

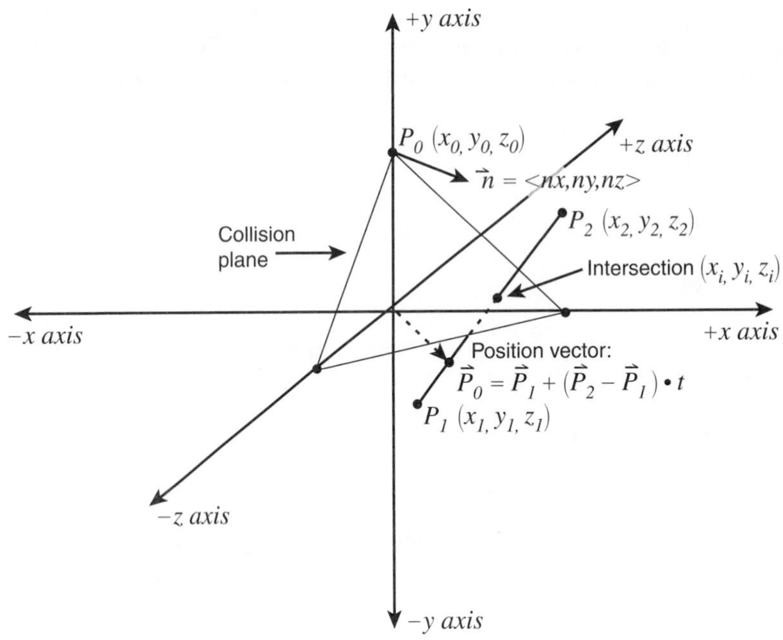

FIGURE 10.10 3D line intersecting a plane.

Now we need to compute the intersection. Once again, this is in Chapter 4, in the section "Computing the Intersection of a 3D Parametric Line and a 3D Plane," but the results are derived basically by plugging in the values for x,y,z of the parametric line into the plane equation and solving for t:

```
nx*(x - x0) + ny*(y - y0) + nz*(z - z0) = 0
```

Now plug x,y,z into the plane equation:

```
nx*(( x1 + (x2 - x1)*t) - x0) +
ny*(( y1 + (y2 - y1)*t) - y0) +
nz*(( z1 + (z2 - z1)*t) - z0) = 0
```

Now solve for t and plug back into the parametric line to solve for x,y,z to find the actual point. We already did this, so I am skipping the math to save space. You get the idea. That's all there is to clipping—once you can intersect a line with a line and a line with a plane, you have the problem beat. All you really need then is to come up with an algorithm that fits your situation. Let's look at some of the more common clipping algorithms with this in mind.

Cohen-Sutherland Clipping

The Cohen-Sutherland algorithm is one of the most popular methods to clip lines to a rectangular region in 2D or a cuboid region in 3D. The algorithm has two distinct phases.

Endpoint Classification Phase

In the classification phase, each line segment in 2D or 3D is classified as being inside or outside the clipping boundary by using bit codes to encode the position of each end point as being inside (`FALSE`) or outside (`TRUE`). This classification code scheme is shown for the 2D case in Figure 10.11.

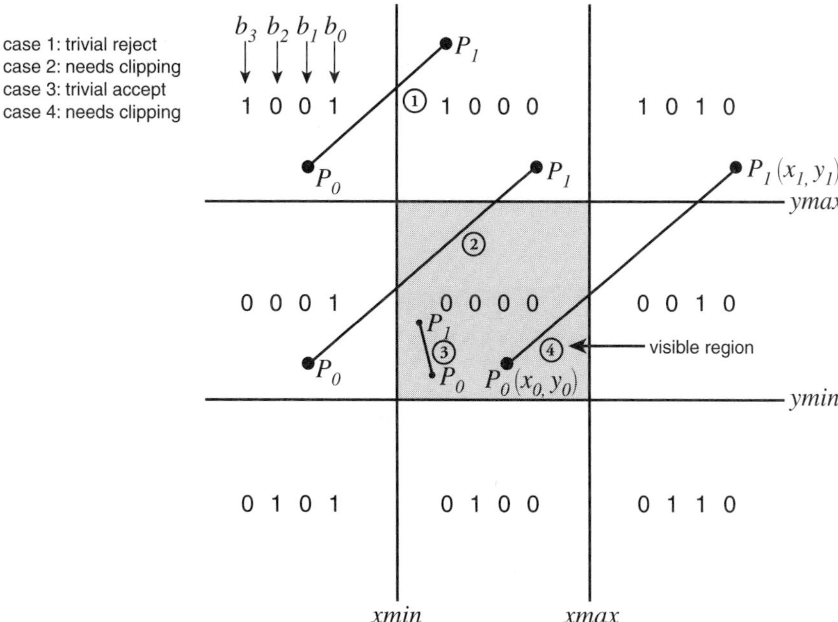

FIGURE 10.11 The bit code classification code system for Cohen-Sutherland clipping.

Each vertex (x,y) of the line **p0**(x0, y0) to **p1**(x1,y1) is classified. A 4-bit (6-bit for 3D) code is derived for the line segment; we'll call it `bitcode0` for vertex **p0**, and `bitcode1` for vertex **p1**. The bits can be encoded any way you want, but generally, given a rectangular bounding region in 2D of {xmin, xmax} to {ymin, ymax}, Table 10.1 lists one possible encoding.

TABLE 10.1 The Bit Encodings for Cohen-Sutherland Algorithm Outcodes

Bit	Meaning when TRUE
b3	y > ymax, above top edge
b2	y < ymin, below bottom edge
b1	x > xmax, to right of right edge
b0	x < xmin, to left of left edge

10

After the end points of the line have been classified, the algorithm moves on to the processing phase, where the actual analysis and clipping occur.

The Processing Phase

The processing phase begins by trying to trivially reject or accept line segments. The cool thing about this algorithm is that it's really doing a precalculation to save us time with writing lots of redundant `if` statements. Because we have a bit-encoding word for each vertex, we can use bitwise logic operations to ask multiple questions at once (like the adversary argument, for you combinatorialists). For example, suppose you want to know whether your line is outside the clipping region. You would have to ask if both vertices are above, below, to the right, to the left—that's a lot of `if` statements! But it's trivial with the bit classification codes, because we can use logical operators to ask questions in parallel. The trivial rejection/acceptance cases are as follows:

Test 1: If (`bitcode0=0`) and (`bitcode1=0`), the line **p0->p1** is totally within the clipping region and no clipping is needed. Refer to Figure 10.11.

Next, we logically `AND` each bit code together and look at the results:

```
bc = (bitcode0 & bitcode1)
```

Test 2: If (bc > 0), both vertices are beyond at least one common boundary and the line can be trivially rejected. Refer to Figure 10.11.

After tests 1 and 2 have been performed and failed, the hard work comes—each line segment can potentially intersect one or two points and must be clipped. This case is also shown in Figure 10.11. There are a number of ways to approach this contingency. One method is to clip the line to both of the lines it goes out of bounds on, creating one or two more segments, and then to reapply the algorithm to the segments. A divide-and-conquer algorithm might be used to compute these intersections, or perhaps through brute force (which isn't bad). Usually I find myself using the classification part of this algorithm and then hybridizing the last part after the two trivial cases have failed.

Cyrus-Beck/Liang-Barsky Clipping

The next algorithm is a little more generalized, and works in terms of both parametric lines, as well as general convex boundaries (2D or 3D) to clip to. The algorithm operates on the premise that it's more natural to think of lines in their parametric form, and uses t values for the intersections rather than explicit (x,y) (or x,y,z) points. Thus, the clipping conditionals and logic can be performed on the intersecting t values at a high level, and the magnitude of the t intersection values, as well as their ranges, can shed light on the intersections and their properties, and clean up the crude low-level details of Cohen-Sutherland a bit.

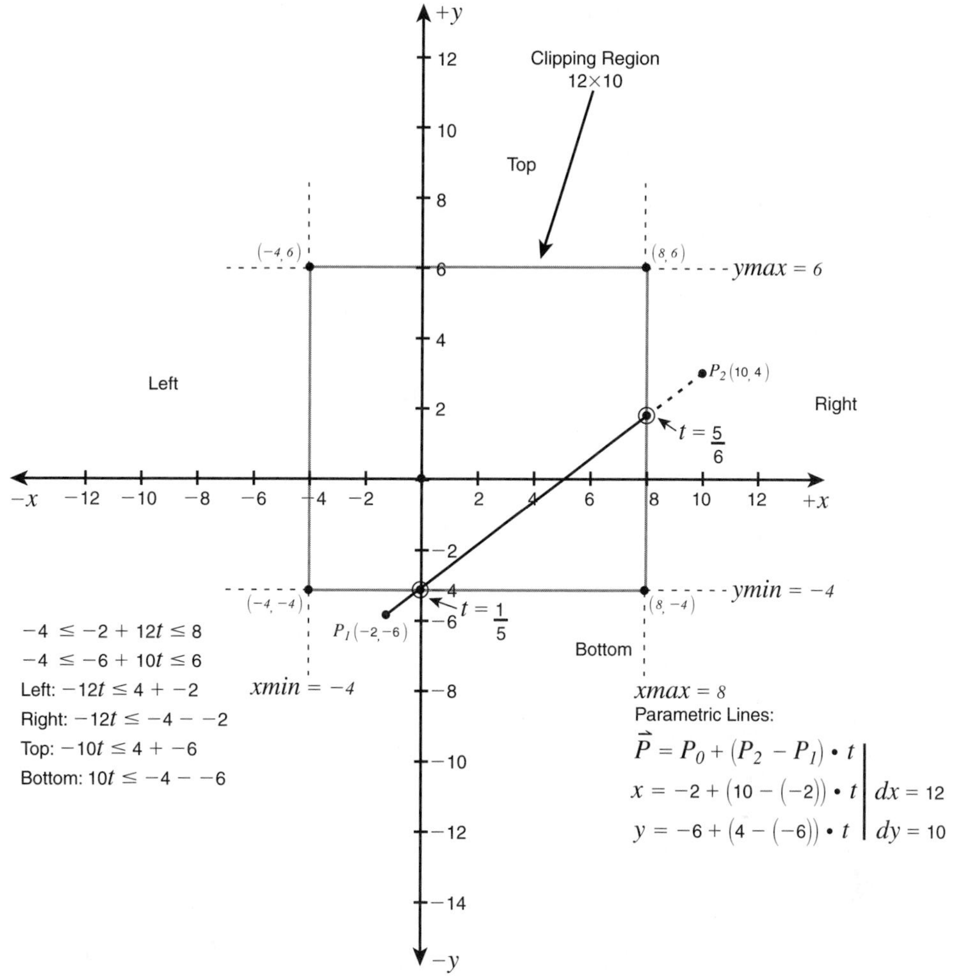

FIGURE 10.12 The setup for Cyrus-Beck/Liang-Barsky clipping.

In Figure 10.12, let's consider the 2D case. We have a boundary defined by {xmin, xmax} to {ymin, ymax} and a parametric 2D line of the form

```
p = p1 + (p2 - p1)*t, {0 <= t <= 1}
```

Or in component form, letting dx = (x2 – x1) and dy = (y2 – y1):

```
x = x1 + dx*t
y = y1 + dy*t
```

10

We want these inequalities to hold true for the line to remain inside the clipping region:

```
Left & Right Side: xmin <= x1 + dx*t <= xmax
Bottom & Top Side: ymin <= y1 + dy*t <= ymax
```

Which further simplifies to these equations:

```
Left:    xmin <= (x1 + dx*t)
Right:    -(x1 + dx*t) >= -xmax


Top:   -(y1 + dy*t) >= -ymax
Bottom:   ymin <= (y1 + dy*t)
```

And finally, we simplify once more to get the dx*t and dx*y terms on the same side of the inequality:

```
Left:    xmin-x1 <= dx*t
Right:    -dx*t >= -xmax + x1


Top:   -dy*t >= -ymax + y1
Bottom:   ymin - y1 <= dy*t
```

Multiplying by (-1) to flip the inequalities:

FORMULA 10.1 The Clipping Inequalities

```
Left side inequality  n=0:    -dx*t <= (-xmin + x1)
Right side inequality n=1:     dx*t <= (xmax - x1)
Top side inequality  n=2:    dy*t <= (ymax - y1)
Bottom side inequality n=3:     -dy*t <= (-ymin + y1)
```

TIP

I had a heck of a time getting these inequalities correct. It's really easy to make a mistake when flipping the direction of the comparison signs, so go slow. Remember the rule: when you divide or multiply either side by a negative number, you must invert the comparison sign.

Assuming that each inequality is of the form p_n*t < q*n*, where *n* means the *n*th inequality as labeled previously, then we have the following cases:

Case 1: If (p_n = 0), the segment is parallel with the boundary and can't possible intersect it.

Case 2: If (p_n >= 0), the segment is inside the boundary.

Case 3: If (p_n < 0), the segment is outside the boundary.

Case 4: If ($p_n < 0$), the segment extends from outside the boundary to inside the boundary intersecting the segment.

Case 5: If ($p_n > 0$), the segment extends from inside the boundary to outside the boundary intersecting the segment.

I know, I know, it's confusing. However, if you review the cases a few times, basically we only need to be concerned with Cases 4 and 5. These are the cases where we need to do some work. We need to solve for the t intersection point for each inequality, but at the same time, keeping track of which case we are dealing with (Case 4 or 5) when we perform the computation of t is done with

$$p_n * t < q_n$$

Therefore,

$$t = q_n / p_n = r_n$$

We perform this computation for each of the four inequalities n = 0,1,2,3, and call each of the results r_n for {n = 0, 1, 2, 3}. So, r_n is the t intersection value when we perform the calculation q_n / p_n, which is one of the inequalities in Formula 10.1.

For the final step, we classify which r_n values were the result of segments *entering* the clipping region ($p_n < 0$), and which were the results of segments *exiting* the clipping region ($p_n > 0$). For those r_n values computed when ($p_n < 0$), we compute the value of t1:

$$t1 = max(0, r_n)$$

For the t values we computed when the segments were exiting (pn > 0), we compute the value of t2:

```
t2 = min(1, rn)
```

So what does this mean? Once again, here's what we are doing: We try the trivial rejection tests, they fail, so now we come to Cases 4 and 5. To solve these, we must compute the intersection values of our line segment with the boundaries of the region. We have four equations that we need to solve for $p_n * t < q_n$, so we compute the t value for each of the four inequalities (which are numbered and listed in Formula 10.1) and call each resulting t value r_n. Then we sort the r_n values based on whether or not they resulted from segments entering or exiting the clipping region. Then we compute two final t values called t1 and t2, which are the final intersections we need to clip this darn line!

If (t1 > t2), the line segment is completely out of the clipping region and we can exit. Otherwise, we need to clip the line by plugging t1 and t2 into the parametric equation of the line and the resulting two vertices **pi1** and **pi2**:

```
pi1 = p1 + (p2 - p1)*t1
pi2 = p1 + (p2 - p1)*t2
```

These are the vertices that define the clipped line. I agree that this algorithm seems like a nightmare, but it's only hard for humans to follow—it really is very straightforward for the computer to solve. This algorithm works perfectly, and is much better than the Cohen-Sutherland algorithm, because it's based on parametric lines and transfers easily to 3D.

An Example of the Algorithm

To solidify our discussion about this algorithm, let's try a simple example to make sure it works, shall we? In Figure 10.12, we see our clipping region in quadrant I, slightly offset, so we have the following setup:

```
xmin = -4, xmax = 8
ymin = -4, ymax = 6

p1=(-2,-6), p2=(10,4)

p = p1 + (p2-p1)*t

x = -2 + (10 - (-2))*t = -2 + 12*t
y = -6 + (4- (-6))*t = -6 + 10*t
```

Therefore, dx = 12 and dy = 10. Now, let's run the algorithm and compute each inequality:

```
Left:    -dx*t <= (-xmin + x1)
Right:     dx*t <= (xmax - x1)
Top:    dy*t <= (ymax - y1)
Bottom:    -dy*t <= (-ymin + y1)
```

Plugging in our values:

```
Left:    -12*t <= (-(-4) + (-2))    = (2)
Right:     12*t <= (8 - (-2))      = (10)
Top:    10*t <= (6 - (-6))      = (12)
Bottom:    -10*t <= (-(-4) + (-6))    = (-2)
```

Extracting out p_n, q_n, and computing r_n for each case:

```
Left:    -12*t <= (2), p0=-12, q0=2, r0=(q0/p0)=-1/6
Right:    12*t <= (10), p1=12, q1=10, r1=(q1/p1)=5/6
Top:  10*t <= (12), p2=10, q2=12, r2=(q2/p2)=6/5
Bottom:  -10*t <= (-2), p3=-10, q3=-2, r2=(q3/p3)=1/5
```

Now we split into two cases. First, when ($p_n < 0$), we compute the value of t1:

```
t1 = max(0, rn) = max(0, -1/6, 1/5) = 1/5.
```

For the t values we computed when the segments were exiting ($p_n > 0$), we compute the value t2:

```
t2 = min(1, rn) = min(1, 5/6, 6/5) = 5/6.
```

Whew! Now we test whether (t1 > t2). If so, the line is totally out of the clipping region. This is obviously not true from the figure, but our math tells us t1 < t2. Thus, we need to plug t1 and t2 into our parametric line equation, and the result will be a shiny new line! Plugging in t1 = 1/5, we get

```
x1' = -2 + 12*(1/5) = -2 + 2.4 = .4
y1' = -6 + 10*(1/5) = -6 + 10/6 = -4.0
```

and plugging in t2 = 5/6, we get

```
x2' = -2 + 12*(5/6) = -2 + 10 = 8
y2' = -6 + 10*(5/6) = -6 + 50/6 = 2.3
```

Thus, the final clipped line segment is **p0**'(0.4, -4.0) to **p1**'(8.0, 2.3), which if you refer to Figure 10.12, looks about right (it better be!)

If you think about the algorithm for a moment, what it's really doing is helping you classify and organize little pieces of information in a clean manner. The ironic thing is that if you look at the code structure of many clippers written by people without knowledge of this algorithm, the code follows the same kind of information flow, so that tells me something—the algorithm is really good!

We won't be formally implementing this algorithm, but maybe later when we get to optimizing, we'll redo the old Cohen-Sutherland algorithm for 2D clipping with this one. Which brings me to a point: can this algorithm be used in 3D? Of course. To convert it to 3D, the exact same procedure is used, except that the inequalities are now whether or not the points are on the positive or negative half space of the planes. Thus, you need to use the dot-product or half-space test.

Weiler-Atherton Clipping

The final algorithm I want to cover fits more of the mindset that polygons are made of vertices, and a vertex is either contained within the clipping region or not. The algorithm is designed to clip any polygon against any other polygon. By this determination, if each vertex that defines a polygon is within the clipping region, the edge that it defines is either leaving or entering the clipping region. In Figure 10.13, the polygon we want clipped is called the *subject polygon*, and the polygon that we are clipping against is called the *clipping polygon*.

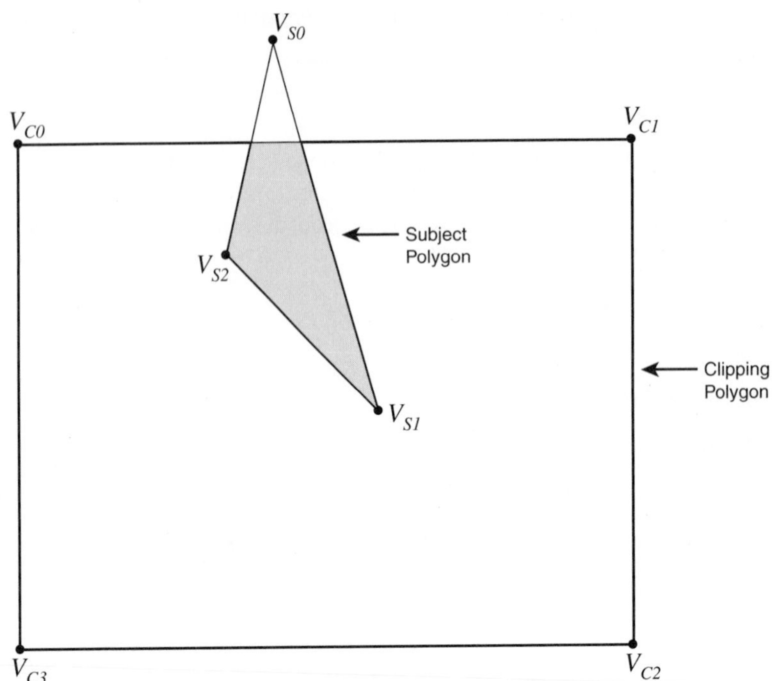

FIGURE 10.13 Weiler-Atherton clipping setup.

To set things up properly, the polygons must be defined by a list of vertices in an array or linked list and be ordered in some consistent manner. Let's assume a clockwise ordering for both. The algorithm begins with the subject polygon vertex 0, and computes its intersection with each edge of the clipping polygon. If an intersection is found, the intersection point is added to *both* the subject polygon list *and* the clipping polygon's vertex list (in between the vertices that make up the edge that the intersection occurred), but marked with an entering or exiting flag, indicating whether the intersection occurred when an edge was entering or leaving the clipping region. After these lists are generated, the following procedure is followed to generate the *resulting polygon*:

1. Find the first intersection in the subject polygon list that is an entering point. Output this point as the first vertex of the resulting clipped polygon.

2. Traverse the subject polygon until another intersection point is found. While you do this, add each point you visit to the final resulting polygon. When you reach this intersection point, it must by definition be the exiting point.

3. Based on the location where you found the intersection point in the subject polygon list, you must now traverse the clipping polygon list until you find the *same* intersection point (to synchronize the lists).

4. Now traverse the clipping polygon list and output each vertex you visit to the resulting polygon until you find another intersection point. You are now at the entering point.
5. If the intersection point from step 4 is not equal to the first point of the result polygon, go back to step 2 (you're trying to close the polygon).
6. If the intersection point from step 4 is equal to the first point of the result polygon, the polygon is closed, but not necessarily complete. If all the entering points in the subject polygon have been included, you are done (use a counter or flags for this); otherwise, traverse to the next entering point on the subject polygon and jump back to step 2.

The preceding algorithm works great and will clip any polygon to any other polygon. Figure 10.14 depicts a flowchart of the actual algorithm working on a simple case for a few steps.

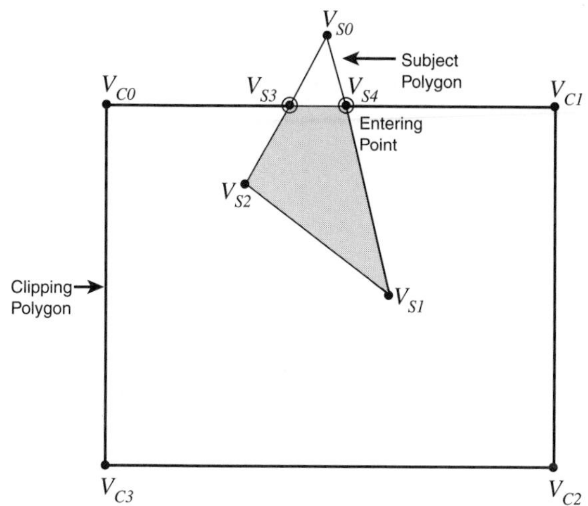

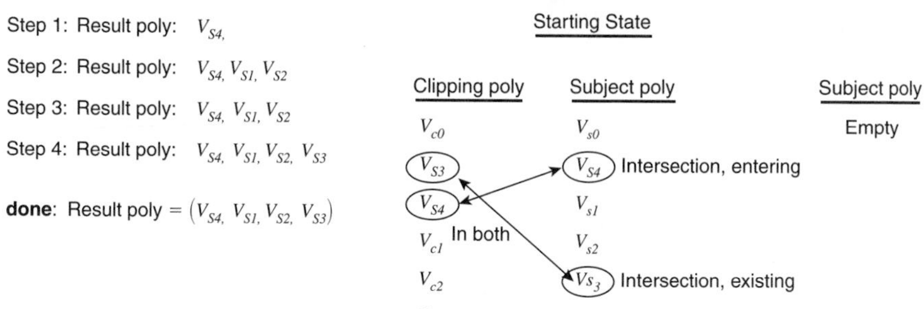

FIGURE 10.14 The Weiler-Atherton algorithm in action.

I personally don't like the thought of all the pre-processing and then making multiple passes over the vertex lists. Also, remember that we are dealing with triangles here, and we can't afford long algorithms in general. In most cases, we just need to hack together a clipping algorithm based on these ideas that is super fast. Anyway, another algorithm based on the Weiler-Atherton algorithm's idea of entering and exiting polygons is as follows:

First, let's just think of one polygon (a triangle) that we want to clip to a single line or plane (we can use multiple lines or planes to make up regions or volumes by repeating the process). You start by classifying the starting vertex as inside or outside the clipping region. If it's inside, you output that vertex, and if it's not, you do nothing and move onto the next vertex. If the start point and end points of an edge have different states (one is inside, one is outside), you find the intersection and output that vertex. Basically you simply traverse the edges that make up a polygon one by one. If you happen to start in the clipping region, great. Anytime you exit out of the clipping region, you emit the intersection point and continue. Then when you finally reach an edge that re-enters the clipping region, you emit that intersection and continue. This is really a simplified version of Weiler-Atherton, but is more real-time and on the fly. It's actually what I use most of the time in one form or another, because it's overkill to create complex clipping vertex lists for the clipping rectangle and subject polygon since I know that they are both so simple. Figure 10.15 illustrates the simplified algorithm working on a simple case.

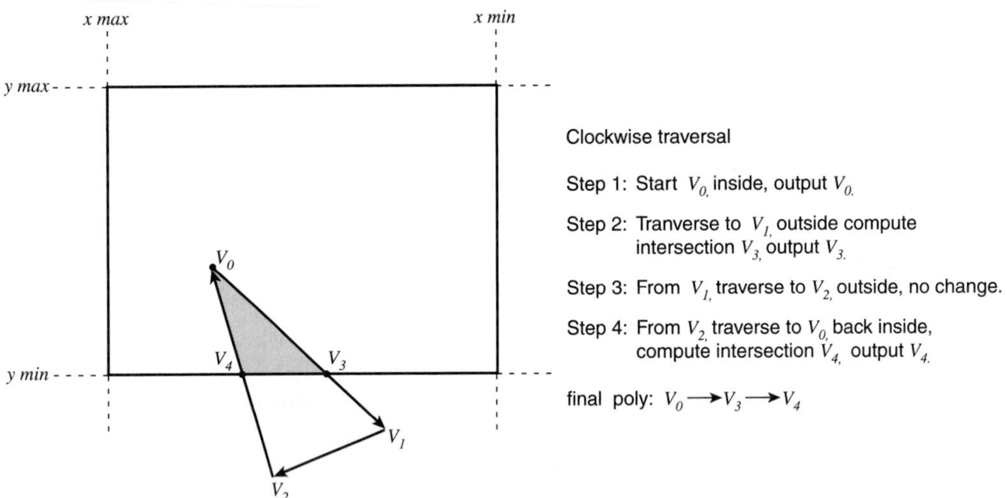

FIGURE 10.15 The simplified Weiler-Atherton algorithm.

Further Studies on Clipping

So that's it, baby! You know how to clip! Seriously, there isn't much to it—you use one of the algorithms or a hybrid and for the most part, just find intersections of your polygons with 2D regions on 3D volumes. Next we are going to actually implement 3D clipping for the engine in a practical way, but if you want to learn more about clipping algorithms, there are some great books on the subject. This is where the academic texts really shine; although academic books are useless for implementing real-time game algorithms, they do at least have full coverage of the algorithms in gory detail. Some of my favorites are the following:

- *Computer Graphics: Principles and Practice* by Foley, van Dam, Feiner, and Hughes (Addison-Wesley)
- *Introduction to Computer Graphics* by Foley, van Dam, Feiner, Hughes, and Phillips (Addison-Wesley)
- *3D Computer Graphics* by Alan H. Watt (Addison-Wesley)
- *Procedural Elements for Computer Graphics* by David F. Rogers (McGraw-Hill)

Those should turn your brains to mush in no time!

Practical View Frustrum Clipping

Alright, now it's time to actually add clipping to our 3D engine! Basically we want to clip polygons to the 3D viewing frustrum at some point in the pipeline. As I mentioned, our plan of attack is to perform a 3D clip on polygons, but to minimize the amount of triangle splitting and to only clip in 3D what absolutely must be clipped.

So when do we absolutely have to clip something? Well, the only time a polygon must be clipped is if it extends beyond the near clipping plane, or worse yet, into z <= 0 space. Projecting polygons with z coordinates that are less than or equal to 0 will cause divides by 0, and inverted (x,y) projections. This is not acceptable.

Up until this point, we have been cheating death by pushing the near clipping plane of the view frustrum far enough in front of the projection plane and the z = 0 barrier that no polygon could ever get past it, because we have been culling whole objects that got too close to the viewpoint and the z = 0 plane. However, at this point, we need to forget about object-level culling and think more in terms of a general list of polygons. These polygons are the problem, because they could be anywhere.

In any event, we are going to write a hybrid clipper/culler that will clip the rendering list polygons to the viewing frustrum—but actual vertex clipping will only occur against the near clipping plane. Polygons that are partially within the to/bottom, right/left, or far clipping planes will simply be left alone, or culled completely if they are beyond those planes. Of course, when projected, these polygons will extend beyond the 2D viewplane, but they will get clipped by the rasterizer and not cause us anymore grief. As we discussed before, this strategy ends up being simpler and faster than clipping every polygon against all six faces of the viewing frustrum, because in the end, all that accomplishes is a lot of wasted time—splitting polygons all over the place, recomputing normals, texture coordinates—all for nothing, because we have to rasterize the darn things anyway! The *only* polygons we *need* to clip are those that are so long that they pierce the near plane and can potentially cause distortions and mathematical errors during projection. What's cool about our approach is that we're not only going to remove back-faces, but cull polygons that are not in the viewing frustrum. We'll remove even more geometry than before, and get better performance! I'm getting excited, so let's get to it!

3D clipping can be performed in a number of places in the 3D pipeline: world space, camera space, or perspective projective space. There are pros and cons of all of these approaches. For example, clipping in world space saves us the work of transforming all the geometry into camera coordinates, but then our nice clean viewing frustrum is located at the viewpoint, and has an arbitrary orientation. Thus, the clipping and culling must be slightly more generalized. On the other hand, if we let the polygons get by the world-to-camera transformation, they're nice and neatly placed relative to the camera, which is at the origin, and the viewing frustrum has its planes all parallel and perpendicular to the axes, which makes the clipping very easy. So we waste the transformation of all the geometry-to-camera coordinates, but the actual clipping/culling process becomes easier. Next, if we wait until the perspective projection (this is actually kinda tricky), the geometry will all be normalized to a canonical viewing volume of the perspective viewing frustrum as a cuboid. In other words, if we perspective-transform all the geometry and *then* clip, we no longer need to clip to a pyramid, but to a cuboid—we covered this a few times in the math and 3D chapters on projection.

So what to do? Well, forget the perspective projection/clipping thing—waiting that long is very bad. Not only would we light polygons that don't need lighting, we would fill the pipeline up with 200% more polygons that will never be rendered, which is a waste. We could clip in world space, but I personally don't cherish the idea of transforming the viewing frustrum all over the place and then performing the clipping (although I am really being a wimp, because it's not that bad). Also, any polygons that are split will be transformed. Thus, assume that we have 1,000 polygons in a scene: We end up with around 1,200 because of clipping and splitting (I am being really biased here, of course). Now we have to transform 1,200 polygons into camera space—ouch! Additionally, the clipping test for each polygon in world space is going to be a little more complex than when the polygons are in camera space, with the camera located at the origin and the viewing frustrum aligned with the positive z-axis.

On the other hand, suppose that we clip in world space and remove approximately half of the polygons. Then we only have to transform 500 polygons into camera space. These two cases show that either approach has its good and bad points. In the end, I have decided to perform the clipping/culling of polygons after the world-to-camera transformation because it's easier to understand, and I really don't think I would gain that much if I did it in world space. However, when we optimize at the end of the book, we might give it a try.

Summing up, we are going to clip/cull after the world-to-camera transformation, removing polygons that are totally outside the viewing frustrum completely, while clipping polygons that pierce the near clipping plane only. Partial piercing on the top/bottom and right/left planes will be tolerated because the image space raster clipping will handle those polygons. Take a look at Figure 10.16 to see our final pipeline with the new clipper added.

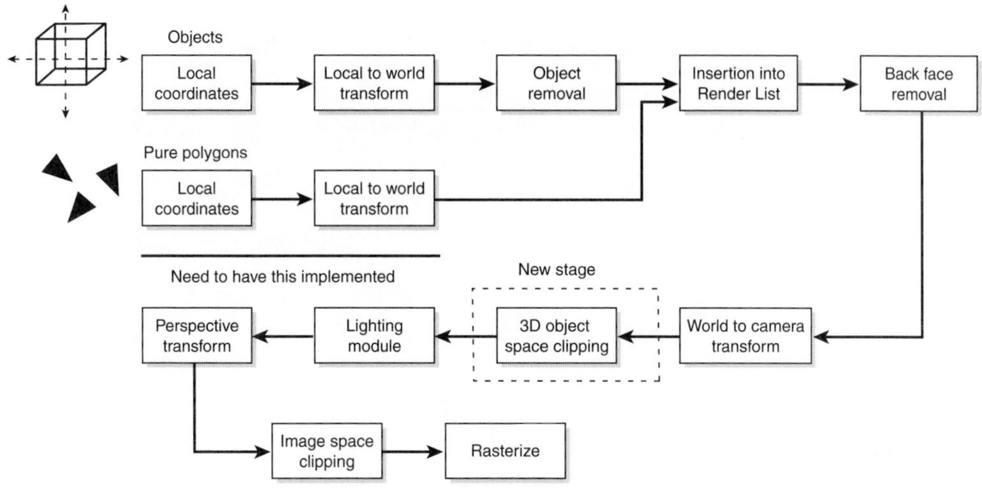

FIGURE 10.16 The final pipeline with 3D clipping added.

The Geometry Pipeline and Data Structures

In Figure 10.16, we see that geometry is loaded into the system via complete objects (or generated as individual polygons), the objects are then transformed, culled, converted into polygons, back-faces removed, transformed some more, clipped, culled, lit, transformed again, and displayed. Lots of transforming going on! The point is that we start with objects—this is great for games with no interior or exterior geometry, but bad for games that have these things.

We need to start loosening our grip on the concept of "objects" and think about new entities that are more suitable for terrain, indoor environments, and so forth. This is exactly why we have been using very little of the object-based calls for lighting and culling. I want you to think in terms of polygons, because very soon we are going to have to come up with some more advanced data structures that support large objects. However, we don't want these objects to be just one big mesh of polygons. We might want them to be ordered, sorted, connected, hierarchical, and so forth.

For example, take a look at Figure 10.17. It depicts an aerial view of an outdoor city game level that we might want to model. Although the level data may be contained in an object-like container, we want to have secondary data structures that enable us to quickly cull away subcomponents of the geometry. This is where the concept of BSP (binary space partitioning) trees, portals, quad-trees, and so forth, come into play.

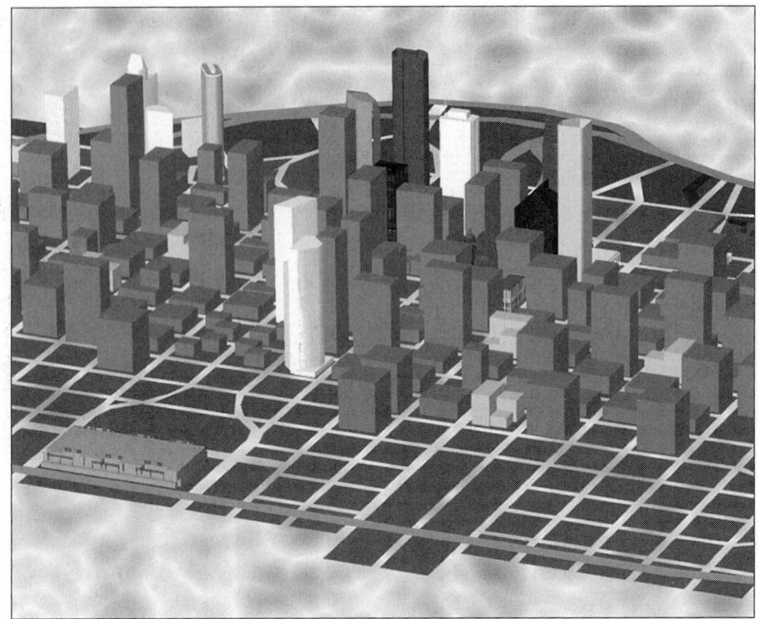

FIGURE 10.17 An aerial view of a game level.

But for all these things to work, we have to be able to get to them efficiently, and at some point turn them all into plain old polygons. My point is that we need to think about what kind of games we are going to make, and realize that in the cases of these interior/exterior kinds of games, clipping is going to be very important (along with culling at the polygon level), so we better be able to do both! That's why we're adding support now for both clipping and culling of polygons in the rendering lists rather than placing the burden in the object code, because we can't assume everything is going to fit into the object data structures for long.

Adding Clipping to the Engine

Let's start from the beginning. The new library module that contains the clipping code is named `T3DLIB8.CPP|H`. It's very short and only has a few functions. As usual, I want to give you a brief overview of the library module without talking about why the functions are there. So, let's review each part of the header file.

The Header File

There are only a few constants used for the clipper, and they have to do with controlling the clipper's logic and what planes are clipped to. Here are those defines:

```
// general clipping flags for polygons
#define CLIP_POLY_X_PLANE    0x0001 // cull on the x clipping planes
#define CLIP_POLY_Y_PLANE    0x0002 // cull on the y clipping planes
#define CLIP_POLY_Z_PLANE    0x0004 // cull on the z clipping planes
#define CLIP_OBJECT_XYZ_PLANES  (CULL_OBJECT_X_PLANE ¦ \
        CULL_OBJECT_Y_PLANE ¦ CULL_OBJECT_Z_PLANE)
```

There are only two functions in the library—one to clip, and the other to generate a terrain (it's a surprise):

```
void Clip_Polys_RENDERLIST4DV2(RENDERLIST4DV2_PTR rend_list,
                // the rendering list to clip
CAM4DV1_PTR cam, // the camera
int clip_flags); // the clipping flags, what to do


int Generate_Terrain_OBJECT4DV2(OBJECT4DV2_PTR obj, // pointer to object
 float twidth,       // width in world coords on x-axis
 float theight,      // height (length) in world coords on z-axis
 float vscale,       // vertical scale of terrain
 char *height_map_file, // filename of height bitmap encoded in 256 colors
 char *texture_map_file, // filename of texture map
 int rgbcolor,       // color of terrain if no texture
 VECTOR4D_PTR pos,     // initial position
 VECTOR4D_PTR rot,     // initial rotations
 int poly_attr);      // the shading attributes we would like
```

That was easy enough, so now let's discuss how the clipping function works.

Building the Clipper

The clipping function needs to operate in camera coordinates on the rendering list, which simply means that we know the viewing frustrum is located at the origin, and the clipping planes are aligned to the positive z-axis, as shown in Figure 10.18.

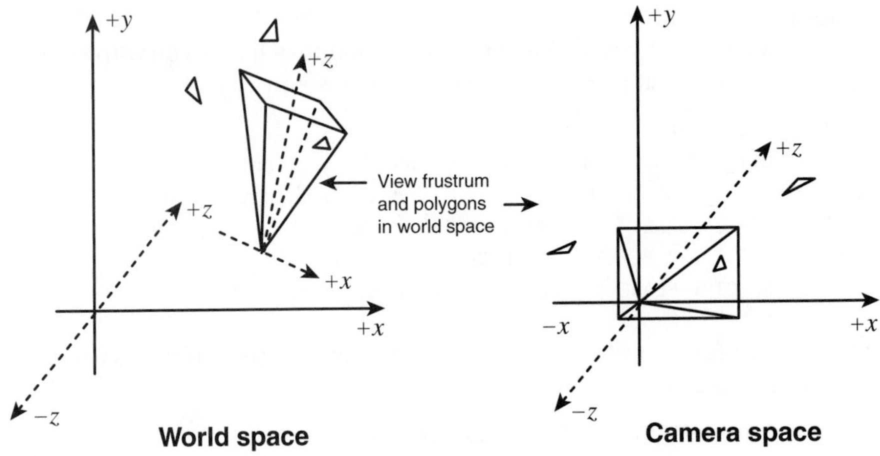

FIGURE 10.18 Clipping in camera coordinates.

The following is a standard code listing of what we have been doing to render a 3D display with our current pipeline:

```
Reset_OBJECT4DV2(&obj);

// build an identity matrix
MAT_IDENTITY_4X4(&mtrans);

// transform the mesh
Transform_OBJECT4DV2(&obj, &mtrans, TRANSFORM_LOCAL_TO_TRANS,1);

// perform world transform
Model_To_World_OBJECT4DV2(&obj, TRANSFORM_TRANS_ONLY);

// insert the object into render list
Insert_OBJECT4DV2_RENDERLIST4DV2(&rend_list, &obj,0);

// remove backfaces
Remove_Backfaces_RENDERLIST4DV2(&rend_list, &cam);

// apply world to camera transform
World_To_Camera_RENDERLIST4DV2(&rend_list, &cam);

//////////////////////////////////////////////////////
// this is where we need to clip the polygons to the viewing frustrum
//////////////////////////////////////////////////////
```

```
// light scene all at once
Light_RENDERLIST4DV2_World16(&rend_list, &cam, lights, 4);

// sort the polygon list (hurry up!)
Sort_RENDERLIST4DV2(&rend_list, SORT_POLYLIST_AVGZ);

// apply camera to perspective transformation
Camera_To_Perspective_RENDERLIST4DV2(&rend_list, &cam);

// apply screen transform
Perspective_To_Screen_RENDERLIST4DV2(&rend_list, &cam);

// lock the back buffer
DDraw_Lock_Back_Surface();

// render the polygons
Draw_RENDERLIST4DV2_Solid16(&rend_list, back_buffer, back_lpitch);


// unlock the back buffer
DDraw_Unlock_Back_Surface();
```

I have bolded where in the pipeline we want to clip the polygons: after the camera transformation, but before the lighting calculations. This is perfect, because after we clip the polygons, not only will there be less of them, but the ones that are totally culled won't be lit.

Let's talk now about what needs to be done to clip the rendering list. The rendering list is composed of two data structures: an array of polygons, and an array of pointers to the polygons. The reason for the indirection, of course, is for fast sorting, and so we don't ever need to reallocate or deallocate space—the storage is always there.

Clipping to the Top/Bottom or Right/Left Clipping Planes We agreed that we are not going to partially clip polygons to the top/bottom or right/left clipping planes that make up the viewing frustrum. We are going to determine whether the test polygon is totally inside the plane or totally outside it. If the polygon is totally inside the plane, we pass on it and move on to the next polygon. If it's outside the plane, we completely cull it (no holds barred clipping, in essence), as shown in Figure 10.19.

To accomplish this task, we only need to know the vertices of the triangle we are testing against the top/bottom-right/left planes, as well as the position and orientation of the clipping planes themselves. There are a couple of ways to approach this. If we've left the clipping in world space coordinates, we would be better off using the plane equations for the planes in point-normal form and then performing a dot product with each vertex to compute the half-space the vertex lies in. If all three vertices are on one side of the plane or the other, we can trivially reject or accept.

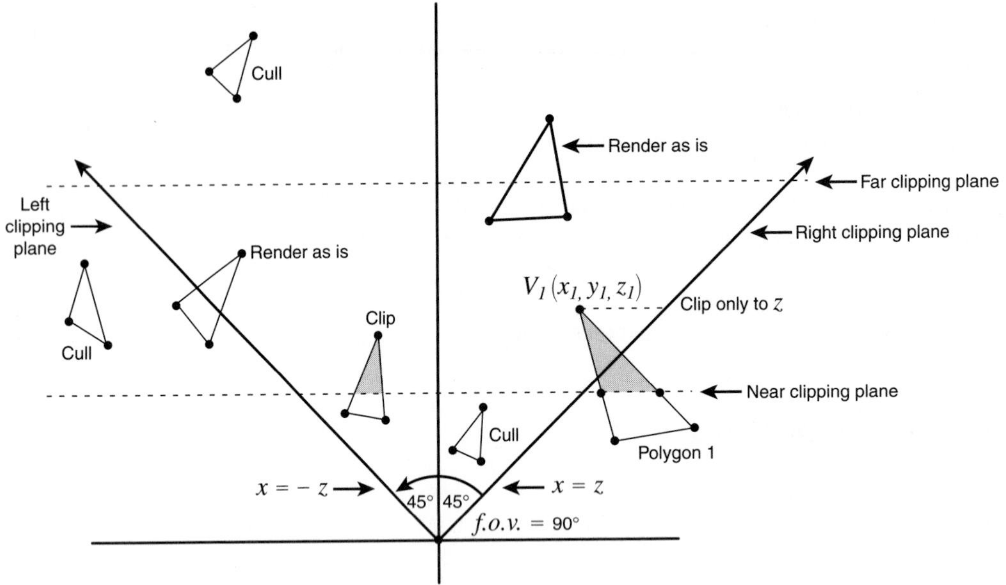

FIGURE 10.19 No-holds-barred 3D clipping.

However, we can cheat a bit because we *know* that the clipping planes are all perpendicular and parallel to the world-axes, so we can use the slope of the planes, or the viewing angle to compute if a point is within the viewing frustrum. Take a look at Figure 10.19 again. You see test polygon 1 being tested against the right-most clipping plane that makes up the viewing frustrum. We can forget about the y-component for a moment and only think about the x-z plane. The question is this: Is the vertex **v1**(x1, y1, z1) inside or outside the right clipping plane? Well, with similar triangles we can find out.

In Figure 10.19, I used a viewing angle of 90 degrees, which means that both the right and left clipping planes make a 45 degree angle with the z-axis, and thus the plane equation is really just x = z (y can be anything). That means if the x-coordinate of the test vertex x1 = z1, the vertex **p1** is on the clipping plane; if x1 > z1, it's outside the clipping plane; and if x1 < z1, the test vertex is inside the clipping plane.

NOTE

I am using the term *inside* to mean in the interior of the viewing frustrum, or the positive half-space of the plane. Similarly, I am using the term *outside* to mean the exterior of the viewing frustrum, or the negative half-space of the plane.

In general, given a test vertex **v**(x,y,z), for a viewing angle of 90 degrees:

- If (x > z), p is outside the right clipping plane.
- If (x < z), p is inside the right clipping plane.
- If (x = z), p is on the right clipping plane.

Similarly, we can perform tests for the left clipping plane:

- If (x > z), p is inside the left clipping plane.
- If (x < z), p is outside the left clipping plane.
- If (x = z), p is on the left clipping plane.

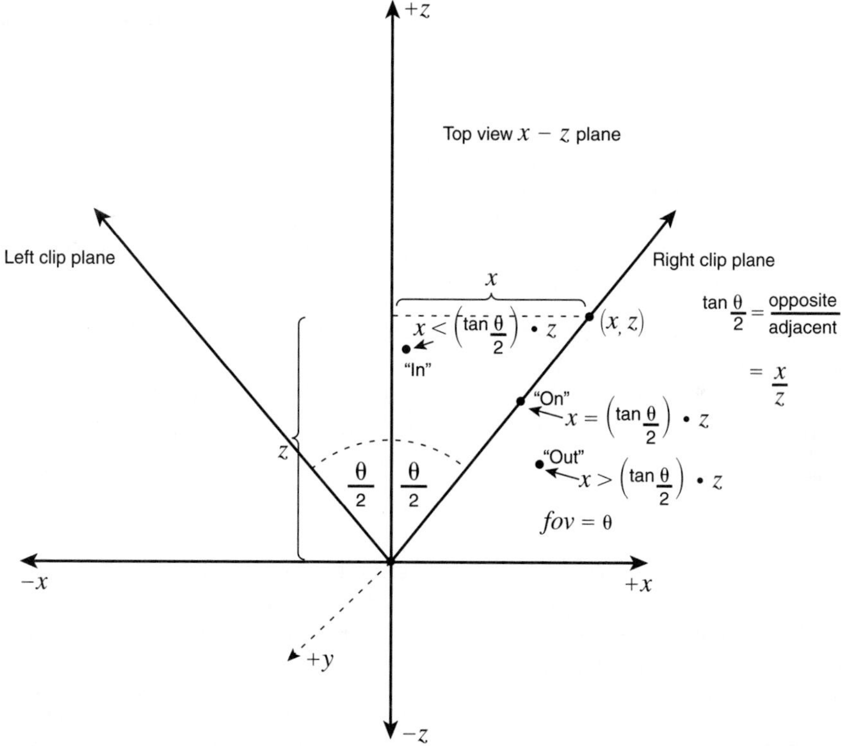

FIGURE 10.20 Computing the clip values based on plane slope projections.

The same process goes for the top and bottom planes: We just replace x with y. Of course, this is a special example, and only works for a viewing angle equal to 90, but if you remember, changing the viewing angle really only changes the slope of the projected planes, so we need only change the formulas slightly to account for this. In Figure 10.20 we see the general case for the right/left clipping planes and the expression

```
tanθ = x/z
```

Therefore,

```
x = tanθ*z
```

In other words, we have these cases:

- When x = tanθ*z, the test vertex is *on* the clipping plane's boundary.
- When x < tanθ*z, the test vertex is in the *positive half-space* of the clipping plane or inside the viewing frustrum.
- When x > tanθ*z, the test vertex is in the *negative half-space* of the clipping plane or outside the viewing frustrum.

The bottom line is that you need to test each vertex to determine whether it's inside each of the four clipping planes (right/left and top/bottom). This means you need to compare the (x,y) coordinates to the z-coordinate of each vertex **v**(x,y,z) based on the viewing angle, which factors in as the tangent function, or a derivative thereof. For example, the viewplane width/height and the viewing distance are related to the field of view, so these can be used as well in the comparison.

We have done all of this about 500 times, so you should feel comfortable with what I am saying at this point. In any event, if a triangle has all three vertices on the interior, we just move on to the next triangle in the list. However, if all three vertices are outside the viewing frustrum, we clip/cull the entire triangle and mark it as "clipped":

```
// clip the poly completely out of frustrum
SET_BIT(curr_poly->state, POLY4DV2_STATE_CLIPPED);
```

I want to wait until we discuss the z clipping before I show you the code listing to save space, but just to see the actual implementation of the tests we designed in the preceding, here's a quick excerpt that tests whether a single vertex of the test polygon is within the right/left or x-axis clipping planes:

```
// since we are clipping to the right/left x-planes we need to use the FOV or
// the plane equations to find the z value that at the current x position would
// be outside the plane
z_factor = (0.5)*cam->viewplane_width/cam->view_dist;

// vertex 0
z_test = z_factor*curr_poly->tvlist[0].z;
```

```
if (curr_poly->tvlist[0].x > z_test)
  vertex_ccodes[0] = CLIP_CODE_GX;
else
if (curr_poly->tvlist[0].x < -z_test)
  vertex_ccodes[0] = CLIP_CODE_LX;
else
  vertex_ccodes[0] = CLIP_CODE_IX;
```

All that explanation for 10 little lines of code! But as I said, we just need to know whether the vertex is on one side of the clipping plane or the other. Based on that, the code sets clipping code flags (something like the Cohen-Sutherland algorithm) that for each vertex tracks whether it's inside the viewing frustrum or outside. This helps with trivial rejection/acceptance later in the algorithm. At this point, let's move on to the near/far z-clipping algorithm, because it's much more complex.

Clipping to the Near/Far Z-Clipping Planes This is where things get a little tricky. Talking about clipping is all fun and games, but when you actually do it in 3D, it's pretty darn hard! Not because the algorithm or the math is hard—it's just the details that kill you, as you will see.... So, assuming we have culled away all the polygons that where beyond the right/left and top/bottom clipping planes, the remaining polygons still must be tested against the near and far z-clipping planes, as we have discussed. Both tests are trivial because the z-clipping planes are parallel to the X-axis, and the camera is already aligned to the positive z-axis. Thus, for each vertex **vi**(xi,yi,zi) (for i = 0, 1, 2) of the test polygon, all we need to do is test zi against the near and far z-clipping planes' z values, which are always within the camera structure and named `near_clip_z`, and `far_clip_z`, respectively.

For example, to test whether a polygon is totally beyond the far clipping plane, we would perform the following algorithm:

```
if (v0.z > far_clip_z) and
  (v1.z > far_clip_z) and
  (v2.z > far_clip_z) then cull polygon (v0, v1, v2).
```

Pretty easy, huh? Similarly, we can test for the near clipping plane:

```
if (v0.z < near_clip_z) and
  (v1.z < near_clip_z) and
  (v2.z < near_clip_z) then cull polygon (v0, v1, v2).
```

We don't care about the cases where the triangle is partially inside and outside the viewing frustrum relative to the far clipping plane, but we *do* care if the triangle pierces the near clipping plane. This is the problem area that we can't avoid. So, here's the deal—we are going to handle this in the following way:

```
for each polygon P in the rendering list
begin
for each vertex v in the current polygon P
  begin

  Record the position of the vertex v:
  1. Is v inside the viewing frustrum?
  2. Is v beyond the far clipping plane?
  3. Is v beyond the near clipping plane?
  end

If all three vertices are beyond the near or far clipping planes then
  cull P completely.

If (any vertex is within the viewing frustrum) and
  (any vertex is beyond the near clipping plane) then
  clip P to the near clipping plane.

end
```

The bolded pseudo-code section is what we need to implement next. The problem is that we need to figure out how to clip a polygon to the next clipping plane, which more or less means that we have to clip each edge that exits the interior of the viewing frustrum with the near clipping plane. Take a look at Figure 10.21 to see the two cases.

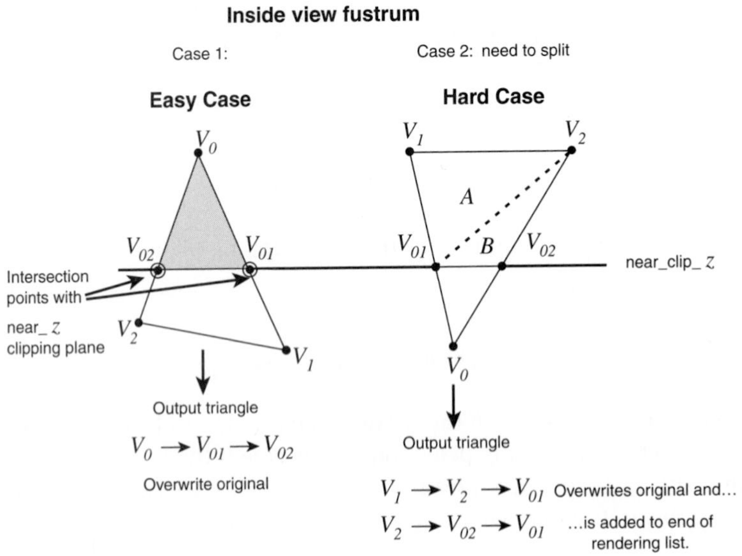

FIGURE 10.21 The two cases of near z-clipping.

Case 1: One interior vertex and two exterior vertices

This is the easy case. In it, we simply clip the two exiting edges to the near z-clipping plane, and then overwrite the new vertices over the old ones in place. Also, if the triangle had a texture map, we need to recompute the texture coordinates. Of course, the normal must be recomputed because its length will change as a result of the smaller size of the triangle. We also store the length of the normal to speed the lighting calculations, and because this has changed it must be recomputed as well.

Case 2: Two interior vertices and one exterior vertex

This is the hard case. Referring to Figure 10.21, when a triangle has two interior vertices and one exterior vertex, there are two intersection points with the near z-clipping plane. This means that the final result polygon is a quadrilateral, or four-sided polygon, which we don't like. Thus, it must be split! The strategy we need to use is to copy all the triangle information from the original triangle into a temporary triangle, then perform the clip, splitting the original triangle into two triangles A and B. Then we overwrite the original triangle with triangle A, and fix up the final vertices with the intersection points of triangle A, while at the same time updating the temporary triangle B with the intersection data as well. The result is that the original polygon in the rendering list is modified in place with one of the resulting split triangles (A), and the second triangle resulting from the split (B) must be inserted into the rendering list at the end of the list.

Please make sure you understand Case 2 before moving on. In a nutshell, when you clip a triangle to a plane, you will end up with one or two triangles after the clip. If you end up with one triangle, you can overwrite the subject triangle with the clipped triangle and cause very little upheaval. If, on the other hand, the subject triangle results in two triangles (A and B) after being clipped, the original triangle can be overwritten, but the new triangle B must be added to the rendering list.

TIP

You might be thinking, "It's too bad we don't have a linked list of polygons rather than an array of pointers to them." The reason is that when we sort the polygons, and the polygon that is split has its clone thrown clear to the end of the polygon list, we know that its z value for sorting is identical to the z value of the original, which will slow the sort down because it will have to move the split poly all the way back up the list. However, later we will optimize this anomaly.

Now that you know the plan of attack, the last detail is the actual clipping code. How will we do it? Well, I decided on an algorithm that's a hybrid of all the algorithms we've discussed. We're already doing the incode/outcode pre-processing step, so that's been discussed. The only problem left is how to intersect the edges of the triangle with the near z-clipping plane. Well, because we know that there are only two cases to deal with (one vertex interior to the clipping region versus two vertices interior to the clipping region), I coded them as separate cases. In each case, I created a parametric line definition of the two exiting edges, something like

```
p = v0 + (v1 - v0)*t
```

where **v0** is the initial vertex, and **v1** is the terminal vertex of an edge.

I then plugged the z value of `near_clip_z` into the parametric line equation for the z component and solved for t:

```
p = v0 + (v1 - v0)*t

x = v0.x + (v1.x - v0.x)*t
y = v0.y + (v1.y - v0.y)*t
z = v0.z + (v1.z - v0.z)*t
```

Plugging in `near_clip_z` for z:

```
near_clip_z = v0.z + (v1.z - v0.z)*t

t = near_clip_z - v0.z/(v1.z - v0.z)
```

Then I plugged this t value back into the equations for x and y of the parametric line, and bam!—I have my intersection point! After doing this for both edges, I'm done. The rest is just housekeeping, making sure to overwrite the proper vertex data with the intersections.

Computing the Texture Coordinates The only remaining detail is computing the new texture coordinates—we have to be careful here. If a polygon has texture coordinates, we have to clip them also, but luckily we can use the same t value to find the clipped texture coordinate values. Here's an example. Suppose that we have a Case 1 triangle, as shown in Figure 10.22, with texture coordinates at each vertex, labeled as shown in the figure.

Now assume that we compute the intersection points, and find that at a value of t = .6, the intersection occurs. We simply use this same t = .6 to linearly interpolate the texture coordinates and find their clipped values, too. Referring to the figure, vertex 0 has the texture coordinate $u_0v_0(3,5)$, and vertex 1 has the texture coordinate $u_1v_1(15,50)$. Therefore, the clipped texture coordinates are

```
u_clipped = u0 + (u1 - u0)*t
v_clipped = v0 + (v1 - v0)*t
```

Plugging in the values, we get

```
u_clipped = 3 + (15 - 3)*(.6) = 10.2
v_clipped = 5 + (50 - 5)*(.6) = 32
```

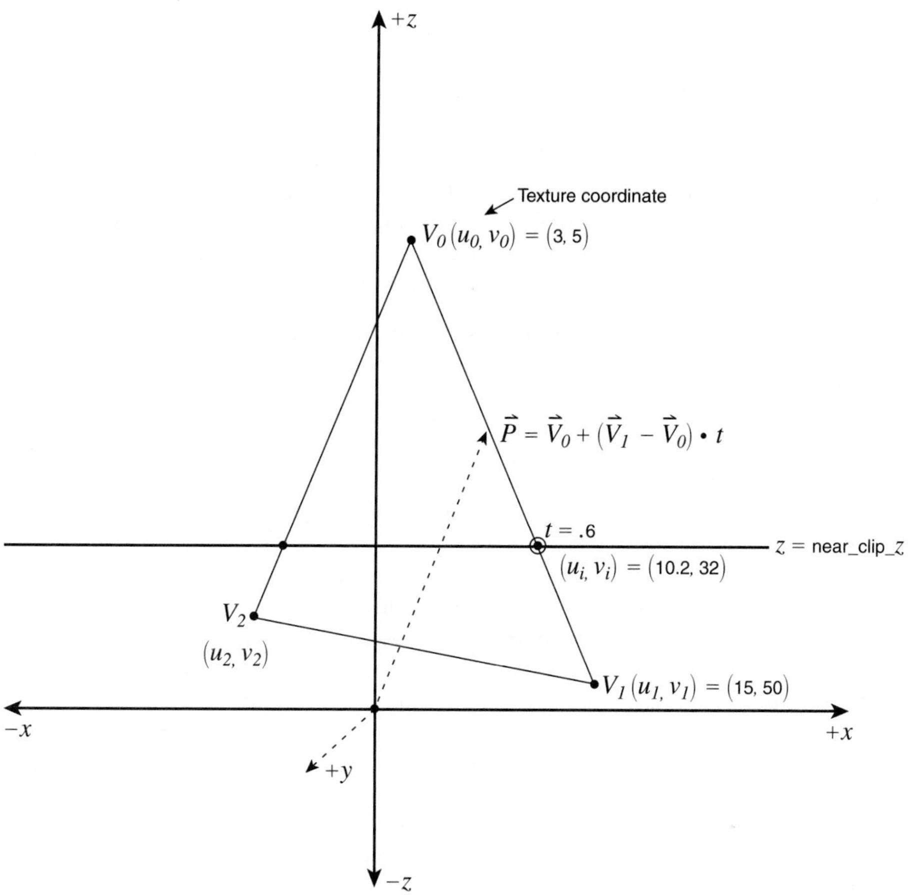

FIGURE 10.22 Computing new texture coordinates for a clipped triangle.

And that's all there is to clipping to the near clipping plane with polygon splitting and texture coordinate recomputation (if needed). Finally, before we go on our merry way, we need to recompute the length of each polygon normal for both cases, because we need this length in the lighting stage and it has unfortunately changed. We simply perform the following code on all clipped polygons, split or not:

```
// build u, v
VECTOR4D_Build(&curr_poly->tvlist[v0].v, &curr_poly->tvlist[v1].v, &u);
VECTOR4D_Build(&curr_poly->tvlist[v0].v, &curr_poly->tvlist[v2].v, &v);

// compute cross product
VECTOR4D_Cross(&u, &v, &n);
```

10

```
// compute length of normal accurately and store in poly nlength
// +- epsilon later to fix over/underflows
curr_poly->nlength = VECTOR4D_Length_Fast(&n);
```

It's a bummer, but hopefully no more than a few hundred polygons per frame will need clipping to the near clipping plane, and I'm using the fast length computation, which is a little raw, but much faster than a square root. Although it's less accurate (about 5–10% error), we won't know about it for too long, because if we are clipping a polygon to the near clipping plane, it's probably on its way by and out of view!

Well, I think I have beaten yet another subject to death, so let's actually look at the function! Here's the code:

```
void Clip_Polys_RENDERLIST4DV2(RENDERLIST4DV2_PTR rend_list,
              CAM4DV1_PTR cam, int clip_flags)
{
// this function clips the polygons in the list against the
// requested clipping planes
// and sets the clipped flag on the poly, so it's not rendered
// note the function ONLY performs clipping on the near and far clipping plane
// but will perform trivial tests on the top/bottom, left/right clipping planes
// if a polygon is completely out of the viewing frustrum , it will
// be culled, however, this test isn't as effective on objects since
// objects that are visible have polygons that are visible, but in the
// case where the polygon list is based on a large object that
// ALWAYS has some portion
// visible, testing for individual polys is worthwhile..
// the function assumes the polygons have been transformed into camera space

// internal clipping codes
#define CLIP_CODE_GZ  0x0001  // z > z_max
#define CLIP_CODE_LZ  0x0002  // z < z_min
#define CLIP_CODE_IZ  0x0004  // z_min < z < z_max

#define CLIP_CODE_GX  0x0001  // x > x_max
#define CLIP_CODE_LX  0x0002  // x < x_min
#define CLIP_CODE_IX  0x0004  // x_min < x < x_max

#define CLIP_CODE_GY  0x0001  // y > y_max
#define CLIP_CODE_LY  0x0002  // y < y_min
#define CLIP_CODE_IY  0x0004  // y_min < y < y_max

#define CLIP_CODE_NULL 0x0000
```

```
int vertex_ccodes[3]; // used to store clipping flags
int num_verts_in;   // number of vertices inside
int v0, v1, v2;    // vertex indices

float z_factor,    // used in clipping computations
   z_test;     // used in clipping computations

float xi, yi, x01i, y01i, x02i, y02i, // vertex intersection points
   t1, t2,              // parametric t values
   ui, vi, u01i, v01i, u02i, v02i;   // texture intersection points

int last_poly_index,  // last valid polygon in polylist
  insert_poly_index; // the current position new polygons are inserted at

VECTOR4D u,v,n;     // used in vector calculations

POLYF4DV2 temp_poly;  // used when we need to split a poly into 2 polys

// set last, current insert index to end of polygon list
// we don't want to clip poly's two times
insert_poly_index = last_poly_index = rend_list->num_polys;

// traverse polygon list and clip/cull polygons
for (int poly = 0; poly < last_poly_index; poly++)
  {
  // acquire current polygon
  POLYF4DV2_PTR curr_poly = rend_list->poly_ptrs[poly];

  // is this polygon valid?
  // test this polygon if and only if it's not clipped, not culled,
  // active, and visible and not 2 sided.
  // Note we test for backface in the event that
  // a previous call might have already determined this, so why work
  // harder!
  if ((curr_poly==NULL) || !(curr_poly->state & POLY4DV2_STATE_ACTIVE) ||
    (curr_poly->state & POLY4DV2_STATE_CLIPPED ) ||
    (curr_poly->state & POLY4DV2_STATE_BACKFACE) )
    continue; // move onto next poly

    // clip/cull to x-planes
    if (clip_flags & CLIP_POLY_X_PLANE)
      {
      // clip/cull only based on x clipping planes
```

```
// for each vertice determine if it's in the
// clipping region or beyond it and
// set the appropriate clipping code
// we do NOT clip the final triangles,
// we are only trying to trivally reject them
// we are going to clip polygons in the rasterizer
// to the screen rectangle
// but we do want to clip/cull polys that are
// totally outside the viewfrustrum

// since we are clipping to the right/left
// x-planes we need to use the FOV or
// the plane equations to find the z value
// that at the current x position would
// be outside the plane
z_factor = (0.5)*cam->viewplane_width/cam->view_dist;

// vertex 0

z_test = z_factor*curr_poly->tvlist[0].z;

if (curr_poly->tvlist[0].x > z_test)
 vertex_ccodes[0] = CLIP_CODE_GX;
else
if (curr_poly->tvlist[0].x < -z_test)
 vertex_ccodes[0] = CLIP_CODE_LX;
else
 vertex_ccodes[0] = CLIP_CODE_IX;

// vertex 1

z_test = z_factor*curr_poly->tvlist[1].z;

if (curr_poly->tvlist[1].x > z_test)
 vertex_ccodes[1] = CLIP_CODE_GX;
else
if (curr_poly->tvlist[1].x < -z_test)
 vertex_ccodes[1] = CLIP_CODE_LX;
else
 vertex_ccodes[1] = CLIP_CODE_IX;

// vertex 2

z_test = z_factor*curr_poly->tvlist[2].z;
```

```
    if (curr_poly->tvlist[2].x > z_test)
     vertex_ccodes[2] = CLIP_CODE_GX;
    else
    if (curr_poly->tvlist[2].x < -z_test)
     vertex_ccodes[2] = CLIP_CODE_LX;
    else
     vertex_ccodes[2] = CLIP_CODE_IX;

   // test for trivial rejections,
   // polygon completely beyond right or left
   // clipping planes
   if ( ((vertex_ccodes[0] == CLIP_CODE_GX) &&
      (vertex_ccodes[1] == CLIP_CODE_GX) &&
      (vertex_ccodes[2] == CLIP_CODE_GX) ) ||

      ((vertex_ccodes[0] == CLIP_CODE_LX) &&
      (vertex_ccodes[1] == CLIP_CODE_LX) &&
      (vertex_ccodes[2] == CLIP_CODE_LX) ) )

     {
     // clip the poly completely out of frustrum
     SET_BIT(curr_poly->state, POLY4DV2_STATE_CLIPPED);

     // move on to next polygon
     continue;
     } // end if

   } // end if x planes

  // clip/cull to y-planes
  if (clip_flags & CLIP_POLY_Y_PLANE)
    {
    // clip/cull only based on y clipping planes
    // for each vertice determine if it's in the
    // clipping region or beyond it and
    // set the appropriate clipping code
    // we do NOT clip the final triangles,
    // we are only trying to trivally reject them
    // we are going to clip polygons in the rasterizer
    // to the screen rectangle
    // but we do want to clip/cull polys that are totally
    // outside the viewfrustrum
```

```
// since we are clipping to the top/bottom y-planes
// we need to use the FOV or
// the plane equations to find the z value that at
// the current y position would
// be outside the plane
z_factor = (0.5)*cam->viewplane_width/cam->view_dist;

// vertex 0

z_test = z_factor*curr_poly->tvlist[0].z;

if (curr_poly->tvlist[0].y > z_test)
 vertex_ccodes[0] = CLIP_CODE_GY;
else
if (curr_poly->tvlist[0].y < -z_test)
 vertex_ccodes[0] = CLIP_CODE_LY;
else
 vertex_ccodes[0] = CLIP_CODE_IY;

// vertex 1

z_test = z_factor*curr_poly->tvlist[1].z;

if (curr_poly->tvlist[1].y > z_test)
 vertex_ccodes[1] = CLIP_CODE_GY;
else
if (curr_poly->tvlist[1].y < -z_test)
 vertex_ccodes[1] = CLIP_CODE_LY;
else
 vertex_ccodes[1] = CLIP_CODE_IY;

// vertex 2

z_test = z_factor*curr_poly->tvlist[2].z;

if (curr_poly->tvlist[2].y > z_test)
 vertex_ccodes[2] = CLIP_CODE_GY;
else
if (curr_poly->tvlist[2].x < -z_test)
 vertex_ccodes[2] = CLIP_CODE_LY;
else
 vertex_ccodes[2] = CLIP_CODE_IY;
```

```
  // test for trivial rejections,
  // polygon completely beyond top or bottom
  // clipping planes
  if ( ((vertex_ccodes[0] == CLIP_CODE_GY) &&
     (vertex_ccodes[1] == CLIP_CODE_GY) &&
     (vertex_ccodes[2] == CLIP_CODE_GY) ) ||

     ((vertex_ccodes[0] == CLIP_CODE_LX) &&
     (vertex_ccodes[1] == CLIP_CODE_LX) &&
     (vertex_ccodes[2] == CLIP_CODE_LX) ) )

    {
    // clip the poly completely out of frustrum
    SET_BIT(curr_poly->state, POLY4DV2_STATE_CLIPPED);

    // move on to next polygon
    continue;
    } // end if

  } // end if y planes

// clip/cull to z planes
if (clip_flags & CLIP_POLY_Z_PLANE)
  {
  // clip/cull only based on z clipping planes
  // for each vertice determine if it's in the
  // clipping region or beyond it and
  // set the appropriate clipping code
  // then actually clip all polygons to the
  // near clipping plane, this will result
  // in at most 1 additional triangle

  // reset vertex counters, these help in classification
  // of the final triangle
  num_verts_in = 0;

  // vertex 0
  if (curr_poly->tvlist[0].z > cam->far_clip_z)
   {
   vertex_ccodes[0] = CLIP_CODE_GZ;
   }
  else
  if (curr_poly->tvlist[0].z < cam->near_clip_z)
   {
```

```
 vertex_ccodes[0] = CLIP_CODE_LZ;
 }
else
 {
 vertex_ccodes[0] = CLIP_CODE_IZ;
 num_verts_in++;
 }

// vertex 1
if (curr_poly->tvlist[1].z > cam->far_clip_z)
 {
 vertex_ccodes[1] = CLIP_CODE_GZ;
 }
else
if (curr_poly->tvlist[1].z < cam->near_clip_z)
 {
 vertex_ccodes[1] = CLIP_CODE_LZ;
 }
else
 {
 vertex_ccodes[1] = CLIP_CODE_IZ;
 num_verts_in++;
 }

// vertex 2
if (curr_poly->tvlist[2].z > cam->far_clip_z)
 {
 vertex_ccodes[2] = CLIP_CODE_GZ;
 }
else
if (curr_poly->tvlist[2].z < cam->near_clip_z)
 {
 vertex_ccodes[2] = CLIP_CODE_LZ;
 }
else
 {
 vertex_ccodes[2] = CLIP_CODE_IZ;
 num_verts_in++;
 }

// test for trivial rejections, polygon completely beyond far or near
// z clipping planes
if ( ((vertex_ccodes[0] == CLIP_CODE_GZ) &&
```

```
     (vertex_ccodes[1] == CLIP_CODE_GZ) &&
     (vertex_ccodes[2] == CLIP_CODE_GZ) ) ||

     ((vertex_ccodes[0] == CLIP_CODE_LZ) &&
     (vertex_ccodes[1] == CLIP_CODE_LZ) &&
     (vertex_ccodes[2] == CLIP_CODE_LZ) ) )

    {
    // clip the poly completely out of frustrum
    SET_BIT(curr_poly->state, POLY4DV2_STATE_CLIPPED);

    // move on to next polygon
    continue;
    } // end if

  // test if any vertex has protruded beyond near clipping plane?
  if ( ( (vertex_ccodes[0] | vertex_ccodes[1] |
      vertex_ccodes[2]) & CLIP_CODE_LZ) )
  {
  // at this point we are ready to clip the polygon to the near
  // clipping plane no need to clip to the far plane since it can't
  // possibly cause problems. We have two cases: case 1: the triangle
  // has 1 vertex interior to the near clipping plane and 2 vertices
  // exterior, OR case 2: the triangle has two vertices interior of
  // the near clipping plane and 1 exterior

  // step 1: classify the triangle type based on number of vertices
  // inside/outside
  // case 1: easy case :)
  if (num_verts_in == 1)
    {
    // we need to clip the triangle against the near clipping plane
    // the clipping procedure is done to each edge leading away from
    // the interior vertex, to clip we need to compute the intersection
    // with the near z plane, this is done with a parametric equation of
    // the edge, once the intersection is computed
    // the old vertex position
    // is overwritten along with re-computing the
    // texture coordinates, if
    // there are any, what's nice about this case,
    // is clipping doesn't
    // introduce any added vertices, so we can overwrite the old poly
    // the other case below results in 2 polys,
```

10

```
// so at very least one has
// to be added to the end of the rendering list -- bummer

// step 1: find vertex index for interior vertex
if ( vertex_ccodes[0] == CLIP_CODE_IZ)
 { v0 = 0; v1 = 1; v2 = 2; }
else
if (vertex_ccodes[1] == CLIP_CODE_IZ)
 { v0 = 1; v1 = 2; v2 = 0; }
else
 { v0 = 2; v1 = 0; v2 = 1; }

// step 2: clip each edge
// basically we are going to generate
// the parametric line p = v0 + v01*t
// then solve for t when the z component
// is equal to near z, then plug that
// back into to solve for x,y of the 3D line,
// we could do this with high
// level code and parametric lines,
// but to save time, lets do it manually

// clip edge v0->v1
VECTOR4D_Build(&curr_poly->tvlist[v0].v,
        &curr_poly->tvlist[v1].v, &v);

// the intersection occurs when z = near z, so t =
t1 = ( (cam->near_clip_z - curr_poly->tvlist[v0].z) / v.z );

// now plug t back in and find x,y intersection with the plane
xi = curr_poly->tvlist[v0].x + v.x * t1;
yi = curr_poly->tvlist[v0].y + v.y * t1;

// now overwrite vertex with new vertex
curr_poly->tvlist[v1].x = xi;
curr_poly->tvlist[v1].y = yi;
curr_poly->tvlist[v1].z = cam->near_clip_z;

// clip edge v0->v2
VECTOR4D_Build(&curr_poly->tvlist[v0].v,
        &curr_poly->tvlist[v2].v, &v);

// the intersection occurs when z = near z, so t =
t2 = ( (cam->near_clip_z - curr_poly->tvlist[v0].z) / v.z );
```

```
// now plug t back in and find x,y intersection with the plane
xi = curr_poly->tvlist[v0].x + v.x * t2;
yi = curr_poly->tvlist[v0].y + v.y * t2;

// now overwrite vertex with new vertex
curr_poly->tvlist[v2].x = xi;
curr_poly->tvlist[v2].y = yi;
curr_poly->tvlist[v2].z = cam->near_clip_z;

// now that we have both t1, t2,
// check if the poly is textured, if so clip
// texture coordinates
if (curr_poly->attr & POLY4DV2_ATTR_SHADE_MODE_TEXTURE)
  {
  ui = curr_poly->tvlist[v0].u0 +
    (curr_poly->tvlist[v1].u0 - curr_poly->tvlist[v0].u0)*t1;
  vi = curr_poly->tvlist[v0].v0 +
    (curr_poly->tvlist[v1].v0 - curr_poly->tvlist[v0].v0)*t1;
  curr_poly->tvlist[v1].u0 = ui;
  curr_poly->tvlist[v1].v0 = vi;

  ui = curr_poly->tvlist[v0].u0 +
    (curr_poly->tvlist[v2].u0 - curr_poly->tvlist[v0].u0)*t2;
  vi = curr_poly->tvlist[v0].v0 +
    (curr_poly->tvlist[v2].v0 - curr_poly->tvlist[v0].v0)*t2;
  curr_poly->tvlist[v2].u0 = ui;
  curr_poly->tvlist[v2].v0 = vi;
  } // end if textured

  // finally, we have obliterated our pre-computed normal length
  // it needs to be recomputed!!!!

 // build u, v
 VECTOR4D_Build(&curr_poly->tvlist[v0].v,
         &curr_poly->tvlist[v1].v, &u);
 VECTOR4D_Build(&curr_poly->tvlist[v0].v,
         &curr_poly->tvlist[v2].v, &v);

 // compute cross product
 VECTOR4D_Cross(&u, &v, &n);

 // compute length of normal accurately and store in poly nlength
 // +- epsilon later to fix over/underflows
 curr_poly->nlength = VECTOR4D_Length_Fast(&n);
```

10

```
  } // end if
else
if (num_verts_in == 2)
  { // num_verts = 2

  // must be the case with num_verts_in = 2
  // we need to clip the triangle against the near clipping plane
  // the clipping procedure is done to each edge leading away from
  // the interior vertex, to clip we need to compute the intersection
  // with the near z plane, this is done with a
  // parametric equation of
  // the edge, however unlike case 1 above,
  // the triangle will be split
  // into two triangles, thus during the first clip,
  // we will store the
  // results into a new triangle at the end
  // of the rendering list, and
  // then on the last clip we will overwrite
  // the triangle being clipped

  // step 0: copy the polygon
  memcpy(&temp_poly, curr_poly, sizeof(POLYF4DV2) );

  // step 1: find vertex index for exterior vertex
  if ( vertex_ccodes[0] == CLIP_CODE_LZ)
   { v0 = 0; v1 = 1; v2 = 2; }
  else
  if (vertex_ccodes[1] == CLIP_CODE_LZ)
   { v0 = 1; v1 = 2; v2 = 0; }
  else
   { v0 = 2; v1 = 0; v2 = 1; }

  // step 2: clip each edge
  // basically we are going to generate the
  // parametric line p = v0 + v01*t
  // then solve for t when the z component is equal to
  // near z, then plug that
  // back into to solve for x,y of the 3D line,
  // we could do this with high
  // level code and parametric lines, but to save time,
  // lets do it manually
```

```
// clip edge v0->v1
VECTOR4D_Build(&curr_poly->tvlist[v0].v,
       &curr_poly->tvlist[v1].v, &v);

// the intersection occurs when z = near z, so t =
t1 = ( (cam->near_clip_z - curr_poly->tvlist[v0].z) / v.z );

// now plug t back in and find x,y intersection with the plane
x01i = curr_poly->tvlist[v0].x + v.x * t1;
y01i = curr_poly->tvlist[v0].y + v.y * t1;

// clip edge v0->v2
VECTOR4D_Build(&curr_poly->tvlist[v0].v,
       &curr_poly->tvlist[v2].v, &v);

// the intersection occurs when z = near z, so t =
t2 = ( (cam->near_clip_z - curr_poly->tvlist[v0].z) / v.z );

// now plug t back in and find x,y intersection with the plane
x02i = curr_poly->tvlist[v0].x + v.x * t2;
y02i = curr_poly->tvlist[v0].y + v.y * t2;

// now we have both intersection points,
// we must overwrite the inplace
// polygon's vertex 0 with the intersection point,
// this poly 1 of 2 from
// the split

// now overwrite vertex with new vertex
curr_poly->tvlist[v0].x = x01i;
curr_poly->tvlist[v0].y = y01i;
curr_poly->tvlist[v0].z = cam->near_clip_z;

// now comes the hard part,
// we have to carefully create a new polygon
// from the 2 intersection points and v2,
// this polygon will be inserted
// at the end of the rendering list,
// but for now, we are building it up
// in temp_poly

// so leave v2 alone, but overwrite v1 with v01,
// and overwrite v0 with v02
```

```
      temp_poly.tvlist[v1].x = x01i;
      temp_poly.tvlist[v1].y = y01i;
      temp_poly.tvlist[v1].z = cam->near_clip_z;

      temp_poly.tvlist[v0].x = x02i;
      temp_poly.tvlist[v0].y = y02i;
      temp_poly.tvlist[v0].z = cam->near_clip_z;

     // now that we have both t1, t2,
     // check if the poly is textured, if so clip
     // texture coordinates
     if (curr_poly->attr & POLY4DV2_ATTR_SHADE_MODE_TEXTURE)
       {
       // compute poly 1 new texture coordinates from split
       u01i = curr_poly->tvlist[v0].u0 +
        (curr_poly->tvlist[v1].u0 - curr_poly->tvlist[v0].u0)*t1;
       v01i = curr_poly->tvlist[v0].v0 +
        (curr_poly->tvlist[v1].v0 - curr_poly->tvlist[v0].v0)*t1;

       // compute poly 2 new texture coordinates from split
       u02i = curr_poly->tvlist[v0].u0 +
        (curr_poly->tvlist[v2].u0 - curr_poly->tvlist[v0].u0)*t2;
       v02i = curr_poly->tvlist[v0].v0 +
        (curr_poly->tvlist[v2].v0 - curr_poly->tvlist[v0].v0) *t2;

       // write them all at the same time
       // poly 1
       curr_poly->tvlist[v0].u0 = u01i;
       curr_poly->tvlist[v0].v0 = v01i;

       // poly 2
       temp_poly.tvlist[v0].u0 = u02i;
       temp_poly.tvlist[v0].v0 = v02i;
       temp_poly.tvlist[v1].u0 = u01i;
       temp_poly.tvlist[v1].v0 = v01i;

       } // end if textured


       // finally, we have obliterated our pre-computed normal lengths
       // they need to be recomputed!!!!

       // poly 1 first, in place
```

```
        // build u, v
        VECTOR4D_Build(&curr_poly->tvlist[v0].v,
               &curr_poly->tvlist[v1].v, &u);
        VECTOR4D_Build(&curr_poly->tvlist[v0].v,
               &curr_poly->tvlist[v2].v, &v);

        // compute cross product
        VECTOR4D_Cross(&u, &v, &n);

        // compute length of normal accurately and store in poly nlength
        // +- epsilon later to fix over/underflows
        curr_poly->nlength = VECTOR4D_Length_Fast(&n);

        // now poly 2, temp_poly
        // build u, v
        VECTOR4D_Build(&temp_poly.tvlist[v0].v,
               &temp_poly.tvlist[v1].v, &u);
        VECTOR4D_Build(&temp_poly.tvlist[v0].v,
               &temp_poly.tvlist[v2].v, &v);

        // compute cross product
        VECTOR4D_Cross(&u, &v, &n);

        // compute length of normal accurately and store in poly nlength
        // +- epsilon later to fix over/underflows
        temp_poly.nlength = VECTOR4D_Length_Fast(&n) ;

       // now we are good to go, insert the polygon into list
       // if the poly won't fit, it won't matter, the function will
       // just return 0
       Insert_POLYF4DV2_RENDERLIST4DV2(rend_list, &temp_poly);

       } // end else

      } // end if near_z clipping has occured

     } // end if z planes

  } // end for poly

} // end Clip_Polys_RENDERLIST4DV2
```

I will admit that I rarely ever read code in books. For one thing, I just can't figure it out because it's so cryptic; code is code, know what I mean? But sometimes I will go line by line and try to understand what the code does. However, I prefer abstract explanations and pseudo-code. Nevertheless, some people learn in the exact opposite way—that's why I list code in my books. The point I am trying to make is that even if you're like me, please try and review this function line by line and understand it. It's the basis for a lot of things, and it's actually really easy because it's mostly redundant.

Using the function is nearly ridiculously simple. You call it like this:

```
Clip_Polys_RENDERLIST4DV2(&rend_list, &cam,
     CLIP_POLY_Z_PLANE | CLIP_POLY_X_PLANE | CLIP_POLY_Y_PLANE);
```

The rendering list, the camera, and the control flags are sent and the function does the rest. Notice that you can enable x,y,z clipping independently. I prefer to enable all three so I can really cull those evil polygons out of my pipeline!

The Clipping Demo

As an example of using the clipping function and just for general principles, I have written yet another demo with some obscure object spinning around in space <BG>. The name of the demo is `DEMOII10_1.CPP|EXE` and it's on the CD. of course. To compile it, you will need `T3DLIB1..8.CPP|H` and all the DirectX .LIB files, as usual. A screenshot is shown in Figure 10.23. The demo basically loads an object and displays it on the screen and slowly spins it. You can move the object closer or farther from the viewplane and rotate it around, forcing it off the screen.

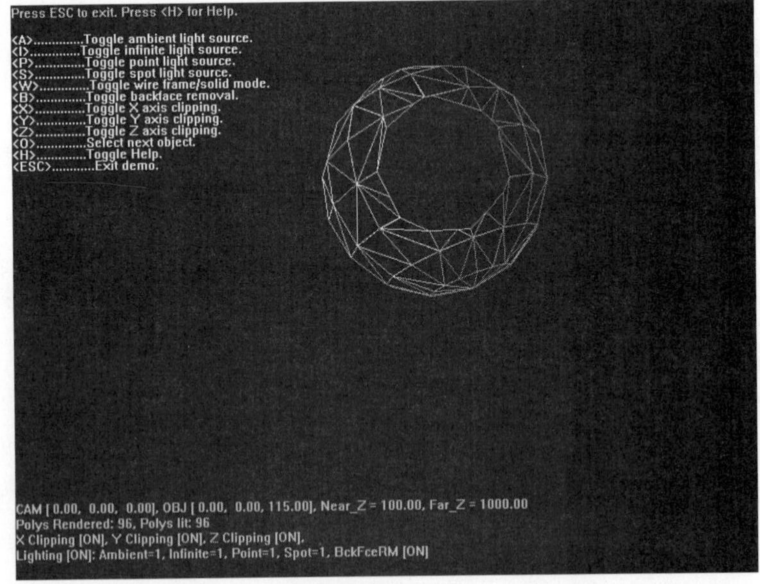

FIGURE 10.23 A screenshot of the clipping demo.

The point of the demo is twofold. First, with only object culling, we could never clip or cull single polygons, so if an object was partially in the viewing frustrum, the entire object was lit and transformed no matter what. Now that's not true, as we'll be clipping/culling on a polygon level. Keep your eyes on the statistical information displays at the bottom of the screen. The controls are listed on the onscreen help, but in general, use the arrow keys to move the object, change objects with the O key, and enable/disable clipping of the x,y,z clipping planes with the X, Y, and Z keys, respectively.

Lighting System Redux

Before we move on, there is a small detail that we need to address in relation to the lighting system. Up until now we have performed lighting in the world coordinate system, thus both the lights and geometry were in world coordinates. However, at this point this is a huge waste of computation. We can hold off lighting until we perform clipping and save lighting polygons that will be clipped! To make this work, we need to transform the lights into camera coordinates (because this is what the geometry will be in after the clipping phase), and perform the lighting calculations there. There are a couple of ways to go about this. We could rewrite the lighting functions and transform the light positions and orientations based on the camera (because it's already a parameter). However, the problem with doing the light transforms on the fly is that if the lighting functions are called on an object-by-object basis, we will transform the lights over and over for nothing. A better strategy is to simply transform the lights themselves into camera coordinates (or whatever).

The only detail we need to consider is that once the positions and orientations of the lights have been transformed into camera coordinates, where do we store the old local lights and orientations? Alas, we must go into the lighting structures and update them from `LIGHTV1` to `LIGHTV2` (version 2.0) and add some storage for the "transformed" versions of their positions and orientation. In addition to this, we will need to rewrite every single function that deals with lights, because internally they will now have to use the `LIGHTV2` struct, rather than the `LIGHTV1` struct. The good news is that there are literally almost no changes to the lighting functions, other than a text replacement of the string `LIGHTV1` to `LIGHTV2`. In any case, let's take a look at the new `LIGHTV2` struct:

```
// version 2.0 of light structure
typedef struct LIGHTV2_TYP
{
int state; // state of light
int id;  // id of light
int attr; // type of light, and extra qualifiers

RGBAV1 c_ambient;  // ambient light intensity
RGBAV1 c_diffuse;  // diffuse light intensity
RGBAV1 c_specular; // specular light intensity
```

```
POINT4D pos;     // position of light world/transformed
POINT4D tpos;
VECTOR4D dir;     // direction of light world/transformed
VECTOR4D tdir;
float kc, kl, kq;  // attenuation factors
float spot_inner;  // inner angle for spot light
float spot_outer;  // outer angle for spot light
float pf;        // power factor/falloff for spot lights

int  iaux1, iaux2; // auxiliary vars for future expansion
float faux1, faux2;
void *ptr;

} LIGHTV2, *LIGHTV2_PTR;
```

I have highlighted the new additions to represent the transformed storage for both the position and orientation. So, when a light is created, the only difference is that the local position and orientation is still stored in pos and dir, but the camera coordinate versions are stored in tpos and tdir. The question is, how do we transform the lights? Well, here's a function that will do it:

```
void Transform_LIGHTSV2(LIGHTV2_PTR lights, // array of lights to transform
            int num_lights,    // number of lights to transform
            MATRIX4X4_PTR mt,  // transformation matrix
            int coord_select)  // selects coords to transform

{
// this function simply transforms all of the lights
// by the transformation matrix
// this function is used to place the
// lights in camera space for example, so that
// lighting calculations are correct if the lighting function is called AFTER
// the polygons have already been trasformed to camera coordinates
// also, later we may decided to optimize this a little by determining
// the light type and only rotating what is needed, however there are thousands
// of vertices in a scene and not rotating 10 more points isn't going to make
// a difference
// NOTE: This function MUST be called even if a transform to the lights
// is not desired, that is, you are lighting in world coords, in this case
// the local light positions and orientations MUST still be copied into the
// working variables for the lighting engine to use pos->tpos, dir->tdir
// hence, call this function with TRANSFORM_COPY_LOCAL_TO_TRANS
// with a matrix of NULL
```

```
int curr_light; // current light in loop
MATRIX4X4 mr;  // used to build up rotation aspect of matrix only

// we need to rotate the direction vectors of the lights also, but
// the translation factors must be zeroed out in the matrix otherwise
// the results will be incorrect, thus make a copy of the matrix and zero
// the translation factors

if (mt!=NULL)
  {
  MAT_COPY_4X4(mt, &mr);
  // zero translation factors
  mr.M30 = mr.M31 = mr.M32 = 0;
  } // end if

// what coordinates should be transformed?
switch(coord_select)
   {
   case TRANSFORM_COPY_LOCAL_TO_TRANS:
      {
      // loop thru all the lights
      for (curr_light = 0; curr_light < num_lights; curr_light++)
      {
      lights[curr_light].tpos = lights[curr_light].pos;
      lights[curr_light].tdir = lights[curr_light].dir;
      } // end for

      } break;

   case TRANSFORM_LOCAL_ONLY:
      {
      // loop thru all the lights
      for (curr_light = 0; curr_light < num_lights; curr_light++)
      {
      // transform the local/world light coordinates in place
      POINT4D presult; // hold result of each transformation

      // transform point position of each light
      Mat_Mul_VECTOR4D_4X4(&lights[curr_light].pos, mt, &presult);

      // store result back
      VECTOR4D_COPY(&lights[curr_light].pos, &presult);
```

```
    // transform direction vector
    Mat_Mul_VECTOR4D_4X4(&lights[curr_light].dir, &mr, &presult);

    // store result back
    VECTOR4D_COPY(&lights[curr_light].dir, &presult);
    } // end for

    } break;

 case TRANSFORM_TRANS_ONLY:
    {
    // loop thru all the lights
    for (curr_light = 0; curr_light < num_lights; curr_light++)
      {
      // transform each "transformed" light
      POINT4D presult; // hold result of each transformation

      // transform point position of each light
      Mat_Mul_VECTOR4D_4X4(&lights[curr_light].tpos, mt, &presult);

      // store result back
      VECTOR4D_COPY(&lights[curr_light].tpos, &presult);

      // transform direction vector
      Mat_Mul_VECTOR4D_4X4(&lights[curr_light].tdir, &mr, &presult);

      // store result back
      VECTOR4D_COPY(&lights[curr_light].tdir, &presult);
      } // end for

     } break;

 case TRANSFORM_LOCAL_TO_TRANS:
    {
    // loop thru all the lights
    for (curr_light = 0; curr_light < num_lights; curr_light++)
    {
    // transform each local/world light and place the
    // results into the transformed
    // storage, this is the usual way the function will be called
    POINT4D presult; // hold result of each transformation
```

```
        // transform point position of each light
        Mat_Mul_VECTOR4D_4X4(&lights[curr_light].pos, mt,
                 &lights[curr_light].tpos) ;

        // transform direction vector
        Mat_Mul_VECTOR4D_4X4(&lights[curr_light].dir, &mr,
                 &lights[curr_light].tdir);
        } // end for

        } break;

    default: break;

    } // end switch

} // end Transform_LIGHTSV2
```

Calling this function with the lights, number of lights, transformation matrix, and finally the coordinate select, is all you need to do. The function is a standard transform like the others you have seen, and it works the same way. In 99 out of 100 cases, you will call it something like this:

```
Transform_LIGHTSV2(lights2, 4, &cam.mcam, TRANSFORM_LOCAL_TO_TRANS);
```

In this case, the array of lights `lights2[]` is transformed with the matrix `cam.mcam`, there are four lights to transform, and the transformation should transform the local lights and store the results in the transformed storage space. Also, now that we have new lights, there is a new array that contains them, declared in `T3DLIB8.CPP|H`:

```
LIGHTV2 lights2[MAX_LIGHTS]; // lights in system
```

Additionally, in the header we need new `#defines` for the lights:

```
// defines for light types version 2.0
#define LIGHTV2_ATTR_AMBIENT    0x0001  // basic ambient light
#define LIGHTV2_ATTR_INFINITE    0x0002  // infinite light source
#define LIGHTV2_ATTR_DIRECTIONAL 0x0002  // infinite light source (alias)
#define LIGHTV2_ATTR_POINT     0x0004  // point light source
#define LIGHTV2_ATTR_SPOTLIGHT1  0x0008  // spotlight type 1 (simple)
#define LIGHTV2_ATTR_SPOTLIGHT2  0x0010  // spotlight type 2 (complex)

#define LIGHTV2_STATE_ON      1     // light on
#define LIGHTV2_STATE_OFF      0     // light off


// transformation control flags
#define TRANSFORM_COPY_LOCAL_TO_TRANS  3 // copy data as is, no transform
```

10

They have the exact same values as the LIGHTV1 versions, just changed the name to LIGHTV2 as the prefix. Also, there is one more transform command specifically for the Transform_LIGHTSV2() function TRANSFORM_COPY_LOCAL_TO_TRANS that simply selects no transform at all and just copies the local lights to the transformed lights.

Finally, all the lighting functions have to be rewritten. However there are no changes for the most part, other than new names,instead of accessing pos and dir for the lights, we need to access tpos and tdir when performing calculations. I am not going to list the code because it's huge, but here are the prototypes from the header file:

```
int Light_OBJECT4DV2_World2_16(OBJECT4DV2_PTR obj, // object to process
     CAM4DV1_PTR cam,    // camera position
     LIGHTV2_PTR lights, // light list (might have more than one)
     int max_lights);    // maximum lights in list


int Light_OBJECT4DV2_World2(OBJECT4DV2_PTR obj, // object to process
     CAM4DV1_PTR cam,    // camera position
     LIGHTV2_PTR lights, // light list (might have more than one)
     int max_lights);    // maximum lights in list

int Light_RENDERLIST4DV2_World2(RENDERLIST4DV2_PTR rend_list,
                // list to process
     CAM4DV1_PTR cam,    // camera position
     LIGHTV2_PTR lights, // light list (might have more than one)
     int max_lights);    // maximum lights in list


int Light_RENDERLIST4DV2_World2_16(RENDERLIST4DV2_PTR rend_list, // list to process
     CAM4DV1_PTR cam,    // camera position
     LIGHTV2_PTR lights, // light list (might have more than one)
     int max_lights);    // maximum lights in list


// lighting system
int Init_Light_LIGHTV2(LIGHTV2_PTR lights, // light array to work with (new)
     int       index,// index of light to create (0..MAX_LIGHTS-1)
     int      _state,// state of light
     int      _attr, // type of light, and extra qualifiers
     RGBAV1    _c_ambient, // ambient light intensity
     RGBAV1    _c_diffuse, // diffuse light intensity
     RGBAV1    _c_specular,// specular light intensity
     POINT4D_PTR _pos,    // position of light
     VECTOR4D_PTR _dir,    // direction of light
```

```
    float     _kc,     // attenuation factors
    float     _kl,
    float     _kq,
    float     _spot_inner, // inner angle for spot light
    float     _spot_outer, // outer angle for spot light
    float     _pf);     // power factor/falloff for spot lights

int Reset_Lights_LIGHTV2(LIGHTV2_PTR lights,// light array to work with (new)
          int max_lights);  // number of lights in system
```

The only difference from these functions and the previous versions is that there is one additional parameter: the pointer to the array of lights as the first parameter. This allows the lighting system to have more than one set of global lights.

CAUTION

When you position a light or give a direction to a light, make sure you send in points or vectors that are VECTOR4D or POINT4D with the last parameter always equal to 1.0. If you forget to do this when the lights are transformed, the translation aspect of the transform matrix will not have any effect!

As an example of making the new calls, simply review the demos. The main point of redoing the lighting functions is simply so we can perform lighting in camera coordinates, so we can put off lighting until we have the absolute minimum number of polygons to light.

A Little Fun with Terrain

The reasons for clipping in 3D are numerous, but the main motivations are to minimize the number of polygons sent down the pipeline, and to make sure that polygons with negative or z = 0 coordinates are not projected, causing potential problems with the perspective calculations. Up until this point in the book, we have made all outdoor object-based demos with no large polygons or interiors, so the chances of these events occurring was nonexistent for the most part. However, we still don't have the capability to load any kind of level or interior models or large polygons worlds, so how can I show this in action? Well, I decided to create a really crude terrain engine function that will generate a very large terrain for us (any size really) and then tessellate it with triangles based on a height map.

We have two problems with this. First, we don't have any 3D object entity except for the OBJECT4DV2, and it isn't really designed to hold such large meshes, but we can still use it for now. However, the real problem is that terrains are notorious for having thousands to millions of polygons. However, with a little design common sense, we can cull out 99% of the polygons by using sectorizing algorithms that create huge terrains by tiling space with terrain patches and then only process the terrain patches that are in view. In essence, each terrain patch becomes an object, and we have a giant array of these patches, as shown in Figure 10.24.

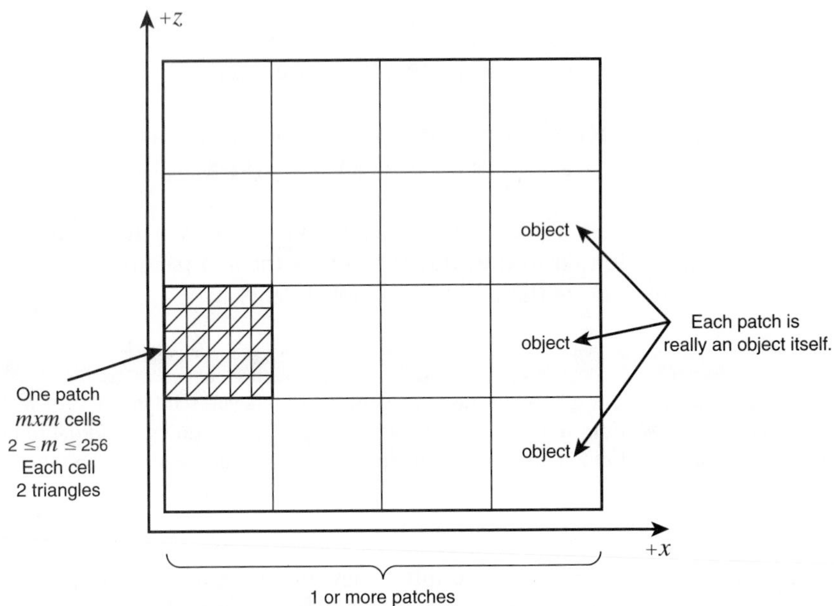

FIGURE 10.24 An example of creating a large world by sectorizing the terrain patches into objects.

We could use multiple objects and stitch them together to make a huge terrain, and then use object culling to cull away terrain patches that aren't visible. But the second problem is more insidious—even after we have a single terrain patch to deal with, it might use 32×32, 64×64, or 256×256 heights, meaning that there would be 31×31, 63×63, or 255×255 tiles, because the number of tiles in each dimension is always one fewer than the number of heights. This is because we are using the heights to define the corners of the bounding quad; thus there would be 31^2*2, 63^2*2, or 255^2*2 polygons in the patch!

Even with clipping and culling, this would kill us. A real terrain engine performs level-of-detail analysis on the fly, combining polygons where they aren't needed and adding them where they are. The result is that when viewing a single patch that was, say, 64×64 tiles, each made up of two triangles, there would be 8,192 triangles in the model. After the reduction, however, there might literally be only a few hundred needed! We aren't going to cover these algorithms because they are another subject that falls under terrain rendering and modeling, but I will give you some references at the end of this section for further study.

Right now, I want to tell you what I did to create a simple terrain that we can generate with a single call that places the terrain into an object that we can work with as usual.

The Terrain Generating Function

There are a number of ways to generate a terrain: with random numbers, from satellite data, with color height maps, or various combinations of these methods. We are going to go with the height map technique. The plan of attack is to load a 256-color bitmap image that will be used to represent a height field that we want to model, along with the color texture that would be stretched over it to show the terrain it represents. Figure 10.25 shows one such height field (greatly scaled so you can see it, of course). Notice the various colors in the height map that indicate different heights.

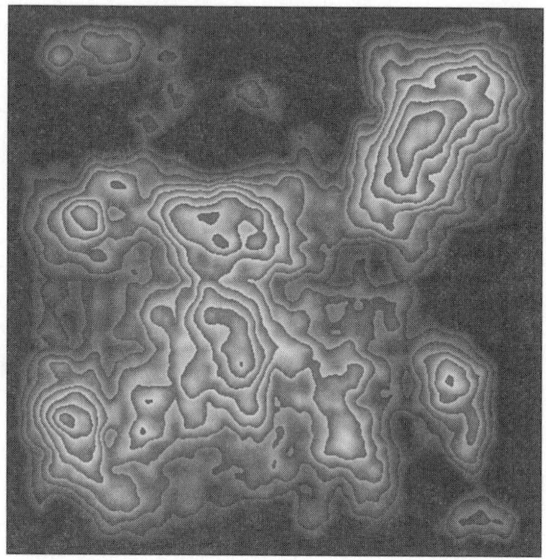

FIGURE 10.25 Using a bitmap to represent terrain height data encoded as color indices.

The height bitmap will be interpreted in the following way: We will generate a regular grid centered at (0,0,0) in world coordinates, and then lay down a matrix of height points where each height point is proportional to the pixel value in the bitmap. For example, color index 0 is the lowest altitude, and color index 255 is the highest. We can generate any height range we desire by multiplying these values. As an example, take a look at Figure 10.26, which is a graphic illustration of a 4×4 bitmap with height values and the generated height matrix with labelings.

Generating the height field mesh from the data is really nothing more than a couple of `for` loops and a lot of being careful about "off by one" errors. The algorithm works by generating two triangles for each height square, which has its height defined by the color index and some scaling factor. Also, we need to know how big to make the height map, meaning its width and height (or maybe you might want to call it the width and length?). The point is that we will generate the height map in the x-z plane and use the bitmap data to define the heights of each of the quads that define each square of the height map. Then for each quad, we will generate two triangles and stuff them into the vertex list of the object.

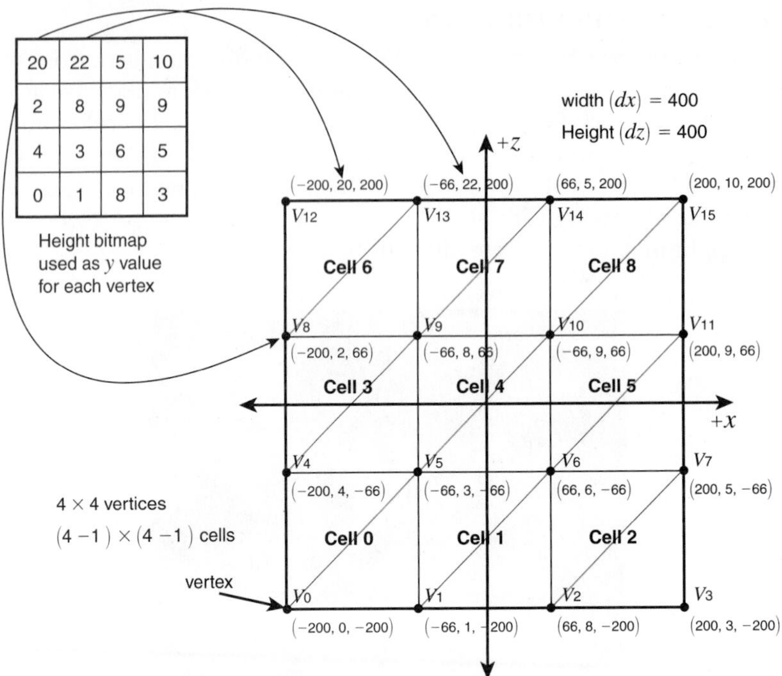

FIGURE 10.26 A fully annotated 4×4 height field construction.

I mentioned that there are lots of "off by one" potential pitfalls when doing this. If you don't know what I mean by that, how many numbers are there from 0 to 10? Well, there are 11! How many parking spaces are there if I draw five lines? There are four. Those are off-by-one errors—you need to make sure to count things correctly. This is really important when doing things like generating meshes artificially because being off by one can push you into memory or cause anomalies and so on. What I like to do is literally run through the algorithm with a really small case. I usually use 1×1, then maybe 4×4 for things like this. That way, I have proven that the base case and the *n*th case work, so I can assume under induction more or less all cases work.

Anyway, building an `OBJECT4DV2` structure artificially isn't too bad. Basically we are just streaming the information that would normally be read off disk in the object we are generating. We need the vertex list, polygon list, the number of each of them, and the attributes for each polygon. Everything is simple except the attributes for each polygon, meaning the lighting and texture information. This information must send in manually to the function using these parameters:

```
// defines for polygons and faces version 2

// attributes of polygons and polygon faces
#define POLY4DV2_ATTR_2SIDED          0x0001
```

```
#define POLY4DV2_ATTR_TRANSPARENT        0x0002
#define POLY4DV2_ATTR_8BITCOLOR         0x0004
#define POLY4DV2_ATTR_RGB16            0x0008
#define POLY4DV2_ATTR_RGB24            0x0010

#define POLY4DV2_ATTR_SHADE_MODE_PURE     0x0020
#define POLY4DV2_ATTR_SHADE_MODE_CONSTANT  0x0020 // (alias)
#define POLY4DV2_ATTR_SHADE_MODE_EMISSIVE  0x0020 // (alias)

#define POLY4DV2_ATTR_SHADE_MODE_FLAT     0x0040
#define POLY4DV2_ATTR_SHADE_MODE_GOURAUD  0x0080
#define POLY4DV2_ATTR_SHADE_MODE_PHONG    0x0100
#define POLY4DV2_ATTR_SHADE_MODE_FASTPHONG 0x0100 // (alias)
#define POLY4DV2_ATTR_SHADE_MODE_TEXTURE  0x0200

// new
#define POLY4DV2_ATTR_ENABLE_MATERIAL  0x0800 // use material for lighting
#define POLY4DV2_ATTR_DISABLE_MATERIAL 0x1000 // use basic color only
                   // for lighting (emulate version 1.0)
```

I have highlighted the attributes we are concerned with. Let's talk about them for a moment. The terrain generator can generate terrain in either 8-bit or 16-bit modes, so you must set either flag, so these defines control that:

```
POLY4DV2_ATTR_8BITCOLOR
POLY4DV2_ATTR_RGB16
```

Next, the function will support constant, flat, or Gouraud shading, because geometrically there is nothing different about these, other than that the normals must be computed. But we don't have to worry about that because once we have the mesh, we make the calls to

```
// compute the polygon normal lengths
Compute_OBJECT4DV2_Poly_Normals(obj);

// compute vertex normals for any gouraud shaded polys
Compute_OBJECT4DV2_Vertex_Normals(obj);
```

to perform any normal calculations that are needed for Gouraud shading (vertex normals), or general polygon normals for back-face removal and polygon lighting.

To set the shade mode, we would select one of these constants:

```
POLY4DV2_ATTR_SHADE_MODE_EMISSIVE
POLY4DV2_ATTR_SHADE_MODE_FLAT
POLY4DV2_ATTR_SHADE_MODE_GOURAUD
```

Then if we want a texture map stretched over the terrain, we need to enable texture mapping with the constant

```
POLY4DV2_ATTR_SHADE_MODE_TEXTURE
```

However, when texture mapping is enabled, we only have rasterizers for emissive or flat shading, so you can't turn on Gouraud shading. So that's it—to create a Gouraud-shaded 16-bit terrain with no texture for example, you would use these constants:

```
(POLY4DV2_ATTR_RGB16 | POLY4DV2_ATTR_SHADE_MODE_GOURAUD  )
```

To create a flat-shaded terrain with texture mapping:

```
(POLY4DV2_ATTR_RGB16 |
POLY4DV2_ATTR_SHADE_MODE_FLAT |
POLY4DV2_ATTR_SHADE_MODE_TEXTURE)
```

As you see, we just logically `OR` the polygon attribute flags together. Alright, now let's talk about the texture mapping support.

Take a look at Figure 10.27. It's a bitmap that we can use to texture our terrain (it was actually generated by a program *as* the texture map for the terrain, so it works out quite nicely). The bitmap is 256×256, but could be any square power of 2 sized down to 8×8 pixels. 256×256 is the largest our system supports in the rasterizer stage as a single texture.

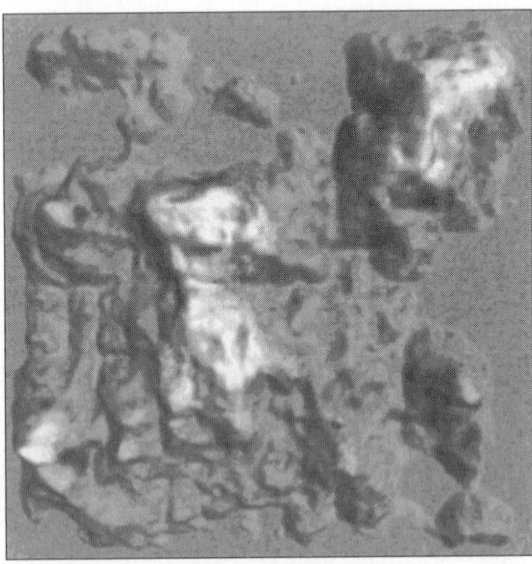

FIGURE 10.27 A sample terrain color map texture.

The approach I took is to compute texture coordinates for the input texture map and then stretch it over the terrain map vertex list. Of course, we could use huge texture maps, break them up into 256×256 size chunks, and then map them to specific polygons, but right now this is simpler, and I don't really care about making a real terrain engine—I just want something with which to do demo clipping. In any event, if you select a texture map, you will send the filename to the function of the texture (along with the filename of the bitmap in 256 color for the height information) and the function will compute the texture coordinates to "skin" the terrain with the single texture map. This is rather simple, and once again just a lot of details with the width, height, and number of cells in the terrain map.

Therefore, if texture mapping is selected for the terrain, you must send in a filename of a 16-bit texture map. The texture map should be square, of course. The terrain function will map the texture onto the terrain via computing texture coordinates that map each triangle of each square that makes up the terrain properly.

That's about it for the terrain generating function—it takes two input files in most cases. One file is the height map in 256 color .BMP format, which should be square if possible, and usually less than 40×40 pixels. This is because anything larger would result in a terrain that has 40×40 heights (39×39 quads, or 39^2*2 triangles = 3,042 polygons), which is getting up there for our little software engine!

Now I want you to review the function itself, and then we will see how to call it with some examples:

```
int Generate_Terrain_OBJECT4DV2(OBJECT4DV2_PTR obj,    // pointer to object
 float twidth,       // width in world coords on x-axis
 float theight,       // height (length) in world coords on z-axis
 float vscale,       // vertical scale of terrain
 char *height_map_file, // filename of height bitmap encoded in 256 colors
 char *texture_map_file, // filename of texture map
 int rgbcolor,       // color of terrain if no texture
 VECTOR4D_PTR pos,     // initial position
 VECTOR4D_PTR rot,     // initial rotations
 int poly_attr)      // the shading attributes we would like
{
// this function generates a terrain of width x height in the x-z plane
// the terrain is defined by a height field encoded as color values
// of a 256 color texture, 0 being ground level 255 being 1.0, this value
// is scaled by vscale for the height of each point in the height field
// the height field generated will be composed of triangles where each vertex
// in the height field is derived from the height map, thus if the height map
// is 256 x 256 points then the final mesh will be (256-1) x (256-1) polygons
// with a absolute world size of width x height (in the x-z plane)
// also if there is a texture map file then it will be mapped onto the terrain
// and texture coordinates will be generated
// the function generates either 8-bit or 16-bit terrains, but make
```

```
// sure to use the correct attributes and match the color texture map
// bit depth!!

char buffer[256]; // working buffer

float col_tstep, row_tstep;
float col_vstep, row_vstep;
int columns, rows;

int rgbwhite;

BITMAP_FILE height_bitmap; // holds the height bitmap

// Step 1: clear out the object and initialize it a bit
memset(obj, 0, sizeof(OBJECT4DV2));

// set state of object to active and visible
obj->state = OBJECT4DV2_STATE_ACTIVE | OBJECT4DV2_STATE_VISIBLE;

// set position of object
obj->world_pos.x = pos->x;
obj->world_pos.y = pos->y;
obj->world_pos.z = pos->z;
obj->world_pos.w = pos->w;

// create proper color word based on selected bit depth of terrain
// rgbcolor is always in rgb5.6.5 format, so only need to downconvert for
// 8-bit mesh
if (poly_attr & POLY4DV1_ATTR_8BITCOLOR)
  {
  rgbcolor = rgblookup[rgbcolor];
  rgbwhite = rgblookup[RGB16Bit(255,255,255)];
  } // end if
else
  {
  rgbwhite = RGB16Bit(255,255,255) ;
  } // end else

// set number of frames
obj->num_frames = 1;
obj->curr_frame = 0;
obj->attr = OBJECT4DV2_ATTR_SINGLE_FRAME;
```

```
// clear the bitmaps out
memset(&height_bitmap, 0, sizeof(BITMAP_FILE));
memset(&bitmap16bit, 0, sizeof(BITMAP_FILE));

// Step 2: load in the height field
Load_Bitmap_File(&height_bitmap, height_map_file);

// compute basic information
columns = height_bitmap.bitmapinfoheader.biWidth;
rows    = height_bitmap.bitmapinfoheader.biHeight;

col_vstep = twidth / (float)(columns - 1);
row_vstep = theight / (float)(rows - 1);

sprintf(obj->name ,"Terrain:%s%s", height_map_file, texture_map_file);
obj->num_vertices = columns * rows;
obj->num_polys    = ((columns - 1) * (rows - 1) ) * 2;

// store some results to help with terrain following
// use the auxilliary variables in the object -- might as well!
obj->ivar1 = columns;
obj->ivar2 = rows;
obj->fvar1 = col_vstep;
obj->fvar2 = row_vstep;

// allocate the memory for the vertices and number of polys
// the call parameters are redundant in this case, but who cares
if (!Init_OBJECT4DV2(obj,   // object to allocate
           obj->num_vertices,
           obj->num_polys,
           obj->num_frames))
  {
  Write_Error("\nTerrain generator error (can't allocate memory).");
  } // end if



// load texture map if there is one
if ( (poly_attr & POLY4DV2_ATTR_SHADE_MODE_TEXTURE) && texture_map_file)
  {
  // load the texture from disk
  Load_Bitmap_File(&bitmap16bit, texture_map_file);
```

```
    // create a proper size and bitdepth bitmap
    obj->texture = (BITMAP_IMAGE_PTR)malloc(sizeof(BITMAP_IMAGE)) ;
    Create_Bitmap(obj->texture,0,0,
           bitmap16bit.bitmapinfoheader.biWidth,
           bitmap16bit.bitmapinfoheader.biHeight,
           bitmap16bit.bitmapinfoheader.biBitCount);

    // load the bitmap image (later make this 8/16 bit)
    if (obj->texture->bpp == 16)
      Load_Image_Bitmap16(obj->texture,
         &bitmap16bit,0,0,BITMAP_EXTRACT_MODE_ABS);
    else
      {
      Load_Image_Bitmap(obj->texture,
         &bitmap16bit,0,0,BITMAP_EXTRACT_MODE_ABS);
      } // end else 8 bit


    // compute stepping factors in texture map for
    // texture coordinate computation
    col_tstep = (float)(bitmap16bit.bitmapinfoheader.biWidth-1)/
          (float)(columns - 1);
    row_tstep = (float)(bitmap16bit.bitmapinfoheader.biHeight-1)/
          (float)(rows - 1);

    // flag object as having textures
    SET_BIT(obj->attr, OBJECT4DV2_ATTR_TEXTURES);

    // done, so unload the bitmap
    Unload_Bitmap_File(&bitmap16bit);
    } // end if

  Write_Error("\ncolumns = %d, rows = %d", columns, rows);
  Write_Error("\ncol_vstep = %f, row_vstep = %f", col_vstep, row_vstep);
  Write_Error("\ncol_tstep=%f, row_tstep=%f", col_tstep, row_tstep);
  Write_Error("\nnum_vertices = %d, num_polys = %d",
        obj->num_vertices, obj->num_polys);

  // Step 4: generate the vertex list,
  // and texture coordinate list in row major form
  for (int curr_row = 0; curr_row < rows; curr_row++)
    {
    for (int curr_col = 0; curr_col < columns; curr_col++)
      {
```

```
    int vertex = (curr_row * columns) + curr_col;
    // compute the vertex
    obj->vlist_local[vertex].x = curr_col * col_vstep - (twidth/2);
    obj->vlist_local[vertex].y = vscale*
  ((float)height_bitmap.buffer[curr_col + (curr_row * columns)]) / 255;
    obj->vlist_local[vertex].z = curr_row * row_vstep - (theight/2);

    obj->vlist_local[vertex].w = 1;

    // every vertex has a point at least, set that in the flags attribute
    SET_BIT(obj->vlist_local[vertex].attr, VERTEX4DTV1_ATTR_POINT) ;

    // need texture coord?
    if ( (poly_attr & POLY4DV2_ATTR_SHADE_MODE_TEXTURE) && texture_map_file)
      {
      // now texture coordinates
      obj->tlist[vertex].x = curr_col * col_tstep;
      obj->tlist[vertex].y = curr_row * row_tstep;

      } // end if

    Write_Error("\nVertex %d: V[%f, %f, %f], T[%f, %f]",
           vertex, obj->vlist_local[vertex].x,
           obj->vlist_local[vertex].y,
           obj->vlist_local[vertex].z,
           obj->tlist[vertex].x,
           obj->tlist[vertex].y);
    } // end for curr_col

   } // end curr_row

// perform rotation transformation?

// compute average and max radius
Compute_OBJECT4DV2_Radius(obj);

Write_Error("\nObject average radius = %f, max radius = %f",
      obj->avg_radius[0], obj->max_radius[0]);

// Step 5: generate the polygon list
for (int poly=0; poly < obj->num_polys/2; poly++)
  {
  // polygons follow a regular pattern of 2 per square, row
```

10

```
// major form, finding the correct indices is a pain, but
// the bottom line is we have an array of vertices mxn and we need
// a list of polygons that is (m-1) x (n-1), with 2 triangles per
// square with a consistent winding order.. this is one one to arrive
// at the indices, another way would be to use two loops, etc.,

int base_poly_index = (poly % (columns-1)) +
          (columns * (poly / (columns - 1)) );

// upper left poly
obj->plist[poly*2].vert[0] = base_poly_index;
obj->plist[poly*2].vert[1] = base_poly_index+columns;
obj->plist[poly*2].vert[2] = base_poly_index+columns+1;

// lower right poly
obj->plist[poly*2+1].vert[0] = base_poly_index;
obj->plist[poly*2+1].vert[1] = base_poly_index+columns+1;
obj->plist[poly*2+1].vert[2] = base_poly_index+1;

// point polygon vertex list to object's vertex list
// note that this is redundant since the polylist is contained
// within the object in this case and its up to the user to select
// whether the local or transformed vertex list is used when building up
// polygon geometry, might be a better idea to set to NULL in the context
// of polygons that are part of an object
obj->plist[poly*2].vlist = obj->vlist_local;
obj->plist[poly*2+1].vlist = obj->vlist_local;

// set attributes of polygon with sent attributes
obj->plist[poly*2].attr = poly_attr;
obj->plist[poly*2+1].attr = poly_attr;

// now perform some test to make sure any secondary data elements are
// set properly

// set color of polygon
obj->plist[poly*2].color = rgbcolor;
obj->plist[poly*2+1].color = rgbcolor;

// check for gouraud of phong shading, if so need normals
if ( (obj->plist[poly*2].attr & POLY4DV2_ATTR_SHADE_MODE_GOURAUD) ||
   (obj->plist[poly*2].attr & POLY4DV2_ATTR_SHADE_MODE_PHONG) )
  {
```

```
    // the vertices from this polygon all need normals, set that in the
➥flags attribute
    SET_BIT(obj->vlist_local[ obj->plist[poly*2].vert[0] ].attr,
        VERTEX4DTV1_ATTR_NORMAL);
    SET_BIT(obj->vlist_local[ obj->plist[poly*2].vert[1] ].attr,
        VERTEX4DTV1_ATTR_NORMAL);
    SET_BIT(obj->vlist_local[ obj->plist[poly*2].vert[2] ].attr,
        VERTEX4DTV1_ATTR_NORMAL);

    SET_BIT(obj->vlist_local[ obj->plist[poly*2+1].vert[0] ].attr,
        VERTEX4DTV1_ATTR_NORMAL);
    SET_BIT(obj->vlist_local[ obj->plist[poly*2+1].vert[1] ].attr,
        VERTEX4DTV1_ATTR_NORMAL);
    SET_BIT(obj->vlist_local[ obj->plist[poly*2+1].vert[2] ].attr,
        VERTEX4DTV1_ATTR_NORMAL);

    } // end if

   // if texture in enabled the enable texture coordinates
   if (poly_attr & POLY4DV2_ATTR_SHADE_MODE_TEXTURE)
    {
    // apply texture to this polygon
    obj->plist[poly*2].texture = obj->texture;
    obj->plist[poly*2+1].texture = obj->texture;

    // assign the texture coordinates
    // upper left poly
    obj->plist[poly*2].text[0] = base_poly_index;
    obj->plist[poly*2].text[1] = base_poly_index+columns;
    obj->plist[poly*2].text[2] = base_poly_index+columns+1;

    // lower right poly
    obj->plist[poly*2+1].text[0] = base_poly_index;
    obj->plist[poly*2+1].text[1] = base_poly_index+columns+1;
    obj->plist[poly*2+1].text[2] = base_poly_index+1;

    // override base color to make poly more reflective
    obj->plist[poly*2].color = rgbwhite;
    obj->plist[poly*2+1].color = rgbwhite;

    // set texture coordinate attributes
    SET_BIT(obj->vlist_local[ obj->plist[poly*2].vert[0] ].attr,
             VERTEX4DTV1_ATTR_TEXTURE);
```

10

```
    SET_BIT(obj->vlist_local[ obj->plist[poly*2].vert[1] ].attr,
                VERTEX4DTV1_ATTR_TEXTURE);
    SET_BIT(obj->vlist_local[ obj->plist[poly*2].vert[2] ].attr,
                VERTEX4DTV1_ATTR_TEXTURE);

    SET_BIT(obj->vlist_local[ obj->plist[poly*2+1].vert[0] ].attr,
                VERTEX4DTV1_ATTR_TEXTURE);
    SET_BIT(obj->vlist_local[ obj->plist[poly*2+1].vert[1] ].attr,
                VERTEX4DTV1_ATTR_TEXTURE);
    SET_BIT(obj->vlist_local[ obj->plist[poly*2+1].vert[2] ].attr,
                VERTEX4DTV1_ATTR_TEXTURE);

    } // end if

  // set the material mode to ver. 1.0 emulation
  SET_BIT(obj->plist[poly*2].attr, POLY4DV2_ATTR_DISABLE_MATERIAL);
  SET_BIT(obj->plist[poly*2+1].attr, POLY4DV2_ATTR_DISABLE_MATERIAL);

  // finally set the polygon to active
  obj->plist[poly*2].state = POLY4DV2_STATE_ACTIVE;
  obj->plist[poly*2+1].state = POLY4DV2_STATE_ACTIVE;

  // point polygon vertex list to object's vertex list
  // note that this is redundant since the polylist is contained
  // within the object in this case and its up to the user to select
  // whether the local or transformed vertex list is used when building up
  // polygon geometry, might be a better idea to set to NULL in the context
  // of polygons that are part of an object
  obj->plist[poly*2].vlist = obj->vlist_local;
  obj->plist[poly*2+1].vlist = obj->vlist_local;

  // set texture coordinate list, this is needed
  obj->plist[poly*2].tlist = obj->tlist;
  obj->plist[poly*2+1].tlist = obj->tlist;

  } // end for poly
#if 0
for (poly=0; poly < obj->num_polys; poly++)
{
Write_Error("\nPoly %d: Vi[%d, %d, %d], Ti[%d, %d, %d]",poly,
      obj->plist[poly].vert[0],
      obj->plist[poly].vert[1],
      obj->plist[poly].vert[2],
```

```
        obj->plist[poly].text[0],
        obj->plist[poly].text[1],
        obj->plist[poly].text[2]);

} // end
#endif

// compute the polygon normal lengths
Compute_OBJECT4DV2_Poly_Normals(obj);

// compute vertex normals for any gouraud shaded polys
Compute_OBJECT4DV2_Vertex_Normals(obj);

// return success
return(1);

} // end Generate_Terrain_OBJECT4DV2
```

The function is based on the .PLG loader. I basically started with the .PLG loader because it had a template for what I needed to do to build an OBJECT4DV2, and then added the algorithm to artificially generate the terrain—cool, huh? Now let's take a look at how to call the function. Here's a call to generate a 32×32 terrain with texture mapping and flat shading for a 4000×4000 size world using the height map EARTHHEIGHTMAP01.BMP and using the texture map (256×256×16) EARTHCOLORMAP01.BMP:

```
VECTOR4D terrain_pos = {0,0,0,0};

Generate_Terrain_OBJECT4DV2(&obj_terrain, // pointer to object
 4000,    // width in world coords on x-axis
 4000,    // height (length) in world coords on z-axis
 700,     // vertical scale of terrain
 "earthheightmap01.bmp", // filename of height bitmap encoded in 256 colors
 "earthcolormap01.bmp", // filename of texture map
 RGB16Bit(255,255,255), // color of terrain if no texture
 &terrain_pos,       // initial position
 NULL,           // initial rotations
 POLY4DV2_ATTR_RGB16 |
 POLY4DV2_ATTR_SHADE_MODE_FLAT | POLY4DV2_ATTR_SHADE_MODE_TEXTURE);
```


The parameters to the function are straightforward. You send in the width and height of the terrain map in world coordinates (this will be the x-z boundaries, 4000×4000 in this case), the height scale of the terrain map, and basically all the heights will be scaled so that the height peak is the value (700 in this case). Next comes the names of the height map and texture map bitmaps on the disk (if there isn't a texture, the texture map should be NULL). Next is the color of the terrain (when the terrain isn't textured, you must tell the function what color to make it). Next is the position of the terrain in world coordinates (usually 0,0,0 is good). Next is the initial rotation of the mesh (use NULL if it's not implemented yet), and finally are the polygon attributes you want to use (in this case, flat-shaded, 16-bit, textured).

You can create as many terrain objects as you want, and if you are so inclined, you could create one huge world with, say, 16×16 of them, each as an object, and then take advantage of the object culling. But as I said, I just wanted something to create really large polygons for an interior or exterior environment that we could fly around in, and this works great.

Generating the Terrain Data

You might be thinking, this is totally cool, but how can I generate the terrain data itself? Well, you can make a program to do it. You also need to make sure that any texture you skin it with looks right. For example, snow caps should be on the mountain tops and blue should be in the water. However, most people use a program to generate terrain that can actually generate both the terrain height map in 256 color .BMP mode, along with a texture map to skin it with. One such program is called VistaPro, which is up to version 4.0, I believe. The problem is, they have licensed the program to everyone, so the best thing to do is go on the Internet and search for *VistaPro* to find the most current publisher. Another program that will generate terrain and height maps is Bryce by Metacreations—but they have also sold the company, and the property is now owned by Corel. Once again, these are just some ideas—there are tons of free terrain generator programs on the Net.

The Dune Buggy Demo

Alright, now let's put this terrain mapping and clipping to use and see if it works! To do this, I have created a little demo in DEMOII10_2.CPP¦EXE (the 8-bit version is in DEMOII10_2_8b.CPP¦EXE) in the form of a dune buggy simulation on a desert island. Figure 10.28 and 10.29 are screenshots from the demo. To compile the demo, you will need the main .CPP file and T3DLIB1-8.CPP¦H, along with the standard DirectX .LIB files.

The demo is pretty straightforward, as usual. It makes a single call to create the terrain with the same parameters as the example you just reviewed, and then dumps the camera down and allows you to drive over the terrain—yes, drive! Alas, I have a little explaining to do about terrain coming up.

The controls for the demo are shown on the onscreen help, which you can toggle with the H key, but the most important things to try are enabling and disabling the 3D clipping planes with the X, Y, and Z keys. Then drive around and try looking at the polygon stats at the bottom of the screen. As you enable/disable different axis clippers, watch the pipeline stats change.

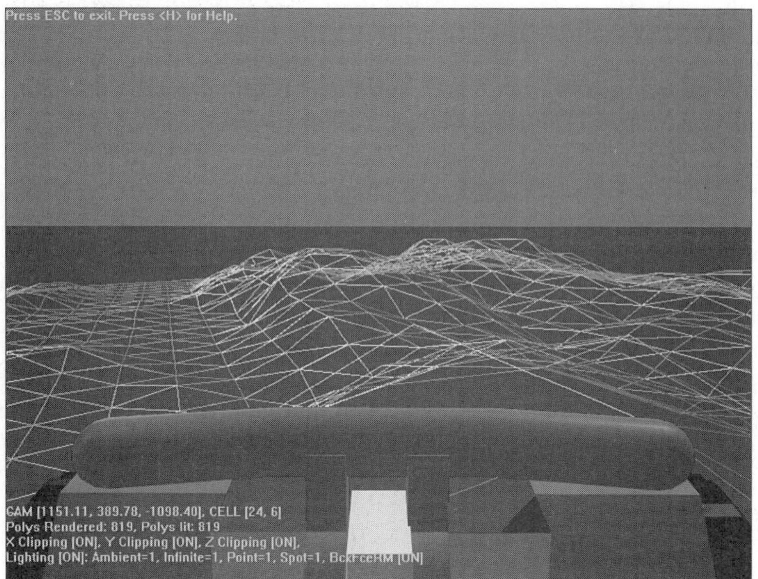

FIGURE 10.28 A screenshot of the terrain demo in wireframe mode.

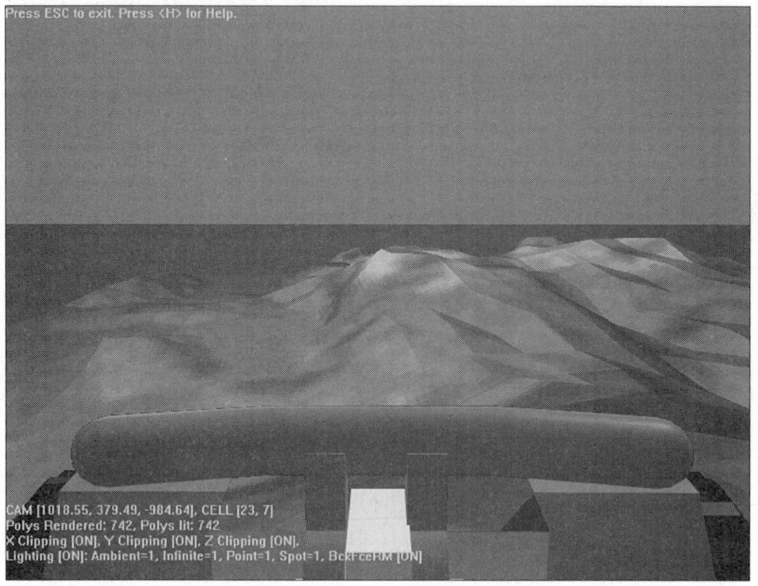

FIGURE 10.29 A screenshot of the terrain demo in solid textured mode.

10

> **CAUTION**
>
> You might cause the application to crash when you disable the near z-clipping plane, because really large polygons will be passed and projected. This could be a bad thing, but of course it won't hurt the computer! Finally, try switching to wireframe mode with the W key to see all the polygons.

The Terrain Following Algorithm

The terrain following algorithm and the simple physics model for the virtual dune buggy are interrelated, so I will discuss both of them at the same time. The problem is this: We have a camera that is used to represent the first-person point of view of the player (with a little prerendered dune buggy front end overlaid, of course). We need the player to be able to drive over the terrain, but not drive through it, so we need to compute the height of the terrain under the camera and move the eye position up appropriately, as shown in Figure 10.30.

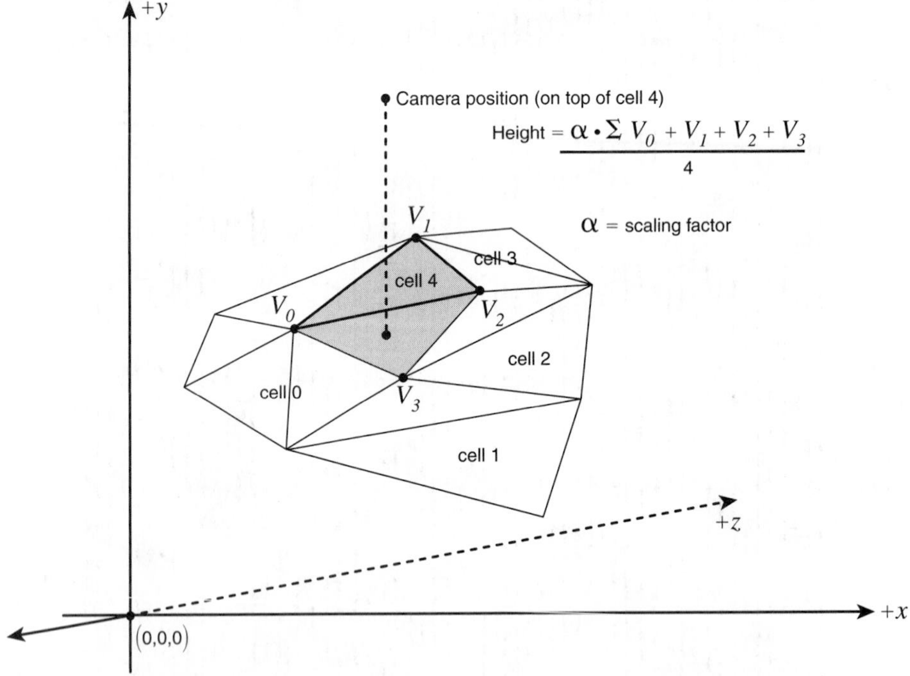

FIGURE 10.30 The terrain following setup.

There are a number of ways to approach this problem. We could make a completely real physics model for the dune buggy with momentum, but that's a lot for such a simple problem. We could also go to the other extreme and just move the camera up to the highest point of any tile cell it's hovering over, but that would suck, so I have come up with a happy medium: A very simplified physics model based on velocity, gravity, and impulse acceleration is attached to the camera's position and orientation, so I will refer to the camera as the dune buggy and vice versa. Here are the physics model highlights:

- The dune buggy has a forward velocity and direction, which are controlled by the arrow keys (the acceleration is constant when the player presses forward or backward).
- There is a downward "gravity" force, which is constantly applied to the dune buggy. The result of this is the y-axis downward velocity of the dune buggy increases as a function of time.
- There is an upward "normal" force applied to the dune buggy. If the dune buggy is ever below sea level, this pushes it upward.
- At every instant of time, the current position of the dune buggy in world space is used to compute which terrain cell the dune buggy is hovering over, and then the four vertices heights are averaged together. This height value is compared to the current height of the dune buggy, and if the current height of the dune buggy is less than the terrain height (minus the ground clearance), the upward velocity of the dune buggy is increased with an impulse acceleration proportional to the delta in the height. Additionally, a stop-limit is applied to the dune buggy height, so when a steep incline or height change is detected, the dune buggy will "skip" up vertically so as not to go through the geometry.
- In addition to changing the height of the dune buggy to track the terrain, the pitch of the dune buggy/camera is changed relative to the gradient of the terrain the dune buggy is traversing. This gives the illusion that the nose of the dune buggy is pitching up and down with the terrain.
- Finally, there is code to force stability in the physics model, so that if the change in position or orientation is small enough, it doesn't oscillate and is zeroed out.

With all that in mind, here are some of the physics constants and variables used in the simulation:

```
// terrain defines
#define TERRAIN_WIDTH      4000
#define TERRAIN_HEIGHT     4000
#define TERRAIN_SCALE      700
#define MAX_SPEED        20


// physical model defines play with these to change the feel of the vehicle
float gravity   = -.40;   // general gravity
float vel_y     = 0;     // the y velocity of camera/jeep
```

```
float cam_speed = 0;      // speed of the camera/jeep
float sea_level = 50;     // sea level of the simulation
float gclearance = 75;    // clearance from the camera to the ground
float neutral_pitch = 10;  // the neutral pitch of the camera
```

And here is the code that runs the entire terrain following/driving simulation:

```
// motion section /////////////////////////////////////////////////////////////

// terrain following, simply find the current cell we are over and then
// index into the vertex list and find the 4 vertices that make up the
// quad cell we are hovering over and then average the values, and based
// on the current height and the height of the terrain push the player upward

// the terrain generates and stores some results to help with terrain following
//ivar1 = columns;
//ivar2 = rows;
//fvar1 = col_vstep;
//fvar2 = row_vstep;

int cell_x = (cam.pos.x + TERRAIN_WIDTH/2) / obj_terrain.fvar1;
int cell_y = (cam.pos.z + TERRAIN_HEIGHT/2) / obj_terrain.fvar1;

static float terrain_height, delta;

// test if we are on terrain
if ( (cell_x >=0) && (cell_x < obj_terrain.ivar1) &&
   (cell_y >=0) && (cell_y < obj_terrain.ivar2) )
  {
  // compute vertex indices into vertex list of the current quad
  int v0 = cell_x + cell_y*obj_terrain.ivar2;
  int v1 = v0 + 1;
  int v2 = v1 + obj_terrain.ivar2;
  int v3 = v0 + obj_terrain.ivar2;

  // now simply index into table
  terrain_height = 0.25 * (obj_terrain.vlist_trans[v0].y +
              obj_terrain.vlist_trans[v1].y +
              obj_terrain.vlist_trans[v2].y +
              obj_terrain.vlist_trans[v3].y) ;

  // compute height difference
  delta = terrain_height - (cam.pos.y - gclearance);
```

```
  // test for penetration
  if (delta > 0)
   {
   // apply force immediately to camera (this will give it a springy feel)
   vel_y+=(delta * (0.025));

   // test for pentration, if so move up immediately,
   // so we don't penetrate geometry
   cam.pos.y+=(delta*.3);

   // now this is more of a hack than the physics model :) let move the front
   // up and down a bit based on the forward velocity and the gradient of the
   // hill
   cam.dir.x -= (delta*.015);

   } // end if

  } // end if

// decelerate camera
if (cam_speed > (0.25) ) cam_speed-=.25;
else
if (cam_speed < (-0.25) ) cam_speed+=.25;
else
  cam_speed = 0;

// make engine sound
DSound_Set_Freq(car_sound_id,8000+fabs(cam_speed)*250);

// force camera to seek a stable orientation
if (cam.dir.x > (neutral_pitch+0.3)) cam.dir.x -= (.3);
else
if (cam.dir.x < (neutral_pitch-0.3)) cam.dir.x += (.3);
 else
  cam.dir.x = neutral_pitch;

// apply gravity
vel_y+=gravity;

// test for absolute sea level and push upward..
if (cam.pos.y < sea_level)
  {
  vel_y = 0;
```

10

```
  cam.pos.y = sea_level;
  } // end if

// move camera
cam.pos.x += cam_speed*Fast_Sin(cam.dir.y);
cam.pos.z += cam_speed*Fast_Cos(cam.dir.y);
cam.pos.y += vel_y;
```

It's actually very small—the inputs to the system are the current camera position and that's about it. From there the system functions.

Well, that's it for my little demo. Please feel free to tweak the variables—you can get everything from a 1,000,000-ton tank to a water craft. Also, with very little work, you should be able to add multiple terrain patches via objects, and make it 3D racing, boating, jet skiing, snowboarding, or whatever—it's up to you. A snowboarding demo would be really easy—you could create, say, 16 or 32 patches of terrain that are each 32×32 tiles, and say 2000×2000 in world space, and then line them up in such a way that they create one large run. Let the object culler remove the patches that are beyond the far clipping plane, have the clipper deal with the one that's in view, throw a snowboard in front of the camera, change the height map, and you're shreddin'!

Summary

I'm glad this chapter is over—I was getting tired of setting the near clipping plane a light year away from the viewplane so that negative projection anomalies didn't occur! But now things are much more stable. In any event, you should now have a good understanding of clipping algorithms, and better yet, that they aren't that complicated at all, just a lot of details. Also, the added culling feature that totally clips polygons that are beyond view out of the viewing frustrum but not back-faces really speeds things up, so now the engine is even faster. Finally, as a added bonus we got to play a little with terrain stuff, and make a little demo that you can easily make into a water or offroad game without much work. It's not going to be *Splashdown* or *V-Rally*, but it's a start! And last but not least—this is the last chapter with 8-bit support.

CHAPTER 11

Depth Buffering and Visibility

IN THIS CHAPTER

- Introduction to Depth Buffering and Visibility
- Z-Buffering Basics
- Creating the Z-Buffer System
- Possible Z-Buffer Optimizations
- Problems with the Z-Buffer
- The Software and Z-Buffer Demos

"I'm not frightened that I don't know …"

—Dr. Richard Feynman, Caltech Physics Lectures

In this chapter, we are going to look at one of the most basic methods of hidden surface removal/visibility—the Z-buffer. And as usual, we'll rewrite our engine to support the technology, make a couple of demos, and that's about it. Believe me, that's enough <BG>. Here's a list of the main topic areas:

- Introduction to depth buffering and visibility
- Z-buffering basics
- The plane equation
- Z interpolation
- 1/z-buffering
- Creating the Z-buffer system
- Adding Z-buffer support to the rasterizers
- Possible Z-buffer optimizations
- The new software and Z-buffer demos

Introduction to Depth Buffering and Visibility

First things first: There is a lot of confusion with the following two concepts:

- Hidden surface removal
- Visible surface determination

The reason is that they are really the same thing in some cases, and different things in others. For example, when we perform the back-face removal step in the 3D pipeline, we are definitely performing hidden surface removal. On the other hand, clipping is both hidden surface removal (clipping away regions that aren't within the viewing frustrum) and at the same time visible surface determination, as we are determining what is visible and not clipped. I can't give you a straight answer myself, because there isn't one. From now on, unless I am specifically removing something, I am just going to refer to the whole business of what to do and what not to draw as *visible surface determination (VSD)*. Many books follow suit, so this shouldn't be any surprise. Moreover, no matter what we do when we talk about z-buffering, the algorithm works down to the pixel level, so there are no surfaces, just components or pieces of surfaces! The moral of the story is the terminology is irrelevant—if it becomes an issue, I will comment on it.

In any case, at this point in the book you should be quite comfortable writing your own 3D engine. We have covered every major aspect of rendering and the 3D pipeline. Of course, physics and gameplay are out of the scope of this book, as we are focusing only how to transform, light, and render polygons. So where are we at this point? Well, we have a fairly advanced lighting system and we can texture map and clip in 2D and 3D, but our polygon models and environments have still been a little simplistic. There are two reasons for this: first, we simply haven't loaded any interior levels because we don't really have a tool or an appropriate file format to do so, but we have the technology to render them nonetheless. The second reason is a little more subtle: We can't sort the polygons or decide what order they should be drawn in with complete accuracy.

Up until now, we have used the painter's algorithm to sort polygons, which does nothing more than use the average, minimum, or maximum z value of each polygon in the rendering list as a sorting key to sort the rendering list. Then we simply draw the polygons from back to front as a painter would, and the display is mostly correct. However, we learned that this algorithm has a number of shortcomings; for example, it doesn't handle long polygons well, or allow interpenetration of polygons, as shown in Figure 11.1.

On the bright side, the painter's algorithm works for 99% of the polygonal data that we have been working with thus far. It works great for scenes that are heavily made up of objects (especially where the objects don't overlap, and themselves are made of small polygons). Additionally, it works fine for rendering meshes such as terrains, which have regularity and non-overlapping geometry. That is, although a terrain is 3D, it's mostly 2D with perturbations in height.

However, the painter's algorithm (or just *z-sorting*, as I will call it from now on) can really look bad when special effects such as interpenetration, complex geometry, large and small geometry, and so forth, come into play. We need another method to resolve the order in which to render the polygons. At first thought, we might decide to rewrite the z-sorting and make it "smarter." This actually is possible. For example, we can look at the problem a pair of polygons at a time and run further tests on them to determine their correct order. This class of algorithms is usually referred to as *list priority algorithms* and there are many names tied to them, but as usual, they are all really just common sense. The bottom line is that if you have a z-sorted list and you want to make sure that no pair of polygons has been incorrectly sorted, you apply some further tests to satisfy this desire. Here is one set of tests derived from the Newell-Sancha algorithm:

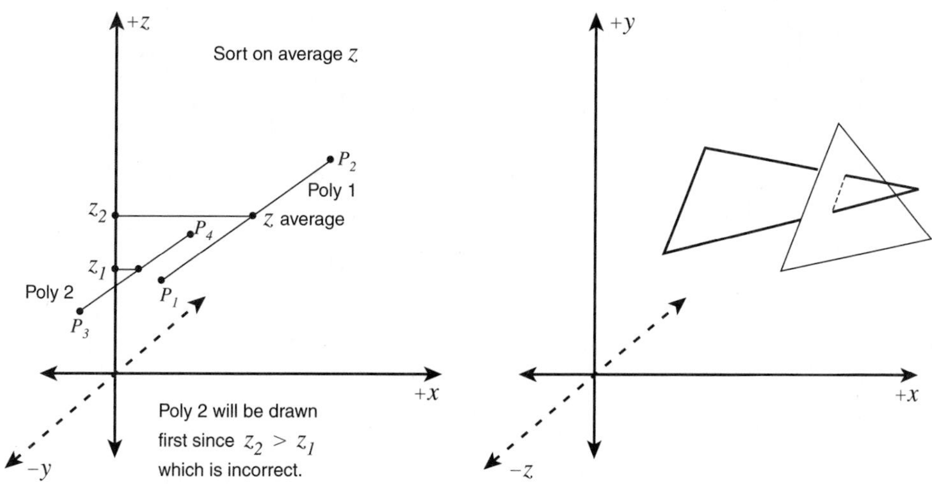

FIGURE 11.1 Z-sorting failure cases.

Look at the two polygons P1 and P2 shown in Figure 11.2. Both have been depth-sorted such that the largest z value of each polygon has been used as the sorting key. Thus, the farthest polygon from the viewpoint is the first in the list.

- Test 1 (z-overlap test): If the z-extents of P1 and P2 do not overlap, no part of P1 can overlap P2 (in other words, if $P1_{min} > P2_{max}$, draw P1 to the frame buffer. This case is shown in Figure 11.2a. On the other hand, if $P2_{max} < P2_{min}$, it's possible that P1 obscures P2 even though P1 has been sorted farthest and will be drawn first. Therefore, a number of tests must be performed to determine this. If any of these tests can be answered affirmatively, the algorithm can exit and P1 can't possibly obscure P2.
- Test 2 (bounding box test): Are the bounding boxes of P1 and P2 disjointed in x or y? That is, if either the x-extents or y-extents of P1 and P2 do not overlap, the polygons can't possibly obscure one another. This is shown in Figure 11.2b.
- Test 3 (half-space test): Is P1 or P2's half-space farther from the viewpoint? If so, draw P1 and exit. This is shown in Figure 11.2c.
- Test 4 (half-space test): Is P2 or P1's half-space nearer to the viewpoint? If so, then draw P1 and exit.
- Test 5 (perspective test): Are the perspective projections of P1 and P2 disjointed? That is, when the polygons are projected, do their projections overlap? If no, draw P1 and exit.

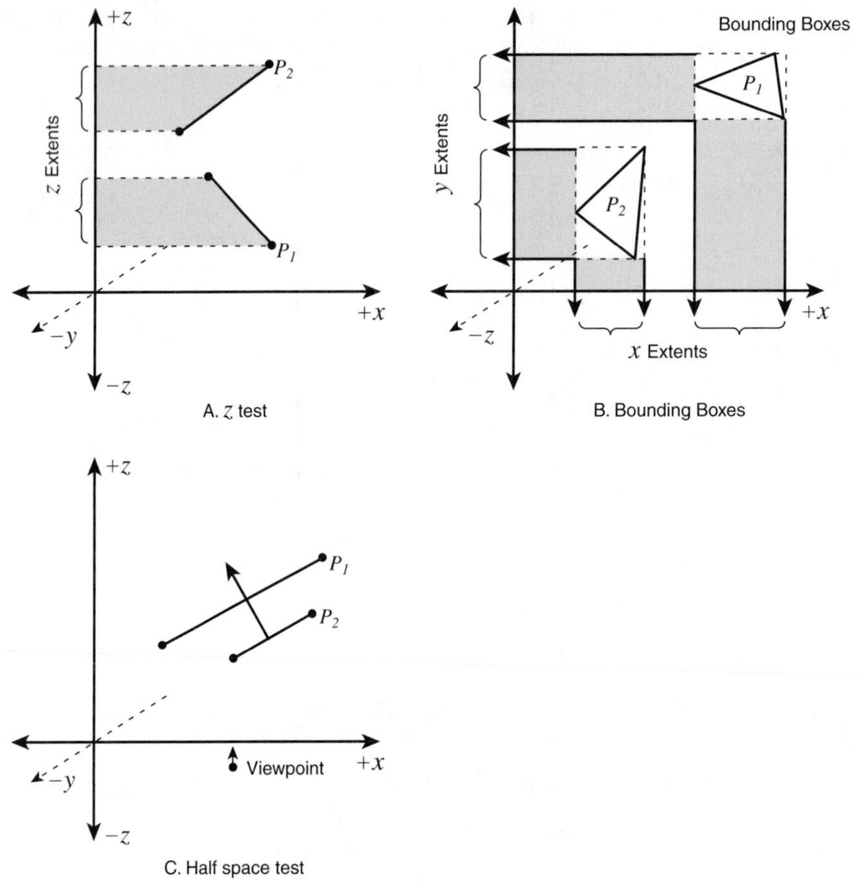

FIGURE 11.2 Polygon sorting setup.

If all the tests fail, swap P1 and P2 and mark them as swapped. If an attempt to swap them is made again, there must be a cyclic overlap, as shown in Figure 11.3. In this case, one of the polygons P1 or P2 must be split to overcome this problem.

If you don't get the algorithm, don't worry—no one uses it! I just wanted you to see the general flow of it. Basically, the problem is that we are trying to solve a problem by asking more and more complex questions until we absolutely pin down the correct order. Is it worth it? The answer is no! If you want perfect order, you would never use that disaster of an algorithm in the first place, and if you didn't care about perfect order, you again wouldn't use the algorithm because the z-sort would look fine in most cases (many games on the PS one and PC use basic z-sorting and you probably never knew!).

So, we need something more elegant (or more simple) that solves the problem of rendering order perfectly without all these complex tests—enter the Z-buffer.

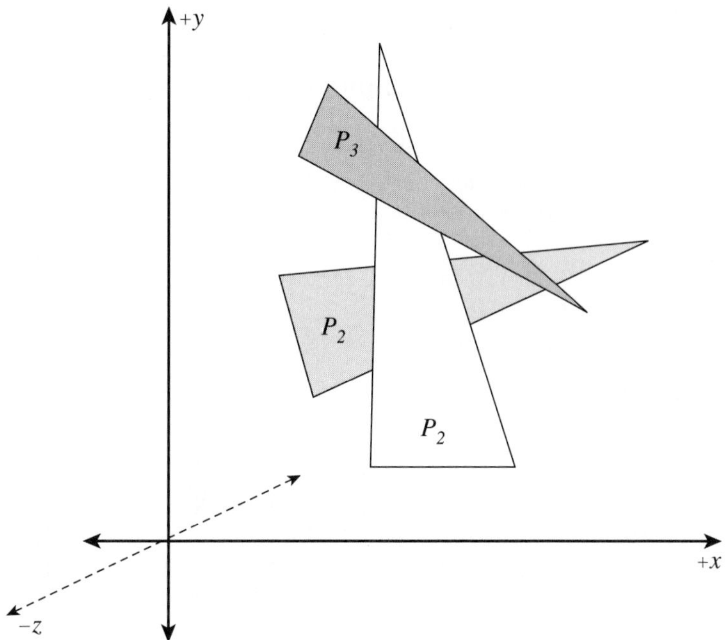

FIGURE 11.3 Polygon cyclic overlap case.

Z-Buffering Basics

The z-sorting algorithm is ironically the solution to all our problems. Remember that it works really well with small polygons, but starts to produce anomalies if the size differential between polygons gets large. This is because of improper sorting (as we saw in some of the algorithm analysis cases in the previous example). However, what if we were to z-sort on a pixel-by-pixel basis? Then there is no possible way that we can get the incorrect order for two polygons, because we are down to the smallest screen unit, the pixel. This is exactly how the Z-buffer works—it's a z-sort on the pixel level, or a pixel-level painter's algorithm, in other words. Try and say that three times!

Amazingly, the idea is so simple, it almost feels like cheating. Historically, the algorithm was originally invented in 1974 by Edwin Catmull (or at least that's what "they" want us to believe). The algorithm is deceptively simple:

> For a screen that is *M*×*N*, create a Z-buffer `zbuffer[x,y]` that contains the z values of each pixel of each polygon as it's being rasterized or scan-converted. The Z-buffer will also be *M*×*N* and will be initialized to the farthest possible z value (infinity, for all intents and purposes).

```
With the Z buffer do

For each polygon in the rendering list begin

   1. Rasterize the polygon and generate xi, yi, zi
    for each value that the polygon's projection on
    the screen would generate during the rasterization.

   2. if (zi < zbuffer[xi, yi]) then write zi into the Z buffer,
      zbuffer[xi, zi] = zi, and then
      write the pixel to the screen, Plot(xi,yi).

end for
```

Simply put, you create an array of floats or integers to track the z values of each polygon as it's being scan-converted. However, instead of just drawing each pixel on the screen, you compare the z value of the pixel to the current z value in the Z-buffer at that position. If the z value of the polygon that is being scan-converted at pixel xi,yi is less than the current z value in the Z-buffer at zbuffer[xi,yi], update the Z-buffer with the new (closer) z value *zi*, and then write the pixel to the screen. Otherwise, do nothing. This algorithm is shown graphically in Figure 11.4.

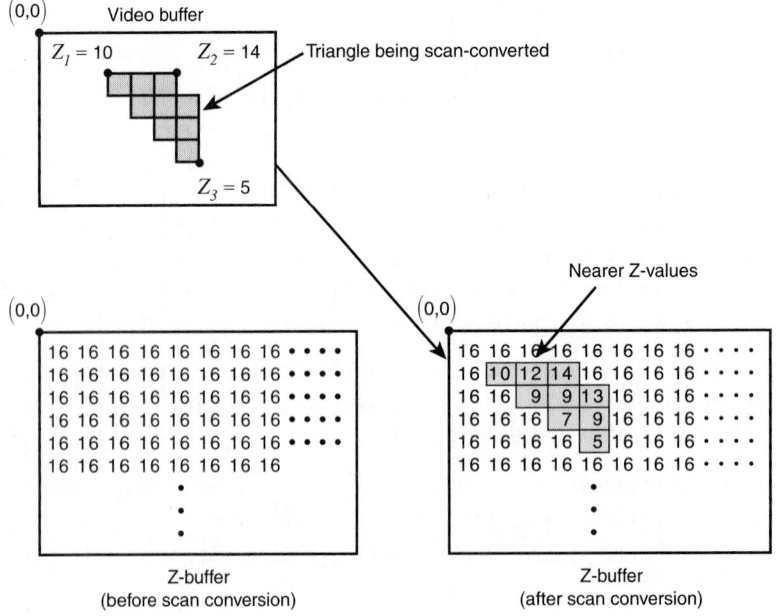

FIGURE 11.4 The Z-buffer algorithm.

This algorithm has the effect of continually drawing closer pixels on top of farther ones, and updating the 2D Z-buffer array with the z value at every x,y position—basically a pixel-level painter's algorithm. Cool, huh? Of course, there are a billion details, and I will get to them, but let's talk about some obvious problems before we go there.

Z-Buffer Problems

First we have to figure out a way to compute the z values of each polygon we are rasterizing. This might be challenging, because by the time the polygons get to the rasterizer, we have usually lost all the z information. This needs to be addressed, as well as what "space" the z values are computing in. Secondly, assuming we can get the z values into the rasterizer, who said we want to compute them? Ouch! That sounds like more work for our poor rasterizer, which is already dying from lighting, texturing, clipping—we're killing that poor thing. Lastly, the Z-buffer is going to take up as much or more storage as the screen buffer, thus we double our memory footprint.

Summing up, by adding z-buffering, we slow down the rasterizer, we overdraw pixels, and we use up at least two times as much memory! That doesn't sound like much help. Ironically, when we get to perspective correct texture mapping we are going to compute z values no matter what, so we need them in the future regardless. As far as the overdraw problem, there are other ways around this, but a pure z buffer will overdraw, that's life, so the best approach is to make it fast. And finally, the average computer these days has at least 128MB of memory, so another 2MB for an 800×600 Z-buffer at 32 bits per element isn't going to kill anyone—maim a little, definitely not kill <BG>.

Z-Buffer Example

To make sure you understand the Z-buffer algorithm before we get to the make and implementation, let's take a quick look at a simple example. Let's assume we have a Z-buffer that is 10×10 pixels (this is a late 70s machine alright!), and that each Z-buffer element is an 8-bit integer, so we will round any fractional values if we see any. Therefore, we might use the following data structure to hold the Z-buffer:

```
UCHAR zbuffer[10][10];
```

Or maybe

```
UCHAR zbuffer[10*10];
```

It doesn't really matter—whatever suits you. For this example, let's assume we can access the array with the notation `zbuffer[xi][yi]`, {0 <= xi <=9}, {0 <= yi <= 9}. To make things interesting, let's assume we have a 10×10 screen that is also an array. We'll call it `screen_buffer[][]`, with the same addressing scheme as the Z-buffer.

Initializing the Z-buffer to a large value that we know will never be written into the Z-buffer, we start off like this:

```
zbuffer[][] =

255 255 255 255 255 255 255 255 255 255
255 255 255 255 255 255 255 255 255 255
255 255 255 255 255 255 255 255 255 255
255 255 255 255 255 255 255 255 255 255
255 255 255 255 255 255 255 255 255 255
255 255 255 255 255 255 255 255 255 255
255 255 255 255 255 255 255 255 255 255
255 255 255 255 255 255 255 255 255 255
255 255 255 255 255 255 255 255 255 255
255 255 255 255 255 255 255 255 255 255
```

And let's initialize the `screen_buffer` to all zeros, which will be black, let's say.

```
screen_buffer[][]=

0 0 0 0 0 0 0 0 0 0
0 0 0 0 0 0 0 0 0 0
0 0 0 0 0 0 0 0 0 0
0 0 0 0 0 0 0 0 0 0
0 0 0 0 0 0 0 0 0 0
0 0 0 0 0 0 0 0 0 0
0 0 0 0 0 0 0 0 0 0
0 0 0 0 0 0 0 0 0 0
0 0 0 0 0 0 0 0 0 0
0 0 0 0 0 0 0 0 0 0
```

Now let's draw a rectangle (these are easier than triangles on paper) from (0,0) to (3,3) with a z value of 100 and a color of 5. Because 100 is always less than 255, the 100 will overwrite the 255 values in the Z-buffer from (0,0) to (3,3), and we will update the screen with the pixel color value 5. Here's what `zbuffer[][]` and `screen_buffer[][]` look like now:

```
zbuffer[][] =

100 100 100 100 255 255 255 255 255 255
100 100 100 100 255 255 255 255 255 255
100 100 100 100 255 255 255 255 255 255
100 100 100 100 255 255 255 255 255 255
255 255 255 255 255 255 255 255 255 255
255 255 255 255 255 255 255 255 255 255
255 255 255 255 255 255 255 255 255 255
255 255 255 255 255 255 255 255 255 255
```

```
255 255 255 255 255 255 255 255 255 255
255 255 255 255 255 255 255 255 255 255

screen_buffer[][]=

5 5 5 5 0 0 0 0 0 0
5 5 5 5 0 0 0 0 0 0
5 5 5 5 0 0 0 0 0 0
5 5 5 5 0 0 0 0 0 0
0 0 0 0 0 0 0 0 0 0
0 0 0 0 0 0 0 0 0 0
0 0 0 0 0 0 0 0 0 0
0 0 0 0 0 0 0 0 0 0
0 0 0 0 0 0 0 0 0 0
0 0 0 0 0 0 0 0 0 0
```

> **NOTE**
>
> I have bolded the affected `zbuffer` and `screen_buffer` locations so you can see them.

Okay, cool, let's go another round. This time, let's write a rectangle from (2,2) to (5,4) with a z value of 150 and a color of 8. The 150 is farther than 100, but nearer than 255, so here's what happens:

```
zbuffer[][] =

100 100 100 100 255 255 255 255 255 255
100 100 100 100 255 255 255 255 255 255
100 100 100 100 150 150 255 255 255 255
100 100 100 100 150 150 255 255 255 255
255 255 150 150 150 150 255 255 255 255
255 255 255 255 255 255 255 255 255 255
255 255 255 255 255 255 255 255 255 255
255 255 255 255 255 255 255 255 255 255
255 255 255 255 255 255 255 255 255 255
255 255 255 255 255 255 255 255 255 255

screen_buffer[][]=

5 5 5 5 0 0 0 0 0 0
5 5 5 5 0 0 0 0 0 0
5 5 5 5 8 8 0 0 0 0
5 5 5 5 8 8 0 0 0 0
0 0 8 8 8 8 0 0 0 0
0 0 0 0 0 0 0 0 0 0
```

```
0 0 0 0 0 0 0 0 0 0
0 0 0 0 0 0 0 0 0 0
0 0 0 0 0 0 0 0 0 0
0 0 0 0 0 0 0 0 0 0
```

NOTE

I have bolded the affected `zbuffer` and `screen_buffer` locations so you can see them.

As you can see, the first rectangle has Z-buffer priority over the new rectangle, so the area of overlap is unaffected by the new rectangle. However, the other portion to the right and below are both updated in `zbuffer[][]` and `screen_buffer[][]`. Last but not least, a final example of a rectangle from (0,0) to (9,9) with a z value of 50 and a color of 1:

```
zbuffer[][] =

50 50 50 50 50 50 50 50 50 50
50 50 50 50 50 50 50 50 50 50
50 50 50 50 50 50 50 50 50 50
50 50 50 50 50 50 50 50 50 50
50 50 50 50 50 50 50 50 50 50
50 50 50 50 50 50 50 50 50 50
50 50 50 50 50 50 50 50 50 50
50 50 50 50 50 50 50 50 50 50
50 50 50 50 50 50 50 50 50 50
50 50 50 50 50 50 50 50 50 50

screen_buffer[][]=

1 1 1 1 1 1 1 1 1 1
1 1 1 1 1 1 1 1 1 1
1 1 1 1 1 1 1 1 1 1
1 1 1 1 1 1 1 1 1 1
1 1 1 1 1 1 1 1 1 1
1 1 1 1 1 1 1 1 1 1
1 1 1 1 1 1 1 1 1 1
1 1 1 1 1 1 1 1 1 1
1 1 1 1 1 1 1 1 1 1
1 1 1 1 1 1 1 1 1 1
```

As you can see, the entire Z-buffer and screen buffer were totally overwritten! This is the worst-case scenario of overwrite. This is something we don't want to see a lot of, because we end up drawing pixels over and over for nothing. However, in defense of the Z-buffer over straight z-sorting, we actually *have* been doing this with the z-sorting, because the z-sort draws entire polygons without considering anything.

NOTE

There is one redeeming quality of the Z-buffer's z-comparison, and that's for cases where the new pixel does not overwrite the previous rasterization calculations, avoiding the pixel plotting step, which makes a difference when texture mapping and lighting are occurring on a per-pixel basis.

Well, that's enough introduction—let's get down to it and see how we are going to actually compute the z values of polygons as we are rasterizing them.

The Plane Equation Method

So how do we compute the z value of each pixel as we are scan-converting each polygon? There are a few ways, but we're going to look at two of the simplest. The first method is to simply use the definition of a plane during the scan conversion. We know that each polygon's vertices lie in a single plane. This is a requirement of all the polygons in our system, and a physical attribute of all triangles. Therefore, if we are scan-converting a triangle, for example, we could first compute the plane equation of the plane the triangle lies in. This can be done by finding the normal to the polygon and then using it in the point-normal form of the plane equation, which looks like

```
nx*(x-x0) + ny*(y-y0) + nz*(z-z0) = 0
```

where `<nx,ny,nz>` is the normal to the polygon being scan-converted, and `(x0,y0,z0)` is a point on the polygon.

This can then be converted into the form

```
a*x+b*y+c*z + d = 0
```

where a = nx, b = ny, c = nz, and d = -(nx*x0+ny*y0+nz*z0)

Then, solving for z by rearranging terms, we see that

```
z = -(a*x + b*y + d)/c
```

which can be computed, since we know the (x,y) of every pixel because the scan converter is generating them. The only drawback to the preceding method is that the plane equation and constants must be computed, and there are two multiplications, one division, and two additions per pixel to find z. Of course, we can trim this down. First off, we can use a precomputed surface normal that is part of each polygon structure, saving us the time of computing the surface normal. Secondly, we can totally simplify the z calculation by using forward differencing and incremental calculations, just as we did for the Gouraud shading and the standard triangle scan converter. To do this, we start by realizing that the change in x in each pixel is exactly 1.0. Therefore, we can come up with the incremental calculations detailed in the following sections.

Z As a Function of x

Noting that

```
z_i    = -(a*x + b*y + d)/c
```

then

```
z_i+1    = -(a*(x+1)+b*y + d)/c
  = -(a*x + a + b*y + d)/c
  = -(a*x + b*y + d)/c + (-a/c)
  =      z_i       + (-a/c)
```

Therefore, we see that the next z value on a horizontal run is simply the previous z value plus the constant term `(-a/c)`. Therefore, we have just cut down the z interpolation to a single addition per pixel. Of course, we still need to compute the very first z value of each line, but this can be done incrementally, because the change in y each line is 1.0. Therefore, carrying out the same incremental calculations on z, we get the following calculation.

Z As a Function of Y

Noting that

```
z_i    = -(a*x + b*y + d)/c
```

then

```
z_i+1    = -(a*x+b*(y+1) + d)/c
  = -(a*x + b*y + b + d)/c
  = -(a*x + B*y + d)/c + (-b/c)
  =      z_i       + (-b/c)
```

which states that as y is incremented down one line, the new value of z is equal to the old value at the beginning of the last line plus the constant `(-b/c)`. Figure 11.5 shows the relationship between both of the incremental calculations and the scan conversion of a polygon.

Although using the plane equation directly to compute the z values of the polygon is correct, there are two reasons not to do it: It's only correct in object space (I will revisit this concept later), and we can compute the z values just as easily with interpolation. Just as we interpolated the intensity levels of the three corners of a triangle to Gouraud shade it, or used the texture coordinates to affine texture map it, we can do the same thing with the z values!

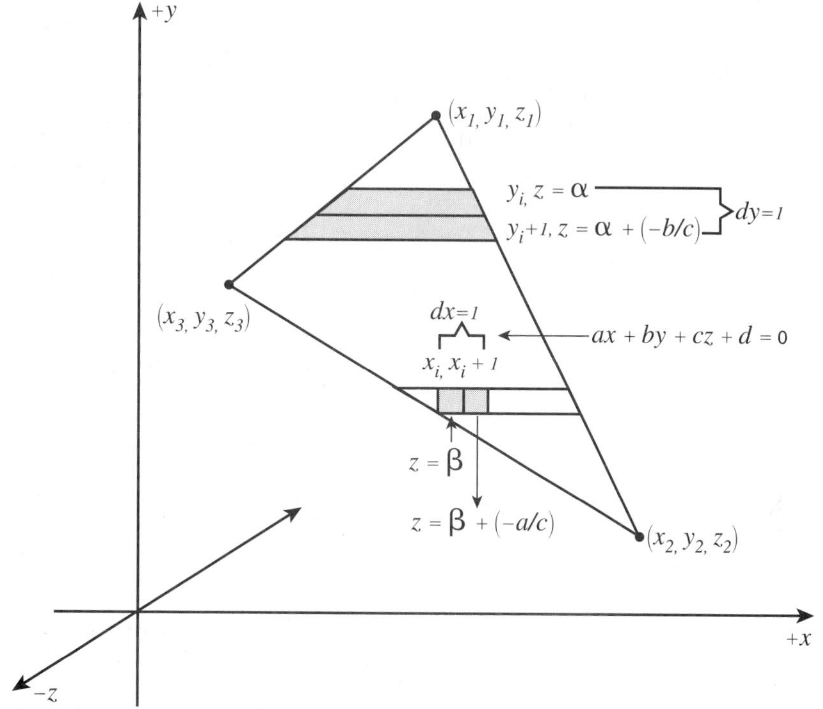

FIGURE 11.5 The planar-based incremental calculations.

Z Interpolation

Take a look at Figure 11.6, which shows the setup we're going to work from for the example. You will notice that the triangle has a flat top, and the calculations are similar for the flat bottom, so we will only derive the flat top version and the final software implementation will handle both.

The interpolation equations for the values of `z_left`, `z_right`, and `z_middle` are

```
z_left = ((y3-y)*z1 + (y-y1)*z3)/(y3-y1);

z_right = ((y3-y)*z2 + (y-y1)*z3)/(y3-y1);

z_middle = ((xe - x)*z_left + (x-xs)*z_right)/(xe-xs);
```

which are a little complex, to say the least, because they are not incremental. We can easily derive versions of these equations that are incremental. First, let's find an incremental version of `z_middle` for changes in x:

```
z_middle(i+1) = ((xe-x-1)*z_left + (x+1-xs)*z_right)/(xe-xs)
       = ((xe-x)*z_left -z_left +
        (x-xs)*z_right + z_right)/(xe-xs)

      = ((xe-x)*z_left + (x-xs)*z_right +
        z_right-z_left)/(xe-xs)

     = ((xe-x)*z_left + (x-xs)*z_right)/(xe-xs) +
        (z_right-z_left)/(xe-xs)

     = z_middle(i) + (z_right-z_left)/(xe-xs)
```

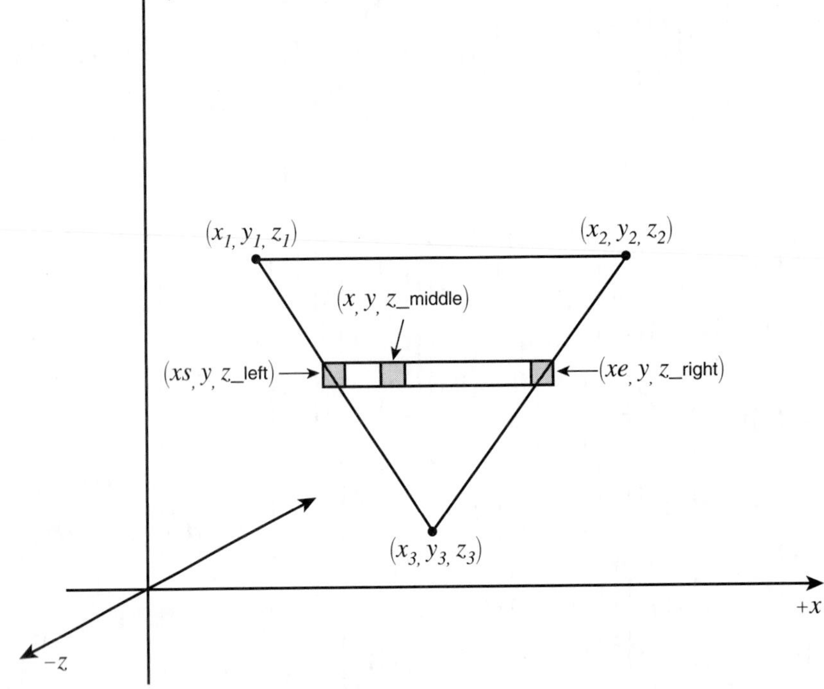

FIGURE 11.6 The setup for interpolating z.

If we let `delta_zx` be equal to the constant `(z_right-z_left)/(xe-xs)`, the next z value pixel to the right of the previous pixel scan-converted is simply the last z value plus `delta_zx`. Or in other words:

```
z_middle(i+1) = z_middle(i) + delta_zx
```

We have again succeeded at finding an algorithm that yields the next value with a single addition. But we still have the problem of determining `z_right` and `z_left` for each scanline, however. Again, we can apply the forward differencing and come up with an incremental algorithm based on the fact that each scanline differs by a change in y of 1.0. Foregoing the long version of the derivation, the results of the calculations are

$$\text{z\_left}_{i+1} = \text{z\_left}_{i} + (z3-z1)/(y3-y1)$$

and

$$\text{z\_right}_{i+1} = \text{z\_right}_{i} + (z3-z2)/(y3-y1)$$

If we let the constants `delta_zyl = (z3-z1)/(y3-y1)` and `delta_zyr = (z3-z2)/(y3-y1)`, the incremental formulas for `z_left` and `z_right` simplify to

$$\text{z\_left}_{i+1} = \text{z\_left}_{i} + \text{delta\_zyl}$$

and

$$\text{z\_right}_{i+1} = \text{z\_right}_{i} + \text{delta\_zyr}$$

which states that the new values of `z_right` and `z_left` can be found with a single addition each per scanline. Pretty cool, huh?

All right, now that we have the interpolation equations, all we need to do is work them into a new triangle scan converter along with the physical Z-buffer, and we're in business. Before we get too ahead of ourselves, I want to bring up a couple of things. First, the previous derivation is basically standard linear interpolation, and thus we don't need to do anything new to the texture mapper or Gouraud shader. Both functions already linearly interpolate values across the triangles, so we can just add one more value to interpolate—the z value—and be done with it. Therefore, the previous derivation is good if you want to start all over, but it's not needed because we already have a code base. However, the more subtle detail that I have been working up to is this: Z-buffering as we have derived it is wrong! Well, sorta ... <BG>.

Z-Buffering Problems and 1/Z Buffering

The reason that our current z-buffering algorithm will be incorrect is that we have been working in world or camera coordinates thus far. We are using (x,y,z) coordinates of triangles and forgetting that we have already projected the triangles, and hence are working with projected (x',y') coordinates in screen space! This is a major problem. Take a look at Figure 11.7 to see what I am talking about.

It does us no good to interpolate across a triangle in 3D space, because we need to draw 2D triangles based on the projection equations:

```
x_screen = d*x/z
y_screen = d*y/z
```

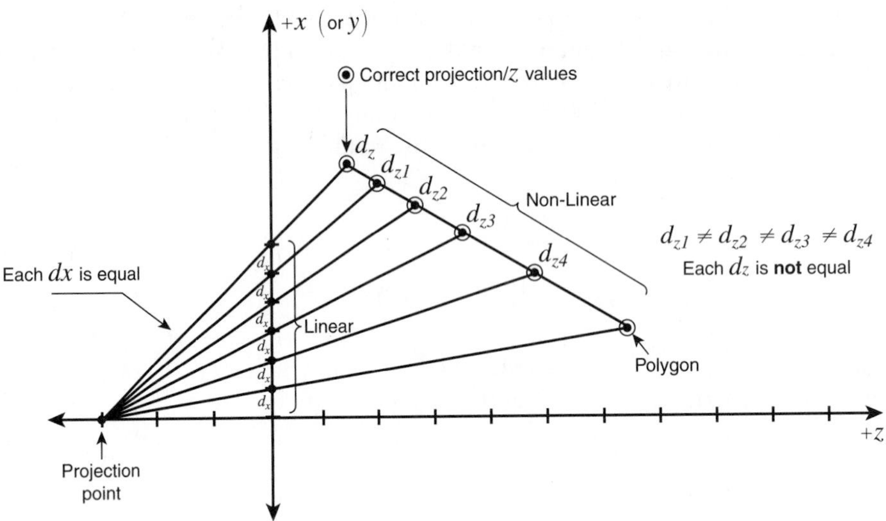

FIGURE 11.7 Screen space Z-interpolation is incorrect.

If you look at Figure 11.7, you see that we're interpolating the z values *from* the original 3D triangle, but using the *projected* 2D (x_screen and y_screen) coordinates. The result is that the z values are not linear in screen space, and there is Z-buffer artifacting, just as we found with Gouraud shading and affine texture mapping. However, it's not that bad with Gouraud shading, and with affine texture mapping, we can live with it if the polygons are reasonably small and parallel to the viewplane. Z-buffering by interpolating the z values from the 3D triangle based on the (x,y) values of the projected triangle will have the same effect. We will end up not correctly computing the z values. You can see this in Figure 11.7. The rays from each one of the polygons' intersections in screen space linearly interpolate the x value down the screen, but those same rays, when traced back to the original un-projected polygon edge, are sampling non-linearly. In fact, they are sampling at a 1/z rate. I will show the math for this in more detail when we implement perspective-correct texture mapping, but for now suffice to say that z is not linear in screen space, but 1/z is.

So, why interpolate z across the polygon? Why not interpolate 1/z because it is linear in screen space? Good idea—that's exactly what we'll do, but later. Right now we are going to interpolate linearly in z, and suck up the distortion, because it turns out that the Z-buffer will still work fine. However, when we get to perspective-correct texture mapping, we will switch to 1/z-buffering and then use the 1/z values for the texture mapping coordinate computation and kill two birds with one stone! For now let's keep it simple—adding z-buffering is enough for one code module.

A Sample Interpolation of Both Z and 1/Z

Now that you know the reasoning behind sticking with a standard Z-buffer and the advantages of the 1/z-buffer, let's run through an example so we know it cold. John Carmack once said (and I am paraphrasing) that the one piece of advice he can give anyone is

> To know it cold, have a deep understanding of the fundamentals.

This has always been my philosophy, too. To this end, I will write it down, graph it, chart it, test it, code it, whatever, and make sure I get it. That's how the feeling of "now I get it" happens. Otherwise, you have an idea of how something works, but not exactly. Anyway, let's try a simple example and see what happens with z-buffering and 1/z-buffering.

In Figure 11.8 we see a typical perspective projection setup. The vertical axis is y, the horizontal is z, and x is coming out of the paper. The viewing distance is 2, and we will assume for simplicity's sake that the x value of all points is 0; that is, this polygon is in the x = 0 plane.

To begin with, we have a triangle that we want to project, rasterize, and z-buffer. The first edge up for processing is **p0**(0,12,4) -> **p1**(0,5,7). The projected points on the viewplane at d = 2 are **p0'**(0,y0',0) -> **p1'**(0,y1',0). We of course need to calculate the y0' and y1' values, but we know that the x and z components are both 0, because both are in the x = 0 plane and the projections are 2D—so there is no z, or we can say it's 0. In any case, here's the fun part: We're going calculate the screen-projected values of **p0'** and **p1'**, then we're going to use them to interpolate to find **pa'**, **pb'**, and the linearly projected pa*, pb* values that are incorrect, as you will see shortly. Let's begin with tabulating what we know:

```
p0 = (0,12,4), p1 = (0,5,7)
```

Then perspective-projecting them with the formula

```
y' = (d/(d+z))*y
```

Note: We would do the same with x, but for this example we assume x = 0.

```
p0' = (0,(2/(2+4))*12,0) = (0, 4, 0)
p1' = (0,(2/(2+7))*5, 0) = (0, 1.111,0)
```

However, we are going to linearly interpolate the z values based on these projected points, so we are going to assign the unprojected z values to the zeroed out z values in **p0'** and **p1'**:

```
p0' = (0, 4, 4)
p1' = (0, 1.111, 7)
```

Now we are ready to interpolate, so let's compute dy and dz:

```
dy = p1'(y) - p0'(y) = (1.11 - 4.0) = -2.89
dz = p1'(z) - p0'(z) = (7 - 4) = 3
```

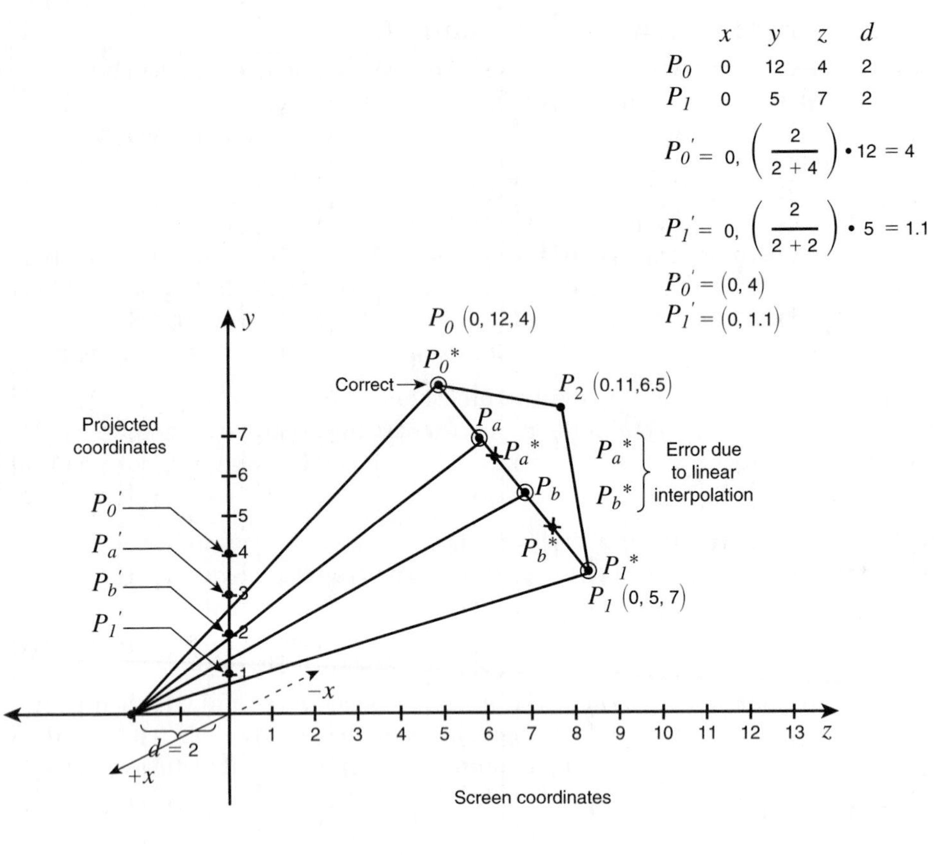

$$(x_s, y_s) \longrightarrow y_s = \frac{D}{(D+z)} \cdot y$$

$$x_s = \frac{D}{(D+z)} \cdot x$$

FIGURE 11.8 Sample perspective projection and z-interpolation error analysis.

Therefore, to rasterize the strip in screen space from **p0'** -> **p1'**, we would simply draw pixels from **p0'** to **p1'** one at a time, but each time we decrement 1.0 pixel rows to the next lower value of y. We would interpolate z by the value of dz/dy; that is, the change in z per the change in y:

```
dz/dy = (3)/(-2.89) = -1.03
```

This is the magic number that shows how linear interpolation fails. We start at **p0'**(0,4) in screen space and then draw three pixels. Table 11.1 shows the action step by step.

TABLE 11.1 The z-Interpolation Example 1

Iteration	x	y	z
[0] Start	x = 0	y = 4	z = 4
[1] dy = -1, dz/dy = -1.03	x = 0	y = 3	z = 4+1.03 = 5.03
[2] dy = -1, dz/dy = -1.03	x = 0	y = 2	z = 5.03+1.03 = 6.06
[3] dy = -1, dz/dy = -1.03	x = 0	y = 1	z = 6.06+1.03 = 7.09

Although we went a little farther than y = 1.1, this is okay. Remember, in a real rasterizer, our filling convention would have stopped us, but I wanted to complete the step so we had enough samples. In any case, the point is this: If you look at Figure 11.8, the rays from **pa** and **pb** to **pa'** and **pb'** are the correct interpolations for perspective. This is easy with graph paper, but our linear interpolations at **pa*** and **pb*** are way off! This is the linear interpolation causing errors for us, because the sample points are linear. The error will die down as the polygon line is increasingly parallel to the viewing plane, and increase as it becomes more skewed.

The problem is really simple if you look at it this way: how can adding a constant value (in this case, dz/dy = -1.03) sample the z value correctly when the relationship from world coordinates to screen coordinates is nonlinear (the division by z makes it that way)? It can't. We need to sample the z value based on something that *is* linear in screen space, such as 1/z, then the projection and interpolation in effect cancel out and then change linearly (via a multiplication constant) with each other.

In any event, I hope you are starting to see that straight z interpolation is incorrect. I bet that if you crack open 10 3D graphics books, they will all do this wrong, or more correctly, not explain this little detail. Now let's try the same experiment, but interpolate 1/z instead. As before, let's start with our points:

```
p0' = (0, 4, 4)
p1' = (0, 1.11, 7)
```

But with 1/z as the last coordinate, we get

```
p0'=(0,4,0.25)
p1'=(0,1.11,.142)
```

Now we are ready to interpolate, so let's compute dy and dz (where we are using 1/z values instead of z values):

```
dy = p1'(y) - p0'(y) = (1.11 - 4.0) = -2.89
dz = p1'(z) - p0'(z) = (1/7 - 1/4) = -.107
```

Once again, to rasterize the strip in screen space from **p0'** -> **p1'**, we would simply draw pixels from **p0'** to **p1'** one at a time, but each time we decrement 1.0 pixel rows to the next lower value of y (subtracting 1.0 in this case). We would interpolate z by the value of dz/dy; that is, the change in z per the change in y:

```
dz/dy = (-.107)/(-2.89) = 0.037
```

This number again illustrates linear interpolation fails. We start at **p0**'(0,4) in screen space and then draw three pixels. Table 11.2 shows the action step by step.

TABLE 11.2 The z-Interpolation Example 2

Iteration	x	y	z
[0] Start	x = 0	y = 4	z = 1/4 = 0.25
[1] dy = -1, dz/dy = -0.037	x = 0	y = 3	z = 0.25-.037 = 0.213
[2] dy = -1, dz/dy = -0.037	x = 0	y = 2	z = .213-.037 = 0.176
[3] dy = -1, dz/dy = -0.037	x = 0	y = 1	z = 0.176+.037 = 0.139

Which is amazingly correct! Although we undershot the last value a bit, this occurred because we rasterized a little too much. If we had rasterized exactly 2.89 pixels rather than 3.0, we would have ended at a 1/z value of exactly 0.142, which would have locked us on the end 1/z value of **p1**'.

Z-buffering makes sense, but how do we use 1/z to compare and update our Z-buffer? We simply flip the sign of our comparison operator. That is, if 1/z is greater than the current 1/z-buffer value, we update the 1/z-buffer and write the pixel—easy!

Creating the Z-Buffer System

Well, enough theory—I'm going nuts with all these little numbers! Let's implement the Z-buffer, shall we? We need some memory storage, the size of the Z-buffer, maybe some flags or attributes to define some of its characteristics, and that's about it. Here's what I came up with for a first version:

```
// defines for zbuffer
#define ZBUFFER_ATTR_16BIT  16
#define ZBUFFER_ATTR_32BIT  32

// structure for zbuffer
typedef struct ZBUFFERV1_TYP
{
int attr;     // attributes of zbuffer
UCHAR *zbuffer; // ptr to storage
int width;    // width in zpixels
int height;    // height in zpixels
int sizeq;    // total size in QUADs
        // of zbuffer
} ZBUFFERV1, *ZBUFFERV1_PTR;
```

This type has storage for the Z-buffer, tracks its size in "words," and its total size in 32-bit QUADS. The width and height fields represent the general width and height of the Z-buffer, but `sizeq` is the actual number of QUADS (each QUAD is four bytes). Also, there is an attribute field `attr`, which at this point only tracks whether the Z-buffer is 16- or 32-bit. Right now, I only foresee us using 32-bit Z-buffers, so this isn't needed as of yet; but later when we optimize, we might need the option. Anyway, we only need to be able to do a few things to the Z-buffer:

- Create the Z-buffer.
- Destroy the Z-buffer.
- Clear/fill the Z-buffer with a value (really fast).

Here's the function that creates a Z-buffer:

```
int Create_Zbuffer(ZBUFFERV1_PTR zb, // pointer to a zbuffer object
          int width,    // width
          int height,    // height
          int attr)     // attributes of zbuffer
{
// this function creates a zbuffer with the sent width, height,
// and bytes per word, in fact the the zbuffer is totally linear
// but this function is nice so we can create it with some
// intelligence

// is this a valid object
if (!zb)
  return(0);

// is there any memory already allocated
if (zb->zbuffer)
  free(zb->zbuffer);

// set fields
zb->width = width;
zb->height = height;
zb->attr  = attr;

// what size zbuffer 16/32 bit?
if (attr & ZBUFFER_ATTR_16BIT)
  {
  // compute size in quads
  zb->sizeq = width*height/2;

  // allocate memory
  if ((zb->zbuffer = (UCHAR *)malloc(width * height * sizeof(SHORT))))
```

```
    return(1);
   else
    return(0);

   } // end if
else
if (attr & ZBUFFER_ATTR_32BIT)
   {
   // compute size in quads
   zb->sizeq = width*height;

   // allocate memory
   if ((zb->zbuffer = (UCHAR *)malloc(width * height * sizeof(INT))))
    return(1);
   else
    return(0);
   } // end if
else
   return(0);

} // end Create_Zbuffer
```

The function simply takes a pointer to a ZBUFFERV1 object that you want to create, along with the width, height, and attributes. For example, to create an 800×600 32-bit Z-buffer, you would make the call

```
ZBUFFERV1 zbuffer; // storage for our Z buffer

Create_Zbuffer(&zbuffer, 800, 600, ZBUFFER_ATTR_32BIT);
```

Here's the interesting part: The ZBUFFERV1 Z-buffer storage is really typeless. It's of the UCHAR type, so you can cast it to anything you like—int, float, and so on, in your algorithms. For the rasterizers we are going to write, we will cast the storage to unsigned integers, but you are free to do as you want.

The next function we need is to clear/fill the Z-buffer with a value. This must be done each frame just as the frame buffer is cleared. Usually you will fill the Z-buffer with the largest value you possibly expect for your numeric range, or infinity for all intents and purposes. Here's the function:

```
void Clear_Zbuffer(ZBUFFERV1_PTR zb, UINT data)
{
// this function clears/sets the zbuffer to a value, the filling
// is ALWAYS performed in QUADS, thus if your zbuffer is a 16-bit
// zbuffer then you must build a quad that has two values each
```

```
// the 16-bit value you want to fill with, otherwise just send
// the fill value casted to a UINT

Mem_Set_QUAD((void *)zb->zbuffer, data, zb->sizeq);

} // end Clear_Zbuffer
```

You will notice that the function uses the call to a function `Mem_Set_QUAD()`. This is actually an inline assembler function located in `T3DLIB1.H`, as shown in the following:

```
inline void Mem_Set_QUAD(void *dest, UINT data, int count)
{
// this function fills or sets unsigned 32-bit aligned memory
// count is number of quads

_asm
  {
  mov edi, dest  ; edi points to destination memory
  mov ecx, count ; number of 32-bit words to move
  mov eax, data  ; 32-bit data
  rep stosd     ; move data
  } // end asm

} // end Mem_Set_QUAD
```

I am using `asm` so I can clear the Z-buffer as fast as possible (actually, I can do better with SIMD instructions). Of course, when you call the function to clear the Z-buffer, you must cast your data without conversion into an unsigned `int`. Also, if your Z-buffer is 16-bit, you must create two maximum value words and concatenate them, as shown in Figure 11.9.

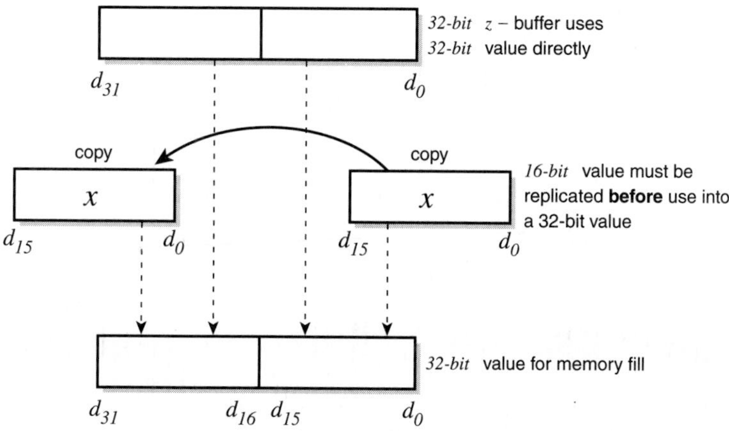

FIGURE 11.9 Preparing for high speed 32-bit Z-buffer memory fills.

For example, if you're using a 16-bit Z-buffer, you can't simply send a 32-bit value version of your maximum 16-bit infinity value. You must build one up, so that as the QUAD memory fills memory, the algorithm fills adjacent cells:

```
USHORT zmax16 = 10000; // say your max is 10000

unsigned int zdata =
 ( ( (unsigned int)zmax16 ) << 16 ¦ (unsigned int)zmax16);
```

As another example, here's how you would set each cell in the 32-bit Z-buffer to the 32-bit fixed-point value of 32000:

```
Clear_Zbuffer(&zbuffer, (32000 << FIXP16_SHIFT));
```

Finally, to destroy the Z-buffer and release the memory call, you would use this function:

```
int Delete_Zbuffer(ZBUFFERV1_PTR zb)
{
// this function deletes and frees the memory of the zbuffer

// test for valid object
if (zb)
  {
  // delete memory and zero object
  if (zb->zbuffer)
   free(zb->zbuffer);

  // clear memory
  memset((void *)zb,0, sizeof(ZBUFFERV1));

  return(1);

  } // end if
else
  return(0);

} // end Delete_Zbuffer
```

Simply call `Delete_ZBuffer()` with a pointer to the Z-buffer object you want to destroy and it will release the memory and clear the object out, too.

TIP

I abstracted Z-buffers into the type ZBUFFERV1 so that we can potentially have multiple Z-buffers later and try some special effects.

Adding Z-Buffer Support to the Rasterizers

To add Z-buffer support to all the rasterizers, first we need to define which rasterizers need support. Currently we have the following rasterizers:

- Class 1: Flat/constant-shaded
- Class 2: Gouraud-shaded
- Class 3: Texture-mapped with constant shading
- Class 4: Texture-mapped with flat shading

The class 1 rasterizers are the oldest we have. In fact, they are from the original *Tricks* core software, and work in mixed integer/floating-point rather than pure fixed-point. That isn't to say they are slower or faster, but simply different that the class 2–4 rasterizers, which all are based on the same core rasterizer/interpolater. In one case, we interpolate colors (the Gouraud shader), in another we interpolate texture coordinates (the texture mapper). So the first decision we have to make is which rasterizers should we upgrade? Well, I want them all! However, I want to rewrite the class 1 rasterizer that rasterizes flat/constant shaded polygons because it has no interpolation capability, and it would be hard to force z-buffering into it. Therefore we are going to redo all of them.

Now for the good news: Redoing them involves only about 10 lines of code each! Maybe a little more, but not much. This is because all of them already have interpolations of two or more variables—either RGB colors for the Gouraud shader, or texture coordinates for the texture mappers. We just need to add the z values of each polygon, interpolate them, add the Z-buffer logic in the inner loops, and we're done. Let's rewrite each function one by one and go from there.

Updating the Flat Shader

Rewriting the flat/constant shader is the hardest of all because we have to completely redo it, but I'm going to use the Gouraud shader as a base and take out the RGB interpolation, use a single color for the pixels, and change one of the interpolants to the z values of each vertex. To do this, we need a couple of things. First we need to make sure that the new function (whatever we call it) is sent a polygon structure with the x,y, and z of each vertex. If you recall, the current rasterizer calls omitted the z coordinates in the setup before the calls to the rasterizer. Bring your attention to `Draw_RENDERLIST4DV2_Solid16()`, which I have copied in the following from `T3DLIB7.CPP`:

```
void Draw_RENDERLIST4DV2_Solid16(RENDERLIST4DV2_PTR rend_list,
               UCHAR *video_buffer,
               int lpitch)
{
  if (!(rend_list->poly_ptrs[poly]->state & POLY4DV2_STATE_ACTIVE) ||
     (rend_list->poly_ptrs[poly]->state & POLY4DV2_STATE_CLIPPED ) ||
     (rend_list->poly_ptrs[poly]->state & POLY4DV2_STATE_BACKFACE) )
    continue; // move onto next poly
```

```
// need to test for textured first, since a textured poly can either
// be emissive, or flat shaded, hence we need to call different
// rasterizers
if (rend_list->poly_ptrs[poly]->attr & POLY4DV2_ATTR_SHADE_MODE_TEXTURE)
  {

  // set the vertices
  face.tvlist[0].x = (int)rend_list->poly_ptrs[poly]->tvlist[0].x;
  face.tvlist[0].y = (int)rend_list->poly_ptrs[poly]->tvlist[0].y;
  face.tvlist[0].u0 = (int)rend_list->poly_ptrs[poly]->tvlist[0].u0;
  face.tvlist[0].v0 = (int)rend_list->poly_ptrs[poly]->tvlist[0].v0;

  face.tvlist[1].x = (int)rend_list->poly_ptrs[poly]->tvlist[1].x;
  face.tvlist[1].y = (int)rend_list->poly_ptrs[poly]->tvlist[1].y;
  face.tvlist[1].u0 = (int)rend_list->poly_ptrs[poly]->tvlist[1].u0;
  face.tvlist[1].v0 = (int)rend_list->poly_ptrs[poly]->tvlist[1].v0;

  face.tvlist[2].x = (int)rend_list->poly_ptrs[poly]->tvlist[2].x;
  face.tvlist[2].y = (int)rend_list->poly_ptrs[poly]->tvlist[2].y;
  face.tvlist[2].u0 = (int)rend_list->poly_ptrs[poly]->tvlist[2].u0;
  face.tvlist[2].v0 = (int)rend_list->poly_ptrs[poly]->tvlist[2].v0;


  // assign the texture
  face.texture = rend_list->poly_ptrs[poly]->texture;

  // is this a plain emissive texture?
  if (rend_list->poly_ptrs[poly]->attr & POLY4DV2_ATTR_SHADE_MODE_CONSTANT)
   {
   // draw the textured triangle as emissive
   Draw_Textured_Triangle16(&face, video_buffer, lpitch);
   } // end if
  else
   {
   // draw as flat shaded
   face.lit_color[0] = rend_list->poly_ptrs[poly]->lit_color[0];
   Draw_Textured_TriangleFS16(&face, video_buffer, lpitch);
   } // end else

  } // end if
else
if ((rend_list->poly_ptrs[poly]->attr & POLY4DV2_ATTR_SHADE_MODE_FLAT) ||
  (rend_list->poly_ptrs[poly]->attr & POLY4DV2_ATTR_SHADE_MODE_CONSTANT) )
  {
```

```
    // draw the triangle with basic flat rasterizer
    Draw_Triangle_2D2_16(rend_list->poly_ptrs[poly]->tvlist[0].x,
              rend_list->poly_ptrs[poly]->tvlist[0].y,
          rend_list->poly_ptrs[poly]->tvlist[1].x,
              rend_list->poly_ptrs[poly]->tvlist[1].y,
        rend_list->poly_ptrs[poly]->tvlist[2].x,
              rend_list->poly_ptrs[poly]->tvlist[2].y,
          rend_list->poly_ptrs[poly]->lit_color[0],
                video_buffer, lpitch);

    } // end if
  else
  if (rend_list->poly_ptrs[poly]->attr & POLY4DV2_ATTR_SHADE_MODE_GOURAUD)
    {
    // {andre take advantage of the data structures later..}
    // set the vertices
    face.tvlist[0].x = (int)rend_list->poly_ptrs[poly]->tvlist[0].x;
    face.tvlist[0].y = (int)rend_list->poly_ptrs[poly]->tvlist[0].y;
    face.lit_color[0] = rend_list->poly_ptrs[poly]->lit_color[0];

    face.tvlist[1].x = (int)rend_list->poly_ptrs[poly]->tvlist[1].x;
    face.tvlist[1].y = (int)rend_list->poly_ptrs[poly]->tvlist[1].y;
    face.lit_color[1] = rend_list->poly_ptrs[poly]->lit_color[1];

    face.tvlist[2].x = (int)rend_list->poly_ptrs[poly]->tvlist[2].x;
    face.tvlist[2].y = (int)rend_list->poly_ptrs[poly]->tvlist[2].y;
    face.lit_color[2] = rend_list->poly_ptrs[poly]->lit_color[2];

    // draw the gouraud shaded triangle
    Draw_Gouraud_Triangle16(&face, video_buffer, lpitch);
    } // end if gouraud

  } // end for poly

} // end Draw_RENDERLIST4DV2_Solid16
```

The function has three main execution paths: flat/constant shaded polygons, Gouraud-shaded, and texture-mapped, not necessarily in that order. For execution path, we set up the function call and then call one of the following functions:

- `Draw_Gouraud_Triangle16()`—The standard Gouraud shader.
- `Draw_Textured_Triangle16()`—The constant-shaded texture mapper.
- `Draw_Textured_TriangleFS16()`—The flat-shaded texture mapper.
- `Draw_Triangle_2D2_16()`—The old flat/constant-shaded polygon rasterizer.

The last one is where we will start, but basically we need to rewrite all of these, including the `Draw_RENDERLIST4DV2_Solid16()` itself. Abracadabra! I'm done. Here's the new function prototype for the flat/constant polygon rasterizer:

```
void Draw_Triangle_2DZB_16(POLYF4DV2_PTR face,  // ptr to face
             UCHAR *_dest_buffer,  // pointer to video buffer
             int mem_pitch,       // bytes per line
             UCHAR *_zbuffer,      // pointer to z-buffer
             int zpitch)        // bytes per line of zbuffer
```

This is different from the old one. The previous version didn't take a `POLYF4DV2_PTR`; it took explicit vertices and a color. However, now we need to unify the calling procedures, so from now on all the rasterizers will have the same calling footprint. The only other additions are pointers to the Z-buffer storage array, and the pitch in bytes of a single line of the Z-buffer. It's up to the rasterizer to access the Z-buffer correctly, and up to the caller to make it big enough. Therefore, to call the function, you would do something like this:

```
// draw as constant shaded
face.lit_color[0] = rend_list->poly_ptrs[poly]->lit_color[0];

// set the vertices
face.tvlist[0].x = (int)rend_list->poly_ptrs[poly]->tvlist[0].x;
face.tvlist[0].y = (int)rend_list->poly_ptrs[poly]->tvlist[0].y;
face.tvlist[0].z = (int)rend_list->poly_ptrs[poly]->tvlist[0].z;

face.tvlist[1].x = (int)rend_list->poly_ptrs[poly]->tvlist[1].x;
face.tvlist[1].y = (int)rend_list->poly_ptrs[poly]->tvlist[1].y;
face.tvlist[1].z = (int)rend_list->poly_ptrs[poly]->tvlist[1].z;

face.tvlist[2].x = (int)rend_list->poly_ptrs[poly]->tvlist[2].x;
face.tvlist[2].y = (int)rend_list->poly_ptrs[poly]->tvlist[2].y;
face.tvlist[2].z = (int)rend_list->poly_ptrs[poly]->tvlist[2].z;

// draw the triangle with basic flat rasterizer
Draw_Triangle_2DZB_16(&face, video_buffer, lpitch,zbuffer,zpitch);
```

In this example, a polygon from the rendering list has its vertices copied into the transport face. The color is set in `lit_color[0]` because flat/constant-shaded polys only need that color defined. Finally, the call is made to rasterize into the sent `video_buffer` storage with its pitch `lpitch`, along with the Z-buffer `zbuffer` and its pitch `zpitch`. This should all look familiar—this is exactly how all the other rasterizers have been working since we wrote the lighting/texture mapping modules.

That's about it for the call to the `Draw_Triangle_2DZB_16()` function and its use. I can't list it out because it's giant, but I am going to excerpt the line rasterizer so you can see the Z-buffer code—it's interesting:

```
// point screen ptr to starting line
screen_ptr = dest_buffer + (ystart * mem_pitch);

// point zbuffer to starting line
z_ptr = zbuffer + (ystart * zpitch);

for (yi = ystart; yi<=yend; yi++)
  {
  // compute span endpoints
  xstart = ((xl + FIXP16_ROUND_UP) >> FIXP16_SHIFT);
  xend  = ((xr + FIXP16_ROUND_UP) >> FIXP16_SHIFT);

  // compute starting points for u,v,w interpolants
  zi = zl + FIXP16_ROUND_UP;

  // compute u,v interpolants
  if ((dx = (xend - xstart))>0)
    {
    dz = (zr - zl)/dx;
    } // end if
  else
    {
  dz = (zr - zl);
  } // end else

  // draw span
  for (xi=xstart; xi<=xend; xi++)
    {
      // test if z of current pixel is nearer than current z buffer value
      if (zi < z_ptr[xi])
       {
      // write textel 5.6.5
       screen_ptr[xi] = color;

       // update z-buffer
       z_ptr[xi] = zi;
       } // end if

     // interpolate z
      zi+=dz;
     } // end for xi

   // interpolate x,z along right and left edge
   xl+=dxdyl;
```

```
    zl+=dzdyl;
    xr+=dxdyr;
     zr+=dzdyr;

    // advance screen ptr
    screen_ptr+=mem_pitch;

    // advance z-buffer ptr
    z_ptr+=zpitch;
    } // end for y
```

The preceding code basically draws the spans from one y value to another. Notice that I have highlighted the Z-buffer code, as it literally follows suit with what we have been talking about. First the current z value is compared with the value in the Z-buffer:

```
if (zi < z_ptr[xi])
{
```

If this is true, the pixel is rasterized:

```
// write textel 5.6.5
screen_ptr[xi] = color;
```

And the Z-buffer is updated:

```
// update z-buffer
z_ptr[xi] = zi;
} // end if
```

> **TIP**
>
> Notice that even after I determine that the Z-buffer should be updated, I do not update it with the value of `zi`. This is an optimization trick. It's usually a bad idea to immediately read and then write the same value—better to put something in between and then write the value.

That is the meat of the entire flat/constant shader. The rest are all the same; I simply add code to interpolate z down the triangles, and then perform the z comparisons to update the Z-buffer.

Updating the Gouraud Shader

The Gouraud shader was a snap to add z-buffering to because we already had three interpolants for R, G, and B. It was just a matter of text additions following the exact interpolation code. Here's the prototype of the new rasterizer. It only differs by name and the addition of the Z-buffer and pitch:

```
void Draw_Gouraud_TriangleZB16(POLYF4DV2_PTR face,  // ptr to face
        UCHAR *_dest_buffer,  // pointer to video buffer
        int mem_pitch,      // bytes per line, 320, 640 etc.
        UCHAR *_zbuffer,     // pointer to z-buffer
        int zpitch)       // bytes per line of zbuffer
```

Calling the function is done exactly as before, except that the additional parameters of the pointer to the Z-buffer storage and the pitch of the Z-buffer in bytes per line must be sent (the same as the flat/constant shader). Now let's look inside the Gouraud shader and see what the inner loop looks like with Z-buffer support:

```
screen_ptr = dest_buffer + (ystart * mem_pitch);

// point zbuffer to starting line
z_ptr = zbuffer + (ystart * zpitch);

for (yi = ystart; yi<=yend; yi++)
   {
   // compute span endpoints
   xstart = ((xl + FIXP16_ROUND_UP) >> FIXP16_SHIFT);
   xend  = ((xr + FIXP16_ROUND_UP) >> FIXP16_SHIFT);

   // compute starting points for u,v,w interpolants
   ui = ul + FIXP16_ROUND_UP;
   vi = vl + FIXP16_ROUND_UP;
   wi = wl + FIXP16_ROUND_UP;
   zi = zl + FIXP16_ROUND_UP;

   // compute u,v interpolants
   if ((dx = (xend - xstart))>0)
  {
  du = (ur - ul)/dx;
  dv = (vr - vl)/dx;
  dw = (wr - wl)/dx;
    dz = (zr - zl)/dx;
  } // end if
   else
  {
  du = (ur - ul);
  dv = (vr - vl);
  dw = (wr - wl);
  dz = (zr - zl);
  } // end else

///////////////////////////////////////////////////////////////////////
```

```
// test for x clipping, LHS
if (xstart < min_clip_x)
{
// compute x overlap
dx = min_clip_x - xstart;

// slide interpolants over
ui+=dx*du;
vi+=dx*dv;
wi+=dx*dw;
zi+=dx*dz;

// reset vars
xstart = min_clip_x;

} // end if

// test for x clipping RHS
if (xend > max_clip_x)
  xend = max_clip_x;

///////////////////////////////////////////////////////////////////////

 // draw span
 for (xi=xstart; xi<=xend; xi++)
 {
   // test if z of current pixel is nearer than current z buffer value
   if (zi < z_ptr[xi])
    {
   // write textel assume 5.6.5
     screen_ptr[xi] = ((ui >> (FIXP16_SHIFT+3)) << 11) +
             ((vi >> (FIXP16_SHIFT+2)) << 5) +
             (wi >> (FIXP16_SHIFT+3));

    // update z-buffer
    z_ptr[xi] = zi;
    } // end if

 // interpolate u,v,w,z
 ui+=du;
 vi+=dv;
 wi+=dw;
 zi+=dz;
 } // end for xi
```

```
    // interpolate u,v,w,z,x along right and left edge
    xl+=dxdyl;
    ul+=dudyl;
    vl+=dvdyl;
    wl+=dwdyl;
    zl+=dzdyl;

    xr+=dxdyr;
    ur+=dudyr;
    vr+=dvdyr;
    wr+=dwdyr;
    zr+=dzdyr;

    // advance screen ptr
    screen_ptr+=mem_pitch;

    // advance z-buffer ptr
    z_ptr+=zpitch;

    } // end for y
```

Again, I have highlighted the Z-buffer comparison. What's interesting now is that if we don't write the pixel, there is actually some savings. Remember, if this had been the old rasterizer, the pixel is rendered and the pixel plot code is executed no matter what. However, in the case of the Z-buffer version, we update the Z-buffer and write the pixel only if the current z value is less than what's currently in the Z-buffer; therefore, we are doing more work to z-buffer the polygon, but we are saving time when the Z-buffer comparison fails. Also, notice that to support the Z-buffer interpolation, we basically have two more additions per outer loop:

```
zl+=dzdyl;
zr+=dzdyr;
```

And only one addition in the span rasterization inner loop:

```
zi+=dz;
```

So all in all, this Z-buffer stuff isn't that bad! In fact, when you see the demos, you will be amazed that it's basically as fast as without a Z-buffer. But we get pixel-perfect rendering!

Updating the Texture Mappers

As you recall, we have two texture mappers. One handles constant-shaded polygons—that is, with no lighting at all; the texture map is simply stretched on the polygon.

The other handles flat-shaded textured polygons. This texture mapper, with the `FS` name appended to it, actually lights the entire polygon using RGB white (255,255,255) as the base color, and then uses the resulting color to modulate the texture map on a pixel-by-pixel basis.

The Constant-Shaded Texture Mapper We need to add Z-buffer support to both. Once again, this is a snap. We just add another interpolant to each, along with the Z-buffer comparison in the inner loop, and we're done! Here's the new prototype of the constant-shaded texture mapper:

```
void Draw_Textured_TriangleZB16(POLYF4DV2_PTR face, // ptr to face
          UCHAR *_dest_buffer, // pointer to video buffer
          int mem_pitch,    // bytes per line, 320, 640 etc.
          UCHAR *_zbuffer,   // pointer to z-buffer
          int zpitch)      // bytes per line of zbuffer
```

The function is called as before; however, the z values of the transport face must be assigned, and of course the pointer to the Z-buffer, along with its bytes per line pitch, must be sent. Once again here is the Z-buffer code from the line rasterizer with the Z-buffer comparison highlighted:

```
// point screen ptr to starting line
screen_ptr = dest_buffer + (ystart * mem_pitch);

// point zbuffer to starting line
z_ptr = zbuffer + (ystart * zpitch);

for (yi = ystart; yi<=yend; yi++)
   {
   // compute span endpoints
   xstart = ((xl + FIXP16_ROUND_UP) >> FIXP16_SHIFT);
   xend  = ((xr + FIXP16_ROUND_UP) >> FIXP16_SHIFT);

   // compute starting points for u,v interpolants
   ui = ul + FIXP16_ROUND_UP;
   vi = vl + FIXP16_ROUND_UP;
   zi = zl + FIXP16_ROUND_UP;

   // compute u,v interpolants
   if ((dx = (xend - xstart))>0)
  {
  du = (ur - ul)/dx;
  dv = (vr - vl)/dx;
  dz = (zr - zl)/dx;
  } // end if
  else
  {
  du = (ur - ul);
```

```
    dv = (vr - vl);
    dz = (zr - zl);
    } // end else

///////////////////////////////////////////////////////////////////////

    // test for x clipping, LHS
    if (xstart < min_clip_x)
    {
    // compute x overlap
    dx = min_clip_x - xstart;

    // slide interpolants over
    ui+=dx*du;
    vi+=dx*dv;
    zi+=dx*dz;

    // reset vars
    xstart = min_clip_x;

    } // end if

    // test for x clipping RHS
    if (xend > max_clip_x)
    xend = max_clip_x;

///////////////////////////////////////////////////////////////////////

    // draw span
    for (xi=xstart; xi<=xend; xi++)
     {
       // test if z of current pixel is nearer than current z buffer value
       if (zi < z_ptr[xi])
       {
      // write textel
      screen_ptr[xi] = textmap[(ui >> FIXP16_SHIFT) +
                   ((vi >> FIXP16_SHIFT) << texture_shift2)];

      // update z-buffer
      z_ptr[xi] = zi;
      } // end if

     // interpolate u,v,z
      ui+=du;
      vi+=dv;
```

```
    zi+=dz;
    } // end for xi

  // interpolate u,v,x along right and left edge
  xl+=dxdyl;
  ul+=dudyl;
  vl+=dvdyl;
  zl+=dzdyl;

  xr+=dxdyr;
  ur+=dudyr;
  vr+=dvdyr;
  zr+=dzdyr;

  // advance screen ptr
  screen_ptr+=mem_pitch;
    // advance zbuffer ptr
    z_ptr+=zpitch;

  } // end for y
```

It's almost criminal that adding Z-buffer support is so easy! Oh well, not everything has to be as hard as writing a real-time colored lighting engine <BG>. Anyway, once again not a single change, other than the addition of a couple of interpolants in both the inner and outer loops of the rasterizer to interpolate the z values of the vertices.

The Flat-Shaded Texture Mapper Now let's take a look at the flat-shaded texture mapper. Actually, the most complex shader code-wise is the z-buffered Gouraud shader, but technically this is the most complex. We just need a new function that enables us to pass the Z-buffer and its pitch. Here's the prototype:

```
void Draw_Textured_TriangleFSZB16(POLYF4DV2_PTR face, // ptr to face
          UCHAR *_dest_buffer, // pointer to video buffer
          int mem_pitch,     // bytes per line, 320, 640 etc.
          UCHAR *_zbuffer,    // pointer to z-buffer
          int zpitch)     // bytes per line of zbuffer
```

Everything works the same as before—just make sure to call the function with valid z coordinates for each polygon, and of course send in the pointer to the Z-buffer memory and its pitch in bytes per line. Finally, here's the code for the rasterization loop with Z-buffer support (I have highlighted the Z-buffer code):

```
// point screen ptr to starting line
screen_ptr = dest_buffer + (ystart * mem_pitch);
```

```
// point zbuffer to starting line
z_ptr = zbuffer + (ystart * zpitch);

for (yi = ystart; yi<=yend; yi++)
   {
   // compute span endpoints
   xstart = ((xl + FIXP16_ROUND_UP) >> FIXP16_SHIFT);
   xend  = ((xr + FIXP16_ROUND_UP) >> FIXP16_SHIFT);

   // compute starting points for u,v interpolants
   ui = ul + FIXP16_ROUND_UP;
   vi = vl + FIXP16_ROUND_UP;
   zi = zl + FIXP16_ROUND_UP;

   // compute u,v interpolants
   if ((dx = (xend - xstart))>0)
  {
  du = (ur - ul)/dx;
  dv = (vr - vl)/dx;
  dz = (zr - zl)/dx;
  } // end if
   else
  {
  du = (ur - ul);
  dv = (vr - vl);
    dz = (zr - zl);
  } // end else

   // draw span
   for (xi=xstart; xi<=xend; xi++)
  {
    // test if z of current pixel is nearer than current z buffer value
    if (zi < z_ptr[xi])
     {
    // write textel
    // get textel first
    textel = textmap[(ui >> FIXP16_SHIFT) +
               ((vi >> FIXP16_SHIFT) << texture_shift2)];

     // extract rgb components
     r_textel = ((textel >> 11)    );
     g_textel = ((textel >> 5) & 0x3f);
     b_textel =  (textel    & 0x1f);
```

```
   // modulate textel with lit background color
   r_textel*=r_base;
   g_textel*=g_base;
   b_textel*=b_base;
   // finally write pixel, note that we did the math such
   // that the results are r*32, g*64, b*32
   // hence we need to divide the results by 32,64,32 respetively,
   // BUT since we need to shift the results to fit into the
   // destination 5.6.5 word, we can take advantage of the shifts
   // and they all cancel out for the most part, but we will need
   // logical anding, we will do it later when we optimize more...
   screen_ptr[xi] = ((b_textel >> 5) +
            ((g_textel >> 6) << 5) +
            ((r_textel >> 5) << 11));

   // update z-buffer
   z_ptr[xi] = zi;
   } // end if

// interpolate u,v,z
ui+=du;
  vi+=dv;
  zi+=dz;
} // end for xi

// interpolate u,v,x along right and left edge
xl+=dxdyl;
ul+=dudyl;
vl+=dvdyl;
zl+=dzdyl;

xr+=dxdyr;
ur+=dudyr;
vr+=dvdyr;
zr+=dzdyr;

// advance screen ptr
screen_ptr+=mem_pitch;

// advance zbuffer ptr
z_ptr+=zpitch;

} // end for y
```

This inner loop is rather complex, and not plotting pixels when the Z-buffer comparison fails is a good thing. We can avoid a lot of code in that case, because we jump over this mess of calculations:

```
// write textel
// get textel first
textel = textmap[(ui >> FIXP16_SHIFT) +
        ((vi >> FIXP16_SHIFT) << texture_shift2)];

// extract rgb components
r_textel = ((textel >> 11)    );
g_textel = ((textel >> 5) & 0x3f);
b_textel =  (textel    & 0x1f);

// modulate textel with lit background color
r_textel*=r_base;
g_textel*=g_base;
b_textel*=b_base;
screen_ptr[xi] = ((b_textel >> 5) +
        ((g_textel >> 6) << 5) +
        ((r_textel >> 5) << 11));

// update z-buffer
z_ptr[xi] = zi;
```

The interesting thing is that as we make more and more complex rasterizers, we think that we are going to slow them down, but we end up speeding them up, because when they are put to use in a real game world, the losses are made up by the gains. In this case, not rasterizing pixels that aren't drawn because of their position in the Z-buffer actually ends up averaging out the performance, and once again we get pixel-perfect rendering for free.

Updating the Rendering List Function

The final function we need to complete the Z-buffer functionality is the rendering list function, which takes a rendering list and makes the calls to the appropriate functions based on the type of polygons in the list. Here's the new version of render list drawing function:

```
void Draw_RENDERLIST4DV2_SolidZB16(RENDERLIST4DV2_PTR rend_list,
                    UCHAR *video_buffer,
                     int lpitch,
                    UCHAR *zbuffer,
                    int zpitch)
{
// 16-bit version
// this function "executes" the render list or in other words
```

```
// draws all the faces in the list, the function will call the
// proper rasterizer based on the lighting model of the polygons


POLYF4DV2 face; // temp face used to render polygon

// at this point, all we have is a list of polygons and it's time
// to draw them
for (int poly=0; poly < rend_list->num_polys; poly++)
  {
  // render this polygon if and only if it's not clipped, not culled,
  // active, and visible, note however the concecpt of "backface" is
  // irrelevant in a wire frame engine though
  if (!(rend_list->poly_ptrs[poly]->state & POLY4DV2_STATE_ACTIVE) ||
     (rend_list->poly_ptrs[poly]->state & POLY4DV2_STATE_CLIPPED ) ||
     (rend_list->poly_ptrs[poly]->state & POLY4DV2_STATE_BACKFACE) )
    continue; // move onto next poly

  // need to test for textured first, since a textured poly can either
  // be emissive, or flat shaded, hence we need to call different
  // rasterizers
  if (rend_list->poly_ptrs[poly]->attr & POLY4DV2_ATTR_SHADE_MODE_TEXTURE)
    {

    // set the vertices
    face.tvlist[0].x = (int)rend_list->poly_ptrs[poly]->tvlist[0].x;
    face.tvlist[0].y = (int)rend_list->poly_ptrs[poly]->tvlist[0].y;
    face.tvlist[0].z = (int)rend_list->poly_ptrs[poly]->tvlist[0].z;
    face.tvlist[0].u0 = (int)rend_list->poly_ptrs[poly]->tvlist[0].u0;
    face.tvlist[0].v0 = (int)rend_list->poly_ptrs[poly]->tvlist[0].v0;

    face.tvlist[1].x = (int)rend_list->poly_ptrs[poly]->tvlist[1].x;
    face.tvlist[1].y = (int)rend_list->poly_ptrs[poly]->tvlist[1].y;
    face.tvlist[1].z = (int)rend_list->poly_ptrs[poly]->tvlist[1].z;
    face.tvlist[1].u0 = (int)rend_list->poly_ptrs[poly]->tvlist[1].u0;
    face.tvlist[1].v0 = (int)rend_list->poly_ptrs[poly]->tvlist[1].v0;

    face.tvlist[2].x = (int)rend_list->poly_ptrs[poly]->tvlist[2].x;
    face.tvlist[2].y = (int)rend_list->poly_ptrs[poly]->tvlist[2].y;
    face.tvlist[2].z = (int)rend_list->poly_ptrs[poly]->tvlist[2].z;
    face.tvlist[2].u0 = (int)rend_list->poly_ptrs[poly]->tvlist[2].u0;
    face.tvlist[2].v0 = (int)rend_list->poly_ptrs[poly]->tvlist[2].v0;
```

```
  // assign the texture
  face.texture = rend_list->poly_ptrs[poly]->texture;

  // is this a plain emissive texture?
  if (rend_list->poly_ptrs[poly]->attr &
    POLY4DV2_ATTR_SHADE_MODE_CONSTANT)
   {
   // draw the textured triangle as emissive
   Draw_Textured_TriangleZB16(&face, video_buffer,
                lpitch,zbuffer,zpitch);
   } // end if
  else
   {
   // draw as flat shaded
   face.lit_color[0] = rend_list->poly_ptrs[poly]->lit_color[0];
   Draw_Textured_TriangleFSZB16(&face, video_buffer,
                lpitch,zbuffer,zpitch);
   } // end else

  } // end if
else
if ((rend_list->poly_ptrs[poly]->attr & POLY4DV2_ATTR_SHADE_MODE_FLAT) ||
  (rend_list->poly_ptrs[poly]->attr &
  POLY4DV2_ATTR_SHADE_MODE_CONSTANT) )
  {
  // draw as constant shaded
  face.lit_color[0] = rend_list->poly_ptrs[poly]->lit_color[0];

  // set the vertices
  face.tvlist[0].x = (int)rend_list->poly_ptrs[poly]->tvlist[0].x;
  face.tvlist[0].y = (int)rend_list->poly_ptrs[poly]->tvlist[0].y;
  face.tvlist[0].z = (int)rend_list->poly_ptrs[poly]->tvlist[0].z;

  face.tvlist[1].x = (int)rend_list->poly_ptrs[poly]->tvlist[1].x;
  face.tvlist[1].y = (int)rend_list->poly_ptrs[poly]->tvlist[1].y;
  face.tvlist[1].z = (int)rend_list->poly_ptrs[poly]->tvlist[1].z;

  face.tvlist[2].x = (int)rend_list->poly_ptrs[poly]->tvlist[2].x;
  face.tvlist[2].y = (int)rend_list->poly_ptrs[poly]->tvlist[2].y;
  face.tvlist[2].z = (int)rend_list->poly_ptrs[poly]->tvlist[2].z;

  // draw the triangle with basic flat rasterizer
  Draw_Triangle_2DZB_16(&face, video_buffer, lpitch,zbuffer,zpitch);
```

```
      } // end if
    else
    if (rend_list->poly_ptrs[poly]->attr & POLY4DV2_ATTR_SHADE_MODE_GOURAUD)
      {
      // {andre take advantage of the data structures later..}
      // set the vertices
      face.tvlist[0].x = (int)rend_list->poly_ptrs[poly]->tvlist[0].x;
      face.tvlist[0].y = (int)rend_list->poly_ptrs[poly]->tvlist[0].y;
      face.tvlist[0].z = (int)rend_list->poly_ptrs[poly]->tvlist[0].z;
      face.lit_color[0] = rend_list->poly_ptrs[poly]->lit_color[0];

      face.tvlist[1].x = (int)rend_list->poly_ptrs[poly]->tvlist[1].x;
      face.tvlist[1].y = (int)rend_list->poly_ptrs[poly]->tvlist[1].y;
      face.tvlist[1].z = (int)rend_list->poly_ptrs[poly]->tvlist[1].z;
      face.lit_color[1] = rend_list->poly_ptrs[poly]->lit_color[1];

      face.tvlist[2].x = (int)rend_list->poly_ptrs[poly]->tvlist[2].x;
      face.tvlist[2].y = (int)rend_list->poly_ptrs[poly]->tvlist[2].y;
      face.tvlist[2].z = (int)rend_list->poly_ptrs[poly]->tvlist[2].z;
      face.lit_color[2] = rend_list->poly_ptrs[poly]->lit_color[2];

      // draw the gouraud shaded triangle
      Draw_Gouraud_TriangleZB16(&face, video_buffer, lpitch,zbuffer,zpitch);
      } // end if gouraud

    } // end for poly

} // end Draw_RENDERLIST4DV2_SolidZB16
```

Please take a moment to see how clean and simple each one of the control paths are. The function checks what kind of polygon we have and then calls the appropriate function. Of course, if this were full-blown C++, we would simply overload the functions, or use virtual functions and not do this case-select stuff. However, C++ is great with a fixed design, and we are all over the map, so it doesn't really help us. We are just writing code here, experimenting with algorithms and seeing what happens. Later you will definitely want to code what we have done and will do in a much more efficient and clean manner. In any event, the `Draw_RENDERLIST4DV2_SolidZB16()` function works just as its predecessor `Draw_RENDERLIST4DV2_Solid16()` did, but with the additional parameters of a pointer to the Z-buffer's memory and the pitch of the Z-buffer's bytes per line.

NOTE

You might wonder why I decided not to send the Z-buffer object itself to each function `ZBUFFERV1_PTR`. Well, I wanted to keep my options open—this way, if we decide to upgrade the Z-buffer object `ZBUFFERV1`, we don't break the rasterizers.

Possible Z-Buffer Optimizations

The computation of the Z-buffer values during the rasterization are about as simple as we are going to get them without resorting to assembly language (SIMD instructions, and so forth). So, we have to look at a higher level to optimize. There are a few possibilities, so let's take a look at them.

Using Less Memory

The first possibility to make the Z-buffer a little faster is to make it smaller; that is, to use a 16-bit Z-buffer rather than a 32-bit buffer. Although this seems like a good idea, it can actually be slower than 32-bit access. The reason is that Pentium processors are 32-bit devices. They like doing things 32 bits at a time. Although you will have better cache coherence with less memory per cache line, you might get a hit from using 16-bit access because of alignment and other subtleties. Additionally, 16 bits is getting close to the minimum you need to represent any decent amount of z resolution to resolve the pixel order of polygons—that's another issue to try out. Personally, I found that because the Z-buffer is part of the inner loop of the rasterizer, the gains made by making it 16-bit were negligible.

Clearing the Z-Buffer Less Often

The memory fill that clears out the Z-buffer takes a little time. Basically, it's the amount of time it takes to write a 32-bit value to memory multiplied by the size of the Z-buffer. As an example, let's say we have a Pentium III+ machine that has an average of four clocks to write to memory because of caching and other effects. Let's also say it's running at 500MHz. Therefore, one clock cycle is 2×10^{-9} seconds, or two nanoseconds. Therefore, at 800×600 we have

```
Total time =
clocks_per_write * width * height * time_per_clock
= 4*800*600*(2x10^-9 s) = 3.84 milliseconds.
```

Although that might not seem like very much time, it really is a lot, considering that a single frame at 60 fps takes 16 milliseconds. This means that roughly 3.84/16 = 24% of your time is spent clearing the Z-buffer! That kinda hurts! This is definitely an area we would like to get rid of. There are a few options: We can use dirty rectangles, track areas of the Z-buffer that aren't touched each frame, and then we simply don't clear them. This sounds good, but doesn't work in reality. The only other option is to not clear the Z-buffer at all. However, this can only be accomplished with 1/z-buffering. Because with 1/z-buffering, the value of 1/z can never be larger than 1.0 as long as z >= 1, we can use a bias each frame and add this "z bias" to every single z value written to the Z-buffer. This way, each frame is a little farther than the rest, but guaranteed not to interfere with the last frame. Additionally, we must change the z-buffering comparisons because each frame the values of z get larger, but this is a simple change to the comparison value. This is shown graphically in Figure 11.10.

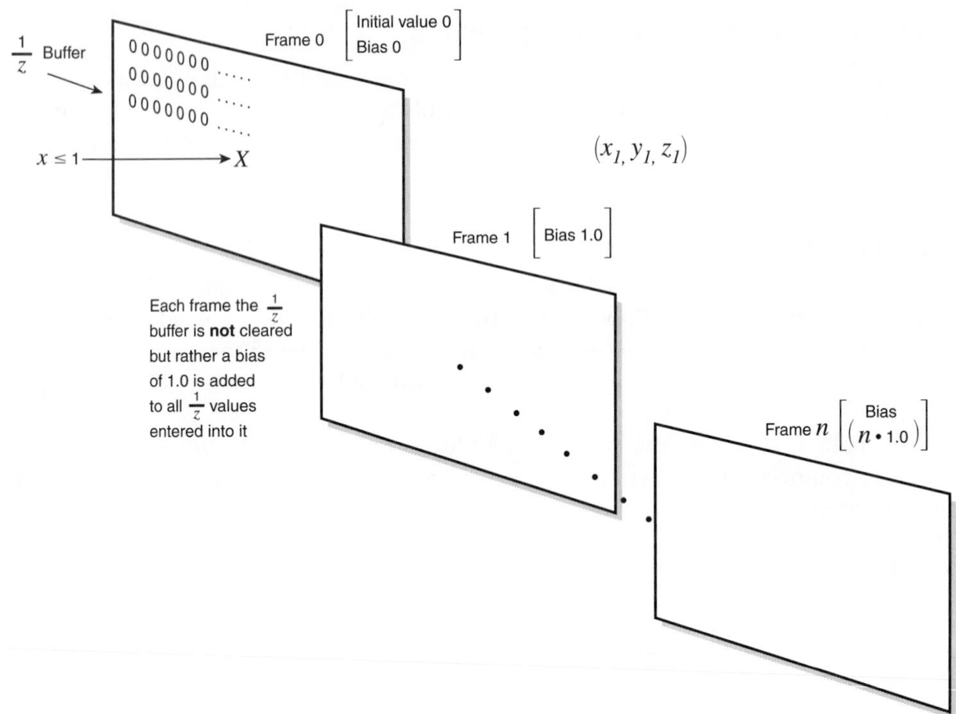

FIGURE 11.10 Avoiding 1/z-buffer clearing.

As an example, here are two frames using this technique. Each pixel's (x,y) is the same, so we will only look at the z value of each. During each frame, we will have a series of pixels plotted on top of each other with different z values to see whether the 1/z buffer is correct at the end. If, when we bias the 1/z buffer, the next frame renders properly. Here's the experiment:

Frame 0: Initial Z-buffer value 0.0

Pixel#	z	1/z	Bias	Final 1/z (with bias)
0	10	.100	0	.100
1	12	.083	0	.083
2	5	.200	0	.200

Analysis of Frame 0:

Z-buffer = 0.0

Pixel 0 has a final 1/z value of .1, which is greater than 0.0. Therefore, the pixel is written to screen and the 1/z buffer is updated to 0.1.

Z-buffer = 0.1

Pixel 1 has a final 1/z value of .083, which is less than .1. Therefore, the pixel is NOT written, and the 1/z-buffer is left alone.

Z-buffer = 0.1

Pixel 2 has a final 1/z value of .2, which is greater than .1. Therefore, the pixel is written to screen and the 1/z-buffer is updated to 0.2.

Reviewing the analysis, the bottom line is that the pixel that is closest to the viewpoint (Pixel 2 with a z value of 5.0) should be the last written to screen and to the Z-buffer, and indeed it was.

Frame 1: Z-buffer value 0.2

Pixel#	z	1/z	Bias	Final 1/z (with bias)
0	5	.200	1.0	1.200
1	2	.5	1.0	1.500
2	3	.333	1.0	1.333

Analysis of Frame 1:

Z-buffer = 0.0

Pixel 0 has a final 1/z value of 1.2, which is greater than 0.2. Therefore, the pixel is written to screen and the 1/z-buffer is updated to 1.2.

Z-buffer = 1.2

Pixel 1 has a final 1/z value of 1.5, which is greater than 1.2. Therefore, the pixel is written and the 1/z-buffer is updated to 1.5.

Z-buffer = 1.5

Pixel 2 has a final 1/z value of 1.333, which is less than 1.5. Therefore, the pixel is NOT written to screen and the 1/z-buffer is NOT updated.

Z-buffer = 1.5

Reviewing the analysis, the bottom line is that the pixel that is closest to the viewpoint (Pixel 1 with a z value of 2.0) should be the last written to screen and to the Z-buffer, and indeed it was.

The 1/z-buffer with delayed writing works fine! The only problem is that at some point, the 1/z-buffer will overflow. Basically, this happens after *n* frames, where *n* is the largest integer that can be represented along with the decimal portion of the 1/z buffer.

Hybrid Z Buffering

The next optimization idea is to use a hybrid Z-buffer. That is, you only z-buffer certain portions of the scene, and you z-sort others. For example, we could filter any polygon that has a z value greater than 30% of the viewing distance and simply z-sort it, because most of the time it will look okay. But for polygons that fall into the first 30% of the viewing distance, we z-buffer them. This actually works very well. First we z-sort the far polygons, render them using the painter's algorithm back to front, and then z-buffer the nearer polygons that need to be perfect. Figure 11.11 illustrates this graphically.

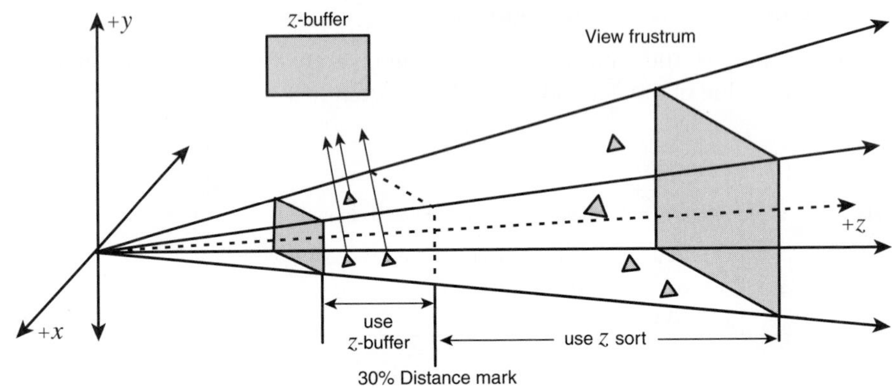

FIGURE 11.11 The hybrid z-buffer/z-sort.

Problems with the Z-Buffer

Lastly I want to talk about problems with the Z-buffer. Obviously, the first problem is that it's totally incorrect. We are interpolating something that's not linear in screen space, so we are going to get those anomalies right off the bat, but that's not the main issue. The main issue with the Z-buffer is that because of the perspective transform and the non-linearity of the z-interpolation, we are going to lose accuracy for large viewing volumes. In other words, imagine that we have a game universe that has a far clipping plane of 1,000,000 units (this is completely reasonable for a space game). To accurately represent 1,000,000 units, we need about 20 bits. Even with a 32-bit Z-buffer, this only leaves us with 12 bits for the decimal portion of the z values. So we waste all the Z-buffer's accuracy spread out over this huge range when we need it up close where it counts. This is another reason why the 1/z-buffer is better.

The Software and Z-Buffer Demos

First, let's talk about the new software modules. Everything in this chapter is contained in the new library files:

- `T3DLIB9.CPP`—The C/C++ source
- `T3DLIB9.H`—The header file for `T3DLIB9.CPP`

Of course, to compile anything you need `T3DLIB1-8.CPP|H`, as well as the new file `T3DLIB9.CPP|H`.

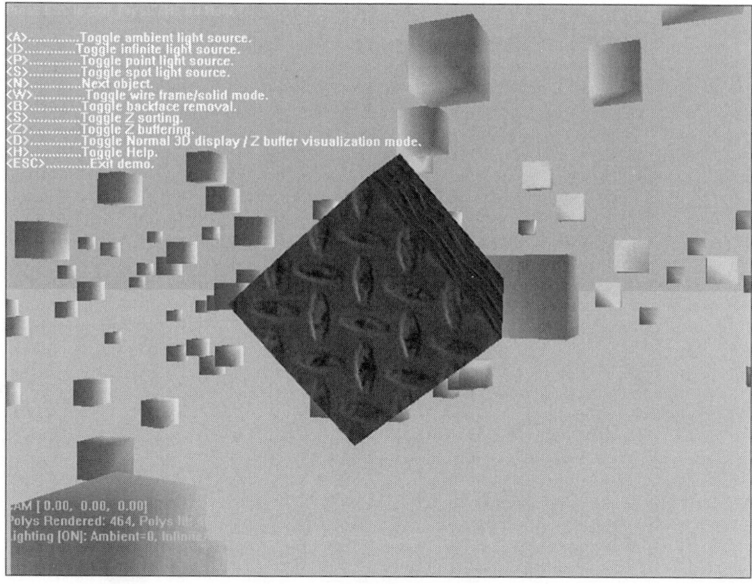

FIGURE 11.12 A screenshot of the first Z-buffer demo.

Demo I: Z-Buffer Visualization

As usual, I like to give an example that leverages the material from the chapter into a game-like or technology demo. I am still not sure what to do for a game, but I will know by the end of this section. The cool thing is that from your point of view, it will be written instantaneously; but from my point of view, I am looking at 4–12 hours of hacking!

Anyway, let's start with a technology demo. Figure 11.12 is a screenshot of `DEMOII11_1.CPP|EXE`. Basically, it enables you to slowly move around the environment with the arrow keys as usual. The cool part is that you can select z-sorting or z-buffering with the Z key. Try selecting each and then moving around causing interpenetrations of the geometry with your player object. Then switch back and forth from z-sorting to z-buffering, and you will see how the Z-buffer version works perfectly. This is all fine and dandy, but I thought it would be cool if you could actually visualize the Z-buffer.

This really isn't very hard. Basically I copy the Z-buffer into the frame buffer through a simple translation filter that takes the 32-bit z depth values and converts them to colors. Because RGB is encoded in 16 bits, with the high bits representing red and the low bits representing blues, this works out in such a way that the Z-buffer is a colored depth map, where red intensities indicate long distances and blue intensities indicate something close to the viewpoint, as shown in Figure 11.13.

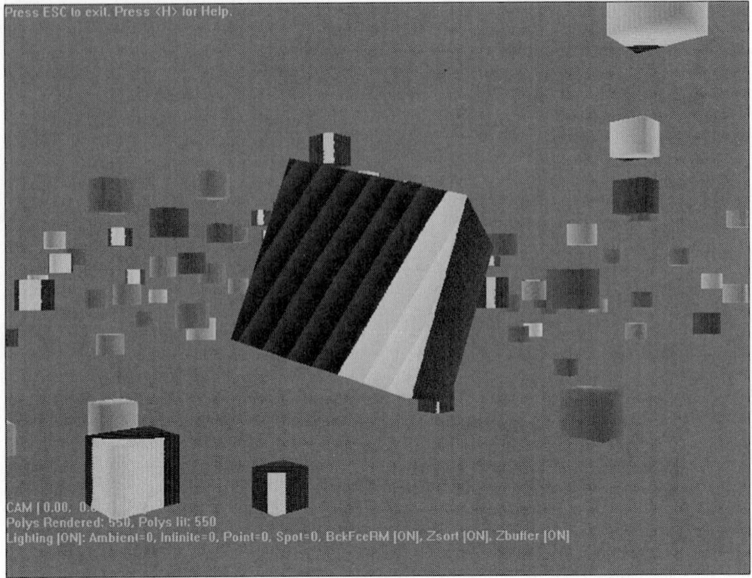

FIGURE 11.13 The Z-buffer demo in Z-buffer visualization mode.

It's very cool, and reminds me of the movie *Predator* <BG>. Anyway, here are the important controls:

- Arrow keys—Movement
- Z—Toggle z-buffering
- S—Toggle z-sorting
- N—Switch objects
- H—Toggle help menu
- D—Toggle normal rendering/Z-buffer filter
- Esc—Exit demo

To compile the demo, you will need the main .CPP file `DEMOII11_1.CPP`, along with all the library modules in `T3DLIB1-9.CPP¦H`. You will also need to link in the DirectX libraries and `WINMM.LIB`, as usual.

CAUTION

When in Z-buffer visualization mode, you will notice the colors cycling. This effect is because z is linear from the viewpoint to infinity. However, colors are encoded as RGB values in 5.6.5 format, and when we map the z values into colors as z increases from 0 to 65536, it will cycle through the lower bits, which represent blue 2048 times, and so forth. Nevertheless, the main point is that the general shade from blue to red indicates depth.

Demo II: *Wave Raider*

For the second demo, I wanted to take our little terrain demo and improve the physics a bit and create a water simulation. Water is the perfect geometry for the Z-buffer because the "water polygons" are drawn at some level and the jet ski or watercraft polygons penetrate the water and go below it, so it looks as though the watercraft is partially above and below the waterline—which is exactly what it should look like! Anyway, take a look at Figure 11.14 for a screenshot of the water demo `DEMOII11_2.CPP¦EXE`; it's pretty cool for the amount of code it took.

FIGURE 11.14 *Wave Raider* putting the Z-buffer to good use with water interpenetration.

Here are the controls, so you can try it out right away.

- Enter/Return—Starts engine
- Right—Turn right
- Left—Turn left
- Up—Throttle

And most of the help and engine controls still work:

- Z—Toggle z-buffering
- S—Toggle z-sorting
- D—Toggle normal rendering/Z-buffer filter

- H—Toggle help menu
- Esc—Exit demo

Now let's talk about a couple of key programming points of the demo.

The Terrain Race Course

I had a miniature nightmare making the race course. The problem is that there are lots of terrain generation programs that will create height maps, but when you are on a schedule like I am, you don't have hours to figure out how to force the tool to create a race course. In the end, I found two incredible programs to help:

- Terragen—`http://www.planetside.co.uk/terragen/`
- Worldmachine—`http://students.washington.edu/sschmitt/world/`

Both have shareware versions that you can use. I actually ended up using Worldmachine to create the height map for this game demo. Figure 11.15 is a screenshot of Worldmachine in action.

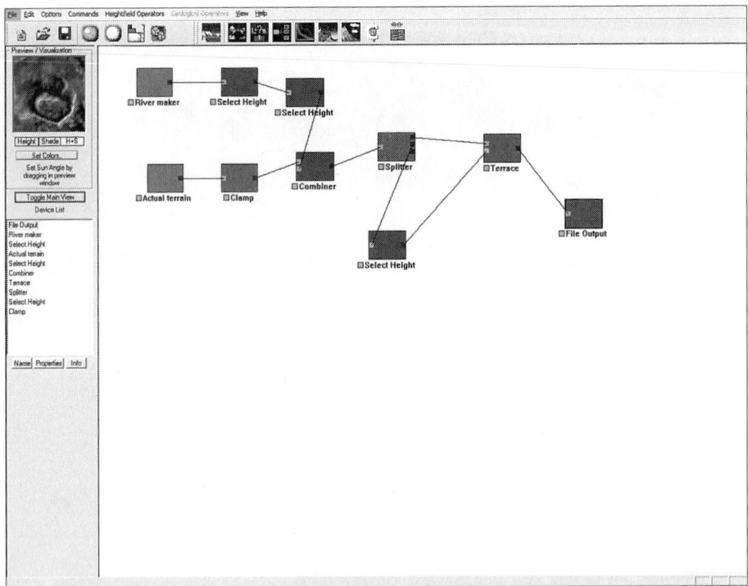

FIGURE 11.15 Worldmachine with my water race track.

For the actual terrain I had to generate a height map with the program along with a texture to stretch over the height map. Figures 11.16 and 11.17 illustrate the height map in grayscale encoding, along with the beautiful texture map that Worldmachine generated for me. The in-game terrain height map is 40×40 and the texture is 256×256, but the figures illustrate the higher resolution versions at 512×512, so you can see them before I mangled them.

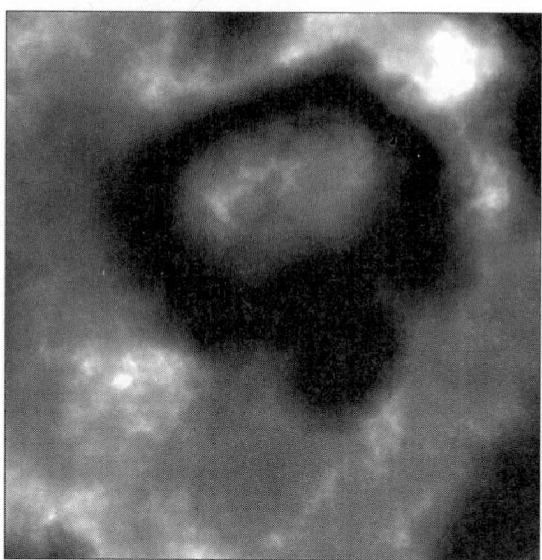

FIGURE 11.16 The height map.

FIGURE 11.17 The texture map of the water raceway.

After I had the terrain ready, I made a single call to our trusty terrain mesh generator and that was it:

```
// generate terrain
Generate_Terrain_OBJECT4DV2(&obj_terrain,       // pointer to object
  TERRAIN_WIDTH,       // width in world coords on x-axis
```

```
TERRAIN_HEIGHT,        // height (length) in world coords on z-axis
TERRAIN_SCALE,         // vertical scale of terrain
"water_track_height_04.bmp", // filename of height bitmap
                  // encoded in 256 colors
"water_track_color_03.bmp",   // filename of texture map
RGB16Bit(255,255,255), // color of terrain if no texture
&terrain_pos,         // initial position
NULL,             // initial rotations
POLY4DV2_ATTR_RGB16 |
POLY4DV2_ATTR_SHADE_MODE_FLAT | /*POLY4DV2_ATTR_SHADE_MODE_GOURAUD */
POLY4DV2_ATTR_SHADE_MODE_TEXTURE );
```

As you can see, the terrain is flat-shaded.

Animating the Water

Getting the water to animate is actually trivial. The idea is to simply modulate the terrain mesh with a sine wave or other related "wave" function. The tricky part is to only modulate the "water" part of the mesh. However, it's not that bad if you think of it this way: As each frame begins, you start off with the initial mesh in local coordinates and then copy that into the transformed mesh so you can alter it. Then you run a wave function (which I will show you in a moment) over the entire terrain mesh; however, you only apply the modulation to vertices that are *below* the virtual water level. This is the trick. Figure 11.18 depicts this concept graphically.

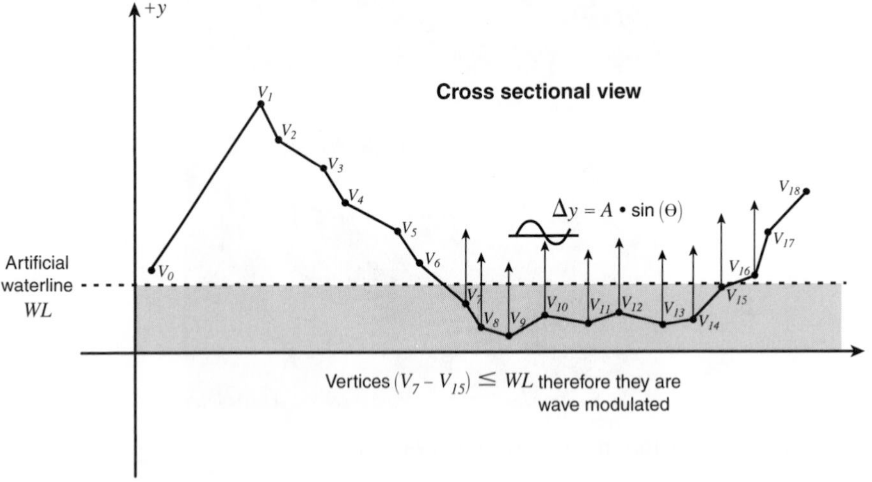

FIGURE 11.18 Modulating the water under the water line.

Here's the entire code that modulates the wave onto the terrain for any vertex that has a height less than the water level:

```
// wave generator ////////////////////////////////////////////////////////////

// for each vertex in the mesh apply wave modulation if height < water level
for (int v = 0; v < obj_terrain.num_vertices; v++)
  {
  // wave modulate below water level only
  if (obj_terrain.vlist_trans[v].y < WATER_LEVEL)
    obj_terrain.vlist_trans[v].y+=
     WAVE_HEIGHT*sin(wave_count + (float)v/(2*(float)obj_terrain.ivar2+0));
  } // end for v

// increase the wave position in time
wave_count+=WAVE_RATE;
```

Kinda disgusting, huh? You probably thought it would have all kinds of complex physics, spring constants, wave functions—Nope! All I need is a little sine wave and a counter. This is not to say writing a real water model isn't important, but sometimes you can get away with really simple code for special effects.

The Physics Model for the Jet Ski

The physics model for the jet ski is identical to the driving model from the last chapter. Basically, I only changed the model constants, making the jet ski more springy and interpenetrate the geometry more to show off the Z-buffer. For the most part, no changes have been made to our physics model. The player accelerates the jet ski, the terrain follower looks at the mesh under it and then pushes the model upward or lets it fall downward. The cool thing is that as the mesh model modulates with the wave, so does the jet ski, so it looks like it's floating and bobbing in the water! Anyway, here's the entire physics model for your review, along with the final jet ski model placement out in front of the camera (this is a bit cheesy, but oh well):

```
// motion section ////////////////////////////////////////////////////////////

// terrain following, simply find the current cell we are over and then
// index into the vertex list and find the 4 vertices that make up the
// quad cell we are hovering over and then average the values, and based
// on the current height and the height of the terrain push the player upward

// the terrain generates and stores some results to help with terrain following
//ivar1 = columns;
//ivar2 = rows;
//fvar1 = col_vstep;
//fvar2 = row_vstep;

int cell_x = (cam.pos.x + TERRAIN_WIDTH/2) / obj_terrain.fvar1;
int cell_y = (cam.pos.z + TERRAIN_HEIGHT/2) / obj_terrain.fvar1;
```

```
static float terrain_height, delta;

// test if we are on terrain
if ( (cell_x >=0) && (cell_x < obj_terrain.ivar1) &&
   (cell_y >=0) && (cell_y < obj_terrain.ivar2) )
  {
  // compute vertex indices into vertex list of the current quad
  int v0 = cell_x + cell_y*obj_terrain.ivar2;
  int v1 = v0 + 1;
  int v2 = v1 + obj_terrain.ivar2;
  int v3 = v0 + obj_terrain.ivar2;

  // now simply index into table
  terrain_height = 0.25 * (obj_terrain.vlist_trans[v0].y +
              obj_terrain.vlist_trans[v1].y +
              obj_terrain.vlist_trans[v2].y +
              obj_terrain.vlist_trans[v3].y);

  // compute height difference
  delta = terrain_height - (cam.pos.y - gclearance);

  // test for penetration
  if (delta > 0)
   {
   // apply force immediately to camera (this will give it a springy feel)
   vel_y+=(delta * (VELOCITY_SCALER));

   // test for pentration, if so move up immediately,
   // so we don't penetrate geometry
   cam.pos.y+=(delta*CAM_HEIGHT_SCALER);

   // now this is more of a hack than the physics model :)
   // let move the front
   // up and down a bit based on the forward velocity
   // and the gradient of the
   // hill
   cam.dir.x -= (delta*PITCH_CHANGE_RATE);

   } // end if

  } // end if

// decelerate camera
if (cam_speed > (CAM_DECEL) ) cam_speed-=CAM_DECEL;
```

```
else
if (cam_speed < (-CAM_DECEL) ) cam_speed+=CAM_DECEL;
else
  cam_speed = 0;

// force camera to seek a stable orientation
if (cam.dir.x > (neutral_pitch+PITCH_RETURN_RATE))
  cam.dir.x -= (PITCH_RETURN_RATE);
else
if (cam.dir.x < (neutral_pitch-PITCH_RETURN_RATE))
  cam.dir.x += (PITCH_RETURN_RATE);
 else
  cam.dir.x = neutral_pitch;

// apply gravity
vel_y+=gravity;

// test for absolute sea level and push upward..
if (cam.pos.y < sea_level)
  {
  vel_y = 0;
  cam.pos.y = sea_level;
  } // end if

// move camera
cam.pos.x += cam_speed*Fast_Sin(cam.dir.y);
cam.pos.z += cam_speed*Fast_Cos(cam.dir.y);
cam.pos.y += vel_y;

// position point light in front of player
lights2[POINT_LIGHT_INDEX].pos.x = cam.pos.x + 150*Fast_Sin(cam.dir.y);
lights2[POINT_LIGHT_INDEX].pos.y = cam.pos.y + 50;
lights2[POINT_LIGHT_INDEX].pos.z = cam.pos.z + 150*Fast_Cos(cam.dir.y);

// position the player object slighty in front of camera and in water
obj_player.world_pos.x = cam.pos.x + 120*Fast_Sin(cam.dir.y);
obj_player.world_pos.y = cam.pos.y - 75 + 7.5*sin(wave_count);
obj_player.world_pos.z = cam.pos.z + 120*Fast_Cos(cam.dir.y);
```

If we were going to write a real game, we would have the camera very loosely locked to watch the player, instead of using the camera as an anchor and then drawing the player in front of it. Additionally, this physics model doesn't model friction, so the jet ski turns on a dime. It would be easy to add, but I have to leave something for other demos!

Sound Effects

I am most proud of the sound in this game. I took a number of samples of the sounds of jet skis, water, the ocean, splashes, and myself (as the announcer) and put them all together to give you a game-like experience. The sound effects have three different aspects—let's cover each briefly, because sound is so important in a game and can make the difference between fun and boring.

The Announcer The game has three primary parts: the introduction from atop mount Aleph One, the in-water instructions, and the normal gameplay. When the game starts, an overview is heard. Then a state change is made and the player is dumped in the water, and the instructions are given.

To make these digital voiceovers, I recorded myself sounding as cheesy as I possibly could in 11KHz 8-bit mono, using Sound Forge to do the recording. I added a bit of noise to make things sound authentic, and finally echoed my voice slightly. The results sound great, and my friend couldn't believe it was me!

The Water Sounds For the water sounds, I sampled water and waves from the Sound Ideas General 6000 sound library. It consists of 40 CDs and cost me around $2,500, but it's worth every penny. In any case, I sampled both a light lake wave sound, and a heavy water wave in a lake sound. Then I played each at different amplitudes and slightly modified their frequencies in the game based on the player's speed. Amazingly, at 8-bit and 11KHz sampling, the sound of the water remained intact. And of course, the water sounds are played as continuous loops.

The Jet Ski Sounds This was the most complex part of the model. I really wanted the sound of a jet ski and the feel of it to come through. This is always a problem when doing sound effects. In real life, lots of things don't make sound—we just think they do. In movies, for example, all the sounds are so exaggerated it's ridiculous. That's why foley artists enhance each event after the movie is complete, so you can hear it as well as see it, even if there isn't anything to hear!

In any event, the jet ski has a number of different states:

- State 1—Engine off
- State 2—Engine start (single shot)
- State 3—Engine idle (loop)
- State 4—Accelerate (single shot)
- State 5—Engine running at RPM (loop)

I needed a good starting sound, and in the end I used a 25-HP outboard motor mixed with a real jet ski starting, because the jet ski was simply too subdued. Next, I used a real jet ski for the idle, acceleration, and running sounds. The tricky part was mixing all of them to sound correctly. I tracked the state of the jet ski, the velocity of the player, and a number of other variables to signal me when to change things. For example, when the player hits the Enter key and starts the jet ski, I turned all the sounds on except the accelerate sound! You can only hear the starting sound for the most part because it's so loud, but the idle is in there under it all. However, the State 5 sound is at zero percent because the jet ski isn't moving.

When the player hits the throttle, I nailed the accelerate sound with a one shot, and you hear the jet ski taking off. At the same time, the player model is accelerating the jet ski. This velocity is used to modulate both the amplitude and frequency of the running engine sound, so the faster you go, the higher its pitch and the louder it is. Still, under it all is the idle sound, waiting for you to let off the throttle.

Of course, there are lots of ways to model these sounds and optimize what really needs to be on at any time rather than turning the volume down, but this seemed to work really well.

CAUTION

The rasterizers still have a divide-by-zero bug in them, and depending on the situation, a degenerate triangle sometimes passes into the rasterizer, causing the demo to crash! Ironically, this occurs in this demo sometimes when passing the highest peak with green grass—you will see it on your left. I have thus named it Zemulda Triangle <BG>.

To compile the demo, you will need the main .CPP file `DEMOII11_2.CPP`, along with all the library modules in `T3DLIB1-9.CPP|H`. You will also need to link in the DirectX libraries and `WINMM.LIB`, as usual.

Summary

Well, another seemingly complex topic beat down and begging for mercy. That's the trick to graphics—just take your time, run the examples on paper, understand it, and everything will work out. The bottom line is that it all starts from plot (x,y). At any rate, we now have a pretty decent 3D engine! It has 16-bit support, lighting, z-buffering, and model loading. And it runs reasonably fast for absolutely no optimization. I am pretty happy at this point. From this point on, we are going to continue adding features to the engine: better lighting, support for hierarchical objects like interior levels, and so forth. However, for the most part, we are done with 90% of everything you need to know about 3D graphics. You should be proud!

PART IV

Advanced 3D Rendering

IN THIS PART

CHAPTER **12**

Advanced Texturing Techniques

IN THIS CHAPTER

"Maybe fun is just fragments of existence with better packaging?"

—Steve Jobs, *Pirates of Silicon Valley*

In this chapter, we are primarily going to discuss rasterization techniques. Although we already have a fairly advanced software rasterizer core, it still has no support for alpha blending, perspective-correct textures, texture filtering, mip mapping, Gouraud-shaded textures, and so forth. Hence, we are going to address these issues here. Finally, we will once again rewrite all the rasterizers. Ouch! You're killing me here ... <BG>. Here are the main areas of interest in this chapter:

- Transparency and alpha blending
- Gouraud-shaded texturing
- Perspective-correct texturing
- 1/z-buffering
- Bilinear texture filtering
- Mip mapping and trilinear texture filtering
- New object loaders
- DirectDraw initialization function revamping
- Multiple pass rendering

Texturing—The Second Wave

I have written so many rasterizers for this chapter that I'm going to explode! I think I've cranked out something like 50,000+ lines of code just for the rasterizers—the reason being that a separate rasterizer is needed for every single permutation of capabilities we add to our engine. This is because I refuse to generalize the rasterizers themselves and take a performance hit.

After writing all these rasterizers and the demos to go along with them, I realized, or rather confirmed, that this chapter wasn't a good place for more lighting and discussions of shadows—that's really a separate topic. Additionally, I really want to show light mapping, environment mapping, and shadows in action, so I need something with which to create levels to do this properly. Thus we are going to hold off on these topics until after the next chapter, which covers spatial partitioning, because after we cover that material, we will have some level editing tools to play with that we can leverage for light mapping demos. At least that's the plan.

Let's talk about what's happening in this chapter. We are going to cover a number of new techniques, such as inverse z-buffering, alpha blending, perspective-correct texturing, mip mapping, bilinear and trilinear texturing, and more. And of course, we will need to rewrite every single rasterizer and then some. This chapter has more than 40 new rasterizers! That's a lot of code, and a lot to debug, so I worked really hard to try and keep everything fast. In the end I think you're going to be amazed at the speed we get without resorting to assembly language and/or any excessive optimization (we will leave that until the end of the book).

So as usual, there's a new library module and header file you will need to compile all the programs from this chapter:

- `T3DLIB10.CPP`—The C/C++ source file
- `T3DLIB10.H`—The header file

You will need to include these, along with the previous library modules `T3DLIB1-9.CPP|H`, to compile any programs from this chapter. You'll also need the DirectX .LIB files, and of course, you'll need to set the compiler up correctly (Win32 .EXE target). I always mention what a program needs to compile at the top of the source code, so you can always look there.

In any case, we're going to cover each topic, review the code, create a demo, and move on. I didn't implement some of the techniques (or did and found them to be too slow), such as trilinear filtering, but we will cover all of them nonetheless.

Additionally, I have updated some of the other functions to support some of our new features—such as the terrain generation function, the Caligari trueSpace .COB file loader, and a redo of the DirectDraw functions that initialize DirectDraw and flip pages because of an anomaly when doing alpha blending and reading from a DirectDraw backbuffer. As usual, I want you to take a quick look at the header file, just to see what's coming. Don't worry if things don't make any sense; it's just to have an idea of what's going on.

The Header File Data Structures

The following text describes the header file T3DLIB10.H. We will cover the functions and structures in more detail throughout the text, but you know I like to start off by showing you everything. Let's begin with the #defines. There's not much here, other than some new fixed-point constants and a set of rendering options we will need later when we write a single all-encompassing rendering function:

```
// DEFINES //////////////////////////////////////////////////////////////////////

// alpha blending defines
#define NUM_ALPHA_LEVELS       8  // total number of alpha levels

// perspective correct/ 1/z buffer defines
#define FIXP28_SHIFT         28 // used for 1/z buffering
#define FIXP22_SHIFT         22 // used for u/z,
                     // v/z perspective texture mapping

// new attributes to support mip mapping
#define POLY4DV2_ATTR_MIPMAP     0x0400 // flags if polygon has a mipmap
#define OBJECT4DV2_ATTR_MIPMAP    0x0008 // flags if object has a mipmap

//////////////////////////////////////////////////////////////////////////////////

// defines that control the rendering function state attributes
// note each class of control flags is contained within
// a 4-bit nibble where possible, this helps with future expansion

// no z buffering, polygons will be rendered as are in list
#define RENDER_ATTR_NOBUFFER          0x00000001

// use z buffering rasterization
#define RENDER_ATTR_ZBUFFER          0x00000002

// use 1/z buffering rasterization
#define RENDER_ATTR_INVZBUFFER          0x00000004

// use mipmapping
#define RENDER_ATTR_MIPMAP          0x00000010

// enable alpha blending and override
#define RENDER_ATTR_ALPHA          0x00000020

// enable bilinear filtering, but only supported for
// constant shaded/affine textures
#define RENDER_ATTR_BILERP          0x00000040
```

```
// use affine texturing for all polys
#define RENDER_ATTR_TEXTURE_PERSPECTIVE_AFFINE  0x00000100

// use perfect perspective texturing
#define RENDER_ATTR_TEXTURE_PERSPECTIVE_CORRECT 0x00000200

// use linear piecewise perspective texturing
#define RENDER_ATTR_TEXTURE_PERSPECTIVE_LINEAR  0x00000400

// use a hybrid of affine and linear piecewise based on distance
#define RENDER_ATTR_TEXTURE_PERSPECTIVE_HYBRID1 0x00000800

// not implemented yet
#define RENDER_ATTR_TEXTURE_PERSPECTIVE_HYBRID2 0x00001000
```

Next we have a single new type, which I refer to as a *rendering context*. Basically, it enables us to initialize it with the desired rendering options. Then a single function call using it as a parameter renders everything, rather than making calls to numerous different rendering functions, as we have been doing in the past. Here's the new structure:

```
// this is a new type to contain the "rendering context" RC, so
// we don't have to keep passing more and more variables to the
// rendering functions, we can fill this structure in with what we
// need and then pass it as a whole
typedef struct RENDERCONTEXTV1_TYP
{
int   attr;           // all the rendering attributes
RENDERLIST4DV2_PTR rend_list; // ptr to rendering list to render
UCHAR *video_buffer;      // ptr to video buffer to render to
int   lpitch;         // memory pitch in bytes of video buffer

UCHAR *zbuffer;        // ptr to z buffer or 1/z buffer
int   zpitch;         // memory pitch in bytes of z or 1/z buffer
int   alpha_override;     // alpha value to override ALL polys with

int   mip_dist;        // maximum distance to divide up into
               // mip levels
               // 0 - (NUM_ALPHA_LEVELS - 1)
int   texture_dist;      // the distance to enable affine texturing
               // when using hybrid perspective/affine mode

// future expansion
int   ival1, ival2;     // extra integers
```

```
float  fval1, fval2;      // extra floats
void  *vptr;          // extra pointer

} RENDERCONTEXTV1, *RENDERCONTEXTV1_PTR;
```

Most of the fields should ring a bell. There are a few new ones to support mip mapping and various optimized texturing techniques, but we will cover them as we broach each topic pertaining to them.

Now for the globals: There is only one, a lookup table to help us with alpha blending:

```
// this table contains each possible RGB value multiplied by some scalar
USHORT rgb_alpha_table[NUM_ALPHA_LEVELS][65536];
```

Lastly, I want to dump the prototypes so you can see the sheer number of them that we have to deal with, and to get an idea of what we are going to be doing in this chapter:

```
// PROTOTYPES ///////////////////////////////////////////////////////////////

// zbuffered versions
void Draw_Textured_TriangleZB2_16(POLYF4DV2_PTR face, // ptr to face
             UCHAR *_dest_buffer, // pointer to video buffer
             int mem_pitch,     // bytes per line, 320, 640 etc.
             UCHAR *zbuffer,     // pointer to z-buffer
             int zpitch);      // bytes per line of zbuffer

void Draw_Textured_Bilerp_TriangleZB_16(POLYF4DV2_PTR face, // ptr to face
         UCHAR *_dest_buffer, // pointer to video buffer
         int mem_pitch,     // bytes per line, 320, 640 etc.
         UCHAR *zbuffer,     // pointer to z-buffer
         int zpitch);      // bytes per line of zbuffer

void Draw_Textured_TriangleFSZB2_16(POLYF4DV2_PTR face, // ptr to face
          UCHAR *_dest_buffer, // pointer to video buffer
          int mem_pitch,     // bytes per line, 320, 640 etc.
          UCHAR *zbuffer,     // pointer to z-buffer
          int zpitch);      // bytes per line of zbuffer


void Draw_Textured_TriangleGSZB_16(POLYF4DV2_PTR face,  // ptr to face
          UCHAR *_dest_buffer, // pointer to video buffer
          int mem_pitch,     // bytes per line, 320, 640 etc.
          UCHAR *_zbuffer,    // pointer to z-buffer
          int zpitch);      // bytes per line of zbuffer
```

```
void Draw_Triangle_2DZB2_16(POLYF4DV2_PTR face, // ptr to face
          UCHAR *_dest_buffer, // pointer to video buffer
          int mem_pitch,    // bytes per line, 320, 640 etc.
          UCHAR *zbuffer,   // pointer to z-buffer
          int zpitch);     // bytes per line of zbuffer


void Draw_Gouraud_TriangleZB2_16(POLYF4DV2_PTR face,  // ptr to face
          UCHAR *_dest_buffer,// pointer to video buffer
          int mem_pitch,   // bytes per line, 320, 640 etc.
          UCHAR *zbuffer,   // pointer to z-buffer
          int zpitch);    // bytes per line of zbuffer


void Draw_RENDERLIST4DV2_SolidZB2_16(RENDERLIST4DV2_PTR rend_list,
        UCHAR *video_buffer, // pointer to video buffer
        int lpitch, // bytes per line, 320, 640 etc.
        UCHAR *zbuffer, // pointer to z-buffer
        int zpitch); // bytes per line of zbuffer



// 1/z versions

void Draw_Textured_TriangleINVZB_16(POLYF4DV2_PTR face, // ptr to face
          UCHAR *_dest_buffer, // pointer to video buffer
          int mem_pitch,    // bytes per line, 320, 640 etc.
          UCHAR *zbuffer,    // pointer to z-buffer
          int zpitch);     // bytes per line of zbuffer

void Draw_Textured_Bilerp_TriangleINVZB_16(POLYF4DV2_PTR face, // ptr to face
          UCHAR *_dest_buffer, // pointer to video buffer
          int mem_pitch,    // bytes per line, 320, 640 etc.
          UCHAR *zbuffer,    // pointer to z-buffer
          int zpitch);     // bytes per line of zbuffer


void Draw_Textured_TriangleFSINVZB_16(POLYF4DV2_PTR face, // ptr to face
          UCHAR *_dest_buffer, // pointer to video buffer
          int mem_pitch,    // bytes per line, 320, 640 etc.
          UCHAR *zbuffer,    // pointer to z-buffer
          int zpitch);     // bytes per line of zbuffer
```

```
void Draw_Textured_TriangleGSINVZB_16(POLYF4DV2_PTR face,  // ptr to face
          UCHAR *_dest_buffer, // pointer to video buffer
          int mem_pitch,      // bytes per line, 320, 640 etc.
          UCHAR *_zbuffer,    // pointer to z-buffer
          int zpitch);       // bytes per line of zbuffer

void Draw_Triangle_2DINVZB_16(POLYF4DV2_PTR face, // ptr to face
          UCHAR *_dest_buffer, // pointer to video buffer
          int mem_pitch,      // bytes per line, 320, 640 etc.
          UCHAR *zbuffer,     // pointer to z-buffer
          int zpitch);       // bytes per line of zbuffer


void Draw_Gouraud_TriangleINVZB_16(POLYF4DV2_PTR face,  // ptr to face
          UCHAR *_dest_buffer, // pointer to video buffer
          int mem_pitch,      // bytes per line, 320, 640 etc.
          UCHAR *zbuffer,    // pointer to z-buffer
          int zpitch);       // bytes per line of zbuffer


void Draw_Textured_Perspective_Triangle_INVZB_16(POLYF4DV2_PTR face,// face
          UCHAR *_dest_buffer, // pointer to video buffer
          int mem_pitch,      // bytes per line, 320, 640 etc.
          UCHAR *_zbuffer,    // pointer to z-buffer
          int zpitch);       // bytes per line of zbuffer


void Draw_Textured_Perspective_Triangle_FSINVZB_16(POLYF4DV2_PTR face,//face
           UCHAR *_dest_buffer,// pointer to video buffer
           int mem_pitch,    // bytes per line, 320, 640 etc.
           UCHAR *_zbuffer,  // pointer to z-buffer
           int zpitch);     // bytes per line of zbuffer

void Draw_Textured_PerspectiveLP_Triangle_FSINVZB_16(POLYF4DV2_PTR face,//face
           UCHAR *_dest_buffer, // pointer to video buffer
           int mem_pitch,     // bytes per line, 320, 640 etc.
           UCHAR *_zbuffer,    // pointer to z-buffer
           int zpitch);      // bytes per line of zbuffer


void Draw_Textured_PerspectiveLP_Triangle_INVZB_16(POLYF4DV2_PTR face, //face
           UCHAR *_dest_buffer, // pointer to video buffer
           int mem_pitch,     // bytes per line, 320, 640 etc.
           UCHAR *_zbuffer,    // pointer to z-buffer
           int zpitch);      // bytes per line of zbuffer
```

```
void Draw_RENDERLIST4DV2_SolidINVZB_16(RENDERLIST4DV2_PTR rend_list,
          UCHAR *video_buffer,
        int lpitch,
          UCHAR *zbuffer,
          int zpitch);

// z buffered and alpha
void Draw_Textured_TriangleZB_Alpha16(POLYF4DV2_PTR face, // ptr to face
          UCHAR *_dest_buffer, // pointer to video buffer
          int mem_pitch,    // bytes per line, 320, 640 etc.
          UCHAR *zbuffer,   // pointer to z-buffer
          int zpitch,      // bytes per line of zbuffer
          int alpha);

void Draw_Textured_TriangleFSZB_Alpha16(POLYF4DV2_PTR face, // ptr to face
          UCHAR *_dest_buffer, // pointer to video buffer
          int mem_pitch,    // bytes per line, 320, 640 etc.
          UCHAR *zbuffer,   // pointer to z-buffer
          int zpitch,      // bytes per line of zbuffer
          int alpha);

void Draw_Textured_TriangleGSZB_Alpha16(POLYF4DV2_PTR face,  // ptr to face
          UCHAR *_dest_buffer, // pointer to video buffer
          int mem_pitch,    // bytes per line, 320, 640 etc.
          UCHAR *_zbuffer,   // pointer to z-buffer
          int zpitch,      // bytes per line of zbuffer
          int alpha);


void Draw_Triangle_2DZB_Alpha16(POLYF4DV2_PTR face, // ptr to face
          UCHAR *_dest_buffer, // pointer to video buffer
          int mem_pitch,    // bytes per line, 320, 640 etc.
          UCHAR *zbuffer,   // pointer to z-buffer
          int zpitch,      // bytes per line of zbuffer
          int alpha);

void Draw_Gouraud_TriangleZB_Alpha16(POLYF4DV2_PTR face,  // ptr to face
          UCHAR *_dest_buffer, // pointer to video buffer
          int mem_pitch,    // bytes per line, 320, 640 etc.
          UCHAR *zbuffer,   // pointer to z-buffer
          int zpitch,      // bytes per line of zbuffer
          int alpha);

void Draw_RENDERLIST4DV2_SolidZB_Alpha16(RENDERLIST4DV2_PTR rend_list,
          UCHAR *video_buffer,
```

```
        int lpitch,
          UCHAR *zbuffer,
          int zpitch,
          int alpha_override);


// 1/z buffered and alpha
void Draw_Textured_TriangleINVZB_Alpha16(POLYF4DV2_PTR face, // ptr to facev
            UCHAR *_dest_buffer, // pointer to video buffer
            int mem_pitch,    // bytes per line, 320, 640 etc.
            UCHAR *zbuffer,   // pointer to z-buffer
            int zpitch,      // bytes per line of zbuffer
            int alpha);

void Draw_Textured_TriangleFSINVZB_Alpha16(POLYF4DV2_PTR face, // ptr to face
            UCHAR *_dest_buffer, // pointer to video buffer
            int mem_pitch,    // bytes per line, 320, 640 etc.
            UCHAR *zbuffer,   // pointer to z-buffer
            int zpitch,      // bytes per line of zbuffer
            int alpha);

void Draw_Textured_TriangleGSINVZB_Alpha16(POLYF4DV2_PTR face,  // ptr to face
            UCHAR *_dest_buffer, // pointer to video buffer
            int mem_pitch,    // bytes per line, 320, 640 etc.
            UCHAR *_zbuffer,   // pointer to z-buffer
            int zpitch,      // bytes per line of zbuffer
            int alpha);


void Draw_Triangle_2DINVZB_Alpha16(POLYF4DV2_PTR face, // ptr to face
            UCHAR *_dest_buffer, // pointer to video buffer
            int mem_pitch,    // bytes per line, 320, 640 etc.
            UCHAR *zbuffer,   // pointer to z-buffer
            int zpitch,      // bytes per line of zbuffer
            int alpha);

void Draw_Gouraud_TriangleINVZB_Alpha16(POLYF4DV2_PTR face,  // ptr to face
            UCHAR *_dest_buffer, // pointer to video buffer
            int mem_pitch,    // bytes per line, 320, 640 etc.
            UCHAR *zbuffer,   // pointer to z-buffer
            int zpitch,      // bytes per line of zbuffer
            int alpha);
```

```
void Draw_Textured_Perspective_Triangle_INVZB_Alpha16(POLYF4DV2_PTR face,
            UCHAR *_dest_buffer, // pointer to video buffer
            int mem_pitch,    // bytes per line, 320, 640 etc.
            UCHAR *_zbuffer,   // pointer to z-buffer
            int zpitch,     // bytes per line of zbuffer
            int alpha);


void Draw_Textured_PerspectiveLP_Triangle_INVZB_Alpha16(POLYF4DV2_PTR face,
            UCHAR *_dest_buffer, // pointer to video buffer
            int mem_pitch,    // bytes per line, 320, 640 etc.
            UCHAR *_zbuffer,   // pointer to z-buffer
            int zpitch,     // bytes per line of zbuffer
            int alpha);

void Draw_Textured_Perspective_Triangle_FSINVZB_Alpha16(POLYF4DV2_PTR face,
            UCHAR *_dest_buffer, // pointer to video buffer
            int mem_pitch,    // bytes per line, 320, 640 etc.
            UCHAR *_zbuffer,   // pointer to z-buffer
            int zpitch,     // bytes per line of zbuffer
            int alpha);

void Draw_Textured_PerspectiveLP_Triangle_FSINVZB_Alpha16(POLYF4DV2_PTR face,
            UCHAR *_dest_buffer, // pointer to video buffer
            int mem_pitch,    // bytes per line, 320, 640 etc.
            UCHAR *_zbuffer,   // pointer to z-buffer
            int zpitch,     // bytes per line of zbuffer
            int alpha);


void Draw_RENDERLIST4DV2_SolidINVZB_Alpha16(RENDERLIST4DV2_PTR rend_list,
            UCHAR *video_buffer,
          int lpitch,
            UCHAR *zbuffer,
            int zpitch,
            int alpha_override);


// non zbuffered versions
void Draw_Textured_Triangle2_16(POLYF4DV2_PTR face, // ptr to face
            UCHAR *_dest_buffer, // pointer to video buffer
            int mem_pitch);    // bytes per line, 320, 640 etc.
```

```
void Draw_Textured_Bilerp_Triangle_16(POLYF4DV2_PTR face, // ptr to face
          UCHAR *_dest_buffer, // pointer to video buffer
          int mem_pitch);     // bytes per line, 320, 640 etc.


void Draw_Textured_TriangleFS2_16(POLYF4DV2_PTR face, // ptr to face
          UCHAR *_dest_buffer, // pointer to video buffer
          int mem_pitch);    // bytes per line, 320, 640 etc.


void Draw_Triangle_2D3_16(POLYF4DV2_PTR face, // ptr to face
          UCHAR *_dest_buffer,// pointer to video buffer
          int mem_pitch);    // bytes per line, 320, 640 etc.


void Draw_Gouraud_Triangle2_16(POLYF4DV2_PTR face, // ptr to face
          UCHAR *_dest_buffer, // pointer to video buffer
          int mem_pitch);    // bytes per line, 320, 640 etc.



void Draw_Textured_TriangleGS_16(POLYF4DV2_PTR face, // ptr to face
          UCHAR *_dest_buffer, // pointer to video buffer
          int mem_pitch);    // bytes per line, 320, 640 etc.

void Draw_Textured_Perspective_Triangle_16(POLYF4DV2_PTR face, // ptr to face
          UCHAR *_dest_buffer, // pointer to video buffer
          int mem_pitch);    // bytes per line, 320, 640 etc.


void Draw_Textured_PerspectiveLP_Triangle_16(POLYF4DV2_PTR face,
          UCHAR *_dest_buffer, // pointer to video buffer
          int mem_pitch);    // bytes per line, 320, 640 etc.

void Draw_Textured_Perspective_Triangle_FS_16(POLYF4DV2_PTR face,
          UCHAR *_dest_buffer, // pointer to video buffer
          int mem_pitch);    // bytes per line, 320, 640 etc.

void Draw_Textured_PerspectiveLP_Triangle_FS_16(POLYF4DV2_PTR face,
          UCHAR *_dest_buffer, // pointer to video buffer
          int mem_pitch);    // bytes per line, 320, 640 etc.
```

```
void Draw_RENDERLIST4DV2_Solid2_16(RENDERLIST4DV2_PTR rend_list,
            UCHAR *video_buffer, // pointer to video buffer
        int lpitch); // bytes per line, 320, 640 etc.


// alpha versions, non-z buffered
int RGB_Alpha_Table_Builder(int num_alpha_levels,  // num levels to create
     USHORT rgb_alpha_table[NUM_ALPHA_LEVELS][65536]); // lookup table


void Draw_Triangle_2D_Alpha16(POLYF4DV2_PTR face, // ptr to face
           UCHAR *_dest_buffer, // pointer to video buffer
           int mem_pitch,    // bytes per line, 320, 640 etc.
           int alpha);

void Draw_Textured_Triangle_Alpha16(POLYF4DV2_PTR face, // ptr to face
           UCHAR *_dest_buffer, // pointer to video buffer
           int mem_pitch,    // bytes per line, 320, 640 etc.
           int alpha);

void Draw_Textured_TriangleFS_Alpha16(POLYF4DV2_PTR face, // ptr to face
           UCHAR *_dest_buffer, // pointer to video buffer
           int mem_pitch,    // bytes per line, 320, 640 etc.
           int alpha);


void Draw_Textured_TriangleGS_Alpha16(POLYF4DV2_PTR face, // ptr to face
           UCHAR *_dest_buffer, // pointer to video buffer
           int mem_pitch,    // bytes per line, 320, 640 etc.
           int alpha);


void Draw_Gouraud_Triangle_Alpha16(POLYF4DV2_PTR face,  // ptr to face
           UCHAR *_dest_buffer, // pointer to video buffer
           int mem_pitch,    // bytes per line, 320, 640 etc.
           int alpha);


void Draw_RENDERLIST4DV2_Solid_Alpha16(RENDERLIST4DV2_PTR rend_list,
           UCHAR *video_buffer, // pointer to video buffer
          int lpitch, // bytes per line, 320, 640 etc.
           int alpha_override); // alpha value
```

```
// new rendering function that works for everything!!! yaaa!!!!!
void Draw_RENDERLISTV2_RENDERCONTEXTV1_16(RENDERCONTEXTV1_PTR rc);

// new model functions
int Load_OBJECT4DV2_COB2(OBJECT4DV2_PTR obj, // pointer to object
             char *filename,    // filename of Caligari COB file
             VECTOR4D_PTR scale, // initial scaling factors
             VECTOR4D_PTR pos,  // initial position
             VECTOR4D_PTR rot,  // initial rotations
             int vertex_flags,  // flags to re-order vertices
                        // and perform transforms
             int mipmap=0);    // mipmap enable flag
                        // 0 means no mipmap, 1 means
                        // generate mip map

int Generate_Terrain2_OBJECT4DV2(OBJECT4DV2_PTR obj,  // pointer to object
    float twidth,      // width in world coords on x-axis
    float theight,      // height (length) in world coords on z-axis
    float vscale,      // vertical scale of terrain
    char *height_map_file, // filename of height bitmap encoded in 256 colors
    char *texture_map_file,// filename of texture map
    int rgbcolor,      // color of terrain if no texture
    VECTOR4D_PTR pos,    // initial position
    VECTOR4D_PTR rot,    // initial rotations
    int poly_attr,      // the shading attributes we would like
    float sea_level=-1,  // height of sea level
    int alpha=-1);      // alpha level for sea polygons

// new directdraw functions
int DDraw_Init2(int width, int height, int bpp,
        int windowed, int backbuffer_enable = 1);
int DDraw_Flip2(void);

// mip mapping functions
int Generate_Mipmaps(BITMAP_IMAGE_PTR source,
          BITMAP_IMAGE_PTR *mipmaps, float gamma = 1.01);

int Delete_Mipmaps(BITMAP_IMAGE_PTR *mipmaps, int leave_level_0);
```

Welcome to my nightmare! That's a ton of prototypes, huh? Imagine writing all the code to go along with them.

Building a New Rasterizer Base

Alright, let's start from the beginning. The first thing we need to rewrite are the core rasterizers. We have been using a set of rasterizers that have a few problems. The major problem is one that you may or may not have noticed. When we wrote the rendering function to call the triangle rasterizer functions, we always truncated the vertices to integers, rather than leaving them as floating-point values to be converted more accurately in the rasterizers themselves into fixed-point. Thus, we lost precision. To refresh your memory, here's what a typical rendering function did to the vertices before passing them into the triangle function:

```
// set the vertices
face.tvlist[0].x = (int)rend_list->poly_ptrs[poly]->tvlist[0].x;
face.tvlist[0].y = (int)rend_list->poly_ptrs[poly]->tvlist[0].y;
```

Truncation was needed primarily because the original fixed point rasterizers that we were using for texturing liked to start with integer coordinates and then work from there. However, this forced us to lose precision with the preceding truncation. This has been fixed—now all the triangle functions can directly take floating-point values, and the functions will round and convert them to fixed-point.

The Final Decision to Go with Fixed-Point

Next I have decided to work with fixed-point numbers. The bottom line is that floating-point is faster for multiplication and division in most cases. The problem is that rasterizing is inherently a "bit twiddling" operation, and we are playing with encoded RGB values, texture coordinates, and memory. Floating-point is horrible at this, and the conversion to int and from int in the rasterization loop's outer and inner line rasterizing code will kill you. Conversion from float to integer is around 70 cycles at worst—totally unacceptable. Additionally, working with 32-bit integers allows us all kinds of optimizations that aren't possible with floating-point formats.

The bottom line is that we will use floating-point for everything but rasterization. This is the best of both worlds: As long as we maintain floating-point calculations, which we do for transformations, lighting, and so on, floating-point is faster and more accurate, but the second we hit the rasterization code, it kills us. I experimented with floating-point—I wrote floating-point, fixed-point, and hybrid versions of everything, and hands down fixed-point 32-bit was much faster for rasterizing each time.

However, the old format of 16.16 fixed-point had to be augmented with other formats like 4.28 and 10.22 to be better suited for high decimal accuracy calculations. However, I will cover that when we get to 1/z-buffering and perspective-correct texturing, where the new formats are needed.

Summing up, we are going to use fixed-point math from here on out for all rasterizers—period! Also, I cleaned up the base rasterizers to follow our upper-left fill convention better. They are sub-pixel accurate now, so the texturing is very clean, as well as the rendering of solids. There are no cracks or pixels being overdrawn on connected meshes because of incorrect fill conventions. With that in mind, let's look at the new base rasterizers that build on these new features.

The New Non-z-Buffered Rasterizers

First let's take a look at the basic non-z-buffered rasterizers. Of course, there are new rasterizers for perspective-correct, alpha blending, and mip mapping, but we are only going to look at the rewrites of the ones we already had at this point so we don't get ahead of ourselves. Here they are one at a time, with explanations:

Function:

```
void Draw_Triangle_2D3_16(POLYF4DV2_PTR face, // ptr to face
        UCHAR *_dest_buffer,// pointer to video buffer
        int mem_pitch);   // bytes per line, 320, 640 etc.
```

Description: `Draw_Triangle_2D3_16()` simply draws a constant or flat-shaded polygon to the screen. There is no z-buffering, of course, so the polygon will be drawn without any consideration for its rendering order. It's up to the caller to presort the polygons. As you see, the function just has a funky name, but that's about the only difference from the previous version 2.0. However, the cool part is that the function is faster, cleaner, and is sub-pixel accurate, with the upper-left hand fill convention maintained. Additionally, the previous version of this function used the top/bottom triangle convention to split all triangles into two cases. This has been unified in this version, so it's just like all the other rasterizers now—one triangle, one leader.

Function:

```
void Draw_Gouraud_Triangle2_16(POLYF4DV2_PTR face, // ptr to face
          UCHAR *_dest_buffer, // pointer to video buffer
          int mem_pitch);   // bytes per line, 320, 640 etc.
```

Description: `void Draw_Gouraud_Triangle2_16()` is a slightly improved version of the previous version of the function, but with sub-pixel accuracy, and more strictly adheres to the upper-left hand fill convention.

Function:

```
void Draw_Textured_Triangle2_16(POLYF4DV2_PTR face, // ptr to face
          UCHAR *_dest_buffer, // pointer to video buffer
          int mem_pitch);    // bytes per line, 320, 640 etc.
```

Description: `Draw_Textured_Triangle2_16()` is a slightly improved version of the previous affine texture mapping function, but with sub-pixel accuracy, and more strictly adheres to the upper left hand fill convention. This improves the texturing and makes it look more solid.

NOTE

To tell you the truth, the affine texturing is so nice and fast that I don't want to use perspective <BG>.

Function:

```
void Draw_Textured_TriangleFS2_16(POLYF4DV2_PTR face, // ptr to face
          UCHAR *_dest_buffer, // pointer to video buffer
          int mem_pitch);    // bytes per line, 320, 640 etc.
```

Description: `Draw_Textured_TriangleFS2_16()` is a slightly improved version of the previous affine texture mapping function that supports flat shading, but with sub-pixel accuracy, and the upper left-hand fill convention is more strictly adhered to. This improves the texturing and makes it look more solid.

Function:

```
void Draw_RENDERLIST4DV2_Solid2_16(RENDERLIST4DV2_PTR rend_list, // render list
           UCHAR *video_buffer, // pointer to video buffer
             int lpitch); // bytes per line, 320, 640, etc.
```

Description: `Draw_RENDERLIST4DV2_Solid2_16()` is the entry point to call the previously listed functions—that is, no z-buffering. The internals of the function are identical to the previous version; however, the integer truncation is removed. Here is the listing of the function for reference:

```
void Draw_RENDERLIST4DV2_Solid2_16(RENDERLIST4DV2_PTR rend_list,
                 UCHAR *video_buffer,
                  int lpitch)
{
// 16-bit version
// this function "executes" the render list or in other words
// draws all the faces in the list, the function will call the
// proper rasterizer based on the lighting model of the polygons

POLYF4DV2 face; // temp face used to render polygon

// at this point, all we have is a list of polygons and it's time
// to draw them
for (int poly=0; poly < rend_list->num_polys; poly++)
  {
  // render this polygon if and only if it's not clipped, not culled,
  // active, and visible, note however the concecpt of "backface" is
  // irrelevant in a wire frame engine though
  if (!(rend_list->poly_ptrs[poly]->state & POLY4DV2_STATE_ACTIVE) ||
     (rend_list->poly_ptrs[poly]->state & POLY4DV2_STATE_CLIPPED ) ||
```

```
     (rend_list->poly_ptrs[poly]->state & POLY4DV2_STATE_BACKFACE) )
    continue; // move onto next poly

 // need to test for textured first, since a textured poly can either
 // be emissive, or flat shaded, hence we need to call different
 // rasterizers
 if (rend_list->poly_ptrs[poly]->attr & POLY4DV2_ATTR_SHADE_MODE_TEXTURE)
    {

    // set the vertices
    face.tvlist[0].x = (float)rend_list->poly_ptrs[poly]->tvlist[0].x;
    face.tvlist[0].y = (float)rend_list->poly_ptrs[poly]->tvlist[0].y;
    face.tvlist[0].z = (float)rend_list->poly_ptrs[poly]->tvlist[0].z;
    face.tvlist[0].u0 = (float)rend_list->poly_ptrs[poly]->tvlist[0].u0;
    face.tvlist[0].v0 = (float)rend_list->poly_ptrs[poly]->tvlist[0].v0;

    face.tvlist[1].x = (float)rend_list->poly_ptrs[poly]->tvlist[1].x;
    face.tvlist[1].y = (float)rend_list->poly_ptrs[poly]->tvlist[1].y;
    face.tvlist[1].z = (float)rend_list->poly_ptrs[poly]->tvlist[1].z;
    face.tvlist[1].u0 = (float)rend_list->poly_ptrs[poly]->tvlist[1].u0;
    face.tvlist[1].v0 = (float)rend_list->poly_ptrs[poly]->tvlist[1].v0;

    face.tvlist[2].x = (float)rend_list->poly_ptrs[poly]->tvlist[2].x;
    face.tvlist[2].y = (float)rend_list->poly_ptrs[poly]->tvlist[2].y;
    face.tvlist[2].z = (float)rend_list->poly_ptrs[poly]->tvlist[2].z;
    face.tvlist[2].u0 = (float)rend_list->poly_ptrs[poly]->tvlist[2].u0;
    face.tvlist[2].v0 = (float)rend_list->poly_ptrs[poly]->tvlist[2].v0;


    // assign the texture
    face.texture = rend_list->poly_ptrs[poly]->texture;

    // is this a plain emissive texture?
    if (rend_list->poly_ptrs[poly]->attr &
      POLY4DV2_ATTR_SHADE_MODE_CONSTANT)
     {
     // draw the textured triangle as emissive
     Draw_Textured_Triangle2_16(&face, video_buffer, lpitch);
     //Draw_Textured_Perspective_Triangle_16(&face, video_buffer, lpitch);
     } // end if
    else
    if (rend_list->poly_ptrs[poly]->attr & POLY4DV2_ATTR_SHADE_MODE_FLAT)
     {
     // draw as flat shaded
     face.lit_color[0] = rend_list->poly_ptrs[poly]->lit_color[0];
```

```
     Draw_Textured_TriangleFS2_16(&face, video_buffer, lpitch);
//Draw_Textured_Perspective_Triangle_FS_16(&face, video_buffer, lpitch);
     } // end else
    else
     {
     // must be gouraud POLY4DV2_ATTR_SHADE_MODE_GOURAUD
     face.lit_color[0] = rend_list->poly_ptrs[poly]->lit_color[0];
     face.lit_color[1] = rend_list->poly_ptrs[poly]->lit_color[1];
     face.lit_color[2] = rend_list->poly_ptrs[poly]->lit_color[2];
     Draw_Textured_TriangleGS_16(&face, video_buffer, lpitch);
     } // end else

    } // end if
  else
  if ((rend_list->poly_ptrs[poly]->attr & POLY4DV2_ATTR_SHADE_MODE_FLAT) ||
   (rend_list->poly_ptrs[poly]->attr & POLY4DV2_ATTR_SHADE_MODE_CONSTANT))
    {
    // draw as constant shaded
    face.lit_color[0] = rend_list->poly_ptrs[poly]->lit_color[0];

    // set the vertices
    face.tvlist[0].x = (float)rend_list->poly_ptrs[poly]->tvlist[0].x;
    face.tvlist[0].y = (float)rend_list->poly_ptrs[poly]->tvlist[0].y;
    face.tvlist[0].z = (float)rend_list->poly_ptrs[poly]->tvlist[0].z;

    face.tvlist[1].x = (float)rend_list->poly_ptrs[poly]->tvlist[1].x;
    face.tvlist[1].y = (float)rend_list->poly_ptrs[poly]->tvlist[1].y;
    face.tvlist[1].z = (float)rend_list->poly_ptrs[poly]->tvlist[1].z;

    face.tvlist[2].x = (float)rend_list->poly_ptrs[poly]->tvlist[2].x;
    face.tvlist[2].y = (float)rend_list->poly_ptrs[poly]->tvlist[2].y;
    face.tvlist[2].z = (float)rend_list->poly_ptrs[poly]->tvlist[2].z;

    // draw the triangle with basic flat rasterizer
    Draw_Triangle_2D3_16(&face, video_buffer, lpitch);

    } // end if
  else
  if (rend_list->poly_ptrs[poly]->attr & POLY4DV2_ATTR_SHADE_MODE_GOURAUD)
    {
    // set the vertices
    face.tvlist[0].x = (float)rend_list->poly_ptrs[poly]->tvlist[0].x;
    face.tvlist[0].y = (float)rend_list->poly_ptrs[poly]->tvlist[0].y;
```

```
    face.tvlist[0].z = (float)rend_list->poly_ptrs[poly]->tvlist[0].z;
    face.lit_color[0] = rend_list->poly_ptrs[poly]->lit_color[0];

    face.tvlist[1].x = (float)rend_list->poly_ptrs[poly]->tvlist[1].x;
    face.tvlist[1].y = (float)rend_list->poly_ptrs[poly]->tvlist[1].y;
    face.tvlist[1].z = (float)rend_list->poly_ptrs[poly]->tvlist[1].z;
    face.lit_color[1] = rend_list->poly_ptrs[poly]->lit_color[1];

    face.tvlist[2].x = (float)rend_list->poly_ptrs[poly]->tvlist[2].x;
    face.tvlist[2].y = (float)rend_list->poly_ptrs[poly]->tvlist[2].y;
    face.tvlist[2].z = (float)rend_list->poly_ptrs[poly]->tvlist[2].z;
    face.lit_color[2] = rend_list->poly_ptrs[poly]->lit_color[2];

    // draw the gouraud shaded triangle
    Draw_Gouraud_Triangle2_16(&face, video_buffer, lpitch);

    } // end if gouraud

  } // end for poly

} // end Draw_RENDERLIST4DV2_Solid2_16
```

Notice all the `float` casts now—the vertices are sent as is, without any loss of precision. I am so happy about this! Now, let's move on to the new z-buffered base rasterizers, omitting anything with new technology, like alpha blending, for now.

The New Z-Buffered Rasterizers

The following lists the new base functions for z-buffering. They are not exhaustive, and thus do not include alpha blending, because we haven't covered that yet. These are just replacements for the previous functions you have been using.

Function:

```
void Draw_Triangle_2DZB2_16(POLYF4DV2_PTR face, // ptr to face
        UCHAR *_dest_buffer, // pointer to video buffer
        int mem_pitch,    // bytes per line, 320, 640 etc.
        UCHAR *zbuffer,   // pointer to z-buffer
        int zpitch);     // bytes per line of zbuffer
```

Description: `Draw_Triangle_2DZB2_16()` is the most basic of the new Z-buffer functions, and simply draws a z-buffered triangle to the screen and updates the Z-buffer while doing so. The function is sub-pixel accurate, and follows the upper left-hand fill convention more strictly. Nothing has changed with the parameters, just the name of the function.

Function:

```
void Draw_Textured_TriangleZB2_16(POLYF4DV2_PTR face, // ptr to face
          UCHAR *_dest_buffer, // pointer to video buffer
          int mem_pitch,    // bytes per line, 320, 640 etc.
          UCHAR *zbuffer,    // pointer to z-buffer
          int zpitch);     // bytes per line of zbuffer
```

Description: `Draw_Textured_TriangleZB2_16()` is the new z-buffered function that draws a constant-shaded affine textured triangle. However, with new sub-pixel accuracy as well as the top-left fill convention, this function works much better. As usual, the calling convention is the same.

Function:

```
void Draw_Textured_TriangleFSZB2_16(POLYF4DV2_PTR face, // ptr to face
          UCHAR *_dest_buffer, // pointer to video buffer
          int mem_pitch,    // bytes per line, 320, 640 etc.
          UCHAR *zbuffer,    // pointer to z-buffer
          int zpitch);     // bytes per line of zbuffer
```

Description: `Draw_Textured_TriangleFSZB2_16()` is the new z-buffered function that draws a flat-shaded affine textured triangle. However, with new sub-pixel accuracy as well as the top-left fill convention, this function works much better. As usual, the calling convention is the same.

Function:

```
void Draw_Gouraud_TriangleZB2_16(POLYF4DV2_PTR face,  // ptr to face
          UCHAR *_dest_buffer,// pointer to video buffer
          int mem_pitch,   // bytes per line, 320, 640 etc.
          UCHAR *zbuffer,   // pointer to z-buffer
          int zpitch);    // bytes per line of zbuffer
```

Description: `Draw_Gouraud_TriangleZB2_16()` is the new z-buffered function that draws a Gouraud-shaded triangle. However, with new sub-pixel accuracy as well as the top-left fill convention, this function works much better. The calling convention is the same.

Function:

```
void Draw_RENDERLIST4DV2_SolidZB2_16(RENDERLIST4DV2_PTR rend_list,
              UCHAR *video_buffer,
           int lpitch,
              UCHAR *zbuffer,
              int zpitch);
```

Description: `Draw_RENDERLIST4DV2_SolidZB2_16()` is the entry point to call the previously listed functions—that is, the function with z-buffering. The internals of the function are identical to the previous version; however, the integer truncation is removed.

Alright, that's about where we were in the last chapter. We could draw solid polygons that are constant-, flat-, or Gouraud-shaded, along with affine textured polygons that are constant- or flat-shaded. The preceding functions do the same thing more or less, but just cleaner, more accurately, and with fewer errors. No point in a demo—it would look the same. Let's move on to something where we can "see" the difference!

Gouraud-Shaded Texturing

The first edition to our rasterization library is support for Gouraud-shaded texturing. Although I originally thought it would be too slow in software, after experimenting with it, I found that it was more than fast enough. Our little fixed-point rasterizer is really fast, so although the inner loop is more complex to support Gouraud shading because I had to add more interpolants, it showed very little slowdown. In any event, let's talk about what's needed to support Gouraud-shaded texturing. In Figure 12.1 we see the two setups for constant-shaded affine texturing and single-colored Gouraud shading. The trick is to merge them.

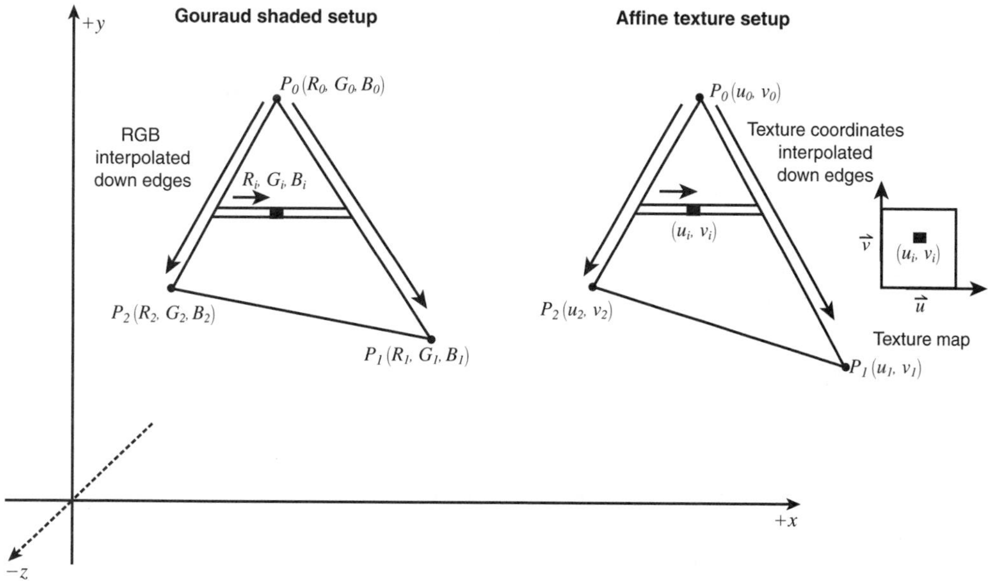

FIGURE 12.1 Merging the setups for constant-shaded texturing and Gouraud-shaded polygons.

My plan of attack is simple: We start with the Gouraud-shading function that draws a single color polygon, add the support to interpolate the u and v coordinates for texturing, and then merge the two using the Gouraud shading function as the base (because it's the larger of the two, and we have added less to it. Let's take a look at what needs to be done, starting with the Gouraud-shading code. Here's an excerpt of the inner loop that draws the polygon (non-z-buffered version):

```
// point screen ptr to starting line
screen_ptr = dest_buffer + (ystart * mem_pitch);

for (yi = ystart; yi < yend; yi++)
   {
   // compute span endpoints
   xstart = ((xl + FIXP16_ROUND_UP) >> FIXP16_SHIFT);
   xend  = ((xr + FIXP16_ROUND_UP) >> FIXP16_SHIFT);

   // compute starting points for u,v,w interpolants
   ui = ul + FIXP16_ROUND_UP;
   vi = vl + FIXP16_ROUND_UP;
   wi = wl + FIXP16_ROUND_UP;

   // compute u,v,w interpolants
   if ((dx = (xend - xstart))>0)
  {
  du = (ur - ul)/dx;
  dv = (vr - vl)/dx;
  dw = (wr - wl)/dx;
  } // end if
  else
  {
  du = (ur - ul);
  dv = (vr - vl);
  dw = (wr - wl);
  } // end else

  // draw span
  for (xi=xstart; xi < xend; xi++)
  {
  // write textel 5.6.5
    screen_ptr[xi] = ((ui >> (FIXP16_SHIFT+3)) << 11) +
            ((vi >> (FIXP16_SHIFT+2)) << 5) +
            (wi >> (FIXP16_SHIFT+3));

  // interpolate u,v,w
  ui+=du;
  vi+=dv;
  wi+=dw;
  } // end for xi

    // interpolate u,v,w,x along right and left edges
  xl+=dxdyl;
```

```
  ul+=dudyl;
  vl+=dvdyl;
  wl+=dwdyl;

  xr+=dxdyr;
  ur+=dudyr;
  vr+=dvdyr;
  wr+=dwdyr;

  // advance screen ptr
  screen_ptr+=mem_pitch;
  } // end for y
```


I have bolded the innermost loop that draws the single span, which is based on the interpolation of red, green, and blue in 16.16 fixed-point format, stored in u, v, and w respectively. This little code snippet builds the RGB 16-bit word up in 5.6.5 format from the fixed-point values and writes it to the screen:

```
screen_ptr[xi] = ((ui >> (FIXP16_SHIFT+3)) << 11) +
         ((vi >> (FIXP16_SHIFT+2)) << 5) +
         (wi >> (FIXP16_SHIFT+3));
```

Other than that, there's nothing else to the Gouraud shader. Now let's look at the affine texture mapper, and see what it's interpolating:

```
// point screen ptr to starting line
screen_ptr = dest_buffer + (ystart * mem_pitch);

for (yi = ystart; yi < yend; yi++)
  {
  // compute span endpoints
  xstart = ((xl + FIXP16_ROUND_UP) >> FIXP16_SHIFT);
  xend  = ((xr + FIXP16_ROUND_UP) >> FIXP16_SHIFT);

  // compute starting points for u,v interpolants
  ui = ul + FIXP16_ROUND_UP;
  vi = vl + FIXP16_ROUND_UP;

  // compute u,v interpolants
  if ((dx = (xend - xstart))>0)
    {
  du = (ur - ul)/dx;
  dv = (vr - vl)/dx;
  } // end if
```

```
else
  {
  du = (ur - ul);
  dv = (vr - vl);
} // end else

// draw span
for (xi=xstart; xi < xend; xi++)
{
// write textel
  screen_ptr[xi] = textmap[(ui >> FIXP16_SHIFT) +
              ((vi >> FIXP16_SHIFT) << texture_shift2)];

// interpolate u,v
ui+=du;
vi+=dv;
} // end for xi

// interpolate u,v,x along right and left edges
xl+=dxdyl;
ul+=dudyl;
vl+=dvdyl;

xr+=dxdyr;
ur+=dudyr;
vr+=dvdyr;

// advance screen ptr
screen_ptr+=mem_pitch;
} // end for y
```

Again, the actual code to write the pixel is rather trivial. `ui` and `vi` are fixed-point texture coordinates that are converted from 16.16 fixed-point format back into integers and then used to access the texture map. The textel (texture pixel) is then written to memory, and that's it. Therefore, merging these two subprograms shouldn't be that hard. The thing we have to remember is that we are Gouraud-shading the texture, but as we did with the flat-shaded version of the texture mapper, we assumed that the color *under* the texture was white. Based on that, we performed the lighting calculations with the white base color and then used the results of that as the color to modulate the texture color. We are going to do the same thing here. Figure 12.2 illustrates the flow of data in this process.

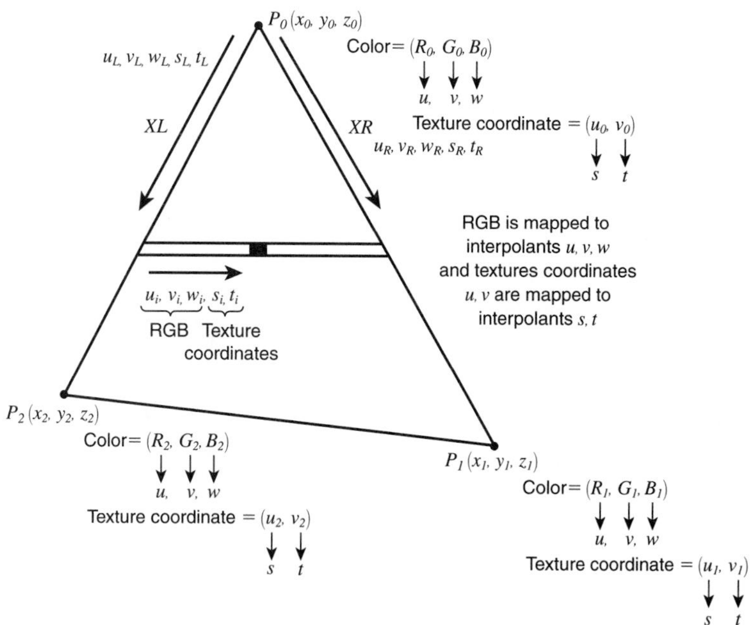

FIGURE 12.2 The interpolation flow of the Gouraud texture mapper.

Basically, the Gouraud shading and texture mapping run side by side simultaneously. The Gouraud shader interpolates r, g, and b (using the interpolants u, v, and w), whereas the texture mapper interpolates u and v (using the interpolants s and t). Then at the last minute the texture access and color modulation step occurs. Review the code excerpt from the completed Gouraud texture mapper and the following:

```
// point screen ptr to starting line
screen_ptr = dest_buffer + (ystart * mem_pitch);

for (yi = ystart; yi < yend; yi++)
  {
  // compute span endpoints
  xstart = ((xl + FIXP16_ROUND_UP) >> FIXP16_SHIFT);
  xend  = ((xr + FIXP16_ROUND_UP) >> FIXP16_SHIFT);

  // compute starting points for u,v,w,s,t interpolants
  ui = ul + FIXP16_ROUND_UP;
  vi = vl + FIXP16_ROUND_UP;
  wi = wl + FIXP16_ROUND_UP;

  si = sl + FIXP16_ROUND_UP;
  ti = tl + FIXP16_ROUND_UP;
```

```
// compute u,v interpolants
if ((dx = (xend - xstart))>0)
{
du = (ur - ul)/dx;
dv = (vr - vl)/dx;
dw = (wr - wl)/dx;

ds = (sr - sl)/dx;
dt = (tr - tl)/dx;
} // end if
else
{
du = (ur - ul);
dv = (vr - vl);
dw = (wr - wl);

ds = (sr - sl);
dt = (tr - tl);

} // end else

// draw span
for (xi=xstart; xi < xend; xi++)
{
  // get textel first
  textel = textmap[(si >> FIXP16_SHIFT) +
           ((ti >> FIXP16_SHIFT) << texture_shift2)];

  // extract rgb components
  r_textel = ((textel >> 11)    );
  g_textel = ((textel >> 5) & 0x3f);
  b_textel =  (textel    & 0x1f);

  // modulate textel with gouraud shading
  r_textel*=ui;
  g_textel*=vi;
  b_textel*=wi;

  // finally write pixel, note that we did the math
  // such that the results are r*32, g*64, b*32
  // hence we need to divide the results by 32,64,32 respectively,
  // BUT since we need to shift
  // the results to fit into the destination 5.6.5 word,
  // we can take advantage of the shifts
  // and they all cancel out for the most part,
```

12

```
        // but we will need logical anding, we will do
        // it later when we optimize more...
        screen_ptr[xi] = ((b_textel >> (FIXP16_SHIFT+8)) +
                ((g_textel >> (FIXP16_SHIFT+8)) << 5) +
                ((r_textel >> (FIXP16_SHIFT+8)) << 11));

      // interpolate u,v
      ui+=du;
      vi+=dv;
      wi+=dw;

      si+=ds;
      ti+=dt;

      } // end for xi

      // interpolate u,v,w,x along right and left edge
      xl+=dxdyl;
      ul+=dudyl;
      vl+=dvdyl;
      wl+=dwdyl;

      sl+=dsdyl;
      tl+=dtdyl;


      xr+=dxdyr;
      ur+=dudyr;
      vr+=dvdyr;
      wr+=dwdyr;

      sr+=dsdyr;
      tr+=dtdyr;

      // advance screen ptr
      screen_ptr+=mem_pitch;

      } // end for y
```

I have highlighted the inner loop as usual. The first step is to extract the textel we want to Gouraud shade. This is accomplished with this code:

```
r_textel = ((textel >> 11)     );
g_textel = ((textel >> 5) & 0x3f);
b_textel =  (textel     & 0x1f);
```

At this point, `r_textel`, `g_textel`, and `b_texel` hold the RGB value of the textel in 5.6.5 format. We need to multiply these values by the red, green, and blue Gouraud interpolants that have been interpolating the "white" ghost polygon under the texture. Here's the code that does this:

```
r_textel*=ui;
g_textel*=vi;
b_textel*=wi;
```

Now, let's stop for a moment here to see what is happening with the fixed-point math. `r_textel`, `g_texel`, and `b_textel` are *not* in fixed-point anymore—they are integers (0..31), (0..63), and (0..31), respectively. However, `ui`, `vi`, `wi`, *are* fixed-point, so multiplying a fixed-point number by a normal integer results in a fixed-point number. Therefore, `r_textel`, `g_textel`, and `b_textel` now have the modulated r,g,b Gouraud-shaded texture. We just need to extract the correct data out of each because they are fixed-point and scaled, shift them into place, and write the final pixel. The following code performs the bit manipulations to achieve this while at the same time formatting the final r, g, and b values into 5.6.5 format to write to the screen:

```
screen_ptr[xi] = ((b_textel >> (FIXP16_SHIFT+8)) +
        ((g_textel >> (FIXP16_SHIFT+8)) << 5) +
        ((r_textel >> (FIXP16_SHIFT+8)) << 11));
```

NOTE

For example, adding fixed-point 10 to fixed-point 10 equals fixed-point 20. That's the same as multiplying fixed-point 10 by 2. Let's see why. Using 16.16 format, fixed-point 10 = (10 * 65536). Therefore, fixed-point 10 added to fixed-point 10 equals

```
(10*65536) + (10*65536) = (20*65536) = (2*10*65536) = 2*(10*65536)
```

So, we can bring integral factors in and out of the fixed-point numbers, and they always remain fixed-point.

Amazing, huh? That's an entire Gouraud-shaded, texture mapped rasterization with three multiplications, a few adds/shifts, and it's *very* fast. This is why we want to stick to fixed-point math—floating-point would kill us in the conversions here.

Now, if you're like me, you're probably trying to think of ways to speed this up. There are many ways, of course, but algorithmically the code is nearly optimal, meaning it's doing nearly the minimum amount of work needed to get the job done. There are a couple of bit-scaling manipulations that could be done, but for the most part, there's no way to do less and get the same results.

Using lookup tables might help, but again, they cause caching problems, and I am not sure that there's much we can use them for. However, the most obvious table to create is something that precomputes all possible products of the textel with the RGB value of the

Gouraud interpolants. That would be a very big table, because we would need to precompute every possible product of two RGB values in 5.6.5 format, which is 65536 * 65536 = 2^{32} = 4 billion, roughly. Way too big! So, another option is to used reduced space computation, maybe scale each down to 12-bit or something, but then we would have $2^{12} * 2^{12} = 2^{24}$ = 16.7 million, roughly. Still too large, and we have lost a lot of color space. I'm not saying it's not possible to use lookup tables, but it's probably not wise. The key to making the preceding code faster is in rearranging a little and other subtle changes—the structure is pretty good as is.

Moving on, here's the actual function that contains the Gouraud-shading texture mapper without z-buffering:

```
void Draw_Textured_TriangleGS_16(POLYF4DV2_PTR face,  // ptr to face
          UCHAR *_dest_buffer, // pointer to video buffer
          int mem_pitch)    // bytes per line, 320, 640 etc.
```

You would call the function as usual with the flat-shaded version, but of course, because it's Gouraud shaded as well as texture mapped, you must set up both the u,v texture coordinates as well as the vertex colors, which must be stored in `lit_colors[0..2]`—remember the vertex color array? Additionally, here is the Z-buffer version of the function:

```
void Draw_Textured_TriangleGSZB_16(POLYF4DV2_PTR face,  // ptr to face
            UCHAR *_dest_buffer, // pointer to video buffer
            int mem_pitch,    // bytes per line, 320, 640 etc.
            UCHAR *_zbuffer,    // pointer to z-buffer
            int zpitch);     // bytes per line of zbuffer
```

Once again, the function needs the transport face to have texture coordinates as well as vertex lighting set, and finally the Z-buffer and Z-buffer pitch must be sent. For example, here's an excerpt from one of the rendering functions setting up to call the Gouraud texturing function:

```
// set up vertex list and texture coordinates
face.tvlist[0].x = (float)rend_list->poly_ptrs[poly]->tvlist[0].x;
face.tvlist[0].y = (float)rend_list->poly_ptrs[poly]->tvlist[0].y;
face.tvlist[0].z = (float)rend_list->poly_ptrs[poly]->tvlist[0].z;
face.tvlist[0].u0 = (float)rend_list->poly_ptrs[poly]->tvlist[0].u0;
face.tvlist[0].v0 = (float)rend_list->poly_ptrs[poly]->tvlist[0].v0;

face.tvlist[1].x = (float)rend_list->poly_ptrs[poly]->tvlist[1].x;
face.tvlist[1].y = (float)rend_list->poly_ptrs[poly]->tvlist[1].y;
face.tvlist[1].z = (float)rend_list->poly_ptrs[poly]->tvlist[1].z;
face.tvlist[1].u0 = (float)rend_list->poly_ptrs[poly]->tvlist[1].u0;
face.tvlist[1].v0 = (float)rend_list->poly_ptrs[poly]->tvlist[1].v0;
```

```
face.tvlist[2].x = (float)rend_list->poly_ptrs[poly]->tvlist[2].x;
face.tvlist[2].y = (float)rend_list->poly_ptrs[poly]->tvlist[2].y;
face.tvlist[2].z = (float)rend_list->poly_ptrs[poly]->tvlist[2].z;
face.tvlist[2].u0 = (float)rend_list->poly_ptrs[poly]->tvlist[2].u0;
face.tvlist[2].v0 = (float)rend_list->poly_ptrs[poly]->tvlist[2].v0;

// assign the texture
face.texture = rend_list->poly_ptrs[poly]->texture;

// set the vertex colors
face.lit_color[0] = rend_list->poly_ptrs[poly]->lit_color[0];
face.lit_color[1] = rend_list->poly_ptrs[poly]->lit_color[1];
face.lit_color[2] = rend_list->poly_ptrs[poly]->lit_color[2];
```

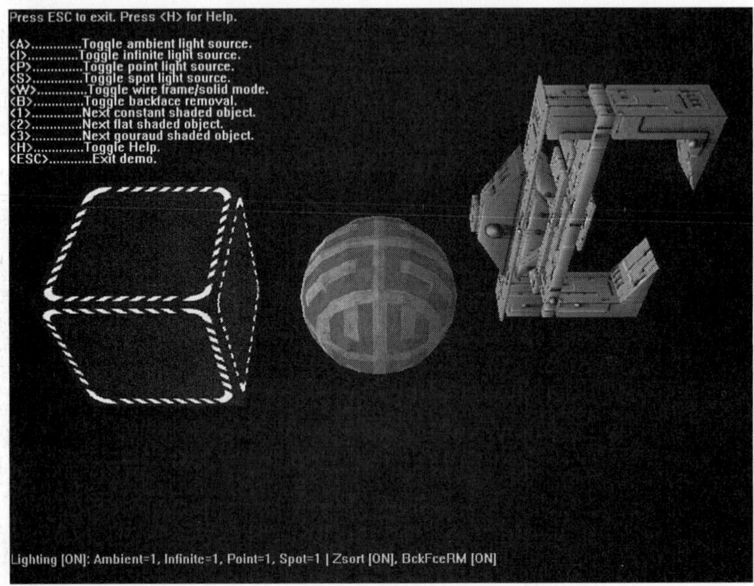

FIGURE 12.3 A screenshot of the Gouraud-shaded texturing rasterizers in action.

That's about all there is to Gouraud texturing. I have moved rather quickly through the material because you have seen each individual technique many times; we simply merged them into one cohesive function.

For a demo of Gouraud texturing, check out DEMOII12_1.CPP¦EXE. Figure 12.3 is a screenshot of the demo in action. It depicts a collection of constant-, flat-, and Gouraud-textured objects on the screen (left to right, respectively), so you can see the difference in quality. Press the 1, 2, and 3 keys to select different objects. Notice how Gouraud texturing doesn't help much on angular objects, but on objects that are smooth, it sure makes a difference!

Transparency and Alpha Blending

To tell the truth, I was a little worried that adding transparency to the engine was going to kill the speed. Theoretically, alpha blending/transparency is nothing more than a simple blending operation. Given two pixels p_source1(r,g,b) and p_source2(r,g,b) and a blending factor we will call alpha (which ranges from 0..1), we want to compute the final pixel p_final(r,g,b), which blends them together. The formula for this is

```
p_final = (alpha)*(p_source1) + (1-alpha)*(p_source2)
```

Each pixel is really made up of three components r, g, and b. Hence, the equations really look like this:

```
p_finalr = (alpha)*(p_source1r) + (1-alpha)*(p_source2r)
p_finalg = (alpha)*(p_source1g) + (1-alpha)*(p_source2g)
p_finalb = (alpha)*(p_source1b) + (1-alpha)*(p_source2b)
```

If alpha = 1, p_source1 is completely opaque and p_source2 is not blended whatsoever. Similarly, if alpha = 0, p_source1 is completely transparent and p_source2 is completely opaque. And finally, if alpha = 0.5, both p_source1 and p_source2 are blended 50/50. This is the basis of our transparency/alpha blending technology. So, we have three major problems:

- How do we perform this complex mathematical operation fast enough?
- How do we support alpha blending in the engine? That is, how do we indicate that polygons have an alpha value?
- How do we deal with DirectX slowing down up to 30 times when reading from a backbuffer surface?

I will defer the second and third problems because they are at a higher level and we'll deal with them later. Right now, let's figure out the first problem.

Alright, so we are looking at something like six multiplications here, plus three additions per pixel. This just kills me for something that we might want to use a lot of and simply isn't feasible to do by brute force. Sure, we could just apply the alpha blending math to each pixel during the rasterization loop and be done with it, but that's not acceptable. There has to be a better way to do this. This is a case where lookup tables can help us.

Using Lookup Tables for Alpha Blending

The problem facing us is this nasty computation to support alpha blending shown here:

```
p_finalr = (alpha)*(p_source1r) + (1-alpha)*(p_source2r)
p_finalg = (alpha)*(p_source1g) + (1-alpha)*(p_source2g)
p_finalb = (alpha)*(p_source1b) + (1-alpha)*(p_source2b)
```

Not only are there six multiplications, but there are three additions and one extra addition to compute the constant (1-alpha), for a total of four additions. This says nothing of the fact that this is pure math—chances are, we won't be able to just perform these calculations to our pixels because many times they are in RGB format and must be extracted. So what we would like to do is create a lookup table that takes two RGB values in 5.6.5 format and an alpha value from 0..255 and gives us the result. This is shown graphically in Figure 12.4. Of course, once again we find ourselves with the same dilemma: a huge lookup table. Here's a calculation to show the size:

```
Inputs to table (3):
Color 1:   RGB 5.6.5 format, 16-bits
Color 2:   RGB 5.6.5 format, 16-bits
Alpha factor: 0..255, 8-bits
```

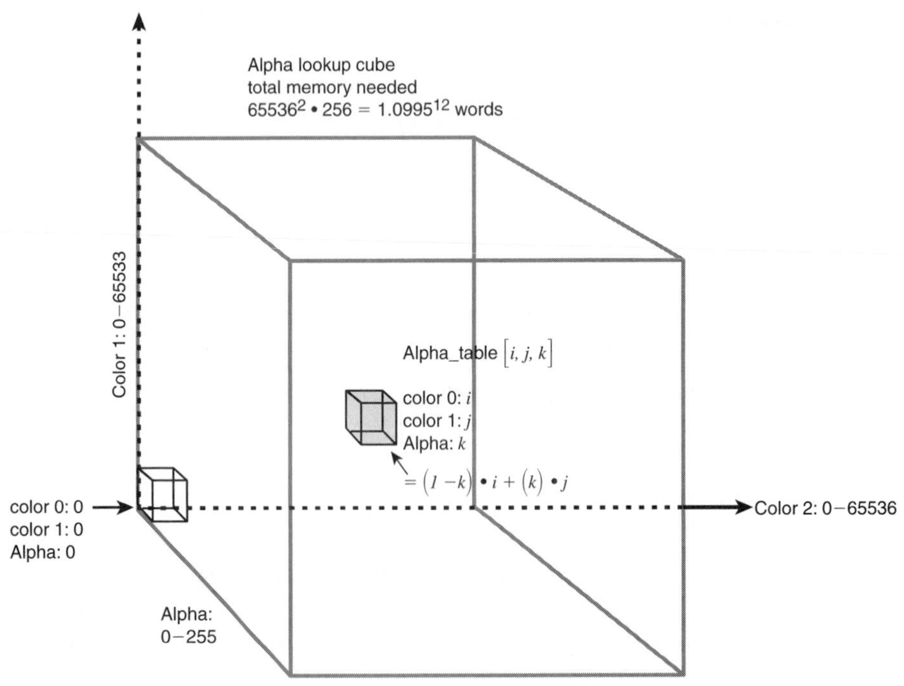

FIGURE 12.4 A potential alpha blending system implemented with tables.

Thus we need the table to precompute all possible products of the two input colors 1 and 2, along with 256 different alpha blending factors. Therefore, we have:

$$65536 * 65536 * 256 = 1.0995^{12}$$

Needless to say, this approach isn't going to work as is. Let's see if we can't look at the problem in another way. Let's look at the math again:

```
p_finalr = (alpha)*(p_source1r) + (1-alpha)*(p_source2r)
p_finalg = (alpha)*(p_source1g) + (1-alpha)*(p_source2g)
p_finalb = (alpha)*(p_source1b) + (1-alpha)*(p_source2b)
```

If we forget about solving the entire problem at once, we can focus on some sub-problems that are worth solving. The major computation is the alpha factor multiplied by each of the `r,g,b` components, and the `(1-alpha)` factor multiplied by the same components—ah ha! What if we create a lookup table that has 65,536 entries, each entry the result of multiplying a specific alpha factor times the entry encoded in 5.6.5 format, say `alpha` = 0.5. Figure 12.5 illustrates this setup.

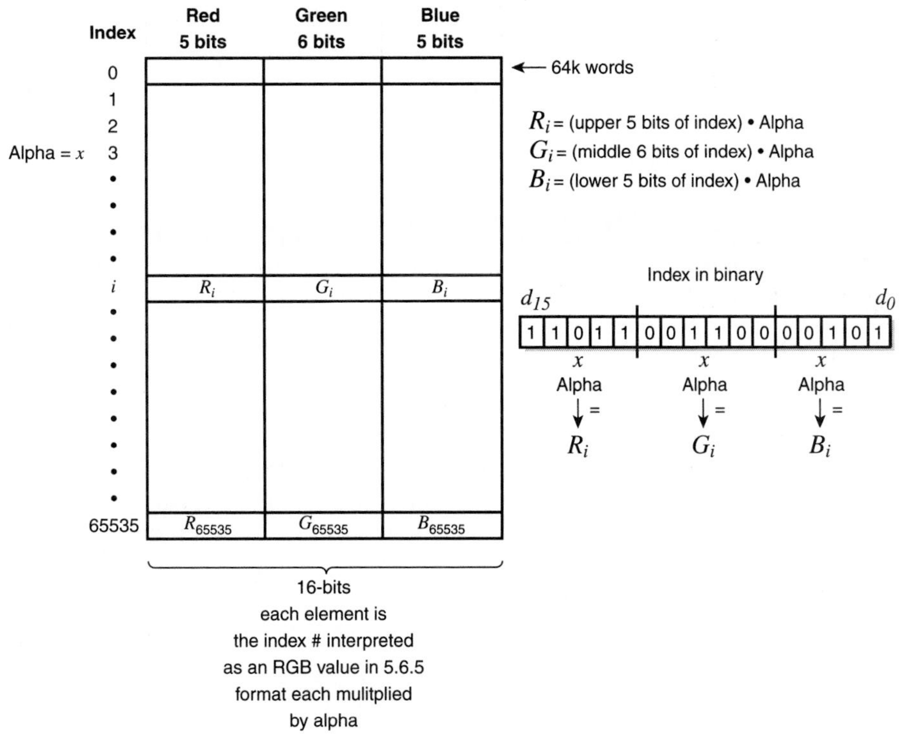

FIGURE 12.5 A more efficient alpha table lookup system.

Assuming we have this table, if we want to know what two pixels blended together with an alpha of 0.5 is (or mathematically):

```
p_final = (0.5)*(p_source1) + (1-0.5)*(p_source2)
```

We could do it with two lookups and one addition:

```
p_final = alphatable[p_source1] + alphatable[p_source2];
```

So with one lookup table that's 65,536 entries long and each entry is 16 bits, we have just turned the following computation:

```
p_finalr = (alpha)*(p_source1r) + (1-alpha)*(p_source2r)
p_finalg = (alpha)*(p_source1g) + (1-alpha)*(p_source2g)
p_finalb = (alpha)*(p_source1b) + (1-alpha)*(p_source2b)
```

into this:

```
p_final = alphatable[p_source1] + alphatable[p_source2];
```

And I will tell you right now, it flies! But you might be asking about other alpha values. Well, each alpha value costs us 64K words, so if we want to support eight equally separated alpha values:

```
0, .125, .250, .375, .5, .625, .75, 1.00
```

We need eight tables for a total of 8*64K = 512K. That I can live with.

NOTE

If you're really clever, you might notice that we don't need the tables for alpha 0 and 1.0. We could use conditional logic for these cases. If the alpha is 0, the pixel is totally transparent, and just use the other pixel without further ado. Similarly, if the alpha is 1.0, draw the pixel as usual without any concern for the alpha, because an alpha of 1.0 is totally opaque. For now, we will just use the extra memory to keep the alpha rasterizers clean and free of special cases.

In summarizing the alpha lookup table, we are going to create a lookup table for a set of alpha values 0..1, where we compute the product of the alpha value with every possible RGB value in the table, but perform the calculations such that we multiply the alpha value by the `r,g,b` components of the input 5.6.5 RGB word in a masked fashion. We do *not* want to multiply alpha by the integral value of each 16-bit value from 0..65535, but by each extracted `r,g,b` value that each integral value from 0..65535 represents. In pseudocode, we have the following algorithm:

```
for each color from 0 to 65535
  begin
    convert the 16-bit encoded color to r,g,b 5.6.5 format

    now multiply each channel by the alpha value

    r=r*alpha
    g=g*alpha
    b=b*alpha
```

```
    finally place the 16-bit color word built up from r.g.b
    into the lookup table at location indexed by color:

    alphatable[value] = r.g.b

  end
```


It really is a simple table to create. The key to understanding it is that we are using each 16-bit index to represent a color that we want multiplied by the alpha value, but *before* we carry out the multiplication, we must extract out the `r,g,b` values of each integral 16-bit value masquerading as a plain number, multiply *each* of them by the alpha value, and then put them back together. Then we need a few of these tables, maybe eight or sixteen, to cover enough alpha values so we can blend things properly. I decided on eight tables, but you can change the constant that controls this. Anyway, here's where the lookup table is stored globally in `T3DLIB10.CPP`:

```
USHORT rgb_alpha_table[NUM_ALPHA_LEVELS][65536];
```

Currently, `NUM_ALPHA_LEVELS` is set to `8`, which gives eight levels of alpha with 0.125 increments. Also, as you see, I have decided to arrange the tables in rows, where each row represents a different alpha value. Figure 12.6 illustrates this.

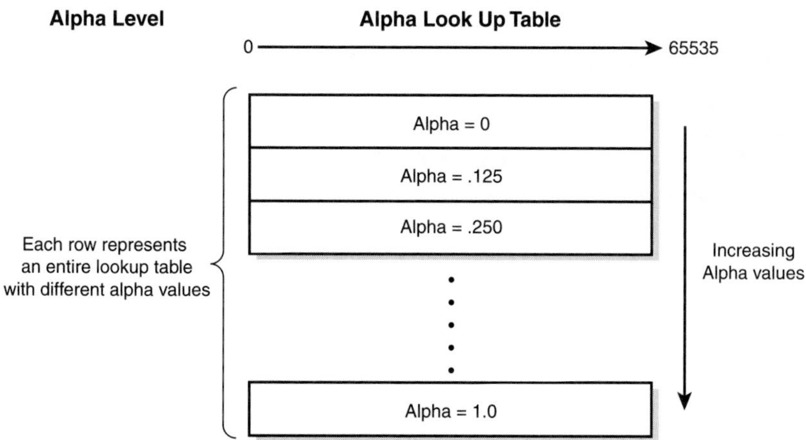

FIGURE 12.6 Using multiple alpha lookup tables.

With all that in mind, here's the function `RGB_Alpha_Table_Builder()` that creates all these tables for us:

```
int RGB_Alpha_Table_Builder(int num_alpha_levels, // numlevels to create
   USHORT rgb_alpha_table[NUM_ALPHA_LEVELS][65536]) // lookup table
{
```

```
// this function creates an alpha lookup table, the purpose of the table is as
// follows; when alpha blending two RGB values,
// one can't simply use the formula:
// final = (alpha)*(source1RGB) + (1-alpha)*(source2RGB)
// the reason of course is that the multiplication
// has to be carried out on R, G, B
// separately, this we first have to extract out
// r,g,b from both sources, then multiply
// both, then add the results, then build
// the result up and store it ! Ouch!
// therefore, we can use a table to speed this
// up in some cases, so if we think of
// the input RGB as a number and then let the
// table extract everything out and do the
// multiplication by the alpha blending factor,
// then we save all that work and in the
// end an alpha blend turns into two accesses,
// and an addition, so we avoid 6 multiplications
// and all the shift. Of course, if the colors are already
// in r,g,b form already then
// another approach may be better.
// In any case, the function works by creating a
// table that consists of num_alpha_levels rows,
// each row consist of 65536 entries which
// represents the scale value of that row times
// each of the 65536 colors in RGB format
// also, the num_alpha_levels must be a power of two,
// so num_alpha_levels of 8 for example
// will result in a table that has 8 rows,
// where the multiplier each row would be
// 8/8, 7/8, 6/8.........1/8, 0/8 is the amount of source pixel to mix

// first check the pointer
if (!rgb_alpha_table)
  return(-1);

int r,g,b; // used to scan colors out of rgbindex

float alpha    = 0;
float delta_alpha = EPSILON_E6 + 1/((float)(num_alpha_levels-1));

// we need num_alpha_level_rows
for (int alpha_level = 0; alpha_level < num_alpha_levels; alpha_level++)
  {
```

```
    // there are 65536 RGB values we need to compute,
    // assuming that we are in RGB: 4.4.4 format
    for (int rgbindex = 0; rgbindex < 65536; rgbindex++)
      {
      // extract r,g,b from rgbindex, assuming an encoding of 5.6.5
      _RGB565FROM16BIT(rgbindex, &r, &g, &b);

      // scale
      r = (int)( (float)r * (float)alpha );
      g = (int)( (float)g * (float)alpha );
      b = (int)( (float)b * (float)alpha );

      // build pixel back up and store
      rgb_alpha_table[alpha_level][rgbindex] = _RGB16BIT565(r,g,b);

      } // end for rgbindex

    // decrease alpha level
    alpha+=delta_alpha;

    } // end for row

// return success
return(1);

} // end RGB_Alpha_Table_Builder
```

To use the function, you call it with the desired number of alpha levels and the storage for the table, which in our case is fixed and global, so we call the function as follows:

```
RGB_Alpha_Table_Builder(NUM_ALPHA_LEVELS, rgb_alpha_table);
```

And we are ready to rock and roll. Now that we have the alpha tables, let's see how use them.

Adding Alpha Blending to the Basic Rasterizers

To add alpha blending to the basic non-z-buffered rasterizers is the path of least resistance, so we will start there. To begin, let's review what we want to alpha blend. The whole point of alpha blending is to be able to see through something that is rendered over something else. Figure 12.7 illustrates this concept.

We have a scene, and then an object is rendered on top of the scene with alpha set to about 20%. Therefore, the background shows through 80%, and the foreground object shows through 20%. This bring us to the first problem with alpha blending and transparency: The object under the transparent object *must* be drawn first. This is a problem for a number of different algorithms. For example, we might have a very optimal rendering algorithm that has zero overdraw. This means that any polygon that's obscured by another polygon is *not* drawn. This is shown in Figure 12.8. The problem is, if we want the polygon on top to be alpha channeled or transparent, there will be nothing under it to see through to!

FIGURE 12.7 Alpha blending in action.

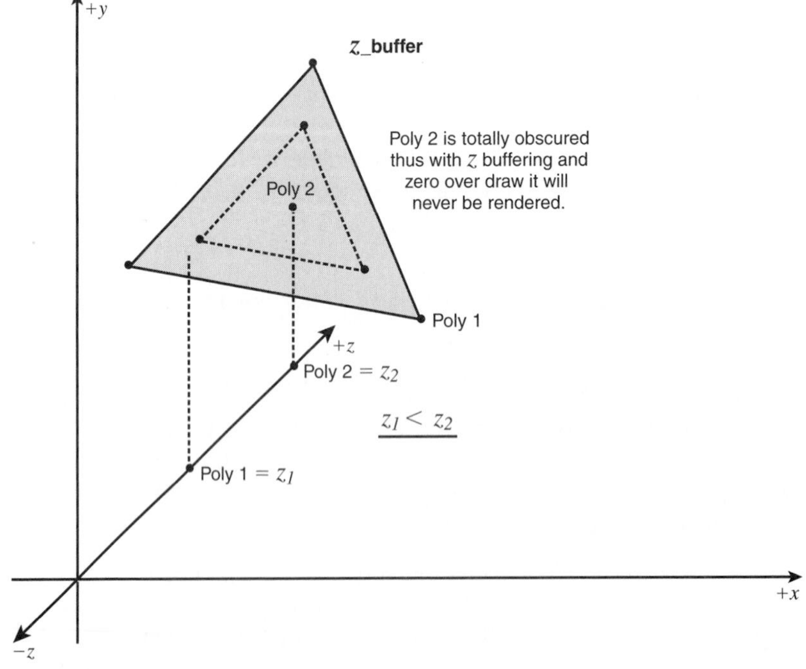

FIGURE 12.8 Obscured polygons are not drawn.

Another problem occurs when you are z-buffering. Suppose that two polygons reach the Z-buffer in front-to-back order; that is, polygon 1 is closer to the viewer than polygon 2, as shown in Figure 12.9.

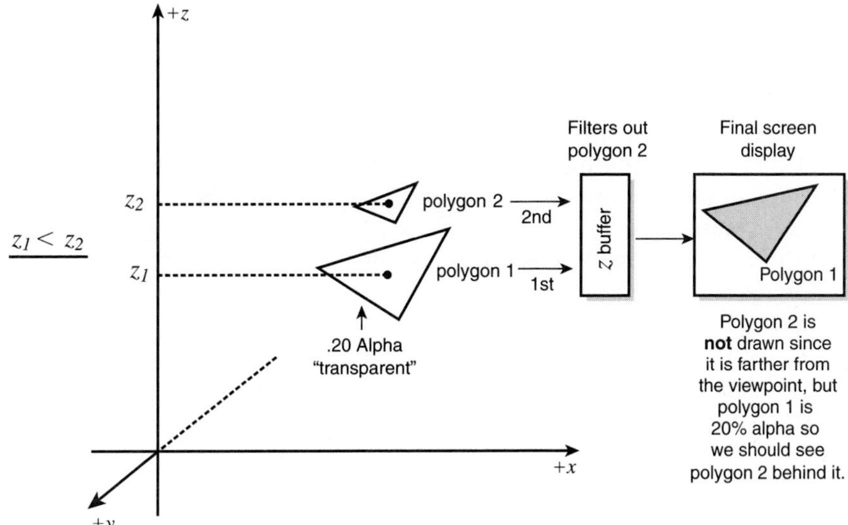

FIGURE 12.9 Problems with alpha blending and z-buffering.

In this case, polygon 1 passes the Z-buffer test and is written to the screen and the Z-buffer with transparency. However, polygon 2 does *not* pass the Z-buffer test and is never drawn at all. However, polygon 1 is transparent, so polygon 2 should be visible under it. Alas, you see the dilemma. There are a number of ways around these problems. For example, if you are trying to get zero overdraw, polygons that are transparent don't count in your calculations—that is, they are drawn regardless. And as for the Z-buffer problem, you can sort polygons back to front to get a rough ordering and *then* Z-buffer to get perfect order with alpha transparency for polygons that are transparent; thus the farther polygons will be drawn first, and the near alpha channeled polygons will be drawn after, so they can blend. If you don't want to waste time by sorting the polygons, you can mark transparent polygons, and then during rendering, if any polygon is determined to be at all within the bounds of a nearer transparent polygon, it is drawn first regardless of Z order.

Now that I have scared you out of your mind about using transparency with software, let's implement it! Let's start with the simplest of all the rasterizers that draw constant-/flat-shaded polygons without a Z-buffer or texturing, the new function `Draw_Triangle_2D3_16()`. If we look at this, we can transform its inner loop and add extra code to make it support alpha transparency as a parameter. Let's first look at the innermost loop again, and come up with a plan:

```
// draw span
for (xi=xstart; xi < xend; xi++)
  {
  // write textel assume 5.6.5
  screen_ptr[xi] = color;
  } // end for xi
```

That looks harmless enough <BG>. So to add transparency, we need to read the current pixel at `screen_ptr[xi]` and blend it with `color` rather than just writing color to `screen_ptr[xi]`. We'll use our mighty lookup table to do this. Let's assume that the table is always global, so we don't have to pass it, and further assume that for generality we will pass an alpha level to the rasterizing function that ranges from `0..(`*`NUM_ALPHA_LEVELS`*` - 1)`. We will then use the alpha level as an index into the *row* of the alpha lookup table, and get a pointer to the row (remember, each row represents a different alpha value multiplied by all possible 5.6.5 RGB values) along with a pointer to the `(1-alpha)` row. If we pick an alpha level of 0, we would want one pointer to row 0 and another pointer to row `(`*`NUM_ALPHA_LEVELS`*` - 1)`. Or in our case with eight alpha levels, if the alpha level is from 0..7, the first row is from 0..7, and the second row selected to blend is from 7..0—get it? The setup code to access the correct table rows for each source would look something like this:

```
// assign both source1 and source2 alpha tables based on polygon alpha level
USHORT *alpha_table_src1 =
    (USHORT *)&rgb_alpha_table[(NUM_ALPHA_LEVELS-1) - alpha][0];
USHORT *alpha_table_src2 =

    (USHORT *)&rgb_alpha_table[alpha][0];
```

At this point, we are done for the most part. All we need to do is blend the pixel that's on the screen with the pixel we want to render on the screen, and that's nothing more than using our mixing algorithm with lookup tables. Here's the new inner loop code for that:

```
for (xi=xstart; xi < xend; xi++)
{
// write textel assume 5.6.5
screen_ptr[xi] = alpha_table_src1[screen_ptr[xi]] + alpha_table_src2[color];
} // end for xi
```

We have reduced the complex problem of alpha blending in real time, 16-bit full color to a single addition and two table lookups! Cool, huh? Based on the preceding formulation, you should see how to add alpha blending to every single rasterizer: You just set the tables up with the alpha level, read the pixel and mix it with the pixel or textel you are about to render, and that's all there is to it!

Alpha Support for Simple Shading Rasterizers The final function with alpha blending support that renders plain constant-/flat-shaded non-z-buffered polygons is called `Draw_Triangle_2D_Alpha16()`, and here's its prototype:

```
void Draw_Triangle_2D_Alpha16(POLYF4DV2_PTR face, // ptr to face
          UCHAR *_dest_buffer, // pointer to video buffer
          int mem_pitch,    // bytes per line, 320, 640 etc.
          int alpha);     // the alpha level to use
```

Other than the addition of the single parameter alpha, the function works in the exact same way as the non-alpha version, and the setup is the same. However, remember that alpha must be from 0. (*NUM_ALPHA_LEVELS*-1)—otherwise, you will cause a memory protection fault accessing memory out of range of the lookup table! Now that you're a pro, let's add alpha support to the other basic rasterizers that support texturing and Gouraud shading.

Alpha Support for Gouraud-Shading Rasterizers Adding alpha support to the Gouraud shader is trivial. We need only setup the look up tables for the sent in alpha level with the lines of code:

```
// assign both source1 and source2 alpha tables based on polygon alpha level
USHORT *alpha_table_src1 =
    (USHORT *)&rgb_alpha_table[(NUM_ALPHA_LEVELS-1) - alpha][0];
USHORT *alpha_table_src2 =

    (USHORT *)&rgb_alpha_table[alpha][0];
```

And then modify the inner loop from this:

```
// draw span
for (xi=xstart; xi < xend; xi++)
  {
  // write textel assume 5.6.5
  screen_ptr[xi] = ((ui >> (FIXP16_SHIFT+3)) << 11) +
           ((vi >> (FIXP16_SHIFT+2)) << 5) +
           (wi >> (FIXP16_SHIFT+3));

  // interpolate u,v,w
  ui+=du;
  vi+=dv;
  wi+=dw;
  } // end for xi
```

To this:

```
// draw span
for (xi=xstart; xi < xend; xi++)
  {
  // write textel assume 5.6.5
  screen_ptr[xi] = alpha_table_src1[screen_ptr[xi]] +
```

12

```
            alpha_table_src2[((ui >> (FIXP16_SHIFT+3)) << 11) +
                    ((vi >> (FIXP16_SHIFT+2)) << 5) +
                    (wi >> (FIXP16_SHIFT+3))];

    // interpolate u,v,w
    ui+=du;
    vi+=dv;
    wi+=dw;
    } // end for xi
```

Notice how the original code's textel access is now a parameter of the alpha blending code's lookup along with the screen pixel. Therefore, the process of converting each of these functions is almost trivial; take the code for generating the pixel value and use it as one parameter in the lookup table, then take the pixel address where the value is to be written and use it as the destination, as well as the other parameter in the other lookup table, and that's all you do. Here's the new Gouraud-shaded function with alpha support:

```
void Draw_Gouraud_Triangle_Alpha16(POLYF4DV2_PTR face,  // ptr to face
            UCHAR *_dest_buffer, // pointer to video buffer
            int mem_pitch,     // bytes per line
            int alpha);      // alpha level
```

Once again, the only difference from the non-alpha version is the alpha parameter, which must be from `0..(NUM_ALPHA_LEVELS-1)`.

Alpha Support for Affine Texture Mapping Rasterizers Adding alpha support for the affine texture mappers is identical to the previous examples, but there are three different versions we need to make. I am simply going to list the prototypes:

```
void Draw_Textured_Triangle_Alpha16(POLYF4DV2_PTR face, // ptr to face
           UCHAR *_dest_buffer, // pointer to video buffer
           int mem_pitch,     // bytes per line, 320, 640 etc.
           int alpha);      // the alpha level

void Draw_Textured_TriangleFS_Alpha16(POLYF4DV2_PTR face, // ptr to face
            UCHAR *_dest_buffer, // pointer to video buffer
            int mem_pitch,     // bytes per line, 320, 640 etc.
            int alpha);      // the alpha level

void Draw_Textured_TriangleGS_Alpha16(POLYF4DV2_PTR face, // ptr to face
          UCHAR *_dest_buffer, // pointer to video buffer
          int mem_pitch,     // bytes per line, 320, 640 etc.
          int alpha);      // the alpha level
```

Now we have the plain constant-shaded, flat-shaded, and Gouraud-shaded texture mappers, all with support for the alpha channel (I have highlighted the new alpha parameters). As an example, let's look at the plain constant-shaded texture mapper's inner loop before and after alpha support. Here's the inner span loop before adding alpha support:

```
// draw span
for (xi=xstart; xi < xend; xi++)
  {
  // write textel
  screen_ptr[xi] = textmap[(ui >> FIXP16_SHIFT) +
               ((vi >> FIXP16_SHIFT) << texture_shift2)];

  // interpolate u,v
  ui+=du;
  vi+=dv;
  } // end for xi
```

And here it is after adding the alpha support via the lookup tables:

```
// draw span
for (xi=xstart; xi < xend; xi++)
  {
  // write textel
  screen_ptr[xi] = alpha_table_src1[screen_ptr[xi]] +
           alpha_table_src2[textmap[(ui >> FIXP16_SHIFT) +
                ((vi >> FIXP16_SHIFT) << texture_shift2)]];

  // interpolate u,v
  ui+=du;
  vi+=dv;
  } // end for xi
```

Again, we simply use the textel and the screen pixel as parameters/indexes into the lookup tables, and then sum the results and write them to the screen. Finally, here's the rendering function to call the alpha-supported rasterizers:

```
void Draw_RENDERLIST4DV2_Solid_Alpha16(
       RENDERLIST4DV2_PTR rend_list, // render list
       UCHAR *video_buffer,  // pointer to video buffer
       int lpitch,       // bytes per line of video buffer
       int alpha_override);  // alpha override for fullscreen alpha
```

The function works like all the rest: You send it a rendering list, pointer to video, and memory pitch, and it renders the rendering list, that is, draws all the polygons in the data structure. However, there is one interesting extra parameter: `alpha_override`. This is to force everything to be drawn with alpha. If `alpha_override` is -1, nothing happens. If `alpha_override` is from `0..(`*NUM_ALPHA_LEVELS*`-1)`, this value will override all real alpha values and render them along with everything else at the sent override value.

CAUTION

I am still leaving something out here: The rasterization functions take an alpha level, but where do they get it? For now, they get it from nowhere—you override it—but soon we will encode it in the polygon base color.

Adding Alpha Blending to the Z-Buffered Rasterizers

Adding alpha blending transparency to the z-buffered rasterizers is exactly the same as the non-z-buffered rasterizers. There are no differences whatsoever, other than the logical difference that because of the Z-buffer pass test, polygons coming into the Z-buffer that are behind a previously z-buffered polygon will not show up under the z-buffered polygon and thus render incorrectly. To solve this, you can presort polygons from back to front with the z-sort and the Z-buffer, or you can add extra logic to the calling function that renders the polygons to force polygons that are under/covered by transparent polygons to always render first in the Z-buffer. However, we will leave that as something to do later, if it becomes an issue. For now, the Z-buffer alpha blending code just blends what comes first.

The addition of alpha blending is identical to all the rest, so once again I will simply show you the final function prototypes, along with a single example of a modified before-and-after function. Here are the prototypes:

```
void Draw_Textured_TriangleZB_Alpha16(POLYF4DV2_PTR face, // ptr to face
          UCHAR *_dest_buffer, // pointer to video buffer
          int mem_pitch,     // bytes per line, 320, 640 etc.
          UCHAR *zbuffer,    // pointer to z-buffer
          int zpitch,       // bytes per line of zbuffer
          int alpha);       // the alpha level

void Draw_Textured_TriangleFSZB_Alpha16(POLYF4DV2_PTR face, // ptr to face
          UCHAR *_dest_buffer, // pointer to video buffer
          int mem_pitch,     // bytes per line, 320, 640 etc.
          UCHAR *zbuffer,    // pointer to z-buffer
          int zpitch,       // bytes per line of zbuffer
          int alpha);       // the alpha level

void Draw_Textured_TriangleGSZB_Alpha16(POLYF4DV2_PTR face, // ptr to face
          UCHAR *_dest_buffer, // pointer to video buffer
          int mem_pitch,     // bytes per line, 320, 640 etc.
          UCHAR *_zbuffer,    // pointer to z-buffer
          int zpitch,       // bytes per line of zbuffer
          int alpha);       // the alpha level


void Draw_Triangle_2DZB_Alpha16(POLYF4DV2_PTR face, // ptr to face
          UCHAR *_dest_buffer, // pointer to video buffer
```

```
        int mem_pitch,     // bytes per line, 320, 640 etc.
        UCHAR *zbuffer,    // pointer to z-buffer
        int zpitch,       // bytes per line of zbuffer
        int alpha);       // the alpha level

void Draw_Gouraud_TriangleZB_Alpha16(POLYF4DV2_PTR face,  // ptr to face
        UCHAR *_dest_buffer, // pointer to video buffer
        int mem_pitch,     // bytes per line, 320, 640 etc.
        UCHAR *zbuffer,    // pointer to z-buffer
        int zpitch,       // bytes per line of zbuffer
        int alpha);       // the alpha level
```

These include every variation of shading and lighting we have so far! As an example, let's take a look at the most complex Z-buffer alpha function's inner loop before and after. This would be the Gouraud-shaded, texture-mapped rasterizer `Draw_Textured_TriangleGSZB_Alpha16()`. Its inner loop before adding alpha is from `Draw_Textured_TriangleGSZB_16()`, which is shown here:

```
// draw span
for (xi=xstart; xi < xend; xi++)
  {
  // write textel assume 5.6.5
  // test if z of current pixel is nearer than current z buffer value
  if (zi < z_ptr[xi])
    {
  // get textel first
   textel = textmap[(si >> FIXP16_SHIFT) +
             ((ti >> FIXP16_SHIFT) << texture_shift2)];

    // extract rgb components
    r_textel = ((textel >> 11)     );
    g_textel = ((textel >> 5) & 0x3f);
    b_textel =  (textel    & 0x1f);

    // modulate textel with gouraud shading
    r_textel*=ui;
    g_textel*=vi;
    b_textel*=wi;

    // finally write pixel
    // note that we did the math such that the results are r*32, g*64, b*32
    screen_ptr[xi] = ((b_textel >> (FIXP16_SHIFT+8)) +
            ((g_textel >> (FIXP16_SHIFT+8)) << 5) +
            ((r_textel >> (FIXP16_SHIFT+8)) << 11));
```

```
    // update z-buffer
    z_ptr[xi] = zi;
    } // end if

   // interpolate u,v,w,z,s,t
   ui+=du;
   vi+=dv;
   wi+=dw;

   zi+=dz;

   si+=ds;
   ti+=dt;

   } // end for xi
```

That's a little nasty, no matter how you look at it! Anyway, here it is with alpha blending added:

```
// draw span
for (xi=xstart; xi < xend; xi++)
  {
  // write textel assume 5.6.5
  // test if z of current pixel is nearer than current z buffer value
  if (zi < z_ptr[xi])
    {
  // get textel first
   textel = textmap[(si >> FIXP16_SHIFT) +
             ((ti >> FIXP16_SHIFT) << texture_shift2)];

    // extract rgb components
    r_textel = ((textel >> 11)    );
    g_textel = ((textel >> 5) & 0x3f);
    b_textel =  (textel    & 0x1f);

    // modulate textel with gouraud shading
    r_textel*=ui;
    g_textel*=vi;
    b_textel*=wi;

    // finally write pixel
    // note that we did the math such that the results are r*32, g*64, b*32
    screen_ptr[xi] = alpha_table_src1[screen_ptr[xi]] +
       alpha_table_src2[((b_textel >> (FIXP16_SHIFT+8)) +
               ((g_textel >> (FIXP16_SHIFT+8)) << 5) +
```

12

```
            ((r_textel >> (FIXP16_SHIFT+8)) << 11))];
    // update z-buffer
    z_ptr[xi] = zi;

    } // end if

   // interpolate u,v,w,z,s,t
   ui+=du;
   vi+=dv;
   wi+=dw;

   zi+=dz;

   si+=ds;
   ti+=dt;

   } // end for xi
```

NOTE

Sorry for all the code, but there is a ton of it—approximately 50,000+ lines, so I am only showing you a fraction of it.

Lastly, there is a rendering function that calls all of the rasterizers with alpha support and z-buffering. It's called `Draw_RENDERLIST4DV2_SolidZB_Alpha16()`, and here's its prototype:

```
void Draw_RENDERLIST4DV2_SolidZB_Alpha16(RENDERLIST4DV2_PTR rend_list,
      UCHAR *video_buffer,
      int lpitch,
      UCHAR *zbuffer,
      int zpitch,
      int alpha_override);
```

The function takes the normal parameter set—rendering list, video buffer, memory pitch, Z-buffer, Z-buffer memory pitch—but it also has the added `alpha_override` parameter to force alpha on the rendering list. This must be from `0..(`*`NUM_ALPHA_LEVELS`*`-1)` or -1 for no effect.

As a demo of alpha blending, check out `DEMOII12_2.CPP|EXE`. A screenshot of it in action is shown in Figure 12.10.

This demo enables you to move around in a world full of basic objects (they are supposed to be Borg ships, so use your imagination), and then the demo slowly increases and decreases the alpha blending via the `alpha_override` variable at a low level (because we still can't set the alpha level at an object level). You can also enable/disable z-sorting, as well as other options. To compile the demo, please make sure to add all the modules `T3DLIB1–10.CPP|H` along with the DirectX .LIB files. And of course, use a Win32 .EXE target!

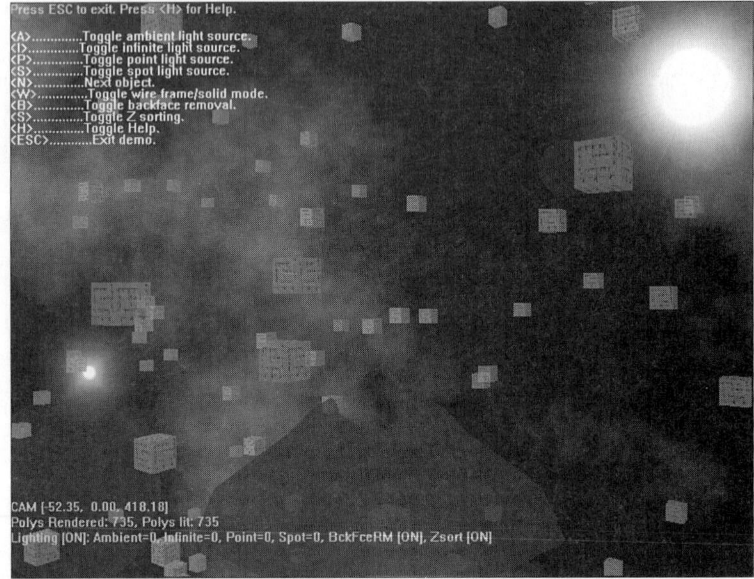

FIGURE 12.10 A screenshot of the alpha blending demo in action.

Supporting Alpha Blending at the Object Level

The next issue we have to deal with is a way to set polygons in our models as having transparency or alpha. Ironically, we thought of this already when we designed the color descriptor back in `T3DLIB6.CPP|H`:

```
typedef struct RGBAV1_TYP
{
union
  {
  int rgba;           // compressed format
  UCHAR rgba_M[4];        // array format
  struct { UCHAR a,b,g,r; }; // explicit name format
  }; // end union

} RGBAV1, *RGBAV1_PTR;
```

The structure represents full 32-bit colors with support for 8 bits of alpha and RGB 8.8.8 format. Unfortunately, the polygon structures don't use this type—they use the base type of a 32-bit integer to hold colors in reduced 16-bit format without any concept of alpha. Nevertheless, we are still okay. Right now, all RGB colors are stored at 16-bit values in the lower 16 bits of the color field in the polygon structures, so we have the upper 16 bits available to do with as we wish. So, we will store the alpha channel in the upper 8 bits of each polygon color. Additionally, we will flag any polygon that has alpha with this attribute:

```
#define POLY4DV2_ATTR_TRANSPARENT        0x0002
```

Which we had already defined in `T3DLIB7.CPP|H` because we were planning on this! So as far as the polygons go, that's all we need to do to support alpha blending: Just set the attribute to `POLY4DV2_ATTR_TRANSPARENT` for the polygon, along with whatever other attributes, and then set the upper 8 bits of the color to the alpha level (`0..(`*`NUM_ALPHA_LEVELS`*`-1)`). Figure 12.11 illustrates this setup.

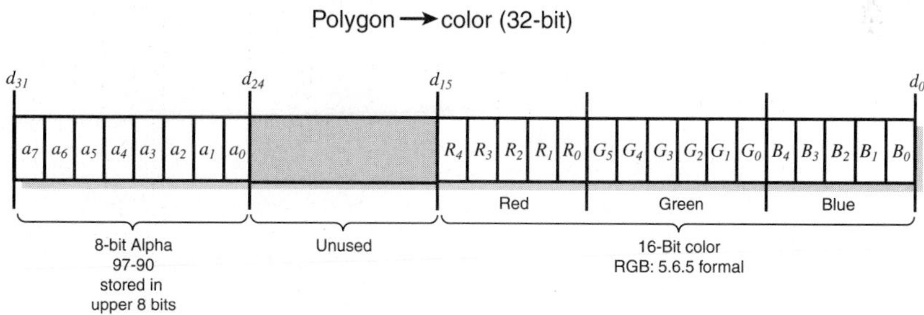

FIGURE 12.11 Encoding the alpha level in the upper 8 bits of the color word.

Now for the hard part—as my friend Mike Perone always says, "It's always something." You never get away with doing anything without a little drama, and here comes ours: We need to rewrite the object loader! Yup, there's no way to avoid this. We must not only rewrite it, but come up with a way to tag polygons as transparent. Well, luckily for us the Caligari trueSpace .COB format already has a transparency class in the file format, so we can just use this. As always, we need to come up with a convention to use the class field to communicate the information we need and to communicate it in a semi-natural way. I don't want to have to resort to using pink to mean transparent!

The first step is to determine what support there is for transparency in all the various versions of the Caligari modeler. It looks like 4.0+ supports what we need right in the interface, so we are good to go. Now, to refresh your memory on how we have been encoding things thus far for shading models, here are our conventions at this point:

1. All polygons must be triangles.
2. A polygon that does not have a texture must have the color class set to `plain color`.

3. A polygon with texture must have the color class set to `texture map`. Also, only one texture per object, and it must be wrapped around the object with repeat factors 1.0, 1.0.
4. The shading mode of a polygon is encoded in the `reflectance` class; `constant` for constant shading or emissive; `matte` for flat shading; and `plastic` for Gouraud shading.

This has worked great, and we can pretty much model naturally and get what we want out of it. Now, to support transparency, we are going to use the transparency class of the Caligari .COB format. Figure 12.12 is an annotated screenshot of me selecting the transparency.

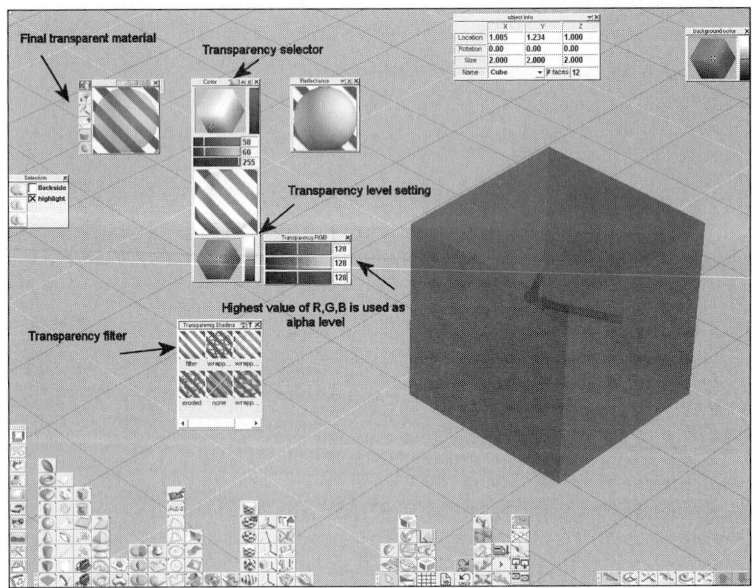

FIGURE 12.12 A detailed screenshot of setting the alpha on a model in Caligari trueSpace.

We are going to set the transparency to "filter" mode, drop down the transparency controls, and then use the slider to control how transparent or how much alpha the polygon or surface has. For example, the blue cube in Figure 12.12 has color class plain color (no texturing), reflectance matte (flat shading), and a transparency of filter mode, along with a setting of RGB 128 out of 256, or 50%. Here's the file the system outputs for what I call `CUBEBLUEALPHA_01.COB` (minus some extraneous data):

```
Caligari V00.01ALH
Name Cube
center 1.08471 1.23355 1
```

```
x axis 1 0 0
y axis 0 1 0
z axis 0 0 1
Transform
1 0 0 1.08471
0 1 0 1.23355
0 0 1 0
0 0 0 1
World Vertices 8
-1.000000 -1.000000 0.000000
-1.000000 -1.000000 2.000000
1.000000 -1.000000 0.000000
1.000000 -1.000000 2.000000
-1.000000 1.000000 0.000000
1.000000 1.000000 0.000000
1.000000 1.000000 2.000000
-1.000000 1.000000 2.000000
Texture Vertices 14
0.000000 0.333333
0.000000 0.666667
0.250000 0.333333
0.250000 0.666667
0.500000 0.000000
0.500000 0.333333
0.500000 0.666667
0.500000 1.000000
0.250000 0.000000
0.250000 1.000000
0.750000 0.333333
0.750000 0.666667
1.000000 0.333333
1.000000 0.666667
Faces 12
Face verts 3 flags 0 mat 0
<0,0> <1,1> <3,3>
Face verts 3 flags 0 mat 0
<0,0> <3,3> <2,2>
Face verts 3 flags 0 mat 0
<0,8> <2,2> <5,5>
Face verts 3 flags 0 mat 0
<0,8> <5,5> <4,4>
Face verts 3 flags 0 mat 0
<2,2> <3,3> <6,6>
```

```
Face verts 3 flags 0 mat 0
<2,2> <6,6> <5,5>
Face verts 3 flags 0 mat 0
<1,9> <7,7> <6,6>
Face verts 3 flags 0 mat 0
<1,9> <6,6> <3,3>
Face verts 3 flags 0 mat 0
<4,10> <5,5> <6,6>
Face verts 3 flags 0 mat 0
<4,10> <6,6> <7,11>
Face verts 3 flags 0 mat 0
<0,12> <4,10> <7,11>
Face verts 3 flags 0 mat 0
<0,12> <7,11> <1,13>
DrawFlags 0
Unit V0.01 Id 18620117 Parent 18620116 Size 00000009
Units 2
ObRQ V0.01 Id 18620121 Parent 18620116 Size 00000121
Object Radiosity Quality: 0
Object Radiosity Max Area: 0
Object Radiosity Min Area: 0
Object Radiosity Mesh Accuracy: 0
Mat1 V0.06 Id 18855732 Parent 18620116 Size 00000099
mat# 0
shader: phong facet: auto32
rgb 0.227451,0.235294,1
alpha 1 ka 0.1 ks 0.1 exp 0 ior 1
ShBx V0.03 Id 18855733 Parent 18855732 Size 00000462
Shader class: color
Shader name: "plain color" (plain)
Number of parameters: 1
colour: color (58, 60, 255)
Flags: 3
Shader class: transparency
Shader name: "filter" (plain)
Number of parameters: 1
colour: color (128, 128, 128)
Flags: 3
Shader class: reflectance
Shader name: "matte" (matte)
Number of parameters: 2
ambient factor: float 0.1
diffuse factor: float 1
Flags: 3
```

```
Shader class: displacement
Shader name: "none" (none)
Number of parameters: 0
Flags: 3
END V1.00 Id 0 Parent 0 Size    0
```

I have highlighted all the material classes we are now using. So, we just need to add support to the .COB parser to read in one more class (`transparency`), and then parse the `colour` field and extract out the alpha level. But before we do that, we need to finalize one more detail. The alpha/transparency in most modelers (including trueSpace) has three channels: red, green, and blue. We have no concept of color-based alpha—we are simply using a monochrome alpha channel. We're simply going to take the largest of the three channels and use it as the alpha value. You can use red, green, or blue, or combinations of all of them, but the parser will take the largest value of each component and make that the alpha value. And finally, as the alpha value from the .COB will be in the range of 0..255, we must scale that to our range of `(0..(`*`NUM_ALPHA_LEVELS`*`-1))`. And that's it—we have model-level support for alpha blending and transparency! Here is the new prototype for the new .COB loader with alpha support:

```
int Load_OBJECT4DV2_COB2(OBJECT4DV2_PTR obj, // pointer to object
             char *filename,    // filename of Caligari COB file
             VECTOR4D_PTR scale, // initial scaling factors
             VECTOR4D_PTR pos,  // initial position
             VECTOR4D_PTR rot,  // initial rotations
             int vertex_flags,  // flags to re-order vertices
                      // and perform transforms
             int mipmap )     // mipmap enable flag
                      // 0 means no mipmap, 1 means
                      // generate mip map
```

For now, just disregard the little mip map parameter—that comes later—and just look at the prototype. You will notice that, other than the mip map parameter, it's identical to the previous version `Load_OBJECT4DV2_COB`*()*. The changes are internal to read the transparency class of the .COB model. So let's take a look at that code:

```
////////////////////////////////////////////////////////////////////////
// ADDED CODE FOR TRANSPARENCY AND ALPHA BLENDING ///////////////////////
////////////////////////////////////////////////////////////////////////
// Now we need to know if there is any transparency for the material
// we have decided to encoded this in the shader class: transparency :)
// also, you must use the "filter" shader, and then set the RGB color to
// the level of transparency you want, 0,0,0 means totally transparent
// 255,255,255 means totally opaque, so we are looking for something like
// this:
// Shader class: transparency
```

```
// Shader name: "filter" (plain)
// Number of parameters: 1
// colour: color (146, 146, 146)
//
// and if there isn't transparency then we will see this:
//
// Shader class: transparency
// Shader name: "none" (none)
// Number of parameters: 0
//
// now, since we aren't doing any kind of RGB transparency,
// we are only concerned
// with the overall value, so the way, I am going to do this is to look at the
// 3 values of R, G, B, and use the highest one as the final alpha/transparency
// value, so a value of 255, 255, 255 with be 100% alpha or totally opaque

// look for the "Shader class: transparency"
while(1)
   {
   // get the next line
   if (!parser.Getline(PARSER_STRIP_EMPTY_LINES | PARSER_STRIP_WS_ENDS))
    {
    Write_Error("\nshader transparency class not found in .COB file %s.",
          filename);
    return(0);
    } // end if

   // look for "Shader class: transparency"
   if (parser.Pattern_Match(parser.buffer,
               "['Shader'] ['class:'] ['transparency']") )
    {
    // now we know the next "shader name"
    // is what we are looking for so, break
    break;
    } // end if

   } // end while

while(1)
   {
   // get the next line
   if (!parser.Getline(PARSER_STRIP_EMPTY_LINES | PARSER_STRIP_WS_ENDS))
    {
    Write_Error("\nshader name ended abruptly! in .COB file %s.",
          filename);
```

```
 return(0);
 } // end if

// get rid of those quotes
ReplaceChars(parser.buffer, parser.buffer, "\"",' ',1);

// did we find the name?
if (parser.Pattern_Match(parser.buffer, "['Shader'] ['name:'] [s>0]" ) )
 {
 // figure out if transparency is enabled
 if (strcmp(parser.pstrings[2], "none") == 0)
   {
   // disable the alpha bit and write 0 alpha
   RESET_BIT(materials[material_index + num_materials].attr,
        MATV1_ATTR_TRANSPARENT);

   // set alpha to 0, unused
   materials[material_index + num_materials].color.a = 0;

   } // end if
 else
 if (strcmp(parser.pstrings[2], "filter") == 0)
  {
  // enable the alpha bit and write the alpha level
  SET_BIT(materials[material_index + num_materials].attr,
      MATV1_ATTR_TRANSPARENT);

  // now search for color line to extract alpha level
  // look for the "Shader class: transparency"
  while(1)
     {
     // get the next line
     if (!parser.Getline(PARSER_STRIP_EMPTY_LINES |
              PARSER_STRIP_WS_ENDS))
      {
      Write_Error("\ntransparency color not found in .COB file %s.",
            filename);
      return(0);
      } // end if

     // get rid of extraneous characters
     ReplaceChars(parser.buffer, parser.buffer, ":(,)",' ',1);
     // look for colour: color (146, 146, 146)
     if (parser.Pattern_Match(parser.buffer,
```

```
                "['colour'] ['color'] [i] [i] [i]") )
        {
         // set the alpha level to the highest value
         int max_alpha = MAX(parser.pints[0], parser.pints[1]);
         max_alpha = MAX(max_alpha, parser.pints[2]);

         // set alpha value
         materials[material_index + num_materials].color.a =
          (int)( (float)max_alpha/255 *
              (float)(NUM_ALPHA_LEVELS-1) + (float)0.5);

         // clamp
         if (materials[material_index + num_materials].color.a
           >= NUM_ALPHA_LEVELS)
       materials[material_index + num_materials].color.a =
              NUM_ALPHA_LEVELS-1;

         break;
         } // end if

       } // end while

      } // end if

    break;
   } // end if

  } // end while
```

I have highlighted the final conversion process of the alpha level for you. The last thing to do is to set the polygon attribute bit to transparent at the end of the file loader, so the rasterizers can know what's up, and they can fork to the alpha blending rasterizers rather than the opaque ones. Here's the code—pay attention to the location of the alpha channel, as it's stored in the upper 8 bits as we outlined:

```
// now test for alpha channel
if (materials[ poly_material[curr_poly] ].attr & MATV1_ATTR_TRANSPARENT)
  {
  // set the value of the alpha channel,
  // upper 8-bits of color will be used to hold it
  // lets hope this doesn't break the lighting engine!!!!
  obj->plist[curr_poly].color +=
      (materials[ poly_material[curr_poly] ].color.a << 24);
```

```
    // set the alpha flag in polygon
    SET_BIT(obj->plist[curr_poly].attr, POLY4DV2_ATTR_TRANSPARENT);
   } // end if
```

That's it. We have already seen alpha blending on a rendering list-wide basis, but we had no local control via the objects themselves—we just set the alpha_override value and called the rendering list function, overriding everything and making every polygon transparent. Now we can support alpha object-to-object on a per-polygon basis. As an example of controlling alpha and transparency, check out DEMOII12_3.CPP|EXE. It loads a number of transparent spheres, along with a solid black and white checkboard textured sphere. The spheres then bounce around in front of a 2D image. Figure 12.13 is a screenshot of the demo in action. The onscreen help is available as usual. Make sure to try disabling the ambient and infinite light sources with the A and L keys, respectively.

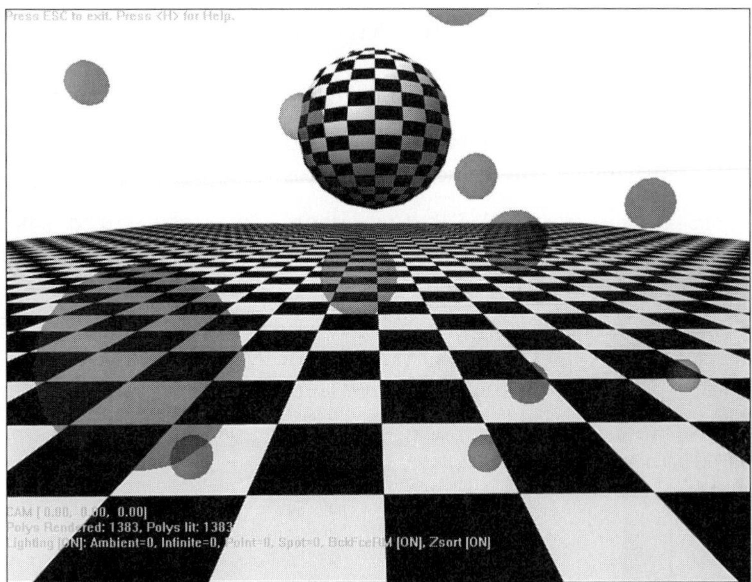

FIGURE 12.13 A screenshot of alpha blending on a per-polygon/object basis.

Adding Alpha to the Terrain Generator for Fun

Now that we can control alpha on a polygon level, let's put it to use with the terrain generator. One of the best examples of transparency is water with terrain under it, so I wanted to test the transparency on a large scale. I thought I would redo the jet ski simulation with support for transparency in the water. To do this, we could go into the color map or height map and encode transparency in some way to mark polygons as being transparent, along with some value for the transparency, but an easier method is to simply set a "sea level" parameter along with a alpha level, and send it to the terrain generation function itself. Then as the function is generating the mesh, any polygon that is below the sea level is set to transparent, with the alpha value encoded in its color. It took all of five minutes to modify the terrain generation function to support this. Here's the new prototype for version 2.0 of the terrain generator:

```
int Generate_Terrain2_OBJECT4DV2(OBJECT4DV2_PTR obj, // pointer to object
    float twidth,      // width in world coords on x-axis
    float theight,      // height (length) in world coords on z-axis
    float vscale,      // vertical scale of terrain
    char *height_map_file, // filename of height bitmap
    char *texture_map_file,// filename of texture map
    int rgbcolor,      // color of terrain if no texture
    VECTOR4D_PTR pos,    // initial position
    VECTOR4D_PTR rot,    // initial rotations
    int poly_attr,      // the shading attributes we would like
    float sea_level,     // height of sea level
    int alpha);      // alpha level to make all polys below sea level
```

`Generate_Terrain2_OBJECT4DV2()` has two new parameters:

- `float sea_level`—The actual level relative to the terrain height that should be the cutoff for transparency. Any value less than this value will be set transparent.
- `int alpha`—A value from 0..255 that represents how transparent to make the water (0 is totally transparent; 255 is totally opaque). This value will be scaled internally to (`0..(`*NUM_ALPHA_LEVELS*`-1)`.

To enable the transparency, set the alpha to a number larger than -1. The `sea_level` (whatever it might be) will then be used as the value to force polygons transparent, as shown in Figure 12.14.

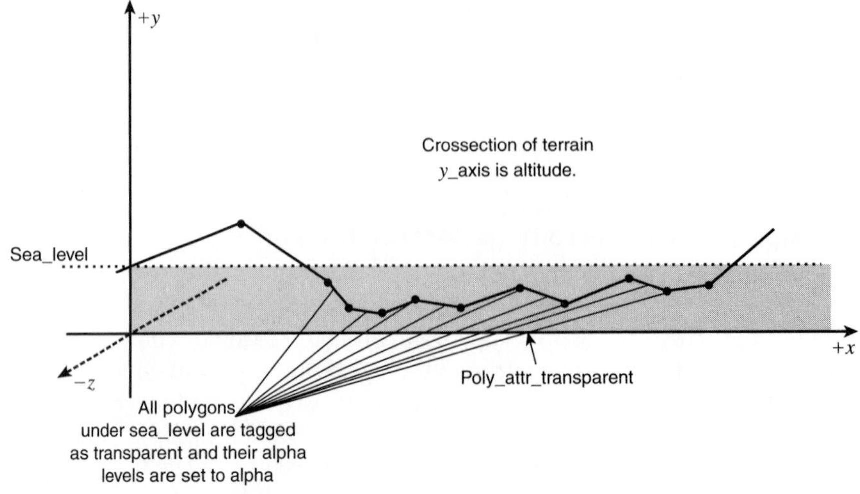

FIGURE 12.14 Adding transparency to the terrain generation via sea level.

Other than this added functionality, there is no difference in the terrain generation—it's still brute force as can be <BG>. The following is the added code that supports the alpha channel. It's excerpted from the vertex generation portion of the terrain generator:

```
// check for alpha enable for sea level polygons to help with water effect
if (alpha >=0 )
  {
  // compute heights of both polygons
  float avg_y_poly1 = (obj->vlist_local[ obj->plist[poly*2].vert[0] ].y +
            obj->vlist_local[ obj->plist[poly*2].vert[1] ].y +
            obj->vlist_local[ obj->plist[poly*2].vert[2] ].y )/3;

  float avg_y_poly2 = (obj->vlist_local[ obj->plist[poly*2+1].vert[0] ].y +
            obj->vlist_local[ obj->plist[poly*2+1].vert[1] ].y +
            obj->vlist_local[ obj->plist[poly*2+1].vert[2] ].y )/3;


  // test height of poly1 relative to sea level
  if (avg_y_poly1 <= sea_level)
   {
   int ialpha = (int)( (float)alpha/255 *
          (float)(NUM_ALPHA_LEVELS-1) + (float)0.5);

   // set the alpha color
   obj->plist[poly*2+0].color+= (ialpha << 24);

   // set the alpha flag in polygon
   SET_BIT(obj->plist[poly*2+0].attr, POLY4DV2_ATTR_TRANSPARENT);
   } // end if


  // test height of poly1 relative to sea level
  if (avg_y_poly2 <= sea_level)
   {
   int ialpha = (int)( (float)alpha/255 *
          (float)(NUM_ALPHA_LEVELS-1) + (float)0.5);

   // set the alpha color
   obj->plist[poly*2+1].color+= (ialpha << 24);

   // set the alpha flag in polygon
   SET_BIT(obj->plist[poly*2+1].attr, POLY4DV2_ATTR_TRANSPARENT);
   } // end if

  } // end if
```

To create the demo, I took the jet ski demo from the last chapter and changed the function call to the new version 2.0 and added the proper call to the rendering function that supports z-buffered alpha channel.

There's also one more feature that slows the demo down a bit, but it's necessary. When the water is transparent, the background skyscape is visible, which is a no-no. Thus I had to place an *extra* terrain mesh under the top terrain to create a sea floor in essence, so when we look through the water, you see the sea bottom rather than the skyscape. In essence, we are rendering two terrains—ouch! However, it doesn't slow down to an unplayable rate (however, I did need to drop the resolution down to 640×480 to make it fast enough). You can toggle the second terrain if you want with the T key to see the difference, but I warn you, you will see the clouds under there! Anyway, Figure 12.15 is a screenshot of `DEMOII12_4.CPP¦EXE` in action.

FIGURE 12.15 The jet ski demo with transparent water and a sea bottom mesh.

When you play the demo, move around and watch the sea bottom under the water level—it's pretty cool. The controls are the same as the previous jet ski demo:

After the announcer is done, he explains how to play:

- Enter/Return—Starts engine
- Right—Turn right
- Left—Turn left
- Up—Throttle
- T—Toggle sea floor terrain

And most of the help and engine controls still work:

- Z—Toggle z-buffering
- S—Toggle z-sorting
- D—Toggle normal rendering/Z-buffer filter
- H—Toggle help menu
- Esc—Exit demo

Try experimenting with turning different light sources on and off, z-buffering, z-sorting, and so forth. To compile the program, you will need the main program `DEMOII12_4.CPP¦H` along with `T3DLIB1-10.CPP¦H` and the DirectX .LIB files as usual.

Perspective-Correct Texturing and 1/z-Buffering

Finally we're ready to deal with our perspective-correct dilemma once again. The reason that we haven't tackled perspective-correct texturing yet is that it relies on a number of fundamental concepts that we still needed to cover, such as z-buffering and affine texture mapping. The reason why we needed to start with affine texture mapping is obvious, but z-buffering might not be so obvious. However, we performed an analysis in the previous chapter where we proved that 1/z is linear in screen space, and contemplated using a 1/z buffer rather than a Z-buffer, but didn't implement it. In essence, we were putting together the tools to not only implement perspective texture mapping, but to really understand it. Sure, I could just dump a totally optimized SIMD (single instruction multiple data—new instructions supported by the Pentium III+) perspective-correct texture mapper on you, but what would that help?

In any event, in this section we are going to cover the mathematical derivation of perspective-correct texture mapping (in a couple of different ways), create 1/z-buffering rasterizers, and then put the ideas together to implement both perfect perspective-correct (as well as piecewise linear perspective-correct) texture mappers. Finally, we will talk about some other approximation techniques and optimizations that can be exploited. Let's start first with the mathematical foundation for perspective texture mapping.

Mathematical Foundations for Perspective Texture Mapping

Affine texture mapping, Gouraud shading and the triangle rasterizer itself are all based on the linear interpolation of values down the triangle edges to be rasterized. This is shown in Figure 12.16.

We have done this many times, and the bottom line is that if you want to linearly interpolate a value from the top of the triangle to the bottom of the triangle, you break it up into equally distanced values and interpolate from top to bottom. So, in general, to interpolate the value `d` from `y0` to `y1`, you would do something like this:

```
float d = y0;
float dy = y1 - y0;

float dxdy = d/dy;

for (y=y0; y <= y1; y++)
  {
  // do something with d

  // interpolate d
  d+=dxdy;

  } // end for
```

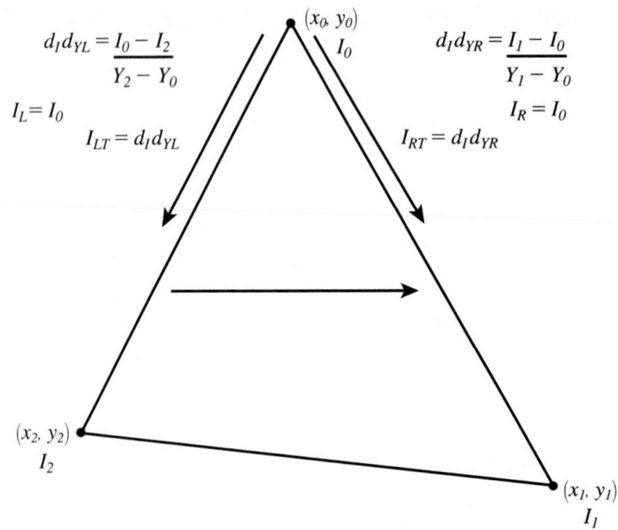

FIGURE 12.16 Standard interpolation flow.

The problem with linear interpolation is that we can't use it to interpolate anything that is not linear in screen space. Therefore, it doesn't work for texturing, z-coordinates, or even color intensities. In all cases, we are warping the data because of the perspective created via the projection-to-screen coordinates; however, it's manageable in all cases. Affine texture mappers look fine at a distance, Gouraud shading with linear interpolation doesn't look too bad, and z-buffering seems to work most of the time—but they are *all* wrong!

Based on our analysis last chapter, we proved that anything we linearly interpolate in screen space *after* the perspective projection is *not* linear, and must be divided by z as well to remain linear. That is, only 1/z is linear in screen space. This is the key to everything. What I would like to do is show you two different derivations of the perspective-correct texturing that are commonly used, so that you get a real grip on why and how it really works.

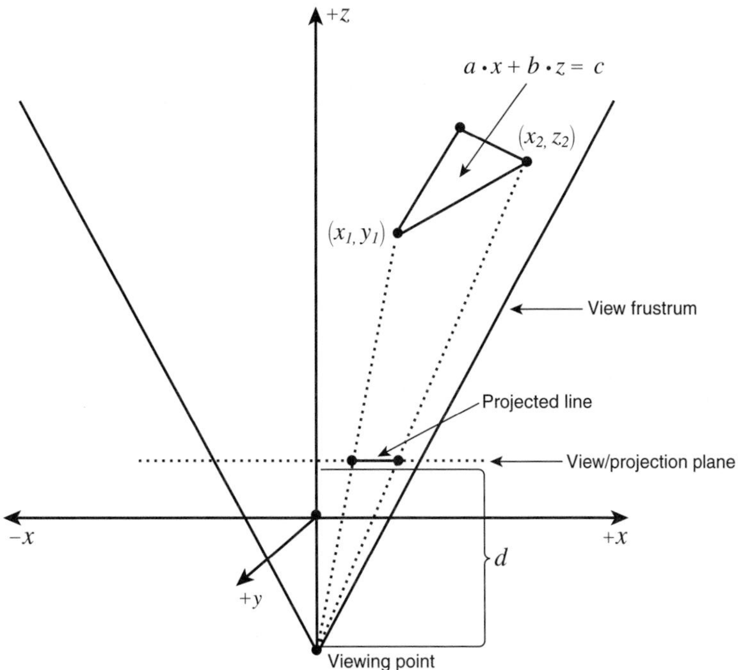

FIGURE 12.17 Projecting a line from 3D to 2D.

Perspective Derivation One

This first proof is a little less robust, but more to the point that the next one, so let's start here. In Figure 12.17, we see a line that we would like to project onto the screen (it's a 2D case, but 3D is the same; just imagine we are in the X-Z plane and y = 0). The line has two endpoints (x1, z1) and (x2,z2). We know that we can write an equation that represents this line as

```
a*x + b*z = c
```

where the coefficients a, b, and c can be found in a number of ways. For example, just plug in (x1, z1) and (x2,z2) and solve for them like this:

```
a*x1 + b*z1 = c
a*x2 + b*z2 = c
```

You can use substitution, matrices, Gaussian elimination, or your TI-92 calculator. But we don't need the coefficients, we are just interested in the form:

```
a*x + b*z = c
```

Now let's imagine that we project a point on the line (x,z) onto the screen using the perspective transformation. That means we just divide by z (of course, the view distance d is multiplied by is a concern, but assume d is 1.0 for now, so it has no effect):

$$x_{per} = x/z$$

Look familiar? Now, if we rearrange this to solve for x:

$$x/z = x_{per}$$

$$x = \mathbf{z*x_{per}}$$

So, we are mapping things backwards, asking the question, "What x in 3D space is equal to what x in screen space?" Now let's plug x into the line equation:

$$a*\mathbf{x} + b*z = c \rightarrow a*(\ \mathbf{z*x_{per}}\ ) + b*z = c$$

Factoring z out, we get

$$(a*x_{per})*z + b*z = c$$

$$(a*x_{per} + b)*z = c$$

Rearranging to solve for z, we get

$$z = c\ /\ (a*x_{per} + b)$$

which is a mess, so let's take the reciprocal of each side:

EQUATION 12.1 The Perspective Linear Equation

$$1/z = (a*x_{per} + b)\ /\ c$$

$$1/z = (a/c)*x_{per} + (b/c)$$

This equation states that 1/z is linear with respect to x_{per}. However, if we plug the value x/z back into x_{per}, we get this back:

$$1/z = (a/c)*\ x/z + (b/c)$$

This says that 1/z is linear with x/z. And that's the proof! What this means is that if we linearly interpolate 1/z, it's linear with x/z. So, if we linearly interpolate x, z, u, whatever, we need to first divide them by z, then linearly interpolate these values. Then at each interpolation interval, we need the original value back, so we must divide by 1/z. For example, let's plug in a texture coordinate u and see what happens:

```
1/z = (a/c)* u/z + (b/c)
```

We start off and compute 1/z and set it equal to z'. Similarly, we compute u/z and call it u'. Then we perform one linear interpolation step. We now have the values u' and z'. u' represents the linearly interpolated value of u/z, and z' represents the linearly interpolated value of 1/z. But we want the real u, not u', so we must divide by z'. Here's the math:

```
u = u'/z' = (u/z) / (1/z) = (u/z) * (z/1) = u
```

We simply interpolate away, and at each step we must divide by z' to compute the real u. Of course, u could be anything—a texture coordinate, light value, and so on. Thus, if u was a texture coordinate, we would need two divisions per pixel to compute u and v from u' and v', and that's where the two divisions per pixel come from with perspective correct texture mapping!

Before we move on to the next derivation, which is a little more robust, let's talk about what is going on from a programming point of view. Without a doubt, we are going to need to interpolate 1/z down the sides of the triangles. Because we are doing this, we can immediately switch from a Z-buffer to a 1/z-buffer and lose nothing. We simply invert the inner loop comparisons from less than to greater than, and use a 1/z-buffer. Practically, we will have to rethink our fixed-point format to get a little more decimal accuracy, because 1/z will never be larger than 1.0. Hence, there is no need to have 16 bits of the whole number part and 16 bits of the fractional number part with the old 16.16 fixed-point format. We should slide the fixed-point way over to give us nearly the entire range—something like a 4.28 format will be good. I will get to this when we implement the 1/z-buffer. Assuming the implementation details will be handled, we are pretty much stuck with two divisions per pixel. There is no way around this—period. We can use optimizations and approximations, of course.

Before moving on, let's do a real example on paper and see what happens with an affine texture mapper and perspective correct. Let's interpolate a single triangle edge with just one coordinate. Let's use points of the form (x,y,z), with **p1**(100,100,20) at u1 = 0 and **p2**(50,110,50) at u2 = 63. This is shown in Figure 12.18.

Here is the algorithm that will perform pure affine/linear interpolation of the texture coordinates:

```
float x1=100, y1=100, z1=20, u1=0,
   x2=50, y2=110, z2=50, u2=63;

float du = u2 - u1;
float dy = y2 - y1;
float dudy = du/dy;
```

```
// initialize interpolant
float u = u1;

// interpolate
for (int y=(int)y1; y <= (int)y2; y++)
  {
  printf("\n@y=%d, u=%f",y,u);

  // interpolate u
  u+=dudy;
  } // end for
```

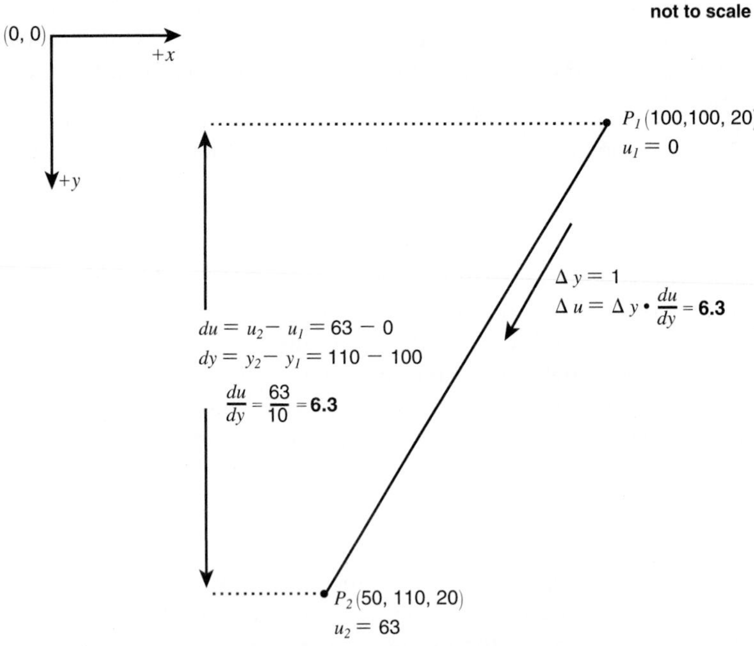

FIGURE 12.18 Triangle edge setup for perspective interpolation.

> **NOTE**
>
> The preceding program is so little, I didn't include it on the CD. Just type it in and make a console application if you want to run it. We really need a quick and dirty C/C++ compiler to do these little programs—hmmm, that gives me an idea ... <BG>.

If you type in this little program, you will get the following run of incorrect data, shown in Table 12.1.

TABLE 12.1 Linear Interpolation of Texture Coordinates

Y Value	Texture Coordinate
100	u = 0.000
101	u = 6.300
102	u = 12.600
103	u = 18.900
104	u = 25.200
105	u = 31.500
106	u = 37.799
107	u = 44.099
108	u = 50.399
109	u = 56.699
110	u = 62.999

Notice the delta between each iteration of the loop is always the same (6.3), so we are blatantly disregarding the z values here! Figure 12.19 shows a plot of this data.

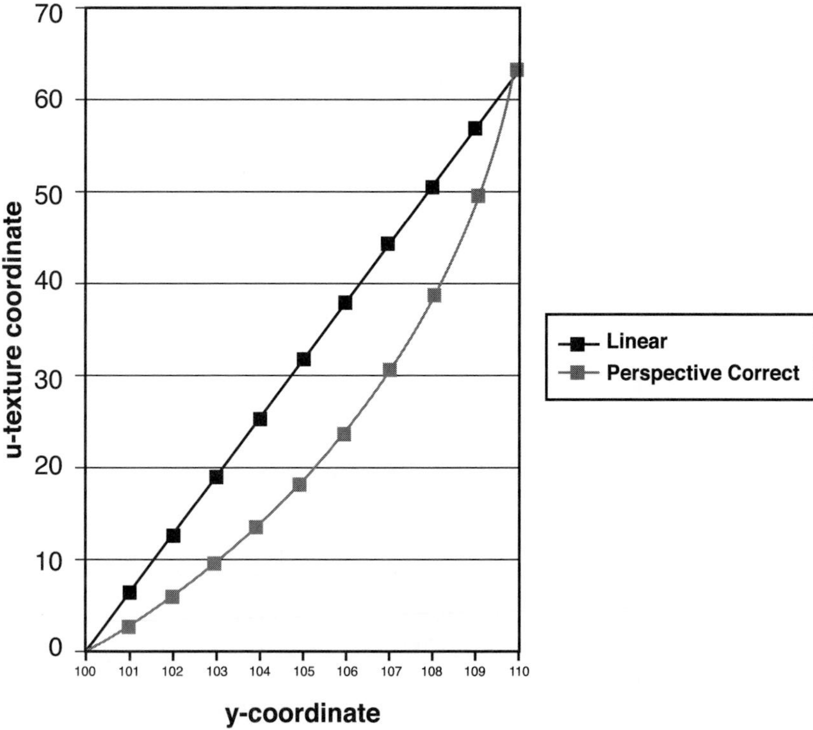

FIGURE 12.19 Data plots of linear and perspective interpolation.

Notice that u varies linearly with z, which we know is incorrect. Now, take a look at the perspective-correct version of the function that interpolates 1/z as well as u/z, and then computes u each iteration by dividing (u/z) by (1/z):

```
float x1=100, y1=100, z1=20, u1=0,
   x2=50, y2=110, z2=50, u2=63;

float du = u2/z2 - u1/z1;
float dy = y2 - y1;
float dz = 1/z2 - 1/z1;

float dzdy = dz/dy;
float dudy = du/dy;

// initialize interpolant
float u = u1/z1;
float z = 1/z1;

// interpolate
for (int y=(int)y1; y <= (int)y2; y++)
  {
  printf("\n@y=%d, 1/z=%f, u/z=%f: u=%f",y, u, z, u/z);

  // interpolate u/z
  u+=dudy;

  // interpolate 1/z
  z+=dzdy;
  } // end for
```

Now take a look at Figure 12.19 and Table 12.2. You can now see that the texture coordinate in not interpolating linearly, but varying with 1/z, as it should.

TABLE 12.2 Perspective-Correct Interpolation of Texture Coordinates

Y Value	1/z	u/z	Texture Coordinate
y = 100	1/z = 0.000	u/z = 0.050	u = 0.000
y = 101	1/z = 0.126	u/z = 0.047	u = 2.680
y = 102	1/z = 0.252	u/z = 0.044	u = 5.727
y = 103	1/z = 0.378	u/z = 0.041	u = 9.219
y = 104	1/z = 0.504	u/z = 0.038	u = 13.263
y = 105	1/z = 0.630	u/z = 0.035	u = 17.999
y = 106	1/z = 0.756	u/z = 0.032	u = 23.624
y = 107	1/z = 0.882	u/z = 0.029	u = 30.413
y = 108	1/z = 1.008	u/z = 0.026	u = 38.769
y = 109	1/z = 1.134	u/z = 0.023	u = 49.304
y = 110	1/z = 1.26	u/z = 0.020	u = 62.999

And as one final example to really make this rock solid, let's set the z coordinates equal to one another. In this case, we should see absolutely no perspective, because the polygon this would represent would be flat to the screen, right? So in this case, the perspective interpolation should be identical to the data from the affine/linear texture mapper—let's see! Setting z1 = 20 and z2 = 20 to get rid of any perspective, we run the program, and Table 12.3 shows the results.

TABLE 12.3 Perspective-Correct Interpolation of Texture Coordinates with z Values Equal

Y Value	1/z	u/z	Texture Coordinate
y = 100	1/z = 0.000	u/z = 0.050	u = 0.000
y = 101	1/z = 0.315	u/z = 0.050	u = 6.300
y = 102	1/z = 0.630	u/z = 0.050	u = 12.600
y = 103	1/z = 0.945	u/z = 0.050	u = 18.900
y = 104	1/z = 1.260	u/z = 0.050	u = 25.199
y = 105	1/z = 1.575	u/z = 0.050	u = 31.500
y = 106	1/z = 1.890	u/z = 0.050	u = 37.800
y = 107	1/z = 2.205	u/z = 0.050	u = 44.100
y = 108	1/z = 2.520	u/z = 0.050	u = 50.400
y = 109	1/z = 2.835	u/z = 0.050	u = 56.700
y = 110	1/z = 3.150	u/z = 0.050	u = 63.000

If you compare the values from Table 12.1 and Table 12.3, you will see that the texture coordinates are the same (with small floating-point errors, of course). Thus proving that our algorithm works in all cases.

Perspective Derivation Two

For the second derivation, we are going to do something similar, but a little more robust that fits into the interpolation equation a little better. This means a little more rigor in the final formulation of the interpolation equation from point to point in the following formula.

EQUATION 12.2 Basic Point-to-Point Interpolation Formula

```
p = (1-t)*p1 + (t)*p2
```

NOTE

p can be vector valued or a single scalar.

Thus, we want to end up with something that illustrates the interpolated relationship from p1 to p2 in terms of z. Let's begin with Figure 12.20, which shows the setup for the derivation.

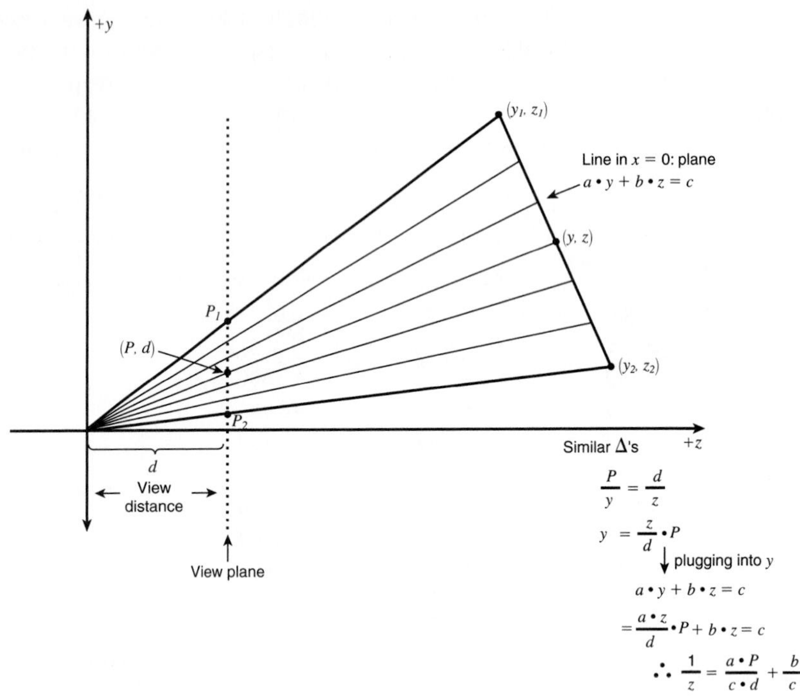

FIGURE 12.20 Line interpolation and perspective projection.

We have two points in world space, with the coordinates (y1,z1) and (y2,z2). These points project and intersect our viewplane at a distance z = d, and at points (p1, d) and (p2, d). Additionally, we have an arbitrary point (x,z) that projects and intersects the viewplane at (p,d).

Let's begin with the equation of the line that represents a polygon edge in 3D space, but in the y-z plane with x = 0. This line has the form

```
a*y + b*z = c
```

Now, referring to Figure 12.20, we can once again use similar triangles to relate the intersection point (p,d) and the 3D point (x,z):

```
p/y = d/z
```

Solving for y, we get

```
y = (p/d)*z
```

Plugging y into the line equation, we get

```
a*y + b*z = c

a*(p/d)*z + b*z = c

(a*p/d)*z + b*z = c
```


Factoring z out, we get

```
((a*p/d) + b)*z = c
```

Then dividing both sides by the term ((a*p/d) + b), we get

```
z = c / ((a*p/d) + b)
```

Taking the reciprocal of both sides, we get

```
1/z = ((a*p/d) + b)/c = (a*p/c*d) + (b/c)
```

And pulling p out to separate constants from variables, we get Equation 12.3.

EQUATION 12.3 Inverse Z-Linear Relationship

```
1/z = (a/c*d)*p + (b/c)
```

This means that at (y1, z1) with projected point (p1,d), we can write

```
1/z1 = (a/c*d)*p1 + (b/c)
```

And at (y2, z2) with projected point (p2,d), we can write

```
1/z2 = (a/c*d)*p2 + (b/c)
```

We have defined the endpoints of the interpolation from p1 to p2, but we still need to see what happens in the middle at the point p. So let's take Equation 12.2 and plug it into Equation 12.3:

Given:

```
1/z = (a/c*d)*p + (b/c)
```

And plugging p = (1-t)*p1 + (t)*p2 into it for p, we get

```
1/z = (a/c*d)*[ (1-t)*p1 + (t)*p2 ] + (b/c)
```

Multiplying terms out, we get

```
1/z = (a/c*d)*p1*(1-t) + (a/c*d)*p2*(t) + (b/c)
```

Now, here's the tricky part algebraically. We need to add (b/c)*t and subtract (b/c)*t to the right-hand side. The results of this will be

```
1/z = [ (a/c*d)*p1 + (b/c) ]*(1-t) + [ (a/c*d)*p2 + (b/c) ]*(t)
```

Now look at the terms I have highlighted. They should look familiar—they are the right-hand sides of

```
1/z1 = (a/c*d)*p1 + (b/c)
1/z2 = (a/c*d)*p2 + (b/c)
```

Therefore, we can substitute the left-hand sides, that is the 1/z1 and 1/z2 terms, giving us the final results:

```
1/z = [(1/z1)]*(1-t) + [(1/z2)]*(t)
```

This says that we can linearly interpolate 1/z1 to 1/z2. Or in other words, anything that we project from 3D space to screen space will only be linear if it's interpolated with a division by z.

Hopefully, you have a good understanding of why interpolating 1/z is linear, and that any x value you interpolate as that value divided by z (x/z) is also linear in screen space! This should also make sense intuitively, because to get the screen projected values, we divide by z.

Adding 1/z-Buffering Support to the Rasterizers

Now that you see the reasoning behind needing 1/z to be interpolated in our rasterizers to support perspective-correct texturing, we need to support it. Doing this is reasonably straightforward, but some work has to be done with the fixed-point format to give us higher accuracy. Currently, we are using a 16.16 format. This allows for signed integers from -32768 to 32767 to be represented, along with a smallest fractional number of $1/2^{16}$, or approximately 1.5258×10^{-5} to be represented—about 4–5 decimal places of accuracy. However, this only holds in relation to the format itself. When operations such as division or multiplication are carried out, this accuracy can be quickly destroyed because of shifting. Alas, we need to come up with another fixed-point format that is more conducive to representing numbers that are less than 1.0, or in other words reciprocals of z. The question is, how far can we go?

The answer is pretty far off, but not too far off. We are using 32-bit integers and we need a sign bit, so that means that we really have only 31 bits to work with. Of course, we could use a 2.30 format, that gives us 1 bit for the sign, 1 bit for the "1" if our number is between 0..1.99999999, but this is too tight. I experimented with it, and it overflows here and there, so in the end I went with a 4.28 format. That's 28 bits of decimal accuracy, three bits of whole part, and the sign bit. So, we can represent -8 to +7 with 28 bits of decimal, which is enough for our 1/z-buffer and any future interpolation we might need to implement. The only `#define` for this new type is found in `T3DLIB10.H`:

```
#define FIXP28_SHIFT 28
```

Based on this, I took the Z-buffer rasterizers and converted them to 1/z. After that, I made versions that were perspective-correct by changing the affine texture interpolation to u/z, v/z interpolation and dividing each pixel by 1/z to compute the real u,z in texture space—whew. But I will get to that shortly—for now, let's take a look at the simplest 1/z-buffering rasterizer that draws constant-/flat-shaded polygons with no alpha. Here's the function prototype:


```
void Draw_Triangle_2DINVZB_16(POLYF4DV2_PTR face, // ptr to face
         UCHAR *_dest_buffer, // pointer to video buffer
         int mem_pitch,    // bytes per line, 320, 640 etc.
         UCHAR *zbuffer,    // pointer to z-buffer
         int zpitch);     // bytes per line of zbuffer
```

The function has identical calling parameters to the z-buffering version, except that internally it works with a 1/z-buffer. Before we get too far, let's back out for a second and review how the 1/z-buffer works. If there's a pixel at z = 100 and another at z = 200, the z = 100 pixel should overwrite the z = 200 pixel. Let's compute 1/z for each:

The z = 100 pixel:

```
1/100 = .01
```

The z = 200 pixel:

```
1/200 = .005
```

So, our normal comparison in the inner loop of

```
if (zi < screen_ptr[x]) then write pixel…
```

needs to be inverted, so that larger 1/z values win out:

```
if (zi > screen_ptr[x]) then write pixel…
```

We covered this already in the previous chapter, so this shouldn't be a surprise. We have to change our initialization of the Z-buffer each frame. With a Z-buffer, we would write the largest potential z value we expect into the Z-buffer, like `32000`. Here's the code we have been using:

```
Clear_Zbuffer(&zbuffer, (32000 << FIXP16_SHIFT));
```

However, now we are not only using a different format for the fixed-point representation, but we need to fill the buffer with `0` anyway! So we need to change the Z-buffer clear to

```
Clear_Zbuffer(&zbuffer, 0);
```

That's convenient, huh?

TIP

Now that we are working on a 1/z-buffer, or *inverse Z-buffer* as I like to call it, we can potentially take advantage of the optimization I mentioned that adds a bias to the z value each frame so the Z-buffer doesn't need to be cleared each frame. However, we can only do this a few times, because we have only three bits to store whole numbers with our 4.28 format. I have decided to omit this optimization for now.

The next issue is the Z-buffer code itself. Do we need to do anything to the data structures and so on? The answer is no—the Z-buffer doesn't care, it's just memory. However, we surely can't mix Z-buffer calls with 1/z-buffer calls, as the Z-buffer memory would be a mess. Nevertheless, even though there are some effects you could get by doing this, I will leave it to you.

Moving on, let's take a look at the 1/z-buffering setup code in the sample rasterizer. Here's what the vertex setup stage looked like before, with normal z-buffering in the simple rasterizer:

```
// extract vertices for processing, now that we have order
x0 = (int)(face->tvlist[v0].x+0.0);
y0 = (int)(face->tvlist[v0].y+0.0);

tz0 = (int)(face->tvlist[v0].z+0.5);

x1 = (int)(face->tvlist[v1].x+0.0);
y1 = (int)(face->tvlist[v1].y+0.0);

tz1 = (int)(face->tvlist[v1].z+0.5);

x2 = (int)(face->tvlist[v2].x+0.0);
y2 = (int)(face->tvlist[v2].y+0.0);

tz2 = (int)(face->tvlist[v2].z+0.5);
```

I have highlighted the z coordinate lines. Now let's look at what it looks like with 1/z-buffering in mind:

```
// extract vertices for processing, now that we have order
x0 = (int)(face->tvlist[v0].x+0.0);
y0 = (int)(face->tvlist[v0].y+0.0);

tz0 = (1 << FIXP28_SHIFT) / (int)(face->tvlist[v0].z+0.5);

x1 = (int)(face->tvlist[v1].x+0.0);
y1 = (int)(face->tvlist[v1].y+0.0);

tz1 = (1 << FIXP28_SHIFT) / (int)(face->tvlist[v1].z+0.5);
```

```
x2 = (int)(face->tvlist[v2].x+0.0);
y2 = (int)(face->tvlist[v2].y+0.0);

tz2 = (1 << FIXP28_SHIFT) / (int)(face->tvlist[v2].z+0.5);
```


There are two things going on that weren't in the previous version. First, we are using fixed-point right off the bat. Notice I am converting 1.0 to fixed-point 4.28 format, and then dividing by the z value. Thus, `tz0`, `tz1`, and `tz2` are now in fixed-point format right from the beginning, whereas they were not in the previous version that supported straight z-buffering. The reason for this is that I can't divide z into 1 without losing everything because we are dealing with integers here, so I had to convert to fixed-point before the division operation. Thus, all the places in the code where there was a shift by `FIXP16_SHIFT` to convert the z interpolants are now gone because they are already in fixed-point format. Performance-wise, I think we might gain a little from this, but I haven't counted it yet—I think it's the same. However, the nice thing is that we start out with `tz0`, `tz1`, and `tz1` as 1/z values in fixed-point 4.28 format. Then the rasterizer proceeds as usual. For example, when we computed all the interpolants for z (I have deleted all the other code here), we used to shift everything by `FIXP16_SHIFT` to convert to fixed-point as we did this:

```
dy = (y2 - y0);
dzdyl = ((tz2 - tz0) << FIXP16_SHIFT)/dy;
dzdyr = ((tz2 - tz1) << FIXP16_SHIFT)/dy;

dy = (min_clip_y - y0);

// computer new LHS starting values
zl = dzdyl*dy + (tz0 << FIXP16_SHIFT);
zr = dzdyr*dy + (tz1 << FIXP16_SHIFT);
```

However, the 1/z-buffering now looks like this in these areas:

```
dy = (y2 - y0);
dzdyl = ((tz2 - tz0))/dy;
dzdyr = ((tz2 - tz1))/dy;

dy = (min_clip_y - y0);

// computer new LHS starting values
zl = dzdyl*dy + (tz0);
zr = dzdyr*dy + (tz1);
```

So we lose all the shifts! Cool, huh? Anyway, in the final inner loop everything is the same, except for the inverted Z-buffer comparison to support 1/z-buffering. This is true because the code doesn't care what we are interpolating, it just interpolates it. The key to this is remembering that the setup is different, and we simply initialize everything to 1/z values rather than z values. With that in mind, here's an excerpt from `Draw_Triangle_2DINVZB_16()` that shows one complete y scan loop. The entire function is way too long to list, but this excerpt shows that the inverse z-buffering is basically identical to z-buffering, and faster if anything. Here's the code:

```
// point screen ptr to starting line
screen_ptr = dest_buffer + (ystart * mem_pitch);

// point zbuffer to starting line
z_ptr = zbuffer + (ystart * zpitch);

for (yi = ystart; yi < yend; yi++)
  {
  // compute span endpoints
  xstart = ((xl + FIXP16_ROUND_UP) >> FIXP16_SHIFT);
  xend   = ((xr + FIXP16_ROUND_UP) >> FIXP16_SHIFT);

  // compute starting points for u,v,w interpolants
  zi = zl;

  // compute u,v interpolants
  if ((dx = (xend - xstart))>0)
      {
    dz = (zr - zl)/dx;
    } // end if
  else
    {
    dz = (zr - zl);
    } // end else

  // draw span
  for (xi=xstart; xi < xend; xi++)
    {
     // test if z of current pixel is nearer than current z buffer value
     if (zi > z_ptr[xi])
      {
      // write textel 5.6.5
      screen_ptr[xi] = color;

      // update z-buffer
      z_ptr[xi] = zi;
      } // end if
```

```
    // interpolate z
    zi+=dz;
    } // end for xi

  // interpolate x,z along right and left edge
  xl+=dxdyl;
  zl+=dzdyl;

  xr+=dxdyr;
  zr+=dzdyr;

  // advance screen ptr
  screen_ptr+=mem_pitch;

   // advance z-buffer ptr
   z_ptr+=zpitch;

  } // end for y
```

Let's briefly review where we are and then take a look at all the rasterizers for 1/z-buffering, minus the perspective-correct one. We need 1/z to perspective-texture map polygons correctly; however, 1/z-buffering turns out to be just as good as z-buffering, so it's a wash, and we lose nothing performance-wise. However, we had to change the fixed-point format to support the reciprocal of z and have enough accuracy. Furthermore, 1/z has more resolution for polygons that are near the viewplane where the Z-buffer spreads the accuracy through the entire viewspace z distance. Thus we get an added bonus of the visibility being more accurate up close. Because we convert all 1/z values to fixed-point from the gate, we save a few shifts during the setup that used to exist in the plain Z-buffer rasterizers. And finally, we need to clear the Z-buffer memory with the value of `0` rather than the farthest possible z value each frame as we did with the Z-buffer. This gives us the opportunity to use the inverse Z-buffer bias techniques, not clearing the buffer each frame for a few frames, and potentially reaping a performance gain. We will look into this later.

NOTE

Last but not least, there is absolutely no difference in supporting the alpha blending with inverse z-buffering: You just take the alpha blending z-buffered rasterizers and convert them to use the inverse Z-buffer. We aren't going to look inside them, but I will show their prototypes.

Here are the prototypes for the new rasterizers that support 1/z-buffering minus the perspective ones, which we are going to cover in a moment:

Function:

```
void Draw_Triangle_2DINVZB_16(POLYF4DV2_PTR face, // ptr to face
         UCHAR *_dest_buffer, // pointer to video buffer
         int mem_pitch,    // bytes per line, 320, 640 etc.
         UCHAR *zbuffer,    // pointer to z-buffer
         int zpitch);     // bytes per line of zbuffer
```

Description: `Draw_Triangle_2DINVZB_16()` draws a standard colored triangle using the inverse Z-buffer.

Function:

```
void Draw_Gouraud_TriangleINVZB_16(POLYF4DV2_PTR face,  // ptr to face
         UCHAR *_dest_buffer, // pointer to video buffer
         int mem_pitch,    // bytes per line, 320, 640 etc.
         UCHAR *zbuffer,   // pointer to z-buffer
         int zpitch);     // bytes per line of zbuffer
```

Description: `Draw_Gouraud_TriangleINVZB_16()` draws a standard Gouraud-shaded triangle using the inverse Z-buffer.

Function:

```
void Draw_Textured_TriangleINVZB_16(POLYF4DV2_PTR face, // ptr to face
          UCHAR *_dest_buffer, // pointer to video buffer
          int mem_pitch,    // bytes per line, 320, 640 etc.
          UCHAR *zbuffer,    // pointer to z-buffer
          int zpitch);     // bytes per line of zbuffer
```

Description: `Draw_Textured_TriangleINVZB_16()` draws an affine-textured triangle with constant shading and an inverse Z-buffer.

Function:

```
void Draw_Textured_TriangleFSINVZB_16(POLYF4DV2_PTR face, // ptr to face
          UCHAR *_dest_buffer, // pointer to video buffer
          int mem_pitch,    // bytes per line, 320, 640 etc.
          UCHAR *zbuffer,    // pointer to z-buffer
          int zpitch);     // bytes per line of zbuffer
```

Description: `Draw_Textured_TriangleFSINVZB_16()` draws an affine-textured triangle with flat shading and an inverse Z-buffer.

Function:

```
void Draw_Textured_TriangleGSINVZB_16(POLYF4DV2_PTR face,  // ptr to face
           UCHAR *_dest_buffer, // pointer to video buffer
           int mem_pitch,    // bytes per line, 320, 640 etc.
```

```
          UCHAR *_zbuffer,    // pointer to z-buffer
          int zpitch);       // bytes per line of zbuffer
```

Description: `Draw_Textured_TriangleGSINVZB_16()` draws an affine-textured triangle with Gouraud shading and an inverse Z-buffer.

Function:

```
void Draw_RENDERLIST4DV2_SolidINVZB_16(RENDERLIST4DV2_PTR rend_list,
          UCHAR *video_buffer, // pointer to video buffer
          int lpitch,     // bytes per line, 320, 640 etc.
          UCHAR *zbuffer, // pointer to z-buffer
          int zpitch);    // bytes per line of zbuffer
```

Description: `Draw_RENDERLIST4DV2_SolidINVZB_16()` is the rendering list function that calls all of the rasterizers based on shading and texturing information per polygon. The function only calls inverse Z-buffer functions.

Next we have all the alpha blending versions of the inverse Z-buffer functions. They are identical to the non-alpha version, except they all have an extra `alpha_override` variable appended to the parameter list (once again, I am leaving out the perspective versions because we haven't covered them yet):

Function:

```
void Draw_Triangle_2DINVZB_Alpha16(POLYF4DV2_PTR face, // ptr to face
          UCHAR *_dest_buffer, // pointer to video buffer
          int mem_pitch,    // bytes per line, 320, 640 etc.
          UCHAR *zbuffer,   // pointer to z-buffer
          int zpitch,      // bytes per line of zbuffer
          int alpha);      // alpha level
```

Description: `Draw_Triangle_2DINVZB_Alpha16()` draws a standard colored triangle using the inverse Z-buffer.

Function:

```
void Draw_Gouraud_TriangleINVZB_Alpha16(POLYF4DV2_PTR face,  // ptr to face
           UCHAR *_dest_buffer, // pointer to video buffer
           int mem_pitch,    // bytes per line, 320, 640 etc.
           UCHAR *zbuffer,   // pointer to z-buffer
           int zpitch,      // bytes per line of zbuffer
           int alpha);      // alpha level
```

Description: `Draw_Gouraud_TriangleINVZB_Alpha16()` draws a standard Gouraud-shaded triangle using the inverse Z-buffer.

Function:

```
void Draw_Textured_TriangleINVZB_Alpha16(POLYF4DV2_PTR face, // ptr to face
            UCHAR *_dest_buffer, // pointer to video buffer
            int mem_pitch,     // bytes per line, 320, 640 etc.
            UCHAR *zbuffer,    // pointer to z-buffer
            int zpitch,       // bytes per line of zbuffer
            int alpha);       // alpha level
```

Description: `Draw_Textured_TriangleINVZB_Alpha16()` draws an affine-textured triangle with constant shading and an inverse Z-buffer.

Function:

```
void Draw_Textured_TriangleFSINVZB_Alpha16(POLYF4DV2_PTR face, // ptr to face
            UCHAR *_dest_buffer, // pointer to video buffer
            int mem_pitch,     // bytes per line, 320, 640 etc.
            UCHAR *zbuffer,    // pointer to z-buffer
            int zpitch,       // bytes per line of zbuffer
            int alpha);       // alpha level
```

Description: `Draw_Textured_TriangleFSINVZB_Alpha16()` draws an affine-textured triangle with flat shading and an inverse Z-buffer.

Function:

```
void Draw_Textured_TriangleGSINVZB_Alpha16(POLYF4DV2_PTR face,  // ptr to face
           UCHAR *_dest_buffer, // pointer to video buffer
           int mem_pitch,     // bytes per line, 320, 640 etc.
           UCHAR *_zbuffer,    // pointer to z-buffer
           int zpitch,       // bytes per line of zbuffer
           int alpha);       // alpha level
```

Description: `Draw_Textured_TriangleGSINVZB_Alpha16()` draws an affine-textured triangle with Gouraud shading and an inverse Z-buffer.

Function:

```
void Draw_RENDERLIST4DV2_SolidINVZB_Alpha16(RENDERLIST4DV2_PTR rend_list,
           UCHAR *video_buffer, // pointer to video buffer
           int lpitch,       // bytes per line, 320, 640 etc.
           UCHAR *zbuffer,    // pointer to z-buffer
           int zpitch,       // bytes per line of zbuffer
           int alpha_override); // alpha override value
```

Description: `Draw_RENDERLIST4DV2_SolidINVZB_Alpha16()` is the rendering list function that calls all of the rasterizers based on shading and texturing information per polygon. The function only calls inverse Z-buffer functions.

DEMOII12_5.CPP|EXE is a demo of the 1/z-buffer technology. A screenshot is shown in Figure 12.21.

FIGURE 12.21 A screenshot of the 1/z-buffer technology.

The demo enables you to switch from Z-buffer to 1/z-buffer to no buffer at all by pressing the Z key. You can also enable and disable z-sorting with the S key. Try moving around and pushing the "probe" into objects with each buffering technique—which looks more accurate to you? To compile the demo, you will need DEMOII12_5.CPP|H, T3DLIB1-10.CPP|H, and the DirectX .LIB files.

> **TIP**
>
> Make sure you disable the ambient light source with the A key—it makes the demo look really cool.

Implementing Perfect Perspective Mapping

Implementing perfect texture mapping at this point involves nothing more than some text editing. We simply need to start with the inverse z-buffering affine texture mapper and make some changes to the interpolants and the final calculation of u,v for each pixel. The changes are in the following areas:

- During entry/initialization, we need to compute the texture coordinates u/z and v/z and interpolate them as well as 1/z.

- In the inner loop of the rasterizer, we need to compute the real u,z texture coordinates. This is accomplished by dividing (1/z) *into* our linearly correct (u/z) and (v/z) values to arrive at the perspective correct (u,v) values at which to sample the texture map.

Of course, the devil is in the details <BG>. First, we need to revisit the fixed-point format once again. The problem is we are no longer interpolating u,v values—we are interpolating (u/z) and (v/z) values. So, we're going to need more than 16 bits of decimal accuracy. However, we can't use the 4.28 format we created for interpolating 1/z because the texture coordinates themselves can range up to 255. We need at least 8 bits to represent 0..255, plus we need a sign bit, so that's 9 bits, plus I hate odd numbers, so that makes a total of 10 bits for the whole part of the texture coordinate. Therefore, we're left with 22 bits of decimal accuracy for the decimal part.

We are going to use a 10.22 fixed-point format to interpolate (u/z) and (v/z), and a 4.22 fixed-point format to interpolate (1/z). This means that when we perform our final division of (1/z) into (u/z) and (v/z), we are going to be dividing a fixed-point 4.22 into fixed-point 10.22, so we need to be careful to shift things properly. Keep that in mind for now.

Let's look at the setup of the vertex and u,v information. Here's an excerpt from the inverse z-buffering, perspective-correct, constant-shaded rasterizer:

```
// extract vertices for processing, now that we have order
x0 = (int)(face->tvlist[v0].x+0.0);
y0 = (int)(face->tvlist[v0].y+0.0);

tu0 = ((int)(face->tvlist[v0].u0+0.5) << FIXP22_SHIFT) /
      (int)(face->tvlist[v0].z+0.5);
tv0 = ((int)(face->tvlist[v0].v0+0.5) << FIXP22_SHIFT) /
      (int)(face->tvlist[v0].z+0.5);

tz0 = (1 << FIXP28_SHIFT) / (int)(face->tvlist[v0].z+0.5);

x1 = (int)(face->tvlist[v1].x+0.0);
y1 = (int)(face->tvlist[v1].y+0.0);

tu1 = ((int)(face->tvlist[v1].u0+0.5) << FIXP22_SHIFT) /
    (int)(face->tvlist[v1].z+0.5);
tv1 = ((int)(face->tvlist[v1].v0+0.5) << FIXP22_SHIFT) /
    (int)(face->tvlist[v1].z+0.5);

tz1 = (1 << FIXP28_SHIFT) / (int)(face->tvlist[v1].z+0.5);

x2 = (int)(face->tvlist[v2].x+0.0);
y2 = (int)(face->tvlist[v2].y+0.0);
```

```
tu2 = ((int)(face->tvlist[v2].u0+0.5) << FIXP22_SHIFT) /
    (int)(face->tvlist[v2].z+0.5);
tv2 = ((int)(face->tvlist[v2].v0+0.5) << FIXP22_SHIFT) /
    (int)(face->tvlist[v2].z+0.5);

tz2 = (1 << FIXP28_SHIFT) / (int)(face->tvlist[v2].z+0.5);
```

And of course, the constant FIXP22_SHIFT is defined as

```
#define FIXP22_SHIFT 22
```

Please take a moment to make sure you see what's going on with the setup. We are doing the same thing with the 1/z calculation, but the (u,v) texture coordinates for each vertex are now being computed as (u/z) and (v/z). First we pre-shift (u,v) into fixed-point 10.22 format and then divide by z. However, as you might recall from a previous math note in this chapter, we proved that a fixed-point number can be divided or multiplied by a normal integer and the number will remain fixed-point, as long as it's not overflowed or underflowed, of course. Therefore, at the end of this initialization, we have (1/z) and all the texture coordinates for each vertex in (u/z), (v/z) format ready to be *linearly* interpolated.

Take my word for it—the code is the same in the rasterizer up until the inner-most loop. This is where the action takes place. We need the real texture coordinates (u,v) to access the texture memory, but to compute them for perfect perspective-correct texturing, we need to divide (1/z) into each (u/z), (v/z) interpolant. In other words:

```
u = (u/z) / (1/z)
v = (v/z) / (1/z)
```

However, (u/z) and (v/z) are in 10.22-fixed point format, and (1/z) is in 4.22 fixed-point format, so a straight division won't work. We need to shift one or both of the operands before performing the division, so we are left with both u,v in straight integral format without any loss of precision. Here's the inner span loop that accomplishes this:

```
for (xi=xstart; xi < xend; xi++)
  {
  // test if z of current pixel is nearer than current z buffer value
  if (zi > z_ptr[xi])
    {
    // write textel
    screen_ptr[xi] = textmap[ ((ui << (FIXP28_SHIFT - FIXP22_SHIFT)) / zi) +
   ( ((vi << (FIXP28_SHIFT - FIXP22_SHIFT)) / zi) << texture_shift2)];

    // update z-buffer
    z_ptr[xi] = zi;
    } // end if
```

```
// interpolate u,v,z
ui+=du;
vi+=dv;
zi+=dz;
} // end for xi
```

I have highlighted the magical code. With normal affine texturing, this code looked like

```
screen_ptr[xi] = textmap[(ui >> FIXP16_SHIFT) +
            ((vi >> FIXP16_SHIFT) << texture_shift2)];
```

Now we see the division by `zi`, as well as the shift by the difference (`FIXP28_SHIFT - FIXP22_SHIFT`). Let's talk about this shift value and why it's `(FIXP28_SHIFT - FIXP22_SHIFT) = (6)`. Take a look at Figure 12.22.

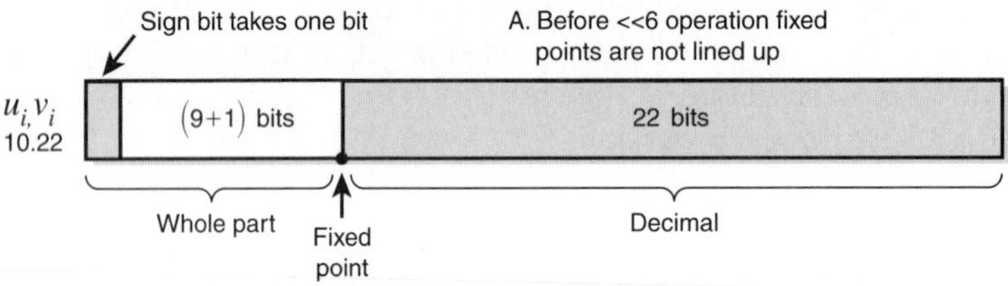

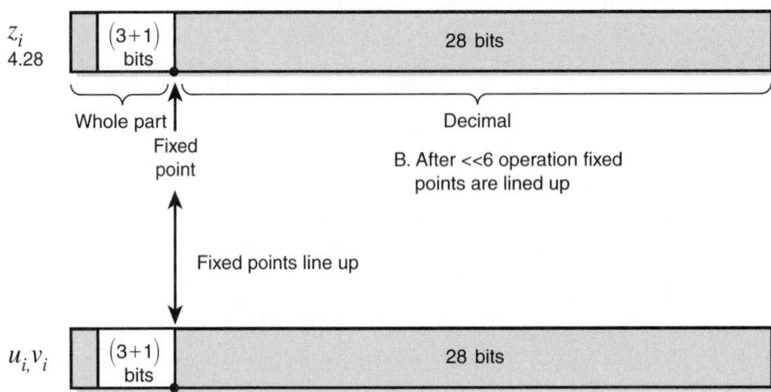

FIGURE 12.22 Getting the fixed points to line up.

Think of it like this: `ui` and `vi` are both in 10.22 format, and `zi` is in 4.28 format. Therefore, we need to line up the fixed points so the division results in no scaling, and thus an integer. To do this, we see that `ui` and `vi` need to be shifted six places to the left to line up with `zi`. This makes sense because the two formats differ by exactly

```
(FIXP28_SHIFT - FIXP22_SHIFT) = (28 - 22) = 6
```

Therefore, the shifting puts both the dividend and divisor into 4.28 format, and the resulting division reduces to a quotient that is integral and non-scaled.

TIP

There is another potential optimization with the texture addressing. If you look at the code, it performs the following texture access:

```
texture[u + (v << n)]
```

where *n* is the $\log_2$ of the texture width, or the number of words per row—so it's a multiplication, more or less. However, if we prescale `vi` by this value, we can avoid the left shift << operator in the final texture address calculation, and therefore speed up the texture address computation by approximately 30% <BG>. But we'll leave that one for later.

And that's simply all there is to perspective-correct texture mapping. Of course, the two divisions per pixel is not acceptable, but we will address that in a number of ways momentarily. At the very least, the division can always be turned into multiplication by computation of the reciprocal of the divisor. For example:

```
float x,y,c;

// some computations are performed with x,y,c...

x = x/c;
y = y/c;
```

Assuming anywhere from 15–40 cycles for each division, we are looking at around 30–80 cycles. Now let's perform this simple transformation:

```
float x,y,c;

// some computations are performed with x,y,c...

float oneoverc = 1/c;

x = x*c;
y = y*c;
```

We have a single division costing us 15–40 cycles, plus two multiplications costing 2–3 cycles each, so that's a total of 34—46 cycles. Of course, I am being brutally pessimistic with all the cycle counting, but we are looking at a savings of nearly 50% by first computing the single reciprocal. Nevertheless, any division at all in the innermost loop is totally unacceptable—we have to do better. Our only algorithmic possibilities are by approximation, and we will explore them shortly, but for now, let's take a look at the new functions that support perspective correct texturing with the inverse Z-buffer.

Function:

```
void Draw_Textured_Perspective_Triangle_INVZB_Alpha16(
                POLYF4DV2_PTR face, // ptr to face
                UCHAR *_dest_buffer, // pointer to video buffer
                int mem_pitch,    // bytes per line, 320, 640 etc.
                UCHAR *_zbuffer,   // pointer to z-buffer
                int zpitch,     // bytes per line of zbuffer
                int alpha);     // the alpha level
```

Description: `Draw_Textured_Perspective_Triangle_INVZB_Alpha16()` draws a perspective-correct triangle with alpha blending and constant shading.

Function:

```
void Draw_Textured_Perspective_Triangle_FSINVZB_Alpha16(
           POLYF4DV2_PTR face, // ptr to face
           UCHAR *_dest_buffer, // pointer to video buffer
           int mem_pitch,    // bytes per line, 320, 640 etc.
           UCHAR *_zbuffer,   // pointer to z-buffer
           int zpitch,     // bytes per line of zbuffer
           int alpha);     // the alpha level
```

Description: `Draw_Textured_Perspective_Triangle_FSINVZB_Alpha16()` draws a perspective-correct triangle with alpha blending and flat shading.

Function:

```
void Draw_Textured_Perspective_Triangle_INVZB_16(
          POLYF4DV2_PTR face, // ptr to face
          UCHAR *_dest_buffer, // pointer to video buffer
          int mem_pitch,    // bytes per line, 320, 640 etc.
          UCHAR *_zbuffer,   // pointer to z-buffer
          int zpitch);     // bytes per line of zbuffer
```

Description: `Draw_Textured_Perspective_Triangle_INVZB_16()` draws a perspective-correct triangle with constant shading.

Function:

```
void Draw_Textured_Perspective_Triangle_FSINVZB_16(
           POLYF4DV2_PTR face,// ptr to face
           UCHAR *_dest_buffer,// pointer to video buffer
           int mem_pitch,   // bytes per line, 320, 640 etc.
           UCHAR *_zbuffer,  // pointer to z-buffer
           int zpitch);    // bytes per line of zbuffer
```

Description: `Draw_Textured_Perspective_Triangle_FSINVZB_16()` draws a perspective-correct triangle with flat shading.

For a demo of the perspective-correct texturing, the best thing is of course a walkthrough interior environment, but we are still without a good tool to build interiors. DEMOII12_6.CPP|EXE instead creates a very flat terrain, with a checkerboard texture on it as the map. This shows the difference between the affine and perspective texture mappers quite significantly. Figure 12.23 is a screenshot of the demo in action.

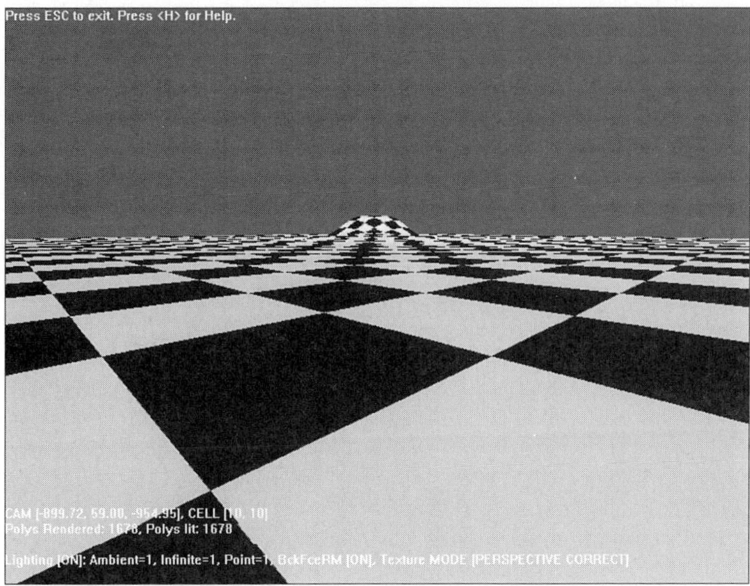
Press ESC to exit. Press <H> for Help.

FIGURE 12.23 The perspective-correct texturing demo.

Use the arrow keys to navigate around as usual, and press the T key to select between affine and perspective texturing. To compile the demo, you will need DEMOII12_6.CPP|H, along with T3DLIB1-10.CPP|H and the DirectX .LIB files.

Implementing Linear Piecewise Perspective Mapping

Although we could probably speed up the perfect texture mapper with some optimization within the two divisions using the product-of-reciprocal trick, a division is a division, and not acceptable for a software engine in most cases. Alas, is there anything we can do to speed this up? Can we make an approximation that is faster, and visually pleasing? The answer is it depends. All approximations are based on the concept of acceptable error, so it really depends on how much error is acceptable with the final rendered image. For example, a first-person shooter might not have the tolerance an outdoor terrain game might have to texture distortion, so these are the kinds of factors you need to take into consideration. So, we are going to implement a type of approximation that we can control to go from totally affine to totally perspective. Unfortunately, my implementation won't have this capability programmed in, but you can add it if you need it.

In any case, the approximation we are going to implement is called *linear piecewise approximation* (or *piecewise linear*, depending on what side of the bed you sleep on). Basically, it's somewhere between affine texture mapping and perspective-correct texture mapping, and is illustrated in Figure 12.24.

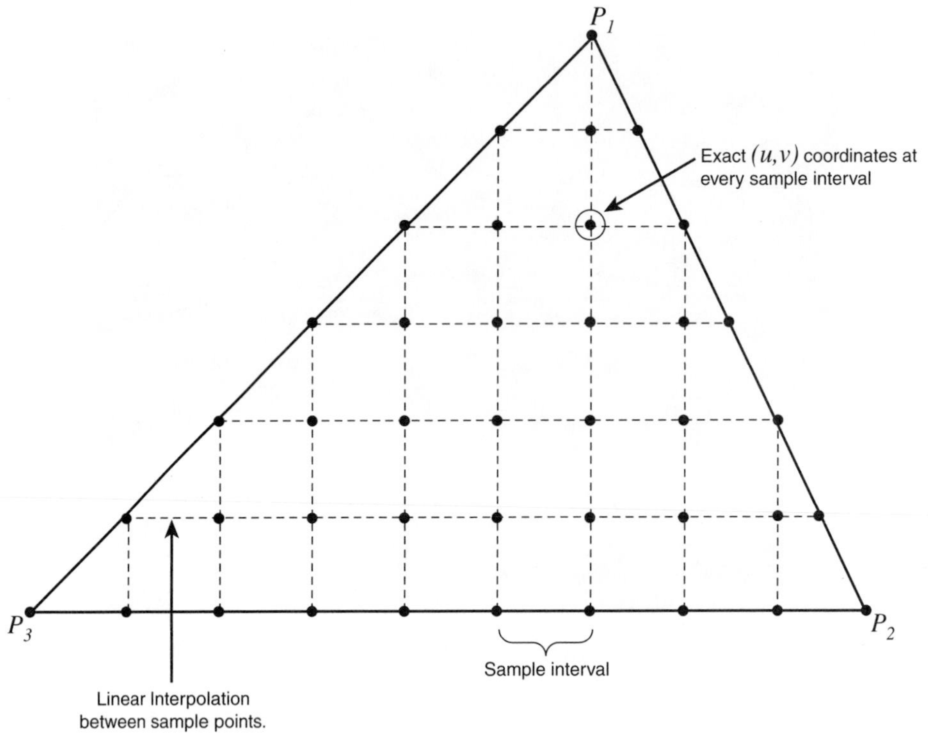

FIGURE 12.24 Linear piecewise approximation sampling points on the triangle.

Here's how it works: Unlike perfect-perspective texture mapping, linear piecewise texture mapping computes the perfect texture coordinates only on specific intervals, such as every 16–32 pixels, and then performs an affine linear texture mapping between these pixels. In Figure 12.25, you see the sampling curve of a perfect and linear piecewise approximation.

Basically, we are computing the correct texture coordinates along the perspective curve and then linearly interpolating between them. As the number of sample points increases, the curve becomes more and more like perfect-perspective texturing, as you can see in the figure. Therefore, this is a perfect technology to use for on-demand texturing. With control over quality and precision, we can save the divisions per-pixel, compute them every *n*th pixel, and then linearly interpolate between them! When objects get close, we can turn up the approximation (make the number of sample points higher), and when polygons are far from the viewplane, we can turn the number of sample points way down so that the texturing is nearly affine.

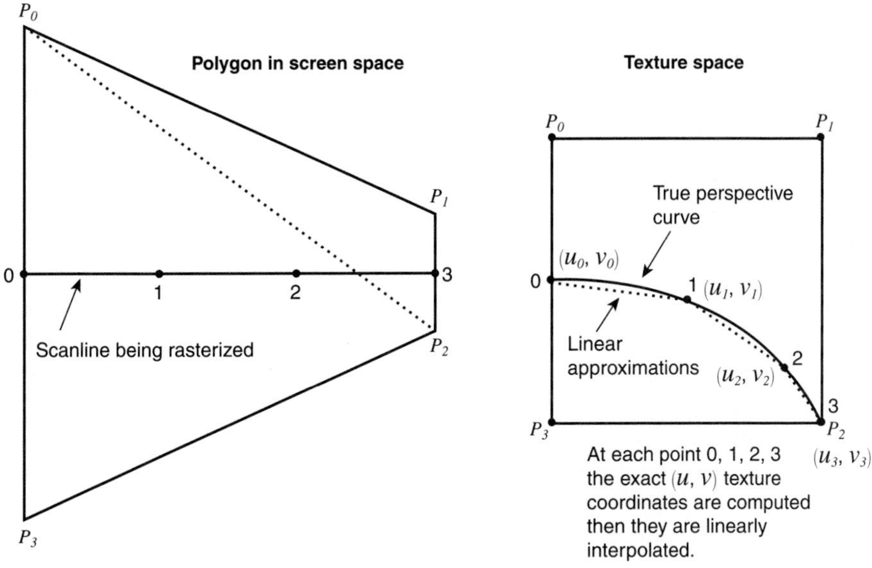

FIGURE 12.25 Linear piecewise approximation relative to the perspective curve.

In practice, I find that recomputing the texture coordinates every 16–32 pixels looks nearly perfect, even when you are on top of the texture. Now for the bad news: The details of implementing the algorithm are a little tricky—more like yucky! So it's a little bit hard to code for the general case every *n*th pixel. What I mean by this is that there are a few ways to implement the piecewise sampling, as shown in Figure 12.26 and listed in the following points.

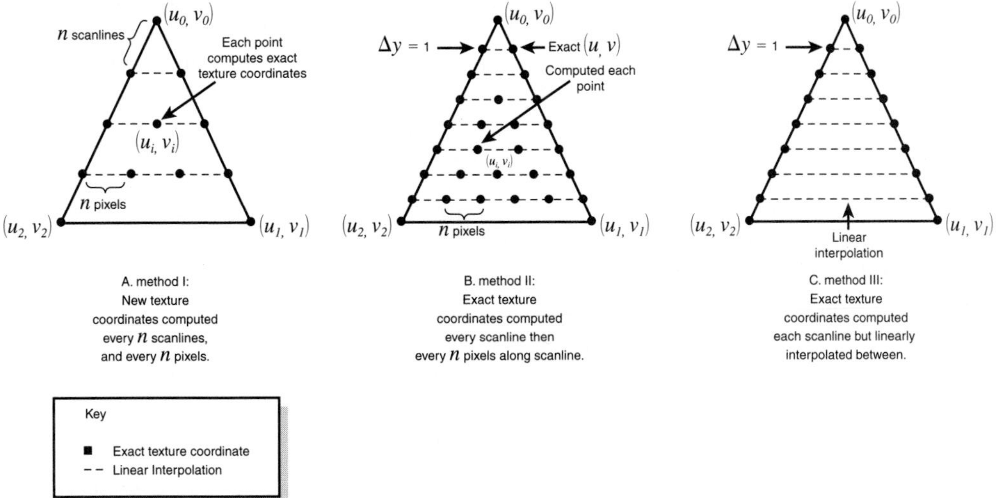

FIGURE 12.26 Methods of computing new texture coordinates for piecewise linear texture mapping.

- **Method 1:** The exact texture coordinates can be computed every *n* scanlines, and then every *n* pixels along each scanline.
- **Method 2:** The exact texture coordinates can be computed every scanline, and then every *n* pixels along that scanline.
- **Method 3:** The exact texture coordinates can be computed every scanline, and then the scanline is linearly interpolated.

We are going to implement method 3 for now, and we might implement method 2 later. The reason is that we already have the logic to compute the exact texture coordinates each scanline with the perfect texture mapper we just wrote, and we can just turn off the perfect texture mapping per pixel and simply linearly interpolate each scanline with the perfect u,v end points. We could implement method 2, but it's got a lot of overhead to get the recomputation of u,v every *n*th pixel along the scanline, and at this point we don't need it. We'll come back to it if we need to when we go more interior with our models and engine. However, you are free to try it yourself, along with traveling to parallel dimensions and hyperplanes via mental telepathy.

In any event, the plan is this: We simply take the perspective-correct texture mapper (any of them) and change it so that instead of computing the exact u,v coordinates of each pixel, we only compute the exact u,v texture coordinates of each scanline at the end points of the scan line. Then, using the perfect u,v coordinates we compute at the endpoints of the scanline, we linearly interpolate the texture coordinates from left to right.

NOTE

The interesting thing about this technique is that if a polygon is flat on the screen, and then it's rotated parallel to the x-axis, the texture mapping will be perfect. Only when it's rotated parallel to the y-axis will distortion occur. Thus, the technique is perfect in one axis. If we were to recompute the perfect u,v coordinates along each scanline, say every 32 pixels, the x-axis rotation would still give zero distortion, but the y-axis rotation would result in less distortion because we are resampling every 32 pixels.

Now let's look at the code that does this. Here's an excerpt from the most basic piecewise linear texture mapper `Draw_Textured_PerspectiveLP_Triangle_INVZB_16()`. This is the main y loop that renders the entire triangle:

```
// point screen ptr to starting line
screen_ptr = dest_buffer + (ystart * mem_pitch);

// point zbuffer to starting line
z_ptr = zbuffer + (ystart * zpitch);

for (yi = ystart; yi < yend; yi++)
  {
```

```
// compute span endpoints
xstart = ((xl + FIXP16_ROUND_UP) >> FIXP16_SHIFT);
xend   = ((xr + FIXP16_ROUND_UP) >> FIXP16_SHIFT);

// compute linear version of ul, ur, vl, vr
ul2 = ((ul << (FIXP28_SHIFT - FIXP22_SHIFT)) / (zl >> 6) ) << 16;
ur2 = ((ur << (FIXP28_SHIFT - FIXP22_SHIFT)) / (zr >> 6) ) << 16;

vl2 = ((vl << (FIXP28_SHIFT - FIXP22_SHIFT)) / (zl >> 6) ) << 16;
vr2 = ((vr << (FIXP28_SHIFT - FIXP22_SHIFT)) / (zr >> 6) ) << 16;

// compute starting points for u,v interpolants
zi = zl + 0; // ????
ui = ul2 + 0;
vi = vl2 + 0;

// compute u,v interpolants
if ((dx = (xend - xstart))>0)
 {
 du = (ur2 - ul2) / dx;
 dv = (vr2 - vl2) / dx;
 dz = (zr - zl) / dx;
 } // end if
else
 {
 du = (ur2 - ul2) ;
 dv = (vr2 - vl2) ;
 dz = (zr - zl);
 } // end else


// draw span
for (xi=xstart; xi < xend; xi++)
{
  // test if z of current pixel is nearer than current z buffer value
  if (zi > z_ptr[xi])
    {
    // write textel
    screen_ptr[xi] = textmap[(ui >> FIXP22_SHIFT) +
                 ((vi >> FIXP22_SHIFT) << texture_shift2)];

    // update z-buffer
    z_ptr[xi] = zi;
    } // end if
```

```
    // interpolate u,v,z
    ui+=du;
    vi+=dv;
    zi+=dz;
    } // end for xi

    // interpolate u,v,x along right and left edge
    xl+=dxdyl;
    ul+=dudyl;
    vl+=dvdyl;
    zl+=dzdyl;

    xr+=dxdyr;
    ur+=dudyr;
    vr+=dvdyr;
    zr+=dzdyr;

    // advance screen ptr
    screen_ptr+=mem_pitch;

      // advance zbuffer ptr
      z_ptr+=zpitch;

    } // end for y
```

I know the code is out of context and a little hard to follow, but take a minute and drudge through it if you can. I have bolded the two main areas where the action occurs. The first bolded area is where the exact u,v coordinates are computed for the current scanline by dividing by 1/z. The results are stored in `ul2`, `vl2`, `ur2`, and `vr2`. After this is done, the rest is trivial. The scanline rasterization's innermost loop is entered (the second bolded section) and the values (`ul2`, `vl2`) and (`ur2`, `vr2`) are linearly interpolated as texture coordinates. Although we are still dividing to compute the exact u,v texture coordinates, we are doing it on a per-scanline basis now, rather than per-pixel. Additionally, adding support to recompute the exact u,v coordinates along the scanline and then linearly interpolating in between isn't that complicated, but it's "unclean" to say the least, and messes up my perfect inner loop; so right now we'll leave that alone.

So that's all there is to piecewise linear perspective correct texture mapping; it's nothing more than computing the perfect texture coordinates every so often and then linearly interpolating between them. Let's see the new functions that support this (note that all the functions work with an inverse Z-buffer *only*):

Function:

```
void Draw_Textured_PerspectiveLP_Triangle_FSINVZB_16(
          POLYF4DV2_PTR face,// ptr to face
          UCHAR *_dest_buffer, // pointer to video buffer
```

```
         int mem_pitch,     // bytes per line, 320, 640 etc.
         UCHAR *_zbuffer,    // pointer to z-buffer
         int zpitch);      // bytes per line of zbuffer
```

Description: `Draw_Textured_PerspectiveLP_Triangle_FSINVZB_16()` draws a linear piecewise perspective-correct texture using flat shading.

Function:

```
void Draw_Textured_PerspectiveLP_Triangle_INVZB_16(
         POLYF4DV2_PTR face, // ptr to face
         UCHAR *_dest_buffer, // pointer to video buffer
         int mem_pitch,     // bytes per line, 320, 640 etc.
         UCHAR *_zbuffer,    // pointer to z-buffer
         int zpitch);      // bytes per line of zbuffer
```

Description: `Draw_Textured_PerspectiveLP_Triangle_INVZB_16()` draws a linear piecewise perspective-correct texture using constant shading.

Function:

```
void Draw_Textured_PerspectiveLP_Triangle_FSINVZB_Alpha16(
          POLYF4DV2_PTR face, // ptr to face
          UCHAR *_dest_buffer, // pointer to video buffer
          int mem_pitch,     // bytes per line, 320, 640 etc.
          UCHAR *_zbuffer,    // pointer to z-buffer
          int zpitch,      // bytes per line of zbuffer
          int alpha);      // the alpha
```

Description: `Draw_Textured_PerspectiveLP_Triangle_FSINVZB_Alpha16()` draws a linear piecewise perspective-correct texture using flat shading with alpha blending.

Function:

```
void Draw_Textured_PerspectiveLP_Triangle_INVZB_Alpha16(
          POLYF4DV2_PTR face, // ptr to face
          UCHAR *_dest_buffer, // pointer to video buffer
          int mem_pitch,     // bytes per line, 320, 640 etc.
          UCHAR *_zbuffer,    // pointer to z-buffer
          int zpitch,      // bytes per line of zbuffer
          int alpha);      // alpha
```

Description: `Draw_Textured_PerspectiveLP_Triangle_INVZB_Alpha16()` draws a linear piecewise perspective-correct texture using constant shading with alpha blending.

> **NOTE**
>
> I am truly sorry about how long these function names are getting, but there's really no way around it—they would be much worse if I spelled out *inverse, Z-buffer, Gouraud,* and so on.

To compare the affine, linear piecewise approximation and perfect-perspective correct texturing, I have updated the previous demo to support the linear piecewise rasterizers. Figure 12.27 is a screenshot of `DEMOII12_7.CPP|EXE` in action.

FIGURE 12.27 Linear piecewise texturing in action.

In the linear piecewise mode, it doesn't look too bad! Anyway, the controls are the same—move around with the arrow keys, and use the T key to switch from affine, linear, and perfect texturing modes.

Exploring Quadratic Approximations for Perspective Texturing

The next approximation technique I want to discuss is called *quadratic approximation*. It's based on the idea of linear piecewise approximation, but instead of linearly interpolating each scanline, we use a quadratic curve to approximate the perspective curve. Now, you might think that sounds worse than two divisions per pixel, but it's not! In fact, we can do it almost as easily as linear piecewise, except that it's nearly identical to perfect-perspective texture mapping. Before you get too excited, we are not going to implement it yet because we don't need it, but you can if you like. However, we are going to cover every detail of how it works, which turns out to be very easy.

First let's state the problem. Let's assume that we are computing the exact u,v texture coordinates per scanline (maybe using the multiplication of reciprocals to compute the divisions). We want a better approximation per scanline than what we are getting with the linear affine interpolation per scanline, but we don't want to resort to breaking the scanline up into more pieces. The solution is to interpolate the scanline from the left to right not linearly, but with a curve that passes through the true perspective curve at three points on the curve, or at the very least closer to the perspective curve than the straight line we are using when we linearly interpolate. Figure 12.28 shows what we are looking for in the abstract.

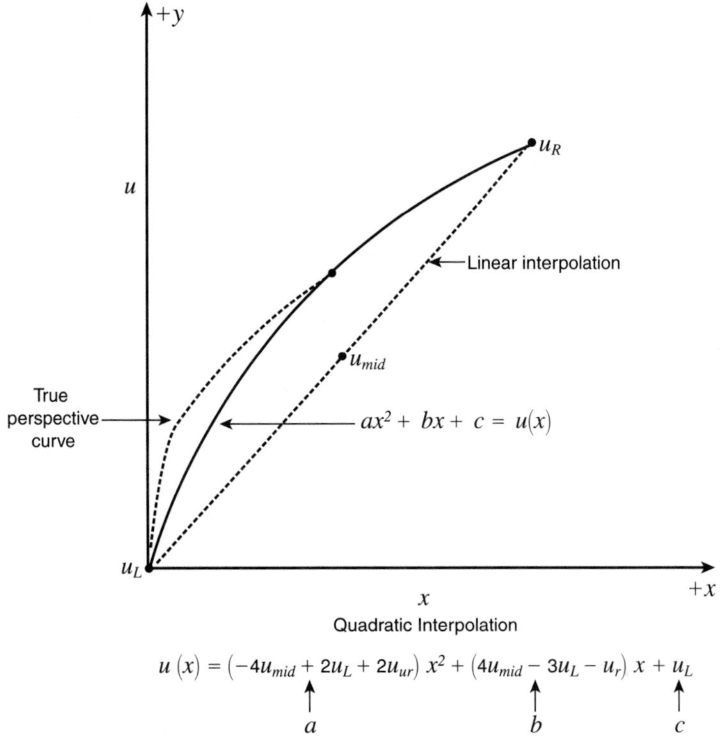

FIGURE 12.28 Quadratic approximation fitting the perspective curve.

Therefore, we need a curve that can look like c/z, where c is a constant, and this is where the quadratic part comes in. We know that functions of the form

```
a*x² + bx + c = 0
```

are parabolas. For example, Figure 12.29 shows what the curve

```
f(x) = 1*x² + 2*x + 3
```

looks like. It's definitely curvy!

We need to figure out a way to map the general quadratic $a*x^2 + bx + c$ to our texture curve c/z. I really want you to understand this, because it's key to so many approximations in computer graphics. Also remember that although the quadratic curve is a parabola, that's only when we plot it from (-∞, +∞). No one ever said we can't take a small range of it in some interval [i,j] and then use that as our approximation, right? This is exactly what we're going to do. We simply need to find the correct coefficients a, b, and c in the formula

```
f(x) = a*x² + b*x + c
```

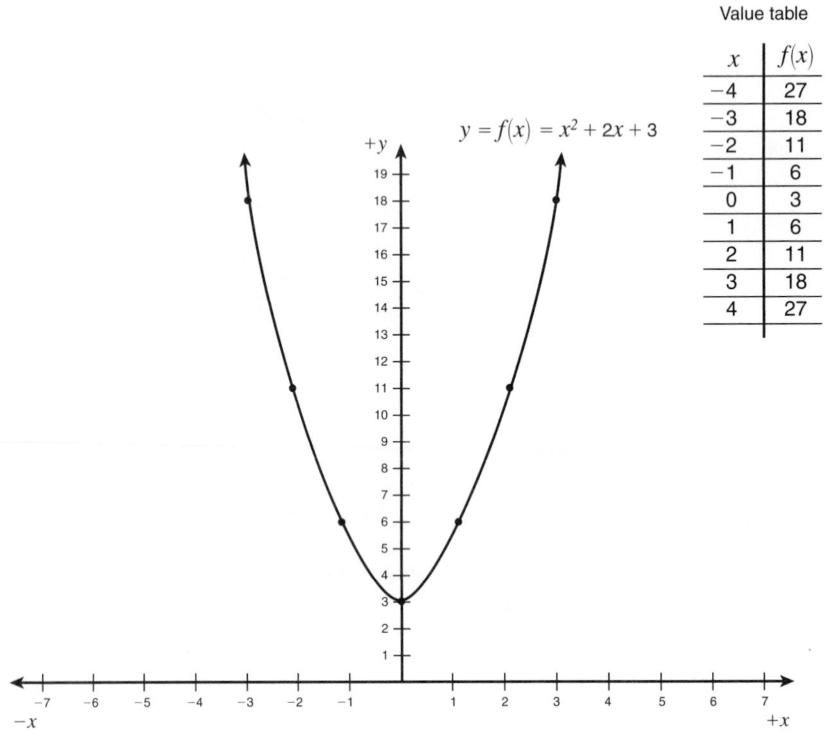

x	$f(x)$
−4	27
−3	18
−2	11
−1	6
0	3
1	6
2	11
3	18
4	27

FIGURE 12.29 A standard parabola.

This will follow the perspective curve as closely as possible. The trick is this: We compute the texture coordinates at each end as we go, and then we use the texture coordinates at each end to solve for a, b, and c. This will force the curve through them, but what will it do in the middle? This is where we need a little more information. We have three unknowns (a, b, and c), and we have only two knowns (ul, ur, (or vl, vr)), which are the endpoints we are trying to interpolate. Remember, both u and v are independent, so they must be interpolated separately. So, we need one quadratic curve to interpolate u, and another to interpolate v. So, after we figure u out, we have figured v out.

Now we have the quadratic polynomial we are going to use as the interpolator:

```
f(x) = a*x² + b*x + c
```

We also have two endpoints ul and ur. We now need at least one more piece of information, because there are three unknowns in the quadratic. We could use the slope as the third; that is, if we differentiate

```
f(x) = a*x² + b*x + c
```

with respect to x, we get

```
f'(x) = (d/dx)(a*x² + b*x + c) = 2*a*x + b
```

If we had the first derivative of the curve at the point ul, we could plug that in, but that still only dictates the slope at a point—we are more interested with the curve interpolating the c/z curve not having the same slope. Alas, we are stuck, and we need one more exact u,v pair to perform the computation to find the coefficients of $a*x^2 + bx + c = 0$. We have the exact u,v at the left and right edge of the scanline we are trying to interpolate, and we are going to compute the exact u,v at the midway point, or at .5 along the scanline. This is shown in Figure 12.30.

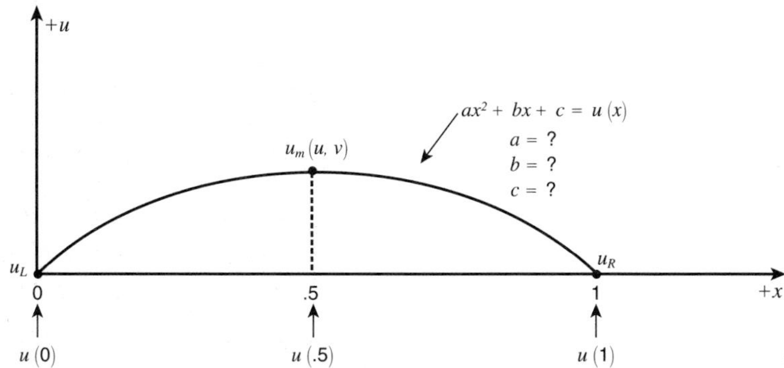

FIGURE 12.30 The setup for computation of endpoints and the midway point of the quadratic curve.

To compute the midpoint u,v we will need to perform two divisions as usual, but that's unavoidable. We simply multiply the scanline interpolants for the current scanline, we'll call them (u_z)i, (v_z)i, by 0.5, followed by a multiplication of the current scanlines dx (0.5*dx). Additionally, we would have to find the (1/z) value at the midpoint because we need it to divide into the (u/z), (v/z) midpoint values to find the real midpoint u,v values. Thus, we need to multiply the current scanline's (1/z)i interpolant by (0.5*dx), and then add those values respectively to ul, vl, and zl (the left-side u/z, v/z, and 1/z values) and then divide to compute the real u,v, as shown in Figure 12.30 and in the following.

Given the following:

- u_zl, v_zl, and zl are the u/z, v/z, and 1/z values at the current scanline's left edge. That is, they are the interpolants for the left side of the current scanline to be drawn.

- $(1\_z)_i$ is the 1/z interpolant at the left side for the current scanline.
- $(u\_z)_i$ is the (u/z) scanline interpolant at the left side for the current scanline.
- $(v\_z)_i$ is the (v/z) scanline interpolant at the left side for the current scanline.
- dx is the distance from the left edge to the right side of the current scanline; that is, $dx = (x_r - x_l)$

We attempt to find the real u,v midpoints.

First compute 1/z at the midpoint, because we need it to divide into the (u/z), (v/z) values at the midpoint to extract the final, real (u,v):

```
1_zmid = 1/zl + [(1_z)i *(0.5*dx)]
```

Now with the 1/z midpoint in hand, compute the real u,v midpoints:

```
umid = u_zl + [(u_z)i *(0.5*dx)] / 1_zmid

vmid = v_zl + [(v_z)i *(0.5*dx)] / 1_zmid
```

Although the explanation of the midpoint computation sounds a little like crop circles, the computation is trivial. We just need the blasted midpoint's real (u,v)! Now that we have it, let's get back to the quadratic approximation. Once again, we need to compute the coefficients for both the u curve and v curve, but they are the same, so we can derive the curve for u, copy it, and then replace u with v to find the coefficients of the v curve. Also, without loss of generality we can assume that the line we are rasterizing goes from 0 to 1, rather than xl to xr for the computation of the coefficients:

Given that at the left side of scanline curve the real u texture coordinate is ul, at the right side the real u texture coordinate is ur, and the midpoint is u_{mid}, we want to find the coefficients a0, b0, and c0 for the quadratic

```
f(x) = a0*x² + b0*x + c0
```

such that when

```
x=0,  f(0)   = ul
x=1,   f(1)   = ur
x=0.5, f(0.5) = umid
```

That is, the curve interpolates ul, u_{mid}, and ur. Begin by plugging in the values x = 0, x = 1 and setting them equal to ul and ur, respectively:

```
At x=0,  f(0) = a0*0² + b0*0 + c0 = ul
      = c0 = ul

At x=1,   f(1) = a0*1² + b0*1 + c0 = ur
      = a0 + b0 + c0 = ur
```

Substituting in ul for c0:

```
a0 + b0 + ul = ur
a0 + b0 = (ur - ul)
```

We're almost there. Let's use our last data point at x = 0.5, remembering the fact that c0 = ul:

```
At x=0.5,  f(0.5)    = a0*0.5² + b0*0.5 + c0 = u_mid
            = a0*0.25 + b0*0.5 + ul = u_mid
            = a0*0.25 + b0*0.5 = (u_mid - ul)
```

We are ready for the last step. Let's take the last two equations and solve for a0 and b0 (rearranging slightly, and writing coefficients first):

```
Line 1: (1)   * a0 + (1) * b0 = (ur - ul)
Line 2: (0.25)* a0 + (0.5)* b0 = (u_mid - ul)
```

Multiplying line 2 by 4, we get

```
Line 1: (1)* a0 + (1)* b0 = (ur - ul)
Line 2: (1)* a0 + (2)* b0 = 4*(u_mid - ul)
```

And subtracting line 1 from line 2, we get

```
Line 1: (1)* a0 + (1)* b0 = (ur - ul)
Line 2:         (1)* b0 = 4*(u_mid - ul) - (ur - ul)
           = (4*u_mid - 3*ul - ur)
```

Therefore, b0 = (4*u_{mid} - 3*ul - ur). Now, substituting b0 into line 1, we get

```
a0 + (4*u_mid - 3*ul - ur) = (ur - ul)

a0   = (ur - ul) - (4*u_mid - 3*ul - ur)
  = ur - ul - 4*u_mid + 3*ul + ur
  = -4*u_mid + 2*ul + 2*ur
```

Collecting our results, we have

```
a0 = (-4*u_mid + 2*ul + 2*ur)
b0 = (4*u_mid - 3*ul - ur)
c0 = ul
```

Therefore, u(x) equals

```
u(x) = a0*x² + b0*x + c0
   = (-4*u_mid + 2*ul + 2*ur)*x² + (4*u_mid - 3*ul - ur)*x + ul
```

Pretty cool, huh? Let's test it out and make sure it's correct. At x = 0, u(0) should be ul:

$$u(x) = (-4*u_{mid} + 2*ul + 2*ur)*0^2 + (4*u_{mid} - 3*ul - ur)*0 + ul$$
$$= ul$$

And at x = 1, u(1) should be ur:

$$u(x) = (-4*u_{mid} + 2*ul + 2*ur)*1^2 + (4*u_{mid} - 3*ul - ur)*1 + ul$$
$$= -4*u_{mid} + 2*ul + 2*ur + 4*u_{mid} - 3*ul - ur + ul$$
$$= ur$$

And finally, at x = 0.5, u(.5) should be umid:

$$u(x) = (-4*u_{mid} + 2*ul + 2*ur)*x^2 + (4*u_{mid} - 3*ul - ur)*x + ul$$
$$= (-4*u_{mid} + 2*ul + 2*ur)*.5^2 + (4*u_{mid} - 3*ul - ur)*.5 + ul$$
$$= -u_{mid} + .5*ul + .5*ur + 2*u_{mid} - 1.5*ul - .5*ur + ul$$
$$= u_{mid}$$

Of course, to interpolate the curve for the v texture coordinate (let's use the coefficients a1, b1, and c1), we simply replace the variables:

$$a1 = (-4*v_{mid} + 2*vl + 2*vr)$$
$$b1 = (4*v_{mid} - 3*vl - vr)$$
$$c1 = vl$$

Now we have everything we need to interpolate the perspective approximation from the left side to the right side for both u and v, and what's more, there are no divisions per pixel! But wait a minute—we have traded two divisions for five multiplications and four additions, because we now need to compute these each pixel along the scanline:

$$u(x) = a0*x^2 + b0*x + c0$$
$$v(x) = a1*x^2 + b1*x + c1$$

NOTE

x^2 can be computed once and then substituted into v(x).

Using Forward Differences to Evaluate the Quadratic Polynomial

Using brute force to evaluate the polynomial is still faster than the two divisions per pixel in practice, but we can do better with a number of techniques, such as forward differencing, because along the curve nothing changes other than x. Therefore, we simply compute u(0) and v(0). To compute the forward difference, we want to find u(x+1). Given that we have u(x), we make the assumption that

```
u(x+1) = u(x) + du
```

That is, du is the forward difference, therefore

```
du = u(x+1) - u(x)
```

Now we must compute du by evaluating u(x+1) – u(x), which is in general for a quadratic:

```
du   = [a*(x+1)² + b*(x+1) + c] - [a*x² + b*x + c]
  = [a*x² + 2*a*x + a+ b*x + b + c ] - [a*x² + b*x + c]
   = a*x² + 2*a*x + a+ b*x + b + c - a*x² - b*x - c
   = 2*a*x + a + b
```

Therefore,

```
u(x+1) = u(x) + (2*a*x+a+b)
```

We can still do better if we want. At this point, we need two multiplications (we might be able to get away with one multiplication because there's a factor of 2 in there) and two additions per pixel, for a total of four multiplications and four additions per pixel. This is compared to the brute-force evaluation of the quadratic, which will take five multiplications and four additions. A little better, but not much. However, we are getting there! Let's do one more iteration of forward differencing with the linear equation of du:

```
du(x) = 2*a*x + a + b
```

So we want to find the forward difference ddu, such that du(x+1) is equal to

```
du(x+1) = du(x) + ddu
```

Therefore, ddu is equal to

```
ddu = du(x+1) - du(x)
```

Plugging into 2*a*x + a + b, we get

```
ddu   = [2*a*(x+1) + a + b  ] - [2*a*x + a + b  ]
  = 2*a*x + 2*a + a + b - 2*a*x - a - b
  = 2*a
```

Thus we have cheated death! It's a constant, so we can compute each new u(x) as follows:

```
u(x+1) = u(x) + du

du = du(x) + ddu
```

So we simply need to find u(0) and du(0), and the forward differences can begin from there, with a total of two additions per pixel times two interpolants, for a total of four additions per pixel, per textel for the interpolation! As *Quake* would say, "I M P R E S S I V E."

Optimizing Texturing with Hybrid Approaches

Now that we have affine piecewise linear perspective and perfect-perspective texture mapping, there's obviously a number of optimizations that can be made by calling different texture mappers, depending on what's being texture mapped, and on how close and or how much distortion you are willing to accept during rendering. For example, one approach might be the following: For really close polygons, only the perfect-perspective correct rasterizer is called; for polygons that are in the midrange, the linear piecewise texture mapper is called; and for polygons that are far away, the affine texture mapper is called. This setup is shown in Figure 12.31.

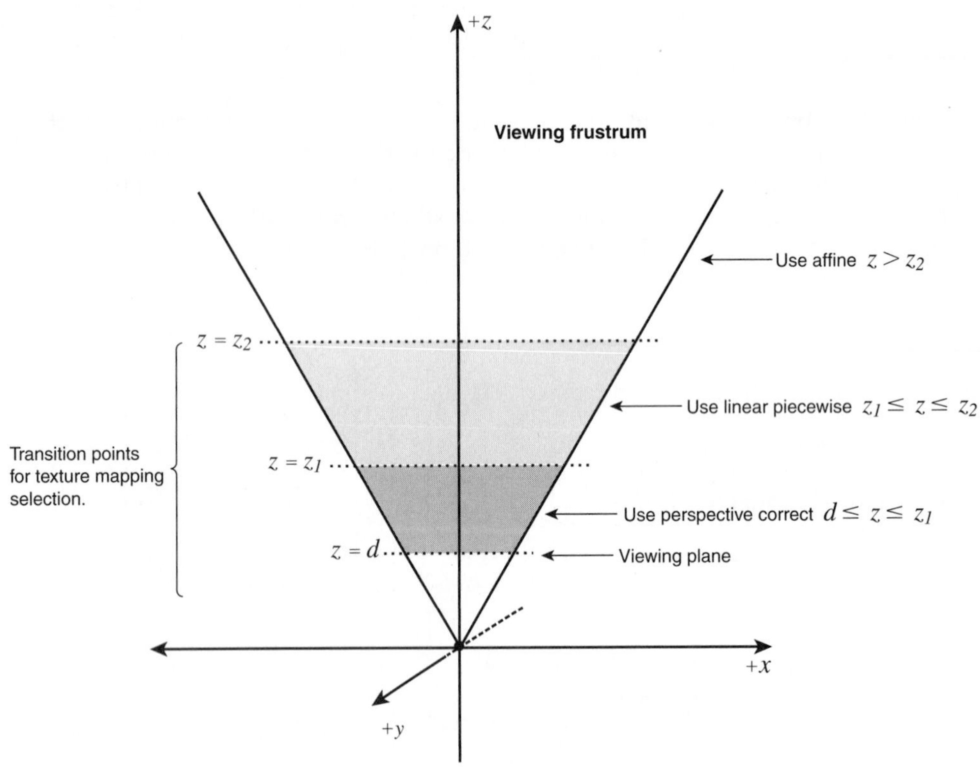

FIGURE 12.31 Hybrid texturing based on distance.

Thus, we get excellent performance, excellent visualization, and the best of all worlds. Setting this optimization up is actually trivial. During the call to the rendering list function (or outside it), the current z position of the polygon being rendered is determined (or the average). This value is then compared against the different quality ranges—perfect, linear, and affine—and the appropriate texture mapper is called! We might have some pseudo-code that looks like this:

```
float perfect_range  = 1000; // use perfect mapping 0-1000 units
float piecewise_range = 2000; // use piecewise linear mapping 1000 - 2000 units
float affine_range  = 2000; // use affine mapping 2000 on
```

```
// rasterizer selection
if (curr_poly->z < perfect_range)
  Perfect_Perspective_Texture_Mapper(curr_poly);
else
if (curr_poly->z > perfect_range && curr_poly->z < linear_range)
  Linear_Piecewise_Perspective_Texture_Mapper(curr_poly);
else
if (curr_poly->z > affine_range)
  Affine_Perspective_Texture_Mapper(curr_poly);
```

Obviously, we have different function names, and accessing the vertex information is different in the real engine, but the preceding algorithm is what's important. This is a really good optimization, and I have implemented it in the final high-level wrapper function. However, I decided to add support for the more simplistic use of just the linear piecewise and affine texture mappers, because they are so much faster. This selection is programmable, so when the call is made to the high-level function, you can select which optimization (or none) to take.

As a demo, I have manually implemented the preceding algorithm because we haven't seen the wrapper function yet, and we need to discuss more concepts before I show it to you. This demo implementation is brute force based on the preceding algorithm. The filename of the program is DEMOII12_8.CPP¦EXE. Figure 12.32 is a screenshot of the demo in action.

Press ESC to exit. Press <H> for Help.

FIGURE 12.32 Hybrid texture mapping in action.

You can change the distance where the perfect, linear piecewise, and affine texture mappers switch in and out with the following controls:

<1> - Decrease first distance cutoff.

<2> - Increase first distance cutoff.

<3> - Decrease second distance cutoff.

<4> - Increase second distance cutoff.

To compile the program, you will need `DEMOII12_8.CPP|H`, along with `T3DLIB1-10.CPP|H` and the DirectX .LIB files.

Bilinear Texture Filtering

Bilinear texture filtering, or *bilerp* for short, is the process of sampling more than one pixel during texture mapping from the source texture and averaging or using some other filter to arrive at the final pixel value for the destination pixel. Currently when we texture map, we use point sampling—that is, we compute the u,v texture coordinates, throw away the decimal fractions (or round them), and then use them to access the texel in the source texture. This is shown in Figure 12.33.

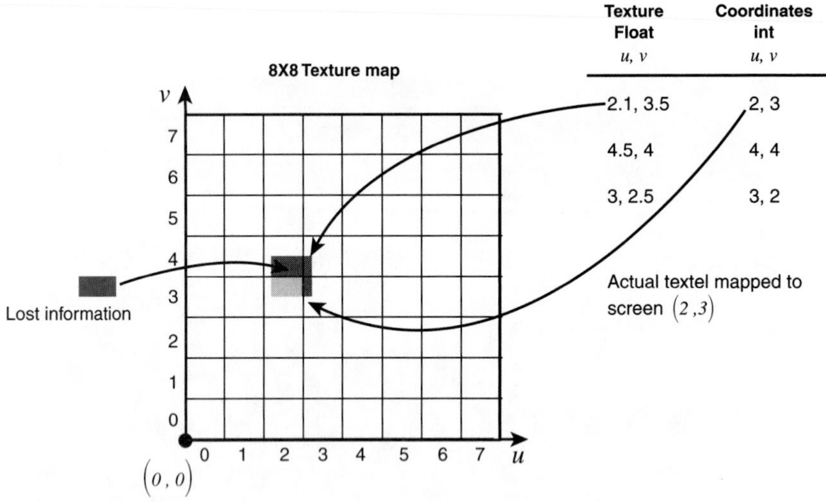

FIGURE 12.33 Point sampling mechanics.

The problem is that information we could use to make a better picture is being thrown away. This is where bilinear interpolation, or filtering, comes in. Instead of throwing away the fractional components of the u,v texture coordinates, we use them to access the textels around our source point in the texture map, and then average or filter them together in a linear fashion.

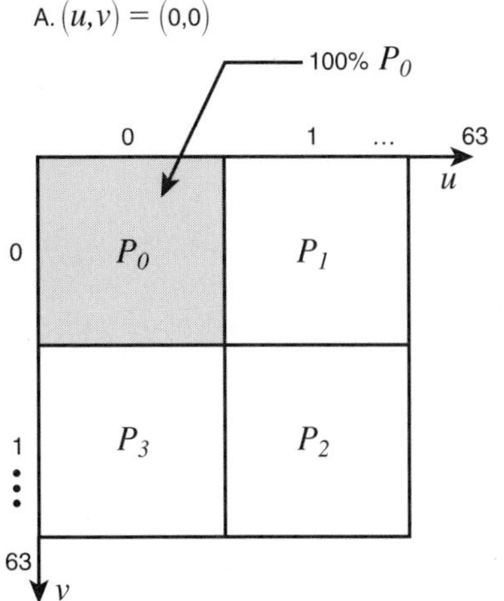

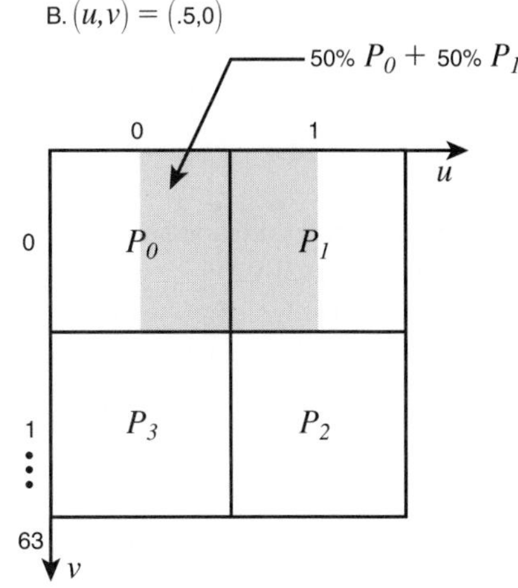

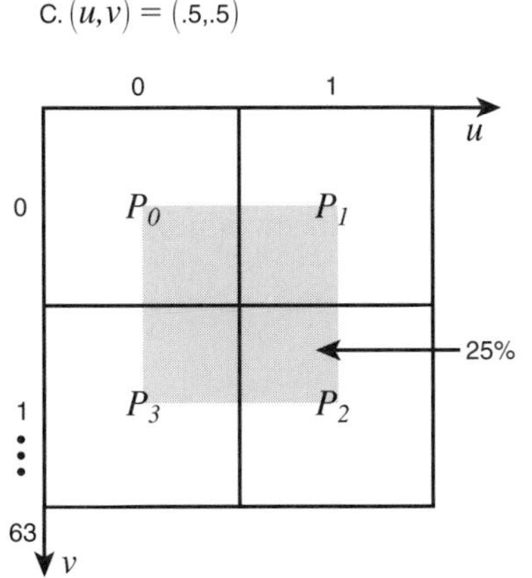

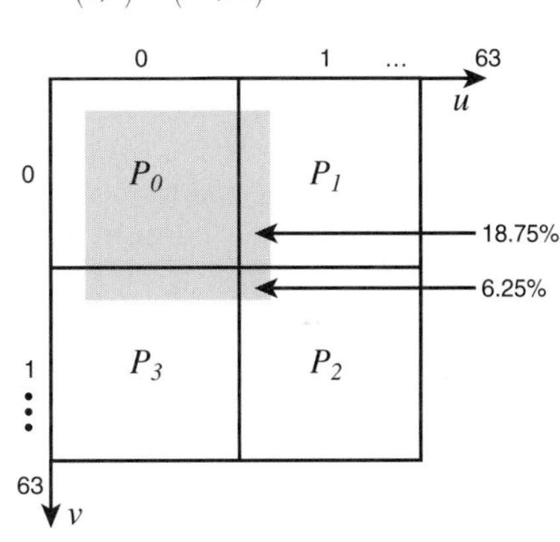

FIGURE 12.34 Bilinear filtering visually.

As an example, let's assume that we have a 64×64 texture map, as shown in Figure 12.34. We want to sample the four surrounding textels and average them together linearly (or we might use linear interpolation plus a weighting function). Figure 12.34 shows the process visually. We want to compute the final pixel pfinal from p1, p2, p3, and p4, which are the pixels surrounding p0 itself. The way to think about the problem is thus: p0 is a sampling box, and we slide it over the 2×2 pixel matrix made up of p1–p4. Then we look at the area of coverage that pfinal makes on p1–p4 and sum them up (in RGB space, of course). Figure 12.34 shows a few examples of this. Let's run through them, shall we?

Without loss of generality, we can assume that the pixel matrix p0–p3 is the upper left-hand corner of the texture. Now let's say that (u,v) were both exactly (0,0)—then we would have the sampling you see in Figure 12.34a. In this case, the sampling box is perfectly coincident with textel (0,0), so you would expect 100% of p0, and 0% of p1–p3. Therefore, our result pfinal would be equal to p0. Mathematically, we would have

$$p_{final} = (1.0)*p0 + (0.0)*p1 + (0.0)*p2 + (0.0)*p3$$

As another example, take a look at Figure 12.34b. Here we see the sampling box slightly shifted on the u axis. In this case, we have (u,v) equal to (0.5, 0). Therefore, the sampling box has a 50% coverage of p0 and a 50% coverage of p1. Thus the final pixel value would be 50% of p0, and 50% of p1, or mathematically:

$$p_{final} = (0.5)*p0 + (0.5)*p1 + (0.0)*p2 + (0.0)*p3$$

Now let's take a look at Figure 12.34c, which is the full 2D bilinear interpolation case. In this case, we have texture coordinates (u,v) of (0.5, 0.5). Therefore, the sampling box is covering exactly 25% of each textel. Mathematically we have

$$p_{final} = (0.5)*(0.5)*p0 + (0.5)*(0.5)*p1 + (0.5)*(0.5)*p2 + (0.5)*(0.5)*p3$$

$$= (0.25)*p0 + (0.25)*p1 + (0.25)*p2 + (0.25)*p3$$

In this case, we not only had to multiply each pixel sample by the u value, but also by the v value, and therefore the "bilinear" interpolation. Let's try one more—take a look at Figure 12.34d. Here we have u = 0.25, v = 0.25. Reviewing the figure (and counting squares to create fractional areas), we see that pfinal is

$$= (9/16)*p0 + (3/16)*p1 + (1/16)*p2 + (3/16)*p3$$

Mathematically, we have

$$p_{final} = (1-0.25)*(1-0.25)*p0 + (0.25)*(1-0.25)*p1 + (0.25)*(0.25)*p2 + (1-0.25)*(0.25)*p3$$

$$= (0.5625)*p0 + (0.1875)*p1 + (0.0625)*p2 + (0.1875)*p3$$

This is identical to the fractional computation we did visually. Thus we can see we simply need to apply the standard one-dimensional interpolation value of

```
(x)*value_1 + (1-x)*value_2
```

to two dimensions.

What we need is a general formula that enables us to plug in any u or v value and bilinearly interpolates the fractional components of u and v, samples the texture map, and gives us the final pixel value we desire. Here's the pseudo-code that will accomplish this for a single monochrome value rather than full RGB:

```
// single channel bilinear texture interpolation

// our monochrome texture
float texture[TEXT_SIZE[TEXT_SIZE];

float u,v; // texture coordinates 0..TEXT_SIZE-1

// compute integral values of u,v
int ui = (int)u;
int vi = (int)v;

// compute fractional components of u,v
float du = u - ui;
float dv = v - vi;

// now we are ready to sample the texture

float pfinal = (1-du)*(1-dv)* texture[u] [v]  +
        (du) *(1-dv)* texture[u+1][v]  +
        (du) *(dv) * texture[u+1][v+1] +
        (1-du)*(dv) * texture[u] [v+1];
```

As you can see, the problem with bilinear interpolation is that there are a lot of computations going on. For a single monochrome channel, we have to first compute the integer values of u and v and the fractions. Then we have to compute one minus the fractional part, so that's like four addition operations, more or less. Then we need to perform eight multiplications, and potentially two more additions to get the u+1, v+1 terms.

That's a total of six additions and eight multiplications per pixel, per channel—now we need three channels, so that's 3*(6 additions) = 18 additions per pixel, and 3*(8 multiplications) = 24 multiplications per pixel. This is a bit much for software. Of course, with tricks and optimizations it can be sped up, but even with lookup tables and such, there is a lot of interpolation and data extraction going on here.

So, the question is, is it worth implementing bilinearly texture mapping/filtering? Well, it's going to be reasonably slow, can only be used in a small amount, and not for everything, so if you want a small number of things to look good, it's worth it. However, you can get some of the same effects by slightly blurring your textures with a blur, Gaussian filter, or whatever to remove high frequencies. Of course, this diminishes the texture definition, so it's a give and take solution.

What I'm going to do is implement bilinear texture mapping on the most basic rasterizers only: constant-shaded with affine texturing for the non-z-buffered, z-buffered, and 1/z-buffered rasterizers (for a total of three new rasterizers). It's pointless to redo all the different versions to support bilerp, because it's just not worth the work at this point because of its speed. Also, to keep things real, I will show at least one of the modifications to one of the texture mappers (because all of them are huge), so you can rip the code to make other versions if you need them.

I think the Z-buffer, constant-shaded, affine texture mapper will be our target for modification. Therefore, I am going to take the function `Draw_Textured_TriangleZB2_16()` and make a bilinear interpolation version of it. This function has the simplest inner loop of all the texture mappers; therefore, if you do want to move ahead and create alternative versions, you can do so. Anyway, the prototype of the new version that supports bilinear interpolation is shown in the following:

```
void Draw_Textured_Bilerp_TriangleZB_16(POLYF4DV2_PTR face, // ptr to face
          UCHAR *_dest_buffer, // pointer to video buffer
          int mem_pitch,    // bytes per line, 320, 640 etc.
          UCHAR *_zbuffer,     // pointer to z-buffer
         int zpitch)     // bytes per line of zbuffer
```

The calling convention is the same, but it just has bilinear texture interpolation inside. I have more or less implemented the pseudo-code algorithm we derived in the preceding with heavy optimizations and fixed-point format. The following is a listing of the inner loop of the texture mapper, so you can see what's going on:

```
// draw span
for (xi=xstart; xi < xend; xi++)
  {
  // test if z of current pixel is nearer than current z buffer value
  if (zi < z_ptr[xi])
    {
    // compute integral values of u,v
    int uint = ui >> FIXP16_SHIFT;
    int vint = vi >> FIXP16_SHIFT;

    int uint_pls_1 = uint+1;
    if (uint_pls_1 > texture_size) uint_pls_1 = texture_size;

    int vint_pls_1 = vint+1;
    if (vint_pls_1 > texture_size) vint_pls_1 = texture_size;

    int textel00 = textmap[(uint+0)    + ((vint+0) << texture_shift2)];
    int textel10 = textmap[(uint_pls_1) + ((vint+0) << texture_shift2)];
    int textel01 = textmap[(uint+0)    + ((vint_pls_1) << texture_shift2)];
    int textel11 = textmap[(uint_pls_1) + ((vint_pls_1) << texture_shift2)];
```

```
// extract rgb components
int r_textel00 = ((textel00 >> 11)    );
int g_textel00 = ((textel00 >> 5) & 0x3f);
int b_textel00 = (textel00    & 0x1f);

int r_textel10 = ((textel10 >> 11)    );
int g_textel10 = ((textel10 >> 5) & 0x3f);
int b_textel10 = (textel10    & 0x1f);

int r_textel01 = ((textel01 >> 11)    );
int g_textel01 = ((textel01 >> 5) & 0x3f);
int b_textel01 = (textel01    & 0x1f);

int r_textel11 = ((textel11 >> 11)    );
int g_textel11 = ((textel11 >> 5) & 0x3f);
int b_textel11 = (textel11    & 0x1f);

// compute fractional components of u,v in fixed 24.8 point format
int dtu = (ui & (0xffff)) >> 8;
int dtv = (vi & (0xffff)) >> 8;

int one_minus_dtu = (1 << 8) - dtu;
int one_minus_dtv = (1 << 8) - dtv;

// each interpolant has 3 terms, (du), (dv), textel, however
// the (du) and (dv) terms repeat during each computation of
// r_textel, g_textel, and b_textel, so we can compute them once
int one_minus_dtu_x_one_minus_dtv = (one_minus_dtu) * (one_minus_dtv);
int dtu_x_one_minus_dtv      = (dtu)      * (one_minus_dtv);
int dtu_x_dtv            = (dtu)      * (dtv);
int one_minus_dtu_x_dtv      = (one_minus_dtu) * (dtv);

// now we are ready to sample the texture
int r_textel = one_minus_dtu_x_one_minus_dtv * r_textel00 +
       dtu_x_one_minus_dtv      * r_textel10 +
       dtu_x_dtv            * r_textel11 +
       one_minus_dtu_x_dtv      * r_textel01;

int g_textel = one_minus_dtu_x_one_minus_dtv * g_textel00 +
       dtu_x_one_minus_dtv      * g_textel10 +
       dtu_x_dtv            * g_textel11 +
       one_minus_dtu_x_dtv      * g_textel01;

int b_textel = one_minus_dtu_x_one_minus_dtv * b_textel00 +
       dtu_x_one_minus_dtv      * b_textel10 +
```

```
            dtu_x_dtv           * b_textel11 +
            one_minus_dtu_x_dtv      * b_textel01;

    // write textel
    screen_ptr[xi] = ((r_textel >> 16) << 11) +
             ((g_textel >> 16) << 5) +
             (b_textel >> 16);

    // update z-buffer
    z_ptr[xi] = zi;
    } // end if
```

More or less, the code computes the fractional values and then carries out the computation in RGB space. The results are written to the screen, and we're done. The problem with this algorithm is not its inherent complexity, but simply that there's a lot to do, and optimization is difficult as a result. In essence, we are performing an image processing algorithm, which is never something that goes down well in real time. If you review the code, you will see a number of optimizations, such as precomputation of common factors, and the use of the 8.24 fixed-point format. This new format was necessary because during the multiplication of each bilinear term, there are three products; two of them being fixed-point 16.16 would overflow the format, so I had to back it off a little and go with 8.24 to keep things in range. However, the results are very impressive, and the bilinear demo looks darn good!

Additionally, here are the prototypes to the other two modified functions, with added bilinear interpolation support: the inverse Z-buffer, and no sorting version (both still affine/constant-shaded):

```
void Draw_Textured_Bilerp_TriangleINVZB_16(POLYF4DV2_PTR face, // ptr to face
             UCHAR *_dest_buffer, // pointer to video buffer
             int mem_pitch,    // bytes per line, 320, 640 etc.
             UCHAR *zbuffer,    // pointer to z-buffer
             int zpitch);     // bytes per line of zbuffer

void Draw_Textured_Bilerp_Triangle_16(POLYF4DV2_PTR face, // ptr to face
             UCHAR *_dest_buffer, // pointer to video buffer
             int mem_pitch);    // bytes per line, 320, 640 etc.
```

As an example of the bilinear interpolation, check out DEMOII12_9.CPP¦EXE. Figure 12.35 is a screenshot of it running. It basically enables you to toggle point-sampling/bilinear-filtered texture mapping for the objects via the B key. You can also use the N key to select different objects. See if you can tell the difference. To compile the program, you need DEMOII12_9.CPP¦H, along with T3DLIB1–10.CPP¦H and the DirectX .LIB files.

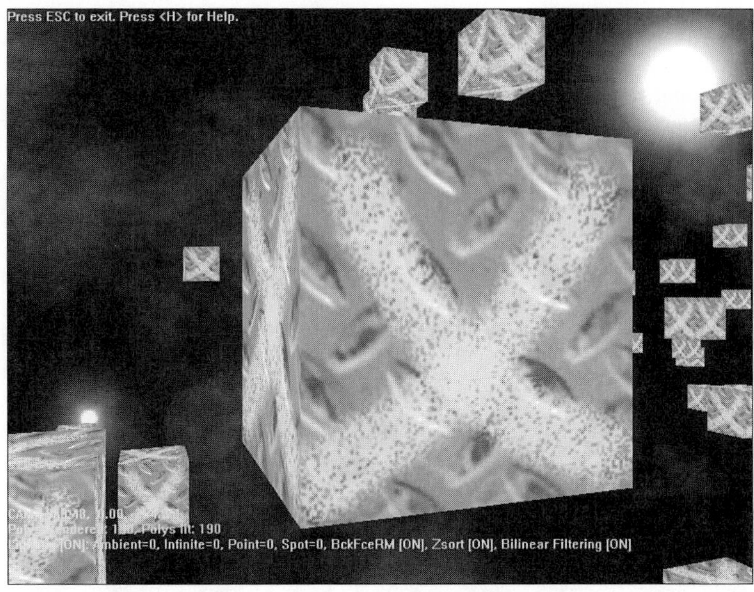

FIGURE 12.35 Bilinear interpolation makes the jaggies go away.

Mip Mapping and Trilinear Texture Filtering

Mip mapping is based on the phrase *multum in parvo*, which means "many things in a small place." The problem that mip mapping solves is that of *aliasing*. The problem is that when you are texture-mapping a texture onto a polygon and sampling the texture (point sampling, bilinear filtering, and so on) you end up with a number of odd effects that are all related to the sampling theory of spatial information. One of the problems you might have seen when texture mapping is *sparkling*. Sparkling occurs when high frequency elements of the texture map (that is, large changes in intensity as a function of position in the map) come in and out of view, and the texture map is being minified (scaled down). Basically, you are seeing the high frequency information come in and out of phase with the sampling frequency.

The second major problem with texture mapping is low frequency aliasing, resulting in moiré patterns. This occurs when low frequency images start forming based on the high frequency original image. Figure 12.36 shows a point-sampled checkerboard image. Notice the sinusoidal pattern that forms in it? Now, take a look at Figure 12.37—it depicts the same scene with mip mapping and texture filtering. The effect is much reduced, and the image is much cleaner

NOTE

When two identical repetitive patterns of lines, circles, or arrays of dots are overlapped with imperfect alignment, the pattern of light and dark lines called a *moiré pattern* appears. The moiré pattern is not a pattern of the images themselves, but rather a pattern in the image formed in your eye. Basically, the patterns show up where there are high areas of contrast, or high frequency components. Moiré patterns also show up when two images are overlaid because of the interference of the light and dark areas.

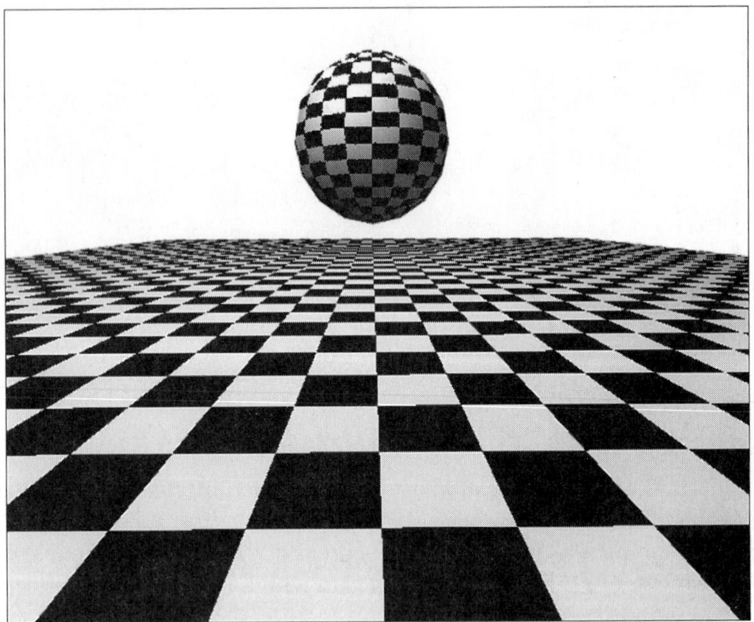

FIGURE 12.36 Point-sampled images look bad.

To implement mip mapping, we are going to create what is called a *mip chain* of textures, each texture half as large as the previous one on each axis, all the way down to 1×1. Additionally, we are going to generate each of these mip textures using a filter (averaging, box, Gaussian, and so on), and then based on some metric, we will select the appropriate mip texture to use, as we are rendering the polygons based on the distance from the view point or the area of the projected polygon (more on this later). This will minimize the amount of sparkling and low frequency aliasing/moiré patterns that will form. So that's the plan from a high level—let's get down to the details.

Introduction to Fourier Analysis and Aliasing

I had first planned to go into a large explanation of Fourier analysis, but after taking many semesters in college in both mathematics and electrical engineering on the subject, there is simply no way I am going to be able to do it any justice in fewer than 100 pages.

Instead, I'm just going to give you some information about why it's important, what it does, what it tells us, and why we care, and then we'll move on.

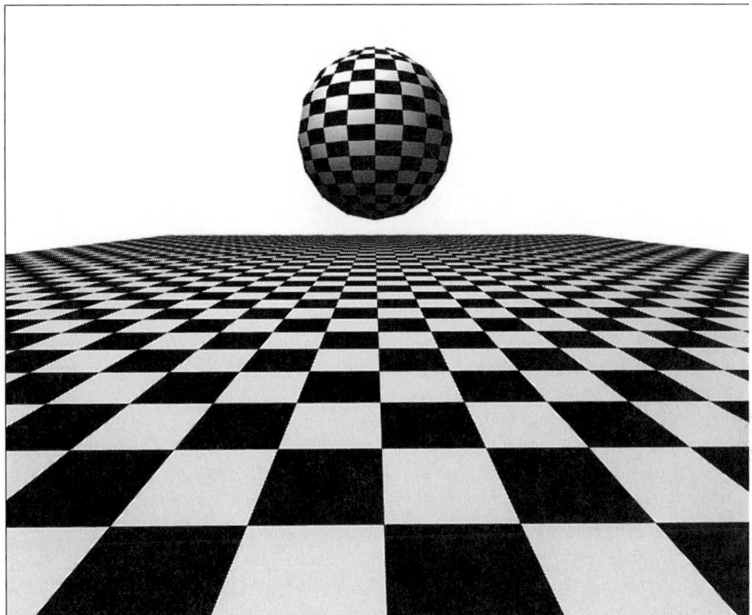

FIGURE 12.37 Mip-mapped images with filtering look good.

NOTE

If you're really interested in more information on Fourier analysis, I highly recommended these texts: *Information, Transmission, Modulation and Noise* by Mischa Schwartz (McGraw Hill), and *Continuous and Discrete Signal and System Analysis* by McGillem and Cooper (Oxford University Press). For more of a computer graphics-based explanation, try *Computer Graphics: Principles and Practice* by Foley et al (Addison-Wesley) and *Digital Image Warping* by George Wolberg (Wiley-IEEE Press).

Fourier analysis is all about the deconstruction of signals in the time domain (or spatial domain, when talking about graphics) into their constituent sinusoidal components. That is, any periodic signal for the most part (the Dirchlet conditions must hold though) can be broken into a sum of sine waves of varying frequency, amplitude, and phase—simple as that. Put another way, any signal has a basis that is a sum of sine waves. So, we can write any signal in the form of a Fourier series, which is more or less a sum of sine terms—that is, the Fourier series is a basis that can represent any signal. I am going in circles, I know <BG>.

The Fourier transform enables us to extract this frequency information from the signal and compute the constituent parts of it. For example, let's say we have a pure sine wave with frequency f and period $T = 1/f$, as shown in Figure 12.38a.

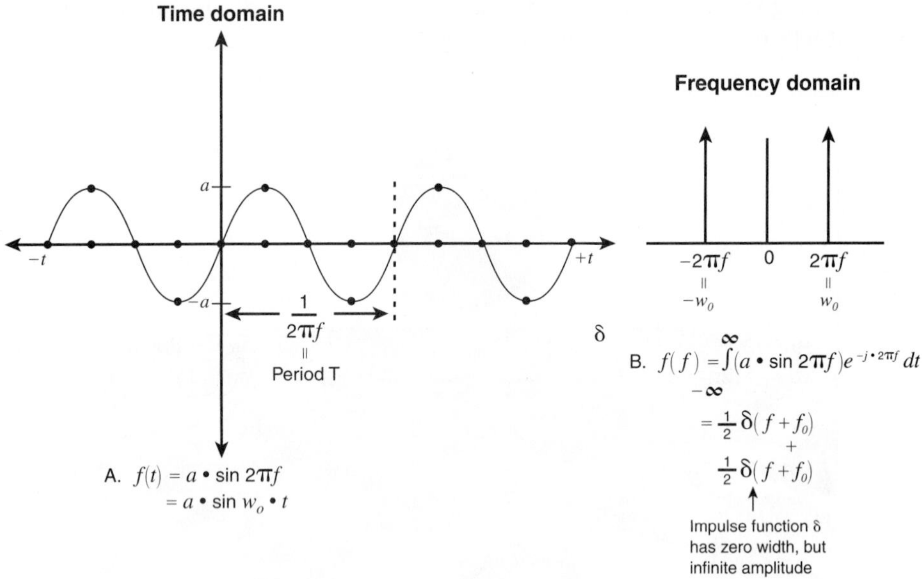

FIGURE 12.38 Your garden variety sine wave and its Fourier transform.

This signal is in the time domain—that is, we have a function of time `t` that looks like this (`t` is time and `T` is the period):

```
f(t) = a*sin(2*π*f*T)
```

> **NOTE**
>
> t is time, and T is period.

Here a is the amplitude, `t` is time, and `f` is the frequency. Now, if we were to take the Fourier transform of this simple sine function, the result would be a single value (plus its imaginary conjugate) located at the frequency `f` of the original sine wave, with an amplitude of a on the frequency axis. Therefore, we graph Fourier transforms not on the time axis, but on the frequency axis. Figure 12.38b shows the single sine Fourier transform as plotted on the frequency axis. If we take the single sine

```
f(t) = 10*sin(100*t) + 20*sin(200*t)
```

and take the Fourier transform of it, we get exactly two frequency pulses at (100, 200) and (-100, -200) in the frequency domain. Sine waves have the same effect. Any signal can be broken into sine waves, and can be reconstructed back into the original. So, the magical operation that performs this transformation and converts a signal from the time domain to the frequency domain is

$$F\{ f(t) \} = \int_{-\infty}^{+\infty} f(t)*e^{-j*2*?*f}\, dt$$

You simply take your function `f(t)` and perform the integration to compute the Fourier transform, where `j` is the imaginary number that's equal to the square root of -1. `j` is also called `i` in many texts. In any case, you hardly need to know how to do this to perform mip mapping. The whole point of the Fourier transform is to have a mathematical way to extract the frequency components of a signal, so this is the tool we would use. However, someone has already done all this work for us (thank God!); now let's talk about the results.

TIP

The graphs for Figure 12.39 were generated with MathGV, a freeware graphing program that's as good as professional packages. Check it out on the CD in the `Applications\` directory, or at `http://www.mathgv.com`.

I want you to take a look at Figure 12.39. In Figure 12.39a, we see a signal that we might want to sample (this could be audio, imagery, or whatever). The signal has a frequency f_0 and a period $T_0 = 1/f_0$. In Figure 12.39b we sample the signal again, along with the sampled version following at some interval T_1 at a frequency $f_1 > 2*f_0$. As you can see from Figure 12.39b, there is no confusion about the reconstructed signal. Now let's slow down the sample rate to exactly $2*f_0$, as shown in Figure 12.39c. Here we see that, by dumb luck, we are sampling right on the zero crossings! Thus our reconstructed wave is a flat line!

Finally, take a look at Figure 12.39d. Here we are sampling the original signal at a frequency f1 < 2*f0, and because we are doing so, the reconstructed wave actually isn't still a signal, but a low frequency *alias* of the original. This is exactly what happens when we are point-sampling information while at the same time minifying it—we are creating low frequency aliases in our final image.

The problem is that there is no way around this for the most part—no matter how much higher a frequency we sample our image at, this alias will always occur. We can only minimize it. To minimize it, the trick is to remove the high frequency components that are causing the aliasing to occur when we are getting heavy texture minification. This is the entire basis of mip mapping: to create a chain of textures based on the original texture with less and less high frequency information, each texture one-fourth the size of the original.

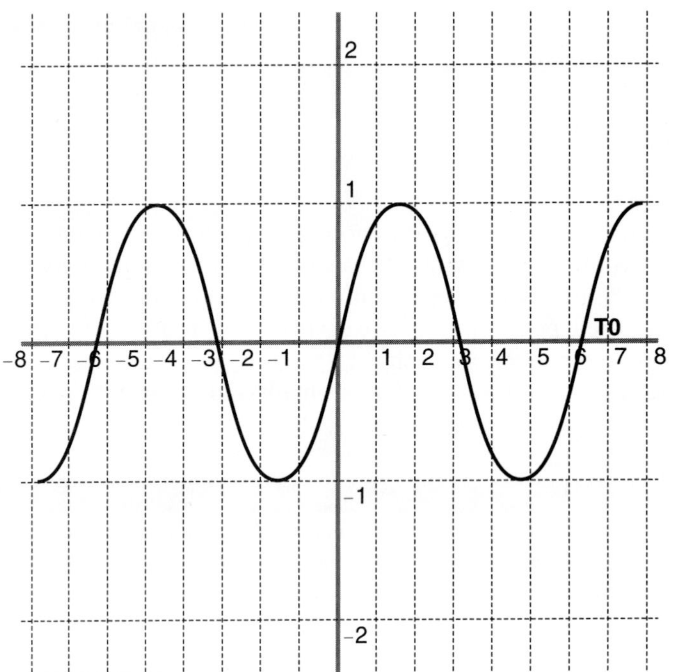

A. The signal we want to sample

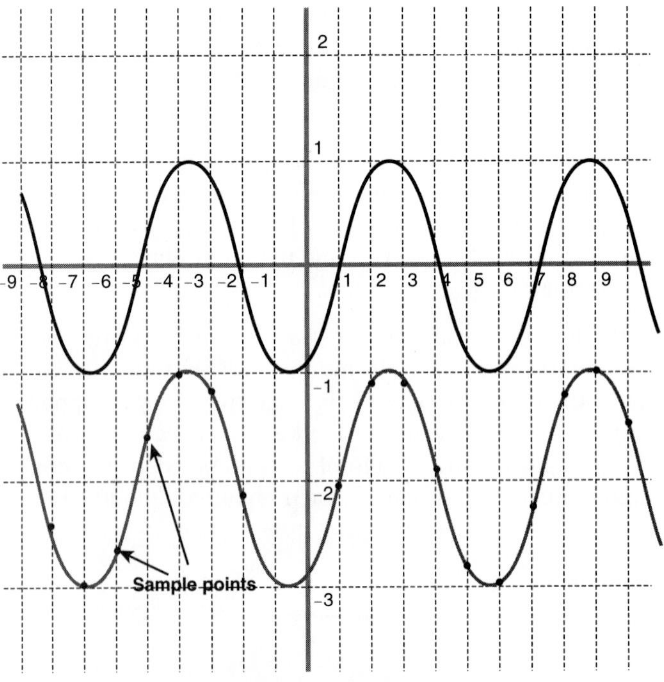

B. Sampling at f1>2*f0

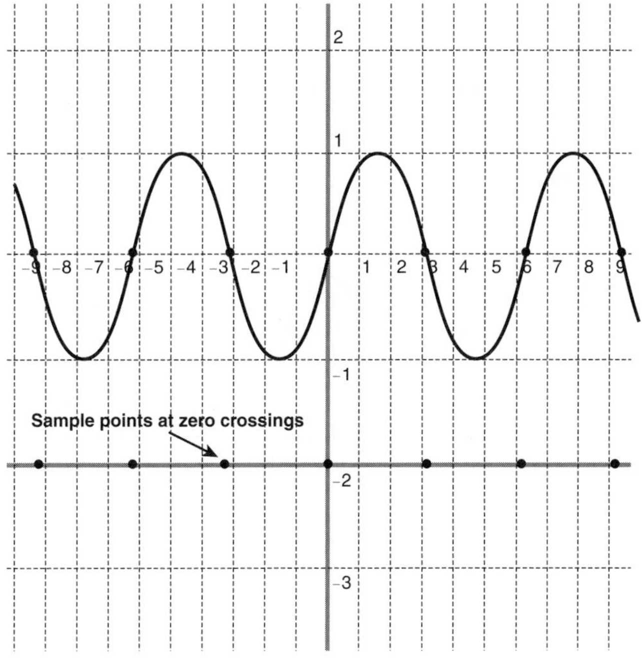

C. Sampling at f1>2*f0

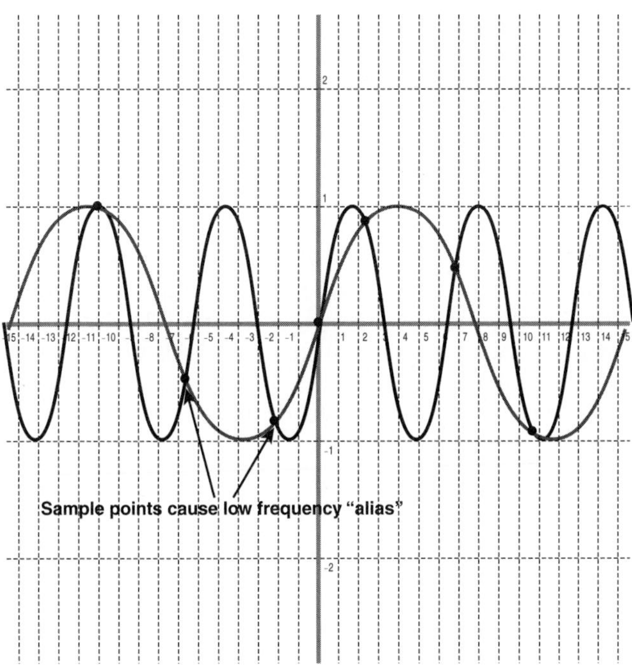

D. Sampling at f1>2*f0

FIGURE 12.39 What happens when a signal is sampled.

Creating the Mip Map Chain

What we want to do is take our base texture, let's call it T0 (which has nothing to do with the period of a signal), and then create a chain of textures derived from T0 (by averaging usually), where each consecutive texture T1, T2, T*n* is one-fourth the original size of T0. That is, for the T*n* texture to create the next smallest texture T*n*+1, we divide the width and height of T*n* by 2. This is shown in Figure 12.40.

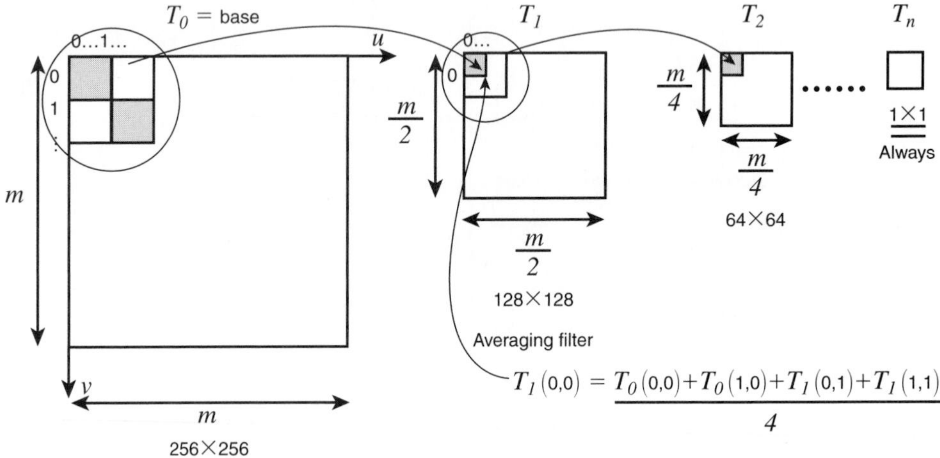

FIGURE 12.40 Down-sampling a base texture to create a mip map chain.

To compute the pixel value in each new texture from the previous mip level, we can use an averaging filter. That is, we take the pixels (x,y), (x+1,y), (x+1, y+1), and (x,y+1), and average them together in RGB space. This is the final pixel we write to the new texture. This operation is shown in Figure 12.41.

Now, there are some rules to create mip map chains. First, all textures must be square and powers of two. This is so that they mip down at the same rate. When we reach the end of the mip chain, the final texture is always 1×1. The convention is to call the original texture mip level 0, and each progressively smaller texture 1,2,3,4...*n*. So as an example, say we have a texture that's 256×256—the mip chain would be the sizes shown in Table 12.4.

TABLE 12.4 Mip Map Texture Size for Base Texture of 256×256

Mip Level	Texture Size
T0	256×256
T1	128×128
T2	64×64
T3	32×32
T4	16×16
T5	8×8

TABLE 12.4 Continued

Mip Level	Texture Size
T6	4×4
T7	2×2
T8	1×1

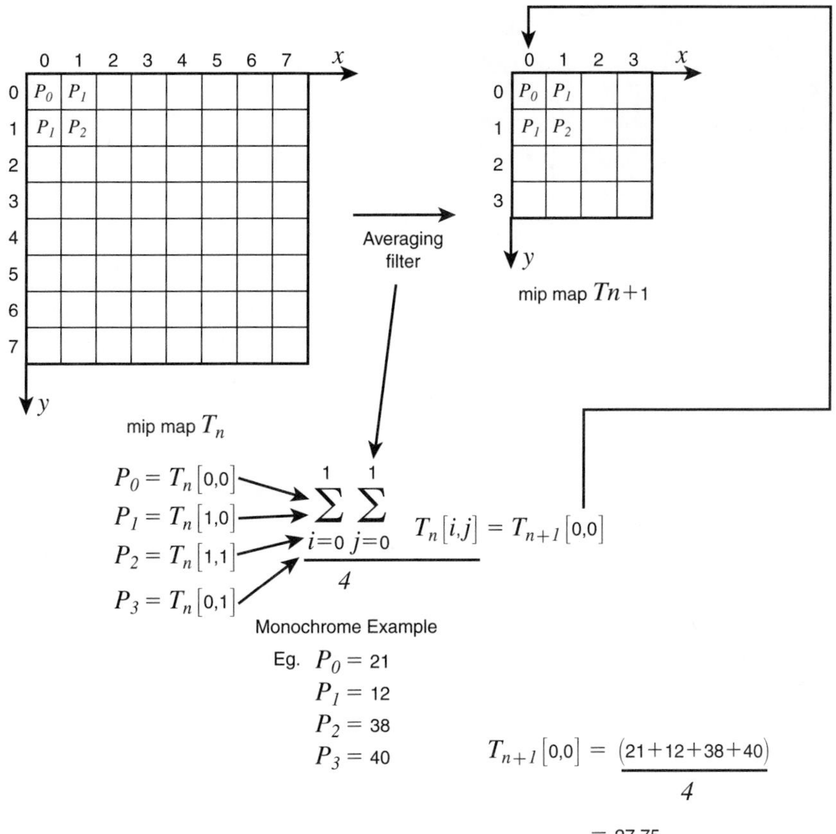

FIGURE 12.41 The averaging filter used to create mip maps.

Therefore, we see that the total number of mip levels excluding the original texture, is computed in Equation 12.4.

EQUATION 12.4 Total Number of Mip Levels Excluding Base Texture

$\log_2 \text{T0}$

In this case, that would be $\log_2 256 = 8$. Moreover, if we wanted the total number of textures, we would just add 1 to account for the base texture we are mipping from. Therefore, the total number of textures is always ($\log_2 \text{T0} + 1$), or 9 in this case.

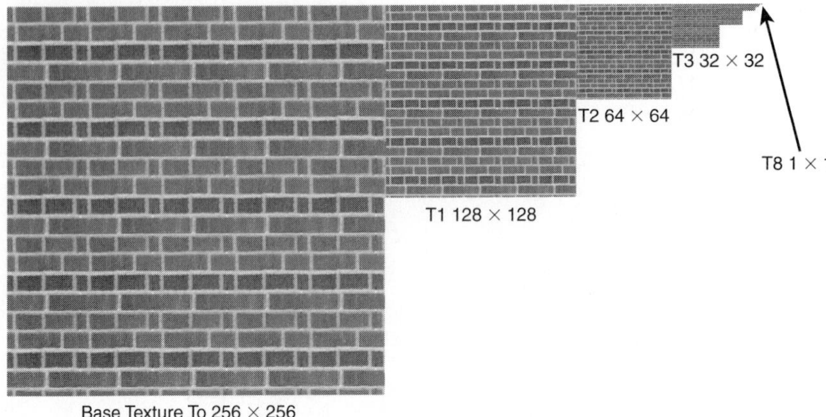

FIGURE 12.42 Actual mip maps.

Cool, but what about memory usage? Well, take a look at Figure 12.42, which is a screenshot of actual mip maps. Notice how each one fits into one-fourth the size of the previous one? We are reducing the size of the texture by a factor of 1/4 each time, so the memory is very small. In fact, let's see what happens if we perform a simple calculation on the preceding example:

If the initial texture size is 256×256, or 256^2 words, let's compute the mip map chain memory requirements such that its memory footprint is always one-fourth as much:

$$x = 128^2 + 64^2 + 32^2 + 16^2 + 8^2 + 4^2 + 2^2 + 1^2$$

And we want to compare the ratio of x with the original memory, so we divide x by 256^2:

$$\frac{x}{256^2} = \frac{128^2 + 64^2 + 32^2 + 16^2 + 8^2 + 4^2 + 2^2 + 1^2}{256^2}$$

$$= 1.333..$$

Or in other words, adding the mip mapping textures adds another 33% to our memory storage per texture. A small price to pay for what it brings to the table.

Now that we know how to create mip maps, and how much memory they take, we just need to figure out a way to add them to the engine! Well, I thought hard about this and was considering changing the object/polygons structures again, but then it dawned on me: We can just point the texture pointer to a mip map chain rather than a single texture. Then we set a flag in each polygon that is mip mapped, and when we go to render a polygon, instead of just using the texture pointer as a pointer to a bitmap, we use it as if it were a pointer to an *array* of pointers to bitmaps! This way, we use all the same structures and nothing is lost. Take a look at Figure 12.43 to see what I'm talking about.

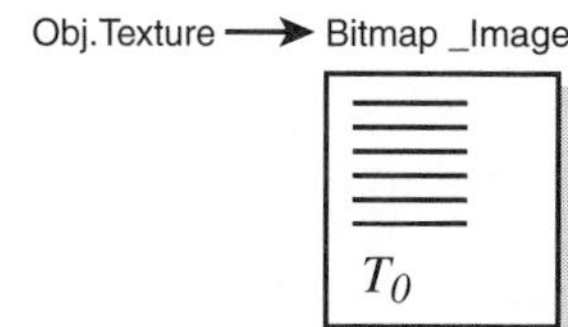

A. Before re-directing the texture pointer to the mip chain array

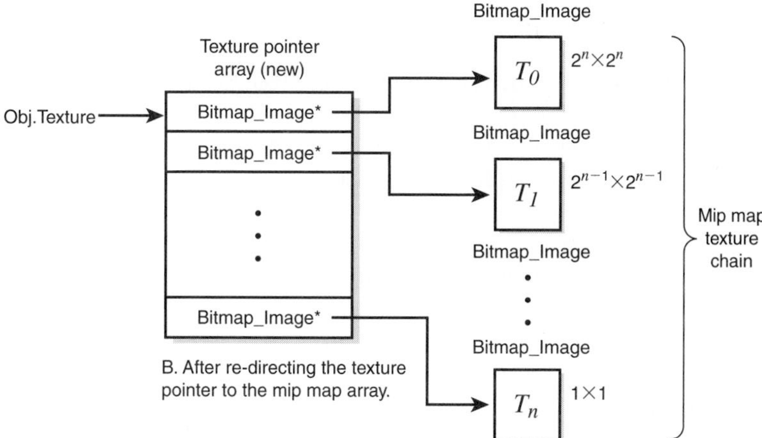

B. After re-directing the texture pointer to the mip map array.

FIGURE 12.43 The new array of texture pointers to support the mip map chain.

When a texture is requested to be mip mapped, the original texture pointer is used at the level 0 mip map. Then from there, the mip map chain is created in two steps. First, we need to allocate an array of pointers to bitmaps, and then point the original texture pointer to that array. Then we need to allocate the memory for each mip texture, generate it, and point each entry in the mip chain array to each respective mip level texture bitmap. Seems confusing, but it's not.

The only problem with this whole scheme is that we are forcing/coercing the bitmap image pointer in the object/polygons to point to something that is *not* a bitmap, but an array of pointers to bitmaps. Therefore, we have to be very careful to ensure that any function that doesn't know a texture has been mip mapped gets tricked into thinking the level 0 texture is the normal texture; of course, any function that does know that a texture is mip mapped must select the correct mip map from the chain.

There are some runtime details to all this, but I will get to that shortly. Right now I want to show you the mip map function in its entirety:

```
int Generate_Mipmaps(BITMAP_IMAGE_PTR source,   // source bitmap for mipmap
    BITMAP_IMAGE_PTR *mipmaps, // pointer to array to store mipmap chain
    float gamma)          // gamma correction factor
{
// this functions creates a mip map chain of bitmap textures
```

```
// on entry source should point to the bottom level d = 0 texture
// and on exit mipmap will point to an array of pointers that holds
// all the mip levels including source as entry 0, additionally the
// function will return the total number of levels or -1 if there
// is a problem, the last param gamma is used to brighten each mip level up
// since averaging has the effect of darkening, a value of 1.01 is usually
// good, values greater that 1.0 brighten each mip map, values less than
// 1.0 darken each mip map, and 1.0 has no effect

BITMAP_IMAGE_PTR *tmipmaps; // local temporary pointer to array of pointers

// step 1: compute number of mip levels total
int num_mip_levels = logbase2ofx[source->width] + 1;

// allocate array of pointers to mip maps
tmipmaps = (BITMAP_IMAGE_PTR *)malloc(num_mip_levels *
      sizeof(BITMAP_IMAGE_PTR) );

// point element 0 (level 0) to entry source
tmipmaps[0] = source;

// set width and height (same actually)
int mip_width = source->width;
int mip_height = source->height;

// iterate thru and generate pyramid mipmap levels using averaging filter
for (int mip_level = 1; mip_level < num_mip_levels; mip_level++)
  {
  // scale size of mip map down one level
  mip_width = mip_width / 2;
  mip_height = mip_height / 2;

  // allocate memory for bitmap object
  tmipmaps[mip_level] = (BITMAP_IMAGE_PTR)malloc(sizeof(BITMAP_IMAGE) );

  // create a bitmap to hold mip map
  Create_Bitmap(tmipmaps[mip_level],0,0, mip_width, mip_height, 16);

  // enable the bitmap for rendering
  SET_BIT(tmipmaps[mip_level]->attr, BITMAP_ATTR_LOADED);

  // now interate thru previous level's mipmap and
  // average down to create this level
  for (int x = 0; x < tmipmaps[mip_level]->width; x++)
    {
```

```
  for (int y = 0; y < tmipmaps[mip_level]->height; y++)
    {
    // we need to average the 4 pixel located at:
    // (x*2, y*2), (x*2+1, y*2), (x*2,y*2+1), (x*2+1,y*2+1)
    // in previous mipmap level, and then write them
    // to x,y in this mipmap level :) easy!
    float r0, g0, b0,    // r,g,b components of 4 sample pixels
       r1, g1, b1,
       r2, g2, b2,
       r3, g3, b3;

    int r_avg, g_avg, b_avg; // used to compute averages

    USHORT *src_buffer = (USHORT *)tmipmaps[mip_level-1]->buffer,
        *dest_buffer = (USHORT *)tmipmaps[mip_level]->buffer;

    // extract rgb components of each pixel
    _RGB565FROM16BIT( src_buffer[(x*2+0)+(y*2+0)*mip_width*2],
             &r0, &g0, &b0);
    _RGB565FROM16BIT( src_buffer[(x*2+1)+(y*2+0)*mip_width*2],
             &r1, &g1, &b1);
    _RGB565FROM16BIT( src_buffer[(x*2+0)+(y*2+1)*mip_width*2],
             &r2, &g2, &b2);
    _RGB565FROM16BIT( src_buffer[(x*2+1)+(y*2+1)*mip_width*2],
             &r3, &g3, &b3);

    // compute average, take gamma into consideration
    r_avg = (int)(0.5f + gamma*(r0+r1+r2+r3)/4);
    g_avg = (int)(0.5f + gamma*(g0+g1+g2+g3)/4);
    b_avg = (int)(0.5f + gamma*(b0+b1+b2+b3)/4);

    // clamp values to max r, g, b values for 5.6.5 format
    if (r_avg > 31) r_avg = 31;
    if (g_avg > 63) g_avg = 63;
    if (b_avg > 31) b_avg = 31;

    // write data
    dest_buffer[x + y*mip_width] = _RGB16BIT565(r_avg,g_avg,b_avg);

    } // end for y

  } // end for x

} // end for mip_level
```

```
// now assign array of pointers to exit
*mipmaps = (BITMAP_IMAGE_PTR)tmipmaps;

// return success
return(num_mip_levels);

} // end Generate_Mipmaps
```

The function begins by taking three parameters, and they are a little tricky. The first is the source bitmap pointer. This can be a pointer to any valid BITMAP_IMAGE object, but remember, it's a pointer. The second parameter is a little more complicated:

```
BITMAP_IMAGE_PTR *mipmaps;
```

This is a pointer to a pointer to a BITMAP_IMAGE. Let me explain: Suppose we have an object (or polygon, for that matter) that has a texture pointer. The texture pointer is pointing to a BITMAP_IMAGE; that is, the structure element itself in the object or polygon is a BITMAP_IMAGE_PTR (a BITMAP_IMAGE *, in other words). Now, the problem is that when the mip map function runs and generates all the mip maps, we want the pointer to point to the mip map chain itself, but to do this, we need the address of the pointer itself so we can modify it. Thus, a ** BITMAP_IMAGE is needed. That's why we have a pointer to a pointer on entry. This is what we are going to point to the mip map chain array of pointers.

I wrote the function to be flexible, so on entry you might send in the same object as both the source *and* the mip map. For the source parameter, you will only send the pointer, but for the mip map object, you will send the address of the pointer so the function can modify it with the new information. Let's say that you called the function like this:

```
Generate_Mipmaps(obj->texture, (BITMAP_IMAGE_PTR *)&obj->texture,1.01);
```

where obj is of the type OBJECT4DV2_PTR, which has an internal field texture that is a pointer to a BITMAP_IMAGE or a BITMAP_IMAGE_PTR, using our types. This is great, but look at that call carefully: We send in the pointer as the first parameter, but we send in the address of it as the second parameter, so any change made will change the actual value that obj->texture was pointing to and potentially lose the original data to which it was pointing. But, wait! The trick is that we aren't going to lose anything, but we are going to use the original bitmap pointed to by obj->texture as the first mip texture in the mip map chain, and then when we are all done. We will fix the pointer back up when we delete the mip maps. Figure 12.44 shows the entire process.

Back to the function—it basically implements our mip mapping function line for line, allocating the memory for the texture pointer array, computing the size of the next mip level, allocating the memory, and then performing an averaging filter in RGB space to create the next mip level. This process is iterated until a mip level of 1×1 is reached when the function exits. Finally, the last parameter of the function (which actually has a default value of 1.01) controls the gamma. It turns out that when you iteratively average down an image, it tends to lose its brightness; therefore, a gamma factor is usually used to brighten up each mip level to keep the overall intensity constant. To show you this, I would like to skip ahead and have you play with a demo program. The demo program `DEMOII12_10.CPP¦EXE` enables you select different texture maps, and the program creates mip maps on the fly and displays them as shown in Figure 12.45. Additionally, you can change the gamma level and see the effects. The controls are shown here:

- RIGHT—Select next texture
- LEFT—Select previous texture
- UP—Increase gamma level
- DOWN—Decrease gamma level

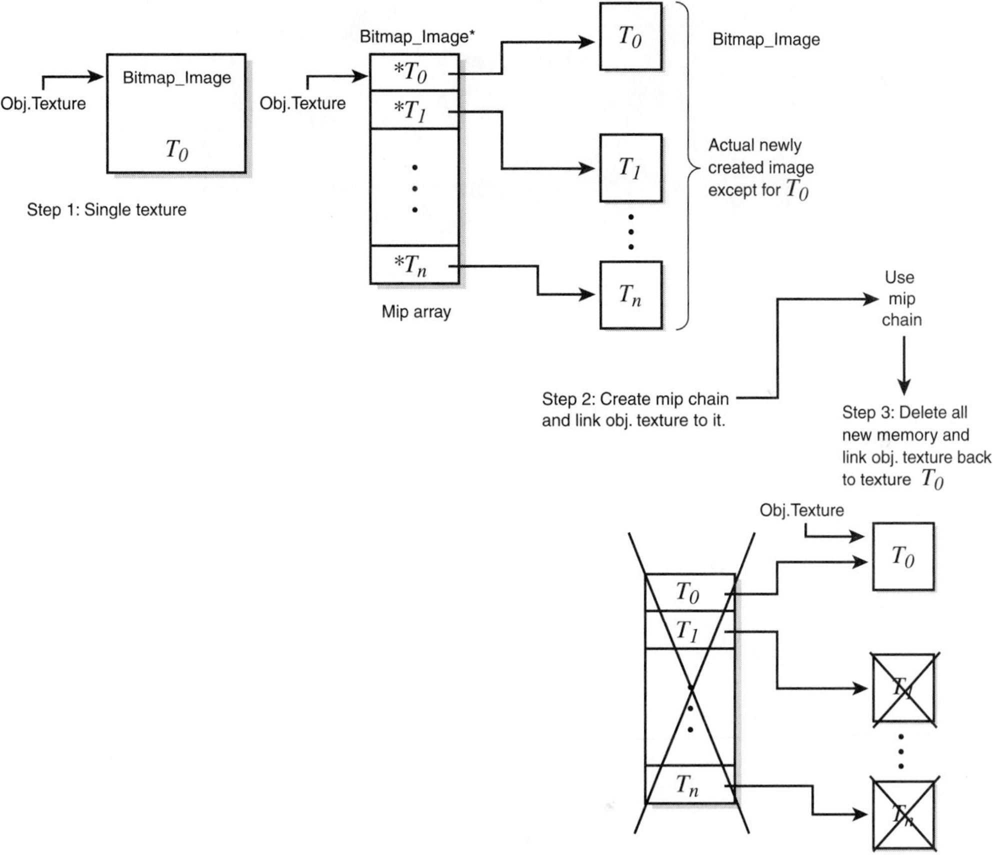

FIGURE 12.44 Linking in and out the mip map chain from the object texture pointer.

TIP

Each mip map is computed by averaging down the previous texture from (m×m) to (m/2×m/2). This has the effect of slowly decreasing the overall intensity of the image. With this in mind, the gamma factor is used as a multiplier during the averaging filter process, so the textels can be slightly brightened to make up for this problem.

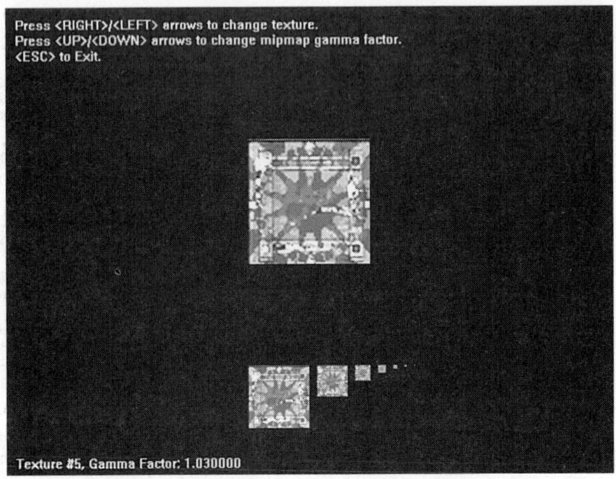

FIGURE 12.45 A screenshot of the real-time mip map generator.

To compile the program, you will need the `DEMOII12_10.CPP|H`, along with the library files `T3DLIB1-10.CPP|H` and the DirectX .LIB files.

Now back to the explanation: `obj->texture`, in the case of the preceding call to `Generate_Mipmaps()`, would now point to a mip chain, rather than a single bitmap texture. Therefore, if you just call a rasterizer, you'll get a big boo-boo! So, we need to tag polygons that are mipped, and we need to take this into consideration *before* calling the rasterizer. To do this, I have created a couple of flags: one for polygons, and one for objects.

```
// new attributes to support mip mapping
#define POLY4DV2_ATTR_MIPMAP     0x0400 // flags if polygon has a mipmap

#define OBJECT4DV2_ATTR_MIPMAP    0x0008 // flags if object has a mipmap
```

If an object that we want mip mapped is loaded, we must set this flag in its attributes. We'll also do it for each polygon that is mip mapped. However, who's going to do this? Yup, you guessed it—we need yet another object-loading function that supports mip mapping. I have only added the functionality to the Caligari .COB reader because I find myself using it the most. Here is the new prototype:

```
int Load_OBJECT4DV2_COB2(OBJECT4DV2_PTR obj,  // pointer to object
       char *filename,     // filename of Caligari COB file
       VECTOR4D_PTR scale,  // initial scaling factors
       VECTOR4D_PTR pos,   // initial position
       VECTOR4D_PTR rot,   // initial rotations
       int vertex_flags,   // flags to re-order vertices
                  // and perform transforms
       int mipmap )      // mipmap enable flag
                  // 0 means no mipmap, 1 means
                  // generate mip map
```

The function is absolutely identical to the previous version, except for the addition of the last parameter mipmap, which is a flag that indicates whether you want mip mapping. If you set the parameter to 1 and there are any textures on the object, they will be mip mapped; if the flag is 0, no mip mapping will be done. The loading function is gigantic, so I can't list it, but there are only two new code blocks inside. The first one sets the mip attribute on the object:

```
// before performing texture application we
// need to determine if the texture on this
// object is mipmapped, if so we need to create
// a mip map chain, and set the proper
// attributes in both the object and the polygons themselves
if (mipmap==1)
  {
  // set the mipmap bit in the object
  SET_BIT(obj->attr, OBJECT4DV2_ATTR_MIPMAP);

  // now with the base texture as level d=0 call the mipmap chain generator
  Generate_Mipmaps(obj->texture, (BITMAP_IMAGE_PTR *)&obj->texture);
  } // end if
```

This code appears right before the final material analysis and cleanup is done. And then in the final attribute setting of all the polygons, there is some mip map code to set the attributes inside the texture case:

```
if (materials[ poly_material[curr_poly] ].attr & MATV1_ATTR_SHADE_MODE_TEXTURE)
  {
  // set shading mode
  SET_BIT(obj->plist[curr_poly].attr, POLY4DV2_ATTR_SHADE_MODE_TEXTURE);

  // apply texture to this polygon
  obj->plist[curr_poly].texture = obj->texture;

  // if the object was mipmapped this above assignment
  // will just point the texture to
```

```
  // the mipmap chain array, however we still need to
  // set the polygon attribute, so
  // we know the poly is mip mapped, since once its in
  // the rendering list we will have
  // no idea
  if (mipmap)
    SET_BIT(obj->plist[curr_poly].attr,POLY4DV2_ATTR_MIPMAP);

  // set texture coordinate attributes
  SET_BIT(obj->vlist_local[ obj->plist[curr_poly].vert[0] ].attr,
      VERTEX4DTV1_ATTR_TEXTURE);
  SET_BIT(obj->vlist_local[ obj->plist[curr_poly].vert[1] ].attr,
      VERTEX4DTV1_ATTR_TEXTURE);
  SET_BIT(obj->vlist_local[ obj->plist[curr_poly].vert[2] ].attr,
      VERTEX4DTV1_ATTR_TEXTURE);

  } // end if
```

And that's the extent of the modifications to the new object loader to create and set the mip map attributes. The trick is in the selection and logic to pass mip maps to the rasterizers, but I will get to that shortly. Right now, I want to show you the last function pertaining to mip maps, the deletion function:

```
int Delete_Mipmaps(BITMAP_IMAGE_PTR *mipmaps, int leave_level_0)
{
// this function deletes all the mipmaps in the chain
// that each pointer in the array mipmaps points to and
// then releases the array memory itself, the function has the
// ability to leave the top level 0 bitmap in place if
// leave_level_0 flag is 1

BITMAP_IMAGE_PTR *tmipmaps = (BITMAP_IMAGE_PTR *)*mipmaps;

// are there any mipmaps
if (!tmipmaps)
  return(0);

// step 1: compute number of mip levels total
int num_mip_levels = logbase2ofx[tmipmaps[0]->width] + 1;

// iterate thru delete each bitmap
for (int mip_level = 1; mip_level < num_mip_levels; mip_level++)
  {
  // release the memory for the bitmap buffer
  Destroy_Bitmap(tmipmaps[mip_level]);
```

```
  // now release the bitmap object itself
  free(tmipmaps[mip_level]);

  } // end for mip_level

// now depending on the leave_level_0 flag delete everything or leave the
// original level 0 in place
if (leave_level_0 == 1)
  {
  // we need a temp pointer to the level 0 bitmap
  BITMAP_IMAGE_PTR temp = tmipmaps[0];

  // and the array storage too
  //free(*tmipmaps);

  // and assign mipmaps to the original level 0
  *tmipmaps = temp;
  } // end if
else
  {
  // delete everything!
  Destroy_Bitmap(tmipmaps[0]);

  // now release the bitmap object itself
  free(tmipmaps[0]);

  // and the array storage too
  //free(*tmipmaps);
  } // end else

// return success
return(1);

} // end Delete_Mipmaps
```

`Delete_Mipmaps()` takes two parameters: a pointer to the pointer of the bitmap image, and a flag to leave or destroy the level 0 mip map. The reason why we need the address of the pointer is similar to the case when we generated the mip map chain itself. We need to modify the pointer on exit; in other words, we need to undo all the damage we have wrought, pointing it to the mip array, rather than a normal `BITMAP_IMAGE` as it was intended to do. For example, suppose you have an object `obj` that has a single texture that's mapped on the object. You then request that it be mip mapped via a call to the new load object function, with a mip map enable of `1`. Now the function takes the texture and creates a mip map chain, but when we are done, we need to put things back to the way they were. The object deletion works because it knows nothing of mip maps, so we need to delete the mip map chain texture elements `1-n`, but we need to point the texture pointer back to texture element 0.

This is why we need the address of the pointer, rather than just the pointer. In any case, `Delete_Mipmaps()` supports all of this via the `leave_level_0` variable. If `leave_level_0` is 1, the level 0 texture will be fixed back up and survive. However, if `leave_level_0` is equal to 0, *everything* will be deleted. The mip array, all the textures including level 0, and the pointers will all be set to `NULL` on exit. If we want be perfect, we need to call `Delete_Mipmaps()` on the object's texture pointer before exiting our program or block when we load an object with mip mapping.

Mip Map Selection and Setup

There are two ways to select the mip map when rendering: per-pixel and per-polygon. Per-pixel uses a metric or algorithm to determine which mip map to select on a pixel-by-pixel basis. There are a few methods to do this, but all of them are much too complex to do in real time with a software engine. We're going to stick with per-polygon mip map selection.

The trick to finding a suitable algorithm to select the proper mip level is to remember why we created mip levels in the first place: to minimize the amount of high frequency aliasing (showing up as low frequency aliases or moiré patterns) by averaging the texture map down by one-fourth each time, and then using a smaller texture map with less high frequency components in it as the projection polygon being rendered gets smaller.

There is no point in using a 256×256 size texture to texture a polygon that is 10×10 pixels—you are going to see all kinds of artifacts, sparkling, and so forth; but if you were to use an 8×8 texture, that would be just right. Therefore, we now see the basis of an algorithm: We simply take the *projected* area of the polygon in screen coordinates and compare it to the level 0 mip map area. This will tell us the ratio of textels to pixels, which we want to be as close to 1:1 as possible. In other words, we don't want to use a 256×256 texture for a 10×10 polygon; we would like to use maybe an 8×8. Likewise, we wouldn't want to use an 8×8 size texture for a 30×30 size polygon; a 32×32 size texture might be more appropriate.

Selection of Mip Level Based on Textel-to-Pixel Ratio

Now that we have a general heuristic, let's see whether we can make a robust formula based on the fact that we know each mip level has one-fourth the information as the previous one. Every time the textel-to-pixel ratio is greater than a factor of 4, we know we need to move another mip level up or down the chain. Mathematically, we have the ratio of textels to pixels as shown in Equation 12.5.

EQUATION 12.5 Computation of Mip Ratio

$$\text{mip\_ratio} = \frac{\text{area of level 0 mip map texture in textels}}{\text{projected area of polygon in pixels}}$$

As an example, let's say our level 0 mip texture is 256×256 (our base texture), and we are texturing it onto a polygon that has area 24×90. We would have a mip_ratio of

```
mip_ratio = 256*256 / 24*90 = 65536 / 2160 = 30.3
```

Rounding off, that means a mip ratio of 30.3:1. We know that for every factor of 4, we need to go to the next mip level. But we need to be careful here on what this means—we need to compute the $\log_4 30.3$ to find the mip level, not divide 4 into 30. Thus, we need to compute the $\log_4 30.3$. That is the number *x*in $4^x = 30.3$. Luckily for us, there is a conversion from one base to another, shown in Equation 12.6.

EQUATION 12.6 Change of Logarithmic Base

$$\log_a x = \mathit{ln}\ x \ / \ \mathit{ln}\ a$$

Where *ln* is the natural log, or the log base e = 2.718.

Applying the change-of-base formula to $\log_4 30.3$, we get

$$\log_4 30.3 = \ln 30.3 \ / \ \ln 4 = 2.46$$

Alrighty then, we have the mip level! It's 2.46—that means we should select the second mip level (rounding or truncating). Referring back to Table 12.4, we see that the second mip level has a size 64×64, or a textel area of 4096. This is within a factor of 4 of the real projected pixel area of 2160, so we have indeed picked out the best matched mip map of 64×64 to the polygon of 24×90. Very cool, huh?

Just to make sure you believe it works, let's do two more quick examples. If the polygon size is 200×170, we would expect that mip level 0 would be selected because it's the closest within a factor of 4. Let's see:

```
mip_ratio = (256*256) / (200*170) = 1.927
```

$$\log_4 1.927 = 0.$$

This suggests we take mip level 0, or the 256×256 texture! Hmmm ... Let's try one more case at the other end of the spectrum. Suppose we have a polygon that has a projected pixel area of 3×4. We would expect a final mip level of 6 or 7, which is 4×4 and 2×2, respectively. Let's see:

```
mip_ratio = (256*256) / (3*4) = 5461.33
```

$$\log_4 5461.33 = 6.2.$$

This suggests we select mip level 6. Are we gods, or what?

The only problem with the preceding outlined textel-to-pixel ratio computation algorithm is that we have to compute the area of each polygon (triangle) and compare it with the texture area, do some logs, and come up with a mip level. Although this can be done in a few instructions, it's really unnecessary. In practice, a far easier method can be employed that looks 99% as good with regard to selecting the mip level, and it actually enables you to tune it more. It's based on a linear falloff from the view point which we will discuss now.

Selection of Mip Map Based on Simple Z Distance

The bottom line is that we want to select from *n* different mip maps as polygons get smaller. Well, they usually get smaller as they get farther from the viewpoint, right? True, a teenie-weenie polygon viewed up close and a huge polygon far away look the same, but that's an extreme case. The point is that we can use a loose heuristic like distance instead of the textel-to-pixel area ratio computation to select mip map levels.

In Figure 12.46, we're going to set a maximum mip distance at which we want the last mip level to be selected. In other words, suppose we set the maximum mip distance to 10,000 units. Then any polygon that has a *z* coordinate (max or average) greater than 10,000 will always select the highest mip level (which is 1×1). Any polygons within the range of 0–10,000 units will select a mip level as a linear function of the range and the maximum distance.

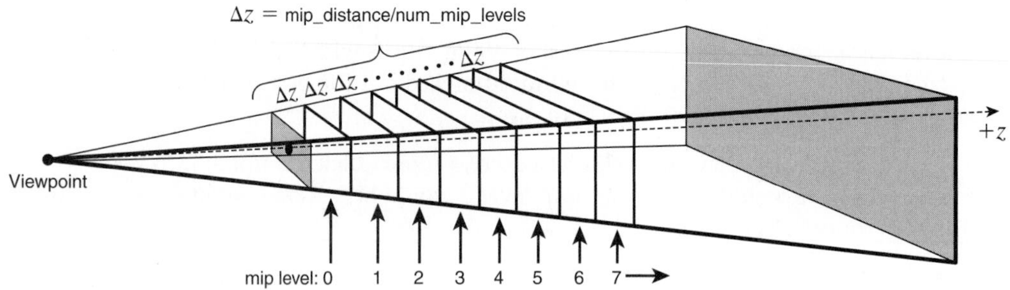

FIGURE 12.46 Selecting mip levels based on distance.

With that in mind, I want to show you the actual code from the rendering context function `Draw_RENDERLIST4DV2_RENDERCONTEXTV1_16()` that performs the mip level selection:

```
// test if this is a mipmapped polygon?
if (rc->rend_list->poly_ptrs[poly]->attr & POLY4DV2_ATTR_MIPMAP)
  {
  // determine if mipmapping is desired at all globally
  if (rc->attr & RENDER_ATTR_MIPMAP)
    {
    // determine mip level for this polygon
    // first determine how many miplevels there
    // are in mipchain for this polygon
    int tmiplevels =
```

```
  logbase2ofx[((BITMAP_IMAGE_PTR *)
       (rc->rend_list->poly_ptrs[poly]->texture))[0]->width];

// now based on the requested linear miplevel fall off distance, cut
// the viewdistance into segments,
// determine what segment polygon is
// in and select mip level -- simple!
// later you might want something more
// robust, also note I only use a single vertex,
// you might want to find the average
// since for long walls perpendicular to view
// direction this might causing mip
// popping mid surface
int miplevel = (tmiplevels * rc->rend_list->poly_ptrs[poly]->tvlist[0].z /
        rc->mip_dist);

// clamp miplevel
if (miplevel > tmiplevels) miplevel = tmiplevels;

// based on miplevel select proper texture
face.texture = ((BITMAP_IMAGE_PTR *)
       (rc->rend_list->poly_ptrs[poly]->texture))[miplevel];

// now we must divide each texture coordinate by 2 per miplevel
// very crude
for (int ts = 0; ts < miplevel; ts++)
  {
  face.tvlist[0].u0*=.5;
  face.tvlist[0].v0*=.5;

  face.tvlist[1].u0*=.5;
  face.tvlist[1].v0*=.5;

  face.tvlist[2].u0*=.5;
  face.tvlist[2].v0*=.5;
  } // end for

} // end if mipmmaping enabled globally
else // mipmapping not selected globally
 {
 // in this case the polygon IS mipmapped,
 // but the caller has requested NO
 // mipmapping, so we will support this
 // by selecting mip level 0 since the
```

```
    // texture pointer is pointing to a mip chain regardless
    face.texture = ((BITMAP_IMAGE_PTR *)
            (rc->rend_list->poly_ptrs[poly]->texture))[0];

    // note: texture coordinate manipulation is unneeded
    } // end else

    } // end if
   else
    {
    // assign the texture without change
    face.texture = rc->rend_list->poly_ptrs[poly]->texture;
    } // end if
```

There's a lot going on here, so let's start at the top. The code block is excerpted from one of the rasterizer entry points where it's being determined whether mip mapping is being requested. There are a number of cases to consider. The first is the polygon has no mip mapping, in which case we can't mip map it. The second is the polygon has mip mapping but we didn't request it with the rendering attributes. Third is the polygon is mip mapped and we requested it. All these cases have to be considered as the code runs. Let's step through it. First the block starts, and the number of mip levels is computed by taking the $\log_2$ of the width of the level 0 texture map:

```
int tmiplevels =
   logbase2ofx[((BITMAP_IMAGE_PTR *)

         (rc->rend_list->poly_ptrs[poly]->texture))[0]->width];
```

This bit of nasty code has all the texture and pointer coercion needed to cast the texture pointer from an array of pointers to a texture pointer, and then access the first texture's width (remember, the first texture is always the texture level 0), so if it's, say, 128×128, we know there are $\log_2 128 = 7$ mip levels. Anyway, we perform the computation and then move on to selecting the mip texture with this code:

```
int miplevel = (tmiplevels * rc->rend_list->poly_ptrs[poly]->tvlist[0].z /

        rc->mip_dist);
```

This is basically scaling our range down based on the `mip_dist` parameter in the rendering context. This is the variable that determines how far to divide mip mapping; or in other words, the point where all mip maps will be at the highest level (1×1). Next we set the face texture with this code:

```
// based on miplevel select proper texture
face.texture = ((BITMAP_IMAGE_PTR *)
        (rc->rend_list->poly_ptrs[poly]->texture))[miplevel];
```

Again, lots of nasty pointer casting because the texture pointer isn't a pointer to a texture anymore, but a pointer to an array of pointers to textures. `face.texture` needs only the pointer, so we have to jump through some hoops here.

Next is a *very* important detail that I haven't mentioned yet. Suppose we have the texture coordinates (u,v) = (63,63), and we have a level 0 texture that is 64×64 pixels. So, (63,63) means the far u,v corner. However, when we select another mip level, the texture is no longer 64×64! It could be 8×8, 2×2, or whatever. Therefore, we need to *scale* the texture coordinates down to make sure they map correctly. This is shown in Figure 12.47.

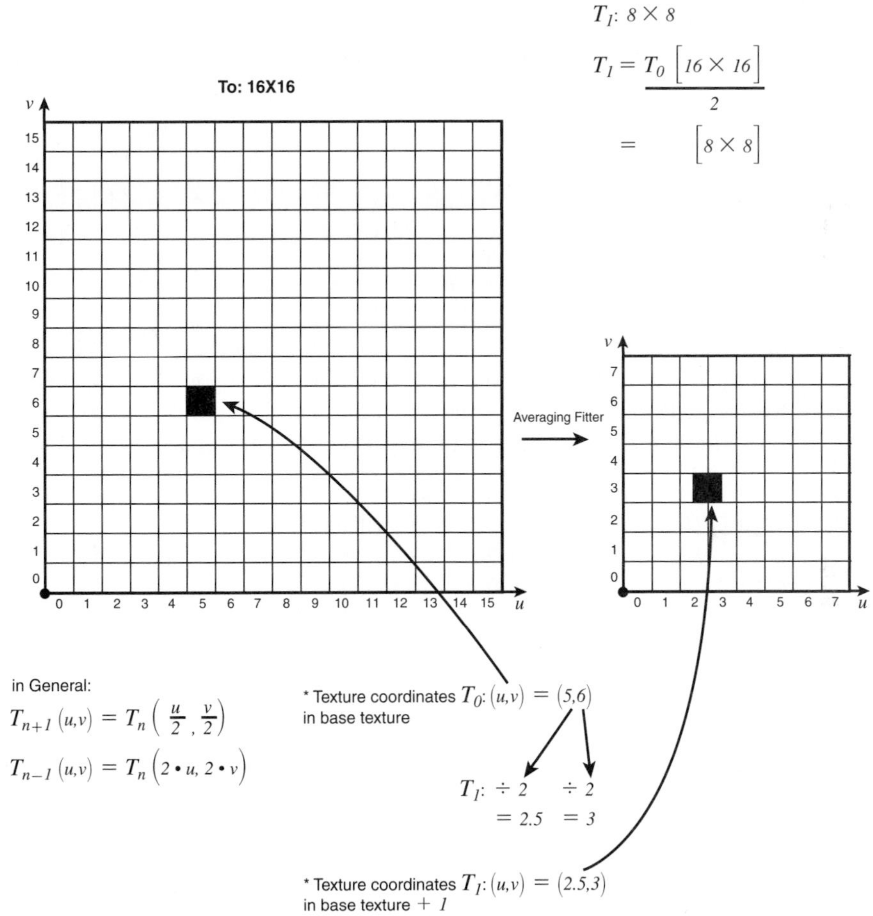

FIGURE 12.47 Scaling texture coordinates down to fit the mipped textures.

The code that does this basically looks at how many mip levels up the chain we need to go, then iteratively divides the texture coordinates by 2 (multiplying by .5) on each axis to match up the texture map with the texture coordinates:

```
for (int ts = 0; ts < miplevel; ts++)
  {
  face.tvlist[0].u0*=.5;
  face.tvlist[0].v0*=.5;
  face.tvlist[1].u0*=.5;
  face.tvlist[1].v0*=.5;

  face.tvlist[2].u0*=.5;
  face.tvlist[2].v0*=.5;
  } // end for
```

There are definitely faster ways to do this, such as using a lookup table with constants of $(0.5)^{mip\_level}$ and then multiplying by that rather than iteratively doing it, but this is easier to understand for now.

NOTE

Everything we do to the texture coordinates, texture, and so on, is performed on the local face object, so we don't have to worry about restoring anything.

That's mip mapping for you! Of course, you might find that you prefer to do the area ratio selection method rather than this faster method, but that's up to you. Anyway, before moving onto a demo, let's see a sample setup of loading an object and then setting up a rendering context. Here's a typical call to load an object with mip mapping enabled:

```
// load in the scenery object that we will place all over the place
Load_OBJECT4DV2_COB2(&obj_scene, "cube_flat_textured_01.cob",
           &vscale, &vpos, &vrot, VERTEX_FLAGS_SWAP_YZ |
           VERTEX_FLAGS_TRANSFORM_LOCAL ,
           ,1); // enable mip mapping
```

Now let's set up the rendering context:

```
// set up rendering context
rc.attr = RENDER_ATTR_ZBUFFER
     | RENDER_ATTR_MIPMAP
     | RENDER_ATTR_TEXTURE_PERSPECTIVE_AFFINE;

  rc.video_buffer  = back_buffer;
  rc.lpitch       = back_lpitch;
  rc.mip_dist      = 1500;
  rc.zbuffer      = (UCHAR *)zbuffer.zbuffer;
  rc.zpitch       = WINDOW_WIDTH*4;
  rc.rend_list     = &rend_list;
```

```
rc.texture_dist   = 0;
rc.alpha_override = -1;

// render scene
Draw_RENDERLIST4DV2_RENDERCONTEXTV1_16(&rc);
```

For an example of mip mapping and bilinear interpolation, check out the DEMOII12_11.CPP¦EXE;files: shown in Figure 12.48. It enables you to move around and enable/disable mip mapping in the 3D world.

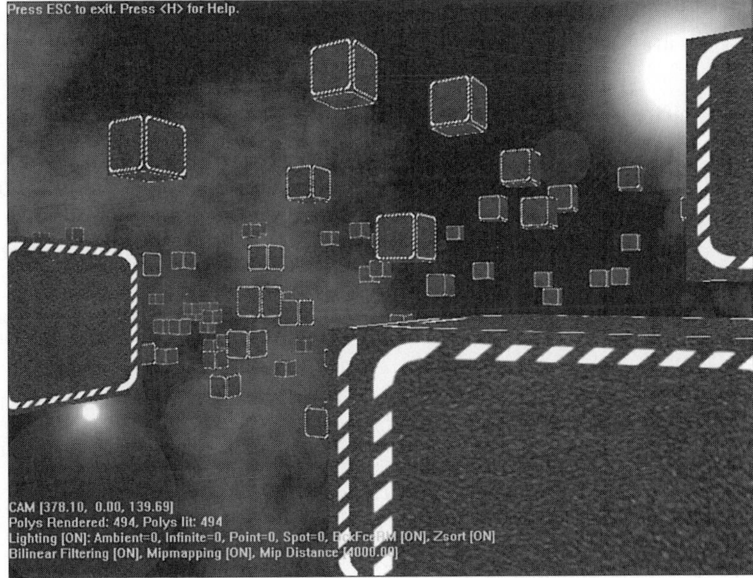

FIGURE 12.48 The mip mapping demo in action.

Notice how much better textures look when mip mapped. Also, the demo has bilinear texturing capability, so it looks really good. The controls are as follows:

- Arrow keys—Move around
- B—Toggle bilinear filtering
- M—Toggle mip mapping
- 1, 2—Decrease/increase mip distance
- N—Select next object to experiment with

Also try adjusting the mip distance so that the texures pop in and out. This is called *mip popping*, and if it occurs within a polygon, it's called *mip banding*. The bottom line is that using the linear distance method to select mip levels works fine and is much cheaper than the more complex area method.

> **TIP**
>
> Use the 1 and 2 keys to change the mip distance. Make it something like 500–1000, and you will really see heavy mipping. Change it to 3500 or so, which is a good in-game value.

Finally, to compile the demo, you will need `DEMOII12_11.CPP|H`, along with `T3DLIB1-10.CPP|H` and the DirectX .LIB files.

Trilinear Filtering

Last but not least, let's talk for a moment about trilinear filtering. *Trilinear filtering* brings bilinear interpolation together with mip mapping for the ultimate in texture filtering. First we select the mip level to render the polygon or pixel by using whatever technique we want (most likely the area technique, because it's more accurate). We end up with a number like 4.3. What this tells us is that we want to use both mip map level 4 and level 5. That is, we want to linearly interpolate the final value from mip map 4 with 5, using this formula:

```
mip_pixel = (1 - 0.3)* mip_level_pixel_4 + (.3)*mip_level_pixel_5
```

So instead of just using one mip level, we linearly interpolate between the pixel from two of them, which is the linear interpolation of the decimal value from the mip level computation. If this looks like linear interpolation, the trilinear part comes in because we first select the pixel from map 4 via bilinear interpolation, then select the pixel from map 5 with bilinear interpolation, and then linearly interpolate the resulting pixels to arrive at a final value of the pixel. This entire process is shown in Figure 12.49.

Now, many engines/hardware don't actually do all this work. Some engines just linearly interpolate between the point-sampled textels from maps 4 and 5, whereas others perform the entire computation. We could actually implement this right now, but it will be just a bit too slow. However, as an exercise, I think you should do it just for fun. The problem is that the final interpolation has to happen *inside* the rasterizers, and this is the rub that gets you in trouble.

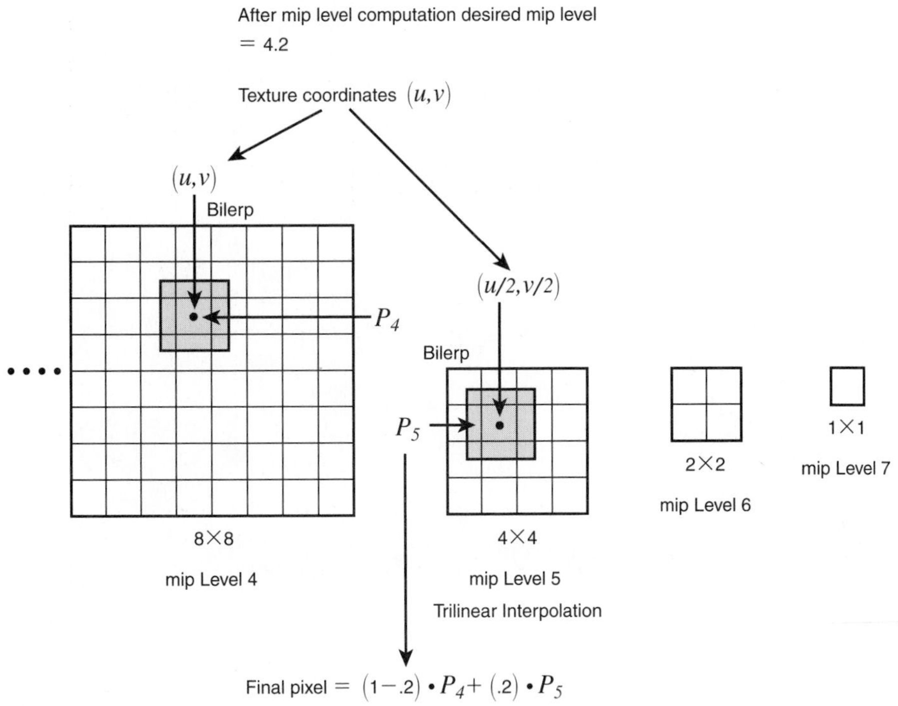

FIGURE 12.49 Trilinear filtering.

Multiple Pass Rendering and Texturing

It's a little hard to believe, but multiple passes with a software rasterizer are possible. Look at it this way: We're able to render about 1,000–3,000 polygons per frame at 15–30 fps right now, depending on the settings. So, I just cut that down by half and perform two passes. There are lots of effects you can get with this. For example, a reflection-in-water effect can be achieved by first rendering the scene right side up, and then rendering it upside down (with transparency), blending it with the ground plane, which is supposed to be a shiny surface.

You can also get shadow and other special effects with multiple rendering passes. However, in our case, two passes is the most you'll want to try, even with a simple world, because it's going to kill your frame rate. As an example of multiple pass rendering, I have created a scene with some simple geometric shapes sitting on a plane. To create the effect, I render the ground plane object without any Z-buffer. Then I render the reflection with the alpha channel and the Z-buffer by inverting the view matrix. Next I render the scene once more with no alpha and the Z-buffer with the normal view matrix. The final results are a shiny surface reflecting the objects. Figure 12.50 shows a screenshot.

FIGURE 12.50 A screenshot of the reflection demo.

To run the demo, check out DEMOII12_12.CPP|EXE. Use the arrow keys to move around the environment, and press the P key to toggle through different passes, so you can see the scene being built up. To compile the demo, you will need DEMOII12_12.CPP|H, along with T3DLIB1-10.CPP|H and the DirectX .LIB files.

Wrapping Things Up with a Single Call

Wow—I began this chapter without thinking it would be this big. Amazingly, this is after deciding to move the lighting and shadow code into a chapter of their own. However, it's turned out to be a nasty chapter nonetheless. This further emphasizes that even a very basic software 3D engine is a complex subject. However, it's amazing how far we have come!

Anyway, the code size is getting out of hand at this point, and we need to add a single layer of indirection on top of the rendering calls to draw the rendering list. Currently, we have a different version of sorted, z-buffered, 1/z-buffered, mip mapped, alpha'ed, perspective, and so on rasterizers; there are quite a few of them. This is totally unacceptable in the long run. Figure 12.51 shows what I am talking about. Of course, if you know what kind of rasterization you want, you don't need another layer. But at this point, creating demos for this book is getting too complicated with all this code.

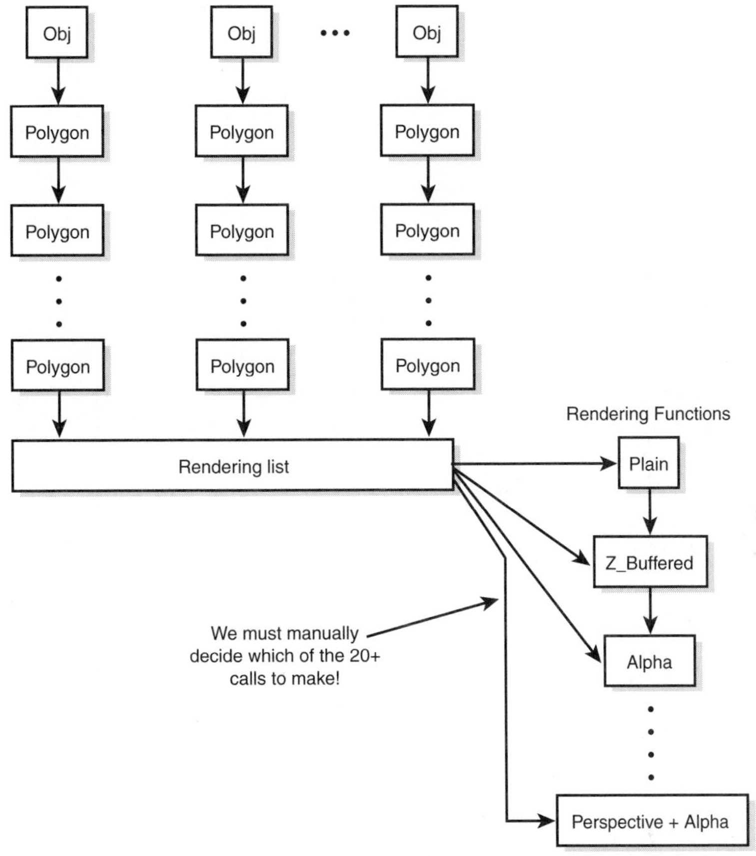

FIGURE 12.51 Our system as it stands without a unified rendering port.

The New Rendering Context

To solve the problem of function call anarchy, I have created a new data structure called a *rendering context* that we set up like a DirectX structure. The point of data structure is to enable us to fill it in with information like the video buffer, Z-buffer, rendering flags, and so forth, and then make a single call to a high-level function that analyzes the rendering context and makes all the calls to the proper triangle. Figure 12.52 shows this abstractly.

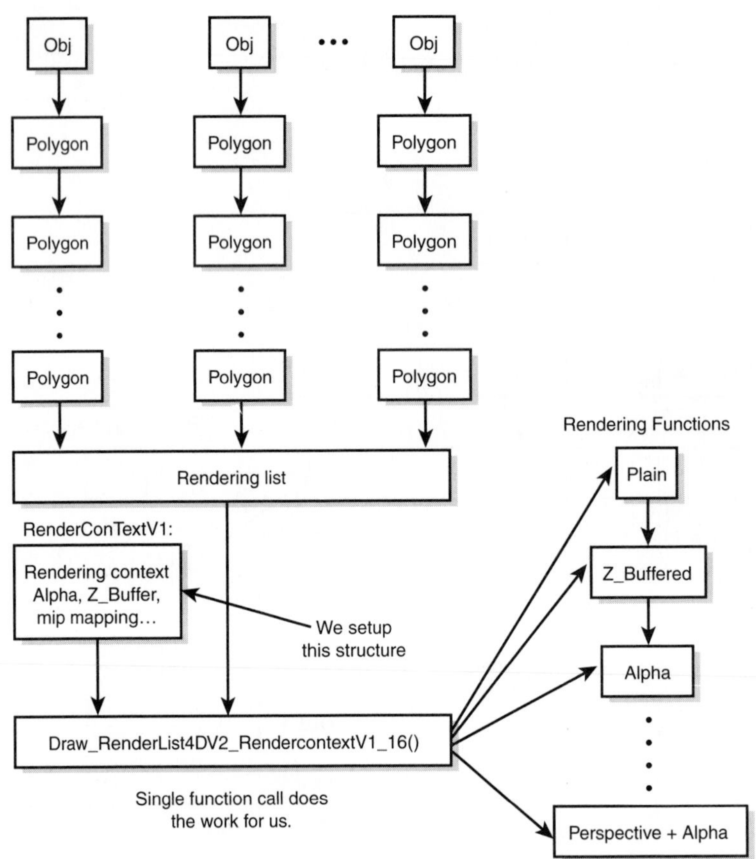

FIGURE 12.52 Our new system with rendering context support.

Here's the new data structure (which is found in T3DLIB10.H):

```
// this is a new type to contain the "rendering context" RC, so
// we don't have to keep passing more and more variables to the
// rendering functions, we can fill this structure in with what we
// need and then pass it as a whole
typedef struct RENDERCONTEXTV1_TYP
{
int   attr;          // all the rendering attributes
RENDERLIST4DV2_PTR rend_list; // ptr to rendering list to render
UCHAR *video_buffer;     // ptr to video buffer to render to
int   lpitch;        // memory pitch in bytes of video buffer

UCHAR *zbuffer;        // ptr to z buffer or 1/z buffer
int   zpitch;        // memory pitch in bytes of z or 1/z buffer
int   alpha_override;    // alpha value to override ALL polys with
```

```
int   mip_dist;        // maximum distance to divide up into
             // mip levels
             // 0 - (NUM_ALPHA_LEVELS - 1)
int   texture_dist,     // the distance to enable affine texturing
    texture_dist2;    // when using hybrid perspective/affine mode

// future expansion
int   ival1, ivalu2;    // extra integers
float  fval1, fval2;     // extra floats
void  *vptr;         // extra pointer

} RENDERCONTEXTV1, *RENDERCONTEXTV1_PTR;
```


In essence, it's nothing more than the parameter list of the union of all the rendering functions. So, it has everything we could possibly need to set up a rendering frame. All the fields are self-explanatory by their name and do what they normally do, but I want to cover them briefly just to make sure we are both on the same page:

- `attr`—This controls how the rendering is carried out; that is, what options are used: z-buffering, no buffering, alpha blending, bilinear interpolation, mip mapping, and so forth. Before the final call to the rendering function is made, you will set this up with the logical `OR` of the requested rendering options. More on this shortly.
- `rend_list`—A pointer to the rendering list your wish rendered.
- `video_buffer`—A pointer to the final video buffer to which you want the scene rendered.
- `lpitch`—The memory pitch of the `video_buffer` in bytes.
- `zbuffer`—A pointer to the Z-buffer storage. You might use a Z-buffer or inverse Z-buffer, but the storage needs are always the same.
- `zpitch`—The memory pitch of the Z-buffer storage in bytes.
- `alpha_override`—If you have enabled alpha blending with the rendering context, you can override the entire scene by placing an integer from `(0..NUM_ALPHA_LEVELS-1)` in this variable—otherwise keep it -1.
- `mip_dist`—This controls the mip range in which to perform mip mapping. The range is from 0 to this value; within this the mip levels will be linearly selected as a function of distance.
- `texture_dist`, `texture_dist2`—These are used to control the range selects when using hybrid texturing modes. You will need to set one or both of them depending on whether you want perfect perspective, linear piecewise, affine, or the simpler linear piecewise affine hybrid modes. More on this shortly.
- `ival1`, `ival2`—These are simply extra integers to do with as you will.

- `fval1`, `fval2`—These are simply extra floats to do with as you will.
- `vptr`—A void `ptr` to do with as you will.

Setting Up the Rendering Context

Now let's talk about setting up the rendering context. First, a rendering context must be created (this will usually be a single global, but you might have more than one):

```
RENDERCONTEXTV1 rc;
```

It's always a good idea to clear out any large structure with some code like this:

```
memset(&rc,0,sizeof(rc));
```

The `attr` field of the rendering context is the key to everything—you simply need to set it up with whatever rendering options you want. The control flags are found in `T3DLIB10.H` and are listed here:

```
// defines that control the rendering function state attributes
// note each class of control flags is contained within
// a 4-bit nibble where possible, this helps with future expansion

// no z buffering, polygons will be rendered as are in list
#define RENDER_ATTR_NOBUFFER            0x00000001

// use z buffering rasterization
#define RENDER_ATTR_ZBUFFER            0x00000002

// use 1/z buffering rasterization
#define RENDER_ATTR_INVZBUFFER            0x00000004

// use mipmapping
#define RENDER_ATTR_MIPMAP            0x00000010

// enable alpha blending and override
#define RENDER_ATTR_ALPHA            0x00000020

// enable bilinear filtering, but only supported for
// constant shaded/affine textures
#define RENDER_ATTR_BILERP            0x00000040

// use affine texturing for all polys
#define RENDER_ATTR_TEXTURE_PERSPECTIVE_AFFINE  0x00000100

// use perfect perspective texturing
#define RENDER_ATTR_TEXTURE_PERSPECTIVE_CORRECT 0x00000200
```

```
// use linear piecewise perspective texturing
#define RENDER_ATTR_TEXTURE_PERSPECTIVE_LINEAR  0x00000400

// use a hybrid of affine and linear piecewise based on distance
#define RENDER_ATTR_TEXTURE_PERSPECTIVE_HYBRID1 0x00000800

// not implemented yet
#define RENDER_ATTR_TEXTURE_PERSPECTIVE_HYBRID2 0x00001000
```


Now let's look at some examples. Suppose you want to set up a rendering context that has no buffering at all (you z-sort the polygons yourself or whatever).

Rendering Context Setup: Example 1

No alpha, no mip mapping, and you want affine texture mapping for everything. This would be the setup:

```
// set up rendering context
rc.attr      = (RENDER_ATTR_NOBUFFER ¦
          RENDER_ATTR_TEXTURE_PERSPECTIVE_AFFINE);

rc.video_buffer = back_buffer; // set video buffer up
rc.lpitch     = back_lpitch;
rc.mip_dist    = 0;
rc.zbuffer    = NULL;
rc.zpitch     = 0;
rc.rend_list   = &rend_list; // rendering list
rc.texture_dist = 0;
rc.alpha_override = -1;
```

That's it!

Rendering Context Setup: Example 2

Z-buffering with alpha support and linear piecewise perspective texture mapping:

```
// set up rendering context
rc.attr      = (RENDER_ATTR_ZBUFFER ¦
          RENDER_ATTR_ALPHA ¦
          RENDER_ATTR_TEXTURE_PERSPECTIVE_LINEAR);

rc.video_buffer = back_buffer; // set up video buffer
rc.lpitch     = back_lpitch;
rc.mip_dist    = 0;
rc.zbuffer    = (UCHAR *)zbuffer.zbuffer; // we need this now
rc.zpitch     = WINDOW_WIDTH*4;
rc.rend_list   = &rend_list;
rc.texture_dist = 0;
rc.alpha_override = -1;
```

Rendering Context Setup: Example 3

Now let's try one with mip mapping and a mip distance of 2000. Full perspective-correct texturing and 1/z-buffer will be needed, of course.

```
// set up rendering context
rc.attr      = (RENDER_ATTR_INVZBUFFER |
          RENDER_ATTR_ALPHA |
          RENDER_ATTR_MIPMAP |
          RENDER_ATTR_TEXTURE_PERSPECTIVE_CORRECT);

rc.video_buffer = back_buffer; // set up video buffer
rc.lpitch     = back_lpitch;
rc.mip_dist    = 2000; // and mip distance
rc.zbuffer    = (UCHAR *)zbuffer.zbuffer; // the storage for the 1/z buffer
rc.zpitch     = WINDOW_WIDTH*4;
rc.rend_list   = &rend_list;
rc.texture_dist = 0;
rc.alpha_override = -1;
```

NOTE

Remember, the `mip_dist` variable is the maximum amount of distance that all the levels of the mip chain will be divided into from the viewing plane.

Rendering Context Setup: Example 4

Let's try one more example using the hybrid texturing. Let's select mode 1, which is only linear piecewise up close and then switches to affine past the first texture distance mark `texture_dist`. We will set the texture distance to 500, so everything from 0–500 will use the linear piecewise texture mapper, and everything beyond 500 on will use affine texture mapping. All the other settings will be the same as the previous example:

```
// set up rendering context
rc.attr      = (RENDER_ATTR_INVZBUFFER |
          RENDER_ATTR_ALPHA |
          RENDER_ATTR_MIPMAP |
          RENDER_ATTR_TEXTURE_PERSPECTIVE_HYBRID1);

rc.video_buffer = back_buffer; // set up video buffer
rc.lpitch     = back_lpitch;
rc.mip_dist    = 2000; // and mip distance
rc.zbuffer    = (UCHAR *)zbuffer.zbuffer; // the storage for the 1/z buffer
rc.zpitch     = WINDOW_WIDTH*4;
rc.rend_list   = &rend_list;
rc.texture_dist = 500;
rc.alpha_override = -1;
```

CAUTION

When using any form of perspective-correct texturing, you MUST use a 1/z-buffer, because it's not supported with plain or Z-buffering rasterizers.

Making the Call to Render the Rendering Context

Now that you have the rendering context set up, it's time to actually do the rendering. We need a function that will take all these options and transparently do our dirty work, and figure out what rasterizer to call for each polygon. This function has a lot of conditional logic, but I do want you to see it, so I am going to list this one.

However, please note that there are better ways to do this. For example, I am executing conditionals in the inner loop for each polygon that could be precomputed. Then we can make the function as optimal as calling the lower-level functions via function pointers. However, then you wouldn't see the real work being done, so I have left it slightly unoptimized for now. Later we will add the function pointer support and make a version that is optimal and faster.

The only problem with the function is that it's rather large (15-30 pages), so I can't list it here. What I'm going to do is partially list one component of it. The function optimizes the conditional logic slightly by first determining whether the caller has requested no buffer, z-buffering, or 1/z-buffering, and then goes from there. Therefore, I am going to list just the first section that takes care of the no-buffering cases; the other cases are similar, but have been deleted to save space.

```
void Draw_RENDERLIST4DV2_RENDERCONTEXTV1_16(RENDERCONTEXTV1_PTR rc)
{
// this function renders the rendering list, it's based on the new
// rendering context data structure which is container for everything
// we need to consider when rendering, z, 1/z buffering, alpha, mipmapping,
// perspective, etc. the function is basically a merge of all the functions
// we have written thus far, so its rather long, but better than having
// 20-30 rendering functions for all possible permutations!

POLYF4DV2 face; // temp face used to render polygon
int alpha;    // alpha of the face

// we need to try and separate as much conditional logic as possible
// at the beginning of the function, so we can minimize it inline during
// the traversal of the polygon list, let's start by subclassing which
// kind of rendering we are doing none, z buffered, or 1/z buffered

if (rc->attr & RENDER_ATTR_NOBUFFER) ////////////////////////////////////
{
// no buffering at all
```

```
// at this point, all we have is a list of polygons and it's time
// to draw them
for (int poly=0; poly < rc->rend_list->num_polys; poly++)
  {
  // render this polygon if and only if it's not clipped, not culled,
  // active, and visible, note however the concecpt of "backface" is
  // irrelevant in a wire frame engine though
  if (!(rc->rend_list->poly_ptrs[poly]->state & POLY4DV2_STATE_ACTIVE) ||
     (rc->rend_list->poly_ptrs[poly]->state & POLY4DV2_STATE_CLIPPED ) ||
     (rc->rend_list->poly_ptrs[poly]->state & POLY4DV2_STATE_BACKFACE) )
    continue; // move onto next poly

  // test for alpha override
  if (rc->alpha_override>= 0)
    {
    // set alpha to override value
    alpha = rc->alpha_override;
    } // end if
  else
    {
    // extract alpha (even if there isn't any)
    alpha = ((rc->rend_list->poly_ptrs[poly]->color & 0xff000000) >> 24);
    } // end else


  // need to test for textured first, since a textured poly can either
  // be emissive, or flat shaded, hence we need to call different
  // rasterizers
  if (rc->rend_list->poly_ptrs[poly]->attr & POLY4DV2_ATTR_SHADE_MODE_TEXTURE)
    {
    // set the vertices
    face.tvlist[0].x = (float)rc->rend_list->poly_ptrs[poly]->tvlist[0].x;
    face.tvlist[0].y = (float)rc->rend_list->poly_ptrs[poly]->tvlist[0].y;
    face.tvlist[0].z = (float)rc->rend_list->poly_ptrs[poly]->tvlist[0].z;
    face.tvlist[0].u0 = (float)rc->rend_list->poly_ptrs[poly]->tvlist[0].u0;
    face.tvlist[0].v0 = (float)rc->rend_list->poly_ptrs[poly]->tvlist[0].v0;

    face.tvlist[1].x = (float)rc->rend_list->poly_ptrs[poly]->tvlist[1].x;
    face.tvlist[1].y = (float)rc->rend_list->poly_ptrs[poly]->tvlist[1].y;
    face.tvlist[1].z = (float)rc->rend_list->poly_ptrs[poly]->tvlist[1].z;
    face.tvlist[1].u0 = (float)rc->rend_list->poly_ptrs[poly]->tvlist[1].u0;
    face.tvlist[1].v0 = (float)rc->rend_list->poly_ptrs[poly]->tvlist[1].v0;

    face.tvlist[2].x = (float)rc->rend_list->poly_ptrs[poly]->tvlist[2].x;
    face.tvlist[2].y = (float)rc->rend_list->poly_ptrs[poly]->tvlist[2].y;
```

```
face.tvlist[2].z = (float)rc->rend_list->poly_ptrs[poly]->tvlist[2].z;
face.tvlist[2].u0 = (float)rc->rend_list->poly_ptrs[poly]->tvlist[2].u0;
face.tvlist[2].v0 = (float)rc->rend_list->poly_ptrs[poly]->tvlist[2].v0;

// test if this is a mipmapped polygon?
if (rc->rend_list->poly_ptrs[poly]->attr & POLY4DV2_ATTR_MIPMAP)
 {
 // determine if mipmapping is desired at all globally
 if (rc->attr & RENDER_ATTR_MIPMAP)
   {
   // determine mip level for this polygon

   // first determine how many miplevels
   // there are in mipchain for this polygon
   int tmiplevels = logbase2ofx[((BITMAP_IMAGE_PTR *)
    (rc->rend_list->poly_ptrs[poly]->texture))[0]->width];

   // now based on the requested linear
   // miplevel fall off distance, cut
   // the viewdistance into segments,
   // determine what segment polygon is
   // in and select mip level -- simple!
   // later you might want something more
   // robust, also note I only use a single vertex,
   // you might want to find the average
   // since for long walls perpendicular to
   // view direction this might causing mip
   // popping mid surface
   int miplevel = (tmiplevels *
     rc->rend_list->poly_ptrs[poly]->tvlist[0].z / rc->mip_dist);

   // clamp miplevel
   if (miplevel > tmiplevels) miplevel = tmiplevels;

   // based on miplevel select proper texture
   face.texture = ((BITMAP_IMAGE_PTR *)
     (rc->rend_list->poly_ptrs[poly]->texture))[miplevel];

   // now we must divide each texture coordinate by 2 per miplevel
   for (int ts = 0; ts < miplevel; ts++)
     {
     face.tvlist[0].u0*=.5;
     face.tvlist[0].v0*=.5;
```

```
      face.tvlist[1].u0*=.5;
      face.tvlist[1].v0*=.5;

      face.tvlist[2].u0*=.5;
      face.tvlist[2].v0*=.5;
     } // end for

    } // end if mipmmaping enabled globally
  else // mipmapping not selected globally
    {
    // in this case the polygon IS mipmapped,
    // but the caller has requested NO
    // mipmapping, so we will support this by
    // selecting mip level 0 since the
    // texture pointer is pointing to a mip chain regardless
    face.texture = ((BITMAP_IMAGE_PTR *)
           (rc->rend_list->poly_ptrs[poly]->texture))[0];

    // note: texture coordinate manipulation is unneeded

    } // end else

  } // end if
 else
  {
  // assign the texture without change
  face.texture = rc->rend_list->poly_ptrs[poly]->texture;
  } // end if

 // is this a plain emissive texture?
 if (rc->rend_list->poly_ptrs[poly]->attr &
   POLY4DV2_ATTR_SHADE_MODE_CONSTANT)
  {
  // draw the textured triangle as emissive

  if ((rc->attr & RENDER_ATTR_ALPHA) &&
    ((rc->rend_list->poly_ptrs[poly]->attr &
     POLY4DV2_ATTR_TRANSPARENT) || rc->alpha_override>=0) )
    {
    // alpha version

    // which texture mapper?
    if (rc->attr & RENDER_ATTR_TEXTURE_PERSPECTIVE_AFFINE)
     {
```

```
    Draw_Textured_Triangle_Alpha16(&face, rc->video_buffer,
                    rc->lpitch, alpha);
    } // end if
   else
   if (rc->attr & RENDER_ATTR_TEXTURE_PERSPECTIVE_CORRECT)
    {
    // not supported yet!
    Draw_Textured_Triangle_Alpha16(&face, rc->video_buffer,
                    rc->lpitch, alpha);
    } // end if
   else
   if (rc->attr & RENDER_ATTR_TEXTURE_PERSPECTIVE_LINEAR)
    {
    // not supported yet
    Draw_Textured_Triangle_Alpha16(&face, rc->video_buffer,
                    rc->lpitch, alpha);
    } // end if
   else
   if (rc->attr & RENDER_ATTR_TEXTURE_PERSPECTIVE_HYBRID1)
    {
    // test z distance again perspective transition gate
    if (rc->rend_list->poly_ptrs[poly]->tvlist[0].z >
      rc-> texture_dist)
      {
      // default back to affine
      Draw_Textured_Triangle_Alpha16(&face, rc->video_buffer,
                      rc->lpitch, alpha);
      } // end if
    else
      {
      // use perspective linear
      // not supported yet
      Draw_Textured_Triangle_Alpha16(&face, rc->video_buffer,
                      rc->lpitch, alpha);
      } // end if

     } // end if

   } // end if
 else
   {
   // non alpha
   // which texture mapper?
   if (rc->attr & RENDER_ATTR_TEXTURE_PERSPECTIVE_AFFINE)
    {
```

```
     Draw_Textured_Triangle2_16(&face, rc->video_buffer,
                   rc->lpitch);
     } // end if
    else
    if (rc->attr & RENDER_ATTR_TEXTURE_PERSPECTIVE_CORRECT)
     {
     // not supported yet
     Draw_Textured_Triangle2_16(&face, rc->video_buffer,
                   rc->lpitch);
     } // end if
    else
    if (rc->attr & RENDER_ATTR_TEXTURE_PERSPECTIVE_LINEAR)
     {
     // not supported yet
     Draw_Textured_Triangle2_16(&face, rc->video_buffer,
                   rc->lpitch);
     } // end if
    else
    if (rc->attr & RENDER_ATTR_TEXTURE_PERSPECTIVE_HYBRID1)
     {
     // test z distance again perspective transition gate
     if (rc->rend_list->poly_ptrs[poly]->tvlist[0].z >
       rc-> texture_dist)
       {
       // default back to affine
       Draw_Textured_Triangle2_16(&face, rc->video_buffer,
                     rc->lpitch);
       } // end if
     else
       {
       // use perspective linear
       // not supported yet
       Draw_Textured_Triangle2_16(&face, rc->video_buffer,
                     rc->lpitch);
       } // end if

     } // end if

    } // end if

 } // end if
else
if (rc->rend_list->poly_ptrs[poly]->attr &
  POLY4DV2_ATTR_SHADE_MODE_FLAT)
 {
```

```
// draw as flat shaded
face.lit_color[0] = rc->rend_list->poly_ptrs[poly]->lit_color[0];

if ((rc->attr & RENDER_ATTR_ALPHA) &&
  ((rc->rend_list->poly_ptrs[poly]->attr &
   POLY4DV2_ATTR_TRANSPARENT) ||
   rc->alpha_override>=0) )
  {
  // alpha version

  // which texture mapper?
  if (rc->attr & RENDER_ATTR_TEXTURE_PERSPECTIVE_AFFINE)
   {
   Draw_Textured_TriangleFS_Alpha16(&face, rc->video_buffer,
                    rc->lpitch, alpha);
   } // end if
  else
  if (rc->attr & RENDER_ATTR_TEXTURE_PERSPECTIVE_CORRECT)
   {
   // not supported yet!
   Draw_Textured_TriangleFS_Alpha16(&face, rc->video_buffer,
                    rc->lpitch, alpha);
   } // end if
  else
  if (rc->attr & RENDER_ATTR_TEXTURE_PERSPECTIVE_LINEAR)
   {
   // not supported yet
   Draw_Textured_TriangleFS_Alpha16(&face, rc->video_buffer,
                    rc->lpitch, alpha);
   } // end if
  else
  if (rc->attr & RENDER_ATTR_TEXTURE_PERSPECTIVE_HYBRID1)
   {
   // test z distance again perspective transition gate
   if (rc->rend_list->poly_ptrs[poly]->tvlist[0].z >
     rc-> texture_dist)
     {
     // default back to affine
     Draw_Textured_TriangleFS_Alpha16(&face, rc->video_buffer,
                      rc->lpitch, alpha);
     } // end if
   else
     {
     // use perspective linear
```

```
          // not supported yet
          Draw_Textured_TriangleFS_Alpha16(&face, rc->video_buffer,
                          rc->lpitch, alpha);
          } // end if

         } // end if

       } // end if
     else
       {
       // non alpha
       // which texture mapper?
       if (rc->attr & RENDER_ATTR_TEXTURE_PERSPECTIVE_AFFINE)
        {
        Draw_Textured_TriangleFS2_16(&face, rc->video_buffer,
                        rc->lpitch);
        } // end if
       else
       if (rc->attr & RENDER_ATTR_TEXTURE_PERSPECTIVE_CORRECT)
        {
        // not supported yet
        Draw_Textured_TriangleFS2_16(&face, rc->video_buffer,
                        rc->lpitch);
        } // end if
       else
       if (rc->attr & RENDER_ATTR_TEXTURE_PERSPECTIVE_LINEAR)
        {
        // not supported yet
        Draw_Textured_TriangleFS2_16(&face, rc->video_buffer,
                        rc->lpitch);
        } // end if
       else
       if (rc->attr & RENDER_ATTR_TEXTURE_PERSPECTIVE_HYBRID1)
        {
        // test z distance again perspective transition gate
        if (rc->rend_list->poly_ptrs[poly]->tvlist[0].z >
          rc-> texture_dist)
          {
          // default back to affine
          Draw_Textured_TriangleFS2_16(&face, rc->video_buffer,
                          rc->lpitch);
          } // end if
        else
          {
```

```
        // use perspective linear
        // not supported yet
        Draw_Textured_TriangleFS2_16(&face, rc->video_buffer,
                       rc->lpitch);
        } // end if

      } // end if

    } // end if

  } // end else
 else
  {
  // must be gouraud POLY4DV2_ATTR_SHADE_MODE_GOURAUD
  face.lit_color[0] = rc->rend_list->poly_ptrs[poly]->lit_color[0];
  face.lit_color[1] = rc->rend_list->poly_ptrs[poly]->lit_color[1];
  face.lit_color[2] = rc->rend_list->poly_ptrs[poly]->lit_color[2];

  if ((rc->attr & RENDER_ATTR_ALPHA) &&
    ((rc->rend_list->poly_ptrs[poly]->attr &
     POLY4DV2_ATTR_TRANSPARENT) ||
     rc->alpha_override>=0) )
    {
    // alpha version

    // which texture mapper?
    if (rc->attr & RENDER_ATTR_TEXTURE_PERSPECTIVE_AFFINE)
     {
     Draw_Textured_TriangleGS_Alpha16(&face, rc->video_buffer,
                       rc->lpitch, alpha);
     } // end if
    else
    if (rc->attr & RENDER_ATTR_TEXTURE_PERSPECTIVE_CORRECT)
     {
     // not supported yet!
     Draw_Textured_TriangleGS_Alpha16(&face, rc->video_buffer,
                       rc->lpitch, alpha);
     } // end if
    else
    if (rc->attr & RENDER_ATTR_TEXTURE_PERSPECTIVE_LINEAR)
     {
     // not supported yet
     Draw_Textured_TriangleGS_Alpha16(&face, rc->video_buffer,
                       rc->lpitch, alpha);
     } // end if
```

```
else
if (rc->attr & RENDER_ATTR_TEXTURE_PERSPECTIVE_HYBRID1)
 {
 // test z distance again perspective transition gate
 if (rc->rend_list->poly_ptrs[poly]->tvlist[0].z >
   rc-> texture_dist)
   {
   // default back to affine
   Draw_Textured_TriangleGS_Alpha16(&face, rc->video_buffer,
                    rc->lpitch, alpha);
   } // end if
 else
   {
   // use perspective linear
   // not supported yet
   Draw_Textured_TriangleGS_Alpha16(&face, rc->video_buffer,
                    rc->lpitch, alpha);
   } // end if

  } // end if

} // end if
else
  {
  // non alpha
  // which texture mapper?
  if (rc->attr & RENDER_ATTR_TEXTURE_PERSPECTIVE_AFFINE)
   {
   Draw_Textured_TriangleGS_16(&face, rc->video_buffer,
                 rc->lpitch);
   } // end if
  else
  if (rc->attr & RENDER_ATTR_TEXTURE_PERSPECTIVE_CORRECT)
   {
   // not supported yet
   Draw_Textured_TriangleGS_16(&face, rc->video_buffer,
                 rc->lpitch);
   } // end if
  else
  if (rc->attr & RENDER_ATTR_TEXTURE_PERSPECTIVE_LINEAR)
   {
   // not supported yet
   Draw_Textured_TriangleGS_16(&face, rc->video_buffer,
                 rc->lpitch);
   } // end if
```

```
      else
      if (rc->attr & RENDER_ATTR_TEXTURE_PERSPECTIVE_HYBRID1)
       {
       // test z distance again perspective transition gate
       if (rc->rend_list->poly_ptrs[poly]->tvlist[0].z >
         rc-> texture_dist)
         {
         // default back to affine
         Draw_Textured_TriangleGS_16(&face, rc->video_buffer,
                       rc->lpitch);
         } // end if
       else
         {
         // use perspective linear
         // not supported yet
         Draw_Textured_TriangleGS_16(&face, rc->video_buffer,
                       rc->lpitch);
         } // end if

       } // end if

      } // end if

    } // end else

   } // end if
else
if ((rc->rend_list->poly_ptrs[poly]->attr &
   POLY4DV2_ATTR_SHADE_MODE_FLAT) ||
   (rc->rend_list->poly_ptrs[poly]->attr &
    POLY4DV2_ATTR_SHADE_MODE_CONSTANT) )
   {
   // draw as constant shaded
   face.lit_color[0] = rc->rend_list->poly_ptrs[poly]->lit_color[0];

   // set the vertices
   face.tvlist[0].x = (float)rc->rend_list->poly_ptrs[poly]->tvlist[0].x;
   face.tvlist[0].y = (float)rc->rend_list->poly_ptrs[poly]->tvlist[0].y;
   face.tvlist[0].z = (float)rc->rend_list->poly_ptrs[poly]->tvlist[0].z;

   face.tvlist[1].x = (float)rc->rend_list->poly_ptrs[poly]->tvlist[1].x;
   face.tvlist[1].y = (float)rc->rend_list->poly_ptrs[poly]->tvlist[1].y;
   face.tvlist[1].z = (float)rc->rend_list->poly_ptrs[poly]->tvlist[1].z;
```

12

```
        face.tvlist[2].x = (float)rc->rend_list->poly_ptrs[poly]->tvlist[2].x;
        face.tvlist[2].y = (float)rc->rend_list->poly_ptrs[poly]->tvlist[2].y;
        face.tvlist[2].z = (float)rc->rend_list->poly_ptrs[poly]->tvlist[2].z;

        // draw the triangle with basic flat rasterizer

        // test for transparent
        if ((rc->attr & RENDER_ATTR_ALPHA) &&
           ((rc->rend_list->poly_ptrs[poly]->attr &
            POLY4DV2_ATTR_TRANSPARENT) || rc->alpha_override>=0) )
         {
         Draw_Triangle_2D_Alpha16(&face, rc->video_buffer, rc->lpitch,alpha);
         } // end if
        else
         {
         Draw_Triangle_2D3_16(&face, rc->video_buffer, rc->lpitch);
         } // end if

        } // end if
      else
      if (rc->rend_list->poly_ptrs[poly]->attr &
        POLY4DV2_ATTR_SHADE_MODE_GOURAUD)
        {
        // {andre take advantage of the data structures later..}
        // set the vertices
        face.tvlist[0].x = (float)rc->rend_list->poly_ptrs[poly]->tvlist[0].x;
        face.tvlist[0].y = (float)rc->rend_list->poly_ptrs[poly]->tvlist[0].y;
        face.tvlist[0].z = (float)rc->rend_list->poly_ptrs[poly]->tvlist[0].z;
        face.lit_color[0] = rc->rend_list->poly_ptrs[poly]->lit_color[0];

        face.tvlist[1].x = (float)rc->rend_list->poly_ptrs[poly]->tvlist[1].x;
        face.tvlist[1].y = (float)rc->rend_list->poly_ptrs[poly]->tvlist[1].y;
        face.tvlist[1].z = (float)rc->rend_list->poly_ptrs[poly]->tvlist[1].z;
        face.lit_color[1] = rc->rend_list->poly_ptrs[poly]->lit_color[1];

        face.tvlist[2].x = (float)rc->rend_list->poly_ptrs[poly]->tvlist[2].x;
        face.tvlist[2].y = (float)rc->rend_list->poly_ptrs[poly]->tvlist[2].y;
        face.tvlist[2].z = (float)rc->rend_list->poly_ptrs[poly]->tvlist[2].z;
        face.lit_color[2] = rc->rend_list->poly_ptrs[poly]->lit_color[2];

        // draw the gouraud shaded triangle
        // test for transparent
         if ((rc->attr & RENDER_ATTR_ALPHA) &&
           ((rc->rend_list->poly_ptrs[poly]->attr &
```

```
        POLY4DV2_ATTR_TRANSPARENT) || rc->alpha_override>=0) )
      {
      Draw_Gouraud_Triangle_Alpha16(&face, rc->video_buffer,
                    rc->lpitch,alpha);
      } // end if
    else
      {
      Draw_Gouraud_Triangle2_16(&face, rc->video_buffer, rc->lpitch);
      } // end if

    } // end if gouraud

  } // end for poly

} // end if RENDER_ATTR_NOBUFFER

else
if (rc->attr & RENDER_ATTR_ZBUFFER) ////////////////////////////////////
{
// z buffer block goes here..

} // end if RENDER_ATTR_ZBUFFER
else
if (rc->attr & RENDER_ATTR_INVZBUFFER)
{
// inverse z buffer block goes here..

} // end if RENDER_ATTR_INVZBUFFER

} // end Draw_RENDERLIST4DV2_RENDERCONTEXTV1_16
```

The code simply iterates through all the possibilities branching on different rendering conditions. Pay close attention the alpha and mip mapping sections, along with the hybrid texture mapping computations. Admittedly, this is slower than just calling the correct rasterizer, as we are losing about 1–3% of our performance from calling the high-level function, but we will get it back and then some, I promise. For now, this is much better than trying to call all those millions of zillions of rendering functions! In any event, let's make a call to the function with one of our setup rendering contexts:

```
// render scene
Draw_RENDERLISTV2_RENDERCONTEXTV1_16(&rc);
```

Now isn't that worth it? I agree <BG>. There's no demo for this function call because that's not much of a demo, but if you look at all the demos thus far, I have secretly been using the new function—he he he!

Summary

This has been another long chapter dealing with seemingly brief material that just seemed to blow up when we got into it! Additionally, we wrote more code than in any other chapter, but it was all worth it. At this point, the engine supports so much stuff that it's ready to make games. We added perspective-correct texturing, alpha blending, mip mapping, 1/z-buffering, optimizations galore, and rewrote the engine rasterization interface to have a single interface. Moreover, we added some features to the .COB model loader, as well as the terrain generator. Last but not least, there were some good demos that are good starting points for you to experiment. Remember, the point of this book is not to teach bleeding-edge techniques, but to give you a solid understanding of 3D algorithms and practical real-time implementations. The funny thing is that this engine is looking pretty good—I had one of the demos running, and someone walked in and thought it was hardware because of the lighting and texturing. The fact is, if we stopped here, you would have more than enough to keep you busy. But we've come this far—why not go totally insane <BG>?

My only regret is that bugs are starting to creep into the system. There is so much software that I hardly get time to test it. Of course, the point of the book and demos is as a teaching aid so you can make your own engine, but it's kind of a bummer when you see flaws. However, I will continue to try and squash them. Right now, the major thing bugging me is that the 3D clipper seems to be having trouble with large polygons, but no one is perfect <BG>. Next we are going to cover spatial partitioning techniques and start dealing with world geometry.

CHAPTER 13

Spatial Partitioning and Visibility Algorithms

IN THIS CHAPTER

- The New Game Engine Module
- Introduction to Spatial Partitioning and Visible Surface Determination
- The Binary Space Partition
- Potentially Visible Sets
- Portals
- Bounding Hierarchical Volumes and Octrees
- Occlusion Culling

"What if you miss?"

"I won't."

—*Halo 2*

In this chapter, we're going to cover spatial partitioning algorithms such as binary space partitions, bounding hierarchical volumes, octrees, portals, and more. Additionally, we are also going to discuss general visibility algorithms such as potentially visible sets, and occlusion culling. Because of the highly technical nature of the material and its sheer volume, we are only going to implement a couple of techniques including BSP trees. However, this will be more than enough to keep you busy. Here's the general outline for this chapter:

- The new game engine library module
- Introduction to spatial partitioning and visible surface determination
- Binary space partitioning
- Potentially visible sets
- Portals
- Bounding hierarchical volumes and octrees
- Occlusion culling

The New Game Engine Module

Once again, there is enough software in this chapter for a separate library module. We are up to `T3DLIB11` now, so to compile any program from this chapter, you will need the main .CPP file for the program, the DirectX .LIB files, and these new library modules:

- T3DLIB11.CPP—The C/C++ source for the spatial partitioning technology, and so on.
- T3DLIB11.H—The accompanying header file.

NOTE

Of course, you must link to T3DLIB1-10.CPP¦H as well.

I would list the library source and header, but we are running out of room and need to be frugal with the listings. However, every function and data structure will be shown within the chapter, either in full or with prototypes.

Introduction to Spatial Partitioning and Visible Surface Determination

Spatial partitioning and visible surface determination go hand in hand. In general, any given 3D world is filled with objects, terrain, interiors, and exteriors. The problem is that all these model meshes can easily represent thousands, if not millions, of polygons (and hundreds of millions very soon). Thus far, we have worked very hard to find ways to remove as many polygons from the rendering pipeline as possible. Our current system is based on objects for the most part, where each object is a collection of polygons. These objects are transformed and then inserted into the global rendering list for more transformations, such as lighting, clipping, projection, and rasterization. However, we learned early on that we can cull entire objects from the viewing frustrum by using the bounding sphere of each object and clipping it to the view frustrum before passing the object into the rendering pipeline. This is shown in Figure 13.1.

Nevertheless, many objects can't be culled with this crude technique, and get passed down the pipeline. For example, long objects, or objects that contain many sub-parts and so on, don't fit well into bounding spheres. However, we didn't give up, and we performed a back-face removal stage, where polygons that are not facing the viewer are removed from the pipeline as well. These techniques are shown in Figure 13.2.

Finally, polygons that we can't cull make it to the 3D clipper and are clipped to the viewing frustrum in object space, and are finally clipped in 2D space during rasterization. The clipping process itself is a form of polygon-based culling, and entire polygons can be culled, as shown in Figure 13.3.

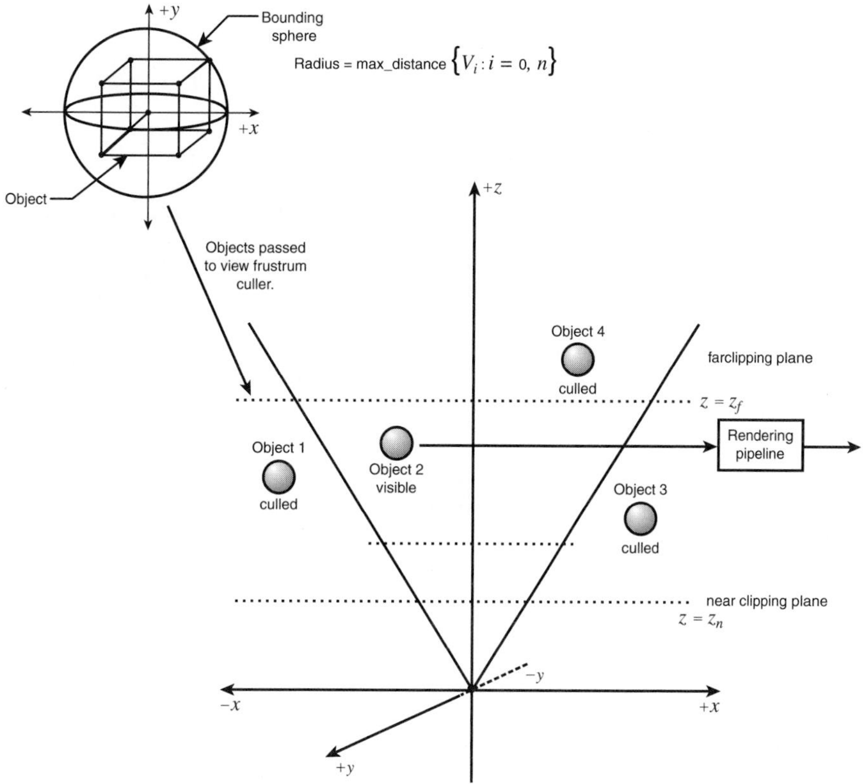

FIGURE 13.1 Bounding sphere culling.

For the most part, this system works fine for sparse, outdoor, object-based scenes, and even works with our crude terrain demos. The point is that we are not taking advantage of any of the geometrical cues of the mesh geometry or common sense. This is the theme of this chapter. We are interested in solutions to two primary problems:

Problem 1: How can we partition space/objects, possibly using preprocessing or other assumptions, so that we can quickly cull large portions of the scene away and or help with rendering and visibility?

Problem 2: Are there ways to determine what polygons are visible from any given viewpoint in the game, and only process polygons that are potentially visible from said viewpoint?

Both of these problems slightly overlap and fall under the concepts of visibility determination, occlusion, and spatial partitioning, which comprise the material we are going to explore in this chapter.

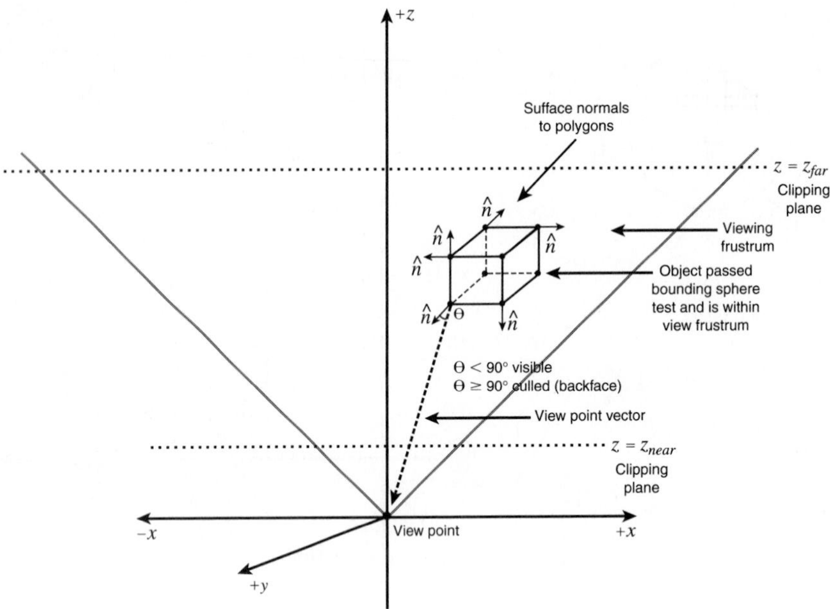

FIGURE 13.2 Back-face culling.

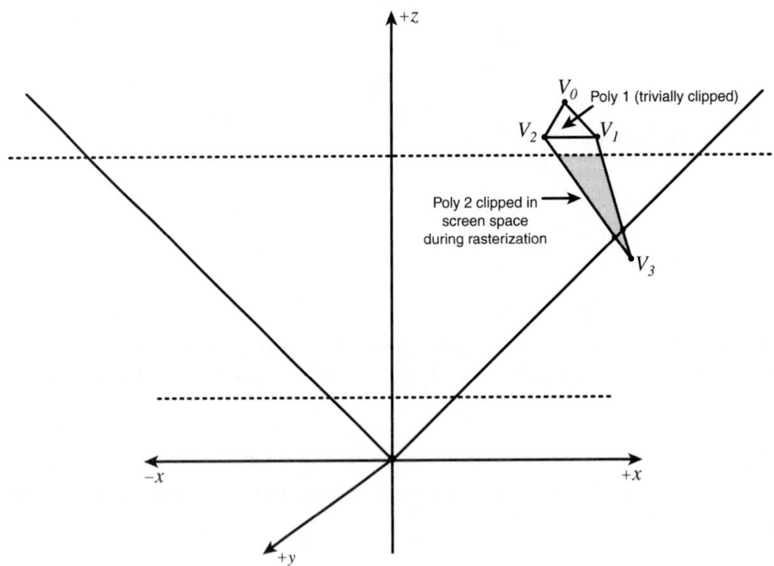

FIGURE 13.3 Polygon clipping.

The largest problem with computer graphics is not rasterization, lighting, or many of the topics we have covered thus far. Doing those things is of course important—they have all been solved by hardware for the most part. However, the problems that we are going to talk about in this chapter have *not* been solved by hardware, and probably never will be solved in closed form. In other words, a single technique will work for a finite number of polygons, but then when we increase that number ten times, we need a new technique. A line-drawing algorithm is a line-drawing algorithm—it doesn't care whether we are drawing a house or a space ship, but spatial portioning and visibility algorithms *do* care about the kind and size of data sets they are working on. And as we make larger and larger worlds, these data sets are going to continually get larger. Thus, the world of visibility determination and culling is of utmost concern, because not rendering something is always the fastest way to draw it!

For example, suppose we want to use our little terrain generator function to create a 1024×1024 terrain. We could use the function to do that, but then huge amounts of polygons would be passed to the culler and clipper because the terrain is a single object. A better technique would be to create a hierarchy of terrains themselves in a cell-based world of 32×32, so each cell itself is a terrain of 32×32 tiles (or 32×32×2 polygons, because there are two triangles per cell) and then we can cull each terrain object as single objects. This is shown in Figure 13.4.

Can we do better? What about grouping terrain cells of 8×8 and placing bounding rectangles around them, or cells of 16×16, or 32×32! See what I'm getting at? We can create hierarchical data structures that contain more or less world data, and then during the culling or visibility determination phase, we can immediately throw away vast amounts of data. This is absolutely necessary for large-scale terrains, indoor worlds, and environments out in space. Can you imagine trying to model a galaxy with 100,000,000 star systems? It's actually possible: We can store the position of each planet in each star system, we can store a procedural algorithm with a set of parameters that can generate the planet terrain on the fly at any level of detail, and we can create records of the buildings, vegetation, and so on, on each planet. However, what we can't do is run through all 100,000,000 star systems each iteration and determine whether they should be rendered. However, with a spatial partitioning system, this can be accomplished in a few iterations—believe it or not!

We're going to cover a number of spatial partitioning techniques, starting with binary space partitioning, because this is one of the most commonly used and powerful algorithms, and the one I decided to implement here for you. Remember though why we need this technology: The point is that we can't simply throw polygons at the pipeline anymore when we are dealing with huge datasets.

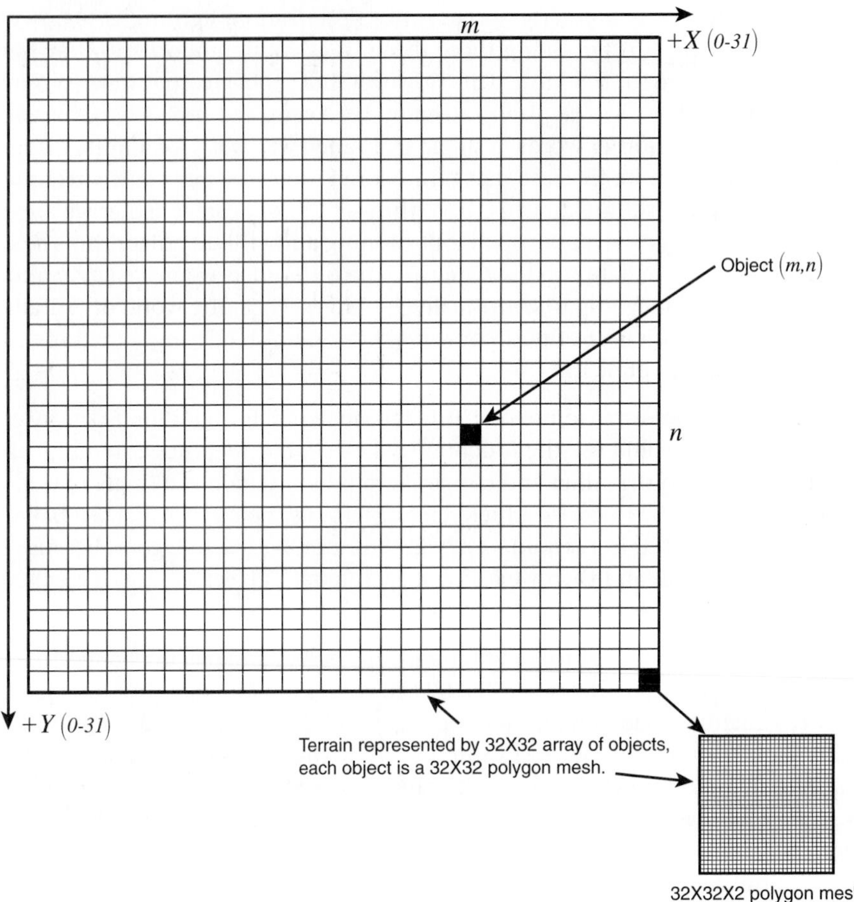

FIGURE 13.4 Object hierarchy representations.

Additionally, when running around in say a first-person shooter, 99% of the time we are going to be in a level with hundreds of rooms, but we can only see the geometry in the current room the viewpoint is in (sure, there might be windows). For the most part, we surely don't want to render all those extra rooms, so we want to find techniques and algorithms to deal with this kind of problem. Figure 13.5 illustrates this visibility problem.

We'll look at a number of techniques, some just in theory, some in practical use, and then you should be able to handle just about any problem with indoor/outdoor rendering, or at least know what you need to do and where to begin.

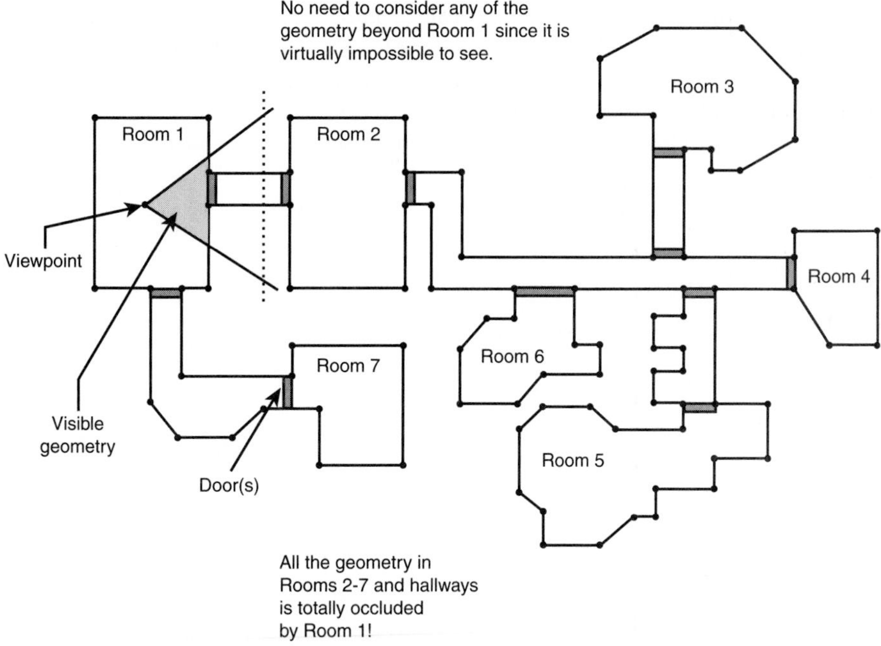
No need to consider any of the geometry beyond Room 1 since it is virtually impossible to see.
Room 1
Room 2
Room 3
Room 4
Room 5
Room 6
Room 7
Viewpoint
Visible geometry
Door(s)
All the geometry in Rooms 2-7 and hallways is totally occluded by Room 1!

FIGURE 13.5 The visibility problem.

The Binary Space Partition

The *binary space partition (BSP)* is a technique that belongs to the class of 3D spatial partitioning algorithms that trade initial space and offline computation time (with some geometrical constraints) for fast runtime performance. In essence, BSP is a method that takes as an input a collection of polygons, and then through a recursive algorithm, the BSP creates a binary tree structure with a number of interesting properties. These properties enable us to walk the tree in perfect back-to-front polygon order, or front to back. We can also use the tree for collision detection, or for large scale culling. This data structure is the basis for games like *Doom*, *Quake*, and many other first-person shooters. The basis of the BSP tree is that it partitions space into convex subspaces using separating planes. These planes can be axis-aligned or co-planar with the polygons themselves, but the point is that the geometry itself is used to partition space.

The BSP sounds too good to be true, so let's take a look at how it works. Refer to the x-z aerial view shown in Figure 13.6 for the following explanation. The figure depicts a collection of polygons that might make up the geometry of a game level. Each polygon defines a plane that it lies in. As you can see, if we were to place the viewer in any position within the figure, it's not too difficult to manually determine the order in which the polygons should be drawn for a given viewing direction and frustrum so that the scene would be rendered correctly.

For example, in Figure 13.7, the rendering order would be back-to-front a, b, c, d, e, f. This is the same problem that we solved in a number of ways, such as the painter's algorithm and with z-buffering before. However, it's possible to solve the problem in another way: by using the BSP tree. From any viewpoint, the BSP can tell us the proper back-to-front and front-to-back order of the polygons, as well as other useful information.

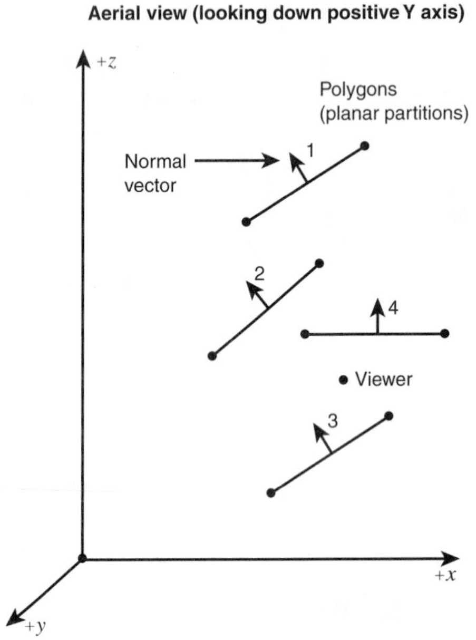

FIGURE 13.6 The basic problem for the BSP to solve.

The BSP algorithm works by simply taking all the polygons in the mesh or environment and then partitioning them into convex subspaces based on splitting planes. These splitting planes can either be axis-aligned, arbitrary, or coplanar with the polygons themselves. Let's take a quick look at each of these techniques and then focus on the most commonly used method.

Axis-Aligned Binary Space Partitioning

Figure 13.8 depicts an initial set of polygons and the subsequent partitioning of the polygons with axis-aligned planes. As you see, the polygons are partitioned into small boxes until each box contains a single polygon. If a partition intersects any polygon, the polygon is split and added to both subspaces of the partitioning plane in most cases. However, another technique is to tag the polygon in both subspaces (or boxes, in this case), and then later during runtime flag the polygon as being "touched." Then when another pass from another subspace tries to access the polygon, it's ignored because it has already been touched. Also, note that by definition, each partitioned space is convex, because any square or cube is convex. Thus, each node of the BSP defines a convex subspace—we will return to this in detail shortly.

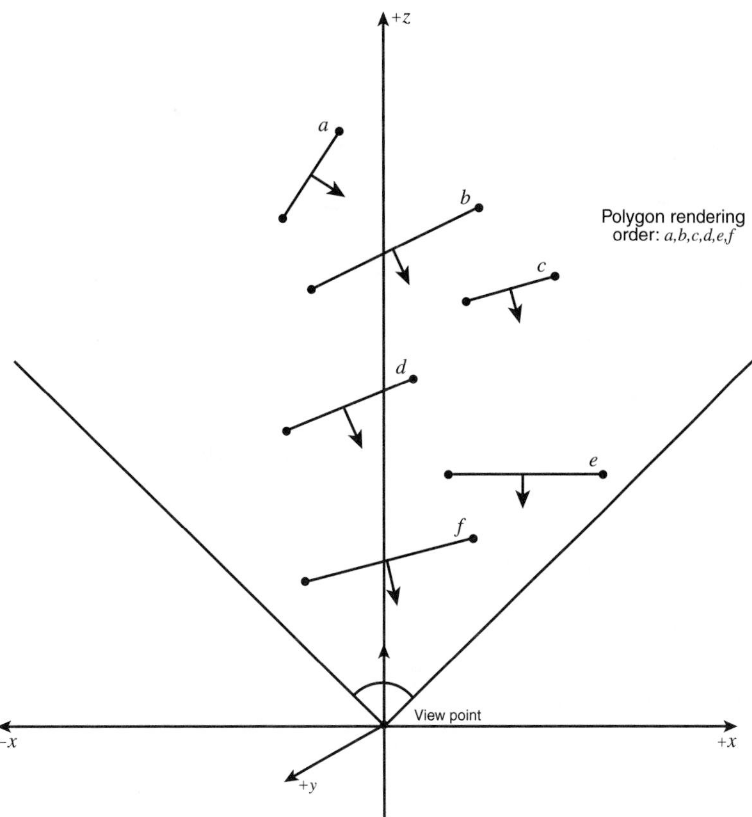

FIGURE 13.7 Rendering order for back-to-front rendering.

Arbitrary Plane Space Partitioning

Figure 13.9 depicts the second method of partitioning the polygons: selecting partitioning planes that divide the polygons up into nice clean partitions. A heuristic or other algorithm might also be invoked to try to find partitioning planes that equally divide the polygons, or cause the least number of splits, and so forth. The result of this type of partitioning is that a BSP tree is generated in which each node defines a subspace, and each terminal leaf defines a convex subspace. Thus, beginning at the root, the right child defines everything behind the partitioning plane, and the left child defines everything in front of the partitioning plane. Then when a terminal lead node is reached in the tree, it defines a convex subspace that contains one or more polygons, as shown in Figure 13.9.

You are probably still wondering how all this partitioning helps, and I am getting there, but first let's get the mechanical stuff out of the way. Let's direct our attention toward the last method of partitioning.

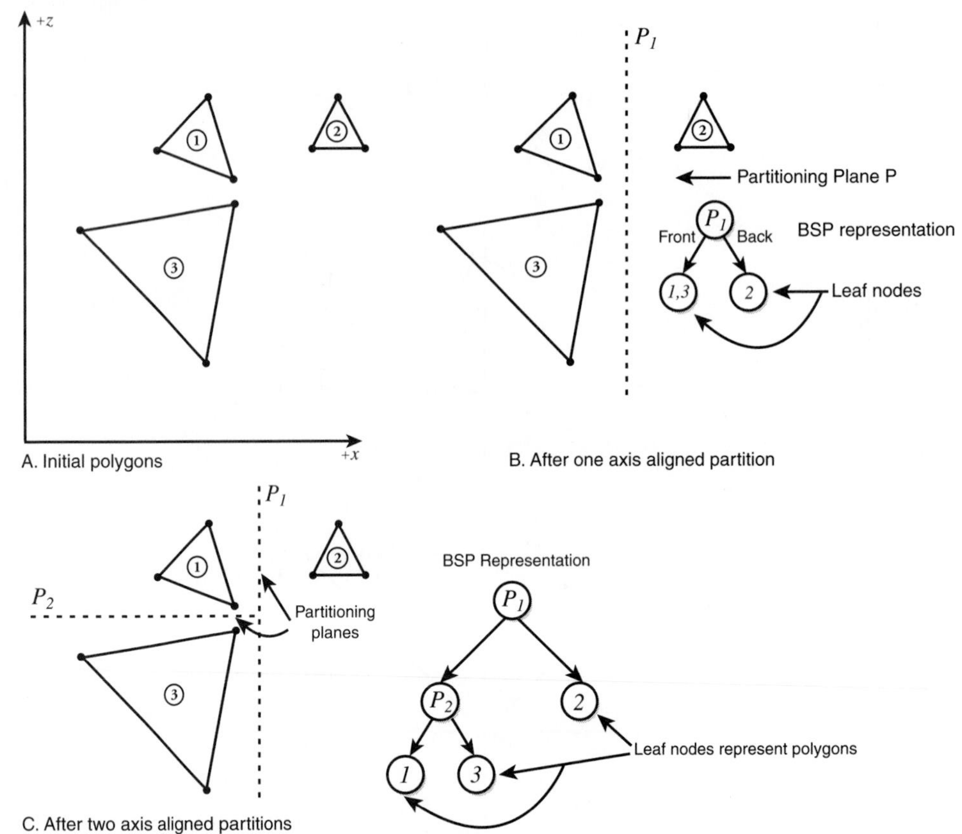

FIGURE 13.8 Axis-aligned polygon partitioning.

Polygon-Aligned Space Partitioning

Polygon-aligned space partitioning works as follows: A polygon is selected from the scene as the partitioning plane (it doesn't really matter which, for now). The plane in which the polygon lies is infinite in nature and is referred to as a *hyperplane*. This then divides space into two half spaces, as shown in Figure 13.10.

Then the algorithm tests each polygon in the scene against the partitioning plane and determines which side the test polygon is on (front or back). If the partitioning plane happens to cut a polygon(s) in half, the polygon is split into two polygons at the intersection point (line), as shown in Figure 13.11.

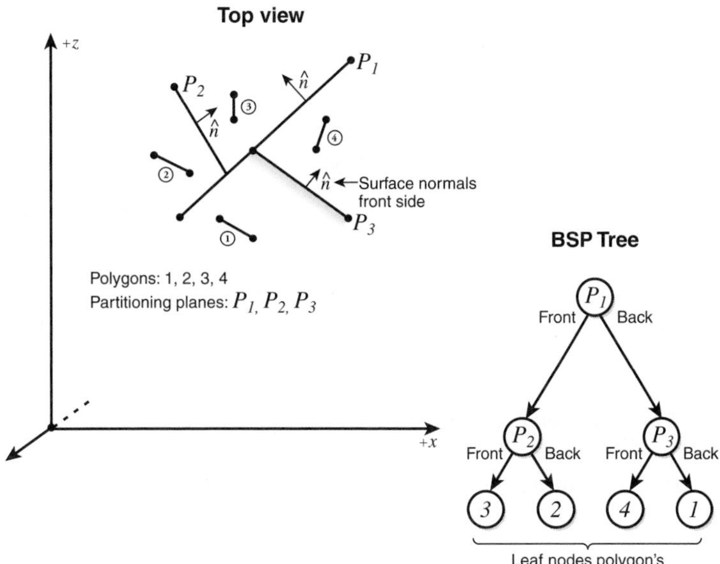

FIGURE 13.9 Arbitrary polygon partitioning planes.

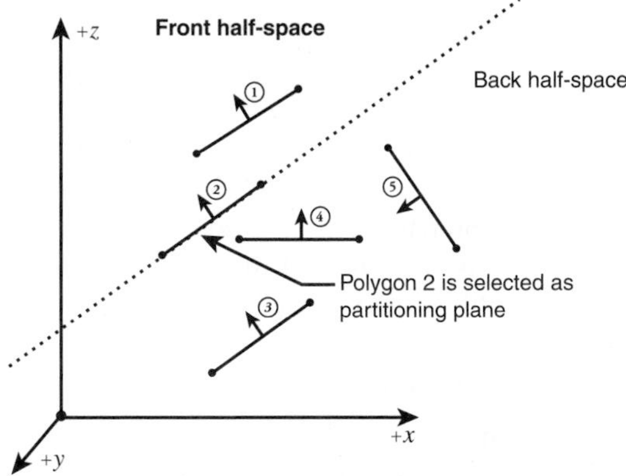

FIGURE 13.10 Using polygons themselves as the partitioning planes.

NOTE

The term *hyperplane* is used in *n*-dimensional geometry to simply describe an object that has one fewer dimension than the space itself. For example, in 3D space a hyperplane would be a 2D sheet or a plane, as you would expect. In *n*-dimensional space, a hyperplane would have the dimension n-1. In reality, it just sounds cool. <BG>

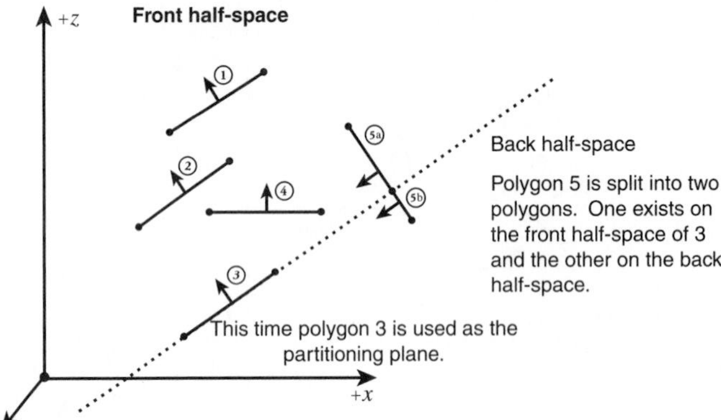

FIGURE 13.11 A polygon-aligned partition partitioning space and dividing geometry.

After the algorithm has completed this first step, each of the polygon lists representing the polygons on the front and back half spaces that were generated by this step (the list of polygons on the front and back sides of the partitioning plane) are recursively processed in a similar fashion. This is continued until all the polygons have been processed and the BSP tree has been built. Thus, the initial polygon-linked list attached to the BSP node is used to "feed" the partitioning system.

As an example, Figure 13.12 illustrates the construction of two similar BSPs from a scene consisting of five polygons using two different starting selections for the initial partitioning plane. The first step of the algorithm is to create a single node that contains the partitioning plane. Then the children of this node become two linked lists: one list represents the front polygons, and the other represents the back polygons relative to the plane itself. Each of these lists are then processed in the same way: The front list has a partitioning plane selected (any will work, for now) and then the polygons in the front list are partitioned. This process continues until finally trees of the form in Figures 13.12b and 13.12e are obtained.

After the BSP tree is constructed, it exhibits a number of special properties that can be leveraged for rendering, collision, or large-scale culling. For example, a modified in-order recursive visitation algorithm can be used to visit the polygon in perfect back-to-front order for any viewpoint. Let me repeat that: For *any* viewpoint in the 3D world, we can use a simple linear time in-order search to determine the exact order in which to render the polygons back to front (like the perfect painter's algorithm). We can do this without polygon sorting and without a Z-buffer!

Additionally, as the search time to visit every node of a *binary search tree (BST)* is always linear, or `O(n)`, because it can be reduced to a linear stack problem. Finding a single key is always $O(\log_2 n)$.

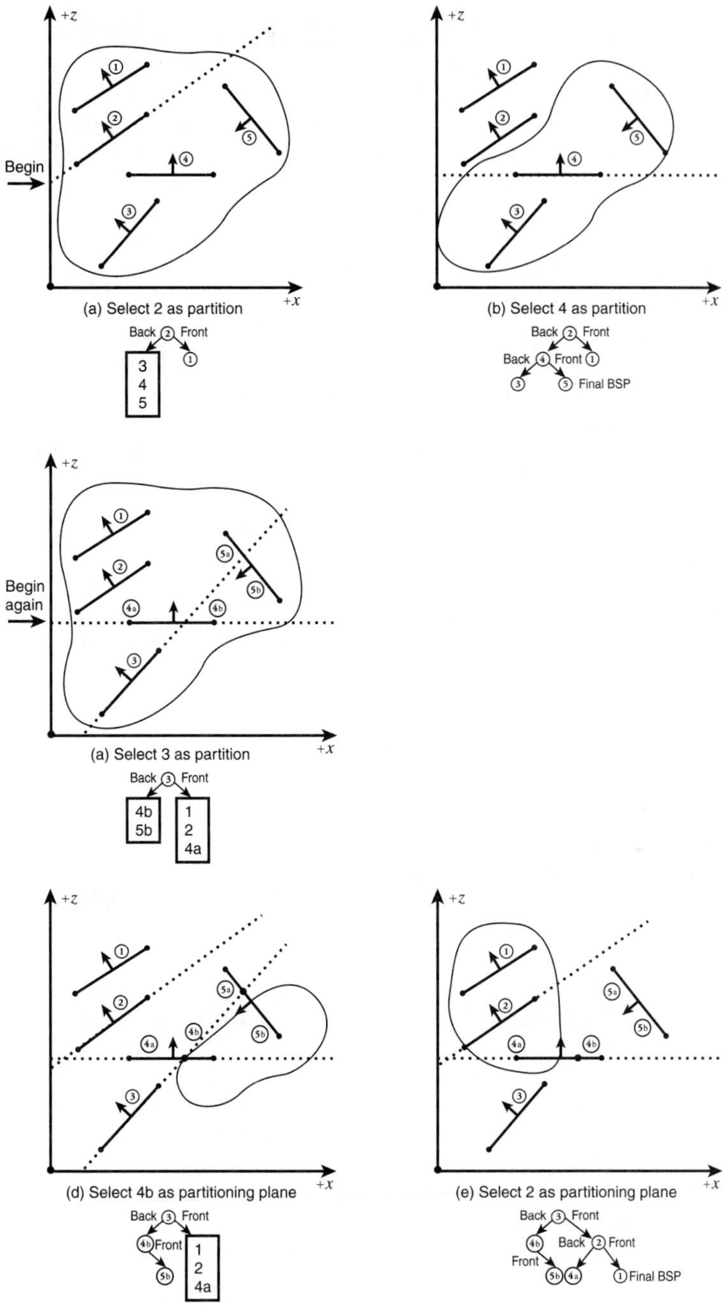

FIGURE 13.12 Step-by-step creation of a BSP tree.

NOTE

The selection of the partitioning plane is important, because poor selection can lead to more polygon splits and/or unbalanced trees. (The former is much more important.) This is definitely an important detail to discuss later. In most cases, a simple heuristic can be used in which 0.1–1% of the potential set of polygons are selected randomly each iteration as potential splitters. The algorithm is run on each, and the results are used to select which polygon to actually use as the splitter, based on the number of splits, and the balance as parameters to an optimization function, and the algorithm continues. So, if you have a world of 10,000 polygons, you will need to test 10–100 polygons at most each iteration to get nearly optimal results.

Now that you have a rough idea of how a BSP tree is created, let's get down to the details and list the steps needed to code it. Assuming that a linked list of polygons that makes up the game universe or level to be partitioned has been created (by some tool or function) and the head of this list is called `root`, then a rough algorithm to create the BSP tree is as follows:

1. Select a polygon in the list based on some heuristic and use it as a partitioning plane. If there are no more polygons in the list, exit.
2. Create two sublists, each attached to the front and back pointers of the partitioning plane BSP node that contain the polygons in front and in back of the partitioning plane, as seen in Figure 13.13.
3. Process the front list recursively.
4. Process the back list recursively.

Of course, there are a million details to be considered, such as how do we determine which side a polygon is on relative to the partitioning plane? Which plane should be selected as the partitioning plane each cycle? (We have made some suggestions on this topic.) What are the best data structures to use?

NOTE

We have been generalizing BSP trees, but now we need to start getting specific. We are going to implement a 2D BSP for the most part. Of course, the BSP will be used in a full 3D engine. However, I don't have time to create a full 3D modeling tool to generate 3D BSPs, and the planar intersection calculations for arbitrary planes intersecting is more complex and has nothing to do with BSP trees. Thus, I'm going to keep it simple and we are going to create BSP worlds that consist of line segments that will be converted into 3D walls. However, all the modeling and BSP will initially be performed in 2D space to ease the complexity of the problem. Generalizing the math to 3D is just that—more math—and you are more than equipped to do it.

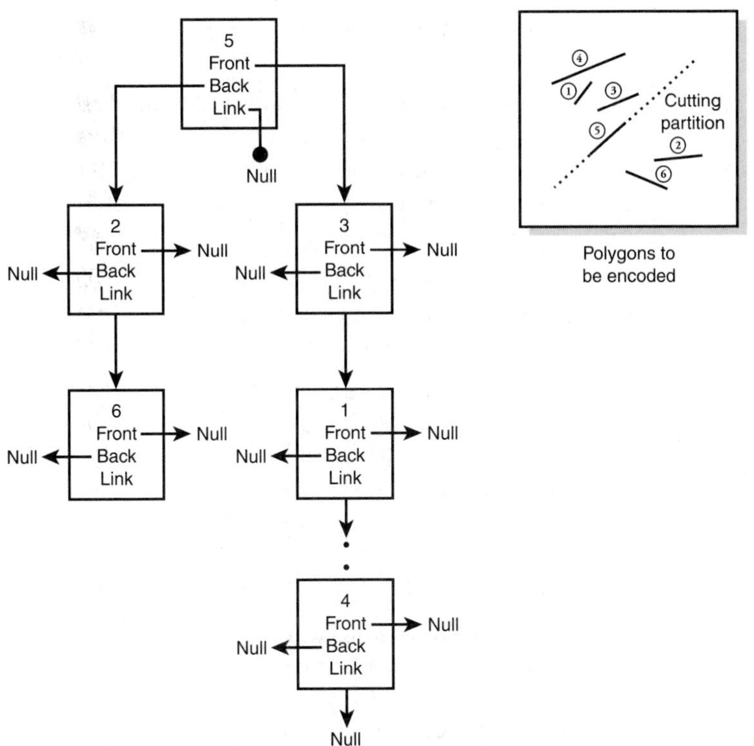

FIGURE 13.13 A detailed view of the BSP data and related data structure.

Displaying/Visiting Each Node of a BSP Tree

As I mentioned, BSP trees can be used for many things: rendering, collision, culling, and so forth. However, in many cases they are used to compute the exact back-to-front or front-to-back rendering order of a level for an arbitrary viewpoint. Let's talk about how this is done.

Thankfully, displaying the BSP tree is much easier than building it. All we need to do is write an algorithm that uses a modified in-order binary tree traversal algorithm, along with a traversal condition that guides the search path branches taken based on which side the viewer is on for each test polygon (partitioning plane).

The algorithm works as follows: We begin at the root of the BSP, as shown in Figure 13.14. Then the viewpoint is tested against the plane equation of the root polygon (which defines a plane in 3D). If the viewpoint is on the front side of the root, the algorithm recursively searches the back branch, visits the polygon (displaying or processing the polygon), and then recursively traverses the front branch.

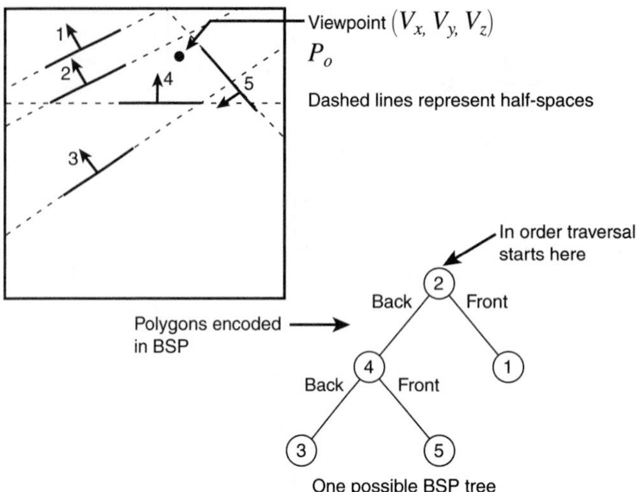

FIGURE 13.14 The polygons and BSP tree used for the sample traversal.

On the other hand, if the viewpoint is on the back side of the partitioning plane, the opposite steps are taken: The front branch is traversed recursively, the polygon is visited, and finally the back branch is recursively traversed.

This might be a little confusing, so let's think about it for a moment and then look at another example. The key to the BSP tree is that after the tree is built, then wherever we place the viewpoint, the subspace that the viewpoint is currently in is guaranteed both to have the closest polygon in it and to be convex. Thus the subspace behind said polygon is guaranteed to be farther away. Therefore, we can take advantage of this by exploiting the BSP's capability to determine the perfect back-to-front rendering order of the polygons. In Figure 13.15, we see the viewpoint located in world coordinates at some location **p**0, along with the polygons that make up the BSP.

Initially, we see that our viewpoint is on the front side of polygon 1. Thus, we know that we must be closest to it, because if we are on the front side of it and there are no more partitioning planes, by definition we are in a convex subspace, and polygon 1 is the closest to us. Based on this property, we know that polygons on the back side of polygon 1 are farther from us, so if we visit those polygons, we can apply this same idea recursively at any point. Thus, if we visit the polygons (always recursing such that we continually search until we are the farthest away from the viewpoint) and then visit each node (drawing it), we are guaranteed to get back-to-front order. Similarly, if we visit each node using the opposite search strategy, the results will be perfect front-to-back order.

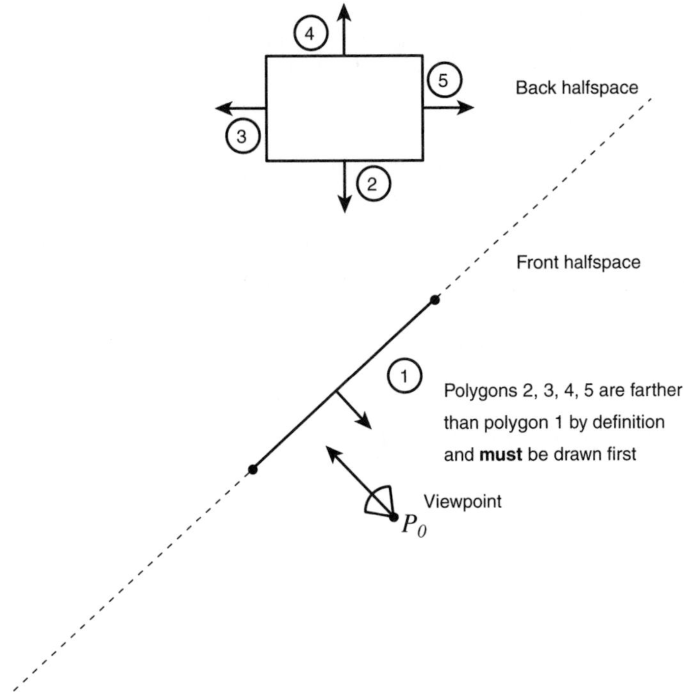

FIGURE 13.15 The polygons in the current subspace are closer to the viewpoint.

Let's take a look at another example to illustrate these concepts and solidify them. Using the BSP tree from Figure 13.14, assume the viewpoint is located as shown in Figure 13.14 also. Let's see whether the algorithm works correctly by applying the algorithm step-by-step to the polygons, as outlined here.

1. Begin at polygon 2. The viewpoint is within the back-half space; therefore, traverse the front-half space of polygon 2.
2. Because polygon 1 has no children, it is rendered and the stack is popped back to polygon 2.
3. Polygon 2 is rendered and the back-half space is traversed.
4. The viewpoint is within the front-half space of polygon 4; therefore, traverse the back-half space of polygon 4.
5. Because polygon 3 has no children, it is rendered and the stack is popped back to polygon 4.
6. Polygon 4 is rendered.

7. The front-half space of polygon 4 is traversed.
8. Because polygon 5 has no children, it is rendered and the stack is popped all the way out.

Therefore, the polygons are drawn in the sequence 1, 2, 3, 4, and 5, which is perfect back-to-front order.

The BSP visitation algorithm will work all the time regardless of the polygon(s) selected as the partitioning planes during construction, and regardless of the viewpoint and orientation. And just to be complete, let's see the traversal algorithm in pseudo-C/C++ code this time, instead of a step-by-step fashion.

Assume each node has both a front and a back pointer:

```
void Bsp_Traverse(BSPNODEV1_PTR root, VECTOR4D viewpoint)
{

if (root==NULL)
  return;

if (viewpoint is on front side of root)
  {
  // perform an inorder traversal
  Bsp_Traverse(root->back, viewpoint);

  Visit_Polygon(root->poly);

  Bsp_Traverse(root->front, viewpoint);
  }
else
  {
  // perform an inorder traversal
  Bsp_Traverse(root->front, viewpoint);

  Display_Polygon(root->poly);

  Bsp_Traverse(root->back, viewpoint);
  }

  } // end else

} // end Bsp_Traverse
```

Simple, huh! Of course, the determination of which side the viewpoint is on relative to each polygon is a dot product computation. I left it out for simplicity here, so you can see the beauty of the search algorithm.

The next thing we're going to do is take a look at what kind of data structures and support we need to create a working BSP demo and integrate it into our existing 3D engine, with support for lighting, texturing, clipping, and so forth.

The BSP Tree Functions and Data Structures

Implementing a BSP tree and supporting functions isn't as simple as it might seem—there are many decisions to make. Even though we are only interested in a demo of the technique, creating such a demo wasn't an easy task. In the end I have tried to make everything as simple as possible so the ideas are understood. Let's begin with the data structure used to represent a single-wall/BSP node, which uncovers our first problem.

Currently, our 3D engine is based completely on triangles and not quadrilaterals. This design decision was made to simplify just about everything from representation, lighting, clipping, and more. However, triangles aren't the best representation when modeling interior models because most interiors are constructed of flat planar surfaces that are mostly quads. With this in mind, I had to punt. Rather than use two triangles to represent a quad, I decided to simply create a new polygon type with four vertices instead of three and do all the BSP work with this new representation. Then, during traversal of the BSP, we can convert each BSP polygon node to two triangles, as shown in Figure 13.16.

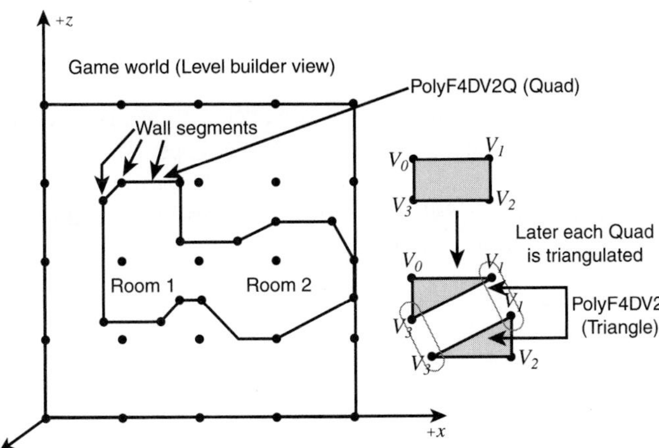

FIGURE 13.16 Using a quadrilateral representation to simplify the creation of the BSP tree.

On the other hand, I wanted to use a structure that was very familiar. Therefore, all I did was take the POLYF4DV2 and add one more vertex to it, along with a "Q" to the name. Here's the new polygon that supports quads:

```
// a self contained quad polygon used for the render list version 2 //////
// we need this to represent the walls since they are quads
typedef struct POLYF4DV2Q_TYP
{
```

```
int   state;      // state information
int   attr;      // physical attributes of polygon
int   color;      // color of polygon
int   lit_color[4];  // holds colors after lighting, 0 for flat shading
             // 0,1,2 for vertex colors after vertex lighting
BITMAP_IMAGE_PTR texture; // pointer to the texture information for
             // simple texture mapping

int   mati;     // material index (-1) for no material

float  nlength;    // length of the polygon normal if not normalized
VECTOR4D normal;    // the general polygon normal

float  avg_z;     // average z of vertices, used for simple sorting

VERTEX4DTV1 vlist[4];  // the vertices of this quad
VERTEX4DTV1 tvlist[4]; // the vertices after transformation if needed

POLYF4DV2Q_TYP *next;  // pointer to next polygon in list??
POLYF4DV2Q_TYP *prev;  // pointer to previous polygon in list??

} POLYF4DV2Q, *POLYF4DV2Q_PTR;s
```

I have bolded the changed fields from the previous POLYF4DV2 structure. We can use the POLYF4DV2Q to represent single quads, but we need to encapsulate it in a BSP node that contains not only one of these quads, which represents both the polygon itself and partitioning plane (implicitly), but it needs to support front and back links to build the BSP structure itself. I call this a general BSP node:

```
// a general bsp node, all bsp trees are built from this
// struct, and the root of a bsp is also this struct
typedef struct BSPNODEV1_TYP
{
int    id;   // id tag for debugging
POLYF4DV2Q wall; // the actual wall quad

struct BSPNODEV1_TYP *link; // pointer to next wall
struct BSPNODEV1_TYP *front; // pointer to walls in front
struct BSPNODEV1_TYP *back; // pointer to walls behind

} BSPNODEV1, *BSPNODEV1_PTR;
```

The BSPNODEV1 is the basic unit that will be contained within the BSP tree. Figure 13.17 depicts the BSPNODEV1 graphically. Each node basically consists of a quadrilateral polygon, an identification number for debugging, and three pointers, two of which we have discussed (the front and back pointers). The last pointer is called `link`, and is used to link all the BSP node walls together in a linked list during construction. This data linked to `link` is the raw input format for the walls to the binary space partitioner algorithm. Therefore, any program can create the linked list of walls that make up the game level to be BSPed. The list is then presented to the binary space partitioner for processing.

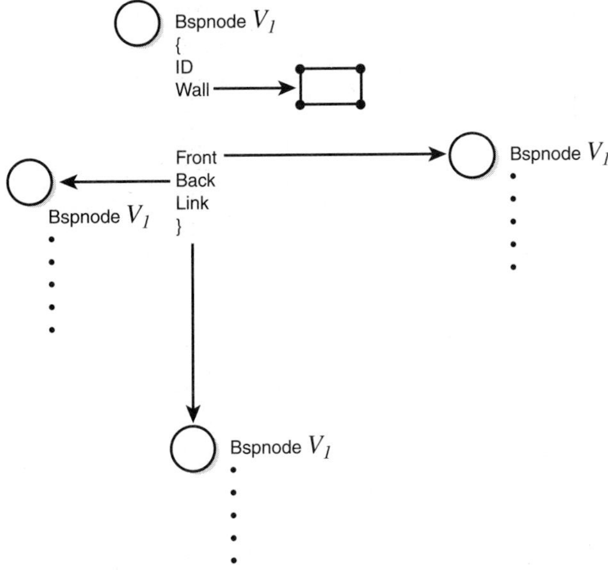

FIGURE 13.17 The `BSPNODEV1` unit graphically represented.

Now, let's assume for a moment that some other program or tool has enabled the user to input a set of walls, and a linked list using the `link` elements to connect each wall has been generated, as shown in Figure 13.18. Let's write a program that takes this as the input and creates the final BSP tree.

Creating the BSP Tree

Theoretically (long pause), building the BSP isn't too hard, but when the pointers start flying, the memory is being allocated, and coplanar walls have points in common, things get uglier faster than an IRS audit of a massage parlor. However, I have tried to make the function as clean as possible. Abstractly, the function works as follows: The wall list is presented to the function, then the first element in the list is used as the partitioning plane, and the walls on the front and back of the plane are placed into two lists that lead from the front and back pointers of the first partitioning node. The individual lists are linked together using the `link` field of the wall structure. Each of these lists are then used as inputs to recursive calls to the BSP creation function again. This process continues until each of the front and back lists have only one polygon or none. At this point, the BSP tree is complete.

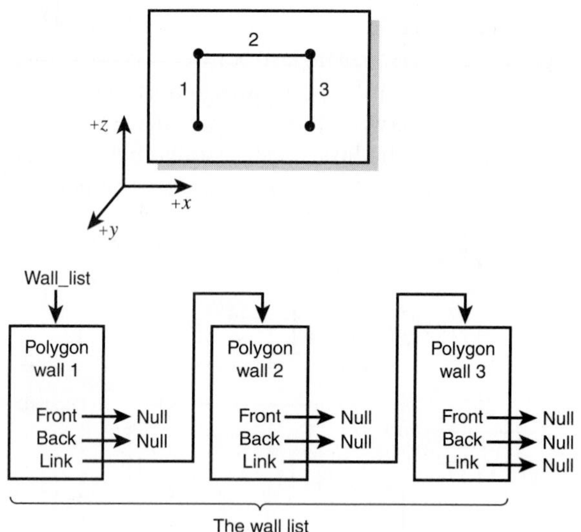

FIGURE 13.18 The wall list before being processed into a BSP tree.

There are a couple of major difficulties during this process, and some special cases that must be considered. First let's talk about the difficulties. The first problem is how to determine which side a polygon is on of the partitioning plane. Figure 13.19 shows the three cases.

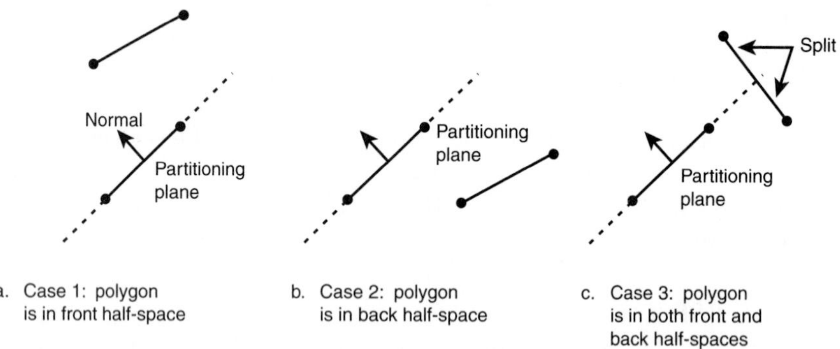

FIGURE 13.19 The geometrical orientation cases that must be considered for each wall.

Case 1: Both endpoints are on the front side on the test partition.

Case 2: Both endpoints are on the back side of the test partition.

Case 3: One endpoint is on the front side and one is on the back side of the test partition, so the polygon must be split into two.

Cases 1 and 2 are easy to test and easy to deal with. In these cases, the surface normal of the partitioning plane and the dot product of the vector to each test vertex of the test polygon's endpoints are used to determine which side each of the endpoints of the test wall are on. Walls on the front side are added to the front list of the partitioning wall, and walls on the back side of the partitioning wall are added to the back of the partitioning plane's linked lists. The problems occur with Case 3.

In this case, we need to extend the partitioning plane and determine where it intersects the test wall. This is easy to do because the walls are represented as 2D segments in the x-z plane. Computing the point of intersection between two walls thus becomes the same as determining the point of intersection between two 2D lines, as shown in Figure 13.20.

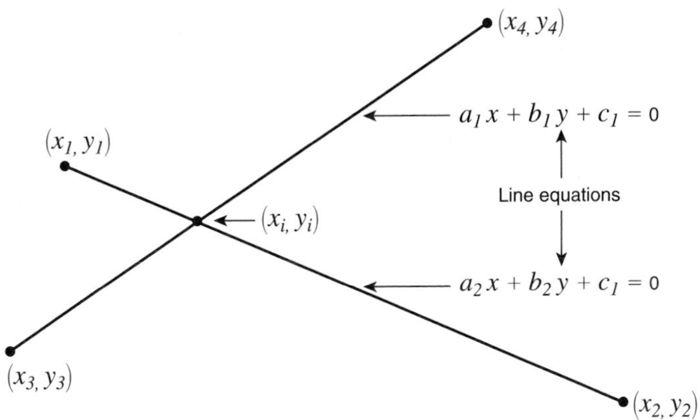

FIGURE 13.20 The mechanics of two intersecting lines.

There are many ways to compute the intersection of the infinite lines, but we are going to use the straightforward method of the line equations rather than parametrics, because it would be extra work to put the line segments into parametric form, as we gain nothing from it, for the most part, in this limited context. In a real BSP engine, I might decide to use parametric lines, but for now the line equations are easier. Also, remember that creating the BSP isn't time-critical (only displaying it is), because after we have the BSP, we can just load it in from disk and use it—so a little extra computation isn't going to kill us here.

Anyway, refer to Figure 13.20 for the derivation of the intersection equations (which should look familiar). What we need are two linear equations of the form

```
a1*x + a1*y = c1
a2*x + a2*y = c2
```

where each equation represents one of the lines in question. Then we can solve the system of equations using Cramer's rule, matrix multiplication, or substitution, as we learned in Chapters 4 and 5. I prefer Cramer's rule, which states in a nutshell that the variables in a system of linear equations can be computed by replacing the column in the coefficient matrix of the desired variable with the constant column vector and then computing the determinant of the matrix. The results of this calculation are then divided by the determinant of the original coefficient matrix. This is done for each variable to be computed. The coefficient matrix of the preceding system is

```
C =    |a1  b1|
       |a2  b2|
```

and Det(**C**) = (a1*b2 - a2*b1)

To find x, we would compute the following:

```
          Det of  |c1  b1|
                  |c2  b2|         (b2*c1 - b1*c2)
xi = ------------------------- = ---------------------
         (a1*b2 - a2*b1)           (a1*b2 - a2*b1)
```

And y can be found with the following:

```
          Det of   |a1  c1|
                   |a2  c2|        (a1*c2 - a2*c1)
yi = ----------------------- = ---------------------
          (a1*b2 - a2*b1)          (a1*b2 - a2*b1)
```

But the only problem is, how do we get the lines into linear equation form? Simple—we can use the point-slope form of a line, which states

```
m*(x-x0) = (y-y0)
```

where m is the slope, and is equal to (y1-y0)/(x1-x0). If we rearrange the equation, we can put it into the linear form we desire:

```
 (m)*x + (-1)* y = (m*x0-y0)
```

Which is of the form:

```
a*x + b*y = c
```

where a = m, b = -1, and c = (m*x0-y0)

Based on the preceding derivation (which should look very familiar, as we covered this same material in Chapters 4 and 5), the following function computes the intersection of two lines, given their endpoints:

```
void Intersect_Lines(float x0,float y0,float x1,float y1,
           float x2,float y2,float x3,float y3,
           float *xi,float *yi)
{
```

```
// this function computes the intersection of the sent lines
// and returns the intersection point, note that the function assumes
// the lines intersect. the function can handle vertical as well
// as horizontal lines. note the function isn't very clever, it simply applies
// the math, but we don't need speed since this is a pre-processing step
// we could have used parametric lines if we wanted, but this is more straight
// forward for this use, I want the intersection of 2 infinite lines
// rather than line segments as the parametric system defines

float a1,b1,c1, // constants of linear equations
   a2,b2,c2,
   det_inv, // the inverse of the determinant of the coefficient matrix
   m1,m2;  // the slopes of each line

// compute slopes, note the cludge for infinity, however, this will
// be close enough
if ((x1-x0)!=0)
  m1 = (y1-y0) / (x1-x0);
else
  m1 = (float)1.0E+20;  // close enough to infinity

if ((x3-x2)!=0)
  m2 = (y3-y2) / (x3-x2);
else
  m2 = (float)1.0E+20;  // close enough to infinity

// compute constants
a1 = m1;
a2 = m2;

b1 = -1;
b2 = -1;

c1 = (y0-m1*x0);
c2 = (y2-m2*x2);

// compute the inverse of the determinate
det_inv = 1 / (a1*b2 - a2*b1);

// use cramers rule to compute xi and yi
*xi=((b1*c2 - b2*c1)*det_inv);
*yi=((a2*c1 - a1*c2)*det_inv);

} // end Intersect_Lines
```

13

The function takes as parameters the x,y endpoints of two lines, and a pair of pointers to floats to return the intersection point in.

> **NOTE**
>
> The function assumes that the lines are not parallel; that is, they intersect. If the lines are parallel, there is a problem and a division by zero will occur, because the determinant of two parallel lines will always be zero. This can easily be remedied by first checking whether the lines are parallel within some tolerance, and then returning some code to signify that there is a problem. However, if the function is called, the lines weren't parallel in the first place. It's good defensive programming to add the test just in case—I leave it to you.

Now that we know how to find the intersection of the partitioning plane with the test wall, we unfortunately must split the test wall into two walls at the intersection point xi, yi (or in 3D: xi, zi in the x-z plane). One half of the split wall is then inserted into the front-linked list, and the other is inserted into the back-linked list of the partitioning plane's node.

Splitting Strategies

Before moving on, let's talk about an optimization. When a wall is split into two sub-walls, instead of splitting the wall, it's possible to add the wall to *both* the front and back sub-trees intact, but with a field that records where the intersection takes place for future reference. This way, we won't get polygon splits. However, we do get two copies of the polygon linked to the front and back partitioning planes.

This might seem like a problem, but it's not. During BSP traversal, any polygon that's visited is tagged or marked as it's visited. So, if a polygon has two links, the first visitation will set the visited flag and any other visitations will be ignored. Additionally, using this technique a polygon might be split numerous times, and therefore have multiple splitting points. Thus, a strategy to track multiple split points in an array or other similar data structure is needed. Nevertheless, the visitation tagging algorithm will continue to work—after a polygon is visited, even if it's visited again, ignore it. This will always maintain the property of perfect back-to-front and front-to-back BSP searching. However, we won't be doing this, because it complicates my already complicated life <BG>.

Moving on, let's get back to building the BSP and talk about special cases, because they always exist. First, we're going to assume that no two walls intersect, as shown in Figure 13.21. This isn't much of a constraint, because if you want a wall to intersect another, you can always use two walls, one on each side of the intersector.

However, the other common case of two walls with a vertex point in common is unavoidable and must be dealt with. Take a look at Figure 13.22. Here we see a set of coplanar polygon wall segments. The problem is that during our calculation, we find that the points in common can neither be classified as on the front side or on the back side of the partitioning planes. So, what should we do?

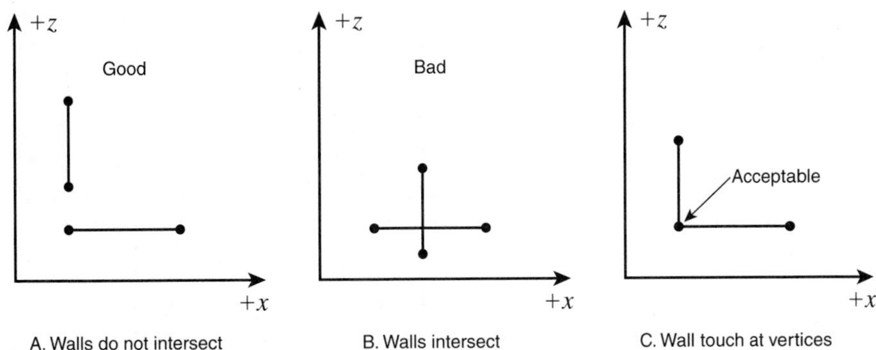

FIGURE 13.21 Walls are not allowed to intersect and interpenetrate.

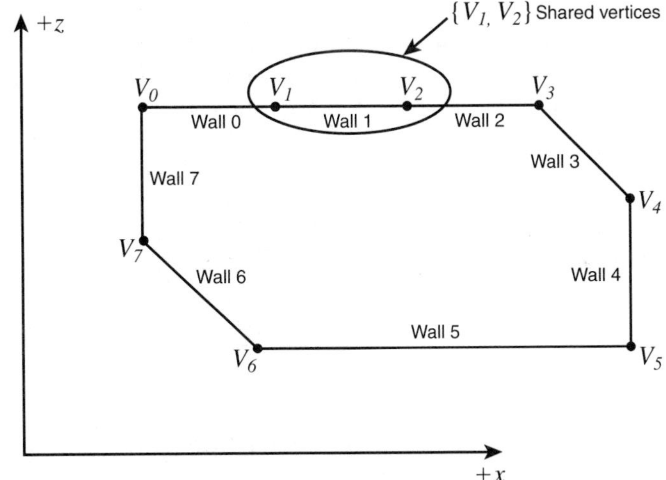

FIGURE 13.22 Coplanar polygons sets with shared vertices.

The answer is to ask ourselves, what exactly does it mean when two walls have an edge in common? This is the key to determining what to do in this case. When two walls have a vertical edge in common, or from the aerial view they have common endpoints, it only means that the point is neither on the front nor the back side of the wall. In essence, the common point is on the plane *itself*; therefore, we must decide where the test wall should be placed in reference to the partitioning plane by analyzing the *second* endpoint.

Hence, after it has been determined that the partitioning plane and the test wall have a common edge or point (however you want to think of it, 3D or 2D), the second vertex point of the test wall is used to resolve which side the test polygon is on relative to the partitioning plane. Alas, there is one little problem: What if the second endpoint or edge is also on the plane of the partitioning plane? Well, this isn't a problem—in fact, in this case it doesn't matter on which side we put the test wall, as either the front or the back will do equally well.

However, there is another optimization or simplification that can be made with coplanar walls, and that is to place them into collections with each other. For example, in Figure 13.22, why even perform any computations with all the individual wall segments? We know that they are all coplanar (or we can compute it), so we can use a single segment or wall to represent all of them, and cases of coplanar wall segments will never occur!

Of course, this comes at the cost of simplicity. The data structure holding the BSP once again becomes more complex, and although we can think of the collection of wall segments as a single wall or plane, we still have to be able to split them on other partitioning planes. So, basically we have to collect them into a linked list of coplanar walls, perform the intersection calculations as if they were a single wall, and then split them as if they were multiple walls and place them appropriately on the front and back links of the partitioning plane at any given iteration of the algorithm. This is shown in Figure 13.23. Again, this is a lot of drama so we are going to pass on it; however, in a real engine, you definitely want to go through the trouble of writing the code for this, because it will be worth it in the end.

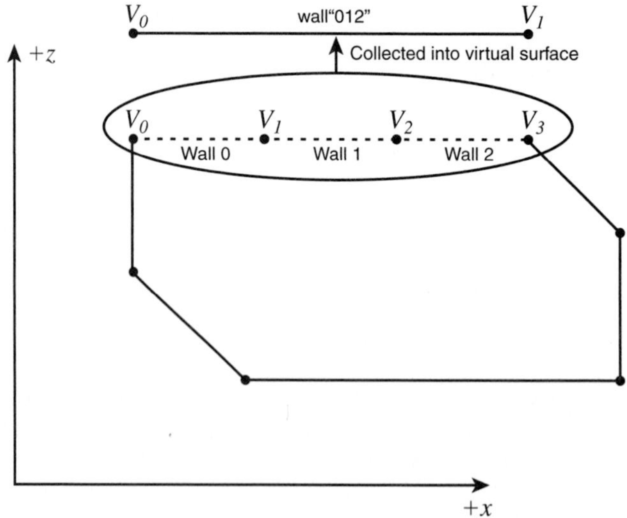

FIGURE 13.23 Joining coplanar walls into single surfaces for ease of computation.

Now that we finally have an outline of the algorithm in implementational terms, let's see the actual function that creates the BSP tree, given a linked list of walls generated by some other source. Here's the code:

```
void Bsp_Build_Tree(BSPNODEV1_PTR root)
{
// this function recursively builds the bsp tree from the root of the wall list
// the function works by taking the wall list which begins as a linked list
// of walls in no particular order, then it uses the wall at the TOP of the list
// as the separating plane and then divides space with that wall computing
// the walls on the front and back of the separating plane. The walls that are
// determined to be on the front and back, are once again linked lists, that
// are each processed recursively in the same manner. When the process is
// complete the entire BSP tree is built with exactly one node/leaf per wall

static BSPNODEV1_PTR next_wall, // pointer to next wall to be processed
         front_wall,  // the front wall
         back_wall,   // the back wall
         temp_wall;   // a temporary wall

static float dot_wall_1,        // dot products for test wall
       dot_wall_2,
       wall_x0,wall_y0,wall_z0, // working vars for test wall
       wall_x1,wall_y1,wall_z1,
       pp_x0,pp_y0,pp_z0,     // working vars for partitioning plane
       pp_x1,pp_y1,pp_z1,
       xi,zi;           // points of intersection when the partioning
                  // plane cuts a wall in two

static VECTOR4D test_vector_1, // test vectors from the partioning plane
        test_vector_2; // to the test wall to test the side
                // of the partioning plane the test wall
                // lies on

static int front_flag = 0,    // flags if a wall is on the front or back
      back_flag = 0,    // of the partioning plane
      index;         // looping index

// SECTION 1 ////////////////////////////////////////////////////////////////////

// test if this tree is complete
if (root==NULL)
  return;
```

13

```
// the root is the partitioning plane, partition the polygons using it
next_wall = root->link;
root->link = NULL;

// extract top two vertices of partioning plane wall for ease of calculations
pp_x0 = root->wall.vlist[0].x;
pp_y0 = root->wall.vlist[0].y;
pp_z0 = root->wall.vlist[0].z;

pp_x1 = root->wall.vlist[1].x;
pp_y1 = root->wall.vlist[1].y;
pp_z1 = root->wall.vlist[1].z;

// SECTION 2 ////////////////////////////////////////////////////////////////////

// test if all walls have been partitioned
while(next_wall)
   {
   // test which side test wall is relative to partioning plane
   // defined by root

   // first compute vectors from point on partioning plane to points on
   // test wall
   VECTOR4D_Build(&root->wall.vlist[0].v,
          &next_wall->wall.vlist[0].v,
          &test_vector_1);

   VECTOR4D_Build(&root->wall.vlist[0].v,
          &next_wall->wall.vlist[1].v,
          &test_vector_2);

   // now dot each test vector with the surface normal and analyze signs
   // to determine half space
   dot_wall_1 = VECTOR4D_Dot(&test_vector_1, &root->wall.normal);
   dot_wall_2 = VECTOR4D_Dot(&test_vector_2, &root->wall.normal);

// SECTION 3 ////////////////////////////////////////////////////////////////////

   // perform the tests

   // case 0, the partioning plane and the test wall have a point in common
   // this is a special case and must be accounted for, shorten the code
   // we will set a pair of flags and then the next case will handle
   // the actual insertion of the wall into BSP
```

```
// reset flags
front_flag = back_flag = 0;

// determine if wall is tangent to endpoints of partitioning wall
if (VECTOR4D_Equal(&root->wall.vlist[0].v ,&next_wall->wall.vlist[0].v) )
 {
 // p0 of partioning plane is the same at p0 of test wall
 // we only need to see what side p1 of test wall in on
 if (dot_wall_2 > 0)
   front_flag = 1;
 else
   back_flag = 1;

 } // end if
else
if (VECTOR4D_Equal(&root->wall.vlist[0].v, &next_wall->wall.vlist[1].v) )
 {
 // p0 of partioning plane is the same at p1 of test wall
 // we only need to see what side p0 of test wall in on
 if (dot_wall_1 > 0)
   front_flag = 1;
 else
   back_flag = 1;

 } // end if
else
if (VECTOR4D_Equal(&root->wall.vlist[1].v, &next_wall->wall.vlist[0].v) )
 {
 // p1 of partioning plane is the same at p0 of test wall
 // we only need to see what side p1 of test wall in on

 if (dot_wall_2 > 0)
   front_flag = 1;
 else
   back_flag = 1;

 } // end if
else
if (VECTOR4D_Equal(&root->wall.vlist[1].v, &next_wall->wall.vlist[1].v) )
 {
 // p1 of partioning plane is the same at p1 of test wall
 // we only need to see what side p0 of test wall in on
```

```
    if (dot_wall_1 > 0)
      front_flag = 1;
    else
      back_flag = 1;

    } // end if

// SECTION 4 ////////////////////////////////////////////////////////////////////

   // case 1 both signs are the same or the front or back flag has been set
   if ( (dot_wall_1 >= 0 && dot_wall_2 >= 0) || front_flag )
    {
    // place this wall on the front list
    if (root->front==NULL)
      {
      // this is the first node
      root->front   = next_wall;
      next_wall     = next_wall->link;
      front_wall    = root->front;
      front_wall->link = NULL;

      } // end if
    else
      {
      // this is the nth node
      front_wall->link = next_wall;
      next_wall     = next_wall->link;
      front_wall    = front_wall->link;
      front_wall->link = NULL;

      } // end else

    } // end if both positive

// SECTION 5 ////////////////////////////////////////////////////////////////////

   else // back side sub-case
   if ( (dot_wall_1 < 0 && dot_wall_2 < 0) || back_flag)
    {
    // place this wall on the back list
    if (root->back==NULL)
      {
      // this is the first node
      root->back   = next_wall;
```

```
      next_wall    = next_wall->link;
      back_wall    = root->back;
      back_wall->link = NULL;

      } // end if
    else
      {
      // this is the nth node
      back_wall->link = next_wall;
      next_wall    = next_wall->link;
      back_wall    = back_wall->link;
      back_wall->link = NULL;

      } // end else

    } // end if both negative

   // case 2 both signs are different, we must partition the wall

// SECTION 6 ////////////////////////////////////////////////////////////

   else
   if ( (dot_wall_1 < 0 && dot_wall_2 >= 0) ||
     (dot_wall_1 >= 0 && dot_wall_2 < 0))
    {
    // the partioning plane cuts the wall in half, the wall
    // must be split into two walls

    // extract top two vertices of test wall for ease of calculations
    wall_x0 = next_wall->wall.vlist[0].x;
    wall_y0 = next_wall->wall.vlist[0].y;
    wall_z0 = next_wall->wall.vlist[0].z;

    wall_x1 = next_wall->wall.vlist[1].x;
    wall_y1 = next_wall->wall.vlist[1].y;
    wall_z1 = next_wall->wall.vlist[1].z;

    // compute the point of intersection between the walls
    // note that the intersection takes place in the x-z plane
    Intersect_Lines(wall_x0, wall_z0, wall_x1, wall_z1,
            pp_x0,  pp_z0,  pp_x1,  pp_z1,
            &xi, &zi);

    // here comes the tricky part, we need to split the wall in half and
    // create two new walls. We'll do this by creating two new walls,
```

```
// placing them on the appropriate front and back lists and
// then deleting the original wall (hold your breath)...

// process first wall...

// allocate the memory for the wall
temp_wall = (BSPNODEV1_PTR)malloc(sizeof(BSPNODEV1));

// set links
temp_wall->front = NULL;
temp_wall->back = NULL;
temp_wall->link = NULL;

// poly normal is the same
temp_wall->wall.normal = next_wall->wall.normal;
temp_wall->wall.nlength = next_wall->wall.nlength;

// poly color is the same
temp_wall->wall.color = next_wall->wall.color;

// poly material is the same
temp_wall->wall.mati = next_wall->wall.mati;

// poly texture is the same
temp_wall->wall.texture = next_wall->wall.texture;

// poly attributes are the same
temp_wall->wall.attr = next_wall->wall.attr;

// poly states are the same
temp_wall->wall.state = next_wall->wall.state;

// add factor denote a split

temp_wall->id = next_wall->id + WALL_SPLIT_ID;
// compute wall vertices
for (index = 0; index < 4; index++)
 {
  temp_wall->wall.vlist[index].x = next_wall->wall.vlist[index].x;
  temp_wall->wall.vlist[index].y = next_wall->wall.vlist[index].y;
  temp_wall->wall.vlist[index].z = next_wall->wall.vlist[index].z;
  temp_wall->wall.vlist[index].w = 1;

 // copy vertex attributes, texture coordinates, normal
 temp_wall->wall.vlist[index].attr= next_wall->wall.vlist[index].attr;
```

```
     temp_wall->wall.vlist[index].n  = next_wall->wall.vlist[index].n;
     temp_wall->wall.vlist[index].t  = next_wall->wall.vlist[index].t;
     } // end for index

    // now modify vertices 1 and 2 to reflect intersection point
    // but leave y alone since it's invariant for the wall spliting
    temp_wall->wall.vlist[1].x = xi;
    temp_wall->wall.vlist[1].z = zi;

    temp_wall->wall.vlist[2].x = xi;
    temp_wall->wall.vlist[2].z = zi;

// SECTION 7 ////////////////////////////////////////////////////////////////

    // insert new wall into front or back of root
    if (dot_wall_1 >= 0)
      {
      // place this wall on the front list
      if (root->front==NULL)
       {
       // this is the first node
       root->front   = temp_wall;
       front_wall    = root->front;
       front_wall->link = NULL;

       } // end if
      else
       {
       // this is the nth node
       front_wall->link = temp_wall;
       front_wall    = front_wall->link;
       front_wall->link = NULL;

       } // end else

      } // end if positive
    else
    if (dot_wall_1 < 0)
      {
      // place this wall on the back list
      if (root->back==NULL)
       {
       // this is the first node
       root->back   = temp_wall;
```

```
        back_wall     = root->back;
        back_wall->link = NULL;

        } // end if
       else
        {
        // this is the nth node
        back_wall->link = temp_wall;
        back_wall     = back_wall->link;
        back_wall->link = NULL;

        } // end else

       } // end if negative

// SECTION 8 ///////////////////////////////////////////////////////////////

    // process second wall...

    // allocate the memory for the wall
    temp_wall = (BSPNODEV1_PTR)malloc(sizeof(BSPNODEV1));

    // set links
    temp_wall->front = NULL;
    temp_wall->back = NULL;
    temp_wall->link = NULL;

    // poly normal is the same
    temp_wall->wall.normal = next_wall->wall.normal;
    temp_wall->wall.nlength = next_wall->wall.nlength;

    // poly color is the same
    temp_wall->wall.color = next_wall->wall.color;

    // poly material is the same
    temp_wall->wall.mati = next_wall->wall.mati;

    // poly texture is the same
    temp_wall->wall.texture = next_wall->wall.texture;

    // poly attributes are the same
    temp_wall->wall.attr = next_wall->wall.attr;
```

```
// poly states are the same
temp_wall->wall.state = next_wall->wall.state;

// add factor denote a split

temp_wall->id = next_wall->id + WALL_SPLIT_ID;
// compute wall vertices
for (index=0; index < 4; index++)
 {
 temp_wall->wall.vlist[index].x = next_wall->wall.vlist[index].x;
 temp_wall->wall.vlist[index].y = next_wall->wall.vlist[index].y;
 temp_wall->wall.vlist[index].z = next_wall->wall.vlist[index].z;
 temp_wall->wall.vlist[index].w = 1;

 // copy vertex attributes, texture coordinates, normal
 temp_wall->wall.vlist[index].attr= next_wall->wall.vlist[index].attr;
 temp_wall->wall.vlist[index].n  = next_wall->wall.vlist[index].n;
 temp_wall->wall.vlist[index].t  = next_wall->wall.vlist[index].t;

 } // end for index

// now modify vertices 0 and 3 to reflect intersection point
// but leave y alone since it's invariant for the wall spliting
temp_wall->wall.vlist[0].x = xi;
temp_wall->wall.vlist[0].z = zi;

temp_wall->wall.vlist[3].x = xi;
temp_wall->wall.vlist[3].z = zi;

// insert new wall into front or back of root
if (dot_wall_2 >= 0)
  {
  // place this wall on the front list
  if (root->front==NULL)
   {
   // this is the first node
   root->front   = temp_wall;
   front_wall    = root->front;
   front_wall->link = NULL;

   } // end if
  else
   {
   // this is the nth node
   front_wall->link = temp_wall;
```

```
        front_wall     = front_wall->link;
        front_wall->link = NULL;

        } // end else


       } // end if positive
    else
    if (dot_wall_2 < 0)
       {
       // place this wall on the back list
       if (root->back==NULL)
        {
        // this is the first node
        root->back    = temp_wall;
        back_wall     = root->back;
        back_wall->link = NULL;

        } // end if
       else
        {
        // this is the nth node
        back_wall->link = temp_wall;
        back_wall     = back_wall->link;
        back_wall->link = NULL;

        } // end else

       } // end if negative

// SECTION 9 /////////////////////////////////////////////////////////////////////

    // we are now done splitting the wall, so we can delete it
    temp_wall = next_wall;
    next_wall = next_wall->link;

    // release the memory
    free(temp_wall);

    } // end else

   } // end while

// SECTION 10 ////////////////////////////////////////////////////////////////////
```

```
// recursively process front and back walls/sub-trees
Bsp_Build_Tree(root->front);

Bsp_Build_Tree(root->back);

} // end Bsp_Build_Tree
```

The function has clear areas of interest that are arranged in highlighted sections. Let's review what each section does:

- **Section 1**—Tests whether the current BSPNODEV1 pointer is NULL. If not, the vertices of the partitioning plane are extracted.
- **Section 2**—The two endpoints of the first wall below the partitioning plane in its wall-linked list are used to determine their relative positions to the partitioning wall by use of dot products.
- **Section 3**—The special case of common endpoints is processed, and flags are set to track this into the next phase.
- **Section 4**—Based on the signs of the dot products, the test wall is determined to be on front side of the partitioning plane and the test wall is added to the front-linked list.
- **Section 5**—Based on the signs of the dot products, the test wall is determined to be on the back side of the partitioning plane, and the test wall is added to the back-linked list.
- **Section 6**—The test wall must have been cut in half by the partitioning plane. Therefore, the coordinates of the two halves are computed.
- **Section 7**—If section 6 was executed, the first half of the wall is inserted into either the front- or back-linked list.
- **Section 8**—If section 6 was executed, the second half of the wall is inserted into either the front- or back-linked list.
- **Section 9**—The next wall to be processed is accessed and the process continues.
- **Section 10**—When all the walls of the list have been processed, the front and back wall lists are recursively processed, and the function processes the front and back lists.

When the function exits, the BSP tree is complete and the original wall list links are mangled. The memory won't be lost, but you can no longer use the `link` element to traverse the wall list. Now that we have the BSP tree, let's see how to display it.

Traversing and Displaying the BSP Tree

We have already seen the algorithm to traverse the BSP tree, but how can we work this into our graphics pipeline? The answer is that we will traverse the BSP tree, and during the traversal, we'll insert the polygons as they are visited into the rendering list, and then simply pass the rendering list on to the remaining pipeline modules as we would any object. Of course, as we traverse the BSP tree and insert each polygon into the rendering list, we must split the quadrilateral into two triangles and compute the proper vertices, texture coordinates, and so on of the two sub-triangles that the original quad composed. This is shown in Figure 13.24.

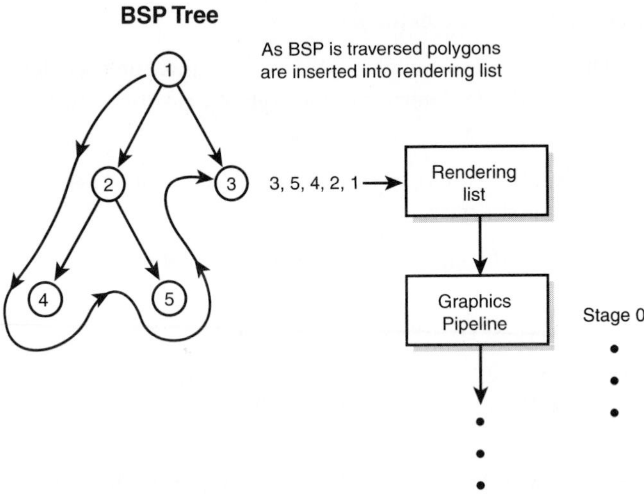

FIGURE 13.24 BSP traversal and insertion into the global rendering list.

The cool part is that we don't need any sorting or z-buffering during rendering. We only need to make sure that we insert the polygons that make up the BSP tree using the modified in-order traversal, so that the polygons are inserted in back-to-front order (like the painter's algorithm). Their ordering will be correct because they will be inserted into the polygon list during the modified recursive in-order traversal of the BSP tree, which is guaranteed to generate the proper order for any viewpoint. Here's the function that traverses the BSP tree and adds the polygons to the rendering list.

```
void Bsp_Insertion_Traversal_RENDERLIST4DV2(
   RENDERLIST4DV2_PTR rend_list, // the rendering list
   BSPNODEV1_PTR root, // root of bsp tree
   CAM4DV1_PTR cam,   // current camera
   int insert_local=0) // which vertices to use

{
// converts the entire bsp tree into a face list and then inserts
```

```
// the visible, active, non-clipped, non-culled polygons into
// the render list, also note the flag insert_local control
// whether or not the vlist_local or vlist_trans vertex list
// is used, thus you can insert a bsp tree "raw" totally untranformed
// if you set insert_local to 1, default is 0, that is you would
// only insert an object after at least the local to world transform

// the functions walks the tree recursively in back to front order
// relative to the viewpoint sent in cam, the bsp must be in world coordinates
// for this to work correctly

// this function works be testing the viewpoint against the current wall
// in the bsp, then depending on the side the viewpoint is the algorithm
// proceeds. the search takes place as the rest in an "inorder" method
// with hooks to process and add each node into the polygon list at the
// right time

static VECTOR4D test_vector;
static float dot_wall;

// SECTION 1 ////////////////////////////////////////////////////////////////

//Write_Error("\nEntering Bsp_Insertion_Traversal_RENDERLIST4DV2()...");

//Write_Error("\nTesting root...");

// is this a dead end?
if (root==NULL)
  {
  //Write_Error("\nRoot was null...");
  return;
  } // end if

//Write_Error("\nRoot was valid...");

// test which side viewpoint is on relative to the current wall
VECTOR4D_Build(&root->wall.vlist[0].v, &cam->pos, &test_vector);

// now dot test vector with the surface normal and analyze signs
dot_wall = VECTOR4D_Dot(&test_vector, &root->wall.normal);

//Write_Error("\nTesting dot product...");

// SECTION 2 ////////////////////////////////////////////////////////////////
```

```
// if the sign of the dot product is positive then the viewer on on the
// front side of current wall, so recursively process the walls behind then
// in front of this wall, else do the opposite
if (dot_wall > 0)
  {
  // viewer is in front of this wall
  //Write_Error("\nDot > 0, front side...");

  // process the back wall sub tree
  Bsp_Insertion_Traversal_RENDERLIST4DV2(rend_list,
                     root->back,
                     cam, insert_local);

  // split quad into (2) triangles for insertion
  POLYF4DV2 poly1, poly2;

  // the only difference from the POLYF4DV2 and the POLYF4DV2Q is that
  // the later has (4) vertices rather than (3), thus we are going to
  // create (2) triangles from the single quad :)
  // copy fields that are important
  poly1.state  = root->wall.state;   // state information
  poly1.attr  = root->wall.attr;    // physical attributes of polygon
  poly1.color  = root->wall.color;   // color of polygon
  poly1.texture = root->wall.texture;  // pointer to the texture
                     // information for simple texture mapping
  poly1.mati  = root->wall.mati;    // material index (-1)
                     // for no material (new)
  poly1.nlength = root->wall.nlength;  // length of the polygon normal
                     // if not normalized (new)
  poly1.normal = root->wall.normal;   // the general polygon normal (new)

  poly2.state  = root->wall.state;   // state information
  poly2.attr  = root->wall.attr;    // physical attributes of polygon
  poly2.color  = root->wall.color;   // color of polygon
  poly2.texture = root->wall.texture;  // pointer to the texture information
                     // for simple texture mapping
  poly2.mati  = root->wall.mati;    // material index (-1) f
                     // or no material (new)
  poly2.nlength = root->wall.nlength;  // length of the polygon normal
                     // if not normalized (new)
  poly2.normal = root->wall.normal;   // the general polygon normal (new)

  // now the vertices, they currently look like this
  // v0   v1
  //
```

```
//
// v3   v2
// we want to create (2) triangles that look like this
//  poly 1      poly2
// v0   v1        v1
//
//
//
// v3        v3   v2
//
// where the winding order of poly 1 is v0,v1,v3 and the winding order
// of poly 2 is v1, v2, v3 to keep with our clockwise conventions
if (insert_local==1)
 {
 // polygon 1
 poly1.vlist[0] = root->wall.vlist[0]; // the vertices of this triangle
 poly1.tvlist[0] = root->wall.vlist[0]; // the vertices of this triangle

 poly1.vlist[1] = root->wall.vlist[1]; // the vertices of this triangle
 poly1.tvlist[1] = root->wall.vlist[1]; // the vertices of this triangle

 poly1.vlist[2] = root->wall.vlist[3]; // the vertices of this triangle
 poly1.tvlist[2] = root->wall.vlist[3]; // the vertices of this triangle

 // polygon 2
 poly2.vlist[0] = root->wall.vlist[1]; // the vertices of this triangle
 poly2.tvlist[0] = root->wall.vlist[1]; // the vertices of this triangle

 poly2.vlist[1] = root->wall.vlist[2]; // the vertices of this triangle
 poly2.tvlist[1] = root->wall.vlist[2]; // the vertices of this triangle

 poly2.vlist[2] = root->wall.vlist[3]; // the vertices of this triangle
 poly2.tvlist[2] = root->wall.vlist[3]; // the vertices of this triangle
 } // end if
else
 {
 // polygon 1
 poly1.vlist[0] = root->wall.vlist[0];  // the vertices of this triangle
 poly1.tvlist[0] = root->wall.tvlist[0]; // the vertices of this triangle

 poly1.vlist[1] = root->wall.vlist[1];  // the vertices of this triangle
 poly1.tvlist[1] = root->wall.tvlist[1]; // the vertices of this triangle
```

```
    poly1.vlist[2] = root->wall.vlist[3];  // the vertices of this triangle
    poly1.tvlist[2] = root->wall.tvlist[3]; // the vertices of this triangle

    // polygon 2
    poly2.vlist[0] = root->wall.vlist[1];  // the vertices of this triangle
    poly2.tvlist[0] = root->wall.tvlist[1]; // the vertices of this triangle

    poly2.vlist[1] = root->wall.vlist[2];  // the vertices of this triangle
    poly2.tvlist[1] = root->wall.tvlist[2]; // the vertices of this triangle

    poly2.vlist[2] = root->wall.vlist[3];  // the vertices of this triangle
    poly2.tvlist[2] = root->wall.tvlist[3]; // the vertices of this triangle
    } // end if

   //Write_Error("\nInserting polygons...");

   // insert polygons into rendering list
   Insert_POLYF4DV2_RENDERLIST4DV2(rend_list, &poly1);
   Insert_POLYF4DV2_RENDERLIST4DV2(rend_list, &poly2);

   // now process the front walls sub tree
   Bsp_Insertion_Traversal_RENDERLIST4DV2(rend_list, root->front,
                     cam, insert_local);

   } // end if

// SECTION 3 ////////////////////////////////////////////////////////////

else
   {
   // viewer is behind this wall
   //Write_Error("\nDot < 0, back side...");

   // process the back wall sub tree
   Bsp_Insertion_Traversal_RENDERLIST4DV2(rend_list, root->front,
                     cam, insert_local);

   // split quad into (2) triangles for insertion
   POLYF4DV2 poly1, poly2;

   // the only difference from the POLYF4DV2 and the POLYF4DV2Q is that
   // the later has (4) vertices rather than (3), thus we are going to
   // create (2) triangles from the single quad :)
   // copy fields that are important
   poly1.state  = root->wall.state;   // state information
```

```
poly1.attr  = root->wall.attr;    // physical attributes of polygon
poly1.color  = root->wall.color;   // color of polygon
poly1.texture = root->wall.texture;  // pointer to the texture
                 // information for simple texture mapping
poly1.mati  = root->wall.mati;    // material index (-1)
                 // for no material (new)
poly1.nlength = root->wall.nlength;  // length of the polygon normal
                 // if not normalized (new)
poly1.normal = root->wall.normal;   // the general polygon normal (new)

poly2.state  = root->wall.state;   // state information
poly2.attr  = root->wall.attr;    // physical attributes of polygon
poly2.color  = root->wall.color;   // color of polygon
poly2.texture = root->wall.texture;  // pointer to the texture
                 // information for simple texture mapping
poly2.mati  = root->wall.mati;    // material index (-1)
                 // for no material (new)
poly2.nlength = root->wall.nlength;  // length of the polygon normal
                 // if not normalized (new)
poly2.normal = root->wall.normal;   // the general polygon normal (new)

// now the vertices, they currently look like this
// v0   v1
//
//
// v3   v2
// we want to create (2) triangles that look like this
//  poly 1      poly2
// v0   v1        v1
//
//
//
// v3        v3   v2
//
// where the winding order of poly 1 is v0,v1,v3 and the winding order
// of poly 2 is v1, v2, v3 to keep with our clockwise conventions
if (insert_local==1)
 {
 // polygon 1
 poly1.vlist[0] = root->wall.vlist[0]; // the vertices of this triangle
 poly1.tvlist[0] = root->wall.vlist[0]; // the vertices of this triangle

 poly1.vlist[1] = root->wall.vlist[1]; // the vertices of this triangle
 poly1.tvlist[1] = root->wall.vlist[1]; // the vertices of this triangle
```

13

```
 poly1.vlist[2] = root->wall.vlist[3]; // the vertices of this triangle
 poly1.tvlist[2] = root->wall.vlist[3]; // the vertices of this triangle

 // polygon 2
 poly2.vlist[0] = root->wall.vlist[1]; // the vertices of this triangle
 poly2.tvlist[0] = root->wall.vlist[1]; // the vertices of this triangle

 poly2.vlist[1] = root->wall.vlist[2]; // the vertices of this triangle
 poly2.tvlist[1] = root->wall.vlist[2]; // the vertices of this triangle

 poly2.vlist[2] = root->wall.vlist[3]; // the vertices of this triangle
 poly2.tvlist[2] = root->wall.vlist[3]; // the vertices of this triangle
 } // end if
else
 {
 // polygon 1
 poly1.vlist[0] = root->wall.vlist[0];  // the vertices of this triangle
 poly1.tvlist[0] = root->wall.tvlist[0]; // the vertices of this triangle

 poly1.vlist[1] = root->wall.vlist[1];  // the vertices of this triangle
 poly1.tvlist[1] = root->wall.tvlist[1]; // the vertices of this triangle

 poly1.vlist[2] = root->wall.vlist[3];  // the vertices of this triangle
 poly1.tvlist[2] = root->wall.tvlist[3]; // the vertices of this triangle

 // polygon 2
 poly2.vlist[0] = root->wall.vlist[1];  // the vertices of this triangle
 poly2.tvlist[0] = root->wall.tvlist[1]; // the vertices of this triangle

 poly2.vlist[1] = root->wall.vlist[2];  // the vertices of this triangle
 poly2.tvlist[1] = root->wall.tvlist[2]; // the vertices of this triangle

 poly2.vlist[2] = root->wall.vlist[3];  // the vertices of this triangle
 poly2.tvlist[2] = root->wall.tvlist[3]; // the vertices of this triangle
 } // end if

//Write_Error("\nInserting polygons...");

// insert polygons into rendering list
Insert_POLYF4DV2_RENDERLIST4DV2(rend_list, &poly1);
Insert_POLYF4DV2_RENDERLIST4DV2(rend_list, &poly2);
```

```
  // now process the front walls sub tree
  Bsp_Insertion_Traversal_RENDERLIST4DV2(rend_list, root->back,
                      cam, insert_local);

  } // end else

//Write_Error("\nExiting Bsp_Insertion_Traversal_RENDERLIST4DV2()...");

} // end Bsp_Insertion_Traversal_RENDERLIST4DV2
```


As usual, the reality of implementing a function is much different from the theoretical version. As you can see, the preceding function is much more complex than the pseudocode version we saw a while ago. Let's take a look at the sections.

- **Section 1**—Tests whether the current node is `NULL`. If so, it exits; otherwise the viewpoint position relative to the current node is computed using a dot product.
- **Section 2**—The sign of the dot product from section 1 is used to determine which side the viewpoint and hence the viewer is on. Based on this, one of two different traversal methods is selected, both of which are identical except for the recursive calls.
- **Section 3**—First a recursive call to process the back walls is made. Then the polygon is split into two triangles, texture coordinates are copied along with vertices and other information, and the two triangles are added to the rendering list. Finally, a recursive call is made to process the back-side walls.

The second block of code works in a similar way, except the order of the recursive calls is reversed.

After the call is made to `Bsp_Insertion_Traversal_RENDERLIST4DV2()`, the rendering list is updated with the BSP mesh, and we can simply continue using the rendering pipeline as we would after inserting an object.

However, there are still a couple of issues we need to address. First, you should have noticed that the preceding function has a flag `insert_local`, which determines whether either the local vertex list `vlist[]` or the transformed vertex list `tvlist[]` is used during the insertion of the wall into the polygon list. The BSP tree is in local space, but because it's a mesh of a level, local space might be the same as world space, so both arrays might have the same data. However, if they don't and you want to perform a transformation on the BSP tree, you simply need to walk it (in any order) and perform the transformation. For example, say you want to translate every vertex in the BSP; you could write something like this:

```
void Bsp_Translate(BSPNODEV1_PTR root, VECTOR4D_PTR trans)
{
// this function translates all the walls that make up the bsp world
```

```
// note function is recursive, we don't really need this function, but
// it's a good example of how we might perform transformations on the BSP
// tree and similar tree like structures using recursion
// note the translation is perform from local to world coords

static int index; // looping variable

// test if we have hit a dead end
if (root==NULL)
  return;

// translate back most sub-tree
Bsp_Translate(root->back, trans);

// iterate thru all vertices of current wall and translate them
for (index=0; index < 4; index++)
  {
  // perform translation
  root->wall.tvlist[index].x = root->wall.vlist[index].x + trans->x;
  root->wall.tvlist[index].y = root->wall.vlist[index].y + trans->y;
  root->wall.tvlist[index].z = root->wall.vlist[index].z + trans->z;
  } // end for index

// translate front most sub-tree
Bsp_Translate(root->front, trans);

} // end Bsp_Translate
```

You simply send the root of the BSP along with a translation vector and the entire BSP will be translated.

NOTE

You might be wondering whether all this recursion is healthy. Well, the fact is that I tried converting many of the functions to pure stack-based data recursion, and found that the compiler is just as good at it as I am. In the end, I found that if the functions have any "body" at all, it's nearly useless to convert them to data recursion via a stack to save the function invocation overhead.

A more generalized transformation function would walk the BSP and apply a matrix transform to the vertices. Additionally, as many of our transformations work, we are able to select which coordinates the transformation is applied to: local coordinates, transformed coordinates, or local-copied-to-transformed. The following function implements this functionality:

```
void Bsp_Transform(BSPNODEV1_PTR root, // root of bsp tree
          MATRIX4X4_PTR mt,  // transformation matrix
          int coord_select)  // selects coords to transform)
{
// this function traverses the bsp tree and applies the transformation
// matrix to each node, the function is of course recursive and uses
// and inorder traversal, other traversals such as preorder and postorder
// will would just as well...

// test if we have hit a dead end
if (root==NULL)
  return;

// transform back most sub-tree
Bsp_Transform(root->back, mt, coord_select);

// iterate thru all vertices of current wall and transform them into
// camera coordinates

// what coordinates should be transformed?
switch(coord_select)
   {
   case TRANSFORM_LOCAL_ONLY:
      {
      // transform each local/model vertex of the object mesh in place
      for (int vertex = 0; vertex < 4; vertex++)
       {
       POINT4D presult; // hold result of each transformation

       // transform point
       Mat_Mul_VECTOR4D_4X4(&root->wall.vlist[vertex].v, mt, &presult);

       // store result back
       VECTOR4D_COPY(&root->wall.vlist[vertex].v, &presult);

       // transform vertex normal if needed
       if (root->wall.vlist[vertex].attr & VERTEX4DTV1_ATTR_NORMAL)
         {
         // transform normal
         Mat_Mul_VECTOR4D_4X4(&root->wall.vlist[vertex].n,
                     mt, &presult);

         // store result back
         VECTOR4D_COPY(&root->wall.vlist[vertex].n, &presult);
         } // end if
```

13

```
      } // end for index
    } break;

  case TRANSFORM_TRANS_ONLY:
    {
    // transform each "transformed" vertex of the object mesh in place
    // remember, the idea of the vlist_trans[] array is to accumulate
    // transformations
    for (int vertex = 0; vertex < 4; vertex++)
     {
     POINT4D presult; // hold result of each transformation

     // transform point
     Mat_Mul_VECTOR4D_4X4(&root->wall.tvlist[vertex].v, mt, &presult);

     // store result back
     VECTOR4D_COPY(&root->wall.tvlist[vertex].v, &presult);

     // transform vertex normal if needed
     if (root->wall.tvlist[vertex].attr & VERTEX4DTV1_ATTR_NORMAL)
       {
       // transform normal
       Mat_Mul_VECTOR4D_4X4(&root->wall.tvlist[vertex].n,
                 mt, &presult);

       // store result back
       VECTOR4D_COPY(&root->wall.tvlist[vertex].n, &presult);
       } // end if
      } // end for index

    } break;

  case TRANSFORM_LOCAL_TO_TRANS:
    {
    // transform each local/model vertex of the
    // object mesh and store result
    // in "transformed" vertex list
    for (int vertex=0; vertex < 4; vertex++)
      {
      POINT4D presult; // hold result of each transformation

      // transform point
      Mat_Mul_VECTOR4D_4X4(&root->wall.vlist[vertex].v, mt,
                 &root->wall.tvlist[vertex].v);
```

```
        // transform vertex normal if needed
        if (root->wall.tvlist[vertex].attr & VERTEX4DTV1_ATTR_NORMAL)
          {
          // transform point
          Mat_Mul_VECTOR4D_4X4(&root->wall.vlist[vertex].n, mt,
                    &root->wall.tvlist[vertex].n);
          } // end if

         } // end for index
      } break;

   default: break;

   } // end switch

// transform front most sub-tree
Bsp_Transform(root->front, mt, coord_select);

} // end Bsp_Insertion_Traversal_RENDERLIST4DV2
```

`Bsp_Insertion_Traversal_RENDERLIST4DV2()` is called with the root to the BSP tree, along with a transformation matrix and the transformation selection flag. The function performs the requested transformation recursively and returns (hopefully). However, in most cases, you will never need to translate, rotate, or transform the BSP, because in all likelihood the BSP will represent static indoor or outdoor level data. The only thing moving in it is the camera.

To release all the memory allocated by the BSP tree, here's a deletion function that will walk the BSP and release all the memory it allocates:

```
void Bsp_Delete(BSPNODEV1_PTR root)
{
// this function recursively deletes all the nodes in the bsp tree and free's
// the memory back to the OS.

BSPNODEV1_PTR temp_wall; // a temporary wall

// test if we have hit a dead end
if (root==NULL)
  return;

// delete back sub tree
Bsp_Delete(root->back);
```

```
// delete this node, but first save the front sub-tree
temp_wall = root->front;

// delete the memory
free(root);

// assign the root to the saved front most sub-tree
root = temp_wall;

// delete front sub tree
Bsp_Delete(root);

} // end Bsp_Delete
```

Just call `Bsp_Delete()` with the root of the BSP tree and the tree will be recursively de-allocated.

Finally, for diagnostics, here's a printing function that will dump the BSP (trust me, take it, you will need it!):

```
void Bsp_Print(BSPNODEV1_PTR root)
{
// this function performs a recursive in-order traversal of the BSP tree and
// prints the results out to the file opened with fp_out as the handle

// test if this child is null
if (root==NULL)
  {
  Write_Error("\nReached NULL node returning...");
  return;
  } // end if

// search left tree (back walls)
Write_Error("\nTraversing back sub-tree...");

// call recursively
Bsp_Print(root->back);

// visit node
Write_Error("\n\n\nWall ID #%d",root->id);

Write_Error("\nstate   = %d", root->wall.state); // state
Write_Error("\nattr  = %d", root->wall.attr); // attributes of poly
Write_Error("\ncolor   = %d", root->wall.color); // color of poly
Write_Error("\ntexture = %x", root->wall.texture); // pnt to texture info
                               // for simple texture mapping
```

```
Write_Error("\nmati  = %d", root->wall.mati); // material index
                       // (-1) for no material (new)

Write_Error("\nVertex 0: (%f,%f,%f,%f)",root->wall.vlist[0].x,
                    root->wall.vlist[0].y,
                    root->wall.vlist[0].z,
                    root->wall.vlist[0].w);

Write_Error("\nVertex 1: (%f,%f,%f, %f)",root->wall.vlist[1].x,
                     root->wall.vlist[1].y,
                     root->wall.vlist[1].z,
                     root->wall.vlist[1].w);

Write_Error("\nVertex 2: (%f,%f,%f, %f)",root->wall.vlist[2].x,
                     root->wall.vlist[2].y,
                     root->wall.vlist[2].z,
                     root->wall.vlist[2].w);

Write_Error("\nVertex 3: (%f,%f,%f, %f)",root->wall.vlist[3].x,
                     root->wall.vlist[3].y,
                     root->wall.vlist[3].z,
                     root->wall.vlist[3].w);

Write_Error("\nNormal (%f,%f,%f, %f), length=%f",root->wall.normal.x,
                         root->wall.normal.y,
                         root->wall.normal.z,
                         root->wall.nlength);

Write_Error("\nTextCoords (%f,%f)",root->wall.vlist[1].u0,
                  root->wall.vlist[1].v0);

Write_Error("\nEnd wall data\n");

// search right tree (front walls)
Write_Error("\nTraversing front sub-tree..");

Bsp_Print(root->front);

} // end Bsp_Print
```

Simply call `Bsp_Print()` with the root of the tree, but make sure you have previously opened an error channel with a call to `Open_Error_File()`. That's about all there is to a complete BSP system—now let's see how we're going to add it to our graphics pipeline.

Integrating BSP Tree into the Graphics Pipeline

Adding the BSP tree technology to the graphics pipeline shouldn't be that hard. We're going to add the BSP system in a similar fashion to how we integrated the Z-buffer system previously. We won't need any of the object functions because the BSP tree contains all the geometry for the static components of the game universe itself. We treat the BSP object the same as any other object, with one caveat: We must insert the BSP into the rendering list *first*, and we must *not* z-sort the rendering list, because it would destroy the BSP ordering.

Of course, if you aren't interested in using the back-to-front in-order visitation property exhibited by the BSP tree and want it for collision detection or culling (which we will get to later), you can insert the BSP tree in any order you want (before or after objects) and enable z-sorting and/or a Z-buffer, or whatever. In fact, 99% of all hardware-based games don't use BSPs to compute render order anymore, but use them only for collision and culling. However, for our demo we are going to use the BSP to show that perfect back-to-front rendering order can be extracted from the BSP tree with a back-to-front in-order walk of the tree.

To integrate the BSP, all you need to do is make a single call to `Bsp_Insertion_Traversal_RENDERLIST4DV2()` at the top of your rendering loop in the same place that you would make your calls to insert objects into the rendering list. However, you must insert the BSP knowing that it is in back-to-front order as is, and anything else added to the rendering list will be in front of it because sorting is out of the question. Of course, you can turn on z-buffering, but that blows the whole point of the BSP in this example (to compute back-to-front rendering order). In any case, here's an example of the order of operations to use the BSP functionality in the rendering pipeline (I have excerpted this from the upcoming demo and removed anything extraneous, so you can see the main calls):

```
// start the timing clock
Start_Clock();

// clear the drawing surface
DDraw_Fill_Surface(lpddsback, 0);

// read keyboard and other devices here
DInput_Read_Keyboard();

// game logic here...

// reset the render list
Reset_RENDERLIST4DV2(&rend_list);

// generate camera matrix
Build_CAM4DV1_Matrix_Euler(&cam, CAM_ROT_SEQ_ZYX);
```

```
// insert the bsp into rendering list
Bsp_Insertion_Traversal_RENDERLIST4DV2(&rend_list,
                    bsp_root, &cam, 1);

// apply world to camera transform
World_To_Camera_RENDERLIST4DV2(&rend_list, &cam);

// clip the polygons themselves now
Clip_Polys_RENDERLIST4DV2(&rend_list,
   &cam,
   ((x_clip_mode == 1) ? CLIP_POLY_X_PLANE : 0) |
   ((y_clip_mode == 1) ? CLIP_POLY_Y_PLANE : 0) |
   ((z_clip_mode == 1) ? CLIP_POLY_Z_PLANE : 0) );

// light scene all at once
if (lighting_mode==1)
  {
  Transform_LIGHTSV2(lights2, 4, &cam.mcam, TRANSFORM_LOCAL_TO_TRANS);
  Light_RENDERLIST4DV2_World2_16(&rend_list, &cam, lights2, 4);
  } // end if

// apply camera to perspective transformation
Camera_To_Perspective_RENDERLIST4DV2(&rend_list, &cam);

// apply screen transform
Perspective_To_Screen_RENDERLIST4DV2(&rend_list, &cam);

// lock the back buffer
DDraw_Lock_Back_Surface();

// set up rendering context for no zbuffer
rc.attr    = RENDER_ATTR_NOBUFFER | RENDER_ATTR_TEXTURE_PERSPECTIVE_AFFINE;

rc.video_buffer  = back_buffer;
rc.lpitch      = back_lpitch;
rc.mip_dist     = 0;
rc.zbuffer     = (UCHAR *)zbuffer.zbuffer;
rc.zpitch      = WINDOW_WIDTH*4;
rc.rend_list    = &rend_list;
rc.texture_dist  = 0;
rc.alpha_override = -1;

// render scene
Draw_RENDERLIST4DV2_RENDERCONTEXTV1_16(&rc);
```

```
// unlock the back buffer
DDraw_Unlock_Back_Surface();

// flip the surfaces
DDraw_Flip2();
```

As you can see, the BSP is inserted with a single call, and the remainder of the 3D pipeline is called as usual. The final version in the demo has both a ceiling and a floor mesh, which are actually OBJECT4DV2s that are inserted into the rendering list first with the BSP following, because by definition the floor and ceiling are always under the walls; or in other words, the walls always occlude the floors and ceiling. Also, the walls and ceilings do not need to be sorted as long as they are all coplanar. Anyway, we will get to that shortly.

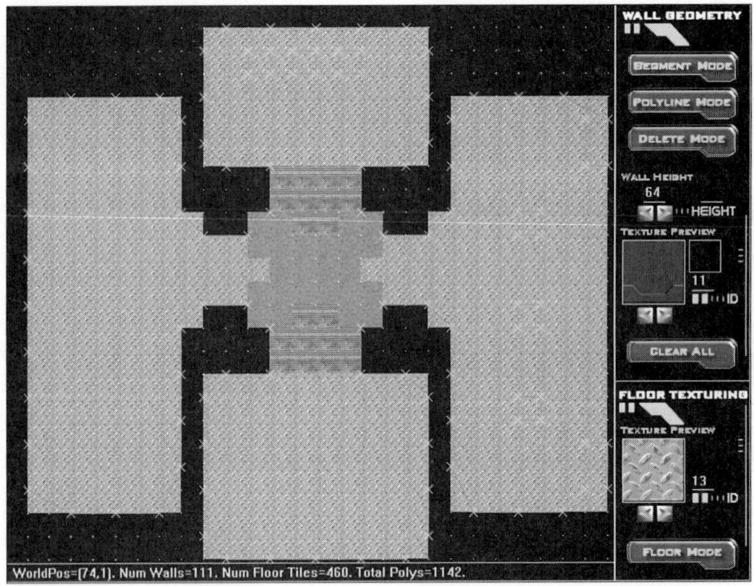

FIGURE 13.25 A screenshot of the BSP demo in action.

The BSP Level Editor

The BSP demo program is about 90% interface code with a few calls to all the BSP functions. This is a perfect example of how complex it is to write interfaces. Most of the time, the interface code is 10 times bigger than the program it encapsulates. Anyway, the demo is named DEMOII13_1.CPP|EXE and enables us to use the mouse to draw a top view of a game level constructed from 2D walls. Figure 13.25 shows a screenshot of the program running. As you can see, there are three main areas of interest. The area on the right is the control area, and the area on the left is the editor area. The top menu bar is used to select various modes and compile, save, load, and so on.

NOTE

To compile the demo yourself, you will need `DEMOII13_1.CPP`, along with all the library modules `T3DLIB1-11.CPP|H` in addition to the DirectX .LIB files. Additionally, you will need the resource file for the menus and so on. This file is named `DEMOII13_1.RC`.

Before getting into how to use the editor, let's talk about a few constraints you will need to adhere to when using it:

- No more than 256 lines.
- When drawing walls, I suggest not making them more than 2–4 grid snaps long. Otherwise, you will get horrible texture mapping artifacts (because of the affine texturing for speed). I find that walls that are 2–3 grid snaps in length with a height of 128 seem to look like a standard FPS.
- Try not to overlap wall segments.
- Try to keep the levels simple—this system is hardly robust, and will crash on you.
- The editor and viewer both work in windowed mode, with a minimum resolution of 800×600×16 necessary on your desktop. Of course, the color depth must be 16-bit, as with all our windowed applications.

The *Doom* Demo

This demo hardly looks like *Doom*, but it's a catchy title, so I used it. Anyway, before we get into the editor's code and functionality, I thought a brief look how to load a level and run around would be a good start. Here are the steps I want you to follow:

1. Launch the executable `DEMOII13_1.EXE` from its working directory. To ensure that all the assets are intact, make sure your desktop is in 16-bit color mode with a resolution of 800×600 or greater—I suggest 1024×768. You should see something like Figure 13.26.
2. Select the File menu on the main menu bar and select File, Load .LEV File. This is shown in Figure 13.28. Now, type in **`DOOM01.LEV`** into file edit box and click OK.
3. The level editor will load the level, and you'll see something like the image shown in Figure 13.25. Now, to compile the level into a BSP tree and view it, simply use to mouse to select the main menu item Build and select the submenu Build, Compile BSP and View. The second you do this, the system will compile the level into a BSP tree and then switch into 3D mode. You should see something like the image shown in Figure 13.29.

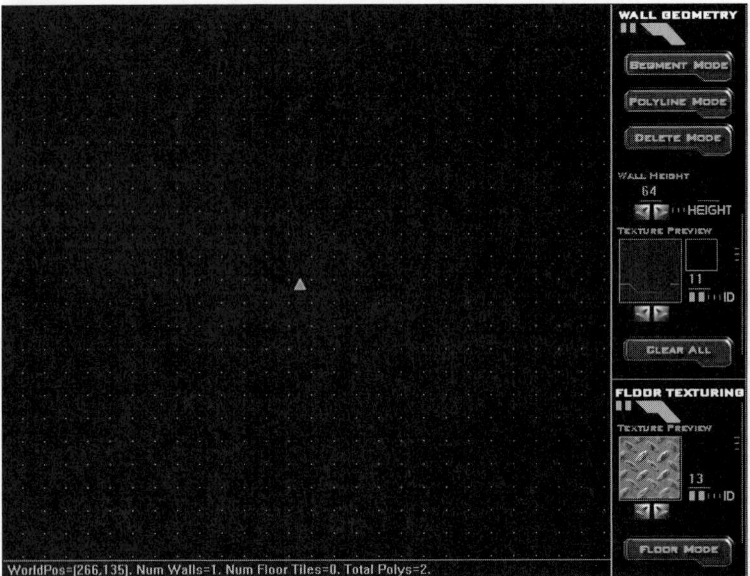

FIGURE 13.26 Launching the level editor.

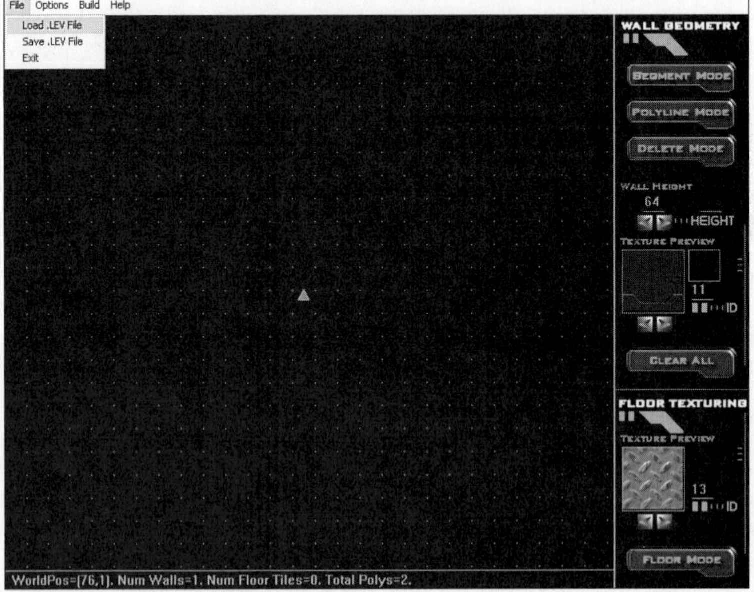

FIGURE 13.27 Loading a level into the editor.

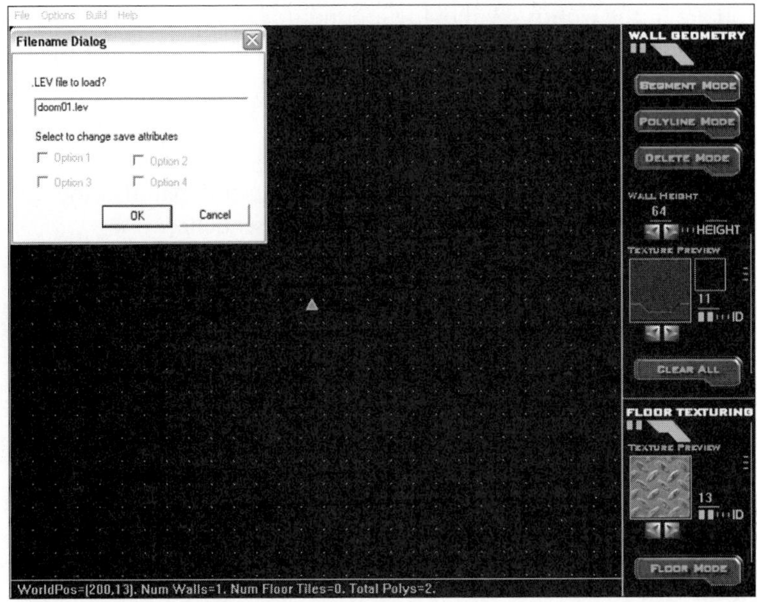

FIGURE 13.28 Entering in the level filename.

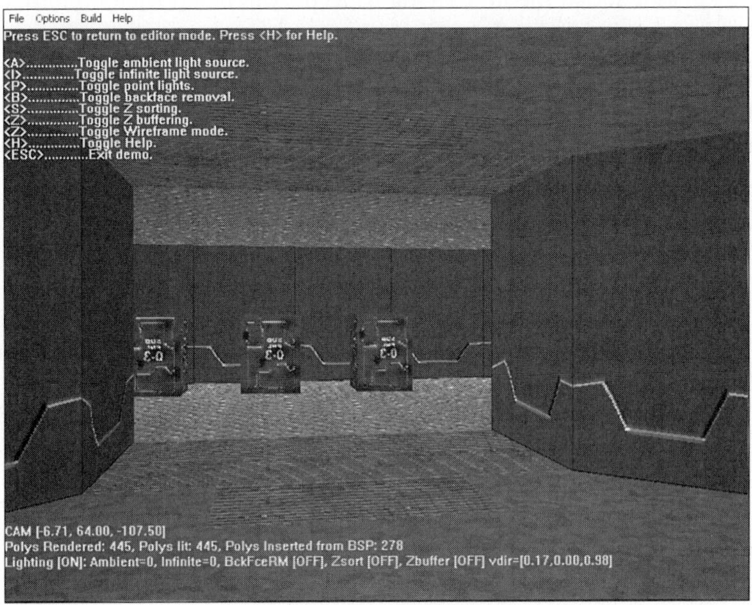

FIGURE 13.29 The level editor in 3D walkthrough mode.

4. Now you are in the world: Try moving around, toggling the lights with the A, I, and P keys. If you have a fast enough machine (1.5GHz or better), the display should be pretty snappy. Try walking through walls and playing around. Also, try enabling and disabling the wireframe mode with the W key and keep your eye on the polygon count per frame.
5. Return to the editor with the Esc key. You can enter and exit 3D mode over and over with steps 3, 4, and 5. This will be your modeling sequence.

CAUTION

At the time I wrote this chapter, there were still a few outstanding bugs with the BSP demo, and sometimes certain walls cause the system to hang, or not display correctly. So keep it simple—otherwise you will be terminating applications <BG>.

Now that you have a rough idea of what the level editor can do, let's review the file format, each of the controls, and how to use the editor.

The Level Editor GUI

When I first decided to make a basic level editor, my first impulse was to try to parse the *Quake* format, but that is simply too complicated. There is too much stuff in it, plus I like really simple file formats, so the underlying concepts can be understood rather than dealing with the complexities of more file formats.

After I bit the bullet and decided to make a level editor (in about one day), I had to decide how to write it: should I use Visual Basic, Visual C++, Borland Builder, DirectX, GDI, and so on? In real life, I would (and do) build all my tools with Builder or Visual Basic, but for this, that's too much work, and you wouldn't be able to play with it and add to it, so I decided to go with straight Visual C++.

Then, of course, the issue of using a real Windows application or a full-screen application comes into play. I need a DirectX application for 3D mode, but for the GUI I need buttons and controls. I decided that I would use Windows controls for the menu only and do everything else manually—that is, make my own buttons for the editor area controls. This is a lot easier than making Windows and DirectX play nice. In any event, it all worked out pretty well, and the editor works well enough for our needs. We'll get back to the software for it later. Right now I want to switch gears to user mode and show you how each of the controls works.

The editor has a simple goal: to enable you to draw wall segments in the x-z plane that represent 3D walls in the 3D world. It also places floor tile textures, which are represented by polygons in the 3D world. So, from a user's point of view, we simply draw wall segments and floor tiles with various textures and then build the BSP and view it—very simple.

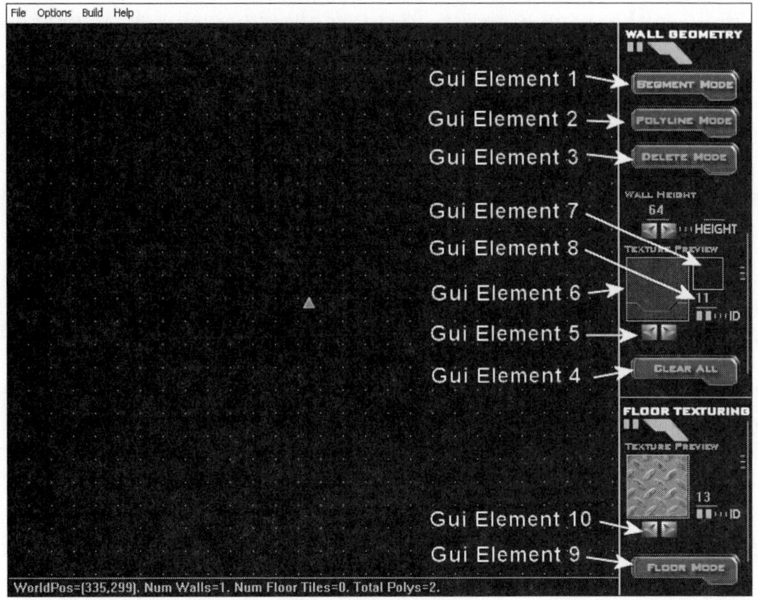

FIGURE 13.30 Detailed level editor interface annotation.

Let's take a look at each of the controls on the right-hand side control panel of the interface. In Figure 13.30, there are two main sub-panels of the control group:

- Wall Geometry
- Floor Texturing

Segment Mode Let's talk about the wall geometry section first. The element labeled 1, SEGMENT MODE, in Figure 13.30 indicates that you want to draw single segments in the editor area to the left. When you left-click on this button, the system will switch into single segment mode. This mode works as follows: When you move the mouse over to the editor area on the left and left-click, a node will be created. Release the mouse button and you will see a dragging line following the mouse pointer. Left-click again and a wall segment will be generated at the current point. This mode is good if you like to do things one at a time. If you decide to terminate the current line segment before finishing the line, right-click and the system will discard the line.

Polyline Mode Polyline mode is more flexible and enables you to draw multiple line segments in succession. Referring to the element labeled 2 in Figure 13.30, if you select POLYLINE MODE by left-clicking on it, the editor will change into polyline mode. This mode works as follows: When you move over to the editor area on the left and left-click, a "starting point" is created. Then you will see a line dragged to the current mouse position that will show you where the next line will be placed. To place the line, simply left-click again. The system will keep allowing you to add segments without terminating the segment, as it did in the segment mode. To stop adding segments to the polyline, simply right-click.

Delete Mode Next is the wall deletion mode. To select deletion mode, place the cursor over the DELETE MODE button, shown in Figure 13.30 as the element labeled 3. Once in this mode, the system tracks the nearest line to the cursor in the editor area and illuminates it with a glow to indicate that it's the "hot" spot. Simply left-click while hovering over any line segment, and the line segment will be deleted from the system.

Clear All The element labeled 4 in Figure 13.30 is the CLEAR ALL button. This is used to clear the entire system, including walls and floors, and resets everything to the initial state. Simply left-click it and say bye bye to your level!

Wall Height and Texture Preview So far we know how to draw lines in the editor, but what do they represent? Well, they represent 3D vertical walls in the x-z plane (world space), each roughly the size of 48 length units between each grid tick. However, we have said nothing yet about the height or texture map that is mapped on each wall. These values are controlled by GUI elements 5 and 6. GUI element 5 is the wall height, and you can change it by clicking the blue arrows under the value to the value you desire. I suggest you start off with walls that are 128 grid marks high and 2 grid marks in length.

For each wall, a texture is mapped onto it and stretched without repeating. The textures are all 128×128, and there are currently about 20 or so of them. The currently active texture is displayed in the texture preview window pointed to by GUI element 6. To change the texture, use the right and left arrows under the preview and click on them. Note that all walls drawn with the current wall height and texture cannot be changed. The only way to modify a wall is to delete it and redo it—sorry!

Wall Height and Texture Scanners In addition to the wall height and texture preview elements, there are some other elements indicated by GUI elements 7 and 8. These are like the eye dropper in a paint program, and show you the texture and wall height for any wall segment that the cursor is hovering over in the editor area to the left. For example, suppose you've drawn a level and can't remember what texture you applied to a wall or its height. Just move the mouse over the wall segment until it highlights with a glow, and the texture and height scanner will display the data. Remember—you can't change it; you must delete the segment and start over.

Floor Mode The last important part of the level editor GUI other than the main menu is the FLOOR MODE button, indicated by GUI label 9. When you draw a level, it will have no floor or ceiling geometry. To add a single floor tile, you must select the floor mode by clicking on it. The current texture depicted in the Floor Texturing texture preview will be applied to any tile that you left-click on in the editor area. This way, you can "paint" floor tiles down. If you make a mistake, you can erase floor tiles by right-clicking on them, but you must be in floor mode for this to work. As with wall texturing, you can select different floor tiles from a palette of 20 or so by clicking the right and left arrows under the floor texture preview, labeled as GUI element 10.

The Main Menu The main menu has a number of menu items on it. Let's take a look at each.

- File—File has three submenu options: Load .LEV File, Save .LEV File, and Exit. Load and Save enable you to load or save a BSP file in ASCII format. Simply enter in the name of the file you want to load or save with the .LEV extension and click OK. Exit, of course, exits the system.
- Options—The Options menu enables you to select what is visible in the editor window. Sometimes you might want to see only the walls, or floors, or disable the grid, and the Options menu enables you to do this. There are three submenu options: View Grid, View Walls, and View Floor. You can toggle them on or off by selecting them.
- Build—The Build menu has two options, but only one is currently active: Compile BSP and View. This single option compiles the BSP level and switches to 3D rendering mode. While in 3D rendering mode, you can use the arrow keys to navigate and use the H key to display help. ESC enables you to exit back to the editor and make changes transparently.
- Help—This menu has a single About submenu.

NOTE

The camera will be positioned at (0,0,0) in the 3D world, which is marked by a green triangle. Additionally, your altitude will always be the current wall height. So before entering your 3D world, make sure to make the wall height less than the highest wall, otherwise your head will poke out from the ceiling.

Final Notes on the Editor and Viewing Levels That wraps it up for using the editor, but I want to mention of few details before moving on to the technical material. In most cases, you will launch the editor and start with a blank level. If you have a level in progress, you would load it by selecting File, Load .LEV File from the main menu. In either case, you will select a wall height and texture and proceed to add walls to the level. Then you might switch to floor mode and add some floor tiles. When you're ready to view the level, change the wall height to the altitude at which you want the player's viewpoint and then select the Build, Compile BSP and View from the main menu to generate the BSP and walk through it. Then you can exit the 3D mode and return to the editor with the Esc key.

You will continue this process until you have a level that you like. Now, there are some things to keep in mind. First, the editor will generate both a floor and a ceiling from the floor tiles you lay down. The ceiling will be a mirror reflection of the floor, but it's rendered with the height of the highest wall in your level. Additionally, I suggest that you save your work before trying to compile it—when dealing with complex levels, it tends to get hung sometimes.

BSP Editor File Format

Now that you have an idea of how to use the editor, let's talk about how the level data is stored. The file format has the extension .LEV, and is an ASCII format that is human-readable for the most part. It is composed of a header, the wall list, and the floors. Here's a sample of the file of a single square room, as shown in Figure 13.31. The name of file is `BSPEXAMPLE01.LEV` and can be found on the CD.

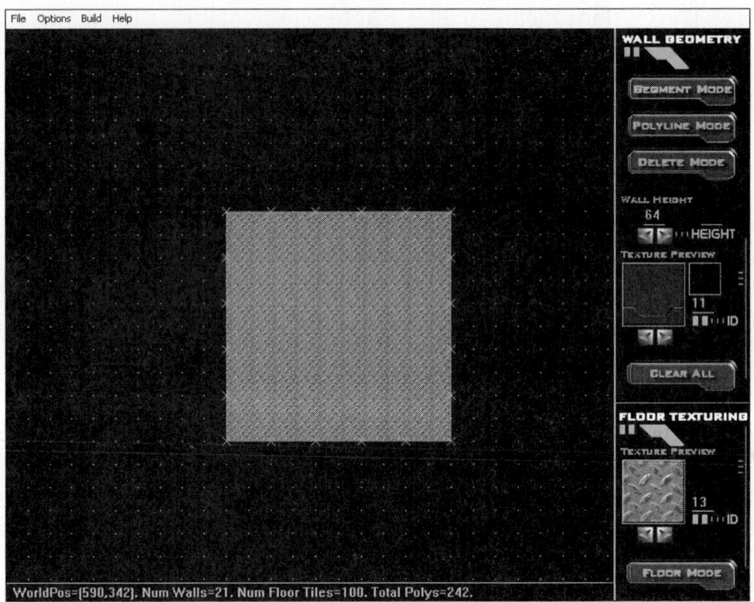

FIGURE 13.31 A sample room file.

```
Version: 1.0

NumSections: 2

Section: walls

NumWalls: 20

240 192 288 192 0 128 11 65535 4169
288 192 336 192 0 128 11 65535 4169
336 192 384 192 0 128 11 65535 4169
384 192 432 192 0 128 11 65535 4169
432 192 480 192 0 128 11 65535 4169
480 192 480 240 0 128 11 65535 4169
480 240 480 288 0 128 11 65535 4169
480 288 480 336 0 128 11 65535 4169
480 336 480 384 0 128 11 65535 4169
```

```
480 384 480 432 0 128 11 65535 4169
480 432 432 432 0 128 11 65535 4169
432 432 384 432 0 128 11 65535 4169
384 432 336 432 0 128 11 65535 4169
336 432 288 432 0 128 11 65535 4169
288 432 240 432 0 128 11 65535 4169
240 432 240 384 0 128 11 65535 4169
240 384 240 336 0 128 11 65535 4169
240 336 240 288 0 128 11 65535 4169
240 288 240 240 0 128 11 65535 4169
240 240 240 192 0 128 11 65535 4169

EndSection

Section: floors

NumFloorsX: 27
NumFloorsY: 24

-1 -1 -1 -1 -1 -1 -1 -1 -1 -1 -1 -1 -1 -1 -1 -1 -1 -1 -1 -1 -1 -1 -1 -1 -1 -1-1
-1 -1 -1 -1 -1 -1 -1 -1 -1 -1 -1 -1 -1 -1 -1 -1 -1 -1 -1 -1 -1 -1 -1 -1 -1 -1-1
-1 -1 -1 -1 -1 -1 -1 -1 -1 -1 -1 -1 -1 -1 -1 -1 -1 -1 -1 -1 -1 -1 -1 -1 -1 -1-1
-1 -1 -1 -1 -1 -1 -1 -1 -1 -1 -1 -1 -1 -1 -1 -1 -1 -1 -1 -1 -1 -1 -1 -1 -1 -1-1
-1 -1 -1 -1 -1 -1 -1 -1 -1 -1 -1 -1 -1 -1 -1 -1 -1 -1 -1 -1 -1 -1 -1 -1 -1 -1-1
-1 -1 -1 -1 -1 -1 -1 -1 -1 -1 -1 -1 -1 -1 -1 -1 -1 -1 -1 -1 -1 -1 -1 -1 -1 -1-1
-1 -1 -1 -1 -1 -1 -1 -1 -1 -1 -1 -1 -1 -1 -1 -1 -1 -1 -1 -1 -1 -1 -1 -1 -1 -1-1
-1 -1 -1 -1 -1 -1 -1 -1 -1 -1 -1 -1 -1 -1 -1 -1 -1 -1 -1 -1 -1 -1 -1 -1 -1 -1-1
-1 -1 -1 -1 -1 -1 -1 -1 -1 -1 13 13 13 13 13 13 13 13 13 13 -1 -1 -1 -1 -1 -1-1
-1 -1 -1 -1 -1 -1 -1 -1 -1 -1 13 13 13 13 13 13 13 13 13 13 -1 -1 -1 -1 -1 -1-1
-1 -1 -1 -1 -1 -1 -1 -1 -1 -1 13 13 13 13 13 13 13 13 13 13 -1 -1 -1 -1 -1 -1-1
-1 -1 -1 -1 -1 -1 -1 -1 -1 -1 13 13 13 13 13 13 13 13 13 13 -1 -1 -1 -1 -1 -1-1
-1 -1 -1 -1 -1 -1 -1 -1 -1 -1 13 13 13 13 13 13 13 13 13 13 -1 -1 -1 -1 -1 -1-1
-1 -1 -1 -1 -1 -1 -1 -1 -1 -1 13 13 13 13 13 13 13 13 13 13 -1 -1 -1 -1 -1 -1-1
-1 -1 -1 -1 -1 -1 -1 -1 -1 -1 13 13 13 13 13 13 13 13 13 13 -1 -1 -1 -1 -1 -1-1
-1 -1 -1 -1 -1 -1 -1 -1 -1 -1 13 13 13 13 13 13 13 13 13 13 -1 -1 -1 -1 -1 -1-1
-1 -1 -1 -1 -1 -1 -1 -1 -1 -1 13 13 13 13 13 13 13 13 13 13 -1 -1 -1 -1 -1 -1-1
-1 -1 -1 -1 -1 -1 -1 -1 -1 -1 13 13 13 13 13 13 13 13 13 13 -1 -1 -1 -1 -1 -1-1
-1 -1 -1 -1 -1 -1 -1 -1 -1 -1 -1 -1 -1 -1 -1 -1 -1 -1 -1 -1 -1 -1 -1 -1 -1 -1-1
-1 -1 -1 -1 -1 -1 -1 -1 -1 -1 -1 -1 -1 -1 -1 -1 -1 -1 -1 -1 -1 -1 -1 -1 -1 -1-1
-1 -1 -1 -1 -1 -1 -1 -1 -1 -1 -1 -1 -1 -1 -1 -1 -1 -1 -1 -1 -1 -1 -1 -1 -1 -1-1
-1 -1 -1 -1 -1 -1 -1 -1 -1 -1 -1 -1 -1 -1 -1 -1 -1 -1 -1 -1 -1 -1 -1 -1 -1 -1-1
-1 -1 -1 -1 -1 -1 -1 -1 -1 -1 -1 -1 -1 -1 -1 -1 -1 -1 -1 -1 -1 -1 -1 -1 -1 -1-1
-1 -1 -1 -1 -1 -1 -1 -1 -1 -1 -1 -1 -1 -1 -1 -1 -1 -1 -1 -1 -1 -1 -1 -1 -1 -1-1

EndSection
```

The file format begins with the version of the file, which in this case is 1.0. The next element is the number of sections. Currently all files have two sections (the walls and floors), but we are going to build on this format, so the number of sections field leaves things open-ended. I hate parsing a file to find out how many things I need to parse! I like to be told. So this is a nice feature for your own file format—tell the reader what's coming. Anyway, next are the sections. They can be anything, and are always of the form

```
Section: "section name"
.
.
.
EndSection
```

where the dots represent the data and can be anything you want. The section name information tells your parser what to look for. In this case, we have two section types, `walls` and `floors`. The wall section is first, and has the field

```
NumWalls: 20
```

This indicates the number of walls that are to be read in line by line. Each wall is composed of seven values (for now) and has this format:

```
x0.f y0.f x1.f y1.f elev.f height.f text_id.d color.d attr.d
```

Where `x0.f`, `y0.f`, `x1.f`, and `y1.f` are the endpoints of the line segment, `evel.f` and `height.f` are the elevation and height of the wall (elevation is currently unused and is always 0), and finally `text_id.d`, `color.d`, and `attr.d` are the texture ID, color, and attributes, respectively.

NOTE

.f means floating point, and .d means integer.

For example, the first wall defined in `BSPEXAMPLE01.LEV` is

```
240 192 288 192 0 128 11 65535 4169
```

which means a wall segment from (240, 192) to (288, 192) with an elevation of 0.0, a height of 128.0, a color of RGB 255.255.255 and attributes of 4169, which means it's flat-shaded, two-sided, and in 16-bit color.

After the wall section is parsed, the `EndSection` keyword is reached and the floor section begins.

```
Section: floors
```

The first two lines define the size of the game world in tiles:

```
NumFloorsX: 27
NumFloorsY: 24
```

The floor tiles are stored as single integers that each represent the texture ID of the tile. If the tile has a value of -1, there is no floor tile there. Values greater than or equal to zero are considered texture indices. The engine parses them, and based on their position in the matrix, generates an `OBJECT4DV2` constructed of a polygon mesh, where each floor tile is a texture-mapped pair of triangles.

That's all there is to the file format. The cool thing is that you can make changes with an ASCII editor, and we can easily add more functionality with the `Section` and `EndSection` commands, so it's very flexible.

The Level Editor Program

The level editor is a typical hacked-together program, and is in no way meant to be an illustration of clean programming. Nevertheless, it gets the job done, and we will use it to add more features for future BSP-related demos (if there are any). The level editor has a set of functions that it needs to perform for the level editing to take place that might seem easy, but are truly a pain to get working. Let's briefly discuss them.

The GUI is the first problem. I had to write a button handler that allows mouse clicks, dragging, and drawing in the editor area. The problem with this is that the mixture of DirectX and GDI/Win32 menus and so forth caused me to have to let Windows handle the mouse. This means that mouse events come into the `WinProc()`, rather than through DirectInput (yuck), so I have to buffer them and then read them out in the `Game_Main()` loop. Additionally, because I am using DirectX to render the display, DirectX and our system like rendering the display 30 times a second. In other words, drawing on the window is really happening in real time, and is being redrawn in real time—it's not static imagery. This is an issue, and when designing an editor, you must decide whether you are going to update your display in real time or not.

The next issue is the drawing of the walls and floors. I used lines, and scaled bitmaps to represent the walls and floor textures, but placing everything and getting the mouse to point to where you think you're pointing it is always a bit troublesome. Additionally, the 2D screen is supposed to represent a 3D top-down x-z view of a left-handed system, and I had to pick a scale and a size to scale the 2D data to when converting to 3D. This was another semi-arbitrary design decision along with the grid size, among other things.

Finally, I needed a secondary data structure to represent the walls and floors while editing, loading, and saving, rather than the more complex `BSPNODEV1`. I used nothing more than this:

```
// the bsp line type that represents single 2d lines
typedef struct BSP2D_LINE_TYP
    {
```

```
int id;       // id of line
int color;     // color of line (polygon)
int attr;     // line (polygon) attributes (shading modes etc.)
int texture_id;  // texture index
POINT2D p0, p1;  // endpoints of line

int elev, height; // height of wall

} BSP2D_LINE, *BSP2D_LINE_PTR;
```

This is totally for the editor and has nothing to do with 3D, but simply helps to represent the 2D editor world. And of course, the floor tiles are nothing more than a 2D array of integers:

```
int floors[BSP_CELLS_Y-1][BSP_CELLS_X-1];
```

When the Build, Compile BSP and View command is executed from the main menu, a couple of things happen. First, the walls are converted from the `BSP2D_LINE` format preceding into a linked list of `BSPNODEV1`s. This is accomplished by the function `Convert_Lines_To_Walls()`, which is too long to list, but basically converts the 2D wall list to a 3D set of polygons and stores them as a single linked list of `BSPNODEV1`s. Then the root is passed to `Bsp_Build_Tree()`, which builds the tree.

Only one thing is left: the floors and ceiling. The floors are the only mesh that needs be generated. As the ceiling is just the floor translated, we can use the same `OBJECT4DV2`. In any case, the function

```
int Generate_Floors_OBJECT4DV2(OBJECT4DV2_PTR obj, // pointer to object
       int rgbcolor,     // color of floor if no texture
       VECTOR4D_PTR pos,  // initial position
       VECTOR4D_PTR rot,  // initial rotations
       int poly_attr);   // the shading attributes we would like
```

generates the floors. It takes a pointer to the output object, along with the base color of the floors under the texture (RGB white usually), a position, rotation, and polygon attributes you want the entire floor mesh to have. Then it generates the floor. For example, if you passed in the floor tiles shown in Figure 13.32, the output would be a mesh something like Figure 13.32b, with the texture coordinates, attributes, the works all set up.

After the floors are generated, the editor switches state to 3D mode and is, more or less, the standard 3D demo model loop we have been using. The only difference is that the loop never uses sorting or z-buffering, and inserts the geometry into the rendering list in this order each frame:

1. Floors
2. Ceiling

3. BSP tree
4. Repeat

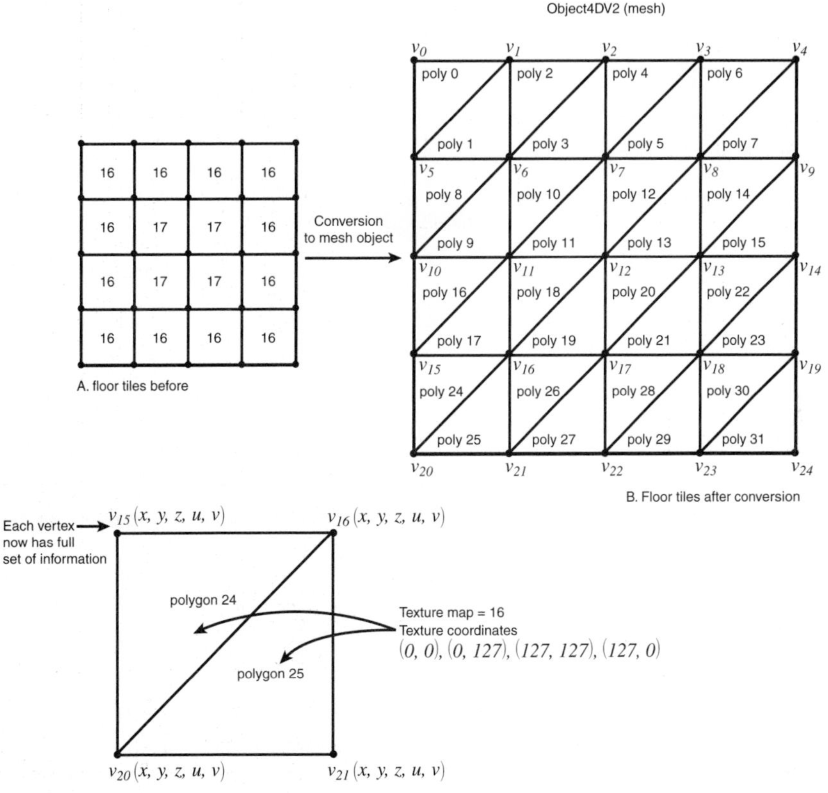

FIGURE 13.32 Floor-to-mesh conversion.

This guarantees the correct ordering because the floors and ceilings are always "behind" the BSP, as long as the BSP has the correct order (which we know it will have, because we are inserting it by walking the tree with an in-order, back-to-front walk).

Limitations of the BSP

Although the BSP tree is an incredibly fast way to determine polygon rendering orders during runtime, it isn't without its limitations. The first limitation is that the universe must be semi-static. This means that polygons can't rotate, but they can translate in some cases. For example, take a look at Figure 13.33. Here we see a view of two walls. If we slide one of the walls upward as in Figure 13.33b, the order remains the same. Thus, a BSP tree can be used if there are polygon translations in the plane that the polygon exists in, but that's it.

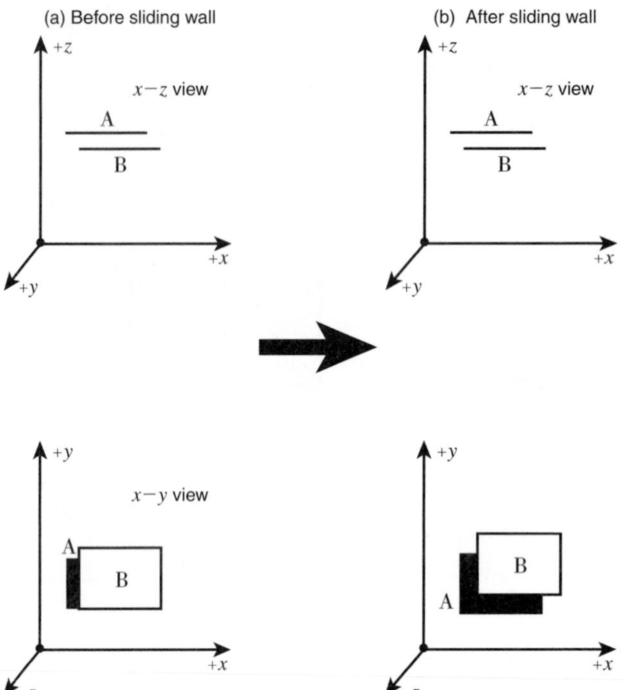

FIGURE 13.33 The BSP tree is invariant for y-axis translations of the walls.

The second main limitation is that BPS trees are definitely not the way to go for simulators or games with a lot of motion, because the BSP would have to be regenerated each frame. But all in all, the BSP tree is a very elegant solution to the rendering problem, and can be used in situations were the player is moving through a generally static environment. However, no one ever said that BSP trees have to be for rendering only.

Zero Overdraw Strategies Using BSP Trees

The BSP can be used to determine the exact back-to-front order of polygons in a scene for a given set of static polygons from any viewpoint. This is determined by walking the BSP tree with a modified in-order recursive search and visiting nodes in a back-to-front order with the painter's algorithm.

The problem with this is that in many cases, the same pixel will get painted over and over. This is a huge problem with any sorting or z-buffering algorithm. The correct rendering order is determined, and the same pixel can be overdrawn many times (in some cases, hundreds of times).

For example, take a look at Figure 13.34. Here we see a set of polygons in the x-z plane. The polygons are already sorted back to front, or they are rendered with a Z-buffer. In the case of using z-sorting, each pixel that makes up the smallest polygon in the set will be overwritten by the remaining polygons. Each pixel in the next largest polygon will be overwritten by each larger polygon, and so forth. In this simple example, we see that each pixel of each of the far z polygons is going to be redrawn by one to (*n*-1), where *n* is the number of polygons in this set.

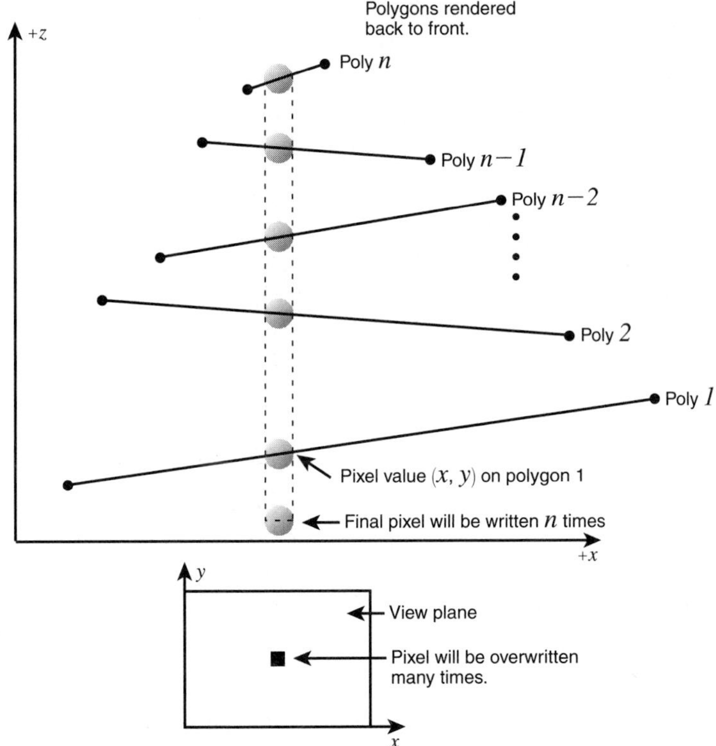

FIGURE 13.34 The worst case of overdraw.

The z-buffered version is equally bad. Not only are the pixels overwritten (if the z values are nearer), but no matter what, the Z-buffer is *always* tested. So although the overdraw isn't as bad in general for a Z-buffer, the Z-buffer read/write is. Again, we're getting killed by drawing pixels, or testing pixels that can't possibly be seen. There must be a solution to this overdraw problem, right?

Here come BSP trees to the rescue. Instead of traversing the BSP tree in a back-to-front order, we traverse it in a front-to-back order. Then for each polygon we visit, we mask data writes to the screen or use the polygons as a stencil buffer of sorts. In theory, this is great, but in reality, we are just z-buffering again, (testing a condition and then writing a pixel if the condition passes or fails). Sure, we don't do the overdraw, but we still perform the test for every single pixel. The question is, can we take advantage of the front and back order in a more intelligent way? The answer is always yes, but I like to have some sort of exciting build-up <BG>. Anyway, one possibility is to use scan line rendering.

Scan line rendering works as follows: Instead of drawing a polygon pixel by pixel, we only compute the endpoints of each scan line and then place them into a linked list or data structure. Basically, we just disable the inner loop that rasterizes each scan line and instead place the endpoint data into a list. Then for each polygon, we insert the scan lines into this list and sort the list on x and y, so we have a collection of scan line buckets for each possible screen row. Thus, we have separated the problem into a collection of scan lines. The process is shown in Figure 13.35. If we can solve the problem for a single scan line, we have solved it for all of them, so let's start there.

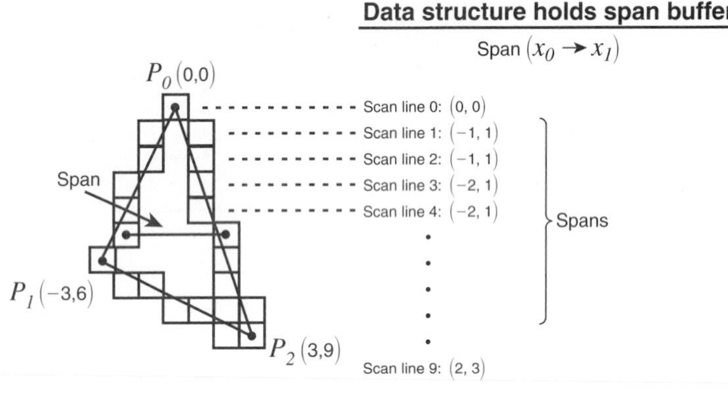

FIGURE 13.35 Storing polygons as scan lines rather than rasterizing them on the fly.

Let's look at a number of cases, as shown in Figure 13.36, of what can happen:

- In case 1, a single scan line is inserted into row n. In this case, that scan line is rasterized, and we are done.
- In case 2, two scan lines are inserted into row n, but they don't overlap in X. Therefore, once again we simply rasterize each of them, because they can't possibly overlap.
- In case 3, one scan line is inserted, followed by another, but the second scan line is completely obscured by the first scan line; thus the second scan line is summarily discarded and there is no overdraw.
- In case 4, one scan line is inserted, followed by another, but this time, the second scan line added is only partially obscured by the first scan line. We therefore clip the second scan line to the first, and then draw only the remaining part of the second scan line—again, zero overdraw.

These cases illustrate the types of conditions that arise and how they might be handled. Using the scan line technique with front-to-back rendering, you can achieve perfect rendering with zero overdraw. However, there is a price to pay, and that's the amount of time it takes to determine whether a scan line is either obscured or clipped and then merging the scan lines. Getting the algorithm to actually work in practice with texture coordinates and so on isn't easy to do. Nevertheless, even a crude version that doesn't remove 100% of the overdraw might be worth the effort.

*Case 1: A single scan line is inserted into Row N buffer

*Case 2: Two scan lines are inserted into Row N buffer

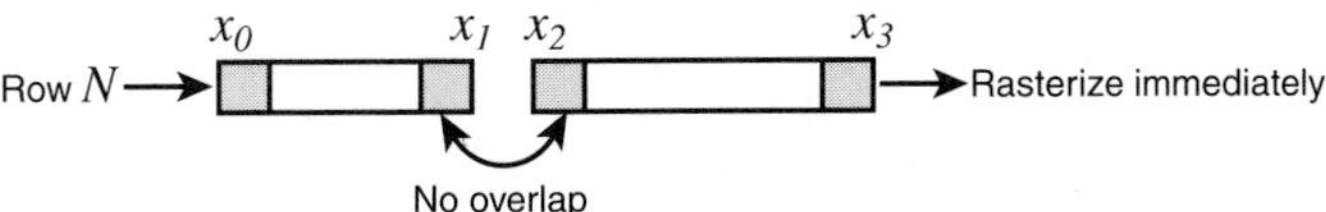

*Case 3: Two scan lines are inserted, but 2nd is occluded by first

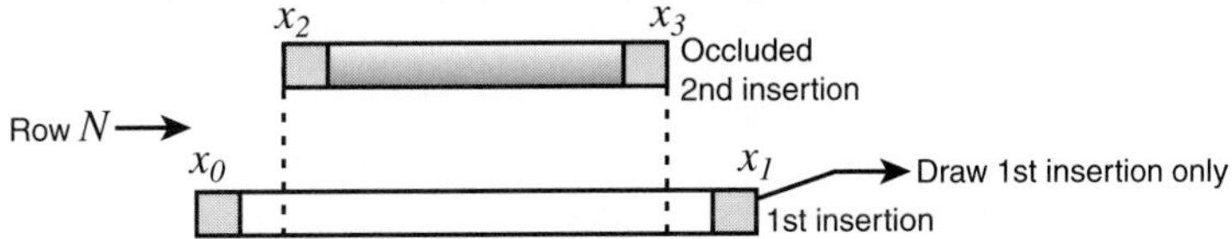

*Case 4: Two scan lines inserted with partial clipping

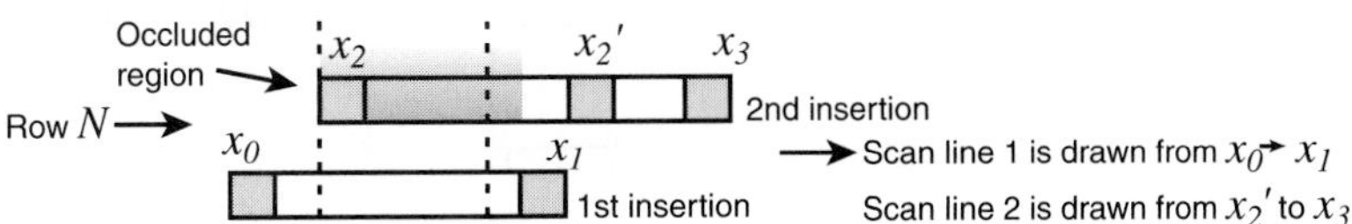

FIGURE 13.36 Potential scan line span cases.

BSP Trees for Culling

One of the most powerful properties of any spatial partitioning algorithm is the capability to quickly cull large amounts of polygonal information from the rendering pipeline. In fact, in most cases, this along with collision detection is the only reason people use BSP trees these days. BSP trees' convex subspace properties, along with their linear time traversal, make them ideal for large-scale culling. We are going to look at two different culling techniques that can be applied to BSP trees: *back-face culling* and *frustrum culling*. The former is more of an atomic culling, whereas the latter is more of a high-level culling that really takes advantage of the BSP structure to shred the polygons that aren't potentially visible.

Back-Face Culling

Even though we simply walked the BSP and inserted the polygons into the rendering list, it's also possible to back-face cull or clip the BSP polygons during the insertion function.

However, in most cases, walls are two-sided, so performing a standard back-face culling operation isn't effective because all faces will pass through the culler. Therefore, a more accurate back-face culling algorithm must be employed if you want to remove back-faces during the insertion scan.

To refresh your memory, take a look at the setup for back-face culling shown in Figure 13.37. As depicted in the figure, the surface normal of the polygon is computed (or referenced, if precomputed), and then the dot product is computed with the normal vector and the vector to the viewpoint. If the angle is greater 90 degrees (the dot product is < 0), the polygon is a back-face. However, as I mentioned, this only works for one-sided polygons.

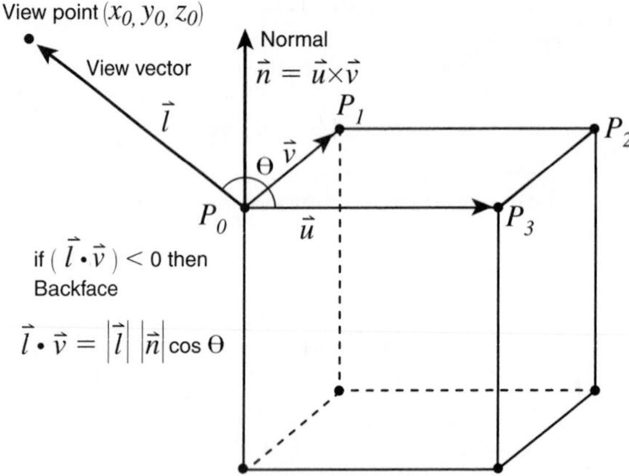

FIGURE 13.37 A detailed analysis of back-face removal.

Additionally, the back-face removal algorithm does *not* take the view direction vector into consideration. For example, take a look at Figure 13.38. Here the angle between the normal and view vector is less than 90 degrees, but if we bring the view direction vector into consideration, we see that even though the standard back-face removal algorithm does not remove the back-face, the polygon is in fact impossible to see.

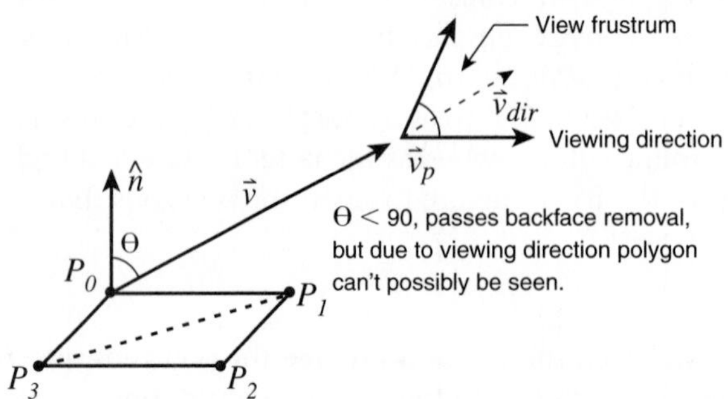

FIGURE 13.38 Back-face removal doesn't take view direction into consideration.

If back-face removal is performed in camera space, this detail disappears, because we know that the orientation of the view vector is always straight down the positive z-axis (0,0,1). So, the back-face cull is correct in this case, and won't let any extra polygons through the pipeline. But the question is, do we want to transform polygons into camera space just to cull them? Of course, the answer is no. Thus we have been culling back-faces in world space, which actually results in extra polygons slipping through behind us that are then trivially removed by the clipping stage.

Therefore, with all that in mind, you see that in the case of a BSP tree where we are for the most part using two-sided polygons, we are going to have to perform a more strict back-face culling if we want it to work during traversal and insertion of the BSP into the rendering list. Of course, we can just ignore this entire optimization, let the rendering list move through the pipeline, and let the rendering list back-face removal function work on it, as usual. However, this is a nice optimization that is going to come in handy in the next section when you cull entire subspaces.

Let's take a look at what we need to know to solve the back-face problem for two-sided polygons in world space based on both the view position and view direction. Figure 13.39 depicts the setup.

We first need to determine what side the viewpoint is on relative to the test polygon. Next we need to compute the angle between the test polygon surface normal and the view vector itself. However, we need to be careful, taking into consideration the field of view of the viewing frustrum. In other words, even if the angle between the positive surface normal and the view direction vector (not to be confused with the view vector, which is the vector from the polygon to the viewpoint) is greater than 90 degrees, the polygon can still be in the field of view. This is true because the field of view "opens" up the valid range of angles that the test polygon can potentially be visible in, as shown in Figure 13.39.

Thus, we need to take the field of view into consideration when carrying out the calculations. We need to compute or use the surface normal of the test polygon, and perform a dot product between it and the view vector to the viewpoint to determine what side the viewpoint is on relative to the polygon's front/back orientation.

After we have determined which side the viewpoint is on, we carry out a second dot product, but this time we perform a dot product with the surface normal of the polygon side we are on and the viewing direction vector. This result is our final determining factor. Moreover, we have two cases: If we are on the front side of the test polygon and (? + FOV/2) > 90, the polygon is visible; otherwise it's a back-face. On the other hand, if we are on the back side of the polygon, then we want to test whether (? - FOV/2) < 90 for visibility. Mathematically, we have the following:

Given:

- $\mathbf{v}_{dir}$ is the view direction vector.
- $\mathbf{v}_{pos}$ is the viewpoint position.

- **n** is the surface normal.
- $\mathbf{v}_{view}$ is the surface to viewpoint vector.
- θ is the angle from the surface normal **n** to the view direction vector $\mathbf{v}_{dir}$.

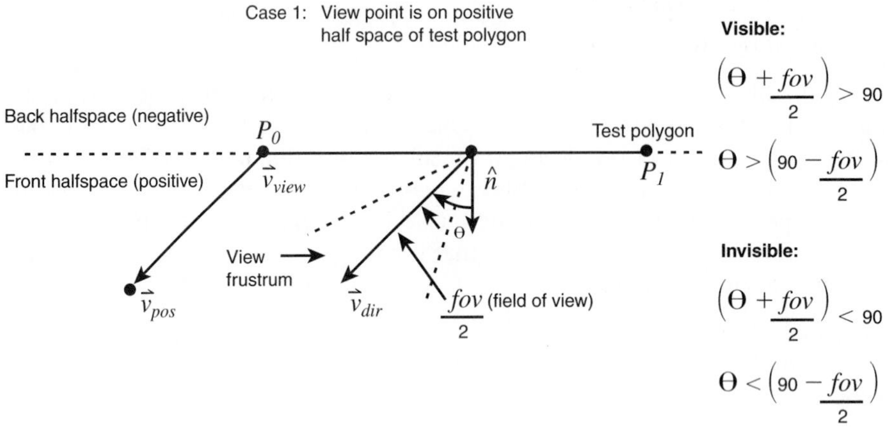

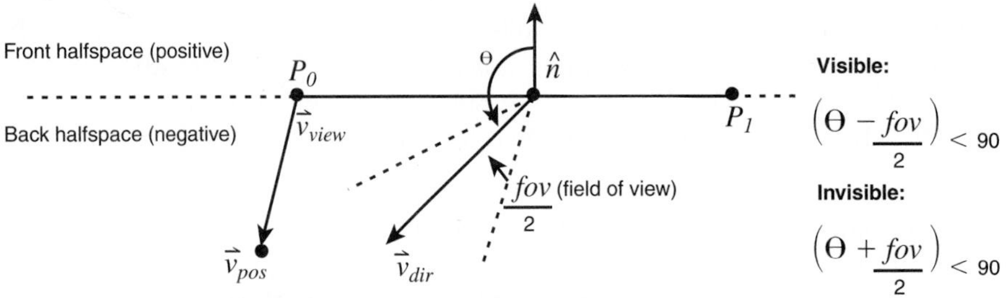

FIGURE 13.39 Setup for full back-face removal with viewpoint and view direction taken into consideration.

Case 1: If the viewpoint v_{pos} is on the front side of the test polygon, that is, if ($\mathbf{n}$. $\mathbf{v}_{view} > 0$), then:

Visibility Condition: (θ + FOV/2) > 90, therefore:

```
n . v_dir = |n| * | v_dir | * cos θ
```

Assume the vectors have been normalized, $|\mathbf{n}| = |\mathbf{v}_{dir}| = 1$, then:

```
n . v_dir = cos θ
```

Taking the inverse cosine of each side, we have:

```
θ = arccosine(n . v_dir)
```

Here we simply compute θ and plug it into the visibility condition, or we can use the converse to detect whether the polygon is culled. However, obviously we can't use `arccosine()` in real time! But I'll get to that in a moment—let's look at the back side case.

Case 2: If the viewpoint v_{pos} is on the back side of the test polygon, that is, if ($\mathbf{n} \cdot \mathbf{v}_{view} < 0$), then:

Visibility Condition: (θ - FOV/2) < 90.

The angle θ is computed similarly to case 1, and simply plugged into the back side visibility condition.

Computing the Inverse Cosine Really, Really Fast If the thought of computing the inverse cosine doesn't make you completely cringe, you must be using a quantum computer, because there is no way we can possibly make a call to the math library function `arccosine()` in real time work. It's time for another trick, or a lookup table, more specifically. Let's talk about what exactly `arccosine()` does first.

`arccosine()` is the inverse cosine, or in other words, given a value x in the interval [-1,1], find a function f(x) such that cos(f(x)) = x. f(x) is said to be the inverse cosine, or *arccosine*. For example:

```
cosine(30) = .866

arccos(.866) = 30 degrees
```

Composing the functions, we get

```
cosine(arccos(.866)) = .866
```

NOTE

These examples are in degrees.

We can create a lookup table to compute arccosine rather easily. We need to map the values [-1,1] into the angles 0–180 using the arccosine as the mapping function. Now, we surely can't use a lookup table with negative or decimal numbers, so we need to shift the range first by adding 1. So, [-1,1] becomes [0,2]. It's then sort of useless to have a table with three elements, so we're going to scale the range so that there's at least one value for each possible angle 0–180. We multiply by 90, for example, and we get the range 90*[0,2] = [0,180]—perfect!

The mapping function is as follows:

```
Input x: [-1,1]
Mapping function f(x) = (x+1)*90 = index
```

Then we use `index` as an index into a lookup table that has the arccosine computed for 180 values equally spaced from [-1,1] but mapped to the range 0–180 always. Figure 13.40 depicts the setup of the lookup table.

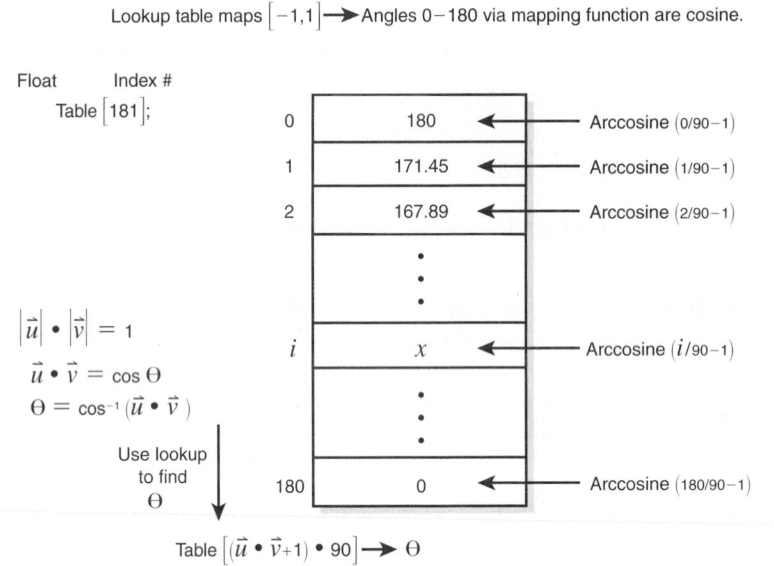

FIGURE 13.40 Inverse cosine lookup table setup.

If we want more accuracy, we increase the mapping; that is, we might break the range of [-1,1] into 360 intervals that still represent the angles 0–180, but now in half-degree angles. I have written software to do all this. First is the storage for the lookup table:

```
float dp_inverse_cos[360+2]; // 0 to 180 in .5 degree steps
          // the +2 for padding
```

So, I am defining a global lookup that has storage for roughly 360 elements (the +2 is so we don't overflow when the 360th or 361st elements are accessed with slight floating-point overflow during the mappings). And to make things easier, I have created the following macro to compute the arccosine of *x*, where *x* is in the range of [-1,1]:

```
#define FAST_INV_COS(x) \
 (dp_inverse_cos[(int)(((float)x+1)*(float)180)])
```

And here is the function that generates the lookup table:

```
void Build_Inverse_Cos_Table(float *invcos,    // storage for table
          int  range_scale) // range for table to span

{
// this function builds an inverse cosine table used to help with
```

```
// dot product calculations where the angle is needed rather than
// the value -1 to 1, the function maps the values [-1, 1] to
// [0, range] and then breaks that interval up into n intervals
// where the interval size is 180/range then the function computes
// the arccos for each value -1 to 1 scaled and mapped as
// referred to above and places the values in the table
// for example if the range is 360 then the interval will be
// [0, 360] therefore, since the inverse cosine must
// always be from 0 - 180, we are going to map 0 - 180 to 0 - 360
// or in other words, the array elements will each represent .5
// degree increments
// the table must be large enough to hold the results which will
// be = (range_scale+1) * sizeof(float)

// to use the table, the user must scale the value of [-1, 1] to the
// exact table size, for example say you made a table with 0..180
// the to access it with values from x = [-1, 1] would be:
// invcos[ (x+1)*180 ], the result would be the angle in degrees
// to a 1.0 degree accuracy.

float val = -1; // starting value

// create table
for (int index = 0; index <= range_scale; index++)
  {
  // insert next element in table in degrees
  val = (val > 1) ? 1 : val;
  invcos[index] = RAD_TO_DEG(acos(val));

  // increment val by interval
  val += ((float)1/(float)(range_scale/2));

  } // end for index

// insert one more element for padding, so that durring access if there is
// an overflow of 1, we won't go out of bounds and we can save the clamp in the
// floating point logic
invcos[index] = invcos[index-1];

} // end Build_Inverse_Cos_Table
```

In the initialization section of your code, make a call to `Build_Inverse_Cos_Table()` with these parameters:

```
// build the inverse cosine lookup
Build_Inverse_Cos_Table(dp_inverse_cos, 360);
```

This tells the function to use the array dp_inverse_cos as storage for the table. The table should cover 360 entries to represent the 0–180 range, or an accuracy of .5 degrees.

To use the function, just use the macro (of course, the macro assumes a table with 362 elements):

```
// x:[-1, 1]
FAST_INV_COS(.5)
```

Now with the macro in hand, we can rewrite the BSP insertion function so that it attempts to cull based on the view direction, as well as the viewpoint.

TIP

Why 362 elements? We need 0–360, so that's 361, but then many algorithms can be sped up if they're not fence posted, and we ignore the case in which they round up to 361 because of floating-point error. However, if the table has a 361st element that's a copy of the 360th element, we get the fence post value for free!

Aligning the View Vector Only one problem remains before we can write the new BSP insertion function: Because we aren't performing the world-to-camera transformation with the world geometry, we don't know the view direction vector. Normally, we use the Euler angles or the UVN representation to transform the world geometry, and then we assume the camera is located at (0,0,0) pointed down the positive z-axis, or in other words, with a direction vector of (0,0,1).

We have a bit of a wrinkle here, because we need the view direction vector. However, we can compute it rather easily on a per-frame basis. We are simply going to transform the vector (0,0,1) by the camera transformation matrix (the inverse, actually), and this will give us the view direction vector. However, we don't need the total transformation including the translation vector—we simply need to rotate the vector (0,0,1) by the rotation angles only. These angles for the Euler model are exactly cam.dir.x, cam.dir.y, and cam.dir.z. Of course, the order of rotation is important, but we have been using the call

```
Build_CAM4DV1_Matrix_Euler(&cam, CAM_ROT_SEQ_ZYX);
```

to build our camera matrix, which means that we need to perform the rotation of the vector in XYZ order (the opposite) in addition to using the non-inverse transformations. In other words, we just take the vector (0,0,1) and rotate it with the XYZ rotation matrix based on the angles cam.dir.x, cam.dir.y, and cam.dir.z. This can be accomplished with a call to

```
MATRIX4X4 mrot;

Build_XYZ_Rotation_MATRIX4X4(cam.dir.x,
              cam.dir.y,
              cam.dir.z
              &mrot);
```

Then we transform the direction vector with the matrix with a call to

```
VECTOR4D vz = {0,0,1,1}; // z = 1, w = 1

Mat_Mul_VECTOR4D_4X4(&vz,
          &mrot,
          &vdir);
```

Finally, we have everything we need. I know this might seem like a lot of work to compute the vectors and remove back-faces when the rendering list back-face removal works perfectly well as is. However, the time lost performing the test is definitely worth the time lost transforming the two extra triangles per quad that will be inserted into the rendering list, not to mention the wasted time performing the world-to-camera transformation on them. Remember, while in the BSP tree, all walls are still quads, and haven't yet been broken into two triangles, so we should leverage that if possible.

In conclusion, although this entire section has been important, it's more of a segue to the next section on frustrum culling, which will enable us to remove entire sub-trees at once in the BSP. In any event, the new function that has the additional capability to remove back-faces during the BSP insertion process is shown here (prototype only):

```
void Bsp_Insertion_Traversal_RemoveBF_RENDERLIST4DV2(
          RENDERLIST4DV2_PTR rend_list, // rendering list
          BSPNODEV1_PTR root, // root of BSP tree to insert
          CAM4DV1_PTR cam,    // camera
          int insert_local=0); // insertion flags
```

The function has the exact same calling convention as the previous version without support for back-face removal, so you can interchange them without worry. The code that performs the back-face removal is identical to the work we have derived in the past few pages, and to save space I have omitted the listing, but it's on the CD with everything else in this chapter.

As a demo of the function, take a look at DEMOII13_2.CPP¦EXE. It's the standard level editor, but when you enter into 3D mode, you'll see a display indicating the number of polygons entering the pipeline from the BSP insertion function at the bottom of the screen. Use the C key to toggle the culling mode between the standard BSP insertion function and the new one, and then look at the number of polygons entering the rendering list decrease as you experiment with different viewpoints.

NOTE

To compile the demo yourself, you will need `DEMOII13_2.CPP`, along with all the library modules `T3DLIB1-11.CPP|H` in addition to the DirectX .LIB files. Additionally, you will need the resource file for the menus and so on—this file is named `DEMOII13_2.RC`. Also, make sure to use the `DOOM01.LEV` file for experimentation.

NOTE

As you run the demo, you might be surprised that when you walk outside, you still see polygons being inserted from the BSP into the rendering list. This is actually correct, because we are culling planes, not finite polygons. If we want to take the culling to the next level, not only do we have test whether the plane is visible, but that the endpoints of the polygon are in the view frustrum. This is a bit much, and starts to result in diminishing returns. However, you might want to try it, as shown in Figure 13.41.

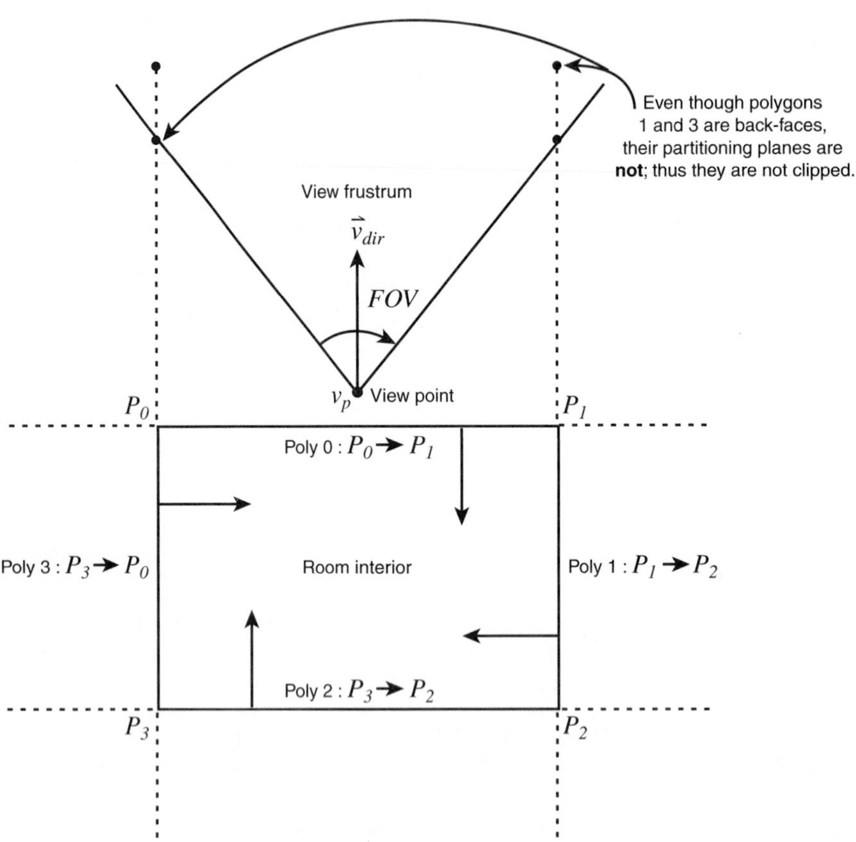

FIGURE 13.41 Polygons can be back-faces, but we are culling partitioning planes.

Frustrum Culling

A more powerful culling operation can be used on BSP trees than trivial back-face culling. The irony is that we already wrote it when we wrote the back-face culling function—we just didn't finish it. Take a look at Figure 13.42 to see what I mean. The viewpoint is on the negative half space of the partitioning plane. Because of the view direction's orientation, the plane is definitely not visible, but more importantly, neither is the entire positive half space behind the partitioning plane!

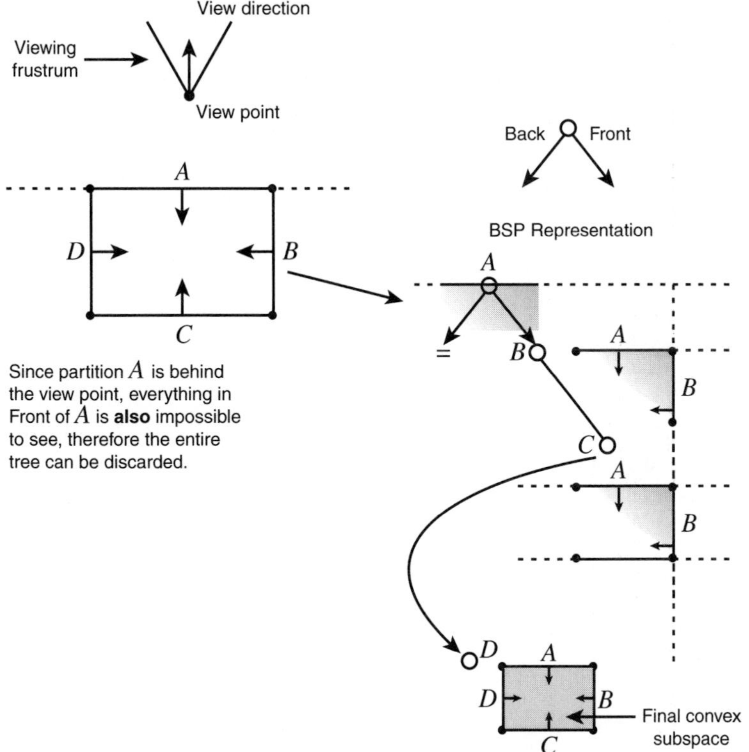

FIGURE 13.42 Full frustrum culling.

In other words, we can kill the entire sub-tree from the current node and not even consider it! Think how powerful this is: After a partitioning plane that we are in front of (or behind) is found, and we can't possibly see the plane from our current orientation, then not only that plane, but the entire sub-tree behind it can be culled. This is the true power of the BSP tree, with its property of representing space carved up into convex subspaces.

To further convince you, take a look at Figure 13.43. Here we see a simple example of two rooms (assume we have constructed a BSP tree, of course). Additionally, we see the viewpoint in room 1, but the wall behind the player and the entire contents of room 2 are invisible. We can determine this immediately by noting that wall 3 is invisible, and thus the entire subspace behind it is, too. Therefore, we no longer need to traverse any further.

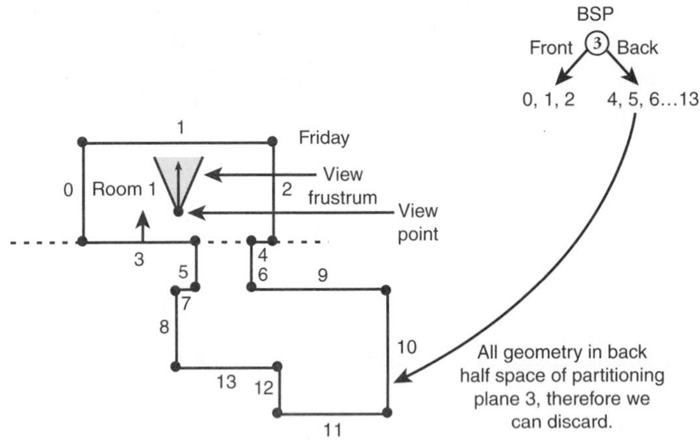

FIGURE 13.43 Frustrum culling entire rooms.

Implementing the frustrum culling is actually pretty easy—we are already done more or less, and we can either write a separate function that tags nodes that are culled and all their children, or we can do it on the fly, as we did with the back-face culler. Because there's really no need to walk the tree twice, we are going to integrate the frustrum culling with the BSP insertion as we did the back-face culling. The strategy will be to simply enclose the recursive calls to visit the front or back trees within the culling operation. In other words, after we have determined that a polygon is culled, then we know that anything behind it is also culled—thus there is no need to make the recursive call to traverse the backfacing sub-tree. This is the only change—a single line of code.

The new function that implements this is the following:

```
void Bsp_Insertion_Traversal_FrustrumCull_RENDERLIST4DV2(RENDERLIST4DV2_PTR
➥rend_list,
                                    BSPNODEV1_PTR root,
                                    CAM4DV1_PTR cam,
                                    int insert_local=0);
```

This is called identically to the previous two; the only difference is that it performs both back-face culling and frustrum culling.

As a demo of the function, take a look at `DEMOII13_3.CPP|EXE`. This is the standard level editor, but when you enter into 3D mode you will see a display indicating the number of polygons entering the pipeline from the BSP insertion function at the bottom of the screen. Use the C key to toggle the culling mode between the standard BSP insertion function and the new one, and then look at the number of polygons entering the rendering list decrease as you experiment with different viewpoints.

You will notice that in this case, the number of polygons are even fewer that that of the back-face culling version, because entire subtrees are being culled, and polygons within the subtrees that have visible planes are not slipping through, as they were with the more simplistic back-face culling function alone.

NOTE

To compile the demo yourself, you will need `DEMOII13_3.CPP`, along with all the library modules `T3DLIB1-11.CPP|H` in addition to the DirectX .LIB files. Additionally, you will need the resource file for the menus and so on. This file is named `DEMOII13_3.RC`. Also, make sure to use the `DOOM01.LEV` file for experimentation.

One final note: It's of course possible to make the frustrum culling even more powerful by both considering just the polygons in the viewing frustrum rather than just the planes they lie in, and by using a finite viewing volume and enabling view frustrum clipping. This way, after you determine that a polygon is beyond the near or far clipping planes, you can discard the entire back-facing subtrees, as shown in Figure 13.44.

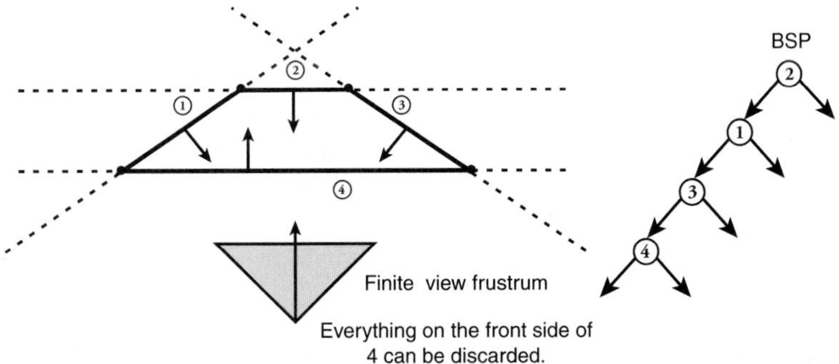

FIGURE 13.44 Using the finite view frustrum for aggressive frustrum clipping.

This stuff really gets me excited—I can't wait to do some more culling! Seriously though, you should be able to see that the possibilities are limitless with BSP trees. They do have their limitations, but if you can use them in your system, they are powerful allies.

BSP Trees for Collision Detection

Last but not least, let's briefly touch on collision detection using BSPs (we will cover the subject in more depth when we discuss collision detection formally). A BSP tree can be used for a quick determination of collision with the player or other objects. In most cases, bounding volumes such as cubes, spheres, or cylinders are used to enclose the player or non-player-character mesh, but the point is that after the collision surface is constructed, the BSP is used for quick determination of potential collisions.

The advantage of the BSP is that it enables very fast traversal of the 3D space by "pushing" the object's origin down the BSP until the object is within the convex subspace of a leaf node. This operation takes an average $\log_2 n$ steps, but can take n steps for a completely unbalanced tree. This is true because during each iteration, as the viewpoint or object center is being compared to nodes, half the volume of the 3D space is discarded until the test node is determined to be within a lead node.

After the test point is within the leaf node, the geometry can be used to test against the BSP geometry to see whether there is (or will be) a collision with the bounding object by expanding the bounding volume, or by expanding the BSP itself along the normal vector lines—that is, by pushing each partitioning plane along its normal until there is a collision.

Anyway, this is just a little bit to get you thinking about it.

Integrating BSP Trees and Standard Rendering

This section is only important if you want to walk BSP trees to compute the exact perfect painter's algorithm back-to-front (or front-to-back) rendering order. If you're not interested in using this property, integration is irrelevant. If you are, read on.

Integration with Z-sorting

Integrating BSP trees with z-sorting is rather tricky because the BSP tree has perfect order, and the z-sorting is going to result in a re-ordering of your already perfect polygon order. However, in the case of the BSP level editor demo, I did something like this. I knew that the floors and ceiling both were always "under" the wall geometry; in other words, like a painter, I could always render them first, then render the walls in BSP order. Thus, for simple layered scenes, you can use z-sorting for the background and the foreground, as long as you don't sort into the BSP polygons.

For example, in the case of the BSP demo, the floor polygons are all coplanar, so it didn't matter what order they were rendered in, because they can't possibly occlude one another. However, let's say that they had some ordering low to the ground (that is, some height to them—maybe they're bumpy). In this case, a near polygon with a bump in it must be drawn after a far polygon without a bump. We can still handle this with a hybrid approach—we simply load the rendering list with all the polygons for the floor, z-sort them, and then insert the BSP tree with its perfect order. As long as none of the BSP geometry is smaller than the floor geometry (meaning there's a tiny BSP wall that could be occluded by something at the floor level), then we can render the rendering list back-to-front and once again get perfect order.

Personally, I don't like to use z-sorting with BSP trees because it's nearly useless for anything but floors, ceilings, or geometry you have tagged as being completely in front or behind the BSP. Z-buffering is the better approach.

Integration with Z-Buffering and Movable Objects

The whole point of BSP tree rendering is to compute the proper back-to-front rendering order (with a perhaps a PVS to minimize polygon overdraw) and then draw the polygons *without* a Z-buffer. However, this approach doesn't work for movable objects because we surely can't recompute the BSP tree every time an object moves around (this could take seconds, minutes, or even hours with complex levels).

> **NOTE**
>
> If a polygon within a BSP plane moves within the same plane that it's defined in and it does not cut into another convex subspace that a different BSP node represents, you can safely move the polygon in said plane. This is great for things like doors, elevators, and so on.

Alas, we must find a way to integrate the BSP rendering with z-buffering. However, if we z-buffer the BSP tree, we have lost out on the whole point of the BSP rendering, which is to use back to front order with an in-order walk. The trick is as follows: We create special rasterizers in which we can turn the z-comparision functions off, and simply always write to the Z-buffer. Instead of doing a *read-compare-write* per pixel, we only do a write per pixel (a *write-through*). Therefore, we get a Z-buffer out of it that we can use at a later stage. The reason we are guaranteed that the Z-buffer is correct is that the back-to-front in-order walk of the BSP gives us the correct image, and thus the correct Z-buffer, because we are always overwriting the Z-buffer back to front. This is shown in Figure 13.45.

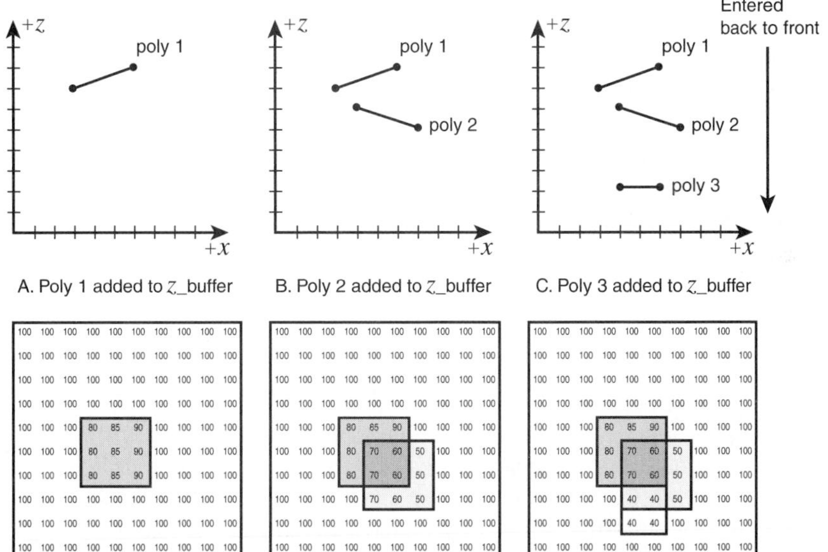

FIGURE 13.45 A back-to-front walk always overwrites the Z-buffer with closer z values.

For example, here's an excerpt from the flat-shaded z-buffering function `Draw_Triangle_2DZB_16()` before the write-through functionality has been added:

```
// draw span
for (xi=xstart; xi<=xend; xi++)
  {
  // test if z of current pixel is nearer than current z buffer value
  if (zi < z_ptr[xi])
    {
    // write textel assume 5.6.5
     screen_ptr[xi] = color;

    // update z-buffer
    z_ptr[xi] = zi;
    } // end if

   // interpolate u,v,w,z
   zi+=dz;
   } // end for xi
```

After removing the z comparison and allowing straight write-through:

```
// draw span
for (xi=xstart; xi<=xend; xi++)
  {
  // write thru z buffer
  // write textel assume 5.6.5
  screen_ptr[xi] = color;

  // update z-buffer
  z_ptr[xi] = zi;


  // interpolate u,v,w,z
  zi+=dz;
  } // end for xi
```

Now we are ready to render in the movable objects using the Z-buffer. In this phase, we actually use the standard read-compare-write algorithm, but we don't clear the Z-buffer. We use the z image that was generated during the BSP pass and then draw our objects and so on as usual, with z-buffering using the z image from the BSP. We get perfect BSP ordering, with movable objects able to hide behind walls, interpenetrate, and more.

The New Write-Through Z-Buffer Software To add z write-through functionality, we need to add this capability to the rasterization functions (just a few of them for demos), and we need a new rendering context constant to select the write-through Z-buffer, along with a new rendering context function to steer the logic to the new rasterization function—ouch! Let's start with the new constant to select a rendering context mode of Z-buffer write-through:

```
// use a Z buffer, but with write thru, no compare
#define RENDER_ATTR_WRITETHRUZBUFFER      0x00000008
```

Next we need some rasterization functions to support z-buffering write-through. In essence, I simply removed the Z-buffer test logic and just let the code write the Z-buffer without testing the Z-buffer. Of course, we have about 40–50,000 lines of rasterizer code, so I didn't want to go nuts—I only supported flat-shaded, Gouraud-shaded, affine textured with constant lighting, and affine textured with flat shading. The following are the new prototypes. They only differ in the string `WT` (which stands for write through) inserted in the middle of the previous function names:

Function:

```
void Draw_Gouraud_TriangleWTZB2_16(POLYF4DV2_PTR face, // ptr to face
       UCHAR *_dest_buffer,   // pointer to video buffer
       int mem_pitch,      // bytes per line, 320, 640 etc.
       UCHAR *_zbuffer,     // pointer to z-buffer
       int zpitch);       // bytes per line of zbuffer
```

Description: `Draw_Gouraud_TriangleWTZB2_16()` draws a Gouraud-shaded triangle with write-through z-buffering. The polygon is not textured and is drawn with pure color only.

Function:

```
void Draw_Triangle_2DWTZB_16(POLYF4DV2_PTR face, // ptr to face
        UCHAR *_dest_buffer,  // pointer to video buffer
        int mem_pitch,     // bytes per line, 320, 640 etc.
        UCHAR *_zbuffer,    // pointer to z-buffer
        int zpitch);      // bytes per line of zbuffer
```

Description: `Draw_Triangle_2DWTZB_16()` draws a constant/flat-shaded triangle with write-through z-buffering. The polygon is not textured and is simply drawn with a single color.

Function:

```
void Draw_Textured_TriangleGSWTZB_16(POLYF4DV2_PTR face, // ptr to face
           UCHAR *_dest_buffer,  // pointer to video buffer
           int mem_pitch,     // bytes per line, 320, 640 etc.
           UCHAR *_zbuffer,    // pointer to z-buffer
           int zpitch);      // bytes per line of zbuffer
```

Description: `Draw_Textured_TriangleGSWTZB_16()` draws a Gouraud-shaded affine texture mapped triangle with write-through z-buffering.

Function:

```
void Draw_Textured_TriangleFSWTZB2_16(POLYF4DV2_PTR face, // ptr to face
           UCHAR *_dest_buffer,   // pointer to video buffer
           int mem_pitch,      // bytes per line, 320, 640 etc.
           UCHAR *_zbuffer,     // pointer to z-buffer
           int zpitch);       // bytes per line of zbuffer
```

Description: `Draw_Textured_TriangleGSWTZB_16()` draws a flat-shaded affine texture mapped triangle with write-through z-buffering.

Function:

```
void Draw_Textured_TriangleWTZB2_16(POLYF4DV2_PTR face, // ptr to face
         UCHAR *_dest_buffer,    // pointer to video buffer
         int mem_pitch,       // bytes per line, 320, 640 etc.
         UCHAR *_zbuffer,      // pointer to z-buffer
         int zpitch);        // bytes per line of zbuffer
```

Description: `Draw_Textured_TriangleWTZB2_16()` draws a constant-shaded affine texture mapped triangle with write-through z-buffering.

Every one of the functions works exactly as the previous version they update, except that they don't test z values, they only overwrite them. It's the caller's responsibility to make sure that polygons are rendered back to front before normal z-buffered movable objects are rendered in.

Last but not least we need a new rendering context function that has a code block to handle the new Z-buffer mode of

```
RENDER_ATTR_WRITETHRUZBUFFER
```

The new function has the following prototype:

```
void Draw_RENDERLIST4DV2_RENDERCONTEXTV1_16_2(RENDERCONTEXTV1_PTR rc);
```

It's also identical to the previous version `Draw_RENDERLIST4DV2_RENDERCONTEXTV1_16()`, except that it has the added support for the new Z-buffer write-through mode and knows how to call the write-through Z-buffer rasterizers.

Finally, here's an example of setting up the rendering context for a write-through Z-buffer pass:

```
// set up rendering context for 1/z buffer
rc.attr = RENDER_ATTR_WRITETHRUZBUFFER |
     RENDER_ATTR_TEXTURE_PERSPECTIVE_AFFINE;
```

```
// clear the z buffer
Clear_Zbuffer(&zbuffer, (32000 << FIXP16_SHIFT));

rc.video_buffer   = back_buffer;
rc.lpitch      = back_lpitch;
rc.mip_dist     = 0;
rc.zbuffer     = (UCHAR *)zbuffer.zbuffer;
rc.zpitch      = WINDOW_WIDTH*4;
rc.rend_list    = &rend_list;
rc.texture_dist  = 0;
rc.alpha_override = -1;

// render scene
Draw_RENDERLIST4DV2_RENDERCONTEXTV1_16_2(&rc);
```

The single change other than the call to `Draw_RENDERLIST4DV2_RENDERCONTEXTV1_16_2()` is the flag `RENDER_ATTR_WRITETHRUZBUFFER` rather than the flag `RENDER_ATTR_ZBUFFER`. However, notice that the Z-buffer is still cleared before the pass. The pass writes through the Z-buffer, but it still needs the Z-buffer to be initialized before writing; otherwise, the *next* pass will be incorrect when objects are inserted with z-buffering on.

That's really all there is to adding objects. The steps are as follows:

1. Initialize the Z-buffer.
2. Render all static geometry with Z-buffer write-through mode. This pass must be back-to-front, because the Z-buffer will not consider an incorrect rendering order.
3. Render all movable geometry with the Z-buffer on.
4. Display the frame.

Example of Moving Objects

As an example of moving objects and the BSP, I have used the demo level editor to make a version that loads a Tron recognizer (at least that's what it's supposed to be) and moves it around the game universe in a circular path. The direction of the moving object is always aligned to the tangent of its circular path, as shown in Figure 13.46.

The only change to the working demo is the addition of the new write-through mode, and in the `Game_Main()` code of the demo is the code to move the object around. This is just a hack and not part of the normal demo, but I added it so you can see that the technique does work. The name of demo is `DEMOII13_4.CPP|EXE`, and Figures 13.47a and b are screenshots of it in action (wireframe and solid modes). It is identical to the level editor demo; however, when you go into 3D mode with the Build, Compile BSP, and View menu item, the object that is z-buffered into the final display will be floating around. You can use any level you have constructed (if any), but just use `DOOM01.LEV` if you don't have any yet. To run the demo, the first step is to select File, Load .LEV File. Then select **Build**, Compile BSP, and View. Also, try toggling the Z-buffer on and off with the Z key.

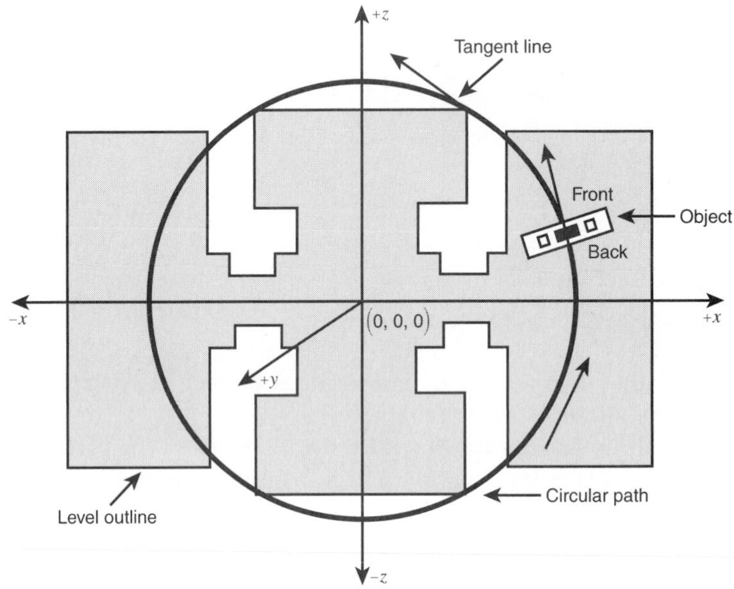

FIGURE 13.46 Z-buffered object path and orientation.

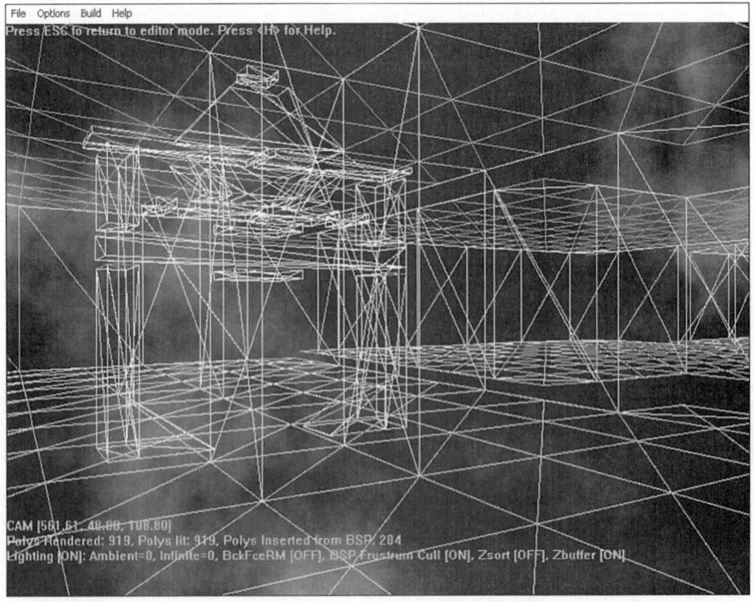

FIGURE 13.47A Screenshot of the wireframe z-buffered demo in action.

FIGURE 13.47B Screenshot of the solid z-buffered demo in action.

NOTE

To compile the demo yourself, you will need `DEMOII13_4.CPP`, along with all the library modules `T3DLIB1-11.CPP¦H` in addition to the DirectX .LIB files. Additionally, you will need the resource file for the menus and so on. This file is named `DEMOII13_4.RC`. Also, make sure to use the `DOOM01.LEV` file for experimentation.

Potentially Visible Sets

The theme that we are seeing repeatedly is that avoiding processing geometry that is invisible to the viewpoint (outside the viewing frustrum) is a good thing. We learned that the BSP tree itself can be used to perform large-scale culling of BSP nodes because at any node if the node is beyond the view frustrum, anything behind the node is also beyond the frustrum and can be culled trivially. This way, huge amounts of geometry can be removed.

However, this still leaves us with the visible geometry. If there are 10,000 polygons in the viewing frustrum, even with zero overdraw, we must still process the polygons and determine that they don't need to be drawn. What if we could determine that we don't need to draw them before we even start? That is, at any given viewpoint, what if we had a list of all the polygons that are *potentially* visible? We can perform whatever culling we want on large-scale geometry, but then when we run down the list of polygons that are still in the view frustrum, we refer to this potentially visible set (PVS) of polygons that uses our viewpoint as the index, and only draw polygons in the list.

There are a billion ways to implement this idea—with BSPs, octrees, or nothing at all—so I will focus on the idea for a moment. Let's say that you have a level editor and have constructed some rooms as shown in Figure 13.48.

A. Room geometry visibility from Room 1

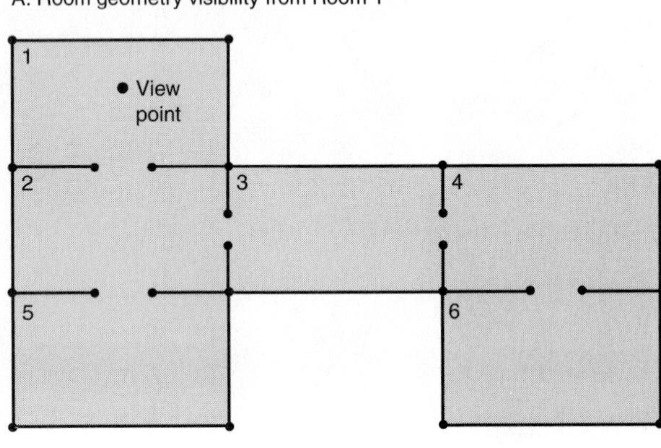

B. Visibility data structure

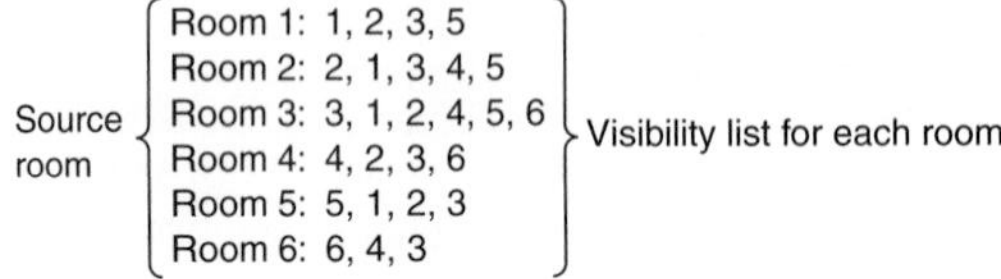

FIGURE 13.48 Room-to-room visibility.

In the figure, there are six different axis-aligned rooms, each room is constructed of a number of different polygons, and there might even be objects in the rooms made of polygons. For simplicity's sake, let's assume that the mesh data is static. Now, let's create a PVS for room 1. The question is, if we were in room 1, what rooms are potentially visible? We can immediately see that from room 1, rooms 1, 2, 3, and 5 can be seen through the doorways.

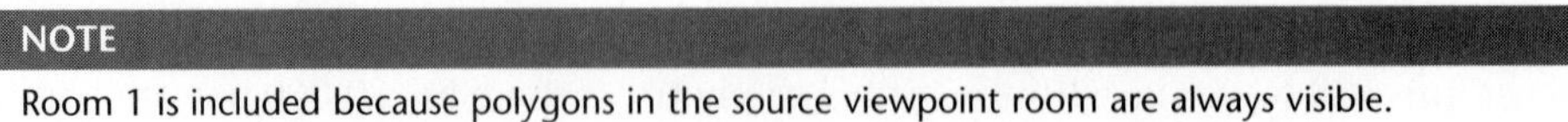

NOTE

Room 1 is included because polygons in the source viewpoint room are always visible.

As a second example, imagine that we have a hierarchical example in which each one of these rooms is stored in a data structure with a list of all rooms potentially visible from each source room, as in Figure 13.48b. In this case, there's a list or array of rooms that are visible from any source room. Of course, another strategy would be to have an adjacency matrix that is m×m, where *m* is the number of rooms and the value in the matrix i,j (*i* is the column, and *j* is the row) determines whether there is visibility from room i to j. For example, recoding our example with an adjacency matrix looks like Figure 13.49.

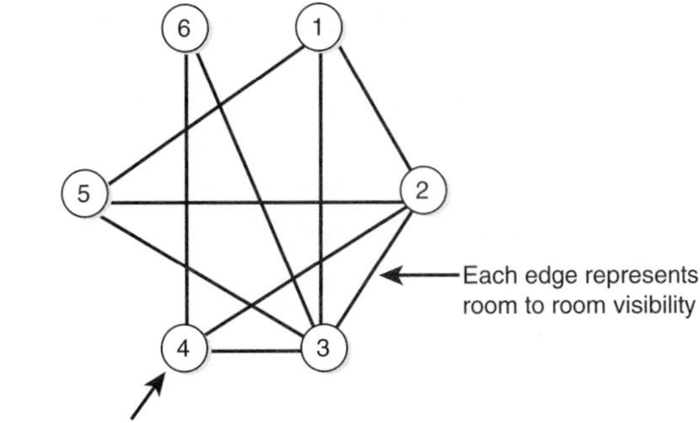

FIGURE 13.49 Adjacency graph for rooms.

Here is the level encoding:

```
    i1 i2 i3 i4 i5 i6


j1  1  1  1  0  1  0

j2  1  1  1  1  1  0

j3  1  1  1  1  1  1

j4  0  1  1  1  0  1

j5  1  1  1  0  1  0

j6  0  0  1  1  0  1
```

For the most part, we see that from any source room, say room i, most of the other rooms in the level are potentially visible. Room 6 seems to have the least number of rooms visible from it. At this point, we have a PVS that has a room "granularity," or in other words, we must include all the polygons from the source room to potentially visible rooms. This is okay, and we will come back to this point in a moment. For now, let's talk about using the PVS.

Using the Potentially Visible Set

Assuming that you have created a level that contains a set of rooms, each room with an encoded visibility of the other rooms that are potentially visible, then PVS is easy to take advantage of to reduce overdraw. For example, suppose you have used a BSP or other spatial partitioning system to represent each individual room. You have culled everything you can to the viewing frustrum, including using BSP culling to remove large parts of the environment. At this point, you are ready to pass polygons down the pipeline for clipping, lighting, projection, back-face removal, and so forth. Here's where the PVS comes into play. You first determine what room you are in—this can be done using the BSP, or simply by sectorizing the game level and determining what cell you are in. Let's say that you are in room 6, with a view frustrum as shown in Figure 13.50.

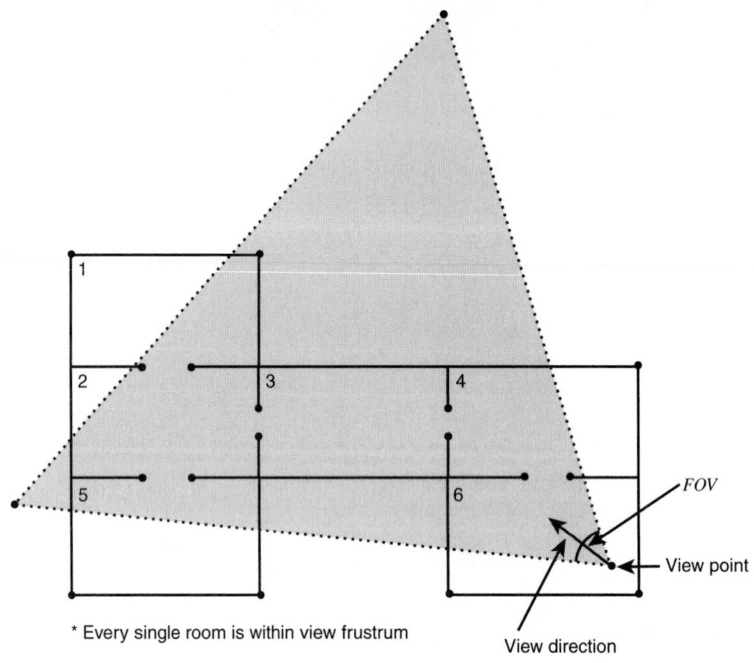
1
2
3
4
5
6
FOV
View point
View direction
* Every single room is within view frustrum
* With PVS only rooms 6,4,3 will be considered.

FIGURE 13.50 Using the PVS to cull geometry.

Even with BSP culling, the entire model database would probably pass into the rendering list. However, by using our PVS, we can remove nearly all the overdraw! It's so easy, it feels like cheating, but all you have to do is look up the current room that you're in—room 6 in this case. The next step is to access your data structure that contains the PVS for the room. In this case, we used an adjacency list, and we need to look at column 6 in the adjacency list and read out all the rooms that are potentially visible, which are rooms 3, 4, and 6 (the source room is always included in the PVS list, of course).

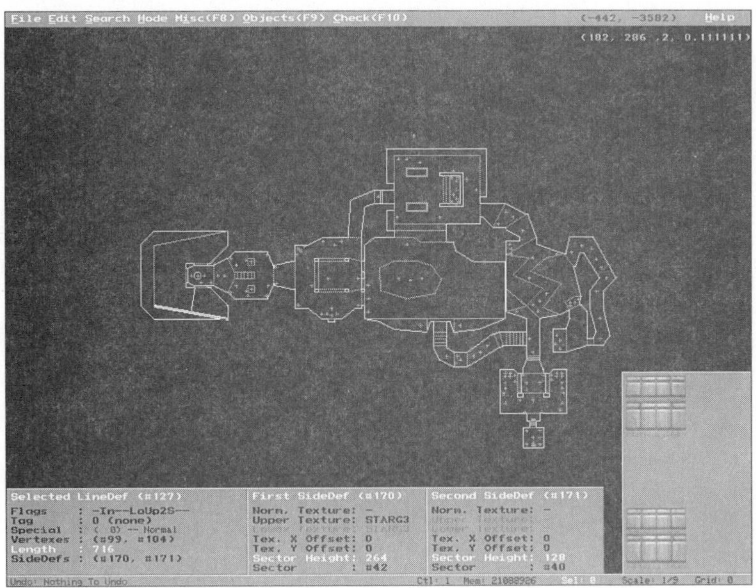

FIGURE 13.51 Even a simple *Doom* level can create an overdraw nightmare.

The amazing thing is that from the viewing frustrum's point of view, every single room is visible, and thus nearly every polygon would be passed into the pipeline. Some would be clipped for sure, but many polygons that are completely occluded by the walls of room 6 would be drawn, or at least z-tested.

This is totally unacceptable, and if you have a level something like that shown in Figure 13.51 (a simple *Doom* level) with many rooms, I think you can see how this overdraw could pile up very quickly, with the screen redrawing many times. Therefore, the use of the PVS is an incredible tool to speed up rendering, and to minimize overdraw to nearly zero.

Some polygons are going to be partially occluded, but will still be included in the PVS. This is totally acceptable, and in my experience, an overdraw of 50–150% is the worst case scenario with a general PVS as we have outlined. Without the PVS, an overdraw of 10–20% can happen very easily with large levels. So, the PVS alone can increase our frame rate or decrease our polygon count by an order of magnitude.

Other Encodings of the Potentially Visible Set

When the size of a level gets large (10,000 to 1,000,000 polygons), the size of the PVS can become rather huge, and its storage and access can likewise become huge. In our simple example, we used two methods: either an explicit list attached to each room, sector, or BSP node, or an adjacency list. Either of these techniques will work fine when you are encoding a room-to-room PVS (a PVS that encodes room visibility rather than individual polygon visibility), but that's the next level of PVS.

If we want to encode specific polygons that are visible from any viewpoint, we can once again use a sectoring technique where we encode the viewpoint as a specific sector and then compute each and every polygon visible from that viewpoint. Finding the visible polygons is a geometry problem that I will return to, but it's more or less based on light and line-of-sight visibility, so it's not that hard. However, let's focus for a moment on the encoding of such large data.

Assuming that we have a level that has 50,000 polygons and there are 100 rooms, then we have a couple of choices. We can encode PVS visibility based on which room the viewpoint is in, or we can compute it based on sectorizing the gameworld into little squares or cubes, and then for each and every room or sector, we construct a list of potentially visible polygons for the entire world. Figure 13.52 illustrates this in the abstract.

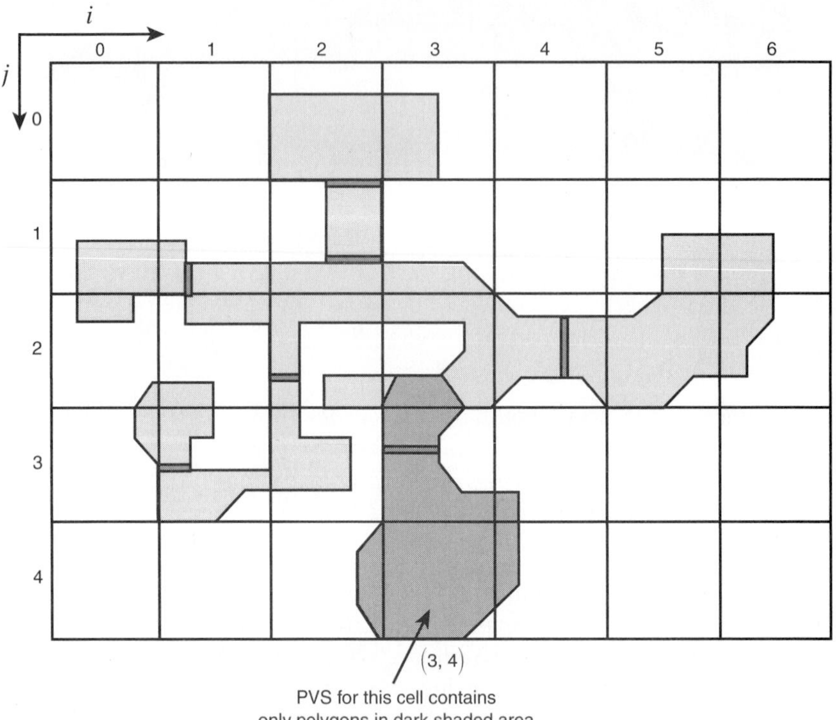

FIGURE 13.52 Sector-based PVS.

Now, there's a definite trade-off here. If we encode the PVS as pointers or indices, we need to have one for each and every polygon that's in the PVS for a given room or sector. For example, with our hundred-room example, out of the 50,000 polygons, on average 1,000 of them are visible from each room. That means that the PVS will have on the order of:

(100 rooms) × (1000 polygons potentially visible) × (4 bytes) = 400K bytes to encode the entire PVS.

This is actually not too bad. Of course, we could do a little better by encoding each index by three bytes, rather than a full 4-byte, 32-bit integer. On the other hand, it might be more productive to encode the PVS in another way.

For example, instead of using the explicit index list, let's use an encoding such that instead of using the polygon index as an element of the PVS, we create an ordered bit list from polygon 0...n, and tag each bit if the polygon is visible. In other words, say there are 10 polygons in the world and I want to say that for room n I can see polygons 0, 5, and 6. The PVS would look like this:

Room n PVS: 0, 0, 0, 0, 0, 1, 1, 0, 0, 0

Of course, with this bit encoding, we can't skip indices because they are in order, but it does save on memory, so let's take a look at what this encoding takes using single bits to encode each potentially visible polygon:

(100 rooms) × (50,000 polygons) × (1 bit per polygon) = 625,000 bytes!

Ouch—but I said it was smaller! It is, but you need to compress it. A simple run-length encoding where you compress runs of zeros or ones can compress the PVS by a factor of 1 to 20 in most cases. Thus, the real storage is around 50KB in most cases.

In conclusion, it's up to you how you store the PVS—as polygon indices, or an explicit list of enabled polygons in an ordered list. Both have their pros and cons. Personally, I am a memory hog, so I like the index list methods.

More Robust Computation of the PVS

So far we have been avoiding the details of computing the PVS, not because it's hard, but because there is no "correct" way to do it. There are a number of approaches, so let's take a look at a couple of the most popular techniques.

Tool-Based PVS

The first and easiest method to create a PVS is to do it manually. For example, let's say you've a created a tool to draw 2D worlds that are extruded into 3D worlds. Each room has a set of polygons that make it up, and after you have modeled the 2D world, you enter another stage of the model where you manually create an adjacency list or other supporting structure that indicates which rooms are visible from which. This could be done via line drawing, flood filling, or whatever. The point is, why make it hard? If you are working with small worlds with 10–50 rooms, you can very quickly draw the adjacency information visually room by room and be done with it, without complex algorithms.

This is the method I suggest when you are starting out. Simply encode the PVS manually or with a tool, so you can work on using the PVS rather than creating it. Because the PVS is usually created offline, time is not an issue. However, if you are continually changing your gameworld, it would be a pain to keep redoing the PVS. Because the PVS is only an optimization, you can wait until the very end when you are totally happy with your gameworld to create the PVS.

Portal-/Light-Based PVS

The next and more common method of generating a PVS is by using cell-to-cell portal visibility, or by using the properties of light to "find" potentially visible polygons from any room, sector, or cell. For example, take a look at Figure 13.53. Here we see a room example with each door marked—these are referred to as *portals*.

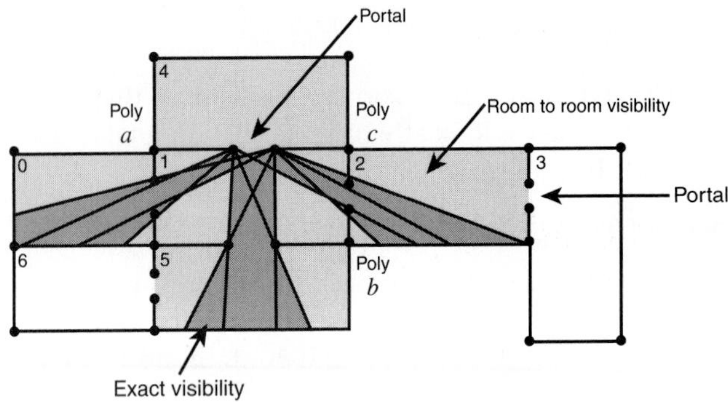

FIGURE 13.53 Portal visibility with polygon resolution.

Additionally, each room is now constructed of separate polygons, so we are looking for a PVS that includes polygons. Referring to the figure, we see the room-to-room visibility originating from room 4 with the lightly shaded areas. We are looking for a more precise visibility, so we can tag individual polygons. This can be obtained by computing every single ray path from room 4 to the remaining shaded rooms that have a completely unobscured path. Doing this manually would nearly be impossible, but if we think of the portal from room 4 as a light source and then trace the light cone using the other portals as occluders, we will get exactly what we are looking for, as shown by the dark areas in Figure 13.53.

As you see, I have ray-traced out the light cones from the portal of room 4 through the adjacent room 1 into the other potentially visible rooms, and where the light strikes is the total volume, or *wedge*, that is potentially visible from room 4. Any polygon edge that falls within the area or volume of these shaded areas is part of the PVS for room 4. Additionally, we must add room 1 to the list in its entirety, because it's immediately adjacent to room 4 and there is no "in-between room" from the portal boundaries.

With this new technique, we have minimized the PVS from room 4 from containing all the geometry from rooms 0, 1, 2, and 5, to containing only the geometry that is intersected or contained within the light cones using the portal of Room 4 as the light source. Thus, in this case, from room 4 there is something like 30–50% fewer polygons we need to include in the PVS. For example, polygons a, b, and c are not in the PVS, even though they would have been included in the room-to-room PVS before with our more crude method.

This technique also extends to objects in the room. They are also simply polygons, and you test to see whether they too are within the light cones (or *anti-penumbras*, as some call them). Of course, the PVS is only good for static objects, and if room objects move around, they might become invisible, but the PVS will continue to keep them in view. However, you can also create "shadow" areas, whereby you take sectors within a room that are shadowed for an object, meaning that an object is only in the PVS while it's in said sector. If it moves out of the sector, it's occluded.

As you can see, you can go crazy with all kinds of cool optimizations, special cases, and so forth with the concept of PVS—only your imagination will stop you. However, the main point to remember is that computation of the PVS is offline, so you can take as long as needed to come up with the polygons that are visible from any given viewpoint or room.

This brings me to another example: What if you don't have a room-based world with cleanly defined portals or doors you can use as light casters? This is no problem—you just have to get creative. One possible technique involves sectorizing the world into squares or cubes (depending on whether it's mostly level-based or completely arbitrary 3D). In either case, you randomly select thousands, tens of thousands, or hundreds of thousands of random viewpoints in the world, or you select them uniformly based on how the player can move. Then for every single viewpoint, you try to cast rays to each and every polygon in the world. If you can cast a ray unobstructed by at least one ray from the sample viewpoint to at least one vertex, you can be quite certain that that particular polygon is visible from that viewpoint, and you can add the polygon to the viewpoint's PVS. This is shown in Figure 13.54.

Final Thoughts on PVS

Potentially visible sets are an absolute necessity for any game with a large polygon database. They are nearly free to use in runtime, and have at most a medium-sized memory footprint, even with the crudest encoding. PVSs work hand in hand with BSP trees, octrees, portals (in particular), and more. Computing the PVS can be quite computationally intensive, depending on how accurate you want the PVS to be. However, I have shown that a simple tool-based PVS, or a portal-based/light casting PVS can be computed with a little geometry and ray tracing. Finally, after the PVS is computed, it can be encoded as an adjacency matrix, list, or one-to-one bit encoding.

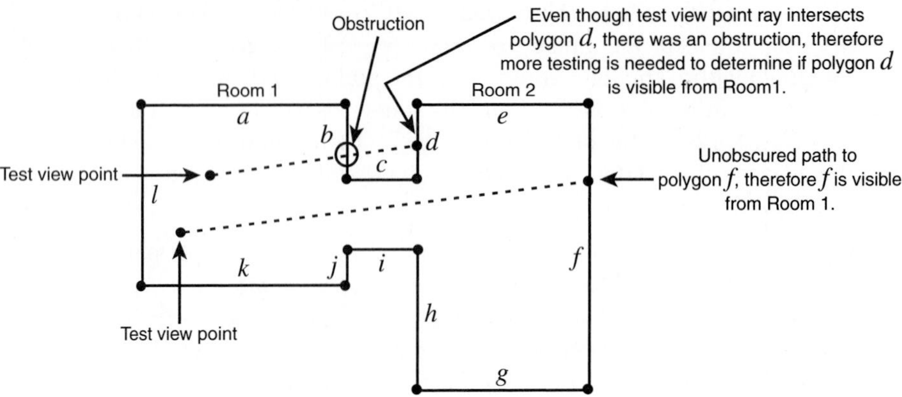

FIGURE 13.54 Ray casting to determine visibility.

Portals

Portals have gotten a lot of attention in the past few years. The funny thing is that they have been around since the 60s more or less, so all you coders that think you invented them—think again <BG>. Two of the most famous portal games are *Descent* and *Duke Nukem 3D*, shown in Figures 13.55 and 13.56. *Descent* is a 3D flying game with six possible directions of flight, and allows the player to fly around a seemingly endless 3D maze of tunnels. There's lighting, texture mapping, and really cool effects. However, what's amazing is that the worlds are rendered so quickly. *Duke Nukem 3D* is another amazing 3D game from the mid-90s. It also features real-time lighting, texture mapping, multiple levels, stairs, moving objects—the list goes on and on—also a product of portal technology. Portals are hardly magical—they are nothing more than a PVS strategy implemented in real time.

The point is, even if you have a level with a billion polygons, if you only need to draw a couple hundred each frame, you will have an amazing game that can seemingly handle enormous amounts of data. The trick is in rendering only what you can see. Portals are based on the fact that if you have a cell- or room-based environment, if you can tag the "portals" to adjacent rooms, you can use a clever technique to compute a PVS on the fly. Here's how it works. Take a look at Figure 13.57, which depicts yet another room example, but this time there are only five rooms and I have marked each doorway as a portal.

FIGURE 13.55 *Descent* uses portals to the max.

FIGURE 13.56 *Duke Nukem 3D.*

Disregarding any objects that might be within the rooms, let's see whether we can compute the visible polygons on the fly using the doorway portals. The first step is to create at the very least a room-to-room visibility list offline. We do this because there's no reason to even invoke the portal logic if we can't see from room 1 to room 5. This time, let's use adjacency lists rather than a matrix, as shown in Figure 13.57b. After we have these lists, we are ready to go in real time. Here are the steps:

1. From the current viewpoint, compute which room/cell the viewpoint is in. Save this information.
2. Render the polygons in the current room using whatever technique (BSP, z-buffering, z-sorting, and so on) you want to use.
3. **IMPORTANT:** For each portal leading out of the current room (we have a list, remember), *adjust the viewing frustrum by adding the clipping planes that define the portal doorway*, and then recurse into the next room in the list and draw the polygons in that room.

A. Room Geometry

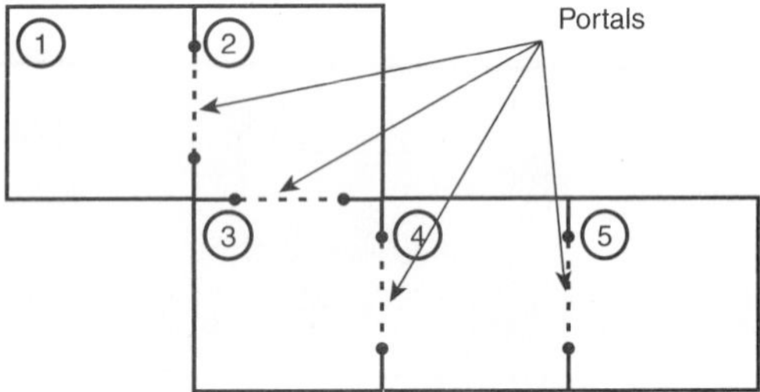

B. Adjacency Lists

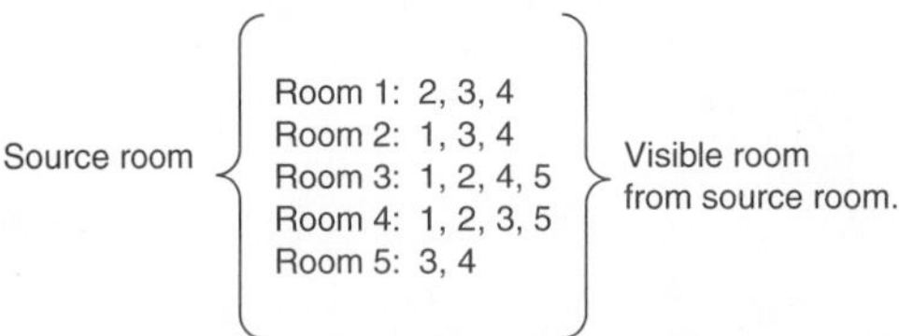

FIGURE 13.57 Offline computation of room-to-room visibility for portals.

I have highlighted the important part, but let's review the process before delving into the clipping details. You begin with the room you're in, then you render it, and then you recursively traverse the room's adjacency list via the portal list, but each time you enter into a room from a previous room, you only render what's visible through the portal from the source room to the destination room. In other words, you clip your view from the source room to the destination room to the exit portal. This is shown in Figure 13.58.

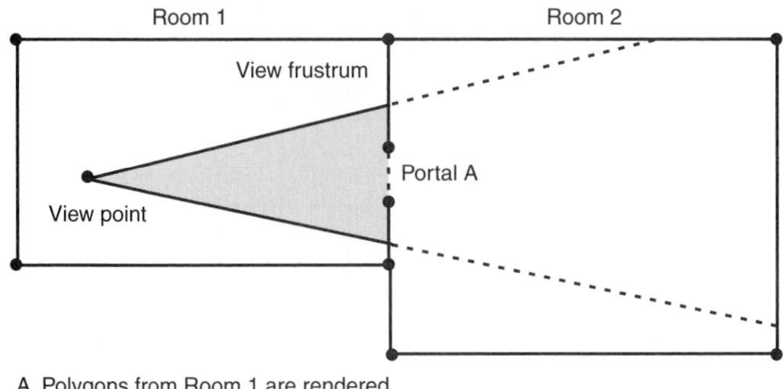

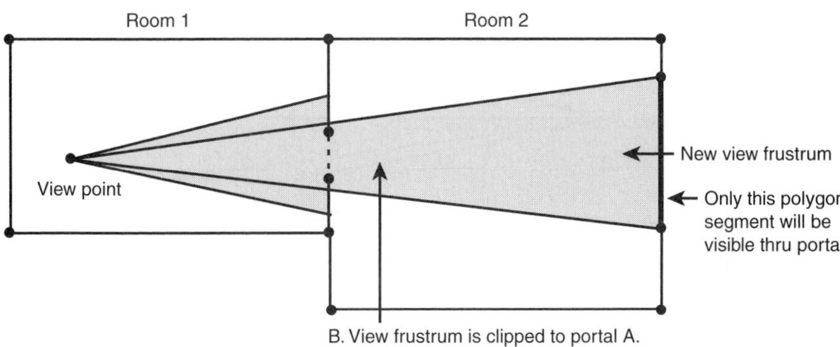

FIGURE 13.58 A simple two-room example of portal clipping and traversal.

Let's try an example with exactly two rooms in 2D to see the process. In Figure 13.58, we begin with an adjacency list from room 1 to room 2, meaning that both rooms are visible to each other through the portal. The viewpoint happens to be in room 1, so we render all the polygons in room 1 with the full viewing frustrum. Now we recurse into room 2, because it's visible through the portal marked A. However, we adjust the viewing frustrum to the clipping planes defined by the original viewpoint clipped by the portal geometry (in this case 2D). The new viewing frustrum is shown in Figure 13.58b. Now only the polygons in this new viewing frustrum are visible to the original viewpoint, and any other polygons are invisible and thus won't be rendered. Therefore, because we are clipping to the portal geometry itself, by definition the viewpoint in room 1 will only see *exactly* what's visible in room 2 through the portal (doorway).

There are two problems with portals that we can see right off the bat. First, the portal technology still doesn't give a PVS; it only creates a new clipping volume or viewing frustrum for us. However, if we have a BSP or octree, we can cull entire rooms or cells to the current portal, which saves time. The second problem is more difficult. Every time we recurse into the next room and add the portal geometry to the current viewing frustrum, we have to adjust the viewing frustrum from a nice four sides (plus near and far) to a potential *n*-sided volume, as shown in Figure 13.59.

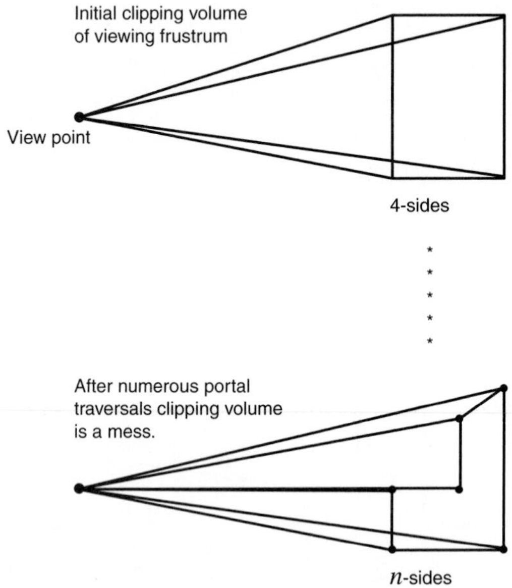

FIGURE 13.59 The viewing frustrum gets ugly after numerous portal clips.

This is reasonable, and can be done with a set of planes, but the real problem is all that clipping after the fact. The clipping starts to eat into the rendering of the polygons—the clipping takes so long that you might as well just render the darn polygons!

In conclusion, portals work well with simple worlds that are connected by hallways or have a very regular geometry. In addition, if you are willing to relax your clipping and portal plane-to-view frustrum merging, you can get away with some very good real-time performance. However, portals still don't beat PVS—how can they? It's always better *knowing* what to draw and what not to draw ahead of time—period.

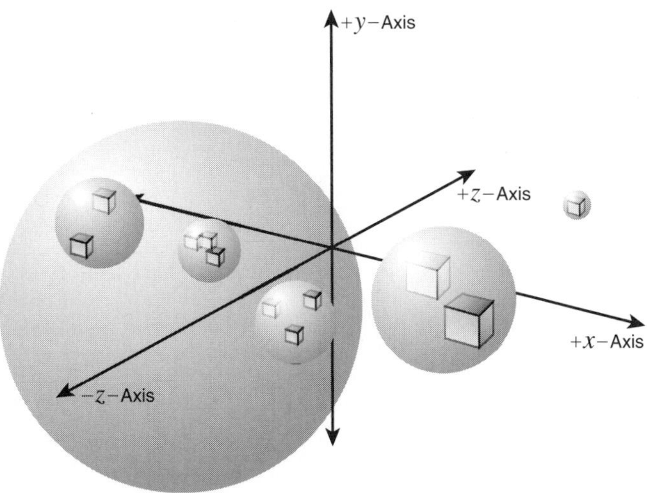

FIGURE 13.60 Grouping objects in bounding hierarchical spheres.

Bounding Hierarchical Volumes and Octrees

Bounding hierarchical volumes (BHVs) are just another method for grouping objects or geometry for fast collision detection or culling. In fact, we have been using bounding spheres since day one to collect the geometry of objects for fast culling. BHV simply takes this idea to the next level and creates a hierarchy of volumes, as shown in Figure 13.60. The volumes might be bounding spheres, as shown in Figure 13.60, or they might be axis-aligned cubic shapes, or object-oriented cubic shapes. The choice is yours. In most cases, people use spheres or axis-aligned cubes.

As an example, imagine you have a collection of objects as shown in Figure 13.61. Each object is represented by its bounding sphere. The point of BHV is to further group the objects in large sets, so that we can trivially cull the entire set, rather than the individual constituents. Figure 13.61b shows the objects collected into a number of smaller spheres, and Figure 13.61c shows one last collection of even smaller spheres.

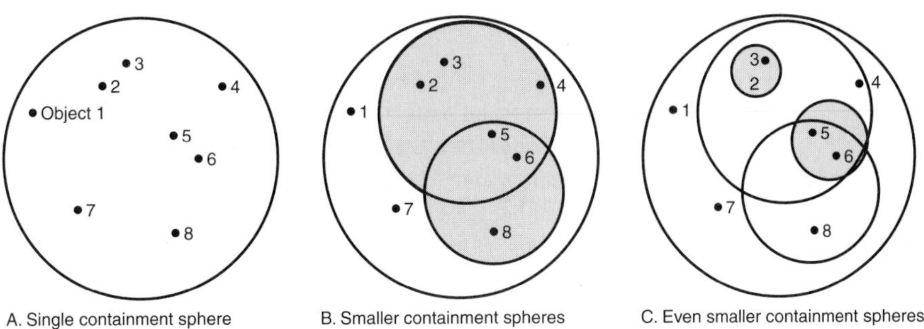

FIGURE 13.61 Layering bounding volumes.

The data structure to hold something similar to what's shown in Figure 13.62 could be anything, but a treelike structure works most naturally. However, because any higher level in the hierarchy could have more than two children, we need to employ an *n*-tree structure, as shown in Figure 13.62.

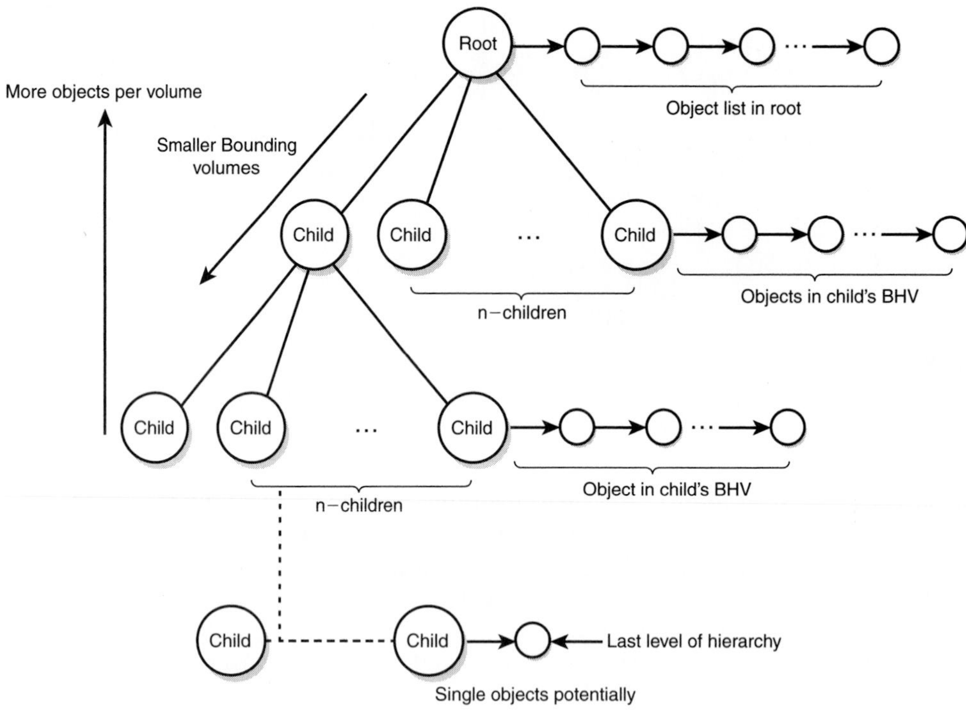

FIGURE 13.62 A possible data structure abstraction for the BHV.

Each node would have a center, radius, an array or linked list of nodes to its children nodes, and an array or linked list of the actual objects contained within the node, along with state information. Here's one possible set of data structures you might employ:

```
// object container to hold any object
typedef struct OBJ_CONTAINERV1_TYP
    {
    int state;      // state of container object
    int attr;       // attributes of container object
    POINT4D pos;     // position of container object
    VECTOR4D vel;     // velocity of object container
    VECTOR4D rot;     // rotational rate of object container
    int auxi[8];     // aux array of 8 ints
    int auxf[8];     // aux array of 8 floats
```

```
    void *aux_ptr;    // aux pointer
    void *obj;      // pointer to master object

    } OBJ_CONTAINERV1, *OBJ_CONTAINERV1_PTR;

// a bounding hierarchical volume node
typedef struct BHV_NODEV1_TYP
    {
    int state;      // state of this node
    int attr;      // attributes of this node
    POINT4D pos;     // center of node
    VECTOR4D radius;  // x,y,z radius of node
    int num_objects;  // number of objects contained in node
    OBJ_CONTAINERV1 *objects[MAX_OBJECTS_PER_BHV_NODE]; // objects

    int num_children; // number of children nodes

    BHV_NODEV1_TYP *links[MAX_BHV_PER_NODE]; // links to children

    } BHV_NODEV1, *BHV_NODEV1_PTR;
```

The preceding structures can handle spheres, cubes, or rectangular solids. Because the radius is VECTOR4D, we can easily have different axial widths. Used in conjunction with the attribute field, BHV_NODEV1 should work for most applications. Also, note that BHV_NODEV1 has been slightly abstracted to hold a generalized object OBJ_CONTAINERV1, rather than an OBJECT4DV2. Moreover, note that OBJ_CONTAINERV1 itself has a void pointer to the object it points to. This way, if we change the object, we can still use these same data structures.

Of course, we need a strategy for how the bounding spheres might be constructed, or in other words, how the objects are selected at each iteration and how the size of the spheres is computed. Right now though, let's discuss how to use the BHV tree.

Using the BHV Tree

Assuming that a BHV has been constructed using bounding spheres (or cuboid shapes), we can now use it during runtime to perform large-scale collision detection or culling. Because they are both related, and the theme of this chapter is rendering, not collision, I will stick with the culling aspects of the BHV.

In any event, the BHV represents all the geometry in the world at varying levels or coarseness. At the topmost root level, there is a single sphere that encloses the entire universe, so the first step is to try to cull the entire sphere to the view frustrum. This is easily accomplished; it's similar to how we cull bounding spheres for objects. If the entire root node can be culled, all objects in the objects[] array are tagged as culled, and there is no further processing. The following simple line of code

```
SET_BIT(obj->state, OBJECT4DV2_STATE_CULLED);
```

suffices to set the culled flag for any object. If the topmost node can't be culled, an algorithm that can be implemented either recursively or explicitly simply runs through each link of the current node and tries to cull the bounding spheres of each node. At each node, the process can continue in either a depth-first or breadth-first manner, as shown in Figure 13.63. In either case, the entire tree will be tested, if need be. The thing to remember is that after a node is culled, all objects in the node are tagged as culled no matter what, and all children from the node are not visited.

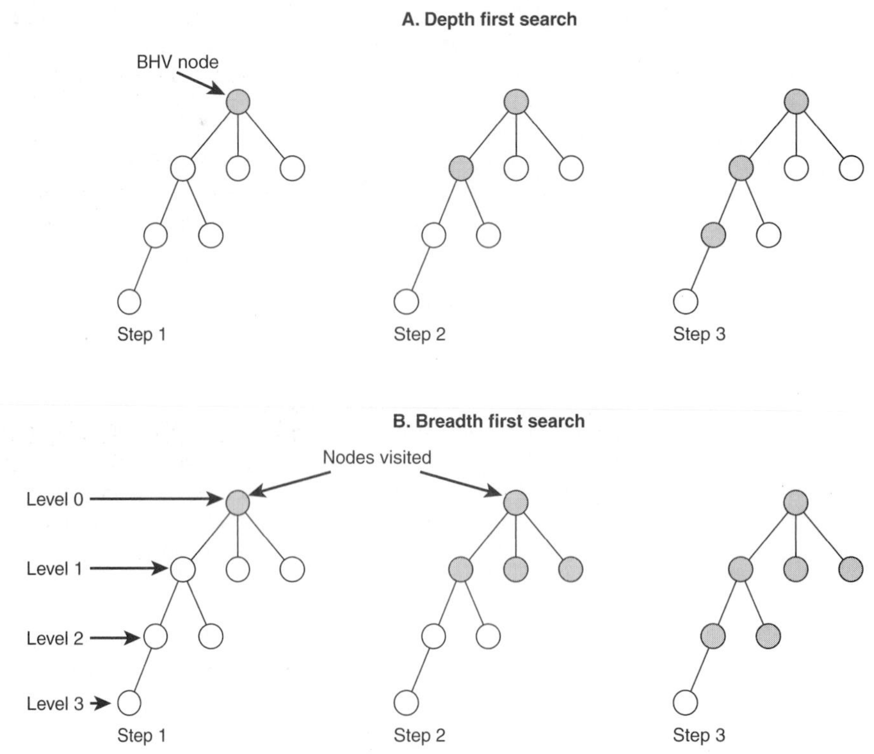

FIGURE 13.63 Depth-first and breadth-first searching of the BHV.

When the process is complete, each culled object will be tagged, so during rendering when the main loop runs through the objects, a simple test can be made to see whether the object has been culled already by checking the `OBJECT4DV2_STATE_CULLED` flag in the object state. If the object hasn't been culled, the standard object culling procedure *must* still be performed, because there is no guarantee that the BHV system created bounding volumes around single objects.

Runtime Performance

Let's talk a moment about runtime performance, and why the BHV helps. Consider a test case with 10,000 objects that are equally distributed in space. Now imagine that we have four levels of bounding volumes. Level 0 is the root that contains all the objects. Level 1 also contains all the objects, but the bounding volumes are at most 50% the size of the root level, and each level continues on.

Let's make up an example:

Root: The BHV has a radius r. All 10,000 objects contained.

Level 1: This level will contain BHVs with a radius <= r/2. There can be one or more Level 1 BHVs. Let's assume this level has five BHVs, each with a radius of r/2. They are equally distributed, so there are 2,000 objects per BHV.

Level 2: This level contains BHVs with a radius <= r/4. There can be one or more Level 2 BHVs. Let's assume this level has 20 BHVs, each with a radius of r/4. They are equally distributed, so there are 100 objects per BHV.

Level 3: This level contains BHVs with a radius <= r/8. There can be one or more Level 2 BHVs. Let's assume this level has 10 BHVs, each with a radius of r/8. They are equally distributed, so there are 10 objects per BHV.

We end up with a tree that looks something like that shown in Figure 13.64. Now we simply push the tree through a frustrum sphere culler, starting at the root (the code from `Cull_OBJECT4DV2()` is exactly what would be used). If we can discard the root from the view frustrum, we are done, and we know that not a single object is visible—we just turned 10,000 bounding sphere tests into one test! However, chances are, the only way the entire game universe is out of view is if hell has frozen over. Alas, we must continue down to the next level of the tree. This is where things get interesting.

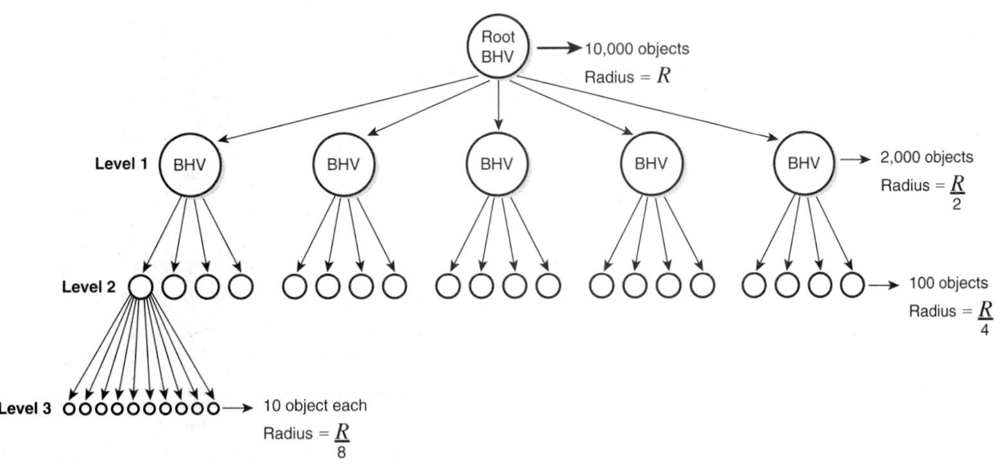

FIGURE 13.64 A visual of the BHV example.

The root has five children, so we traverse the five children either depth-first or breadth-first. Let's just stick to breadth-first for now, meaning we will process each of the five children and determine whether the BHVs are culled. If so, we tag all the objects in that node as culled, and tag the node's BHV as visited so none of its children are visited. Let's assume that four of the five children BHVs are culled during the pass. We then traverse to the next level and process the its BHVs—in this case there are 20. The process continues as before until each necessary BHV node has been visited.

When the traversal is complete, all possible objects will have been culled. On average, we are talking about a few dozen tests compared to 10,000, so this is quite significant. This is the power of BHV techniques.

However, there are some obvious optimizations that can be applied. First, when traversing the BHV tree, it's quite possible that one object exists in overlapping nodes, and thus may be culled at a high level and then culled (or attempted to be culled) more than once. This is acceptable in most cases, and has to do more with the percentage overlap any two BHVs possess. In other words, two BHVs may have objects in both sets.

The second major optimization is a counter that simply counts the number of objects that are uniquely culled. If this counter reaches the total number of possible objects, the traversal algorithm can stop.

Selection Strategies

The final piece of the puzzle is the initial algorithm to select the BHVs. In a later section, we will contrast general BHVs to the more specific case of octrees, which are very deterministic. However, general BHVs can be deterministic or heuristic in nature. For example, you might use a tool to select the BHVs manually, or you might write a loose heuristic algorithm, or you might write a very deterministic algorithm. So, what I'm going to do is throw out some ideas that I have used.

Additionally, many people use BHVs for real-time collision and the culling of *moving* objects. This means the BHV tree must be regenerated whenever an object moves out of a node, or each frame—whichever is more appropriate. Thus, simple schemes that have few levels 3–8 are usually employed. Remember, we just want some help here—we don't need it to be perfect. Speed is always the most important concern.

Divide and Conquer

This strategy is based on sectorizing the 3D space into cubes, spheres, or whatever, but doing it in a consistent basis, where the size of each sector is the same. For example, the first step is always to contain the entire space in the root BHV. The second step could be to divide space into cubelets that all have some size—perhaps it's always 16×16×16, or maybe 4×4×4, and space is equally divided up. Then the BHVs are sized around them. Any sector that doesn't contain any objects isn't included in the BHV for that level. Then at each level, each BHV that makes up the level (the children BHVs) are once again sectorized into cubelets (or other geometry). This process is shown in Figures 13.65a and b. The nice thing about the divide and conquer technique is that it's easy to implement. However, we are walking a fine line with octrees using this strategy (in fact, we are building an octree—he he he!).

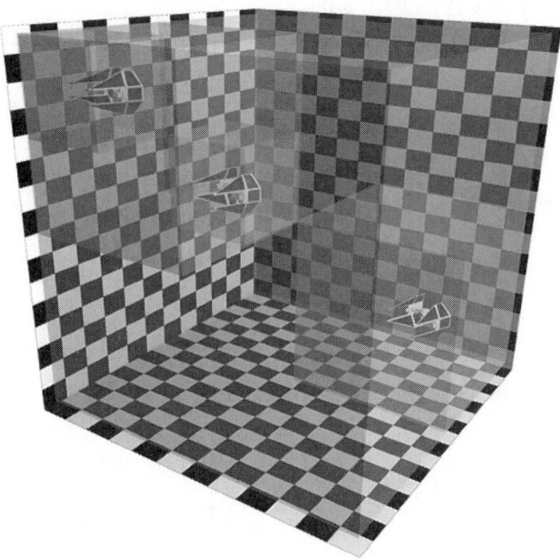

FIGURE 13.65a 3D sectorization solid view.

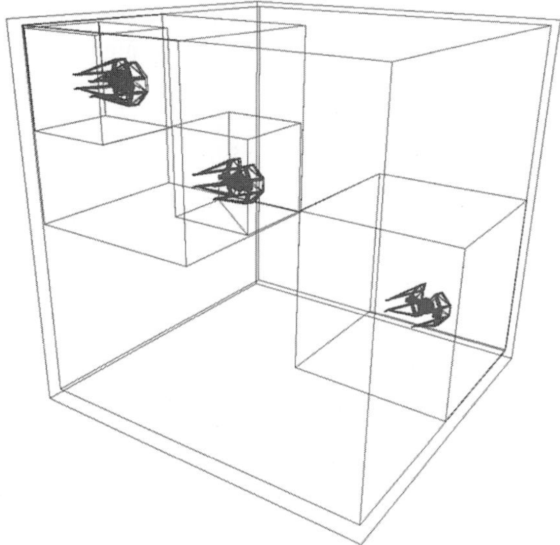

FIGURE 13.65b 3D sectorization wireframe view.

Clustering

Although the divide and conquer technique is easy to implement, it's not very smart. For example, take a look at Figure 13.66. I can immediately see that sectorizing this universe is a waste of time, when I can immediately just circle the three clusters of objects and start there.

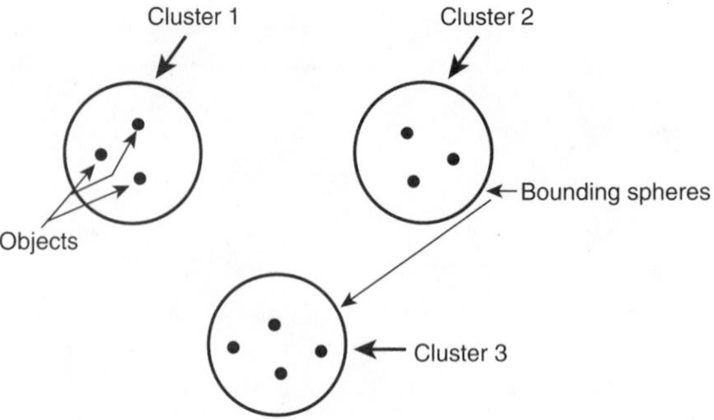

FIGURE 13.66 Sectorization is wasteful in this case.

Thus, clustering works on a heuristic algorithm based on randomly selecting a single object. For that object, the average distance to every other object is determined. Objects that are within a specific maximum cluster range are included in the cluster. That is one potential clustering. The algorithm continues and selects yet another random cluster seed and performs the same logic.

The process continues until some stopping condition is met, maybe *n* seeds and so on. The best seed object is used, the BHV is used, and the process continues, finding other BHVs in a similar manner. Figure 13.67 shows the process highly simplified for six objects. Each object is tested as a potential seed, but during the first pass, it's found that object A is the best overall seed, and its average distance to the objects in its cluster is the minimum. Thus, the first BHV is created using object A as the center. Then the next BHV is centered on the remaining objects, and shrunk to fit it more tightly.

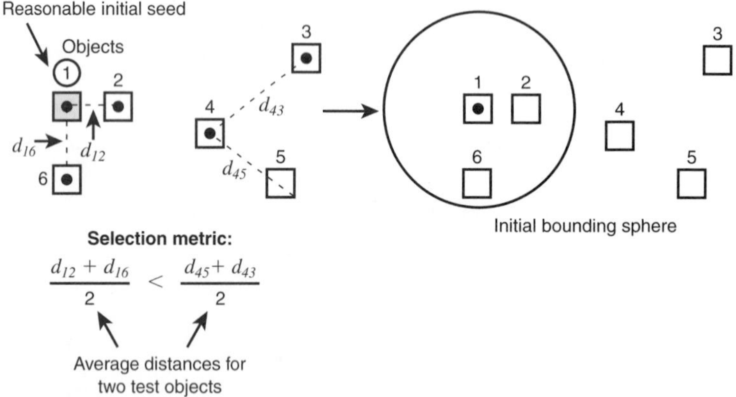

FIGURE 13.67 Initial selection of the seed object is based on the average minimum distance to all other neighbors.

Implementing BHV

As an example of BHV, I have written a demo that creates a 3D universe, loads a few hundred objects, and places them randomly in the universe. Then a divide and conquer algorithm is employed to group the objects in each level of the BHV. The algorithm continues *n* levels, where *n* is programmable. The function that performs the BHV analysis is specifically designed for the way the objects are represented. If you have been reviewing the multiple object demos, in most cases a single OBJECT4DV2 is loaded, and then an array is defined that positions a set of objects, each pointing to the single root object. Thus, for our BHV to work, we once again must use this technique, so we are going to create an array of virtual objects, then render the array by using each position, and so on. This setup is shown in Figure 13.68.

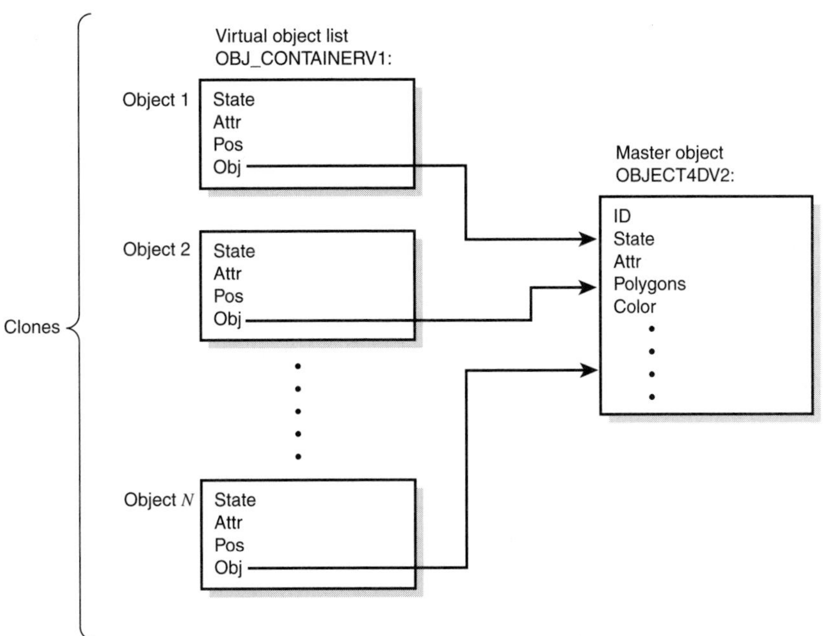

FIGURE 13.68 Single master object cloned.

Here is the basic object container:

```
typedef struct OBJ_CONTAINERV1_TYP
{
int state;      // state of container object
int attr;       // attributes of container object
POINT4D pos;     // position of container object
OBJECT4DV2_PTR obj; // pointer to master object

} OBJ_CONTAINERV1, * OBJ_CONTAINERV1_PTR;
```

Of course, I used the previously defined BHV_NODEV1 as the basic BHV node. There are only two functions involved in the entire BHV process: one to create the BHV, and one to cull the BHV to the viewing frustrum. The creation function is shown here:

```
void BHV_Build_Tree(BHV_NODEV1_PTR bhv_tree, // tree to build
   OBJ_CONTAINERV1_PTR bhv_objects,// ptr to all objects in intial scene
   int num_objects,        // number of objects in initial scene
   int level,           // recursion level
   int num_divisions,       // number of division per level
   int universe_radius)       // initial size of universe to enclose
{
// this function builds the BHV tree using a divide and conquer
// divisioning algorithm to cluster the objects together

Write_Error("\nEntering BHV function...");

// are we building root?
if (level == 0)
  {
  Write_Error("\nlevel = 0");

  // position at (0,0,0)
  bhv_tree->pos.x = 0;
  bhv_tree->pos.y = 0;
  bhv_tree->pos.z = 0;
  bhv_tree->pos.w = 1;

  // set radius of node to maximum
  bhv_tree->radius.x = universe_radius;
  bhv_tree->radius.y = universe_radius;
  bhv_tree->radius.z = universe_radius;
  bhv_tree->radius.w = 1;

  Write_Error("\nnode pos[%f, %f, %f], r[%f, %f, %f]",
           bhv_tree->pos.x,bhv_tree->pos.y,bhv_tree->pos.z,
           bhv_tree->radius.x,bhv_tree->radius.y,bhv_tree->radius.z);

  // build root, simply add all objects to root
  for (int index = 0; index < num_objects; index++)
    {
    // make sure object is not culled
    if (!(bhv_objects[index].state & OBJECT4DV2_STATE_CULLED))
     {
     bhv_tree->objects[bhv_tree->num_objects++] =
```

```
         (OBJ_CONTAINERV1_PTR)&bhv_objects[index];
     } // end if

    } // end for index

  // at this point all the objects have been inserted into the root node
  // and num_objects is set to the number of objects
  // enable the node
  bhv_tree->state = 1;
  bhv_tree->attr = 0;

  // and set all links to NULL
  for (int ilink = 0; ilink < MAX_BHV_PER_NODE; ilink++)
    bhv_tree->links[ilink] = NULL;

  // set the number of objects
  bhv_tree->num_objects = num_objects;

  Write_Error("\nInserted %d objects into root node", bhv_tree->num_objects);
  Write_Error("\nMaking recursive call with root node...");

  // done, so now allow recursion to build the rest of the tree
  BHV_Build_Tree(bhv_tree,
         bhv_objects,
         num_objects,
         1,
         num_divisions,
         universe_radius);
  } // end if
else
  {
  Write_Error("\nEntering Level = %d > 0 block, number of objects = %d",
       level, bhv_tree->num_objects);

  // test for exit state
  if (bhv_tree->num_objects <= MIN_OBJECTS_PER_BHV_CELL)
   return;

  // building a child node (hard part)
  // we must take the current node and split it
  // into a number of children nodes, and then
  // create a bhv for each child and then insert
  // all the objects into each child
  // the for each child call the recursion again....
```

```
// create 3D cell temp storage to track cells
BHV_CELL cells[MAX_BHV_CELL_DIVISIONS]
       [MAX_BHV_CELL_DIVISIONS]
       [MAX_BHV_CELL_DIVISIONS];

// find origin of bounding volume based on radius and center
int x0 = bhv_tree->pos.x - bhv_tree->radius.x;
int y0 = bhv_tree->pos.y - bhv_tree->radius.y;
int z0 = bhv_tree->pos.z - bhv_tree->radius.z;

// compute cell sizes on x,y,z axis
float cell_size_x = 2*bhv_tree->radius.x / (float)num_divisions;
float cell_size_y = 2*bhv_tree->radius.y / (float)num_divisions;
float cell_size_z = 2*bhv_tree->radius.z / (float)num_divisions;

Write_Error("\ncell pos=(%d, %d, %d) size=(%f, %f, %f)",
      x0,y0,z0, cell_size_x, cell_size_y, cell_size_z);

int cell_x, cell_y, cell_z; // used to locate cell in 3D matrix

// clear cell memory out
memset(cells, 0, sizeof(cells));

// now partition space up into num_divisions (must be < MAX_BHV_CELL_DIVISIONS)
// and then sort each object's center into each cell of the 3D sorting matrix
for (int obj_index = 0; obj_index < bhv_tree->num_objects; obj_index++)
  {
  // compute cell position in temp sorting matrix
  cell_x = (bhv_tree->objects[obj_index]->pos.x - x0)/cell_size_x;
  cell_y = (bhv_tree->objects[obj_index]->pos.y - y0)/cell_size_y;
  cell_z = (bhv_tree->objects[obj_index]->pos.z - z0)/cell_size_z;

  // insert this object into list
 cells[cell_x][cell_y][cell_z].obj_list
  [cells[cell_x][cell_y][cell_z].num_objects ]= bhv_tree->objects[obj_index];

  Write_Error("\ninserting object %d /
  located at (%f, %f, %f) into cell (%d, %d, %d)",
       obj_index,
       bhv_tree->objects[obj_index]->pos.x,
       bhv_tree->objects[obj_index]->pos.y,
       bhv_tree->objects[obj_index]->pos.z,
       cell_x, cell_y, cell_z);
```

```
  // increment number of objects in this cell
  if (++cells[cell_x][cell_y][cell_z].num_objects >=
    MAX_OBJECTS_PER_BHV_CELL)
cells[cell_x][cell_y][cell_z].num_objects = MAX_OBJECTS_PER_BHV_CELL-1;

  } // end for obj_index

Write_Error("\nEntering sorting section...");

// now the 3D sorting matrix has all the information we need, the next step
// is to create a BHV node for each non-empty

for (int icell_x = 0; icell_x < num_divisions; icell_x++)
  {
  for (int icell_y = 0; icell_y < num_divisions; icell_y++)
    {
    for (int icell_z = 0; icell_z < num_divisions; icell_z++)
      {
      // are there any objects in this node?
      if ( cells[icell_x][icell_y][icell_z].num_objects > 0)
        {
        Write_Error("\nCell %d, %d, %d contains %d objects",
              icell_x, icell_y, icell_z,
              cells[icell_x][icell_y][icell_z].num_objects);

        Write_Error("\nCreating child node...");

        // create a node and set the link to it
        bhv_tree->links[ bhv_tree->num_children ] =
         (BHV_NODEV1_PTR)malloc(sizeof(BHV_NODEV1));

        // zero node out
        memset(bhv_tree->links[ bhv_tree->num_children ],
           0, sizeof(BHV_NODEV1) );

        // set the node up
        BHV_NODEV1_PTR curr_node =
          bhv_tree->links[ bhv_tree->num_children ];

        // position
        curr_node->pos.x = (icell_x*cell_size_x + cell_size_x/2) + x0;
        curr_node->pos.y = (icell_y*cell_size_y + cell_size_y/2) + y0;
        curr_node->pos.z = (icell_z*cell_size_z + cell_size_z/2) + z0;
        curr_node->pos.w = 1;
```

13

```
        // radius is cell_size / 2
        curr_node->radius.x = cell_size_x/2;
        curr_node->radius.y = cell_size_y/2;
        curr_node->radius.z = cell_size_z/2;
        curr_node->radius.w = 1;

        // set number of objects
        curr_node->num_objects =
          cells[icell_x][icell_y][icell_z].num_objects;

        // set num children
        curr_node->num_children = 0;

        // set state and attr
        curr_node->state    = 1; // enable node
        curr_node->attr     = 0;

        // now insert each object into this node's object list
        for (int icell_index = 0;
          icell_index < curr_node->num_objects; icell_index++)
          {
          curr_node->objects[icell_index] =
          cells[icell_x][icell_y][icell_z].obj_list[icell_index];
          } // end for icell_index

       Write_Error("\nChild node pos=(%f, %f, %f), r=(%f, %f, %f)",
        curr_node->pos.x,curr_node->pos.y,curr_node->pos.z,
        curr_node->radius.x,curr_node->radius.y,curr_node->radius.z);

       // increment number of children of parent
       bhv_tree->num_children++;

       } // end if

     } // end for icell_z

   } // end for icell_y

 } // end for icell_x

 Write_Error("\nParent has %d children..", bhv_tree->num_children);

 // now for each child build a BHV
 for (int inode = 0; inode < bhv_tree->num_children; inode++)
```

```
    {
    Write_Error("\nfor Level %d, creating child %d", level, inode);

    BHV_Build_Tree(bhv_tree->links[inode],
         NULL, // unused now
         NULL, // unused now
         level+1,
         num_divisions,
         universe_radius);

    } // end if

  } // end else level > 0

Write_Error("\nExiting BHV...level = %d", level);

} // end BHV_Build_Tree
```


Here's the BHV frustrum culling function:

```
int BHV_FrustrumCull(BHV_NODEV1_PTR bhv_tree, // the root of the BHV
     CAM4DV1_PTR cam,     // camera to cull relative to
     int cull_flags)     // clipping planes to consider
{
// NOTE: is matrix based
// this function culls the BHV from the viewing
// frustrum by using the sent camera information and
// the cull_flags determine what axes culling should take place
// x, y, z or all which is controlled by ORing the flags
// together. as the BHV is culled the state information in each node is
// modified, so rendering functions can refer to it

// test for valid BHV and camera
if (!bhv_tree || !cam)
  return(0);

// we need to walk the tree from top to bottom culling

// step 1: transform the center of the nodes bounding
// sphere into camera space

POINT4D sphere_pos; // hold result of transforming center of bounding sphere

// transform point
Mat_Mul_VECTOR4D_4X4(&bhv_tree->pos, &cam->mcam, &sphere_pos);
```

```
// step 2: based on culling flags remove the object
if (cull_flags & CULL_OBJECT_Z_PLANE)
{
// cull only based on z clipping planes

// test far plane
if ( ((sphere_pos.z - bhv_tree->radius.z) > cam->far_clip_z) ||
   ((sphere_pos.z + bhv_tree->radius.z) < cam->near_clip_z) )
  {
  // this entire node is culled, so we need to set the culled flag
  // for every object
  for (int iobject = 0; iobject < bhv_tree->num_objects; iobject++)
    {
    SET_BIT(bhv_tree->objects[iobject]->state, OBJECT4DV2_STATE_CULLED);
    } // end for iobject

  // this node was visited and culled
  bhv_nodes_visited++;

  return(1);
  } // end if

} // end if

if (cull_flags & CULL_OBJECT_X_PLANE)
{
// cull only based on x clipping planes
// we could use plane equations, but simple similar triangles
// is easier since this is really a 2D problem
// if the view volume is 90 degrees the the problem is trivial
// buts lets assume its not

// test the the right and left clipping planes
/ against the leftmost and rightmost
// points of the bounding sphere
float z_test = (0.5)*cam->viewplane_width*sphere_pos.z/cam->view_dist;

if ( ((sphere_pos.x - bhv_tree->radius.x) > z_test) || // right side
   ((sphere_pos.x + bhv_tree->radius.x) < -z_test) )
            // left side, note sign change
  {
  // this entire node is culled, so we need to set the culled flag
  // for every object
  for (int iobject = 0; iobject < bhv_tree->num_objects; iobject++)
    {
```

```
    SET_BIT(bhv_tree->objects[iobject]->state, OBJECT4DV2_STATE_CULLED);
    } // end for iobject

  // this node was visited and culled
  bhv_nodes_visited++;

  return(1);
  } // end if
} // end if

if (cull_flags & CULL_OBJECT_Y_PLANE)
{
// cull only based on y clipping planes
// we could use plane equations, but simple similar triangles
// is easier since this is really a 2D problem
// if the view volume is 90 degrees the the problem is trivial
// buts lets assume its not

// test the the top and bottom clipping planes
// against the bottommost and topmost
// points of the bounding sphere
float z_test = (0.5)*cam->viewplane_height*sphere_pos.z/cam->view_dist;

if ( ((sphere_pos.y - bhv_tree->radius.y) > z_test) || // top side
   ((sphere_pos.y + bhv_tree->radius.y) < -z_test) )
    // bottom side, note sign change
  {
  // this entire node is culled, so we need to set the culled flag
  // for every object
  for (int iobject = 0; iobject < bhv_tree->num_objects; iobject++)
    {
    SET_BIT(bhv_tree->objects[iobject]->state, OBJECT4DV2_STATE_CULLED);
    } // end for iobject

  // this node was visited and culled
  bhv_nodes_visited++;

  return(1);
  } // end if

} // end if

// at this point, we have concluded that this BHV node is too large
// to cull, so we need to traverse the children and see if we can cull them
```

```
for (int ichild = 0; ichild < bhv_tree->num_children; ichild++)
  {
  // recursively call..
  BHV_FrustrumCull(bhv_tree->links[ichild], cam, cull_flags);

  // here's where we can optimize by tracking the total number
  // of objects culled and we can exit early if all the objects
  // are already culled...

  } // end ichild

// return failure to cull anything!
return(0);

} // end BHV_FrustrumCull
```

BHV_FrustrumCull() walks the BHV as outlined before, and simply applies the bounding sphere-to-frustrum culling algorithm from the Cull_OBJECT4DV2() function. In essence, we're using the center of the BHV, along with its radius, to create a bounding sphere, and then testing whether the bounding sphere is within the viewing frustrum.

CAUTION

Using a bounding sphere is great if the volume is a sphere, but in the default case that the bounding volume is a cube, you'll see objects culled early in some cases. This is an easy fix: You just need to write a culler that supports cubes. I will leave this to you, because you might need many shapes depending on how you use the technology, but the sphere is easy for demonstrative purposes.

TIP

Implementing the cube cull is relatively simple: Instead of finding the six tangent points to the sphere, simply use the eight vertex points of the bounding cube!

After BHV_FrustrumCull() runs, the array of objects are updated via their state field (with the culled bit is set or not). Then during the object rendering loop, the array of objects is simply tested. Objects that are culled are ignored; objects that are not culled are processed as usual, which includes standard bounding sphere culling!

Figure 13.69 depicts a screenshot of the DEMOII13_5.EXE¦CPP running. It doesn't look that exciting because all the action is behind the screen, but the status and information display is interesting. The display indicates the number of objects culled, the number of BHV nodes visited, and the number of objects passed to the rendering loop (not culled by the BHV). You can enable and disable the BHV with the B key.

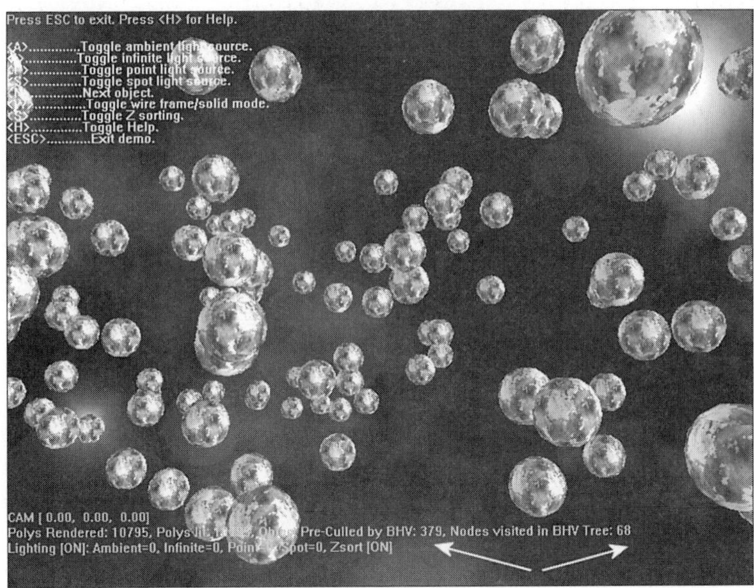

FIGURE 13.69 A screenshot of the BHV demo.

> **NOTE**
>
> To compile the demo yourself, you will need `DEMOII13_5.CPP`, along with all the library modules `T3DLIB1-11.CPP|H` in addition to the DirectX .LIB files. Additionally, you will need the resource file for the menus and so on. This file is named `DEMOII13_5.RC`.

Octrees

Octrees are simply a special case of the more generalized BHV system we just developed. In fact, when the number of divisions is equal to two, a call to `BHV_Build_Tree()` actually creates an octree! I wrote the BHV code first because it's more general.

To reiterate, an octree is simply a BHV that is axis-aligned and has children per node. Each node is exactly the same size, and is always shaped like a cube. The BHV system enables non-cubic bounding objects like spheres and so on because we track the radius as a vector, and have an attribute word for each node that could potentially describe each bounding volume type.

With that in mind, we already have an octree system, and there's nothing else to write. However, there are some points I want to mention about generating an octree.

Octrees (and BHVs, for that matter) can operate at the object or polygon level. In our case, we have worked with objects rather than polygons (but we used polygons for the BSP demo, so I thought this would be a nice change) because octrees and BHVs are really useful for huge outdoor worlds with thousands of objects.

Octrees always have up to eight equally sized children per node in 3D. However, there is no rule that says each child must be contained in the octree.

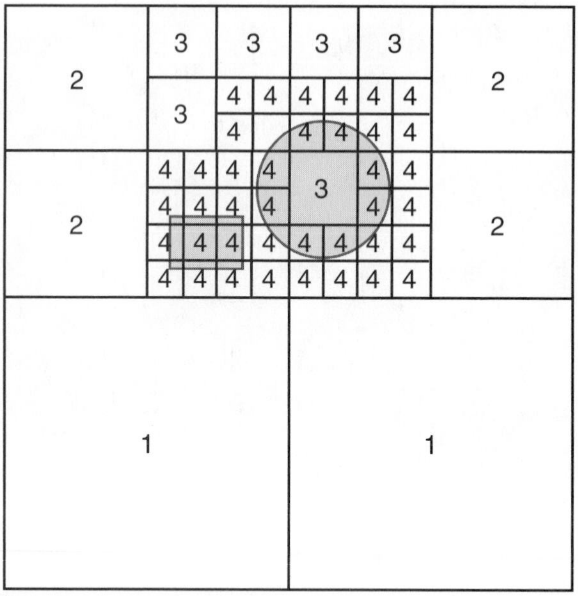

FIGURE 13.70 A 2D representation of an octree division (technically a quadtree).

For example, take a look at Figure 13.70. Here we see a few iterations of an octree BHV algorithm running and partitioning space (a 2D projection with numbering indicating the level of the iteration). However, the partitioning does not partition space equally—the partitioning only occurs where polygons or objects are actually contained within the node. This is to save memory. If you like, you can surely create eight nodes each iteration and place nothing in them, but I prefer to create the eight nodes virtually (like our BHV does), and then if there is something in the node, it's committed to the data structure, otherwise the octant is NULLed.

When creating an octree, as with a BHV, there are a number of stopping conditions. You might decide to stop when an octant has reached a certain size, or when a certain recursive depth has been reached, or maybe when there is a minimum number of polygons in each node. The choice is up to you.

In conclusion, octrees are simply specific cases of BHVs. The algorithms we have written create an octree with the build function when the division is set to two, like this:

```
BHV_Build_Tree(&bhv_tree,
        scene_objects,
        NUM_SCENE_OBJECTS,
        0,
        2);
```

The frustrum culling works the exact same. Cool, huh! The only reason to use an octree rather than some bizarre division scheme (with 10 divisions per node for 100 little sectors with spheres, for example) is that the eight octants mimic the eight octants of a 3D system very well, which has some nice properties and is easier to work with.

Occlusion Culling

The last topic I want to talk about is again related to drawing what you can see. We saw with PVS technology that we can generate lists of polygons from any viewpoint in the game, and then refer to these lists to determine what polygons should be considered during any particular frame. However, what if you aren't using a PVS, or it's just not feasible, or doesn't help because of the type of world?

There is yet another class of techniques that work from the other end of the problem called *occlusion culling*. In essence, occlusion culling is a technique used when you may or may not want a static solution to your visibility (maybe your world changes frequently, and PVS, BSP, and octrees are out of the question). Nevertheless, there are some key geometrical elements in your world that are simply invisible, because they are so large they occlude much of the scene.

For example, take a look at the screenshot of *Unreal 2003* in Figure 13.71. Now take a look at the screenshot in Figure 13.72. I did nothing but rotate, but all of a sudden there is a giant object in front of me occluding my vision, so PVS isn't going to help here (unless we do it based on view angle, which would be huge). Portals are useless, but there has to be something we can do to take this ridiculously simple case into consideration and not render or even consider polygons occluded by this object. This is the basis of occlusion culling.

Occlusion Volumes

Let's break the problem down into a really simple case that comes up in outdoor-based games with cityscapes, for example. Take a look at Figure 13.73a. Here we see a top view of a cityscape (Houston, actually) where the little blocks represent building meshes. There is no sense of rooms, portals, and so on. We could do a PVS, but without any bounding indoor geometry, we would have to use the viewing frustrum as the containment cell to build the PVS for each viewpoint. Forget about that, and let's focus on the obvious. In Figure 13.73a, take a look at where the viewpoint is placed and the viewing frustrum around it. Notice the large shaded building in front of the viewpoint. Now, take a look at Figure 13.73b—you can see this building occludes 90% of the potentially visible polygons!

Therefore, if we create an occlusion volume and objects that are within the shadow of the volume are not visible, we are done. Of course, creating these bounding volumes generally isn't easy. There are many algorithms to find the silhouette edges of a 3D object, and from the silhouette, you can project a number of planes, which then define an occlusion frustrum.

FIGURE 13.71 An open view in *Unreal 2003*.

FIGURE 13.72 The same position after rotation.

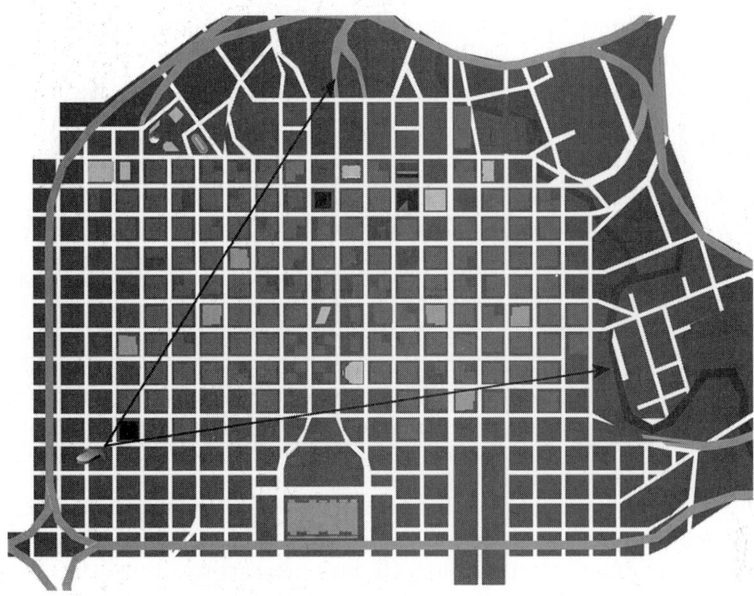

FIGURE 13.73a Cityscape setup for occlusion.

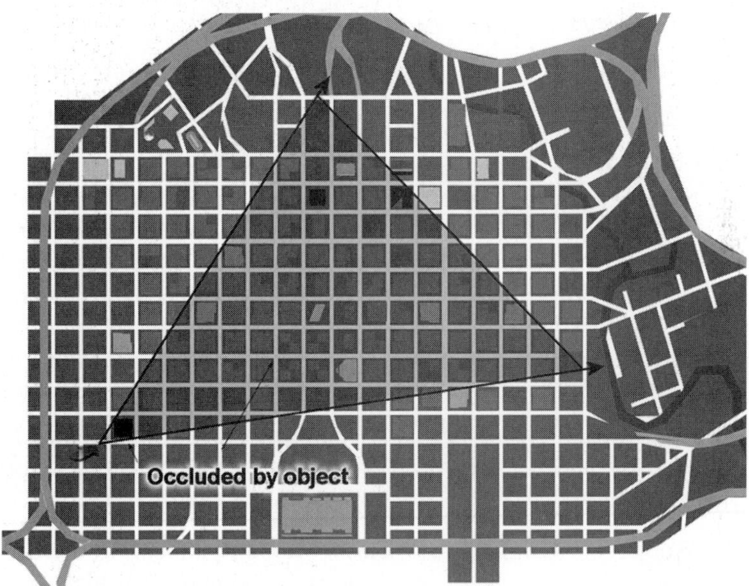

FIGURE 13.73b Cityscape after rendering occlusion shadow volume.

Anything within the frustrum is clipped. You can take this idea further and have multiple occluders and create multiple occlusion volumes. Of course, there is a point of diminishing returns, when the complexity of determining whether a polygon is within the occlusion volume takes longer than simply drawing the polygon. However, no one said that we have to use polygons as the smallest unit to occlude. We can occlude objects, BSP trees, octree cells, and so on, just as well.

Selection of Occluders

The next step in getting occlusion to work is occluder selection. We still need some method to select what objects are potential occluders (which we might even perform some preprocessing on to compute the bounding silhouette). There are a number of strategies people use to select occluders, but they all fall into one of two broad categories: offline and runtime. In the case of offline occluder selection, a modeler might tag specific objects as potential occluders. These are tagged because they are large, or they will continually occlude the player's viewpoint during game play. Additionally, a set of potential occluders might be selected on a sector-by-sector basis.

For the online category of occluders, there is usually an offline phase, or at least the tagging of potential occluders. During runtime, the system determines whether the occluder is worth adding to the occlusion list, and hence converting it into an occlusion volume and the clipping/culling that will be introduced as such. The heuristic might be based on the size of each occluder, meaning that only objects that are large and movable, or perhaps large terrain or environment objects will be tagged as potential occluders. Then during runtime, the system determines a projected screen space of the occluder, and decides whether it's worth using as an occluder. This brings me to a hybrid technique that I like to use.

Hybrid Occluder Selection

Occluders can be selected during an offline processing or modeling step (or algorithmically); they can be selected during runtime from a potential occluder set; or they can be selected completely on the fly by computing the volume of large projected objects (or polygons) and then deciding whether it's worth using the object as an occluder. Taking all these techniques into consideration takes a bit of work in your modeling and rendering pipeline. However, there are lots of simple opportunities to select occluders that are either polygons are object-based. The steps are as follows:

1. For all the objects and geometry that are definitely within the viewing frustrum and potentially visible, make a pass through them and select the n nearest objects that have the largest size.

2. Project the objects or geometry into screen space and look at the area of the projected region(s). Select the m <= n objects or geometry that make up the largest screen space. Then compute bounding rectangles that are contained within each of the occluders. (Although this will miss some potential occlusions, the bounding rectangles are much easier to project than the arbitrary polygons or meshes.)

3. Now add the small set of occlusion rectangles to the occlusion volumes, and pass all objects and all polygons through the occlusion volumes, removing all occluded geometry.

In essence, the algorithm is quite straightforward—you make a quick pass and select a few of the nearest largest objects or geometry, assuming that these will probably be occluders. Then you project their volumes/areas into screen space, and a set of these occluders are selected because they have the potential to occlude a great deal of the viewspace. However, instead of using complex geometry, bounding inscribed rectangles are used that are wholly inside each occluder as the basis of the occluder volume. Then any object that has z values farther than the occluder object plane and is within the occlusion volume is disregarded. Of course, this works best when there is still some hierarchy left in the object/world representation, such as BSP, rooms, octrees, and so on, so large chunks can be occluded and disregarded.

Summary

This has been a really cool chapter. We covered all the important spatial partitioning algorithms, got down to the nitty gritty on many of them and implemented the most important ones. With this knowledge, you now have a framework to create your own visibility algorithms as hybrids of what I have covered here. In fact, you will find yourself with a surplus of ideas on this topic.

However, before you start coding anything, make sure to read everything you can get your hands on about the subject, so you don't reinvent the wheel too many times—people have tried just about everything. Of course, you know that I am a proponent of trying everything just for the experience of it, but if you have a finite schedule, it's worth reading through previous works on the subject.

Finally, a word of warning: Many of the algorithms are recursive, so take your time and program defensively, because debugging recursion is a nightmare, because debugging recursion is a nightmare, because debugging recursion is a nightmare, because debugging recursion is a nightmare...

```
Stack Overflow: Instruction Pointer = 0x00fff564
```

See what I mean?

CHAPTER 14

Shadows, Lighting, and Secrets of the id

IN THIS CHAPTER

- The New Game Engine Module
- Introduction and Game Plan
- The Physics of Shadows
- Simulating Shadows with Projective Images and Billboards
- Planar Mesh Shadow Mapping
- Introduction to Light Mapping and Surface Caching
- Putting Everything Together

"If we knew what it was we were doing, it would not be called research, would it?"

—Albert Einstein

In this chapter, we are going to cover some material that will add a little more realism to our scenes: shadows and light mapping. As usual, our coverage is going to be down and dirty, focusing on software techniques because we aren't cheating with hardware, but interesting nonetheless. Here's what's in store:

- The new game engine library module
- Introduction and game plan
- The physics of shadows
- Simulating shadows with projective images and billboards
- Planar mesh shadow mapping
- Light mapping and surface caching
- Putting everything together
- Lots of demos!

The New Game Engine Module

Once again, there is enough software in this chapter for a separate library module. We are up to `T3DLIB12.CPP|H` now, so to compile any program from this chapter, you will need the main .CPP program file for the program, the DirectX .LIB files, and the following new library modules:

T3DLIB12.CPP—The C/C++ source for the added shadow and light mapping software.

T3DLIB12.H—The accompanying header file.

Of course, you must link to T3DLIB1-11.CPP¦H, as well.

Introduction and Game Plan

We have held off on this chapter for a long time. The reason was that I wanted to build up enough technology, demos, and techniques, so that by the time we got here, you could do it yourself, more or less. Of course, I am not going to leave you hanging, but the point I want to make is that we have already more or less covered light mapping. Didn't we blend textures with light textures in Chapter 8, "Basic Lighting and Solid Modeling"? And as for shadows, haven't we written alpha blending rasterizers that could potentially be used to draw shadow projections? Absolutely! Thus, what we are going to do in this chapter is *systems integrate* what we already have, and add a couple of things to make the demos possible. But for the most part, you will probably finish each one of my sentences, because you know how to do this already, I bet!

In any event, I think the best approach to the main topics of this chapter is to start off with some physics relating to shadows, and then implement a couple of shadowing techniques (there are many more, but they work better for hardware, so I will leave that to Direct3D/OpenGL books). Then we'll move on to light mapping and surface caching in a very simplified case, rather than adding total support to the engine for it. I made this decision because adding general light mapping to the engine would take about ten times more code than an example of it. Plus, if you're like me, a simple example is more meaningful than a long implementation.

This will be the theme throughout the remainder of the book. We are getting near the end, and at this point, you should be able to create a software engine capable of rendering *Quake*/*Unreal*-like worlds. When we finish this chapter, you will have a few more special effects, but for the most part you are ready. Let's get started.

The Simplified Physics of Shadows

The exact details of the photons and the interactions of surfaces is far beyond what we need to model shadows, but we do want to model or at least understand how shadows are generated, and why they have the "soft" and "hard" edges you see, or if you recall, what are called the umbra and penumbra, from when we discussed lighting earlier in the book.

In Figure 14.1, we see a cylinder resting on a plane with a point light source above it. There is a bit of ambient light, so the cylinder is visible from all sides, but the cylinder casts a shadow on the plane because it obscures the line of sight of the point light source to the ground plane—this is a shadow. However, there is an interesting second-order effect if you look at the rendering closely.

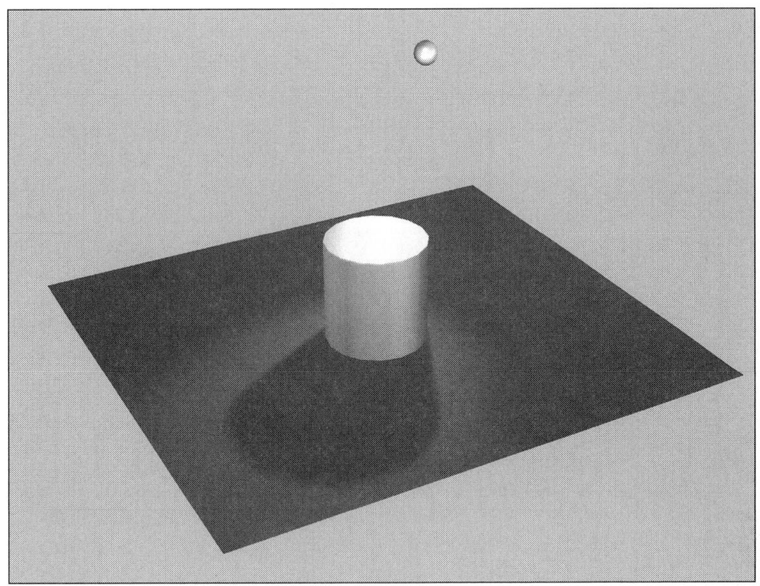

FIGURE 14.1 A simple shadow cast by a cylinder.

Analyzing the shadow itself, it has a solid dark area in the middle (the *umbra*), but near the edges where the shadow falls off, the area is brighter (or less shadowed). This is called the *penumbra*. Also, notice that the existence of the penumbra is only pronounced at the far boundaries of the shadow, and not at the base of the cylinder.

Inspecting the base of the cylinder and the shadow in this area, you will notice that the shadow is very "hard" and strong. These are the kinds of details we want to simulate, model, or otherwise implement in our engine. Let's take a look at what is happening from the photon's point of view.

Ray Tracing Photons and Computing Intensity

Take a look at Figure 14.2a. Here we see a side view of our cylinder example, with a single point light source. Tracing the ray from the light source and intersecting it with the ground plane, we see that the results are trivial. A single point of light illuminates everything not in the shadowed area (occluded by the cylinder). Therefore, we get a hard-edged shadow, as shown in Figure 14.2b.

Here's where things get interesting. What if the point light source wasn't a point at all, but a small sphere? Figure 14.3 illustrates this setup. The interesting thing about the situation in Figure 14.3 is that for any point $\mathbf{p}_i$ located on the x-axis in the shadow cast by the cylinder, the amount of light intensity is different for each position x, and is directly proportional to the area of the projectors from the point of interest to the two points that intersect the point light sphere.

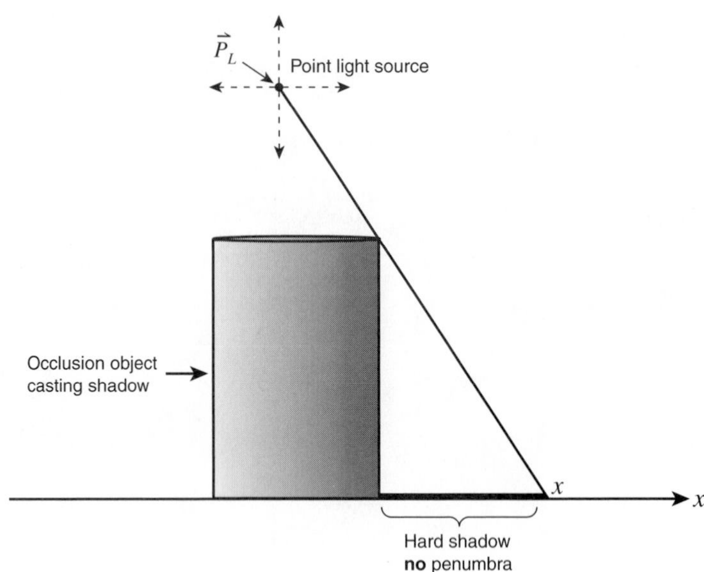

FIGURE 14.2a Ray tracing a point light source.

FIGURE 14.2b Ray tracing a point light source.

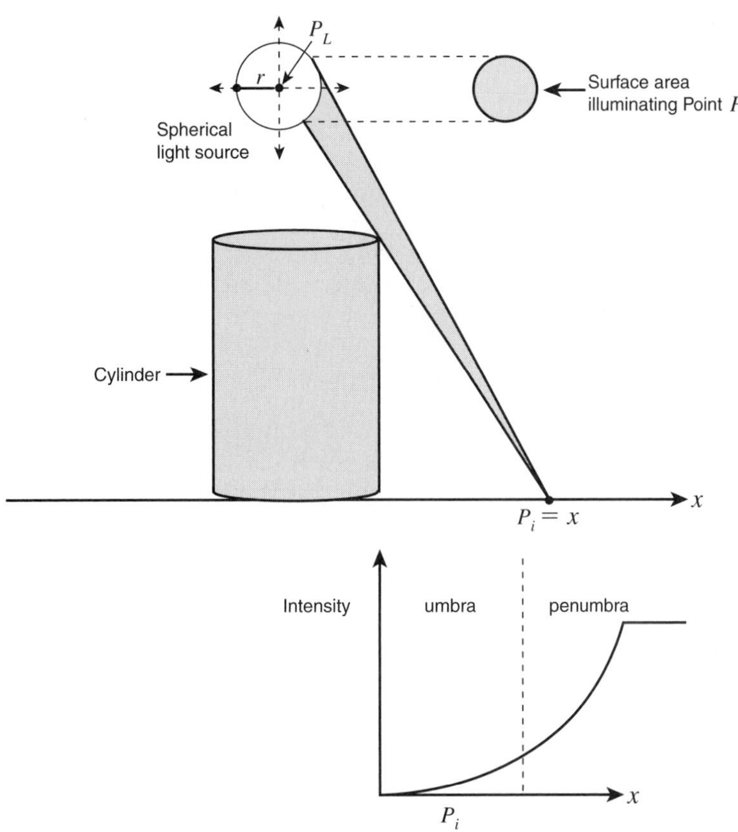

FIGURE 14.3 Ray tracing a spherical light source.

These points generate an "area" on the sphere. This is the total illumination that the receiver point(s) receive, and as the receiver point moves on the x-axis, the amount of area increases or decreases. This effect generates the penumbra, and that's why as we move the test point away from the edges of the shadow, the intensity of light increases or the shadow diminishes—because there is more surface area illuminating the position (Figure 14.4b is actually a rendering of this situation). Finally, maintaining the position of the point and increasing the size of the point light source sphere size softens the shadow. This is illustrated in Figures 14.4a and b.

The bottom line is that if we want to correctly model the umbra and penumbra, we need to take into consideration the size of the light source, and we need to do a little ray tracing. However, this could be very computationally intensive. That's not to say you couldn't do it, but is it really needed? Well, the answer is no. As of the writing of this book, many games still do not have shadows—sure, many do, but the shadows are hard with no penumbra. However, some games do have soft shadows, and they look great (usually implemented with multitexturing, pixel shaders, and stencil buffers).

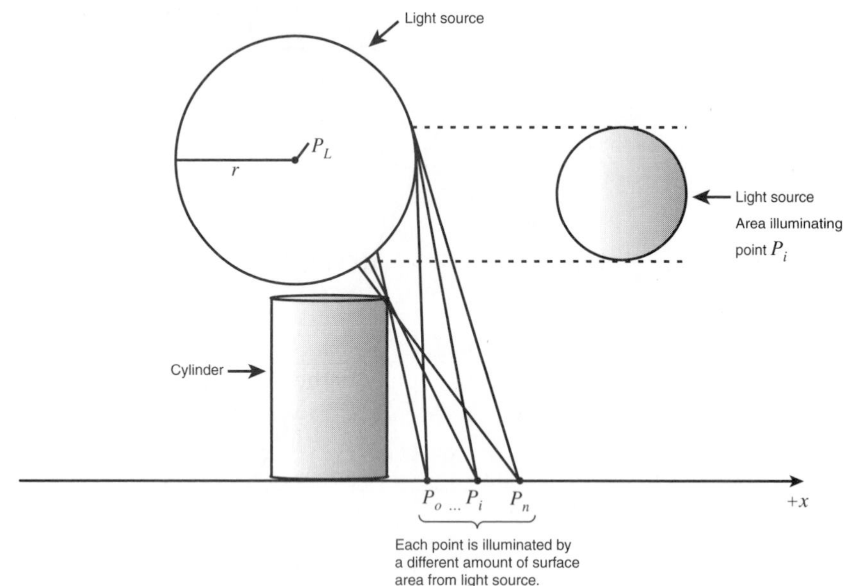

FIGURE 14.4a Increasing the size of the point light source creates softer shadows.

FIGURE 14.4b Increasing the size of the point source light creates softer shadows.

The point is that for nearly a quarter century, video games have lived without shadows (or physically correct ones, at least), so any shadow at all is better than nothing. Hence, even if we don't compute the exact light intensity at every pixel, we can basically create an artificial soft shadow with an alpha blending pass, or other tricks. And in software, this is more than enough.

Now that you know what generates shadows from an optical point of view and how the umbra and penumbra are generated, let's get down to creating some shadows in steps, from really simple-looking to reasonably realistic.

Simulating Shadows with Projective Images and Billboards

The first type of shadow technology is hardly a real shadow, as far as the geometry of the occluder is concerned, but looks very convincing nonetheless until you really focus on it. The technology I am referring to is simply drawing a shadow bitmap right under the object that is supposed to be generating a shadow. Take a look at Figure 14.5 where we see a good example of a billboard or projective shadow under the character object (Mario in this case). The shadow is nothing more than a circular blur located under the character.

FIGURE 14.5 An example of a 2D shadow being rendered under a character with a bitmap or billboard.

In the simplest case, the shadow will stay exactly under the character and not take any light source into position. The next level of detail would be to scale the size of the shadow as the character moves up and down in the y-axis (changed height), and thus the shadow would get larger or smaller. This is pretty common as well.

Additionally, many games use a bitmap projection of the object for the shadow, rather than a circle. For example, take a look at Figure 14.6a. Here we see a 3D space fighter, and in Figure 14.6b, we see a shadow bitmap projected from a top-down view (of course, the final bitmap would be resized). This is the bitmap we might use if we want a little more detail.

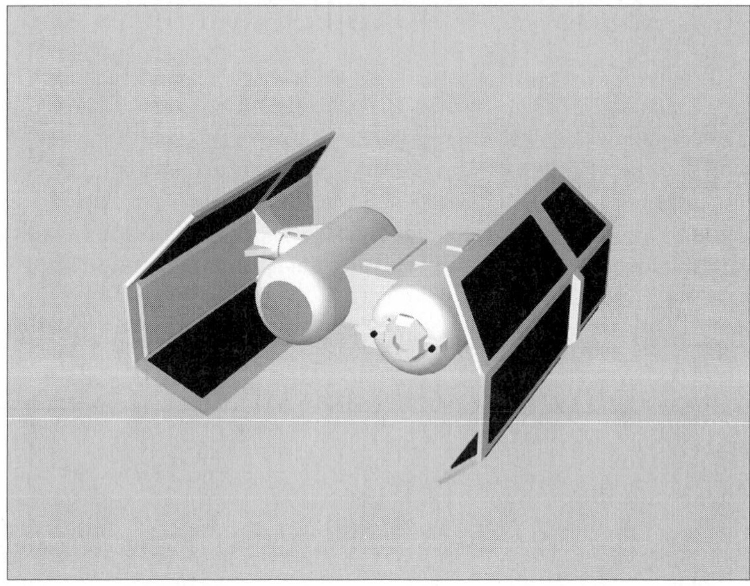

FIGURE 14.6a A space fighter.

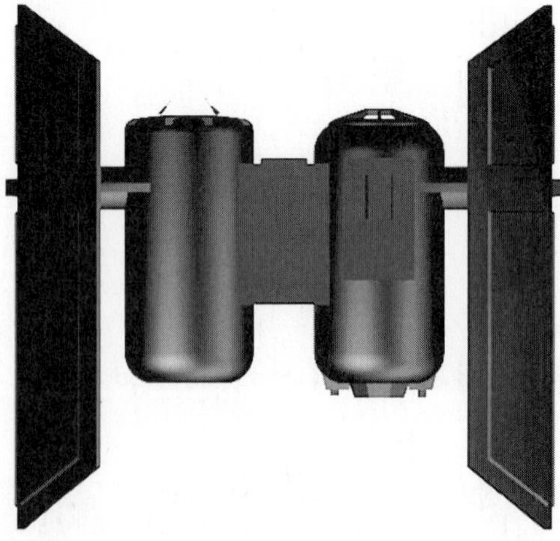

FIGURE 14.6b The 2D bitmap projection of the fighter to be used as the billboard shadow texture.

However, there are problems with this: Every object will need a shadow bitmap. That's not too bad, but the fact that the shadow is a bitmap of the object means that it is orientation-dependent, and as the object rotates, the bitmap must be rotated as well. This isn't a problem if the bitmap is textured onto a polygon billboard, as shown in Figure 14.7, because we can rotate the mesh, which will rotate the texture. However, a first attempt at shadows is best made with a single "shadow" bitmap for everything. Later you can try using a shadow bitmap for each object, properly tracking the rotational orientation of the shadow object and rotating or transforming the shadow appropriately.

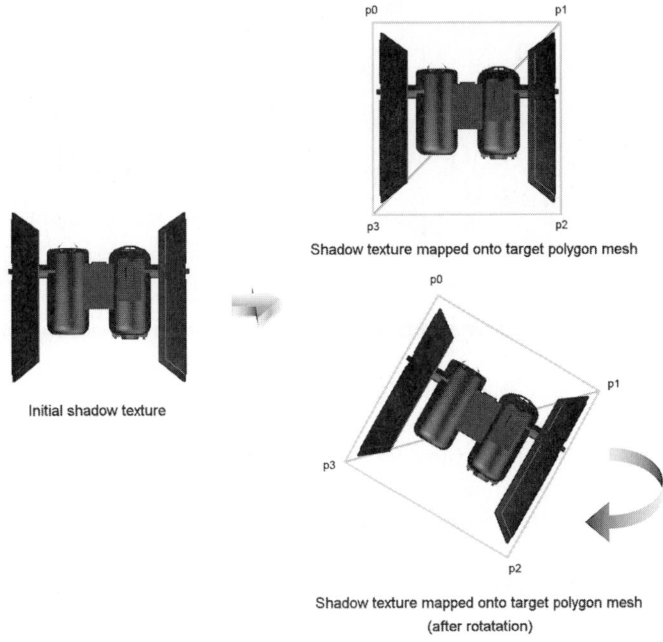

FIGURE 14.7 Mapping the shadow texture onto a polygon mesh, simplifying rotation.

Moving on, the next detail we can implement in the shadow model is to not only change the scale of the shadow with the height of the shadow occluder, but to actually use one of the light sources in the calculations, look where the light would project through the shadow object, and then cast a shadow on the ground. Figure 14.8 illustrates this idea briefly. Again, this is a bit of a hack, because we are only going to use the center of the shadow occluder object—the center of the light source—to look at where the projector pierces the ground plane and then simply draw the circular shadow there. Even so, it looks pretty good. The only thing we are missing is the shearing of the shadow, as we are always drawing the same bitmap (perhaps rotated). We'll implement shearing in the next section on planar shadows; for now, let's keep it simple.

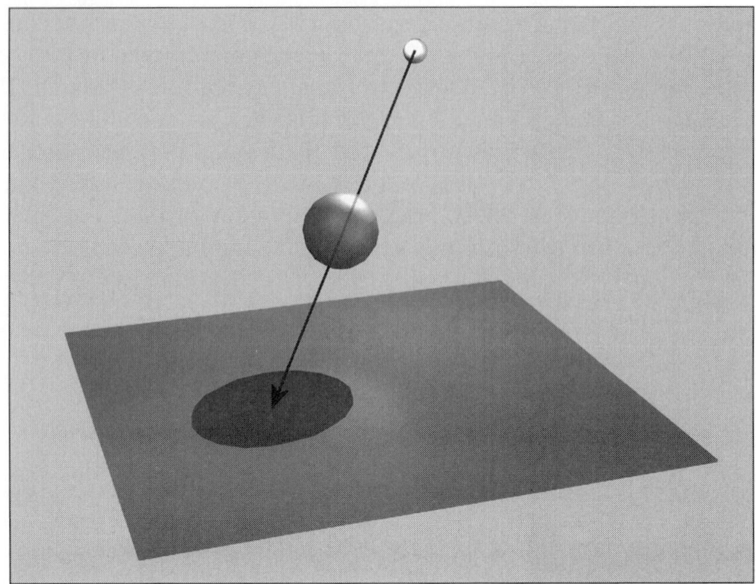

FIGURE 14.8 Scaling the shadow and projecting its location on the ground plane.

What we're going to do now is implement the preceding ideas one by one. But before we can do that, we need to be able to draw *billboards*, or flat square polygons with textures mapped onto them, where the textures have a transparent value. We will need this capability to implement the actual rendering of the shadow. The plan is to create a square from two triangles, and then texture-map the texture of a black circular area as a shadow. But where there is the transparent pixel, we need to see through it. This is a bit of a problem, because we don't have support for transparency in the rasterizers. So, we're going to have to once again rewrite some of them to add this support.

Implementing Rasterizers with Transparency Support

To draw shadows, or billboards in general, we have almost everything we need already. We are going to create a simple two-polygon mesh, as shown in Figure 14.9, and then texture-map a shadow texture onto it. The only problem is that right now, all of our texture mappers only deal with opaque textures—there is no way to "see through" any portion of the texture.

TIP

Billboard is a common term used in 3D programming to mean a polygon that has a 2D image textured onto it. The polygon that is textured usually keeps its orientation parallel to the view-plane, or some other plane. Billboarding is used to "draw" the 2D projections of 3D objects on a 2D plane in such a way that they look real. You will see billboards in many 3D games representing trees, houses, or other objects that don't need a full 3D polygonal mesh (fire and explosions are good examples of billboards—they're almost never made from polygons; they're just 2D images that are always oriented toward you). In our case, we are going to implement billboards informally just to draw shadows on them, and then we'll draw the billboards on the ground plane with the texture shadow.

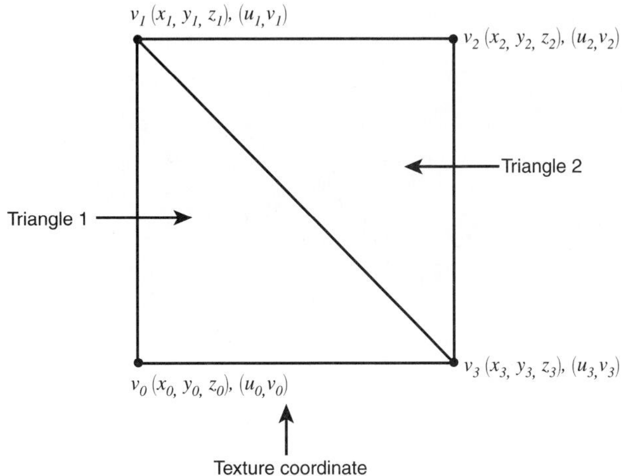

FIGURE 14.9 Our billboard is based on a simple two-polygon mesh.

Adding support for transparency is rather simple with the rasterizers we currently have. However, I want to make sure that we are on the same page: transparency is *not* alpha blending. Transparency in this context means *completely* transparent. That means if a pixel has value i_{rgb}, that pixel is not rendered or rasterized. So, if there is a texture that has holes in it with the pixel value i_{rgb} in the area of the holes, we will see through it to the background. Figure 14.10 illustrates this with a rod iron fence and a Terragen rendering.

Because I'm a fiend about speed, I don't want to use a general value for the transparent color. Let's just use RGB (0,0,0) so the `SHORT` value of the 16-bit color in the texture will be 0. Therefore, we can add a single comparison to the inner loops of our code that looks like this:

```
if (pixel)
   {
   // render pixel
   } // end if
```

FIGURE 14.10 An example of transparent texture mapping.

Or, if negative logic is more appropriate:

```
if (!pixel)
  {
  // don't draw
  } // end if
```

In either case, 0 is a great number to test for, and there are numerous optimizations that can be made with it. The only downfall to using RGB(0,0,0) for the transparent color is that it's totally black. What if there is black in the texture that we want to be opaque? Well, too bad—make it (0,0,1) or (1,1,1) and I guarantee your eyes won't see it. Although many people use pink RGB(255,0,255), we're going to use black.

With all that in mind, I'm not going to redo every single rasterizer, because we need transparency for the shadows and lighting, and advanced shading isn't needed for a shadow. However, I don't want to be cheap, so I will redo enough of the rasterizers to give you the ability to use transparent textures for at least z-buffered renderings. If you want 1/z support, you will have to redo them yourself (it takes about five minutes to modify each rasterizer). Anyway, before I show you all the new function prototypes, here's the main loop from the constant-shaded affine texture mapping rasterizer, with support for transparent RGB(0,0,0) values:

```
// draw span
for (xi=xstart; xi < xend; xi++)
  {
  // write thru the z buffer always
  // write textel
```

```
// test for transparent pixel
textel = textmap[(ui >> FIXP16_SHIFT) +
        ((vi >> FIXP16_SHIFT) << texture_shift2)];

if (textel)
  {
  // update z-buffer
  z_ptr[xi] = zi;
  // write pixel
  screen_ptr[xi] = textel;
  } // end if


// interpolate u,v,z
ui+=du;
vi+=dv;
zi+=dz;
} // end for xi
```

I have highlighted the single line of code we need to make this work. Also, for reference, here's the old function's code before adding support for transparency:

```
// draw span
for (xi=xstart; xi < xend; xi++)
  {
  // write thru the z buffer always
  // write textel
  screen_ptr[xi] = textmap[(ui >> FIXP16_SHIFT) +
              ((vi >> FIXP16_SHIFT) << texture_shift2)];

  // update z-buffer
  z_ptr[xi] = zi;

  // interpolate u,v,z
  ui+=du;
  vi+=dv;
  zi+=dz;
  } // end for xi
```

If you compare the preceding old code and the new code fragment with transparency support, you will see that basically the new texture mapper simply reads the textel and compares it to RGB(0,0,0). If it's not (0,0,0), rendering proceeds along with a Z-buffer update.

TIP

It's very important that the Z-buffer is *not* updated on transparent pixels. They are not there, so they shouldn't have an effect on the Z-buffer.

The New Software Library

The new software and rasterizers are located within T3DLIB12.CPP|H. Here's the header file for your reference:

```
// T3DLIB12.H - header file for T3DLIB12.H

// watch for multiple inclusions
#ifndef T3DLIB12
#define T3DLIB12

// EXTERNALS ///////////////////////////////////////////////////////////////////

extern HWND main_window_handle; // save the window handle
extern HINSTANCE main_instance; // save the instance

// MACROS ///////////////////////////////////////////////////

// PROTOTYPES //////////////////////////////////////////////////////////////////

// new rendering context function that calls the transparent rasterizers
void Draw_RENDERLIST4DV2_RENDERCONTEXTV1_16_3(RENDERCONTEXTV1_PTR rc);

// normal z-buffered, with write thru z and transparency support on textures
void Draw_Textured_TriangleGSWTZB2_16(POLYF4DV2_PTR face, // ptr to face
          UCHAR *_dest_buffer,   // pointer to video buffer
          int mem_pitch,      // bytes per line, 320, 640 etc.
          UCHAR *_zbuffer,     // pointer to z-buffer
          int zpitch);       // bytes per line of zbuffer

void Draw_Textured_TriangleFSWTZB3_16(POLYF4DV2_PTR face, // ptr to face
          UCHAR *_dest_buffer,   // pointer to video buffer
          int mem_pitch,      // bytes per line, 320, 640 etc.
          UCHAR *_zbuffer,     // pointer to z-buffer
          int zpitch);       // bytes per line of zbuffer


void Draw_Textured_TriangleWTZB3_16(POLYF4DV2_PTR face, // ptr to face
          UCHAR *_dest_buffer,    // pointer to video buffer
```

```
          int mem_pitch,       // bytes per line, 320, 640 etc.
          UCHAR *_zbuffer,      // pointer to z-buffer
          int zpitch);         // bytes per line of zbuffer

// normal z-buffered, and transparency support on textures

void Draw_Textured_TriangleZB3_16(POLYF4DV2_PTR face, // ptr to face
       UCHAR *_dest_buffer, // pointer to video buffer
       int mem_pitch,    // bytes per line, 320, 640 etc.
       UCHAR *_zbuffer,   // pointer to z-buffer
       int zpitch);     // bytes per line of zbuffer


// normal z-buffered, with write thru z and
// transparency support on textures and alpha
void Draw_Textured_TriangleWTZB_Alpha16_2(POLYF4DV2_PTR face, // ptr to face
       UCHAR *_dest_buffer, // pointer to video buffer
       int mem_pitch,    // bytes per line, 320, 640 etc.
       UCHAR *_zbuffer,   // pointer to z-buffer
       int zpitch,     // bytes per line of zbuffer
       int alpha);

void Draw_Textured_TriangleZB_Alpha16_2(POLYF4DV2_PTR face, // ptr to face
       UCHAR *_dest_buffer,  // pointer to video buffer
       int mem_pitch,     // bytes per line, 320, 640 etc.
       UCHAR *_zbuffer,    // pointer to z-buffer
       int zpitch,      // bytes per line of zbuffer
       int alpha);

void Draw_Textured_Triangle_Alpha16_2(POLYF4DV2_PTR face,  // ptr to face
       UCHAR *_dest_buffer,    // pointer to video buffer
       int mem_pitch, int alpha); // bytes per line, 320, 640 etc.

#endif
```

Referring to the header file, you see that there are six new rasterizers that are identical to the previous versions they each build on, but with the one added feature of transparency support. I reworked enough of the functions to make sure we could draw alpha blended textures with transparency support with or without z-buffering. However, if you are keeping up with current events, you know that we stopped calling the rasterizers manually, and have been using a "rendering context" function that we set up and then call. We were on version 2.0, and now we are on version 3.0:

```
void Draw_RENDERLIST4DV2_RENDERCONTEXTV1_16_3(RENDERCONTEXTV1_PTR rc);
```

There is absolutely no difference, other than the name has a "3" in it. And of course, within the function there is support for the transparent rasterizers. There is a slight speed hit for using transparency. I could have added a flag in the polygon attributes to indicate that a texture was transparent, and then used a switch case on which rasterizer to use and fork, but that's not worth the trouble at this point. Additionally, you would have to set something in the modeler to indicate transparency for the attached texture, and we have enough weird settings for lighting and alpha blending as it is!

That's all there is to the software—the rest is just math, and we will implement each technique in the context of a demo.

Simple Shadows

Implementing simple shadows involves nothing more than drawing a bitmap shadow with alpha blending directly under the object that is supposedly casting the shadow. To implement this effect, first we need two things: the shadow texture, and the shadow polygon mesh for the billboard. Let's start with the shadow texture: Its name is `shadow64_64.bmp`; it's 64×64 pixels, and basically a very dark disk RGB(16,16,16) with a RGB(0,0,0) fill color. Figure 14.11 is a negative version of the texture, because you can't see the black on the printed side, but you can at least see the shape. Just imagine it black on black!

FIGURE 14.11 Our shadow texture (inverted negative image).

The next step is to model a square made of two triangles and then apply the shadow texture to the mesh. Additionally, to make the nontransparent parts of the texture look more realistic as shadows, the alpha should be enabled in the model. If you recall, we have support for this with the Caligari .COB file format. We just set the transparency to filter mode, and then set the level of transparency to whatever. In this case, I used a level that makes the shadow texture look dark—but not too much, so it doesn't look black. Finally, the lighting model on the shadow model billboard model should be constant shading; we don't want light reflecting off the shadow!

The final model for the shadow billboard model is named `shadow_poly_01.cob` and can be found on the CD in this chapter's directory. I would show you a screenshot of it, but there's nothing to show—just two triangles! Anyway, now that we have the shadow polygon mesh and the transparent texture with alpha set on the polygons to blend on nontransparent textures, we are ready to write a demo.

Writing the demo is rather easy. The steps to creating a shadow for any object are the following:

1. Render all objects in the world with normal z-buffering.
2. Make a second pass, and for each object that a shadow should be projected from, render the shadow mesh directly under the object and above the terrain (if there's any below it) with alpha blending and the transparent texture mappers.

The reason why a second pass is needed is because to alpha blend the shadow with the terrain or geometry under it, we need an image in the buffer with which to alpha blend. Also, because the shadow is supposed to be on the ground, we need to figure out not only where the ground is, but at what altitude to draw the shadow above the ground. Figure 14.12 illustrates these considerations.

For the demo, I used our trusty terrain generator to make an icy planet with a little planet/moon orbiting around the center of the terrain (I have no idea what I was thinking!). The rendering process goes as follows: The terrain and planet are rendered as usual, and then a second pass is made, but this time, a single object is rendered—the shadow mesh. The position of the shadow mesh is located directly under and centered relative to the planet mesh object (which is projecting the shadow), and at a height that takes the terrain into consideration, so the shadow doesn't "z-fight" the Z-buffer. Of course, for really rough terrain, this won't look good, because the shadow is planar and will end up intersecting the geometry no matter what you do!

In any case, here's a code snippet from the demo illustrating the shadow pass:

```
// shadow object

// reset the render list
Reset_RENDERLIST4DV2(&rend_list);

// reset the object (this only matters for backface and object removal)
Reset_OBJECT4DV2(&shadow_obj);
```

```
// compute terrain cell shadow is over
cell_x = (obj_work->world_pos.x + TERRAIN_WIDTH/2) / obj_terrain.fvar1;
cell_y = (obj_work->world_pos.z + TERRAIN_HEIGHT/2) / obj_terrain.fvar1;

// compute vertex indices into vertex list of the current quad
int v0 = cell_x + cell_y*obj_terrain.ivar2;
int v1 = v0 + 1;
int v2 = v1 + obj_terrain.ivar2;
int v3 = v0 + obj_terrain.ivar2;

// now simply index into table
terrain_height = MAX(  MAX(obj_terrain.vlist_trans[v0].y,
               obj_terrain.vlist_trans[v1].y),
             MAX(obj_terrain.vlist_trans[v2].y,
               obj_terrain.vlist_trans[v3].y) );

// update position
shadow_obj.world_pos   = obj_work->world_pos;
shadow_obj.world_pos.y = terrain_height+10;

// create identity matrix
MAT_IDENTITY_4X4(&mrot);

// transform the local coords of the object
Transform_OBJECT4DV2(&shadow_obj, &mrot, TRANSFORM_LOCAL_TO_TRANS,1);

// perform world transform
Model_To_World_OBJECT4DV2(&shadow_obj, TRANSFORM_TRANS_ONLY);

// insert the object into render list
Insert_OBJECT4DV2_RENDERLIST4DV2(&rend_list, &shadow_obj,0);
```

Further down in the complete code, the rendering context is set up and a full render pass is made. Figure 14.13 is a screenshot of the demo in action. It's quite cool, but it's going to get a lot cooler by the end of the chapter—he he he! The name of the demo is DEMOII14_1.CPP¦EXE, and to compile it you will need all the usual DirectX .LIB files, along with all the library modules T3DLIB1–12.CPP¦H. The controls for the demo are on the screen, but you can basically move around with the keyboard and try toggling the lights and wireframe modes so you can see what's going on.

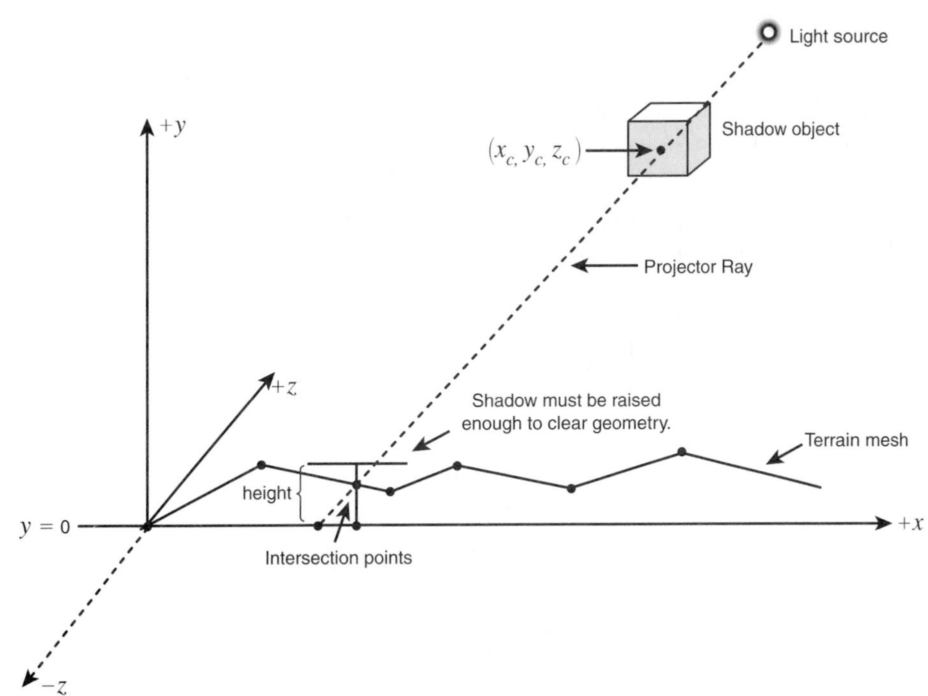

FIGURE 14.12 Computing the height at which to render the shadow polygon.

FIGURE 14.13 A screenshot of the simple shadow demo.

14

Shadows that Scale

Now that we have something that resembles a shadow, let's take it to the next level. We need to scale the shadow based on three things: the size of the object, the position of the object relative to the ground (its altitude), and the position of the light source creating the fictional shadow.

The size of the object is constant in the calculations, so we don't need to worry about that. We can use a scaling factor later to account for this, but we must consider the height of the object and the height/position of the light source in real time. A mathematical relationship must be derived that takes at least the height of the object above the ground and the height of the light source above the ground into account. Take a look at Figure 14.14 to see a derivation.

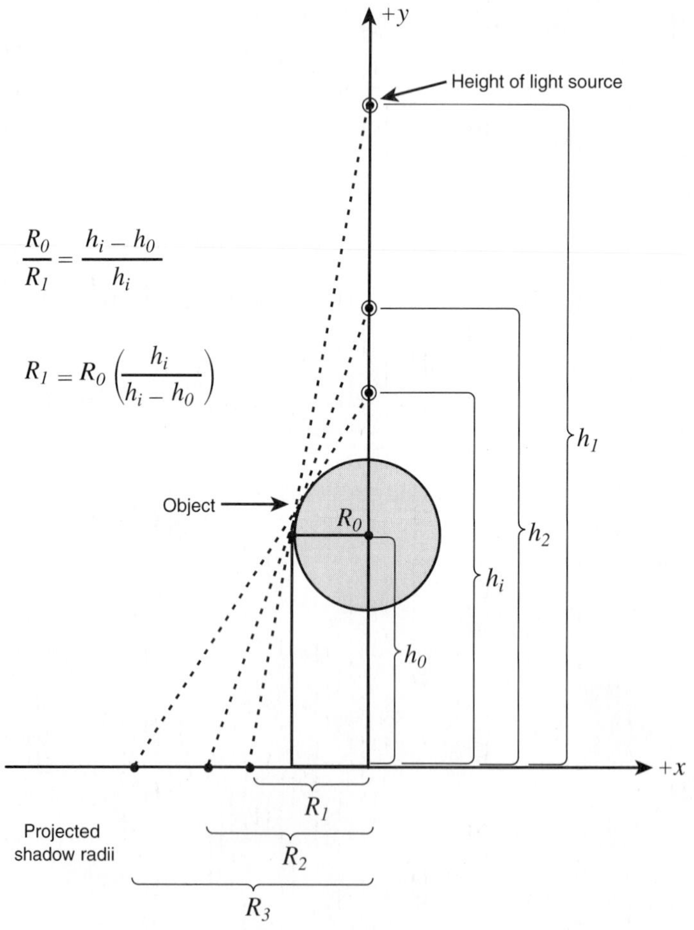

FIGURE 14.14 The geometrical setup for scaling shadows.

In Figure 14.14, we see a 2D dimensional version of the problem. Without loss of generality, we can position the object on the y-axis some height h_0 with radius r_0. We can then position the light source above the object at a position h_i. Also in the figure, there are a number of other rays plotted out. You can see that a light with position h_1 will leave everything in shadow from the origin to r_1. Similarly, a light with position h_2 will leave everything in shadow from the origin to position r_2, and so forth. In general, when the light source is at position h_i, the radius of the shadow will be r_i. The googleplex question is, what is the relationship between r_0, r_i, h_0, and h_i?

Similar triangles to the rescue! Noting that the triangle formed by the origin, h_i, and r_i, is similar to the triangle formed by $(h_i - h_0)$, and r_0, we can write this relationship:

$$\frac{r_0}{r_i} = \frac{(h_i - h_0)}{(h_i)}$$

Rearranging and solving for r_i, we have:

$$r_i = r_0 * (h_i / (h_i - h_0))$$

Let's try this out with some common sense. What if the light source is like the sun, and infinitely far away? We would expect that the light rays would be nearly parallel, and thus the shadow would approach the radius r_0 in the limit. Let's check it out:

$$\lim_{h_i \to \infty} r_i = \lim_{h_i \to \infty} r_0 * (h_i / (h_i - h_0))$$

$$= r_0 * \lim_{h_i \to \infty} (h_i / (h_i - h_0))$$

Dividing top and bottom by h_i, we get

$$= r_0 * \lim_{h_i \to \infty} ((h_i/h_i) / (h_i/h_i - h_0/h_i))$$

$$= r_0 * \lim_{h_i \to \infty} (1 / (1 - h_0/h_i))$$

As h_i approaches infinity, the quotient h_0/h_i approaches 0. Therefore, we have

$$= r_0 * (1 / (1 - 0)) = r_0$$

from which we conclude that as the light source altitude gets larger and larger (y tends toward positive infinity), the shadow radius approaches the object radius, and the converse is true as well. Now let's implement our findings.

The next demo will take the shadow scaling math into account, along with the actual position of one of the point light sources we are so used to seeing floating around.

14

However, only the altitude of the light source will be used in the calculations (the green point light will be our source). The process to render the shadow is exactly the same as before, only the final scale is factored in, and the shadow mesh is scaled before rendering. Here's the code fragment that accomplishes this task:

```
// now make second rendering pass and draw shadow(s)

// reset the render list
Reset_RENDERLIST4DV2(&rend_list);

//////////////////////////////////////////////////////////////////////////
// shadow object

// reset the object (this only matters for backface and object removal)
Reset_OBJECT4DV2(&shadow_obj);

// compute terrain cell shadow is over
cell_x = (obj_work->world_pos.x + TERRAIN_WIDTH/2) / obj_terrain.fvar1;
cell_y = (obj_work->world_pos.z + TERRAIN_HEIGHT/2) / obj_terrain.fvar1;

// compute vertex indices into vertex list of the current quad
int v0 = cell_x + cell_y*obj_terrain.ivar2;
int v1 = v0 + 1;
int v2 = v1 + obj_terrain.ivar2;
int v3 = v0 + obj_terrain.ivar2;

// now simply index into table
terrain_height = MAX(  MAX(obj_terrain.vlist_trans[v0].y,
               obj_terrain.vlist_trans[v1].y),
             MAX(obj_terrain.vlist_trans[v2].y,
               obj_terrain.vlist_trans[v3].y) );

// update position
shadow_obj.world_pos   = obj_work->world_pos;
shadow_obj.world_pos.y = terrain_height+25;

// now compute the size of the shadow radius based on the
// calculations shown in the book
// the size of the projected shadow, assuming a sphere as the
// occluder with a point lightsource
// height hl above the ground plane, a spherical object
// with radius ro, and height above
// the groundplane ho, the radius of the shadow is rs:
//
//  rs = ro * (hl)/(hl - ho)
```

```
// set height to altitude of green light for fun
hl = lights2[POINT_LIGHT_INDEX].pos.y;

// use the average radius of the object to base calcs on, better than nothing
float rs = ks * ( obj_work->avg_radius[0] *
        (hl/ (hl - obj_work->world_pos.y)) );

// generate scaling matrix bases on shadow scale
MAT_IDENTITY_4X4(&mrot);

// set scaling values to scale in X-Z plane
mrot.M00 = rs;
mrot.M11 = 1.0;
mrot.M22 = rs;

// scale the local coords of the object via the matrix
Transform_OBJECT4DV2(&shadow_obj, &mrot, TRANSFORM_LOCAL_TO_TRANS,1);

// perform world transform
Model_To_World_OBJECT4DV2(&shadow_obj, TRANSFORM_TRANS_ONLY);

// insert the object into render list
Insert_OBJECT4DV2_RENDERLIST4DV2(&rend_list, &shadow_obj,0);
```


TIP

You will notice a constant ks being multiplied against the scale computation. This is just a "fudge factor" to make the size of the shadow look good. Sometimes correct doesn't look as real as real.

I have highlighted the new code, which is almost identical to the math we derived. The only interesting fact is that I opted to use a matrix transform to scale the mesh. If you recall, to scale any vertex point **p** via a matrix $\mathbf{M}_s$, the scaling matrix should look like this:

```
     |sx  0   0  0|
     |0   sy  0  0|
Ms = |0   0   sz 0|
     |0   0   0  1|
```

In this case, we only want to scale in the x-z plane, of course.

Figure 14.15 is a screenshot of `DEMOII14_2.CPP|EXE` in action. To compile the demo, you will need `T3DLIB1-12.CPP|H`, in addition to the DirectX .LIB files. The controls of the demo are identical to the previous demo, with the addition of controlling the altitude of the green point light with the 1 and 2 keys. Try changing the height of the light and see what happens to the shadow, but don't raise the light too high, or the illusion will break down! Also, make sure to toggle to wireframe mode with the W key to see the mesh being rendered for the shadow to confirm that it's just a square.

FIGURE 14.15 A screenshot of the shadow demo that supports scaling shadows.

Tracking the Light Source

Now we are starting to get somewhere. The shadow is starting to look like a shadow. It's always a disk—I could use a minibus as the occluder and we would still see disk for the shadow—but that's easy enough to fix. The real issue here is that the shadow is always directly under the object casting the shadow, and this is not correct. In the previous demo, we used the green point light as the shadow light source, but only used its height to help compute how large to make the projected shadow's radius. However, what we really need to do is the full mathematical projection of where the shadow would be in the x-z plane, given the position of the object and the light source.

Take a look at Figure 14.16 for the setup of the problem we need to solve. For a change, I thought I would solve the problem using parametric vector equations rather than similar triangles (I feel cheap and dirty when I use similar triangles). In the figure, the position of the point light source is $\mathbf{p}_l$, the center of the object is located at position $\mathbf{p}_o$, and the projected point on the ground plane is $\mathbf{p}_s$.

Let's write these equations out and see what we can find. The parametric line in 3D space from the light source piercing the center of the shadow object and intersecting the ground plane is

$$\mathbf{p}_s = \mathbf{p}_l + t * (\mathbf{p}_o - \mathbf{p}_l)$$

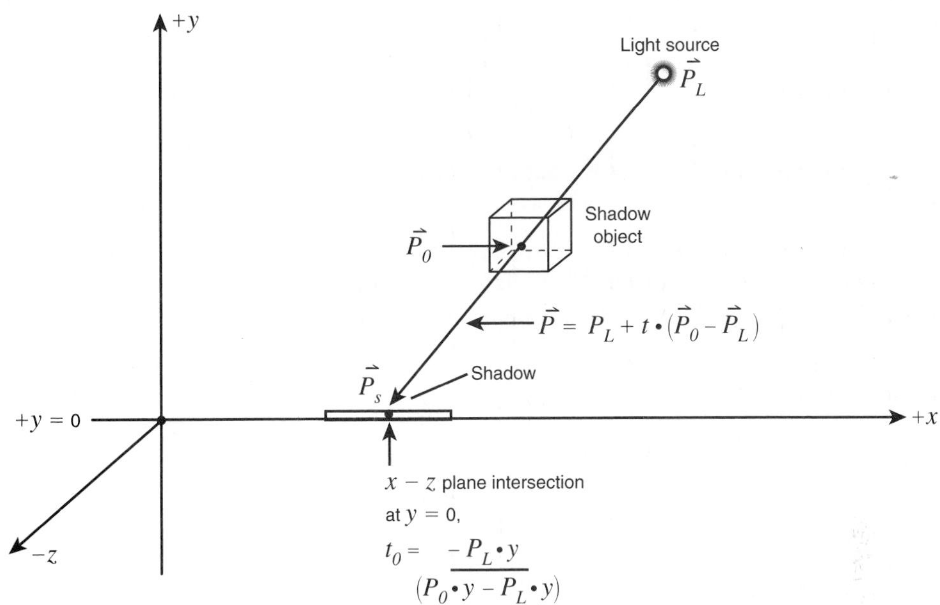

FIGURE 14.16 The geometrical setup for computing the shadow position based on a light source.

Writing $\mathbf{p}_s$ as components, we have

```
ps.x = p1.x + t * (po.x - p1.x)
ps.y = p1.y + t * (po.y - p1.y)
ps.z = p1.z + t * (po.z - p1.z)
```

We are interested in the x and z components when y = 0. Thus we can set p_s.y to 0.0 and solve for t, then plug t back into p_s.x and p_s.z, and solve for the x and z components. Solving for t is easy:

```
ps.y = p1.y + t * (po.y - p1.y) = 0
```

Therefore,

```
p1.y + t * (po.y - p1.y) = 0

t = -p1.y / (po.y - p1.y)
```

With the point $\mathbf{p}_s$ in hand, we simply render the shadow object centered at $\mathbf{p}_s$ (y = 0, of course) and we are done! The shadow will follow the light source properly, as if the object were occluding it. Moreover, we will add the scaling effect to complete the system.

Once again, implementing the rendering pipeline is identical to the previous demo—there are no changes: The terrain and the object are rendered, then the shadow objects are positioned using the math we just outlined, and a second rendering pass alpha blends the shadow objects (with transparent textures) on the ground plane of the terrain, for a fairly realistic shadow demo.

Of course, we still have two things that we need to address: the shape of the shadow has nothing to do with the object, as we are always using a circular disk; and the shadow always has the same dimension—there is no shearing or skewing—but we will get to that.

With that in mind, let's take a look at the new shadow code that computes the position of the shadow based on the position of the light source, the object, and the y = 0 plane. Here's the code fragment from the next demo that does this:

```
// reset the render list
Reset_RENDERLIST4DV2(&rend_list);

// reset shadow image for car, if in shadow change to 0
cockpit.curr_frame = 0;

int v0, v1, v2, v3; // used to track vertices

VECTOR4D pl, // position of the light
     po, // position of the occluder object
     vlo, // vector from light to object
     ps; // position of the shadow

float  rs, // radius of shadow
     t;  // parameter t

//////////////////////////////////////////////////////////////////////////
// shadow object

// reset the object (this only matters for backface and object removal)
Reset_OBJECT4DV2(&shadow_obj);

// compute terrain cell shadow is over
cell_x = (obj_work->world_pos.x + TERRAIN_WIDTH/2) / obj_terrain.fvar1;
cell_y = (obj_work->world_pos.z + TERRAIN_HEIGHT/2) / obj_terrain.fvar1;

// compute vertex indices into vertex list of the current quad
v0 = cell_x + cell_y*obj_terrain.ivar2;
v1 = v0 + 1;
v2 = v1 + obj_terrain.ivar2;
v3 = v0 + obj_terrain.ivar2;

// now simply index into table
terrain_height = MAX(  MAX(obj_terrain.vlist_trans[v0].y,
```

```
          obj_terrain.vlist_trans[v1].y),
         MAX(obj_terrain.vlist_trans[v2].y,
          obj_terrain.vlist_trans[v3].y) );

// update position
//shadow_obj.world_pos  = obj_work->world_pos;
shadow_obj.world_pos.y = terrain_height+25;

// using point light source 1 as the projector, compute target projection
// position, use local variables to make the math easier to understand

// assign light position from point light
pl = lights2[POINT_LIGHT_INDEX].pos;

// assign object position
po = obj_work->world_pos;

// create vector from lightsource to object
VECTOR4D_Build(&pl, &po, &vlo);

// now, comes the fun part, solve for t when y=0 of the projector line
// technically, we are placing the shadow slightly higher in the math above,
// so if you like, you can change the solution of t,
// to take that into consideration
// but this is cleaner for now
t = -pl.y / vlo.y;

// now compute x,z of projected shadow position
// (scale t by .5 to keep the shadow close)
shadow_obj.world_pos.x = pl.x + t*vlo.x;
shadow_obj.world_pos.z = pl.z + t*vlo.z;

// now compute the size of the shadow radius based on the calculations
// shown in the book the size of the projected shadow, assuming a sphere
// as the occluder with a point lightsource height hl above the
// ground plane, a spherical object with radius ro, and height above
// the groundplane ho, the radius of the shadow is rs:
//
//  rs = ro * (hl)/(hl - ho)

// set height to altitude of light
hl = lights2[POINT_LIGHT_INDEX].pos.y;
```

14

```
// use the average radius of the object to base calcs on, better than nothing
rs = ks * ( obj_work->avg_radius[0] * (hl/ (hl - obj_work->world_pos.y)) );

// generate scaling matrix bases on shadow scale
MAT_IDENTITY_4X4(&mrot);

// set scaling values to scale in X-Z plane
mrot.M00 = rs;
mrot.M11 = 1.0;
mrot.M22 = rs;

// scale the local coords of the object
Transform_OBJECT4DV2(&shadow_obj, &mrot, TRANSFORM_LOCAL_TO_TRANS,1);

// perform world transform
Model_To_World_OBJECT4DV2(&shadow_obj, TRANSFORM_TRANS_ONLY);

// insert the object into render list
Insert_OBJECT4DV2_RENDERLIST4DV2(&rend_list, &shadow_obj,0);

//////////////////////////////////////////////////////////////////////////

// test if camera is in shadow
VECTOR4D vd;
VECTOR4D_Build(&cam.pos, &shadow_obj.world_pos, &vd);
float d = VECTOR4D_Length_Fast(&vd);

// test if distance is within 1.5 times the radius of the shadow,
// the 1.5 makes it a little more noticeable
if (d < 1.5*rs)
  cockpit.curr_frame = 1; // cockpit with lower brightness
else
  cockpit.curr_frame = 0; // cockpit with higher brightness
```

The code implements the parametric projection and intersection almost verbatim; the only added feature is some code to swap out cockpit bitmaps when the camera is in the virtual shadow. If you have ever played a first-person game, when you walk into a dark area, the lighting of the mesh is diminished, either by the light model or by manually decreasing the ambient factor for the mesh to simulate the effect of the shadow. For fun, I did the same thing here. I used a little cockpit from a jeep vehicle rendering and have two versions of it: full intensity and dark. When I detect that the camera is in a shadow, I swap out the bright image for the dark image and vice versa, thus creating the illusion (and I am pushing it with that euphemistic word to say the least) that the car is in the shadow.

In a real first-person game, you probably would use real 3D geometry for the cockpit, player, gun, or whatever, and let the lighting model drive the shading for real. However, the lighting model doesn't know about shadows, so at very least, you still have to determine whether the mesh is in a shadow and then decrease the ambient term or something to make the mesh get darker. Anyway, I highlighted the code fragment that performs this little test and bitmap swap.

The only other extra code you will find in the final demo is that it renders a shadow for every single point light source (there are two of them), and this is a key point when performing shadow calculations. More or less, you must render a shadow for each object, for all light sources. Even with simple shadow algorithms, this can spin out of control quickly. Imagine 50 objects with three lights—that's an added 150 renderings! Sure, each is just a two-polygon mesh with a texture on it, but they are alpha blended, so they hurt performance somewhat. Just something to think about.

Last but not least, just to make sure we are on the same page with the rendering algorithm, take a look at the flow chart in Figure 14.17. It illustrates the pipeline:

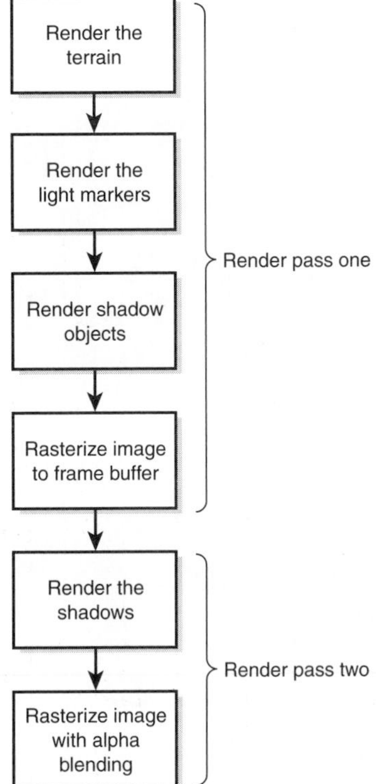

FIGURE 14.17 A flowchart of the rendering process for shadows.

1. Render the terrain.
2. Render the light markers.
3. Render the shadow object itself.
4. Rasterize the image.
5. Render each of the shadows.
6. Rasterize the image with alpha blending.

Take a look at Figure 14.18 for a screenshot of `DEMOII14_3.CPP¦EXE` in action. Once again, the controls are the same, but this time you can control the height of both the green and red point lights with the 1 and 2 keys (for the green points) and the 3 and 4 keys (for the red points). But watch out—if you make the lights too low, you will cause an inverted projection, and the shadows will do weird things—try it! Also, experiment by making the points' lights very high above the ground plane to simulate sun light. You will notice that not only do the positions of the projections stay near the planet object, but the size of the shadows are the same, because their radius will tend toward the radius of the occluder object, as we derived in our calculations.

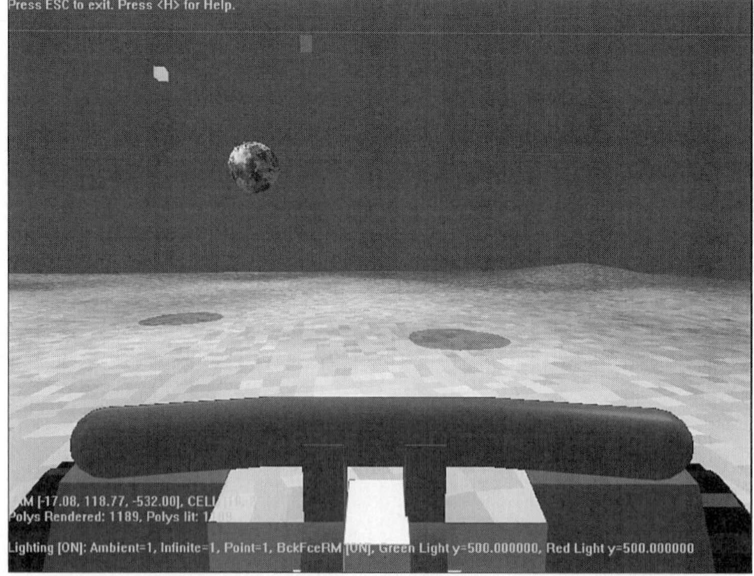

FIGURE 14.18 A screenshot of the shadow demo with scaling, and positioning.

To compile the demo, you will need the library modules `T3DLIB1-12.CPP¦H`, as well as the main program `DEMOII14_3.CPP¦H` and the DirectX .LIB files.

Final Thoughts on Simulated Shadows

Even with what we have now, we can do some pretty cool shadow effects. In fact, positional, scaling, and alpha blended shadows are middle-of-the-road for most hardware accelerated games, so we aren't doing bad.

One last feature you might want to add is using a bitmap image of the 3D mesh projected from a light source point of view. This way, the shadow looks like it has something to do with the object. The only problem, of course, is that if the object rotates, the shadow mesh must be rotated also. However, this is easily solved if the rotation is parallel to the y-axis, as shown in Figure 14.19.

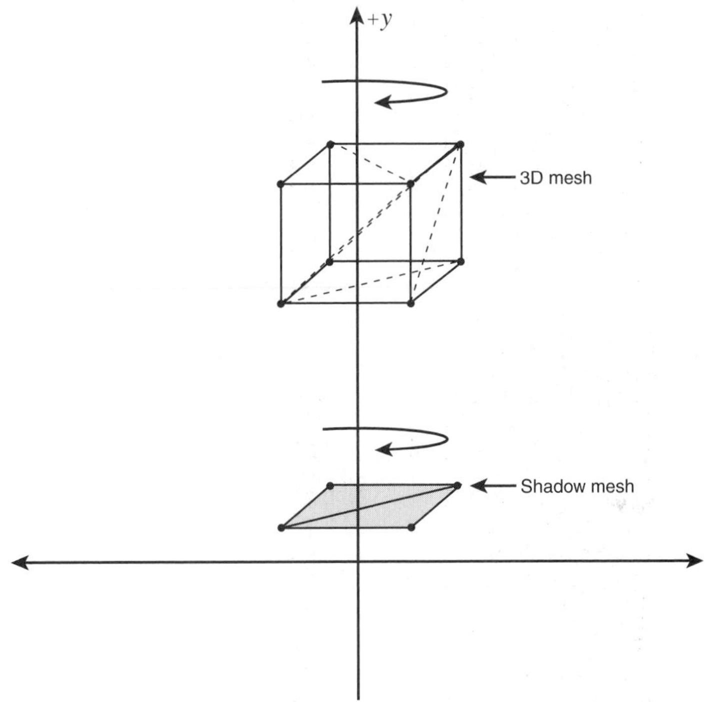

FIGURE 14.19 Rotation of the bitmap shadow billboard tracking the object.

If the object rotates in the y-axis, simply rotate the shadow mesh the exact same amount and use the projected bitmap image of the object as the texture. Of course, the system will look wrong if the object rotates on the other axis, but for many games and objects, you can get away with this. It's an easy thing to add (two to five lines of code), and an extra bitmap really makes the shadow look more convincing.

Planar Mesh Shadow Mapping

We are now ready for the next level of shadow technology. This involves actually projecting the mesh geometry on the ground plane and then drawing the mesh with gray color and alpha to make it look like a shadow. We'll basically model how a single photon would trace from the light source through a given vertex on the object mesh we want as the shadow generator and onto the ground. This is shown in Figure 14.20.

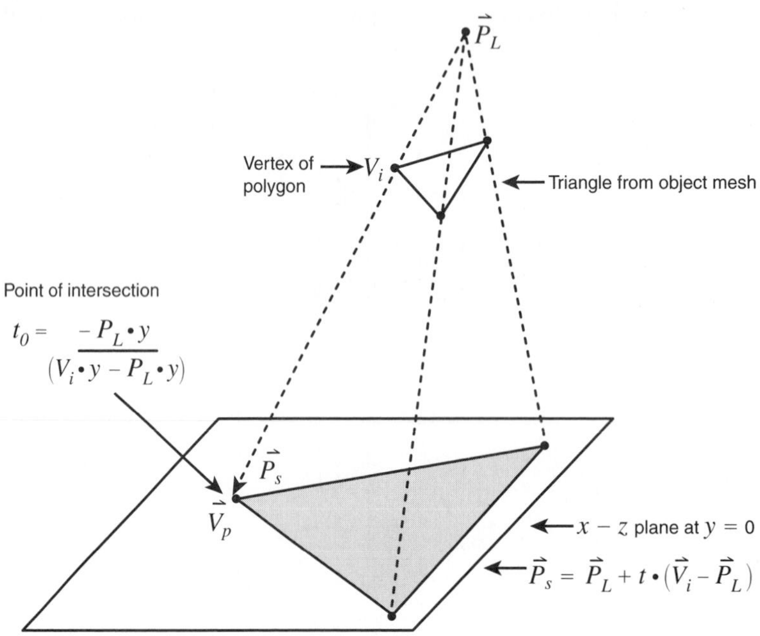

FIGURE 14.20 Planar mesh shadow mapping.

We've solved this problem in the previous example—we just need to generalize it a bit. What we really need to do is find a transformation that will "project" a 3D mesh intact onto a flat plane (the x-z in this case), and then we will render this flattened mesh with shading set so it looks like a shadow (disabling textures and lighting, more or less). In other words, we are going to render the object itself projected onto the ground plane as a shadow!

Computing the Vector Transformations for Projection

Let's work through the algorithm. What we need is a transformation that will take any vertex from the source mesh and then project it onto the ground plane based on the position of the light source. Let's derive the math with a slightly different notation:

We want to project the vertex $\mathbf{v}_i$ from the mesh, and $\mathbf{v}_i$ is really a vertex from a polygon $\mathbf{p}_i$. The light source we are projecting from is at $\mathbf{p}_l$, and the ground plane is located at y = 0. The projected point on the ground plane we will call $\mathbf{p}_s$; it is computed as follows:

```
ps = pl + t * (vi - pl)
```

Writing $\mathbf{p}_s$ as components, we have

```
ps.x = pl.x + t * (vi.x - pl.x)
ps.y = pl.y + t * (vi.y - pl.y)
ps.z = pl.z + t * (vi.z - pl.z)
```

Once again, we know that $p_s.y = 0$ in the x-z plane. Thus, we can solve $p_s.y = 0$ for t (calling it t_0), and then plug the solution back into the system to solve for the x,z components:


```
ps.y = pl.y + t0 * (vi.y - pl.y) = 0
```

Therefore,

```
pl.y + t0 * (vi.y - pl.y) = 0

t0 = -pl.y / (vi.y - pl.y)
```

Then plugging back in, we have

```
ps.x = pl.x + (-pl.y / (vi.y - pl.y)) * (vi.x - pl.x)
ps.y = 0
ps.z = pl.z + (-pl.y / (vi.y - pl.y)) * (vi.z - pl.z)
```

If you play with the math for a minute, you will arrive at the general vector equation:

```
ps = pl + t0 * (vi - pl)
   = pl + t0 * vi - t0*pl

   = t0*vi + pl*(1-t0)
```

Or in other words, for every point $\mathbf{v}_i$ in the initial mesh, the projected point equals that point scaled by the constant t_0 plus the sum of $\mathbf{p}_l$ scaled by $(1\text{-}t_0)$. This is perfect for a matrix operation to perform the operation. Here's the matrix:

```
      |t0              0              0              0|
Mps = |0               t0             0              0|
      |0               0              t0             0|
      |pl.x*(1-t0)     pl.y*(1-t0)    pl.z*(1-t0)    1|
```

If you take the planar shadow matrix and pre-multiply by the vertex $\mathbf{v}_i$, you will get

$$\mathbf{v}_i * \mathbf{M}_{ps} = [t_0 * v_i.x + p_1.x * (1 - t_0),\ t_0 * v_i.y + p_1.y * (1 - t_0),\ t_0 * v_i.z + p_1.z * (1 - t_0)]$$

which is correct, but there is one little problem with this—can you guess? It only works with one vertex! The computation of t_0 used $\mathbf{v}_i$ in it; therefore, although the matrix operation is valid, it's only valid for $\mathbf{v}_i$. We need this to recompute t_0 for the next $\mathbf{v}_i$, and so on.

Alas, using a matrix transform isn't as good an idea as it seemed. The best approach is to simply compute the vector equation manually for each vertex in a loop, solving for t_0 at $y = 0$, plugging it back in, and solving for x and z for each transformed vertex. But on a positive note, because we are doing all this transformation and computing in world space, we can perform the local-to-world transform right in the shadow calculation and omit the step to position the shadow mesh—this is a nice gain.

Now let's assume that we have the shadow mesh flattened out based on the shadow object and the light source. We are ready to render it, but rendering a flattened-out version of the object (car, planet, and so on) isn't going to look like a shadow—we need to change its shading properties. Here are the steps we will follow to change the shading properties, so the object's shadow looks like a shadow:

1. Take the object mesh that we want to project a shadow for, transform it, project the local coordinates to the planar projection, and store them in the transformed coordinates. (Remember, no matter what we do to a mesh, it doesn't hurt it as long as we don't mess with the local coordinates for the model. We can always transform them and copy them in the transformed vertex list.)
2. With the new flattened mesh in hand, change the lighting and shading of the mesh, so that the mesh will look like a shadow. Simply save each color and the attributes for each polygon and then overwrite into each polygon constant shading, alpha blending, an alpha value at roughly 50%, and disable the texture.
3. Send the mesh into the pipeline, and restore the color and attributes previously saved.

In essence, if an object is supposed to cast a shadow, we use the object itself to generate the shadow by projecting its mesh on the ground plane, then we modify the shading parameters of the mesh to make it look like a shadow would, render it, and then restore it! Cool, huh?

So without further ado, here's the code fragment from the next demo that does all this:

```
// reset the render list
Reset_RENDERLIST4DV2(&rend_list);

//////////////////////////////////////////////////////////////////////
// project shaded object into shadow by projecting its vertices onto
// the ground plane
```

```
// reset the object (this only matters for backface and object removal)
Reset_OBJECT4DV2(obj_work);

// save the shading attributes/color of each polygon, and override them with
// attributes of a shadow then restore them
int pcolor[OBJECT4DV2_MAX_POLYS],  // used to store color
  pattr[OBJECT4DV2_MAX_POLYS];   // used to store attribute

// save all the color and attributes for each polygon
for (int pindex = 0; pindex < obj_work->num_polys; pindex++)
  {
  // save attribute and color
  pattr[pindex] = obj_work->plist[pindex].attr;
  pcolor[pindex] = obj_work->plist[pindex].color;

  // set attributes for shadow rendering
  obj_work->plist[pindex].attr  = POLY4DV2_ATTR_RGB16 |
                  POLY4DV2_ATTR_SHADE_MODE_CONSTANT |
                  POLY4DV2_ATTR_TRANSPARENT;
  obj_work->plist[pindex].color  = RGB16Bit(0,0,0) + (2 << 24);

  } // end for pindex

// create identity matrix
MAT_IDENTITY_4X4(&mrot);

// solve for t when the projected vertex intersects ground plane
pl = lights2[POINT_LIGHT_INDEX].pos;

// transform each local/model vertex of the object mesh and store result
// in "transformed" vertex list, note
for (int vertex=0; vertex < obj_work->num_vertices; vertex++)
  {
  POINT4D presult; // hold result of each transformation

  // compute parameter t0 when projected ray pierces y=0 plane
  VECTOR4D vi;

  // transform coordinates to worldspace right now...
  VECTOR4D_Add(&obj_work->vlist_local[vertex].v, &obj_work->world_pos, &vi);

  float t0 = -pl.y / (vi.y - pl.y);
```

14

```
    // transform point
    obj_work->vlist_trans[vertex].v.x = pl.x + t0*(vi.x - pl.x);
    obj_work->vlist_trans[vertex].v.y = 25.0; // pl.y + t0*(vi.y - pl.y);
    obj_work->vlist_trans[vertex].v.z = pl.z + t0*(vi.z - pl.z);
    obj_work->vlist_trans[vertex].v.w = 1.0;

    } // end for index

// insert the object into render list
Insert_OBJECT4DV2_RENDERLIST4DV2(&rend_list, obj_work,0);
```

Then the next light source is used to create yet another mesh, and so on until all the light sources have been projected to cast shadows (in this case, there are only two). Then the old attributes and colors are restored and the mesh is back to normal:

```
// restore attributes and color
for (pindex = 0; pindex < obj_work->num_polys; pindex++)
  {
  // save attribute and color
  obj_work->plist[pindex].attr = pattr[pindex];
  obj_work->plist[pindex].color = pcolor[pindex];
  } // end for pindex
```

The rendering order is exactly the same as before: first the terrain is rendered, then the light markers, and the object itself. Then a second pass is made where the shadows are rendered, because they need to alpha blend in with the background image.

The results of the planar mesh projection is rather stunning—I leave it to you to implement. Just kidding! Figure 14.21a is a screenshot of the demo in wireframe mode, and 14.21b is another screenshot, but in solid mode. The point I want to make is that the shadows are indeed complete 3D meshes—they're simply squished (yes, that's a technical term).

The name of the demo is DEMOII14_4.CPP¦EXE. To compile it, you will need the library modules T3DLIB1–12.CPP¦H, along with the DirectX .LIB files. To control the demo, everything is the same as the previous demo, but I highly suggest you play with the wireframe mode (toggle it with the W key) to see all the skewing that goes on to create this geometrically correct shadow.

Optimizing Planar Shadows

Now for the bad news—we are rendering a lot of geometry we don't need to render. We have basically compressed a complete volumetric model into two dimensions. Thus, we are possibly rendering back-faces or geometry that is overlapping, and so on. What we really want to do is project only the silhouette of the occluder object as a shadow mesh.

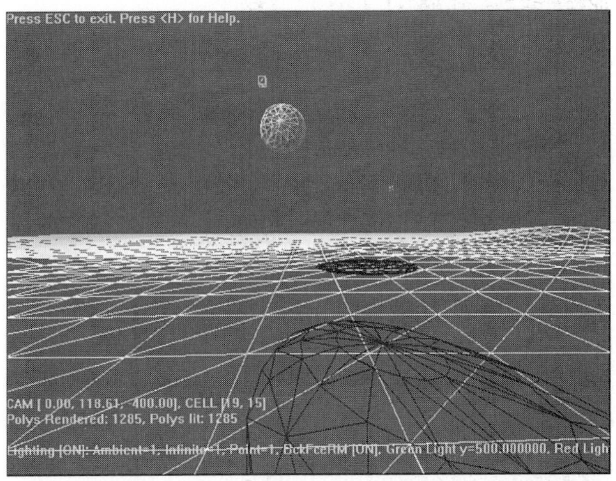

FIGURE 14.21a A wireframe screenshot of the planar shadow demo.

FIGURE 14.21b A solid-shaded screenshot of the planar shadow demo.

Take a look at Figure 14.22, which depicts a simple cube and outlines the silhouette. The trick is finding the silhouette, and there are many tricks and techniques to do this. The silhouette is composed of edges shared by polygons that are both back-faces and front-faces relative to the light source.

The edge labeled $\mathbf{e}_i$ in the figure is a silhouette edge. If you inspect it, it is a common edge for polygon $\mathbf{P}_0$ and $\mathbf{P}_1$. Polygon $\mathbf{P}_0$ is a back-face, whereas polygon $\mathbf{P}_1$ is a front-face relative to the light source. Therefore, we can algorithmically detect edges this way and create a silhouette. The problem is that this will only work for objects without holes and non-intersecting geometry. This is okay too, but in the end, is it worth it?

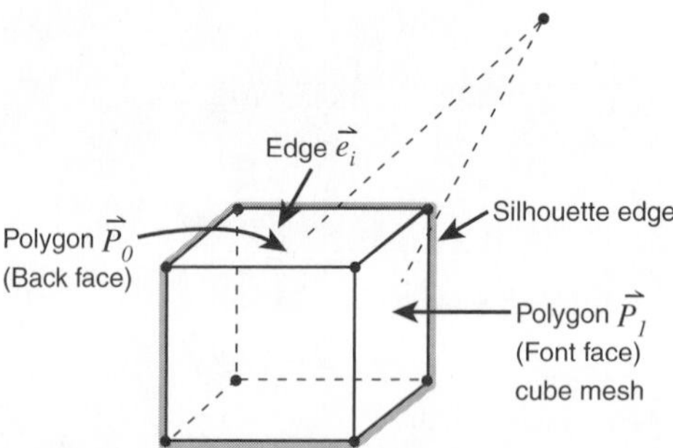

FIGURE 14.22 The silhouette of a cube.

Maybe it is—I have found that using silhouette edges is more suited to different algorithms based on stencil buffers or volume shadows. The problem is that in many cases, the time it takes to save yourself some time is longer than just drawing the polygons! Therefore, another trick is to project a simplified mesh (a *really* simplified mesh) for each object when generating the shadow and be done with it. This simplified mesh might have 10% of the polygons that the full model has or less, so the hit is an extra 10% for shadows—not bad.

Introduction to Light Mapping and Surface Caching

This is a bit hard to explain, so before I say anything, I want you to look at a 3D scene without light mapping. Take a look at Figure 14.23a.

FIGURE 14.23a A *Quake* level without light mapping.

Now take a look at Figure 14.23b. See the difference? Big difference, huh! You might wonder what the big deal is—our Gouraud shaders and other lighting systems can generate something like that. The truth is that they can't for two reasons. First, Gouraud shading is vertex based, so we can never get anything detailed. Secondly, we have no way to create shadows on walls, objects, self shadowing, and so on. This is what light mapping is all about.

FIGURE 14.23b A *Quake* level with light mapping.

The technique of light mapping is rather old—from the 8-bit days, or probably earlier (basically drawing textures in textures). The trick is simply this: Instead of doing lighting in real time, lighting computations are performed offline to compute the illumination, shadows, and so on in a scene. An artist can do this manually and just draw what the lighting would look like. This computation or drawing is a 2D image called a *light map.*

For example, on a very small scale, if we take the texture shown in Figure 14.24a and then multiply the light map texture shown the Figure 14.24b, the results are what is shown in Figure 14.24c. This is something we already did when we covered lighting models much earlier in the book. However, now we are going to just scale the technique up to entire rooms and meshes.

Therefore, the idea of light mapping is to use a light map texture to modulate the textures that are mapped on the geometry of the worlds and objects in our games. Thus, the lighting is just a mirage—it's just "drawn in."

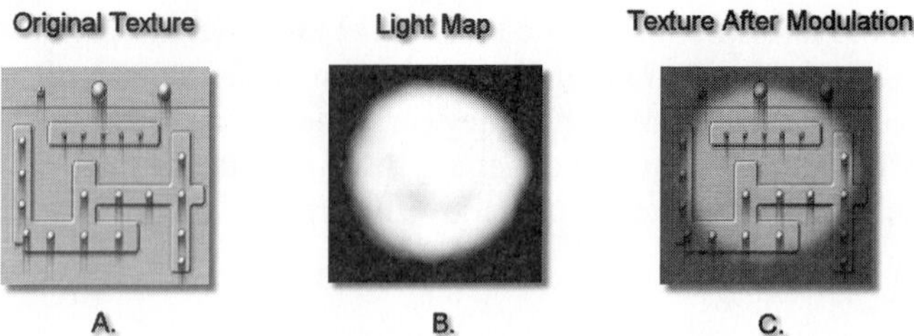

FIGURE 14.24 Light mapping a single texture.

The first thing you might say is cool, but why not just create pre-lit textures? You could, but what if you have a large environment with 1,000 walls/surfaces, and each wall has a 256×256 texture on it? If the base texture is similar to the image in Figure 14.25, you would need 1,000 copies of it, all pre-lit! This is definitely a waste of memory. On the other hand, you might argue that if you use the same texture, you still need 1,000 light maps! This is true, but not entirely so. The key is that the light maps don't need to have the same resolution as the textures. For example, we can use light maps that are 32×32 textels for textures that are 256×256 and it would hardly be noticeable.

FIGURE 14.25 A possible wall texture.

Figure 14.26 shows an example of using low-resolution light maps to modulate a texture. The figure shows the original texture, the 32×32 light map, and the modulated texture. Sure, it's looks a little rough, but if we pass the light map through a filter and buffer the results before modulating, we can get a perfect image. That is, we store our light maps at a resolution many times smaller than the target textures (32×32 and so on), then we decompress the light maps into a buffer and average or blur them. Next we take the final results, say 256×256, and use that light map to modulate the texture, which is also possibly 256×256. Therefore, each one of our light maps only takes 32×32 = 1024 bytes (monochrome) in the worst case rather than 65536 bytes—a 64× savings!

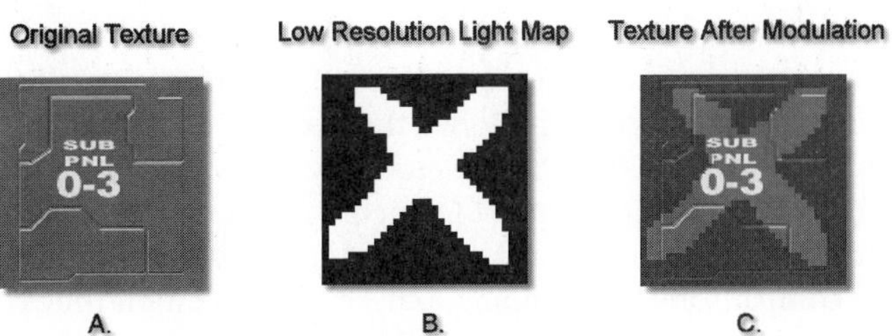

FIGURE 14.26 Using low-resolution light maps.

However, the results look the same because we have a decompression and averaging step. Of course, if you are astute, you can see that the decompression is really nothing more than interpolation of the light maps. The point is that light is something that bleeds and blurs by nature, and soft shadows look better than harsh edges. Using low-resolution light maps and an averaging filter to reduce the jaggies from the light map before modulating will do the trick.

The overall process for light mapping is shown in Figure 14.27. The light map is brought in and decompressed from its low resolution and copied out to a higher resolution buffer (this step is optional, of course). Then the light map is used to modulate the texture map. Remember, all that means is that the light map values are multiplied by the texture map values, and the results are buffered and used as the final texture to map onto the polygon or polygons.

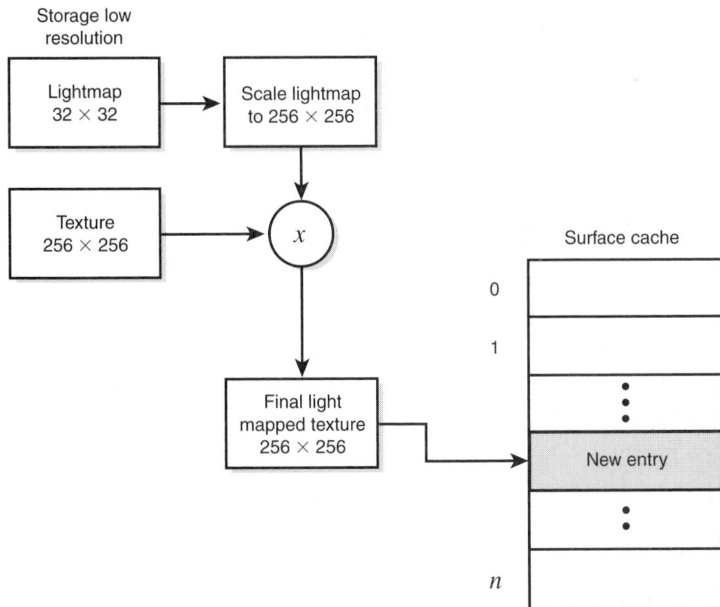

FIGURE 14.27 The light mapping pipeline.

That's all there really is to light mapping. You take a 2D light map texture, use it to modulate a solid texture in 2D space, and then use the results to texture the geometry. The technique is great, because the only computation is the overhead of generating the light mapped texture from the source. This can be considerable, because for a 256×256 texture, there are at least 64,000 calculations, each of which consists of 1–3 multiplications (depending on whether you are using monochrome or full RGB color), along with additions and possible comparisons for clamping. Call the computation time constant per pixel c_m. Therefore, for an m×n texture and an m×n light map, a total of c_m*m*n calculations must be done, at the very least. This is a lot of work, and every time we light-map a texture and render it, we throw it away—ouch! This is where surface caching comes into play.

Surface Caching

Surface caching is nothing more than remembering the results of previous light-mapping calculations. For example, suppose you have 10 textures that are to be light mapped for a room. You are not leaving the room, so why not compute all the light-mapped versions of the textures and cache them for the next frame? Then if the light-mapped texture is available in the cache, you don't need to recompute it. This way, not only do you not throw away light-mapping calculations, you amortize your computations: As a texture needs light mapping, the calculations are performed; and as light-mapped textures get old and are no longer needed, they are flushed. The light mapping surface cache works as follows:

```
Surface Caching Algorithm:

Initialize Texture Cache, and flush all textures

Begin Scene

For each texture T in scene Begin

if T exists in surface cache then render polygon(s) with T
else
  Begin
  Find light map for T, light map texture T store in cache
  if cache is full, delete least recently used texture
  End else

End Scene

Repeat
```

Very simple. Basically, we just cache every single light-mapping computation until the cache is full, and use the results whenever the same request is made. Therefore, once you enter a room and the modulated textures are computed based on the light maps, you get the beautiful light mapping and shadows absolutely free! It can't be true, but it is.

Of course, with anything this cool, there are problems, such as the following:

- How large will the light maps be?
- Will the light maps be on a per-polygon basis or on a per-surface (coplanar polygon set) basis?
- Will the light maps be compressed?
- Will the light maps be monochrome or full RGB for colored effects, as well as for general shadowing?
- How large will the surface cache (if any) be?

And the list goes on and on. However, these are the kind of decisions only experience and your particular situation will be able to answer. For now, our goal is simply to implement the technology to show how simple and how amazing it is.

Generating the Light Maps

I hinted earlier that you could generate the light maps either algorithmically or via a human artist. If you decide to generate the light maps algorithmically, chances are the whole idea of light mapping is to show nice shadows, dark crevices, and so on. The only way you are going to get this look is with an offline lighting system that either ray traces or performs some other global illumination algorithms, such as photon mapping or radiosity.

Ray tracing isn't too hard to implement, but doesn't look as nice as radiosity, which is essentially the computation of the energy flow in a scene. Figure 14.28 is an image of a radiosity-illuminated scene—it looks almost real, as you can see. But in our case, all we want is the lighting portion of the computation for the light maps. Radiosity is something I am not going to cover, because it's not real-time (yet), but there are many good books on it, as well as on photon mapping and ray tracing.

Your second choice still related to using the aforementioned techniques is to simply take your geometry into a 3D modeling tool such as Pov-Ray, trueSpace, or 3D Studio Max and use the tool to create a fully lit monochrome scene that you can cut up into light maps by changing the position of the camera.

Finally, you can simply have an artist "draw" light maps as textures, and through trial and error come up with light maps that look as good or better than the real thing. The choice is up to you—in most cases, I find I use a mixture of these techniques. id Software, for example, has its own tools to compute light maps, but many other companies use tools like Pov-Ray or 3D Studio Max that already exist, and just make an interface or plug-in to leverage the ray tracing or radiosity systems rather than waste time writing one. Nonetheless, when you are just getting the hang of the technique, I suggest that you just draw your light maps and be done with it, as I have for these examples.

FIGURE 14.28 A scene illuminated with radiosity.

Implementing the Light Mapper

You're going to hate me when you read this. Here we go.

Done.

Yup, we already wrote the light mapping code! Remember, all the algorithm does is modulate (multiply) one texture with another. Of course, it has to do a lot of computations for large textures, but DEMOII8_4.CPP|EXE did exactly this. I took the code from that demo, optimized it a bit, and created an inline fragment that uses the texture source, the light map, and a buffer to modulate the texture source by the light map. The results are very fast and look great. However, an algorithm like this is dying to be optimized using a SIMD (single instruction multiple data) architecture, such as that featured in Pentium III+ processors. Maybe we will do this in the last chapter on optimization, but for now, here's the code fragment that performs the light mapping to the source texture:

```
// perform lightmapping here ///////////////////////////////////////////////

// the idea is to take the source lightmap and use it to modulate the texture
// that is being mapped onto the target polygons and then write the results
// into the texture for rendering

/////////////////////////////////////////////
// our little image processing algorithm :)

// Pixel_dest[x,y]rgb = pixel_source[x,y]rgb * light_map[x,y]rgb
```

```
USHORT *sbuffer = (USHORT *)texture_copy.buffer;
USHORT *lbuffer = (USHORT *)lightmaps[curr_lightmap].buffer;
USHORT *dbuffer = (USHORT *)obj_terrain.texture->buffer;


// perform RGB transformation on bitmap
for (int iy = 0; iy < texture_copy.height; iy++)
  for (int ix = 0; ix < texture_copy.width; ix++)
     {
     int rs,gs,bs;  // used to extract the source rgb values
     int rl, gl, bl; // light map rgb values
     int rf,gf,bf;  // the final rgb terms

     // extract pixel from source bitmap
     USHORT spixel = sbuffer[iy*texture_copy.width + ix];

     // extract RGB values
     _RGB565FROM16BIT(spixel, &rs,&gs,&bs);

     // extract pixel from lightmap bitmap
     USHORT lpixel = lbuffer[iy*texture_copy.width + ix];

     // extract RGB values
     _RGB565FROM16BIT(lpixel, &rl,&gl,&bl);

     // compute modulation term
     rf = ( (rs*rl) >> 5 );
     gf = ( (gs*gl) >> 6 );
     bf = ( (bs*bl) >> 5 );

     // rebuild RGB and test for overflow
     // and write back to buffer
     dbuffer[iy*texture_copy.width + ix] = _RGB16BIT565(rf,gf,bf);

     } // end for ix
```

The algorithm is very straightforward—it takes the source texture in `sbuffer`, modulates it with the light map in `lbuffer`, and stores the results in `dbuffer`. The calculations are performed in RGB space for each pixel. Thus, there are two loops, one for x and one for y, that iterate over the texture space, extract the RGB values for both the source texture and the light map, multiply them together, and store the results back into the destination buffer, `dbuffer`, which is then used as the final texture to map onto the polygon mesh.

Before I show you the light mapping demo, let's see what we could have done without light mapping. Take a look at Figure 14.29.

14

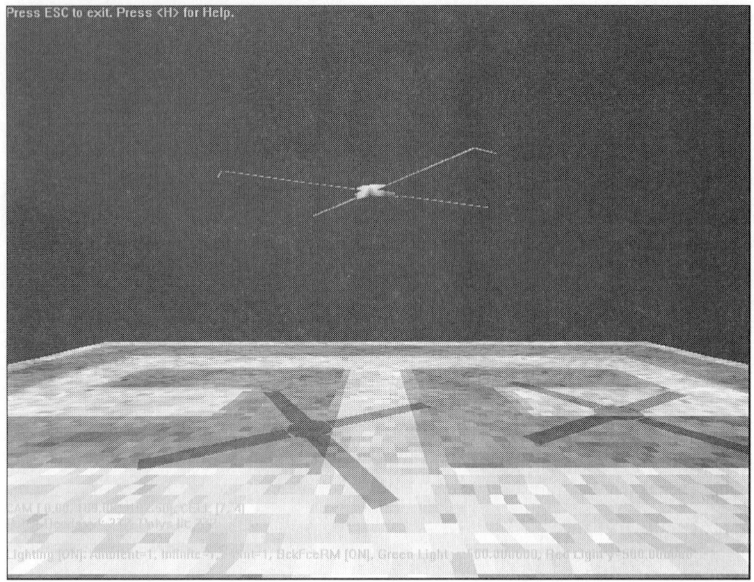
Press ESC to exit. Press <H> for Help.

FIGURE 14.29 A screenshot of the planar shadow demo with an overhead fan.

It's a screenshot of `DEMOII14_5.CPP¦EXE`, which is a prelude to the light mapping demo. Basically, it's nothing more than `DEMOII14_4.CPP¦EXE` with an overhead fan model for the object to be shadowed. The fan is shown in Figure 14.30.

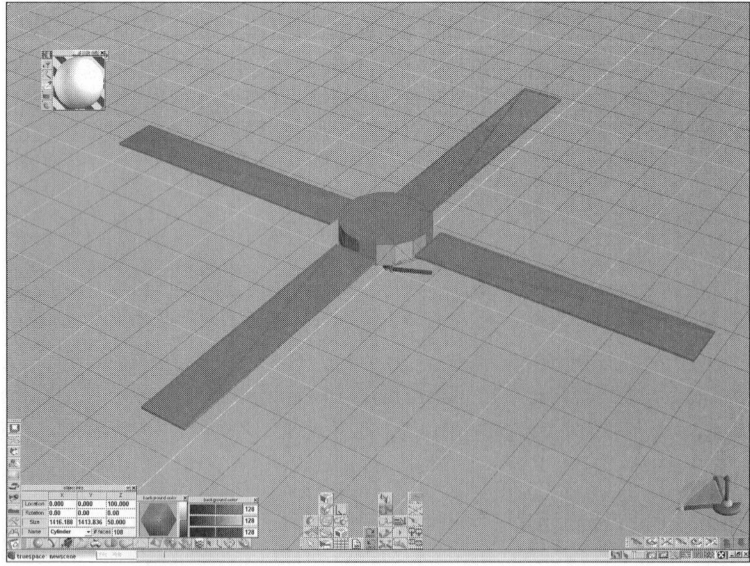

FIGURE 14.30 The model used for the overhead fan.

Now that you have something for comparison, let's take a look at how the light mapping demo works. The first light mapping demo DEMOII14_6.CPP¦EXE has a number of pieces to build this demo. First I needed the fan model, which I made in trueSpace in about 5–10 minutes. It's just a cylinder and four blades. The name of the file model file is fan_01b.cob. Then I needed a texture to map onto the floor (which is a terrain object generated on the fly), shown in Figure 14.31.

FIGURE 14.31 The floor texture for the demo.

Finally I needed the light maps. This was really the only tricky part. I used the modeler to create a top view of the fan, and then rendered it at 256×256 in full 16-bit color. The setup is shown in Figure 14.32.

FIGURE 14.32 The setup for rendering the light map for the fan object.

After I had the 2D bitmap rendering, I brought the bitmap of the fan into Paint Shop Pro and rotated the image in 10-degree increments to create the light map animations. This is shown in Figure 14.33. Now, with model and light maps in hand, the actual program is simple to create.

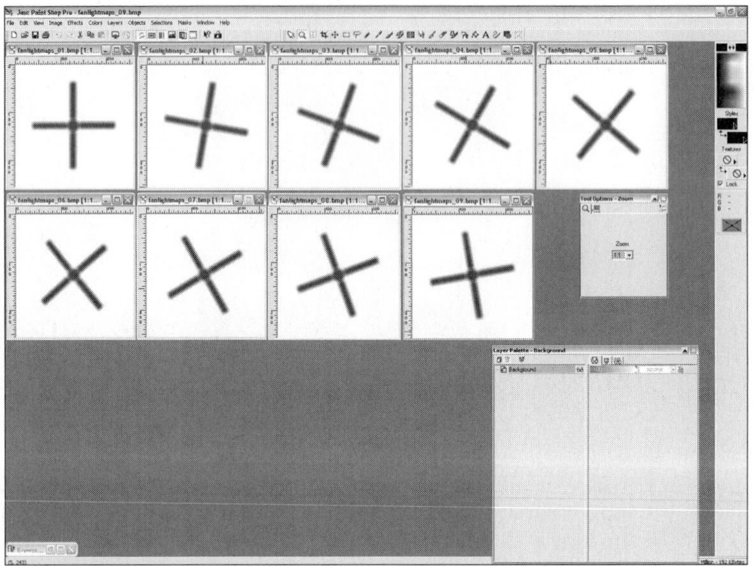

FIGURE 14.33 The light maps after rotation and image processing.

DEMOII14_16.CPP is a very simple loop—it begins by taking the current light map (1 of 9), selecting a light map, modulating the base terrain texture with it, and moving along to the rendering phase. The terrain is rendered with the light-mapped texture, and then the 3D model of the overhead fan is rendered in a single pass, because there is no alpha blending step here. And that's it! Amazing, huh? All the work is done offline, and during the texture modulation step to perform the actual light mapping. The results are pretty cool, and you can see them for yourself in Figure 14.34. To compile the demo, you will need T3DLIB1–12.CPP¦H, along with the main file DEMOII14_6.CPP, and don't forget to link in the DirectX .LIB files.

Dark Mapping

No one said that we have to draw shadows—we can draw light just as well. In fact, the term *light mapping* is really a misnomer, because what we are really doing is mapping darkness, not light—we are using a modulation algorithm that at best doesn't change a pixel's value, but in most cases darkens it.

In any case, for a demo that is more to the point, I modified DEMOII14_6.CPP¦EXE to load in light maps that have the opposite polarity. That is, I took the nine light maps and inverted their images, as shown in Figure 14.35.

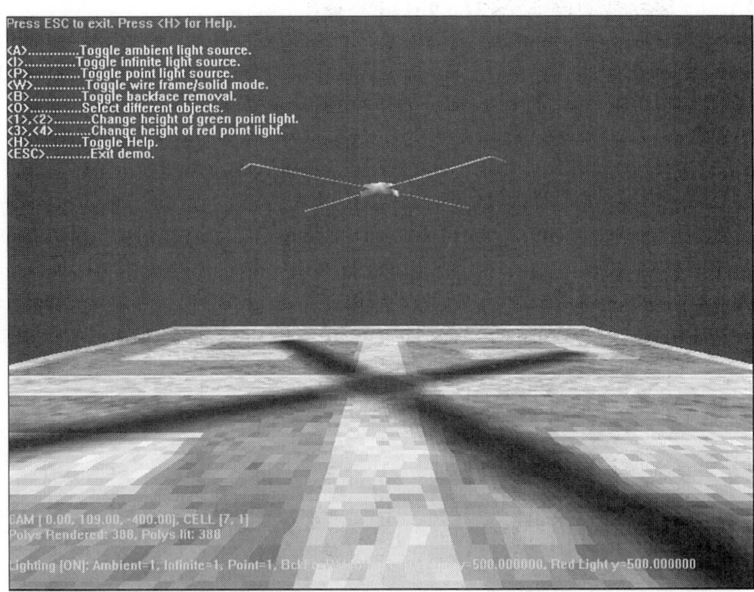

FIGURE 14.34 A screenshot of the light mapping demo in action.

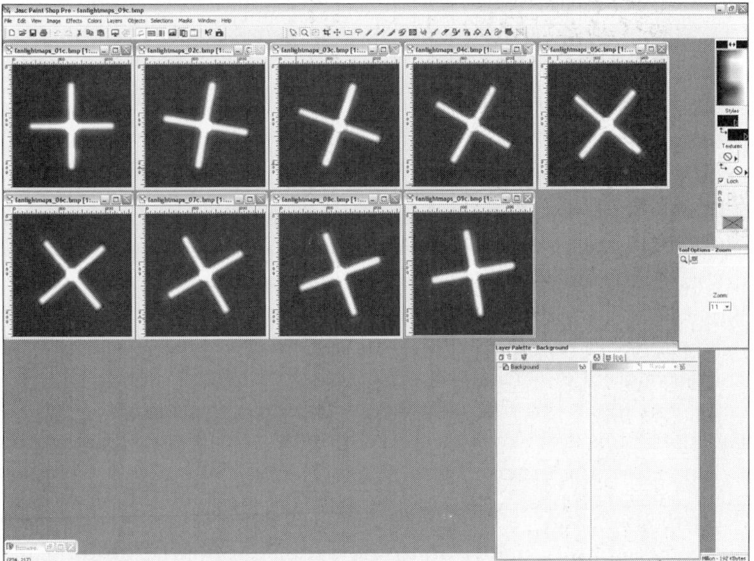

FIGURE 14.35 The inverted dark maps.

Then I took a little artistic license and blurred them a bit to make the light parts look a little more caustic. I then dropped them into the demo, and the results are in

DEMOII14_6b.CPP¦EXE. Figure 14.36 is a screenshot of the demo in action. Pretty cool, huh? Make sure to try both demos out—notice that the light sources don't have too much to do with the final lighting, because it's being done via light mapping.

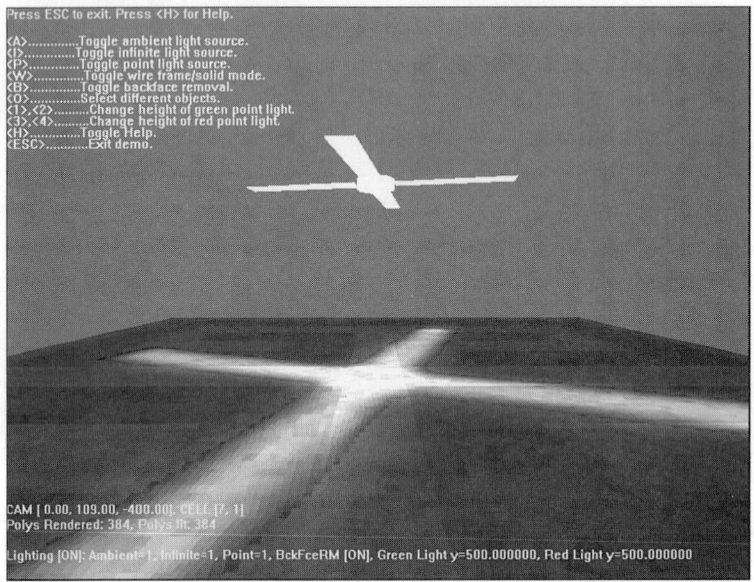

FIGURE 14.36 A screenshot of the dark mapping demo in action.

Special FX with Light Maps

Before finishing up the chapter, let's talk about some ideas and cool things that can be achieved with light maps. First, the biggest challenge with light maps is that they are for the most part static. However, this isn't really a big deal—no one said you can't have animated light maps. Of course, you want to be cognizant of the memory footprint, but a few areas with animated light maps is easy to do. For example, you can have flickering light (like in *Quake*), color effects, and more by using multiple light maps. Additionally, suppose you have a large room that is broken up into four quadrants—as long as you make sure the light maps don't overlap, you can have lights turning on and off in one section that don't effect the others.

Another light map effect that's really cool is complex shadows animation. For example, when a door opens, you use a light map to show the light pouring into the darkened room, then when the light is at a maximum, you just turn on the normal lighting. You can also use light maps to project animations of light on other objects. For example, you can take a cylinder with a plastic transparent wrap around it and put a light in it. (Of course, this is all done in model space.) You rotate the model in 3D, and then take the texture itself and use it as the light map (this is actually called *projective textures*, but the idea is the same, and is based on light mapping).

Finally, one area that hasn't had much done with it is procedural light maps. Using a mathematical formula to generate light map textures and then using these textures for the light maps themselves, you can get really cool clouds, smoke, and other effects that always look different, but somehow modulate the light in the scene.

Optimizing the Light Mapping Code

The light mapping code is algorithmically pretty optimal, but of course there are always ways to make it faster. The first is to use a lookup table instead of multiplications. However, these days cache coherence can really slow things down and multiplication only takes a single cycle, so I don't see much help there. The other opportunity is in using the SIMD instructions and performing the light mapping calculations four at a time. This is definitely doable, and the first thing you should do.

However, putting aside the actual modulation code for a moment, the real problem is working the light mapping into an engine in a way that it doesn't hurt anything or cause a speed loss when it's not being used (and when it is used, the speed hit should be minimized). We have already discussed the surface caching technique to generate light-mapped textures once and then reuse them, so this is the best optimization I can suggest. However, it's also worth using smaller light map textures in the 32×32 size, or at least 1/16 to 1/32 of the resolution of the texture maps, just so that they fit into the cache all at once or nearly so, and the texture modulation phase can run very quickly.

In conclusion, I think a simple system with a surface cache, low-resolution light maps that have both full RGB and monochrome support, along with support for animation to the light maps is a very robust system.

Putting Everything Together

Now that you have the tools to perform real-time shadows and light mapping, I bet you are going nuts with cool ideas—I know I am. However, keep in mind that you only have so many CPU cycles per frame, so although full polygonal projective shadows for each light source looks cool, you can probably get away with the billboards for many objects, especially if they are far away. Also, when in doubt, use light mapping, especially for interior scenes. No amount of lighting will even come close to the look of light-mapped geometry in a software or hardware engine.

As a final experiment, try doing some two-pass stuff, where you render your scene from one angle and then from another. Maybe the top, and then use the rendering as the light map for the floor? That way, you get fully animated shadows that look very real! The possibilities are limitless.

Summary

This chapter has been one of the coolest, as we got a lot of visual mileage out of a little code. More importantly, this chapter illustrates how thinking outside the box is a powerful tool.

We learned that amazing special effects can be achieved using surface caching techniques—shadows, lighting, animation, and more. Remember this and see whether you can apply the same techniques to other aspects of your games and engines—that is, doing things completely backwards, sideways, or nonconventionally.

Finally, this chapter brings into the spotlight another more subtle aspect of game development—asset generation and tool paths. As game programmers, we have to write code where needed, but also think about letting artists and other tools do work for us offline. If an artist can do it nearly as well with art, and in half the time, who cares if something is mathematically correct? The key is knowing when to give in and cheat, and when to do it for real.

PART V

Advanced Animation, Physics Modeling, and Optimization

IN THIS PART

CHAPTER **15**

3D Character Animation, Motion, and Collision Detection

IN THIS CHAPTER

- The New Game Engine Module
- Introduction to 3D Animation
- The *Quake II* .MD2 File Format
- Simple Non-Character-Based Animation
- 3D Collision Detection

"As far as the laws of mathematics refer to reality, they are not certain; and as far as they are certain, they do not refer to reality."

—Albert Einstein

In this chapter, we're going to discuss (for the most part) the loading and displaying of 3D animated models of the *Quake II* .MD2 file format. We will also cover some motion techniques in 3D, along with formalizing basic collision detection techniques for model-to-model collision and model-to-environment collision. Here's the outline:

- The new library module
- Introduction to 3D animation
- Loading *Quake II* .MD2 files
- Animating *Quake II* .MD2 files
- Rotational and linear motion
- Parametric and curved motion
- Using scripts for motion
- 3D collision and terrain-following techniques

The New Game Engine Module

Once again, there is enough software in this chapter for a separate library module. We are up to `T3DLIB13.CPP|H` now, so to compile any program from this chapter, you will need the main .CPP program file for the program, the DirectX .LIB files, and the following new library modules:

- `T3DLIB13.CPP`—The C/C++ source for the added shadow and light mapping software
- `T3DLIB13.H`—The accompanying header file

Of course, you must link to `T3DLIB1-12.CPP¦H` as well.

Introduction to 3D Animation

The primary focus of this chapter is animation, with an emphasis on character animation. I had hoped to have time to cover skeletal animation and motion files (such as Biovision and so on), but it'll have to wait until the next volume. For now, we are to have to settle for key-framed animation and interpolation. Even so, key-framed animation looks great, and if it's good enough for *Quake* and *Quake II*, it's good enough for our experimental uses. Thus, we're going to focus on three primary topics as they relate to animation: the definition, loading, and rendering of *Quake II* .MD2 models; the movement and positioning of 3D models and objects in general; and collision detection techniques for 3D models that represent characters.

The majority of code and examples in this chapter will be related to the first topic—that is, the loading and rendering of 3D models based on id Software's *Quake II* .MD2 format. This is by far the most complex aspect of this chapter. We'll discuss the remaining subjects theoretically for the most part, concentrating on ideas rather than implementations because there's nothing more I can teach you at this point—we have covered so many things in so many ways, that it's really up to you from here on out.

The *Quake II* .MD2 File Format

The *Quake II* .MD2 file format, which I will refer to as .MD2 from here on, was developed by id Software for the blockbuster game *Quake II* (shown in Figure 15.1). *Quake II* brought hardware acceleration to the forefront of gaming, and showed the world what could be accomplished with the technology. The end of the software acceleration era for commercial products was upon us with *Quake II*. In any event, many cool technologies were explored and exploited in *Quake II*, and one of them was better character animation via key-framed animation and interpolation.

Although .MD2 files don't have skeletons or support inverse/forward kinematics, the file format is relatively easy to parse and easy to understand. However, the best aspect of .MD2 files is that there are a zillion of them on the Internet, and a bazillion tools to go along with them! Thus, you will have no trouble finding models, tools, and other applications.

FIGURE 15.1 A screenshot of *Quake II* in action.

NOTE

One of the best places to look for *Quake II* models is Planet Quake:

`http://www.planetquake.com/polycount/`

There are also plenty of tools you can use to manipulate .MD2 files. Many can be found here:

`http://www.planetquake.com/polycount/resources/quake2/tools.shtml`

Finally, the technical specs for the format can be found here:

`http://www.planetquake.com/polycount/resources/quake2/q2frameslist.shtml`

I have downloaded a few models from Planet Quake, which are all free to use as long as you don't make money from them. However, the author of every model is listed, so if you want to use them in a commercial game, I am sure you can contact the developer and ask. So, without further ado, let's talk about the format itself.

Let me begin by saying that I have never had so much trouble trying to find a decent description of anything on the Internet as when I was trying to find out about the .MD2 format. I looked at every single article and book that discusses the .MD2 format, and in every example, the authors always leave out some really important detail, so I'm really going to try to be very thorough about the file format so you don't have any lingering questions.

Let's start with a high-level description and drill down to the details. The .MD2 file format consists of two main sections: a header and the data, as shown in Figure 15.2.

- Header section—Contains a description of the model, number of polygons, vertices, animation details, and so on.
- Data section—The actual data that makes up the polygon mesh of the model, including all the polygon, vertex, and texture data.

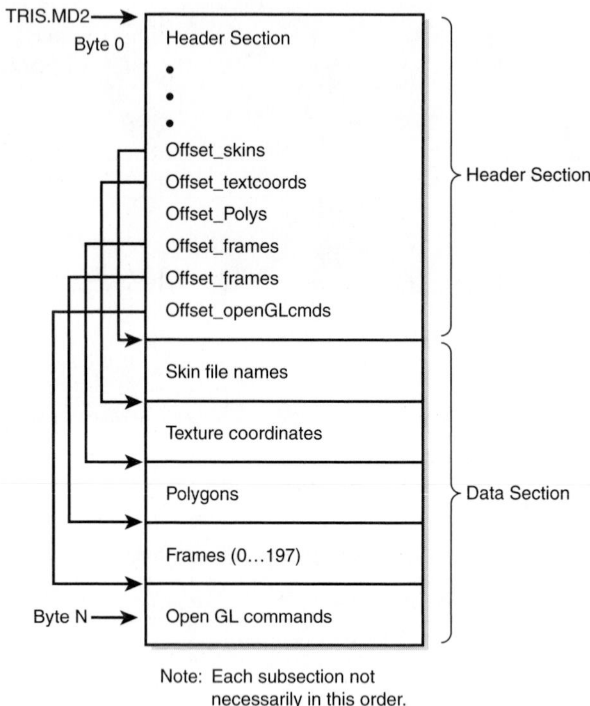

FIGURE 15.2 The general structure of a *Quake II* .MD2 file.

TIP

All polygons in the .MD2 file are triangles, and there are no other entities—just triangles, baby!

The header is a standard header without anything out of the ordinary, but the data is rather interesting, in that the vertex data (which we will get to in a moment) doesn't define a single frame of animation, but many. In fact, there are 198 frames of animation in a .MD2 file, numbered 0...197.

CAUTION

You might find models with 199, 200 or more frames of animation that are malformed from the original definition. Nonetheless, the original id Software spec calls for 198 frames. This only matters for the animation frames because indices are used to define what is a walk, run, death, and so on.

These frames are defined as polygon meshes consisting of collections of vertices in model space, with the origin at (0,0,0) in a right-hand coordinate system featuring a counter-clockwise winding order (this will be important later, so keep this in mind). These vertices define what the mesh looks like for each frame of animation, and each of these animation frames might consist of a number of frames per each specific animation: walk, run, jump, and so on. We will cover all this in detail of course, but for now, just keep in mind that there is a header at the beginning of the file that defines the model, and based on the header information, you load the frame data, which is a pure binary stream.

Animation is performed by sequencing through the frames of animation. For example, the "standing idle" animation is defined as consisting of frames 0–39, so you would display these frames in succession, and you would see the "standing idle" animation. However, these frames are key frames, meaning that if you want to, you can linearly interpolate between them to get a smoother animation. For example, you might decide to interpolate at a rate of 0.25 from frame i to i+1; thus, you would blend the vertex (x,y,z) positions together from frame i to i+1, with the interpolation values 0, 0.25, 0.50, 0.75, 1.0.

The next important thing is the texture map, or *skin*, as the guys at id Software like to call it. Figure 15.3 depicts a standard skin texture for a .MD2 model (this one is Warhammer from Polycount, designed by Joe "Ebola" Woodrell). The skin is 256×256 in 256 colors, and comes in the .PCX file format for the most part. Thus, we will have to convert all skins to 16-bit color and .BMP format.

FIGURE 15.3 A *Quake II* skin.

In any case, the idea of the skin is that it is used as a texture for the model. Each model may have many skins (for different colors and styles). The interesting thing is that skins are *not* part of the .MD2 file. They are only referenced in the .MD2 file as filenames in the path of the *Quake II* game directory. Thus, during parsing of the file header to the .MD2 file, you might find that there are three skins for the model (maybe a blue, a camouflaged, and blood red). In that case, you would use the file path and name to load the .PCX file and thus the texture—more on this later.

The .MD2 Header

Now let's take a detailed look at the header section of the .MD2 file format. First, most .MD2 models that you will find on the Internet will be located in a single directory when you decompress them. You will typically find a number of files related to the model that have to do with the model itself, weapons, the art, and the sound. We are only interested in the model and the skins, so let's focus on that. When you download a model from the Internet or look at the ones I placed on the CD for you to play with, you will list out the directory and find, at the very least, the following:

- `TRIS.MD2`—This is always the file that contains the actual model data for the character.
- `WEAPON.MD2`—This may or may not be present, but usually is. This file contains the weapon model, which is also a .MD2 file. We aren't going to consider the weapons in this chapter, but you can load them similarly to the character models.

Next you will find a number of texture files in the 256×256 256-color .PCX file format. Simply browse them with your favorite painting application (Paint Shop Pro, Photoshop, and so on). The images you'll see are mostly the skins used for texturing for the model. They are 256×256 because all texture coordinates are from 0...255 for both u and v in the data part of the .MD2 file. However, to use any of the textures, we need to convert them to 16-bit color and save them as .BMP files. (Even though we have a .PCX loader, .BMP is easier.)

You will also see a number of small images used for icons, as well as a number of .WAV files used for sound effects. We don't care about this stuff, either. All we really want is the `TRIS.MD2` file and one or more of the skins converted to 16-bit .BMP format. In most cases, I download a .MD2 model from Polycount or some other site and decompress it into a directory. Then I browse the images in the directory and look for the skins. When I find a couple of skins I like, I increase the color depth to 16-bit, brighten the textures by 10–20%, and then save them as .BMP files with whatever name I like. The name is irrelevant, because we are going to override the built-in texture skin names in the header and use our own with our own paths. This will work out because all the texture coordinates are still the same in 256×256 u,v space, and the texture(s) are still the same, so nothing will look incorrect.

TIP

The texture skin support is natively designed to load from the paths to the *Quake II* .EXE file, so we aren't going to bother trying to extract only the filename from the paths, because we can just as well supply the name of our .BMP version of the texture to the .MD2 loader and override it.

Of course, we can't supply just any skin—we must use one of the real skins from the model itself, because we need the texture coordinate to match up and map correctly. We can at least simplify the texture access on the disk media by placing them where we want them, and with the names we like.

Okay, now that you know what to look for on the hard drive when you download a .MD2 file, let's take a look at the header and data. First, note that the .MD2 file is totally binary, and the data must be read as bytes. Here is the header, which always comes first in the .MD2 file from byte 0 on:

```
// this if the header structure for a Quake II .MD2 file by id Software,
// I have slightly annotated the field names to make them more readable
// and less cryptic :)
typedef struct MD2_HEADER_TYP
{
int identifier;    // identifies the file type, should be "IDP2"
int version;      // version number, should be 8
int skin_width;    // width of texture map used for skinning
int skin_height;   // height of texture map using for skinning
int framesize;    // number of bytes in a single frame of animation
int num_skins;    // total number of skins
          // listed by ASCII filename and are available
          // for loading if files are found in full path
int num_verts;    // number of vertices in each model frame, the
          // number of vertices in each frame is always the
          // same
int num_textcoords; // total number of texture coordinates in entire file
          // may be larger than the number of vertices
int num_polys;    // number of polygons per model, or per frame of
          // animation if you will
int num_openGLcmds; // number of openGL commands which can help with
          // rendering optimization
          // however, we won't be using them

int num_frames;    // total number of animation frames

// memory byte offsets to actual data for each item

int offset_skins;    // offset in bytes from beginning of file to the
           // skin array that holds the file name for each skin,
           // each file name record is 64 bytes
int offset_textcoords; // offset in bytes from the beginning of file to the
           // texture coordinate array
```

15

```
int offset_polys;    // offset in bytes from beginning of file to the
            // polygon mesh

int offset_frames;    // offset in bytes from beginning of file to the
            // vertex data for each frame

int offset_openGLcmds; // offset in bytes from beginning of file to the
            // openGL commands

int offset_end;    // offset in bytes from beginning of file to end of file

} MD2_HEADER, *MD2_HEADER_PTR;
```

Depending on where you learn about .MD2 files and the header, you will see slightly different field names, but for the most part, everyone tries to stick to names that are representative of id's original definition. However, the data types and their order must be identical to the preceding structure; otherwise, you won't be able to reference the header data when you load the `TRIS.MD2` file. Let's cover each field in detail:

`int identifier`—This magic number field identifies the file type as .MD2 and should be `IDP2` in little endian format. In other words, on a PC with an Intel processor (big endian), you should look for this value (notice the `I` is the low byte):

```
#define MD2_MAGIC_NUM (('I') + ('D' << 8) + ('P' << 16) + ('2' << 24))
```

`int version`—This is the version number, and should always be 8. Again, I have defined a constant to compare it to:

```
#define MD2_VERSION     8
```

If either the magic number or version are not correct, you either have a bad .MD2 file or your computer was just hit by a lot of high energy particles. In either case, check it out.

`int skin_width`—This is the width of the texture map used for skinning the model in pixels. This is usually 256 for models created by third parties; however, it might be different, so if you really want to be robust, take this into consideration.

`int skin_height`—This is the height of the texture map used for skinning the model in pixels. This is usually 256 for models created by third parties; however, it might be different, so if you really want to be robust, take this into consideration.

Note that *all* the texture maps for any particular model will have skins that are the same size, so on the disk, you will never have to worry about them changing size after you determine the size of the textures. However, in 99% of the cases, the textures are 256×256.

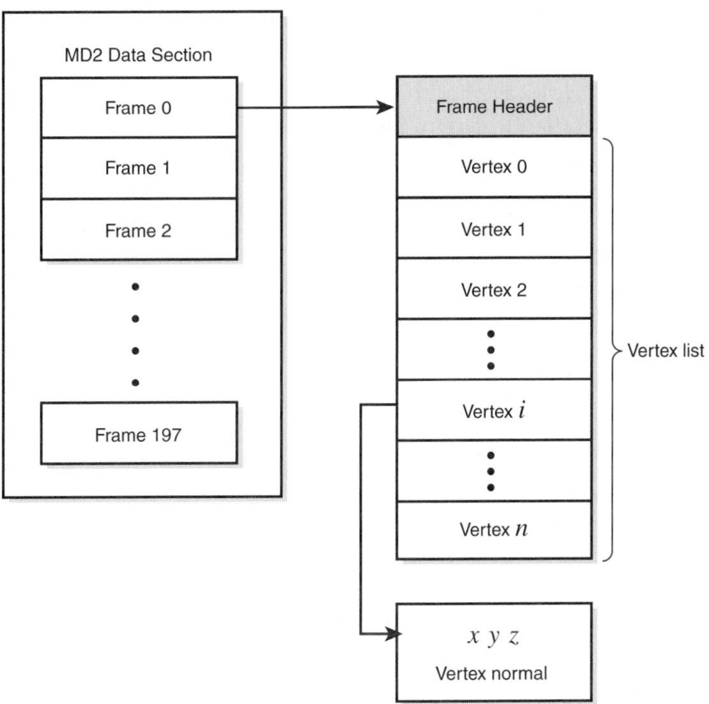

FIGURE 15.4 The details of a single animation frame.

`int framesize`—This field is very tricky. It's the size in bytes of a single frame of animation for the model, as shown in Figure 15.4. Each frame consists of a header and vertex information for each vertex of the model. We will revisit this shortly, but for now, keep in mind that a single frame consists of all the vertices for the model and a header, which instructs us how to scale and position the vertices. There are 198 of these frames in most cases for id Software-compliant .MD2 files.

`int num_skins`—This field defines the total number of skins defined by ASCII filenames that are available with the model files on the disk. Each skin name is located in an array of strings at the end of the header (at a specific position, of course). Each skin name is 64 bytes exactly. Any white space is `NULL`, (padded with 0). The model might have one or more skin names. These names will in most cases have path information that is *Quake II*-specific; that's why we're going to ignore them and just manually look at the skins in the directory of the model, rename them, and then when loading the model, pass a string with the path and filename of the skin we like (in 16-bit .BMP format).

`int num_verts`—This field is the number of vertices in a single model frame—not the total number of vertices in the entire file, but the number of vertices in a single frame of animation. This is very important. Also, because the model always has the exact same polygons that make it up, the number of vertices is *always* the same frame to frame. Thus,

15

the only thing that changes frame to frame is the position of the vertices. This is how animation is achieved with the .MD2 format.

`int num_textcoords`—This is another tricky field. It defines the total number of texture coordinates in the model file. Be careful here: you might think that we need a texture coordinate for each vertex. This is not necessarily true. Remember, a texture coordinate is a pair of u,v coordinates in texture space; however, many times you might have more or fewer texture coordinates than you have vertices, because you can map multiple vertices to the same texture coordinate and so on. Think of the texture coordinates as all the possible texture coordinates needed by the model in any frame of animation. In most cases, there are a few hundred texture coordinates. Moreover, there is only *one* set or pool of these coordinates shared by all animation frames. This is shown in Figure 15.5.

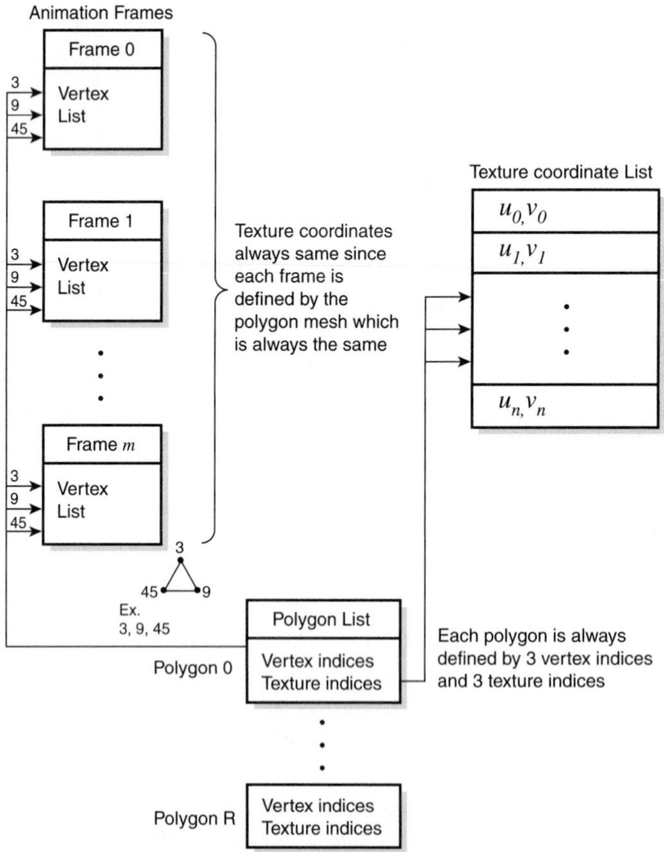

FIGURE 15.5 Texture coordinates are shared by all animation frames.

`int num_polys`—This field is the number of polygons in the model, or per frame of animation. This number is always the same for every frame of animation, so if a model has 800 polygons, it means that every frame of animation has 800 polygons—period.

`int num_openGLcmds`—We are going to ignore this field, but it's the number of OpenGL commands that can help with rendering optimization for hardware. When rendering with hardware, better performance can be achieved by rendering polygon fans or strips—these commands dictate when to use which, how many, and so on.

`int num_frames`—This field is the total number of animation frames. It should be 198 for most .MD2 models.

The next fields are the memory offsets to the actual data streams. Keep in mind that the .MD2 file is a pure binary file, so this should all make sense. These offsets indicate how many bytes from the beginning of the .MD2 file to skip to find each particular data item. The data structure(s) are then simply overlaid, and the data is accessed. This overall format is shown in Figure 15.6.

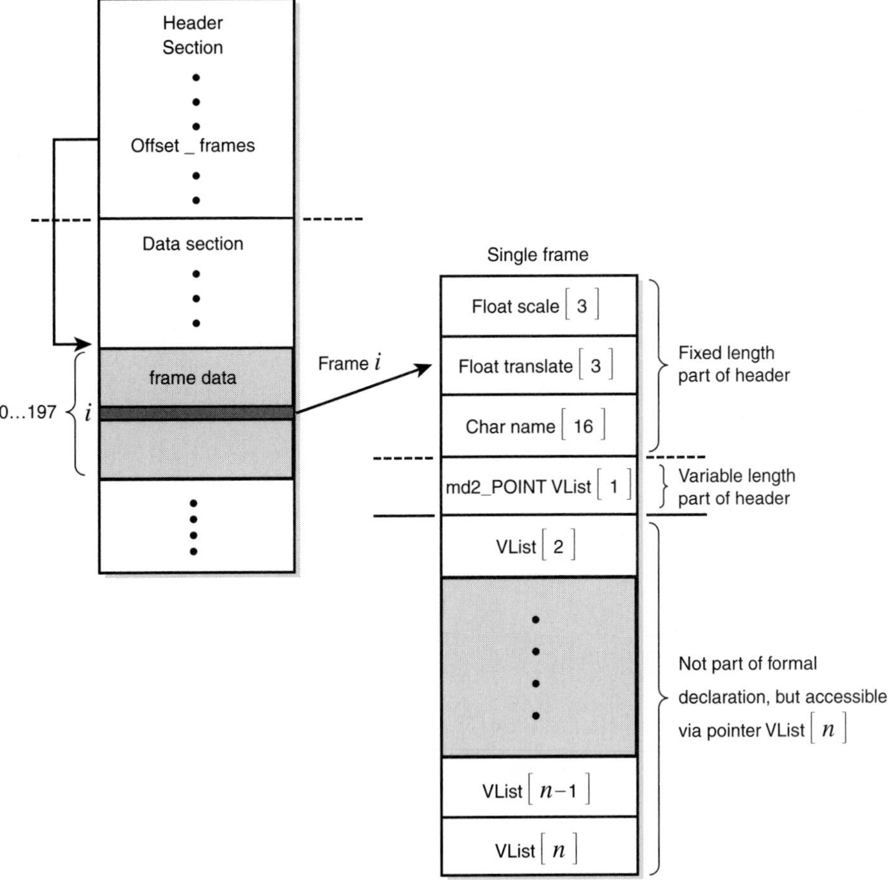

FIGURE 15.6 Overlaying a variable-size data structure template.

`int offset_skins`—This is the offset in bytes from the beginning of the file to the skin array that holds the filename for each skin. Each filename record is 64 bytes.

`int offset_textcoords`—This is the offset in bytes from the beginning of the file to the texture coordinate array. Each texture coordinate is a `SHORT`, and is defined as follows:

```
// this is a single u,v texture
typedef struct MD2_TEXTCOORD_TYP
{
short u,v; // texture coordinate
} MD2_TEXTCOORD, *MD2_TEXTCOORD_PTR;
```

Thus, each texture coordinate is 32 bits, or four bytes total. We use the `num_textcoords` along with the preceding structure to access each texture coordinate.

`int offset_polys`—This field is the offset in bytes from the beginning of the file to the polygon mesh data. Each polygon is defined as a set of indices to the vertices that make up the polygon. Now, we need to be careful here: Suppose that polygon 0 has vertex indices (12,56,99). This means that polygon 0 always has vertices (12,56,99)—it doesn't matter what vertex set or frame is being used. So, the end result is that we only need one polygon definition for the model that describes the relationship of polygons to vertex indices. For animation, we swap vertex sets in and out, but the same vertex indices are always used. Figure 15.7 illustrates this.

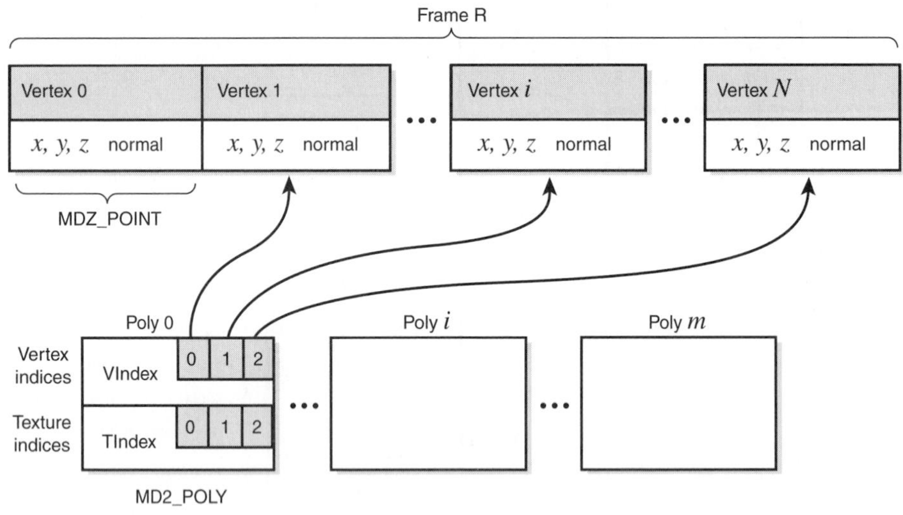

FIGURE 15.7 The relationship between polygons and vertices.

The data format of each polygon definition is as follows:

```
// this is a data structure for a single md2 polygon (triangle)
// its composed of 3 vertices and 3 texture coordinates, both indices
typedef struct MD2_POLY_TYP
{
unsigned short vindex[3];  // vertex indices
unsigned short tindex[3];  // texture indices
} MD2_POLY, *MD2_POLY_PTR;
```

The polygon list is an array of polygons, each with six elements. The first three are unsigned shorts that define the vertex indices, and the second set of three unsigned shorts define the texture coordinate indices. Thus, the polygon is totally defined indirectly, as shown in Figure 15.8.

`int offset_frames`—This is the offset in bytes from the beginning of the file to the vertex data for each frame. This is probably the data that gives people the most trouble, because it's not very clear what each frame consists of, so let's start here. An `offset_frames` is an array of frames. Each frame consists of a small header and an array of vertices that define the animation frame. Figure 15.9 depicts this.

The header for each frame is defined as

```
// this is a single frame for the md2 format, it has a small header portion
// which describes how to scale and translate the model vertices, but then
// has an array to the actual data points which is variable, so the definition
// uses a single unit array to allow the compiler to address up to n with
// array syntax
typedef struct MD2_FRAME_TYP
{
float scale[3];     // x,y,z scaling factors for the frame vertices
float translate[3];  // x,y,z translation factors for the frame vertices
char name[16];      // ASCII name of the model, "evil death lord" etc. :)
MD2_POINT vlist[1];  // beginning of vertex storage array
```

Following the header is the actual vertex data array, but let's hold off on that for a moment and talk about the frame header. The frame header has four fields, all within `float scale[3]`.

`float scale[3]`—This is an array of three floats that are the x, y, and z scaling factors by which to scale every single vertex, so when you load the .MD2 frame, you must scale each vertex by this value. The x scaling factor is stored in `scale[0]`, the y scaling factor in `scale[1]`, and the z scaling factor is in `scale[2]`. The reason for the scaling factor is twofold: First, each vertex is compressed to fit into 8 bits to save space (similar to wavelet compression), so you have to scale each vertex back to its normal size position; secondly, to help achieve animation. Suppose you want to scale a frame as part of the animation—this is how you would do it.

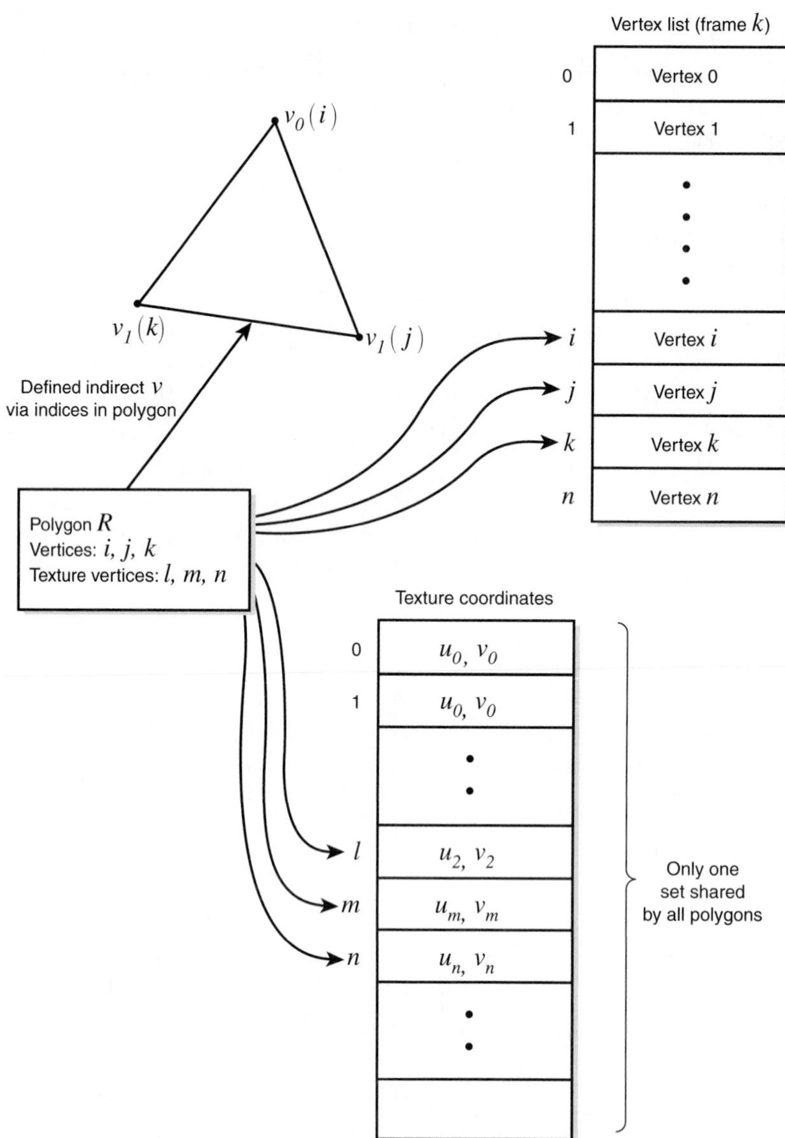

FIGURE 15.8 Each polygon is defined indirectly.

`float translate[3]`—This is an array of three floats that are the x, y, and z translation factors by which to translate every single vertex, so when you load the .MD2 frame, you must translate each vertex by this value. The x translation factor is stored in `translate[0]`, the y translation factor in `translate[1]`, and the z translation factor is in `translate[2]`. The reason for the translation factor is once again to save space because each vertex is stored in an 8-bit value, but more importantly, this is done to move each frame around in model space to achieve animation. For example, this is how a "jump" motion is achieved—by translating the model coordinates, rather than translating the world position and performing a local-to-world transformation.

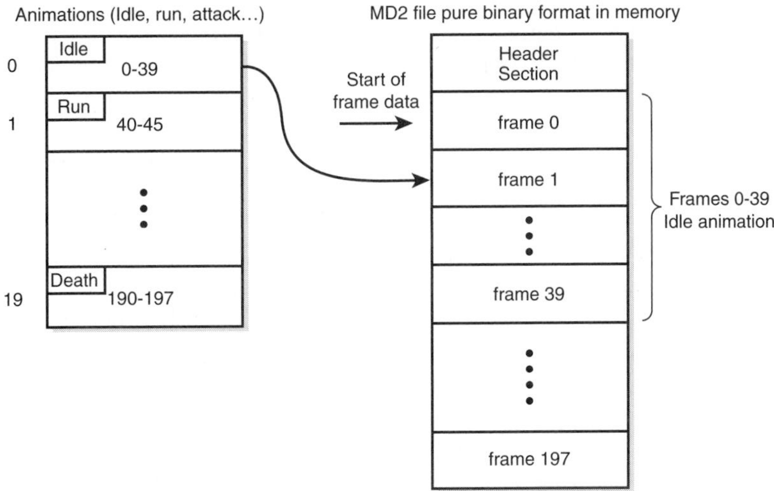

FIGURE 15.9 The animation frames array.

Figure 15.10 illustrates the transformations that the frame header defines as they relate the each vertex, and here's some pseudo-code that performs the transformations:

Given a vertex **v** with `scale[]` and `translate[]` arrays to scale and position any vertex:

```
v.x = v.x * scale[0] + translate[0];
v.y = v.y * scale[1] + translate[1];
v.z = v.z * scale[2] + translate[2];
```

`char name[16]` This field is nothing more than an ASCII name of the model—"Terminator T1000," and so on.

Finally, here's the actual frame data:

`MD2_POINT vlist[1]` This is a pointer, more or less, to an array of vertices. However, we don't know how many vertices, so the trick of defining an array of size 1 is used. Hence, if you access `vlist[2]`, and so on, the compiler will allow it—just make sure there is something there to access, or you will get an access violation! This is a common trick used with variable size data structures: You overlay a pointer or an array, and then index into it with knowledge of how long it is. However, you can use a single data structure template for any size. With that in mind, the vertex list `vlist[]` is the list of vertices for a particular frame of animation. There will always be exactly `num_verts` vertices, and they will always be in the format shown here:

```
// this is a single point for the md2 model, contains an 8-bit scaled x,y,z
// and an index for the normal to the point that is encoded as an
// index into a normal table supplied by id software
typedef struct MD2_POINT_TYP
{
unsigned char v[3];     // vertex x,y,z in compressed byte format
unsigned char normal_index; // index into normal table from id Software (unused)
} MD2_POINT, *MD2_POINT_PTR;
```

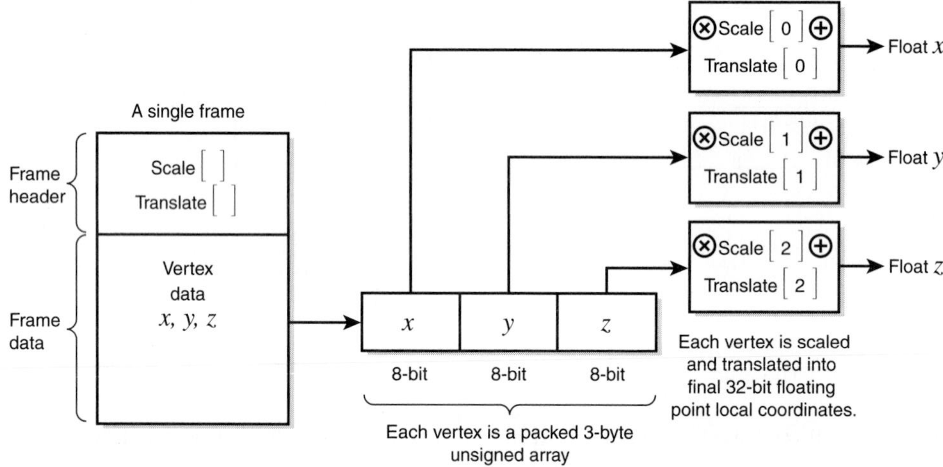

FIGURE 15.10 The frame header transformations to apply to each vertex set.

Notice that the x,y,z of each point is defined as an `unsigned char`—that's only 8 bits! Now you see why the scale and translate support is necessary in the header section of each frame. Each vertex is composed of three bytes, followed by another byte called the `normal_index`. The `normal_index` is used for another trick/compression scheme. For every vertex of every frame, the vertex has a normal to it, as shown in Figure 15.11.

The normal is once again in model space, but is encoded as an index into an array of precomputed normals. id Software created a table located in the *Quake II* source code that has the values for each normal. However, even though we aren't going to use this value because we are going to compute normals only on a per-polygon basis, once again we see optimization and indirection to save space and speed computation.

Summing up, at the beginning of the frame data at `offset_frames` is an array of frames (198 of them). Each frame consists of a header and an array of vertices. The header has a scaling factor and a translation factor, along with an ASCII frame name, all followed by the frame's vertex data. The data consists of an array of 4-byte values, the first three of which are the x,y,z vertex positions in model space. The last item is an index to a 256-element table of vertex normals (which we aren't supporting).

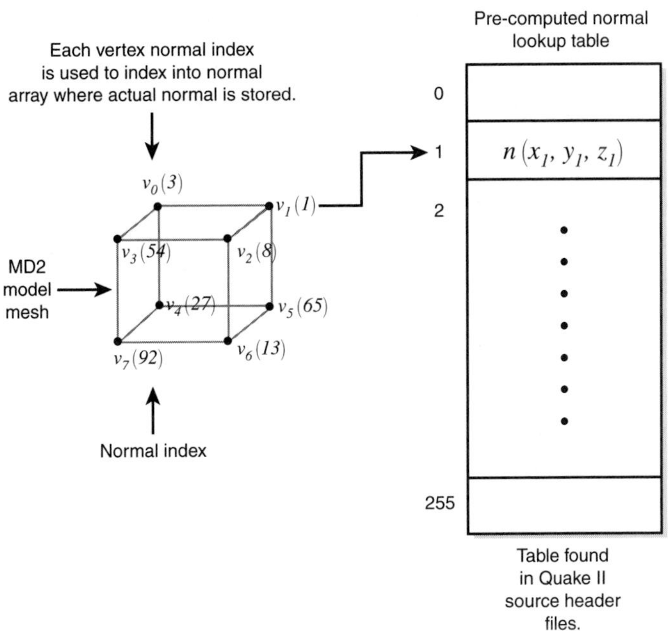

FIGURE 15.11 The *Quake II* lighting normals.

`int offset_openGLcmds`—This field is the offset in bytes from the beginning of file to the OpenGL commands. We aren't using OpenGL, so this is ignored.

`int offset_end`—Last but not least is the offset in bytes from the beginning of the file to the end of file. This is not necessary because we can query the filesystem for the length of the file, but it's here if you need it.

Now let's write some code to load the .MD2 files.

Loading *Quake II* .MD2 Files

You might recall that we originally thought that the `OBJECT4DV2` structure would be used to support animation, and actually wrote a bunch of code to support multiple frames. However, it dawned on me that the `OBJECT4DV2` is just a "container" class that renders a mesh—why make it support animation, .MD2 files, or whatever? A better approach is to simply write extraction functions that "fill" an `OBJECT4DV2` object with polygon data and then pass the object to the rendering engine and leverage all the software we already have. This is the approach I ended up using, so all that animation support we wrote was pretty much an exercise in typing, but it built a lot of character <BG>.

In any event, the general plan of attack to load and render .MD2 files is as follows:

1. Load the .MD2 file and convert it into a more easily accessible format and from which frames can be extracted and loaded into an `OBJECT4DV2`.
2. Write a couple of support functions to prepare `OBJECT4DV2`s to be used as "hosts" for .MD2 frames.
3. Write an extraction function to extract a given frame from the .MD2 model animation, load it into an `OBJECT4DV2` host, and then do whatever you want with the `OBJECT4DV2` as usual, leveraging the entire engine.

At first, I thought I could extract frames directly from the native .MD2 file loaded as pure data in memory, but that would mean performing the frame scaling, translations, and so on. Plus, all the bizarre compressed and indirect data structures make this a bad idea. A better idea is to create yet another container class or structure that's really good at holding .MD2 data, but one that uses a lot of our data structures for points, vertices, textures, and so on. This way, we can access this container class and extract frames from it very quickly.

This is the main point here—speed. We want to be able to render any frame almost instantly, and we don't want much overhead when switching frames. Also, we need to have some forward thinking when designing the container class to support animation, motion, and general state information, like a blitter object, or BOB. In the end, I came up with the following structure:

```
typedef struct MD2_CONTAINER_TYP
{
int state;      // state of the model
int attr;       // attributes of the model
int color;      // base color if no texture
int num_frames;   // number of frames in the model
int num_polys;    // number of polygons
int num_verts;    // number of vertices
int num_textcoords; // number of texture coordinates

BITMAP_IMAGE_PTR skin;  // pointer to texture skin for model

MD2_POLY_PTR polys; // pointer to polygon list
VECTOR3D_PTR vlist; // pointer to vertex coordinate list
VECTOR2D_PTR tlist; // pointer to texture coordinate list

VECTOR4D world_pos; // position of object
VECTOR4D vel;     // velocity of object

int  ivars[8];    // integer variables
float fvars[8];    // floating point variables
int counters[8];  // general counters
```

```
void *link;      // A generic void pointer
int anim_state;    // state of animation
int anim_counter;  // general animation counter
int anim_mode;    // single shot, loop, etc.
int anim_speed;    // smaller number, faster animation
int anim_complete; // flags if single shot animation is done
float curr_frame;    // current frame in animation

} MD2_CONTAINER, *MD2_CONTAINER_PTR;
```

All the fields are clearly marked, and many are copies of the data found in the .MD2 header, but let's review all of them so we are on the same page:

- `int state`—This is the state of the model—if it's alive, dead, and so on.
- `int attr`—This is the attributes of the model's polygons; that is, how we want the polygons rendered, or the shader attributes. We need this because the .MD2 format doesn't have any kind of shading or lighting information, so we need to define how we would like the model rendered. This field is used to store these flags and is then inserted into the `OBJECT4DV2` for each polygon later. In most cases, the attributes will be as follows:

  ```
  (POLY4DV2_ATTR_RGB16 | POLY4DV2_ATTR_SHADE_MODE_FLAT |
  POLY4DV2_ATTR_SHADE_MODE_TEXTURE)
  ```

  which indicates 16-bit color, flat shading, and texture support.
- `int color`—This is the base color if no texture is supplied. However, a single color model is pretty boring, so in most cases, this will be set to `RGB(255,255,255)` for maximum reflectivity of the texture skin.
- `int num_frames`—This is the total number of frames in the .MD2 model for all the animations (198 usually). This element is copied from the .MD2 header.
- `int num_polys`—This is the total number of polygons that make up a single frame of animation. This is the same as in the .MD2 header, and is always the same for each frame of animation because the polygon mesh is the template, and the only things that change each frame of animation are the vertices themselves.
- `int num_verts`—This is the number of vertices for a single frame of animation (there are usually hundreds of vertices in a .MD2 animation frame). This is always the same for every frame of animation. The only things that change to animate the model are the positions of the vertices.
- `int num_textcoords`—This is the number of texture coordinates available for all vertices. Each frame of animation references texture coordinates as indices into the texture coordinate array. In most case, there are a couple hundred texture coordinates in a .MD2 model.

- `BITMAP_IMAGE_PTR skin`—This is a pointer to the texture skin for the model. This bitmap is derived by taking the 256×256 256-color skin from the model directory and increasing the color depth to 16-bit, saving as a .BMP, and loading and storing it here as the texture to be mapped onto the model.

The following fields define where the actual geometrical storage is, but unlike the raw .MD2 file, this data is all ready to go for rendering—it's been scaled, translated, and so forth. Moreover, it's all stored using our native data structures, so they can easily be manipulated.

- `MD2_POLY_PTR polys`—This is a pointer to polygon list, which is composed of an array of structures. Each structure is a record that contains the vertex indices and texture indices for each vertex. This is the same as in the .MD2 file. There is no need for this to have a different format, because it's basically an indirection array.

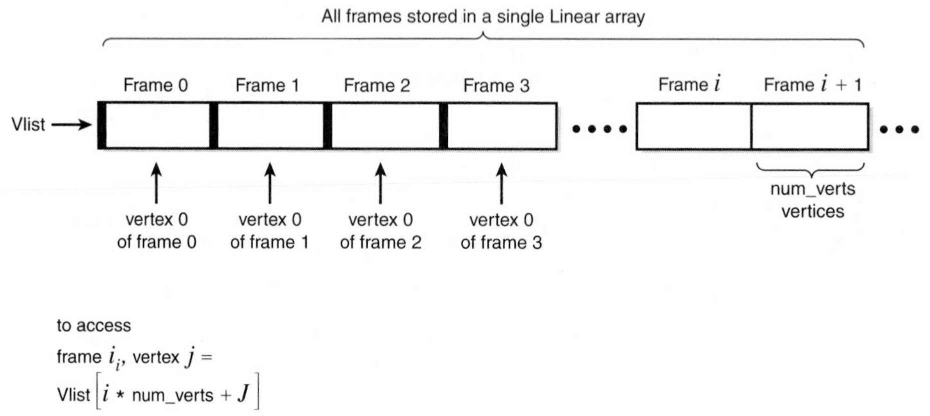

FIGURE 15.12 The vertex list in frame set order.

- `VECTOR3D_PTR vlist`—This is a pointer to the vertex coordinate list. Each vertex is a standard `VECTOR3D`. The interesting thing about this array is that it has every single vertex for every single frame of animation (thousands of vertices!). The data is stored as shown in Figure 15.12—that is, frame 0, frame 1 ... frame *n*. Each frame is composed of `num_verts` vertices, each of which is a `VECTOR3D`. There is no other structure, so to access a specific frame of animation and gain access to the vertices for that frame, the frame number must be multiplied by `num_verts` and this result used as a base index.
- `VECTOR2D_PTR tlist`—This is a pointer to the texture coordinate list. Each texture coordinate is stored as a floating-point value in a `VECTOR2D`. The entire texture coordinate list is stored in this array. There are `num_textcoords` elements.

These next two fields are used to help position and move the model in 3D space:

- `VECTOR4D world_pos`—This is the position of the model in world coordinates.
- `VECTOR4D vel`—This is the velocity of model.

These next fields are just for fun and to help store state information, perform logic, or whatever:

- `int ivars[8]`—Some generic integer variables.
- `float fvars[8]`—Some generic floating point variables.
- `int counters[8]`—Some generic counters.
- `void *link`—A generic void pointer.

These fields are rather important, and are used to help animate and track the state of the model:

- `int anim_state`—This is the state of the animation, which in this context means which animation is currently being played. Basically, the guys at id Software came up with a list of animations that they wanted to support for each model. The list features walking, running, dying, shooting, and so on. However, over the past few years many people have taken creative license on this list and created more animations, so in the end I had to go to the *Quake II* source code itself and figure out exactly how many animations there are supposed to be, what they are called roughly, and what frame indices they are. My findings were as follows:
    - There are 198 total frames in a .MD2 file.
    - There are 20 different animations.
    - Each animation consists of a number of frames, and these frame numbers are always the same.

Table 15.1 lists the animations by name and frame indices. I derived this list by reviewing the *Quake II* source code, and by looking at the file `M_PLAYER.H` in the headers directory of the *Quake II* source code, which can be found at `http://www.fileplanet.com/files/80000/83000.shtml`.

However, a search at Google.com or Yahoo.com will work just as well if that link dies.

TABLE 15.1 Animation Specification for the Animation Frames of the .MD2 File Format

Animation #	Text Name	Frame Indices
0	`STANDING_IDLE`	0–39
1	`RUN`	40–45
2	`ATTACK`	46–53

TABLE 15.1 Continued

Animation #	Text Name	Frame Indices
3	PAIN 1	54–57
4	PAIN 2	58–61
5	PAIN 3	62–65
6	JUMP	66–71
7	FLIP	72–83
8	SALUTE	84–94
9	TAUNT	95–111
10	WAVE	112–122
11	POINT	123–134
12	CROUCH STAND	135–153
13	CROUCH WALK	154–159
14	CROUCH ATTACK	160–168
15	CROUCH PAIN	169–172
16	CROUCH DEATH	173–177
17	DEATH BACK	178–183
18	DEATH FORWARD	184–189
19	DEATH SLOW	190–197

Most of the text descriptions describe what the animation represents. For example, `Pain 1`, `Pain 2`, and `Pain 3` are the animations for when the model is hit and feels "pain"; `ATTACK` is the animation when the model fires its weapon, and so on. However, the most important data is the frame numbers: They do not change, and they are always the same. The problem is that many models you will find on the Internet are not correct, and there might be too many or too few frames for a particular animation. This is not a big problem, but one you will have to deal with sooner or later, because you will see problems with animations. The best approach is to use a table of frame indices that's programmable, so you can change them on the fly on a per-model basis if need be. In any case, I have created a set of `defines` to help select the *`anim_state`* in your code:

```
// md2 animation states
#define MD2_ANIM_STATE_STANDING_IDLE  0 // model standing and idling
#define MD2_ANIM_STATE_RUN       1 // model running
#define MD2_ANIM_STATE_ATTACK     2 // model firing weapon/attacking
#define MD2_ANIM_STATE_PAIN_1     3 // model being hit version 1
#define MD2_ANIM_STATE_PAIN_2     4 // model being hit version 2
#define MD2_ANIM_STATE_PAIN_3     5 // model being hit version 3
#define MD2_ANIM_STATE_JUMP      6 // model jumping
#define MD2_ANIM_STATE_FLIP      7 // model using hand gestures :)
#define MD2_ANIM_STATE_SALUTE     8 // model saluting
#define MD2_ANIM_STATE_TAUNT      9 // model taunting
#define MD2_ANIM_STATE_WAVE      10 // model waving at someone
#define MD2_ANIM_STATE_POINT     11 // model pointing at someone
```

```
#define MD2_ANIM_STATE_CROUCH_STAND  12 // model crouching and idling
#define MD2_ANIM_STATE_CROUCH_WALK  13 // model walking while crouching
#define MD2_ANIM_STATE_CROUCH_ATTACK 14 // model firing weapon while crouching
#define MD2_ANIM_STATE_CROUCH_PAIN  15 // model being hit while crouching
#define MD2_ANIM_STATE_CROUCH_DEATH  16 // model dying while crouching
#define MD2_ANIM_STATE_DEATH_BACK   17 // model dying while falling backward
#define MD2_ANIM_STATE_DEATH_FORWARD 18 // model dying while falling forward
#define MD2_ANIM_STATE_DEATH_SLOW   19 // model dying slowly (any direction)
```

NOTE

You might notice that there is no timing information. Basically, we are left to our own devices to decide how fast to play and interpolate the frames; however, I have added support to simplify this when we get to implementing animation.

- `int anim_counter`—This is a general animation counter used to count frames until the animation is updated to the next frame.
- `int anim_mode`—This defines how the animation in `anim_state` is to be played: single shot or in a loop. Usually `anim_mode` will be one of these two defines:

  ```
  // modes to run animation
  #define MD2_ANIM_LOOP       0 // play animation over and over
  #define MD2_ANIM_SINGLE_SHOT  1 // single shot animation
  ```

- `int anim_speed`—This is the actual animation speed that `anim_counter` counts up to before updating the animation. The smaller the number, the faster the animation.
- `int anim_complete`—This flags whether single shot animation is complete (1 is complete, 0 is pending). Use this to poll the model from the main line code to control logic based upon when an animation is complete. For example, when a "jump" completes, you might make a landing sound, and so forth.
- `float curr_frame`—This is a the current frame of animation to render. Notice that it's floating-point, not an integer—this is very important. We are supporting interpolation between frames, so fractional frame numbers are allowed. For example, frame 5.4 would mean to interpolate between frame 5 and 6 at 40%, and so on. We will go into more detail when discussing animation and vertex interpolation later in the chapter.

That was a lot of setup! Let's implement the loader function first. We need to load a .MD2 file from disk into a memory buffer, overlay the MD2 header, extract all the information and store it into the container class `MD2_CONTAINER`, and then release the temp buffer. Normally, I wouldn't list such a large function, but I think it's warranted in this case. I am going to modify it from the function in `T3DLIB13.CPP` by removing extraneous error handling/output code, but you can always review the actual function on the CD. Anyway, here's the function, with lots of inline comments. Please review the function slowly and read the comments—they proceed in a very linear fashion. When you're done, I'll meet you at the end of the function:

```
int Load_Object_MD2(MD2_CONTAINER_PTR obj_md2, // storage for md2 model
      char *modelfile,  // the filename of the .MD2 model
      VECTOR4D_PTR scale, // initial scaling factors
      VECTOR4D_PTR pos,  // initial position
      VECTOR4D_PTR rot,  // initial rotations (not implemented)
      char *texturefile, // the texture filename for the model
      int attr,      // the lighting/model attributes for the model
      int color,     // base color if no texturing
      int vertex_flags)  // control ordering etc.
{
// this function loads in an md2 file, extracts all the data
// and stores it in the container class which will be used
// later to load frames into a the standard object
// type for rendering on the fly

FILE *fp   = NULL; // file pointer to model
int  flength = -1;  // general file length
UCHAR *buffer = NULL; // used to buffer md2 file data

MD2_HEADER_PTR md2_header;  // pointer to the md2 header


// begin by loading in the .md2 model file
if ((fp = fopen(modelfile, "rb"))==NULL)
  {
  Write_Error("\nLoad_Object_MD2 - couldn't find file %s", modelfile);
  return(0);
  } // end if

// find the length of the model file
// seek to end of file
fseek(fp, 0, SEEK_END);

// where is the file pointer?
flength = ftell(fp);

// now read the md2 file into a buffer to analyze it

// re-position file pointer to beginning of file
fseek(fp, 0, SEEK_SET);
```

```
// allocate memory to hold file
buffer = (UCHAR *)malloc(flength+1);

// load data into buffer
int bytes_read = fread(buffer, sizeof(UCHAR), flength, fp);

// the header is the first item in the buffer, so alias a pointer
// to it, so we can start analyzing it and creating the model
md2_header = (MD2_HEADER_PTR)buffer;


// test for valid file
if (md2_header->identifier != MD2_MAGIC_NUM ||
  md2_header->version != MD2_VERSION)
  {
  fclose(fp);
  return(0);
  } // end if

// assign fields to container class
obj_md2->state     = 0;          // state of the model
obj_md2->attr      = attr;         // attributes of the model
obj_md2->color     = color;        // base color of mesh
obj_md2->num_frames   = md2_header->num_frames; // num frames in model
obj_md2->num_polys   = md2_header->num_polys; // num polygons
obj_md2->num_verts   = md2_header->num_verts; // num vertices
obj_md2->num_textcoords = md2_header->num_textcoords; // num texture coords
obj_md2->curr_frame   = 0;            // current frame in anim
obj_md2->skin      = NULL;           // ptr to texture skin
obj_md2->world_pos   = *pos;            // pos of object in world

// allocate memory for mesh data
// pointer to polygon list
obj_md2->polys = (MD2_POLY_PTR)malloc(md2_header->num_polys*sizeof(MD2_POLY));
// pointer to vertex coordinate list
obj_md2->vlist = (VECTOR3D_PTR)malloc(md2_header->num_frames *
   md2_header->num_verts* sizeof(VECTOR3D));
// pointer to texture coordinate list
obj_md2->tlist = (VECTOR2D_PTR)malloc(md2_header->num_textcoords *
          sizeof(VECTOR2D));

for (int tindex = 0; tindex < md2_header->num_textcoords; tindex++)
  {
  // insert texture coordinate into storage container
```

```
  obj_md2->tlist[tindex].x =
    ((MD2_TEXTCOORD_PTR)(buffer+md2_header->offset_textcoords))[tindex].u;
  obj_md2->tlist[tindex].y =
    ((MD2_TEXTCOORD_PTR)(buffer+md2_header->offset_textcoords))[tindex].v;
  } // end for vindex


for (int findex = 0; findex < md2_header->num_frames; findex++)
  {

  MD2_FRAME_PTR frame_ptr =
     (MD2_FRAME_PTR)(buffer + md2_header->offset_frames +
             md2_header->framesize * findex);

  // extract md2 scale and translate,
  // additionally use sent scale and translate
  float sx = frame_ptr->scale[0],
     sy = frame_ptr->scale[1],
     sz = frame_ptr->scale[2],
     tx = frame_ptr->translate[0],
     ty = frame_ptr->translate[1],
     tz = frame_ptr->translate[2];

  for (int vindex = 0; vindex < md2_header->num_verts; vindex++)
    {
    VECTOR3D v; // temp vector

    // scale and translate compressed vertex
    v.x = (float)frame_ptr->vlist[vindex].v[0] * sx + tx;
    v.y = (float)frame_ptr->vlist[vindex].v[1] * sy + ty;
    v.z = (float)frame_ptr->vlist[vindex].v[2] * sz + tz;

    // scale final point based on sent data
    v.x = scale->x * v.x;
    v.y = scale->y * v.y;
    v.z = scale->z * v.z;

float temp; // used for swaping

    // test for vertex modifications to winding order etc.
    if (vertex_flags & VERTEX_FLAGS_INVERT_X)
      v.x = -v.x;

    if (vertex_flags & VERTEX_FLAGS_INVERT_Y)
      v.y = -v.y;
```

```
      if (vertex_flags & VERTEX_FLAGS_INVERT_Z)
        v.z = -v.z;

      if (vertex_flags & VERTEX_FLAGS_SWAP_YZ)
        SWAP(v.y, v.z, temp);

      if (vertex_flags & VERTEX_FLAGS_SWAP_XZ)
        SWAP(v.x, v.z, temp);

      if (vertex_flags & VERTEX_FLAGS_SWAP_XY)
        SWAP(v.x, v.y, temp);

      // insert vertex into vertex list which is laid out:
      // frame 0, frame 1,..., frame n
      // frame i: vertex 0, vertex 1,....vertex j
      obj_md2->vlist[vindex + (findex * obj_md2->num_verts)] = v;
      } // end vindex

   } // end findex


 MD2_POLY_PTR poly_ptr = (MD2_POLY_PTR)(buffer + md2_header->offset_polys);

 for (int pindex = 0; pindex < md2_header->num_polys; pindex++)
   {
   // insert polygon into polygon list in container
   if (vertex_flags & VERTEX_FLAGS_INVERT_WINDING_ORDER)
      {
      // inverted winding order

      // vertices
      obj_md2->polys[pindex].vindex[0] = poly_ptr[pindex].vindex[2];
      obj_md2->polys[pindex].vindex[1] = poly_ptr[pindex].vindex[1];
      obj_md2->polys[pindex].vindex[2] = poly_ptr[pindex].vindex[0];

      // texture coordinates
      obj_md2->polys[pindex].tindex[0] = poly_ptr[pindex].tindex[2];
      obj_md2->polys[pindex].tindex[1] = poly_ptr[pindex].tindex[1];
      obj_md2->polys[pindex].tindex[2] = poly_ptr[pindex].tindex[0];
      } // end if
   else
      {
      // normal winding order
```

```
    // vertices
    obj_md2->polys[pindex].vindex[0] = poly_ptr[pindex].vindex[0];
    obj_md2->polys[pindex].vindex[1] = poly_ptr[pindex].vindex[1];
    obj_md2->polys[pindex].vindex[2] = poly_ptr[pindex].vindex[2];

    // texture coordinates
    obj_md2->polys[pindex].tindex[0] = poly_ptr[pindex].tindex[0];
    obj_md2->polys[pindex].tindex[1] = poly_ptr[pindex].tindex[1];
    obj_md2->polys[pindex].tindex[2] = poly_ptr[pindex].tindex[2];

    } // end if

  } // end for vindex

// close the file
fclose(fp);

////////////////////////////////////////////////////////////////////////////////
// load the texture from disk
Load_Bitmap_File(&bitmap16bit, texturefile);

// create a proper size and bitdepth bitmap
obj_md2->skin = (BITMAP_IMAGE_PTR)malloc(sizeof(BITMAP_IMAGE));

// initialize bitmap
Create_Bitmap(obj_md2->skin,0,0,
       bitmap16bit.bitmapinfoheader.biWidth,
       bitmap16bit.bitmapinfoheader.biHeight,
       bitmap16bit.bitmapinfoheader.biBitCount);

// load the bitmap image
Load_Image_Bitmap16(obj_md2->skin, &bitmap16bit,0,0,BITMAP_EXTRACT_MODE_ABS);

// done, so unload the bitmap
Unload_Bitmap_File(&bitmap16bit);


// finally release the memory for the temporary buffer
if (buffer)
  free(buffer);

// return success
return(1);

} // end Load_Object_MD2
```

To call `Load_Object_MD2()`, we need to send in a pointer to the container to hold the MD2 model, along with the name of the .MD2 file on disk, a scaling factor, position, rotation (only the scale and position are used currently), filename for the .BMP file holding the 16-bit 256×256 texture skin, the polygon attributes to be used for the model, the base color, and finally `vertex_flags` to implement changing winding order, coordinate systems, and so on.

If you look closely at the function prototype, I have tried to make this .MD2 file loader look something like all our other file loaders, so the parameters should be reasonably familiar. The function begins by searching for the .MD2 file on the disk, and then it opens and loads the file into one large memory buffer. Then the function begins the analysis stage: It scans the header's information and, based on this, extracts all the important information from the .MD2 model. At the same time, the code inserts all the data into the container class in a cleaner, noncompressed format, and initializes all the fields of the container class as well.

One of the most important code fragments is the `vertex_flags` code that allows the caller to perform simple coordinate transformations with the axes and winding order. If you recall, we are using a left-hand coordinate system, with a clockwise winding order. .MD2 files, on the other hand, use a right-hand system with a counterclockwise winding order. To fix this, we only have to swap the y-z axes. This little detail can be a huge pain if it's not supported with a simple flag. In any case, after the model is loaded and extracted into the `MD2_CONTAINER` class, we are almost ready to go. All we have to do is write a function that can extract a single frame from the container and insert it into the `OBJECT4DV2` host. Along with this, we also need support functions to control the selected animations and perform timing. Let's take a look at this now.

Animating .MD2 Files

Animation is a snap once you understand the .MD2 file format, and have extracted and massaged the data into a format more palatable than its native compressed format. This is the function of the loader and the `MD2_CONTAINER` class. The loader is called with a container class with something like the following:

```
// some working vectors
static VECTOR4D vs = {4,4,4,1};
static VECTOR4D vp = {0,0,0,1};

// load the md2 object
Load_Object_MD2(&obj_md2,  // the loaded md2 file placed in container
   "./md2/q2mdl-tekkblade/tris.md2", // the filename of the .MD2 model
   &vs, // scale and position
   &vp,
   NULL,
   "./md2/q2mdl-tekkblade/blade_black.bmp", //texture filefor the model
   POLY4DV2_ATTR_RGB16 |
```

```
POLY4DV2_ATTR_SHADE_MODE_FLAT |
POLY4DV2_ATTR_SHADE_MODE_TEXTURE,
RGB16Bit(255,255,255),
VERTEX_FLAGS_SWAP_YZ);     // control ordering etc.
```

NOTE

This model is called "Tekkaman Blade" and can be found on Polycount. This is a good example of the quality of the models found on Polycount. The author of this particular model is Michael "Magarnigal" Mellor.

We would have the .MD2 model loaded into the `MD2_CONTAINER obj_md2` from the file `"./md2/q2mdl-tekkblade/tris.md2"` with the texture found in the file `"./md2/q2mdl-tekkblade/blade_black.bmp"`.

All we need to do is extract the vertex list for any given frame and insert it into the vertex list of an `OBJECT4DV2`. However, the cool thing is that the polygon list and the texture coordinates, and so on of the `OBJECT4DV2` never change, because they are indirection arrays and refer to indices of vertices, not the vertices themselves. Basically, we create a "host" `OBJECT4DV2` and fill it with everything except the vertices of the mesh.

We set up the attributes, color, the polygon list, the texture coordinates, the texture map, and so on, but we don't insert any vertices. This is called *preparation*. When we are ready to render a frame, we make a call to a function that, given a specific frame of animation, extracts the vertices from the `MD2_CONTAINER` (`obj_md2` in this case) and then inserts them in to the "host" `OBJECT4DV2`. Then we pass the `OBJECT4DV2` to the rendering engine, and it has no idea what it is rendering!

Preparing an `OBJECT4DV2` Host for the .MD2 Model

Let's start with the function that prepares an `OBJECT4DV2` to be a host for the `MD2_CONTAINER`. Here's the function that does that (minus some extraneous error display code to save space):

```
int Prepare_OBJECT4DV2_For_MD2(OBJECT4DV2_PTR obj, // ptr to dest obj
      MD2_CONTAINER_PTR obj_md2) // md2 obj to extract frame from
{
// this function prepares the OBJECT4DV2 to be used as a vessel to hold
// frames from the md2 container, it allocated the memory needed, set fields
// and pre-computes as much as possible since each new frame will change only
// the vertex list

// clear out the object and initialize it a bit
memset(obj, 0, sizeof(OBJECT4DV2));
```

```
// set state of object to active and visible
obj->state = OBJECT4DV2_STATE_ACTIVE | OBJECT4DV2_STATE_VISIBLE;

// set some information in object
obj->num_frames  = 1;  // always set to 1
obj->curr_frame  = 0;
obj->attr     = OBJECT4DV2_ATTR_SINGLE_FRAME | OBJECT4DV2_ATTR_TEXTURES;

obj->num_vertices = obj_md2->num_verts;
obj->num_polys  = obj_md2->num_polys;
obj->texture   = obj_md2->skin;

// set position of object
obj->world_pos = obj_md2->world_pos;

// allocate the memory for the vertices and number of polys
// the call parameters are redundant in this case, but who cares
if (!Init_OBJECT4DV2(obj,
           obj->num_vertices,
           obj->num_polys,
           obj->num_frames))
  {
  Write_Error("\n(can't allocate memory).");
  } // end if

// compute average and max radius using the vertices from frame 0, this isn't
// totally accurate, but the volume of the object hopefully does vary wildly
// during animation

// reset incase there's any residue
obj->avg_radius[0] = 0;
obj->max_radius[0] = 0;

// loop thru and compute radius
for (int vindex = 0; vindex < obj_md2->num_verts; vindex++)
  {
  // update the average and maximum radius (use frame 0)
  float dist_to_vertex =
     sqrt(obj_md2->vlist[vindex].x * obj_md2->vlist[vindex].x +
        obj_md2->vlist[vindex].y * obj_md2->vlist[vindex].y +
        obj_md2->vlist[vindex].z * obj_md2->vlist[vindex].z );

  // accumulate total radius
  obj->avg_radius[0]+=dist_to_vertex;
```

15

```
    // update maximum radius
    if (dist_to_vertex > obj->max_radius[0])
      obj->max_radius[0] = dist_to_vertex;

    } // end for vertex

  // finallize average radius computation
  obj->avg_radius[0]/=obj->num_vertices;


  // copy texture coordinate list always the same
  for (int tindex = 0; tindex < obj_md2->num_textcoords; tindex++)
    {
    // now texture coordinates
    obj->tlist[tindex].x = obj_md2->tlist[tindex].x;
    obj->tlist[tindex].y = obj_md2->tlist[tindex].y;
    } // end for tindex

  // generate the polygon index list, always the same
  for (int pindex=0; pindex < obj_md2->num_polys; pindex++)
    {
    // set polygon indices
    obj->plist[pindex].vert[0] = obj_md2->polys[pindex].vindex[0];
    obj->plist[pindex].vert[1] = obj_md2->polys[pindex].vindex[1];
    obj->plist[pindex].vert[2] = obj_md2->polys[pindex].vindex[2];

    // point polygon vertex list to object's vertex list
    // note that this is redundant since the polylist is contained
    // within the object in this case and its up to the user to select
    // whether the local or transformed vertex list is used when building up
    // polygon geometry, might be a better idea to set to NULL in the context
    // of polygons that are part of an object
    obj->plist[pindex].vlist  = obj->vlist_local;

    // set attributes of polygon with sent attributes
    obj->plist[pindex].attr  = obj_md2->attr;

    // set color of polygon
    obj->plist[pindex].color  = obj_md2->color;

    // apply texture to this polygon
    obj->plist[pindex].texture = obj_md2->skin;
```

```
// assign the texture coordinates
obj->plist[pindex].text[0] = obj_md2->polys[pindex].tindex[0];
obj->plist[pindex].text[1] = obj_md2->polys[pindex].tindex[1];
obj->plist[pindex].text[2] = obj_md2->polys[pindex].tindex[2];

// set texture coordinate attributes
SET_BIT(obj->vlist_local[ obj->plist[pindex].vert[0] ].attr,
    VERTEX4DTV1_ATTR_TEXTURE);
SET_BIT(obj->vlist_local[ obj->plist[pindex].vert[1] ].attr,
    VERTEX4DTV1_ATTR_TEXTURE);
SET_BIT(obj->vlist_local[ obj->plist[pindex].vert[2] ].attr,
    VERTEX4DTV1_ATTR_TEXTURE);

// set the material mode to ver. 1.0 emulation
SET_BIT(obj->plist[pindex].attr, POLY4DV2_ATTR_DISABLE_MATERIAL);

// finally set the polygon to active
obj->plist[pindex].state = POLY4DV2_STATE_ACTIVE;

// point polygon vertex list to object's vertex list
// note that this is redundant since the polylist is contained
// within the object in this case and its up to the user to select
// whether the local or transformed vertex list is used when building up
// polygon geometry, might be a better idea to set to NULL in the context
// of polygons that are part of an object
obj->plist[pindex].vlist = obj->vlist_local;

// set texture coordinate list, this is needed
obj->plist[pindex].tlist = obj->tlist;

// extract vertex indices
int vindex_0 = obj_md2->polys[pindex].vindex[0];
int vindex_1 = obj_md2->polys[pindex].vindex[1];
int vindex_2 = obj_md2->polys[pindex].vindex[2];

// we need to compute the normal of this polygon face, and recall
// that the vertices are in cw order, u=p0->p1, v=p0->p2, n=uxv
VECTOR4D u, v, n;

// build u, v
u.x = obj_md2->vlist[vindex_1].x - obj_md2->vlist[vindex_0].x;
u.y = obj_md2->vlist[vindex_1].y - obj_md2->vlist[vindex_0].y;
u.z = obj_md2->vlist[vindex_1].z - obj_md2->vlist[vindex_0].z;
u.w = 1;
```

```
    v.x = obj_md2->vlist[vindex_2].x - obj_md2->vlist[vindex_0].x;
    v.y = obj_md2->vlist[vindex_2].y - obj_md2->vlist[vindex_0].y;
    v.z = obj_md2->vlist[vindex_2].z - obj_md2->vlist[vindex_0].z;
    v.w = 1;

    // compute cross product
    VECTOR4D_Cross(&u, &v, &n);

    // compute length of normal accurately and store in poly nlength
    // +- epsilon later to fix over/underflows
    obj->plist[pindex].nlength = VECTOR4D_Length(&n);

    } // end for poly

// return success
return(1);

} // end Prepare_OBJECT4DV2_For_MD2
```

`Prepare_OBJECT4DV2_For_MD2()` takes two parameters: a pointer to the `OBJECT4DV2` host that will receive the `MD2_CONTAINER` mesh information, and a pointer to the `MD2_CONTAINER` holding the actual .MD2 model we want to animate and render. `Prepare_OBJECT4DV2_For_MD2()` more or less initializes the `OBJECT4DV2` object and then copies everything it can from the `MD2_CONTAINER` class that won't change frame to frame. Only the vertices are not copied. This function isn't required to be fast because it's called during initialization, so speed isn't important. The function basically creates the polygon list, texture list, and performs all needed calculations on the object, such as computation of surface normal lengths, and average and maximum radius.

CAUTION

The length of all polygon normals is calculated based on frame 0 as a reference. As the model animates, the normals of the precomputed length of polygon normals will stay the same. This is mostly unnoticeable, but is a factor for lighting. A more detailed model would be to store a normal length for every polygon for each vertex set; however, that would mean for each polygon, we would need an array 198 elements long, each with a normal, and then we would have to copy that as well when we extract a frame. In the end, you can't tell the difference. Also, the average radius is also computed using only frame 0.

Extracting Frames from the `MD2_CONTAINER` Class

After the `OBJECT4DV2` is prepared to be a host for the `MD2_CONTAINER` vertex information, the rest is a snap. Simply select a frame from 0…198, figure out where in the vertex list the vertices are, and then copy them into the vertex storage of the `OBJECT4DV2`, tricking it into thinking it's always the same frame. Here's the code that does that:

```
int Extract_MD2_Frame(OBJECT4DV2_PTR obj, // ptr to dest obj
   MD2_CONTAINER_PTR obj_md2) // md2 obj to extract frame from
{
// this function extracts a single frame of animation
// from the md2 container and stores in into the object4dv2 container,
// this is so we can leverage the library to transform,
// light, etc. the mesh rather than writing new functions,
// granted the process of extraction is an unneeded overhead,
// but since we will only have a few MD2 object running around
// the rendering swamps the time to extract by many orders of magnitude,
// so the extraction is negligible the function also interpolates frames;
// if the curr_frame value is non-intergral then
// the function will blend frames together based on the decimal fraction

// test if frame number is greater than max frames allowable,
// some models are malformed
int frame_0,  // starting frame to interpolate
  frame_1;  // ending frame to interpolate


// step 1: decide if this is an interpolated frame?

float ivalue = obj_md2->curr_frame - (int)obj_md2->curr_frame;

// test for integer?
if (ivalue == 0.0)
  {
  // single frame, no interpolation
  frame_0 = obj_md2->curr_frame;

  // check for overflow?
  if (frame_0 >= obj_md2->num_frames)
    frame_0 = obj_md2->num_frames-1;

  // copy vertex list for selected frame, vertex list begins at
  // base index (obj_md2->num_verts * obj_md2->curr_frame)
  int base_index = obj_md2->num_verts * frame_0;

  // copy vertices now from base
  for (int vindex = 0; vindex < obj_md2->num_verts; vindex++)
    {
    // copy the vertex
    obj->vlist_local[vindex].x = obj_md2->vlist[vindex + base_index].x;
    obj->vlist_local[vindex].y = obj_md2->vlist[vindex + base_index].y;
```

15

```
        obj->vlist_local[vindex].z = obj_md2->vlist[vindex + base_index].z;
        obj->vlist_local[vindex].w = 1;

        // every vertex has a point and texture attached,
        // set that in the flags attribute
        SET_BIT(obj->vlist_local[vindex].attr, VERTEX4DTV1_ATTR_POINT);
        SET_BIT(obj->vlist_local[vindex].attr, VERTEX4DTV1_ATTR_TEXTURE);

        } // end for vindex

      } // end if
    else
      {
      // interpolate between curr_frame and curr_frame+1 based
      // on ivalue
      frame_0 = obj_md2->curr_frame;
      frame_1 = obj_md2->curr_frame+1;

      // check for overflow?
      if (frame_0 >= obj_md2->num_frames)
        frame_0 = obj_md2->num_frames-1;

      // check for overflow?
      if (frame_1 >= obj_md2->num_frames)
        frame_1 = obj_md2->num_frames-1;

      // interpolate vertex lists for selected frame(s), vertex list(s) begin at
      // base index (obj_md2->num_verts * obj_md2->curr_frame)
      int base_index_0 = obj_md2->num_verts * frame_0;
      int base_index_1 = obj_md2->num_verts * frame_1;

      // interpolate vertices now from base frame 0,1
    for (int vindex = 0; vindex < obj_md2->num_verts; vindex++)
    {
    // interpolate the vertices
    obj->vlist_local[vindex].x =((1-ivalue)*obj_md2->vlist[vindex+base_index_0].x
                   + ivalue*obj_md2->vlist[vindex+base_index_1].x);
    obj->vlist_local[vindex].y =((1-ivalue)*obj_md2->vlist[vindex+base_index_0].y
                   + ivalue*obj_md2->vlist[vindex+base_index_1].y);
    obj->vlist_local[vindex].z =((1-ivalue)*obj_md2->vlist[vindex+base_index_0].z
                   + ivalue*obj_md2->vlist[vindex+base_index_1].z);
    obj->vlist_local[vindex].w =1;
```

```
    // every vertex has a point and texture attached,
    // set that in the flags attribute
    SET_BIT(obj->vlist_local[vindex].attr, VERTEX4DTV1_ATTR_POINT);
    SET_BIT(obj->vlist_local[vindex].attr, VERTEX4DTV1_ATTR_TEXTURE);
} // end for vindex

    } // end if

// return success
return(1);

} // end Extract_MD2_Frame
```

`Extract_MD2_Frame()` once again simply takes a pointer to both the host `OBJECT4DV2` that receives the vertex information, and a pointer to the `MD2_CONTAINER` sourcing it. The frame that's extracted is `curr_frame` within the `MD2_CONTAINER`. However, there is a catch: The extraction function performs key-frame interpolation. Let's talk about this for a moment.

15

If you review `Extract_MD2_Frame()`, you will see that the function begins with an `if` statement:

```
// test for integer?
if (ivalue == 0.0)
...
```

This tests whether there is a fractional or decimal component to the current frame. If not, the exact frame is extracted from the vertex list. For example, suppose that `curr_frame` is equal to 26. The vertex list from the 26th frame would then be copied to the host `OBJECT4DV2`. This would be accomplished by multiplying 26 by the number of vertices per model, which is `num_verts`, and then using that product as the base index into the vertex list and copying `num_verts` vertices from there out into the host `OBJECT4DV2`, as shown in Figure 15.12. Nothing strange about that, but when the `curr_frame` is not an integral value, we need to vertex blend/interpolate between key frames.

Take a look at Figure 15.13. Here we see a number of key frames of a stick figure walking. Suppose that we want the animation to look smoother. We can artificially compute what the value/position of each vertex would be between any frame i and i+1. As long as nothing too weird happens, and as long as each vertex follows a linear motion, interpolation will look reasonable. This is the philosophy behind .MD2 files. Even though there are 198 frames of animation, they are used for 20 different animations. This might seem like a lot, but if you were to run a game at 60 frames a second, and on average, each animation has 198/20, or roughly 10 frames, each animation would occur in 10/60 = .16 seconds, or 160 milliseconds. Not much time to see anything!

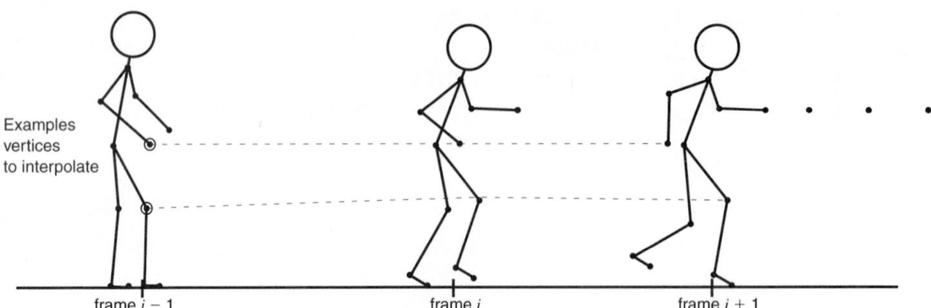

FIGURE 15.13 Key-frame animation.

To slow the animation, we can do two things: insert delays before we switch frames, or interpolate. If we insert delays and render a new frame each 10 frames for example, we slow it down 10 times. However, the animation still looks jerky because there are so few frames per animation. A better solution is to interpolate between frames, or more specifically, to interpolate between vertices for each frame. This is exactly what the second code block of `Extract_MD2_Frame()` does.

Implementing Frame/Vertex Interpolation

The second code block of `Extract_MD2_Frame()` is a little more complicated than the first. This is because it's performing a full vertex interpolation between two frames of animation. The two frames are selected based on `curr_frame`. Basically, if `curr_frame` is non-integral (say it's 5.1), it means we need to blend the vertices from frame 5 and frame 6 such that we get 90% of frame 5 and 10% of frame 6. Read that again: 90% of frame 5, and 10% of frame 6—not the other way around!

The math for an interpolated vertex is given that $\mathbf{v_0}$ is a vertex from frame 0 and $\mathbf{v_1}$ is a vertex from frame 1, and that we want to interpolate between the two based on the interpolant i value from 0...1.0, which is the decimal portion of `curr_frame`, then

$$\mathbf{v_i} = \mathbf{v_0} * (1 - \text{ivalue}) + \mathbf{v_1} * (\text{ivalue})$$

This is exactly what the code does. The only reason I create special cases on the integral values is for speed. That is, when the `curr_frame` is a whole number, there is no interpolation, and thus no need to perform the multiplication and addition.

We can send in any frame value 0...198 with a decimal fraction, and the `Extract_MD2_Frame()` function will interpolate between frames if need be, extract the vertices and place them in the `OBJECT4DV2` host, and save the day!

The last piece to the puzzle is a little logic to drive the actual selection of animation, or *state*, and to animate the model (select the frames).

Adding State-Based Animation to the .MD2 Support

At this point, we can load an .MD2 file from disk, convert it into a more easily accessible MD2_CONTAINER class, extract frames with vertex animation, and store them in a host OBJECT4DV2 object. We could stop right here, call a rendering function with the OBJECT4DV2 object and be done. However, think of all those cool animations frames listed in Table 15.1. It would be nice to be able to call a function that would allow us to initialize and control the animation of the model with single-shot and looped animation. That way, from our game we could tell the model to run, jump, idle, or whatever based on game logic, and not have to hard-code it. So, let's write one last set of functions to accomplish this task—it's really simple.

We need two things: a simple data structure to hold animations, and a couple of functions to drive the animation and update the MD2_CONTAINER's fields. Let's start with the animation. An animation consists of the starting frame, the ending frame, an interpolation rate, and an animation speed:

```
// holds a simple animation start-end plus interpolation rate
typedef struct MD2_ANIMATION_TYP
    {
    int  start_frame; // starting and ending frame
    int  end_frame;
    float irate;     // interpolation rate
    int  anim_speed;  // animation rate
    } MD2_ANIMATION, *MD2_ANIMATION_PTR;
```

The start_frame and end_frame fields are simply going to hold the indices from Table 15.1, but irate and anim_speed need a little explanation. irate is the interpolation rate, or in other words, how many steps are interpolated between frames. For example, if irate is set to 0.1, interpolation from frame 5 to 6 would look like this:

5.0, 5.1, 5.2, 5.3 ... 5.9, 6.0

In most cases, an interpolation rate of .25 or .50 works fine. Try to use nonrepeating decimals; for example, .33 would be bad. The next field of interest is anim_speed. This is simply the counter value used to perform the animation or interpolation logic as the game runs, so setting it to 0 means update the animation each frame, setting it to 1 means update the animation after one frame, and so forth. Between all these values, we can create any timings we want. The next thing to do is to create an array of these structures, each containing the animation indices from Table 15.1:

```
// the animations, the frames, and timing look good on most
// models, but tweak them to suit your needs OR create a table
// for every character in your game to fine tune your animation
MD2_ANIMATION md2_animations[NUM_MD2_ANIMATIONS] =
{
// format: start frame (0..197), end frame (0..197),
```

15

```
// interpolation rate (0..1, 1 for no interpolation),
// speed (0..10, 0 fastest, 1 fast, 2 medium, 3 slow...)

{0,39,0.5,1},  // MD2_ANIM_STATE_STANDING_IDLE    0
{40,45,0.5,2},  // MD2_ANIM_STATE_RUN          1
{46,53,0.5,1},  // MD2_ANIM_STATE_ATTACK        2
{54,57,0.5,1},  // MD2_ANIM_STATE_PAIN_1        3
{58,61,0.5,1},  // MD2_ANIM_STATE_PAIN_2        4
{62,65,0.5,1},  // MD2_ANIM_STATE_PAIN_3        5
{66,71,0.5,1},  // MD2_ANIM_STATE_JUMP         6
{72,83,0.5,1},  // MD2_ANIM_STATE_FLIP         7
{84,94,0.5,1},  // MD2_ANIM_STATE_SALUTE        8
{95,111,0.5,1}, // MD2_ANIM_STATE_TAUNT         9
{112,122,0.5,1}, // MD2_ANIM_STATE_WAVE         10
{123,134,0.5,1}, // MD2_ANIM_STATE_POINT         11
{135,153,0.5,1}, // MD2_ANIM_STATE_CROUCH_STAND     12
{154,159,0.5,1}, // MD2_ANIM_STATE_CROUCH_WALK      13
{160,168,0.5,1}, // MD2_ANIM_STATE_CROUCH_ATTACK     14
{169,172,0.5,1}, // MD2_ANIM_STATE_CROUCH_PAIN      15
{173,177,0.25,0}, // MD2_ANIM_STATE_CROUCH_DEATH     16
{178,183,0.25,0}, // MD2_ANIM_STATE_DEATH_BACK      17
{184,189,0.25,0}, // MD2_ANIM_STATE_DEATH_FORWARD     18
{190,197,0.25,0}, // MD2_ANIM_STATE_DEATH_SLOW      19
};
```

In most cases, I use a .5 for the interpolation and a 1 for the animation update. Given this data structure, we need a couple of functions to start an animation and run it. Here's a function to set up for a particular animation:

```
int Set_Animation_MD2(MD2_CONTAINER_PTR md2_obj, // md2 object
       int anim_state,        // which animation to play
       int anim_mode = MD2_ANIM_LOOP) // mode of animation single/loop
{
// this function initializes an animation for play back
md2_obj->anim_state  = anim_state;
md2_obj->anim_counter = 0;
md2_obj->anim_speed  = md2_animations[anim_state].anim_speed;
md2_obj->anim_mode  = anim_mode;

// set initial frame
md2_obj->curr_frame  = md2_animations[anim_state].start_frame;

// set animation complete flag
md2_obj->anim_complete = 0;
```

```
// return success
return(1);

} // end Set_Animation_MD2
```

`Set_Animation_MD2()` takes a pointer to the `MD2_CONTAINER` of the model you want to animate, along with the animation state and the mode for the animation. For example, assume a model has been loaded and prepared from the `MD2_CONTAINER` object `obj_md2`. To select the run animation for loop mode, you would make the call

```
Set_Animation_MD2(&obj_md2,
         MD2_ANIM_STATE_RUN,
         MD2_ANIM_LOOP);
```

and that's it. However, we need something to update the animation and change `curr_frame` in the `MD2_CONTAINER` class, so here's the final animation function that does this:

```
int Animate_MD2(MD2_CONTAINER_PTR md2_obj) // md2 object
{
// animate the mesh to next frame based on state and interpolation values...

// update animation counter
if (++md2_obj->anim_counter >= md2_obj->anim_speed)
  {
  // reset counter
  md2_obj->anim_counter = 0;

  // animate mesh with interpolation, algorithm is straightforward interpolate
  // from current frame in animation to next and blend vertex positions based
  // on interpolant ivalue in the md2_container class, couple tricky parts
  // are to watch out for the endpost values of the animation, etc.
  // if the interpolation rate irate=1.0 then there is no interpolation
  // for all intent purposes...

  // add interpolation rate to interpolation value, test for next frame
  md2_obj->curr_frame+=md2_animations[md2_obj->anim_state].irate;

  // test if sequence is complete?
  if (md2_obj->curr_frame > md2_animations[md2_obj->anim_state].end_frame)
   {
   // test for one shot, if so then reset to last frame, if loop, the loop
   if (md2_obj->anim_mode == MD2_ANIM_LOOP)
     {
     // loop animation back to starting frame
```

15

```
      md2_obj->curr_frame = md2_animations[md2_obj->anim_state].start_frame;
      } // end if
    else
      {
      // MD2_ANIM_SINGLE_SHOT
      md2_obj->curr_frame = md2_animations[md2_obj->anim_state].end_frame;

      // set complete flag incase outside wants to take action
      md2_obj->anim_complete = 1;
      } // end else

    } // end if sequence complete

  } // end if time to animate

// return success
return(1);

} // end Animate_MD2
```

You simply call `Animate_MD2()` with a pointer to the container class and it does the rest. Notice that it knows nothing about interpolation. It only cares about timing, and whether it's performing a single-shot or a looped animation.

Well, that's about it for the .MD2 file format—we can load them, convert them to `OBJECT4DV2` format, animate, and render them. Let's actually see all this in action with a demo.

.MD2 Demo

As a demo of loading, rendering, and animating .MD2 files, take a look at the screenshots in Figure 15.14. They depict `DEMOII15_1.CPP¦EXE` in action in both wireframe and solid mode. The demo basically loads a .MD2 file from the CD/hard drive and then animates it in place. The controls are as follows:

- 1—Previous animation
- 2—Next animation
- 3—Play the current animation single-shot
- 4—Play the current animation looped
- H—Onscreen help
- Arrow keys—Move the camera around
- Esc—Exit

FIGURE 15.14 A screenshot of the .MD2 demo in action.

The rest of the controls are shown in the onscreen help. If you don't like the timings, try playing around with the `irate` and `anim_speed` values in the `md2_animations[]` array. Finally, to compile the program, you will need `DEMOII15_1.CPP|H`, along with all the library files, including this chapter's `T3DLIB1-13.CPP|H` and a link with the DirectX .LIB files. Of course, there is a precompiled .EXE file on the CD.

CAUTION

This demo, like the rest, uses files within a subdirectory that contains the assets (the .MD2 files and textures), so if you want to copy it all to the hard drive, make sure you copy the subdirectories, and don't flatten them out—the paths are relative, but still need the subdirectories relative to the .EXE's root directory.

Simple Non-Character-Based Animation

Up until now, this entire book has been an exercise in overheating the warp core. In this last section, we are going to really slow down and just talk about the remaining topics rather than dig down deep. The reason why, of course, is that I've covered this stuff in the first *Tricks* and throughout this book in one way or another. Nevertheless, I just want to make sure that we at least touch upon these concepts, because so many people make simple things hard. I want you to realize that none of this stuff is hard—you just have to know how to approach it. With that in mind, let's take a look at moving objects around and animating them.

Of course, we already know how to perform character animation based on the .MD2 coverage, so the following material is going to simply cover moving objects as if they're points or objects. You would use the character animation techniques along with the following ideas to complete the animation system—that is, to make an object look like it's walking or turning while the animation frame the character is displaying is the walking sequence, and so on.

Rotational and Translational Motion

Let's begin with the two most basic types of animation you can perform on a 3D object: rotation and translation. Rotational animation is used when you want to turn an object as it's moving from one point to another, or for objects that are stationary that need to simply rotate, such as a turret, for example. Translational animation is the only way you're going to move something from point A to point B.

Rotating Objects

To rotate any object, we simply need to perform a rotation transformation with an x,y,z rotation matrix, and then apply the transformation to the object. We have done this many times in many demos, so nothing interesting there. What is interesting is creating a higher-level functionality to drive the rotation.

There's also the consideration of transforming the local or transformed coordinates of the model. If you recall, all models have a set of local or model vertices stored in the `vlist[]` array. This is the only "fresh" copy of the model. Then when we transform the object, we can perform the transformation on these local coordinates, or make a copy of them and store the results in the transformed coordinate `tvlist[]`. This works out great—however, any transformation you perform is lost each frame; the object doesn't "remember" anything about what you did.

Nonetheless, this is usually a better approach that transforming the model coordinates themselves because once they are transformed, the model's vertex coordinates will be altered, and moreover, errors will slowly creep into the vertex positions, so that after thousands or tens of thousands of transformations, the model will degrade.

Thus, the best approach is to use a rotation variable or state that tracks the current rotation angles of the object, and then for each frame, you should use this variable to transform the local coordinates and store them into the transformed coordinates for rendering. This is shown in Figure 15.15.

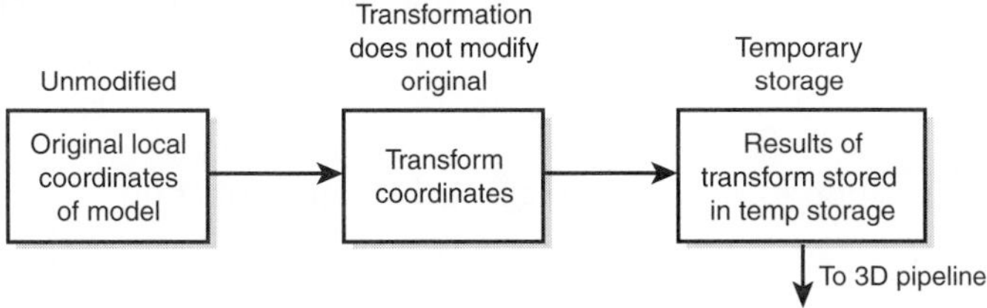

FIGURE 15.15 Transforming local coordinates and storing results into other storage.

Of course, the downside to this approach is that you must perform a transformation on your model each frame. For example, suppose you load your model into the system such that its major axis is pointing toward the positive z-axis. You would then create a variable to track its rotation around the y-axis (call it `rot_y`). Each frame, you will update `rot_y` and use it to generate the transformation matrix for y-axis rotation and rotate the local coordinates, but you'll store them in the transformed vertex list. Thus, if you have a model with 1,000 vertices, you are going to perform 1,000 transformations per frame to transform it from model space to world space. This is the price you pay, but your original model will never be destroyed.

TIP

If you are really trying to save time and can't perform all these transformations per frame, you can surely directly modify the model coordinates. However, after every 10,000 transformations, you might want to "refresh" the model's local coordinates with a copy of the original model's vertices to minimize degradation because of numeric inaccuracies.

In conclusion, I suggest that you try both and see what works best. Additionally, it will be definitely worth your time to create some software with which you can command an object to rotate some angle over some amount of time or number of frames and then stop. Similarly to how we wrote the animation code for the .MD2 system, you might want to write some helper functions, so you can simply start a rotation on an object and the object will rotate each frame at some rate.

Moving Objects in Lines

Moving an object in a straight line is rather trivial, as it's nothing more than translation. However, once again, there are a number of ways to achieve this. One way is to use a simple velocity vector **v**, and then given a position vector **p** of the object, just apply the transformation

```
p = p + v
```

each frame. This will move the object in a straight line starting from **p** along the vector **v**. But what if you want to move an object from point $\mathbf{p_0}$ to point $\mathbf{p_1}$? Again, this is easy—we simply set up a vector equation and parametrically translate the object along the vector path. Here's how:

Given $\mathbf{p_0}$, $\mathbf{p_1}$:

Set object's world position to $\mathbf{p_0}$, and then apply this transformation:

$$p = p_0 + t*(p_1 - p_0)$$

```
for t = 0 to 1.0
```

As you can see, the position vector **p** will trace a line from $\mathbf{p_0}$ to $\mathbf{p_1}$ as t ranges from 0 to 1.0. The rate of the motion is controlled by the change in t per unit of time. This is a *parametric* equation. Figure 15.16 illustrates this motion setup.

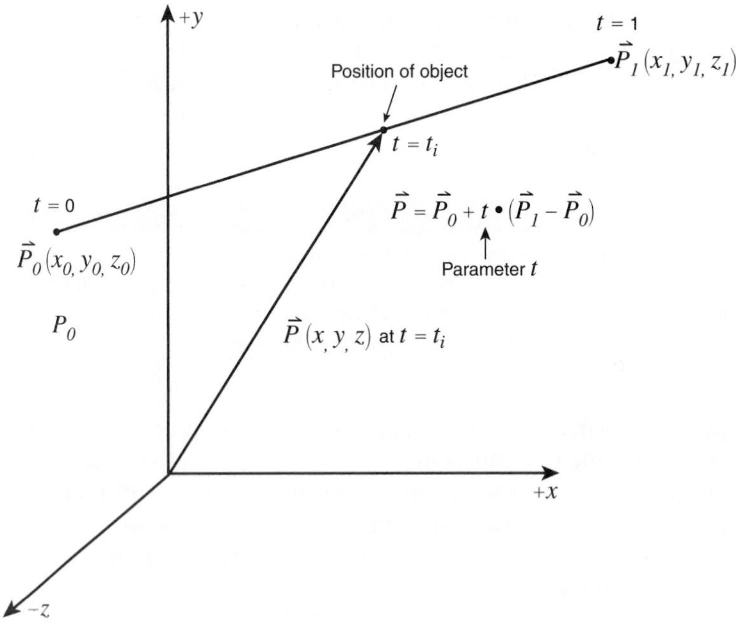

FIGURE 15.16 The parametric motion setup for a line.

Complex Parametric and Curved Motion

Although straight lines are very elegant, geometrically, they are rather boring! The next step up the translational ladder of motion is to move objects in curved paths, or along more complex parametric curves in general.

> **NOTE**
>
> All motion can be implemented with real-time physics models that drive motions, and the results are totally realistic, based on the object's mass, acceleration, and the environment. Here we are more concerned with simple deterministic motions for arcade-like games with little physics support.

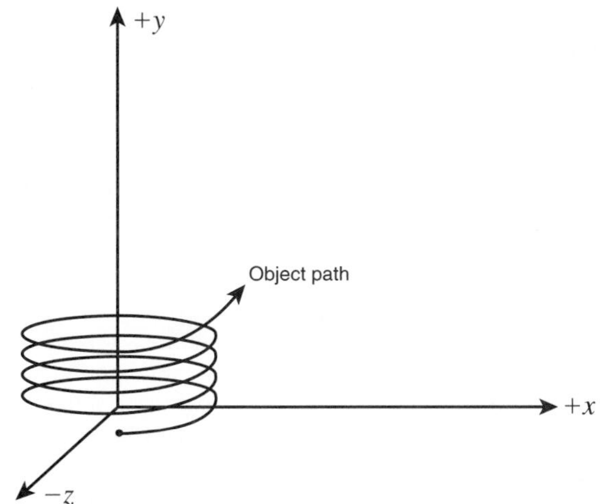

FIGURE 15.17 A winding corkscrew path.

Creating curved paths is just as easy as the straight line parametric path; we simply need to use more complex parametric equations. For example, let's say that you want to move an object in a circular path that slowly spirals up, as shown in Figure 15.17. To accomplish this, we could use lookup tables, but a better approach would be to use the formula for a circle or curve and then create a parametric version of it for our needs to move a position vector **p**. Here's one such derivation:

Given the position vector **p**, we want to move **p** such that it follows a circular or elliptical path around center $\mathbf{p_0}$ in the x-z plane with some radius r, at some rate related to a parameter t.

```
p.x = p0.x + r1*cos(2*PI*c*t)
p.z = p0.z + r2*sin(2*PI*c*t)
p.y = p0.y + b*t;
```

The above parametric equations will do the job. Let's analyze the equations: r_1 and r_2 are the radii on the x- and z-axes of the path, c is a rate constant that scales the rate or frequency, t is the parameter, and b is the rate scale for the vertical motion. If we let b = c = r_1 = r_2 = 1, and the location vector $\mathbf{p_0}$ = [0,0,0], let's see what we get as the parameter t ranges from 0 to 1.0:

```
p.x = cos(2*PI*t)
p.z = sin(2*PI*t)
p.y = t;
```

This is clearly a circle located at the origin that corkscrews upward from 0 to 1.0.

This is really all there is to creating complex curved paths. Most of them can be created with sine/cosine curves, but you can surely follow more complex curves by using polynomial, Bezier, or spline curves. If you recall when we did the perspective transformations, we used quadratic curves to follow the perspective curve and interpolate points $\mathbf{p_0}$ and $\mathbf{p_1}$. You can use this same derivation to interpolate curves for motion: Simply decide what kind of curve you want (I suggest simple spline curves), create a parametric version of the curve in x,y,z, and then compute the points along the curve and make your object follow it. Of course, you will have to stitch a number of curve segments together, but that's no big deal.

NOTE

When an object is in 3D space, not only are we concerned with moving it along a path, but we also have to rotate it simultaneously as it's moving. For example, if a space fighter is following a path, we might want to make it roll as it follows the path. This is easy—just perform a rotation parallel to the vector path line from the last position to the next position or parallel to the derivative of the curve at the object's current position.

Using Scripts for Motion

The final motion technique I want to cover is scripting. The idea is to create a small program that has an instruction set that directs the motion and animation of a game character. The idea of a scripting system is that you create small scripts or behaviors for your characters, and a scripting engine parses these instructions and instructs the character to take action. Figure 15.18 illustrates this concept.

Using scripts, you can create extremely complex behaviors that enable game characters to move and act in very complex ways that would normally be nearly impossible with hard-coded logic or paths. Moreover, you can create very high-level, C-like scripting languages that allow you to program the characters themselves.

NOTE

If you're interested in learning more about game scripting, check out *Game Scripting Mastery* by Alex Varanese and John Romero (Premier Press)—it's the best book on the market on this subject.

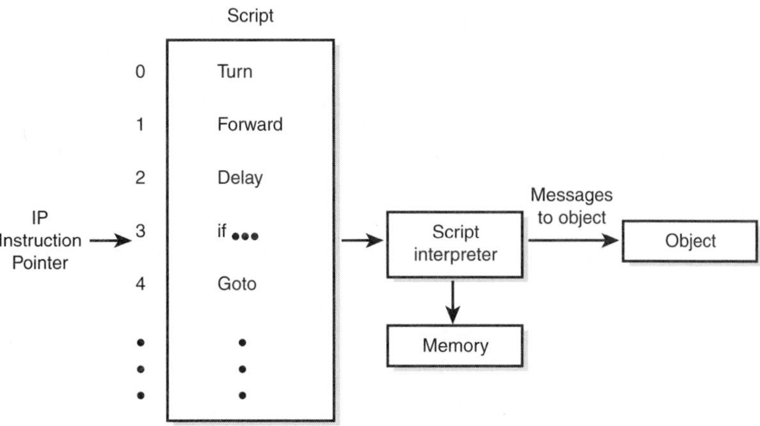

FIGURE 15.18 The architecture of a scripting engine.

As an example, let's define a language that supports straight-line motion and rotation around any axis with support for delays. Each instruction is encoded as a record or structure. We'll create small script programs as an array or list of these instructions, and then write a parser/engine that reads and executes the instructions. First, here's a possible data structure to hold each instruction, or *opcode*:

```
// a possible instruction format
typedef struct OPCODE_TYP
{
int   opcode; // the opcode for this instruction
float  op1;  // a simple floating point operand
VECTOR3D op2;  // a vector operand
} OPCODE, *OPCODE_PTR;
```

Each instruction has an opcode and two operands that may or may not be necessary. Here are some opcodes:

```
#define OP_MOVE       0 // move opcode
#define OP_ROTATE_X     1 // rotate parallel to x
#define OP_ROTATE_Y     2 // rotate parallel to y
#define OP_ROTATE_Z     3 // rotate parallel to z
#define OP_DELAY      4 // delay
#define OP_END       -1 // end program
```

For each opcode, we have to decide how we are going to encode the operands in `op1` and `op2` fields. Here's one possible methodology:

- `OP_MOVE`—The new position is stored in `op2`, and the rate or speed in `op1` (0 might be very slow, 1 might be very fast).

- OP_ROTATE_*—For all the rotation opcodes, the angle of rotation in degrees will be encoded in op1. Positive angles and negative angles are supported.
- OP_DELAY—The number of frames to delay will be stored in op1; it must be integral.
- OP_END—When the pattern engine reads this instruction, it will stop running the pattern.

That was easy enough, so now we can implement a simple state machine that executes a program something like this:

```
int  instruction_ptr = 0; // instruction pointer
int  fetch           = 1; // used to fetch instructions
OPCODE instr;             // next instruction

// this while would really be part of a function or your
// main loop, etc.

while(1)
{
// fetch next instruction if we are ready for one
if (fetch)
  {
  instr = pattern[instruction_ptr];
  fetch = 0;
  } // end if

// now switch on the opcode
switch(instr.opcode)
   {
   case OP_MOVE:      // move opcode
   {
   // move the object to instr.op2

   } break;
   case OP_ROTATE_X:   // rotate parallel to x
   {
   // rotate the object instr.op1 in x-axis
   } break;
   case OP_ROTATE_Y:   // rotate parallel to y
   {
   // rotate the object instr.op1 in y-axis
   } break;
   case OP_ROTATE_Z:   // rotate parallel to z
   {
```

```
// rotate the object instr.op1 in z-axis
} break;

case OP_DELAY:     // delay
{
// count down from instr.op1
} break;

case OP_END:      // end program
{
// break out of loop, end program, etc.
} break;

default: break;

} // end switch

} // end while
```


Very minimal, but you get the idea. Of course, when each behavior is complete, it sets the `fetch` flag back to 1, so another instruction is fetched. We also need a program, so here's a "square" example:

```
OPCODE program[] = {
{OP_MOVE, 1, 100,0,0 },
{OP_MOVE, 1, 100,100,0 },
{OP_MOVE, 1, 0,100,0 },
{OP_MOVE, 1, 100,0,0 },
{OP_DELAY,100, 0,0,0 },
};
```

Although this example is greatly simplified, the point is to use high-level scripts or commands to drive low-level motion control of the game characters.

3D Collision Detection

Although I had hoped to write an entire chapter on collision detection, I spent my page count describing graphics algorithms and rendering, which are more important, especially for this book. Collision detection is nothing more than a geometry problem at the lowest level, and there are a lot of interesting algorithms to solve the problem of determining whether two objects intersect or collide. What I want to do here is encourage you to keep it simple: 99% of the time, simple bounding spheres, boxes, and so on work just as well as some really complicated collision algorithm, so let's review some ideas.

Bounding Spheres and Cylinders

The first method of collision detection is to use bounding spheres or cylinders around each object and test whether these bounding volumes collide. Let's assume we have two objects A and B, as shown in Figure 15.19.

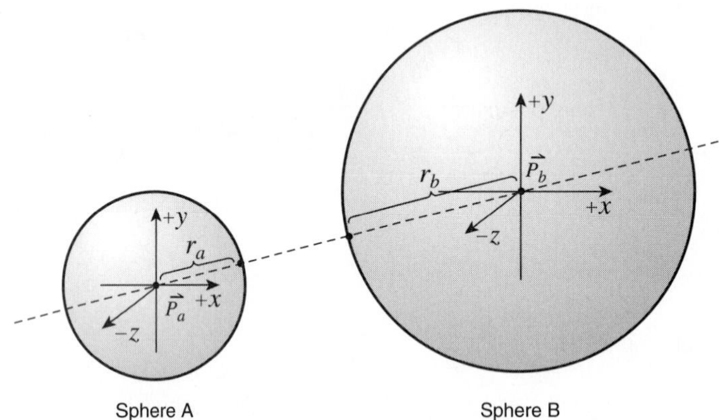

FIGURE 15.19 The setup for bounding spheres collision detection.

Each object is contained by a bounding sphere with radii r_a and r_b to detect whether a collision has occurred. We simply ask whether the distance between the two centers is less than $(r_a + r_b)$, or

```
if (dist_xyz(p_a, p_b) < (r_a + r_b) )
  {
  // collision has occurred
  } // end if
```

where `dist`$_{xyz}$`()` computes the full distance between the points $\mathbf{p_a}$ and $\mathbf{p_b}$ in 3D space.

Of course, if the objects are not very spherical in nature, such as a long pipe and a board, bounding spheres aren't going to work too well. However, in my experience with writing fast action games, you can get away with "tight" bounding spheres in these cases. In other words, you shrink the bounding spheres up to 50–70% of the actual size they would normally be.

Additionally, you can use other bounding volumes, such as cylinders, for objects that have longitudinal geometry. As long as the cylinders are oriented the same way, then the test for collision is similar. Take a look at Figure 15.20 for an example.

In the figure we see two objects A and B with radii r_a and r_b, respectively. However, to test for a collision, we need to test two things: whether the objects overlap in the y-axis (as in this case), and whether their circular radii overlap. Here's the test:

```
if (dist_xz(p_a, p_b) < (r_a + r_b) &&
  (fabs(p_a.y - p_b.y) < (h_1+h_2)/2))
  {
  // collision has occured
  } // end if
```

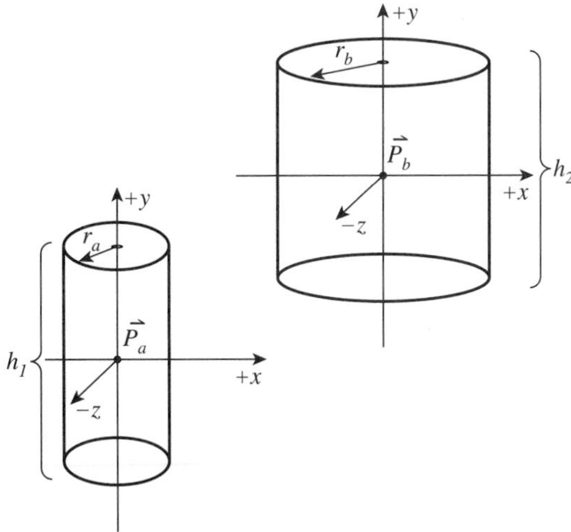

FIGURE 15.20 The setup for cylindrical bounding volume collision detection.

In which `dist_xz()` computes the 2D distance between the points $\mathbf{p_a}$ and $\mathbf{p_b}$ in the x-z plane in 2D space.

Of course, you can continue using various bounding volumes to help better fit the problem, such as axis- or object axis-aligned bounding boxes. The collision tests are similar for the each—you simply need to compute whether the objects overlap with a battery of geometrical tests.

NOTE

Some great books for collision detection geometry are *Geometric Tools for Computer Graphics* by Philip J. Schneider and David H. Eberly (Morgan Kaufmann), as well as the *Graphics and Game Programming Gems* series.

Using Data Structures to Speed Collision Detection

The final point I want to make about collision detection is related to optimization. Collision detection techniques are like formulas—we all know them, there are a lot of books that show them, and everyone uses the same math. The difference between a real-time game and a theoretical collision detection algorithm is speed.

15

As an example, imagine you have 1,000 objects in a game universe (object, bullets, and so on)—this is very easy to imagine in any first-person shooter or space game. Now imagine that you want to perform collision detection on these 1,000 objects: that's 1000×1000 = 1,000,000 calculations! Now imagine that all these objects are shooting, particles are flying, and the number of objects goes up to 10,000. Now you are talking about 10,000×10,000 = 100,000,000 calculations! Obviously, a faster line intersector or bounding box collider isn't going to help with this. The point I am making is that you have to approach the collision detection problem from a different angle, and that is with spatial partitioning.

We discussed spatial partitioning when we covered BSP trees and octrees, and I mentioned that these data structures are not only useful for graphics but for collision as well, and you can see why. Using these data structures, we can partition our objects into cells or regions so that within each region, there are perhaps only a couple hundred or fewer objects. Our calculations then go way down.

For example, using the 10,000 object example, let's say that after we sector, octree, or BSP the game universe, we find that in each cell, there are at most 50 objects. Thus, we have to process 10,000/50 cells = 200 cells, and for each cell, we have to perform 50×50 calculations, for a total of 200×(2500) = 500,000 computations.

This is much better than 100,000,000! Put another way, with clever use of partitioning, we solved a problem that made 100,000,000 calculations with only 500,000 calculations (500,000/100,000,000 = .5% of the computational work).

This is the kind of out-of-the-box thinking you need to use when performing collision detection. Don't focus on the low-level algorithms that test for bounding boxes or polygons intersecting—start with the general collision algorithm and work your way down.

Terrain-Following Techniques

The last topic I want to discuss is one that I get a lot of questions on. When you are writing a game with any kind of terrain, you must follow the terrain with your tanks, game characters, or whatever. In the majority of terrain demos in the later half of this book, we have been using a very simple (but effective) physics model that scans the polygon mesh under the center of the moving object, finds the height of the vertices making up the patch, and then lifts or drops the object proportionally to the general gradient of the change in distance from the current position to the new position.

This looks great, feels great, and comprises 10 lines of code. However, the problem is that the object is still not following the terrain. In other words, if we were looking at the object and it had wheels, for example, it would be lifting up and dropping down correctly, but it wouldn't be following the terrain. Let's talk about how to fix this.

Referring to Figure 15.21, we see a patch of terrain that we want to follow. One possible terrain-following algorithm is illustrated in the following steps:

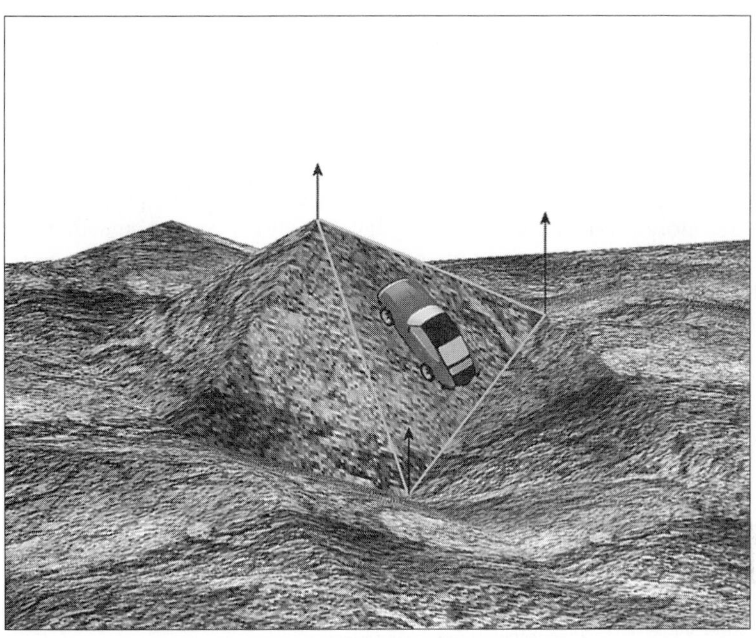

FIGURE 15.21 The problem to solve for terrain following.

1. The current height or position of the object following the terrain is computed as the average height of the vertices of the patch, or if you want to be more accurate, you must drop a line from the center of the object and compute where it pierces the plane of the polygon from the current patch it's hovering over. Of course, if you *really* want to be accurate, you should project these piercing rays from the wheels or points of contact of the object, rather than its center. In any case, this value is what you will use to lift or drop the object.
2. The rotational orientation of the object is the next concern. There are a couple of approaches to solving this problem based on the points of contact of the object. However, a quick and dirty method is as follows: Compute the normal vector to the terrain patch. Then rotate the object such that its normal vector is in alignment with the normal vector of the patch. To do this, you must compute the angles between the normal of the patch and the normal of the object. This can be accomplished in a number of ways—using the dot product, for example. After you have these rotation angles, you must generate a matrix and transform the object, thus aligning it with the normal to the patch.

I leave the details up to you—I'm out of paper, but those are the steps: First translate the object to the proper height, and simply rotate the object so the normal of the object aligns with the normal to the terrain patch.

Summary

This chapter has been a lot of fun. Finally, we can animate 3D character models and see them move around. As far as motion and general animation, we have done lots of it in previous chapters, but it was good to review it a bit, even if the material was basic. Finally, we covered some basic 3D collision tests, and discussed ideas for more advanced systems.

By now you are more than well equipped to develop all this stuff yourself. You have all the fundamentals of 3D graphics and rasterization down, and that's about all there is to it. Now the rabbit hole just gets deeper, but I have at least shown you the rabbit hole! In the next and last chapter, we are going to take a look at some optimization techniques we can apply to our engine, and the new Pentium III+ processors that support SIMD (single instruction multiple data) instructions.

CHAPTER 16

Optimization Technologies

IN THIS CHAPTER

- Introduction to Optimization Technologies
- Profiling Your Code with Microsoft Visual C++ and Intel VTune
- Using the Intel C++ Compiler
- Single Instruction Multiple Data (SIMD) Programming Primer with SSE
- General Optimization Tricks

"The speed of light sucks."

—John Carmack, id Software

I think the preceding quote really sets the mood for this chapter: Fast is never really fast enough. In fact, the speed of light is a joke as far as velocities go—you couldn't possibly hope to travel anywhere of any appreciable distance in our galaxy at light speed. But I like to think of it as a "governor." When a species is sufficiently evolved enough to figure out how to get around the speed of light, then hopefully they are smart enough not to ruin the rest of the galaxy.

Anyway, in this chapter, we are going to take a look at some optimization technologies that aren't quite as complex as breaking the lightspeed barrier. We are going to avoid low-level optimization techniques because they are too time-consuming to implement, and instead concentrate on taking advantage of new technologies and tools to help with the optimization phase of game development. Also, by the end of this chapter, I will show you how to get $250 worth of free books from Intel! Here are the topics we are going to discuss:

- Introduction to optimization technologies
- Profiling your code with Visual C++ and Intel VTune
- Using the Intel C++ compiler
- Single Instruction Multiple Data programming primer
- General optimization tricks

Introduction to Optimization Technologies

In preparation for this chapter, I did a lot of thinking and research, and decided to completely recast what I had originally planned based on an entirely new point of view. Originally, I was going to do the standard stuff; show you loops, code examples, and so forth, and then show you how to optimize them. However, not only have I done this before, but I am not quite sure that information would have as much impact these days as other information (which I will discuss in a moment). I wanted to give you some information that's really a "trick" or uncommon knowledge, so you would walk away from this chapter really trying something different. Therefore, I turned my sights on technology rather than on specifics, and asked myself, what tools do I use when optimizing code? Then I conducted a survey and, amazingly, found some startling and disturbing statistics about many game programmers—they had never used the tools/technologies, or had never heard about them! I was very happy—I had finally found something that everyone didn't know about, so I thought this would be really good information to cover.

I'm going to ask you a few questions. If you answer no to any of them, you will definitely get something out of this chapter.

- **Question 1:** Have you ever actually used Microsoft's Visual C++ built-in profiling tools?
- **Question 2:** Have you ever actually used Intel's VTune optimization tool?
- **Question 3:** Have you ever installed and used Intel's Optimizing C++ compiler plug-in for Microsoft Visual C++?
- **Question 4:** Have you ever programmed SSE or SSE2 code? These acronyms stand for Streaming Single Instruction Multiple Data Extensions, versions 1 and 2, for the Pentium III and Pentium 4, respectively. (And yes, that's the way Intel refers to the Pentium III and 4.)
- **Question 5:** Have you read the Intel Pentium III/4 architecture and software development manuals that are freely available online, and which will be sent to your house free of charge?

In a quick study of 20 or so game developers, I found that 90% of hobbyists answered no to almost all of these questions. That I expected—what was more shocking was that 50% of professional game programmers also answered no to most of them. What this means is that not only are most game developers not using real optimization tools, but they are running Pentium III/4 processors in slow motion, and not taking full advantage of the super scalar architecture that SIMD and the parallel execution units provide. As Darth Vader said, "your lack of faith disturbs me." With all that said, my goal in this chapter is simply to show you how *easy* it is to try these tools and technologies out—you will have a whole new world open up to you afterward.

And of course, last but not least, I will throw a little voodoo your way at the end of chapter to finally make good on the "tricks" part of the book's title! So without further ado, let's get going—I am very excited!

Profiling Your Code with Microsoft Visual C++ and Intel VTune

Back in the old days, you could get away with placing timing function calls at the beginning of a function, and timing how long the function took to run by calling it thousands of times. Or maybe you simply tried an optimization and then recompiled, ran it, and empirically tested your program. Of course, this technique still works, and for small programs, you can get a lot done. However, with advanced processors, optimizing compilers, and software systems containing system calls, .DLLs, APIs, and your own code, trying to drill down and figure out where to even begin optimizing can be tedious and nearly impossible.

For example, suppose you are writing a rasterizer application. You might optimize the inner loop of the rasterizer, thinking that this is where most of the work is being done. However, you don't realize that the call to a C runtime function above the rasterizer code to `memcpy()` uses a byte-wide move that you could speed up 4×! The point being—how can you optimize something if you don't know it's slow? Therefore, what we need are some tools (visualization tools in particular) that help tabulate and graph the amount of processing time on specific functions, memory usage, and other related factors, so at a glance, you can look at your entire program's "profile" and see exactly where you should be spending your time. This is the point of profiling your program.

16

Now, there are a lot of tools with which to profile your program, but of the two I'm going to talk about, you probably have one already, and the other is free (for the demo version, at least).

Profiling with Visual C++

Microsoft Visual C++ has built-in profiling tools in both the Professional and Enterprise editions. If you have the educational or standard edition, you will not be able to use this feature (.NET has similar profiling capabilities, too). In any case, profiling under Visual C++ is rather simple, and will immediately give you some decent results to start your optimization analysis and find hot spots to recode. For the following example, we are going to use `DEMOII16_1.CPP|EXE` as the program to profile. It's basically the character demo from the last chapter, except that it runs in a window so we can move it around, and if it crashes, we can still gain control of the computer. To begin, I want you to compile the program and get that all squared away.

To compile `DEMOII16_1.CPP|EXE`, set up a workspace or project, or use one you already have. At this point, you should be able to do this with ease. Of course, you will need to include `T3DLIB1-13.CPP` in the project, as well as the DirectX .LIB files, as you did in the previous chapter to compile this demo. When you have a clean compile and running demo, you should see the character demo in a window when you execute the program, as shown in the screenshot of Figure 16.1.

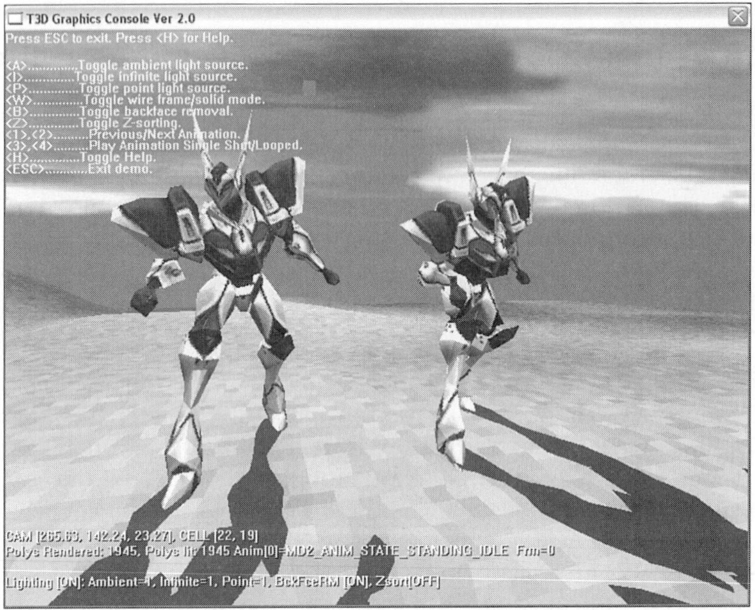

FIGURE 16.1 A screenshot of the character demo running in windowed mode for ease of profiling.

Now that you have a working demo and can compile it, let's set the compiler up for profiling. Here are the steps:

1. On the main menu bar of Visual C++, select Project, Settings. On the property sheets, select Link, and then select General in the Category field. You should see something like that shown in Figure 16.2. Take a look at the check boxes, and check the Enable Profiling and Generate Debug Info check boxes, as shown in the figure. Now click OK and close the dialog box.

2. Now you must rebuild your application with the new settings. From the main menu, select Build, Rebuild All to rebuild the application with profiling enabled.

3. Now you are ready to profile! That was too easy, huh? To begin your profiling run, select Build, Profile on the main menu bar of Visual C++, and the application will launch a small dialog to ask you what kind of profiling options you want. This dialog is shown in Figure 16.3. Select Function Timing for this run and click OK. At this point, the application will launch and run at an incredibly slow rate—this is because of the sampling of the application.

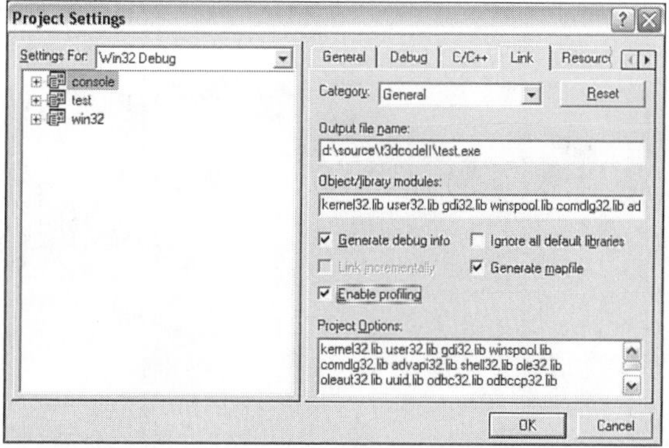

FIGURE 16.2 Enabling profiling with Visual C++.

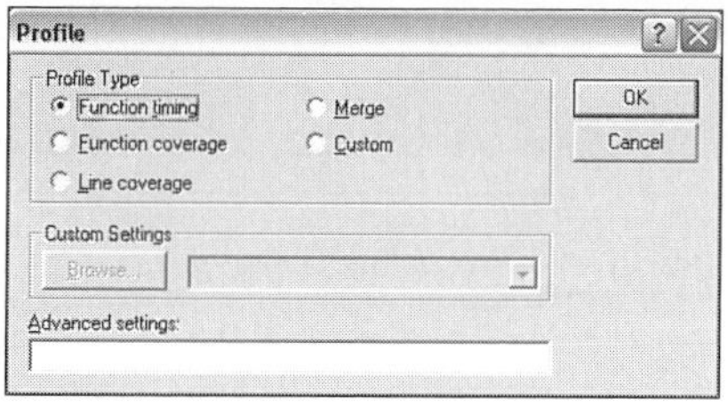

FIGURE 16.3 Selecting options in the profiling dialog.

4. Let the analysis run for 30–60 seconds, and then kill the application by hitting the close window icon or pressing the Esc key.

5. In one of your workspace views, there will be a new property selection tab called Profile. In most cases, the compiler will switch to it automatically, but if not, click it with the mouse as shown in Figure 16.4. Resize the window so you can see more information as shown in Figure 16.5, and let's see what we see.

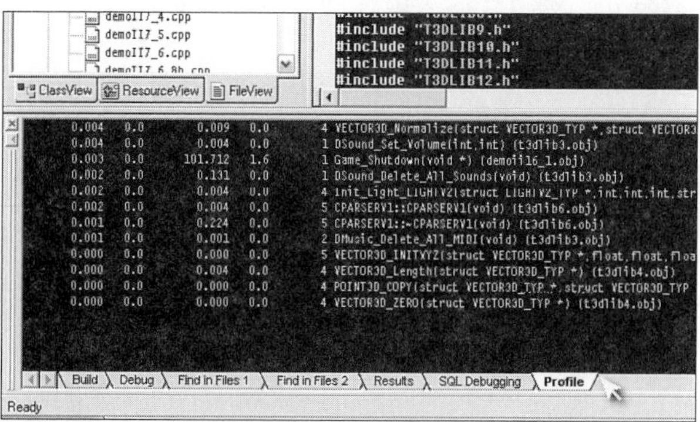

FIGURE 16.4 Selecting the profiling output window in Visual C++.

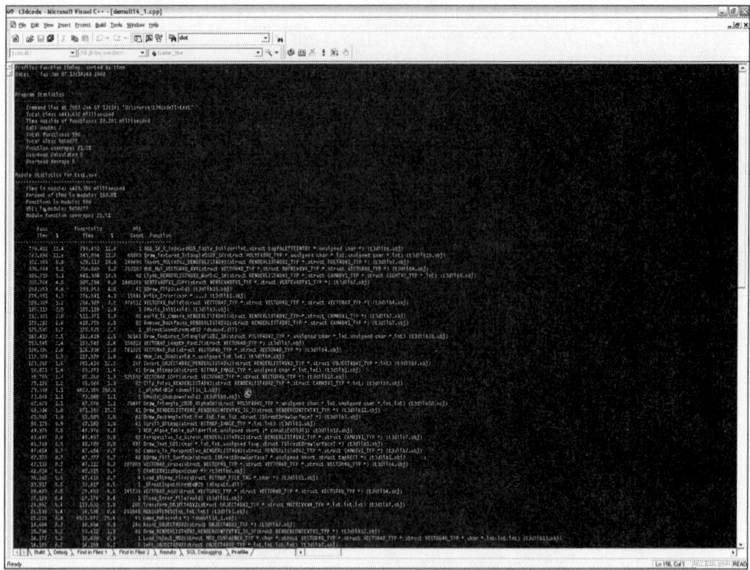

FIGURE 16.5 Opening up the profiling view to analyze the data.

Analyzing the Profile Data

After you run the profiler in Function Timing or Function Coverage Mode, you will see the profiler output window:

```
Profile: Function timing, sorted by time
Date:  Fri Jan 03 18:57:23 2003


Program Statistics
------------------
  Command line at 2003 Jan 03 18:55: "D:\source\t3dcodeII\test"
  Total time: 12949.659 millisecond
  Time outside of functions: 3.581 millisecond
  Call depth: 6
  Total functions: 574
  Total hits: 12775605
  Function coverage: 20.6%
  Overhead Calculated 5
  Overhead Average 5

Module Statistics for test.exe
------------------------------
  Time in module: 12946.078 millisecond
```

```
  Percent of time in module: 100.0%
  Functions in module: 574
  Hits in module: 12775605
  Module function coverage: 20.6%

    Func      Func+Child      Hit
    Time  %     Time    %   Count Function
---------------------------------------------------------
  2751.804 21.3   2751.804 21.3  164604 Draw_Textured_TriangleGSZB_16(
struct POLYF4DV2_TYP *,unsigned char *,int,unsigned char *,int) (t3dlib10.obj)
  1115.720  8.6   1115.720  8.6     158 DDraw_Flip2(void) (t3dlib10.obj)
  1041.832  8.0   1484.683 11.5     316 Light_RENDERLIST4DV2_World2_16(
struct RENDERLIST4DV2_TYP *,struct CAM4DV1_TYP *,
struct LIGHTV2_TYP *,int) (t3dlib8.obj)
   653.307  5.0   1334.972 10.3     316 Remove_Backfaces_RENDERLIST4DV2(
struct RENDERLIST4DV2_TYP *,struct CAM4DV1_TYP *) (t3dlib7.obj)
   631.246  4.9    631.246  4.9  962220 Insert_POLY4DV2_RENDERLIST4DV2(
struct RENDERLIST4DV2_TYP *,struct POLY4DV2_TYP *) (t3dlib7.obj)
```

…

The header is general information, but the interesting part is each line of the profile:

- `Func Time`—This is the amount of time spent in the function itself.
- `Func Time+Child Time`—This is the amount of time spent in the function plus all the calls to the functions within the parent function.
- `Hit Count`—The number of times the function was called.

Although the information isn't very robust, it's definitely a start. You would have to do a lot of work to get the same information. As a quick example, take a look at the first line of the profile (it's highlighted). This is the call to the polygon rasterizer, and we see that it is responsible for approximately 21% of the compute cycles of this application. Wow! The bottom line is that if we make this function 2× as fast, the performance of the entire application will go up quite a bit because the section that took 21% of the time now would only take 10.5% of the time.

In conclusion, profiling your code is a powerful way to find out what functions are taking up the most time in your program, so you can focus your optimization efforts there. Although you might think your lighting function is slow, you might realize that the Z-buffer clear (which is only a few lines of code) is taking up all the time, and you can focus on these few lines to get a much better speed gain than by reworking 500–1,000 lines of lighting code for the same gain. So—pick your fights.

Optimizing with VTune

Everyone has heard of it, but who really uses it? People who want absolute power, that's who! Intel's VTune is without a doubt one of the coolest tools I have ever used, but with all that power comes complexity. However, Intel has made great efforts to make the tool very easy to use for beginners, so anyone can immediately get something out of the tool within minutes of installing and launching it.

Now if you haven't heard of VTune, it's basically Intel's premier software optimization tool. It enables you to view, analyze, and optimize any program. With it, you can analyze everything from function timing, memory usage, cache access—the list goes on and on. Of course, I could write a whole book on the subject, so rather than do that, let's actually install the thing and try it out.

Installing VTune

The first thing you need to do is download the latest version of VTune from Intel's Web site at

```
http://developer.intel.com/software/products/VTune/
```

Look around the Web site page and find the Free Evaluation Download link and download the software. Make sure to select either the Visual C++ or the .NET version, depending on which compiler you are using. After you download the application, launch the installer and install the default version of the application onto your computer. The installation is very straightforward, but you might have to reboot after the application installs.

Preparing for Profiling

After you have successfully installed the application, you are ready to profile. However, before we launch VTune, let's get our test application ready. Once again, we are going to use `DEMOII16_1.CPP|EXE`, so launch Visual C++, load up the project or workspace with this application ready to compile. First we need to make sure of a few compiler settings. Here are the steps:

1. Because you are preparing to profile runtime code, it's best to set the compiler for release mode. This is done by selecting the main menu item Build, Set Active Configuration and then selecting the release version of your application, as shown in Figure 16.6.

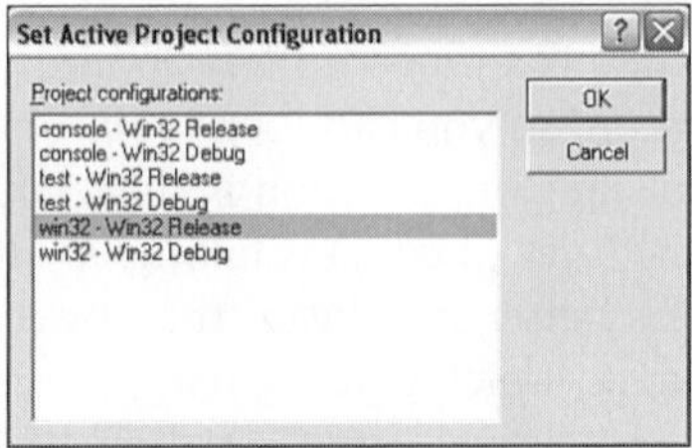

FIGURE 16.6 Selecting the release version of your application.

2. The next step is to ensure that all the symbols are available for VTune to show you "code views" of your code, so let's make sure all the browse database information is enabled on the compiler. Once again, select from the main menu Project, Settings, and under the C++ tab, select General in the Category box. Then make sure that the Generate Browse Info check box is checked and that you have selected Program Database in the Debug Info box. This will ensure that the profiler can see all the symbols and source code. Figure 16.7 shows the dialog and the selections. Leave the dialog open—we aren't done with it.

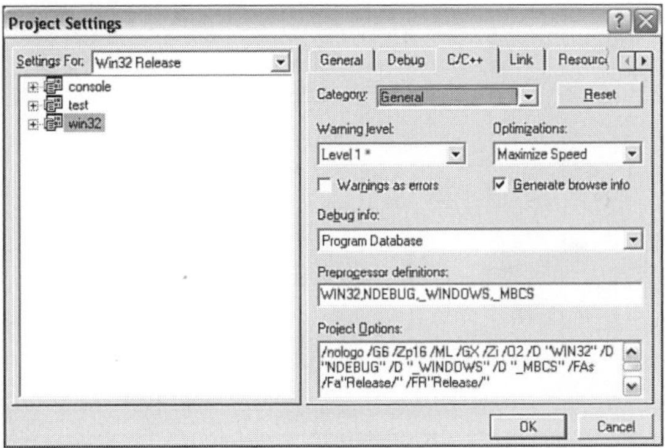

FIGURE 16.7 Making sure the browsing symbols and source are available to VTune.

3. We still need to check some items on the Link tab, so select it and then select the General category. Now make sure that the Generate Debug Info check box is checked, and if you have the Professional or Enterprise edition of Visual C++, you might as well check the Enable Profiling check box, in case you want to compare profiling results later. These selections are shown in Figure 16.8.

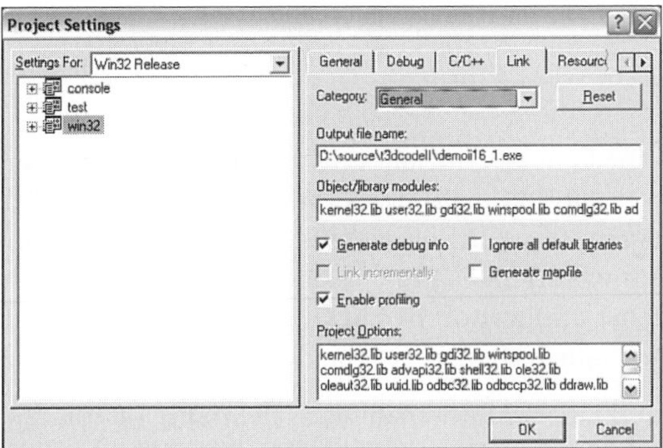

FIGURE 16.8 Enabling more debug and profiling settings.

4. Now you are ready to build the application, so select Build, Rebuild All from the main menu and rebuild everything.

That's it—now you have a final .EXE (whatever you named it and a workspace to feed to VTune).

Let the Games Begin: Running VTune

With Visual C++ minimized and the test application `DEMOII16_1.CPP¦EXE` compiled, it's time to launch VTune and get down to business. You should see a link on your desktop to VTune, or you can use the Programs, Intel VTune Performance Analyzer link. Either way, launch the application, and you should see the dialog shown in Figure 16.9.

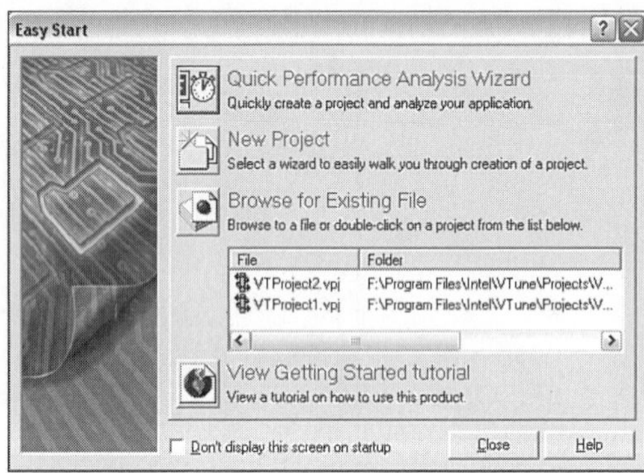

FIGURE 16.9 Launching VTune.

This dialog is the wizard that enables you to create or load profiling projects. For now, click the Quick Performance Analysis Wizard button to create a quick and dirty project. Here are the steps to get started:

TIP

Note the button at the bottom of the dialog View Getting Started Tutorial. I highly recommend taking 20–30 minutes and going through this entire tutorial—I had to do it, so it's only fair you do it, too!

1. After you select the Quick Performance Analysis Wizard button, you will be presented with yet another dialog, as shown in Figure 16.10. This dialog enables you to select the program to profile along with setting up its runtime environment. In this case, we want to run `DEMOII16_1.EXE` (or whatever you called it), so navigate and select the demo application by clicking the "..." browse button, which will invoke a file find dialog. Then select the .EXE application, as shown in Figure 16.10.
2. Now the original dialog will populate with the name of your application, its path, and so on, but you need to select what kind of profiling to perform. We are going to select both the Collect Sampling with Counter Monitor Data and Collect Call Graph Data check boxes. The former is for timing, and the latter is to generate a full call graph of all the functional calling trees.

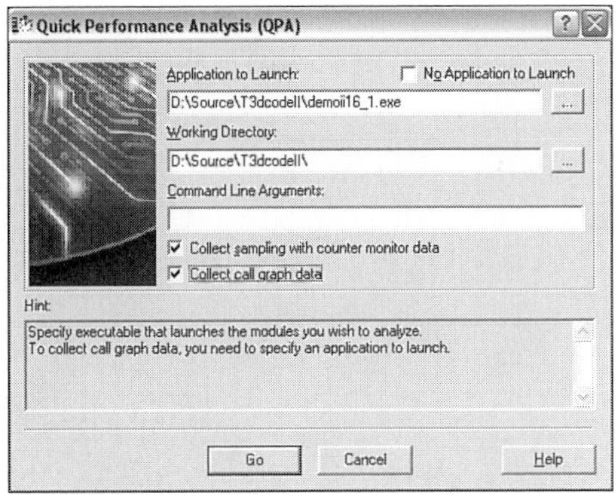

FIGURE 16.10 Selecting the application to profile.

3. Click the Go button and the profiling will begin. The application will launch and stop multiple times. On the last run, you will notice it running really slowly. This is the final timing analysis, and you can let it run forever if you like—I suggest 1–2 minutes or so—then manually hit the Esc key, or kill the demo application by clicking the close window box. VTune will start working, and finally a little dialog that enables you to select an activity will appear—just cancel it.

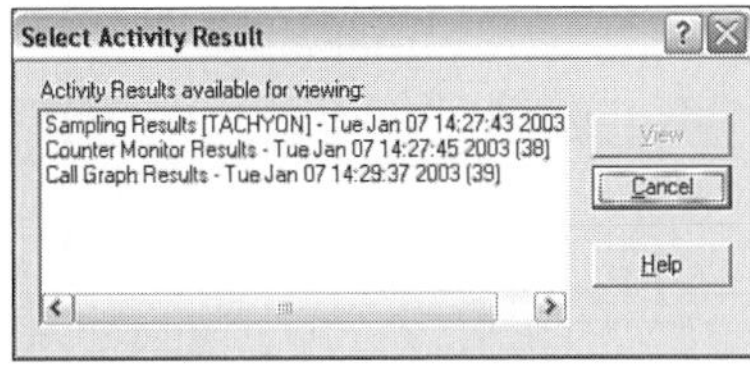

FIGURE 16.11 Activity selection dialog.

You have a complete profile now, so let's take a quick look at some of the cool information you can get out of it.

Viewing VTune's Data

I can hardly do this subject any justice—you absolutely must study the VTune tutorial to see all the amazing methods of analysis this product supports. I will show you some of the main areas to get you started.

The first view after the initial profiling has been performed presents you with the entire application GUI and four main windows, as shown in Figure 16.12: a pane to the left (the project pane), and two vertical panes (the Counter Monitor Runtime Data and the Legend for it), along with a small output pane to the bottom. This first view simply shows the system timing information on a system-wide basis. If you double-click any of the rows in the Legend pane, the data will highlight in the data pane. Not very interesting—let's take a look at the Clockticks data.

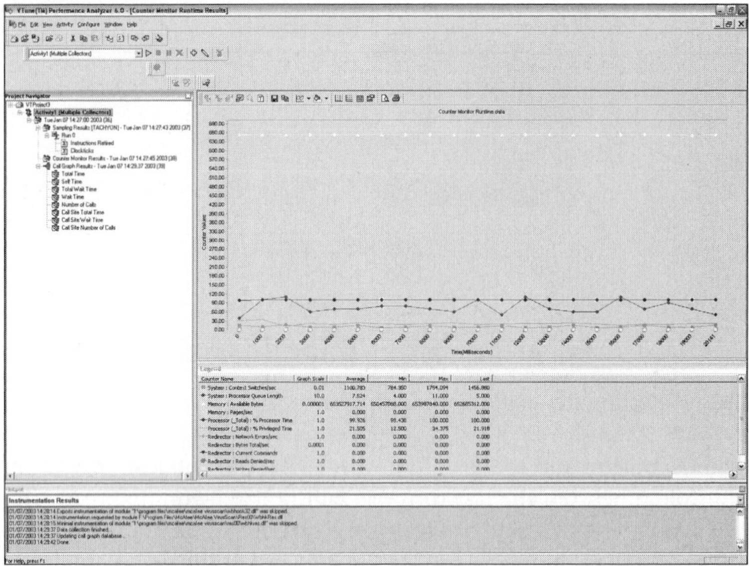

FIGURE 16.12 The main VTune view.

Viewing the Clockticks View The Clockticks data shows you how each application/process running on the system took up system resources on your PC. To select it, double-click the Clockticks item under Run 0 in the leftmost project pane, as shown in Figure 16.13.

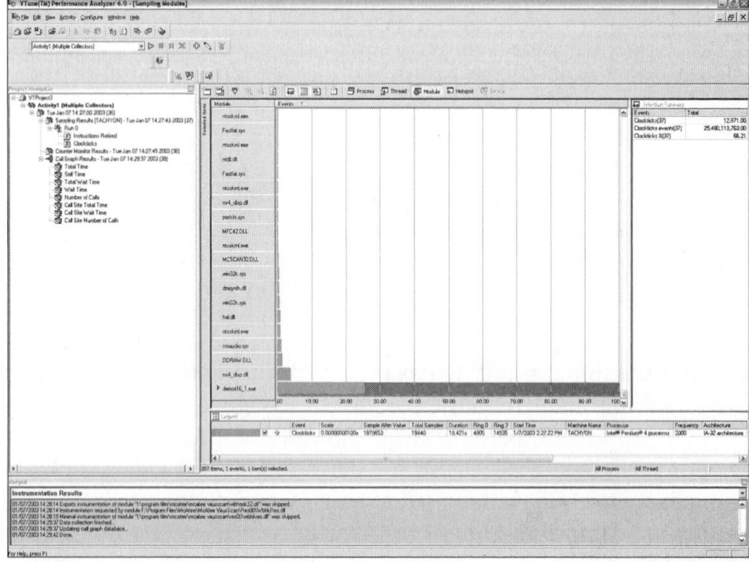

FIGURE 16.13 Reviewing processor time on a process-by-process basis with the Clockticks view.

Also in this figure, you see what the results will be: a bar graph of all the processes that were running during the analysis and their respective times. If you look closely, you will see our application `DEMOII16_1.EXE` (or whatever you named it) highlighted at the bottom. Double-click the text and you will see a more detailed view of our application. Figure 16.14 shows this.

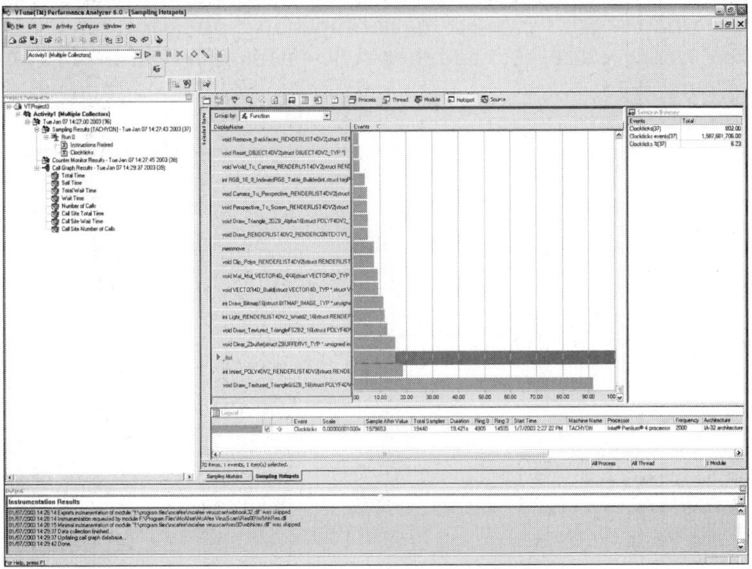

FIGURE 16.14 Analyzing our application at the functional level.

Now we're getting somewhere! This is an amazing view—here we can see on a function-by-function basis exactly which functions are taking up the time. Try single-clicking on different functions in the bar graph and highlighting them when you do so—you will see the Selection Summary change in the right-most pane of the view. This shows the total clock ticks spent in the function, and the percentage of processor time spent in the function relative to the other functions. If you double-click a function, you will open a new window with its source code. Just close the window, or press Ctrl+Tab to sequence back to the function list view.

At this point, I want to show you something that should make your head spin. Take a look at the fifth function from the bottom of the bar chart; I have highlighted it in Figure 16.14. This is the `_ftol()` function that converts floats to integers. What's going on? Well, the sad thing is that a single C runtime function is taking nearly as long as the 3D engine code! This is one of the most misunderstood math problems. To make a long story short, when you assign a `float` to an `int`, like this

```
float f;
int i = (int)f;
```

the compiler generates a function call to convert the floating-point value to an integer (in some cases)! So in all of our nicely optimized code, we are getting killed by this! I have actually touched on this in many books, and later I will show you some optimizations for it. However, the point is that with this view, we see that finding a way around this function call can save us roughly 5% of the computing time.

Also, as a sanity check, let's compare the results from the built-in profiler in Visual C++ to VTune, and see what we can see. Select the last function in the bar chart `Draw_Textured_TriangleGSZB_16()` and then review its summary in the right-hand pane, as shown in Figure 16.15.

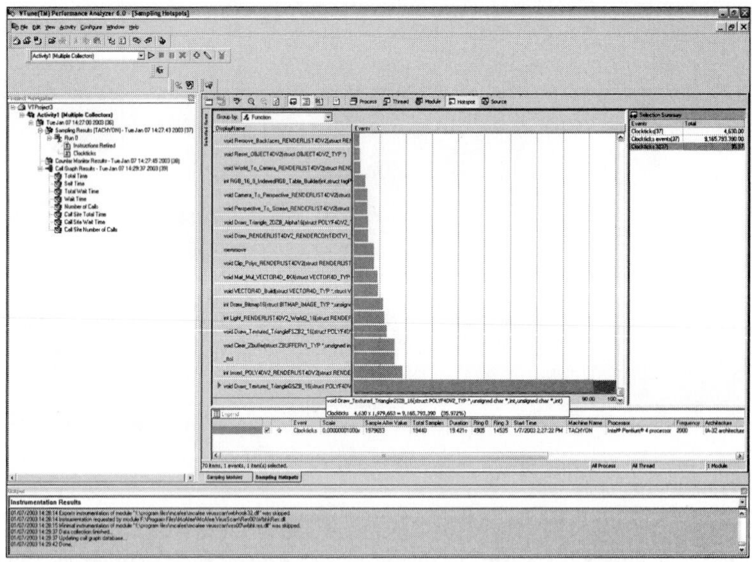

FIGURE 16.15 Selecting a particular function to see its performance.

Notice the last line that details the percentage of time: it's 35.9%. If you take a look back at the information from the Visual C++ profiling, we found that the same function took 21.3% of the time. The two data points are out of agreement a little bit—this is because of many factors, such as how the tests were performed and so on, so don't worry about it. With this bar chart, you can really drill down on each function, and at a glance, figure out where to focus your optimization efforts. Of course, there is much more you can do from this view, but this is enough for now. If you are interested in going further, the VTune tutorial is your best bet.

Viewing the Call Graph Moving on, let's take a look at another very important view based on the call graph of the program that analyzes what's calling what. To select the

Call Graph, double-click Call Graph Results in the left-most project pane, and you should see something like what's shown in Figure 16.16. This is a graphical tree that enables you to see the call "flow" of both the *caller* and the *callee* of each function. Simply click on the little < and > icons at the end of each function to open or collapse the call list. The more red a function is, the more time that is spent in it. Our application is `thread_13A4` in Figure 16.16.

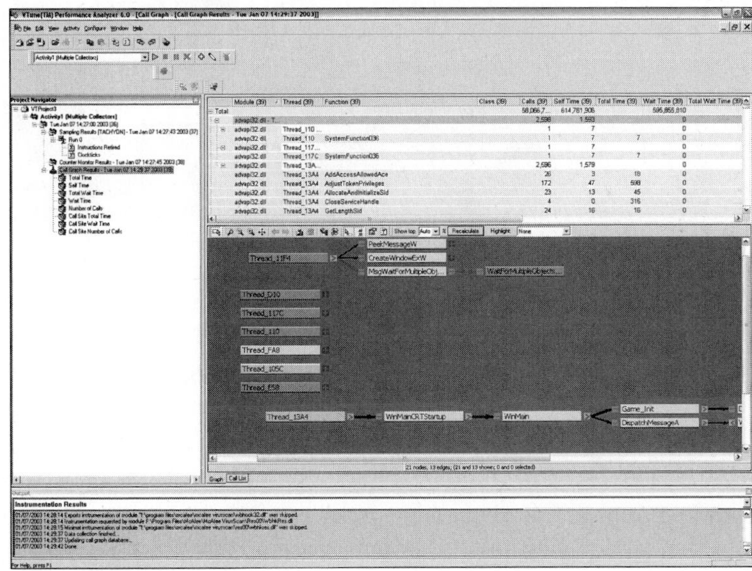

FIGURE 16.16 Viewing the Call Graph.

Figure 16.17 shows me drilling down to the `Light_RENDERLIST4D()` function and noting that, once again, it's calling that pesky `_ftol()` function a lot! In fact, that's where a great deal of the time is spent. Let's flip the script and see what functions are calling `_ftol()`. To do this, we click the left icon on the function label of `_ftol()`, also shown in Figure 16.17. This will show the incoming call graph of `_ftol()` (if it isn't already visible), so we can see all the functions we need to purge this call from with some other coding technique.

In conclusion, VTune is incredibly powerful. I suggest you play with it for hours—try clicking everything, see what happens, and please review the tutorial at the beginning of the application.

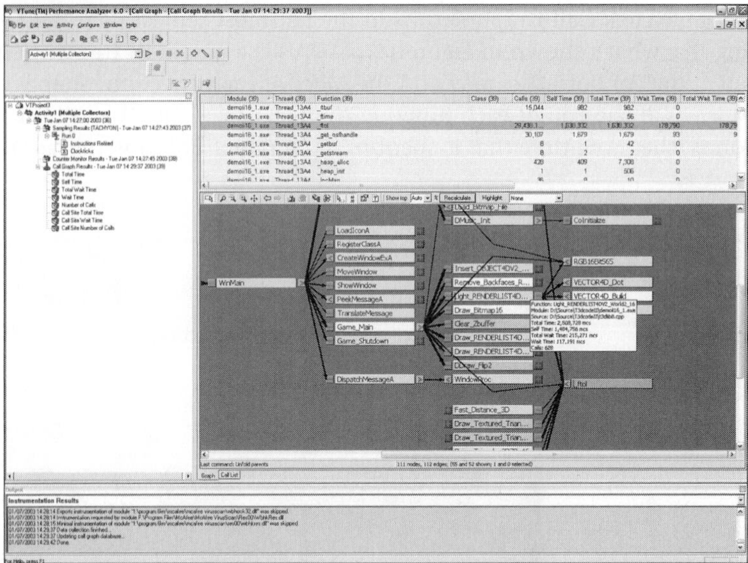

FIGURE 16.17 Drilling down on the lighting function to see what's taking so long!

Using the Intel C++ Compiler

The next big thing I want to talk about is the Intel optimizing compiler. The reason I mention this is that 95% of all games for PCs are written with Visual C++—can you believe that? Well, it's not hard to believe, because Microsoft makes really good tools, and has integrated them very well into so many systems. Visual C++ is an amazing product, and .NET is even more amazing.

Nevertheless, there was a time when other companies made compilers for PCs that were used quite a bit. Remember Borland and Watcom? Well, the bottom line is that they went out of business or were acquired because they couldn't compete with Microsoft. However, Microsoft is such a large company now that it's hard for it to keep up with the state of the art in everything (even though it tries), and compilers are something for which it actually doesn't have the most advanced product on all fronts.

This makes sense because Microsoft makes software, not microprocessors, so how could it know everything about the Pentium processors to write the absolute best compiler? It doesn't, and that's the point. The Microsoft compiler is the best tool for creating a huge cross-section of software from applications to .DLLs to ActiveX components, but it's not the very best optimizer for Intel Pentium processors—the Intel optimizing compiler is.

Many people don't even realize that Intel makes a compiler. You might have hypothesized that they have internal tools and so on, but a commercial compiler? They do, and it's the most advanced optimizing compiler for the Intel series of processors in the world—that means you'll want to compile your games with it if you can afford to do so. Sometimes your code might not be any faster and sometimes it will, but it's an option at least; if you're building a commercial product, a few hundred dollars for more speed is surely worth the tens or hundreds of man-hours needed to get the same performance increase with hand optimization with Visual C++.

The thought of learning a new tool after spending years with Visual C++ makes me ill, but Intel realized this and made their C++ compiler plug right into Visual C++ Studio/.NET, so you literally only have to click a single check box and it's game time. Now that I have your attention, it's possible that simple recompilation with the Intel compiler can give you speed gains of 0% to 200%! Definitely worth a few minutes of learning curve—so let's get started.

Downloading Intel's Optimizing Compiler

The first step is to download the compiler itself. You can find the latest version online at Intel's site at

```
http://developer.intel.com/software/products/compilers/
```

Navigate around and find the Intel compiler for Windows free evaluation link and download the product onto your hard drive.

> **TIP**
>
> Intel also has Linux versions of the compiler, and Fortran compilers for you scientists!

After you have downloaded the compiler, make sure you close all applications such as Visual C++ and VTune, and then launch the installer. Run through the installation process as you would anything else. At some point, you will see a dialog asking you to select Itanium processor support—do *not* install this. Also, use the Typical installation files. The installation will go very smoothly if all goes well, almost like nothing happened. Now comes the fun part.

Using the Intel Compiler

Go ahead and launch Visual C++ and load in the test workspace with `DEMOII16_1.CPP|EXE` that you have been using (of course, I have no idea what you named this). Visual C++ will load up and display the workspace as usual. Now comes the fun part: On the main menu, select the Tools, Select Compiler option, and the dialog shown in Figure 16.18 will be displayed. You will notice a little check box titled Intel® C++ Compiler—check this box, and you are now using the Intel optimizing compiler! Click OK to exit the dialog.

Ninety-nine percent of all the compiler options work the same with the Intel compiler, so you shouldn't have to change anything. However, the Intel compiler has a ton of new optimization options that aren't supported/standard in Visual C++ that you will have to add in manually with flags.

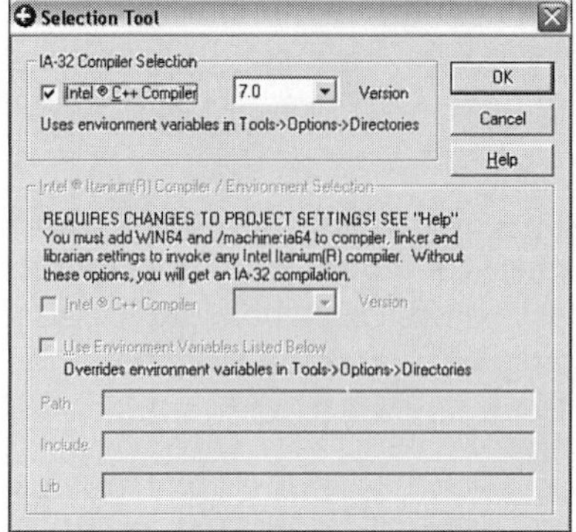

FIGURE 16.18 Selecting the Intel compiler is really easy!

I will show you that in a moment, but for now, let's just try to compile and run our demo application `DEMOII16_1.CPP` and see whether it works. Select Build, Rebuild All from the main menu to compile the project. When the build begins, you might see weird warnings or compiler output that you haven't seen before—this is a good thing, as it means that the Intel compiler is working. When the application is compiled, we will continue.

CAUTION

It might take 2–3 times longer than usual because the Intel compiler is attempting all kinds of optimization strategies. I will wait for you in the next paragraph...

If you compiled successfully, you should get a few warnings because of my "throw caution to the wind" programming style, but hopefully no errors. Let's run the program and see whether it works. At the main menu, select Build, Execute... or press Ctrl+F5 and you should see the mechs doing their thing. If you're astute and have good eyes, you will notice that the animation looks a little faster—that's because it is! The demo is already running about 5–10% faster, depending on your hardware, just with a plain recompilation without any tweaking. This is amazing!

Taking Advantage of Compiler Options

The Intel optimizing compiler has a lot of added optimization features that you can control via compiler flags, entering them in manually. Take a look at Table 16.1 for a small list of some of the more interesting ones.

TABLE 16.1 Interesting Intel Optimizing Compiler Options

Option	Meaning
Option Optimizes for:	
`-G5`	Pentium processor
`-G6`	Pentium Pro, Pentium II, and Pentium III processors
`-G7`	Pentium 4 and Xeon processor

TABLE 16.1 Continued

Option	Meaning
Option-Specific Optimization for:	
`-Qxi`	Intel Pentium Pro, and Pentium II processors (uses the CMOV, FCMOV, and FCOMI instructions)
`-QxM`	Pentium processors with MMX technology instructions (does not imply i instructions)
`-QxK`	Pentium III processor with the Streaming SIMD Extensions (implies i and M instructions)
`-QxW`	Pentium 4 and Xeon processor with the Streaming SIMD Extensions 2 (implies i, M, and K instructions)
Option Optimizes for:	
`-Qaxi`	Intel Pentium Pro and Pentium II processors (uses the CMOV, FCMOV, and FCOMI instructions)
`-QaxM`	Pentium processors with MMX technology instructions
`-QaxK`	Pentium III processor with Streaming SIMD Extensions (implies i and M instructions)
`-QaxW`	Pentium 4 and Xeon processor with Streaming SIMD Extensions 2 (implies i, M, and K instructions)
`-Qax{i¦M¦K¦W}`	Enables the vectorizer and generates specialized and generic IA-32 code (slower)
`-Qx{i¦M¦K¦W}`	Turns on the vectorizer and generates processor-specific specialized code (faster)
General Optimization Levels:	
`-O1`	Optimize for speed, but disable some optimizations that increase code size for small speed benefit
`-O2`	Optimizes for speed
`-O3`	Enables high-level optimization (This level does not guarantee higher performance)
`-Og`	Enables global optimizations
`-Os`	Enables most speed optimizations, but disables optimizations that increase code size for a small speed benefit
`-Ot`	Enables all speed optimizations

There are a lot more options than these, but these will get you started. Try setting the compiler to target your specific processor, turning optimization all the way up, and make sure to try the vectorization options. However, when you enable vectorization options, you *might* break your code. If this happens, you can always compile each source file with different options, or you can simply use the Microsoft compiler for those files. To select which compiler to use on a source file-by-source file basis, you can force Visual C++ to use either the Microsoft or Intel compiler using the following technique.

Selecting Compiler Manually on a Source File Basis

Let's assume that you have selected the Intel compiler in the Select Compiler dialog. However, a specific source file is giving you too many errors, and simply won't compile. If you would like to force that specific source file (or any other) to use the standard Microsoft compiler, use the following procedure.

1. In the source tree window, right-click the source file and select Settings.
2. You will see the dialog shown in Figure 16.19. Select the C/C++ tab and under Category, select General.

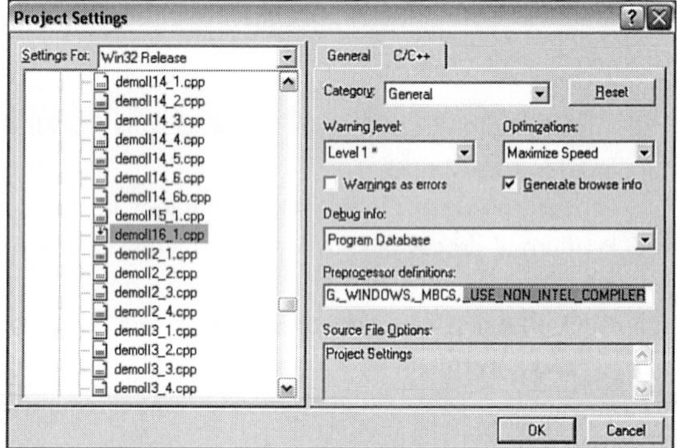

FIGURE 16.19 Selecting the Intel/Visual C++ compiler on a source file basis.

3. Down in the Preprocessor Definitions edit box, add the following constant:

```
_USE_NON_INTEL_COMPILER
```

This will force Visual C++ to use the Microsoft compiler rather than the Intel compiler.

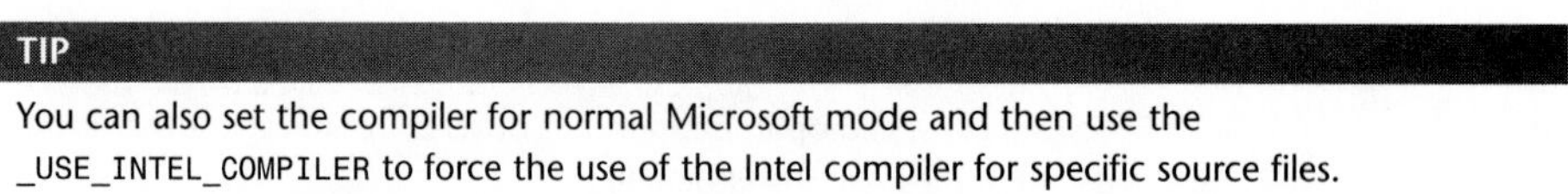

TIP

You can also set the compiler for normal Microsoft mode and then use the `_USE_INTEL_COMPILER` to force the use of the Intel compiler for specific source files.

Optimization Strategies

After you get the compiler working and you can compile your programs with it, simply try everything: Turn the optimizations way up, way down, target specific processors, and then use profiling or VTune to find where the bottlenecks are located. Of course, you should do this in a consistent and logical manner—play with a single compiler option at a time, and then record the results. If you make multiple changes each experiment, you will never track down what is doing what, so only change one option at a time and then test the results.

Single Instruction Multiple Data (SIMD) Programming Primer with SSE

Alrighty then! It's been a long time since I said that, huh? In any event, the next subject I want to cover is something for which I feel like I am evangelizing the second coming: SIMD (single-instruction multiple data) programming. If you have heard of SIMD and used it, skip this section; if not, you are probably in for a shocking enlightenment.

First, let's get our terminology, chronology, and history straight. After the initial release of the Pentium processor, Intel came out with Multimedia Extensions, otherwise known as MMX. The new MMX technology was supposed to change the world, accelerate 3D graphics, and speed up the Internet—you know, the usual marketing stuff; just imagine music and some dancing girls to make the image complete.

Alas, MMX didn't gain popularity or meet expectations. The reason was that MMX was shoehorned into the Pentium processor's architecture. Basically, the MMX technology added a few more instructions to the Pentium's instruction set to allow parallel or SIMD integer operations to take place.

The problem with this little plan was that Intel didn't have any register real state for the MMXs working registers, so it decided to alias them onto the floating-point registers and use 64 bits of the 80 bits allocated to each FPU register, as shown in Figure 16.20a.

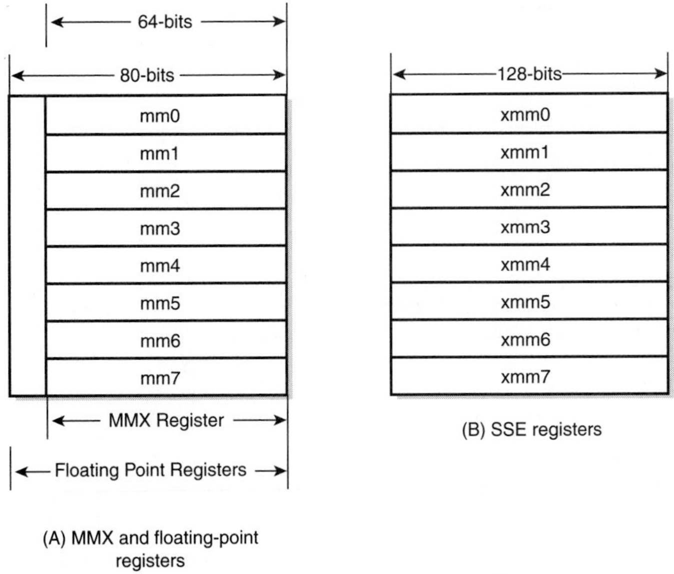

FIGURE 16.20 Allocation of MMX registers from the FPU stack.

This was probably the biggest goof in microprocessor architecture history. The problem was that when you wanted to use the MMX instructions, you had to switch processor states, save the FPU registers, do the math, and then restore everything. So, although you could perform parallel additions and so on with MMX, by the time you got done switching, doing the work, and restoring everything, it was slower! So, MMX didn't quite work out.

However, with the advent of the Pentium III, they got it right, and implemented what is known as Streaming SIMD Extensions (SSE)—yes, it's an acronym within an acronym.

With SSE, Intel created an entirely new set of eight 128-bit registers labeled XMM0 to XMM7, as shown in Figure 16.20b. Moreover, SSE can function in parallel with the FPU and even integer MMX, and there is no context switching, no saving, no problems. Each one of these registers can hold up to four 32-bit, single-precision floating-point numbers. Thus, SSE is SIMD for floating-point and enables you to process four 32-bit floating-point values at once. You can add, multiply, take square roots, compare—the list goes on and on. In fact, there are approximately 70 new instructions added to the instruction set for SSE—it's like having another processor in there!

Before I move forward, I want to mention Streaming SIMD Extensions 2 (SSE2). These are new additions to the Pentium 4 processor that add a total of 150 new instructions that support double-precision floating-point operations rather than single-precision. If you have a Pentium 4, you can perform two operations in parallel on two 64-bit floating-point double values, rather than four 32-bit single-precision floating-point values. Figure 16.21 should clarify this conundrum.

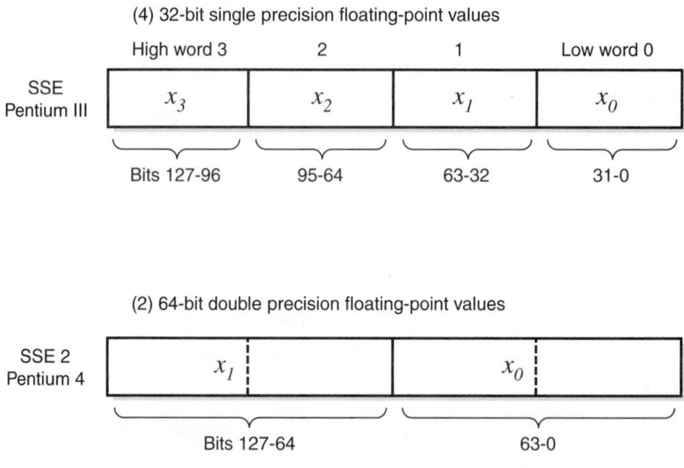

FIGURE 16.21 The breakdown of a single 128-bit SSE/SSE2 register.

SSE2 is great, but unless you are doing scientific programming or something of that nature, where you need 64-bit accuracy, I don't see the need to use double values in games as of yet, and I would rather perform four operations at once with SSE instead of two operations with twice the precision via SSE2. However, the Pentium 4 supports both SSE and SSE2, so your code that's written for the Pentium III will work perfectly on the Pentium 4.

Moreover, the SIMD registers XMM0–XMM7 are still 128-bit in both SSE and SSE2 implementations, so everything works the same. We're only going to talk about SSE on the Pentium III; or in other words, we only want single-precision 32-bit, four-way parallel SIMD processing.

I think you can see why no one uses SSE/SSE2—first you need a darn interpreter to figure out what all the acronyms mean! Anyway, from now on, I am going to refer to SSE/SSE2 simply as SIMD, and you need a Pentium III or better for everything to work.

Basic SIMD Architecture

The basic SIMD architecture consists of eight 128-bit registers, as shown in Figure 16.20b. Each register holds four 32-bit single-precision values, and operations are carried out on these values in parallel. Each SIMD register XMM0–XMM7 is laid out as shown in Figure 16.21: Bits 0–31 represent the least significant element, and bits 96–127 represent the most significant element. Remember, each element or value is unaware of the others, and operations are performed in parallel on these data items; hence the term *single* instruction, *multiple* data.

SIMD is uniquely applicable to 3D graphics because many operations can be parallelized, such as dot products, matrix multiplication, lighting, rasterization, and so forth. However, don't get your hopes up too much, because although with SIMD you can perform four floating-point operations at once, getting your data into and out of the registers and transforming data representations in your programs to be SIMD-friendly creates a performance hit. In the best case scenario, you will get about 200% better performance, with 150–170% being average for reasonable intelligent programming of SIMD. Thus, all of your math code will in most cases run twice as fast, at minimum!

16

Working with SIMD in the Real World

Using SIMD can be very easy if you know the steps, so let's cover that now. First, you need an operating system that supports it, in addition to a Pentium III+ processor. Windows 2000, XP, and later all support SSE/SSE2 in most cases. However, even if you have a Pentium III+ that supports SIMD, you should always check out the operating system to determine whether SSE is supported. Under Windows, you can use the following code to check for both MMX and SSE:

```
if (IsProcessorFeaturePresent(PF_MMX_INSTRUCTIONS_AVAILABLE))
  printf("\nMMX Available.\n");
else
  printf("\nMMX NOT Available.\n");

if (IsProcessorFeaturePresent(PF_XMMI_INSTRUCTIONS_AVAILABLE))
  printf("\nXMMI Available.\n");
else
  printf("\nXMMI NOT Available.\n");
```

The code uses the Windows API call `IsProcessorFeaturePresent()`, which reports back `TRUE` or `FALSE` to the query for the requested feature. The function has many other features you can request, I suggest referring to your API help to review them.

Once you know that the OS and processor support SSE, which in this case is the `PF_XMMI_INSTRUCTIONS_AVAILABLE`, then you have to write some code, or have some that uses it! Of course, we saw that the Intel compiler can actually target the Pentium III and 4, so it intrinsically uses SIMD code during optimization. However, we are interested in writing our own code, so let's see what we need to do to accomplish this.

Setting Up the Compiler to Support SIMD

The Intel optimizing compiler already has SIMD support and the appropriate headers and libraries within it. However, if you're using Microsoft's Visual C++, you are going to have to download the new processor pack upgrade for it. This will install all the headers, libraries, and so on. You will need Visual C++ Professional or Enterprise, along with Service Pack upgrade 4 or 5 (I suggest 5 or the latest, of course). The processor pack can be found at

`http://msdn.microsoft.com/vstudio/downloads/tools/ppack/default.asp`

> **TIP**
>
> You also get MASM when you install the processor pack!

I highly recommend that you first install the latest Service Pack for Visual C++ Studio, at

`http://msdn.microsoft.com/vstudio/downloads/updates/sp/vs6/sp5/default.asp`

> **TIP**
>
> If you do not have Visual C++ Professional or Enterprise but still want to try out the SIMD instructions, don't worry: The Intel compiler has it built in, so just download the free evaluation of Intel's compiler and you are good to go—for 30 days, at least!

Assuming that you download the processor pack, simply install it onto your machine and follow the instructions. When installation is complete, you might be asked to restart your machine. Now you are ready to go!

Let's test out your new processor pack or SIMD support with a simple program. First create a simple `CONSOLE` application, and then type in the following code from `DEMOII16_2.CPP` (or use the source from the CD):

```
// DEMOII16_2.CPP - Hello world SIMD demo

// I N C L U D E S ///////////////////////////////////////////////////////////////
```

```
#define WIN32_LEAN_AND_MEAN
#include <windows.h>  // include important windows stuff
#include <windowsx.h>
#include <stdio.h>
#include <math.h>
#include <xmmintrin.h> // <-- this is needed for SIMD support (SSE I)

// MAIN ////////////////////////////////////////////////////////////////

void main()
{
// print out os/processor support
if (IsProcessorFeaturePresent(PF_MMX_INSTRUCTIONS_AVAILABLE))
  printf("\nMMX Available.\n");
else
  printf("\nMMX NOT Available.\n");

if (IsProcessorFeaturePresent(PF_XMMI_INSTRUCTIONS_AVAILABLE))
  printf("\nXMMI Available.\n");
else
  {
  printf("\nXMMI NOT Available.\n");
  return;
  } // end if

// define 3 SIMD packed values, remember always must be 16byte aligned
__declspec(align(16)) static float x[4] = {1,2,3,4};
__declspec(align(16)) static float y[4] = {5,6,7,8};
__declspec(align(16)) static float z[4] = {0,0,0,0};

// lets do a little SIMD to add X and Y and store the results in Z
_asm
  {
  movaps xmm0, x // move the value of x into XMM0
  addps xmm0, y // add the value of y to XMM0
  movaps z, xmm0 // store the results from XMM0 into z
  } // end asm

// print the results
printf("\n x[%f,%f,%f,%f]", x[0], x[1], x[2], x[3]);
printf("\n+y[%f,%f,%f,%f]", y[0], y[1], y[2], y[3]);
printf("\n____________________________________");
printf("\n=z[%f,%f,%f,%f]\n", z[0], z[1], z[2], z[3]);

} // end main
```

16

Compile your program with the Intel compiler or Visual C++ with the processor pack extensions installed. You should get a clean compile. Run the program and you will see a simple output that adds two sets of four floating-point values at once. The output should look like that shown in Figure 16.22.

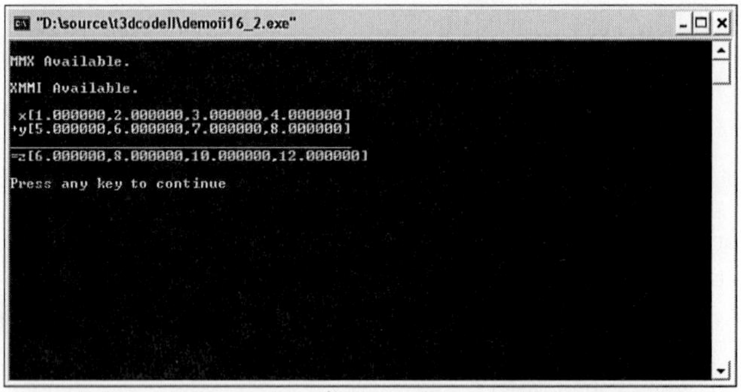

FIGURE 16.22 The output of the SIMD demo program `DEMOII16_2.CPP`¦`EXE`.

NOTE

You might notice the use of the `_asm` command. This is how you instruct the compiler that you want inline assembly language. Simply enclose the instructions as you would any other block with { and } and you are good to go. For more information on the capabilities of the inline assembler, consult your compiler's help file. However, you can more or less use variable names from your C/C++, pointers, constants, macros, and so on. The inline assembler is reasonably intelligent.

The demo program basically creates three arrays of floats. Each array has four elements—these elements are the units that the SIMD architecture processes in parallel. The program then uses the SIMD instruction `movaps` to move the 128-bit value as a whole from array `x[]` into SIMD register `XMM0`. The program then adds the value of `y[]` to `XMM0` with the instruction `addps`, and finally stores the results in the floating-point array `z[]`. I will detail what the instructions mean and how they work shortly, but for now, realize that in a single addition instruction, we perform four addition computations of 32-bit floating-point values at once! That's pretty amazing. Try some benchmarking for fun: Run the loop 1,000,000 times and time it, and then write it with straight C/C++ or even straight FPU assembler to see whether you can beat SIMD—I bet you can't!

NOTE

You can also use the source from `DEMOII16_2.CPP` on the CD if you don't want to type it in.

Data Types, Packing, and SOA/AOS Strategies

SIMD has assembly language support via the SIMD instructions, but there is also an "intrinsic" library written by Intel that is supported by both Visual C++ and the Intel compiler. The first important thing about this is the new 128-bit data type `__m128`. This new data type is basically a packed array of four floats and it's always 16-byte aligned. When using the intrinsic functions, you must use the `__m128` data type; otherwise, you will need to cast results in and out. However, it's basically equivalent to:

```
__declspec(align(16)) float __m128[4
```

In essence, SIMD uses what's referred to as a *packed* data type; that is, four 32-bit floats packed adjacently, starting on a 16-byte boundary. You can either use the built-in `__m128` data type, or an aligned `float[4]` array; however, the `float[4]` array might be more convenient because you can access each individual element by indexing. Nonetheless, if you want to use the built-in intrinsic libraries for SIMD, you must use the `__m128` type or cast to it. We will get to intrinsics shortly.

The next important decision to make when using SIMD is the layout of data structures. SIMD is capable of processing four data elements at once and performing simple logical or mathematical operations on them. However, as efficient as SIMD is, you might find that the process of transforming your data into SIMD-packed words and extracting your data after the calculations might waste time. Therefore, consider using both the *array-of-structures (AoS)* or *structure-of-arrays (SoA)* formats when defining your data structures, as shown in Figure 16.23.

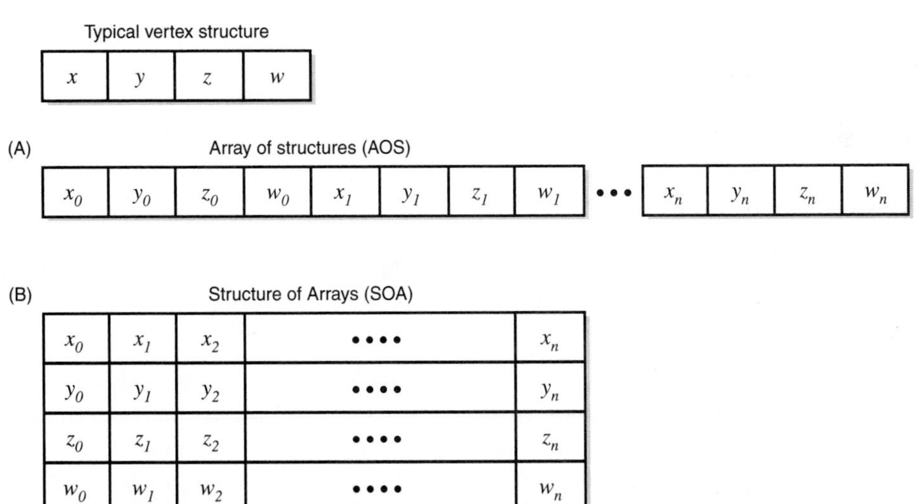

FIGURE 16.23 Array of structures versus structure of arrays.

As an example, let's say that we want to perform operations on homogeneous 3D vectors/points/vertices. A typical data structure might look like this:

```
typedef struct VECTOR4D_TYP
{
__declspec(align(16)) float x,y,z,w;
} VECTOR4D, *VECTOR4D_PTR;
```

With this structure, we might define 1,000 vertices like this:

```
VECTOR4D vertex_list[1000];
```

This would be an array-of-structures data structure. Now, let's say that we want to simply add up all the vectors. Sounds simple: We would load a `VECTOR4D` into a SIMD register, add it to another `VECTOR4D` and then store the result, summing over all 1,000 vertices.

Now forget about the details for a moment, and let's think about what we are doing. We load a single `VECTOR4D` into one register in the format $x_i y_i z_i w_i$ (low to high) and then add it to another $x_j y_j z_j w_j$. However, we are wasting an entire computation slot with the w slot. w is used for other things, and when performing vector addition, w is assumed to always be 1.0 (in most cases). This is just one example showing that perhaps a different format is in order.

Using a structure of arrays solves this. Instead of defining a vertex and then creating an array of them, we do this:

```
typedef struct VERTEXLIST4D_TYP
{
__declspec(align(16)) float x[1000];
__declspec(align(16)) float y[1000];
__declspec(align(16)) float z[1000];
__declspec(align(16)) float w[1000];
} VERTEXLIST4D, * VERTEXLIST4D_PTR;
```

Then in our loops, we load four `x` values at once, add them to the next set of `x` values, and then run through the entire list 1000/4 times. We do the same thing with `y` and `z` and we're done.

These issues are related to what you want to do with SIMD. For example, if you're going to be doing a lot of dot products, a SoA format might work better, but if you are doing a lot of summation of simple four-value 32-bit words, the AoS might work out well. The point is that this is an important consideration when doing SIMD programming, and something for which you will have to design your data structures. For example, using the SoA data structure works faster for the addition example, but this is definitely not conducive to how our engine likes to store data.

Some Simple SIMD Examples

SIMD is a huge topic. In fact, it's basically a whole new language and processor assembly language, because there are 70+ instructions supported, so I can't explain in a few pages. I can show you how to perform basic mathematic operations with SIMD and you can work from there. Also, at the end of the examples, I will show you the Intel intrinsic versions.

The intrinsic library is basically a wrapper around much of the SIMD assembly language instructions. Using intrinsics is probably easier than straight assembly language SIMD, but is slightly slower, so you might want to stick to assembly language. It goes without saying that to make any of the code in the following examples, you must have the processor pack installed into Visual C++ or be using the Intel compiler. Additionally, you must include the following header file:

```
#include <xmmintrin.h>
```

TIP

If you want support for Pentium 4 SSE2 with double-precision SIMD, you must include `emmintrin.h` also.

Finally, when reviewing the examples, realize that these are just a fraction of the instructions, and simply representatives of each primary class of instructions.

16

For all the examples, assume the following data structures:

```
__declspec(align(16)) float x[4], y[4], z[4];
__m128 m0, m1, m2;
```

Data Movement and Shuffling There are many, many ways to get a SIMD value into a SIMD register using assembly language or intrinsics. In general, the inline assembler knows the type of each variable and the difference between a pointer and a value. Thus, you can always use variables that hold SIMD values directly and assign them to XMM registers with the single-precision move-aligned `movaps` instruction, which has two basic forms:

```
movasp xmm_dest, xmm_src/memory
```

or

```
movasp xmm_dest/memory, xmm_src
```

Basically, you can always move from a XMM register to another XMM register. Additionally, you can move from memory to an XMM register, or an XMM register to memory, but not memory to memory. Let's try some examples.

Given:

```
__declspec(align(16)) float x[4], y[4], z[4];
__m128 m0, m1, m2;
```

Example: Move `x[]` into `xmm0`

```
_asm
  {
  movaps xmm0, x
  }
```

You can also use pointer coercion to make sure that the source operand doesn't cause a compiler warning:

```
_asm
  {
  movaps xmm0, XMMWORD PTR x
  }
```

Of course, you could also use one of the data pointers `esi`, `edi`, `edx`, and so on, like this:

```
_asm
  {
  lea esi, x
  movaps xmm0, [esi]
  }
```

Similarly, to store a result from an XMM register, you simply use a pointer to the destination memory:

Example: Move `xmm0` into `z[]`

```
_asm
  {
  movaps z, xmm0
  }
```

The intrinsic functions for storing and setting are:

```
// stores the SIMD intrinsic type __m128 into the float array *v
void _mm_store_ps(float *v, __m128 a);

// assigns a,b,c,d to the packed intrinsic type __m128
__m128 _mm_set_ps(float a, float b, float c, float d);
```

Example: Initialize `m0` to `[1,2,3,4]`

```
m0 = _mm_set_ps(1,2,3,4);
```

Example: Store `m0` into `x[]`

```
_mm_store_ps(x, m0);
```

Of course, there are many other intrinsic movement, initialization, and assignment functions, but the preceding should get you started.

Now that you can move data around and assign SIMD data to registers, let's take a look at something you will really need to have a handle on once you actually try doing stuff with SIMD, and that's data shuffling, or *swizzling*. The movement of words within a SIMD registers in other locations within a SIMD register. There are numerous instructions within the SIMD instruction set to perform these operations, but we are only going to look at the most representative instruction `shufps`, shown graphically in Figure 16.24 and following:

```
shufps xmm_dest, xmm_src, control8
```

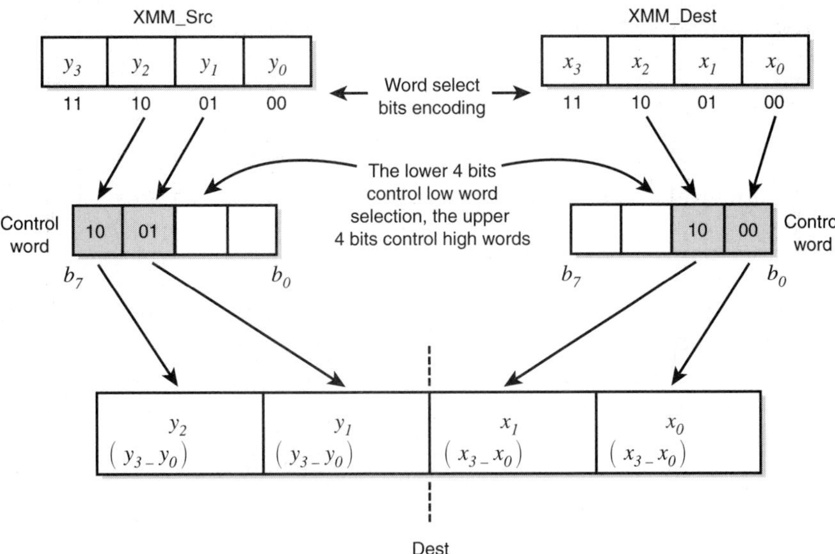

FIGURE 16.24 The `shufps` data movement instruction.

To make a long story short, the instruction has three operands: a source, destination, and an 8-bit control word. The instruction's purpose is to take two of the four words from the destination operand, along with two of the four words of the source operand, and then store them in the destination operand. Thus, the destination operand is used as a source operand also. It's best to think of the operation in two steps, in which both operands are source operands, and the final results are simply overwritten into one of them. In this case, it's the first operand, or `xmm_dest`, in my instruction prototype. Let's quickly discuss the details of the instruction.

`xmm_dest` is the destination SIMD register, and `xmm_src` is the source SIMD register. The tricky part is how the instructions work (refer to the Intel manuals for more detail).

Basically, the instruction takes two of the four words from the source register and places them in the destination register high words, and also takes two of the four words from the destination register and places them in the low words of the destination register (refer to Figure 16.24)! So, the destination is used as a source *and* a destination as mentioned before—but just think of the source and destination registers as both being sources, and the final result just happens to be stored in one of the source registers at the end of the process. In any case, the bit encoding of the select control word for a particular 32-bit word from either the source or destination is shown in Table 16.2.

TABLE 16.2 Control Word Encoding for `shufps`

2-Bit Value	Meaning
00	Selects word 0 (low word, bits 0–31)
01	Selects word 1 (bits 32–63)
10	Selects word 2 (bits 64–95)
11	Selects word 3 (high word, bits 96–127)

And the `control8` word has the following encoding:

(high bit) A_1A_0 B_1B_0 C_1C_0 D_1D_0 (low bit)

So each 2-bit subword controls the selection of one word from the source operands. Table 16.3 describes the encoding of each subcontrol bit word.

TABLE 16.3 2-Bit Control Word Encodings for `shufps`

Bits	Operation
D_1D_0	Selects the 32-word from the destination operand and places it in the (low) word 0 of the result.
C_1C_0	Selects the 32-word from the destination operand and places it in word 1 of the result.
B_1B_0	Selects the 32-word from the source operand and places it in word 2 of the result.
A_1A_0	Selects the 32-word from the source operand and places it in the (high) word 3 of the result.

Using `shufps`, instruction can take a little work, and figuring out the bits to move a word to and from can be error-prone. A macro can help us out here:

```
// srch - A1A0
// srcl - B1B0

// desth - C1C0
// destl - D1D0
#define SIMD_SHUFFLE(srch,srcl,desth,destl) (((srch) << 6) | ((srcl) << 4) \
                        | ((desth) << 2) | ((destl)))
```

Basically, all the macro does is take four parameters (the source and destination selection control words) and shift them into place. The comments show the that the encoding of the parameters basically maps directly to our bits in Table 16.3.

General SIMD Operation Flow In the next sections, we'll discuss some basic operations that SIMD can perform. In general, they all follow the same parallel flow, as shown in Figure 16.25; that is, a single operation is applied to the two SIMD source registers, and one of the source registers is used as the final destination.

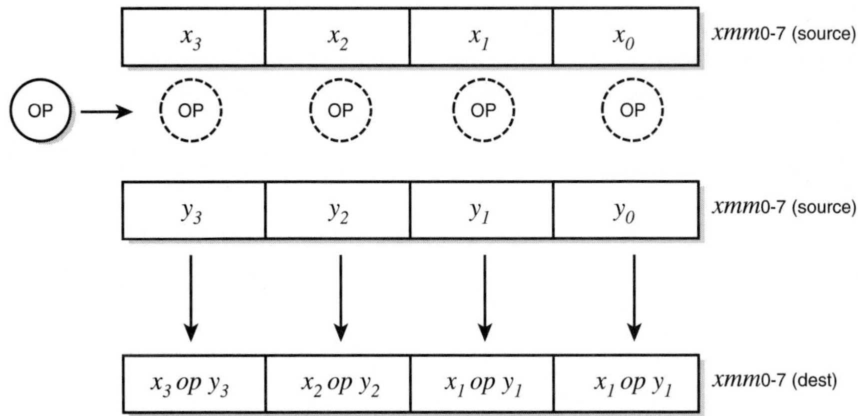

FIGURE 16.25 General SIMD operations.

Addition and Subtraction The instructions for packed single-precision aligned SIMD addition and subtraction add and subtract four 32-bit values in parallel. Let's begin with addition:

```
addps xmm_dest, xmm_src/memory
```

`addps` adds either an XMM register or a 128-bit memory operand to the destination XMM register.

Example: Compute `x0+y0, x1+y1, x2+y2, x3+y3`

```
_asm {
   movaps xmm0, x // move contents of x into xmm0
   addps xmm0, y // add contents of y to xmm0
   movaps z, xmm0 // store results (x0+y0, x1+y1, x2+y2, x3+y3) in z
   }
```

The subtraction instruction has the format

```
subps xmm_dest, xmm_src/memory
```

subps subtracts either a XMM register or a 128-bit memory operand from the destination XMM register.

Example: Compute x0-y0, x1-y1, x2-y2, x3-y3

```
_asm {
   movaps xmm0, x // move contents of x into xmm0
   subps xmm0, y // subtract contents of y to xmm0
   movaps z, xmm0 // store results (x0-y0, x1-y1, x2-y2, x3-y3) in z
   }
```

Multiplication and Division The instructions for packed single-precision aligned SIMD multiplication and division multiply and divide four 32-bit values in parallel. Let's begin with multiplication:

```
mulps xmm_dest, xmm_src/memory
```

mulps multiplies either an XMM register or a 128-bit memory operand and the destination XMM register.

Example: Compute x0*y0, x1*y1, x2*y2, x3*y3

```
_asm {
   movaps xmm0, x // move contents of x into xmm0
   mulps xmm0, y // multiple contents of y to xmm0
   movaps z, xmm0 // store results (x0*y0, x1*y1, x2*y2, x3*y3) in z
   }
```

The division instruction has the format

```
divps xmm_dest, xmm_src/memory
```

divps divides either an XMM register or a 128-bit memory operand into the destination XMM register.

Example: Compute x0/y0, x1/y1, x2/y2, x3/y3

```
_asm {
   movaps xmm0, x // move contents of x into xmm0
   divps xmm0, y // divide contents of y into xmm0
   movaps z, xmm0 // store results (x0/y0, x1/y1, x2/y2, x3/y3) in z
   }
```

Square Roots The instruction for packed single-precision aligned SIMD square root computes the square root of four 32-bit values in parallel:

```
sqrtps xmm_dest, xmm_src/memory
```

sqrtps computes the square root of the four 32-bit values, each stored in either a XMM register or a 128-bit memory operand, and stores the results in the destination XMM register.

Example: Compute $x0^{1/2}$, $x1^{1/2}$, $x2^{1/2}$, $x3^{1/2}$

```
_asm {
   sqrtps xmm0, x // compute square root of x0,x1,x2,x3
   movaps z, xmm0 // store results (x0^1/2, x1^1/2, x2^1/2, x3^1/2) in z
   }
```

Logical Operations SIMD has full support for every logical operation you could ever want. The basic logical instructions AND, OR, and XOR all work with single-precision packed 32-bit values and have the format

```
andps xmm_dest, xmm_src/memory
orps xmm_dest, xmm_src/memory
xorps xmm_dest, xmm_src/memory
```

where each logical operation applies the operation from either memory or an XMM register and the destination register. The results are always stored in the destination register.

Example: Compute z = ((x AND y) OR z)

```
_asm {
   mov xmm0, x // move contents of x into xmm0
   mov xmm1, y // move contents of y into xmm1
   mov xmm2, z // move contents of z into xmm2

   andps xmm0, xmm1 // xmm0 = x AND y
   orps xmm0, xmm2 // xmm0 = (x AND y) OR z
   movps z, xmm0  // z = xmm0
   }
```


Comparison Operations Lastly, there are many comparison instructions, but the basic cmpps instruction is similar to the standard cmp IA-32 instruction you are used to. The cmpps instruction means single-precision packed comparison, and has the following format:

```
cmpps xmm_dest, xmm_src, immediate_8
```

Each of the four 32-bit packed values is compared, and the results are stored in xmm_dest as four 32-bit strings of continuous 0s or 1s, depending on the results. immediate_8 controls the comparison to apply. The possible comparisons are shown in Table 16.4.

TABLE 16.4 Comparison Operators

Bits 0–2	Comparison
0	Equal
1	Less than
2	Less than or equal to
3	Unordered
4	Not equal
5	Not less than
6	Not less than or equal to
7	Ordered

Note: Bits 4–7 are reserved.

Example: Test whether `x[] < y[]`

```
_asm {
   mov xmm0, y
   cmpps xmm0, x
   // xmm0 has comparison bits, branch appropriately…
   }
```

Intrinsic Support The intrinsic support is very similar to the instructions themselves. The best thing to do is peruse the file `xmmintrin.h` to see for yourself, but here are some key intrinsics.

Arithmetic Operations:

```
__m128 _mm_add_ps(__m128 a, __m128 b); // a+b
__m128 _mm_sub_ps(__m128 a, __m128 b); // a-b
__m128 _mm_mul_ps(__m128 a, __m128 b); // a*b
__m128 _mm_div_ps(__m128 a, __m128 b); // a/b
__m128 _mm_sqrt_ps(__m128 a); // square root of a
__m128 _mm_rcp_ps(__m128 a); // reciprocal a
__m128 _mm_rsqrt_ps(__m128 a); // reciprocal of a
__m128 _mm_min_ps(__m128 a, __m128 b); // min(a,b)
__m128 _mm_max_ps(__m128 a, __m128 b); // max(a,b)
```

Example: `m0 = m1+m2`

```
m0 = _mm_add_ps(m1, m2);
```

Logical Operations:

```
__m128 _mm_and_ps(__m128 a, __m128 b); // a AND b
__m128 _mm_andnot_ps(__m128 a, __m128 b); // a NAND b
__m128 _mm_or_ps(__m128 a, __m128 b); // a OR b
__m128 _mm_xor_ps(__m128 a, __m128 b); // a XOR b
```

Example: `m0 = m1 AND m2`

```
m0 = _mm_and_ps(m1, m2);
```

Comparison Operations:

```
__m128 _mm_cmpeq_ps(__m128 a, __m128 b); // a == b
__m128 _mm_cmplt_ps(__m128 a, __m128 b); // a < b
__m128 _mm_cmple_ps(__m128 a, __m128 b); // a <= b
__m128 _mm_cmpgt_ps(__m128 a, __m128 b); // a > b
__m128 _mm_cmpge_ps(__m128 a, __m128 b); // a >= b
__m128 _mm_cmpneq_ps(__m128 a, __m128 b); // a!=b
__m128 _mm_cmpnlt_ps(__m128 a, __m128 b); // !(a < b)
__m128 _mm_cmpnle_ps(__m128 a, __m128 b); // !(a <= b)
__m128 _mm_cmpngt_ps(__m128 a, __m128 b); // !(a > b)
__m128 _mm_cmpnge_ps(__m128 a, __m128 b); // !(a >= b)
__m128 _mm_cmpord_ps(__m128 a, __m128 b);
__m128 _mm_cmpunord_ps(__m128 a, __m128 b);
```

Example: `m0 = m1 < m2`

```
m0 = _mm_ cmplt_ps(m1, m2);
```

16

You are free to use intrinsics and inline assembly as you want; however, keep in mind that many intrinsics actually represent more than one atomic SIMD instruction, so you might want to review the assembly language output when optimizing to make sure that you can't do a better job with inline assembly SIMD in performance hotspots.

Where to Find More Information When I was a teenager, I used to get thousands of dollars of free chips, books, and software from companies just by calling up and asking. These days, you can still do that, but it's really hard to find the right person; however, Intel has a lot of free stuff on its site that I think you would be very interested in. I want to bring to your attention the fact that you can get the entire Pentium III/4 software development, programming, and optimization manuals for free from Intel's site. And I don't mean in PDF format—I mean real books, with a $250+ value, sent to your house! All you have to do is read these books and you will be a Pentium optimization guru. Here's the URL where you can order within Intel's Literature Center:

`http://developer.intel.com/design/pentium4/manuals/index2.htm`

You will find the following manuals on the site:

- "IA-32 Intel Architecture Software Developer's Manual Volume 1: Basic Architecture"
- "IA-32 Intel Architecture Software Developer's Manual Volume 2: Instruction Set Reference"

- "IA-32 Intel Architecture Software Developer's Manual Volume 3: System Programming Guide"
- "Intel Pentium 4 and Intel Xeon Processor Optimization Manual"

TIP

This is one of the best kept secrets in the world, so don't order these free books unless you plan to read them.

Nothing beats free stuff! Also, Intel's site has a ton of articles and white papers on Pentium optimization in general. If you're going to make games, you must know this stuff, so take the time and read all of it. I'm glad I did.

A SIMD 3D Vector Class

Now that you have a little SIMD theory under your belt, and some idea of how to use some of the basic math instructions, let's put it all together and start on a little C++ class that supports 3D vectors with w, and uses SIMD to perform calculations.

The class is just a start and nowhere near done, but it's a good place to experiment and try coding SIMD. The class supports 4D vectors of the format [x,y,z,w], so each object has the same layout as a SIMD register. Also, I have implemented addition, subtraction, dot product, length, printing, array access, and a couple other housekeeping functions. Additionally, I have implemented many functions with conditional compilation, allowing pure assembly SIMD or intrinsic SIMD. The defines that control conditional compilation are as follows:

```
// enable the final output type by setting one of these to 1
// (the other MUST be 0!)
#define SIMD_INTRINSIC   0
#define SIMD_ASM         1
```

The following is the entire class. it's extremely well commented, so please take your time and read all of it, and try to follow each SIMD operation. Most of them should be very easy to follow. The only operation that will give you some grief is the dot product. The reason is that when performing a dot product, it's easy to multiply two vectors in parallel, but it's hard to sum the results of an XMM register "horizontally." This takes some shuffling via the `shufps` instruction, along with some `addpss` to get the final results. Anyway, here is the class:

```
// this is the new vector class that supports SIMD sse
// note the numerous ways we can access the data members,
// this allows transparent support of assignments,
// data access, and intrinsic library use without lots of casts
```

```
class C_VECTOR4D
{
public:

union
  {
  __declspec(align(16)) __m128 v;  // SIMD data type access
  float M[4];                  // array indexed storage
  // explicit names
  struct
     {
     float x,y,z,w;
     }; // end struct
  }; // end union

// note: the declspec is redundant since in the type __m128 forces
// the compiler to align in 16-byte boundaries, so as long as __m128 is
// part of the union declspec is NOT needed :) But, it can't
// hurt and when you are defining locals and globals, always put
// declspec(align(16)) to KNOW data is on 16-byte boundaries

// CONSTRUCTORS //////////////////////////////////////////////////////////////

C_VECTOR4D()
{
// void constructor
// initialize vector to 0.0.0.1
x=y=z=0; w=1.0;
} // end C_VECTOR4D

//////////////////////////////////////////////////////////////////////////////

C_VECTOR4D(float _x, float _y, float _z, float _w = 1.0)
{
// initialize vector to sent values
x = _x;
y = _y;
z = _z;
w = _w;
} // end C_VECTOR4D

// FUNCTIONS /////////////////////////////////////////////////////////////////
```

```
void init(float _x, float _y, float _z, float _w = 1.0)
{
// initialize vector to sent values
x = _x;
y = _y;
z = _z;
w = _w;
} // end init

////////////////////////////////////////////////////////////////////////////

void zero(void)
{
// initialize vector to 0.0.0.1
x=y=z=0; w=1.0;

} // end zero

////////////////////////////////////////////////////////////////////////////

float length(void)
{
// computes the length of the vector
C_VECTOR4D vr = *this;

// set w=0
vr.w = 0;

// compile pure asm version?
#if (SIMD_ASM==1)

// begin inline asm version of SIMD dot product since we need its
// results for the length since length = sqrt(v*v)
_asm
  {
  // first we need dot product of this*this
  movaps xmm0, vr.v  // move left operand into xmm0
  mulps xmm0, xmm0  // multiply operands vertically

  // at this point, xmm0 =
  // [ (v1.x * v2.x), (v1.y * v2.y), (v1.z * v2.z), (1*1) ]
  // or more simply: let xmm0 = [x,y,z,1] =
  // [ (v1.x * v2.x), (v1.y * v2.y), (v1.z * v2.z), (1*1) ]
  // we need to sum the x,y,z components into a single scalar
```

```
    // to compute the final dot product of:
    // dp = x + y + z == x1*x2 + y1*y2 + z1*z2

    // begin
    // xmm0: = [x,y,z,1] (note: all regs in low to hight order)
    // xmm1: = [?,?,?,?]
    movaps xmm1, xmm0 // copy result into xmm1
    // xmm0: = [x,y,z,1]
    // xmm1: = [x,y,z,1]

    shufps xmm1, xmm0, SIMD_SHUFFLE(0x01,0x00,0x03,0x02)
    // xmm0: = [x,y,z,1]
    // xmm1: = [z,1,x,y]

    addps xmm1, xmm0
    // xmm0: = [x ,y ,z ,1]
    // xmm1: = [x+z,y+1,x+z,y+1]

    shufps xmm0, xmm1, SIMD_SHUFFLE(0x02,0x03,0x00,0x01)
    // xmm0: = [y ,x ,y+1,x+z]
    // xmm1: = [x+z,y+1,x+z,y+1]

    // finally we can add!
    addps xmm0, xmm1
    // xmm0: = [x+y+z,x+y+1,x+y+z+1,x+y+z+1]
    // xmm1: = [x+z ,y+1 ,x+z  ,y+1]
    // xmm0.x contains the dot product
    // xmm0.z, xmm0.w contains the dot+1

    // now low double word contains dot product, let's take squaroot
    sqrtss xmm0, xmm0

    movaps vr, xmm0 // save results

    } // end asm

#endif // end use inline asm version

// compile intrinsic version?
#if (SIMD_INTRINSIC==1)

#endif // end use intrinsic library version
```

16

```
// return result
return(vr.x);

} // end length

// OVERLOADED OPERATORS //////////////////////////////////////////////////////

float& operator[](int index)
{
// return the ith element from the array
return(M[index]);
} // end operator[]

/////////////////////////////////////////////////////////////////////////////

C_VECTOR4D operator+(C_VECTOR4D &v)
{
// adds the "this" vector and the sent vector

__declspec(align(16)) C_VECTOR4D vr; // used to hold result
                   // aligned on 16 bytes

// compile pure asm version?
#if (SIMD_ASM==1)

// begin inline asm version of SIMD add
_asm
  {
  mov esi, this    // "this" contains a point to the left operand
  mov edi, v     // v points to the right operand

  movaps xmm0, [esi] // esi points to first vector, move into xmm0
  addps xmm0, [edi] // edi points to second vector, add it to xmm0

  movaps vr, xmm0   // move result into output vector

  } // end asm

#endif // end use inline asm version

// compile intrinsic version?
#if (SIMD_INTRINSIC==1)

vr.v = _mm_add_ps(this->v, v.v);
```

```
#endif // end use intrinsic library version

// always set w=1
vr.w = 1.0;

// return result
return(vr);

} // end operator+

////////////////////////////////////////////////////////////////////////////////

C_VECTOR4D operator-(C_VECTOR4D &v)
{
// subtracts the "this" vector and the sent vector

__declspec(align(16)) C_VECTOR4D vr; // used to hold result
                   // aligned on 16 bytes

// compile pure asm version?
#if (SIMD_ASM==1)

// begin inline asm version of SIMD add
_asm
  {
  mov esi, this    // "this" contains a point to the left operand
  mov edi, v     // v points to the right operand

  movaps xmm0, [esi] // esi points to first vector, move into xmm0
  subps xmm0, [edi] // edi points to second vector, subtract it from xmm0

  movaps vr, xmm0   // move result into output vector

  } // end asm

#endif // end use inline asm version

// compile intrinsic version?
#if (SIMD_INTRINSIC==1)

vr.v = _mm_sub_ps(this->v, v.v);

#endif // end use intrinsic library version
```

```
// always set w=1
vr.w = 1.0;

// return result
return(vr);

} // end operator-

////////////////////////////////////////////////////////////////////////////

float operator*(C_VECTOR4D &v)
{
// the dot product will be * since dot product is a more common operation
// computes the dot between between the "this" vector and the sent vector

__declspec(align(16)) C_VECTOR4D vr; // used to hold result
                  // aligned on 16 bytes

// compile pure asm version?
#if (SIMD_ASM==1)

// begin inline asm version of SIMD dot product
_asm
  {
  mov esi, this    // "this" contains a point to the left operand
  mov edi, v     // v points to the right operand

  movaps xmm0, [esi] // move left operand into xmm0
  mulps xmm0, [edi] // multiply operands vertically

  // at this point, xmm0 =
  // [ (v1.x * v2.x), (v1.y * v2.y), (v1.z * v2.z), (1*1) ]
  // or more simply: let xmm0 = [x,y,z,1] =
  // [ (v1.x * v2.x), (v1.y * v2.y), (v1.z * v2.z), (1*1) ]
  // we need to sum the x,y,z components into a single scalar
  // to compute the final dot product of:
  // dp = x + y + z where x = x1*x2, y = y1*y2, z = z1*z2

  // begin
  // xmm0: = [x,y,z,1] (note: all regs in low to hight order)
  // xmm1: = [?,?,?,?]
  movaps xmm1, xmm0 // copy result into xmm1
```

```
  // xmm0: = [x,y,z,1]
  // xmm1: = [x,y,z,1]

  shufps xmm1, xmm0, SIMD_SHUFFLE(0x01,0x00,0x03,0x02)
  // xmm0: = [x,y,z,1]
  // xmm1: = [z,1,x,y]

  addps xmm1, xmm0
  // xmm0: = [x ,y ,z ,1]
  // xmm1: = [x+z,y+1,x+z,y+1]

  shufps xmm0, xmm1, SIMD_SHUFFLE(0x02,0x03,0x00,0x01)
  // xmm0: = [y ,x ,y+1,x+z]
  // xmm1: = [x+z,y+1,x+z,y+1]

  // finally we can add!
  addps xmm0, xmm1
  // xmm0: = [x+y+z,x+y+1,x+y+z+1,x+y+z+1]
  // xmm1: = [x+z ,y+1 ,x+z  ,y+1]
  // xmm0.x contains the dot product
  // xmm0.z, xmm0.w contains the dot+1
  movaps vr, xmm0
  } // end asm

#endif // end use inline asm version

// compile intrinsic version?
#if (SIMD_INTRINSIC==1)
vr.v = _mm_mul_ps(this->v, v.v);
return(vr.x + vr.y + vr.z);

#endif // end use intrinsic library version

// return result
return(vr.x);

} // end operator*

//////////////////////////////////////////////////////////////////////////////

void print(void)
{
```

16

```
// this member function prints out the vector
printf("\nv = [%f, %f, %f, %f]", this->x, this->y, this->z, this->w);
} // end print

//////////////////////////////////////////////////////////////////////////////

}; // end class C_VECTOR4D
```

In a moment, I will show you some simple examples of using the class, but before that, you might notice the use of the `SIMD_SHUFFLE()` macro we discussed earlier in the section on data movement. Once again, this macro does nothing more than move one SIMD word from one position in a source operand to another position in a destination operand, enabling you to move things around to order things in such a way that the data is easier to work with.

The final stage of the dot product needs a *horizontal* addition, meaning that after the initial computation u*v, the results of the first parallel SIMD multiply are

```
[ux*vx, uy*vy, uz*vz, 1*1]
```

The problem is, we need to add up (ux*vx + uy*vy + uz*vz) to arrive at the final dot product result. This can't be accomplished with normal SIMD instructions because there's no horizontal addition instruction. Thus, we need to copy the results, shift them, and add them in an accumulator to derive the final results of

```
(ux*vx + uy*vy + uz*vz)
```

So, let's put the class to use. Let's define two SIMD vectors:

```
C_VECTOR4D v1(1,2,3), v2(4,5,6), result;
```

Here's an addition:

```
result = v1+v2;
```

Let's print out the result:

```
result.print();
```

Now let's compute the length of this result vector and print it out:

```
length = result.length();
cout << "\nlength";
```

And finally, computing the dot product of `v1` and `v2`:

```
float dp = v1*v2;
```

Doesn't get much easier than that! For a demo of the class in action, take a look at DEMOII16_3.CPP|EXE. It contains the entire class and a short demo similar to the preceding examples. The program, like the previous demo, must be compiled as a CONSOLE application, and you must have an SSE-compatible operating system, as well as a Pentium III+ processor. Try experimenting with the conditional assembly flag, and set it for intrinsic or assembly mode via the defines we covered earlier in the section.

If you're feeling creative, try adding matrix multiplication and everything else you can think of. Take your time and think of the fastest way in and out of each operation. Good SIMD programming takes some thought—similar to writing a class. If you just brute-force it, you will find it's not much better than straight C++.

General Optimization Tricks

In this next section, I am just going to throw out a few interesting optimization tricks that you might find useful. They vary from tips to magical incantations. Some are my own, others I've picked up from the references at the end of this chapter.

Trick 1: Getting Rid of `_ftol()`

When assigning a `float` to an `int`, the compiler will many times call the internal function `_ftol()`, which can slow things down to a crawl. For example:

```
float f = 10.5;
int i = f;
```

To avoid this, use inline assembly and FPU instructions, such as `fistp/fst`:

```
_asm
  {
  fld f;
  fistp i;
  }
```

Or, use the compiler flag `/QIfist` to force the rounding mode to chop, and no call to `_ftol()` will be made.

However, watch out for second-order effects and loss of accuracy throughout your code. Try this on a module-to-module basis. However, the `_ftol()` call is one of the biggest performance bottlenecks there is. You think you're writing totally optimal code, you simply assign a `float` to an `int`, and unbeknownst to you, a function call is being made!

Trick 2: Setting the FPU Control Word

The floating-point processor has a control word that dictates rounding mode, accuracy, and denormalization. You can control the FPU control word with assembly language;

however, there is a C/C++ runtime function that does the job for you called `_control87()` and shown here:

```
unsigned int _control87( unsigned int control, unsigned int mask );
```

Table 16.5 contains some of the more useful control flags you can manipulate to gain more performance.

TABLE 16.5 *_control87()* Parameters

Mask	Hex Value	Control Constant	Hex Value
_MCW_DN (Denormal control)	0x03000000		
		_DN_SAVE	0x00000000
		_DN_FLUSH	0x01000000
_MCW_RC (Rounding control)	0x00000300		
		_RC_CHOP	0x00000300
		_RC_UP	0x00000200
		_RC_DOWN	0x00000100
		_RC_NEAR	0x00000000
_MCW_PC (Precision control)	0x00030000		
		_PC_24 (24 bits)	0x00020000
		_PC_53 (53 bits)	0x00010000
		_PC_64 (64 bits)	0x00000000

For example, when calculations are made and numbers are very small, this can cause exceptions. However, if you set the denormal control to flush, processing will speed up. Also, try lowering the precision of your calculations and see whether everything still works. This will speed things up. Here's the code to set both properties:

```
// set single precision
_control87( _PC_24, _MCW_PC );

// set to flush mode
_control87( _DN_FLUSH, _MCW_DN );
```

Trick 3: Fast Zeroing of Floating-Point Values

The binary encoding of an integer and floating-point value in general are completely different. That is, `(int)1` does not equal `(float)1` in binary. However, `(int)0` does happen to equal `(float)0`, so if you need to quickly clear out a large area of memory and set them with floating-point 0, you can replace this code:

```
float x[1000];

for (int i=0; i < 1000; i++)
  x[i] = 0;
```

with this code:

```
memset(x, 0x0, sizeof(float)*1000);
```

Or better yet, use some inline assembly language and a QUADword fill, like this:

```
_asm
  {
  mov edi, x    ; edi points to destination memory
  mov ecx, 1000/4 ; number of 32-bit words to move
  mov eax, 0    ; 32-bit data
  rep stosd    ; move data
  } // end asm
```

Trick 4: Fast Square Root

Here's a fast square root algorithm that computes the square root of the sent number within a 5% margin of error:

```
float Fast_SquareRT(float f)
{
float result; // used to send out result
_asm
  {
  mov eax, f
  sub eax, 0x3f800000
  sar eax, 1
  add eax, 0x3f800000
  mov result, eax
  } // end asm

// return result
return(result);

} // end Fast_SquareRT
```

Trick 5: Piecewise Linear Arctangent

We have seen the use of lookup tables and other tricks to compute the arctangent. However, all our techniques are special cases. There is an interesting piecewise solution to the problem that for any (dx, dy) will output the arctangent and have a very small amount of error.

The algorithm works by first using a decision tree to figure out the octant of (dx, dy) and then uses an output function to give the final result in the range [0,8], which you can scale or remap to any value you like: 0–360 degrees, or 0–2PI radians, for instance. Figure 16.26 illustrates the algorithm graphically. Simply use the conditional code in each octant as steering logic and output the value.

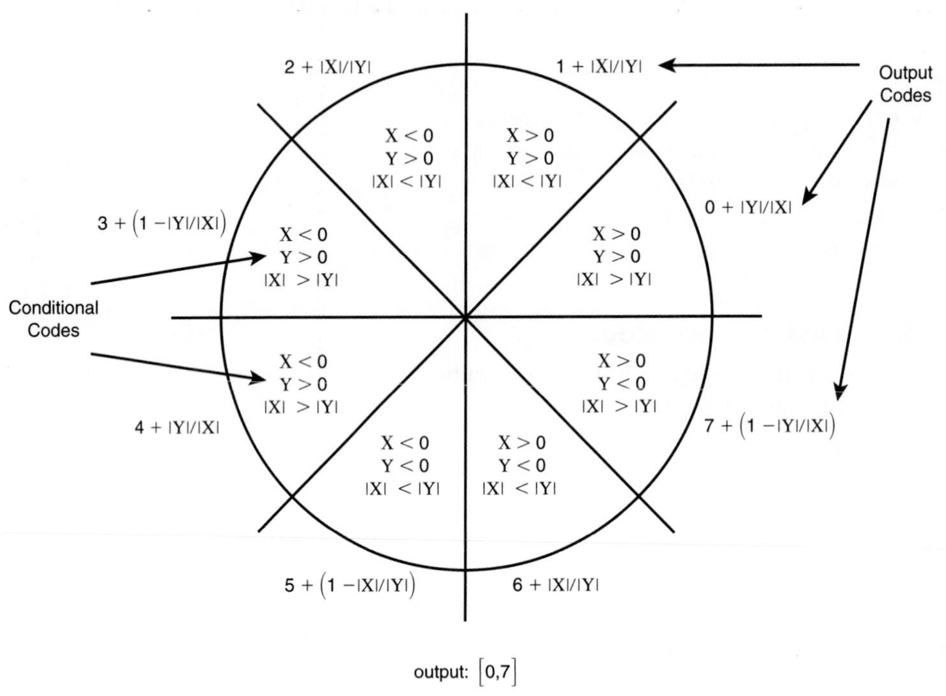

FIGURE 16.26 A graphical approximation to the arctangent.

Trick 6: Pointer Increment

When accessing arrays with pointers, don't do this:

```
int *p = base;

*p = 5;
p++;

*p = 6;
p++;

*p = 7;
```

Instead, try this:

```
p[0] = 5;
p[1] = 6;
p[2] = 7;
```

Accessing data with array notation is faster than incrementing the pointer and then accessing it.

Trick 7: Take `if`s Out of Loops

This is common sense, but I see it all the time in code, so I thought I would mention it. Suppose you have a loop, and within the loop, you need to perform an operation every *n*th iteration. So, you do something like this:

```
for (int i=0; i < 256; i++)
  {
  // test for special case
  if ((i % 64) == 0)
    {
    // special case code
    }
  else
    {
    // normal case code
    } // end else
  } // end for
```

This is a disaster. Why not just break the loop up into four loops like this, so the `if` statement is never needed:

```
// special case code for i = 0

// 1-63 loop
for (i = 1; i < 64; i++)
  // normal code

// special case code for i=64

// 65 - 127 loop
for (; i < 128; i++)
  // normal code

// special case code for i=128
```

```
// 129 - 192 loop
for (; i < 192; i++)
  // normal code

// special case code for i=192

// 193 - 255 loop
for (; i < 256; i++)
  // normal code
```

Now there are no more `if` statements.

Trick 8: Branching the Pipeline

Pentium III/4 processors have very deep instruction pipelines (up to 20 instructions), so when a mispredicted branch occurs, the entire pipeline is flushed; hence, mispredictions should be avoided. Moreover, when the processor is executing code, it usually executes the code it thinks you are going to need next, so not only does a misprediction stall the pipeline, it also processes code that will never be needed! To avoid mispredictions, you should code such that a conditional `if` should be taken *most* of the time, and only skipped over *some* of the time.

Trick 9: Data Alignment

The Pentium processors work best with 16-/32-byte alignment, so if possible, align all data structures to these boundaries, and/or pad data structures so they are multiples of these numbers. You can control alignment in both the compiler options, and with the `__declspec(align(value))` methods.

Trick 10: Inline All Short Functions

Any function that is 10–20 lines of code that is called often should be inlined. To inline a function, you must move it from the C/C++ source file to a header file, because the compiler literally needs the source of the function, not just the header. As an example, through profiling I found that the vector dot product and matrix multiplier were being called more than any other math functions. I inlined these functions and gained about 3–5% in performance—all that from a single keyword.

References

The following is a list of references used for this chapter, and are great sources for more optimizations:

- The *Graphics Gems Series* (Academic Press)
- "IA-32 Intel Architecture Software Developer's Manual Volume 1: Basic Architecture" (Intel Press)

- "IA-32 Intel Architecture Software Developer's Manual Volume 2: Instruction Set Reference" (Intel Press)
- "IA-32 Intel Architecture Software Developer's Manual Volume 3: System Programming Guide" (Intel Press)
- "Intel Pentium 4 and Intel Xeon Processor Optimization Manual" (Intel Press)
- *The Software Optimization Cookbook* by Richard Gerber (Intel Press)

Summary

In this chapter, we didn't cover much hard-core optimization. Instead the focus was on technology and empowering you with tools and technologies that you've probably never used. I can't impress upon you how important it is for you to embrace all the technologies discussed in this chapter—they really can change your entire outlook on programming next-generation processors and game applications. Long gone are the days of using stop-watches to optimize code—you really have to leverage every bit of technology out there.

PART VI

CD-ROM Appendixes

IN THIS PART

Index

Note: **Pages prefixed by *CD:* are located on the accompanying CD-ROM. For example, *CD:1629* would be located on page 1629 on the CD.**

Symbols

A

B

C

D

E

F

G

H

I

J-K

L

M

O

P

Q

R

S

U

V

W

X

Y-Z

Other Related Titles

DirectX 8 and Visual Basic Development
Keith Sink
0-672-32225-0
$39.99 U.S./$62.99 CAN

Open GL SuperBible, Second Edition
Richard S. Wright, Jr.
Michael R. Sweet
1-571-69164-2
$49.99 U.S./$77.99 CAN

Sams Teach Yourself Game Programming with Visual Basic in 21 Days
Clayton Walnum
0-672-31987-X
$39.99 U.S./$62.99 CAN

Sams Teach Yourself Game Programming with DirectX in 21 Days
Clayton Walnum
0-672-32419-9
$39.99 U.S./$62.99 CAN

Microsoft Direct 3D Programming Kick Start
Clayton Walnum
0-672-32498-9
$34.99 U.S./$54.99 CAN

Tricks of the Windows Game Programming Gurus
André LaMothe
0-672-32369-9
$59.99 U.S./$93.99 CAN

.NET Game Programming with C#
Justin Rogers
0-672-32435-0
$44.99 U.S./$69.99 CAN

The Art of Photoshop
Daniel Giordan
0-672-32270-6
$49.99 U.S./$62.99 CAN

Sams Teach Yourself Game Programming with DirectX in 24 Hours
Michael Morrison
0-672-32461-x
$29.99 U.S./$46.99 CAN

SAMS
www.samspublishing.com

Sams Teach Yourself C++ in 21 Days, Fourth Edition
Jesse Liberty
0-672-32072-X
$34.99 U.S./$54.99 CAN

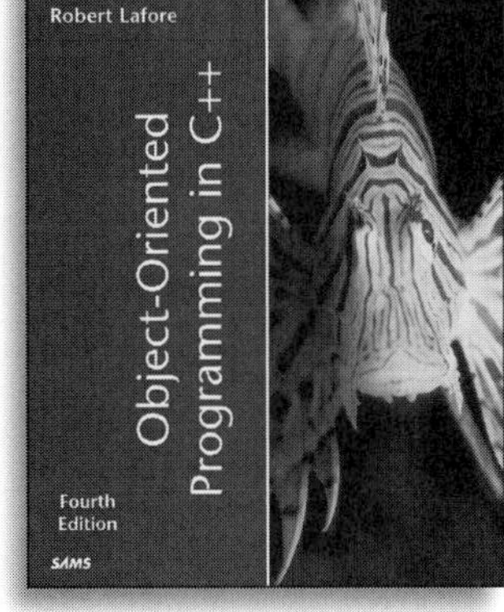

Object-Oriented Programming in C++, Fourth EditionJ
Robert Lafore
0-672-32308-7
$44.99 U.S./$67.95 CAN

C++ Primer Plus, Fourth Edition
Stephen Prata
0-672-32223-4
$49.99 U.S./$74.95 CAN

All prices are subject to change.